NEW TESTAMENT APOCRYPHA
(Volume Two)

EDGAR HENNECKE

NEW TESTAMENT APOCRYPHA

Edited by
WILHELM SCHNEEMELCHER

English translation edited by
R. McL. Wilson

VOLUME TWO

WRITINGS RELATING TO THE APOSTLES;
APOCALYPSES AND RELATED SUBJECTS

INDEX TO VOLUMES I AND II

THE WESTMINSTER PRESS
PHILADELPHIA

This book originally appeared as E. Hennecke, *Neutestamentliche Apokryphen*, Volume II (ed. W. Schneemelcher), and was published in 1964 by J. C. B. Mohr, Tübingen, Germany. The English translation has been made by Ernest Best, David Hill, George Ogg, G. C. Stead, and R. McL. Wilson

LIBRARY OF CONGRESS CATALOG CARD NO. 63–7492

PUBLISHED BY THE WESTMINSTER PRESS®
PHILADELPHIA, PENNSYLVANIA

PRINTED IN THE UNITED STATES OF AMERICA
9 8 7 6 5 4

5

ABBREVIATIONS

AA	= Acta Andreae (Acts of Andrew)
Aa	= Acta apostolorum apocrypha 1, ed. Lipsius 1891: 2, 1 & 2, ed. Bonnet 1898 & 1903
ABA	= Abhandlungen der Berliner Akademie der Wissenschaften, Phil.-hist. Klasse
AJ	= Acta Johannis (Acts of John)
Altaner	= Berthold Altaner, Patrologie ⁵1958 (ET 1960)
AP	= Acta Pauli (Acts of Paul)
Apa	= Apocalypses apocryphae ed. Tischendorf, 1866
Apokr. 1	= Neutestamentliche Apokryphen, hrsg. von E. Hennecke, ¹1904
Apokr. 2	= Neutestamentliche Apokryphen, hrsg. von E. Hennecke, ²1924
APt	= Acta Petri (Acts of Peter)
AR	= Archiv für Religionswissenschaft
ATh	= Acta Thomae (Acts of Thomas)
AThANT	= Abhandlungen zur Theologie des Alten und Neuen Testaments
Bardenhewer Lit. gesch.	= Otto Bardenhewer, Geschichte der altkirchlichen Literatur I, ²1913: II, ²1914: III, ²1923: IV, ¹⁺²1924: V, 1932 (Reprint 1962) (ET 1908)
Bauer	= W. Bauer, Das Leben Jesu im Zeitalter der neutestamentlichen Apokryphen, 1909
BHG	= Bibliotheca Hagiographica Graeca, ³1957
BZAW	= Beihefte zur Zeitschrift für die alttestamentliche Wissenschaft
BZNW	= Beihefte zur Zeitschrift für die neutestamentliche Wissenschaft und die Kunde der älteren Kirche
CCh	= Corpus Christianorum. Series latina
CSCO	= Corpus Scriptorum Christianorum Orientalium
CSEL	= Corpus Scriptorum Ecclesiasticorum Latinorum
DB	= A Dictionary of the Bible, ed. J. Hastings, 5 vols., 1898–1904
Ea	= Evangelia apocrypha ed. Tischendorf ²1876
FHG	= Fragmenta Historicorum Graecorum, 5 vols., 1841–70
FRLANT	= Forschungen zur Religion und Literatur des Alten und Neuen Testaments
GCS	= Die griechisch-christlichen Schriftsteller der ersten Jahrhunderte
GGA	= Göttingische Gelehrte Anzeigen

Handb.	=Handbuch zu den neutestamentlichen Apokryphen, hrsg. von E. Hennecke, 1904
Harnack, Lit. gesch.	=Adolf Harnack, Geschichte der altchristlichen Literatur, ²1958
HTR	=The Harvard Theological Review
James	=The Apocryphal New Testament ed. M. R. James, 1924 (reprint 1955)
JBL	=Journal of Biblical Literature
JTS	=Journal of Theological Studies
KlT	=Kleine Texte für Vorlesungen und Übungen, hrsg. von H. Lietzmann
Lipsius	=R. A. Lipsius, Die apokryphen Apostelgeschichten und Apostellegenden, 2 vols., 1883f.: supplementary vol. 1890
LThK	=Lexikon für Theologie und Kirche, ¹1930–38: ²1957ff.
Michaelis	=Die apokryphen Schriften zum Neuen Testament, übersetzt und erläutert von W. Michaelis, ²1958
NGA	=Nachrichten der Akademie der Wissenschaften zu Göttingen
NkZ	=Neue Kirchliche Zeitschrift
OrChr	=Oriens Christianus
OrientLZ	=Orientalistische Literaturzeitung
PA	=Patrum apostolicorum opera ed. O. von Gebhardt, A. Harnack, Th. Zahn I, ²1876–77: II, 1876: III, 1877
PG	=Migne, Patrologia Graeca
PL	=Migne, Patrologia Latina
PO	=Patrologia Orientalis, ed. Graffin-Nau
Quasten	=Johannes Quasten, Patrology I, 1950: II, 1953: III, 1960
RAC	=Reallexikon für Antike und Christentum, 1941ff.
RE	=Realencyklopädie für protestantische Theologie und Kirche, ³1896–1913
Rev.Bén.	=Revue Bénédictine
Rev.Bibl	=Revue Biblique
RGG	=Religion in Geschichte und Gegenwart, ³1957–62
RHE	=Revue d'Histoire Ecclésiastique
RHPR	=Revue d'Histoire et de Philosophie Religieuses
RQS	=Römische Quartalschrift
Santos	=Los Evangelios Apócrifos ed. A. De Santos Otero, 1956: ²1963
SB Berlin	=Sitzungsberichte der Berliner Akademie der Wissenschaften, Phil.-hist. Klasse

ABBREVIATIONS

SHA	=Sitzungsberichte der Heidelberger Akademie der Wissenschaften, Phil.-hist. Klasse
Schürer	=E. Schürer, Geschichte des jüdischen Volkes im Zeitalter Jesu Christi, 3 vols. and index vol., [4]1901–11 (ET 1890ff.)
ThLBl	=Theologisches Literaturblatt
ThLZ	=Theologische Literaturzeitung
ThWtb	=Theologisches Wörterbuch
TSt	=Texts and Studies, Contributions to biblical and patristic literature
TU	=Texte und Untersuchungen zur Geschichte der altchristlichen Literatur
Vig. Chr.	=Vigiliae Christianae
Zahn, Forsch.	=Forschungen zur Geschichte des neutestamentlichen Kanons und der altkirchlichen Literatur, ed. T. Zahn, 1881–1929
ZDMG	=Zeitschrift der Deutschen Morgenländischen Gesellschaft
ZKG	=Zeitschrift für Kirchengeschichte
ZkTh	=Zeitschrift für katholische Theologie
ZNW	=Zeitschrift für die neutestamentliche Wissenschaft und die Kunde der älteren Kirche
ZRGG	=Zeitschrift für Religions- und Geistesgeschichte
ZThK	=Zeitschrift für Theologie und Kirche
ZwTh	=Zeitschrift für wissenschaftliche Theologie

8

CORRIGENDA TO VOLUME I

Page 26, line 22, *c. Faust.* II, 2, should be: *C. Faust.* XI, 2.

Page 29, line 1, add at end: E.T. The Origins of the New Testament, London, 1925.

Page 75, Section 2, line 4, 1960 should be 1963.

Page 96, line 17, Jeremias' book *Unbekannte Jesusworte* has now appeared in a third edition (1962). References here and elsewhere to the second edition are not always applicable to the third.

Page 119, line 8, Dibelius: E.T. A Fresh Approach to the NT and Early Christian Literature, London 1937.

Page 138, line 12, Vilmart should be: Wilmart.

Page 150, No. 24, Is. 53:2 should be: Is. 53:12.

Page 151, No. 27, line 5, and page 152, No. 30, line 5: Clem. should be Clm.

Page 170, Section (*l*), Epiph. *Haer.* 62, 4 should be: Epiph. *Haer.* 62, 2.

Page 286, note 1, read: W. Bauer, Vol. II, pp. 59f.

PREFACE TO THE ENGLISH EDITION

OUR AIM IN this second volume is the same as in the first, to present "an English version of Hennecke, checked and corrected to make it in every way possible an adequate tool for the use of the English-speaking reader". Such an undertaking presents problems entirely of its own. The several introductions, of course, are direct translations from the German, and here it has been our primary concern to keep faith with our German colleagues. With the texts, however, it is quite another matter. Simply to translate the German version would have entailed a certain remoteness from the original, not to speak of the possibility of errors arising in the process. On the other hand, completely fresh and independent translations could not have been placed under the names of the German contributors. Our solution was to check the texts so far as possible against the original sources, so as to ensure that the translations really were English translations and not merely mediated at second hand through the German.

It is necessary to emphasize this point, since one reviewer wrote that "unfortunately" the translations of the extracts in our first volume were not made from the original, with a few exceptions, but mediated through the German. His comments merely revealed his complete misunderstanding of the preface to that volume, and his failure to do us the elementary courtesy of checking a few passages against the German and against the originals. In point of fact, his "exceptions"—namely translations from Latin, Greek and Coptic—account for the greater part by far of the extracts contained in the volume, the only text of any considerable length in another tongue being the Ethiopic *Epistula Apostolorum*, the Coptic parallel version of which was checked in detail. In short, the possibility of such criticism was anticipated from the outset, and everything possible has been done in both volumes to eliminate any justification for it.

The first volume on the whole has met with a cordial reception. Those who would have wished a complete translation of the Gospel of Truth and other documents from Nag Hammadi may be referred to Professor Schneemelcher's remarks about the legal difficulties encountered, while those who complained that only extracts were given from such documents as the Pistis Sophia may be invited to reflect that this is a volume in itself. Moreover, in some cases the first volume presents not merely excerpts but all the fragments that have survived. Some reviewers, again, would have done well to consider the problems involved for Professor Schneemelcher and his collaborators in selecting the material from the bulk available and reducing it to manageable compass.

This book contains, with one exception, all the material in the German volume. Professor Schneemelcher suggested that the bulk of the volume might be reduced by the omission of the Sibylline Oracles and the Odes of Solomon, but on investigation it was found that there is no recent and accessible English translation of the Christian Sibyllines (the selection in Charles, *Apocrypha and Pseudepigrapha*, contains only the Jewish) and this section was accordingly retained. The Odes, however, are available in the Harris-Mingana edition, and their omission here was therefore more readily acceptable, especially since in the German volume they figure in an appendix. Unfortunately this involves the sacrifice of Bauer's apparatus, but his introduction has been retained.

That it has been possible to produce this English version within a comparatively short interval after the publication of the German edition is due to the collaboration and courtesy of the German publishers, who made copies of the page-proofs available so that the work of translation could begin. The whole has been checked against the published German volume, and the texts against the originals. Some of us, in fact, have worked with both the German and the original text before us from the outset.

In this connection thanks are due to Dr. J. W. B. Barns and the editors of the *Journal of Theological Studies* for permission to reproduce Dr. Barns's translation of a Coptic fragment of the Acts of Andrew, originally published in that Journal: to Professor G. Quispel and Dr. J. Zandee, who revised and corrected the translation of the Coptic papyrus of the same Acts, now in Utrecht: and to Professor R. Kasser, who revised the translation of a fragment of the Acts of Paul from the Bodmer collection. Principal Matthew Black has checked the translation of the Hymn of the Pearl in the Acts of Thomas against the Syriac.

In one respect this volume differs from its predecessor; since it appears that some English-speaking scholars do not make use of Harvey's divisions of Irenaeus, and the numbering of earlier editors is given in the margins of Harvey's edition, references to Irenaeus in this volume have been left unchanged. English translations of books in other languages have of course been noted wherever possible.

Finally, it is a pleasure for the editor once more to express his thanks to those who have co-operated in the preparation of the book; first of all to his collaborators in the work of translation, and secondly to the staff of the Lutterworth Press. Among them two deserve special mention: Dr. Hill took over the responsibility for his section at short notice when the original translator, for good and sufficient reason, found himself unable to fulfil the assignment, and has also undertaken the considerable burden of preparing the index. Only the editor can fully appreciate the service rendered by Miss H. M. Wilson in seeing the book through the press. Suffice it to say that the news of her impending retirement provided further stimulus to the expeditious completion of the second volume. It is a very great pleasure to record that the tradition has been faithfully maintained by her successor.

R. McL. W.

St. Andrews
 1964

THIS SECOND VOLUME of the *Neutestamentliche Apokryphen* has been rather longer in making its appearance than the contributors, the editor and the publishers would have liked. The reasons for this regrettable delay lie partly in the editor's heavy burden of other responsibilities, partly in the difficulty of setting proper limits to the material here to be presented, and of securing its correct selection and arrangement, and partly in the expectation, unfortunately not fulfilled, that it might be possible to include in this collection new texts from the great Coptic Gnostic library of Nag Hammadi which were relevant to the subject. Since the publication of these texts is making only slow progress we finally had to abandon any consideration of the "Apocalypses" and "Acts" discovered at Nag Hammadi, unless we were prepared to wait for at least another five years.

It may however be observed that the titles used in the reports about the Nag Hammadi discovery which have so far appeared, titles which indeed for the most part correspond to the Coptic titles, are not to be utilized without further ado for the form-critical classification of the documents concerned. Rather must we await their publication before we can say whether the "Coptic Gnostic Apocalypses" are Apocalypses in the sense in which this term has hitherto been used. The same holds for the "Acts of Peter and the Twelve Apostles" in Codex VI. Cf. the survey by Martin Krause, Der koptische Handschriftenfund bei Nag Hammadi, Umfang und Inhalt, *Mitteilungen des Deutschen Archäologischen Instituts*, Abt. Kairo, 18, 1962, pp. 121–132. This contains also further literature which appeared after Puech's contribution to volume I (pp. 158ff.; English ed., pp. 231ff.), together with a concordance to the numbering of the Codices in Puech, Doresse and Krause-Labib. The last named is now probably to be regarded as the standard numbering. Of importance are the four volumes of texts so far published;

1. *Die koptisch-gnostische Schrift ohne Titel aus Codex II von Nag Hammadi im Koptischen Museum zu Alt-Kairo.* Herausgegeben, übersetzt und bearbeitet von Alexander Böhlig und Pahor Labib, Berlin 1962 (=Deutsche Akademie der Wissenschaften zu Berlin, Institut für Orientforschung, Veröffentlichung Nr. 58).

2. *Koptisch-gnostische Apokalypsen aus Codex V von Nag Hammadi im Koptischen Museum zu Alt-Kairo.* Herausgegeben, übersetzt und bearbeitet von Alexander Böhlig und Pahor Labib, Halle-

Wittenberg 1963 (=Sonderband der wissenschaftlichen Zeit-schrift der Martin-Luther-Universität Halle-Wittenberg) (so far not available to me).

3. *Die drei Versionen des Apokryphen des Johannes im Koptischen Museum zu Alt-Kairo.* Herausgegeben von Martin Krause und Pahor Labib, Wiesbaden 1962 (=Abhandlungen des Deutschen Archäologischen Instituts in Kairo, Koptische Reihe Bd. I).[1]

4. *Das Evangelium nach Philippos.* Herausgegeben und übersetzt von Walter C. Till, Berlin 1963 (Patristische Texte und Studien, Bd. 2).[2]

We can only wish and hope that the publication of the texts, found in 1945-46, may proceed somewhat more rapidly than hitherto, in order that the evaluation of this material may be undertaken. In this connection, and particularly for the field of the New Testament Apocrypha, questions of *Formgeschichte* ought not to be pushed unduly into the background in comparison with those of *Religionsgeschichte*. But only then will it be possible to decide whether and to what extent these texts are to be reckoned among the New Testament Apocrypha at all.

The present volume is considerably more bulky than the first. In particular the complete translations of the five great Acts have contributed to its inflation. That it thus became impossible to include the Apostolic Fathers, for which some reviewers of the first volume expressed a wish, may be readily understood. Whether these texts ought to be associated at all with the New Testament Apocrypha seems to me to be questionable.

The first volume in general met with a cordial reception. Many reviewers, however, complained that in H. C. Puech's contribu-tion the complete text of the Gospel of Thomas and the Gospel of Philip was not provided. Reference has already been made in the preface to volume I to the considerable legal difficulties with which we had to contend. It need only be added here that H. C. Puech has faithfully abided by certain agreements which for others have evidently been of no consequence. In the meantime the two texts mentioned have appeared in several German translations (cf. Krause, *op. cit.*). The English edition of volume I includes the Gospel of Thomas as an appendix. A supplementary volume does not secm to me at present to be appropriate. On the other hand, a later revision of the work, which for the moment is not possible, will require to take the whole Nag Hammadi library into account and present more texts than we can do as

---

[1] An edition of the Coptic text from Codex II, with an English translation, has been published by S. Giversen, *Apocryphon Johannis*, Copenhagen 1963.

[2] English translations of the text have been published by C. J. de Catanzaro (JTS 13 (1962) 35ff.) and by R. McL. Wilson, *The Gospel of Philip* (with Introduction and Commentary: London and New York 1962).

yet. For the progress of scientific work on the New Testament Apocrypha the interested reader may be referred to the annual *Bibliographia Patristica* (Bd. I/1956, 1959ff., ed. W. Schneemelcher).

For volume II also I have to thank many friends and helpers. In particular mention should be made of the contributors, who placed their work at our disposal and have often shown much patience. Of their number Walter Bauer and Hugo Duensing have in the interval passed away. Both were especially closely associated with our work. We shall keep their memory thankfully in honour. A. Kurfess was prevented by serious illness from preparing his manuscript for the press and correcting the proofs, and these tasks had to be taken over by the editor. Here and elsewhere Knut Schäferdiek, Siegfried Helmer, Jürgen Regul and Christoph Bizer have helped untiringly to bring the work to a satisfactory conclusion. In this volume also I have to thank my friend P. Vielhauer for his manifold counsel. Finally, cordial thanks are due to the publisher, Herr H. G. Siebeck, for all his patience and understanding.

WILHELM SCHNEEMELCHER

Bonn,
10*th September,* 1963

CONTENTS

19

CONTENTS

B. WRITINGS RELATING TO THE APOSTLES

NON-BIBLICAL MATERIAL ABOUT THE APOSTLES

INTRODUCTION

(*W. Schneemelcher*)

1. APOSTLE AND APOSTOLIC

LITERATURE (only a selection from the more recent literature): O. Linton, *Das Problem der Urkirche in der neueren Forschung*, 1932; K. H. Rengstorf, Art. ἀπόστολος, *ThWtb* I, pp. 406–448 (ET *Apostleship*, 1952); W. Bauer, *Rechtgläubigkeit und Ketzerei im ältesten Christentum*, 1934; E. Käsemann, "Die Legitimität des Apostels", *ZNW* 41, 1942, pp. 33–71; W. G. Kümmel, *Kirchenbegriff und Geschichtsbewusstsein in der Urgemeinde und bei Jesus*, 1943; H. von Campenhausen, "Der urchristliche Apostelbegriff", *Studia Theol.* 1, 1948, pp. 96–130; J. Munck, "Paul, the Apostles and the Twelve", *Studia Theol.* 3, 1950, pp. 96–110; R. Bultmann, *Theologie des Neuen Testaments*, 1953 ([3]1958) (ET 1952, 1955); H. von Campenhausen, *Kirchliches Amt und geistliche Vollmacht in den ersten drei Jahrhunderten*, 1953; A. Ehrhardt, *The Apostolic Succession in the first two Centuries of the Church*, 1953; E. Lohse, "Ursprung und Prägung des christlichen Apostolats", *Theol. Zeitschr.* 9, 1953, pp. 259–275; E. M. Kredel, "Der Apostelbegriff in der neueren Exegese", *Zeitschr. f. kath. Theologie* 78, 1956, pp. 169–193 and 257–305; G. Klein, *Die zwölf Apostel, Ursprung und Gehalt einer Idee*, 1961; E. Haenchen, *Die Apostelgeschichte*, [13]1961; W. Schmithals, *Das kirchliche Apostelamt, Eine historische Untersuchung*, 1961.

"At present the question as to the origin and the idea of the apostolate is one of the most intricate and difficult problems of New Testament scholarship." Such was the judgment of E. Haupt (*Zum Verständis des Apostolats im NT*, p. 1) as early as 1896, and today in fact that judgment still holds good. "The discussion of our problem is, I admit, not yet nearly concluded. . . . In the extensive literature on our subject all the sources have been investigated in all their aspects: the points of view that have been put forward keep repeating with no prospect of an end to the discussion. It can be carried further only with the help of new sources, which are however hardly to be expected, or of essentially new ideas." That is the opinion given in 1961 by W. Schmithals (*Das kirchliche Apostelamt*, p. 12). It needs doubtless to be added that even "essentially new ideas" (to make no mention of dogmatic prejudices which, precisely in this problem, are a grievous hindrance to the historical comprehension of the phenomenon) are perhaps not the right way to a satisfactory and recognized solution. Certainly the somewhat fantastic hypotheses in Schmithals' brilliant book hardly entice us to pursue the way of "essentially new ideas".

In this necessarily concisely worded introduction to the apocrypha that are bound up with the names of apostles, it cannot of course be our task to discuss in a comprehensive way the problem of the genesis and character of the early Christian apostolate. We must be satisfied with a few observations introductory to the literature assembled in this volume and to its problems. Also it is not possible to present an assessment, documented and supported by a cloud of witnesses for and against, of all the theses that have been brought forward in recent decades. We would merely attempt in a brief outline to indicate the problems so far as they are of importance for our literature. In this connection the first question that must be asked is whether the tendency towards a special appreciation of the apostles that comes to light in the pseudapostolic literature, and also in the works which deal with the life and work of one or more of the apostles, can be observed already in the early period and from what time and to what extent that is the case.[1]

(a) The word ἀπόστολος occurs in profane Greek in different senses. As all recent lexicons and special investigations show, it can mean "a naval expedition, the leader of such an undertaking". It is difficult to decide whether the neuter form τὸ ἀπόστολον in the sense "a ship ready to set sail or already dispatched" is older than the masculine. In the papyri ἀπόστολος crops up as "bill of delivery", once also as "passport". Besides this usage, which belongs to the field of maritime commerce, we come sporadically, from the time of Herodotus on, upon the meaning "emissary, messenger".[2] This general sense is also to be assumed in some New Testament passages: Jn. 13:16; Phil. 2:25; 2 Cor. 8:23. Besides these there may also be mentioned the New Testament passages (Lk. 11:49; Hebr. 3:1) in which likewise the term is not used in the specific sense of a particular group of "apostles". The question whether the particular use is to be explained on the basis of this general usage must be answered in the negative. Throughout the area in which Greek was spoken the word was known, but it did not have associated with it the distinctive meaning which ἀπόστολος now has in most New Testament

[1] That in this connection we must not operate with the apocryphal Acts of the 2nd and 3rd centuries would hardly need to be said, were it not that in Schmithals we read the astonishing sentence, "The title of apostle remains preserved in the Gnostic literature, as can be understood, in the Acts of Apostles, for, although their conception of the apostle is Gnostic, they are concerned throughout with characters from the circle of the Twelve" (p. 180). Let alone the vagueness that prevails in this sentence, it must be underlined that there can be no talk whatever of a uniform conception of the apostle in these Acts and that at least the earliest apocryphal Acts (APt and AP) have nothing or very little to do with Gnosis.

[2] Instances in Bauer, *Wörterbuch zum NT s.v.*, and in the literature that has been cited.

passages. In the field of Hellenism no actual continuity can be shown from the general to the particular sense of the word.

It has been supposed that for the New Testament apostolate there is a Jewish prototype, the institution of the *Schaliach*, which was taken over and designated by the well-known Greek word ἀπόστολος (on this thesis cf. among others Rengstorf). But especially of late years considerable objections have been raised to this hypothesis (Munck, Ehrhardt, Klein, Schmithals, etc.). These need not be repeated here. Decisive on the one hand is the fact that the Jewish establishment of the "envoy" is supported only by quite late evidence in respect of those details of the institution which are important for this question, and on the other hand the fact that especially in Paul, who is for us an essential and above all the earliest witness for the early Christian apostolate, nothing of the Jewish legal institution of the *Schaliach* is to be found. Undoubtedly the linguistic derivation and the historical explanation of the New Testament apostolate from the Jewish institution of the *Schaliach* cannot be maintained. "And thus the question as to the possible sources of the apostolate in the environment of the NT, which since Rengstorf seemed to be definitely disposed of, has once again become a problem" (Klein, *op. cit.*, p. 27).

(*b*) The problem of the origin of the apostolate is further complicated by the fact that to date there is no consistent view as to when for the first time in the Christian sphere there can have been talk of apostles—in the specific sense. The question has first to be narrowed down to this: Is this phenomenon rooted in the life of Jesus? The answer to that is certainly rendered difficult by the fact that with the problem of the "apostle" in the life-time of Jesus there is closely bound up the other problem of the "twelve" and their call by Jesus. But these two must be kept apart. It cannot be disputed that through his preaching Jesus gathered a circle of followers. In the Synoptic Gospels it is reported how he was accompanied and surrounded by his disciples. At the same time it is evident that often these notes have so stereotyped and schematic a ring that they may be assigned to the later redaction of the Evangelists.[1] But the fact that in the Synoptics the disciples are often introduced into an earlier tradition which was originally concerned with Jesus alone, naturally makes no difference to this, that there was a circle of followers of Jesus which it is now difficult indeed to comprehend or circumscribe. The tradition

---

[1] Cf. also Bultmann, *Geschichte der synopt. Tradition*,[3] pp. 368f. (ET 1963, 343f.), where it is also pointed out how the idea of the regular accompanying of Jesus by the disciples is enhanced into the dogmatic idea of the twelve as the authoritative witnesses of the gospel.

regarding this circle was first moulded into fixed forms in the post-Easter community, i.e. at a time when this circle had already a quite definite position in the community or else had dispersed. The assembling of the 'twelve apostles' (e.g. in Mt. 10:2; Lk. 6:13) is thus a later formulation. The early formula in 1 Cor. 15:3ff. still separates the twelve from the apostles.

Wellhausen (*Einleitung in die drei ersten Evangelien*, 2nd ed. 1901, pp. 138ff.) has already alluded to the difficulties which confront the assumption that the twelve belonged to the life-time of Jesus. Vielhauer has in my opinion brought forward conclusive proof that the twelve are a phenomenon of the post-Easter community, which indeed soon disappeared again (P. Vielhauer, Gottesreich und Menschensohn, *Dehn-Festschrift* 1957, pp. 62ff.; cf. also Klein, *op. cit.* pp. 34ff.). The arguments need not be repeated here in detail. 1 Cor. 15:3–5 seems to me decisive, since here reference is made to the twelve, although according to the Gospels we ought to speak only of eleven disciples.

If now the twelve do not go back to the life-time of Jesus, there still remains the other question whether Jesus designated a group of his followers as apostles. That the institution of the *Schaliach*, which in this connection readily comes to mind, is of no assistance, has already been stated. And here other alleged proofs also break down (cf. Klein, *op. cit.*, pp. 28ff.). Consequently we are obliged to say: The institution and conception of the apostles do not have their roots in the *historia Jesu*.

(*c*) How does it stand now with the twelve and the apostles in the primitive church, i.e. in the first circle of Christian believers after the events of Easter? This circle, which was brought together and held together by belief in the risen Christ, understood itself as the eschatological people of God, as the church of the last time (the term ἐκκλησία implies that). According to 1 Cor. 15:5 the first appearances of the risen Christ were granted to Peter and the twelve. There is much other evidence that Peter was in fact the first witness of the resurrection and that he, who already in the life-time of Jesus had followed the Lord, occupied on that account a leading position in the nascent community. It may be presumed that he was first of all the head of the twelve. These twelve were an institution which was closely connected with the primitive church's apocalyptic world of ideas (cf. Mt. 19:28), but this institution was not of long duration; the authority of Peter certainly outlasted it. Paul no longer knew the twelve as an established institution functioning in his time. On the occasion of his first visit to Jerusalem, so he reports in Gal. 1:18f., he spent 14 days with Peter, but "other of the apostles" he did not see, save James. At the time of this visit, then, the group of the twelve was already detached from that of the apostles, among whom Peter was now again the leader. Moreover at this time James, the brother of the Lord, appears already to play a certain part in the church, without indeed belonging to the apostles.[1] Whether besides Peter any other member of the circle of the twelve was added to the group of the apostles is not known. But it is improbable, for the apostles belong to another context. Even if we cannot say with certainty how this institution came into being, it nevertheless seems clear that the apostles did not belong to the apocalyptically minded Christian believers (probably of Jewish extraction). We prefer to reckon to the circle of the Hellenists (Acts 6) those who in 1 Cor. 15:7 are named after James as witnesses of the resurrection. At all events that seems to me the explanation that lies nearest to hand. According to the fragmentary information about them which can still be gathered from Acts these Hellenists were the people who first applied themselves to missionary work. From the term ἀπόστολος it may be supposed that this title came into vogue in this circle and that thus first of all it denoted simply a special group of missionaries.[2]

The apostolate was certainly in existence *before* Paul (cf. Gal. 1:17). As has already been stated, he no longer knew the twelve as an authority, but the apostles (and moreover the στῦλοι, a treatment of whom is not needed here), who now exercised the function of proclamation outside Jerusalem.

(*d*) It is only indirectly that we can form an idea of the activity of these apostles. Above all it was missionary in character (cf. e.g. 1 Cor. 9:3ff.; in *Didache* 11 this function of the apostles is still clear). Paul certainly wrought in many respects exactly as did the other apostles, but he gave the office a distinctive theological foundation and great theological importance. That cannot be entered into here (cf. e.g. Schmithals, *op. cit.*, pp. 13ff.; also the additional literature there). Only this may be pointed out: according to Paul the apostle is called directly by Christ (in his own case that took place outside Damascus) and he has now to proclaim the word in accordance with this call. But he is not an apostle—and this is important for our context—because he was an eyewitness of the life and deeds of Jesus. Luke gives this stipulation in his account of the choice of Matthias (Acts 1:21–22). Moreover the requirement that a candidate for the college of

[1] It is clear that the very difficult problem of Gal. 1:15ff. cannot be discussed here.

[2] The relation to the seven spoken of in Acts 6 remains questionable. These seven were obviously not apostles. The chronological questions are also difficult: according to 1 Cor. 15:7 the apostles were witnesses of the resurrection before Paul. Therefore the "Hellenists", if the apostles came from their circle, must very early have constituted themselves as a special group. Now that is quite possible since already in the life-time of Jesus the body of his followers was not composed merely of Jews (cf. W. Bauer, Jesus der Galiläer, *Festgabe für A. Jülicher*, 1927, pp. 16–34).

apostles must have been in contact with the earthly Jesus from the time of his baptism by John up to the time of his ascension is bound up with the idea of the apostolate of the twelve.[1] G. Klein has sought to show that Luke may have been the person who devised the combination 'the twelve apostles'. But against that, as Haenchen (*Die Apostelgeschichte*, p. 679) shows, there speaks among other things the fact that this combination of the twelve with the apostles is already made in the logia source (Q; cf. Mt. 19:28 and Lk. 22:47).

Be that as it may, the differences between Paul and Luke in their conception of the office of the apostle are manifest; and in spite of Klein's work it remains an open question when this momentous narrowing of the apostle-concept to the twelve came about. For it cannot be denied that here an alteration took place. To bring the matter to a point, it may be stated that Paul sees in the apostles the messengers of the gospel, whilst Luke sees in them the witnesses of the *historia Jesu* and so the guarantors for the truth of the church's preaching. To be sure it may be disputed whether already in the time of Paul the twelve and the apostles were not set in a close relation to one another (cf. Haenchen, p. 680). But the theological valuation of the apostolate is in Luke quite certainly other than it is in Paul.

Moreover it ought assuredly not to be overlooked that the view that the apostle should be a witness of the resurrection (Acts 1:22) is probably connected with the fact that from the beginning this office was bound up with Christophanies. The apostle is called by the risen Lord; therefore Paul declares himself to be the last in the enumeration 1 Cor. 15:8. It is quite possible that in this fact there was given the starting point for the evolution of the Lukan idea of the apostle. Further there also lies here the reason why all apostles were missionaries but not all missionaries were apostles, just as on the other hand not all those to whom a Christophany was granted became apostles.

(*e*) It is striking that in Acts a considerable dignity is bestowed on the twelve apostles, but that the adjective ἀποστολικός does not occur. 'Apostolic' as a designation for a special doctrine or for the church occurs nowhere in the whole of the NT. In it the apostles are spoken of merely as persons. Whenever Paul or Luke speaks of apostles, the background is never some abstract 'apostolicity'; rather the measure for this office rests in the case of Paul in the event of the call by the risen Christ and in the case of Luke in personal connection with the *historia Jesu*. It is questionable whether Luke still knew apostles. The *Didache* by this title

---

[1] After all, if we follow the Gospels, no disciple would have fulfilled the requirement set out in Acts 1:21f.

means wandering missionaries. It is perhaps possible that Luke wanted to deny this title to such wandering preachers since among them there may well have been many a noteworthy prophet, and that his conception of the apostle is to be explained from that. But that makes no difference to the fact that in Luke what is 'apostolic' is still understood from the point of view of the person. Certainly we see in Acts the start of the evolution which led to the dogmatic abstraction according to which what was 'apostolic' became the guarantee of the genuine tradition. The appearance of the adjective ἀποστολικός in Ignatius and in the *Martyrdom of Polycarp*[1] is a sign of the view, by then firmly rooted, that what is 'apostolic' is of special worth in various respects, especially in reference to doctrine. The exhortations in the Pastoral Epistles to hold fast 'the sound teaching' (cf. 1 Tim. 1:10, also the excursus on the passage by Dibelius in the *Handbuch zum NT*) are further examples of this evolution, which then debouches into the idea, developed in the conflict with Gnosticism, that the apostles are the bearers of the tradition (see also Hornschuh, pp. 74ff. below).

2. THE ORIGIN OF THE PSEUDAPOSTOLIC LITERATURE

The literature assembled in the following pages is very diverse in form and in content, but is held together by its connection with the apostles, whether it be a question of apostolic pseudepigrapha or whether individual apostles and their fortunes are the substance of what is presented. The origin of this literature cannot be expounded in a single sentence, but has very diverse causes and motives. That will be made clear in detail. Here at the outset attention will be paid only to two general points of view.

(a) The short sketch of the evolution of the institution and conception of the apostle has already made manifest to us some of the assumptions that were decisive for the origin of the pseudapostolic literature. Only because the thesis was arrived at that the apostles were the guarantors for the true and pure tradition was it possible to come by pseudapostolic writings. Not until what was 'apostolic' had become the standard—assuredly in very different ways—had the writing or circulation of books in the names of apostles any significance. The earliest example is *The Teaching of the Twelve Apostles*, *The Didache*, of which the title probably was "The Teaching of the Lord for the Gentiles by the

---

[1] Ignatius, *Trall. Praescr.*, salutes the church after the apostolic fashion (ἐν ἀποστολικῷ χαρακτῆρι); in *Mart. Pol.* 16. 2 Polycarp is described as an "apostolic and prophetic teacher".

Twelve Apostles". It is characteristic that it was precisely a treatise specially concerned with Church order that was composed as a pseudapostolic writing. In the literature of the early church devoted to canonical law it had many successors. The Pastoral Epistles also, which belong to the same context as the early pseudapostolic literature, have an emphatically judicial purpose.

Further, as the apocryphal letters of apostles show, there was a desire through such concoctions to intensify and above all to legitimate the conflict against the heretics. The authority of the apostles was so consolidated dogmatically that works originated in the "apostolic" church which turned this authority to account for the questions of the day.

On the other hand, this sense of what is 'apostolic' had this further consequence in the church that people wanted to learn more about the persons of the apostles than is given in the New Testament. Already in the Acts of the Apostles Luke has used many legends which exhibit the marks of a pious curiosity about the life and work of the apostles (cf. Acts 5:15: the shadow of Peter; Acts 19:11f.: Paul's handkerchief). At the same time the apostles easily turned into miracle-workers such as were then known in heathendom. "Here we see the danger by which the popular tradition regarding the apostolic miracles was threatened: it converted the μάρτυς Ἰησοῦ Χριστοῦ into a man who is full of miraculous power even as far as his shadow and through this fullness makes the divine authority immediately observable" (Haenchen, *Apostelgeschichte*, p. 202). That is of course absolutely at variance with the picture of the apostle which Paul has sketched (cf. E. Käsemann, *ZNW* 41, 1942, pp. 33ff.). Here undoubtedly Luke follows popular tradition. It may however be said that for him these folk-legends were not the main thing, but are intended merely to underscore the edifying character of his theologically orientated work.

In the course of the 2nd century legendary traits come more and more largely into the foreground. The stabilizing of the church as an "apostolic" institution, the conflict with the Gnostics who appealed to the apostles for their esoteric doctrine, the more vigorous propagation of Christianity, the coming into vogue of the veneration of the martyrs, and many other motives, brought it about that the life and doings of the apostles were dealt with in greater detail and at the same time that a more and more coloured picture of them was formed.

In the environment there were literary models of diverse sorts for stories of the life of the apostles, and in different ways these may have had an effect on the oral tradition as upon its fixation in writing in the apocryphal Acts. But the process with which we have here to do must not be understood onesidedly on the basis of the literary history. These Acts are indeed literary documents, but above all they are popular stories in regard to which questions as to style and type certainly do not stand in the foreground (see pp. 167ff. below).

In the pseudapostolic literature too a relation to the canonical writings is to be observed. In this literature also as in the apocryphal Gospels there are works which came into being at a time when the canon was still not closed or was not yet fully established. Admittedly the number of pseudapostolic apocrypha which have here to be counted is very small. In the case of most of the works which are to be dealt with in this volume it must be assumed that they originated at a time later than the canonical writings and also than the formation of the canon. This means that the question whether the apocryphal writings of apostles were intended to supersede or supplement the canonical writings cannot be answered so simply as in the case of the apocryphal Gospels. In the case of most of the texts with which we have to do it should be assumed that by means of them the authors meant to supplement the canon or particular documents that were respected and valued. In the case of a portion of them a connection with the types and forms that lie before us in the New Testament is notorious. An epistle such as the apocryphal Epistle to the Laodiceans, which is in fact merely an omnium-gatherum of passages from the epistles of Paul, has been conformed to the pattern of his epistles. On the other hand, it is questionable whether and to what extent the Lukan pattern was decisive for the apocryphal Acts (cf. on this pp. 169ff. below). Very much more significant here has been the influx of pre-Christian and non-Christian literary forms and types. For this process what has already been said in the General Introduction (Vol. I, pp. 63f.) holds good: we are not concerned here with a purely formal problem of literary history. But this process is connected with the whole development of ecclesiastical history, the multifariousness of which comes to expression in the apocryphal writings connected with the apostles in the same way as it does in the apocryphal Gospels. That in quite a distinct way the later Acts are tendency literature, in which the canonical pattern plays no part at all, may at least be noted.

(b) Already in the case of the apocryphal Gospels we can hardly speak of a uniform literary type. In Vol. I, pp. 8off. we have attempted to distinguish three different types of apocryphal Gospels, taking their relation to the canonical Gospels as the important matter in differentiating them. It is much more difficult to arrange according to type the material with which we have to do in the case of the apostolic apocrypha. Special groups certainly stand out, such as the pseudapostolic Epistles or the apocryphal Acts, for which we have also patterns or resemblances in the types and forms of the New Testament. But in addition there are works which evade a clear classification or belong to a type which has nothing to do with the types that occur in the New Testament (e.g. the *Kerygma Petrou*).

The reason why we have here to do with much more varicoloured material is that the concept 'what is apostolic' played so significant a part. On that account things the most dissimilar were bound up with the names and figures of the apostles. Dogmatic, polemic and apologetic intentions were brought into connection with the apostles in the same way as canonical purposes or edifying and entertaining aims. The literary genus of which use was made was in each case determined by the end in view. It is characteristic that the correspondence between the Corinthian church and Paul (3 Cor., cf. pp. 373ff. below), which is a part of the Acts of Paul, has as its purport the warding off of the Gnostic heretics, i.e. a dogmatic theme, whilst the remaining Acts of Paul scarcely permit us to detect such a polemic, but are intended rather to be edifying and entertaining. For such edifying purposes, however, the form of the fictitious or legendary folk-story was more suitable than the epistolary form. Of course in the case of our literature, which, it is clear, had its origin in circles which cannot be considered intellectually leading classes, the types and forms do not permit their being worked out tidily. On the whole, however, the distinction just sketched may be used.

It thus becomes clear once more that the questions of type- and form-history never present purely formal problems, but that form and content belong closely together. That certainly also holds good for the narrative material which, before it was fixed in writing or worked together by a redactor, was already handed down orally. On the other hand, it is significant that it is precisely in the discourses of the apocryphal Acts, which are the work of the redactors or authors of these histories of the apostles, that the real intentions of these authors come best to expression.

All these observations amount to this, that the methods of type- and form-history, which have so much proved their value in the investigation of the Gospels, can and must be applied to the pseudapostolic literature also. Only with their help can these documents be correctly opened up as sources for the history of Christianity in the 2nd and 3rd centuries. Here lie tasks which must be set about in the future.

34

XI

THE PICTURE OF THE APOSTLE IN EARLY CHRISTIAN TRADITION

1. ACCOUNTS[1]

(W. Bauer)

I. NUMBER: LISTS OF THE APOSTLES. It is early evangelic information that Jesus chose for himself out of the multitude of his followers twelve men who were particularly intimate with him, who assisted him in his work and continued it. Whether their appointment actually goes back to the historical Jesus[2] or whether the twelve are an institution of the post-Easter church,[3] is a disputed question. In any case the number twelve stands so fast that exceedingly often *twelve* disciples are spoken of where actually only *eleven* can be meant,[4] e.g. *Gospel of Peter* 59; *Ascension of Isaiah* 3. 17; 4. 3; 11. 22 (see pp. 642ff. below); *Kerygma Petrou* (see pp. 94ff. below).[5] It is a closed circle which retains its name even when there are losses. In the same way Xenophon (*Hell.* 2. 4. 23) speaks of the *thirty* although Critias and Hippomachus are already dead (2. 4. 19). The practice of making comparisons and speculations in which the twelve is the significant factor shows how little doubt can be thrown on the number: thus in Rev. (21:14); in Justin; Tertullian; Irenaeus; *Excerpta ex Theodoto* in Clement of Alexandria; Hippolytus.[6] The more remarkable in the face of that is the uncertainty of the opponents of Christianity: Celsus:

---

[1] The following section was gone over by the late W. Bauer, but had then to be revised by M. Hornschuh. In spite of the pains taken by Hornschuh (and also by K. Schäferdiek and J. Regul) the literature has by no means been brought up everywhere to its latest state. Nevertheless I did not wish to give up this contribution, which as it stands is remarkable for the wealth of the material which it presents. *W. Sch.*

[2] See among others Rengstorf, Art. δώδεκα, *ThWtb* II, 1935, pp. 325ff.; Oepke, *Das neue Gottesvolk*, 1950, pp. 165ff.; v. Campenhausen, *Kirchliches Amt und geistliche Vollmacht in den ersten drei Jahrhunderten*, 1953, p. 15; G. Bornkamm, *Jesus von Nazareth*, 1956, p. 138 (ET 1960, p. 150).

[3] So among others, following Schleiermacher and Wellhausen, Bultmann, *Theologie des NT*, [3]1958, §6, 1 (ET 1952); cf. also *Geschichte der synoptischen Tradition*, [3]1957, pp. 368ff. (ET 1963, 343ff.); Vielhauer, *Festschr. für G. Dehn*, ed. by W. Schneemelcher, 1957, pp. 62f.; encyclopaedic: G. Klein, *Die zwölf Apostel, Ursprung und Gehalt einer Idee (Forsch. z. Rel. und Lit. des A.u.NT*, NF 59), 1961.

[4] Thus correctly Mt. 28:16; Mk. 16:14; Lk. 24:9, 33; Acts 1:26.

[5] Cf. also Aristides, *Apol.* 2 (Hennecke, *TU* 4. 3, 1893); Justin, *Apol.* 1. 39.

[6] Justin, *dial. c. Tryph.* 42. – Tertullian *adv. Marc.* IV. 13. 3 (*Corpus Christianorum ser. lat.* 1, 1954, p. 572). – Irenaeus, *adv. haer.* I. 3, 2; 18, 4; II. 21, 1; IV. 21, 3. – Clem. Alex., *Exc. ex Theod.* 25, 1f. (*GCS* 17, Stählin, p. 115, 10–14); Hippol., *Exposition of the Blessings of Moses on the 12 Tribes*, XV 6 (G. N. Bonwetsch, *Drei georgisch erhaltene Schriften des Hippolyt*, *TU* 26. 1, 1904, pp. 67f.).

ten or eleven (in Origen, *c. Cels.* I. 62), also only ten (II. 46); the Babylonian Talmud speaks of five pupils of Jesus with the names Matthai, Naqai, Nezer, Buni, Thoda (Sanhedrin 43a; cf. *Handb.*, p. 62); Hierocles mentions the number 900 (Lactantius, *div. inst.* V.3.4.).

Whilst the number stands fast, the names by no means completely agree even in the New Testament lists of the apostles, and there are variations also in their sequence. The most serious difference is that a member of the college of the apostles is called *Lebbaeus* in Mt. (10:2–4), *Thaddaeus* in Mk. (3:16–19) and *Judas son of James* in Lk. (6:16; Acts 1:13).[1] The *Act. Thom.* 1 repeats in essentials the catalogue of the canonical Acts. On the other hand, the earliest period still has at its disposal a complete catalogue which to a considerable extent is constructed otherwise than the Biblical lists. Both *The Apostolic Church Order*[2] and the *Epistula Apostolorum* 2(13); see Vol. I, p. 192) contain an enumeration of eleven names of apostles, and the peculiarities that these have in common show that they belong very closely to one another, despite a difference in one name (*Apostolic Church Order*: Simon; *Epistula Apostolorum*: Judas Zelotes) and changes in the sequence. In both John stands at the beginning and Nathanael and Cephas—the latter in addition to Peter—appear as apostles. Whilst Baumstark (*ZNW* 14, 1913, pp. 232ff.) assumes a common source, most probably the *Gospel of the Egyptians*, and in that has met with the agreement of F. Haase (*ZNW* 16, 1915, p. 106), C. Schmidt[3] explains the connections that undoubtedly exist with the help of the assumption of a dependence of the *Apostolic Church Order* on the *Epistle*.[4]

In addition to the lists which comprise all the twelve or eleven units there are others which show only a portion of the names. We refer here less to John 21:2 or to the abrupt conclusion of the *Gospel of Peter* (see Vol. I, p. 187) than to Papias (see pp. 78f. below) and to the *Gospel of the Ebionites* (see Vol. I, p. 156) where Jesus, after he has mentioned eight names, of which John is again the first, proceeds:

You I will to be twelve apostles for a testimony unto Israel.

There is much to be said for the view that the shortening of the list is not a charge on the apocryphal Gospel but on Epiphanius

[1] On the attempt, which can be traced back to Tatian (Hjelt, *Die altsyrische Evangelienübersetzung und Tatians Diatessaron*, 1901, pp. 34; 124f.), to hold together what strives apart, see Th. Zahn, *Das Evangelium des Matthäus*, ³1910, pp. 390–392.
[2] Ed. Hilgenfeld, *Novum Testamentum extra canonum receptum*, 4th part, ²1884, p. 111; A. Harnack, *Die Lehre der zwölf Apostel* (*TU* 2. 1–2), 1884, p. 225.
[3] *Gespräche Jesu mit seinen Jüngern nach der Auferstehung*, *TU* 43, 1919, p. 244.
[4] Cf. also Th. Schermann, *Die allgemeine Kirchenordnung, frühchristliche Liturgien und kirchliche Überlieferung* (*Studien zur Geschichte und Kultur des Altertums* 3) 3, 1916, pp. 601ff.

or one of his copyists. On the other hand Papias in his enumeration, which certainly illustrates the truth that the sequence need not always have a deep significance, gathers the rest of the apostles together in a general phrase. The sentence in the *First Book of Jeû* (c. 3; see Vol. I, p. 262):

All the apostles answered with one voice, Matthew and John, Philip and Bartholomew and James, saying . . .

is to be judged in the same way.

Regarding this Schmidt[1] rightly observes, "There are thus only five names mentioned and yet they are put down as the totality of the apostles; but we are not in the least justified in drawing from that the conclusion that the author did not know or had not read the names of the others. Rather, he has given prominence only to the most distinguished of them as, we find, is frequently the case in the church fathers. Names such as James the son of Alphaeus, Lebbaeus, Judas Iscariot or Matthias were of no interest whatever; in the post-apostolic period they step almost entirely into the background." In the writing edited as Book IV of the *Pistis Sophia* (*GCS* 45, p. 232) Thomas, Andrew, James, Simon "the Canaanite", Philip and Bartholomew are named and then there are mentioned summarily *the remaining disciples and women disciples*. In the *Manichaean Psalm-book*[2] we find two catalogues that do not altogether agree, each of eleven names from the circle of the twelve.

The one (p. 192, 5–20) makes of James the son of Alphaeus an *obedient disciple Alphaeus*, completely omits Thaddaeus (Lebbaeus, Judas son of James), and then recovers the number twelve by adding the apostle Paul. The other (p. 194, 7–17) does without him and likewise has no Thaddaeus, also it has no Matthew the tax-gatherer but a Levi with no indication of his calling (see p. 64 below).

As a sort of list of the apostles there can be counted the enumeration of the twelve apostles who in pseudo-Clement, *Rec.* I. 55–62, debate with the Jews and Samaritans in the temple at Jerusalem. Here we have the following sequence: 1. Matthew (55), 2. Andrew (56), 3. and 4. James and John (57), 5. Philip (58), 6. Bartholomew (59), 7. James the son of Alphaeus (59), 8. Lebbaeus (59), 9. Simon Cananaeus (60), 10. Barnabas who is also called Matthias (60), 11. Thomas (61), 12. Peter (62). That Peter, who is the speaker, names himself last is not surprising.

On apostle-registers belonging to later times see R. A. Lipsius,

---

[1] *Gnostische Schriften in koptischer Sprache, TU* 8. 1/2, 1892, p. 451.
[2] *A Manichaean Psalm-book*, ed. by C. R. C. Allberry, Stuttgart 1938 (=Manichaean Manuscripts in the Chester Beatty Collection, Vol. II).

Die apokryphen Apostelgeschichten und Apostellegenden I, 1883, pp. 22–25, 192–206, 210–215; II, 2, pp. 416ff.; supplementary vol., pp. 2–4, 14f., 16f., 19; Th. Schermann, *Propheten- und Apostellegenden nebst Jüngerkatalogen, TU* 31. 3, 1907, pp. 198ff.

2. THE APOSTLES IN THE RETINUE OF JESUS are described for the most part in pursuance of the New Testament statements or in connection with them. Yet the *Acts of John*, e.g., gives a presentation of their call which is designed to serve its peculiar conception of the person of Jesus (c. 88f., cf. 113: see p. 225 and p. 257 below). The chosen apostles are the true witnesses of the evangelic history. They have always been with the Lord and know everything that he has done and said: Irenaeus, *adv. haer.* II. 22. 5; Origen, *c. Cels.* VI. 8; Paul to the Corinthians in the *Acts of Paul* (see p. 375 below); pseudo-Clement, *hom.* XVII. 7; the Syriac *Didascalia* (p. 67, J. Flemming *TU* 25. 2, 1904). The Lukan Acts of the Apostles already formulates in 1:21f. the fundamental requirement for entrance into the college of the twelve apostles in these terms, that the claimant must have been a witness of the entire public ministry of Jesus beginning from the baptism of John. That in conformity with this the *Gospel of the Ebionites* makes the call of the disciples precede the baptism of the Lord, is likely, yet not altogether certain (cf. Vielhauer in Vol. I, p. 154).

Were now the disciples themselves baptized? The New Testament gives no clear information. It does not record a baptism of the disciples. On the other hand the Gospels underline the necessity of baptism for salvation (Jn. 3:5; Mt. 28:19; Mk. 16:16) and mention that the apostles on their part baptized (Jn. 4:2) and that at least a portion of them had belonged to the followers of the Baptist (Jn. 1:35, 40). Perhaps Jn. 13 may explain the matter to him who looks deeply into it. Tertullian attacks people, doubtless Marcionites, who, from the assumption that the apostles had not received Christian baptism, draw the conclusion that they missed salvation, but he shares the pre-supposition (*de bapt.* 12); for Jesus did not baptize and there was no Christian baptism until after the resurrection (c. 11). On the other hand Hermas (*sim.* IX. 16. 5) and pseudo-Cyprian (*de rebapt.* 6) are persuaded that the apostles were baptized in the name of Jesus. From the two passages we learn nothing further. Ephraem, however, in his *Commentary on the Diatessaron*[1] explains that Jesus rebaptized those who had been baptized by John. His text of the Gospels

---

[1] Edited by L. Leloir, *CSCO* 137, 1953, Armenian text; 145, 1954, Latin translation. In what follows citations are made, except where otherwise noted, only according to this edition, the page given first referring to the volume containing the Armenian text, the second to the one containing the Latin translation.

may to some extent have given him a right to do so, at least if the harmonizing reading of the Sinaitic Syriac in Jn. 4:2 *not our Lord alone baptized, but also his disciples* goes back to Tatian. It brings this passage into conformity with Jn. 3:22, 26; 4:1, and thereby delivers the christening-activity from all doubt. Also in the *Pistis Sophia* (c. 122, *GCS* 45, p. 202) Jesus appears baptizing. Therewith the condition is given for the information which Johannes Moschus has extracted from the 5th Book of the *Hypotyposes* of Clement of Alexandria (*GCS* 17, p. 196) that the apostles were baptized: Peter by Jesus, Andrew by Peter, James and John by Andrew, whilst the sons of Zebedee passed baptism on to the rest.[1]

That the disciples were of Jewish extraction is so obvious that it is mentioned only by the way, e.g. in the Syriac *Didascalia* (Flemming, p. 133). Sometimes still more particularly they are described jointly and severally as Galilaeans: Acts 2:7; *Acta Petr. et Andr.* 8 (Aa 2. 1, p. 121); Ephraem, *Commentary on the Diatessaron* (p. 57; p. 42, 22). Only of Matthew is it occasionally asserted that he had belonged to the uncircumcised (*Altercatio Simonis et Theophili* 20, Harnack, *TU* I. 3, pp. 26f., 47, 53), and this seems already to have been Marcion's opinion (Tertullian, *adv. Marc.* IV. 11, *Corp. Christ.* I, p. 565).

In opposition to the enemies of Christianity, who could not do enough in disparagement of the social class to which the disciples belonged (Celsus in Origen I. 62, 63; II. 46; Julian *c. Christianos* 199, 200, 226 Neumann), it is emphasized that the apostles were by no means sprung from wholly impecunious circles. Indeed the tax-gatherer Matthew could be called 'rich' (Clement of Alexandria, *quis div. salv.* 13), and in the *First Book of Jeû* 2 (*GCS* 45, p. 258) the apostles say:

We . . . have forsaken father and mother . . . have forsaken goods, have forsaken the splendour of a king and have followed thee.[2]

On the other hand, however, pseudo-Clement, *hom.* XII. 6, lets Peter and Andrew grow up as orphans in poverty and indigence.

Statements regarding the calling and the education of the apostles are tied up entirely with the New Testament: fishermen and tax-collectors, on the other hand unlearned and common men (Acts 4:13). That they were without even the rudiments of knowledge is a thought on which their opponents dwell with

---

[1] Cf. Th. Zahn, *Forschungen zur Geschichte des neutestamentlichen Kanons* III, pp. 69f.; later this statement is often repeated and still further elaborated, cf. A. Berendts, *Studien über Zacharias-Apokryphen* 1895, p. 104, n. 1; F. Diekamp, *Hippolytos von Theben* 1898, pp. 27, 120f.
[2] Cf. also 2 *Book of Jeû* 44, p. 306.

relish (Celsus in Origen, *c. Cels.* I. 62; Porphyry in pseudo-Jerome, *brev. in psalt.* on Ps. 81; Hierocles in Eusebius *c. Hierocl.* 2, *PG* 22, 800B). The Christians admit it in view of the New Testament, in particular Origen (*c. Cels.* I. 62; VI. 7; VIII. 47; *de princ.* II. 6. 1; *hom.* I. 13 *in Gen.*) does so willingly and already before him Justin (*Apol.* I. 39) and Clement of Alexandria (*Strom.* I. 45. 1f.). Origen (*c. Cels.* I. 62) openly admits that the occupations of the majority of the disciples were not known. Only incidentally do we learn once, for example, about Thomas, that he had been a carpenter (*Act. Thom.* 2).

The high esteem in which the younger generation holds the apostles naturally expresses itself in the way in which their life is spoken of, cf. the description of them put into the mouth of the Lord in the *Kerygma Petrou* (fragment in Clement of Alexandria, *Strom.* VI. 48. 1f.; see p. 101 below). In cod. D of Lk. 22:28 Jesus says in praise of the disciples:

You have grown up in my service as the one who serves.

Indeed, under the influence of Eph. 1:4 there has come about the logion (Ephraem, *Commentary on the Diatessaron*[1]):

I have chosen you before the world was.

That the apostles possessed all gifts of grace is a positive fact for Clement of Alexandria (*Strom.* IV. 133. 3). Above all there are to be named here the Gnostic writings preserved in Coptic. In the Fourth Book of the *Pistis Sophia* and in the *Books of Jeû* the disciples of Jesus, "his brothers and beloved", receive high praise. They have kept all and every commandment of the Master (*Pistis Sophia* c. 138, *GCS* 45, pp. 235f.; c. 142, pp. 243ff.; 2 *Book of Jeû* c. 43, pp. 304f.; c. 44, p. 306). They are declared worthy of all knowledge and mysteries (*Pistis Sophia* c. 138, pp. 235f.; 2 *Book of Jeû* c. 43f., pp. 304ff.). Jesus invites them to rejoice because all sin has been forgiven them and they belong to the Father's kingdom (*Pistis Sophia* c. 142, pp. 243ff.). The only human element in them is that they have a consciousness of guilt and accordingly wish that through the Redeemer they may be freed from their carnal infirmity (*Pistis Sophia* c. 136, pp. 232ff.; c. 141, pp. 241ff.; c. 142, pp. 243ff.; 1 *Book of Jeû* c. 1ff., pp. 257ff.; 2 *Book of Jeû* c. 45ff., pp. 308ff.). Much more exalted are the statements of the other three books of the *Pistis Sophia*, which in fact present "the most extreme and eccentric allusion to the importance of the twelve apostles".[2] The disciples are perfect

[1] P. 57; p. 42, 22.
[2] A. Harnack, *Die Mission und Ausbreitung des Christentums in den ersten drei Jahrhunderten* I[4], p. 360, n. 5 (ET *The Expansion of Christianity* I. 439, n. 1).

(c. 96, pp. 144ff.), have the spirit of Jesus (c. 46, pp. 49ff.; c. 49, pp. 55ff.), are sprung from the Redeemer himself (c. 110, pp. 180f.). Indeed, Jesus explains that the souls of his apostles pre-existed on high, wherefore they are not of this world (c. 7 and 8, pp. 6ff.). Cf. in addition Carpocrates in Irenaeus, *adv. haer.* I. 25. 2. Perhaps they are Gnostics whom Origen has in view when he controverts the opinion that the apostles had become perfect even before the passion of Jesus (*in Mt.* tom. XII. 40; *GCS* 40 Klostermann, p. 158).

It was not possible, however, everywhere to free oneself so much from history as to be able to extol the perfection of the apostles, and indeed their superiority to all earthly things. Too numerous were the occasions on which the Gospels showed them to be weak, void of understanding and sinful. It was also remembered that Jesus had come to call sinners. Thus the *Epistle of Barnabas* declares that Jesus chose his disciples from the most depraved of all existences (5. 9). That was water for the mill to the opponents of Christianity (Celsus in Origen, *c. Cels.* I. 62f.; II. 46). Yet Origen ventures no serious objection, but thinks merely that under the influence of Jesus the disciples became converted to a virtuous course of life (*c. Cels.* I. 63, 64; *hom.* I. 13 *in Gen.*), to be sure not without relapses of many kinds, as e.g. the denial and such words as those in Mt. 16:22, 17:4 show (*Comm. in Mt.* tom. XII. 40f.). The attacks of the anti-Christian and the task of expounding the Gospel in its context allowed Origen no choice. Where one did not come under the control of such a need, one preferred to overlook the passages in the Gospels which give unfavourable accounts of the disciples (the Apostolic Fathers, Irenaeus, Clement of Alexandria, Tertullian). This commended itself the more since the heretics frequently manifested a certain contempt of the apostles: the Gnostic Marcus (Irenaeus, *adv. haer.* I. 13. 6), the Carpocratians (*ib.* I. 25), the 'Gnostics' of Irenaeus (*ib.* I. 30. 13). The magician Simon lets Jesus himself illustrate his relation to the apostles in the words: "those who are with me have not understood me" (*Act. Petr. c. Sim.* 10). In the original apostles Marcion can see only people who in their indiscretion have adulterated the teaching of Jesus with Judaism (Irenaeus, *adv. haer.* III. 2. 2; 12. 12; 13. 1; Tertullian, *adv. Marc.* I. 20; IV. 3; V. 3; *de praescr. haer.* 23). In another way Montanus was persuaded of the incompetence of the apostles. For the men of the church in contrast with these heretics the apostles counted as the guarantors and bearers of the genuine revelation. They were taught by Jesus in a unique way. And in this the orthodox concur with those heretics who, in the interest of their own peculiar views, sought in mysterious fashion to establish a connection with Jesus through the apostles or individual disciples (on this see pp. 79ff. below). Over against the tendency, met with in many heretics, but also in Clement of Alexandria (*Strom.* I. 11. 3; *Hypotyp.* 7, in Eusebius, *HE* II. 1. 4) and Origen (c. *Cels.* II. 64; IV. 16;] VI. 77; *comm. in Mt.* tom. XII. 36f.; 41), to single out certain personalities from the circle of the apostles, there prevailed in ecclesiastical circles the tendency to view the apostles as a uniform entity of even texture (Polycarp, *Phil.* 9. 1). Only the statements of Scripture occasionally lead back to reality. The best of intentions are imputed to them, and their short-comings are excused as well as may be. Justin is already of opinion that after the resurrection the disciples made atonement for having disowned their Lord at the time of the crucifixion (*dial. c. Tryph.* 106). And where this delicate theme was not rather left wholly untouched, all kinds of arguments were brought into play to allow the failure of the disciples on particular occasions to be seen in a more subdued light. Yet the apostles also, in the interest of apologetics, have to consent to shadows being cast at times on their character. All that the New Testament says in this direction is far surpassed by the obstinacy with which the disciples in *Epist. Apost.* 10 (21); 11 (22) (see Vol. I, pp. 195f.) refuse to believe in the resurrection of the Lord.

3. THE APOSTLES AFTER THE ASCENSION. We also hear all sorts of things about the views and the activities of the apostles after the ascension, and the content of the apocryphal Acts may practically be left at that. That all proclaim the same doctrine is from Acts onward so much a matter of course for the Church that proofs are almost unnecessary.[1] Clement of Alexandria, who was persuaded that no gift of grace was wanting to the disciples (*Strom.* IV. 133. 3), also has them work especially as prophets (V. 38. 5). Regarding the participation of the twelve in the conversion of Paul see below on Paul (pp. 71ff.). On their journeys they had their wives with them not as mates but as collaborators (*Strom.* III. 53. 3; on the wife of Peter: *Strom.* VII. 63. 3; cf. on Peter pp. 45ff. below). Tertullian to be sure will hear nothing of any one of the apostles having been married except Peter (*de monog.* 8. 4, *Corp. Christ.* 2, p. 1239).

The apostles also appear as authorities in certain writings of which they pass as the authors. The *Didache* does not indeed put in a claim to have been written by the apostles; and how things stood in this respect with the different apocryphal writings circulating under the designation 'Gospel of the Twelve Apostles' can be established with certainty only in one instance: the Gospel of this title originating from the Manichaeans claims to have been

---

[1] Cf. C. Schmidt, *Gespräche Jesu*, TU 43, 1919, pp. 190, 255.

written by the twelve apostles (cf. Vol. I, pp. 268ff.). The *Epistula Apostolorum*, the *Syriac Didascalia* and the *Apostolic Church Order* name the twelve disciples as their authors. And also in the Gospel fragment of the Strassburg Coptic papyrus (see Vol. I, pp. 227ff.) the apostles are the speakers or writers. On the literary activity of individual apostles see pp. 45ff. below.

As regards the death of the disciples, Heracleon (*Com. on Lk.;* in Clement of Alexandria, *Strom.* IV. 71. 3) knows of four disciples who did not become martyrs, whilst the *Manichaean Psalm-book* (p. 142. 18ff., Allberry) can name only five or six apostolic blood-witnesses. After their death the apostles visited Hades in order to preach there to such as had not heard the gospel and to baptize the righteous (Hermas, *sim.* IX. 16. 5–7; following this but going further, Clement of Alexandria, *Strom.* II. 43. 5–44. 4; VI. 48. 3).

On earth the churches were soon proudly shown in which the chairs of the apostles had stood and in which the original texts of their correspondence were still read (Tertullian, *de praescr. haer.* 36. 1, *Corp. Christ.* 1, p. 216), in some towns the graves of the apostles as well: in Rome on the Vatican that of Peter and on the way to Ostia that of Paul (Gaius in Eusebius, *HE* II. 25. 7) or of both apostles on the Via Appia,[1] in Ephesus that of the beloved disciple John (Polycrates in Eusebius, *HE* V. 24. 2–7; cf. III. 39. 6), in Hierapolis that of Philip and his daughters (Polycrates, *loc. cit.*).

4. DEPARTURE TO MISSIONARY WORK. The most important task that the apostles undertook after the departure of their Master was an exodus to missionary work. Here also the NT yielded possible connections. It is acquainted with missionary orders (Mt. 28:19f., Mk. 16:16, Lk. 24:47f., Acts 1:8, 10:42) which we again and again come upon afresh in the pronouncements of the mission church, be it that they are repeated or that allusion is made to them or that in some other way their influence can be traced. As a rule a requirement that there be some national limitation is not advanced. The *Syriac Didascalia* (translation of J. Flemming, *TU* 25. 2, 1904, p. 77) expressly states the universality of the missionary command: "Jesus Christ has sent out us, the twelve, to teach the (chosen) people and the Gentile peoples." Likewise the *Kerygma Petrou*[2] and the *Epistula Apostolorum* 30 (41)

---

[1] Compilation of the evidences and memorials of the Roman apostle-tradition in Lietzmann, *Petrus und Paulus in Rom* (*Arbeiten z. Kirchengeschichte* I.)[2], 1927. For the relation of the shrines on the Vatican and the Via Ostia on the one hand and on the Via Appia on the other (no translation) see Th. Klauser, *Die römische Petrustradition im Lichte der neuen Ausgrabungen unter der Peterskirche* (*Arbeitsgemeinsch. d. Landes Nordrhein-Westf., Geisteswissensch.*, no. 24) 1956. Further literature in E. Dinkler, 'Die Petrus-Rom-Frage', *Theol. Rundschau* NF 25, 1959, pp. 189–230, 289–335.

[2] According to Clement of Alexandria, *Strom.* VI. 48, 1; see p. 101 below.

(Vol. I, p. 212); *Go and preach to the twelve tribes of Israel and to the Gentiles.* . . . Basically not different are already the short conclusion of Mk., the *Diatessaron*, 1 Clement 42. 3, Aristides, Justin, Irenaeus, the *Ascension of Isaiah*, the *Apostolic Church Order*, the fragment of an apocryphal Gospel-ending in the first volume of the Coptic Gnostic writings, *Pistis Sophia*.[1] Eusebius (*HE* III. 1) communicates a tradition according to which there fell by lot Parthia to Thomas, Scythia to Andrew and Asia Minor to John as missionary territories. We are concerned here with a fragment of a plan of partition of the earth among the twelve apostles.[2]

Certainly there also stands alongside the universalistic conception the view that as the twelve apostles are on the whole connected with the twelve tribes (Mt. 19:28; Lk. 22:30; Barn. 8. 3), so also they are destined as missionaries only to them (cf. Mt. 10:5). That was clearly the view of the Jewish Christians, of the *Gospel of the Ebionites* (see Vol. I, p. 156), yet not less that of the followers of the Gnostic Marcus (Irenaeus, *adv. haer.* I. 20. 2) and of the Naassenes (Hippol. *ref.* V. 8). A contrary opinion seeks to restrict the apostles more or less clearly to the Gentiles: pseudo-Clement (*hom.* XVII. 7, VIII. 22, *rec.* II. 33; IV. 35); *Acta Joh.* 112; the *Gospel of Mary* (see Vol. I, p. 342); also Justin (*dial.* 53). The Jews are most decidedly excluded from the consideration of the apostles in the pseudo-Cyprianic writing *Adv. Judaeos* (5), and indeed by Jesus himself, who bears witness to the disobedience of Israel and on account of it declares his will to send the disciples to the ends of the earth in order at length to invite all Gentiles without exception to the wedding-banquet.

The *Kerygma Petrou* (see pp. 94ff. below) has so apportioned the duty of the apostles among Jews and Gentiles that during the first twelve years they should hearken to the longing for repentance and forgiveness of sins in Israel, and should then turn to the 'world'. So ran the Lord's commission to the disciples. These twelve years during which the disciples stay in Jerusalem before they go out into the world also play a role elsewhere in the Christian tradition: Apollonius (in Eusebius, *HE* V. 18. 14);

---

[1] Diatessaron: Ephraem, *Commentary on the Diatessaron*, p. 276; p. 198, 22f.; also p. 350; p. 248, 24–26; H. Hill, *A Dissertation on the Gospel Commentary of S. Ephrem*, 1896, p. 118; Aphraates, *hom.* ed. Wright 12 – Aristides, *Apol.* 2 (p. 10, Hennecke *TU* 4. 3, 1893) – Justin, *apol.* 1. 31, 39, 45, 50; *dial.* 53 – Iren., Fragment XXXI (p. 843 Stieren); *Epideixis* 41 – Ascension of Isaiah 3, 17f.; 11, 22 – Apostolic Church Order 1 – Coptic-Gnost. Gospel Fragment, *GCS* 45, p. 254 – *Pistis Sophia*, Bks. I–III (*GCS* 45, c. 111, pp. 181ff.; c. 106, pp. 174f.; c. 100, pp. 158ff.; c. 125, pp. 205ff.).

[2] Cf. A. v. Harnack, *Die kirchengeschichtliche Ertrag der exegetischen Arbeiten des Origenes* 1 (*TU* 42. 3), 1918, p. 16: "At all events there was here at the bottom a complete register of the mission territories."

Acta Petri, c. 5 (see. p. 284 below); the *Acta Johannis* of Prochorus (ed. Zahn, 1880, pp. 3f.). Certainly not because they are historical, as Harnack[1] will have it. The number of the years—pseudo-Clement, however (*rec.* I. 43: IX. 29), puts forward the number seven, whilst a Sahidic fragment (Fragm. IV. 26, F. Robinson, *Texts and Studies* IV. 2, 1896, p. 28) has fifteen—fits too well with that of the apostles. Moreover certain Gnostics let Jesus dwell with the disciples throughout the twelve years before his final return home (*Pistis Sophia* I, GCS 45, p. 1; 2 *Book of Jeû* 44, *ib.* pp. 305ff.).[2] Other Gnostics reckoned the time during which the risen Christ remained with his disciples at eighteen months: Valentinians (Irenaeus, *adv. haer.* I. 3. 2), the 'Gnostics' of Irenaeus (*ib.* I. 30. 14), similarly the *Ascension of Isaiah* 9. 16: 545 days (18 × 30 = 540) and the *Apocryphon Jacobi* (see Vol. I, p. 336). Frequently the idea that they divided the whole world into twelve parts, of which each was to take one, is connected with the departure of the apostles: *Acta Thomae* 1; *Syriac Didascalia* (p. 120 Flemming), indeed already Origen (Eusebius, *HE* III. 1). Later authorities in *Handb.*, p. 564 and in Lipsius, *Die apokryphen Apostelgeschichten und Apostellegenden* I. 1883, pp. 11 to 16 and often.

5. THE INDIVIDUAL APOSTLES. A position of superiority is already assigned to Peter and the sons of Zebedee in the canonical Gospels (Mk. 9:2 and parallels; 14:33 and parallels). Connected with that is what Eusebius (*HE* II. 1. 3) has to communicate from the sixth book of the *Hypotyposes* of Clement of Alexandria, "that after the ascension of the Redeemer Peter and James and John did not enter a claim for honour since before then they had been honoured by the Redeemer, but chose James the Just to be bishop of Jerusalem." These three disciples have also an exceptional position as recipients and transmitters of esoteric revelation in Clement of Alexandria (on this see pp. 79ff. below); James and Peter have the same position in the *Apocryphon Jacobi* (see Vol. I, pp. 336f.).

Following the NT *Peter* counts overwhelmingly as the first of the apostles, above all to the Jewish Christians, cf. pseudo-Clement (*hom. Ep. Clem. ad Jac.* 1, *hom.* I. 15). Schahrastani (*Religionsparteien*, ed. Haarbrücker I. 261) after Jewish Christian sources: *Simon Cephas was his (Jesus') representative and he was the most excellent of the apostles as regards knowledge, piety and education.* In the same way he is here the only recipient of a revelation of the risen Christ: *And after he was dead and crucified he descended and was seen of Simon Cephas and he spake with him and handed over the*

[1] *Gesch. d. altchristl. Lit.* II. 1, p. 244.
[2] *Gnostische Schriften in koptischer Sprache* (*TU* 8. 1/2), 1892, pp. 493f.

dominion to him, then he left the world and ascended into heaven. Nevertheless his prestige was by no means confined to Jewish Christians. In the *Gospel of Bartholomew* Peter counts as the *chiefest of the apostles* (II. 7, 14; Vol. I, pp. 492, 493) and as the *strongest pillar* (II. 7; Vol. I, p. 492). Bartholomew, his fellow-apostle, makes use of the address *Father Peter* (II. 3; Vol. I, p. 492). The hero of the pseudo-Clementine fictions (cf. pp. 532ff. below), he is also the hero of a widely-branching literature of Acts of Peter (cf. pp. 259ff. below). Not only the two canonical Epistles of Peter but also the *Gospel of Peter* (cf. Vol. I, pp. 179f.), the *Apocalypse of Peter* (cf. pp. 663ff. below) and indeed the *Kerygma Petrou* (cf. pp. 94ff. below) as well profess to be his. On his relation to the Gospel of Mark see below on Mark. He has his place in the *Gospel of Mary* (see Vol. I, pp. 341, 342f.), in the *Epistula Apostolorum* (11 [22], see Vol. I, p. 197), in the Fragment from Fajjum (cf. Vol. I, p. 116), in the conversations of Jesus in 2 Clement (5. 2–4), in the *Apocryphon Jacobi* (cf. Vol. I, p. 336), in Ignatius (*Smyrn.* 3. 1f., cf. Vol. I, pp. 128f.) and is also met with in the *Acta Johannis* (88, 90, 91). 1 Clement (5) and Ignatius (*Rom.* 4. 3) name him beside Paul with high respect, and even the *Ascension of Isaiah* (4. 3) seems to allude to him (see p. 648 below). The general position is that to which Clement of Alexandria (*quis div. salv.* 21) gives expression when he speaks of the blessed Peter, the chosen one, the superior one, the first of the disciples, for whom alone, besides himself, the Lord paid the tribute money.

Nevertheless here and there Peter enjoys less respect. It is not merely in Marcion and those who have the catalogue of the apostles beginning with John (see p. 36 above) that this is the case. In the two books of Jeû he is not named at all, and in the 4th book of the *Pistis Sophia* (c. 136, p. 232, *GCS* 45 Till), after Thomas, Andrew, James, Simon the Canaanite, Philip and Bartholomew have been mentioned individually, he disappears among the *remaining disciples*. Already in the Fourth Gospel Peter had been set back behind the beloved disciple.

When the Lord called him, Peter forsook wife and child besides his business (Origen, *Comm. in Matth.* tom. XV. 21, *GCS* 40, p. 411 Klostermann). He was married (cf. Mk. 1:29–31 and pars.; 1 Cor. 9:5) and had children (cf. Mk. 10:29 and pars.; 1 Pet. 5:13). The wife of Peter is spoken of by pseudo-Clement (*hom.* XIII. 1, 11; *rec.* VII. 25, 36; IX. 38) and Clement of Alexandria (*Strom.* VII. 63. 3; see below), and the latter also speaks of children (III. 52. 5); a daughter is spoken of particularly in the *Acts of Peter* (C. Schmidt, *Die alten Petrusakten*, *TU* 24. 1, 1903, pp. 3–10, cf. pp. 276ff. below), in the *Acts of Philip* (c. 142, Aa 2. 2, p. 81) as also in the *Acts of Nereus and Achilleus* (c. 15, ed. Achelis *TU* 11. 2, 1893, pp. 14ff.). The view deduced from 1 Pet. 5:13 that Mark was Peter's own son is found only later, and not yet in Clement of Alexandria.[1] The *Acts of Philip* reports (*loc. cit.*) yet further that, mindful of Mt. 5:28, Peter fled from every place which housed a woman, cf. also pseudo-Clement, *Epistle to Virgins* 11. 15 (Funk, p. 26). Peter appears as a woman-hater of another kind in the Gnostic literature. In the *Pistis Sophia* he opposes the forwardness, felt as inadmissible, of the women among the followers of Jesus (c. 72, p. 104). The Gnostic *Gospel of Mary* also knows of a difference between Peter and Andrew on the one hand and Mary on the other, with whom Levi sides (see Vol. I, p. 343; cf. *Gospel of Thomas*, logion 114).[2] To Peter's cautiousness in reference to women there corresponds the simplicity of his conduct (pseudo-Clement, *hom.* XII. 6; *rec.* VII. 6; Gregory of Nazianzus, *orat.* 14. 4). Regarding Peter's extraction, business and education see pp. 39f. above. What we learn about his life in the company of Jesus' followers that is somewhat beyond the NT belongs mainly to the history of the exposition of the Biblical text, what more is recorded e.g. about his confession of Christ, his position as the rock-bed of the church, the power of the keys conveyed to him, his denial and the like. As independent tradition there comes into question perhaps only Schahrastani's story (I. 261 Haarbrücker) which goes back to Jewish-Christian sources. It lets the risen Christ appear only to Peter: *And after he was crucified, he descended and was seen of Simon Cephas, and he spoke with him and handed over all dominion to him; then he left the world and ascended into heaven.*

After his departure from Jerusalem (see above, pp. 43ff.) an early tradition makes Peter proclaim the gospel to the Jews of the Diaspora in Pontus, Galatia, Bithynia, Cappadocia and Asia (Eusebius, *HE* III. 1. 2, doubtless following Origen, see *ib.* III. 1. 3). The influence of 1 Pet. 1:1 is quite clear (cf. *ib.* III. 4. 2). According to Origen (*hom. 6 in Luc.*) he founded the Antiochean bishopric (Eusebius, *HE* III. 36. 2; cf. pseudo-Clement, *rec.* X. 69–72). Regarding his work in company with Paul in Corinth and Rome cf. Dionysius of Corinth (in Eusebius, *HE* IV. 23. 3; cf. Eusebius, *HE* II. 25. 8; III. 4. 10). The earlier witnesses for a stay of Peter in Rome are not absolutely unambiguous (see *I Clement* 5. 4; Ignatius, *Rom.* 4). In later times, on the other hand, the authorities increase: Irenaeus, *adv. haer.*

---

[1] So Zahn, *Neue kirchl. Zeitschr.* 1901, p. 745; against that K. Heussi, *Zeitschr. f. wissensch. Theol.* 1902, pp. 481ff.

[2] Cf. A. Harnack, *Über das gnostische Buch Pistis Sophia* 1891, pp. 16f.; C. Schmidt, *Gnostische Schriften in koptischer Sprache* (*TU* 8. 1/2) 1892, p. 455; L. Zscharnack, *Der Dienst der Frau in den ersten Jahrhunderten der christlichen Kirche* 1902, p. 161.

III. 1; Tertullian, *de praescr. haer.* 36. 3 (*Corp. Christ.* 1, p. 216); Clement of Alexandria, *Hypotyposes* VI (according to Eusebius *HE* II. 25. 8 and VI. 14. 5–7, Tradition of the 'Elders'); Gaius (*ib.* II. 25. 7). Also it can hardly be doubted that Rome is concealed behind Babylon in 1 Pet. 5:13 (so already Clement of Alexandria and Papias in Eusebius, *HE* II. 15. 2). Witness is borne to the martyr death of Peter by 1 Clement 5. 4; 2 Pet. 1:14(?); Dionysius of Corinth (in Eusebius, *HE* II. 25. 8); the *Muratori Canon* 37 (see Vol. I, p. 44) and generally by many onwards from the end of the second century, yet already also by Jn. 21:18f., the words of which Tertullian (*scorp.* 15. 3, *Corp. Christ.* 2, p. 1097) already correctly interpreted as a prophecy of Peter's crucifixion. That this took place head-downwards is said, in accordance with the proceedings of the *Acts of Peter* (see p. 319 below), first by Origen (in Eusebius, *HE* III. 1. 2), who carries it back to the express wish of the apostle; so also the *Manichaean Psalm-book* (p. 142, 18f. Allberry). Whilst Clement of Rome, Ignatius and Clement of Alexandria make no definite statements concerning the relation of Peter to the church of Rome, Dionysius (in Eusebius *HE* II. 25. 8), Irenaeus (*adv. haer.* III. 1. 1) and Gaius (in Eusebius, *HE* II. 25. 7) name Peter as a mission preacher who in conjunction with Paul had founded the Roman church; cf. Epiphanius (*haer.* 37. 6) and the Peter-Paul-Acts. Tertullian also (*de praescr. haer.* 36), although he has Clement ordained only by Peter (c. 32), nevertheless sets Paul at Peter's side in the founding of the Roman church. In *de pudic.* 21, however, he indicates that the Roman bishop Calixtus described himself as the occupant of Peter's episcopal chair.[1] In the middle of the 3rd century the idea that the seat of the Roman bishop is the *cathedra Petri* is clearly attested: Cyprian (*epist.* 55. 8; 59. 14), also Firmilian (*ib.* 75. 17); pseudo-Cyprian (*de aleat.* 1); pseudo-Clement, *hom.* (Epistle of Clement to James 2. 6).[2] Eusebius in his *Chronicle* is the first who knows of a definite decades-long duration of Peter's administration as bishop of Rome. His dependence on the *Chronicle* of Sextus Julius Africanus, which was completed in 220, is doubtless certain.[3] How far, however, the statements that are accepted for Peter have been taken from there eludes more accurate investigation. Anyhow he has certainly already, and indeed not as the first (cf. *Acta Petri* 41), put the death of Peter under Nero[4]—Tertullian (*scorp.* 15), Lactantius

---

[1] Cf. G. Esser, Tertullian de pudic. 21 und der Primat des römischen Bischofs, *Katholik*, 3rd Series 26, 1902, pp. 193–220.
[2] Cf. H. Koch, Kathedra Petri, *BZNW* 11, 1930.
[3] Harnack, *Gesch. d. altchrist. Lit.* II. 1, pp. 123ff., 201, 704ff.; E. Schwartz, *Eusebius, Die Kirchengeschichte* III (*GCS* 9, 3) 1909, pp. CCXXIff.
[4] Harnack, *ibid.*, p. 201.

(*div. inst.* IV. 21) and the later *Acts of Peter* also mention Nero by name as the author of the martyrdom of Peter—and he has assumed an activity of the apostle in Rome of many years duration. But this is contradicted not only by the statements of the NT but also by the anti-Christian in Macarius Magnes (*c.* 400), *apocrit.* III. 22 (Porphyry?):

> It is related that Peter was crucified after that he had fed the little sheep for only a few months.

So also the *Acts of Peter* (see pp. 282ff. below).

The tradition of a stay of Peter in Rome has been disputed from very different sides, e.g. by Neander, F. C. Baur, Mangold, Zeller, Lipsius; further by P. W. Schmiedel (art. "Simon Peter" in *Encyclopaedia Biblica*, ed. Cheyne and Black iv, 4559ff.), K. Erbes ("Petrus nicht in Rom, sondern in Jerusalem gestorben", *ZKG* 22, 1901, pp. 1ff., 161ff.), C. Guignebert (*La primauté de Pierre et la venue de Pierre à Rome*, 1909), A. Bauer ("Die Legende von dem Martyrium des Petrus und Paulus in Rom", *Wiener Studien* 38, 1916, pp. 270ff.), H. Dannenbauer ("Die römische Petruslegende", *Historische Zeitschrift* 146, 1932, pp. 239 ff.; 159, 1938, pp. 81ff.), most vigorously by K. Heussi (*War Petrus in Rom?* 1936; *War Petrus wirklich römischer Märtyrer?* 1937; *Neues zur Petrusfrage* 1939; *Die römische Petrustradition in kritischer Sicht*, 1955. For further works of Heussi on this subject see *ThLZ* 86, 1961, cols. 545f.).

On the other hand, the tradition is endorsed among others by Bleek, Credner, H. Ewald, Hilgenfeld, Renan, Lightfoot, Harnack, Clemen, C. Schmidt, F. Sieffert (*RE* 15, pp. 199ff.), Th. Zahn (*Einl. in das NT*, ³, 1906, 2, pp. 22ff.), F. H. Chase (art. "Peter (Simon)" in Hastings, *Dictionary of the Bible* iii, 1909, pp. 765 ff.), H. Lietzmann, *Petrus und Paulus in Rom*, ²1927); among the more recent works O. Cullmann (*Petrus. Jünger, Apostel, Märtyrer*, 1952, ²1960; ET 1953, ²1962), K. Aland (*Histor. Ztschr.* 183, 1957, pp. 497f.), and among Catholic research workers H. Schmutz ("Petrus war dennoch in Rom", *Benediktinische Monatsschr.* 22, 1946, pp. 128ff.), Th. Klauser (*Die römische Petrustradition im Lichte der neuen Ausgrabungen unter der Peterskirche*, 1956) and E. Kirschbaum (*Die Gräber der Apostelfürsten*, 1957 (ET 1959)). On the whole matter cf. E. Dinkler's account of the research, "Die Petrus-Rom-Frage", *Theol. Rdsch.* NF 25, 1959, pp. 189–230; 289–335.

In Papias, who in this matter appeals to the "elders", Mark is reckoned the "interpreter" of Peter (see Eusebius *HE* III. 39. 15). In a noteworthy way Basilides asserts that he had had as his teacher an *interpreter* of Peter, who bore the name Glaucias

(Clement of Alexandria, *Strom.* VII. 106. 4). Clement of Alexandria (*Strom.* VII. 63. 3, GCS 17, p. 46) reports an incident in the later life of Peter:

> When the blessed Peter was obliged to see how his own wife was led to death, he rejoiced because she partook of her call and returned home, and shouted to her the name (of the Lord) that he might truly encourage and comfort her, and said to her: Think, beloved, on the Lord!

This story would belong to the traditions about Peter even if it be assumed that a scribe erroneously converted his going to martyrdom into his wife's going there.[1]

Andrew appears occasionally in association with his brother: *The Gospel of the Ebionites* (see Vol. I, p. 156, no. 1), the *Gospel of Peter* (see Vol. I, p. 187), the *Gospel of Mary* (see Vol. I, pp. 342f.), *Epistula Apost.* 2 (13) (see Vol. I, p. 192), *Pistis Sophia* (repeatedly), Papias, who names him before Peter (in Eusebius, *HE* III. 39. 3f., see p. 78 below), *Acta Johannis* 88, pseudo-Clement, *hom.* XII. 16. According to the *Muratori Canon* 14 (see Vol. I, p. 43) Andrew received the divine revelation which gave the decisive impulse to the composition of the Gospel of John (see also under John). Origen (in Eusebius *HE* III. 1. 1) knows that at the partition of the world Scythia fell to him as his mission territory. From the missionary activity of the apostle the so-called *Epistola Titi discipuli* reports the following:

> Finally when Andrew came to a wedding, that he might show the glory of God he there parted the spouses, the men and the women, who were destined for one another, and taught them to remain holy in single state (see p. 161 below).

It is not certain that this fragment belongs to the *Acts of Andrew*. Andrew died by crucifixion in Patrae in Achaia (see pp. 416ff. below). So also in the *Manichaean Psalm-book* (Allberry, p. 142, 20f.), according to which his pupils shared his fate. If further (p. 194, 8) Andrew is there called *the first sacred statue*, that must relate to a story communicated by Epiphanius Monachus (9th cent.), according to which there was extant in his day in Sinope a house of prayer with a marble statue of Andrew that had been made in his own lifetime.[2] The *Gospel of Andrew* mentioned in the *Decretum Gelasianum* (see Vol. I, p. 47) probably never existed.[3]

[1] Cf. Hort and Mayor, *Clement of Alexandria* (Miscellanies Book 7) 1902, p. 293. 27.
[2] Epiphanius Monachus, ed. Dressel, pp. 47. 24, 50. 23. Cf. Lipsius, *Die apokryphen Apostelgeschichten* I, 1883, pp. 570, 576. See further p. 37 above, and Th. Zahn, *Forschungen* VI, pp. 220f.
[3] Cf. E. v. Dobschütz, "Das Decretum Gelasianum", *TU* 38. 4, 1912, p. 293. On the rôle of Andrew in the Andrew-Matthias-Acts see below on Matthias. Cf. also

John is mentioned in a fragment of the *Gospel of the Nazaraeans* in which it is said:

As he was the son of the poor fisherman Zebedee, he had often brought fish to the palace of the high priest Annas and Caiaphas (Fragm. 33, Vielhauer, Vol. I, p. 152).

Again there is talk of him in the Gospel of the Ebionites and in Papias,[1] also in an anonymous prologue to the Gospel of John.[2] He is the recipient of the revelation in the *Apocryphon of John* (see Vol. I, pp. 321ff.), and the favoured disciple in the *Acts of John* as in the *Pistis Sophia* (c. 96, GCS 45, p. 148, 25f.):

Mary Magdalene and John, the immaculate, will surpass all my disciples.

John plays the same role in the Greek form of the *Assumption of the Virgin Mary* (see Vol. I, p. 429).[3]

The Christian writers from the end of the 2nd century report this and that about his person and his life. According to the *Act. Joh.* 113 (see p. 257 below) the Lord called him as a young man. His chastity is underlined again and again by Tertullian and Methodius of Olympus, in the *Questions of Bartholomew*, in the so-called monarchian Prologue to the Gospel of John, in the pseudo-Clementine writing *Ad Virgines*, by the Manichaean Faustus, in the *Manichaean Psalm-book*, in the *Pistis Sophia* and especially in the *Act. Joh.* Epiphanius extends his abstemiousness to the whole sphere of his life.[4] In the *Apostolic Church Order* (c. 26, Schermann, p. 32) it is John who recalls how at the time of the

---

P. M. Peterson, *Andrew, Brother of Simon Peter, His History and his Legend*, 1958; F. Dvornik, *The Idea of Apostolicity in Byzantium and the Legend of the Apostle Andrew* (Dumbarton Oaks Studies IV) Cambridge (Mass.) 1958. On Peterson and Dvornik see also M. Hornschuh, *ZKG* 71, 1960, pp. 138ff.

[1] *The Gospel of the Ebionites*, Fragm. 1, Vielhauer, Vol. I, p. 156. Papias in the preface to the κυριακῶν ἐξηγήσεις, in Eusebius, *HE* III. 39. 4 (*GCS* 9. 1, p. 286, 16–20); further in a fragment from the 2nd Book of the same work in Philip of Side, *Church History* (?) (ed. Boor, *TU* 5.2, 1888, p. 170; Funk-Bihlmeyer, *Die apostolischen Väter*, ²1956, p. 138).

[2] *Patrum apostol. opera*, ed. O. v. Gebhardt, A. v. Harnack, Th. Zahn, ed. minor, ⁶1920, p. 77; Funk-Bihlmeyer², pp. 139f.

[3] Cf. further the registers of the apostles (see p. 36 above).

[4] Tertullian, *De monog.* 17. 1 (*Corp. Christ.* 2, p. 1252). – Methodius of Olymp., *De resurrect.* I. 59. 6 (*GCS* 27, p. 323. 16f.). – *Questions of Bartholomew* II. 14 (Vol. I, p. 493). — monarchian Prologue to John (Lietzmann, *Kleine Texte* 1, p. 13. 13–15). – ps.–Clement, *Epist. de virg.* I. 6. 3 (Funk, *Patres Apostolici* II, 1901, p. 5. 11–14). – Faustus, in August., *Contr. Faust.* XXX. 4 (*CSEL* 25, p. 175. 26f.). – Manich. Psalm-b. (Allberry, pp. 142. 23; 192. 7). – *Pistis Sophia* 41 and 96 (*GCS* 45, pp. 42. 27 and 148. 25f.). – *Act. Joh.* 113 (see p. 257 below) – Epiphanius, *haer.* 78. 13. 1–4 (*GCS* 37, pp. 463. 26–464. 7).

Last Supper the Lord had excluded Mary and Martha from the sacrament of the eucharist.[1]

That John the son of Zebedee wrought in Ephesus is a view often repeated from the second half of the 2nd century.[2] In Clement (*Quis div. salv.* 42. 2, *GCS* 17, p. 188, 3–7) he appears as the highest authority in all the district belonging to Ephesus, he organizes the churches, he replenishes the clergy as needed, and appoints bishops; similarly the *Muratori Canon* 10 (see Vol. I, p. 43), which in reference to John speaks of *his bishops*.[3] Neither Polycarp nor the "elders" of Irenaeus are able to secure this point of view for still earlier times.[4]

The above-mentioned testimonies of Clement of Alexandria and Jerome agree in the opinion that John attained a very great age. So also the *Acts of John* and Irenaeus, who has him live up to the time of Trajan's reign (*adv. haer.* II. 22. 5; III. 3. 4).[5] Tertullian (*de anima* 50, *Corp. Christ.* 2, p. 856) also shares the view that John became very old, for he records that it was believed of John that he would live to see the second coming of Christ. According to the view shared by the vast majority the apostle's earthly course ended in a peaceful death: so manifestly Irenaeus (*adv. haer.* II. 22. 5; III. 3. 4), Polycrates (in Eusebius, *HE* III. 31. 3 = V. 24. 2), Tertullian (*loc. cit.*), the *Act. Joh.* (115) and, in dependence on them, the so-called monarchian Prologue to the Gospel of John (*KlT* 1, p. 14). The *Acts* are the first to advocate the idea that John had a grave selected before the gate of Ephesus, put himself into it and gave up the ghost.[6] This view of a bloodless death need not necessarily exclude another which speaks of a martyrdom of John. For the desire to square Jesus' prediction in Mk. 10:39 = Mt. 20:23, which had already pointed antiquity to a martyrdom that was in prospect, with the tradition that the apostle had lived long and had not died a violent death, led to the result that extreme deductions were not drawn from his activity as a *witness*. Origen (*Comm. in Mt.*, tom. XVI. 6) speaks of a tradition which discerned the fulfilment of the Lord's

[1] Cf. A. Harnack, *Die Quellen der sog. Apostolischen Kirchenordnung, TU* 2. 5, 1886, pp. 28ff. – L. Zscharnack, *Der Dienst der Frau in den ersten Jahrhunderten der christlichen Kirche*, 1902, p. 161.

[2] *Act. Joh.* (*passim*, see pp. 188ff. below). – Irenaeus (*adv. haer.* III. 1. 1). – Polycrates of Ephesus, Epistle to Victor of Rome (in Eusebius, *HE* III. 31.3 = V. 24. 3). – Clement of Alexandria, *Quis div. salv.* 42 (*GCS* 17, pp. 187f.).

[3] Cf. also the so-called monarchian Prologue to the Gospel of John (*KlT* 1, p. 14), Apollonius (in Eusebius, *HE* V. 18. 14), Tertullian (*de praescr.* 32. 2, *Corp. Christ.* 1, p. 213) and Jerome (*Commentary on Gal.* 6: 10, *PL* 26, col. 462 BC). Cf. Th. Zahn, *Forsch.* VI, p. 207.

[4] W. Bauer, *Das Johannesevangelium, Handb. z. NT* 6, [3]1933, pp. 242f.

[5] Further details in Th. Zahn, *Acta Joannis*, 1880, pp. CXXXIIf.

[6] The so-called monarchian Prologue to the Gospel of John also follows the *Acts of John* in this point.

prophecy in the banishment to Patmos. His teacher Clement of Alexandria had already spoken of the exile to Patmos, which is doubtless derived from Rev. 1:9 (*Quis div. salv.* 42. 2, *GCS* 17, p. 188). Tertullian connects with the banishment to the island a tradition that previously, and indeed in Rome, John had been dipped in burning oil without suffering harm (*de praescr.* 36. 3, *Corp. Christ.* 1, pp. 216/17). According also to Hippolytus (*de antichr.* 36) John seems to have been in Rome in order to receive there the sentence of banishment. This information is not fixed chronologically by those who have been named—Jerome (*adv. Iovin.* I. 26, PL 23, col. 259B) only reads into Tertullian that the oil-martyrdom had taken place in Nero's time; Eusebius also advocates the Nero tradition in *demonstr. evang.* III. 5. 65—the statements which put the exile in the time of Domitian thus begin with Victorinus of Pettau (on Rev. 10:11, Haussleiter, *CSEL* 49, 1916, p. 92) and Eusebius in the *Ecclesiastical History* (III. 17; 18; 20. 8, 9; 23. 1; so also in the *Chronicle*).

We find a quite divergent tradition in Papias (in Philip of Side, *hist. eccl.* [?], Funk-Bihlmeyer, *Die Apostolischen Väter*, 2nd ed., 1956, p. 138). According to his statement there was an actual bearing of witness by the shedding of blood, and indeed Jerusalem in Palestine has to be thought of as its theatre. Heracleon indirectly confirms the martyrdom in that he asserts expressly only of Matthew, Philip, Thomas and Levi that they died a natural death (*Commentary on Lk.* 12, 8ff. according to Clement of Alexandria, *Strom.* IV. 71. 3). In the matter with which we are here concerned Aphraates 417. 10 (ed. Bert, *TU* 3. 3/4, pp. 347ff.) seconds him in that he observes that besides Stephen, Peter and Paul there were only two apostolic martyrs, namely James and John. Correspondingly the Syriac martyrology of 411 (Lietzmann *KlT* 2, p. 9) names for 27 December (similarly the Armenian for 28 December) *John and James, the apostles in Jerusalem.* The *Manichaean Psalm-book* also must have a violent death in mind when in 142. 18–29 it names John in the midst of the martyr apostles and enframes the holy five, Peter, Andrew, John, James and Thomas, with Jesus. It is curious that in this case John should be starved in prison.[1]

For Irenaeus in his *Epistle to Florinus* (Eusebius, *HE* V. 20. 6) John counts as the teacher of Polycarp, whom, according to Tertullian, *de praescr. haer.* 32, he also appointed to be bishop of Smyrna. Papias also is said to have been a hearer of the son of Zebedee: Irenaeus, *adv. haer.* V. 33. 4. But Eusebius (*HE* III. 39. 2) disputes that, appealing to Papias' own words.

[1] For a conjectural derivation and understanding of this tradition see Schäferdiek, *Act. Joh.*, pp. 199f. below.

Ecclesiastical tradition names John as the writer of five of the New Testament writings.

1. For Papias he counts as the author of the Fourth Gospel, if the anonymous Prologue (see Th. Zahn, *op. cit.*, p. 127 and Funk-Bihlmeyer, p. 139) is to be trusted: *the Gospel of John was published and given to the churches by John whilst he was still in the body*. That was certainly the opinion widely held in the last third of the 2nd century: Irenaeus, *adv. haer.* III. 1. 1; 11. 1; Clement of Alexandria, *Hypotyposes* 6 (in Eusebius, *HE* VI. 14. 7); the *Muratori Canon* 9–34 (see Vol. I, p. 43); Theophilus, *ad. Autol.* II. 22. The Roman church, it is true, at first exercised caution in relation to a Gospel which within its area stood in high favour with the heretics Ptolemaeus, Heracleon and Tatian. Here one either held one's peace as did Justin or allowed a presbyter Gaius, whose orthodoxy in its hostility to the heretics was beyond doubt, to dismiss not only the Revelation but also the Fourth Gospel as forgeries of the Gnostic Cerinthus. Not until the beginning of the 3rd century does the opposition dwindle; Hippolytus, it is true, still aims at a categorical refutation of Gaius and his supporters, whom Epiphanius, *haer.* 51, gathers up as the *Alogi*.[1] But the view of the Johannine-apostolic authorship of the Fourth Gospel, about which the *Muratori Canon* was already in no doubt (9–16), prevailed in the Church onwards from the time of Tertullian (*de praescr. haer.* 22. 5, *Corp. Christ.* 1, p. 203; *adv. Marc.* IV. 2. 3, *ib.* p. 547).

Almost as far back as the assertion of the Johannine-apostolic authorship of the Fourth Gospel there can be traced the tradition that here we are concerned with the latest of the canonical Gospels: Irenaeus, *adv. haer.* III. 1. 1; Clement of Alexandria, *Hypotyposes* 6 (in Eusebius, *HE* VI. 14. 7) and the tradition in Origen (according to Eusebius, *HE* VI. 25. 3–6). With Ephesus as the residence of the Evangelist the place of the Gospel's origin is also given. It is expressly noted as Asia or Ephesus in Irenaeus (*ibid.*) and in the so-called monarchian Prologue to the Fourth Gospel; according to the latter the writing of the Gospel took place only after John had written the Revelation in the isle of Patmos. According to a fragment of Ephraem John wrote his Gospel in Greek in Antioch.[2] The purpose of the Evangelist in

---

[1] See W. Bauer, *Rechtgläubigkeit und Ketzerei im ältesten Christentum*, 1934, pp. 208–211.

[2] [Bauer follows here the Latin translation which J. Aucher made from the Armenian edition of the Mechitarist fathers (Venice 1836) and which G. Moesinger revised and edited (Venice 1876). Aucher-Moesinger translate: . . . *Lucas* (*sc. scripsit*) *graece, Joannes etiam graece scripsit Antiochiae* . . . and observe that the words *etiam graece Antiochiae* are found only in one of the two Armenian manuscripts (p. 276). Harnack (*ZKG* 4, 1881, p. 497) and Conybeare (*ZNW* 3, 1902, p. 193) make this translation the basis of their investigations. But recently Leloir in his translation has attached

his work is according to Irenaeus (*adv. haer.* III. 11. 1) to combat
Cerinthus and the Nicolaitans, according to Victorinus of Pettau
(on Rev. 11, 1, pp. 94, 96 Haussleiter) to combat Valentinus,
Cerinthus and Ebion. Victorinus adds that John was incited to his
undertaking by the urgent desires of bishops who had come from
the farthest regions. Bishops who encouraged him are also mentioned in the *Muratori Canon* 10 (see Vol. I, p. 43). Another early
story about the genesis of the Gospel of John is communicated by
Clement of Alexandria in his *Hypotyposes* (in Eusebius, *HE* VI.
14. 7):

> Last of all John, perceiving that the external facts had (already)
> been dealt with in the Gospels, being urged by his pupils and
> inspired by the Spirit, composed a spiritual Gospel.

2. The Revelation is cited by Justin (*dial. c. Tryph.* 81) as a
book of the apostle John. Onwards from the time of Irenaeus,
who invokes the testimony of the "elders" (*adv. haer.* V. 30. 1, 3),
Tertullian[1] and the *Muratori Canon* 48f., 71 (see Vol. I, pp. 44f.)
that is the opinion of the Westerners: Hippolytus,[2] Cyprian,[3]
Victorinus (*de fabrica mundi* 10, p. 9 Haussleiter), as also of the
Orientals: Clement of Alexandria (see Zahn, *Forsch.* I, p. 205),
Origen (see Bousset, *Offb.*, p. 22), Methodius (see Bousset, *op.
cit.* pp. 19, 28 n. 1). The fact that the Revelation was used and
highly esteemed by other early Christians such as Papias, Melito
of Sardis, Theophilus of Antioch and Apollonius does not
necessarily prove belief in its apostolic origin. Here then that
matter may be let rest together with the remaining numerous
evidences which more or less certainly prove an early existence of
the Revelation. It must nevertheless be mentioned briefly that
objection was raised to the equating of the John of the Revelation
with the apostle, and indeed on the part of the Alogi already
mentioned above (more details on their attitude to the apostle
are given in Bousset, *op. cit.*, pp. 22–25), the Roman presbyter
Gaius (in Eusebius, *HE* III. 28. 2) and Dionysius of Alexandria
(in Eusebius *HE* VII. 25). Regarding the time when the Revelation originated the *Muratori Canon* 48ff. (see Vol. I, p. 44) expounds the remarkable idea that John wrote before Paul. Still
more curious is what is given in Epiphanius, *haer.* 51. 12, 33.

Antiochiae to *Lucas* (*CSCO* 145, p. 248, 9) probably on the ground of the statement
repeated again and again since the time of Eusebius (*HE* III. 4. 6) that Luke came
from Antioch.] (*Regul*).

[1] The passages are in Zahn, *Forsch.* I, pp. 203f.

[2] Cf. W. Bousset, *Die Offenbarung Johannis* (Krit-exeget. Komm., initiated by
H. A. W. Meyer, 16[6]), 1906, pp. 25, 30, 50f.

[3] See Lücke, *Versuch einer vollständigen Einleitung in die Offenbarung des Johannes* [2]II,
1852, p. 597.

On the other hand, Irenaeus (*adv. haer.* V. 30. 3), Hippolytus[1] and Victorinus (p. 118 Haussleiter) put the composition of the Revelation in the time of Domitian (81–96), the last putting it in Patmos. Hippolytus (*c. Noet.* 15) sets it in point of time after the Gospel, the so-called monarchian Prologue to the Fourth Gospel (*KlT* 1, p. 13) before it. Tertullian (*de fuga* 9; *scorp.* 12) assumes that it was written before the First Epistle of John. In his capacity as the writer of an apocalypse John is readily called a *prophet:* Clement of Alexandria (*Strom.* III. 106. 1?); Origen (*Comm. in Joh.* tom. II. 5). For two late apocalypses under the name of John see James, pp. 504f.

3. Of the Johannine Epistles the first two are certainly held as apostolic about 200: Irenaeus (*adv. haer.* III. 16. 5, 8), Clement of Alexandria (*Strom.* II. 66. 4 and *Adumbrationes, GCS* 17 Stählin, pp. 209–215), the *Muratori Canon* 27–34, 68f. (see Vol. I, pp. 43, 44); Tertullian, who certainly quotes only the large epistle (*scorp.* 12, *de pud.* 2, 19, *de anima* 17, *de idol.* 2), but calls it the *prior epistula* (*de pud.* 19).[2] Origen (in Eusebius, *HE* VI. 25. 10) tells of doubt as to the Johannine-apostolic origin of the two small epistles of John; so also Eusebius, *HE* III. 24. 17; 25. 3. But in the 3rd century the disposition towards these becomes more and more favourable.[3]

James, the other son of Zebedee, is met with, outside the NT, in the *Gospel of the Ebionites* (see Vol. I, p. 156), the *Apocryphon of John* (see Vol. I, p. 321), the *Acts of John* (c. 88, 89, 91) and the Coptic Gnostic writings (*GCS* 45 Till passim). Whether the *Epistle of James* contained in Codex II of the Gnostic library of Nag Hammadi (on this see Vol. I, pp. 333ff.) was ostensibly composed by the son of Zebedee or by the Lord's brother, remains open to question; H-Ch. Puech regards it as more likely that the Lord's brother is referred to (see Vol. I, p. 335). On the two writings in Codex VII from Nag Hammadi which are described as apocalypses of James, cf. Puech in Vol. I, p. 334. Papias also mentions James the son of Zebedee in the preface to the κυριακῶν ἐξηγήσεις (in Eusebius, *HE* III. 39. 4 and in the above-mentioned fragment preserved in Philip of Side, where his bloody death at Jewish hands is spoken of, cf. Acts. 12, 1f.). According to Eusebius (*HE* II. 9. 2f.) Clement of Alexandria in the 7th Book of his *Hypotyposes* related, as *tradition received from his predecessors,* a story about James,

---

[1] Cf. Th. Zahn, *Einleitung in das NT*, §64, 14.

[2] [Bauer here follows the reading *in priore quidem epistola*. The reading *in primore quidem epistola* seems to be better.]

[3] On the Johannine problem cf. also F. M. Braun, *Jean le Théologien et son Évangile dans l'Église ancienne, Études bibliques,* 1959.

that (the soldier) who led him to the law court, moved by his firm confession, confessed himself a Christian. They were now both led away, he relates, and on the way he begged that James would forgive his sins. After a brief consideration he said: Peace be with thee! and kissed him. After this both were beheaded at the same time.

On the other hand, the *Manichaean Psalm-book* (pp. 142, 25f.; 192, 9 Allberry) professes to know of a stoning of James.

. *Philip* is referred to in Papias (in the above-mentioned prologue to the κυριακῶν ἐξηγήσεις), in the *Sophia Jesu Christi* (see Vol. I, p. 247) and in detail in the *Pistis Sophia* (cf. Vol. I, pp. 271f.) where he receives the role of a *writer of all the discourses which Jesus spoke and of all that he did* (ch. 42, *GCS* 45, p. 44, 21f.). In conformity with this Philip passes for the author of Gospels which were respected in Gnostic circles. The existence of a *Gospel of Philip* is attested by Epiphanius, who communicates to us a fragment from it (*haer.* 26. 13. 2–3, see Vol. I, pp. 271ff.). A *Gospel of Philip* is also found among the writings of the Gnostic library of Nag Hammadi.[1] The later *Acts of Philip* (Aa II. 2, pp. 1ff.) describes Philip as quick-tempered and vindictive and persistently calls him *son of thunder*.[2] Whilst Tertullian (*de bapt.* 12. 9, *Corp. Christ.* 1, p. 228) describes as an apostle the man who was commanded by Jesus to follow him instead of burying his father (Mt. 8:21f., Lk. 9:59f.), Clement of Alexandria (*Strom.* III. 25. 3) identifies him more closely with the apostle Philip. That the Marcionites had already done this does not follow with certainty from Clement's words.[3] Whilst in the fragment of the *Gospel of Philip* cited by Epiphanius (see Vol. I, p. 273) an encratitic tendency discloses itself, in Clement (*Strom.* III. 52. 5 = Eusebius, *HE* III. 30. 1) Philip has children and allows his daughters to marry. The apostle Philip seems to have passed as a married man and as a father of daughters already in Papias, who, according to Eusebius (*HE* III. 39. 9), asserted that *he had got to know a wonderful story from the daughters of Philip. He relates namely a rising from the dead which had taken place at that time.* It is likely that Papias also learned from Philip's daughters the miracle story (see p. 67 below) which he communicates about Justus Barsabbas (Eusebius, *HE* III. 39. 9). In his *Epistle to Victor of Rome* (in Eusebius, *HE*

[1] See H. Ch. Puech in Vol. I, p. 275ff.; H. M. Schenke, *ThLZ* 84, 1959, cols. 1ff. English translations by C. J. de Catanzaro, *JTS* 13 (1962) 35ff., and R. McL. Wilson, *The Gospel of Philip*, London and New York, 1962. Text and German translation in W. C. Till, *Das Evangelium nach Philippos*, Berlin 1963.

[2] Th. Zahn, *Forsch.* VI, pp. 24–27.

[3] Th. Zahn, *op. cit.*, p. 26, n. 2; Th. Zahn, *Geschichte d. ntl. Kanons* II. 2, p. 766, n. 1; Harnack, *Marcion* (*TU* 45), ²1924, p. 254*, n. 1.

III. 31. 3) Polycrates of Ephesus speaks of Philip one of the apostles,

who sleeps in Hierapolis with his two aged virgin daughters, whilst another daughter, who lived in the Holy Spirit, fell asleep in Ephesus.

The daughters of Philip the apostle are doubtless derived from Acts 21: 8f., where, however, the evangelist Philip (6:5; 8:5ff.) is their father.[1] The same mistake also presents itself in the *Martyrdom of Andrew* (Aa II. 1, p. 47), where the apostle Philip is turned into the missionary to Samaria. John of Asia also seems through confusion with the son of Zebedee to have come by apostolic dignity (Papias in Eusebius, *HE* III. 39. 4, also Eusebius, *ib.* 39. 1–7). According to the earliest tradition Philip did not become a martyr (Heracleon on Lk. 12:8ff., in Clement of Alexandria, *Strom.* IV, 71. 3). On his grave see p. 43 above. Further literature: P. W. Schmiedel, 'Philip the Apostle and Philip the Evangelist', *Encyclopaedia Biblica* 3697–3701; Th. Zahn, *Forsch.* VI, p. 369b; Paul Corssen, 'Die Töchter des Philippus', *ZNW* 2, 1901, pp. 289ff.; H. Waitz, 'Die Quellen der Philippusgeschichten in der AG 8, 5–40', *ZNW* 7, 1906, pp. 340ff.; E. Schwartz, 'Zur Chronologie des Paulus', *Nachr. d. kön. Gesellsch. der Wissensch. zu Göttingen, phil-histor. kl.* 1907, pp. 263ff., especially 279ff.; against that H. Waitz, *ZKG* 55, 1936, p. 260, n. 40; Joh. Jeremias, *Das Evangelium des Diakonen Philippus*, 1933; E. Barnikol, 'Die drei Phasen der Formgeschichte der Petrus-Philippus-Quelle um 75–135 n. Chr.', *Theol. Jahrbücher* edit. by Barnikol, Halle 1957; W. C. van Unnik, 'Der Befehl an Philippus', *ZNW* 47, 1956, pp. 181–191.

Bartholomew counts in the *Sophia Jesu Christi* as one of the recipients of the esoteric revelation (see Vol. I, p. 247). Eusebius (*HE* V. 10. 3) tells of an early tradition according to which Pantaenus, when on his journey to India, came upon Christian churches whose founder was said to have been Bartholomew. To him these Christians were also supposedly indebted for the Hebrew Gospel of Matthew.[2] A series of later apocryphal texts are associated with the apostle Bartholomew.[3] In the *Gospel of Bartholomew* Bartholomew passes as one called by Jesus from the custom-house (c. 49; see Vol. I, p. 499; cf. note 4), he is the spokesman of the disciples at the time of the reception of the

[1] Cf. Th. Zahn, *Forschungen zur Geschichte d. ntl. Kanons VI*, pp. 158ff.
[2] On the question of the Hebrew Gospel of Matthew cf. Ph. Vielhauer, Vol. I, pp. 117ff.
[3] See on this W. Schneemelcher, Vol. I, pp. 484ff.; 503f.

revelation after the resurrection, and plays the part of one of the Lord's interrogators (see Vol. I, pp. 488ff.).

Thomas is mentioned by name by Papias in the preface to the κυριακῶν ἐξηγήσεις, in the *Epist. Apost.* 2 (13); 11 (22) (see Vol. I, pp. 192, 197), and in the *Sophia Jesu Christi* (see Vol. I, p. 247). In the *Pistis Sophia* (c. 42f., see Vol. I, p. 272) he is appointed along with Philip and Matthew *to write all the discourses of the kingdom of light and to testify thereto.* He seems to have been reckoned as the authority for and the writer of the *Apocalypse of Thomas.*[1] The *Acts of Thomas* introduces him as the author (see pp. 425ff. below); cf. further on the *Gospel of Thomas* Vol. I, pp. 278ff. A fragment that goes back to Irenaeus (in de Lagarde, *Catenae in evang. aegyptiacae* 1886, p. 220) relates how Thomas was not present at the crucifixion of Jesus, but without more ado believed his fellow-disciples regarding the wonder wrought by the spear-thrust. Their assertion, however, that Jesus was risen met with his unbelief.[2] According to the *Acts of Thomas* the apostle always kept himself aloof from women (c. 144). The earlier tradition (Origen in Eusebius, *HE* III. 1. 1; pseudo-Clement, *rec.* IX. 29) describes Thomas as the apostle of the Parthians. On his calling see pp. 39f. above, on his natural death Heracleon on Lk. 12:8ff. (according to Clement of Alexandria, *Strom.* IV. 71. 3). Nevertheless in the *Manichaean Psalm-book* (p. 142. 28f., Allberry), entirely as in the *Acts of Thomas* (c. 164, 168), he is pierced through by four soldiers with a spear. Among the Syrians Thomas also bears the name Judas. They have besides the traitor two further disciples of his name: Judas Thomas and Judas Jacobi.[3] The *Gospel of Thomas* included in Codex III from Nag Hammadi names him Didymus Judas Thomas (see Vol. I, p. 285); the *Acts of Thomas* also confers upon its hero the surname Didymus (see Vol. I, p. 286, and pp. 425ff. below), which, however, is nothing other than the Greek equivalent of the Aramaic *taumā, tomā = twin.* For further designations of Thomas in the *Acts of Thomas* see Vol. I, p. 286. Thomas is also met with in the Abgar legend, in which it is recorded that after the ascension he sent Thaddaeus to Edessa (Eusebius, *HE* I. 13. 4, 11; II. 1. 6), so also in Ephraem (Burkitt, *Evangelium da-Mepharresche* 2, pp. 146f.) and elsewhere.[4] Ephraem distinguishes Judas Thomas

[1] See *Decretum Gelasianum*, Vol. I, p. 48, l. 10; James, pp. 555ff. (further literature there); de Santos, p. 798 below.

[2] Cf. Manucci, "Ein unbeachtetes Irenäusfragment", *Theologie und Glaube* 1, 1909, p. 291; Vogels, *Bibl. Zeitschr.* 10, 1913, p. 404.

[3] Cf. syr. cur. at Jn. 14: 22. Thomas besides Judas Jacobi in the Syriac lists of the apostles: Tatian in Isho'dadh of Merv, Hjelt, *Altsyrische Evangelienübersetzungen*, p. 34; syr. sin. at Mt. 10:2-4 and Lk. 6:15f.; *Acta Thom.* 1.

[4] Cf. A. Merx, *Die vier kanonischen Evangelien nach ihrem ältesten bekannten Texte. Übersetzung und Erläuterung der syrischen im Sinaikloster gefundenen Palimpsesthandschrift* II. 1, 1902, p. 173.

alike from Judas Jacobi and from Judas the Lord's brother, the two last being for him one and the same person.[1] On the other hand the *Acts of Thomas* regards Judas Thomas as the brother of the Lord and indeed as a twin-brother (so quite clearly c. 31, 39). Thomas and Jesus are evidently both sons of the carpenter Joseph (c. 2). The occasion of this conception of the apostle as a twin-brother lies clearly in the meaning of his name indicated above. Attempts have been made to secure for him still other twin brothers and sisters: e.g. in pseudo-Clement, *hom.* II. 1, a brother Eliezer.

Matthew is met with in the *Gospel of the Ebionites* (Fragm. 1, Vol. I, p. 156), in the *Sophia Jesu Christi* (see Vol. I, p. 247), in the *Pistis Sophia* (see Vol. I, p. 256), the *Books of Jeû* (see Vol. I, pp. 261, 262), and in Papias in the preface to the κυριακῶν ἐξηγήσεις (in Eusebius, *HE* III, 39. 4) and in other passages of the same work (in Eusebius, *HE* III. 39. 16). On his wealth, see p. 39 above, likewise on the view that he belonged to the uncircumcised. Usually he passes as a Jew as do the other apostles, cf. the so-called monarchian Prologue to the Gospel of Matthew (*KlT* 1, p. 12); Eusebius also is not in doubt about that since, following Julius Africanus, he calls Matthew *a Syrian man, a tax-collector by occupation and, to judge by his speech, a Hebrew* (*quaest. ad Steph.*, in A. Mai, *Nova Patr. Bibl.* IV. 1, p. 270). In the tax-gatherer Matthew the especially gross sins are readily seen: Origen (*hom.* I. 13 *in Gen.*), the *Syriac Didascalia* (p. 54 Flemming). The view that he was a strict vegetarian (Clement of Alexandria, *paed.* II. 1. 16) has its basis in a confusion with the apostle Matthias, to whose encratitic views prominence is given by Clement of Alexandria (*Strom.* III. 26. 4). On his peaceful death see Heracleon (*ib.* IV. 71. 3). Not until a later time was every possible martyrdom falsely attributed to him. As a missionary Matthew is said to have worked first of all among the Hebrews and then to have migrated (Eusebius, *HE* III. 24. 6). His activity among the Hebrews is related to the conviction that Matthew composed in the Hebrew tongue the Gospel which has been assigned to him from early times and without objection being raised; so first of all Papias (in Eusebius, *HE* III. 39. 16) and then Irenaeus (*adv. haer.* III. 1. 1, with a more exact statement of time). The latter connects with that the view that Matthew wrote as the first of the Evangelists, an opinion which very soon prevailed in the church; cf. below on Mark. Pantaenus is said to have found the Hebrew Gospel of Matthew among the Indians see p. 58 above; Vol. I, p. 123). On the question of the Hebrew proto-Matthew cf. Vielhauer in Vol. I, pp. 118ff. With Matthew's

[1] See J. R. Harris, *Four Lectures on the Western Text*, 1894, p. 37.

position as a Gospel writer there is certainly connected the fact
that the catalogue of the apostles in the *Apostolic Church Order*
assigns to him the second place—after John and before Peter
(cf. A. Jülicher, *RE* 12, pp. 428ff.). According to the *Book of
Thomas the Athlete* Matthew heard and wrote down the words
of the Lord that were made known to Thomas (see Vol. I,
p. 307).

James, the son of Alphaeus, is wanting in the list of the apostles
in the *Apostolic Church Order* and in the *Epistula Apostolorum*.
Numerous witnesses for Mk. 2:14, as e.g. Cod. D, certain Old
Latin manuscripts (see A. Jülicher–W. Matzkow, *Itala. Das NT
in altlateinischer Überlieferung* II, 1940, p. 14), minuscules, the
supposed *Commentary on Mark* of Victor of Antioch I. 34 (ed.
C. F. Matthäi, Moscow 1775, or I. A. Cramer, *Catenae in Evang.
Mti. et Mci.*, Oxford 1840, cf. Altaner, p. 479) have equated the
tax-gatherer who was won by Jesus and who was indeed also a
son of Alphaeus with our James, and accordingly have altered
the name Levi. Tatian already gave the name James to the tax-
gatherer whose conversion is related in his *Gospel Harmony*.[1] In
his catalogue, however, he has withheld the title of tax-collector
from *James the Lebbaean, who is called the son of Alphaeus* (Isho'dadh
in Hjelt, pp. 34, 124f.) in favour of Matthew. James the Just
was early identified with the son of Alphaeus.[2]

Simon. Ordinarily the catalogues of the apostles carry a second
Simon, who is called *the Canaanean* in Matthew and Mark, also
in the *Act. Thom.* 1, *the Canaanite* by some witnesses to Mt. 10:4,
Mk. 3:18, and the *Manichaean Psalm-book* (pp. 192. 14; 194. 15,
Allberry), on the other hand *the Zealot* in Luke, in the Acts of the
Apostles and in the *Gospel of the Ebionites* (Fragm. 1, Vol. I,
p. 156). As regards the Acts of the Apostles no second Simon can
actually be spoken of since in it the first is merely called Peter.
The *Epistula Apostolorum* has besides Peter a Judas Zelotes (2 (13),
Vol. I, p. 192). Has the pronounced opposition to the heretic
Simon—without a distinguishing surname (1 (12), *ib.*, p. 191)—
here brought it about that the name Simon completely disappeared from the list of the apostles, whilst Simon Zelotes and
Judas Jacobi coalesced? For the rest *Judas the Zealot* occurs in
early Old Latin manuscripts in Mt. 10:3 in place of Lebbaeus
(see Jülicher-Matzkow, *Itala* I, 1938, p. 56).

The name *Judas Jacobi* is in the NT a characteristic of the
writer to Theophilus, but it occurs also in the list of the *Acts of
Thomas* (c. 1) and is probably to be equated with the apostle

[1] Ephraem, *Comm. on the Diatessaron*, p. 67; p. 50.1.
[2] Cf. Holtzmann, 'Jakobus der Gerechte und seine Namensbrüder', *Zeitschr. f.
wissenschaftl. Theol.* 23, 1880, pp. 198–221.

Judas (Jn. 14:22). Origen (*Comm. in ep. ad Rom.* praef. VI. 8 Lommatzsch) was already of opinion that the apostle Judas Jacobi had at the same time borne the names Thaddaeus and Lebbaeus. His opinion was based on the fact that the name Judas Jacobi is lacking in the lists of Matthew and Mark and that in place of it the latter has a Thaddaeus and the former a Lebbaeus.

Thaddaeus is entered among the twelve in the *Gospel of the Ebionites* (Frg. 1; Vol. I, p. 156). On the other hand, the Abgar legend knows a Thaddaeus whom it reckons to the seventy (Eusebius, *HE* I. 13. 4, 11, also I. 12. 3). Later that led to two disciples of the same name being distinguished: the one of them had to belong to the narrower, the other to the wider circle (Lipsius, *Die apokryphen Apostelgeschichten* I, 1883, p. 20). Thaddaeus is the hero of the Greek Acts, the content of which joins on to the Edessene Abgar legend; on this see James, p. 471.

Lebbaeus is in pseudo-Clement, *rec.* I. 59, a member of the college of the twelve (see p. 37 above).

Judas Iscariot occupies the last place in the catalogues of the canonical Gospels. The *Gospel of the Ebionites* (Frg. 1; Vol. I, p. 156) also counts him alongside of other apostles; so also the *Manichaean Psalm-book* (Allberry, pp. 192. 18; 194. 17). What is thought to be known about him, his person, his work, his motives, his fate, often ties up with the New Testament statements: avarice as his guiding principle (Origen, *c. Cels.* II. 11; *Comm. in Mt. ser.* 75, 78; *Acta Thom.* 84). Jesus knew the weakness of his pupil from the beginning (Origen, *in Cant. Cant.* IV) and was also aware what consequences it would have (Origen, *Comm. in Mt. ser.* 80; Tertullian, *de pat.* 3. 7, *Corp. Christ.* 1, p. 301). Nevertheless he suffered him about himself (*Syriac Didascalia* p. 21 Flemming), indeed he appointed him treasurer (Tertullian, *de anima* 11. 5, *Corp. Christ.* 2, p. 797). He desired even to better him, and that was altogether within the reach of possibility since Judas was not predestined to commit his crime (Origen, *in Cant. Cant.* IV). He did not need to be an evil-doer; rather he could have been equal to Peter (Origen, ex tom. III. *in Gen.* 6, 7). His association with Jesus must also have had an influence upon him, and prevented him from going altogether to the bad (Origen, *c. Cels.* II, 11; *Comm. in Mt. ser.* 117; *Comm. in Joh.* XXXII. 19 (12), *GCS* 10, p. 458). In the *Syriac Didascalia* (pp. 110f. Flemming) we find the account of Judas's atrocious deed amplified with material that goes beyond what the canonical writings provide. Here the betrayal is transferred to the night of Tuesday. Judas had already obtained his reward on Monday 10th Nisan. Christendom early saw in Judas the embodiment of all the anti-godly instincts that are in man and imputed to him faults of which the New Testament knows nothing. Thus Irenaeus (*adv. haer.* V. 33. 3f.) communicates to us from the writing of Papias a fragment, the main content of which is a word of the Lord regarding the untold fertility that there is to be in the new kingdom, but to it he adds the remark that Jesus met with unbelief in the case of Judas and that the Lord indicated to him that he would not see the kingdom of heaven. The same story is told us more briefly and with some differences by Hippolytus, *Comm. on Daniel* IV. 60 (*GCS* 1. 1 Bonwetsch p. 338): Judas is counted among the unworthy.[1] In early Christian times the view already expressed in the NT that Satan had helped the evil in Judas to prevail was repeated extremely often: *Act. Petr.* 8; *Act. Thom.* 32; Tertullian, *de anima* 11; *adv. Marc.* III. 7; Origen, *Comm. in Mt. ser.* 75; *de princ.* III. 2. 1. Since the anti-christ has Dan, *the serpent in the way* (Gen. 49:17), as progenitor (Hippol. *de antichr.* 14, *GCS* 1. 2 Bonwetsch p. 11), Judas, his relative, must also belong to this breed (Hippol. frg. *in Gen.* no. XXXf., *ib.* pp. 64f.). Yet there were Christians who did not join in the general judgment of condemnation because they assessed the character and conduct of Judas in another way. Irenaeus (*adv. haer.* I. 31. 1) records that the Cainites discerned in Judas an instrument of Sophia and therefore an object of hatred to the Demiurge. He alone recognized the truth and accomplished the mystery of the betrayal. What importance that has is shown in the *Syntagma* of Hippolytus, in so far as the relevant contents of it can be restored from pseudo-Tertullian (*adv. omn. haer.* 2) and Epiphanius (*Haer.* 38. 3). According to them the Cainites fall into two groups which certainly agree in describing Judas as wonderful and great, yet are not at one as regards the significance of Jesus. The members of the one group declare him to be of inferior worth and see the merit of Judas especially in this, that when Christ would have destroyed the truth, he betrayed him and thus put a stop to his destructive doings. Those of the other group do not see the incentive of Judas in the wickedness of Jesus. Rather they think that the powers of this world strove with all their might to hold back catastrophe in the Saviour's life in order to make away with salvation. Wherefore Judas accomplished the betrayal and wrested the possession of blessedness for mankind. In view of such a valuation we are not surprised to find a Gospel carried back to Judas (see on this Vol. I, pp. 313f.).

Quite early Christendom followed up the history of the traitor

[1] On the relation of Hippolytus to Irenaeus and Papias see Zahn, *Forsch.* VI. p. 128, n. 2.

with an interest that was mingled with dread. The NT already contains two different stories about the death of Judas (Mt. 27:3–10; Acts 1:16–26). Yet another account of the end of Judas is given by Papias in Book IV of his work (preserved in Apollinaris of Laodicea in Cramer's *Catenae*, Oxford 1838 and 1840, on Mt. 27 and Acts 1; German in *Apokr.* 2, p. 130). There it is said that Judas swelled out so enormously that he could no longer come through where a vehicle could pass easily. Finally his belly burst asunder and his bowels were scattered.[1]

Levi. Whilst in Mt. 9:9 a tax-gatherer Matthew is called and in this Gospel the apostle Matthew is expressly named a *tax-gatherer* (10:3), Mark and Luke have likewise a Matthew in their catalogues, but give Levi as the name of the tax-gatherer whose winning for Christ they also relate (Mk. 2:14ff.; Lk. 5:27ff.). Easy as it must have been for early Christendom to identify Matthew and Levi, a thing that perhaps was also done in the *Manichaean Psalm-book* (194. 7–17 Allberry), nevertheless quite early we find the two side by side, namely in Heracleon (in Clement of Alexandria, *Strom.* IV. 71. 3) and the *Gospel of Peter* 60 (Vol. I, p. 187), where a Levi, son of Alphaeus, accompanies Simon Peter and Andrew. The *Syriac Didascalia* (p. 107 Flemming) relates how in the early morning of Easter Sunday the risen Christ entered the house of Levi. Moreover the name Levi was clearly intruded quite early into the catalogues of the apostles. At least Origen, who did not identify the tax-gatherer Levi with Matthew but excluded him from the college of the twelve, reports that some exemplars of the Gospel of Mark included Levi in the twelve (*c. Cels.* I. 62). Evidently he has in mind manuscripts in which in Mk. 3:18 a Levi, son of Alphaeus, from Mk. 2:14 was substituted for James, the son of Alphaeus. The *Gospel of Peter* (see Vol. I, p. 187) also clearly includes Levi, son of Alphaeus, among the most intimate.

Cephas. The registers of the apostles in the *Epistula Apostolorum* and the *Apostolic Church Order* include a Cephas distinct from Peter and also Nathanael. This distinction also occurs in Clement of Alexandria. According to Eusebius (*HE* I. 12. 2) he reports in Book V of the *Hypotyposes that Cephas, regarding whom Paul says . . . (Gal. 2:11), was one of the 70 disciples and bore the same name as the apostle Peter.* In the Epistle to the Galatians there is

---

[1] Cf. F. Overbeck, *Zeitschr. f. wissenschaftl. Theol.* 10, 1867, pp. 39ff.; A. Hilgenfeld, *ib.* 15, 1872, pp. 262ff.; Th. Zahn, *Theol. Studien und Kritiken*, 39, 1866, pp. 68off.; Th. Zahn, *Forsch.* VI, pp. 153ff.; 126, n. 2; W. Wrede, *Vorträge und Studien*, 1907, pp. 140ff. – On *Iscariot* cf. F. Schulthess, *ZNW* 21 1922, pp. 250ff.; C. C. Torrey, *HTR* 36, 1943, pp. 51ff.; B. Gärtner, *Die rätselhaften Termini Nazoräer und Iskariot*, Lund 1957; C. Colpe, review of Gärtner, *ThLZ* 86, 1961, cols. 31–34.

thus given the motive or at least one of the motives for this juxtaposing of Peter and Cephas.[1]

Nathanael appears to have been described in the *Diatessaron* as a scribe,[2] a tradition which is found again in Chrysostom's exposition of the Gospel of John (*hom.* 20) and in Augustine (*tract.* VII. 17). Epiphanius (*Haer.* 23. 6. 5) assumes as generally known that Nathanael was the unknown Emmaus disciple.[3] In the apocryphal Gospel-fragment of the Berlin papyrus 11710 (not earlier than the 6th century), which Lietzmann published in *ZNW* 22, 1923, pp. 153f., Jn. 1:49 and 29 are united in a dialogue between Nathanael and the rabbi (Jesus), and there is added this admonition to Nathanael: Walk in the sun! (perhaps in contrast with his recorded sitting in the shadow of the fig-tree vv. 48, 50?). Regarding Nathanael in the catalogue of the apostles see p. 36 above.

Matthias. Finally there may be included among the twelve the substitute Matthias. Origen (*c. Cels.* II. 65) thus explains the number twelve of the disciples in 1 Cor. 15:5. That does not exclude the possibility that earlier in his life Matthias may have belonged to the 70 (tradition in Eusebius, *HE* I. 12. 3). Th. Zahn (*Forschungen* II, p. 759) conjectures, whilst A. Harnack (*Gesch. der altchristl. Lit. bis Eusebius* II. 1, pp. 597f.) legitimately denies, that the Matthew mentioned repeatedly in the *Pistis Sophia* (see Vol. I, p. 256) arose through confusion with Matthias. Rather the vegetarian Matthias, whose encratitic tendency is emphasized by Clement of Alexandria (*Strom.* III. 26. 3) may be at the back of the preference for vegetable food which Clement repeats for Matthew (*Paed.* II. 1. 16). Clement also alleges that the occurrences in the story of Zacchaeus the tax-gatherer (Lk. 19) were referred by others to Matthias. Into that there fits well the fact that in a Coptic Bartholomew-text Matthias is represented as one *who was rich and forsook all to follow Jesus* (James, p. 185). Matthias also plays a part in another Coptic fragment (see Vol. I, p. 505). According to the Andrew-Matthias Acts (Aa II. 1, pp. 65ff.), at the time of the partition of the world, the land of the cannibals fell to Matthias as his missionary territory. On his arrival in that land Matthias was blinded and cast into prison. But after his eyesight had been restored by God, he was delivered

---

[1] Cf. F. Overbeck, *Über die Auffassung des Streites des Paulus mit Petrus in Antiochien* (*Gal.* 2:11ff.) *bei den Kirchenvätern, Baseler Programm* 1877; G. Krüger, *ZNW* 7, 1906, p. 190; further literature in W. Bauer, *Griech.-deutsches Wörterbuch zu den Schriften des NT*, 1958, s.v. *Petrus.*

[2] Ephraem, *Commentary on the Diatessaron*, p. 58; p. 43, 7f.; H. Hill, *A Dissertation on the Gospel Commentary of St. Ephraem the Syrian*, 1896, p. 81; Th. Zahn, *Forsch.* I, pp. 126f.

[3] On this see also scholia on Lk. 24:18 in Tischendorf, *Nov. Test. Graece*, editio octava crit. maior I, 1896, p. 726; Th. Zahn, *Forsch.* VI, p. 350 n. 1.

from his imprisonment in a wonderful way by Andrew. On the rôle of Matthias as the authority of Basilides and his followers, as also on the question of the Matthias-Gospel, see Vol. I, pp. 308ff.

The seventy disciples. Of the persons named thus far Thaddaeus, Cephas (see above) and Matthias were often counted among the 70 disciples. In the NT only Lk. 10:1 knows this wider circle of disciples, to which the textual witnesses allow sometimes 70 members (אAC and the majority of the uncials, the Old Latin a b c e l f q, Irenaeus, Tertullian, Hippolytus, Origen, Eusebius, Ulfilas, the Peshitta and the Late Syriac), sometimes 72 members (BD Diatessaron, Syr. sin. cur., the majority of the Vetus-Latina-manuscripts (cf. Jülicher, *Itala* III, 1954, p. 116), the Vulgate, pseudo-Clement, *rec.* I. 40, Origen (lat.), Adamantius, Jerome, Augustine, Epiphanius). According to Hippolytus (Arabic Fragments on the Pentateuch XVII, *GCS* I. 2, p. 105 Achelis) Jesus sent these men as messengers to the Gentiles that 40 days later (the statement of time comes from Num. 13:25), after their return to him, he might receive their report. On their initiation into the knowledge of the truth see p. 79 below. Origen (*c. Cels.* II. 65) sees in them *all the apostles* who according to 1 Cor. 15:7 had seen the risen Christ. Eusebius (*HE* I. 12. 1) still did not know any list which comprised the names of every personality forming this circle. But he knew that there had been reckoned to that college this and that celebrity of the first times. He begins (*loc. cit.*) his comments on the 70 with the observation that Barnabas and Sosthenes (1 Cor. 1:1) had belonged to them. Although it does not clearly emerge from his own words, it is overwhelmingly likely that he owes this knowledge to the *Hypotyposes* of Clement of Alexandria, which is cited immediately afterwards (cf. Zahn, *Forschungen* III, pp. 68, 148f.). At all events as regards Barnabas it is certain that Clement included him among the 70. He does that not merely in the *Hypotyposes* (VII.) but likewise in the *Stromateis* (II. 116. 3). So also he reckons a Cephas who is distinct from Peter to the wider circle of disciples (see above on Cephas) and also, if an unknown Latinist is to be trusted, and that in spite of Th. Zahn (*ib.*, pp. 70, 148f.) is certainly doubtful (Th. Schermann, *Propheten- und Apostelle-genden, TU* 31. 3, 1907, pp. 296f.), the eunuch of queen Candace (Acts 8:26–40). What further information Eusebius (*HE* I. 12. 3) is able to give about the circle of the 70 certainly does not come from the Alexandrian. But the generally worded phrase *it is reported* shows that what he communicates is older than himself. According to it Matthias and Joseph Barsabbas, his rival contestant, belonged to the 70; also—introduced by *it is said—*

66

Thaddaeus (see above). Origen (*Comm. in Rom.* X. 21) would regard Andronicus and Junias, who are named with respect by Paul in Rom. 16:7, as members of the college of the 70 (or 72). In his *Dialogue* Adamantius defends against the contradiction of Megethius (I. 5 *GCS* 4, pp. 8ff. van de Sande Bakhuyzen) the thesis that Mark and Luke belonged to the 72 disciples (10. 14). Very many other celebrities of the first Christian period were naturally assigned to this group, but, in my opinion, demonstrably only at a later time. For whether, in calling them *disciples of the Lord*, Papias wishes to enrol among the 70 the Aristion mentioned in the preface to the κυριακῶν ἐξηγήσεις (in Eusebius, *HE* III. 39. 4) and the 'elder' John remains questionable. The complete registers which were sketched out (on them see Th. Schermann, *op. cit.* pp. 292ff.) also belong to a later time. In what follows something will be said about some of the members who have been named.

Barnabas, who is called an apostle by Clement of Alexandria (*Strom.* II. 31. 2, cf. 116. 3) and already in Acts 14:14 (cf. also verse 4), is in pseudo-Clement, *hom.* I. 9–16; II. 4, a personal disciple of Jesus, a strict servant of the law, a Palestinian by birth, but residing in Alexandria, where he comes to know Clement that soon afterwards he may journey before him to Judaea and there bring about his acquaintance with Peter. The *Recognitions*, which identify Barnabas with Matthias (I. 60; cf. Th. Zahn, *Forschungen* II, p. 562) and thus enrol him as substitute for the betrayer in the band of the twelve, have the meeting between Clement and Barnabas take place in Rome, whither the latter had brought the gospel already in the life-time of Jesus (1. 6f.). The *Acts of Peter* (c. 4) also knows of a stay of Barnabas in Rome. For Tertullian (*de pud.* 20. 2, *Corp. Christ.* 2, p. 1324) and the *Tractatus Origenis* (*PL* Suppl. I, 417) the Epistle to the Hebrews counts as a work of Barnabas. And the so-called *Epistle of Barnabas* also has likewise been carried back to our Barnabas ever since it was cited, i.e. since the time of Clement of Alexandria (*Strom.* II. 31. 2; 35. 5 and often). In the *Decretum Gelasianum* (see Vol. I, p. 47) as also in the *List of the 60 Books* (see Vol. I, p. 52) there appears a *Gospel of Barnabas* which baffles us.

Joseph Barsabbas, called Justus, is mentioned by Papias (in Eusebius, *HE* III. 39. 9). As Eusebius reports, Papias tells the story of a miracle which befell Justus Barsabbas, who drank deadly poison without taking hurt from it (cf. Mk. 16:18). Philip of Side brings forward the same story from Papias (Funk-Bihlmeyer, *Die apostolischen Väter*, [2]1956, p. 139). In the *Acta Pauli* (*Martyrdom of Paul* II; Aa I, p. 108) a Barsabbas Justus appears among Nero's celebrities.

67

Mark, according to the monarchian Prologue to the Gospel of Mark (*KlT* 1, p. 15), was a Levite—clearly as the cousin of the Levite Barnabas (Acts 4:36)—and was converted and baptized by Peter—doubtless because of 1 Pet. 5:13—and later was bishop of Alexandria. The latter statement also stood in the *Chronography* of Julius Africanus (A. Harnack, *Geschichte der altchristlichen Literatur bis Eusebius* II. 1, pp. 123f.); cf. Eusebius, *HE* II. 16. 1; II. 24. Of the description of Mark as *stump-fingered*, which is treated by Hippolytus (*Ref.* VII. 30) as widely spread abroad, the so-called antimarcionite Prologue to Mark[1] gives the explanation: because his fingers were too small in comparison with the length of the rest of his body.[2] Moreover the Prologue defends the view which already lies before us in the NT (cf. Phlm. 24; Col. 4:10; 2 Tim. 4:11; 1 Pet. 5:13, see p. 49 above), that Mark was in Rome: *he wrote his Gospel in Italy*. For tradition there never counts as the Gospel composed by Mark any other than our second one. Tradition also asserts unanimously that Peter had an indirect share in the work. Mark is in fact nothing other than the *interpreter* of Peter (so already Papias in Eusebius, *HE* III. 39. 15). In Tertullian (*adv. Marc.* IV. 5. 3f., *Corp. Christ.* 1, p. 551) we read:

> (The Gospel) which Mark published can be regarded as that of Peter, whose interpreter Mark was. . . . We do well in ascribing to teachers what their pupils have published.

As regards the extent of Peter's participation there are different opinions. As the legend grows, it tends to make the relation between Peter and the Gospel of Mark closer and closer. Papias (see above) stands at the beginning of this development so far as we are able to trace it.[3] Irenaeus (*adv. haer.* III. 1. 1) follows. Origen may not have gone any farther than Irenaeus, only he takes the series Matthew, Mark, Luke, John as quite definitely chronological (Eusebius, *HE* VI. 25. 4–6), as the *Muratori Canon* (see Vol. I, p. 43) and certainly the so-called monarchian Prologue already do. According to Clement of Alexandria, *Hypotyposes* VI (in Eusebius, *HE* VI. 14. 5–7) the Gospel of Mark came into being on the following occasion:

> After Peter had proclaimed the word publicly in Rome and preached the gospel in the Spirit, the numerous (hearers) who were present requested Mark, since he had already for a long time accompanied

---

[1] Text in de Bruyne, *Rev. Bén.* 40, 1928, pp. 193ff.; Huck-Lietzmann, *Synopse der drei ersten Evangelien*, [10]1950, p. VIII.

[2] Cf. on this A. Harnack, *ZNW* 3, 1902, p. 165 n. 1; E. Nestle, *ib.* 4, 1903, p. 347.

[3] On the origin of this tradition cf. E. Haenchen, *Die Apostelgeschichte* (Krit-exeget. Kommentar zum NT, initiated by H. A. W. Meyer) [12]1959, p. 414 n. 2. Cf. *ib.*, p. 8 n. 3, on the problem of the so-called antimarcionite Prologues.

Peter and remembered his words, to write down his preaching. Mark did this and delivered the Gospel to those who had requested it. When Peter learned of this, he neither hindered it with a word of admonition nor encouraged it.

Eusebius gives an account of his own in his *hist. eccl.* II. 15. It contains trimmings to the account of Clement of Alexandria that are characteristic of Eusebius and his time. Peter had learned of the matter through the Holy Spirit, rejoiced over the zeal of the Romans and authorized the Gospel for the churches (see also Eusebius, *demonstr. evang.* III. 5. 89–95 and cf. Justin, *dial. c. Tryph.* 106; *Act. Petr.* 20; Victorinus of Pettau, *Comm. on the Rev.* 4. 4, p. 50 Haussleiter). On Mark as Peter's own son see p. 47 above.

Luke, according to the *Muratori Canon* lines 6f. (see Vol. I, p. 43), *did not see the Lord in the flesh.* In the dialogue of Adamantius, *De recta in Deum fide* (*GCS* 4, 1901, van de Sande Bakhuyzen pp. 8ff.) Megethius asserts on the other hand that Luke had indeed not been a disciple of the Lord (in the narrow sense), but had belonged to the 72 disciples. Col. 4:14 describes Luke as a physician, and that posterity often repeated (*Muratori Canon* line 3, Vol. I, p. 43; the so-called monarchian Prologue to the Gospel of Luke, *KlT* 1, p. 14; Irenaeus, *adv. haer.* III. 14. 1; Eusebius, *HE* III. 4. 6); Marcion has, it is true, completely struck out the epithet *beloved.*[1] The *Muratori Canon* also reports what had occasioned Paul to take him with him (lines 4f.: Vol. I, p. 43). Overstating the closeness of the relation to the apostle, Irenaeus (*adv. haer.* III. 14. 1) says that Luke *was inseparable from Paul and was his colleague in the gospel.* The relations between the two must have been represented in the same way by those also who would have Luke report in the Acts only what he himself had experienced (*Muratori Canon* lines 35ff., Vol. I *loc. cit.*; Eusebius, *HE* III. 4. 6).

That does not prevent Luke from appearing on occasion as the pupil of a number of apostles (Irenaeus, *adv. haer.* III. 10. 1; 14. 2 and the so-called monarchian Prologue to the Gospel of Luke). After all in his second book he deals with other apostles besides Paul. Already before Origen (*hom.* I in Luc.) Paul's helper Luke was found in the brother of 2 Cor. 8:18, and later many repeated that. Many held that as a term that would give prominence to, and make honourable mention of, his accomplishments in the service of the gospel even the title *apostle* was not too high (Hippol., *de antichr.* 56; cf. Th. Zahn, *Forsch.* VI, p. 7 n. 2). The so-called monarchian Prologue and Eusebius (*HE* III. 4. 6) describe Luke as a Syrian, in particular as an Antiochean, and

[1] See Zahn, *Forsch.* I, p. 647; II, p. 528; Harnack, *Marcion,* p. 50; 124*.

that was perhaps also the opinion of Julius Africanus (in Eusebius, *quaest. evang. ad Stephanum* in Mai, *Nova. patr. bibl.* 4. 1, p. 270).[1] The reading (Cod. D and the Old Latins, among them Augustine)[2] which permits the we-report to set in for the first time at Acts 11:28 certainly also testifies to the existence of this view. Like Luke, Theophilus also, to whom he dedicates his two-volumed work, is early thought of as resident in Antioch (pseudo-Clement, *rec.* X. 71). The so-called monarchian Prologue to the Gospel of Luke reports further particulars from his life (*KlT.* 1, p. 14). The *Martyrdom of Paul* (see p. 383 below) mentions a journey of Luke to Gaul, and Epiphanius speaks of his preaching there (*Haer.* 51. 11). This doubtless assumes the reading Γαλλίαν instead of the better attested Γαλατίαν in 2 Tim. 4:10, a reading which is given in the codd. ℵ C, minuscules, several Vulgate manuscripts and was already known to Eusebius (*HE* III. 4. 8). Luke was unanimously described by Christian antiquity as the author of the 3rd Gospel (already by Marcion?, see however Harnack, *Marcion*, pp. 40f., 124*, 249*f.) and of Acts (*Muratori Canon* 35f.; the so-called monarchian Prologue; Irenaeus, *adv. haer.* III. 13. 3; 15. 1; Clement of Alexandria, *Strom.* V. 82. 4), but in ever increasing measure he is made dependent in his literary work on Paul (Irenaeus, *adv. haer.* III. 1. 1; Tertullian, *adv. Marc.* IV. 5. 3), just as Mark is on Peter (see p. 68 above). According to Eusebius (*HE* VI. 14. 4) Clement of Alexandria defends in his *Adumbrationes* (on 1 Pet. 5:13, *GCS* 17, p. 206) the view that Luke translated for the Greeks the Epistle to the Hebrews composed by Paul in Hebrew, whilst Origen (in Eusebius, *HE* VI. 25. 14) even mentions a tradition which regarded Luke as the author of that epistle.[3]

The Emmaus Disciples. In later times Luke was occasionally identified with the unnamed Emmaus disciple (Zahn, *Forsch*, VI, p. 351 n. 1) and thus shared the lot of Nathanael (see p. 65 above). Much earlier than this identification is another. Origen (*c. Cels.* II. 62, 68; *hom. XX in Jerem.*, *GCS* 6 Klostermann, p. 191. 12–15; p. 192. 12f.; *Johanneskommentar* I. 5. 8, *GCS* 10 Preuschen, p. 10. 16f.; pp. 13f.) without the least hesitation names the two Emmaus disciples Cleopas and Simon. A marginal note in Cod. S on Lk. 24:18 (see Tischendorf *in loc.*) does the same, yet in such a way that Simon—Origen leaves this open—is expressly

---

[1] Cf. on this among others Spitta, *Der Brief des Julius Africanus an Aristides*, 1877, pp. 70–73; 111.

[2] Cf. Haenchen, *Die Apostelgeschichte, in loc.*

[3] Further Lk-accounts in R. A. Lipsius, *Die apokryphen Apostelgeschichten und Apostellegenden* II. 2, 1884, pp. 354ff.; on the problem of the Lk-accounts see also Haenchen, *Die Apostelgeschichte*, [12]1959, pp. 1ff.

distinguished from Peter. Ambrose is also a witness to this tradition, since he repeatedly names the two travellers Amaon or Ammaon and Kleopas; the name Simon was clearly subject to the influence of the place-name Emmaus (cf. Zahn, *Forsch.* IV, p. 313; VI, p. 351, n.; A. Loisy, *Les Évangiles synopt.* 2, p. 764 n. 4).

In early Christendom *Paul* underwent a discordant judgment, and the opinion that was entertained of his person and his life corresponded to that. The Jewish Christians dismissed the apostle to the Gentiles (Irenaeus, *adv. haer.* I. 26. 2; III. 15. 1; Origen, *c. Cels.* V. 65; *hom. XIX* 12 *in Jerem.*; Eusebius, *HE* III. 27. 4; see also Cerinthus in Filastrius of Brescia, *de haer.* 36 (according to Hippolytus, *Syntagma*?); Epiphanius, *Haer.* 38. 5). How in several particulars they thought about him is shown above all by the pseudo-Clementine writings. In them Paul is sometimes pushed into the background as a *certain hostile man* (*rec.* I. 70, 73; *Epist. Petr. ad Jac.* 2, see p. 112 below)—the observation that this man came to Damascus as an envoy of Caiaphas to persecute the Christians there (*Rec.* I. 71) leaves us in no doubt as to who is meant—sometimes slandered as Simon Magus. This mask is also transparent: *rec.* III. 49 Simon as a *chosen vessel* (Acts 9:15) of the devil; IV 34f. Peter advises the Tripolitans to trust no teacher who has not been attested by James, the Lord's brother. Apart from the twelve there are no genuine prophets and apostles. Cf. *hom.* XI. 35; XVII. 19: Peter denies that Simon = Paul had ever actually seen the Lord. Otherwise he would not have opposed and reviled as one *condemned* (Gal. 2:11) him whom Jesus named the solid rock-bed of the church. How strong an effect such antagonism could have on the view of Paul and his life we learn from the Jewish-Christian *Ascension of James* (Epiphanius, *Haer.* 30. 16):

Paul was a man of Tarsus and indeed a Hellene (=Gentile), the son of a Hellenist mother and a Hellenist father. Having gone up to Jerusalem and having remained there a long time, he desired to marry a daughter of the (high) priest and on that account submitted himself as a proselyte for circumcision. When nevertheless he did not obtain the girl, he became furious and began to write against circumcision, the sabbath, and the Law. (Cf. also *ib.* 30. 25[1].)

Much higher was the esteem that Paul enjoyed among the Gentile Christians. Not only is he the apostle par excellence for Marcion, but also 1 Clem. (5. 5ff.; 47. 1), Ignatius (*Eph.* 12:2;

[1] For the picture of Paul in the ps.-Clementines cf. also G. Strecker, *Das Judenchristentum in den Pseudoklementinen,* TU 70, 1958, pp. 187ff.

Rom. 4:3) and Polycarp (*ad Phil.* 3. 2; 9. 1; 11. 2f.) name him with the greatest respect as the apostle of Corinth, Ephesus and Philippi. The *Acts of Peter* and above all the *Acts of Paul* are documents of a veneration that is intensified to the utmost. Clement of Alexandria (*Strom.* I. 94. 4; V. 5. 1 and often) and others speak of the *divine* apostle to the Gentiles. Later he invades the list of the apostles and indeed secures in it the place immediately beside Peter (Th. Schermann, *Propheten- und Apostellegenden, TU* 31. 3, 1907, pp. 212, 209, 227). On this ground also the life of Paul is altered in respects which have only a loose hold on the NT or none at all. According to a tradition which, it is true, is attested only by Jerome (*de vir. ill.* 5: *in ep. ad Philem.* 23), Paul was born in the small town of Gischala in Galilee and only when a youth removed with his parents to Tarsus. The *Acts of Paul* (c. 3; see p. 354 below) contain a (not altogether invented?) description of the apostle in his prime. In the *Epistula Apostolorum* (31 (42); 33 (34), see Vol. I, pp. 213, 214) the risen Christ informs his disciples what part Paul is to play in the early history of his church. And indeed the twelve, who also pass as the founders of the Christian church of Damascus (33 (44), Vol. I, p. 214), are to take a decisive part in his conversion. Through the sign of the cross they restore him to sight, baptize him and initiate him into the teaching which they have received from the Lord. In that there is declared the conviction of the church, already prepared for in Acts, that the apostles as a body all expound the same gospel (Irenaeus, *adv. haer.* III. 13; Tertullian, *de praescr. haer.* 23, *Corp. Christ.* 1, pp. 204ff.); and certainly by the side of that the other conviction that the twelve, as the personal pupils of the Lord, are the only sure mainstays of the Christian teaching.[1] For Clement of Alexandria (*Strom.* III. 53. 1) Paul was a married man—because of Phil. 4:3—but did not take his wife with him on his journeys—because of 1 Cor. 9:5. Pierius has the married apostle separate himself from his wife and dedicate her to the service of the church (see C. de Boor, *Neue Fragmente des Papias, Hegesippus and Pierius, TU* 5. 2, 1888, pp. 170, 180).

Later Christians know also of some pupils, friends and companions of Paul whom the NT does not know, as Theodas, the teacher of Valentinus (Clement of Alexandria, *Strom.* VII. 106. 4). The life of the Christian emissary Paul, as we know it from the NT, is fitted out and refashioned above all in the fictions and fables of the *Acts of Paul.* Here also there perhaps belongs what the *vita Polycarpi per Pionium* 1f. professes to know from old manuscripts about a visit of Paul to the Christians in Smyrna. At all events—

---

[1] See on this W. Bauer, *Rechtgläubigkeit und Ketzerei im ältesten Christentum,* 1934, pp. 89; 117; 235; G. Klein, *Die zwölf Apostel, passim.* Further literature there.

however one may judge this Pionius—the Paul who speaks about the correct celebration of Easter must belong to the end of the 2nd century.[1]

At the end of the 1st and in the course of the 2nd century the view is sometimes expressed and assumed that the imprisonment of Paul mentioned in the conclusion of Acts ended with his liberation and that he then made a journey to Spain (1 Clem. 5. 7; *Act. Petr.* 1, 6; *Muratori Canon* 38f., Vol. I, p. 44). As regards other authors some hold their peace about these happenings, and some through their narrative make them appear impossible (the author of the *Acts of Paul;* Origen in Eusebius, *HE* III. 1. 3; see *Handb.*, p. 368).

The martyr death of Paul in Rome takes place in the reign of Nero, without the apostle being clearly described as a victim of the Neronian persecution: *Act. Petr.* 1; *Mart. Pauli;* Clement of Alexandria, *Strom.* VII. 106. 3; Tertullian, *scorp.* 15. 3 (*Corp. Christ.* 2, p. 1097); Origen (in Eusebius, *HE* III. 1. 3); Lactantius, *div. inst.* IV. 21, *de mort. pers.* 2; Eusebius, *HE* II. 25. 5. Where the manner of his death is spoken of it is said that Paul was beheaded: *Mart. Pauli* (see pp. 383ff. below); Tertullian, *de praescr. haer.* 36, 3 (*Corp. Christ.* 1, p. 216); Eusebius, *HE* II. 25. 5; *demonstr. evang.* III. 5. 65. Onwards from the end of the 1st century we find Peter and Paul often set together and their activity as also their destiny closely bound together: 1 Clem. 5; Ign., *Rom.* 4. 3; Dionysius of Corinth (in Eusebius, *HE* II. 25. 8); Irenaeus, *adv. haer.* III. 1. 1; 3. 2; *Act. Petr.* 23; Tertullian, *adv. Marc.* IV. 5; *de praescr. haer.* 36; Hippolytus (Arabic Fragments on the Pentateuch 17); the Preaching of Paul in pseudo-Cyprian, *de rebaptismate* 17. That, however, did not prevent it coming about at the end of the 2nd century "that an effective recasting of the tradition in Rome took place by virtue of which Paul was eliminated as regards the Roman bishopric and the office fastened on Peter".[2] The *Muratori Canon* (64, see Vol. I, p. 44) names an Epistle to the Laodiceans and an Epistle to the Alexandrians which were falsely ascribed to Paul. Marcion regarded Ephesians as the Epistle to the Laodiceans. On the other hand, there has been since at the latest the 4th century an apocryphal Epistle of Paul to Laodicea.[3] The *Acts of Paul* hand down a correspondence between the apostle to the Gentiles and the Corinthians (see pp. 373ff. below). The correspondence between Paul and Seneca (see pp. 133ff. below) belongs only to a later time. Polycarp (*Phil* 3. 2), however, seems to be

---

[1] Cf. on the Pionius question Altaner, p. 89 and J. Quasten, *Patrology* I, 1950, p. 79.
[2] Harnack, *Gesch. der altchrist. Literatur bis Eusebius*, II, 1, p. 703. Cf. W. Bauer, *Rechtgläubigkeit und Ketzerei im ältesten Christentum*, pp. 116ff. A collection of accounts of Paul in R. A. Lipsius, *Die apokryphen Apostelgeschichten* II, 1, 1887, pp. 11ff.
[3] Text in Harnack, *KlT* 12, 1931. On the whole question see pp. 128ff. below.

of opinion that the apostle to the Gentiles had written repeatedly to the church of Philippi. In the 2nd and 3rd century the Gnostics esteemed a book with the title *The Ascension of Paul* (after 2 Cor. 12:4). Subsequently there appeared an *Apocalypse of Paul* (O. Bardenhewer, *Gesch. d. altkirchlichen Literatur* I, 1913, pp. 615–620; see pp. 755ff. below). On a *Preaching of Paul* see pp. 92f. below.

2. THE APOSTLES AS BEARERS OF THE TRADITION

(*M. Hornschuh*)

LITERATURE. K. H. Rengstorf, ἀπόστολος, *ThWtb* I, 1933, pp. 406ff. (ET *Apostleship* 1952); A. Friedrichsen, *The Apostle and his Message*, 1947; H. Frhr. v. Campenhausen, "Der urchristliche Apostelbegriff", *Studia theologica* 1, 1948, pp. 96ff.; J. Munck, "Paul, the Apostles and the Twelve", *Studia theologica* 3, 1950, pp. 96ff.; E. Lohse, "Ursprung und Prägung des christlichen Apostolats", *Theol. Zeitschrift* 9, 1953, pp. 259ff.; H. Frhr. v. Campenhausen, *Kirchliches Amt und geistliche Vollmacht in den ersten drei Jahrhunderten*, 1953, pp. 13ff.; R. Bultmann, *Theologie des Neuen Testaments*, ³1958, §§ 52, 3; 55, 5 (ET 1955); H. Riesenfeld, art., "Apostel", *RGG³* I, 1957, cols. 497ff.; G. Klein, *Die zwölf Apostel. Ursprung und Gehalt einer Idee* (FRLANT, NF 59), 1961; W. Schmithals, *Das kirchliche Apostelamt* (FRLANT, NF 61), 1961.

I. IN EARLY CATHOLICISM. In view of the existing differences in doctrine, of the great number of tendencies and opinions, as also of the increasing Gnostic peril, recourse to the beginnings of the Christian faith seemed to provide the only sure guarantee of a verdict as to the truth. This thought took for granted the supposition that originally Christianity had been of a dogmatically uniform mould. In the beginning there was unity; subsequently multiplicity developed as a depravation of what was historically original. The recovery and full establishment of unity could therefore take place only through a return to what was early, i.e. by way of a faithful bringing back of the original mould, consequently of the Christian faith in the form in which it was revealed by the Lord. To ask what was the original mould was the same as to ask what was the reliable tradition. Here, however, complete certainty did not seem to be attainable unless at the same time the question was raised as to the authority which guaranteed the reliability of the tradition. As the bearers and guarantors of the tradition the apostles alone were involved. By tradition is now to be understood what the apostles received from Christ, whether before or after his resurrection, and did not then write down but transmitted orally.

If the conception of the apostle as the herald sent forth by the risen Christ was originally determined primarily by the idea of authorization—the apostle is accordingly the representative of Christ, whose word is legitimated by the Lord—in the second and third generation the idea of tradition comes gradually to prevail. The thought of tradition becomes the impulse that determines the conception of the apostle.[1] References to the oral apostolic tradition are already found in Acts 2:42; 2 Pet. 3:2; Jude 17; Ign. *Mag.* 13. 1; Ign. *Trall.* 7. 1; cf. Pol. *Phil.* 6. 3; 1 Clem. 42. 1. In each case we are concerned with the teaching of the circle of the twelve apostles represented as a uniform entity of homogeneous character, in which individual differences do not come into consideration.[2]

The chief marks of the apostolic tradition are its catholicity, i.e. its universal validity destined for the whole church, its definitive exclusiveness and its plain sufficiency. Cf. Irenaeus, *Adv. haer.* III. 4. 1:

> (In the church) as in a wealthy treasury the apostles have lodged most copiously all that pertains to the truth so that every man, whosoever will, may draw from it the water of life.

On the basis of the conception of tradition thus characterized there grew up in the second century the doctrine of an apostolic succession of bishops. An attempt was made to connect the tradition backwards by drawing up a series of bishops for each of the chief places, and so to bind the present to the beginning. Irenaeus and Tertullian see in the existing lists of bishops the guarantee of an actual connection of the doctrine with the apostles; these lists prove that the church is the place where the original truth is taught. As regards the question of the apostolic succession of bishops the suggestions given here must suffice; cf. on the origin and development of the early catholic principle of succession the expositions of H. Frh. von Campenhausen, *Kirchliches Amt*, pp. 178ff.[3]

2. IN GNOSTICISM. Not only the "orthodox" but also the Gnostics appealed to apostolic tradition,[4] that is to say to esoteric revelations as the bearers of which there came into consideration either the totality of the apostles or—this much more commonly—only

---

[1] Cf. Bultmann, *op. cit.*

[2] Cf. Bultmann, *op. cit.*, § 55, 5; Bauer, pp. 35ff. above.

[3] On the structure of the early catholic conception of tradition cf. also G. Ebeling, *Die Geschichtlichkeit der Kirche und ihrer Verkündigung als theologisches Problem*, 1954, pp. 31ff.; R. P. C. Hanson, *Tradition in the Early Church*, 1962.

[4] Cf. Origen, *Hom. in Ezech.* II. 5.

individual apostles who had been specially honoured by the Lord. Thus in Irenaeus (*adv. haer.* II. 27. 2) it is said of the Gnostics that they asserted that "the Saviour secretly taught these same things not to all but only to some of his disciples who could comprehend them and who were capable of understanding what was indicated by the scenes, enigmas and parables that he brought forward". Tertullian (*de praescr.* 25) also asserts that in the opinion of the Gnostics the apostles "had not revealed everything to every one. That is to say they had entrusted some things publicly to all, but some in secret to a few. . . ." According to the *Exc. ex Theod.* 66 "the Saviour taught the apostles in the first place typically and mystically, then parabolically and enigmatically, and then in the third place only clearly and openly".[1] The idea of a secret oral tradition underwent development in connection with the doctrine that only a numerically small religious élite was, thanks to its pneumatic quality, capable of accepting 'gnosis'. A consistent assessment of the teaching tradition of the great church did not result from this approach. That tradition either met with radical rejection—in which case Gnosis had to supplant and supersede it—or it was accorded conditional recognition—in which case Gnosis was understood as a supervening complement. The claim of the church tradition to be, in the form under consideration, of absolute sufficiency and definitive completeness, was rejected by the Gnostic secret tradition in every case, i.e. even when, strictly speaking, it did not stand in opposition to the church tradition.

On 1. The early catholic conception of tradition as the tradition mediated by the whole college of the apostles and vested with absolute and universal validity, is assumed in the early compilations of canonical law[2]: the *Didache* ("The Teaching of the Lord for the Gentiles by the Twelve Apostles"), the Church Order of Hippolytus ("The Apostolic Tradition"), the *Syriac Didascalia* ("The Doctrine of the Apostles") and the *Apostolic Constitutions* ("The Instructions of the Apostles by Clement (of Rome)").[3] In the circles of the great church appeal was made by preference to the apostles as the bearers and guarantors of the tradition when it was a matter of justifying or enforcing a particular church

---

[1] See further Irenaeus, *adv. haer.* I. 25. 5 (Carpocratians), I. 30. 14 (so-called 'Gnostics'); the *Gospel of Bartholomew* 66–68 (Vol. I, pp. 501f.); the *Testamentum Domini* (ed. J. Cooper and A. J. Maclean, *The Testament of our Lord*, Edinburgh 1902); cf. Liechtenhan, *Die Offenbarung im Gnostizismus*, 1901, p. 70; C. Barth, *Die Interpretation des NT in der valentinianischen Gnosis*, TU 37. 3, 1911, pp. 52ff.

[2] Cf. also A. Walls, "A Note on the Apostolic Claim in the Church Order Literature," *Studia Patristica* II, TU 64, 1957, pp. 83–92.

[3] The *regula fidei* also was understood as apostolic tradition. Since it does not belong to the works judged to be "apocryphal", it cannot be discussed in this context, any more than the church orders that have been mentioned.

practice,[1] consequently in questions in dispute regarding the cult, morality and ecclesiastical law.[2]

Appeal to the apostolic tradition played a significant part when controversy arose in the second century between the Roman bishop and those of Asia Minor over the determination of the date of Easter. Those in Palestine who sided with the Roman standpoint asserted against those of Asia Minor "the tradition (παράδοσις) regarding the passover that had reached them through the succession (διαδοχή) of the apostles" (Eusebius, *HE* V. 25). On his part Polycrates of Ephesus in a writing to the Roman church sets forth "the tradition (παράδοσις) that had come down to him" (Eusebius, *HE* V. 24. 1). In the Epistle of Polycrates handed down by Eusebius (*HE* V. 24. 2–7) the bishop attempts to defend the existing quartodeciman passover practice by referring to the great number of apostles, holy men and martyrs whose graves are in Asia Minor. In this manner the bishop of Ephesus is able to refer to Philip, one of the twelve apostles, who had lived with his daughters in Asia Minor and lay buried in Hierapolis, and finally to John also, the disciple "who reclined on the bosom of the Lord", a "witness and teacher" who now rests in Ephesus.[3] Doubtless Polycrates does not speak of some special traditions of Philip and John; for him, to be sure, the apostles mentioned come into the picture as representatives of the whole circle of the twelve and as witnesses of the one truth advocated by all the apostles. Not otherwise ought we to understand Irenaeus, who in *Adv. haer.* III. 3. 4 sets this forth:

[1] Origen described the practice of infant baptism as apostolic tradition: *Ecclesia ab apostolis traditionem suscepit, etiam parvulis baptismum dare* (*Comm. in Rom.* V, 9).

[2] Basil asserts (*de Spiritu Sancto* 27, PG XXXII, cols. 188f.) that of the dogmas and practices that hold good in the church "the one" has come down "by virtue of written teaching", whereas we have received "the other by virtue of the tradition of the apostles, it having been handed over to us in secret (ἐν μυστηρίῳ)". Through this tradition there have been transmitted to the church among others the following practices: the turning to the east in prayer (cf. on this F. J. Dölger, *Sol Salutis*, pp. 170f.), the marking with the sign of the cross, the formula of the *epiclesis* in eucharistic worship, and also various baptismal practices: the anointing with oil, the blessing of the water, of the consecrated oil, and of the child to be baptized, the three-fold immersing of the same and the renunciation of the devil and his angels. This secret tradition of the great church refers principally to τῶν μυστηρίων τὸ σεμνόν, which the fathers knew "to preserve in silence". The Gnostic terminology in which this tradition is described as σιωπωμένη καὶ μυστικὴ παράδοσις points merely to a mystic apprehension of the sacraments and is to be understood from the church's secret discipline. The apostolic secret tradition of which Basil speaks is accessible not merely to the small circle of a spiritual élite, the "hylic" and "psychic" or "pistic" being excluded on principle, but to all those who have been received into the church by baptism as full Christians, as distinct from catechumens and also from unbelievers. The traditions were not committed to the holy scriptures by the apostles out of fear of their being profaned.

[3] That the Quartodecimans carried back their practice direct to the apostle John is asserted by Socrates, *hist. eccl.* V. 22. The Romans correspondingly appealed to Peter and Paul.

John remained with them (the Ephesians) up to the time of Trajan; he is a true witness of the tradition of the apostles.

Appeal was also made to the apostles when it was a matter of occupying certain theological positions in arguing with the heretics. An example of this is given in the *Epistula Apostolorum*,[1] whose author acknowledges truth and validity only in what can be carried back directly to the instance of the circle of the apostles and beyond them to the Lord himself. There is no legitimate approach to Christ and his revelation other than the one that goes by the original apostles. Paul is consistently subordinated to them.

It is clearly a matter of dogmatic questions also in the anti-montanist *Dialogue with Proclus* of the Roman Christian Gaius (fragment in Eusebius, *HE* II. 25. 7). Gaius urges that in Rome there are the graves of the apostles "who founded this (Roman) church", those therefore of Peter and Paul,[2] who passes here as an apostle of equal standing.

Bishop Papias of Hierapolis, in a fragment of his κυριακῶν ἐξηγήσεις preserved in Eusebius (*HE* III. 39. 4) in which he speaks of his own endeavours to obtain trustworthy information about the words of the Lord, says:

> When any one came who had been a disciple of the elders (πρεσβύτεροι), I questioned (him) regarding the words of the elders (πρεσβύτεροι): what Andrew or what Peter or Philip or Thomas or James or John or Matthew or any other of the disciples of the Lord had said and what Aristion and the elder (πρεσβύτερος) John, the disciples of the Lord, say.

Aristion and the presbyter John are the representatives of the second generation of the bearers of the tradition still living in the time of Papias. Papias proceeds:

> I did not think that what was taken from books would profit me so much as what came from the living and abiding voice.

Papias therefore knows an oral apostolic tradition which he prefers to all written documents of the evangelic tradition. He states that "he had received the words of the apostles from those who had followed them (as disciples); he says that he had been a disciple of Aristion and of the elder (πρεσβύτερος) John" (Eusebius, *HE* III. 39. 7). Among what "had come to him as springing from the oral tradition" there were among other things "some strange parables of the Lord and teachings of his" (Eusebius, *HE* III. 39. 11), finally also eschatological statements, the chiliasm of which is denounced by Eusebius as "mythical".

[1] See Vol. I, pp. 189ff.   [2] On the Peter-Rome-question see pp. 47ff. above.

The eschatological theme is also discussed in a larger fragment which Irenaeus communicates in *adv. haer.* V. 33. 3. According to the information supplied by Irenaeus we are concerned here with teaching given by the Lord himself ("how the Lord himself had taught and spoken about these times", V. 33. 1), which was handed down by John, repeated by the "elders" and also mentioned by Papias in the fourth Book of his work[1]:

> The days will come when vines will grow every one of which will have ten thousand branches, and on each branch there will be ten thousand twigs and on each twig ten thousand shoots and on each shoot ten thousand clusters will grow and on each cluster ten thousand grapes, and every single grape, when pressed, will yield five and twenty barrels of wine. And when any one of the saints lays hold of a cluster, another cluster shall cry out: I am better, take me, praise the Lord through me. In like manner a grain of wheat will bring forth ten thousand ears, and every ear will have ten thousand grains and every grain will yield ten pounds of clean, fine flour. And all other (plants) also, fruit-bearing trees, seed and grass will bring forth in exactly the same measure as these. And all animals that feed only on what they obtain from the earth, will be peaceable and live harmoniously with one another and be in complete subjection to man.

On 2. We meet with the Gnostic tradition principle in Clement of Alexandria, who in *Strom.* I. 11. 3; VI. 61. 3; VI. 131. 5 and the *Hypotyposes* Book VII (according to Eusebius, *HE* II. 1. 4) sets the 'gnosis' taught by him under the protection of apostolic authority. As he insists in *Strom.* I. 11, his "miscellanies" are meant to be nothing other than an artlessly constructed "copy and outline" of the instructive lectures (λόγοι) of those holy and remarkable men whom it was his privilege to hear and who held fast the true "tradition of the blessed doctrine" originating directly from the holy apostles Peter, James, John[2] and Paul, and received by them "as by a son from his father". "And by God's grace they reach into our time to sow in us those apostolic seeds inherited from the fathers" (*ibid.*).

According to Eusebius (*HE* II. 1. 4) Clement wrote in Book VII of his *Hypotyposes*:

> After his resurrection the Lord imparted knowledge to James the Just and John and Peter, they imparted it to the remaining apostles, and the remaining apostles gave it to the seventy, of whom Barnabas was one.

---

[1] According to Irenaeus, *adv. haer.* V. 33. 4.

[2] Origen also has lifted Peter and the sons of Zebedee out of the circle of the apostles, asserting that only they belong to the true Gnostics (*c. Cels.* II. 64; IV. 16; VI. 77; *Comm. in Mt.* tom. XII. 36, 37, 41).

According to *Strom.* VI. 61. 2 "vision" (θεωρία), which is the highest aim of the wise man, can only be attained when through instruction we get to know how "the present, the future and the past" are related. Clement adds:

> This knowledge (γνῶσις) has descended from the apostles in unbroken sequence (κατὰ διαδοχάς) to a few (only) through oral tradition (61. 3).[1]

Clement thus claims to have access to secret teaching traditions, which he usually calls "knowledge" (γνῶσις) and sometimes "tradition" (παράδοσις).[2] The Lord has committed this Gnosis not to any written documents but only to the oral word.[3] Only few of the believers of the succeeding generations, those namely "who are capable of grasping it" (*Strom.* I. 13. 1) were found worthy of initiation into the secret wisdom. To the rank and file of Christians the approach to it is closed.[4]

Any attempt to discover traces and reflexions of the orally transmitted wisdom in the early Christian literature and to determine its content (or at least its themes and motifs) in whole or in part, has as a matter of course to reckon with the greatest difficulties, it being a question of esoteric traditions which for reasons of secret discipline, i.e. for protection from profanation, were given no setting in writing and which only quite occasionally and very rarely—so to say by a lucky inconsequence—could leave a trace behind them in the literature of the early church. Elements of the Gnosis transmitted under the authority of the apostles John and James permit of their being ascertained by us with a relatively high degree of probability.

In the *Adumbrationes* (*GCS* 17, p. 210, Stählin) Clement of Alexandria on 1 Jn. 1:1 mentions expressly "traditions" which were associated with the name of John:

> In the traditions it is reported that John touched the outward body (of Jesus) and put his hand deep within and that the solidity of the flesh in no wise offered resistance but yielded to the disciple's hand.

---

[1] To this context there does not belong the notice in Eusebius, *HE* VI. 13. 9 that Clement in his (missing) writing "On the Easter Feast" falls back upon tradition which he had received orally "from the ancient presbyters". For there is no indication that it is a matter of a pseudapostolic tradition, it being altogether unlikely that the Alexandrian "presbyters" were transmitters of esoteric traditions.

[2] Cf. P. Th.Camelot, *Foi et gnose. Introduction à l'étude de la connaissance mystique chez Clément d'Alexandrie*, 1945, pp. 90ff.; R. P. C. Hanson, *Origen's Doctrine of Tradition*, 1954, pp. 53ff.

[3] Cf. *Strom.* I. 13. 2: τὰ δὲ ἀπόρρητα, καθάπερ ὁ θεός, λόγῳ πιστεύεται οὐ γράμματι.

[4] Assuredly it is not the case that the oral apostolic tradition stands in opposition to the church principles of knowledge and its norms of doctrine. It is strictly the case, as R. P. C. Hanson has shown, that "Clement identifies his secret tradition with the Church's rule of faith, that there is no evidence at all that he kept them separate in his thought" (p. 59).

Further traces of the John-tradition can be recognized by us in the Coptic Gnostic *Apocryphon of John* and the *Acts of John*. The narrative framework of the Apocryphon shows us John, the brother of James, as the recipient and transmitter of the secret revelation.[1] The framework can be detached without more ado from the main content of the document as a later secondary addition, since it does not stand in any real inner connection with the content of the revelation proper. It shows a conspicuous agreement, which extends even to details, with the *Act. Joh.* 88–105. According to the *Apocryphon* John, aghast at the questions and assertions of a Pharisee, betakes himself "in great sadness" (20. 6) to the Mount of Olives. According to the *Act. Joh.* 97 the same disciple fled "weeping" from the place of the crucifixion and indeed likewise to the Mount of Olives. The *Apocryphon* knows of a vision John had of Christ on the Mount of Olives; so also does the *Acts of John* (97). Both sources know of a receiving and transmitting by John of esoteric revelation (cf. *Apocryphon of John*, Pap. Berol. 8502, 76. 18–77. 5 Till; *Act. Joh.* 105). The assumption may well seem obvious that the *Acts of John* are in literary dependence on the earlier *Apocryphon*. The following considerations, however, exclude any assumption of the kind. In spite of the later date of the origin of the *Acta Johannis* the Mount of Olives story in this work gives us an impression of much greater primitiveness than does the framework of the *Apocryphon*. The elements we have to consider in any comparison form a uniform whole with the narrative in general, and in particular with the content of the revelation that follows: whilst above the pneumatic Christ appears to the apostle, the true Gnostic, on the Mount of Olives, down below a blinded Jerusalem in ignorance and folly executes the senseless act of the crucifixion. The revelation which John receives refers to the present moment and includes an explanation of the situation. In the *Apocryphon of John* on the other hand the framework is artificial and, in comparison with the rest of the document, heterogeneous. The content of the revelation has no reference to the situation. The salvation events, the passion and resurrection of the Lord, are not once mentioned, although according to the introduction that was strictly speaking to be expected. That the author of the *Acta Johannis* spun his story out of the meagre framework in the *Apocryphon* is out of the question. The motifs which form the elements of this framework must have been taken over from other contexts, i.e. the author must have reverted to an earlier tradition. And indeed it is a matter of the self-same tradition which, in a form possibly already considerably modified, was given a late literary fixation in the *Acta Johannis*,

[1] cf. H. Ch. Puech, Vol. I, p. 320.

but continued also to be handed down orally; for it is oral tradition and not a written source to which Clement has recourse. Both sources, the framework in the *Apocryphon* and the corresponding sections of the *Acta Johannis*, go back independently of one another to oral tradition which consequently reaches back to the beginnings of the second century. Nothing points to a literary source of the two. There was then an oral tradition in which John passes as the favoured disciple and as the mediator to his fellow disciples of the revelation received from the risen Christ on the Mount of Olives. The circle in which this tradition originated and was fostered seems to continue in the circle to which the author of the *Acta Johannis* belonged and for which he wrote.

We must, however, beware of drawing from the content of the *Acta Johannis* far-reaching conclusions as to the material of the oral tradition. As an element of the early John-tradition we can identify with certainty only what can be verified as such on the strength of parallels in Clement and in the *Apocryphon of John*. Thus the following sentences from the *Acts* can be carried back with more or less certainty to the early oral tradition, since they show a strong resemblance to the tradition communicated by Clement in the *Adumbrationes*:

> Sometimes when I wished to lay hold of him I encountered a material and solid body, sometimes again when another time I touched him, the substance was immaterial and incorporeal and altogether as nothing (93).

In *Act. Joh.* 88–90 mention is made of a continuous mutation of Christ's condition; similarly, according to the information given in the *Apocryphon* (Pap. Berol. 8502, p. 26. 3–6 Till), the revealed Christ appears at one time as a child, at another time as a hoary old man. It is thus for good reasons to be supposed that this common trait also goes back to the oral John-tradition. The docetic character of this tradition is in any case conspicuous: the Christ who revealed himself on the Mount of Olives had no ordinary human body, but an immaterial body. How far one is justified in describing this tradition as 'gnostic' is a question to which the meagre sources permit no answer. But it will not have been a matter of a Gnosis of extreme tendency, for otherwise Clement would not explicitly have embraced the special revelation handed down under the name of John.

James, as has already been mentioned, is also named among the apostles who are described by Clement of Alexandria as recipients and mediators of the secret tradition. Whether we have to do here with the son of Zebedee or with the brother of the Lord cannot be learned clearly from the brief statements of the Alexandrian. The bringing of James into relief as the bearer of an oral secret tradition is probably connected with the preferential placing in which, according to the Synoptic accounts,[1] James the son of Zebedee participated together with Peter and his brother John. But if we are justified in bringing the *Apocryphon Jacobi* of Cod. II of the Gnostic library of Nag Hammadi (cf. Vol. I, pp. 335ff.) into association with the Jacobean tradition mentioned by Clement, then it follows that the Lord's brother must be meant, the picture of James in the apocryphal Epistle being clearly connected with the part which the Lord's brother played in the Jewish-Christian tradition. The question cannot, however, be answered with certainty. After all it is very unlikely that these two persons were always consciously distinguished the one from the other by later generations.

If we enquire as to the themes and motifs of the Gnosis handed down under the authority of James, we are again wholly dependent on inferences, there being no source which gives us clear and direct information. Above all we have to stick to Clement, whose 'miscellanies' aim at being nothing more than a "copy and outline" of the early apostolic secret tradition. Since James is also among the four apostles named by Clement to whom special prominence is given, we may rightly seek for traces of the Jacobean tradition in his *Stromateis*. But since Clement avoids any special exposition or clear definition in individual cases of the origin of the motifs from the early traditions that are worked up in the *Stromateis*, enquiry as to what is "Jacobean" can only be taken in hand by pointing out in other early Christian works of literature parallel thoughts which are there expressly declared to be "Jacobean". Here the already mentioned *Apocryphon Jacobi* alone comes into consideration. The fact has of course to be reckoned with that the early wisdom handed down under the name of James has been put into written form in this *Apocryphon*. Assuredly we may not without more ado claim its content wholesale for the early James-traditions, and yet precisely here it is very natural to look for traces of it, in view of the following considerations: the traditions to which Clement refers can have been neither Gnostic in the proper sense nor yet catholic. The traditions handed down under the names of individual apostles cannot have originated and been disseminated in catholic circles, for it was the normal catholic procedure to place the accepted church practices and doctrines under the protection of *all* the apostles. On the other hand, we may not expect in these traditions any expressions of a mythological and dualistic Gnosis of an extreme stamp, for

[1] Mk. 9:2 par.; 14:33 par.

Clement, who accepted the esoteric traditions, opposed the consistently dualistic Gnosis. In the early traditions we have then to see manifestations of a semi-gnosis standing in the midst between early Catholicism on the one hand and extreme Gnosis on the other. Here also the Gnostic understanding of existence declares itself, although it is hampered by inadequate forms of expression. Gnostic elements push against the barriers of a Jewish-Christian tradition which was stubbornly immovable; that prevents the step to consistent cosmological dualism and to the Gnostic *blasphemia creatoris*. In its fundamental attitude or in its religio-historical general character the *Apocryphon* mentioned agrees with the picture of the early pseudapostolic traditions which we have to make for ourselves on the basis of the foregoing considerations.

What in particular is to be carried back from the content of this writing to the esoteric traditions, we must learn from a thorough comparison of it with the *Stromateis*. Such a comparison is not possible so long as the apocryphal Epistle is not published in full. But from the survey and the extracts which Puech and Quispel have put before us in a French translation[1] some things already emerge. So far as we as yet can see there are some conspicuous agreements between many thoughts in the pseudapostolic Epistle and certain orders of statement in the *Stromateis*, so that it is permissible to infer traditions which both assume—the one independently of the other. That here it is a matter of 'Jacobean' traditions, should be likely.

What is the point at issue? The *Apocryphon Jacobi* deals among other things with the question of the right attitude of Christians to persecution. Jesus exhorts his disciples to be ready for affliction and martyrdom.[2] Persecution not merely foreseen but also willed by God should be willingly accepted by believers, that they may find opportunity through martyrdom to become like the Lord. The same question is also discussed more extensively and completely in the *Stromateis* (IV. 76. 1–88. 5). Clement, however, brings forward other conceptions; his own standpoint is much less radical than that of the *Apocryphon Jacobi:* persecution is not willed by God, but merely permitted. The circumstance that differences of the kind are met with debars us from drawing a sure conclusion as to what were the statements of the tradition on this theme. In our investigations, then, all we have come by is merely this, that we are now able to name one of the themes

---

[1] H. Ch. Puech and G. Quispel, "Les écrits gnostiques du Codex Jung", *Vig. Chr.* 8, 1954, pp. 7–22.

[2] Cf. the passage: "And if you are pursued and you accomplish His will, I tell you, He will love you and will make of you my equals, and He will think of you that you have become well-beloved in His providence according to your free decision (προαίρεσις)" (so the translation of H. Ch. Puech and G. Quispel, *op. cit.*, p. 12).

and problems with which the Jacobean traditions were concerned. Neither from the Coptic Epistle of James nor from Clement can we expect with certainty an unaltered reproduction of the early traditions.[1]

We may, however, assert with greater confidence that if we want to obtain a reliable impression of the character of the early Jacobean traditions (as of the oral pseudapostolic traditions generally), then we may well devote ourselves to the reading of the Coptic Epistle of James, which in respect of its general religio-historical character does not differ from the orally transmitted wisdom of the apostles.

As bearer of the oral tradition James was known also to the Naassenes whom Hippolytus describes for us in *Refut.* V. 1–11. The Naassenes carry back their secret doctrines to traditions passed on by the Lord's brother to Mariamne, i.e. Mary of Magdala: *This is the principal matter of very many words which—so they say—James, the brother of the Lord, handed down to Mariamne* (V. 7. 1). It is however also possible that the supposed James-Mariamne tradition lay before the author, i.e. the Christian interpolator of the basically pre-Christian text, in a form fixed in writing.[2] The James-tradition mentioned in the 'Naassene preaching' must be other than that which was known to Clement of Alexandria, the trend of the tradition expounded by Clement (regarding the whole circle of the apostles and the seventy) being certainly a different one.

Whilst the task of getting on the track of the Gnosis handed down as Johannine or Jacobean involves great difficulties, an investigation of the traditions ascribed to the apostles Peter and Paul is meanwhile completely impossible. It is not indeed out of the question that traditions of the kind stand behind the *Acta Petri* and the *Acta Pauli*, but there is nothing to prove that. For the time being we can only content ourselves with the observation that such traditions were in circulation. That there were traditions regarding doctrine handed down under the name of Peter must also have been asserted by Basilides, who is said to have established a connection with the apostle through a certain Glaucias, an alleged interpreter of Peter (Clement of Alexandria, *Strom.* VII. 106. 4). In exactly the same way Valentinus appealed to an alleged disciple of Paul, Theodas by name (Clement of Alexandria, *Strom.* VII. 106. 4). Whether Basilides and Valentinus

---

[1] A point in common, which goes beyond mere agreement in themes and problems and links Clement with the Apocryphon in terms of "dogma", is the emphasis in both on free will. May we see here also the oral James-tradition standing in the background? In any case we must be cautious in judgment and say too little rather than too much.

[2] Cf. Vol. I, p. 334.

THE APOSTLE IN EARLY CHRISTIAN TRADITION

actually knew of any traditions whatever derived from Peter or Paul and whether, if there were such, they stood in any connection with the traditions mentioned by Clement in *Strom.* I. 11, are matters that elude our control.

Ptolemy, the disciple of Valentinus, also states that he had received an apostolic tradition. Since he does not bring it into association with the names of particular apostles, it seems as if he had had recourse to a general apostolic tradition. Towards the end of his *Epistula ad Floram* (in Epiphanius, *Haer.* 33. 7. 9) it is said:

> Thou wilt, so God will, shortly attain to knowledge regarding the origin and creation of the same (namely of what has emerged from the good and imperishable divine basic principle of all being, but is yet not the same as it in essence, which is to say is of an inferior "nature", 33. 7. 8), since thou wilt be found worthy (to receive) the apostolic tradition (παράδοσις) which we also have received by succession (ἐκ διαδοχῆς)[1].

Again it remains an insoluble problem whether Ptolemy actually knew a definite pseudapostolic tradition or whether the "succession" (διαδοχή) in which he claims to stand is nothing more than a fiction intended to impart a higher degree of authority to his words.

The traditions handed down under the name of Matthias need not be discussed here, since they are dealt with in Vol. I, pp. 311ff.

A single (oral?) tradition carried back to the apostle Philip has been fixed in writing in the *Gospel according to Philip* of Cod. III of Nag Hammadi (pl. 121. 8; section 91):

> The apostle (ἀπόστολος) Philip said: Joseph the carpenter planted a garden (παράδεισος) since he needed (-χρεία) wood for his trade (τέχνη). He it is who made the cross (σταυρός) out of the trees which he had planted. And his seed hung on what he had planted. His seed was Jesus, but the plantation the cross (σταυρός).[2]

In the context of their statements regarding the apostolic traditions Clement and Ptolemy make use of a terminology that is distinctive for the theme. It is a matter above all of the frequently recurring expressions παράδοσις, παραδιδόναι and διαδοχή. As H. Frh. von Campenhausen (*Kirchliches Amt*, pp. 174f.) in particular has pointed out, the same expressions for centuries play a great part in the philosophical schools of antiquity

---

[1] Cf. on this B. Reynders, "Paradosis, Le progrès de l'idée de tradition jusqu'à saint Irenée", *Rech. de Theol. anc. et médiév.* 5, 1933, pp. 172f.

[2] Translated after H. M. Schenke, *ThLZ* 84, 1959, col. 18. (Cf. also p. 57 n. 1 above).

"to elucidate the genealogical propagation, so to speak, of the teaching tradition from the original teacher to his pupils and later leaders of the school. Ancient philosophy knows as little as does the Church of a mediation of doctrine without the idea of a community that bears it or at least of a personal contact of the forerunner with his successors". διαδοχή denotes not (as does παράδοσις) the teaching-content, but "the connection itself, brought about by the process of handing over and taking over, thus the school. . . ." (v. Campenhausen, *op. cit.*, p. 175). Therewith we stand in the sphere in which Gnostics such as Valentinus and Ptolemy felt themselves at home: they regarded themselves as philosophers just as much as did Clement of Alexandria on the side of the Church (cf. v. Campenhausen, *ibid.*). Only, the peculiar esoteric character of these traditions is not to be understood from the philosophical conception of παράδοσις and διαδοχή, but goes back to the influence of the mystery religions. After all Jesus is understood as no other than the revealer of a new doctrine and the founder of a school; the apostles are the teachers and mystagogues who pass on the tradition and initiate those who are worthy into the secret revelation.

XII

APOSTOLIC PSEUDEPIGRAPHA

(W. Schneemelcher)

1. Under the designation Apostolic Pseudepigrapha there are
collected here a series of pseudapostolic writings the only common
feature of which is the claim to apostolicity in their title, but
which for the rest cannot be comprised in a uniform category.
These writings also differ in form and cannot be reckoned to the
other types of New Testament apocrypha. We are concerned here
in the first place with works which are labelled apostolic
"kerygma" (*Kerygma Petrou* and *Kerygmata Petrou*) and are of a
type that can be classified only with difficulty. It may be said
that in the case of these writings we are concerned with something
intermediate between the Gospel book and the theological
treatise. At the same time, however, the apostolic authority that
comes to expression in their discourses so stands in the foreground
that a relationship to parts of the apocryphal Acts is not to be
disregarded. In view of the fragmentary character of the *Kerygma
Petrou* and of the touched-up state of the *Kerygmata* the question
as to their type can be given no precise answer.

The *Letter to the Laodiceans*, in itself an altogether insignificant
document, is an instance of a pseudapostolic epistle which intentionally, on very superficial grounds (the absence of the letter to
the Laodiceans mentioned in Col. 4:16), ties up with the type of
the New Testament letter, but in its artificiality shows that it is
no letter but an epistle (on this distinction cf. J. Schneider's
comprehensive article "Brief" in *RAC* II, cols. 564 ff.; also the
further literature there). Undoubtedly the *Correspondence between
Paul and Seneca* also belongs to this literary type of the epistle, i.e.
these letters also are not letters but literature which has made
choice of the letter-form in the interest of a definite purpose
(propaganda among the educated). Here, however, it has to be
observed that this correspondence hardly ever claimed to have
canonical worth like the letters of the NT. It is then only very
conditionally that it can be reckoned to the New Testament
apocrypha. The same holds good of the *Pseudo-Letter of Titus*,
which is to be regarded as a theological treatise to which the title
of a pseudapostolic letter was given either at the time of its
publication or in general only later. In any case it follows from
the "letter" itself that we have to do here with a fragment of the

ascetic literature, which so far as its type is concerned exhibits a certain affinity to a homily, but on the whole is an essay on the subject of celibacy.

Under the general designation Apostolic Pseudepigrapha there are thus assembled very heterogeneous texts, which however should not be omitted in this work although they are not all New Testament apocrypha in the strict sense of the word. Not only can we observe in them the problems raised alike by the further development of New Testament literary forms and by the influx of other forms in their association with the idea of what is apostolic (cf. on this Vol. I, pp. 6off.), but also particular attention can be directed in dealing with them to a special problem, that namely of anonymity and pseudonymity in early church literature.

2. PSEUDONYMITY AND APOSTOLIC PSEUDEPIGRAPHA. "A comprehensive 'treatment of the problem of literary pseudonymity in early Christianity' (Wrede in *ZNW* 1, 1900, p. 78 n. 1) is still outstanding" (Hennecke, *Apokr.* 2, p. 140). Today there is still not much in this observation that can be altered. It is true that F. Torm (*Die Psychologie der Pseudonymität im Hinblick auf die Literatur des Urchristentums, Studien zur Luther-Akademie* 2, 1932) and Arnold Meyer (" Religiöse Pseudepigraphie als ethisch-psychologisches Problem," *ZNW* 35, 1936, pp. 262–279) have applied themselves to this problem. The two works do not really carry us forward. Torm's book presents an inadequate attempt to account, with the help of psychology, for the origin of pseudonymous writings, without distinguishing clearly enough between anonymous and pseudonymous works. In Meyer also the problem is not formulated with sufficient clarity or in the right categories, i.e. those that are appropriate to early Christianity. Nevertheless Meyer points to the significance of the Holy Spirit in early Christianity, and in doing so has mentioned the central point of the whole question. That is very clear in the latest contribution on this subject by K. Aland ("The Problem of Anonymity and Pseudonymity in Christian Literature of the First Two Centuries," *JThSt* XII, 1961, pp. 39–49), in which he develops the view that in Christian literature up to the middle of the 2nd century anonymity and pseudonymity were to a great extent connected with the fact that writings of the kind were the fixations of oral prophetic discourses and were intended to count as works of the Holy Spirit. There can be no question that many anonymous or pseudonymous writings of the NT came into being in this way, and a portion of the New Testament apocrypha ought also to be understood from this point of view. In particular it was for these reasons that the earlier apocryphal Gospels appeared and spread abroad anonymously and pseudonymously.

In dealing with the writings which are here assembled as pseudepigrapha we must make a distinction (hence in what follows only the problem of pseudepigraphy will be discussed, since anonymity does not come into question). The *Kerygma Petrou* was probably a writing in the case of which the apostolic name was intended to guarantee that it was a composition wrought by the Spirit. It can no longer be determined with certainty, but is to be conjectured, that the work was spread abroad pseudonymously for this reason. In the case of the *Kerygmata Petrou* there seems to be another reason for the pseudonymity. Here pseudonymity has probably been deliberately chosen in order to secure respect for certain tendencies with the help of an apostolic name. The *Letter to the Laodiceans* certainly belongs to the pseudonymous writings in the case of which the author's name has of set purpose been falsely given to lend to the concoction the requisite weight; in this case, in other words, we have to do not with discourse of the Spirit or with apostolic teaching but simply with an attempt to fill in a gap in the Corpus Paulinum. The letters of Paul and Seneca need to be discussed in this connection as little as does the so-called *Letter of Titus*.

In these five texts then we can detect a development of pseudonymity within the Christian sphere which started from the use, already rooted in early Christian thought, of the name of an apostle as the token of an authority wrought by the Spirit, and led on to the utilization of a false name in the manner of the pseudonymity that obtained generally. In respect of the *Kerygma Petrou* this statement admittedly needs to be modified, inasmuch as we cannot say with certainty whether this work actually was pseudonymous in the early Christian sense. But at least it may be said that it represents a half-way house between the early Christian pseudonyma and the later form of pseudonymous writing. In agreement with that is the fact that in its content the *Kerygma Petrou* obviously represents the transition from the early Christian literature to apologetic writing, which is certainly no longer anonymous or pseudonymous.

In this connection there belongs yet another question. It is striking that the number of the pseudapostolic letters is comparatively small. The few texts which are presented below, and the small number of pseudapostolic letters of which only reports have reached us, show that the letter-form did not in fact belong to the favoured types of the apocryphal literature. The reason for this state of affairs lies above all in this, that the letter-type, like that of the epistle, did not lend itself to the purposes of the apocryphal literature (cf. Vol. I, pp. 6off.). Letter and epistle are types which (apart from the purely private letter, which however in our context at any rate can be left aside) in a special way make literary claims, but are less suitable for the purpose which the apocryphal writings are intended to serve, namely the proclamation of the gospel. It is a fact, to which in my opinion sufficient attention has not yet been paid, that the (real) letters of the NT do not live on in the apocryphal literature, that the epistles of the NT shade into the theological treatise literature, and that the few apostolic pseudepigrapha (in the sense given above) which we possess represent no pure type, but are either theological treatises which make use of certain elements of the letter, or literary experiments that have deliberately been made pseudonymous. The *Kerygma Petrou* may be an exception.

3. LOST AND LATER PSEUDEPIGRAPHA. Besides the texts named hitherto there are some reports of works which would belong to our context, but of which, apart from brief notices, nothing is known.

(*a*) Letter of Paul to the Alexandrians. We know of this apocryphon only through the statement of the *Muratori Canon* (l. 64: Vol. I, p. 44), which rejects this letter, as also the *Letter to the Laodiceans*, as Marcionite. Every further discussion of its content or purpose (Harnack: perhaps forged to further Marcionite propaganda in Egypt? *Marcion*,[2] p. 134*) leads us into the domain of phantasy. The conjectures of Th. Zahn (*Gesch. des ntl. Kanons* II. 2, pp. 586ff.) also carry us no farther. The *Lectionarium Bobbiense* mentioned there speaks of an *epistola Pauli ad Colos.*, but denotes by that a section from a later homily. Cf. Harnack, *Gesch d. altchr. Lit.* I. 1, p. 33; L. Vouaux, *Les Actes de Paul*, 1913, pp. 327–332.

(*b*) Letter of Paul to the Macedonians. Clement of Alexandria mentions once such a letter: "In this sense the apostle of the Lord also exhorted the Macedonians and became an interpreter of the divine word. 'The Lord is at hand,' he says, 'wherefore take care that we be not overtaken empty (in vain)'" (*Protr.* IX. 87. 4). The citation recalls Phil. 4:5. Since otherwise nothing is known of a Macedonian letter of Paul, either free citation or a mistake can be assumed. Cf. Harnack, *Gesch. d. altchr. Lit.* I. 2, p. 788.

(*c*) Letter of Peter. In Optatus of Milevis it is said: "Since we have read in the Letter of the Apostle Peter: 'Judge not your brother according to prejudice'" (*De schism. Donat.* I. 5). Harnack conjectures that Optatus combined Jas. 2:1 and 4:11 and then erroneously attributed this saying to Peter (*Gesch. d. altchr. Lit.* I. 2, p. 788). But it is also possible that we are concerned here with a citation from some lost apocryphon of Peter about which we can say nothing at all.

(*d*) A quotation from a letter of John is met with in ps. Cyprian,

De Montibus Sina et Sion, c. 13: Christ "instructs and exhorts us in the letter of his disciple John to the people: 'So see me in you as one of you sees himself in water or in a mirror.' " Zahn has maintained that we are concerned here with a quotation from a letter of John which had belonged to the *Acts of John (Forsch. zur Gesch. d. ntl. Kanons* VI, 1900, p. 196 n. 1; literature also there). He refers above all to a passage from the hymn of Christ in c. 95 of the *Acts of John:* "A mirror am I to thee who perceivest me" (see p. 230 below). Hennecke (*Apokr.* 2, p. 172 n. 1) has recourse to c. 15 of the *Acts of Andrew* (see p. 414 below) where also a mirror is spoken of. In spite of all our admiration of the ingenious combinations proposed by Zahn, we must still state the fact that from the quotaion in ps. Cyprian nothing precise can be learned about the assumed letter of John. Its attribution to the *Acts of John* is pure hypothesis; cf. also Schäferdiek, pp. 201f. below.

(*e*) A *Praedicatio Pauli* (Homily of Paul) is mentioned in ps. Cyprian, *de rebaptismate* 17 (3rd cent.?). This is said to have been forged by heretics to give support to their false doctrine: "In this book one discovers how Christ, who alone had committed no kind of sin, contrary to all (the assertions of) Scripture confessed his own sins and almost against his own will was constrained by his mother to receive the baptism of John. Further (it is related) that when he was baptized, fire appeared upon the water, a thing that is written in no Gospel. And after the agreement regarding the gospel come to in Jerusalem and consultation and debate together and after arrangements had been made as to what was to be done, after so long a time Peter and Paul finally came to know one another in Rome, as it were for the first time. And there are some other things of the kind (it is stated), absurd, improper and fictitious, all of which are found collected in that book." We shall not here enter into a discussion as to which heretics are referred to and as to whether the statement of ps. Cyprian that the *Praedicatio Pauli* was composed by them is true. That ps. Cyprian had a definite writing before him, seems to me to be certain. It is likewise clear that the *Praedicatio* mentioned here had nothing to do with the *Acts of Paul*, as Th. Zahn supposed (*Gesch. d. ntl. Kanons* II. 2, p. 881; against that Dobschütz, *Das Kerygma Petri*, p. 127). The statement that Jesus had received the baptism of John only when constrained, and that at the time of his baptism fire was seen upon the water, is striking. It has rightly been concluded that here our text is connected with a fragment of the *Gospel of the Nazaraeans* (Vol. I, pp. 146f., no. 2) and another of the *Gospel of the Ebionites* (Vol. I, p. 157, no. 4) (cf. Dobschutz, *op. cit.*, pp. 128ff.). A use of two different Jewish-Christian Gospels in the *Praedicatio Pauli* is unlikely. But above all hardly more than the possibility of a use of Jewish-Christian Gospels can be made out, the basis for more far-reaching hypotheses being in fact too small. The other statement that Peter and Paul came to know one another properly only in Rome—earlier meetings, it is true, seem according to the text not to be altogether excluded (!!)—is singular. Here also the short text allows of no far-reaching conclusion. With regard also to the composition, content and form of this *Praedicatio* nothing can be said. Only this seems to be certain, that the writing has nothing to do with the *Kerygma Petrou* and nothing with the *Acts* of Paul.

(*f*) A *Praedicatio Petri et Pauli* (Homily of Peter and Paul) has been inferred from a passage in Lactantius. He writes: "And he (*sc.* Jesus) has revealed to them (*sc.* the disciples) all the future; Peter and Paul have preached this in Rome and this discourse of theirs remains in writing for a memorial. In it, besides many other wonderful things, it is also said that in the future it would come to pass that after a short time God would send a king who would conquer the Jews, make their cities level with the ground and besiege them themselves, exhausted by hunger and thirst. Then it would come to pass that they would live on the bodies of their own and consume one another. At last they would fall as prisoners into the hands of their enemies and would see before their eyes their wives disgracefully ill-treated, their maidens violated and deflowered, their youths deported, their small children dashed to the ground. Finally everything would be devastated by fire and sword, and they would be exiled for ever as prisoners from their own land because they had gloated over the most beloved and most acceptable Son of God" (Lact., *divin. instit.* IV. 21. 2-4. Dobschütz, *op. cit.*, p. 132, translates the conclusion: "over the (reviled) most beloved Son of God, in whom he is well pleased"). In Lactantius the text stands in the context of the account of the ascension and the command to *praedicatio evangelii*. On this occasion Jesus also revealed the future, and this future is now described more closely in traditional apocalyptic traits (in this connection accounts of the Jewish War may also be used). But with not a single word does Lactantius say that he goes back to a particular writing. In any case all conjectures about such a *Praedicatio Petri et Pauli* are pure hypotheses without support of any kind. Cf. Dobschütz, *op. cit.*, pp. 131-134.

(*g*) A Discourse of Simon Cephas in the City of Rome preserved in Syriac (edited by W. Cureton, *Ancient Syriac Documents*, 1864, pp. 35-41) hardly belongs to our context. It is a late work which is doubtless connected with the *Acts of Peter* and has been enriched with all sorts of other legends about Peter. The dogmatic statements in this discourse refer it to the 5th century. Cf. R. A.

Lipsius, *Die apokryphen Apostelgeschichten und Apostellegenden*, II. 1, 1887, pp. 206f.; Bardenhewer I, p. 550.

(*h*) Finally it may be noted that some surviving texts which profess to be apostolic letters do not need to be considered more closely here since they belong to another context. Thus the apocryphal correspondence of Paul with the church at Corinth is part of the *Acta Pauli*, and therefore, in spite of its letter-form, it must be regarded as a literary stratagem on the part of the author of the *Acts of Paul* (cf. on this pp. 340ff. below). The same holds good of the *Epistula Petri* which belongs to the *Kerygmata Petrou* (see pp. 102ff. below) and cannot be separated from it. The so-called *Epistula Apostolorum* (see Vol. I, pp. 189ff.) is not a letter, but a dialogue of Jesus with his disciples after the resurrection and thus belongs to a special type of revelation-writing, even if the title *epistula apostolorum* should be original (cf. C. Schmidt, *Gespräche Jesu, TU* 43 (1919), pp. 156ff.). The so-called *Epistle of Barnabas* also can hardly be labelled a letter. "Strictly speaking only the sections 1 and 21. 7–9 bear the character of a letter" (H. Windisch, *Hbd. z. NT*, supplementary vol. *Die apostolischen Väter* III, 1920, p. 411). On the whole, the Epistle of Barnabas is a theological treatise in which only a few epistolary elements are used.

1. THE KERYGMA PETROU

(*W. Schneemelcher*)

LITERATURE. E. von Dobschütz, *Das Kerygma Petri kritisch untersucht* (*TU* 11. 1), 1893 (fundamental).—The texts are assembled in Klostermann, Apokrypha I (KlT 3) 1933.—Harnack, *Litgesch.* I, pp. 25ff.; II. 1, pp. 472ff.—R. Seeberg, *Die Apologie des Aristides* (*Forsch. z. Gesch. d. ntl. Kanons* V. 2) 1893, pp. 216–220.—Hennecke in *Hdb.*, pp. 239–247.—James, pp. 16–18. G. Quispel and R. M. Grant, "Note on the Petrine Apocrypha", (*Vig. Chr.* VI, 1952, pp. 31f.).

1. ATTESTATION AND TIME OF COMPOSITION. In Clement of Alexandria we find a series of quotations from a writing κήρυγμα Πέτρου (KP). There can be no doubt that Clement regards this work as composed by Peter. Certainly, without expressing himself more nearly about the origin, genuineness or any other problem of the writing, he quotes from it with the words: "Peter says in the Kerygma" or the like. Unhappily the contexts in which Clement quotes the writing give no clue to its composition and origin (cf. the analysis of Hennecke in the *Handbuch*, pp. 241f.). Origen apparently no longer shares the high opinion that Clement had of the KP. For in his *Commentary on John* (XIII. 17) he quotes Heracleon, who had used the KP, but at the same time indicates that he is in doubt as to whether it is "genuine, not genuine or

mixed". Origen's comments on this passage (see fr. 2c below) allow it to appear questionable whether on the whole he himself had known the KP. It is quite possible that here he merely reproduces what he has found in Heracleon. At any rate the KP for him no longer belongs to the uncontested sources of Christian tradition. On the other hand it is clear from this passage in Origen that the Gnostic Heracleon (middle of the 2nd century) made use of it, probably in the conviction that the KP was a genuine work of Peter. The apologist Aristides seems to have used this work, at least considerable connection between his apology and the KP can be pointed out (cf. R. Seeberg and Dobschütz). Whether Theophilus of Antioch made use of the KP is not certain, but permits of its being assumed (cf. Quispel and Grant; of most importance are the connections between Fragment 2 and Theoph. *ad. Autol.* I. 10 and II. 2). The KP is certainly not named either in Aristides or in Theophilus. In Eusebius (*HE* III. 3. 2) and Jerome *de vir. ill.* 1) the KP is definitely reckoned to the non-canonical writings.

The attestation and conjectured use of the KP refer this writing to the 2nd century and indeed to its first half. Dobschütz sets it between 80 and 140 (*op. cit.*, p. 67). Egypt has doubtless to be accepted as its homeland, even although this conjecture is not strictly demonstrable.

2. TITLE. The title *Κήρυγμα Πέτρου* attested by Clement has doubtless to be understood in the sense that this writing is intended to be a compendium of the preaching of Peter and yet, over and above that, a compendium of the whole apostolic proclamation. Here *κήρυγμα* is certainly not to be understood as *actus praedicandi*, but ought to be taken as indicating the content: it is a matter of the gospel which was preached by Peter, as the representative of the apostolic activity, and which mediates salvation.[1] Accordingly the title is interpreted too narrowly when it is rendered merely "The Missionary Preaching of Peter" (so Hennecke, *Apokr.* 2, pp. 144f.). Rather the title that has been handed down is best translated "The Proclamation of Peter". By that it is not said that the work claimed to be written by Peter. The title certainly makes no statement regarding that. It may be that Peter is named in the title merely as authority for the apostolic preaching (at any rate he obviously often discoursed in the plural). On the other hand, the possibility that Peter was meant to be regarded as the author is of course not to be excluded. From the title nothing further results that in any way can have a bearing on a relation to the Gospel of Mark. Dobschütz (*op. cit.*, pp. 68ff.) has conjectured that the KP may have been written as a *δεύτερος λόγος*

---

[1] On *κήρυγμα* cf. G. Friedrich, art. *κῆρυξ* etc., in *ThWtb* III, pp. 682ff.

to the Gospel of Mark. But neither the title nor the contents of the fragments admit such an hypothesis.

3. COMPOSITION AND CONTENTS. The scanty remains of the KP that have come down to us do not permit us to make precise statements of any sort about the composition of the work. In particular it can on no account be concluded from fr. 4 that the KP also contained an account of the life of Jesus and therefore was designed as a parallel or as a sequel to a Gospel. This assumption is superfluous since both fr. 4 and fr. 6 can have a place entirely within the compass of the preaching of Peter. Such being the state of affairs, the attempt to set the fragments once again in what was probably their original sequence must as a matter of course be abandoned. We present them here in the order in which they appear in Clement of Alexandria.

With regard also to the contents of the whole work hardly anything can be said; we can only interpret the fragments that have been preserved. When we do so nothing can be gathered naturally from fr. 1 for the content and tendency of the KP. On the other hand, fr. 2 shows that the KP contained discourses of Peter which in many respects remind us of the apologetic literature. Here it is a matter of the proclamation of the one God, the warding off of polytheism and the rejection of the false Jewish worship of God. Frgs. 3 and 4 seem to belong to a discourse of Jesus after the resurrection, without its being said therewith that this discourse belongs to the beginning of the work; it can just as well be a portion of a report or a sermon by Peter. Whether fr. 5 belongs or not to the KP cannot be said with certainty. The context in which it stands in Clement of Alexandria indicates that it belongs to the KP. Fr. 6 shows that the work was not limited to general monotheistic and antipolytheistic expositions, but also comprised christological passages in which the conformity to the Scriptures of the passion and the resurrection of Jesus was emphasized. Dobschütz has provided a detailed commentary on the individual fragments (*op. cit.*, pp. 27–64).

Dobschütz was of opinion that the writing "marks the transition from the early Christian to the apologetic literature" (*op. cit.*, p. 66). This characterization is correct to the extent that considerable material contacts with the early Christian apologists (above all Aristides) do in fact lie before us. It must, however, be restricted to this extent, that these agreements of the fragments with 2nd-century apologetic ought not to be understood as if in the apologists something entirely new appears and this new element is met with for the first time in the KP. It is assuredly no accident that the few passages in the surviving fragments which can be regarded as reminiscences of the Gospels point to the

Gospel of Luke, and further that certain contacts with Luke's Acts of the Apostles cannot be overlooked. Moreover the fact is not to be overlooked that monotheistic preaching is by no means only an apologetic phenomenon; manifestly it was already for Paul an essential part of every Christian missionary discourse (cf. the summary, 1 Thess. 1:9). It must therefore be said that the surviving fragments of the KP have only given currency in a particularly distinctive way to certain tendencies in early Christian missionary preaching, and on that account should not be reckoned to the apologetic literature in the strict sense. On the other hand, even the apologetic theology had its beginnings entirely in the early Christian proclamation of the gospel in the 1st century. The significance of the KP seems now to lie in the fact that here there is to be seen a middle term in the proclamation tradition between early Christian missionary preaching, as it has left traces for example with Luke in the Acts of the Apostles, on the one hand and Greek apologetic on the other. It is thus the more regrettable that so few fragments of this important document have survived.

4. THE KERYGMA PETROU AND OTHER APOCRYPHAL WRITINGS. Attempts have been made to enlarge the number of the fragments of the KP by adding to them some other assumed quotations from this work. Thus in the prologue to his *De principiis* (preserved only in a Latin translation) Origen mentions a *doctrina Petri*:

> And if any one should confront us with (a section) from that book which is called the "Doctrine of Peter", in which the Saviour seems to say to the disciples: "I am not a bodiless daemon", then the answer must be given him, in the first place, that this book is not included among the books of the church, and further it must be pointed out that this writing comes neither from Peter nor from any other person inspired by the Spirit of God. (Orig., *De princ.* praef. 8.)

Now in the first place it is remarkable that here Origen rejects the work named by him much more decisively than he does in his *Commentary on John* (see fr. 2c below). Further, the question must evidently be asked whether *doctrina* in the translation of Rufinus actually renders the word $K\acute{\eta}\rho\nu\gamma\mu\alpha$ or whether $\delta\iota\delta\alpha\sigma\kappa\alpha\lambda\acute{\iota}\alpha$ is not rather to be regarded as its Greek equivalent, and whether therefore a writing other than the KP is meant here. Finally, the cited word of Jesus has also been handed down elsewhere: from Ignatius (*Smyrn.* 3. 1f.) it reached Eusebius, and Jerome—wrongly—ascribed it to a Jewish-Christian Gospel (cf. Vielhauer, Vol. I, pp. 128f.). All this makes it very questionable whether here Origen actually refers to the KP.[1]

---

[1] I take no notice at all of the passages Origen, *hom. X in Lev.* and Optatus Mil., *de schism. Don.* I. 5 discussed in Dobschütz, *op. cit.*, pp. 84–105. They have certainly nothing to do with the KP.

The problem is further complicated by the fact that there may possibly have been such a *doctrina Petri*. Certainly in Gregory of Nazianzus and in John of Damascus we come upon quotations from a διδασκαλία Πέτρου. Gregory of Nazianzus twice quotes a logion:

> God is near a soul that toils and moils. (Gregory Naz., *ep.* 20; *or.* 17. 5.)

In *ep.* 20 he adds to this word: "Peter says somewhere in an admirable way". Elias of Crete (12th cent.), in commenting on this passage, suggests that it comes from the διδασκαλία Πέτρου (*PG* 36, 395). Now we cannot do much with this "beautiful, pithy dictum" (Dobschütz, p. 109), and the suggestion of Elias of Crete affords us no further help, since it is not to be assumed that he was at all acquainted with the work which he mentions. To judge then by this quotation, it cannot be said whether the saying belongs to the KP or whether there was a *doctrina Petri* and the sentence comes from it.

In the *Sacra Parallela* of John of Damascus there are two passages which are ascribed in the lemmata to a διδασκαλία Πέτρου:

> I, unhappy one, did not reflect that God sees the heart and has regard to the voice of the soul. I consented to sin, saying to myself: God is merciful and will suffer me; and since I was not struck at once, I did not discontinue but still more despised the forgiveness and exhausted the patience of God. (Joh. Dam. in Holl, *TU* 20. 2, 1899, p. 234, no. 502.)

> Rich is that man who has compassion on many and who in imitation of God gives of what he has. For God has given to all all of that which he has made. Understand then (ye) rich men that ye must serve since ye have received more than ye yourselves need. Learn that others lack what ye have in abundance. Be ashamed to retain other people's property. Imitate God's equity, and no one will be poor. (Holl, *op. cit.*, p. 234, no. 503.)

Now these two texts are so general—they are exhortations to repentance such as are frequently met with in Christian literature —that it would hardly be possible to assign them to some one particular work. Dobschütz (*op. cit.*, pp. 110-121) has conjectured that they come from a writing of Peter of Alexandria. This hypothesis is, however, just as undemonstrable as the one that the *doctrina Petri* mentioned here is to be identified with the KP of Clement of Alexandria.

TEXTS

1. (*a*) In the "Preaching of Peter" we find the Lord called *Law and Word* (*Logos*). (Clem. Alex., *Strom.* I. 29. 182; Dobschütz no. Ia.)

(*b*) In the "Preaching" Peter called the Lord *Law and Word* (*Logos*). (Clem. Alex., *Strom.* II. 15. 68; Dobschütz no. Ib.)

(*c*) The Lord himself is called *Law and Word* (*Logos*), so Peter in the "Preaching". (Clem. Alex., *Ecl. proph.* 58; Dobschütz no. Ic.)

2. (*a*) And that the most notable of the Greeks know (about) God not by positive knowledge, but (only) by roundabout expression, Peter says in the "Preaching":

Recognize now that there is one God who created the beginning of all things and who has the power to set an end;

and

the Invisible who sees all things; the Incomprehensible who comprehends all things; the One who needs nothing, of whom all things stand in need and for whose sake they are; the Inconceivable, the Everlasting, the Imperishable, the Uncreated, who has made all things by the word of his power[1] (who is discernible through Scripture, that is to say through the Son).[2]

Then he proceeds:

Worship not this God in the manner of the Greeks;

by which it is obviously said that the notables among the Greeks also worship the same God as we, but not with perfect knowledge since they have not learned to know what was delivered by the Son. Therefore he says: "Worship not!" He does not say: "the God whom the Greeks (worship)", but "(worship) not in the manner of the Greeks". In doing so he gives another direction to the way of worshipping God, but does not proclaim another (God). What now "not in the manner of the Greeks" means, Peter himself makes clear, adding:

For actuated by ignorance and not knowing God—as we do according to the perfect knowledge[3]—they have fashioned into figures that over which he has given them the power of disposal for use, (namely) stocks and stones, brass and iron, gold and

[1] Cf. Heb. 1:3.
[2] The words in brackets are probably an addition made by Clement. The translation rests upon a conjecture of Früchtel.
[3] *as . . . knowledge:* an addition made by Clement?

silver; and forgetting their material and use, have set up and worshipped (as gods) that which should have served them as subsistence. That also which God has given them for food, the fowls of the air and the fishes of the sea, the creeping things of the earth with the four-footed beasts of the field, weasels and mice, cats, dogs and apes; and that which should serve them as food they sacrifice to (animals) that can be eaten up; and offering what is dead to the dead as though they were gods, they are unthankful toward God since thereby they deny his existence.[1]

And since he thinks that we ourselves and the Greeks know the same God, although not in the same way, he adds the following:

Neither worship him in the manner of the Jews; for they also, who think that they alone know God, do not understand, worshipping angels and archangels, the months and the moon.[2] And when the moon does not shine, they do not celebrate the so-called first Sabbath, also they do not celebrate the new moon or the feast of unleavened bread or the feast (of Tabernacles) or the great day (of atonement).

He then inserts the keystone to his own inquiry:

Learn then, ye also, holily and righteously what we deliver to you and keep it, worshipping God through Christ in a new way. For we have found in the Scriptures, how the Lord says: 'Behold, I make with you a new covenant, not as I made (one) with your fathers in Mount Horeb'.[3] A new one has he made with us. For what has reference to the Greeks and Jews is old. But we are Christians, who as a third race worship him in a new way. (Clem. Alex., *Strom.* VI. 5. 39–41; Dobschütz no. IIa; IIIa; IVa; V.)

(b) For truly God who made the beginning of all things is one, writes Peter, whilst (at the same time) he refers to the first-born Son, accurately understanding the word: In the beginning God created the heaven and the earth.[4] (Clem. Alex., *Strom.* VI. 7. 58; Dobschütz no. IIb.)

(c) Now much is to be adduced from the words quoted by Heracleon from the so-called "Kerygma of Peter" and in reference to them

[1] Cf. on the whole section Theophilus, *ad Autol.* I. 10 and II. 2, as also the coments on that in *Sources Chrét.* 20, 1948, pp. 81 and 97.
[2] Cf. Gal. 4:10; Col. 2:16, 18. [3] Cf. Jer. 31 (38): 31f; Deut. 29:1. [4] Gen. 1:1.

inquiry has to be made regarding the book, whether it is genuine or not genuine or mixed. For that very reason we would willingly pass by it and merely refer to the fact that it states that Peter had taught:

(God) should not be worshipped in the manner of the Greeks, who take material things and serve stocks and stones. Also the Divine ought not to be worshipped in the manner of the Jews, for they, who believe that they alone know God, rather do not know him and worship angels, the month and the moon. (Origen, *in Joh.* XIII. 17; Dobschütz no. IIIb.)

3. For that reason Peter records that the Lord had said to the disciples:

If now any one of Israel wishes to repent and through my name to believe in God, his sins will be forgiven him.[1] And after 12 years go ye out into the world that no one may say, "We have not heard (it)".[2] (Clem. Alex., *Strom.* VI. 5. 43; Dobschütz no. VI.)

4. Therefore (*sc.* to adduce a similar example) in the "Preaching of Peter" the Lord says to his disciples after the resurrection:

I have chosen you twelve[3] because I judged you worthy to be my disciples (whom the Lord wished).[4] And I sent them, of whom I was persuaded that they would be true apostles, into the world to proclaim to men in all the world the joyous message that they may know that there is (only) one God, and to reveal what future happenings there would be through belief on me (Christ), to the end that those who hear and believe may be saved[5]; and that those who believe not may testify that they have heard it and not be able to excuse themselves saying, "We have not heard". (Clem. Alex., *Strom.* VI. 6. 48; Dobschütz no. VII.)

5. But concerning all reasonable souls it has been said from the beginning: All sins which any one of you has committed in ignorance, because he did not know God accurately, will be forgiven him if he comes to know (God) and repents.[6] (Clem. Alex., *Strom.* VI. 6. 48; Dobschütz no. VIII.)

6. Wherefore Peter also in the "Preaching" speaks about the apostles as follows:

But we opened the books of the prophets[7] which we had, which

[1] Cf. Lk. 24:47; Acts 5:31; 10:43.
[2] On the 12 years cf. W. Bauer, pp. 44f. above. [3] Cf. Lk. 6:13; Jn. 6:70.
[4] *whom the Lord wished*: addition made by Clement? [5] Cf. Rom.10:14f.
[6] Cf. Acts 3:17; 17:30. [7] Cf. 1 Pet. 1:10–12.

partly in parables, partly in enigmas, partly with certainty and in clear words name Christ Jesus, and found his coming, his death, his crucifixion and all the rest of the tortures which the Jews inflicted on him, his resurrection and his assumption to heaven before the foundation (? *better doubtless:* before the destruction) of Jerusalem, how all was written that he had to suffer and what would be after him.[1] Recognizing this, we believed God in consequence of what is written of (in reference to) him.

And somewhat later he adds the following, stating that the prophecies have taken place through the divine providence:

For we recognize that God enjoined them, and we say nothing apart from Scripture. (Clem. Alex., *Strom.* VI. 15. 128; Dobschütz nos. IX and X.)

2. THE KERYGMATA PETROU*

(G. Strecker)

1. LITERATURE. The literature is most extensively assembled in G. Strecker, *Das Judenchristentum in den Pseudoklementinen* (*TU* 70), 1958. In addition cf. also O. Cullmann, 'Ο ὀπίσω μου ἐρχόμενος, *Coniect. Neotestament.* XI (*in honorem A. Fridrichsen*), 1947, pp. 26–32; A. Salles, "La diatribe antipaulinienne dans le 'Roman pseudoclémentin' et l'origine des 'Kérygmes de Pierre'," *RevBibl* 64, 1957, pp. 516–551; H. J. Schoeps, "Bemerkungen zu Reinkarnationsvorstellungen der Gnosis", *Numen* 4, 1957, pp. 228–232; A. Salles, "Simon le Magicien ou Marcion", *VigChr* 12, 1958, pp. 197–224; G. Quispel, "L'Évangile selon Thomas et les Clémentines", *VigChr* 12, 1958, pp. 181–196 (against the theses presented here cf. E. Haenchen in *Theol. Rundsch.*, NF 27, 1960, pp. 162ff., especially 165, 168; see also B. Gärtner, *The Theology of the Gospel of Thomas*, London 1961, pp. 61ff.); H. J. Schoeps, "Die Pseudo-Klementinen und das Urchristentum", ZRGG 10, 1958, pp. 3–15; H. J. Schoeps, "Das Judenchristentum in den Pseudoklementinen", *ib.* 11, 1959, pp. 72–77; H. J. Schoeps, "Ebionitische Apokalyptik im NT", *ZNW* 51, 1960, pp. 101–111; G. Strecker, article "Ebioniten" in *RAC* IV, cols. 487–500; G. Strecker, Supplement to W. Bauer, *Rechtgläubigkeit und Ketzerei*[2] (1964).

---

[1] Cf. 1 Pet. 1:11.

* In what follows the following abbreviations are regularly used: Cont. =*Contestatio* (Διαμαρτυρία); Ep. P. =*Epistula Petri* (Ep. P. and Cont. =introductory writings handed down in the Greek recension of the Clement romance); G =pseudo-Clementine basic writing (reconstructable from H and R); H =the *Homilies* (first, Greek recension of the Clement romance, ed. B. Rehm, GCS 42, 1953); ΚΠ =Κηρύγματα Πέτρου; ΠΠ =Πράξεις Πέτρου; R =the *Recognitions* (second recension of the Clement romance, originally in Greek, to hand in the Latin translation of Rufinus, ed. E. G. Gersdorf, 1838). On questions of introduction see also Irmscher, pp. 532ff. below.

2. HISTORY OF RESEARCH. Since the time of Ferdinand Christian Baur ("Die Christuspartei in der korinthischen Gemeinde", *Tüb. Zeitschr. f. Theol.* 1831, pp. 76ff.) the question of Jewish–Christian elements has occupied the central place of interest in the pseudo-Clementines. The so-called (later) Tübingen School names the Clement romance as a witness for the thesis that the catholic church arose out of Petrinism and Paulinism. According to this thesis the Jewish-Christian colouring is an expression of an Ebionitism which, in spite of its anti-Pauline attitude, has taken over from Paulinism its universalistic tendency, and so represents a step in Ebionitic thought in the direction of catholicism. Later scholars linked with the question as to the character and significance of the pseudo-Clementine Jewish Christianity a consideration, much more thorough than that of the Tübingen School, of literary-critical arrangement in the Clement romance: Adolf Hilgenfeld (*Die clementischen Recognitionen und Homilien nach ihrem Ursprung dargestellt*, Jena 1848) reconstructed from R I. 27–72, according to the "table of contents" in R III. 75, a Jewish-Christian source writing which was originally joined to the *Epistula Petri* and the *Contestatio* and is called the Κηρύγματα Πέτρου. The Jewish Christianity of the kerygmata was associated with the Essenes. That was followed by further Ebionite adaptations (R II.–III., R IV.–VII. and R VIII.–X.). Finally the Homilist reviewed the romance that had thus grown together and gave to it an anti-Marcionite alignment. Gerhard Uhlhorn (*Die Homilien und Recognitionen des Clemens Romanus*, Göttingen 1848) maintained against Hilgenfeld that, as compared with the *Recognitions*, the *Homilies* were primary. Nevertheless he had to recognize that in some passages the *Recognitions* have primitive features. He was thus forced to assume a pseudo-Clementine basic writing which had lain before the Homilist and the Recognitionist, who used the *Homilies* as well. The basic writing and the *Homilies* represent a Jewish Christianity the ultimate root of which reaches back to the Elkesaites. In the *Recognitions*, on the other hand, the Jewish-Christian element steps into the background.

Richard Adelbert Lipsius (*Die Quellen der römischen Petrussage*, Kiel 1872) had asserted the existence of Ebionite Πράξεις Πέτρου, which depicted the discussions between Peter and the magician Simon from Palestine to Rome and must have been accessible to the author of the basic writing through the likewise Ebionite Kerygmata. In opposition to him Hans Waitz (*Die Pseudo-klementinen, Homilien und Rekognitionen*, Leipzig 1904) for the first time clearly distinguishes between catholic and Jewish-Christian originals in the Clement romance: the author of the basic writing used a catholic-antignostic source in the Πράξεις Πέτρου, a

Jewish-Christian anti-Pauline source that was independent of that in the Kerygmata. The *KΠ*-source found entrance into the basic writing in a form that had been touched up by Marcionites. The (according to R III. 75) 'Seventh' Book of the Kerygmata R I. 54–69, which delineates Jerusalem disputations of the apostle with the Jews, was originally independent. The genuine Kerygmata are a product of syncretistic Jewish Christianity; their author was of Elkesaite extraction.

A return to the Tübingen School in recent times is marked by the names Cullmann and Schoeps. Oscar Cullman (*Le problème littéraire et historique du roman Pseudo-Clémentin*, Paris 1930) understands the *ΠΠ*-writing as Περίοδοι Πέτρου, which on literary-historical grounds he files between the Kerygmata and the basic writing. The *KΠ*-writing, as he sees it, stands in the sphere of influence of Jewish gnosis and of the Baptist sects. From this point of view numerous parallels to the earliest literary pronouncements of early Christianity can be pointed out. The explanation of these is found by going back to an environment that was common to the early church and the Kerygmata. For his presentation of the *Theologie und Geschichte des Judenchristentums* (Tübingen 1949) Hans Joachim Schoeps draws essentially upon the pseudo-Clementine romance. The *KΠ*-source, which is to be reconstructed in a measure beyond what Waitz allows on the basis of R III. 75, originated in the conflict against the Marcionite gnosis and defends early church traditions. With these it associates Essene ideas. Schoeps seeks to deduce from the Kerygmata literary units that lie still farther back; as such there are mentioned a Commentary of Symmachus on the *Gospel of the Ebionites* and also an "Ebionite Acts of Apostles", which combined with a narrative of the occurrences in Jerusalem according to R I. 27–72 a Jewish-Christian description of the conversion of Saul and other anti-Pauline material.

In this way it was claimed that there is a close connection between the pseudo-Clementine circle of writings and early Christianity, and so a significance was given to the Clementines such as hitherto had been given them only by the Tübingen scholars. But a counter-stroke did not fail. John Chapman *On the Date of the Clementines*, *ZNW* 9, 1908, pp. 21ff., 147ff.) had already disputed the presence of Ebionite elements in the Clementines, and Eduard Schwartz (*Unzeitgemässe Betrachtungen zu den Clementinen*, *ZNW* 31, 1932, pp. 151ff.) reinforced the negative-critical position by referring to parallel literary phenomena in the Greek romances. Bernhard Rehm (*Zur Entstehung der pseudo-clementinischen Schriften*, *ZNW* 37, 1938, pp. 77ff.) strove in a special way to secure a foundation for the critical trend in research, going back to Uhlhorn in his approach to source-analysis and assuming for the Recognitionist a double dependence, both upon the basic writing and upon the *Homilies*. Ebionite elements in the Clementines are not denied, but Rehm understands them on the basis of his own source-critical approach as interpolations, which intruded into the *Homilies* and from there influenced the *Recognitions* also; for the orthodox Recognitionist succeeded only imperfectly in restoring by means of omissions and polishings the orthodox character of the Clement romance. The table of contents R III. 75 is fictitious and cannot be used for the reconstruction of the Jewish-Christian elements; nevertheless the Ebionite interpolations can be recognized by their manner of speech, and accordingly the introductory writings (Ep. P., Cont.), the James motive in H XI. 35. 3–36. 1 par., the anti-Pauline section H XVII. 13–19 and the like can be identified as Ebionite.

3. THE STARTING-POINT FOR RECONSTRUCTION. The presence of Jewish-Christian elements in the pseudo-Clementines has not been doubted any more since Rehm made his investigations. On the other hand, the literary-historical classification is disputed. It must proceed from a settlement of the relation of the two recensions H and R to one another and to the basic writing. Since Rehm's attempt to prove a double dependence of the *Recognitions* on G and H must be regarded as having failed (see Strecker, *op. cit.*, pp. 35ff.), it is to be assumed as more likely that H and R go back independently of one another to the basic writing. On the basis of this source-analytical starting-point it can be concluded, from the fact that H and R hand down Jewish-Christian ideas, that the basic writing already comprised Jewish-Christian elements.

The author of the basic writing did not himself create the genuine "Ebionitisms". From him comes the *Epistula Clementis*, which was fashioned after the Jewish-Christian *Epistula Petri*. But if the *Letter of Peter* lay before the author of the basic writing, then that is also to be assumed for the *Contestatio*, which is placed after the *Epistula Petri*, and further for all Jewish-Christian elements of the Clementines which together with the *Epistula Petri* and the *Contestatio* constitute an entity. In conformity with what is mentioned in Ep. P. 1. 2; Cont. 1. 1 and frequently, this source-writing bears the name Κηρύγματα Πέτρου.

If R III. 75, the so-called Table of Contents of the Kerygmata, is to be recognized (with Rehm) as a literary fiction, then in reconstructing the *KΠ*-source we must proceed only from the introductory writings, the *Epistula Petri* and the *Contestatio*, isolating on the basis of conceptual and material parallels those contexts in the pseudo-Clementines which display the same trend or tendency. Admittedly it is always only portions of the basic writing that are thus laid hold of; statements regarding the Kerygmata cannot be wholly freed from the relativity that is theirs through their having been selected and interfered with by the author of the basic writing.

This approach to reconstruction does not allow of the section R I. 33–44. 2 and 53. 4b–71 being connected with the Kerygmata. Since as compared with the *KII* it has an independent character, it is to be regarded as a second Jewish-Christian source-writing which the author of the basic document worked up side by side with his remaining texts. This writing comprised a sketch of the history of salvation—from Abraham to the church in Jerusalem—disputations of the twelve apostles and of James with the factions of Judaism and a discussion with Paul. Because of its parallelism with the 'Αναβαθμοὶ 'Ιακώβου according to Epiphanius (=AJ I; Epiph. *haer.* 30. 16. 6–9), with which it has a basis (=AJ) in common, it is called the AJ II-source (cf. on this Strecker, *op. cit.*, pp. 221ff.).

4. CONTENTS. The *Epistula Petri* and the *Contestatio* were prefixed to the *KII* writing. According to the statements of the *Epistula Petri* Peter forwarded the books of his Kerygmata to 'bishop' James and asked for special precautionary measures in connection with their transmission to prevent a falsification of their doctrine by the followers of the 'hostile man'. The following *Contestatio* describes the disclosure of the letter to the seventy presbyters and the establishment of the required precautions, and below that is the text of the engagement pledge.

There can be no doubt as to the fictitious character of the introductory writings. Not only are the statements about the sender and the recipient imaginary, but the same literary trend also shows itself much more in the archaizing style: it determines among other things the reference to the college of the seventy in the Jerusalem church (Ep. P. 2. 1; Cont. 1. 1ff. following Lk. 10:1; Num. 11:25; cf. Ep. P. 1. 2), the requirement of a probation period of six years (Cont. 1. 2), the prohibition of swearing, which is in fact abandoned in what follows (cf. Cont. 1. 2 with 4. 3). It is, however, in the literary motives that the real concern of the author comes to expression. The introductory writings are intended to arouse the interest of the reader and make good the claim which the 'proclamation of Peter' makes. Moses has already made known the 'word of truth' and by Jesus it was confirmed (Ep. P. 2. 5, cf. 2. 2). Peter now testifies to the true "lawful proclamation" in opposition to the 'lawless doctrine' of the "hostile man" (Ep. P. 2.3). The tradition of the Jews provides a precedent; they have preserved a uniform norm of exposition which is employed in dealing with the "ambiguous utterances of the (Biblical) prophets", and in that they can serve the Christians by way of example (Ep. P. 1. 3ff.). Such statements permit us to recognize the outline of a theological system which is to be defined exactly in what follows on the basis of the original *KΠ*-sections within the basic writing.

The dominating entity in the Kerygmata is "the true prophet" (cf. above all H III. 17–28), the bearer of the divine revelation, who has manifested himself since the beginning of the world in a continuous series of changing characters (H III. 20. 2). Adam represents the first incarnation of 'the prophet'; he was anointed with the oil of the tree of life (R I. 47) and possessed the Spirit of God (H III. 17. 3); accordingly, contrary to the report in Genesis, he committed no sin (H III. 17, 21. 2; II. 52. 2). Beside him as figures in whom the true prophet was manifested prominence is given to the lawgiver Moses (H II. 52. 3) and the Lord Jesus (H III. 17–19; cf. Ep. P. 2. 5). The true prophet has the task of proclaiming the "lawful knowledge" which shows the way to the future aeon (H XI. 19. 3).

Female prophecy appears as the opponent of the true prophet (cf. also H II. 15–17); she accompanies him as a negative, left-hand syzygy-partner in his passage through time. Her first representative is Eve, the mother of mankind, who was created at the same time as Adam (H III. 22. 25). What she proclaims suits the taste of the transitory cosmos (H II. 15. 2); she pretends to possess knowledge, but leads all who follow her into error and to death (H III. 24. 3f.).

The knowledge which the true prophet brings to men is identified with the law (on the following, see: H II. 37–52; III. 39, (42), 43–56; H. XVI. 5–15 ~ R II. 38–46). Adam already taught an eternal law (H VIII. 10. 3). It is identical with the law of Moses. Moses transmitted it orally to the seventy elders (H III. 47. 1). Thus it is preserved on the "chair of Moses" through the ages (Ep. P. 1. 2ff.). Now it rests in the hands of the Pharisees and scribes to whom Jesus has expressly referred (Mt. 23:2f.). But the representatives of Judaism have failed in passing it on (Mt. 23:13). Consequently the sending of the true prophet has become necessary (H III. 18f.). He points out the false pericopes (H III. 49. 2) which were worked into the written formulation of the law in the Pentateuch (H II. 38. 1). He who is instructed by him is able to recognize that those Scripture passages which speak of God as a being afflicted with human passions cannot be original (H II. 43f.; III. 39. 43ff.), and likewise those pericopes which speak of many gods (H XVI. 5ff.).

A portion also of the utterances of the Old Testament prophets (Ep. P. 1. 4; H. III. 53. 2), the references to sacrifice (H. II. 44. 2; III. 52. 1), to the temple (H II. 44. 1f.) and to kingship (H. III. 52. 1; 53. 2) are to be reckoned to the falsified elements of Scripture.

The consequence of the "lawful proclamation" of the true prophet is an anti-Paulinism. That is how the Kerygmata, directly or indirectly, have expressed it (cf. H II. 15–17; H XI. 35. 3–6 ~ R. IV. 34. 5–35. 2; H XVII. 13–19). It is true that in the basic writing the statements in question are directed against Simon Magus, and in this way veiled; nevertheless the allusions to citations from the Pauline letters, above all to the discussion between Paul and Peter in Antioch (Gal. 2:11ff.: H XVII. 19), the inapposite designation of the magician as a missionary to the Gentiles (H II. 17. 3; XI. 35. 4–6), and not least the scarcely disguised attitude of the *Epistula Petri* (2. 3f.) show that in the *KΠ* source they are levelled against Paul.

Paul is Peter's antagonist; the two are mentioned as the last pair of the series of syzygies, Paul as the representative of female prophecy (H II. 17. 3). There is also a polemical emphasis in the discussion about revelation, in which the possibility of genuine visions is disputed (cf. Acts 9; Gal. 2:2; 1 Cor. 15:8; 2 Cor. 12:1ff.), and over against that the true apostolicity of Peter is substantiated by the promise of Jesus (Mt. 16:17: H XVII. 18f.). From the fact that Jesus chose only twelve apostles it is to be concluded that Paul does not rightly call himself an apostle (cf. R IV. 35). Since moreover his proclamation of the dissolution of the law cannot be approved by James, it is to be recognized as false doctrine (cf. H XI. 35. 4–6; Ep. P. 2. 3f.).

The teaching about baptism presents a confirmation of this standpoint (cf. on this H XI. 21–33 ~ R IV. 6–14). The *KΠ* author attaches himself to the Christian Gnostic school of thought. In baptism "rebirth" comes about (H XI. 26. 1), "likeness to God" being attained (H XI. 27. 2) through "living water" (H XI. 26. 4). In the teaching about baptism, however, the emphasis lies on the requirement of good works; the *pneuma* associated with the water of baptism has the task of offering the good works of the person baptized as gifts to God (H XI. 26. 3). Stress is laid on the exhortation to the candidate for baptism to perform good works analogous to the sins that were passed over in the time of "ignorance". This counsel is based on the instructions of the Sermon on the Mount (Mt. 5: H XI. 32. 1). In addition observance of the Jewish law of purity is called for (H XI. 28f.). The requirements apply generally to Jews and Gentiles and in this respect are in conformity with the universalistic tendency of the Kerygmata, of which there is independent evidence (cf. Ep. P. 2. 3 and often).

5. RELIGIO-HISTORICAL CHARACTER. The religio-historical position of the *KΠ* source can be recognized fairly exactly in spite of the literary setting. The milieu in which this writing came into being presupposes Gnostic influence. The anthropological statements (e.g. H III. 27. 3; 28. 1f.) point to that. The baptism terminology comprises Gnostic elements. The true prophet's appearance in different manifestations has parallels in Gnostic literature. The dualism of the two prophecies, which is determinative for the whole of the Kerygmata, also points on its materialistic-cosmological side to a Gnostic background (cf. H II. 15. 3; XIX. 23. 3).

Side by side with that there are found close contacts with Judaism. That the *KΠ* author was in contact with Jewish theology follows no doubt from his emphatically positive estimation of the religion of Moses (Ep. P. 1. 2ff.). But actual connections can also be observed. To the rational substantiating of the false pericope theory (H II. 40. 1: "All that is said or written against God is lies") the interpretation of Scripture in late Judaism presents similar tendencies and, especially in the Targumim, near parallels. Admittedly the radicalism of the Kerygmata can no longer be understood on the basis of Jewish presuppositions, and only in the Gnostic sphere are there parallels to it (cf. e.g. Ptolemy, *ad Floram* 4. 1f.). If here elements of Jewish origin have been worked in under Gnostic influence, on the other hand the nomism of the Kerygmata interprets the originally Gnostic dualism in a Jewish or Jewish-Christian light. The opposition of two cosmic principles is interpreted as opposition between the true prophet, the content of whose proclamation is the law, and the female prophecy, which teaches the dissolution of the law (H III. 23. 3). A Jewish or Jewish Christian environment also determines the detailed instructions of the true prophet, for example in the ceremonial-legal requirements of the counsel given at baptism. The anti-Paulinism, which is attested for different kinds of Jewish-Christian groups ("Ebionite": Iren., *haer.* I. 26. 2; "Cerinthian": Epiph., *haer.* 28. 5. 3; "Elkesaite": Eusebius, *HE* VI. 38; "Encratite": Origen, *c. Cels.* V. 65 and often), certainly comes from Jewish-Christian tradition. To this there belongs the corresponding understanding of Peter and James respectively. That the author stood in a Jewish-Christian tradition follows from the motif of different manifestations, which evidently already lay before him as fixed tradition, the identification of the true prophet with Jesus being assumed as a matter of course. This idea—parallels are found in the doctrine of Mani and in Mandaeism—is attested for the Elkesaites among others (Hippol. *ref.* IX. 14. 1). There is also a reminder of Elkesaitism in the wording of the oath in Cont. 2. 1; 4. 1 (cf. Hippol. *ref.* IX. 15. 2; Epiph. *haer.* 19. 1. 6; 6. 4), which, however, serves only literary ends in the *Contestatio* and therefore does not permit more than a passing acquaintance with the Elkesaite system to be inferred. Since important differences from the Elkesaite theology can be pointed out, a relationship of dependence cannot be concluded from the remaining analogies, but it must be assumed that the author of the Kerygmata and Elkesai, the founder of the sect, worked in similar circumstances. The author writes in a Jewish-Christian-Gnostic milieu. His work is influenced by a universalistic tendency and presupposes the writings of the New Testament canon: in the land of its origin the great church and heresy do not yet appear to have been marked off the one from the other.

6. COUNTRY OF ORIGIN AND DATE. Recent researchers are at one in the opinion that the *KΠ*-writing cannot have originated in the West, but only in the East. Since the author of the basic writing came from Coele-Syria and the Kerygmata do not seem to have been widely disseminated, the home country of the *KΠ*-author must be sought in the neighbourhood of the land of origin of the basic writing. Something more exact can be inferred from the citation of the New Testament writings. The use of a canon which did not contain the catholic epistles and the Revelation of John points to Syria (on the Syrian form of the canon cf. Zahn, *Geschichte des neutestamentlichen Kanons* I, Erlangen 1888, pp. 373ff.). This locating may also be concluded from the fact that the *KΠ*-author quotes from the Pauline letters only Galatians and the First Letter to the Corinthians (indirectly), and the Syrian corpus of the Pauline letters began with just these two letters—granted that an abridged canon lies behind the Kerygmata. The Kerygmata-source was composed in the Greek, not in the Aramaic tongue; hence as its land of origin there may be reckoned the Greek-speaking Syria that bordered on Osrhoene. Numerous Jewish Christians lived there—in the time of Epiphanius (*haer.* 20. 7) and of Jerome (*de vir. ill.* 3) they were still doing so in Beroea.

For the determination of the date there can be mentioned as *terminus ad quem* the pseudo-Clementine basic writing, which was written *c.* 260 (between 220 and 300). To the fixing of the *terminus a quo* there is no certain clue. We should not go too far up into the second century, for then we should not be able to understand why there is no evidence for the Kerygmata outside the basic writing. In addition a clue to the dating can be secured through comparison with the date of the remaining sources of the basic writing: besides the *KΠ*-source there underlies it *inter alia* the Bardesanian dialogue *Περὶ Εἱμαρμένης*, which was composed probably in the year 220. An ordination schema which the author of the basic writing used came into being *c.* 200. For the Kerygmata the same dating may be assumed.

TEXTS*

(1.) The Epistle of Peter to James

(*Epistula Petri*)

1. 1. Peter to James, the lord and bishop of the holy church: Peace be with you always from the Father of all through Jesus Christ.

2. Knowing well that you, my brother, eagerly take pains about what is for the mutual benefit of us all, I earnestly beseech you not to pass on to any one of the Gentiles the books of my preachings which I (here) forward to you, nor to any one of our own tribe before probation. But if some one of them has been examined and found to be worthy, then you may hand them over to him in the same way as Moses handed over his office of a teacher to the seventy[1]. 3. Wherefore also the fruit of his caution is to be seen up to this day. For those who belong to his people preserve everywhere the same rule in their belief in the one God and in their line of conduct, the Scriptures with their many senses being unable to incline them to assume another attitude. 4. Rather they attempt, on the basis of the rule that has been handed down to them, to harmonize the contradictions of the Scriptures, if haply some one who does not know the traditions is perplexed by the ambiguous utterances of the prophets. 5. On this account they permit no one to teach unless he first learn how the Scriptures should be used. Wherefore there obtain amongst them one God, one law and one hope.

2. 1. In order now that the same may also take place among us, hand over the books of my preachings in the same mysterious way to our seventy brethren[2] that they may prepare those who are candidates for positions as teachers. 2. For if we do not proceed in this way, our word of truth will be split into many opinions. This I do not know as a prophet, but I have already the beginning

---

* A selection. Translation based on the Greek recension (H).
[1] Cf. Num. 11:25.   [2] Cf. Lk. 10:1.

of the evil before me. 3. For some from among the Gentiles have rejected my lawful preaching and have preferred a lawless and absurd doctrine *of the man who is my enemy.*[1] 4. And indeed some have attempted, whilst I am still alive, to distort my words by interpretations of many sorts, as if I taught the dissolution of the law and, although I was of this opinion, did not express it openly.[2] But that may God forbid![3] 5. For to do such a thing means to act contrary to the law of God which was made known by Moses and was confirmed by our Lord in its everlasting continuance. For he said[4]: *The "heaven and the earth will pass away, but one jot or one tittle shall not pass away from the law".* 6. This he said *that everything might come to pass.* But those persons who, I know not how, allege that they are at home in my thoughts wish to expound the words which they have heard of me better than I myself who spoke them. To those whom they instruct they say that this is my opinion, to which indeed I never gave a thought. 7. But if they falsely assert such a thing whilst I am still alive, how much more after my death will those who come later venture to do so?

3. 1. In order now that that may not happen I earnestly beseech you not to pass on the books of my preachings which I send you to any one of our own tribe or to any foreigner before probation, but if some one is examined and found to be worthy, let them then be handed over in the way 2. in which Moses handed over his office of a teacher to the seventy, in order that they may preserve the dogmas and extend farther the rule of the truth, interpreting everything in accordance with our tradition and not being dragged into error through ignorance and uncertainty in their minds to bring others into the like pit of destruction.

3. What seems to me to be necessary I have now indicated to you. And what you, my lord, deem to be right, do you carry fittingly into effect. Farewell.

(2.) Testimony regarding the Recipients of the Epistle
(*Contestatio*)

1. 1. Now when James had read the epistle he called the elders together, read it to them and said: "As is necessary and proper,

---

[1] Cf. Mt. 13:28.   [2] Cf. Gal. 2:11–14.
[3] Cf. Gal. 2:17.   [4] Mt. 24:35; 5:18.

our Peter has called our attention to the fact that we must be cautious in the matter of the truth, that we should pass on the books of his preachings that have been forwarded to us not indiscriminately, but only to a good and religious candidate for the position of a teacher, a man who as one who has been circumcised is a believing Christian, and indeed that we should not pass on all the books to him at once, so that, if he shows indiscretion in handling the first, he may not be entrusted with the others. 2. He ought therefore to be proved for not less than six years. Thereafter, according to the way of Moses, let him be brought to a river or a fountain where there is living water and the regeneration of the righteous takes place; not that he may swear, for that is not permitted,[1] but he should be enjoined to stand in the water and to vow, as we also ourselves were made to do at the time of our regeneration, to the end that we might sin no more.

2. 1. And let him say: 'As witnesses I invoke heaven, earth and water, in which everything is comprehended, and also in addition the all-pervading air, without which I am unable to breathe, that I shall always be obedient to him who hands over to me the books of the preachings and shall not pass on to any one in any way the books which he may give to me, that I shall neither copy them nor give a copy of them nor allow them to come into the hands of a copyist, neither shall I myself do this nor shall I do it through another, and not in any other way, through cunning or tricks, through keeping them carelessly, through depositing them with another or through underhand agreement, nor in any other manner or by means of any other artifice will I pass them on to a third party. 2. Only if I have proved someone to be worthy—proving him as I myself have been proved, or even more, in no case for less than six years—if he is a religious and good candidate for the position of a teacher, I will hand them over to him as I have received them and certainly in agreement with my bishop.

3. 1. Otherwise, though he be either my son or a brother or a friend or any other relation, if he is unworthy, I shall keep information away from him since it does not befit him. 2. I shall

---

[1] Cf. Mt. 5:34; Jas. 5:12.

allow myself neither to be frightened by persecutions nor to be deceived by gifts. And even if I should ever come to the conviction that the books of the preachings which have been handed to me do not contain the truth, then also I shall not pass them on but shall hand them back. 3. When I am on a journey, I shall carry with me all the books that are in my possession. And if I purpose not to take them with me, I shall not leave them behind in my house, but shall consign them to the care of my bishop, who is of the same faith and of like extraction. 4. If I am sick and see death before me, I shall, if I am childless, proceed in the same way. I shall do the like if at the time of my death my son is not worthy or is not yet of age. I shall deposit the books with my bishop that he may hand them to my son when he has come of age and provided he is worthy of the trust, as a father's legacy according to the terms of the vow.

4. 1. And that I shall proceed in this way, I again invoke as witnesses heaven, earth and water, in which everything is comprehended, and also in addition the all-pervading air without which I am unable to breathe: I shall be obedient to him who hands over to me the books of the preachings, I shall keep them in every respect as I have vowed and even beyond that. 2. If now I observe the agreements, then will my portion be with the saints; but if I act against my vow, then may the universe and the all-pervading ether and God, who is over all and is mightier and more exalted than any other, be hostile to me. 3. And if even I should come to believe in another god, then I swear also by him, whether he now is or is not, that I shall not proceed otherwise. In addition to all that, if I am false to my word, I shall be accursed living and dead and suffer eternal punishment.'—And thereupon let him partake of bread and salt with him who hands over the books to him."

5. 1. When James had said this, the elders were pale with fright. Accordingly, observing that they feared greatly, James said, "Hear me, brethren and fellow-servants. 2. If we pass on the books to all without discrimination and if they are falsified by audacious men and are spoiled by interpretations—as indeed you have heard that some have already done—then it will come to pass that even those who earnestly seek the truth will always be

led into error. 3. On this account it is better that we keep the books and, as we have said, hand them with all caution only to those who wish to live and to save others. But if any one, after that he has made such a vow, does not adhere to it, then will he rightly suffer eternal punishment. 4. For why should he not go to ruin who has been guilty of the corruption of others?" Then were the elders pleased with James's conclusion and said, "Praised be he who has foreseen all things and destined you to be our bishop".—And when we had said this, we rose up and prayed to God the Father of all, to whom be glory for ever. Amen.

(3.) The True Prophet

H III. 17

1. "If any one denies that the man (=Adam) who came from the hands of the Creator of all things possessed the great and holy Spirit of divine foreknowledge, but acknowledges that another did this who was begotten of impure seed, how does he not commit a grievous sin? 2. I do not believe that such an one will find pardon even if he has been misdirected to this affront to the Father of all things by a forged passage of Scripture. . . .

20. 2. On the other hand, he executes a godly work who acknowledges that no other possesses the Spirit but he who from the beginning of the world, changing his forms and his names, runs through universal time until, anointed for his toils by the mercy of God, he comes to his own time and will have rest for ever.

21. 1. He, who alone is the true prophet, has, in the place of its Creator, given a suitable name to every living thing according to the measure of its nature;[1] for if he gave a name to anything, then that was also the name given it by him who had created it. 2. How then was it yet necessary for him to eat of a tree that he might know what is good or evil? (Assuredly it stands written:) 'He commanded'.[2] But this undiscerning men believe, who think that a dumb brute is more generous than God, who created them and all things."[3]

H III. 26

1. "He who is among the sons of men has prophecy innate to his

---

[1] Cf. Gen., 2:20.   [2] Gen. 2:16.   [3] Cf. Gen. 3:1 ff.

soul as belonging to it, and as a male being he announces in clear words the hopes of the world to come. Therefore he called his son by the name Abel, which without any ambiguity is translated 'grief'. 2. For he directs his sons to grieve over their deluded brethren. With no deceit he promises them consolation in the world to come.[1] 3. He exhorts them to pray to one God alone. He neither speaks himself of gods nor does he believe any other who speaks of them. He keeps and increases the good that he has.[2] He hates sacrifices, bloodshed and sprinklings, he loves pious, pure and holy men, he puts out the altar fire, 4. puts a stop to wars, preaches peace, commends temperance, does away with sins, orders marriage, permits abstinence and leads all men to purity. 5. He makes men compassionate, commends justice, seals the perfect, publishes the word of peace. He prophesies what is intelligible and speaks what is certain. 6. He frequently calls attention to the eternal fire of punishment, he constantly proclaims the kingdom of God. He makes reference to the heavenly riches, promises imperishable glory and indicates the forgiveness of sins by what he does."

H XI. 19

1. "When the prophet of the truth knew that the world had fallen into error and associated itself with wickedness, he did not cherish peace[3] with it, whilst it continued in error; but to the end he occasions wrath against all those who consent to wickedness. 2. Thus he brings knowledge in place of error; he kindles wrath, as a firebrand[4] among those who are sober, against the insidious serpent. He draws the word like a sword and by knowledge slays ignorance, cutting and separating the living from the dead. 3. Whilst wickedness is vanquished by lawful knowledge, war fills the universe. For the sake of salvation the son who is obedient is separated from his obstinate father, or the father from the son, or the mother from the daughter, or the daughter from the mother, relatives from their people and friends from their companions."[5]

---

[1] Cf. Mt. 5:4. [2] Cf. Mt. 25:14ff. [3] Cf. Mt. 10:34.
[4] Cf. Lk. 12:49. [5] Mt. 10:35; Lk. 12:53

(4.) Female Prophecy

H III. 22

1. "Along with the true prophet there has been created as a companion a female being who is as far inferior to him as *metousia* is to *ousia*, as the moon is to the sun, as fire is to light. 2. As a female she rules over the present world, which is like to her, and counts as the first prophetess; she proclaims her prophecy with all *amongst those born of women.* . . ."[1]

H II. 15

2. "The present world is temporal, on the other hand that which is to come is eternal. First ignorance appears, as second knowledge. 3. In the same way has God set in order the leaders of prophecy. For whilst the present world is female and as a mother brings forth the life of her children, the aeon to come is male and as a father expects his children. . . ."

H III. 23

1. "There are two kinds of prophecy, the one is male . . . 2. the other is found *amongst those who are born of women.* Proclaiming what pertains to the present world, female prophecy desires to be considered male. 3. On this account she steals the seed of the male, envelops them with her own seed of the flesh and lets them—that is, her words—come forth as her own creations. 4. She promises to give earthly riches gratuitously in the present world and wishes to exchange ⟨the slow⟩ for the swift, the small for the greater. 24. 1. She not only ventures to speak and hear of many gods, but also believes that she herself will be deified; and because she hopes to become something that contradicts her nature, she destroys what she has. Pretending to make sacrifice, she stains herself with blood at the time of her menses and thus pollutes those who touch her. 2. When she conceives, she gives birth to temporary kings and brings about wars in which much blood is shed. 3. Those who desire to get to know the truth from her, are led by many opposing and varied statements and hints to seek it perpetually without finding it, even unto death.

[1] Cf. Mt. 11:11.

4. For from the beginning a cause of death is certain for blind men; for she prophesies errors, ambiguities and obscurities, and thus deceives those who believe her. 25. 1. Therefore has she also given an ambiguous name to her first-born son; she named him Cain, which word has a two-fold meaning; for it is interpreted both 'possession' and 'envy' (and indicates) that later he was to envy (his brother Abel) a woman, or a possession, or the love of his parents. 2. But if it be none of these, then it was well ordered that he should be called 'possession', for he was her first possession; which was profitable for her (=false prophecy). For he was a *murderer* and a *liar*[1] and did not wish to cease to sin once he had begun to do so. 3. Moreover, his descendants were the first adulterers. They made harps and lyres and forged instruments of war.[2] 4. Therefore also is the prophecy of his descendants full of adulterers and harps, and secretly and sensually excites to war."

(5.) The Law and False Pericopes

H III. 47

1. . . . . "Moses delivered the law of God orally to seventy wise men[3] that it might be handed down and administered in continuous sequence. After the death of Moses, however, it was written not by Moses himself, but by an unknown person; 2. for in the law it is said: '*And Moses died and was buried near the house of Phogor, and no one knows of his sepulchre unto this day.*'[4] 3. But how, after his death, could Moses write: '*And Moses died . . .*'? And as in the time after Moses—about five hundred or more years later—it was found in the temple that had lately been built,[5] after a further five hundred years it was carried away, and in the reign of Nebuchadnezzar it was consumed by fire.[6] 4. And since it was written in the time after Moses and was repeatedly destroyed, the wisdom of Moses is shown in this; for he did not commit it to writing, foreseeing its disappearance. But those who wrote the law, since they did not foresee its destruction, are convicted of ignorance and were not prophets."

[1] Gen. 4:6ff.; Jn. 8:44.   [2] Cf. Gen. 4:21f.   [3] Num. 11:16ff.
[4] Deut. 34:5f.
[5] Cf. 1 Kgs. 8f. (Solomon's temple), contaminated with 2 Kgs. 22:8; 2 Chron. 34:14.
[6] Cf. 2 Kgs. 24:11-13; 25:8f.

H II. 38

1. "The prophet Moses having by the order of God handed over the law with the elucidations to seventy chosen (men) that they might prepare those who were willing among the people, after a short time the law was committed to writing. At the same time some false pericopes intruded into it. These defamed the only God, who made heaven and earth and all that is in them. The wicked one dared to do this for a good purpose, 2. namely, that it might be ascertained which men are shameless enough to hear willingly what is written against God and which, out of their love of him, not only do not believe what is said against him, but also at the outset do not bear to hear it for a moment, even should it be true, (men therefore) who are of the opinion that it is safer to expose oneself to danger on the ground of a well-meaning belief than in consequence of defamatory words to live with a bad conscience."

H III. 48

2. .... "In the providence of God a pericope was handed down intact in the written law so that it might indicate with certainty which of the things written are true and which false." 49. 1. .... "In the conclusion of the first book of the law it stands written: "*A ruler shall not fail from Judah nor a leader from his loins, until he come whose it is, and him will the Gentiles expect.*"[1] 2. Now he who sees that the leaders out of Judah are past and that a ruler and leader has appeared and is expected by the Gentiles, is able on the ground of the fulfilment to recognize that the passage of Scripture is true and that the promised one has appeared. And if he accepts his doctrine, then will he learn which portions of the Scriptures answer to the truth and which are false."

50. 1. And Peter said: "That what is true is mixed with what is false, follows also from this, that when on one occasion—as I remember—he was attacked by the Sadducees, he answered: '*Wherefore ye do err, because ye do not know the true things of the Scriptures, and on this account also ye know nothing of the power of God.*'[2] If then he assumes that they did not know the true things of the Scriptures, then clearly there are false portions contained in

---

[1] Gen. 49:10.   [2] Cf. Mk. 12:24 (Mt. 22:29).

them. 2. Also his utterance, '*Be ye good money changers*',[1] refers to the genuine and non-genuine words of Scripture. And in saying: '*Wherefore do ye not understand what is reasonable in the Scriptures?*'[2] he strengthens the understanding of him who already on his own reflection judges prudently. 51. 1. That he alluded to the scribes and the teachers of the existing Scriptures[3] because they knew about the true, genuine law, is known. 2. And in saying: '*I am not come to destroy the law*,[4] and yet destroying something, he indicated that what he destroyed had not belonged originally to the law. 3. His declaration: '*The heaven and the earth will pass away, but one jot or one tittle shall not pass from the law*'[5] shows that what passes away earlier than heaven and earth does not belong to the true law. 52. 1. For whilst heaven and earth still exist, sacrifices, kingdoms, prophecies of those who are *among them that are born of women*[6] and such like, have passed away, not going back to the ordinance of God.''

H II. 43

1. "On this account be it far from us to believe that the Lord of all, who has made heaven and earth and all that is in them, shares his authority with others or that he *lies*[7] (for if he lies, who then is truthful?) or that he *puts to the test*[8] as if he was ignorant (for who then has foreknowledge?). 2. If he *is grieved*[9] or *repents*,[10] who then is perfect and of immutable mind? If he is *jealous*,[11] who then is satisfied with himself? If he *hardens hearts*,[12] who then makes wise? 3. If he *makes blind*[13] and *deaf*,[14] who then has given sight and hearing? If he counsels robberies,[15] who then requires that justice be done? If he *mocks*,[16] who then is without deceit? If he is powerless, who then is omnipotent? If he acts unjustly, who then is just? If he *makes what is wicked*,[17] who then will work what is good? 44. 1. If he longs for a *fertile hill*,[18] to whom then do all things belong? If he *lies*,[19] who then is truthful? If he

[1] A frequently attested uncanonical saying; cf. Resch, Agrapha[2], *TU* 30.2, 1906, pp.112 to 122; cf. Vol. I, p. 88.
[2] Non-canonical, instanced only here in the patristic literature,   [3] Mt. 23:2f.
[4] Mt. 5:17.   [5] Mt. 24:35; 5:18; cf. Ep. P. 2. 5.   [6] Mt. 11:11.
[7] Ps. 89:35; 1 Kgs. 22:22f.   [8] Gen. 22:1; Ex. 15:25; 16:4 and often.
[9] Gen. 6:6f.   [10] 1 Sam. 15:35; 1 Chron. 21:15; Ps. 110:4.
[11] Deut. 32:19; Ex. 20:5 and often.   [12] Ex. 4:21; 7:3 and often.
[13] Ex. 4:11; 2 Kgs. 6:18.   [14] Ex. 4:11.   [15] Ex. 3:21f. and often.
[16] Ex. 10:2.   [17] Is. 45:7.   [18] Ps. 68:15f.   [19] Cf. note 7.

dwells in a *tabernacle*,[1] who then is incomprehensible? 2. If he craves after the steam of fat, *sacrifices*,[2] *offerings*,[3] *sprinklings*,[4] who then is without need, holy, pure and perfect? If he takes delight in *lamps* and *candlesticks*,[5] who then set in order the luminaries in the firmament? 3. If he dwells in *shadow, darkness, storm* and *smoke*,[6] who then is light and lightens the infinite spaces of the world? If he draws near with *flourish of trumpets, war-cries, missiles* and *arrows*,[7] who then is the rest that all long for? 4. If he loves *war*,[8] who then desires peace? If he *makes what is wicked*,[9] who then brings forth what is good? If he is cruel,[10] who then is kind? If he does not make good his promises,[11] who then will be trusted? 5. If he loves the unjust, *adulterers* and *murderers*,[12] who then is a just judge?"

(6.) Polemic against Paul

H II. 16

1. "As in the beginning the one God, being as it were a right hand and a left, created first the heavens and then the earth, so also has he assembled in pairs everything that follows. In the case of man, however, he has no longer proceeded in this way, but has reversed every pair. 2. For whereas he created what was stronger as the first and what was weaker as the second, in the case of man we find the opposite, namely, first what is smaller and in the second place what is stronger. 3. Thus from Adam, who was created in the image of God, there sprang as the first the unrighteous Cain, as the second the righteous Abel. 4. Again from him whom you call Deucalion there were sent forth two prototypes of spirits, one clean and one unclean, namely, the black raven and as second the white dove.[13] 5. And from Abraham, the forefather of our people, there issued two firsts,[14] Ishmael first and then Isaac, who was blessed of God. 6. From Isaac again there originated two, the godless Esau and the pious Jacob. 7. According to this order there followed as a first-born in the world the high priest (=Aaron), then the lawgiver (=Moses).[15]

[1] Ex. 40:34.　　[2] Gen. 4:3 and often.　　[3] Ex. 29:28 and often.
[4] Cf. Ex. 24:6 and often.　　[5] Ex. 25:31ff.
[6] Deut. 4:11; Ex. 10:22; 19:18; 20:21.
[7] Ex. 19:13, 16; Num. 24:8; Deut. 32:23, 42 and often.
[8] Ex. 15:3; Deut. 21:10.　　[9] Is. 45:7.　　[10] Cf. Job 30:21; Is. 13:9.
[11] Cf. Gen. 18:13ff.　　[12] 2 Sam. 12:13; Gen. 4:15; Ex. 2:12ff.　　[13] Gen. 8:6ff.
[14] Ishmael and Elieser; not adduced in what follows; but cf. R I. 33f.
[15] Ex. 6:20; 7:7; 1 Chron. 23:13f.

17. 1. Similarly—for the pair with respect to Elias was, as it would seem, set aside for another time . . .—2. there came as the first the one who was *among those that are born of women*,[1] and after that there appeared the one who was among the sons of men. 3. He who follows this order can discern by whom Simon (= Paul), who as the first came before me to the Gentiles, was sent forth, and to whom I (= Peter) belong who appeared later than he did and came in upon him as light upon darkness, as knowledge upon ignorance, as healing upon sickness."

H XVII. 13

1. When Simon heard this, he interrupted with the words: ". . . You have stated that you have learned accurately the teaching of your master because you have heard and seen him directly (ἐναργείᾳ) face to face, and that it is not possible for any other to experience the like in a dream or in a vision.[2] 2. I shall show you that this is false: The person to whose hearing something comes is by no means certain of what is said. For he must check whether he has not been deceived because, whatever befalls him, he is only a man. On the other hand, vision creates together with the appearance the certainty that one sees something divine. Give me an answer first to that."

16. 1. And Peter said: ". . . 2. We know . . . that many idolaters, adulterers and other sinners have seen visions and had true dreams, and also that some have had visions that were wrought by demons. For I maintain that the eyes of mortals cannot see the incorporeal being of the Father or of the Son, because it is enwrapped in insufferable light. 3. Therefore it is a token of the mercy of God, and not of jealousy in him, that he is invisible to men living in the flesh. For he who sees him must die. 6. . . . . No one is able to see the incorporeal power of the Son or even of an angel. But he who has a vision should recognize that this is the work of a wicked demon.

17. 5. . . . . For to a pious, natural, and pure mind the truth reveals itself; it is not acquired through a dream, but is granted to the good through discernment. 18. 1. For in this way was the Son revealed to me also by the Father.[3] Wherefore I know the

---

[1] Mt. 11:11.　　[2] Cf. H XVII. 5, 6b.　　[3] Mt. 16:17.

power of revelation; I have myself learned this from him. For at the very time when the Lord asked how the people named him[1]—although I had heard that others had given him another name—it rose in my heart to say, and I know not how I said it, '*Thou art the Son of the living God*'.[2] 6. You see now how expressions of wrath have to be made through visions and dreams, but discourse with friends takes place from mouth to mouth, openly and not through riddles, visions and dreams as with an enemy. 19. 1. And if our Jesus appeared to you also and became known in a vision and met you as angry with an enemy, yet he has spoken only through visions and dreams or through external revelations. But can any one be made competent to teach through a vision? 2. And if your opinion is, 'That is possible', why then did our teacher spend a whole year with us who were awake? 3. How can we believe you even if he has appeared to you, and how can he have appeared to you if you desire the opposite of what you have learned? 4. But if you were visited by him for the space of an hour and were instructed by him and thereby have become an apostle,[3] then proclaim his words, expound what he has taught, be a friend to his apostles and do not contend with me, who am his confidant; for you have in hostility *withstood*[4] me, who am a firm rock, the foundation stone of the church.[5] 5. If you were not an enemy, then you would not slander me and revile my preaching in order that I may not be believed when I proclaim what I have heard in my own person from the Lord, as if I were undoubtedly *condemned*[6] and you were acknowledged. 6. And if you call me '*condemned*',[6] then you accuse God, who revealed Christ to me, and disparage him who called me blessed on account of the revelation.[7] 7. But if you really desire to co-operate with the truth, then learn first from us what we have learned from him and, as a learner of the truth, become a fellow-worker with us."

[1] Mt. 16:13f.   [2] Mt. 16:16.   [3] Cf. Acts 9:3ff.; 1 Cor. 15:8.
[4] Gal. 2:11.   [5] Cf. Mt. 16:18.   [6] Gal. 2:11.   [7] Mt. 16:17.

(7.) The Doctrine of Baptism

H XI. 25

1. "Wherefore come readily as a son to a father that God may reckon your ignorance as the original cause of your transgressions. But if, after you have been invited, you will not come or delay to do so, then by the just judgment of God you will perish because you have not been willing. 2. And do not believe that you will ever have hope if you remain unbaptized even if you are more pious than all the pious have been hitherto. Rather you will then suffer a punishment all the more severe because you have done good works not in a good way. 3. For to do good is good only when it takes place as God has commanded. But if in opposition to his will you will not be baptized, then you serve your own will and despise his decree.

26. 1. But someone may say: 'What good results to piety when a man is baptized with water?' In the first place, that you do the will of God. And in the second place, when you are born again for God of water, then through fear you get rid of your first birth which came of lust, and thus can attain to salvation. But that is not possible in any other way. 2. For thus has the prophet appealed to us with an oath: *'Verily I say unto you, if you are not born again of living water . . . you cannot enter into the kingdom of heaven'.*[1] 3. Wherefore come! For from the beginning there has been associated with the water something that shows mercy;[2] it knows those who are baptized in the thrice holy name and delivers them from future punishment, bringing as gifts to God the good works of the baptized done after baptism. 4. Wherefore flee to the water; for that alone can quench the violence of fire. He who has not yet been willing to come still bears in himself the spirit of passion and for that reason does not desire to approach the living water for his own salvation. 27. 1. Come then now, be you a righteous or an unrighteous man. For if you are righteous, you need only to be baptized for salvation, but an unrighteous man ought not only to submit to baptism for the forgiveness of the sins he has committed in ignorance, but should also do good according to the measure of his past godlessness, as baptism

[1] Jn. 3:5.   [2] The Spirit of God; cf. Gen. 1:2.

124

requires. 2. Therefore hasten, be you at present righteous or unrighteous, that soon you may be born unto God the Father, who
begets you of water. For postponement brings danger with it,
because the hour of death is hidden. Prove your likeness to God by
good works, loving the truth and honouring the true God as a
father. To honour him means to live as he, who himself is
righteous, desires you to live. 3. The will of a righteous man is
directed to the doing of nothing that is wrong. But wrong is
murder, adultery, hatred, avarice, and the like; and there are
many kinds of wrongdoing. 28. 1. Besides these instructions there
is to be observed what is not for all men in common, but is
peculiar to the worship of God. I mean the keeping of one's self
pure, that a man should not have intercourse with his wife during
her monthly courses, for so the law of God commands.[1] 2. But
what? If the keeping of one's self pure ($\kappa a \theta a \rho \epsilon \acute{v} \epsilon \iota \nu$) did not
belong to the (true) worship of God, would you wallow gladly in
filth like dung-beetles ($\kappa \acute{a} \nu \theta a \rho o \iota$)? Therefore cleanse your hearts
from wickedness by heavenly thoughts, as men who as rational
beings stand above dumb brutes, and wash your bodies with
water. 3. For to keep one's self pure is truly worth aspiring after
not because purity of the body precedes purity of the heart, but
because purity follows goodness. 4. Therefore our teacher convicted some of the Pharisees and scribes among us, who are
separate and as scribes know the law better than others, and
(described) them as hypocrites because they kept clean only what
is visible to men, but neglected purity of the heart, which is
visible to God alone.

29. 1. The following expression he rightly used with reference
to the hypocrites among them, not (however) with reference to
them all; for of some he said that they should be heard because
to them *the seat of Moses*[2] had been assigned. 2. But to the hypocrites he said: '*Woe unto you, ye scribes and Pharisees, hypocrites, for
ye make clean only the outside of the cup and the platter, but the inside is
full* of dirt. *Thou blind Pharisee, cleanse first the inside of the cup and
the platter that their outside may be clean also.*[3] 3. And truly: for if
the mind is enlightened by knowledge, he who has been instructed
can be good, and then purity follows thereupon. For out of the

---

[1] Lev. 15:24; 18:19.   [2] Mt. 23:2f.   [3] Mt. 23:25f.

mental attitude within there comes right care for the body without, as indeed out of neglect of the body care for one's mental attitude cannot come. 4. Thus the man who is pure can cleanse both what is within and what is without. But he who cleanses only what is without, does this to obtain praise of men; and whilst lookers-on lavish praise upon him, he obtains nothing from God.[1]

30. 1. But to whom does it not seem to be better not to have intercourse with a woman during her monthly course, but only after purification and washing? And one should also wash himself after intercourse. 2. If you hesitate to do this, recall to mind how you observed a portion of the purification instructions when you served inanimate idols. Be ashamed that you now hesitate when you ought to commit yourselves, I do not say to more but to the whole of purity. Remember him who made you, and you will recognize who he is who now puts hesitation in your way with respect to purity. 31. 1. But some one of you may ask, 'Is it necessary that we now do everything that we did in the service of the idols?' I answer you, Not everything; but what you did in a good way, that you should do now even more. For whatever is done well in error comes from the truth, just as (conversely) if anything is done badly in the truth, it comes of error. 2. Receive then from every quarter what belongs to you, not what is alien to you, and say not: 'If those who are in error do something good, then we are not under an obligation to do it.' For according to this contention, if any one who worships idols does not kill, then we ought to kill because he who is in error does not become a murderer.

32. 1. No; but (we should do) more: if those living in error *do not kill*, let us never *be angry*;[2] if he who is in error *does not commit adultery*, let us avoid even the beginning and never *lust*.[3] If he who is in error *loves his friends*, let us also love those who *hate* us.[4] If he who is in error *lends* to those who have possessions, let us do so to those also who have no possessions.[5] 2. In a word: we who hope to inherit the endless age are under obligation to complete better works than those who know only this present world.

[1] Cf. Mt. 6:1ff.; 23:4ff.   [2] Mt. 5:21f.   [3] Mt. 5:27f.
[4] Mt. 5:43ff.; Lk. 6:27ff.   [5] Cf. Lk. 6:34f.

3. For we know that if in the day of judgment their works, being compared with ours, are found equal in well-doing, we shall then suffer shame, but they perdition, because in consequence of error they have done good not to their own benefit.[1] But we shall be ashamed, as I said, because we have done no more than they although we have had a greater knowledge. 4. And if we are ashamed because we are equal to them in well-doing and do not surpass them, by how much more shall we be so if we have not so many good works to show as they have? 33. 1. That in truth in the day of judgment the deeds of those who have known the truth will be found equal to the good works of those living in error, the infallible (prophet) has taught us, saying to those who did not wish to come to him and hear him: '*The queen of the south shall rise up with this generation and shall condemn it, because she came from the ends of the earth to hear the wisdom of Solomon. And behold! here is more than Solomon*, and ye believe not.'[2] 2. And to those among the people who, confronted with his preaching, would not repent he said: '*The men of Nineveh will rise up with this generation and will condemn it, because they repented at the preaching of Jonah; and behold! here is more than Jonah*, and no one believes.'[3] 3. And thus he set over against their godlessness the Gentiles who have done (good)—in condemnation of all who possess the true religion and never have so many good works to show as they have who live in error. And he exhorted the judicious to accomplish good works not only in the same way as the Gentiles, but to do more than they.

4. I have adduced this because of the necessity of observing the monthly courses and of washing after sexual intercourse and of not making objection to such purity, though it is practised by those living in error. For the men who do good in error will judge those who have the true religion without however being saved themselves. 5. For they observe purity because of error, and not as service rendered to the true Father and God of the universe."

[1] Cf. H XI. 27, 1 above.   [2] Mt. 12:42, Lk. 11:31.   [3] Mt. 12:41, Lk. 11:32.

3. THE EPISTLE TO THE LAODICEANS

(*W. Schneemelcher*)

LITERATURE. R. Anger, *Über den Laodicenerbrief, eine biblisch-kritische Untersuchung*, 1843.—J. B. Lightfoot, *St. Paul's Epistles to the Colossians and to Philemon*, 1879, pp. 274–300 (text).—Th. Zahn, *Gesch. d. ntl. Kanons* II, pp. 566ff.—A. Harnack, *Apokrypha* IV: *Die apocryphen Briefe des Paulus an die Laodicener und Korinther* (*KlT* 12), 1931².—E. Jacquier, *Le Nouveau Testament dans l'église chrétienne* I, 1911, pp. 345–351.—A. von Harnack, *Marcion. Das Evangelium vom fremden Gott*, 1924², pp. 134*–149*.—K. Pink, "Die pseudo-paulinischen Briefe II", *Biblica* VI, 1925, pp. 179–192.—John Knox, *Marcion and the New Testament*, Chicago 1942.—G. Quispel, "De Brief aan de Laodicensen een Marcionitische vervalsing", *Nederlands Theologisch Tijdschrift* V, 1950, pp. 43–46.

1. ATTESTATION AND TRADITION. In the *Muratori Canon* (cf. Vol. I, p. 44) two Marcionite forgeries, an epistle to the Laodiceans and one to the Alexandrians, are mentioned and rejected. Apart from the suggestion that these books were "forged in Paul's name for the sect of Marcion" (lines 64f.), the passage provides no sort of clue to any closer identification of this epistle. Tertullian reports (*Adv. Marc.* V. 11 and 17) that the heretics, i.e. the Marcionites, regarded Ephesians as the Epistle to the Laodiceans and that Marcion himself had made this change in the title. This note is confirmed to some extent by Epiphanius of Salamis (*haer.* 42. 9. 4 and 42. 12. 3), who, it is true, gives no clear information as to whether the source which he copies here (Hippolytus) recognized Ephesians as the Epistle to the Laodiceans or whether in addition to Ephesians an Epistle to the Laodiceans also stood in the Marcionite canon. Filastrius (*haer.* LXXXIX.), who briefly mentions the Epistle to the Laodiceans in the context of his discussion of Hebrews, likewise goes no farther. Other references (assembled in Pink, *op. cit.*) also contribute little to our knowledge of the Epistle to the Laodiceans. The so-called *Speculum* (Ps. Augustine, *De divinis scripturis*, 5th or 6th cent.) is unambiguous: here verse 4 of the Epistle to the Laodiceans preserved in Latin is quoted (*CSEL* 12, 516); Gregory the Great must also be reckoned among the positive witnesses for this epistle handed down in Latin (*Moralia* 35. 20. 48; PL 76, 778C).

This Latin Epistle to the Laodiceans is found in many Bible manuscripts (cf. among others Jacquier, *op. cit.* I, pp. 345ff.; S. Berger, *Histoire de la vulgate*, pp. 341f.). Although there are no complete Old Latin manuscripts of the Pauline epistles (except the *Book of Armagh*, Dublin Tr. Coll. 52), yet it is evidently true that this Epistle to the Laodiceans is one of the Old Latin components with which the whole Vulgata-tradition has been contaminated in different ways.[1] Here, however, we cannot enter into this whole problem more closely. Only it may be stated that the Latin Epistle to the Laodiceans early met with considerable dissemination in the West. Then on top of that there came later a series of translations into Western vernaculars (cf. Anger, *op. cit.*, and Lightfoot, *op. cit.*).

2. CONTENTS, OCCASION, DATE. When we consider this small apocryphon, we are amazed that it ever found a place in Bible manuscripts. For this pretended epistle of Paul is nothing other than a "worthless patching together of Pauline passages and phrases, mainly from the Epistle to the Philippians" (Knopf-Krüger, *Apokr.* 2, p. 150). A suggestive statement of its contents can scarcely be given, and we seek in vain for a definite theological intention. The author seems to have gathered verses from Paul's epistles, worded in as general terms as possible, that with his patch-work he might close a gap in the Pauline corpus, which could indeed be noticed by any Bible reader. There can be no doubt that Col. 4:16 was the occasion of this forgery. There it is said: "And when this letter has been read among you, have it read also in the church of the Laodiceans, and have the one from Laodicea come to you that you may read it also." Here we do not need to inquire more closely what is to be understood by the ἐπιστολὴ ἐκ Λαοδικείας. What still lies nearest at hand is that Paul refers to a letter to Laodicea which, however, has not come into the Pauline corpus. This want was to be met by the elaborate work of an unknown person who had a knowledge of the Bible, but in other respects had not exactly had a theological training.

The epistle has been known hitherto only in a Latin version (and also in the later translations that have been referred to). No evidence of a Greek text has so far been found. On the other hand, later Greek sources speak of an epistle to the Laodiceans (cf. the compilation in Pink, *op. cit.*), so that it must at least be assumed that the existence of such an epistle was known in the East. The epistle probably came into being in the West (in spite of verse 5, the corrupt text of which perhaps permits of its being remedied through translation back into Greek).

The dating of the Epistle to the Laodiceans is difficult for the

---

[1] I am indebted for this reference to P. Bonifatius Fischer, OSB, Beuron, who refers above all to H. Frede, *Pelagius, der irische Paulustext, Sedulius Scottus*, 1961; cf. also B. Fischer in *Theol. Revue* 57, 1961, cols. 162ff. It is important that the Priscillianist Peregrinus received the Epistle to the Laodiceans into his edition, not indeed in the canons, but in the text. On Peregrinus cf. E. Dekkers, *Clavis Patrum Latinorum*, 1961[2] p. 178 (no. 786) and above all the article by B. Fischer in *Archivos Leoneses* 1961 that is mentioned there.

reason that it depends on the question of the identity of this apocryphon with the one mentioned in the *Muratori Canon*, and this again is closely connected with the problem of its Marcionite derivation. Either the *Muratori Canon* means the Epistle to the Ephesians, the name of which was changed by Marcion into the Epistle to the Laodiceans (so Tertullian)—that, however, is unlikely, since Ephesians is mentioned in the *Muratori Canon*—or it had actually in view a separate Epistle to the Laodiceans, and then it must be the Latin Epistle to the Laodiceans that has come down to us, if no other pseudo-Pauline epistles to Laodicea are to be assumed. Certainly the Latin Epistle to the Laodiceans shows no sort of Marcionite character such as ought to be expected according to the statement of the *Muratori Canon*.

3. THE PROBLEM OF THE MARCIONITE DERIVATION OF THE EPISTLE TO THE LAODICEANS. Whilst for a long time it was widely agreed that the Epistle to the Laodiceans was a colourless and dull compilation of Pauline sentences, A. von Harnack put forward the thesis that the Epistle is a Marcionite forgery: "In the Epistle to the Laodiceans we salute the only complete writing which has been preserved to us from the Marcionite church of the earliest time" (*Marcion*[2], p. 149*). Harnack would like to see a proof of that in the fact that the Epistle to the Laodiceans begins with Gal. 1:1, i.e. with 'monumental, anticatholic words in Marcion's sense' (p. 141*) from the epistle which stood at the head of the Marcionite apostolos. In the departure from Phil. 1:3 (gratias ago *deo* meo; Ep. to the Laodiceans verse 3: *Christo*), in the idea of *veritas evangelii* and in the addition *quod a me praedicatur* (verse 4), in the *ex me* (= οἱ ὄντες ἐξ ἐμοῦ; in Phil. 1:12 we read τὰ κατ᾽ ἐμέ), in the elimination of the ἀπουσία of Phil. 2:12 in Laod. verse 10 and in the twice-repeated appearance of *vita aeterna* (verses 5 and 10) Harnack sees the sagacity and the artfulness of Marcion at work. The Ep. to the Laodiceans must however have come not from the master himself but from a pupil who, between 160 and 190, after the title "Epistle to the Laodiceans" had again become free (Ephesians had been given back its early name), produced it simultaneously in Latin and Greek. From the same workshop there also came the Marcionite Arguments on the Epistles of Paul.

Now the hypothesis of the Marcionite character of the Prologue to Paul is just as problematic as that of the antimarcionite Prologues to the Gospels.[1] That the Roman church unknowingly took over Marcion's Prologue to Paul into its 'counter-canon' (so de Bruyne and Harnack) is—to put it mildly—a fantastic idea. But here it can be left aside; it merely shows us on how

---

[1] Cf. also E. Haenchen, *Die Apostelgeschichte*, 1961,[13], p. 8 n. 3.

precarious ground Harnack's construction stands. Anyhow, it has of itself no convincing power. The passages adduced can be drawn upon only with violence as strict proof of a Marcionite origin of the Ep. to the Laodiceans. That the Marcionite forger—it certainly cannot have been the master himself—satisfied himself with such trifles and did not use the opportunity to give clearer expression to his theology does not go to prove his "sagacity". Further, from the fact that the epistle begins with Gal. 1:1 no far-reaching conclusions can be drawn. Harnack has here got on to a wrong track.

G. Quispel (*op. cit.*) has recently taken up Harnack's hypothesis and attempted to support it from another side. He thinks that the beginning of the Ep. to the Laodiceans (= Gal. 1:1) answers to a stylistic expedient that was conventional in antiquity: in literary counterfeits it was made clear to the readers and hearers through the opening words which model was to be imitated. The beginning of the Ep. to the Laodiceans ought then to draw the reader's attention to the fact that really there speaks here the Paul who—according to Marcion—had expounded in Galatians the decisive points of his theology. Consequently we should here have a case similar to the one in Jn. 1:1, where also a connection is intentionally made with Gen. 1:1. But this reasoning also may hardly carry conviction. For the Ep. to the Laodiceans does not purpose to be a rhetorical performance, and the author had obviously no literary ambitions. Too much honour is done the author of this paltry and carelessly compiled concoction when we judge him by the yardstick of ancient literary practices.

To sum up, it may be said that the Marcionite origin of the Latin Epistle to the Laodiceans is an hypothesis that can neither be proved nor sustained. It is rather a clumsy forgery the purpose of which is to have in the Pauline corpus the Epistle to the Laodiceans mentioned in Col. 4:16. Whether the Epistle to the Laodiceans mentioned in the *Muratori Canon* is identical with this apocryphon remains unsettled. With that the possibility of an accurate dating also falls out. As the time of composition there comes into question the period between the second century and the fourth.

*To the Laodiceans

* The numbers of the notes refer to the verses of Laod.

1. Paul, an apostle not of men and not through man, but through Jesus Christ, to the brethren who are in Laodicea:

1 Gal. 1:1.

2. Grace to you and peace from God the Father and the Lord Jesus Christ.

3. I thank Christ in all my prayer that you are steadfast in him and persevering in his works, in expectation of the promise for the day of judgment. 4. And may you not be deceived by the vain talk of some people who tell (you) tales that they may lead you away from the truth of the gospel which is proclaimed by me. 5. And now may God grant that those who come from me for the furtherance of the truth of the gospel (. . .) may be able to serve and to do good works for the well-being of eternal life.

6. And now my bonds are manifest, which I suffer in Christ, on account of which I am glad and rejoice. 7. This ministers to me unto eternal salvation, which (itself) is effected through your prayers and by the help of the Holy Spirit, whether it be through life or through death. 8. For my life is in Christ and to die is joy (to me).

9. And this will his mercy work in you, that you may have the same love and be of one mind. 10. Therefore, beloved, as you have heard in my presence, so hold fast and do in the fear of God, and eternal life will be your portion. 11. For it is God who works in you. 12. And do without hesitation what you do. 13. And for the rest, beloved, rejoice in Christ and beware of those who are out for sordid gain. 14. May all your requests be manifest before God, and be ye stedfast in the mind of Christ. 15. And what is pure, true, proper, just and lovely, do. 16. And what you have heard and received, hold in your heart and peace will be with you.

[17. Salute all the brethren with the holy kiss.] 18. The saints salute you. 19. The grace of the Lord Jesus Christ be with your spirit. 20. And see that this epistle is read to the Colossians and that of the Colossians among you.

---

[2] Gal. 1:3; Phil. 1:2. [3] Phil. 1:3. [4] Cf. Col. 2:4; Gal. 1:11. [5] Verse 5 has been corrupted in transmission; the translation rests on conjecture; cf. Phil. 1:12. [6] Phil. 1:13, 18. [7] Phil. 1:19f. [8] Phil. 1:21. [9] Phil. 2:2. [10] Phil. 2:12. [11] Phil. 2:13. [12] Cf. Phil. 2:14. [13] Cf. Phil. 3:1. [14] Phil. 4:6; cf. 1 Cor. 15:58; 2:16. [15] Phil. 4:8. [16] Phil. 4:9. [17] Lacking in some MSS., doubtless a secondary addition; 1 Thess. 5:26. [18] Phil. 4:22. [19] Phil. 4:23; Gal. 6:18. [20] The words *this epistle* and *to the Colossians* are lacking in some MSS.; cf. Col. 4:16.

4. THE APOCRYPHAL CORRESPONDENCE BETWEEN SENECA AND PAUL

(A. Kurfess)

INTRODUCTION: I. LITERATURE: Edition by Claude W. Barlow, *Epistolae Senecae ad Paulum et Pauli ad Senecam quae vocantur* (Papers and Monographs of the American Academy in Rome, vol. 10), Rome 1938 (with a bibliography down to 1937); print of this edition in *PL*, supplementum I, cols. 673–678. A complete bibliography (1883–1938) is given by J. Haussleiter: Literatur zu der Frage "Seneca und das Christentum", in *Bursians Jahresbericht über die Fortschritte der klassischen Altertumswissenschaft* 281, 1943, pp. 172–175. Only P. de Labriolle, *La réaction païenne*, Paris 1934, pp. 25–28, is lacking. In addition there may be mentioned severally: E. Westerburg, *Der Ursprung der Sage, dass Seneca Christ gewesen sei*, Berlin 1881 (reviewed by A. Harnack, *ThLZ* 6, 1881, cols. 444–449). E. Liénard, "Sur la correspondance apocryphe de Sénèque et de St. Paul", *Revue belge de philologie et d'histoire* 11, 1932, pp. 5–23. A. Kurfess, "Zum apokryphen Briefwechsel zwischen Seneca und Paulus", *Theologie und Glaube* 19, 1937, pp. 317–322; A. Kurfess, "Zum apokryphen Briefwechsel zwischen Seneca und Paulus", *Theologische Quartalschrift* 119, 1938, pp. 318–331; A. Kurfess, "Der Brand Roms und die Christenverfolgung im Jahre 64 n. Chr.", *Mnemosyne* 3. ser. 6, 1938, pp. 261–272 (on Letter 11); A. Kurfess, "Zum apokryphen Breifwechsel zwischen Seneca und Paulus", *ZRGG* 2, 1949/50, pp. 67–70. H. Leclercq, "Sénèque et Paul", *Dictionnaire d'archéol. chrét. et de liturgie* 15, 1, 1950, cols. 1193–1198. E. Franceschini, "Un ignoto codice delle Epistolae Senecae et Pauli", *Mélanges J. de Ghellinck* I, Gembloux 1951, pp. 149–170. A. Kurfess, "Zu dem apokryphen Briefwechsel zwischen dem Philosophen Seneca und dem Apostel Paulus", *Aevum* 26, 1952, pp. 42–48. J. N. Sevenster, *Paul and Seneca*, Leiden 1961 (on the correspondence: pp. 11–14).

2. ORIGIN, PURPOSE, DATE. On these matters Ernst Bickel, *Lehrbuch der Geschichte der römischen Literatur*, Heidelberg 1937, p. 245, expresses himself as follows: "In the darkness of the 3rd century lesser writings in the common speech of the Itala passed from hand to hand among the Italian people, the Epistles of Paul and the Gospel Books. The spurious correspondence between the philosopher Seneca and the apostle Paul best informs us how at first Christianity became literary material in Italy. This correspondence was already reckoned as genuine by the church father Jerome and originated in the 3rd century.[1] It was born of reflection on the extent to which the mentor and minister of the

---

[1] C. W. Barlow dates the correspondence shortly before 392; but in *Das Altertum* 5, 1959, p. 94, E. Bickel abides by his own statement.

emperor Nero, the philosopher Seneca, could by putting his great literary skill at the service of the Pauline revelation have created for it its fitting place in Latin literature. This correspondence presents a mythical expression of the historical process of fusion which came about in Italy, onwards from the end of the period of the Antonines, of Christianity on the one hand and, on the other, the ancient culture of the rhetoricians (*Rhein. Mus.* LX, 1905, p. 512). From the popular literary form of this correspondence it can be learned in the first place what part of the contents of the Bible stood to the fore in the mission of those days among the lower classes of the Italian population: the epistles of the apostles and the texts that stood closest to them. But this correspondence, which brought together the moral philosopher Seneca and the apostle Paul, is also of fundamental importance for the general frame of mind in which the Italian people turned to Christianity. Such was the Christianity of the Italian people that it was not sufficient when the ordinations and sacramental forms of the foreign cult were brought them. It was evidently the social tenets of Christianity which provided the presupposition for the association of Seneca and Paul."

3. TESTIMONY FROM ANTIQUITY. The most important testimony, on which Augustine (ep. 153. 14) is dependent (Harnack, *ThLZ* 6, 1881, 447), is Jerome, *de vir. ill.* 12 (of the year 392). The passage, which in the manuscript is prefixed as a prologue to the epistles, runs in translation as follows: "L. Annaeus Seneca from Corduba . . . lived a very abstemious life. I would not receive him into the list of the saints were I not made to do so by those epistles which are read by very many, (the epistles) of Paul to Seneca and of Seneca to Paul. In these epistles he who was the teacher of Nero and the most influential man of that time declares that he wishes to occupy among his own people the same place that Paul had among the Christians. This (Seneca) was put to death by Nero two years before the glorious martyrdom of Peter and Paul." Here the conclusion of the 12th epistle is quoted, i.e. the last epistle of the collection which lay before Jerome. The two last epistles were added only later, as the difference in style proves. Had the last (the 14th) epistle lain before the church father, he would undoubtedly have made full use of it and by means of it have justified the reception of Seneca into the *catalogus Sanctorum.*— A further testimony from antiquity is found in the *Passio sancti Pauli apostoli* c. 1 (ps. Linus; Aa I, p. 24. 3ff.): "From the house of the emperor there came to him many who believed on the Lord Jesus Christ, and great gladness and joy increased daily among the believers. Even the emperor's tutor, recognizing the divine wisdom that was in him, became so united to him in

friendship that he could scarcely refrain from conferring with him. As oral discussion was not possible, they frequently entered into mutual correspondence, and he (Seneca) enjoyed his amiability, his friendly talk and his counsel; and so very much was his teaching disseminated and loved through the working of the Holy Spirit that now he taught with express permission and was gladly heard by many. For he disputed with the philosophers of the heathen and refuted them, for which reason also very many followed his teaching. The emperor's teacher also read some of his writings in his presence over and over again and brought it about that all admired him. The senate also thought very highly of him."

4. SURVIVAL IN THE MIDDLE AGES. For the time that followed the edition of Alcuin was important. The epistles are preserved in very many manuscripts (from the 9th century), admittedly in nothing short of a shocking state of corruption. Peter of Cluny (*Tractatus adversus Petrobrusianos, P.L.* 189, 737C) and Peter Abelard (*Introductio ad Theologiam* I. 24 and *Sermo* XXIV = *Expositio in epistolam Pauli ad Romanos* I. 1) show acquaintance with this correspondence. Even Petrarch in his *Epistola ad Senecam* refers to the epistles. The passages are printed together in Barlow's excellent edition. Mention may also be made of the *editio princeps* of Erasmus (Basel 1515); by the way, it was he who first transposed epistles 11 and 12, as then was usually done in the editions that followed down to that of Haase, Barlow being the first to restore the sequence of the manuscripts.

The Correspondence between Seneca and Paul

1. Seneca greets Paul

Paul, you have been told, I believe, that yesterday we had a conversation with our Lucilius about the "Apocrypha" and other things. There were with me some members of your school. For we had retreated into Sallust's garden, where, by a happy chance for us, the people I have just mentioned, although they meant to go elsewhere, caught sight of us and joined us. We certainly longed for your presence, and I would like you to know that after the reading of your booklet, i.e. of a number of letters which you have addressed to city churches or to the chief cities of provinces and which contain wonderful exhortations for the moral life, we are thoroughly refreshed; and I believe that these statements have been uttered not by you but through you, although indeed at some time they were expressed (both) by you and through you. For so great is the majesty of these things and by such an excellent character are they distinguished that, in my opinion, generations of men would scarcely suffice to be instructed and perfected by them. Brother, I wish you prosperity.

2. Paul greets L. Annaeus Seneca

Yesterday I received your letter with joy. I would have been able to answer it at once had the young man whom I purposed to send to you been at hand. You well know when and through whom and at what moment and to whom a thing ought to be given for transmission. I beg you, therefore, not to look upon it as negligence that in the first place I have regard to the trustworthiness of the person. But since you write that you were somehow agreeably touched by my letter, I consider myself honoured by this judgment of a sincere man. For being the censor, philosopher and teacher of so distinguished a prince and also at the same time of the public, you would not say that if what you say was not true. I wish you prolonged prosperity.

3. Seneca greets Paul

I have arranged some scrolls and have brought them into a definite order corresponding to their several divisions. Also I have decided to read them to the emperor. If only fate ordains it favourably that he shows new interest, then perhaps you too will be present; otherwise I shall fix a day for you at another time when together we may examine this work. And if only it could be done safely, I would not read this writing to him before meeting you. You may then be certain that you are not being overlooked. Farewell, most beloved Paul.

4. Paul greets Annaeus Seneca

As often as I hear your letters, I think of your presence and imagine nothing other than that you are always with us. As soon then as you set about coming, we shall see one another and do so at close quarters. I wish you prosperity.

5. Seneca greets Paul

Your staying away, being all too long, distresses us. What then is wrong? What keeps you away? If it is the empress's displeasure because you have wandered away from the ancient rites and beliefs (of Judaism) and become a convert elsewhere, then may you find opportunity to convince her that this has resulted from deliberation and not from levity. Farewell.

6. Paul greets Seneca and Lucilius

I may not express myself with pen and ink[1] regarding the matters about which you have written to me, of which the first indicates something distinctly whilst the last shows it too apparently, especially as I know that under you, i.e. among you and in your midst, there are people who understand me. We must treat all with respect, particularly when they strain after an opportunity to express their displeasure. If we have patience with them, we shall overcome them in every way and in every respect, provided only they are men who can show that they regret what they have done. Farewell.

7. Annaeus Seneca greets Paul and Theophilus

I frankly confess that the reading of your epistles to the Galatians, to the Corinthians and to the Achaians (=2 Cor.; cf. 1:1 there) has touched me agreeably, and we desire to live together even as also with sacred awe you act in them. For the Holy Spirit is in you, and moreover through your elevated speech brings to expression high and truly reverend thoughts. Wherefore I desire that when you utter such high thoughts, a beautiful form of discourse answering to the elevation of the thoughts may not be lacking. And that nothing may be concealed from you, beloved brother, or burden my conscience, I confess that your thoughts have made an impression on Augustus (=the emperor Nero). When I had read to him in the beginning (of your letter) about the power that is in you, he expressed himself in the following way: he could only wonder how a man who had not had the

---

[1] Cf. 2 Jn. 12; 3 Jn. 13.

usual education was capable of such thoughts. I answered him that the gods are wont to discourse through the mouths of the guiltless[1] and not through those of such as pride themselves ever so much on their erudition,[2] and as an instance I mentioned to him Vatienus, a wholly uneducated man, to whom two men appeared in the region of Reate, who later were called Castor and Pollux, and with that he (the emperor) seemed to be sufficiently informed. Farewell.

8. Paul greets Seneca

Whilst I well know that when he is despondent, our emperor (Nero) occasionally finds delight in what is wonderful, yet he does not admit that he is displeased, but (only) that he is admonished. For I believe that your design to bring to his notice what contradicts his belief and tenets was misplaced. Since he worships the gods of the heathen, I do not see what purpose you can have in view in desiring that he should know this; I am thus obliged to believe that you do it all out of a love of me that is much too great. I beg you for the future not to do any such thing again. For you must be wary lest in loving me you offend his mistress (the empress Poppaea Sabina); her disfavour will indeed do no harm if she continues in it, nor will it avail anything if that does not happen; as queen she will not feel displeasure, but as a woman she will take offence.

9. Seneca greets Paul

I know that you are not so much excited for your own sake over the letter which I have addressed to you regarding the edition of your epistles for the emperor as you are over the nature of the things which withhold the minds of men from all the arts and from real culture, and so it is that today I do not wonder, especially since this is now known to me quite definitely from pieces of evidence of many sorts. Let us then set to work afresh; and if in the past a mistake has been made, you will grant me forgiveness. I have sent you a book on 'verbosity' (*de verborum copia*). Farewell, most beloved Paul.

[1] Cf. Ps. 8:3; Mt. 11:25 (Lk. 10:21.)   [2] Cf. 1 Cor. 1:19, 26–29.

10. Paul greets Seneca

As often as I write to you and set my name behind yours,[1] I make a grievous mistake, one that is in fact out of keeping with my status (in the Christian church). Certainly I ought, as I have often explained, to be all things to all men,[2] and as concerns your person I ought to have respect to what Roman law has conceded for the honour of the Senate, namely after the perusal of a letter to choose the last place;[3] else I could wish (only) with embarrassment and shame to carry through what conforms to my own judgment. Farewell, my highly revered teacher. Given on 27 June in the consulate of Nero iii and Messala (=A.D. 58).

11. (12.) Seneca greets Paul

Greetings, my dearest Paul! Can you possibly think that I am not distressed and grieved that capital punishment is still visited upon you innocent persons? As also that all the people are convinced of your cruelty and criminal malignity, believing that all evil in the city is owing to you? But let us bear it with equanimity and make use of favourable circumstances, as fate provides us with them, until invincible good fortune makes an end of evildoers. The time of the ancients suffered the Macedonian, the son of Philip, the Cyruses, Darius and Dionysius, and our own time the emperor Gaius (=Caligula), men to whom everything they wished was legitimate. As regards fire, it is clear as the day at whose hands the Roman capital has to suffer it so often. But if human baseness could state what the first cause of it is, and in this darkness was free to speak with impunity, then no doubt all would see everything. Christians and Jews are—worse luck!— executed as fire-raisers, as commonly happens. This rowdy, whoever he is that finds pleasure in murder and uses lies as a disguise, is destined for his own time; and as the best is sometimes sacrificed as one life for many,[4] so also will this accursed one be burned in the fire for all. 132 palaces, 4,000 apartment houses

---

[1] Only in the unctuous farewell letter (14) is Paul set in front.
[2] 1 Cor. 9:22; 10:33.
[3] When the letter has been completed and read through once more, the address is put on the outside.
[4] Cf. Virgil, *Aen.* V. 815: *unum pro multis dabitur caput.*

were burned down in six days; the seventh day brought a pause. I wish you good health, brother. Written on 28 March in the consulate of Frugi and Bassus (=A.D. 64).

12. (11.) Seneca greets Paul

Greetings, my dearest Paul! If you, a man so distinguished and in every way beloved by God, are I say not united but necessarily incorporated with me and my name, then it will go very well with your Seneca. Being now the crown of the head and the highest peak of all mountains, do you not wish me to rejoice if I am so very near to you that I count as your second self? You can believe then that you are not unworthy to be named first in the letters; otherwise it might look as if you desired to tempt rather than to praise me; all the more since you are a Roman citizen. For I desire that my place be yours with you (in your letters) and that yours be as mine.[1] Given on 23 March in the consulate of Apronianus and Capito (A.D. 59).

13. Seneca greets Paul

Everywhere you join together many subjects (*opera*) allegorically and enigmatically, and therefore the power granted to you, that is in your material and in your office, ought to be adorned not with verbal trappings, but with a certain refinement. And be not afraid because of what, so far as I recollect, I have often said already, that many who strive after this sort of thing debase the thought and weaken the power of the material. May you at least make me the concession that you have regard to the Latinity and that you make use of outward form for beautiful words, so that you may worthily accomplish the work of a noble service. Good-bye! Written on 6 July in the consulate of Lurco and Sabinus (=A.D. 58).

14. Paul greets Seneca

When you engage in thorough reflection, things are revealed to you which the Deity has granted only to few. Entertaining no doubts, I sow in a field that is already fertile most powerful seed,

[1] Cf. Gal. 4:12.

not stuff that seems to be decaying, but the unshakeable word of God, the well-head from him that grows and remains for ever.[1] What your discernment has appropriated will unfailingly hold good, namely that (superficial) observances of the Gentiles and of the Israelites must be avoided. Make yourself a new herald of Jesus Christ and in your rhetorical proclamations bring the irrefutable wisdom to expression. Having already almost attained to this, you will procure an access for it to the temporal king and his servants and true friends, although what you are persuaded of will be to them hard and incomprehensible and the majority of them will not in the least be brought round by your expositions, through which the instilled word of God brings about the blessing of life,[2] namely a new man without corruption, an imperishable soul that hastens from here to God. Good-bye to you, our most beloved Seneca! Written on 1 August in the year of the consulate of Lurco and Sabinus (=A.D. 58).

5. THE PSEUDO-TITUS EPISTLE

(A. de Santos Otero)

INTRODUCTION. As the "Epistle of Titus, the Disciple of Paul, on the State of Chastity" there has survived a noteworthy document which was discovered in 1896 in a Latin manuscript of the eighth century (fol. 84–93v of the 'Codex Burchardi' Mp. th. f. 28 of the University of Würzburg) among the *Homilies* of Caesarius of Arles (cf. D. G. Morin, *Revue Bénédictine* 13, 1896, pp. 97–111). Only in 1925 after lengthy study was this document published in full by D. de Bruyne (*Rev. Bén.* 37, 1925, pp. 47–72). This "Epistle" is composed in barbarous language, the solecisms of which are not to be explained simply through the clumsiness of some scribe, but also go back in large part to the author himself. The hypothesis put forward by de Bruyne that we are concerned here with a Latin translation from the Greek, made apparently by a man who knew neither Latin nor Greek sufficiently (*Rev. Bén.* 25, 1908, p. 150; M. R. James on his part even attempted to restore the presumably original Greek text in the light of some *indicia* of the "Epistle", cf. *ibid.*, p. 151), is today no longer tenable, especially after the investigations of A. von Harnack (cf. *SBA* 17, 1925, p. 191). To this there has to be added the close connection

---

[1] Cf. 1 Pet. 1:23, 25. On this see A. Kurfess in *ZNW* 35, 1936/37, p. 307.
[2] Cf. 1 Cor. 15:42 Vetus Latina.

of our "Epistle" with other like-minded Latin writings about which we have still to speak.

Since we are dependent on a single manuscript the reading of which presents considerable linguistic difficulties, the last word cannot yet be spoken regarding the origin of the Epistle of Titus. Nevertheless much can already be stated about the character and the content of this "Epistle". What is most striking is not only the external apocryphal guise of the "Epistula Titi", but also the liberal use that is made in it of all sorts of apocrypha, especially of the Acts of Apostles and of some Apocalypses. In the course of half a century these numerous quotations from the apocrypha have most of all aroused the interest of scholars, and they have led to many arguments regarding the origin of the "Epistle". But this clue (which is especially valuable for the judgment of a writing which contains no dogmatic statements) ought not to be considered apart from the ostensible aim of the Epistle. The author seems to have had above all a concrete ascetic aim in view, namely to commend the life of chastity. Those whom he addresses belong to a special circle of ascetics of both sexes (*spadones* and *virgines*), who have vowed to live in the state of celibacy, but in whose life several abuses (among them that of "spiritual marriage") have been naturalized. That he may combat this impropriety and give prominence to the worth of chastity, the author has recourse to all the means that are at his disposal. The mere enlistment of Titus as the reputed author of the epistle (as is well known, his authority in the sphere of ascetic matters was very great because of his close connection with Paul) goes to prove the ascetic interests which pseudo-Titus wishes to support.

But the wealth of quotations from the Holy Scriptures with which the author accompanies his enthusiastic exclamations on the state of celibacy reveals a distinct leaning on other ascetic writings which originated above all in literary circles about Jerome and Cyprian and pursued a similar aim. Reference may be made among others to ps.-Cyprian, *De Singularitate Clericorum* (ed. Hartel, *CSEL* 3, 1871) and *De centesima, sexagesima, trigesima* (ed. Reitzenstein, *ZNW* 15, 1914, pp. 6off.); Jerome, *Epistula* 117 (ed. Hilberg, *CSEL* 55, pp. 422ff.); ps.-Jerome, *Epistula* 42 *ad Oceanum* (*PL* 30, 288ff.); Bachiarius, *De reparatione lapsi*(*PL* 20. 1038–1062).

The fact that pseudo-Titus also has recourse to apocryphal quotations which are distinguished by their misogamy not only goes to prove his own naïve enthusiasm, but also suggests the conjecture that this writing may have originated in an environment where the ascetic life especially flourished and the apocryphal writings (above all the strictly ascetic Acts of Apostles) enjoyed a great reputation. This environment is most probably to be sought in connection with the Priscillianist movement in the ascetic circles of the Spanish church in the course of the 5th century. In favour of that there is first the fact that in this land there was from the beginning a rigorous ascetic tendency, which absorbed with a special enthusiasm both the ascetic writings that have been named and the apocryphal Acts of Apostles. To this there have to be added the official documents of the Spanish hierarchy, which denounce the improprieties combated by pseudo-Titus as something typically Priscillianist and condemn them in similar terms. In the author of this "Epistle", however, we certainly do not need to see a Priscillianist. It is quite conceivable that a member of the catholic church, carried away by his ignorant enthusiasm, composed this document and had it circulated under the banner of Titus.

Among the different contributions to the study of pseudo-Titus reference may first be made to works which deal on occasion with some of the problems of this "Epistle" (mainly with the quotations from the apocrypha): E. Schürer, *ThLZ* 33, 1908, p. 614.— J. Weiss, *Der I Korintherbrief*, 1910, pp. 58ff.—M. R. James, *The Lost Apocrypha of the OT*, 1920, p. 55—M. R. James, *The Apocryphal NT*, 1924, pp. 265, 303, 349.—Hennecke, pp. 227/228.—C. Schmidt, *ZKG* 43, 1924, pp. 334ff.

D. G. Morin (*Rev. Bén.* 13, 1896, pp. 97–111) and von Eckhart (*Commentarii de rebus Franciae orientalis* I, pp. 837–847) have described the Würzburg manuscript in detail.

D. de Bruyne first published the quotations made in pseudo-Titus from the apocrypha (*Rev. Bén.* 25, 1908, pp. 149–160) and then edited the whole text with some corrections and elucidations (see above). The most important contribution to the study of pseudo-Titus has been made by A. von Harnack in his investigation "Der apokryphe *Brief des Paulusschülers Titus*", *SBA* 17, 1925, pp. 180–213. H. Koch has discovered a partnership in catchwords between pseudo-Titus and other ascetic writings (*ZNW* 32, 1933, pp. 131–144). Bulhart has suggested some corrections to the Latin text (*Rev. Bén.* 62, 1952, pp. 297–299). For justification of the views regarding the Epistle of Titus advocated by us in the foregoing introduction, we refer to the article "Der apokryphe Titusbrief", *ZKG* 74, 1963, pp. 1-14.

A complete translation of the "Epistle" is here set forth for the first time. We have endeavoured to solve as far as possible the linguistic puzzles which crop up again and again, so as to be able to present a readable and coherent text. In so doing we have had regard not only to the corrections suggested by de Bruyne and Bulhart but also to the peculiar style of pseudo-Titus.

Epistle of Titus, the Disciple of Paul[1]

Great and honourable is the divine promise which the Lord has made with his own mouth to them that are holy and pure: *He will bestow upon them what eyes have not seen nor ears heard, nor has it entered into any human heart.* And from eternity to eternity there will be a race incomparable and incomprehensible.[2]

Blessed then are those who have not polluted their flesh by craving for this world, but are dead to the world that they may live for God! To whom neither flesh nor blood has shown deadly secrets, but the Spirit has shone upon them and shown some better thing so that even in this ⟨ . . . ⟩ and instant of our ⟨pilgrimage on the earth⟩ they may display an angelic appearance. As the Lord says, *Such are to be called angels.*[3]

Those then *who are not defiled with women*[4] he calls an angelic host. Those who have not abandoned themselves to men, he calls virgins, as the apostle of Christ says: *the unmarried think day and night on godly things,*[5] i.e. to act properly and to please Him alone, and not to deny by their doings what they have promised in words. Why should a virgin who is already betrothed to Christ be united with a carnal man?

It is not lawful to cling to a man and to serve him more than God. Virgin! Thou hast cast off Christ, to whom thou wert betrothed! Thou hast separated thyself from Him, thou who strivest to remain united to another! O beauteous maidenhood,

---

[1] In the translating of this difficult text the suggestions of W. Schneemelcher and K. Schäferdiek were of great value to me.

[2] This saying, to which Paul himself appeals (1 Cor. 2:9) and which for its part recalls Is. 64:4, has had a great after-effect in later tradition. Origen already discussed the problem of its origin and came to the conclusion that Paul borrowed this sentence from the *Apocalypse of Elias*, "in nullo enim regulari libro hoc positum invenitur, nisi in secretis Eliae prophetae" (*In Matth.* 27:9: *PG* 3, 1769). Both the *Martyrium Petri* (c. 10, cf. Aa I, p. 98 and pp. 320f. below) and the *Gospel according to Thomas* found at Nag Hammadi (pl. 84, 5–9, log. 17, ed. Brill, Leiden 1959, p. 12) ascribe this saying expressly to Jesus. There is another parallel in the Manichaean Turfan-Fragment, cf. Vol. I, p. 300. PsT puts the words of this promise into the mouth of the *Lord* and adds to the usual text a concluding sentence, to the affinity of which with Clement of Alexandria (*Protrept.* 9. 94) Harnack (*op. cit.* p. 193) has referred. The question to what immediate source this quotation should be carried back is not easy to answer. Resch (cf. *Agrapha*, 1st ed., pp. 102, 154–167, 281) suggested that this saying is to be conceived as a logion; but the assumption that PsT wished in this place to cite nothing other than 1 Cor. 2:9 seems to me much more likely. The naming in both passages of the author of the promise in question also goes to prove that. Cf. Vol. I, p. 300.

[3] Mk. 12:25 par.   [4] Rev. 14:4.   [5] 1 Cor. 7:34.

at the last thou art stuck fast in love to a male being! O (holy) ascetic state, thou disappearest (when) the saints match human offences!

O body, thou art put to the yoke of the law of God, and ever and again committest fornication! Thou art crucified to this world[1] and continuest to act up to it! If the apostle Paul forbade communion to a woman caught in an adulterous relation with a strange man,[2] how much more when those concerned are saints dedicated to Christ! Thou art caught in the vile fellowship of this world, and yet regardest thyself as worthy of the blood of Christ or as united with his body! But this is not the case: if thou eat of the flesh of the Lord unworthily, then thou takest vainly instead of life the fire of thine everlasting punishment! O virgin: if thou strivest to please (another), then thou hast already committed a sin of volition, for the Evangelist says: *one cannot serve two masters, for he obeys the one, and despises the other.*[3] O virgin! so is it also with thee. Thou despisest God, whilst striving to please a man.

Wherefore contemplate the footprints of our ancestors! Consider the daughter of Jephthah: willing to do what had been promised by her father and vowing her own self as a sacrifice to the Lord, she first manifested her connection with God and took other virgins with her *that in the mountains throughout sixty days they might bewail her virginity.*[4] O luminous secrets which disclose the future in advance! Virgin is joined with virgin, and in love to her she bewails the peril of her flesh until the day of her reward comes! Rightly does he say "sixty days", since he means the sixtyfold reward of holiness which the ascetic can gain through many pains, according to the teaching of the apostle: *Let us not lose courage,* he says, *in the hardest labours, in affliction, in grief, in suffering abuse: we suffer persecution, but we are not forsaken, because we bear in our body the passion of Christ. Wherefore we are by no means overcome.*[5] And again the same apostle left an example behind him, describing his own disasters and saying: *I have laboured much, I have frequently been imprisoned, I have suffered extremely many*

---

[1] Cf. Gal. 6:14.
[2] This happening is recorded in detail in the *Actus Petri cum Simone* (c. 2, Aa I, p. 46 and p. 280 below). The name of the woman concerned is there given as Rufina.
[3] Mt. 6:24.   [4] Judg. 11:38.   [5] 2 Cor. 4:8ff.

floggings, I have often fallen into deadly peril. Of the Jews, he says, I have five times received forty stripes save one, three times have I been beaten with rods, once have I been stoned; thrice have I suffered shipwreck, a day and a night I have spent in the depth of the sea; I have often journeyed,[1] often been in peril of rivers, in peril of robbers, in peril among unbelievers in manifold ways, in peril in cities, in peril among Gentiles, in peril in the wilderness, in peril among false brethren; in trouble and labour, frequently in sorrow, in many watchings, in hunger and thirst, in many fastings, in cold and nakedness, in inward anxieties, besides the cares which do not have direct reference to my personal suffering. And in all these I have not lost courage, because Christ was and still is with me.[2]

Oh, through how much trouble does man attain to glory! Besides there is the word of the Lord, who says: *Whom I love,* he says, *I rebuke and chasten*[3] that the righteous man may be tested as gold in the crucible. What bodily joy can there be then in the life to come if the word of the Lord runs: *Oh! as a virgin, as a woman, so is the mystery of resurrection (which) you have shown to me, you who in the beginning of the world did institute vain feasts for yourselves and delighted in the wantonness of the Gentiles and behaved in the same way as those who take delight therein.*[4] Behold what sort of young maidens there are among you! But come and ponder over this, that there is one who tries the soul and a last day of retribution and persecution.

Where then art thou now, thou who hast passed the time of thy youth happily with a sinner, the apostle testifying moreover that *neither flesh nor blood will possess the kingdom of God?*[5]

And again the law runs: *Let not a man glory in his strength, but rather let him trust in the Lord,*[6] and Jeremiah says: *Accursed is he who puts his hope in man.*[7] And in the Psalms it is said: *It is better to trust in the Lord than to rely on men.*[8] Why then art thou not afraid to abandon the Lord and to trust in a man who in the last judgment will not save thee but rather destroy? Consider and take note of the happening about which the following account

---

[1] The correction "in (ex)pedicionibus" instead of "in pedicionibus" proposed by Bulhart is apposite.
[2] 2 Cor. 11:23ff.   [3] Rev. 3:19.
[4] Harnack regards this quotation as a logion of unknown origin (*op. cit.*, p. 195).
[5] 1 Cor. 15:50.   [6] Jer. 9:23.   [7] Jer. 17:5.   [8] Ps. 118:8.

informs us: *A peasant had a girl who was a virgin. She was also his only daughter, and therefore he besought Peter to offer a prayer for her. After he had prayed, the apostle said to the father that the Lord would bestow upon her what was expedient for her soul. Immediately the girl fell down dead.* O reward worthy and ever pleasing to God, to escape the shamelessness of the flesh and to break the pride of the blood! *But this distrustful old man, failing to recognize the worth of the heavenly grace, i.e. the divine blessing, besought Peter again tha his only daughter be raised from the dead. And some days later, after she had been raised, a man who passed himself off as a believer*[1] *came into the house of the old man to stay with him, and seduced the girl, and the two of them never appeared again.*[2]

For the man who dishonours his own body makes himself like the godless. And therefore the dwelling-place of the godless cannot be found out, as David says: *I sought him but he was nowhere to be found,*[3] as also in the (mentioned) case of death those two did not dare (to appear) any more. Thou oughtest then, O virgin, to fear the judgment of this law: *If,* says Moses, *a betrothed virgin is caught unawares with another man, let the two of them be brought before the court of the elders and be condemned to death.*[4]

These happenings have been recorded for us on whom the end of this age has come. One thing stands fast: should a virgin who is betrothed to Christ be caught unawares with another man, let them both be committed for final sentence before the court of the elders, i.e. of Abraham, Isaac and Jacob, whose charge it is to investigate the case of their children. Then will the fathers disown their own children as evildoers. And finally the malefactors will cry amidst the torment of their punishment: Hear us, O Lord God, for our father Abraham has not known us, and Isaac and Jacob have disowned us! Thus then let the children conduct themselves that (some day) they may find themselves in

---

[1] The text runs: "homo vinctus fidelis". Our translation is based on Harnack's assumption that a scribe erroneously replaced the original "fictus" by "vinctus". Hennecke (*Apokr.* 2, p. 228) understands the "homo vinctus" as "the slave of a believer" or "a bewitched Christian man".

[2] Augustine ascribes this story to the Manichaean apocrypha: "In apocryphis legunt . . . hortulani filiam ad precem ipsius Petri esse mortuam" (*Contra Adimantum* 17. 5: *PL.* 42, 161). Unhappily he does not give the title of this apocryphon. This story is not found in the extant *Actus Petri Vercellenses*. Ficker (*Apokr.* 2, p. 227) is of opinion that it never belonged to them, even if it be assumed that these *Actus* are due to mutilations. Cf. p. 270 below.

[3] Ps. 37:36.   [4] Deut. 22:23.

the bosom of father Abraham. That is to say, that they may remain praiseworthy in his remembrance and be not as the daughters of Zion whom the Holy Spirit reproaches through Isaiah: *They moved together through the streets, dancing with their heads erect. And they engaged themselves to men in the villages of Jerusalem, and heaped up iniquity to the sky, and the Lord was angry and delivered them up to king Nebuchadnezzar to slavery for seventy years.*[1]

You also are disobedient and undisciplined, you who do something even worse than the first committed. In the end you also will be delivered up to the wicked king Nebuchadnezzar, as he says, i.e. to the devil who will fall upon you. And as they (the Jews), after they had spent seventy years in anguish, returned to their own places of abode, so a period of seven years is (now) appointed under Antichrist. But the pain of these seven years presents eternal anguish. And as, after their return to their homeland, they henceforth experienced much evil, so is it also now with (these): after death the soul of each one will be tormented unto the judgment day. And again, after the slaughter of the beast, the first resurrection will take place; and then will the faithless souls return to their dwellings; and according to the increase of their (earlier) evil-doings will their torment (now) be augmented beyond the first punishment.

Therefore, beloved, we must combat the works of the flesh because of the coming retribution. In order then that ye may escape eternal torment, ye must struggle, daughters, against flesh and blood so long as a period for that continues and a few days still remain wherein ye may contend for life. Why should the man who has renounced the flesh be held fast in its lust? Why, O virgin, thou who hast renounced a man, dost thou hug his physical beauty? Why (ascetic) givest thou up to a strange woman (i.e. one belonging to Christ) thy body which was not made for that? Why strivest thou against thine own salvation to find death in love? Hear the apostle who says to you: *See*, he says, *that ye give not place to the flesh through the liberty of God.*[2] And again: *Fulfil not the lusts of the flesh. For the flesh lusteth against the Spirit and the Spirit against the flesh. These are opposed to one another. Therefore,* he

---

[1] The source of this apocryphal quotation cannot be traced.
[2] Gal. 5:13.

says, *do not what ye would. Otherwise the Spirit of God is not in you.*[1]
O inherently false one, to despise the commandments of the
holy law and (through) a deceitful marriage to lose in secret the
life everlasting! O honeyed cheat, to draw on torment in the
future! O unbridled passion for glory, to offend against the
devotion that has been vowed to God! O steps that lead astray
from the way, that a virgin is fond of the flesh of another! O
faith(less) craving, theft of fire, honour entangled in crime![2] O
broken promise, that the mind blazes up for a stranger! O pledge
of lust, beauty inclined to crime! O alluring symbol of vice that
brings disdain! O seminari da membra vicinacio tenebrarum![3]
O concealed thievery, to give an appearance of humility and
chastity! O gloom of the dark deed which plunders the glory of
Christ for ever! O fleeting remembrance of holiness which strives
after death in the name of beauty! O *silver that has been refused,*
which according to the saying of Isaiah *is not worthy of God!*[4]
O dishonoured Sabbath in which the works of the flesh come to
light in the last days and times! O foot, that failest on the way to
holiness and dost not arrive at a sure habitation! O ship burst
open by pirates, thou that gettest away empty and miserable!
O house that is undermined by burglars whilst the watchmen sleep
and lose the costly treasure! O maidenly youth, thou that fallest
off miserably from right conduct! O enlargement of trust in this
world which turns into desolation in eternity![5] O consequence of
unchastity which brings down upon itself the malady of melancholy! O fountain of sweet poison which springs up from the
flesh as inextricable entanglement! O wretched house founded on
sand! O despicable crime of (this) time, that corruptest not thine
own members but those of a stranger! O fleeting enjoyment on

---

[1] Gal. 5:16.

[2] The text runs: "O fida cupiditas et ignis praerogativa dignitas sceleris apta".
Bulhart suggests that "fida" and "dignitas" should either be understood ironically
or replaced by "(per)fida" and "(in)dignitas". The present translation, which has
as its basis only the correction of the "fida", seems to me to render clearly the right
sense of the sentence. PsT lays emphasis on the worthiness ("dignitas") of these
"honorary ascetics" in order to describe more realistically the seriousness of their
sins.

[3] In spite of the correction proposed by Bulhart: "O seminari da(re) membra
vicinacio tenebrarum", the passage remains unintelligible to me.

[4] Is. 1:22 or the *Apocryphon of Isaiah.*

[5] The text runs: "O locupletacio secularis fiducia egere in aevo caeleste". De
Bruyne suggests "fiduciae" instead of "fiducia". Bulhart translates: "Sinful gain in
the earthly life has as its consequence lack of hope for the endless life".

the brink of collapse! O parcel of deceit! O unsleeping ardour for the perdition of the soul! O tower that is in building to be left unfinished! O shameful work, thou art the scorn of them that pass by! Why, O virgin, dost thou not ponder over it and estimate the heavenly charges before laying the foundation? In the beginning thou hast acted too hastily, and before the house was completed, thou hast already experienced a terrible collapse![1] In your case the saying of the law has been fulfilled, the prophecy has come to pass: *Many a tract of land*, it says, *is built upon and soon it grows old; temples and cities are built in the land and soon they are abandoned!*[2] O flames of lust! The unclean profane with their lust the temple of God and by Him are condemned to destruction! Oh, a contest is entered upon in the stadium, and when it has hardly come to grappling, the shields fall to the ground! O city captured by enemies and reduced to a wilderness!

Against this whorish behaviour the Lord turns through Ezekiel saying: *Thou hast built thee thy brothel, thou hast desecrated thy beauty and thy comeliness in every by-way, thou hast become an unclean woman, thou who hast heaped up shamelessness for thyself. Thy disgrace in the unchastity which thou hast practised with thy lovers will yet come to light.* And again, *As I live, saith the Lord, Sodom has not so done as thou Jerusalem and thy daughters. But the iniquity of Sodom, thy sister, is fulfilled. For Samaria has not committed the half of thy sins. Thou hast multiplied iniquities beyond thy sisters in all that thou hast done. Wherefore be ashamed and take thy disgrace upon thy head.*[3]

O how frequently the scourgings and beatings of God are not spared, and yet no one takes to heart the word of the Lord to be concerned about the future life! Has not Jerusalem, possessing the law, sinned more than Sodom and Gomorrah, which possessed no law? And have not the crimes of Jerusalem, whose sons and daughters have stood under the banner of faith, outweighed those of Samaria, which already from the beginning was worldly-minded?

On the unprecedented crime of this new people the apostle says: *One hears commonly of unchastity among you and indeed of such unchastity as is never met with among the Gentiles, that one lives with his*

[1] Cf. Lk. 14:28ff.
[2] The source of this apocryphal quotation cannot be determined.
[3] Cf. Ezek. 16:24, 25, 31, 36, 48, 49, 51, 52.

father's wife. And ye are yet puffed up, and do not rather mourn, that such an evil-doer may be removed from your midst. I am indeed absent in the body, but in the spirit am among you and already, as if I were present, I have passed sentence on the evil-doer: to hand over that man to Satan in the name of Christ.[1]

O invention of the devil, sport for those about to perish! Oh poison instead of honey, to take a father's wife in the same way as any bride dedicated to Christ whom in thine heart thou hast craved for! O man, thou hast lent no ear to the wisdom that says to thee: the lust of the ascetic dishonours the virgin.[2] So also did the first created man fall because of a virgin: *when he saw a woman giving him a smile, he fell.*[3] His senses became tied to a craving which he had never known before;[4] assuredly he had not experienced earlier its flavour and the sweetness that proved his downfall. O man who fearest not the face of this criminal person, passing by whom many have lost their lives. The disciple of the Lord, Judas Jacobi, brings that to our remembrance when he says: *Beloved, I would bring to your remembrance, though ye know, what happened to them* who were oppressed by the corruption of the flesh, as for instance the genuine persons (*veraces*) *who did not preserve their dignity, but abandoned their heavenly abode* and, enticed by lust, went to the daughters of men to dwell with them.[5]

Today also they forfeit the angelic character who crave to dwell with strange daughters, according to the word of the Lord who proclaimed by Isaiah: *Woe unto you who join house to house and add field to field that they may draw nigh one another.*[6] And in Micah it is said: Bewail the house which you have pulled on yourselves and endure of yourselves the punishment of indignation.[7] Does the Lord mean perhaps the house or the field of this time when he warns us against pressing them together? (No) rather it is a matter here of warnings in reference to holiness, in which the separation

---

[1] 1 Cor. 5:1ff.   [2] Sir. 20, 4?

[3] This allusion to the fall of Adam is regarded by Harnack (*op. cit.*, p. 192) as a remnant of a lost Book of Adam. Since it is the seduction of Adam by a woman that is spoken of, I am inclined to understand the "irrisio" as "the giving of a smile" rather than as "derision".

[4] The words "rursus haberet" of the original have been left out in the translation because they seem to have no suitable sense in the context.

[5] The allusion to Gen. 6:2 (cf. Jude 1:5f.) is typical of many ascetic writings which deal with the theme of PsT. Cf. *De Singularitate Clericorum* 28 (Hartel, *CSEL* 3, p. 204. 10); Bachiarius, *De reparatione lapsi* c. 4 (*PL* 20, 1059).

[6] Is. 5:8.   [7] Mic. 1:10?

of man and woman is ordered. So the Lord also admonishes us through Jeremiah, saying, *It is an excellent thing for a man that he bear the yoke in his youth; he will sit alone when his hope is real; he will keep quiet and have patience.*[1] 'To bear the yoke' is then to observe God's order. And in conclusion the Lord says: *Take my yoke upon you.*[2] And further, 'in his youth' means in his hope. Thus he has commanded that salvation be preserved in lonely celibacy, so that each one of you may remain as a lonely tower according to the saying of the Evangelist that house should not remain upon house, but should come down at once. Why then, O man, dost thou make haste to build you a ruin upon a strange house and thus to occasion not only your own destruction but also that of the bride of Christ who is united to you?

And also if thou art free from unchastity, already thou committest a sin in keeping up connections with women;[3] for finally, thus says the Lord in the Gospel: *"He who looks upon a woman to lust after her hath committed adultery with her already in his heart."*[4] On this account a man must live for God sincerely and free from all lust. In Daniel also we read: As these false old men, who had craved for the beauty of Susanna, were unable to practise any unchastity with her, they slandered her. Susanna was brought before their court, and these rogues had her stand before them with her head uncovered so that they might satisfy their craving at least in looking on her beauty. And thus they were unable to escape capital punishment.[5] How much more when the last day comes! What, thinkest thou, will Christ do to those who have surrendered their own members to rape? The apostle has already shown the future in advance, saying: *Let no temptation take hold of you,* he says, *save what is human!*[6] O temptation to sensuality! Man is not able to control himself, and inflicts on himself the predicted fatal wounds! O exhalations of the flesh! The glowing fire hidden deep in the heart nourishes a conflagration! O ignoble fight, to strike root in a dark night! O tree of seducing fruit that shows thick foliage! O false lips, out of which honey drops and

---

[1] Lam. 3:27–28.   [2] Mt. 11:29.

[3] The text runs: "Licet inmunis a scelere stupri, et in hoc ipsut peccati eo quod in conplexum foeminarum teneris". I do not regard Bulhart's correction 'licet a scelere stupri (s)et . . . peccati' as necessary, since the passage is understandable without it.

[4] Mt. 5:28.   [5] Cf. Sus.   [6] Cf. 1 Cor. 10:13.

which in the end are as bitter as poison! O charming eloquence, the words of which shoot arrows into the heart! O madness of love: death fetters the young as a chain, whilst wisdom announces the future, this is what it always orders: *Avoid, my son, every evil and everything that resembles it.*[1] And further: *And every man who takes part in a foot-race abstains from all things that he may be able to obtain the crown that is prepared for him.*[2]

Why takest thou, O man, a woman as a servant? Consider the conduct of (our) holy ancestors. Thus Elias, a noble man who still lives in the body, took a young man as servant, to whom also he left his mantle as a holy keepsake when he was taken up into paradise in a chariot of fire.[3] There Enoch also lives in the body, who was carried away (there) in the first age.[4] O holy dispensation of God, who has provided for the coming age! Enoch, the righteous, from among the first people, was commissioned to commit to writing the history of the first men, and the holy Elias (was given the task) of registering the new deeds of this later people![5]

All that has thus to be construed according to the condition of (our) time: each of the two springs from his own age, Enoch (as a symbol) of righteousness and Elias (as a symbol) of holiness. But we must comply with the rule of our holiness, as the apostle says: *In body and spirit genus must resemble genus and the disciple the master.*[6] And the spirit of Elias rested finally on Elisha. He also begged of him that he might immediately receive from him a double blessing like the one which (later) the Lord gave to his advanced disciples, saying, *He that believes on me will also do the works that I do, and will do greater works than these.*[7] But such grace is granted only to those who fulfil the commandments of the Master. What should we now say? If Elisha served in the house

---

[1] Although this quotation agrees verbally with *Didache* 3, 1, it may yet be asked whether PsT has quoted the *Didache* itself or one of the sayings of Sirach that are similar in content. The introduction of 'prudentia' occurs again and again in this and similar quotations (e.g. lines 209 and 420). Cf. Harnack, *op. cit.*, p. 195.

[2] 1 Cor. 9:25.   [3] 2 Kgs 2:15.

[4] This statement is attested in the surviving *Book of Enoch*. Cf. Flemming-Rademacher, *Das Buch Henoch*, Leipzig 1901.

[5] Harnack (p. 193) is of opinion that this statement goes back to the *Apocalypse of Elias*. Bulhart and De Bruyne have proposed many corrections of the text. But the sense of the passage is clear without them.

[6] The source of this Paul-saying is unknown.

[7] Jn. 14:12.

of Elias to comply with the rule of propriety and the boy Gehazi assisted the (prophet) Elisha as Baruch (the prophet) Jeremiah, in order to leave us an (instructive) remembrance, why does a man today take a woman as servant[1] under a semblance of holiness? If it is a matter of a close relative, then that will do; but not if she is a strange woman. After the flood the sons of Noah looked for places for themselves where they might build cities, and they named them after their wives.[2] Precisely so do these (men) now behave who are united (to women).

O ascetics of God who look back at women to offer them gifts, to give them property, to promise them houses, to make them presents of clothes, to surrender to them their own souls and yield to their name all that belongs to them! If thou then, O man, behavest rightly and innocently, why dost thou not take thine own sister with thee? Why dost thou not give her all that belongs to thee, and thou wilt possess every thing? Further and further thou separatest thyself from her: thou hatest her, thou persecutest her. And yet thy greatest safety is in her. Nay, separated from her thou attachest thyself to another. And thus dost thou think to remain wealthy in body and not be controlled by any lust, and dost say that thou possessest the heavenly hope. Hear a word that holds good for thee. Consider what the Lord in the Gospel says to Mary: *Touch me not*, says he, *for I am not yet ascended to my Father!*[3] O divine examples which have been written for us! And Paul, the chosen vessel (of the Lord) and the impregnable wall among the disciples,[4] admonishes us when in the course of

---

[1] The text runs: "Cur . . . mascel sive vir feminam sumit?". The "sive vir" is regarded by Bulhart as a gloss on the strange "mascel", which was constantly rejected by the grammarians and is to be found only in the Vetus Latina of the Codex Lugdunensis.

[2] In this passage Harnack finds the starting-point for the assumption that an apocryphal History of Noah is the source of these allusions.

[3] Jn. 20, 17.

[4] As a parallel to this passage ("Eciam et vas electionis Paulus, vere datus inexpugnabilis murus ex discentibus, exortatur missus") Harnack (p. 198) has referred to the *Epistula Apostolorum* c. 31 (cf. trans. of R. E. Taylor, Vol. I, p. 213), where it is said: "And he will be among my elect a chosen vessel and a wall that does not fall". In view of the numerous parallel passages which the ascetic literature presents (cf. *De Centesima* [ed. Reitzenstein, *ZNW* 15, 1914] lines 191, 278; Cyprian, *De habitu Virg.* 23 [ed. Hartel, *CSEL* 3, p. 204. 11]; Jerome, *Ep.* 22. 5 [ed. Hilberg, *CSEL* 54, p. 149. 11]; Bachiarius, *De fide* [*PL* 20, 1023]), I am inclined to carry back the description of Paul as *vas electionis*, which goes back ultimately to Acts 9:25, to the influences of the ascetic literature just mentioned rather than to the *Epistula Apostolorum*.

his mission the virgin Thecla, full of innocent faithfulness to Christ wished to kiss his chain—mark thou what the apostle said to her: *Touch me not*, he said, *because of the frailty of (this) time.*[1] Thou dost see then, O young man, what the present Lord and the recorded testament of the disciple have said against the flesh. For they did not order the women to withdraw for their own sakes, for the Lord cannot be tempted and just as little can Paul, his vicar, but these admonitions and commands were uttered for the sake of us who are now members of Christ.

Above all the ascetic should avoid women on that account and see to it that he does (worthily) the duty entrusted to him by God. Consider the rebuilding of Jerusalem; at the time of this laborious work every man was armed and mail-clad, and with one hand he built whilst in the other he held fast a sword, always ready to contend against the enemy. Apprehend then the mystery, how one should build the sanctuary of celibacy: in ascetic loneliness one hand must be engaged in the work that an extremely beautiful city may be built for God, whilst the other grasps the sword and is always ready for action against the wicked devil. That is then to be interpreted in this way: both hands, i.e. the spirit and the flesh, have in mutual harmony to bring the building to completion, the spirit being always on the lookout for the enemy and the flesh building on the bedrock of good conduct. Therefore it is said in the Gospel: *Let your works shine before men that they may glorify your Father in heaven.*[2] Behold what a splendid structure is built in the heavenly Jerusalem. In this city one contends rightly in a lonely position, without any intercourse with the flesh, as it stands in the Gospel: *In the coming age*, says the Lord, *they will neither marry nor be given in marriage, but will be as the angels in heaven.*[3] Thus we must endeavour through blameless conduct to gain for ourselves everlasting honour in the future age. O man, who understandest nothing at all of the fruits of righteousness, why has the Lord made the divine phoenix and not given it a little wife, but allowed it to remain in loneliness? Manifestly only on purpose to show the standing of virginity, i.e. that young men, remote from intercourse with women, should

---

[1] The scene is described in the surviving *Acta Pauli cum Thecla* c. 18 (Aa I, p. 247, and see p. 358 below), but there the word of Paul is lacking.
[2] Mt. 5:16.   [3] Mk. 12:25 and pars.

remain holy. And its resurrection points finally to life. In this connection David says in the Psalms: *I will lay me down and sleep in peace for thou, O Lord, makest me to dwell lonesome in hope.*[1] O peaceful rest given without interruption! O great security, when a man lives lonesome in the body! *Thou canst not expect to bind glowing coals on thy garment, and not set the robe alight.*[2] Should you do such a thing, then you will remain naked and your shame will be manifest. Add to this the word of the prophet: *All flesh is grass.*[3] That a man then may not go up in flames, let him keep far from fire. Why exposest thou thine eternal salvation to loss through a trifle? Hast thou not read in the law this word that holds good for thee: *The people sat down to eat and to drink; and they rose to make merry; and of them 23,000 fell there?*[4] For they had begun to have intercourse with the daughters of men, i.e. they allowed themselves to be invited by them to their unclean sacrifices, *and the children of Israel dedicated themselves to Baalpeor.*[5]

Behold, what a godless play it was in which (the children of Israel) allowed themselves to be entangled, and perished! Seeing in advance how such criminal doings would multiply until the end, Christ the Saviour was grieved, and he said: *Woe, woe unto the souls that despise their own judgment! For I see men who delight their souls in vanity and abandon themselves to the unclean world. I see also how all that is for the benefit of the enemy! Therefore I can stand by them and say: O souls that apply yourselves to unchastity and have no fear before God!*[6] The Gibeonites also in the time of the Judges moved the Lord to indignation. Twelve thousand strong men arose to overthrow the city, and only three hundred and two virgins who had had no sexual intercourse with men came forth alive.[7] The name Gibeonites signifies *children of confusion,* who received the body of Christ in the form of a woman, and prosti-

---

[1] Ps. 4:8.

[2] Cf. Prov. 6:27. The use of this metaphor is typical of the anti-syneisactic writings. Cf. *De singul. Cler.* 2 (ed. Hartel, *CSEL* 3, p. 175. 10); Jerome, *Ep.* 22, c. 14 (ed. Hilberg, *CSEL* 54, p. 161); Bachiarius, *De reparatione lapsi* c. 21 (*PL* 20, 1060).

[3] Is. 40:6.   [4] Exod. 32:6, 28.   [5] Ps. 106:28.

[6] The source of this unknown logion cannot be determined. The words "euge me, euge me contemptores suae sentencia animae" provide a typical example of the grammatical anarchy of the text. Harnack suggests that *sentencia* be struck out. Bulhart writes, "Instead of the senseless *sentencia* I suggest *sine paenitencia*". In spite of the obscurity of the expression the sense can in my opinion be clearly recognized. Harnack finds the expression "et plurimum esse ad inimicum" unintelligible. Bulhart translates it "to be much with the enemy, to attempt much devil's work".

[7] Cf. Judg. 21:12.

tuted it to their amusement, and made it an object of derision and mockery. Dost thou not do likewise in venturing to ridicule the members of Christ with a virgin? For all of us, both men and women, who have been baptized into Christ have put on Christ.[1] It is then a matter of the violation not of earthly flesh but of the body of Christ. And rightly was that city taken by the attacking twelve legions, which were a symbol of the twelve apostles. Rightly have they sprung from a strong race, for they are called sons of thunder.[2] In the last judgment they will appear, equipped with might, to perform miracles against the Gentiles. And they will judge the twelve tribes of Israel, sitting on twelve thrones. And no one from the church will then be able to get away, apart from the virgins dedicated to God, whose members have not been defiled by the enemy with the infection of his evil will. The number also suggests the sign of the cross: for 300 is written with the Greek letter T, and T is the figure of the cross, which makes its appearance in the life of virginity. Rightly also is the kingdom of heaven to be arrived at through five virgins, by which he means that the promises can be certain only through purity and wisdom. And therefore the promise was not fulfilled to Abraham through fleshly procreation, but it was through divine inspiration that he received the blessing. What should we then say to this? Can virginity not perhaps itself lead to eternal torment? (Oh yes!), but these five virgins were foolish, precisely as are those who today have not watched over their flesh but have marred their readiness for battle through desire for the male sex. Wherefore also David says in the Psalms: *Those who mounted on horses fell asleep.*[3] In body indeed they went on horseback, but they were unable to persist in their virgin watchfulness, just like the children of confusion who were again thrown from their horses. O dark cringing of the flesh which has turned into torment! Finally they will reprove themselves for their past doings with the following words: O wretched flesh, which has brought us to ruin! Had we not suffered ourselves to be misled by thee, then we also could have been numbered among the saints!

O man, who believest that all these things shall be! Thou knowest that different judgments must be passed on sinners. In

[1] Cf. Gal. 3:27.   [2] Mk. 3:17.   [3] Ps. 76:6.

the member with which each man has sinned, in the same also shall he be tormented.

The prophet Elias bears witness to a vision: *The angel of the Lord*, he says, *showed me a deep valley, which is called Gehenna, burning with brimstone and pitch. In this place the souls of many sinners dwell and are tormented in different ways. Some suffer hanging from the genitals, others by the tongue, some by the eyes, others head downwards. The women are tormented in their breasts, and the young hang from their hands. Some virgins are roasted on a gridiron, and other souls undergo an unceasing torment. The multiplicity of the torments answers to the diversity of the sins of each. The adulterers and the corrupters of such as are under age are tormented in their genitals. Those who hang from their tongues are the blasphemers and false witnesses. They have their eyes burned who have stumbled through their glances and who have looked at foul things with craving for them. Head downwards there hang those who have detested the righteousness of God, who have been evil-minded, quarrelsome towards their fellows. Rightly then are they burned according to the punishment imposed on them. If some women are punished with torment in their breasts, then these are women who for sport have surrendered their own bodies to men, and for this reason these also hang from their hands.*[1] Solomon took these things into account, saying: *Blessed is the eunuch who has committed no offence with his hands.*[2] And again, *If thou controllest the craving of thy heart, then art thou an athlete.*[3]

And through wisdom he admonishes in the following way: *Of what benefit to an idol is an offering when it can neither taste nor smell it? Just as little does it benefit an eunuch to embrace a virgin. O my son, thou shouldest not make her the object of your pleasure!*[4] Thou seest clearly that thou hast become a stranger to God.

In another passage we read: *I abhor such sport*, he says, *unclean heresy, lust of the ascetic, bodies entwined in one another!*[5] I am ashamed to bring forward the further final doings, which the enemy has instigated and to which the apostle has prudently called our

---

[1] This fragment of the *Apocalypse of Elias* is not otherwise attested, although texts which engage in descriptions of the torments of hell are very numerous. Above all reference may be made to the *Apocalypsis b. Dei Genitricis de poenis* (ed. M. R. James *Apocrypha Anecdota*, Cambridge 1893, pp. 115ff.), which circulated particularly in the Slavic area under the name "Choždenie Bogorodicy po mukam". Cf. E. Schürer *ThLZ* 33, 1908, p. 614; M. R. James, *The Lost Apocrypha of the Old Testament*, 1920, p. 55. Cf. also the *Apocalypse of Paul*, pp. 779ff. below.
[2] Cf. Wisd. 3:14.   [3] Apocryphon of Solomon?
[4] Ecclus. 30, 19ff.   [5] An apocryphon that cannot be identified.

attention, saying: *I am afraid concerning you lest ye be seduced by the enemy, as (in those days) Eve was cunningly tempted by the serpent.*[1]

Therefore, watching craftily, let us arm ourselves with spiritual weapons that we may be able to defeat the giant, as the discourse of the Lord by his prophet runs: *He who defeats a giant*, says he, *takes his spoil.*[2] That means to bridle the desires of the flesh that, as its spoil, we may be able to carry away the everlasting resurrection. (That can only take place) after we have been renewed to the glory of God. How wilt thou then be capable of defeating a giant if thou art prevented by women? Hear the thanksgiving[3] rendered by John, the disciple of the Lord, when praying before his death: *O Lord, thou who from my infancy until this age hast preserved me untouched by woman, thou who hast kept my body from them so that the mere sight of a woman excites abhorrence in me.* O gift (of God), to remain untouched by the influence of women! By the grace of this holy state thou canst love what is abominable to the flesh. But thou honorary ascetic, how canst thou believe that thou canst remain free from sordid deed if willingly thou hast women always before thee? Does what we teach (here) stand perhaps outside the law? Compare with this what even the demons declared when they made confession before the deacon Dyrus on the arrival of John:[4] *In the last times many will attempt to dispossess us, saying that they are free from women and from craving after them and clean. And yet if we desired it, we could possess even them themselves.*

Thou seest then, O man, how the strange spirits, i.e. the deeds of the devil, testify to thee that one can be overcome by womanly beauty. How then canst thou set free the bodies possessed by them if thou thyself art possessed by them? To conquer them one must have in oneself the necessary power. *Beware then of being possessed by the evil one or of being conquered by the adulterer;*[5] i.e. *keep thyself*

<hr>

[1] Cf. 2 Cor. 11:3.
[2] An apocryphon that cannot be identified. It may perhaps have developed out of Lk. 11:22.
[3] This *gratulacio* is to be regarded as a free quotation from the *Acts of John*. Cf. Aa II, 1, pp. 212, 213, and below p. 209.
[4] The text runs: "Aut numquid extra legem est quod docemus ut et ipsi daemones cum confiterentur dyro diacono in adventu Johannis considera quid dixerint". Bulhart rightly suggests that the words "considera quid dixerint" should be regarded as a dittography. The deacon Dyrus mentioned here is identical with the "Berus Diakon" who appears in the *Acts of John* (c. 30) (cf. Aa II. 1, p. 167 and p. 209 below). But the whole fragment has not survived.
[5] An apocryphon that cannot be identified.

far from association with women and from pleasantry with them during meal-times. Thus runs the word of Holy Scripture: *Suffer not thy heart to be enticed by her lest thou also come to death. Thus, my child, beware of her, as of a serpent's head.*[1] Receive into thine heart the admonitions of the blessed John, who, when he was invited to a wedding, came only for the sake of chastity. And what did he say? *Little children, whilst your flesh is still pure and you have a body that is still untouched and are not in a state of moral corruption and are not besmirched by Satan, the extremely hostile and shame⟨less⟩ (opponent) of chastity, understand in fuller measure the mystery of the matrimonial association: it is an attempt of the serpent, ignorance of doctrine, violence done to the seed, a gift of death, an office of destruction, instruction in division, an office of moral corruption, a tarrying ⟨ . . . ⟩, a sowing between them of the enemy, an ambush of Satan, a device of the malevolent one, dirty fruit of birth, a shedding of blood, a passion of the heart, a desertion of reason, the earnest of punishment, a deed of torment, a work of fire, a sign of the enemy, the deadly malice of eagerness, a kiss of deceit, an association in bitterness, an excitement of the heart, an invention of corruption, a craving for a phantom, a worldly course of life, the devil's stage-play, an enemy of life, a fetter of darkness, intoxication ⟨ . . . ⟩, mockery by the enemy, a stumbling-block to life which separates from the Lord, a beginning of disobedience, the end of life, and death. Hearing this, little children, bind yourselves each one in an inseparable, true and holy marriage whilst ye await the one incomparable and true bridegroom from heaven, Christ the eternal bridegroom.*[2]

If the apostle allowed marriage itself to be dissolved that it might not occasion a heaping up of offences,[3] what should we say of the state of the ascetic, which most of all should be free from fleshly lust? O bodies separated from one another and already dedicated to Christ! O carnal glow of youth, difficult to quench! O dew that, flowing down from heaven, warms the cold vessel! O those who have ventured to call back to life the lost heavenly dignity! O endless glory of the saints, from death set free! O field pleasing to Christ, which brings forth eternal fruits!

[1] Ecclus. 9:9; 25:22?
[2] The translation of this missing fragment from the *Acts of John* comes from K. Schäferdiek.
[3] The text runs: "Si utique matrimonium deiunxit apostolus ne sit occasio delicti comulando." Bulhart replaces *comulando* by *copulando*.

O denial of the flesh, spiritual nuptials with eternal marriage-ties in the heavenly habitations! O how much one can do in the conflict for chastity when one is discerning!

When finally the apostle Andrew came to a wedding to show the glory of God, he separated the spouses intended for one another, the women and the men, and taught them to remain holy in celibacy.[1] O glory of the one-horned lamb that separates the sheep from the goats, whilst the Lord himself admonishes us: Hear me, my chosen sheep, and fear not the wolf.[2] Not to fear the wolf means to flee from the offence of death. To separate the sheep from the goats means to keep oneself free from foul sins, to live in solitude as one of God's ascetics. So also it is said in Ezra in reference to the future: *Come ye from all cities to Jerusalem to the mount and bring with you cypress and palm leaves and build you detached booths!*[3]

Thou seest then, O holy man, that the hope described by the authors named holds good for us that, pure in body, we may live in solitude in our booths and that no one of us suffer himself to be fettered by carnal love. *For,* according to the question and answer of Christ, our Lord, *the cypress is a mystery of chastity.*[4] Its spike on a single stalk rightly aims at the sky. By the palm leaves also he signifies the victory, the glory of martyrdom. Out of these two kinds of trees are the booths built, which are the bodies of the saints. And since he added *out of the mount,* i.e. from the body of Christ, he meant doubtless the *substancia conexa.*[5] Blessed then are those who preserve this *substancia*! These the Lord praises through Isaiah: *Every one that does not profane the Sabbath but keeps it and takes hold of my covenant, them will I bring to my holy mountain and make them joyful in my house of prayer, and their offering and burnt offering will be accepted on my altar. So saith the Lord.*[6] The keeping holy of the Sabbath clearly means not to defile the pure flesh. And therefore was it ordered in the books of the patriarchs that

---

[1] That this passage belongs to the *Acta Andreae* seems to be clear. But this fragment is not found among the remnants of that work that have been preserved. Cf. Aa II. 1, pp. 38ff. and pp. 390ff. below.

[2] This logion may be a free citation from the Gospels (cf. Mt. 10:16 and Mk. 13:9).

[3] Neh. 8:15.

[4] The source of this logion is unknown. The cypress must already at this time have counted as a symbol of the ascetic-monastic life.

[5] What PsT means by this *substancia conexa* is not clear to me.

[6] Is. 56. 6, 7.

no unprofitable work should be done on the Sabbath.[1] Clearly then it is a positive fact that God forbids the doing of the works of this world in the flesh that is dedicated to Him.

Once upon a time on a Sabbath two men were surprised collecting wood, and God in indignation ordered that the two of them should be put to death.[2] That took place in the past, but it is to be interpreted in the following way: the two collectors of wood signify those who are committing sin, their evil-doings being symbolized by the collected foliage. And therefore the bundle of wood could not be made by one person alone, but it was two together who defiled the Sabbath. Rightly does the Lord give warning by Ezekiel: *Behold the princes of Israel, they have despised my sanctuary and defiled my sabbaths; adulterous men have shed blood in thy midst, O Jerusalem.*[3]

O most beautiful city, in the midst of thy beauty they have exposed their father's nakedness! O priceless holiness of God rejected by all evil-doers! O sabbaths dedicated to Christ, desecrated by burglars! O priceless city, redeemed by the blood of Christ and overwhelmed with most filthy indecencies! The exposing of the father's nakedness means assuredly the violation of the virginity that has been consecrated to God. Finally the Lord urges him on, namely the prophet, to lodge the following reproach: *Each one of you has defiled a wife not his own in shameless act, and each one of you has ravished his father's daughter.*[4] O error of judgment! The devil entices many minds to ravish not their own but the bride of Christ! O imitation of the animal way of life, when a man sleeps with his father's daughter and with one born of the self-same mother!

Therefore, under the inspiration of the Holy Spirit, the voice of the lawgiver sounds:[5] *Cursed be he who lies with his own sister. And the people said, Amen, Amen.*[6] Why art thou not afraid to lie

---

[1] We do not know what books of the patriarchs are referred to here. On this occasion Harnack (p. 193) has referred to the "lost work τῶν τριῶν Πατριαρχῶν". This book, which is composed in the form of a conversation about the last things between the "three patriarchs" (Basil the Great, Gregory of Nazianzus and John Chrysostom) and was widely disseminated especially in the Slavic area, as is to be learned from the numerous surviving Slavic manuscripts, is in my opinion not involved. Cf. I. Ja. Porfirjev, *Pamjatniki otreč. russk. Literatury*, Vol. II, pp. 429–438.

[2] Cf. Num. 15:32ff.   [3] Cf. Ezek. 22:6ff.   [4] Cf. Ezek. 22:11.

[5] The text runs: "Unde legislatoris vox sancto spiritu cecinitante". Here (in my opinion without reason) Bulhart reads "cecinit ante".

[6] Deut. 27:22.

with this sister, daughter of (thy) father and of (thy) mother—here Christ is meant as father and the church as mother—as if thou couldest evade the punishment that is to be imposed by the court? Consider the by-gone doings recorded in the Books of the Kings, e.g. when Adonijah craved for the Shunammite Abishag, his father's girl (*puella*), who was a symbol of the virginity that is dedicated to Christ, (was) he not because of a mere thought ⟨ . . . ⟩?[1] And if Adonijah was punished with death without having realized his purpose, how much more today he who is found guilty of such a deed? If Adonijah perished because of a word, what punishment, thinkest thou, will be measured out for the act? It is hard for a man controlled by lust to come forth unsullied, as the word of the Lord through the prophet Haggai indicates, saying: *Ask the priests concerning the law and say: if one bear holy flesh in the skirt of his garment and after that do touch with his skirt bread, wine, oil, or any other food, will it thereby be holy or not? And the priests answered and said, No. And Haggai said: if one who is defiled touches all this, will it thereby be unclean? And the priests answered and said: It will be unclean. Then answered Haggai and said: So is it also with this people and with this nation before me, saith the Lord.*[2] Now it is the sanctified flesh, dedicated to chastity, that was touched by the skirt of the baptismal robe. But he showed that had it come into contact with what is despicable, (this) food would not thereby become holy; for the material food signifies the transient wishes of the human mind. That is carnal food, and it is not pleasing to the Holy Spirit. Therefore he decreed that the king's garment should not be considered as holy thereby. And further he has likewise shown that there is a state of defilement whereby the creature also is defiled. What Moses had already previously said has been made clear to us by the author of (this) saying: *Everything that an unclean person touches shall be unclean.*[3] And what says Haggai (in addition)? *Even so this people and this race, saith the Lord.* The city governor orders that the city dwellers be like him! O thou that turnest far aside from holiness and usurpest honour for thyself, putting thyself on a par with that priest![4] O unreasonable king, thou that exploitest the people

---

[1] I Kgs 2:13–25. [2] Haggai 2:11–14. [3] Num. 19:22.
[4] The text runs: "O imper sancto ut aequiperetur illi sacerdoti". Bulhart gives "imper(are)".

to rebellion! O the resemblance of an insincere course of life;
many step in and out without justice! O vain, strange prophecy
which has no validity for the future! O worldly reckoning which
is rejected by Christ! In conclusion he reproves them on the last
day with the words: *Depart from me, ye evil-doers, I know you not:
so will I speak to those who go into destruction.*[1]

Thou seest how those who counterfeit holy celibacy, the enemies
of chastity, the unjust, the ⟨ . . . ⟩ of belief, the destroyers of the
flock of God will be rejected. He shows that no one will escape
punishment. Why thinkest thou, O foolish man, that what thou
committest in secrecy is not forbidden, when God is Lord of the
night and of the day, saying ⟨ . . . ⟩. If one knows that it is not
lawful to comply with the divers desires of the flesh and does what
he regards as contrary to belief, can that not be described as
obstinate offence? And it is that even if he does not give a thought
to the fact that, although no one is present, contempt of the law
weighs more heavily than unchastity. The lusts of the flesh must
be deplored; this greediness must be expelled from the mind; but
thou repentest not of this offence, and passest thyself off as guiltless when on the threshold of the glory that is due to (guiltlessness),
and praisest thyself! But consider what David prophesies and
what the Holy Spirit says through his mouth: *I said*, he says,
*ye are gods and altogether children of the Highest, but ye will die like
men and perish like one of the princes.*[2] O gods who die a human
death! O glory of princes that falls from the height into the
depth! That will take place some day, there being a separation
between the righteous and the profane, and no fellowship of the
believer with the (un)righteous, of death with life. Or else consider what lies between destruction and salvation![3] Today the
prophecy of the Lord through Ezekiel has finally come to fulfilment: *My house*, he says, *has for me turned into such dross as brass,
iron, tin, lead in the midst of silver.*[4] Into such a mixture have you
turned.[5] For in the state of the ascetic, which is silver, there have

---

[1] Mt. 25:41.   [2] Ps. 82:6f.

[3] The text runs: "Haec ergo facient cum sit separacio inter iustum et prophanum,
nec est participacio inter fidelem et iustum, et nulla sit segregacio inter mortem et
vitam, vel considera quid sit inter perditum et saluum". Harnack suggests "inter
fidelem et (in)iustum". Bulhart thinks that "*ut* should be read instead of *et*".

[4] Cf. Ezek. 22:18.

[5] According to the text "id ergo commixti estis omnes" the *id* is to be construed as
an accusative, and perhaps it ought not to be replaced by *ideo* as Bulhart suggests.

emerged in the end alloys of different sorts, bad ingredients.
Now these are the elements of this mixture. The iron signifies the
hardness of the heart in which the wisdom of the spiritual mind
has taken no root. Reuben was rightly characterized by Jacob as
the hardness of iron, for he is reckoned the hardest among those
who belong to the Jewish people[1] The lead signifies the heaviness
of the flesh, which is extremely heavy. By this is signified the
offence which submerges men in the destruction of death, for the
submerging of Pharaoh and his people as lead in the sea according
to the account in Scripture[2] was (only) a sign (for us). And
similarly we are admonished through Zechariah: *The mouth of a
shameless woman is stopped up with lead,*[3] whereby crime is clearly
meant. The brass signifies the stench of the sinful flesh, after
which the sons of Israel craved in Egypt when they longed for the
fleshpots.[4] And on that account they died and were unable to
come into possession of the ancestral promises, precisely as those
also who suffer themselves to be enticed by the human ⟨ . . . ⟩
of the flesh will not attain to the possession of the kingdom of
God! The interpretation of the tin is this: They are tin who
dazzle our eyes with the wisdom of God and who in the matter
of chastity exhibit an appearance of polluted silver, but who are
in no wise of great value in the church. They will be rejected
according to the saying of Solomon: *In secrecy they carry out abortions and at the same time think that they will live for ever.*[5] That is then
the mixture that has come to be in the house of God. O seducers
of women who concoct new doctrine! Burglars in strange houses,
corrupters of maidens, violators of chastity, apostates from belief,
resisters of the truth, rebels to the discipline of God! O outrageous
mixture! Thou hast turned into silver, i.e. to chastity, and
therefore these will be melted in the furnace of burning judgment, and then will the Lord purify for himself precious, pure,
sterling, fine silver for that holy Jerusalem with a view to preparing for himself the paternal throne. But the others, of whom we
have spoken above, who have apostatized from belief, these will
go into eternal torment! *Blessed then are those who have remained
holy in body and united in spirit, for they will often speak to God! Blessed*

[1] Cf. Gen. 49:3.   [2] Exod. 15:10.   [3] Cf. Zech. 5:8.   [4] Cf. Exod. 16:3.
[5] According to Harnack's assumption we have to reckon here with a lost Apocryphon of Solomon.

are those who have kept themselves from the unchastity of this world, for they will be pleasing to Christ, the Son of God, and to the Father, the Lord! Blessed are those who have kept the baptism of salvation, for they will enjoy eternal delight.[1] He who has the hearing of the heart, let him hear what God promises: *To the victor,* he says, *will I give to eat of the tree of life which stands in the paradise of my God.*[2] O incorruptible nourishment that comes from the tree of wisdom, the leaves of which are destined for the healing of the nations, where there shall be no curse and where no unclean flesh can enter, where no spite from unrighteous works and no lie will find a place, but only God and the Lamb will be enthroned. Their servants will render them homage for ever and ever![3] These then are the servants of God who always minister to His will and please Him, who live not for the flesh but for the Holy Spirit. These are they who will not be overtaken by the second death and who will eat of the hidden manna, the food of the heavenly paradise.[4] They will receive the white stone, the helmet of eternal salvation, upon which is written the ineffable name of God, which no man knows save he who has received it. O host most white, legions of sanctity, precious to God, to whom Christ the Lord orders royal powers to be given for the judging of all! Like the potter's useless vessels will they smash them! *I will give them,* he says, *the eternal morning star, as I myself received (it) from my Father.*[5] Likewise will he grant those victors to be clad in splendid clothing, nor will their name ever be deleted from the book of life. *I will confess them,* he says, *before my Father and his angels in heaven.*[6] Blessed therefore are they who persevere even unto the end, as the Lord says: *To him that overcometh will I grant to sit at my right hand in my throne, even as I have overcome and sit on the right hand of my Father in his throne to all ages for ever and ever. Amen.*[7]

HERE ENDETH THE EPISTLE OF TITUS, THE DISCIPLE OF PAUL, ON THE ESTATE OF CHASTITY.

[1] Cf. *Acta Pauli* c. 5 (cf. Aa I, p. 238 and p. 354 below).
[2] Rev. 2:7.   [3] Cf. Rev. 22:2, 3.
[4] "Caelestis ortus esca." De Bruyne has rightly understood *ortus* as the genitive of *hortus* by contamination. But Bulhart thinks that "*ortus* indicates *origin*: one makes do with this interpretation".
[5] Cf. Rev. 2:26-28.   [6] Mt. 10:32f.   [7] Rev. 3:21.

XIII

SECOND AND THIRD CENTURY ACTS OF APOSTLES

INTRODUCTION

(W. Schneemelcher and K. Schäferdiek)

TEXTS AND DISCUSSIONS: Lipsius-Bonnet, *Acta Apostolorum Apocrypha,* I (1891), II/1 (1898), II/2 (1903); reprinted 1959. W. Wright, *Apocryphal Acts of the Apostles, edited from Syriac MSS. in the British Museum and other libraries,* I. II, 1871. M. R. James, *Apocrypha Anecdota (Texts and Studies* II. 3, 1893; V, 1897). I. Guidi, "Gli Atti apocrifi degli apostoli nei testi copti arabi ed etiopici" *(Rendiconti della R. Accademia dei Lincei* Notes I–VII, Vol. III, 1897, I, pt. 2; II, pts. 2, 4, 8, 10, 11; Vol. IV, 1888, I, pt. 2: text; Italian translation in *Giornale della Società Asiatica Italiana* II, 1888; German summary in Lipsius, *Apostelgeschichten,* Supplementary Volume, pp. 89ff.). O. von Lemm, "Koptische apokryphe Apostelacten" *(Mélanges asiatiques tirés du Bull. Impériale des Sciences de St. Pétersbourg* X, 1890, pp. 99–171). A. Smith Lewis, *The Mythological Acts of the Apostles* (Arabic; *Horae Semiticae* IV, 1904). E. A. Wallis Budge, *The Contendings of the Apostles* (Ethiopic) I. II, 1898–1901. P. Vetter in *Oriens Christianus* 1901, pp. 217ff.; 1903, pp. 16ff. and 324ff.; *Theol. Quartalschrift* 1906, pp. 161ff. (Armenian). W. H. P. Hatch, "Three Hitherto Unpublished Leaves from a MS. of the Acta Apostolorum Apocrypha in Bohairic" *(Coptic Studies in honor of W. E. Crum = Bulletin of the Byzantine Institute* II, 1950, pp. 305–317). C. Khurcikidze, *Recensions géorgiennes des Actes apocryphes des Apôtres d'après des manuscrits des IXe–XIe siècles,* Tiflis 1959 (not available to me). A. Siegmund, *Die Überlieferung der griechischen christlichen Literatur in der lateinischen Kirche bis zum 12. Jh.,* 1949, pp. 33–40. G. Graf, *Geschichte der christlichen arabischen Literatur,* Bd. I, 1944 *(Studi e Testi* 118), pp. 257ff.

Apokr. 2, pp. 163–289; Michaelis, pp. 216–438; James, pp. 228–438.

Lipsius, *Apostelgeschichten.* H. Ljungvik, *Studien zur Sprache der apokryphen Apostelgeschichten (Uppsala Univ. Årsskrift* 8) 1926. K. Kerényi, *Die Griechisch-Orientalische Romanliteratur in religionsgeschichtlicher Beleuchtung,* 1927. R. Söder, *Die apokryphen Apostelgeschichten und die romanhafte Literatur der Antike* (Würzburger Studien zur Altertumswiss. 3) 1932. M. Blumenthal, *Formen und Motive in den apokryphen Apostelgeschichten* (TU 48. 1) 1933. K. L. Schmidt, *Kanonische und apokryphe Evangelien und Apostelgeschichten* (AThANT 5) 1944. R. Helm, *Der antike Roman,* 1948, pp. 53–61. C. L. Sturhahn, *Die Christologie der ältesten apokryphen Apostelakten* (Theol. Diss. Heidelberg 1951). L. Fabricius, *Die Legende im Bild des ersten Jahrtausends der Kirche. Der Einfluss der Apokryphen und Pseudepigraphen auf die altchristliche und byzantinische Kunst*, 1956. See also the bibliography by H. Kraft in Lipsius-Bonnet, Aa, Second Edition 1959, Vol. II. 2, pp. 397-402.

Abbreviations: AJ = the Acts of John; AP = the Acts of Paul; APt = the (ancient) Acts of Peter; AA = the Acts of Andrew; AT = the Acts of Thomas.

I. GENERAL SURVEY. There is no simple method of characterizing the second- and third-century Acts of Apostles, most of which have come down to us in an incomplete state, and which have been imitated and developed in various ways in later periods. Starting from the general definition of the New Testament Apocrypha given on pp. 26f. of Volume I, we may consider these apocryphal Acts as works whose primary aim was to supplement the New Testament, especially St. Luke's Book of Acts, and whose authors made use of well-defined literary forms that were familiar and widely used in the cultural world of early Christianity. Whether the Greek novel served as their pattern, or some other type of writing, or a mixture of types, is a disputed question which calls for discussion, as well as the question whether these works were written in connection with the Lucan Acts. At this stage we must only insist that these questions are important, since they partly determine our answer to the further question, whether these apocryphal books claimed to be given an equal status with the writings of the New Testament Canon, and particularly the canonical Acts. As far as we can see, the texts are silent on this point. We cannot indeed regard them as an attempt to *displace* the canonical Acts; so much is evident from the history of the distinct types of writing, since (in contrast with the Gospels) we are here dealing with works which, as we now know them, have the formal characteristics of literature. But one could well suppose a desire to *supplement* the canonical Acts as explaining the contents of some of the apocryphal books, where they deal with individual Apostles.

But is it indeed possible to consider the apocryphal books of Acts as a single whole, when one approaches them as a literary critic, or as an historian of religion? One can hardly give a straightforward answer. It must first be remarked that the various apocryphal Acts derive from different periods and different environments, and that they are sharply contrasted in their theological standpoint and in their devotional ideals. There have certainly been repeated attempts to consider these Acts as a unity, regarding them either as products of Gnosticism or of primitive popular Catholicism; but these have too often overlooked the differences of viewpoint which rule out any such simple derivation from Gnosticism or primitive Catholicism; while the boundaries between these two movements, at least in the second century, were by no means so distinct as later historians easily suppose. Secondly, there is no justification for any great emphasis on the unity of the apocryphal Acts on the score of literary affinity. These works are "not even formally homogeneous".[1] An exact analysis of the narrative technique also shows considerable differences. Nevertheless one can speak of a certain unity, that is, if one understands these apocryphal Acts as "narratives coming from the people for the people",[2] which made use of a variety of stylistic devices drawn from hellenistic literature. Only by adopting such a widely-drawn definition, but keeping the varieties of form and content constantly in view, can one associate these apocryphal Acts in a single complex. This general definition, which embodies a number of problems, will be briefly explained in the pages that follow; though for brevity's sake a great deal will have to be treated in quite general terms. It will not be possible to take account of all the criteria which may be of value in dealing with individual books of this type. But even at the risk of allowing certain discrepancies to appear in our estimate of them a general summary has to be attempted; and here it is essential to compare them with the Acts of the Apostles written by Luke.

2. LUKE'S ACTS OF THE APOSTLES AND THE APOCRYPHAL ACTS. Previous researches have differed considerably over the relationship of the apocryphal Acts to the Lucan work that obtained a place in the Canon. Thus C. Schmidt held that the apocryphal Acts, which he took to have arisen out of an attempt to repel the Gnostic assault on the Church, derived their literary form from the Lucan Book of Acts: "Not only the title, $\pi\rho\acute{\alpha}\xi\epsilon\iota\varsigma$, is derived from this source, but the whole method of composition, the thought and diction, just as a general dependence on the canonical literature is very strongly apparent".[3] The apocryphal and the Lucan Acts are closely related, they are "in point of literary $\epsilon\tilde{\iota}\delta o\varsigma$ entirely comparable".[4] On the other hand Pfister, though citing a few instances which pointed to a possible affinity of the apocryphal Acts with the canonical work, went on to insist on an important distinction. The historical description attempted in the canonical book, though hampered by inadequate source-material, contrasts with the luxuriant fancy and extremely free composition of the apocryphal works. "The pattern of the canonical Acts remains a mere shadowy trace in the background."[5] The two positions thus briefly sketched make it obvious that clear understanding of the relationship of the apocryphal

---

[1] R. Söder, *Die apokr. Apostelgeschichten*, 1932, p. 216.   [2] Söder, *op. cit.*, p. 216.
[3] C. Schmidt, *Die alten Petrusakten*, TU 24. 1 (1903), p. 154.
[4] *Ib.*, p. 155.   [5] *Apokr.* 2, p. 169.

to the canonical Acts cannot be attained until the character of the Lucan work has been clearly grasped. Mere general references to "historical writing" or to the title πράξεις do not achieve their end.

Historical and critical investigation of the Acts was for a long time dominated by the critical method which explored the writer's aims, and then by one focused on literary sources. M. Dibelius, who applied the form-critical method to the canonical Acts, was the first to achieve a proper examination and valuation not only of the "smaller units", the blocks out of which the work is built, but also of the method of their compilation. By this means he established a point of primary importance: that Luke belonged to the tradition of ancient historiography, and so aspired to be an historian, not indeed in the modern sense of the word, but as the ancients understood it; and that he also aspired to be a preacher demonstrating the theme of divine judgement in history, which was regarded as the accomplishment of the divine plan of salvation.[1] Since Dibelius' time German scholars have built upon the foundations which he laid and so have increasingly become aware of the theological problems of Luke's conception.[2] An important event was that after a long interval a comprehensive specialist commentary on Acts was at last produced by E. Haenchen, which both summed up previous researches and decisively developed them. Luke's place as a theologian, a historian and a man of letters was now established.

Acts is the work of a theologian who, without writing a doctrinal treatise, nevertheless deals with definite theological questions in his presentation of history. Two contemporary theological problems particularly concern the author: the expectation of an imminent end, and the mission to the Gentiles unimpeded by the Jewish Law. Luke answers the first question by his sketch of the history of salvation, which divides into three epochs;[3] and solves the second problem by means of his presentation of history. Here because of his theological conception of history he has to present the history of early Christianity at one decisive point—namely the question of the Gentile mission—quite otherwise than it actually developed. "Luke the historian does not show us the zig-zag line of the actual development of the Christian mission, but its idealized curve."[4] However, if the author, even in his

---

[1] For the history of these researches, see E. Haenchen, *Die Apostelgeschichte* (Meyers Kommentar, pt. 3), 13th edn. 1961, pp. 13–47; full bibliography.

[2] We should mention here P. Vielhauer, H. Conzelmann, G. Klein and especially of course Haenchen himself.

[3] Cf. H. Conzelmann, *Die Mitte der Zeit*, 2nd edn. 1957 (ET: *The Theology of St. Luke*, London 1960); Haenchen, pp. 84ff.

[4] Haenchen, *op. cit.*, p. 93. Luke's theology has now become the burning question. Nevertheless I believe there will have to be further investigation of the relationship

work as a historian, is tied to his theological conception, and his work is conditioned by these contemporary questions, it must not be overlooked that Acts has also a practical end in view: it was intended to "edify"; it must itself assist the work of evangelism. Dibelius had clearly recognized this already: Luke appears as a historian, but also as an evangelist, who uses the historian's methods to attain his end, that is, evangelism. Haenchen has developed and slightly varied this train of thought: "What Luke could offer his readers, particularly as a sequel to a gospel, had to be a work of edification" (p. 93). This intention therefore determines the method and style in which the material is presented: "A narrative need not then describe an event with the accuracy of a police report, but must impress what has happened on the hearer or reader so that they cannot forget" (p. 99).

If then we have rightly grasped the intention of the author of Acts, as a theologian who intends to write history in order to evangelize, then we can attempt a more accurate characterization of the work itself. Luke's Acts of the Apostles is a work of edification shaped by a definite theological conception and set in the form of a historical narrative. It need hardly be stressed that this comprehensive description does not include everything that has to be said about Acts. For example, it does not mention the apologetic motive, which certainly plays quite an important part in Acts. In this context, however, we must content ourselves with this definition, which provides a point of view which is of real significance for the comparison with the apocryphal Acts. The theme of the Lucan Acts could alternatively be briefly described as "The progress of the 'Word of God' up to the end of the world". This progress is God's work, and he uses his witnesses to perform it. As a description of the contents of the work verse 8 of Chapter I is in its own manner completely appropriate.[1] The chief characters whose deeds are related (Peter and the Apostles in the first part, Paul in the second)[2] are thereby made the instruments of God's plan, whose intention is that the salvation which was manifested in the earthly life of Jesus, the real moment

of Acts to ancient historiography, on which M. Dibelius laid such impressive emphasis. At least the problem must not be minimized as against the theological questions, important as these are. Haenchen, who was under the necessity of writing a commentary and not a special study, seems to emphasize the influence of the Old Testament and of the Gospel tradition rather than making classical models responsible for the style; op. cit., p. 96 n. 1.

[1] Cp. Haenchen, op. cit., p. 112.

[2] The division of Acts into two parts is problematical and so should not serve as a basic principle. Certainly the part concerned with Paul begins at Chapter 13; but the way is prepared for it by a number of passages—a sign of the author's literary skill. Haenchen therefore in his Commentary has dispensed with an analysis into main sections. Nevertheless it must not be overlooked that Luke repeatedly gives a single individual the central place in his narrative.

of salvation, should be preached to all nations. Thus this account is not primarily interested in the journeyings of the messengers, their miracles, etc., but in the march of the Gospel from Jerusalem to Rome. The account of this march is to inspire faith, trust and confidence and so point out to the readers the way to salvation.

But this characterization clearly shows that a comparison between Acts and the apocryphal Acts cannot lead to the conclusion that the latter are to be assigned to the same class as the former. No doubt the Acts of Peter, and also the Acts of Paul, can be described in some sense as narratives running parallel to the canonical Acts.[1] But even if this description of the two apocryphal books we have mentioned were perfectly appropriate, one could not even consider similar theories about the other apocryphal Acts; indeed I am very doubtful whether the two I have named can be described in this way. One or two features or statements may point to a connection with the canonical Acts; but this in no way explains the literary character and the intention of the apocryphal Acts. Without wishing to anticipate the discussion of their literary genre in the next section, the following points must here be noted:

(a) The apocryphal Acts are likewise based on a definite theological position. But one of the most distinctive features of these works is that they are not determined by theological reflexions, but rather directed by practical intentions. Thus the encratite strain that occurs in different forms in the several apocryphal Acts should undoubtedly be understood as showing that the authors of these Acts took sexual continence to be an essential feature, or sometimes indeed the authentic content, of the Christian message. We may think what we like about the beginnings of such an attitude in the New Testament, but it cannot be denied that at this point the aims disclosed in the apocryphal Acts have definitely altered as compared with the canonical book. Other theological questions (e.g. Christology) also provide evidence of the great difference in theological judgment. A still more important point is that, unlike the canonical book, the apocryphal Acts do not intend to execute an explicit theological programme. This can be explained in terms of the change in the Church's situation: thus the frustrated expectation of the End has obviously ceased to be an urgent problem. A more striking point is that the interests of the apocryphal Acts are no longer primarily theological. Exceptions such as certain passages in the Acts of Paul, for instance the apocryphal corres-

---

[1] C. Schmidt has so interpreted them: Studien zu den alten Petrusakten II, *ZKG* 45, 1927, p. 509.

pondence with the Corinthians, really confirm the rule. Entertainment and propagandist activity are their real objects; and this difference of content as compared with the canonical Acts finds its expression in a different literary form.

(b) Beside such general questions of theology, their understanding of history presents a problem of special importance for a comparison between the apocryphal and the canonical Acts. It has already been indicated that St. Luke wrote with the intention of answering definite concrete theological questions through his account of the history of the Christian mission, and uses this to forward his own work of edification and evangelism. He can do this because he is convinced of the continuity of God's action in the history of our salvation. So the account of "the progress of God's Word" gains theological relevance and can itself summon men to believe. It is useless to search the apocryphal Acts for such an interpretation of past history, which for St. Luke continues into the present through the work of evangelism. The apocryphal Acts do indeed describe the effects of the Christian preaching, they are concerned with the missionary work conducted by the Apostles in the different regions. But the problem of the delay of the Parousia no longer affects them; on the other hand the problem of the connection with the People of the Old Covenant is no longer a burning one, so that the distinctive axioms of Luke's theology of history are not to be found. A further and more important point is that in the apocryphal Acts the apostle with whom we are concerned is sometimes given such prominence that we can no longer describe them in terms of missionary history, conceived as the history of the Word of God and its publication throughout the world. The apocryphal Acts, in marked contrast to the canonical book, are determined by the description of the characters involved. This also entails that from a literary point of view a different form must be adopted: one "work" succeeds another, and in conclusion there is the martyrdom or death of the apostle, a feature which Luke actually avoids, although he knew of the death of Paul, as is apparent from Acts 20:17ff. In fine, one may say that the difference between the apocryphal and the canonical Acts appears in the fact that the interest of the apocryphal Acts depends upon the personal fortunes and deeds of the Apostles, and not on the history of the Church as a new period in the divinely appointed history of salvation.

(c) Lastly it has to be remarked that the "edificatory" trend of the apocryphal Acts must certainly be distinguished from Luke's intention to write a work for edification. No doubt the canonical Acts is not devoid of legendary and miraculous stories of every

173

kind (for instance Peter's shadow, 5:15, or Paul's handkerchiefs, 19:12). But these legends are subordinated to the principal themes and made to subserve Luke's theological programme. The case is different in the apocryphal Acts. Here miraculous stories are not only much exaggerated, producing fantastic and bizarre effects, but they often follow one from another as isolated units and are retailed for their own sake. The intention of this is clearly not that of demonstrating the wonderful advance of the Word of God and of underlining God's co-operation with the Church's mission by particular miracles, but rather that of using these stories to glorify the apostles as miracle-workers. Hence one can hardly speak of an "edificatory" trend; their intention is better described as entertainment. It must at once be added that such a decisive difference in content requires a different form. To sum up, we may say that the apocryphal Acts are essentially different from the Lucan Acts in genre and literary form as much as in content and theology, and despite many borrowings of details and points of connection the apocryphal works cannot be put on a level with the Lucan work. That being so, how can the character of the apocryphal Acts be more accurately defined?

3. THE APOCRYPHAL ACTS AS POPULAR LITERATURE. An attempt was made by F. Pfister, in Apokr. 2, pp. 163ff., to establish an overall definition of the literary genre of the apocryphal Acts and also to disclose their connection with ancient literature. Pfister starts from the name πράξεις, which is borne by the apocryphal books as well as the canonical book of Acts and indeed corresponds with the name of a particular genre of ancient literature, the πράξεις, concerned with the actions of some prominent personality, whether historical or mythical. Certain elements which appear both in the ancient "Praxeis" and in the apocryphal books of Acts demonstrate the connections. Thus one can establish the element of "aretalogy", the portrayal of the hero's exceptional abilities and powers, together with the geographical (or "ethnological") interest which finds expression in the travel-narratives, or περίοδοι. Next comes the religious interest, which equally connects the apocryphal Acts with the "Praxeis" of antiquity. Thus according to Pfister the literary genre of the apocryphal Acts can be given a comprehensive description: they are Christian "aretalogies" set in the context of missionary travels. In this way the apocryphal Acts can be integrated with the history of ancient literature, which itself contains a whole series of works which can be also described as aretalogical missionary narratives.

Here Pfister has adopted ideas which already appear in the work of R. Reitzenstein,[1] who emphasized in particular the pattern of the aretalogies concerned with prophets and philosophers. Here he was resisting the tendency to treat the apocryphal Acts as a special form of hellenistic novel, as later represented by R. Helm.[2]

The conception and character of the apocryphal Acts has been further clarified by Rosa Söder's book, *Die apokryphen Apostelgeschichten und die romanhafte Literatur der Antike* (1932).[3] In this work the several themes of the apocryphal Acts are elucidated, and in particular five principal features:

(1) The travel-theme.
(2) The aretalogical element, which stresses the ἀρεταί and the δυνάμεις, the marvellous aspect of the hero's powers.
(3) The teratological element, exhibiting the world of wonders which the apostles encounter: cannibals, talking animals, etc.
(4) The persuasive element, displayed especially in the speeches.
(5) The erotic element, which finds expression in actual lovers' tales, but also in ascetical and encratite features.

This makes it possible in certain cases to trace the lines of connection with hellenistic literature. An important point is that the differences between the individual apocryphal books of Acts can thus be clearly seen. And this thoroughgoing investigation leads to a conclusion which can hardly be refuted. The apocryphal books are not formed on the pattern of the canonical book of Acts; but they are not simply a development of the classical aretalogies. Further, the pattern of the hellenistic novel can hardly be regarded as determinative, principally because the novel almost entirely lacks the themes of teratology and aretalogy. Nor is their source a mixture which combines the aretalogy and the novel as developed by the sophists of the hellenistic age, with other elements incorporated. There is, it is true, no presumption against a new literary form having been created within Christian circles out of the most diverse elements; but the pronounced differences among the various apocryphal Acts tell against this view.

[1] R. Reitzenstein, *Hellenistische Wundererzählungen*, 1906.
[2] R. Helm, *Der antike Roman*, 1948, pp. 53–57; for the history of research, see the notice in R. Söder, *op. cit.*, pp. 1–5, and works there cited.
[3] M. Blumenthal's book *Formen und Motive in den apokr. Apostelgeschichten*, *TU* 48. 1 (1933), which appeared about the same time, is unfortunately not very helpful. The author offers a number of particular observations which are valuable, but his treatment is in my opinion too schematic. Further the "Law of duality", which he assumes is debatable, and the dependence of the apocryphal Acts on the canonical book is too simply conceived.

Thus in order to define the literary genre of these works correctly, their intention must be taken as a starting-point. This intention may be defined as the entertainment, instruction and edification of the common people, rather than of the educated classes. We may therefore say that the apocryphal Acts are "evidence of ancient popular narratives of the adventures, exploits and love-affairs of great men, as now fixed in literary form and in a Christian spirit".[1] They are "popular narratives differing from the novel in being designed for the people rather than for the educated".[2] This of course does not preclude the possibility of their authors' using the stylistic methods that were customary at their time. On the contrary: how else could they write, if they were to gain a hearing among the common people? These considerations explain the various affinities with the hellenistic novel as well as with the philosophical aretalogies, which however do not justify us in actually assigning the apocryphal Acts to these stylistic categories. This characterization, I believe, provides a firm basis for a proper comprehension of the apocryphal Acts, on which further work can proceed. I shall now briefly indicate the way in which this definition is to be developed and the probable nature of further research work to be done by students of the apocryphal Acts.

(a) The composition of the apocryphal Acts must obviously be understood as a literary activity on the part of their authors; they gave their own individual arrangement and form to the material, but in doing so they were able to rely in many respects on older material. This category of apocryphal works thus appears to exhibit certain similarities with the Synoptic Gospels in respect of the processes by which they originated. Here as with the Synoptic Gospels we have to do with the fixation in writing of popular tradition. This explains the fact that the apocryphal Acts are often composed of single stories of actions strung together. Some sort of a connection is indeed generally provided, but one is often led to suspect a basis in units of tradition that originally circulated separately: legends about personalities, local tales and the like. At all events one must assume (and the assumption can be proved in particular cases, e.g. in the Acts of John, as shown below, pp. 212f.) that many passages in the apocryphal Acts already existed as separate legends before their fixation in written form.

(b) The circles from which the apocryphal Acts took their origin have been, as already mentioned, a subject of sharp dispute. The controversy on this problem has been handicapped by the fact that Gnosticism and primitive Catholicism have been contrasted as if they were fixed quantities, and the origin of the

[1] R. Söder, op. cit., p. 187. [2] Ib., p. 216.

apocryphal Acts has been sought in terms of an "Either-Or". But the boundaries between the two phenomena, Gnosticism and primitive Catholicism, remained fluctuating for a considerable period[1]; further the apocryphal Acts themselves, if indeed one regards them as a single whole, manifest strongly contrasting interests; indeed theological unity is not always preserved even within one and the same writing. If one sees in them the precipitation and the literary fixation of an oral tradition of legendary material, it is not surprising that these writings present no single and uniform theological attitude, and that in some cases one passage can be related to Gnosticism, another to primitive Catholic Christianity It therefore seems to me proper to give up the older method of inquiring into the origin of the apocryphal Acts (as a whole); the question must be raised in connection with each and considered separately; furthermore the separate units of tradition must be investigated to discover their origin. This will fully establish, inter alia, that a simple reference to primitive Catholicism or to Gnosticism cannot be made. It is a mark of this popular literature, and one which heightens its importance for the historian, that it can combine in itself both Catholic and Gnostic elements.

(c) Lastly some mention must be made of a task which I believe to be important for future work on the apocryphal Acts. Previous research has had to concern itself primarily with the problems raised by the text, its transmission and the method of composition. This is bound up with the fact that these apocryphal Acts have been handed down in such a fragmentary state, so that the first task always had to be that of establishing the content and arrangement of the ancient apocryphal works. Meanwhile much progress has been made through new discoveries of all kinds and also through intensive research, and this suggests the possibility of proceeding to form-critical investigation of particular passages. Attempts in this direction are of course already available.[2] But the investigation must be carried farther; it will be important for the history of the oral tradition of legend which underlies the apocryphal Acts in their literary form; but further it will enable us to assign to them and to their material their rightful place in the history of religion and that of the Church. The apocryphal Acts are the most important witnesses to the religious ideals of a great part of the Christian race, ideals which did not always follow the paths which were later considered acceptable to the Christian Church. An acquaintance with these religious ideals, however, is beyond question of the utmost

[1] See especially W. Bauer, *Rechtgläubigkeit und Ketzerei im ältesten Christentum*, 1934.
[2] Cp. the works of R. Söder and M. Blumenthal mentioned above.

177

importance for the historical understanding of conditions in the Church of the Second and Third Centuries.

4. THE MANICHAEAN COLLECTION OF ACTS AND LEUCIUS CHARINUS

(*K. Schäferdiek*). Photius in his Bibliotheca describes a collection of five apocryphal books of Acts of Apostles: ". . . a book, the so-called journeyings (περίοδοι) of the Apostles, in which are contained the Acts of Peter, John, Andrew, Thomas, Paul. These were written, as the book itself makes clear, by Leucius Charinus. The style is thoroughly uneven and corrupt, for in places it uses well-turned constructions and expressions, but for the most part common and hackneyed ones, while it shows no trace of the plain artless style and native grace which characterizes the diction of the evangelists and the apostles. It is stuffed with foolishness, inconsistency and incongruity; for it says that there is One who is God of the Jews, who is evil, whose servant Simon Magus became; and another is Christ, whom it calls good[1]; but it mixes and confuses everything by calling him both Father and Son.[2] It also says that he was not truly made man, but only appeared to be, and that he often appeared to his disciples in many forms, as a young man, as an old man, as a child, as an old man again and again as a child, as larger and smaller and then of great size, so that sometimes his head even reached up to heaven.[3] It also invents many foolish absurdities about the Cross,[4] saying that it was not Christ that was crucified, but another in his place, and that for this reason he derided those who crucified him.[5] It rejects lawful marriages[6] and says that every birth is evil and a work of the evil one[7]; and it absurdly states that the creator of the demons is another,[8] and it concocts senseless and childish (stories

---

[1] On this point see M. R. James, *Apocrypha Anecdota* II (= *Texts and Studies* V. 1), Cambridge 1897, pp. xviiif.; C. Schmidt, *Die alten Petrusakten*, pp. 68ff.

[2] Cf. Acts of John 98; the Cross of Light is called *inter alia* "sometimes Father, sometimes Son"; see also cc. 22, 24, 77, 82, 107f., 112.

[3] Cf. Acts of John, 87–93; Acts of Peter (the Vercelli Acts) 21.

[4] Cf. Acts of John, 97–100.

[5] Cf. Acts of John, 97 and 102; though it is John who derides the multitude.

[6] Photius may have drawn this inference from the encratite tendencies which are common to all the various Acts of Apostles which we have mentioned; perhaps he has also pressed the interpretation of sayings such as are found e.g. in the Acts of Paul and Thecla 11; Acts of Andrew, the fragment from Codex Vatic. 808 (below pp. 409ff.) 4ff.; Acts of Thomas 88. A passage in the apocryphal Epistle of Titus (below, pp. 209f.) which may derive from the Acts of John certainly seems to contain an explicit general rejection of marriage.

[7] Cf. Acts of John 98: "There are . . . Satan and the inferior root from which the nature of transient things proceeded"; *ib.*, 99: the Cross "which has separated off what is transitory and inferior".

[8] M. R. James, *op. cit.*, p. xix, refers to Acts of John 98f.; but this hardly suffices to justify the charge of thoroughgoing dualism brought by Photius; while it is not impossible that Photius had in view some (possibly Manichaean) gloss on some passage in the collection of Acts.

about) resurrections of dead men and of cattle[1] and other animals. And the Iconoclasts believe that in the Acts of John there is teaching directed against the (holy) pictures (or icons).[2] In short this book contains innumerable childish, improbable, ill-conceived, false, foolish, self-contradictory, profane and godless things; and if anyone called it the source and mother of all heresies he would not be far from the truth." (Cod. 114: Henry, Vol. II, pp. 84–86.)

Information provided by Eusebius might give the impression that Origen already knew a similar collection of five apocryphal books of apostolic Acts: in his Church History[3] he writes as follows: "The holy Apostles and Disciples of our Saviour were dispersed about the whole world. Thomas, as the tradition has it, was allotted Parthia, and Andrew Scythia, and John Asia; and here he remained till he died at Ephesus. Peter must have preached in Pontus, Galatia, Bithynia, Cappadocia and Asia, among the Jews of the Dispersion; and when at last he came to Rome he was crucified head downwards, since he had requested that he might suffer in this manner. What need is there to speak of Paul, who 'accomplished the Gospel of Christ from Jerusalem as far as Illyria' (Rom. 15:19) and afterwards was martyred at Rome under Nero?—These are the express terms which Origen uses in the third book of his Commentaries on Genesis." However, this text has been analysed by Harnack,[4] who has shown that the quotation from Origen very probably does not include the reports about all five Apostles who are mentioned, but only those about Peter and Paul, and that the statements about Thomas (whose sphere of activity is given as Parthia, not India, as in the Acts of Thomas) and those about Andrew and John should certainly not lead us to postulate corresponding books of Acts as their respective sources.

On the other hand we may refer to the *Manichaean Psalm-Book* preserved in a Coptic translation, which according to C. R. C. Allberry[5] came into being about A.D. 340. There is a passage in its sixth part ($\psi\alpha\lambda\mu\omega\iota\ \Sigma\alpha\rho\alpha\kappa\omega\tau\hat{\omega}\nu$) in an account of the sufferings of holy men (see Allberry, pp. 142, 17–143, 14) which makes it clear that the author knew (certain) Acts of

[1] The miracle of a resurrection of the dead occurs in all the apocryphal Acts of Apostles; however a resurrection of dead animals is not related in the surviving Acts, if one excludes the reanimation of a dried fish in the Acts of Peter (the Vercelli Acts), 13. In the Acts of Thomas 41 the resurrection of a dead donkey is refused, but is in principle declared to be possible.
[2] Acts of John 26–29.　　[3] III. 1: Schwarz I, p. 188, 1–12.
[4] A. von Harnack, *Der kirchengeschichtliche Ertrag der exegetischen Schriften des Origenes* I (*TU* 42. 3), Leipzig 1918, pp. 14ff.
[5] *A Manichaean Psalm-Book, Part II*, ed. by C. R. C. Allberry (= *Manichaean Manuscripts in the Chester Beatty Collection* II), Stuttgart 1938, p. xx.

Peter, Andrew, John, Thomas and Paul,[1] and some characters which appear in these Acts are also mentioned in other contexts. There is an allusion to the same five Apostles in Faustus of Mileve (in Augustine, *C. Faust.* XXX. 4: Zycha, *CSEL* 25, pp. 751, 24–752, 5). When combined with these two references, two further statements acquire value. Philaster of Brescia mentions Acts of Andrew, John, Peter and Paul in the hands of the Manichaeans (*De haer.* 88. 6: Heylen, *CCh* 9, p. 256, 23f.), and the Manichaean Agapius,[2] according to an observation of Photius (*Bibl.* cod. 179: Henry II, p. 186), attributed special authority to the "so-called Acts of the twelve Apostles, especially those of Andrew". Both statements indicate the use of a collection of apocryphal Acts of Apostles by the Manichaeans. There is not much significance in the fact that they represent the content of this collection as different in some points from that presupposed by the Manichaean Psalm-Book and Faustus of Mileve. Philaster's omission of the Acts of Thomas in his account of the Acts used by the Manichaeans only means that he was insufficiently informed; and with regard to Agapius' "Acts of the Twelve Apostles" we may suppose, with C. Schmidt,[3] that perhaps it is only an inflated version of a title given to the collection of five books of apostolic Acts, "Acts of the Apostles", just as the Lucan "Acts of the Apostles" is called "Acts of all the Apostles" in the Muratorian Canon (l. 34: Preuschen, *Analecta*[1] II, 1910, p. 29; see above, Vol. I, p. 43) and "Acts of the twelve Apostles" in Cyril of Jerusalem (*Catech.* IV. 36: Preuschen, *op. cit.*, p. 81, 72f.). In any case it is sufficiently clear that the collection described by Photius appeared in the 4th century as a clearly defined corpus

---

[1] In the same account there certainly appears also a reference to the cup of poison drunk by the two sons of Zebedee (Allberry, p. 142, 22) and the stoning of "James" (*ib.*, p. 142, 25f.) who is not further defined but is probably to be taken as the son of Zebedee (cp. the confusion of him with James the Lord's brother in the Psalms of Heracleides, *ib.*, p. 192, 8f.). Between these references stand the remarks about John (*ib.*, p. 142, 23f.), to which they have very probably been added in order to supplement them by information about his brother, whereas immediately before this there was a reference to Peter and Andrew, the other pair of brothers among the Apostles (*ib.*, p. 142, 18–21). There is no occasion to postulate particular books of Acts as their source; the first reference must be derived from Mk. 10:38f. and parallels, the second from the tradition of Hegesippus about the Lord's brothers (see Volume I, p. 419).

[2] His name is first attested in the 6th century (the Shorter Greek Anathemas: *PG* 100, 1321 C), but he must have lived earlier, since by that time his "Heptalogus" seems to have been accorded classical authority among the Manichaeans of the Byzantine Empire. His appearance in a list of the twelve apostles of Mani given by Photius (*C. Manich.* I. 14: *PG* 102, 41 B) and Peter of Sicily (*Hist. Manich.* XVI: *PG* 104, 1265 C)—with which compare also the Longer Greek Anathemas: *PG* 1, 1468 B—can hardly be regarded as a trustworthy report which enables us to fix his date; nor can the supposition, which Photius makes in his analysis of the "Heptalogus", that Agapius appears to have disputed with Eunomius (*Bibl.*, cod. 179: Henry II, p. 186).

[3] *Die alten Petrusakten*, p. 30, note 1.

of apocryphal Acts in use among the Manichaeans; which prompts the assumption that it was the initiative taken by Manichaean circles that was responsible for uniting within this corpus the Acts which they found and took over, which had been circulating separately or in loose association among Christian sects, and in the case of the Acts of Paul within the Church itself (below pp. 323ff.).

As the Latin version of this collection gained currency Manichaeism seems to have presented the knowledge at least of the Acts of Andrew, of John and of Thomas as a "Greek gift" to the Latin-speaking world; these books first appear in the West with Philaster (minus the Acts of Thomas, see above) and Augustine[1] as writings used by the Manichaeans. However the corpus as a whole has not left clear traces either in the West, where it seems to have been adopted by the Priscillianists, nor in the East in reports from orthodox circles, apart from the account given by Photius. It may be accepted as almost certain that Augustine knew it as a fixed quantity, even if this cannot be clearly established by C. Felic. II. 6 (see below, pp. 184ff.); Evodius of Uzala may also be assumed to have known it in this form (below, pp. 183ff.); but otherwise we find only various combinations of individual units of the five Acts which, even if they may in some degree be seen as resulting from a diffusion of the Manichaean collection, may derive either from a knowledge of mere fragments of the corpus, or from a merely fragmentary knowledge of the corpus itself. The account of Philaster of Brescia has already been mentioned above. Innocent I, in a list of writings to be rejected, names among others those "under the names of Peter and John, which were composed by a certain Leucius: and that under the name of Andrew, (composed) by the philosophers Xenocarides and Leonidas, and that under the name of Thomas" (Ep. 6. 7: ed. H. Wurm, Apollinaris 12, 1939, p. 77, 34–37; PL 20, 205); the name Leucius (see below) shows that Acts are in question. Turribius of Astorga (mid-5th century) mentions Acts of Andrew, John and Thomas used by the Manichaeans and Priscillianists (Ep. ad Idacium et Ceponium 5: PL 54, 694). Finally

---

[1] Acts of Thomas: De serm. dom. in monte I. 19. 65 (PL 34, 1263); C. Adim. 17. 2 (Zycha, CSEL 25, p. 166, 6–17; C. Faust XXII. 79 (ib., p. 681, 6–20); all referring to a single episode, Acts of Thomas c. 6 and 8.—Acts of John: Ep. 237. 2 (Goldbacher IV, CSEL 57, p. 526, 14–24; reference to the hymn in the Acts of John c. 94ff. (for details of the lines from this hymn quoted in Ep. 237. 5–9, see below p. 227 n. 5); In Joh. tract. 124. 2 (Willems, CCh 26, ll. 24–34, p. 681): reference to the Departure, Acts of John, 106ff. All the passages cited refer to their source quite generally as "apocryphal writings"; however in C. adv. legis et proph. I. 20 (PL 42, col. 626) there are mentioned apocrypha "which are composed under the names of the Apostles Andrew and John", which may refer to the Acts of Andrew and the Acts of John; cp. the introduction to the account of the Acts of Thomas in C. Faust. XXII. 79 which mentions "apocryphal writings . . . composed under the names of Apostles". The Acts of Andrew are probably quoted in C. Felic. II. 6 (see below, p. 394 n. 2).

the pseudo-Gelasian Decree refers to apocryphal Acts of Andrew, Thomas, Peter and Philip in the same context (V. 2. 2—5; von Dobschütz, *TU* 38. 4, pp. 49f.) and elsewhere to the Acts of Paul and Thecla (V. 4, 9: *op. cit.*, p. 52); here too possibly the grouping together of Acts of Andrew, of Thomas and of Peter ultimately depends upon their association in the Manichaean corpus. Knowledge of this corpus appears to find its last feeble reflection in the assertions, of no value in themselves, about Leucius as the author of a whole complex of apocryphal literature which are made in the pseudo-Gelasian Decree, in pseudo-Melito and in two spurious letters of Jerome (below, p. 183).

Among the writers of the Greek Church perhaps two reports of narratives of the travels of four or five Apostles may be claimed as showing traces of a corpus of travel-narratives. The first is given by John of Thessalonica (d. abt. A.D. 630); he had prepared an edition of the Dormitio Mariae, because he held that this writing had been corrupted by heretics, and appealed in his Preface to the example of similar works: "We have indeed established that our most recent predecessors and the holy Fathers long before them used this procedure, the former with the various so-called Travels of the holy Apostles, Peter, Paul, Andrew and John, the latter with most of the writings about the Christ-bearing martyrs" (Jugie, *PO* 19, p. 377, 5–12); he seems to have regarded the later "ecclesiastical" Acts of Apostles (on which see below, pp. 571ff.) as revisions of ancient travel-narratives, of which, therefore, he clearly has no independent knowledge. Another list is given by the Stichometry of Nicephorus (above, Vol. I, p. 51); in its account of New Testament apocrypha it gives the first four places to the Travels of Paul, Peter, John and Thomas (ed. Th. Zahn, *Geschichte d. ntl. Kanons* II. 1, p. 300, 63–66). Lastly we may mention the combination of Travels of Peter, John and Thomas in a secondary compilation, the so-called Synopsis of pseudo-Athanasius (*PG* 28, 432 B).

Of the five apostolic travel-narratives belonging to the Manichaean corpus Photius observes that "as the book itself makes clear, Leucius Charinus wrote them". C. Schmidt—like Th. Zahn[1] before him—assumed that this formula expressed a mere personal judgment on the part of Photius; that is, he had not found this name attached to the whole corpus in his MS, but had inferred from the contents that this was the author's name, and had in fact taken it from the Acts of John; for these, together with the Acts of Peter, were the only books of the corpus which

---

[1] C. Schmidt, *Die alten Petrusakten*, pp. 27ff.; Th. Zahn, *Acta Joannis*, Erlangen 1880, pp. lxviif., lxxii; *Geschichte d. ntl. Kanons* II. 2, p. 856. Against this view cp. R. A. Lipsius I, p. 87.

he had read,—a point which Schmidt tries to support in an analysis of Photius' account, *op. cit.*, pp. 68ff.—and again, other witnesses to the tradition about Leucius refer to the Acts of John. This, then, was the only work to which Leucius' name originally belonged[1]; and it was used, as J. C. Thilo, Th. Zahn and R. A. Lipsius have also assumed, by the narrator speaking in the first person to designate himself. Yet it is hardly justifiable to treat the Acts of John as the source of all the references to Leucius that are found (the name Charinus occurring only in Photius; but see below, pp. 187f.). There is indeed no value in the attribution to Leucius of a whole series of apocryphal Acts (and sometimes other writings) in pseudo-Mellitus, or Melito, Preface to the *Passio Johannis* (*PG* 5, 1239), in the Preface of pseudo-Melito to an edition of the *Transitus Mariae* (*PG* 5, 1231) and in two spurious letters of Jerome (Tischendorf, *Ea*, p. 53; *PL* 20, 371; *PL* 30, 297); for here we have only developments of reports received at second hand.[2] Nor is the pseudo-Gelasian Decree decisive, for it only mentions "all the books which Leucius, the disciple of the devil, has made" (V. 4. 4: von Dobschütz, *TU* 38. 4, p. 52), giving no further particulars of these books, and perhaps indeed lacking any clearer impression of them. However, some valuable evidence is found in the first half of the 5th century. Turribius of Astorga says of the Acts of John, and of these only, that Leucius wrote them (*loc. cit.*). In Innocent I he appears as author not only of these, but also of the Acts of Peter: "*Cetera autem, quae uel sub nomine Matthiae siue Iacobi minoris uel sub nomine Petri et Johannis, quae a quodam Leucio scripta sunt . . .*" etc.[3] (*Ep.* 6, 7: ed. H. Wurm, *loc. cit.*, lines 34f.; *PL* 20, 205). Schmidt (*op. cit.*, p. 55) has indeed argued that the relative clause *quae a quodam Leucio scripta sunt* is not meant to include the Acts of Peter; but its inclusion must seem probable to any unprejudiced reader.[4] Lastly Evodius of Uzala connects Leucius with the Acts of Andrew: see his *De fide c. Manich.* 38 (Zycha, *CSEL* 25, pp. 968, 24–969, 6), where he tells of an episode that certainly derives

---

[1] J. C. Thilo, *Colligunter et commentariis illustrantur fragmenta actuum S. Joannis a Leucio Charino conscriptorum, particula I* (no more appeared), Halle (*Universitatis Literariae Fridericianae Halis consociatae programme paschale* 1847, p. 5 n.; Th. Zahn, *Acta Joannis*, pp. lxviii f.; *Gesch. d. ntl. Kanons* II. 2, pp. 859f.; R. A. Lipsius I, p. 117; C. Schmidt, *Die alten Petrusakten*, pp. 73ff.

[2] See Lipsius I, pp. 104ff. and 408ff. C. Schmidt, *op. cit.*, pp. 59ff.

[3] The account continues: ". . . *uel sub nomine Andreae, quae a Xenocaride et Leonida philosophis . . .*" (Wurm, *op. cit.*, p. 78, l. 36). J. A. Fabricius (*Codex apocryphus Novi Testamenti*, Hamburg 1703 [1719]², II, pp. 767f.) assumed that Xenocarides (which he read as Nexocarides; see Wurm's apparatus criticus) and Leonidas were distortions of Charinus and Leucius, and Th. Zahn (*Acta Johannis*, p. 209, App. to l. 10) and R. A. Lipsius (I, p. 84) followed him in this opinion; Gutschmid was probably right in distrusting it (see Lipsius II. 2, p. 430).

[4] Cp. W. Bousset, *ZNW* 18, 1917/18, p. 37.

from them which may be found "in the Acts of Leucius, which he wrote under the name of Apostles" (*op. cit.*, p. 968, 24f.).

Schmidt (*op. cit.*, p. 54) rejects the assumption that Evodius could have known the whole Manichaean corpus of Acts under the name of Leucius, and thinks it more probable that his wording is based on a misunderstanding of a remark of Augustine. For Augustine mentions Leucius and his work in his controversy with the Manichaean Felix. He wishes to establish that Manichaeism itself, by admitting the possibility of moral decision, treats its own dualistic view as questionable; and in this connection we read: "You have this also in apocryphal writings, which indeed the canon of the Catholic Church does not admit, but which are all the more pleasing to you for being excluded from the Catholic canon. Let me mention a point from them; their authority is not binding for me, but you shall be convinced by it. In the Acts written by Leucius (spelt "Leutius"), which he writes as if they were the Acts of the Apostles, you have it set down: 'indeed glittering deceptions and false appearance and the compulsion of visible things do not proceed from their proper nature, but from that man who through his own fault is corrupted by temptation'."[1] (*C. Felic.* II. 6: Zycha, *CSEL* 25, p. 833, 8–17). The same quotation, with the same indication of its source, occurs in Evodius (*De fide* 5: *ib.*, p. 952, 16–20), who possibly draws it from Augustine. Schmidt (*op. cit.*, pp. 50f.) thinks the most probable view is that Augustine, in writing against Felix, did not refer to the Manichaean collection of Acts as a whole, but to the particular Acts from which he quotes. The quotation cannot be further verified[2]; but Schmidt assumes, agreeably to his hypothesis, that it comes from the Acts of John. In that case Evodius misunderstood Augustine as connecting the name Leucius with the corpus as a whole, and therefore wrongly claimed it for the author of the Acts of Andrew, which he also cites. But this is a very disputable theory, and W. Bousset opposes it thus[3]: "It is hardly convincing to begin by referring (Augustine's) brief and ambiguous mention of Leucius' Acts of Apostles to the Acts of John, and then to claim that the valuable and detailed statements of Evodius are a misunderstanding of Augustine's evidence, as thus interpreted". Besides it is still the most obvious probability that Augustine, in describing the Leucian Acts as pretended Acts of the Apostles, meant to indicate the work that would be regarded by his opponent as the Acts of the Apostles, and possibly even bore this title: that is, the Manichaean corpus as a whole.[4] The

---

[1] On the passage quoted by Augustine see *Handb.*, p. 550.
[2] It perhaps derives from the Acts of Andrew; see below, p. 394 n. 2).
[3] *Op. cit.*, p. 37.   [4] Cf. Lipsius I, pp. 73 and 79.

other reasons advanced by Schmidt likewise cannot carry the burden of proof for his view. If, he argues, in *C. Felic.* II. 6 the name Leucius were assigned to the whole collection, and Augustine therefore regarded him as the author of the whole corpus, it is surprising that he never mentions him again, although he often refers to apocryphal Acts (Schmidt, *op. cit.*, pp. 50f.). But if Augustine knows of Leucius as the author of the Acts of John in particular, the question still remains why, even when clearly referring to these very Acts, he only writes in quite general terms of "apocryphal writings" and does not quote the author's name (see *Ep.* 237. 2: Goldbacher IV, *CSEL* 57, p. 526, 14–16; *In Jo. tract.* 124. 2: Willems, *CCh* 26, p. 681, 24f.). Schmidt also refers (*op. cit.*, p. 49) to *C. Faust.* XXII. 79 (Zycha, *CSEL* 25, p. 681, 6–26). Augustine here refers to an episode from the Acts of Thomas and gives as its source Manichaean "apocryphal writings" which are composed "by some fable-mongers or other under the name of Apostles". Had he known of Leucius as author of the whole corpus of Acts "he could certainly not have spoken in such a vague and general way of 'fable-mongers'." (Schmidt, *loc. cit.*) But this does not necessarily follow; it is quite possible that Augustine's wording represents an affected ignorance intended to indicate his contempt for the supposed author of the collection of Acts.[1] The student who wishes to learn anything about Leucius from Augustine must continue to be guided by the text of *C. Felic.* II. 6, the only passage in which he mentions this name; and according to the interpretation which suggests itself for this passage, the statement of Evodius that the incidents retailed by him from the Acts of Andrew are found "in the Acts written by Leucius", etc., must certainly be taken as a reference to the corpus of Acts as a whole.

Such is the extent of the slender thread of tradition about Leucius in relation to the apocryphal Acts of Apostles. The picture it offers may be briefly outlined as follows: Leucius appears at all events as author of the Acts of John (and of these alone only in Turribius); also of the Acts of Peter, according to Innocent I, and yet again of the whole Manichaean corpus, in Augustine and Evodius. If we now revert to the testimony of Photius, we shall hardly be able to expect a precise answer to the question where he could have found the name Leucius (Charinus), unless it actually stood in the title of his copy of the collection of Acts.[2] In any case it is an incontestable fact that he took Leucius to be the author of the whole corpus on the strength of the MS. that he

---

[1] Cf. W. Bousset, *op. cit.*, p. 38 n. 1.

[2] J. C. Thilo (*Colliguntur*, p. 5 n.) supposed that the name stood in the title, but was added by another hand on the basis of tradition about Leucius.

had before him; and the assumption that this was only a faulty judgment based on cursory inspection can hardly be sufficiently established. It must thus be concluded that three witnesses out of five ascribe the whole collection to Leucius. Hence W. Bousset has proposed[1] to regard Leucius as the "collector and reviser of a series of apocryphal Acts of Apostles" moving in Manichaean circles—that is, in effect, the creator of the Manichaean corpus. The remark about Leucius, the "disciple of the Devil", in the pseudo-Gelasian Decree would square with this (above, p. 183). But if this assumption means that the name Leucius, as denoting the author of a collection of Acts, appeared for the first time along with it, then to that extent it still needs to be modified or supplemented; the case for Leucius as the pseudonymous reporter of the Acts of John, even if the reasons for it given by Schmidt must be disputed, is in itself too probable to be easily excluded.

Epiphanius' account of the Alogi includes the statement that a series of psilanthropist heretics had frequently been attacked by "St. John and his companions, Leucius and many others" (*Pan.* 51. 6. 9: Holl. II, *GCS* 31, p. 255, 23f.). Nowhere else in the tradition do we find a disciple of John named Leucius, yet Epiphanius could hardly have invented him *ad hoc*; which suggests that we may look to the Leucius of the apocryphal Acts to account for this statement. Th. Zahn's assertion that Epiphanius owes the statement to his own perusal of the Acts of John has indeed been convincingly refuted by R. A. Lipsius and C. Schmidt,[2] but Epiphanius, or his informant, must have possessed some sort of information indirectly derived from this source. What can this have stated which could prompt the opinion that John's associates included a Leucius? It was certainly more than a general note about a certain Leucius who was the author of apostolic Acts; even a notice of their content, saying that a man of this name had recorded the travels of John, would not sufficiently explain Epiphanius' pronouncement. He must have already heard of a Leucius among John's associates. But suppose, first, that one Leucius was held by tradition to be the author of the Acts of John, or at least of those Acts amongst others, and secondly, that these Acts suggested the statement that John's associates included one Leucius; then it was absolutely bound to be supposed that the two must be identical, in other words, that the author of the Acts of John called himself Leucius and represented himself as a companion of the Apostle.[3] We may supplement this point by

[1] *Op cit.*, p. 38.
[2] Th. Zahn, *Acta Joannis*, p. lxf.; *Gesch. d. ntl. Kanons* II. 2, p. 857. R. A. Lipsius I, pp. 95ff. C. Schmidt, *Die alten Petrusakten*, pp. 31ff.
[3] On this point cf. J. C. Thilo, *Colliguntur . . .*, p. 5 n., and C. Schmidt, *op. cit.*, pp. 76f.

the following suggestion: if it be correct that the description of Leucius as a follower of the Apostle is derived from the Acts of John, this would indicate a particularly prominent position assigned to Leucius in the Acts; however, his name is nowhere mentioned in the very considerable portion of the work which survives (see below, pp. 193ff.); but this inconsistency is removed if it is concealed beneath expressions in the first person used by the narrator, who has introduced himself in the first portion of the Acts, which no longer survives. In that case the name of Leucius was originally connected with the Acts of John; therefore its reference to the whole Manichaean corpus is a later extension, attributable to the author of this collection, who appropriated the name for his work as a whole in order to invest it with the authority of one who was supposedly a follower of the Apostle, The name Leucius would thus cover two persons; it is first the pen-name of the author of the Acts of John who purports to come from John's circle, but secondly it was usurped by the originator of the Manichaean corpus of apostolic travel-narratives. If the Manichaeans could thus claim a fictitious apostolic authority, we see why Augustine with one exception never mentions Leucius, though he often refers to the apocryphal Acts of Apostles. He silence deliberately ignores, and thereby contests, the claim connected with this name. Again, our suggested interpretation of the statements offered by tradition embodies the beginnings of an explanation of the conflict of testimony between Augustine, Evodius and Photius on the one hand, and Innocent I and Turribius on the other, about the Acts which are to be attributed to Leucius. In the manuscript tradition the name Leucius must always have remained firmly connected with the Acts of John, since it occurred in the text of these Acts; but the labelling of the remaining Acts as "Leucian", being no doubt merely an inference drawn from external indications, in the form of titles or prefaces, perhaps, could easily be lost completely, as with Turribius, or in part, as with Innocent I.

In conclusion, and for the sake of completeness, we may refer to two further occurrences of the name Leucius. The first is found in Pacian of Barcelona (d. before 392). In his short account of the Montanists (*Ep. ad Sympronianum* I. 2: *PL* 13, 1053 B), distinguished by its complete ignorance of the facts,[1] he observes that the "nobler Phrygians" falsely pretended "to be inspired by Leucius". His source for this name cannot be determined, but the fact that he makes him combat the heretics suggests that he saw in him a person who could claim some authority, so that here he may be following some obscure piece of information about a

---

[1] See the analysis of R. A. Lipsius, I, pp. 93ff.

supposed disciple of the Apostles named Leucius.[1] Lastly the name occurs again in the Latin versions of the *Descensus*: the two resurrected men who write down the account of the *Descensus* are given the names Karinus and Leucius (A I. 3, *Ea* pp. 390 *et al.*; B I. 1, *Ea* pp. 416 *et al.*; see above, Volume I, p. 476). It may be assumed that there is some connection with the double name, Leucius Charinus, attested by Photius. Leucius' second name Charinus became known in the Latin-speaking world, and before the time of Photius. The fact that this double name could be regarded as a guarantee of valuable ancient tradition—which is how the *Descensus* was meant to appear—represents an echo, though weak and barely recognizable, of some knowledge of a legendary disciple of the Apostle named Leucius.

1. THE ACTS OF JOHN
(*K. Schäferdiek*)

INTRODUCTION

1. BIBLIOGRAPHY

Editions are listed below, pp. 193f. (Greek tradition) and pp. 201f. (ancient versions).

Translations: German, by G. Schimmelpfeng, in *Apokr.* 1, pp. 432ff.; partial German translation including summaries of the passages not translated: E. Hennecke in *Apokr.* 2, pp. 175ff. (revision of Schimmelpfeng's translation). W. Michaelis: *Die apokryphen Schriften zum Neuen Testament* (Sammlung Dieterich 129), Bremen 1956 (2nd edn. 1958), pp. 222ff.

English version: James, pp. 228ff.

Commentary by G. Schimmelpfeng and E. Hennecke, in *Handb.*, pp. 492ff.

Further Literature: Earlier works are listed by G. Schimmelpfeng, *Handb.*, pp. 492ff. and E. Hennecke, *Apokr.* 2, pp. 171ff.; see also the researches of J. C. Thilo, Th. Zahn and M. R. James in the editions of the text given on pp. 193f.—E. Amann, *Dictionnaire de la Bible, Supplément I*, Paris, 1928, cols. 491ff.—P. Corssen, *Monarchianische Prologe zu den vier Evangelien*, *TU* 15. 1, Leipzig, 1896, passim.—C. F. M. Deeleman, "Acta Johannis" (*Geloof en Vrijheid* 46, 1912, pp. 22ff. and 123ff.—A. F. Findlay, *Byways in Early Christian Literature*, Edinburgh, 1923, pp. 179ff.—E. Frhr. von der Goltz, *Das Gebet in der ältesten Christenheit*, Leipzig, 1901 (see Index 2d, s. v. Acta Johannis).—A. Harnack, *Geschichte der altchristlichen Literatur*, 2nd edn., Leipzig, 1958, Vol. I. 1, pp. 116ff.; Vol. II. 1, pp. 541ff.; Vol. II. 2, pp. 169ff.— B. Krivocheine, '*Ο ἀνυπερήφανος Θεός* (*Studia Patristica* II, *TU* 64, Berlin 1957, pp. 485ff.).—R. A. Lipsius, *Die apokryphen Apostelgeschichten und Apostellegenden*, Vol. I, Brunswick 1883, passim; *Nachträge* (Supplements), Vol. II. 2, *ib.* 1884, pp. 413ff.—H. Ljungvik, *Studien*

---

[1] See R. A. Lipsius I, pp. 94f.; C. Schmidt, *op. cit.*, pp. 40f.

zur Sprache der apokryphen Apostelgeschichten, = *Uppsala Universitets Årsskrift* 1926, *Filosofi, Språkwetenskap och Historiska Vetenskaper* 8.—W. von Loewenich, "Das Johannesverständnis im zweiten Jahrhundert", Beih. *ZNW* 13, Giessen 1932, pp. 102ff.—R. L. P. Milburn, "A docetic passage in Ovid's Fasti" *JTS* 46, 1945, pp. 68ff.—Δ. I. Πάλλας, ʽΟ ὕμνος τῶν πράξεων τοῦ Ἰωάννου κεφ. 94–97, *Mélanges offerts à Octave et Melpo Merlier* II =*Collection de l' Institut français d'Athènes* 93, Athens 1956, pp. 221ff.—F. Piontek, *Die katholische Kirche und die häretische Apostelgeschichten bis zum Ausgange des* 6 *Jahrhunderts (Kirchengeschichtliche Abhandlungen* 6, Breslau 1908, pp. 1ff.).—M. Pulver, "Jesu Reigen und Kreuzigung nach den Johannesakten", *Eranos-Jahrbuch* 9, 1942, pp. 141ff.—F. Rostalski, *Sprachliches zu den apokryphen Apostelgeschichten, Wissenschaftliche Beilage zum Jahresbericht des Gymnasiums Myslowitz,* Myslowitz, Upper Silesia, 1909-10.—H. Schlier, *Religionsgeschichtliche Untersuchungen zu den Ignatiusbriefen,* Beih. *ZNW* 8, Giessen 1929, pp. 97ff. passim.—C. Schmidt, *Die alten Petrusakten im Zusammenhang der apokryphen Apostelliteratur, TU* 24. 1, Leipzig 1903.—C. L. Sturhahn, *Die Christologie der ältesten apokryphen Apostelakten,* Heidelberg 1951 (Duplicated theological dissertation; also issued in micro-film, Göttingen 1952).—G. P. Wetter, *Altchristliche Liturgien: Das christliche Mysterium (Forschungen zur Relig. & Lit. d. A. & NT, NF* 13), Göttingen 1921, pp. 110ff.—Th. Zahn, *Geschichte des Neutestamentlichen Kanons,* Vol. II. 2, Erlangen, Leipzig 1892, pp. 856ff.—*id.,* "Die Wanderungen des Apostels Johannes" (*Neue kirchl. Ztschr.* 10, 1899, pp. 191ff.—*id., Forschungen zur Geschichte des neutestamentlichen Kanons* VI, Leipzig 1900, pp. 14ff., 194ff.

2. ATTESTATION

As the earliest witness for the existence of the Acts of John a sentence from the Adumbrationes of Clement of Alexandria has often been quoted.[1] Commenting on 1 John 1:1, he says: "It is reported in the traditions that John, when he touched (Jesus') outward body, put his hand deeply in; and that the solidity of the flesh did not resist him, but made room for the hand of the disciple" (Stählin III, *GCS* 17, p. 210, 12–15). This sentence corresponds to a passage in c. 93 of the Acts of John: John says that when he felt Jesus he sometimes encountered a solid body, but that sometimes "his substance was immaterial and incorporeal", "just as if it existed not at all". But for all their agreement in content the two passages differ so largely in detail that we can hardly assume direct literary relationship; we have rather the product of an esoteric oral tradition concerned with John.[2] Origen likewise cannot be adduced as a witness for the Acts of

[1] Thilo, pp. 20f.—Zahn, *Acta Jo.,* pp. cxl f.; *Neue Kirchl. Ztschr.* 10, 1899, p. 192, etc.—Lipsius I, pp. 512ff.—James, *Apocr. anecd.* II, pp. x and xvi—Schmidt, pp. 120f.—Hennecke, *Apokr.* 2, p. 173.
[2] Cp. Harnack, *Gesch. d. altchristl. Lit.* II. 1, pp. 541ff.; II. 2, p. 174; Piontek, pp. 25f.; but esp. see M. Hornschuh, above, pp. 80ff.

John (see above, p. 179); so that the earliest attestation[1] is still
its mention by Eusebius (*HE* III. 25. 6: Schwartz I, p. 252, 17),
who names it together with the Acts of Andrew "and of the other
Apostles" as an example of apocryphal Acts. Next to be considered is the indirect attestation by the *Manichaean Psalm-
Book*, which uses it as a part of the Manichaean corpus of Acts
(above, pp. 179f.). According to Epiphanius the Encratites used
"the so-called Acts of Andrew, of Thomas and of John" (*Pan.*
47. 1. 5: Holl II, p. 216, 5f.). Amphilochius of Iconium criticized
the content of the Acts of John. In a fragment[2] preserved in the
Acts of the Nicene Council of 787 there are the words: "This
would not have been said by the Apostle John, who wrote in the
Gospel that the Lord spoke from the Cross saying, 'Behold, thy
Son' (Jn. 19:26), so that from that day St. John took her to
himself. How does he then say here that he was never present
with her?" (Conc. Nic. II, section V: Mansi XIII, 176 B). He
here also alludes to c. 97 of the Acts, a reference which is confirmed
by the fact that his words were quoted during a discussion in the
Council about these Acts, in the course of which, *inter alia*, this
chapter was read shortly before.

Further Greek accounts do not appear till considerably later
(see below), whereas with the end of the 4th century the attestation by Latin writers begins. In Philaster of Brescia the Acts of
John occur in an incomplete account of the Manichaean corpus
(see above, p. 180). Faustus of Mileve treats the work as part of
this corpus (p. 180) and Augustine certainly knows of it from
the same source; he once names it expressly (*C. adv. legis et proph.*
I. 20: PL 42, 626; on which see above, p. 181 n. 1) and twice
uses the generally phrased reference "in apocryphal writings".
In his letter to Ceretius[3] (*Ep.* 237) he quotes some passages from
the hymn of cc. 94ff.,[4] which Ceretius had found in a Priscillianist
work, and in his 124th *Tractate* on the Fourth Gospel refers to

[1] On a supposed use of the Acts of John in ps-Cyprian, *De montibus Sina et Sion*, see below, pp. 210f.

[2] On the question whether this is a fragment of an independent work with the title "On the Pseudonymous Writings used by Heretics", or whether it belongs to the "Attack on False Ascetical Practice", of which parts are preserved, see G. Ficker, Amphilochiana I, Leipzig 1906, pp. 137ff.

[3] Piontek (pp. 47, 71) would identify this Ceretius with the Bishop of Grenoble of this name who is mentioned in the lists of those attending the Synods of Orange in 441 and Vaison in 442 (F. Maassen, *Geschichte der Quellen und Literatur des canonischen Rechts*, Graz 1870 [reprinted 1956], pp. 952–3); Ceretius of Grenoble could also be the man who with the two other bishops Salonius (who was present at Orange and Vision as Bishop of Geneva, *ib.*, pp. 951, 953) and Veranus sent a letter to Leo the Great in 450 (No. 68 in Leo's correspondence, PL 54, 587ff.) and who is mentioned once again in a letter written to Leo by Eusebius of Milan (*ib.* 97, 2; PL 54, 946 B). To have been a correspondent of Augustine's he must have been made a bishop in his late twenties, at the latest: but this is not impossible.

[4] A conspectus of the lines cited by Augustine is given below, p. 227 n. 5.

John's Departure (Acts of John 106ff.: *In Jo. tract.* 124, 2: Willems, *CCh* 26, ll. 24–34, pp. 681f.); he also mentions the legend of John's sleep in the grave and of the dust that poured out of it (see below, pp. 258f.); yet this legend is clearly not connected with the text of the Departure as known to him, but forms an independent tradition.[1] A probable allusion to the Acts of John, which will be discussed later (pp. 205f.) is found in Evodius of Uzala (*De fide c. Manich.* 40, Zycha, *CSEL* 25, p. 971, 1). Their apparent use in a few passages of pseudo-Titus, *De dispositione sanctimonii* (below, pp. 209f.) is not perhaps direct evidence, like Augustine's letter to Ceretius, of their currency among the Priscillianists, but brings them into close geographical and spiritual proximity with them.[2] Whether in this connection the so-called Monarchian Gospel-Prologues may also be quoted in evidence must remain uncertain, since the question of their origin and date of writing has by no means been convincingly solved[3] and further this evidence bears only on the Departure,[4] which was handed down independently of the ancient Acts of John. The Acts of John were mentioned by Innocent I (*Ep.* 6, 7: ed. H. Wurm, *Apollinaris* 12, 1939, p. 77, l. 35; *PL* 20, 502) and, about the middle of the 5th century, by Turribius of Astorga (*Ep. ad Idacium et Ceponium* 5: *PL* 54, 694), of whom Turribius at any rate must have known them himself. The pseudo-Gelasian Decree (see above, Vol. I, pp. 46ff.) does not specify the Acts of John, but it should perhaps be included under the rubric "All books which Leucius, the disciple of the devil, has made" (V. 4, 4: v. Dobschütz, *TU* 38. 4, p. 52)[5] so far as the author had any real conception at all of these books. The Acts of John were also drawn upon by the redactor of the Virtutes Johannis handed down in the so-called Collection of pseudo-Abdias.

---

[1] Cf. Zahn, *Acta Joh.*, p. xcviii; Corssen, pp. 100f.

[2] For a description of this work see A. de Santos Otero, above, pp. 141ff.

[3] Corssen (pp. 63ff.) thought they were produced at Rome in the first third of the 3rd century; but J. Chapman attributed them to Priscillian (see his *Notes on the early history of the Vulgate Gospels*, 1908, pp. 238ff.) and E.-Ch. Babut modified this theory to suggest a Priscillianist of the 5th century ("Priscillien et le Priscillianisme", *Bibliothèque de l'école des hautes études* 169, 1909, pp. 294ff.). Harnack at first followed Corssen (*Gesch. der altchristl. Lit.* II. 2, pp. 204ff.) but afterwards also accepted the later date (*Sitzungsber d. preuss. Akad. d. Wissensch.* 1928, phil.-hist. Kl., p. 322). A. Baumstark however has again argued for an early dating, Roman provenance, and for Greek as the original language ("Liturgischer Nachhall der 'monarchianischen' Evangelienprologe": *Jahrb. f. Liturgiewissensch.* 12, 1932, pp. 194ff.). However the pattern of the tradition of the Acts of John disclosed by the other witnesses (below, pp. 192f.) suggests a late dating of the Prologues, especially if they may be taken to have been originally written in Latin.

[4] Two passages of the Prologue to St. John are in question: the first (Lietzmann, *KlT* 1, p. 13, 12–15) corresponds to John's description of himself at the beginning of Acts of John c. 113 (cf. Corssen, pp. 92ff.); the second (*ib.*, p. 14, 1–6) relates the essential part of the Acts of John cc. 111f. (cf. Corssen, pp. 96ff.).

[5] See Schmidt, p. 56; v. Dobschütz, p. 290; on Leucius, see above, pp. 182ff.

Here, in the 6th century, the series of western witnesses is interrupted, but Greek attestation begins again, perhaps with Ephraim of Antioch, Patriarch from 527 to 545; but this must remain an open question, for although in a fragment preserved by Photius (Bibl., cod. 229; *PG* 103, 985–988) he briefly reproduces the content of the Departure as expanded by the legend of John's empty grave and the dust pouring out of it, and names as his source "the Acts of the beloved John and the Life which is used by not a few", he may be referring to a recension of the late Acts of John by pseudo-Prochorus expanded at the close. The ancient Acts are however mentioned by John of Thessalonica (d. abt. 630; see above, p. 182). But it is the Nicene Council of 787, already mentioned, which produces the most important evidence of all; its fifth session, among other matters, dealt with the Acts of John, which had been turned to account by the Iconoclastic Council of 754. Here, with the preface "From the pseudonymous Travels of the Holy Apostles", there were read out c. 27 and the first half of c. 28 of the Acts of John (*Aa* II. 1, pp. 165, 17–166, 12) as a document of iconoclastic sympathies, together with a great part of cc. 93–98 (*ib.*, pp. 196, 19–198, 4 and 199, 7–200, 9) as a general indication of the book's heretical character: see Mansi XIII, 168 D–172 C. In conclusion the evidences from the 9th century should be mentioned. The Stichometry of Nicephorus in its account of the apostolic travel-narratives (above, p. 182) assigns 2,500 lines to the Acts of John (variant readings are 2,600, 3,600), i.e. the same amount as to Matthew (ed. Th. Zahn, *Gesch. d. ntl. Kanons* II. 1, pp. 300, 65 and 298, 25). There is no significance in the mention in the Synopsis of pseudo-Athanasius (see above, p. 182). Lastly Photius in his Bibliotheca gives an analysis of the whole Manichaean corpus of Acts, which however seems to depend primarily upon the Acts of John (above, pp. 178f.).

The general picture produced by this attestation may be briefly outlined as follows: the Acts of John first come into view in the 4th century. Known to the earliest Church authorities only as a sectarian work, they may have belonged to the distinctive tradition of Encratite sects, probably located in Syria and Asia Minor, and must have been adopted from them by the Manichaeans. In the West they became known by the 4th century through the Manichaean corpus of Acts, and seem to have met with approval primarily among the Priscillianists and other representatives of rigorous ascetic discipline, especially in Spain. Here they can only be traced down to the 6th century; whereas in the East they long survived in traditions underlying or running parallel to the literature of the Church. It is true that the late Greek evidences we have quoted might give the impression of a merely antiquarian interest in the Acts of John; their use by the Iconoclasts might also be explained by the concern to produce ancient proof-texts at any cost. Nevertheless it must be observed that not only did sequences of stories from the ancient Acts of John find their way in various forms into copies of the "ecclesiastical" Acts of John of pseudo-Prochorus (and thereby secure their survival), but that even the passage from the Acts of John which is of the greatest interest for the historian of religion and theology but was most disconcerting for the theologians of the Church, John's "preaching of the Gospel" in cc. 87–105, found a copyist as late as 1324 (in the Codex Vindob. hist. gr. 63).

3. CONTENTS OF THE TRADITION

At its fifth session the Nicene Council of 787 pronounced on the Acts of John: "No one is to copy (this book): not only so, but we consider that it deserves to be consigned to the fire" (Mansi XIII, 176 A). In the West, three hundred years earlier, Leo the Great had given a similar verdict on the entire compass of apocryphal works concerned with the Apostles: "The apocryphal writings, however, which under the names of the Apostles contain a hotbed of manifold perversity, should not only be forbidden but altogether removed and burnt with fire." (*Ep.* 15. 15; *PL* 54, 688A.) These judgments sufficiently explain why the Acts of John have only come down to us in an incomplete state, and it is astonishing that so large a portion has nevertheless survived, about 70 per cent. of the whole work, assuming that the Stichometry of Nicephorus is correct in ascribing to it a length equal to that of St. Matthew's Gospel (above, p. 192).

(a) THE SEQUENCES OF STORIES PRESERVED IN GREEK. (aa) *Editions.* Systematic endeavour to reconstitute the Acts of John begins with the work of J. C. Thilo: *Colliguntur et commentariis illustrantur fragmenta actuum S. Joannis a Leucio Charino conscriptorum, particula I* (no more appeared), Halle (*Universitatis Literariae Fridericianae Halis consociatae programma paschale*) 1847, in which the fragments preserved in the Acts of the Nicene Synod were printed (pp. 14ff.) and discussed. Next C. Tischendorf, in *Acta apostolorum apocrypha*, Leipzig 1851, pp. 266–276, published the piece appearing in Bonnet as cc. 1–14 (below, pp. 195f.), and also the Departure (cc. 106–115), using MSS. P and W (below, p. 194 n. 1). Further progress was made by Th. Zahn's edition, *Acta Joannis*, Erlangen 1880, which presents the complete text of the late Acts of John of pseudo-Prochorus (below, p. 575), and the following parts of the ancient Acts: the fragments derived from the Council proceedings of 787 (pp. 219–224); the Departure, using here for the first time MSS. M and Q, together with the Syriac version found in Wright and the Armenian after Katergian (below, p. 202; Zahn's pp. 238–250), and the further material presented by M (pp. 225–234). The parallels to cc. 37–54 in Bonnet which appear in Q and the story about the partridge which follows them in this MS. (c. 56*f. in Bonnet; below, p. 197) are printed among the supplements to pseudo-Prochorus (pp. 187, 2–190, 22; cf. cxv, cxxxvf.). Knowledge of the Acts of John was materially advanced by the publication of the fragment preserved in Codex C by M. R. James: *Apocrypha anecdota II* (Texts and Studies V. 1), Cambridge 1897, pp. 2–25. Finally M. Bonnet, in *Acta apostolorum apocrypha* II. 1, Leipzig 1898 (reprinted Hildesheim 1959), pp. 151–216, has produced the normative edition and further enlarged the material already known.

(*bb*) *Content of the text.* Bonnet's edition presents the following series of narratives:

1. Journey to Rome, exile on Patmos, return to Ephesus: cc. 1–17* (which however cannot be assigned to the ancient Acts of John; below, pp. 195f.).

2. Journey from Miletus to Ephesus, and first events of the stay in Ephesus: cc. 18–37, init.

3. John's preaching of the Gospel: cc. 87–105. (For this departure from Bonnet's arrangement of the text, see below, pp. 198ff.)

4. Concluding events of the stay in Ephesus, and summons to Smyrna: cc. 37–55.

5. The partridge incident: c. 56*f.

6. Journey from Laodicea to Ephesus: Drusiana and Callimachus: cc. 58–86.

7. The Departure: cc. 106–115.

The transmission of the various sections is best shown by a table. Column I sets out the chapters as numbered by Bonnet, indicating with an * those chapters which are not printed in his text proper but only, where they occur, in the parallel versions printed below it. Column II contains the page and line numbers of the main text, showing the larger breaks which must be assumed by ***. Column III gives in italics the page and line numbers for the parallel versions. Lastly, Column IV exhibits the MS. evidence for the respective passages, that for the parallel versions being printed in italics.[1]

---

[1] The MSS. will be indicated by the symbols used by Bonnet:

A = Ambros. A 63 inf. (10th–11th cent.)
B = Athos Vatop. 379 (12th cent.)
C = Vindob. hist. gr. 63 (1324)
M = Venet. Marc. gr. 363 (12th cent.)
P = Paris. gr. 520 (11th cent.)

I	II	III	Γ	R/C	Δ	M	Q	Σ
1 – 2	151, 3–152, 4		Γ					
2 – 14	152, 5–160, 4	152, 22–160, 11	ΓV					
15*– 17*	* * *	160, 12–36	V					
18 – 26	160, 5–165, 16			R				
27 – 28	165, 17–166, 12			R				Σ
28 – 37	166, 12–169, 23			R				
	* * *							
87 – 92	193, 23–196, 18			C				
93 – 95	196, 19–198, 4			C				Σ
95 – 96	198, 4–199, 6			C				
97 – 98	199, 7–200, 9			C				Σ
98 –105	200, 10–203, 7			C				
	* * *							
37	169, 23–30			R				
38 – 54	170, 1–178, 15	169, 31–178, 30		R			Q	
55	178, 16–179, 5			R				
56*– 57*	* * *	178, 31–179, 30					Q	
58 – 80	179, 6–191, 2			R		M		
81 – 86	191, 3–193, 22			R				
106 –107	203, 8–206, 5	203, 15–206, 15	Γ		Δ		Q	
108 –109	206, 6–208, 10		Γ		Δ			
110 –111	208, 11–210, 8		Γ		Δ	M		
111 –114	210, 8–214, 14		Γ		Δ			
115	215, 1–4		Γ		Δ	M		

Of the MSS. named here, V, R, M and Q present their material as included in texts of pseudo-Prochorus. To establish the text of the Departure, Bonnet has also adduced the edition of it by Symeon Metaphrastes from Paris MSS., as well as the ancient versions to which he had access (on which see below). As a glance at the table shows, C and R occasionally exhibit the context in which *Σ*, the fragments read out at the Synod of 787, originally stood, and conversely this sequence presented by R and C, that is cc. 18–105 excluding 56*f., is shown by the Council fragments to be genuine texts of the ancient Acts of John. Unsolved problems remain over cc. 1–17* and 56*f.

(*cc*) *Chapters 1–17** have been rightly omitted by modern translators. This section contains, in two recensions, a narrative of a journey to Rome made by John, his banishment to Patmos and the return to Ephesus: this narrative was formerly connected with the Leucianic Departure-narrative. *Γ*'s recension is provided with its own introduction and so forms a self-contained narrative, while that of V is included in the Acts of pseudo-Prochorus. Its content is as follows: John is summoned from

Q = Paris. gr. 1468 (11th cent.)
R = Patm. 198 (14th cent.)
U = Vatic. gr. 866 (13th cent.)
V = Vatic. gr. 654 (11th cent.)
W = Vindob. hist. gr. 126 (15th cent.)
Γ = PWA
Δ = VRUB
Σ = Acts of the Council of 787. (For collation of the relevant passages of Bonnet with the MSS. cf. *Aa* II. 1, p. xxxi.)

Ephesus to Rome to see the Emperor (in Γ, Domitian, in V Hadrian, adopted from pseudo-Prochorus); on the way he dismays his entourage by his meagre diet of dates (one date a week according to Γ); on arrival he kisses the Emperor on the breast and the head, in God's honour, since (*Aa* II. 1, p. 155, 29f.) "it is written, 'The heart of the King is in the hand of the Lord' (Prov. 21:1) and again, 'The hand of the Lord is upon the head of the King' " (quotation of unknown origin); to prove the truth of his preaching he then drinks a cup of poison without suffering harm, allows the effectiveness of the poison to be demonstrated on a condemned man, and when he dies of the poison proceeds to revive him, but is then nevertheless exiled to Patmos, having, in Γ, meanwhile restored to life one of the royal chambermaids who had suddenly died; after the Emperor's death he returns to Ephesus, V making him float on a piece of cork to Miletus and travel thence to Ephesus. Bonnet himself (*Aa* II. 1, p. xxviii), following Lipsius (I, p. 482), pointed out that this narrative of journeys to Rome and Patmos in both its recensions shows too evident signs of a later date to be ascribed to the ancient Acts of John. But further, it cannot be supposed to consist of later revisions of a narrative in the ancient Acts, to judge by the impression of their structure given by the surviving fragments. In what context could such a narrative have occurred? It certainly does not fit the place which Bonnet assigned to it, as Zahn has clearly demonstrated (*Neue kirchl. Ztschr.* 10, 1899, pp. 194ff.); for the following chapters, 18ff., describe John's first arrival in Ephesus; he cannot therefore already have travelled from there to Rome. According to Zahn (*op. cit.*, p. 198 n. 2) it would fit best before the Departure, yet there is no reason to assume a break there (see below, pp. 200f.). There remain therefore the breaks at c. 37 and after c. 55; but neither can be considered. After c. 55 a travel-narrative has been lost, which did not place John in Ephesus (below, p. 242), whereas he starts from there in the narrative of the journeys to Rome and Patmos. To place this narrative in the break at the beginning of c. 37, which recounts the activity of John in Ephesus (see below, p. 224), is impossible because the journey to Ephesus reported in cc. 58ff. must then have been the third journey to that place and not the second, as stated in the heading preserved in Codex M; while the return from Patmos would have been the second journey thither. The whole narrative of the journey to Rome and Patmos is not based on the ancient Acts of John; it must rather be an elaboration of the tradition of John's banishment to Patmos, intended to serve as an introduction to a narrative of the Departure handed down independently of the Acts.

(*dd*) *Chapters* 56**f.* The passage given by Bonnet as cc. 56* and 57* is the incident of the partridge. This is found in MS. Q of pseudo-Prochorus, which replaces the end of that text by material derived from the Leucian Acts of John, presented in a form which is obviously later and diverges from the remaining witnesses. The transition from pseudo-Prochorus to this material is made by a summary: "After three days (viz. since his return from Patmos to Ephesus recounted by pseudo-Prochorus) John showed himself to the Ephesians and began to teach them, and some gave heed to his words, but others mocked him and went away" (*Aa* II. 1, p. 169, 31–33).[1] Bonnet's placing of this transition in parallel with cc. 30–37, the narrative of the healing of an old woman according to Codex R, is misleading. It is followed in both witnesses, R and Q, by the account of the destruction of the temple, where Q diverges considerably from R. Then in c. 45, according to R, John explains to the Ephesians that he will not leave them yet, although desirous of going to Smyrna, whereas Q shows the Apostle at work in Smyrna. The ensuing narrative of the raising up of the priest of Artemis (cc. 46f.) which in R is clearly connected with the destruction of the temple, is told in Q in another form as taking place in Smyrna, and concludes with a statement that John returns to Ephesus. R and Q then agree fairly closely in the account of the parricide (cc. 48–54). Following on this is R's account (c. 55) of John's being urgently summoned to Smyrna, and then follows a large break. Q on the other hand goes straight from the story of the parricide to the incident of the partridge, passing thence to the Departure. Since this incident does not come from Prochorus and is found in a context formed by narratives that certainly derive from the Leucian Acts of John, we are justified in assuming that it too comes from these Acts, especially since internal evidence does not conflict with this attribution. Since the transference of the action back to Ephesus in Q's c. 47 does not correspond with the course of events in the ancient Acts (it being necessary in Q because Ephesus is used as the scene of the Departure which is recounted as following directly from c. 57*), the position of the partridge incident in Q suggests that it belongs to the travel-narrative, which has disappeared but is to be inferred, coming between cc. 55 and 58 (below, p. 242); Bonnet has indeed indicated this by the numbering of his chapters. In any case the legend had a history of its own outside the Acts of John, for it appears as an "antiqua narratio" in an altered form and with a different moral in John Cassian (*Coll.* XXIV. 21: Petschenig, *CSEL* 13, pp. 697, 10–698, 3).

[1] On the passages immediately preceding this in Q's text of Prochorus see Zahn, p. 156, apparatus to l. 1, and p. 158, 22ff.

(*ee*) *The arrangement of the text.* Bonnet has inserted the passage preserved in C (c. 87–105) into the context of narrative presented by R between the story of Drusiana and Callimachus and the Departure; but this arrangement must be questioned. It is suggested by the beginning of c. 87: "Now those that were present inquired the cause, and were especially perplexed, because Drusiana had said, 'The Lord appeared to me in the tomb in the form of John, and in that of a young man'." The assumption is that the announcement of an appearance of the Lord to Drusiana in the tomb refers to the story of Drusiana and Callimachus in cc. 63–86, the most important part of which takes place in a sepulchre, and which further relates that John and his companions found there a heavenly being in the form of a handsome young man (c. 73), and also makes Callimachus tell of an appearance of the same being that he experienced there (c. 76). It is therefore of course necessary to assume a break between the story of Drusiana and Callimachus and the beginning of c. 87, in which an account was given of Drusiana's telling John and the others of this appearance.[1] However, some objections present themselves against making the story of Drusiana and Callimachus continue thus with cc. 87ff. Whereas Callimachus at the moment when the appearance came to him was present in the sepulchre alive and fully conscious, the appearance of Christ to Drusiana must have taken place when only her corpse was in that place, not her real self, as indeed it is said that it was her dead corruptible body (cc. 70, 77), her mortal remains (cc. 74, 76) that were involved. In such circumstances it is difficult to imagine an appearance of Christ having been granted to her in the tomb. Further, when she is raised up by John, she shows herself to be entirely perplexed and in no way prepared for this (c. 80). In her prayer in c. 82 she does indeed address Christ with the words "thou who hast revealed thyself to me with thy many-formed countenance". Yet in all likelihood this does not refer at all to an appearance that took place fairly shortly before; rather the prayer relates, in a clearly chronological sense, the proofs of grace which Drusiana has received from Christ, and presents the following points in order: (1) Christ has allowed her to see wonders and signs; (2) he has made her a Christian; (3) he has revealed himself to her as many-formed and has had mercy upon her in many ways; (4) he has protected her from the urgency of her husband Andronicus— it may be inferred from c. 63 that she had withdrawn herself from marital intercourse; (5) he has converted Andronicus; (6) he has kept her pure since then; (7) he has through John's agency raised her from death; (8) he has shown her Callimachus as a

---

[1] Cf. Schimmelpfeng, *Handb.*, pp. 520f.

converted man, to whom she no more causes offence; (9) he has given her inward peace. In this recital the revelation of the many-formed Christ, point (3), is widely separated from the events of cc. 63–86, points (7)–(9), and comes shortly before the argument with Andronicus before his conversion, which must be placed in the break at the beginning of c. 37 (below, p. 224).

We should have to content ourselves with establishing these inconsistencies if the narrative of Callimachus' attempted outrage upon a corpse in cc. 63–86 were the only event related in the Acts of John which shows Drusiana in a sepulchre. This however is not the case; in fact in c. 63 the friends who wish to dissuade Callimachus from pursuing Drusiana reproach him as follows: "Are you the only one who does not know that Andronicus, who formerly was not the god-fearing man he is now, shut her up in a tomb and said, 'Either I must have you as the wife whom I had before, or you must die'." That this is not an incidental remark, but a reference back to an episode already recounted, is shown by the *Manichaean Psalm-book*. This contains an account of the sufferings of holy men (Allberry, p. 142, 17ff.) which certainly draws upon the Acts of Apostles belonging to the Manichaean corpus, and which continues a description of the adventures of Thecla with the words: "Even so the holy Drusiana also suffered in like manner, being imprisoned for fourteen days like her master the Apostle" (*ib.*, p. 143, 11ff.); and in another passage (p. 192, 25ff.) which extols a number of women figuring in the apocryphal Acts it is said of Drusiana "A . . . who loves (her) Master is Drusiana, lover of God, who was shut in for fourteen days, during which she questioned her Apostle" (*ib.*, pp. 192, 33–193, 1). The Acts of John therefore included a narrative which told of Drusiana imprisoned alive in a sepulchre and which confirms the supposition we have made, and thereby renders the introduction to c. 87 more intelligible than does the context assigned to it by Bonnet.

But apart from this introduction, another passage in the section whose position is under discussion, cc. 87–105, can easily be explained on these lines. The exhortations concluding John's preaching of the Gospel, c. 103, contain the words "as He (the Lord) is everywhere, he hears us all, and now also myself and Drusiana. being the God of those who are imprisoned, bringing us help through his own compassion." This sentence becomes clear if we bear in mind that the first of the two passages just cited from the *Manichaean Psalm-book* presupposes an imprisonment both of Drusiana and of John, and that similarly in an account of his own sufferings John says that he was imprisoned for fourteen days so that he should die of hunger (*ib.*, p. 142, 24).

Obviously therefore the narrative told how Andronicus not only imprisoned his wife in the sepulchre but also caused John to be confined; and a miraculous release of them both, which is to be placed not long before the preaching of the Gospel in cc. 87ff., is the subject of the words we have quoted from the Apostle's address. Lastly, if the appearance of the many-formed Christ to Drusiana in the grave was related in the course of this sequence of narrative which is to be inferred, this would correspond with the order of the statements given in Drusiana's prayer in c. 82. The whole narrative must have stood in the break at the beginning of c. 37 (see below, p. 224); while the introduction in c. 87 and John's observation in c. 103 show that the preaching of the Gospel, that is the whole text of cc. 87–105, presented by Codex C, must be its continuation and therefore must also be placed in this break.

Bonnet's misplacing of this passage may lastly be shown by investigating the connection of the Departure narrative (cc. 106ff.) with what preceded it. In Codex R it follows immediately on the story of Drusiana and Callimachus, and the transition reads as follows: "John therefore kept company with the brethren and rejoiced in the Lord. But on the following day, being a Sunday . . ." (c. 106). Bonnet having inserted the text from Codex C between the two sections was faced with the question whether the sentence "John therefore kept company with the brethren and rejoiced in the Lord" belonged to the end of the story of Drusiana and Callimachus or to the beginning of the Departure. Bonnet with good reason decided for the latter alternative; for this sentence is presented with minor variations by U as the introduction to the Departure, and so also in a somewhat altered form by V, while the Syriac, Armenian and Coptic versions of the Departure have something corresponding, and the form taken by the next sentence in the parallel recension of Q is clearly influenced by this beginning: "As it was Sunday and he was keeping company with the brethren . . ." (*Aa* II. 1, p. 203, 16). In pseudo-Abdias (see below) the narrative of Drusiana and Callimachus concludes with the words "And he spent that day joyfully with the brethren" (Fabricius II, p. 557), which in view of the fact that pseudo-Abdias by no means gives a consistently literal translation may be regarded as completely corresponding with the sentence "John therefore kept company . . . .". This sentence certainly appears to be widely separated from the Departure by the narratives of Craton, Atticus and Eugenius, the destruction of the temple and the high priest Aristodemus (below, pp. 204ff.). But the following point must be borne in mind; after the story of Drusiana and Callimachus has concluded as described, pseudo-Abdias joins it to the story of Craton and its sequel with the words, "But on the following day . . ." (Fabricius **II**, p. 557); his wording therefore corresponds exactly with the beginning of the Departure in Bonnet's text,[1] running as it does, "And he spent that day joyfully with the brethren. But on the following day . . .". But this means that the whole sequence of narrative which begins with the story of Craton does not separate the sentence "And he spent . . ." from the Departure, but is rather inserted into the next sentence, which certainly belongs with it, "But on the following day . . .". This view of the matter is confirmed by the fact that the very largely re-edited Departure-narrative found in pseudo-Abdias, after an introduction which is of a secondary nature compared with the ancient Acts, begins with the words: "When the Sunday came (so ps.-Mellitus; Fabricius has "dawned") the whole multitude assembled" (ps.-Abdias: Fabricius II, p. 581; ps.-Mellitus: *PG* 5, 1249C), and that Bonnet's text agrees with this by reading "But on the following day"—at this point ps.-Abdias inserts the story of Craton and its sequel—"being a Sunday when all the brethren were assembled" (c. 106). Thus as regards the connection of the Departure with what precedes it, the source of pseudo-Abdias can be pictured in the same form as is presented by Codex R: the Departure follows in both witnesses immediately and without a break upon the narrative of Drusiana and Callimachus. On this hypothesis, however, Bonnet's arrangement of the text would necessitate the following assumption: both the Greek and the Latin tradition must have known the same sub-form which omitted the passage given by Codex C, which ostensibly fits between the story of Drusiana and Callimachus and the Departure, together with the transitional passages preceding and following it, between exactly the same limits; this presupposes that a shortened Greek recension found its way into the Latin-speaking world alongside the complete one which is also attested in the West by Augustine's Letter 237 (see above, pp. 190f.). But if we may assume that the Departure originally followed directly upon the story of Drusiana and Callimachus, and that the text presented by Codex C was originally placed in the position indicated for it by internal evidence, in the break at the beginning of c. 37, then no such improbable supposition is needed to resolve the difficulty.

(*b*) THE ANCIENT VERSIONS. A *Latin* translation of the Acts of John is shown by the attestation (above, pp. 190f.) to have been current by the end of the 4th century at the latest. Apart from the

---

[1] In the original this correspondence is clearer than in translation. Bonnet has: συνῆν οὖν τοῖς ἀδελφοῖς ὁ Ἰωάννης ἀγαλλιώμενος ἐν κυρίῳ · τῇ δὲ ἑξῆς . . . Ps.-Abdias: *et illam diem cum fratribus laetus* (Fabricius: *laetum*) *exegit. altera vero die* . . .

few lines cited by Augustine in *Ep.* 237 (see below, p. 227 n. 5) only two sections of it are preserved in a revised form, namely the story of Drusiana and Callimachus (cc. 63–86) and the Departure (cc. 106–115). They are found in the *Virtutes Johannis* in the so-called Collection of pseudo-Abdias (on which see Lipsius I, pp. 408ff.), in cc. IV.–XIII. and XXIf.; for the text see J. A. Fabricius, *Codex apocryphus Novi Testamenti*, Hamburg 1703 (2nd edn. 1719), Vol. II, pp. 542–557 and 581–590.

However, the source-material at present available affords no proof that the Leucian Acts of John as a whole was current in other versions than the Latin;[1] whereas the Departure-narrative, as a separate document, found its way into all the languages of the Eastern church, as is shown by the following synopsis:

In *Syriac* it is transmitted as an appendix to a life of St. John originally composed in Syriac; see W. Wright, *Apocryphal Acts of the Apostles*, London, 1871; text in Vol. I, pp. 66–72; English translation, Vol. II, pp. 61–68. The Syriac translation has a secondary version in Arabic (see below).

An *Armenian* translation of the 5th century, based on a Greek original, enjoyed a wide circulation and has made its way into Armenian biblical manuscripts. It has often been printed—a survey is given in *Bibliotheca hagiographica orientalis*, ed. P. Peeters, Brussels 1910, No. 474—including the Armenian bible edited by the Mechitharist J. Zohrab, Venice 1805, Appendix, pp. 27–29: ET by S. C. Malan, *The Conflicts of the Holy Apostles*, London 1871, pp. 244–248; and the separate edition with Latin translation by J. Katergian, *Dormitio beati Johannis apostoli*, Vienna 1877. The Armenian translation formed the basis of a secondary Georgian version.

Two *Georgian* versions, one derived from the Armenian, are mentioned by M. Tarchnišvili, *Geschichte der kirchlichen georgischen Literatur (Studi e Testi* 185), Rome 1955, pp. 342f., q.v. for editions.

Old Slavonic manuscripts containing the Departure of John are listed by N. Bonwetsch in Harnack, *Geschichte der altchristlichen Literatur*, 2nd edn. 1958, Vol. I. 2, p. 903.

A version in *Coptic* (Sahidic dialect) of the 5th or 6th century is preserved in a complete text and in six fragments. Textual variants which point to development within the Coptic tradition give evidence of a vigorous circulation. There are available

---

[1] The assumption that there may have been a Coptic translation of the whole Manichaean corpus of Acts including the Acts of John is not inherently unlikely, but cannot be proved. We know of Coptic fragments of four out of the five books of Acts that belonged to this corpus, namely the Acts of John (see below), of Andrew (see below, p. 391), of Peter (pp. 269f.), and of Paul (p. 326); but those of the Acts of John are useless in this connection, since without exception they belong to the Departure-narrative, which circulated widely in separation from the other Acts; so also those of the Acts of Paul, since this work was also popular with churchmen.

(a) a complete Coptic text in Cod. Brit. Mus. Orient. 6782, edited by E. A. Wallis Budge, *Coptic Apocrypha in the Dialect of Upper Egypt*, London, 1913, pp. 51–58, with ET, pp. 233–240.— (b) A fragment corresponding to Bonnet p. 203, 8–11, in Cod. Borgian. 274, printed by I. Guidi, *Di alcune Pergamene saidiche della collezione Borgiana (Rendiconti della Reale Accademia dei Lincei, classe di scienzi morali, stori e filologiche*, Ser. V, Vol. II. 7, Rome 1893), pp. 4f., Italian trans. *ib.*, pp. 5f.—(c) A fragment corresponding to Bonnet pp. 204, 1–206, 6, in Cod. Brit. Mus. Orient. 3581 B, printed by W. E. Crum, *Catalogue of the Coptic Manuscripts in the British Museum*, London 1905, p. 130, No. 295.—(d) A fragment corresponding to Bonnet pp. 204, 9–206, 7, in Cod. Vindob. K 9410f., printed by C. Wessely, *Studien zur Palaeographie und Papyruskunde* XV: *Griechische und Koptische Texte theologischen Inhalts* IV, Leipzig 1914, pp. 131f., No. 242 c. d.—(e) A fragment corresponding to Bonnet pp. 207, 1–214, 5, in Cod. Borgian. 136; edition in I. Guidi, "Frammenti copti, nota III" (*Rendiconti*, Vol. III. 2, Rome 1888), pp. 42–46; Italian transl., *id.*, "Gli atti apocrifi degli Apostoli nei testi copti, arabi ed etiopici" (*Giornale della Società Asiatica Italiana* 2, 1888), pp. 38–41.—(f) A fragment corresponding to Bonnet pp. 210, 9–212, 12, on Pap. Berol. 8772, edited by J. Leipoldt in *Ägyptische Urkunden aus den königlichen Museen zu Berlin* (published by the Directorate (*Generalverwaltung*) of the Berlin Museum): *Koptische Urkunden*, Vol. I, Berlin 1904, pp. 173–175, No. 182.—(g) A fragment corresponding to Bonnet pp. 211, 5–213, 3, in Cod. Borgian. 274, printed by I. Guidi, *Di alcune pergamene*, pp. 6f.

In the *Arabic* language are two secondary versions of the Departure edited by A. Smith Lewis, *Acta mythologica Apostolorum (Horae Semiticae* III), London 1904; ET *id.*, *The mythological Acts of the Apostles (Horae Semiticae* IV), London 1904. One of these (Arabic text, *op. cit.*, pp. 144–146, ET, *op. cit.*, pp. 168–171) has been translated from the Syriac along with the Syriac life of St. John; the other (text, *op. cit.*, pp. 46–51; ET, pp. 54–59) is based on a Coptic original and is connected with a homogeneous collection of late apocryphal Acts. On this collection see I. Guidi, *Gli atti apocrifi degli Apostoli nei testi copti, arabi ed etiopici (Giornale della Società Asiatica Italiana* 2, 1888), pp. 1ff.; R. A. Lipsius, *Die apokryphen Apostelgeschichten und Apostellegenden, Ergänzungsheft*, Brunswick 1890, pp. 89ff.; W. Grossouw, "Die apocriefen van het Oude en Nieuwe Testament in de koptische letterkunde" II (*Studia Catholica* 11, 1934–35), pp. 22ff.; G. Graf, *Geschichte der christlichen arabischen Literatur* I (*Studi e Testi* 118), Rome 1944, pp. 258f. Whether the Coptic original of the Departure-narrative was identical with the Coptic version mentioned above has still to be investigated; according to Graf (*op. cit.*, p. 259) the Arabic text was current in the second half of the 13th century; he gives a list of Arabic MSS. including the Departure independently of this collection, *ib.*, pp. 263f.

Lastly the translation of the Departure into *Ethiopic* was made from the Arabic as part of the whole Egyptian and Arabic corpus of apostolica not earlier than the first half of the 14th century. Text in E. A. Wallis Budge, *The Contendings of the Apostles*, Vol. I, London 1899, pp. 214–222; ET Vol. II, 1901, pp. 253–263. An older ET based on one MS. by S. C. Malan, *The Conflicts of the Holy Apostles*, London 1871, pp. 137–145.

Bonnet was able to use the following versions in producing his text: the Latin passages from the Abdias Collection, from MSS.; the Syriac text of the Departure, in Wright's edition; the Armenian translation, in Katergian's edition; fragment (*e*) of the Coptic version in Guidi's Italian translation; Malan's ET of the Ethiopic Departure-narrative.

(*c*) QUESTIONABLE MATERIAL IN PSEUDO-ABDIAS. Two narratives transmitted only in the Latin, found in pseudo-Abdias and pseudo-Mellitus who depends upon him, have often been attributed to the ancient Acts of John.[1] The first of them (ps.-Abdias, *Virtutes Johannis* 14–18: Fabricius II, pp. 557–573 = ps.-Mellitus, *PG* 5, 1242 B–1247 A) is connected to the story of Drusiana and Callimachus in the manner already described. It tells how Craton, a philosopher, gave in the forum at Ephesus a demonstration of the contempt for riches; he had persuaded two brothers to sell their inheritance and buy each of them a jewel, and then publicly to destroy these jewels; John pronounces this demonstration an act of vanity and quotes Mk. 10:21 (or parallels); Craton replies that he should restore the jewels in God's honour; the Apostle invokes Christ, and the jewels are reconstituted, upon which Craton with his disciples is converted and preaches Christ (c. 14) and the two brothers sell the gems to help the poor. Two prominent Ephesians follow their example and attach themselves to the Apostle, but upon seeing richly dressed slaves in Pergamum regret their action; John realizes their change of mind, tells them to fetch bundles of sticks and pebbles and after calling upon the Lord changes them into gold and jewels (c. 15); he then dismisses the back-sliders with a long speech, saying that they now have perishable riches again, but have lost the eternal; he quotes the story of Lazarus, Lk. 16:19ff., as expanded by an apocryphal narrative of the raising of a dead man, and refers to the resuscitations and healings which he has performed, saying that the back-

---

[1] Zahn, *Act. Jo.*, pp. cxiiff.; 235ff.—Lipsius I, pp. 427ff.—Hennecke, *Apokr.* 1, pp. 430f.; *Apokr.* 2, p. 175—James, pp. 257ff.—Deeleman, pp. 41f.

sliders have lost these spiritual gifts; and the speech concludes with pronouncements about the service of Mammon (c. 16). At this point there comes a widow whose son Stacteus, married only thirty days before, is dead; supported by the funeral procession she begs that he be resurrected. The Apostle performs this also, and causes the resurrected man to impress upon the backsliders that their one remaining hope of salvation is another resurrection from their spiritual death performed by the Apostle (c. 17). Thereupon the people, Stacteus and the backsliders, whose names are now given as Atticus and Eugenius, implore John's intercession; he counsels them to do penance for thirty days and then to pray that the gold and jewels revert to their former state. Meeting with no success they entreat John to intercede for them: his petition is heard, the gold and jewels are transformed and Atticus and Eugenius receive their spiritual gifts again (c. 18).

At this point there follows pseudo-Abdias' version of the Destruction of the Temple, and then the second narrative for which an origin in the Acts of John has been claimed (ps.-Abdias cc. 20f.: Fabricius II, pp. 575–580 = ps.-Mellitus, *PG* 5, 1247 C–1249 B). The high priest at Ephesus, Aristodemus, incites the people to violence; on being questioned by John he demands of him an ordeal by a poisoned cup. He then requests of the pro-consul two condemned men who are compelled to drink the poison and die on the spot. Then John, after calling upon Christ, drinks up the poisoned cup himself; when after three hours he remains unharmed, the people call out "There is (but) one true God, he whom John worships" (c. 20). Even so Aristodemus does not yet believe, but demands that the two poisoned men be first resurrected, at which the people threaten to burn him; but John quietens them and gives Aristodemus his cloak, instructing him to lay it upon the dead men and say, "The Apostle of our Lord Jesus Christ has sent me so that in his name you may rise again, that all may know that life and death are servants to my Lord Jesus Christ.". This is done, and the dead men stand up, where-upon Aristodemus hastens to the proconsul and tells him every-thing, and both are converted and receive baptism. They build a church (basilica)—c. 21—and this forms the scene of the Depar-ture, which is narrated immediately afterwards.

Evodius of Uzala seems to provide an indication that the story of Atticus and Eugenius with the transformation of the faggots into gold is an adaptation of the ancient Acts of John. In *de fide c. Manich.* 40 he brings a series of arguments against his opponents' denial of corporeal resurrection, and then writes: "And yet, though flesh itself is called grass (*foenum*, lit. 'hay') because of its present weakness, you believe that John made gold out of grass.

but you do not believe that almighty God can make a spiritual body out of a carnal body" (Zycha, *CSEL* 25, pp. 970, 31–971, 2). Evodius here clearly presupposes that the story of the Apostle's miraculous deed was generally known to those Manichaeans at least who shared his environment; it may therefore be taken as fairly certain that it belonged to a work which they regarded as authoritative, and that would be the Acts of John in the Manichaean corpus of the Acts. Evodius says that grass was transformed, not sticks as in pseudo-Abdias; and Lipsius (I, p. 428) sees this confirmed as preserving the original detail by the fact that some Greek authors speak of a transformation of grass, namely Theodore of Studios (acc. to Cod. Paris. gr. 1197; in Lipsius *loc. cit.*); Simeon Metaphrastes (*Comm. in div. Apost. Joh.* VI, *PG* 116, 701 D–704 A) and the Menaia for September 26 (*Synaxarion Ecclesiae Constantinopolitanae*, ed. H. Delehaye (= *Acta Sanctorum* LXII: *Propyl. Nov.*), coll. 81, 18–82, 10). Of these, Theodore of Studios gives no more than Evodius, namely a statement that John performed this miracle. In the other two witnesses, however, the miracle concludes a narrative of some length, which is quite unrelated to the context given by pseudo-Abdias. This suggests that the transformation of valueless material into gold is a motif, developed perhaps from Acts 3:6, which has attached itself to various parts of the legend of John, and therefore the narrative presented by pseudo-Abdias cannot immediately be regarded as an adaptation of the episode attested by Evodius; in this case, indeed, the fact that pseudo-Abdias does not mention grass, as Evodius does, tells rather against such an assumption. Naturally one must entirely disregard the stories combined with the narrative of Atticus and Eugenius, namely those of Craton and of the resurrection of Stacteus; there is no reason at all to attribute these to the Acts of John.

We must also suspend judgment on the possible derivation of the narrative of Aristodemus from the Acts of John, upheld by Lipsius (I, pp. 428f., 484ff.) supported by James (pp. 262ff.). The *Manichaean Psalm-book* (Allberry, p. 142, 23) certainly suggests that the Acts of John had a story about a poisoned cup; but this motif too, which derives from Mk. 10:38, is used several times in different contexts in the legend of St. John (see Lipsius I, p. 428f.).

(*d*) ISOLATED FRAGMENTS. (*aa*) *The Greek Oxyrhynchus Papyrus No.* 850 (Grenfell and Hunt, Vol. VI, pp. 12–18; Wessely, PO 18, 3, pp. 483–485) combines the fragments of two episodes.

Verso

f]or him[
]groans and[
]but John[
to Zeux]is, having arisen and taken[
5]who didst compel me . . . [
](him) who thought to hang himself; who the desper[ate
]dost convert to thyself; who what to no one is kno[wn
]dost make known; who weepest for the oppre[ssed
]who raisest up the dead[
10]of the powerless, Jesus, the comforter [of the
]we praise thee and worship (thee) an[d give
than]ks for all thy gift(s) and thy present dispen[sation
and] service. And to Zeuxis alone of (at?) the euchar[ist
]he gave to those who wished to receive[
15 beh]olding they did not dare. But the proconsul[
]in (into?) the midst of the congregation to [John
](and) said: Servant of the unnameable[
]has brought letters from Caes[ar
]and with[

Recto

20 went] forth (?)
A]ndronicus and (his) w[ife(?)][1]
When a few [days] had passed (then) w[ent Jo
hn wit]h many of the brethren to[
pa]ss over a bridge under which a river flowed[
25 and as] John went to the breth[ren
. . .] came to him in soldie[r's clo-
t]hing and stood in his presence and said, "John, i[n
to my] hands (*or*, into combat with me) thou shalt
shortly come." And John[
said, "t]he Lord shall quench thy threatening and
thine anger a[nd thy
30 transgr]ession." And behold, that man disappeared.
So when John c[
ame] to them whom he was visiting and fou[nd

[1] Line 21 is boldly written as the title to what follows.

them] gathered together, he said, "Rise up, m[y
brethren] and let us bow our knees before the Lord,
  who the gre[at en
emy's un]seen activity has brought to nothi[ng
35]bowed their knees together with th[em
  ]God[

That this fragment belongs to the Acts of John is suggested
both by the style[1] and by the name Andronicus, which occurs
among the characters found in the Acts (cc. 31, 105, 37, 46, 59,
61–63, 65f., 70, 72–74, 76, 79f., 82f., 86).[2] The order verso-recto
derives from Grenfell and Hunt, who are followed by Wessely
(*loc. cit.*) and Hennecke (*Apokr.* 2, pp. 178ff.). Grenfell and Hunt
argue (p. 13) that the incident involving Zeuxis found on the
verso must have been preceded by a description of the circumstances at some length which, if we make the recto precede the
verso, cannot have been fitted into the lines that are lost between
the end of the recto and the beginning of the verso. Wessely
(p. 485) adds that the text on the recto also requires an extended
sequel, since according to the title (l. 21) we have here a story
in which Andronicus plays an important part, yet in the papyrus
fragment he is not mentioned again. James (pp. 264f.) adopts the
order recto-verso, since he considers that the emperor's letter at
the end of the verso and its message requires more space than
merely a few lines. He starts from the premiss that this letter is
essential for the development of the story and that it led up to
John's exile, or to the martyrdom in boiling oil, or both. However,
the tradition of such a martyrdom of John, which is confined to
the West (above, p. 53) should not be claimed as belonging to
the ancient Acts of John (cf. Deeleman, p. 41); neither do they
seem to have recognized any such story of John's exile (cf. pp.
195f. above; Hennecke, *Apokr.* 1, pp. 428f.). It is better, therefore,
to retain the editor's arrangement verso-recto, arrived at on
internal evidence of the papyrus text itself. Where in the Acts of
John the fragment belongs cannot be determined. It can hardly
have stood before c. 31, since at that point Andronicus seems to
be introduced for the first time. In c. 37 he appears as a loyal
disciple of John. Hennecke therefore assigned the fragment to the
break at the beginning of c. 37 (*Apokr.* 2, pp. 175, 178f.) and
Sturhahn agrees (p. 16 n. 2). If we could assume that the title
"Andronicus and his wife" (the word "wife" being uncertain)

[1] Parallels indicated by Grenfell and Hunt, pp. 16ff.

[2] Blumenthal, *Formen und Motive in den apokryphen Apostelgeschichten*, TU 48. 1, 1933,
p. 26, gives reasons based on the method of composition to prove the attribution of
this fragment; but their cogency may be contested.

is prefixed to the incident referred to in c. 63, this would certainly be the right context; but it remains entirely uncertain whether this assumption is correct.

(*bb*) *The Latin work entitled "The apocryphal Epistle of Titus"* (see above, pp. 141ff.), contains two fragments of speeches attributed to John (ll. 437–440 and 460–477: see D. de Bruyne, *Rev. Bénéd.* 37, 1925, pp. 58f.) and one similar fragment which must have been uttered in connection with John (ll. 446–449: *op. cit.*, p. 59).[1] All three passages have been attributed to the Acts of John.[2] The first of them is certainly derived from the Departure.

Hearken to the thanksgiving of John, the disciple of the Lord, how in the prayer at his passing he said:

"Lord, who hast kept me from my infancy until this time untouched by woman, who hast separated my body from them, so that it was offensive to me (even) to see a woman."

(Lemma, ll. 436f.: Citation, ll. 437–440)

This is a shortened paraphrase of the beginning of Act. Jn. 113 (*Aa* II. 1, pp. 212, 6–213, 5). The two other passages have no parallel in the surviving text of the Acts:

Or is it outside the Law when we teach that even the demons when they confessed to the deacon Dyrus (= Verus?—see Act. Jn. 30, 61, 111) about John's coming—consider what they said:

"Many will come to us in the last times to drive us out of our vessels [viz. the demoniacs], saying that they are clean and undefiled by women, and not possessed by desire for them. If we wished we would gain possession of them also."

(Lemma, ll. 444–446; Citation, ll. 446–449)

Take also to heart the warnings of blessed John, who when he was called to a marriage went there only for the sake of chastity. And what did he say?

"Children, while your flesh is still clean and you have a body that is untouched, and you are not caught in corruption nor soiled by Satan, that most adverse and shame⟨less⟩ (enemy) to chastity, know now more fully the mystery of conjugal union: it is a device of the serpent, a disregard of the teaching, an injury to

---

1 The passages were first published without their context in the apocryphal Epistle of Titus by D. de Bruyne, *Rev. Bénéd.* 25, 1908, pp. 155f; they are also printed by A. v. Harnack, *Sitzungsber. d. preuss. Akad. d. Wissensch., phil.-hist. Kl.* 1925, p. 197.

2 D. de Bruyne. *Rev. Bénéd.* 25, 1908, pp. 149–160; 37, 1925, footnotes to text on pp. 58f. C. Schmidt, *ZKG* 43, 1924, pp. 337f. A. v. Harnack, *op. cit.*, pp. 187f., 197.

the seed, a gift of death, a work of destruction, a teaching of division, a work of corruption, a lingering . . . a second sowing of the enemy, an ambush of Satan, a device of the jealous one, an unclean fruit of parturition, a shedding of blood, a passion in the mind, a falling from reason, a token of punishment, an instruction of pain, an operation of fire, a sign of the enemy, the deadly malice of envy, the embrace of deceit, an union with bitterness, a morbid humour of the mind, an invention of ruin, the desire of a phantom, a converse with matter, a comedy of the devil, hatred of life, a fetter of darkness, an intoxication . . . a derision of the enemy, a hindrance of life, that separates from the Lord, the beginning of disobedience, the end and death of life. Hearing this, my children, bind yourselves each one of you in an indivisible, true and holy matrimony, waiting for the one incomparable and true bridegroom from heaven, even Christ, who is a bridegroom for ever."

(Lemma, ll. 458–460; Citation, ll. 460–477)

Hennecke (*Apokr.* 2, p. 171 n. 2) cautions us against the assumption that these two sections also are based on freely adapted passages of the Acts of John, on the grounds that the eschatological references given in both fragments would not be appropriate there. But one must not ignore the point that it *is* only free adaptation that is being considered. The complete rejection of marriage expressed in the third fragment is attested by Photius (above, p. 178) as a feature of the Manichaean corpus of apostolic acts. The assumption that ancient material drawn from the Acts of John makes its appearance here can certainly still be considered defensible; beyond this one cannot go. James (p. 266) has indeed supposed that the fragment ll. 446ff. comes from the lost beginning of the Acts; but other possibilities can hardly be excluded; and although Schmidt[1] ascribes the passage in ll. 46off. to the episode of Andronicus and Drusiana, there are no clear indications to go by.

(*cc*) It should be mentioned that a passage from the treatise *De montibus Sina et Zion* wrongly ascribed to Cyprian, which was produced in Africa before 240, has frequently been claimed as coming from the Acts of John.[2] However the various attempts to

---

[1] *ZKG* 43, 1924, p. 338.
[2] James, *Apocr. anecd.* II, pp. 153ff. Harnack, *Gesch. d. altchristl. Lit.* II. 2, p. 384. Zahn, *Forschungen z. Gesch. d. ntl. Kanons* VI, 1900, p. 196 n. 1. Corssen, *ZNW* 12, 1911, pp. 35ff. The passage in question, *De montibus Sina et Zion* 13, arises from a discussion of Wisdom 7:26 (Hartel, *CSEL* 3. 3, p. 117, 2–6): "For we too, who believe

find such a context for it rest so largely on mere hypotheses and
have so little inherent probability that they could only be undertaken at all on the assumption, which is no longer tenable, that
the Acts of John were already current in the West at the beginning
of the 3rd century. The picture of their circulation which the
attestation presents (above, p. 192) shows that these attempts
must be abandoned.

4. STRUCTURE OF THE BOOK

Enough of the text of the Acts of John has come down to us to
allow its whole structure to be shown in a table; items resting on
inference or conjecture are printed in italics; further details are
inserted at corresponding points in the translation.

First Travel-Narrative:
Journey from Jerusalem (?) in several stages, ending with
From Miletus to Ephesus (c. 18).
First Stay in Ephesus:
Lycomedes and Cleopatra (cc. 19–25)
The portrait of John (cc. 26–29)
Healing of an old woman (incomplete; cc. 30–36).
Conversion of Drusiana, and her dispute with Andronicus.
Imprisonment of Drusiana (in a tomb), and that of John.
Conversion of Andronicus, and release of Drusiana and John.
John's Preaching of the Gospel (cc. 87–105)
Introduction (cc. 87–88).
Christ's earthly appearance (cc. 88–93).
The Hymn of Christ (cc. 94–96).
Revelation of the Mystery of the Cross (cc. 97–102).
Concluding Exhortation (cc. 103–105).
Break, whose length and content cannot be determined.
Destruction of the Temple of Artemis (cc. 37–45).
Resurrection of the Priest of Artemis (cc. 46–47).
Encounter with a parricide (cc. 48–54).
Call to Smyrna (c. 55).
Second Travel-Narrative:
Journey from Ephesus to Smyrna (Pergamon, Thyatira, Sardis,
Philadelphia [?]) and to Laodicea; during this journey (?)
John and the Partridge (cc. 56*–57*).
Journey from Laodicea to Ephesus (cc. 58–59).
The obedient Bugs (cc. 60–61).

in Him, see Christ within us as if in a mirror, as He himself instructs and teaches us
in an epistle of his disciple John to the people: 'You see me in yourselves in like
manner as one of you sees himself in water or in a mirror'." Cf. Acts of John 95
(l. 25 of the hymn): "I (viz. Christ) am a mirror to you who know me," as well as
cc. 96 and 100f. Note that the image of a mirror is differently applied in ps.-Cyprian
and in the Acts of John.

Second Stay in Ephesus and Death of John.
  Arrival in Ephesus (c. 62).
  Drusiana and Callimachus (cc. 63–86).
  The Departure (cc. 106–115).
    John's last Act of Worship (cc. 106–110).
    Death of John (cc. 111–115).

5. CHARACTER

The literary character of the Acts of John places it as a whole in the class of "Apostelromane", or novels concerned with the Apostles (see above, pp. 174ff.). Unlike the other works of this sort, however, it does not make its hero suffer a martyr's death: the martyr's testimony that it describes—on the evidence of the *Manichaean Psalm-book* (Allberry, p. 142, 23f.)—consists in his being compelled to take a poisoned cup (above, p. 206) and being imprisoned for fourteen days to die of hunger (above, p. 199), whereas he survived both ordeals unharmed. It is also distinguished by the fact that besides the kind of speeches[1] that are common in this literature it includes in cc. 88–102 a long revelation-discourse delivered by John, which incorporates in its turn a revelational hymn (cc. 94–96), probably of cultic origin, and a revelation-discourse delivered by Christ (cc. 97–101); in respect of their form cc. 88–102 approximate to the Johannine type of Gospel. It is this "Gospel", which must be described as Gnostic, which gives the Acts of John its theological character. Christ's revelation-discourse, cc. 97ff., teaches the Gnostic to recognize that he may know himself to be akin to the Revealer, who as such is the Redeemer; and that the redemption introduces him into a cosmic process which fulfils itself in and through the Cross of Light (cc. 98–100); it is this that is symbolically represented by the earthly event of the Passion of Jesus, which thereby ceases to have any independent significance (cc. 99 and 102). The earthly form of Jesus has of itself no more importance than the Passion, and diversity of form is therefore the appropriate and distinctive manner of His self-manifestation (cc. 88–93). The dualism characteristic of the Gnostic world-view can be recognized in the separative function ascribed to the Cross of Light (c. 99; cf. 98) and is not as such the subject of further reflection in the Acts; though its anthropological aspect appears in the separation between the primordial Man who finds his form in the Cross of Light and the formless multitude standing apart from this Cross (cc. 98 and 100). Apart from its "Gospel",

---

[1] Missionary sermons, cc. 33–36, 39. Homilies, cc. 29, 103–104, 67–69, 106f. Prayers of various types, cc. 22, 41, 82, 85, 108, 109 (an eucharistic consecration), 112–114. An anathematism, c. 84.

Sturhahn has shown that the other material in the Acts of John admits an interpretation in terms of a Gnostic view of the world and of existence. He has further attempted to show that this material in its present form is shaped by Gnostic thought no less than the "Gospel" and so becomes the expression of a complete independent theological design; but this must remain an open question. Thus he regards the pronounced Monarchianism of the Acts of John (e.g. cc. 22, 24, 77, 82, 107f., 112) as resulting from the Gnostic view of revelation, according to which the Revealer continues in the state of transcendence and is not part of the content of his revelation (Sturhahn, p. 26; cf. p. 27); but he has failed to provide evidence for this assertion. Furthermore he poses a false alternative in contrasting his own view with one other possibility, that of interpreting the monarchian pronouncements as voicing a general "devotional (religiöse) modalism" (p. 26): modalism also took the form of deliberate theological pronouncement, and there still remains the obvious possibility that the monarchian features of the Acts of John accrued to it along with its narrative material as a non-Gnostic theological construction and that, with its "Gospel" on the one side and the narrative material on the other, quite different traditions have from the first been combined within it.

Earlier discussion of the Gnostic character of the Acts of John repeatedly attempted to relate it to Valentinian Gnosticism.[1] Two passages in the text serve to indicate such an origin. The most important evidence is provided by ll. 14f. of the Hymn of Revelation:

The one Ogdoad (i.e. the Eight) sings praises with us. Amen.
The twelfth (dōdecatos) number dances on high. Amen. (c. 95)

The Ogdoad and the "twelfth number" would then mean the Ogdoad and the Dodecad of the Valentinian system of Aeons. However this system of thirty Aeons includes also a Decad (cf. Irenaeus, *Haer.* I. 1. 3) which is not mentioned here. James (*op. cit.*, p. xx) has accounted for its omission by supposing that the relevant line has been lost. Sturhahn (p. 25 n. 2) also sees here an echo of the Valentinian system, holding that ll. 12–17 of the hymn, including the irregular phrase before l. 12 (below, p. 229), are an interpolation deriving from a circle "approximating to Valentinian Gnosticism". On the other side Schmidt (pp. 127ff.) has assumed that the Dodecad refers to the signs of the Zodiac and the Ogdoad to "the seven planets (or heavens) with the

---

[1] Lipsius I, pp. 523ff.; James, *Apocr. anecd.* II, pp. xx f.; Zahn, *Neue Kirchl. Ztschr.* 10, 1899, pp. 211ff.; Hilgenfeld, *Ztschr. f. wiss. Theol.* 43, 1900, p. 31 nn. 3 and 4; pp. 36ff.

Ruler of this World (or Satan) at their head"; he justifies this on the ground that the Acts of John presents no developed speculation about a system of Aeons, and here he is followed by Schlier (p. 163). In the second place, the pronouncements about the Cross of Light in the revelation-discourse of cc. 98ff. have been cited as showing the connections between the Acts of John and Valentinian Gnosticism, since they exhibit striking agreements with Valentinian speculation about the Cross as the Boundary (Stauros-Horos). Schlier (pp. 102ff., 175) sees here the appearance of an element "which can be described as a prelude to Valentinian Gnosticism" (p. 175). Sturhahn (p. 26 n. 4) has indeed shown by his interpretation of particular pronouncements that Schlier has regarded the Acts of John as approximating much too closely to the Valentinian system; but it must be insisted that the figure of the Cross of Light and its separating and stabilizing function (c. 98), as found in the Acts of John, reproduces a motif which is also found in Valentinian Gnosticism and is developed in their speculation; though this does not mean that we can assert direct connections between the Acts of John and the Valentinian system.

6. CIRCUMSTANCES OF COMPOSITION

Any attempt to indicate the circumstances in which the Acts of John was composed conducts us into the realm of pure supposition. It may possibly be the case that its "Gospel", as the fixation in written form of Gnostic traditions about John, originated from Gnostic Christianity in Syria; this might be confirmed by the fact that the puzzling $\tau\hat{\omega}$ $\dot{\alpha}\rho o\nu\beta\dot{\alpha}\tau\omega$ in c. 97 is perhaps to be interpreted as a rendering of the Aramaic or Syriac '^{a}rūbtā' (see below, p. 231 n. 4). The Acts as a whole, however, are possibly to be assigned to Asia Minor, which they make the scene of their Apostle's activity; the pronounced Monarchianism may also point to that district, which was the homeland of Praxeas and Noetus; however the information that has come down to us, setting aside a general tradition of the activity of John in Asia Minor and his death at Ephesus, contains nothing which can stand as genuine local tradition: on the contrary the picture of the Apostle's activity at Ephesus can hardly be thought to have an Ephesian origin itself, for the destruction of the Temple of Artemis in a Gothic incursion in 263 makes it extremely improbable that the legend of its destruction by John (cc. 38ff.), perhaps created by the Acts of John, could have gained a foothold there. The date of composition is equally uncertain. The fact that it is first attested by Eusebius and was received by the Manichaeans round about the same time (above, p. 190) suggests the 3rd century; there are certainly no compelling reasons for assuming an earlier date, even though the esoteric traditions connected with John, which are elaborated in the "Gospel" section of the Acts, are already detectable in the 2nd century, in the Apocryphon of John and in Clement of Alexandria (above, pp. 8off.).

THE ACTS OF JOHN

The beginning of the Acts of John is lost. The passage printed by Bonnet as Chapters 1–17* does not belong here, and is not derived from the Acts of John at all (above, pp. 195f.); besides, it is unlikely that there should be an account of legal action against John and of its consequences before his first arrival on the proper scene of his activity, as reported in Chapter 19ff.; though James (p. 228) makes this assumption. If we presume that the lost portions of the Acts of John came to less than half the length of the surviving material (above, p. 193) and that the episodes missing at the beginning of Chapter 37 and after Chapter 55 must have been fairly considerable (below, pp. 224 and 242), there is not very much space left for the opening part. There is some probability in the assumption that it told of John's departure from Jerusalem and his journey to Miletus (cf. Chapter 18). Also the narrator (Leucius, above, pp. 182ff.) must have been introduced, as well as Demonicus and the wife of Marcellus, at least, among the characters mentioned in Chapter 18. James further supposes that the second of the pieces which are reproduced with alterations in the apocryphal Epistle of Titus belonged to the lost beginning of the Acts (above, p. 210).

* The bad textual tradition calls for a considerable number of emendations and conjectures; these are noticed in the translation that follows by pairs of asterisks enclosing all departures from the text printed by Bonnet in Aa II. 1 (e.g. *wealthy* at the beginning of Chapter 19); a single asterisk * marks an omission from Bonnet's text; for conjectures on which no comments are made see Bonnet's apparatus criticus and Schimmelpfeng's Commentary in *Handb*. The German translator is responsible for the titles assigned to individual sections. ⟨⟩ denotes the restoration of a missing word, ( ) an explanatory addition.

From Miletus to Ephesus

18. Now John was hastening to Ephesus, prompted by a vision; so that Demonicus and his kinsman Aristodemus and a very wealthy (man named) Cleobius and the wife of Marcellus prevailed upon him with some difficulty to remain for one day

at Miletus and rested with him. And when they departed very early in the morning and some four miles of their journey were already accomplished, a voice came from heaven in the hearing of us all, saying "John, you shall give glory to your Lord in Ephesus, (glory) of which you shall know, both you and all your brothers that are with you and some of those in that place who shall believe through you." Then John joyfully considered with himself what was to happen at Ephesus, saying, "Lord, behold I go according to thy will. Thy will be done."

First Stay in Ephesus (Chapters 19–55)
Lycomedes and Cleopatra

19. And as we approached the city Lycomedes met us, a *wealthy*man who was praetor of the Ephesians; and he fell at John's feet and entreated him, saying "Is your name John? The God whom you preach has sent you to help my wife who has been *paralysed* for the past seven days and is lying there unable to be cured. But glorify your God by healing her, and have pity upon us. For while I was considering *with myself* what conclusion to draw *from this* someone came to me and said, '*Lycomedes*, enough of this thought which besets you, for it is harmful. Do not submit *to it*! For I have had compassion on my servant Cleopatra and have sent from Miletus a man named John, who will raise her up and restore her to you in good health.' Do not delay then, servant of God who has revealed you [or *himself*] to me; come quickly to my wife, who is only just breathing." Then John went at once, and the brothers who were with him, and *Lycomedes*, from the gate to that man's house. But Cleobius said to his servants, "Go to my kinsman Callippus and let him give you a *comfortable* lodging—for I am coming there with his son—so that we may find everything convenient."

20. But when Lycomedes came with John into the house in which the woman was lying, he grasped his feet again and said "See, my Lord, this faded beauty; look at her youth; look at the famous flower(-like grace) of my poor wife, at which all Ephesus was amazed! Wretched man, I am the victim of envy, I am humbled, my enemies' eye has fallen upon me! I have never

216

wronged anyone, although I was able to injure many, for I had
just this in view and was on my guard, so as not to see any evil
or *misfortune like this.* What use then, Cleopatra, was my
care? What have I gained by being known as a pious man until
today? I suffer worse than a heathen seeing you, Cleopatra, lying
there so. The sun in its course shall no more see me, if you cease
to *be my companion*. I will go before you, Cleopatra, and
despatch myself from life. I will not spare my vigorous health,
though it be still youthful. I will defend myself before Justice,
as *one* that has served (her) justly, though I might indict *her*
for judging unjustly. I will call her to account when I come (before
her) a (mere) phantom of life. I will say to her 'You have forced
me ⟨to leave⟩ the light[1] by tearing away Cleopatra; you have
made me a dead man by bringing this upon me; you have
forced me to anger Providence by cutting off my joy.' "

21. And Lycomedes still speaking to Cleopatra approached her
bed and lamented with a loud voice.

But John pulled him away and said, "Cease from these lamentations and from these unfitting words of yours. It is not proper
for you who saw the vision *to be unbelieving*; for you *shall*
receive *your* consort again. Stand then with us, who have come
on her behalf, and pray to the God whom you saw as he manifested ⟨himself⟩ *to you* in dreams. What is it, then, Lycomedes?
You too must wake up and open your soul. Cast off this heavy
sleep of yours! Call on the Lord, entreat him for your consort
and *he shall revive her*." But he fell upon the ground and
lamented *with all his soul.*[2]

John therefore said with tears, "Alas for the fresh betrayal of
my vision! Alas for the fresh temptation that is prepared *for
me*! Alas for the fresh contrivance of him that is contriving
against me! The voice from heaven that came to me on the way,
did it intend this for me? Did it forewarn me of this that must
happen here, *betraying* me to this great crowd of citizens
because of Lycomedes? The man lies there lifeless, and I know
very well that they will not let me leave the house alive. Why
tarriest thou, Lord? Why hast thou withdrawn from us thy

---

[1] Or, "You have robbed me of my light".—Translator.
[2] James by a simple emendation reads "fainting".—Translator.

gracious promise? No, Lord, I pray thee; do not let him exult who delights in the misfortunes of others; do not let him dance who is always *deriding* us! But let thy holy name and thy mercy make haste! Raise up the two dead who (have brought enmity) against me!"

22. And while John was crying aloud the city of the Ephesians came running together to the house of Lycomedes, (supposing him) dead. But John, seeing the great crowd that had come together, said to the Lord, "Now is the time of refreshment[1] and of confidence in thee, O Christ. Now is the time for us who are sick to have help from thee, O physician *that healest* freely. Keep thou my entrance to this place free from derision. I pray thee, Jesus, *help* this great multitude to come to thee who art Lord of the universe. Look at the affliction, look at those who lie here! Do thou prepare, even from those gathered here, holy vessels for thy service, when they have seen thy gracious gift. For thou thyself hast said, O Christ, 'Ask, and it shall be given you.'[2] We therefore ask of thee, O King, not gold or silver, not substance or possessions, nor any of the perishable things upon earth, but two souls, through whom thou *shalt convert ⟨those who are present⟩* to thy way (and) to thy teaching, to thy confidence, to thine excellent promise; for some of them shall be saved when they learn thy power through the resurrection of (these) who are lifeless. So now thyself grant hope in thee. I am going, then, to Cleopatra and say, 'Arise in the name of Jesus Christ'."[3]

23. And he went to her and touched her face and said "Cleopatra, He speaks, whom every ruler fears, and every creature, power, abyss and all darkness, and unsmiling death, the height of heaven and the circles of hell, the resurrection of the dead and the sight of the blind, the whole power of the prince of this world and the pride of its ruler: Arise (he says), and be not an excuse for many who wish to disbelieve, and *an affliction to souls who are able* to hope and be saved." And Cleopatra cried out at once with a loud voice, "I arise, Master, save thou thine handmaid."

---

[1] Cf. Acts 3:19.   [2] Mt. 7:7 and parallels.
[3] Acts 9:40 in the Old Latin and Sahidic versions and in the Peshitta of Thomas of Heraclea (the Harklean Syriac version).

And *when she had arisen* after seven days ⟨mortal sickness⟩ the city of the Ephesians was stirred at that amazing sight.

But Cleopatra asked after her husband Lycomedes. But John said to her, "Cleopatra, keep your soul unmoved and unwavering, and then you shall have your husband *standing* here with you; if you are not disturbed nor shaken by what has happened, but have come to believe in my God, who through me shall give him (back to you) alive. Come then with me to your other bedroom, and you shall see him dead (indeed), but rising again through the power of my God." 24. And when Cleopatra came with John into her bedroom and saw Lycomedes dead on *her* account she lost her voice, and ground her teeth and bit her tongue, and closed her eyes, raining down tears; and she quietly attended to the Apostle.

But John had pity upon Cleopatra when he saw her neither raging nor distraught, and called upon the perfect and condescending mercy, and said, "Lord Jesus Christ, thou seest (her) distress, thou seest (her) need, thou seest Cleopatra *crying* out her soul in silence; for she contains within her the intolerable raging (of her sorrow); and I know that for Lycomedes' sake she will follow him to death." And she quietly said to John, "That is in my mind, Master, and nothing else". Then the Apostle went up to the couch on which Lycomedes lay, and taking Cleopatra's hand he said, "Cleopatra, because of the crowd that is present,[1] and because of your relatives who have come here also, speak with a loud voice to your husband and say, 'Rise up and glorify the name of God, since to the dead he gives (back) the dead'." And she went near and spoke to her husband as she was instructed, and immediately raised him up. And he arose and fell to the ground and kissed John's feet; but he lifted him up and said "It is not my feet, man, that you should kiss, but those of God in whose power you both have been raised up".

25. But Lycomedes said to John, "I beg and entreat you in God's name through whom you raised us up, to stay with us, both you and your companions". Likewise Cleopatra grasped his feet and said the same. But John said to them, "For tomorrow I will be with you". And they said to him again, "There is no

---

[1] Cf. Jn. 11:42.

hope for us in your God, but we shall have been raised in vain, if you do not stay with us". And Cleobius together with Aristodemus and also *Demonicus* in distress of soul said to John, "Let us stay with them, that they may stay free of offence before the Lord". And he remained there with the brethren.

The Portrait of John

26. Then there *came* together a great gathering of people because of John. And while he was addressing those who were present Lycomedes, who had a friend who was a skilful painter, went running to him and said, "You see how I have hurried to come to you: come quickly to my house and paint the man whom I show you without his knowing it." And the painter, giving someone the necessary implements and colours, said to Lycomedes, "Show me the man and for the rest have no anxiety". Then Lycomedes pointed out John to the painter, and brought him near and shut him up in a room from which the Apostle of Christ could be seen. And Lycomedes was with the blessed man, feasting upon the faith and the knowledge of our God, and rejoiced even more because he was going to have him in a portrait.

27. So on the first day the painter drew his outline and went away; but on the next day he painted him in with his colours, and so delivered the portrait to Lycomedes, to his great joy; and he took it and put it in his bedroom and put garlands on it; so that when John saw it afterwards, he said to him, "My dear child, what is it you are doing when you come from the bath into your bedroom alone? Am I not to pray with you and with the other brethren? Or are you hiding (something) from us?" And saying this and joking with him he went into the bedroom; and he saw there a portrait of an old man crowned with garlands, and lamps and *an altar* set before it. And he called him and said, "Lycomedes, what is it that you (have done) with this portrait? Is it one of your gods that is painted here? Why, I see you are still living as a pagan!" And Lycomedes answered him "He alone is my God who raised me up from death with my wife. But if besides that God we may call our earthly benefactors gods, it is you, my father, whose portrait I possess, whom I crown

and love and reverence, as having become a good guide to me".

28. Then John, who had never beheld his own face, said to him, "You are teasing me, child; am I so (gracious) in form as ⟨ . . . ⟩ your Lord? How can you persuade me that the portrait is like me?" And Lycomedes brought him a looking-glass, and when he had seen himself in the glass and gazed at the portrait, he said, "As the Lord Jesus Christ liveth, the portrait is like me; yet not like me, my child, but like my image in the flesh; for if the painter who has copied my face here wants to put me in a portrait, then *he needs* the colours that were given you and boards [and an appointment (?) and . . . ?] and the shape of (my) figure, and age and youth and all (such) visible things.

29. But do you be a good painter for me, Lycomedes. You have colours which he gives you through me, that is, Jesus, who paints us all (from life) for himself, who knows the shapes and forms and figures and dispositions and types of our souls. And these are the colours which I tell you to paint with: faith in God, knowledge (*gnosis*), reverence, kindness, fellowship, mildness, goodness, brotherly love, purity, sincerity, tranquillity, fearlessness, cheerfulness, dignity and the whole band of colours which portray your soul and already raise up your members that were cast down and level those that were lifted up, which cure your bruises and heal your wounds and arrange your *tangled* hair and wash your face and instruct your eyes and cleanse your heart and purge your belly and cut off that which is below it; in brief, when a full ⟨set⟩ and mixture of such colours has come together into your soul it will present it to our Lord Jesus Christ undismayed and *undaunted*[1] and rounded in form. But what you have now done is childish and imperfect; you have drawn a dead likeness of what is dead."

Healing of the Old Women

30. Then he commanded Verus, the brother who attended him, to bring the old women (that were) in the whole of Ephesus, and he and Cleopatra and Lycomedes made preparations* to care for them. So Verus came and said *to John*, "Out of the

---

[1] So the German. But the Greek text might mean "unworn", "undamaged", cf. the metaphor continued in the next word.—Translator.

old women over sixty that are here, I have found only *four* in good bodily health; of the others ⟨some are . . .⟩ and some paralytic and others sick." And John on hearing this kept silence for a long time; then he rubbed his face and said, "Oh, what slackness among the people of Ephesus! What a collapse, what weakness towards God! O devil, what a mockery you have made all this time of the faithful at Ephesus! Jesus, who gives me grace and the gift of confidence in him, says to me now in silence, 'Send for the old women who are sick, and be with them in the theatre and through me heal them; for some of them who come to see this sight I will convert through these healings, *which may be to some useful purpose*'." (?)

31. Now when the whole crowd had come together to Lycomedes on John's account, he dismissed them all, saying, "Come tomorrow into the theatre, all you who wish ⟨to see⟩ the power of God!" And on the next day the crowds were coming while it was *still* night into the theatre, so that the proconsul heard of it and came quickly and took his seat with all the people. And a certain Andronicus who was praetor, and was the leading citizen of Ephesus at that time, spread the story that *John had promised* what was impossible and incredible. "But if he *can do* any such thing as I hear," he said, "let him come naked into the public theatre, when it is open, holding nothing in his hands; neither let him name that magical name which I have heard him pronounce."

32. So when John heard this and was disturbed by these words, he commanded the old women to be brought into the theatre. And when they were all brought into the midst, some lying on beds and others in a deep sleep,[1] and when the city had come running together, a great silence ensued; then John opened his mouth and began to say,

33. "Men of Ephesus, you must first know why I am visiting your city, or what is this great confidence of mine towards you,[2] (which is) so great that it becomes *evident* (or, I show myself) to this general assembly, (and) to you all. I have been sent, then, on no human mission, nor on a useless journey; nor am I a merchant that makes bargains or exchanges; but Jesus Christ, whom

---

[1] The text is probably corrupt.   [2] Cf. 2 Cor. 7:4.

I preach, in his mercy and goodness is converting you all, you who are held fast in unbelief and enslaved by shameful desires; and through me he wills to deliver you from your error; and by his power I will convict even your praetor's disbelief, by raising up these women who are lying before you—you see what a ⟨state⟩, and what sicknesses they *are* in. And I cannot do this if they *perish*; and (so) they shall all *be helped* by healing. (?)

34. But first I would sow this (word) in your ears, *to take thought* for your souls, which is the reason for my coming to you; not to think that this time is for ever, which is the time of bondage;[1] nor to lay up treasures upon earth[2] where all things wither away. Do not think if children come to you, *you can rest* on them, and do not try to defraud and swindle for their sakes. *Do not be grieved*, you who are poor, if you *have not* (the means) to serve your pleasures; for even those who have them, when they fall ill, pronounce (you) happy. And do not rejoice in possessing much wealth, you who are rich; for by possessing these things you lay up endless (or, inevitable) distress if you lose them, and again while *you have them* you are afraid that someone may *attack you* because of them. 35. But you who are proud of your handsome figure and give haughty looks, you shall see the end of this promise in the grave. And you who delight in adultery, be sure that *law* and nature alike *take vengeance* ⟨on you,⟩ and conscience before these. And you, adulterous woman, you *rebel* against the law without knowing where *you will end*. And he who gives nothing to the needy, although he has money *put away*, when he departs from this body and is burning in the fire, begging for mercy, he shall find no one to pity him. And you, hot-tempered and savage man, be sure that you are living like the brute beasts. And you, drunkard and trouble-maker, must learn that *you take leave* of your senses when you are enslaved to a shameful and filthy desire. 36. You who delight in gold and *ivory* and jewels, do you see your loved (possessions) when night comes on? And you who give way to soft clothing, and then depart from life, *will these things be useful* in the place where you are going? And let the murderer know that the punishment he has earned awaits him

---

[1] Lit. "of the yoke".   [2] Mt. 6:19.

in double measure after he leaves this (world). So also the poisoner, sorcerer, robber, swindler, and sodomite, the thief and all of this band, guided by your deeds you shall come to unquenchable fire and utter darkness and the pit of torments and eternal doom. So, men of Ephesus, change your ways; for you know this also, that kings, rulers, tyrants, boasters and warmongers shall go naked from this world and come to eternal misery and torment."

37. So saying, John healed all (their) diseases through the power of God.

* * *

The summary statement of the first sentence of c. 37 covers the disappearance of a considerable section. It must have concluded the story of the healing of the old women. Moreover a fairly lengthy narrative concerned with Drusiana and Andronicus can be inferred to have stood in this lost section, and Hennecke would assign to it the fragment of Pap. Ox. 850 recto (see above, pp. 206–209). Andronicus is mentioned for the first time in c. 31, where he figures as an unbeliever; he appears next in c. 37, but now as a loyal disciple of John. The lost section, therefore, must have told of his conversion. Further, his conversion must have been preceded by the narrative which can be inferred from c. 63 and from the *Manichaean Psalm-book* (above, pp. 198f.), which told how Drusiana was imprisoned in a sepulchre by her husband Andronicus, who wished to force her to abandon her vow of continence, and how the many-formed Christ appeared to her (cf. c. 87). Connected with this narrative, in all probability, there was also the account, attested by the *Manichaean Psalm-book*, of John's imprisonment for fourteen days for the purpose of starving him to death. An account of the miraculous release of both must then have been followed by John's preaching of the Gospel, cc. 87–105 in Bonnet's numbering. Since in c. 105 it assumes that Andronicus is a convert, it may be supposed that his conversion was in some way connected with the release of the Apostle and of Drusiana. Lastly, this sequence of narrative must also have contained a report of John's removal to the house of Andronicus which is presupposed in c. 46. The only part of this whole section which is preserved, apart from the doubtful possibility of including Pap. Ox. 850, is John's Preaching of the Gospel.

John's Preaching of the Gospel (cc. 87–105)
Introduction to the Preaching

87. Now those that were present enquired the cause, and were especially perplexed, because *Drusiana* had said, "The Lord

appeared to me in the tomb *in the form of John* and in that of a young man." So since they were perplexed and in some ways not yet established in the faith, John took it patiently and said, (88) "Men and brethren, you have experienced nothing strange or incredible in your perception of the ⟨Lord⟩, since even we whom he chose to be his apostles have suffered many temptations; and I cannot ⟨either⟩ *speak* or write to you the things which I have seen and heard. *Yet* now I must adapt myself to your hearing and according to each man's capacity I will impart to you *those things* of which you can be hearers, that you may know the glory which surrounds him that was and is both now and evermore.

Christ's Earthly Appearance

For when he had chosen Peter and Andrew, who were brothers, he came to me and to my brother James, saying 'I need you; come with me!'[1] And my brother said this to me, 'John, what does he want, this child on the shore who called us?' And I said, 'Which child?' And he answered me, 'The one who is beckoning to us.' And I said 'This is because of the long watch we have kept at sea. You are not seeing straight, brother James. Do you not see the man standing there who is handsome, fair and cheerful-looking?' But he said to me, 'I do not see *that man*, my brother. But *let us go*, and we will see what this means.'

89. And when we had brought the boat *to land* we saw how he also helped us to beach the boat. And as we left the place, wishing to *follow* him, he appeared to me again as rather bald-⟨headed⟩ but with a *thick* flowing beard, but to James as a young man whose beard was just beginning. So we *wondered* both of us about the meaning of the vision we had seen. Then as we both followed him we became gradually ⟨more⟩ perplexed about this matter.

But then there appeared to me a yet more amazing sight; I tried to see him as he was, and I never saw his eyes *closing*, but always open. But he sometimes *appeared* to me as a small man with no good looks, and *then again* as looking up to heaven. And he had another strange (property); when I reclined

[1] Cf. Mk. 1:16–20 and pars.

at table he *would take* me to his own breast,[1] and I held him (fast); and sometimes his breast felt to me smooth and soft, but sometimes *hard* like rock; so that I was perplexed in my (mind) and *said,* 'Why do I find it *so*?' And as I thought about it, he . . .

90. Another time he took me and James and Peter to the mountain where he used to pray, and we saw ⟨on⟩ him a light[2] such that a man, *who uses* mortal speech, cannot describe what it was like. Again he took us three likewise up the mountain, saying 'Come with me'. And again we went; and we saw him at a distance praying. Then I, since he loved me,[3] went quietly up to him, as if he (*)could not *see*, and stood looking(*) at his hinder parts; and I saw him not dressed in clothes at all, but stripped *of those* ⟨that⟩ we (usually) *saw* (upon him), and not like a man at all. (And I saw that) his feet (*) were whiter than snow, so that the ground there was lit up by his feet; and that his head stretched up to heaven, so that I was afraid and cried out; and he, turning about, appeared as a small man and *caught hold of* my beard and pulled it and said to me, 'John, do not be faithless, but believing,[4] and not inquisitive.' And I said to him, 'Why, Lord, what have I done?' But I tell you, my brethren, that I suffered such pain for *thirty* days in the place where he touched my beard, that I said to him, 'Lord, if your playful tug has caused such pain, what (would it be) if you had dealt *me* a blow?' And he said to me, '*Let it be* your concern from now on not to tempt him that cannot be tempted.'

91. But *Peter* and *James* were *vexed* as I spoke with the Lord, and beckoned me to come to them and leave *the Lord alone*. And I went, and they both said to me, 'Who *was* it who spoke with the Lord when *he was* on the (mountain-) top? For *we heard* them both speaking.' And when *I considered* his abundant grace and his unity within many faces and his unceasing wisdom that *looks* after us, I said, 'You shall learn this *from him* if you ask him.'

92. And again when we—that is, all his disciples—*were sleeping* in one house at Gennesaret, I wrapped myself *in*

---

[1] Cf. Jn. 13:23, 25.   [2] Cf. Mk. 9:2f. and pars.
[3] Jn. 20:2.   [4] Jn. 20:27.

my cloak and watched by myself (to see) what he was doing.
And first I heard him say, 'John, go to sleep'. Then I pretended
to sleep; and I saw another like *him coming down*,[1] *and I
heard* him also saying to my Lord, 'Jesus, the men you have
chosen still disbelieve you'. And my Lord said to him, 'You are
right; for they are *men*.'

93. I *will tell* you another glory, brethren; sometimes when
I meant to touch him I encountered a material, solid body; but
at other times again when I felt him, his substance was immaterial
and incorporeal, and as if it did not exist at all.

And if ever he were invited by one of the Pharisees and went
(where) he was invited,[2] we went with him; and one loaf was
laid before each one of us by those who had invited (us), and so
he also would take one; but he would bless his and divide it
among us; and every man was satisfied by that little (piece),[3]
and our own loaves were kept intact, so that those who had
invited him were amazed.

And I often wished, as I walked with him, to see his footprint
in the earth, whether it appeared—for I saw him raising himself
from the earth—and I never saw it. And I tell you this much,
my brethren, so as to encourage your faith in him: for his miracles
and wonderful works must not be told for the moment, for they
are unspeakable and, perhaps, can neither be uttered nor heard.

The Hymn of Christ

94. But before he was arrested by the lawless Jews, whose lawgiver is the lawless serpent, he assembled us all and said, 'Before
I am delivered to them, let us sing a hymn to the Father,[4] and
so go to meet what lies before (us).' So he told us to form a circle,
holding one another's hands, and himself stood in the middle and
said, 'Answer Amen to me'. So he began to sing the hymn and
to say,[5]

[1] For the Lord's double cf. Pistis Sophia 61 (Schmidt–Till, *GCS* 45, pp. 77f.); see
above, Vol. I, p. 257.
[2] Cf. Lk. 7:36; 11:37; 14:1.   [3] Cf. Mk. 6:35–44 and pars.
[4] Cf. Mk. 14:26 and pars.
[5] The hymn which now follows has been thoroughly investigated by Pallas to
determine its formal structure, and this investigation has suggested the division into
lines of verse which is adopted in the translation, with sequences of three units in the
prologue and the concluding doxology and of two units in the rest of the hymn.
Pallas has gone farther and arranged the whole hymn in regular stanzas; but this

1. 'Glory be to thee, Father.'

And we circled round him and answered him, 'Amen'.[1]

'Glory be to thee, Logos:
Glory be to thee, Grace.'—'Amen.'

2. 'Glory be to thee, Spirit:
Glory be to thee, Holy One:
Glory be to thy Glory.'—'Amen.'

3. 'We praise thee, Father:
We thank thee, Light:
In whom darkness dwelleth not.'[2]—'Amen.'

95. 'And why we give thanks, I tell you:[3]

4. 'I will be saved,
And I will save.'[4]—'Amen.'

5. 'I will be loosed,
And I will loose.'—'Amen.'

6. 'I will be wounded,
And I will wound.'—'Amen.'

7. 'I will be born,
And I will bear.'—'Amen.'

8. 'I will eat,
And I will be eaten.'—'Amen.'

arrangement has not been adopted here, since it does not seem possible to execute it neatly throughout. The (German) translator is responsible for the numbering of the lines of verse.

Some fragments of the hymn are quoted by Augustine in *Ep.* 237, 5-9 (see above, pp. 190f.) and may be collected here: the numbers preceding them denote the lines of the hymn, those following them in brackets give the context of quotation in Goldbacher IV, *CSEL* 57:

4b, a: I will save, and I will be saved (p. 530, 17).
5b, a: I will loose, and I will be loosed (p. 529, 3 and 29).
7a: I will be born (p. 531, 4).
12: I will sing, dance all of you (p. 531, 7 and 9).
13: I will lament, beat you all yourselves (p. 531, 12).
19: I will adorn, and I will be adorned (p. 531, 13f.).
24: I am a lamp to you who see me (p. 531, 18).
26: I am a door to you who knock on me (p. 531, 20f.).
30: You who see what I do, keep silence about my works (p. 531, 26).
48: By the Word I mocked at all things, and I was not mocked at all (p. 532, 17f.).

[1] This line is due to the insertion of the hymn into the Acts and its "Gospel".
[2] Cf. 1 Jn. 1:5; James 1:17.
[3] Pallas (p. 226 n. 1) would emend λέγω to λέγε, "tell (me)!", regarding the line as a liturgical direction. However if one interprets it as an introduction to the hymn's first main section, which follows here, the first person is perfectly possible.
[4] The word "will" in this and the following verses has its full significance; "it is my will to be saved"; not simply "I shall be saved."—Translator.

9. 'I will hear,
   And I will be heard.'—'Amen.'
10. 'I will be thought,
   Being wholly thought.'—'Amen.'
11. 'I will be washed,
   And I will *wash*.'[1]—'Amen.'

Grace dances.[2]

12. 'I will pipe,
   Dance, all of you.'—'Amen.'
13. 'I will mourn,
   Beat you all your breasts.'[3]—'Amen.'
14. '(The) one Ogdoad[4]
   sings praises with us.'—'Amen.'
15. 'The twelfth number
   dances on high.'—'Amen.'
16. '*To the Universe*
   belongs *the dancer*.'[5]—'Amen.'
17. 'He who does not dance
   does not know what happens.'[6]—'Amen.'
18. 'I will flee,
   and I will remain.'—'Amen.'
19. 'I will adorn,
   and I will *be adorned*.'—'Amen.'
20. 'I will be united,
   and I will *unite*.'—'Amen.'
21. 'I have no house,
   and I have houses.'—'Amen.'

[1] λοῦσαι is to be read here, with Pallas, instead of λούειν; cf. the aorist infinitive of the preceding lines.
[2] The line interrupts the structure of the hymn, both in form and content. Pallas (p. 227 n. 1) takes it as a liturgical direction. Grace (χάρις) on this theory would be "perhaps an ecclesiastical office"; but this is very doubtful.
[3] Cf. Mt. 11:17 and pars.
[4] I.e. the number eight, or the eightfold power (cf. above, p. 213)—(Translator).— Lines 14–17 do not display the progressive and antithetical parallelism of the preceding and following lines; Pallas (pp. 224f.) would assume that originally they did not belong here, but were inserted after lines 12f. owing to an association of ideas, namely self-expression through music and rhythm.
[5] Cod. C: τῷ δὲ ὅλων ᾧ χορεύειν ὑπάρχει. Pallas conjectures, τῷ δὲ ὅλῳ ὁ χορεύων ὑπάρχει. Other suggestions in Bonnet's notes ad loc.
[6] Pallas (p. 227) reads, metri gratia, ἀγνοεῖ τὸ γινόμενον instead of τὸ γιν. ἀγν. (Cod. C), and moreover would transpose ll. 16 and 17.

22. 'I have no place,
    and I have places.'—'Amen.'

23. 'I have no temple
    and I have temples.'—'Amen.'

24. 'I am a lamp[1] to you (sing.)
    who see me.'—'Amen.'

25. 'I am a mirror to you
    who know me.'—'Amen.'

26. 'I am a door[2] to you
    ⟨who⟩[3] knock on me.'—'Amen.'

27. 'I am a way[4] to you
    ⟨the⟩ traveller.'—⟨'Amen'⟩[5].

96. 28. 'Now *if you follow*
    my dance,

29. see yourself
    in Me who am speaking,

30. and when you have seen what *I do*,
    keep silence about my mysteries.[6]

31. You who dance, consider
    what I do, for yours is[7]

32. This passion of Man[8]
    which I am to suffer.

33. For you *could* by no means
    have understood what you suffer

34. unless to you as Logos
    I had been sent by the Father.

---

[1] Cf. Rev. 21:23. In ll. 24–50 the pronoun "you" and the imperatives are all to be taken as singular.

[2] Cf. Jn. 10:9.   [3] Word supplied by Pallas, p. 228.   [4] Cf. Jn. 14:6.

[5] ὁδός εἰμί σοι <τῷ> παροδίτῃ. <ἀμήν)> : τῷ being supplied on Pallas' suggestion (p. 228), ἀμήν on Bonnet's. But perhaps l. 27 is not an original part of the hymn but an addition deriving from Jn. 14:6 which was suggested by the Johannine allusion in l. 26. This is indeed borne out by the structure of the hymn: ll. 21–23 give three antithetical parallelisms ("having" and "not having"), ll. 24–26 three progressive parallelisms, each developing from the Revealer's statement about himself; l. 27 would make a fourth parallelism of this kind and thus be superfluous.

[6] Pallas (p. 228) completely rearranges the received text and would reconstruct ll. 28–30 as follows: "He who performs (*) the mysteries *keeps silence*" (as a title). "*By following* my dance,/see yourself/in Me who am speaking,/and if you see, <be still>." In view of the text furnished by Augustine (above, p. 227 n. 5) he has to assume the Greek text was corrupted before it passed to the Latin-speaking world.

[7] Pallas' division into half-lines has been altered here.

[8] Cod. C.: τοῦτο τοῦ ἀνθρώπου πάθος; according to Schlier (p. 162 n. 1) τὸ should be read instead of τοῦ; ἀνθρώπου being used without the article in the sense of Anthropos, the primordial man.

35. You who saw what I suffer
    saw ⟨me⟩ as *suffering* (yourself)[1],

36. and seeing it you did not stay
    but were wholly moved.

37. Being moved towards wisdom
    you have *me* as a support (*lit.* couch);
    rest in me.[2]

38. Who I am,[3] *you shall know*
    when I go forth.

39. What I now am seen to be,
    that I am not;

40. ⟨What I am⟩[4] you shall see
    when you come yourself.

41. If you knew how to suffer
    you would be able not to suffer.

42. Learn how to suffer
    and you shall be able not to suffer.

43. What you do not know
    I myself will teach you.

44. I am your God,
    not (the God) of the traitor.

45. I will that there be prepared
    holy souls for me.[5]

46. Understand the word
    of wisdom!

47. As for me,
    if you would understand *what I was*:

---

[1] Cod. C.: ὡς πάσχοντα εἶδες, "saw (me) as a sufferer"; but in this case the two half-lines express a tautology; hence πάσχοντα should be emended to πάσχων, following Schlier (p. 162) and conforming to the thought of ll. 31f. The insertion of με before εἶδες by Pallas (p. 229) is justified both by the metre and by the thought.

[2] Line 37 with its three members interrupts the series of verses each consisting of two half-lines: hence Pallas supposes (p. 229) that there were originally four half-lines, of which the second has been lost. But there seems to be no break in the train of thought.

[3] Pallas (p. 229) would delete ἐγώ (in τίς εἰμι ἐγώ) on metrical grounds.

[4] Pallas (p. 229) supplies the phrase ὅ εἰμι (Bonner having already suggested ὃ δέ εἰμι), which is required on formal grounds and gives quite possible sense; its omission is to be explained by homoioteleuton.

[5] Cod. C: ῥυθμίζεσθαι θέλω ψυχαῖς ἁγίαις ἐπ' ἐμέ. Liechtenhan (*Die Offenbarung im Gnosticismus*, 1901, p. 128) translates "I will be attuned to the souls that are holy in me", but prefers to connect ἐπ' ἐμέ with the next sentence; so also James, who emends to ἐπ' ἐμοί. Pallas' conjecture (p. 230) seems preferable, reading ψυχὰς ἁγίας for ψυχαῖς ἁγίαις.

48. By the word (?Word) I (*) mocked at all things
and I was not *mocked* at all,
49. I exulted: (*lit.* leaped)
but do you understand the whole,
50. and when you have understood it, say,
Glory be to thee, Father.

Say again with me,[1]

51. Glory be to thee, Father,
Glory be to thee, Word.
Glory be to thee, [holy] Spirit.'[2]—'Amen.'

Revelation of the Mystery of the Cross

97. After the Lord had so danced with us, my beloved, he went out. And we were like men amazed or fast asleep, and we fled[3] this way and that. And so I saw him suffer, and did not wait by his suffering, but fled to the Mount of Olives and wept at what had come to pass. And when he was hung (upon the Cross) on Friday,[4] at the sixth hour of the day there came a darkness over the whole earth.[5] And my Lord stood in the middle of the cave and gave light to it and said, 'John, for the people below in Jerusalem I am being crucified and pierced with lances and reeds[6] and given vinegar and gall to drink.[7] But to you I am speaking, and listen to what I speak. I put into your mind to come up to this mountain so that you may hear what a disciple should learn from his teacher and a man from God.'

98. And when he had said this he showed me a Cross of Light

---

[1] Text arranged after Pallas (p. 230). In Codex C the invitation with the doxology that follows comes between lines 46 and 47, and the final "Amen" at the end of line 50; but here we clearly have the doxology which concluded the hymn.
[2] Cod. C: δόξα σοι πνεῦμα ἅγιον; Pallas (p. 230) proposes to read τὸ πνεῦμα and regard ἅγιον as an accretion, in conformity with l. 2.
[3] Mk. 14:50 and pars.
[4] In most of the MSS. of Σ used by Bonnet the text reads τῷ ἀρουβάτῳ, in Cod. C τῇ ἀρούβα. Hilgenfeld (*Ztschr. f. wiss. Theol.* 40, 1897, p. 470; 43, 1900, p. 14 note ad loc.) suggests seeing here a reproduction of the Aramaic 'ᵃrūbā' or 'ᵃrūbtā', preparation-day, Friday. James (*JTS* 7, 1906, pp. 566–568) agrees, having found a 13th-century example of the Christian use of this word; however there are numerous examples of the use of 'ᵃrūbtā' in Christian Syriac. Duensing however (according to Hennecke, *Apokr.* 2, p. 172 n. 2) has contested this interpretation on the ground of the superfluous second α.
[5] Cf. Mk. 15:33 and pars.
[6] Cf. Mk. 15:19 and pars.; Jn. 19:34; Gospel of Peter 9.
[7] Mt. 27:34; Gospel of Peter 16.

firmly fixed, and around the Cross a great crowd, which had no
single form; and in it (the Cross) was one form and the same
likeness.[1] And I saw the Lord himself above the Cross, having
no shape but only a kind of voice; yet not that voice which we
knew, but one that was sweet and gentle and truly (the voice)
of God, which said to me, 'John, there must (be) one man (to)
hear these things from me; for I need one who is ready to hear.
This Cross of Light is sometimes called Logos[2] by me for your
sakes, sometimes mind, sometimes Jesus, sometimes Christ, some-
times a door,[3] sometimes a way,[4] sometimes bread,[5] sometimes
seed,[6] sometimes resurrection,[7] sometimes Son, sometimes Father,
sometimes Spirit,[8] sometimes life,[7] sometimes truth,[9] sometimes
faith, sometimes grace; *and so* (it is called) for men's sake.

But what it truly is, as known in *itself* and spoken to us,
(is this): it is the distinction of all things, and the *strong uplifting*
of *what is firmly fixed* out of what is unstable, and the harmony
of wisdom, being wisdom in harmony (?). ⟨But⟩ there are
⟨places⟩ on the right and on the left, powers, authorities, principalities and demons, activities, threatenings, passions, devils,
Satan and the inferior root *from which* the nature of transient
things proceeded.

99. This Cross then (is that) which has united all things by
the word and which has separated off what is transitory and
inferior, which has also *compacted*all things into ⟨one⟩. But
this is not that wooden Cross which you shall see when you go
down from here; nor am I the (man) who is on the Cross, (I)
whom now you do not see but only hear (my) voice. I was taken
to be what I am not, I who am not what for many others I was;
but what they will say of me is mean and unworthy of me. Since
then the place of (my?) rest is neither (to be) seen nor told, much
more shall I, the Lord of this (place), be neither seen ⟨nor told⟩.

100. The multitude around the Cross that is ⟨not⟩[10] of one
form is the inferior nature. And those whom you saw in the Cross,
even if they have not (yet) one form—not every member of him

---

[1] See below, n. 10.   [2] Jn. 1:1.   [3] Jn. 10:9.   [4] Jn. 14:6.
[5] Jn. 6:33, 35, 48.   [6] Mk. 4:26 and pars.   [7] Jn. 11:25.
[8] Jn. 4:24; 2 Cor. 3:17.   [9] Jn. 14:6.
[10] Emended and interpreted in the light of c. 98 init. after Schimmelpfeng (*Handb.*,
p. 532, q.v. for the textual difficulties and other proposed emendations).

who has come down has yet been gathered together. But when
human nature is taken up, and the race that comes to me and
obeys[1] my voice, then *he who* now *hears* me shall be united
with this (race) and shall no longer be what he now is, but
(shall be) above them as I am now. For so long as you do not call
yourself mine, I am not what I am; but if you hear me, you also
as hearer *shall be* as I am, and I shall be what I was, when
you[2] (are) as I am with myself; for from *me* you are ⟨what
I am⟩.(?) Therefore ignore the many and despise those who are
outside the mystery; for you must know that I am wholly with the
Father, and the Father with me.[3]

101. So then I have suffered none of those things which they
will say of me; even that suffering which I showed to you and to
the rest in my dance, I will that it be called a mystery. For what
you *are*, that I have shown you, (as) you see; but what I am is
known to me alone, and no one else. *Let me* have what is mine;
what is yours *you must see* through me; but me *you must see*
truly—not ⟨that which⟩ I am, (as) I said, but that which you,
as (my) kinsman, *are able* to know. You hear that I suffered,
yet I suffered not; and that I suffered not, yet I did suffer; and
that I was pierced,[4] yet I was not wounded; that I was hanged,
yet I was not hanged; that blood *flowed* from me,[4] yet it did
not flow; and, in a word, that what they say of me, I did not
endure, but what they do not say, those things I did suffer.
Now what these are, I secretly show *you*; for I know that you
will understand. You must know me, then, as the *torment* of
the Logos, the *piercing* of the Logos, the blood of the Logos,
the wounding of the Logos, the fastening of the Logos, the death
of the Logos. And so I speak, discarding the man(hood). The
first then (that) you must know (is) the Logos; then you shall
know the Lord, and thirdly the man, and what he has suffered.'

102. When he had said these things to me, and others which
I know not how to say as he wills, he was taken up,[5] without any
of the multitude seeing him. And going ⟨down⟩ I laughed at
them all, since he had told me what they had said about him;
and I held this one thing fast in my (mind), that the Lord had

---

[1] Cf. Jn. 18:37.   [2] Conjecture following Schlier, p. 97.   [3] Cf. Jn. 14:10.
[4] Cf. Jn. 19:34.   [5] Cf. Mk. 16:19; Acts 1:2; Gospel of Peter 19.

performed everything as a symbol and a dispensation for the conversion and salvation *of man*.

Concluding Admonitions

103. Now, my brothers, since we have seen the grace of the Lord and his affection towards us, *let us worship him*, since we have obtained mercy from him; not with (our) fingers, nor with (our) mouths nor with (our) tongue nor with any member of (our) body at all, but with the disposition *of our soul*; (let us worship) him *who was made man* ⟨apart from⟩ this body. And let us watch, since he is at hand even now in prisons for our sakes, and in tombs, in bonds and dungeons, in reproaches and insults, by sea and on dry land, in torments, *sentences*, conspiracies, plots and punishments; in a word, he is with all of us, and with the sufferers he suffers himself, (my) brethren. If he is called upon by any of us he does not hold out against hearing us, but being everywhere he *hears* us all, and now also myself and Drusiana, being the God of those who are imprisoned, bringing us help through his own compassion.

104. You therefore, beloved, (must) also be persuaded, that it is not a man that I *exhort* you *to worship*, but God unchangeable, God *invincible*, God who is higher than all authority and all power and elder and stronger than all angels and (all) that are called creatures and all aeons. So if you hold fast to *him* and are built up upon *him*, you shall possess your soul indestructible."

105. And when John had delivered these things to the brethren, he went out with Andronicus to walk. And *Drusiana* followed at a distance with (them) *all* to see the things performed by him and to hear his word at all times in the Lord.

* * *

The Destruction of the Temple of Artemis

37. Now the brothers from Miletus said to John, "We have remained a long time in Ephesus; if you agree, let us go to Smyrna. For already we hear that the great works of God[1] have arrived there also." And Andronicus said to them, "When our teacher

[1] Acts 2:11.

wishes, then let us go." But John said, "Let us first go into the Temple of Artemis; for perhaps if we are seen (there), the servants of the Lord will be found there also."

38. Now two days later there was the dedication-festival of the idol-temple. So while everyone was wearing white, John alone put on black clothing and went up to the temple; and they seized him and tried to kill him. But John said, "You are mad to lay hands on me, *a man who serves* the one true God." And he went up on a high platform, and said to them,

. 39. "Men of Ephesus, you are liable to behave like the sea; every river at its outfall, every spring that flows down, the *rains* and incessant waves and stony torrents, are all made salt by the bitter *brine*(?) that is in it. You likewise have remained to this day unchanged (in your attitude) towards the true religion, and are being corrupted by your ancient rituals. How many miracles (and) cures of diseases have you seen (performed) through me? And yet you are blinded in your hearts, and cannot recover your sight. What is it then, men of Ephesus? I have ventured to come up now into this very idol-temple of yours. I will convict you of being utterly godless and dead *through human reasoning*. See, here I stand. You all say that you have Artemis as your goddess(*) [or, that Artemis has *power*]; *so* pray in her (name) that I, and I alone, may die; or if you cannot do this, then I alone will call upon my own God and because of your unbelief I will put you all to death."

40. But since they had long experience of him and had seen dead men raised (by him), they cried out, "Do not destroy us like that, we implore you, John; we know that you can do it!" And John said to them, "If you do not wish to die, then your religion must be convicted; and why *convicted?*—so that you may abandon your ancient error. For now is the time! Either you must be converted by my God, or I myself will die at the hands of your goddess; for I will pray in your presence and entreat my God that you may find mercy."

41. So saying he uttered this prayer: "O God, who art God above all that are called gods; yet rejected till this day in the city of the Ephesians; who *didst put* me in mind to come to this place, of which I never thought; who dost convict every form of

worship, by converting (men) to thee; at whose name every idol
takes flight, and every demon and every unclean power: now
let the demon that is here *take flight* at thy name, the deceiver
of this great multitude; and show thy mercy in this place, for
they have been led astray."

42. And while John was saying this, of a sudden the altar of
Artemis split into many pieces, and all the offerings laid up in
the temple suddenly fell to the floor and its goodness(?)[1] was
broken, and so were more than seven images; and half the temple
fell down, so that the priest was killed at one stroke as *the
roof*(?)[2] came down. Then the assembled Ephesians cried out,
"(There is but) one God, (the God) of John! (There is but) one
God who has mercy upon us; for thou alone art God! We are
converted, now that we have seen thy marvellous works! Have
mercy upon us, O God, according to thy will, and save us from
our great error!" And some of them lay on their faces and made
supplication, others bent their knees and prayed; some tore their
clothes and wept, and others tried to take flight.

43. But John stretched out his hands and with uplifted heart
said to the Lord, "Glory be to thee, my Jesus, the only God of
truth, for thou dost gain thy servants by elaborate means." And
having said this he said to the people, "Rise up from the ground,
men of Ephesus, and pray to my God, and acknowledge his invisible power that is openly seen, and the wonderful works that
were done before your eyes. Artemis should have helped *herself*; her servant should have been helped by her, and not have
died. Where is the power of the demon (i.e. the goddess)? Where
are her sacrifices? Where are her dedication-festivals?—her
feasts?—her garlands? Where is all that sorcery and the poisoner's
art that is sister to it?"

44. And the people rising from the ground went running and
threw down the rest of the idol temple, crying out, "The God of
John (is the) only (God) we know; from now on we worship him,
since he has had mercy upon us!" And as John came down from

[1] τὸ δόξαν αὐτῷ. Hennecke (Apokr. 2, p. 174 n. 1) suggested τὰ δόκανα αὐτῶν
"their substructure", but this is hardly acceptable; τὰ δόκανα being a cultic object
specifically belonging to the Spartan cult of the Dioscuri.
[2] κατερχομένου τοῦ στυμόνος. Schimmelpfeng (Handb., p. 507) reads στέγους;
Hennecke's suggestion (Apokr. 2, p. 174 n. 1) of τῆς σταμίνης, properly the rib of a
ship, is no more satisfactory.

that place a great crowd took hold of him, saying, "Help us, John; stand by us, for we perish in vain. You see our purpose; you see the people following after you, hanging in hope upon your God. We have seen the way which we followed in error when we lost (Him); we have seen that our gods were *set up* in vain; we have seen their great and shameful derision. But let us, we beg you, come to your house and receive help without hindrance. Accept us, for we are desperate!"

45. But John said to them, "Friends, you must believe that it was on your account that I remained at Ephesus, although I was eager to go to Smyrna and the other cities, that the servants of Christ who are there may be converted to him. But since *I was about to depart* without being fully at ease about you(?), I have waited, praying to my God, and asked him that I should leave Ephesus (only) when I have confirmed you (in the faith); and now that I see this *has come* and is still *increasing*, I will not leave you until I have weaned you like children from the nurse's milk and set you upon a solid rock."

Resurrection of the Priest of Artemis

46. So John remained with them and received them (*) in the house of Andronicus. And one of those who were assembled there laid down the dead body of the priest of Artemis before the door [MS. *wrongly adds* "of the temple"], for he was his kinsman, and came in quickly with the rest, telling no one. Therefore John, after he had addressed the brethren, and after the prayer and the thanksgiving (eucharist), and after he had laid hands on each of those who were assembled, said in the Spirit, "*There is one* of those present who is moved by faith in God, ⟨who⟩ has laid down the priest of Artemis before the door and has come in; ⟨and⟩ in the longing of his soul he has put the concern for himself first, reasoning thus with himself; 'It is better that I should take thought for the living than for my dead kinsman; for I know that if I turn to the Lord and save my own soul, John will not refuse even to raise up the dead'." And John rising from ⟨his⟩ place went where the priest's kinsman, who had thought this, came in; and he took him by the hand, and said, "Had you these thoughts when you came in to me, my son?"

And *he*, overcome with trembling and fright, said, "Yes, my Lord," and threw himself at his feet. And John (said), "Our Lord is Jesus Christ, and he will show his power on your dead kinsman (*) by raising him again."

47. And he made the young man rise and took his hand and said, "It is no *great matter* for a man *who has power* over great mysteries to be still concerned with small things. Or is it any great matter (*) if bodily sicknesses are cured?" And still holding the young man by the hand he said, "I tell you, my son, go and raise up the dead man yourself, saying nothing but only this: 'John, the servant of God, says to you, Arise!'" And the young man went to his kinsman and said just this, while a great crowd of people were with him, and came in to John bringing him alive.

And when John saw the man who was raised up, he said, "Now that you have risen, you are not really living, nor are you a partner and heir to the true life; will you belong to him by whose name and power you were raised up? So now, believe, and you shall live for all eternity." And then and there he believed on the Lord Jesus, and from that time kept company with John.

Encounter with a Parricide

48. On the next day John saw in a dream that he was to walk three miles outside the gates, and he did not ignore it, but rose up at dawn and started with the brothers along the road. And (there was) a countryman who was warned by his father not to possess himself of the wife of his fellow-labourer, while he threatened to kill *him* (*or*, *himself*); (but) the young man could not put up with his father's warning, but kicked him and left him speechless. [*The parallel account in Cod. Q reads*, "immediately laid him dead on the ground".] But when John saw what had happened, he said to the Lord, "Lord, was it because of this that you told me to come here today?"

49. But the young man, seeing (his) sudden death and fearing arrest, took out the sickle that was in his belt and began running towards his cottage; but John met him and said, "Stand still, you ruthless demon, and tell me where you are running with (that) bloodthirsty sickle." And the young man in his confusion

239

let his weapon fall to the ground and said to him, "I have committed a monstrous and inhuman act, and I know (it), so I resolved to do something worse and more cruel to myself, and to die at once. My father was always urging me to live a chaste and honourable life, yet I could not put up with his reproofs, but kicked him to death. And when I saw what had happened I was hurrying to the woman for whom I murdered my father, and I meant to kill her and her husband and last of all myself. I could not bear the woman's husband to see me suffer the death-penalty."

50. Then John said to him, "I will not go away and leave you in danger, or I shall give place to him who would laugh and scoff at you. No, come with me and show me where your father is lying. And if I raise him up for you, shall I keep (you) apart from the woman who has become (so) dangerous to you?" And the young man said, "If you raise me up my father himself alive and I see him whole and *continuing* in life, I will keep away (from her) in future."

51. And as he said this, while they talked they came to the place where the old man lay dead, and there were a number of passers-by standing by the place. And John said to the young man, "You wretch, did you not even spare your father's *old age*?" But he wept and tore his hair and said he was sorry for it. And John the servant of the Lord said, "(Lord,) who didst show me today that I was to come to this place, who knewest that this would happen, since *nothing* that is done in this life can escape thee, *who* dost grant me *every* (kind of) cure and healing by thy will; grant even now that this old man may live, seeing that his *murderer* has become his own judge. Spare him, thou (who art) Lord alone, *though he did not spare* his father, ⟨because he⟩ gave him counsel for the best."

52. With these words he went to the old man and said, "My Lord will not be slack to extend his good pity and his condescending heart even to you; rise up and give glory to God for the work that has been *revealed*(?)" And the old man said, "I arise, my Lord." And he arose. And seating himself he said, "I was released from a terrible life (in which) *I suffered* many grievous insults from my son, and his *lack of* affection, and you

called me back, servant (*lit.* man) of the living God—for what purpose?" ⟨And John answered him, "If⟩ you are arising to this same (life), you should rather be dead; but rouse yourself to a better (one)!" And he took him and brought him into the city and proclaimed the grace of God to him, so that before they reached the gate the old man believed.

53. But when the young man saw the marvellous resurrection of his father and his own deliverance, he took the sickle and took off his private parts; and he ran to the house where he kept his adulteress and threw them down before her, and said, "For your sake I became my father's murderer, and of you two, and of myself. There you have the pattern and cause *of all* this! As for me, God has had mercy on me and shown me his power." 54. And he went and told John before the brethren what he had done.

But John said to him, "Young man, the one who tempted you to kill your father and commit adultery with another man's wife, he has also made you take off the unruly (members) as if this were a virtuous act. But you should not have destroyed the place (of your temptation), but the thought which showed its temper through those members; for it is not those organs which are harmful to man, but the unseen springs through which every shameful emotion is stirred up and comes to light. So, my son, if you repent of this fault and recognize the devices of Satan, you have God to help you in everything that your soul *requires*." And the young man kept quiet, repenting of his former sins to obtain pardon from the goodness of God; and he would not separate from John.

The Call to Smyrna

55. Now while he was doing these things in the city of the Ephesians, the people of Smyrna sent messengers to him, saying, "We hear that the God whom you preach is bountiful, and has charged you not to show favour by staying in one place. Since then you are the preacher of such a God, come over to Smyrna and to the other cities, so that we may come to know of your God and knowing him may set our hopes on him."

* * *

A considerable break must be assumed between cc. 55 and 58. In c. 55 there reaches the apostle the call "to Smyrna and to the other cities", in c. 58 he begins the journey back to Ephesus, as stated in the heading preserved in Cod. M.; and he begins it from Laodicea. Accordingly a travel-narrative must have disappeared, which took him from Ephesus to Smyrna and other cities, and then to Laodicea. These names and their order suggested to Zahn (*Neue kirchl. Ztschr.* 10, 1899, p. 198; *Forschungen zur Gesch. d. ntl. Kanons* VI, 1900, pp. 197ff.) that a journey round the seven cities of Asia Minor of Rev. 1:11 was involved, and that therefore the author of the Acts of John knew the Apocalypse. Such a use of the Apocalypse however would not necessarily imply that the author of these Acts appreciated it as a whole, and so must have included in his narrative an account of John's writing it and his exile on Patmos (cf. Schmidt, pp. 122f.); to all appearances the Acts of John contained no such account (see above, pp. 195f. and 215). However, whether the lost travel-narrative depends for its setting upon Rev. 1:11 or not, in any case as told in Leucius' longwinded narrative style it must have been fairly lengthy. Possibly there also belongs to it the episode of John and the Partridge, which cannot be located with any certainty (see above p. 197).

John and the Partridge

56*. Now one day as John was sitting (there) a partridge flew by and came and played[1] in the dust before him; and John was amazed as he saw it. But a certain priest, who was one of his hearers, came and went in to John and saw the partridge playing in the dust before him. And he was offended and said to himself, "Can such a man, at his age, take pleasure in a partridge *playing in the dust*?" But John knew in the spirit what he was thinking, and said to him, "It would be better for you, my son, to watch a partridge playing in the dust and not to foul yourself with shameful and impious practices. For he who waits for the conversion and repentance of all men has brought you here for this purpose. For I have no need of a partridge playing in the dust; for the partridge is your own soul."

57*. When the elder heard this and saw that he was not unknown but that the Apostle of Christ had told him all that was in his heart, he fell on his face to the ground and cried out, saying, "Now I know that God dwells in you, blessed John! How happy is the man who has not tempted God in you; for the man who

[1] The German has "bathed", which is good ornithology but perhaps does not suit the tale; the partridge which apparently fouls itself symbolizes the priest's soul.— Translator.

tempts you tempts the untemptable." And he begged him to pray for him; and (John) instructed him and gave him injunctions (*or*, "canons") and sent him away to his house, and glorified God who is (Lord) over all.

* * *

Departure from Laodicea for Ephesus
(Cod. M. has the heading: From Laodicea to Ephesus the second time.)

58. Now when some considerable time had gone by, and none of the brethren had ever been distressed by John, they were distressed at that time because he had said, "Brethren, it is time for me now to go to Ephesus; for so I have agreed with those who live there, so that they do not grow slack through having no one to encourage them all this time; and you all must set your minds upon God, who does not desert us." When the brethren heard this from him they were grieved, because they were parting from him. But John said, "Even if I am parting from you, yet Christ is with you always; and if you love him purely, you shall possess continually the fellowship (that comes) from him; for where he is loved, he first (loves) those who love him."[1] 59. And when he had said this and given them instructions [*Cod. R has*, "said farewell to them"] and had left large sums of money with the brethren for distribution, he set out for Ephesus, to all the brethren's grief and lamentation.

Now there went with him, (of those) from Ephesus, Andronicus and Drusiana and the household of Lycomedes and of Cleobius. Also there followed him Aristobula, who had learnt that her husband Tertullus had died on the way, and Aristippus together with Xenophon, and the virtuous prostitute and several others, whom he continually charged to (follow) the Lord and who would not be parted from him.

The Obedient Bugs
60. And on the first day we arrived at a lonely inn; and while we were trying to find a bed for John we saw a curious thing.

[1] Cf. 1 Jn. 4:19.

There was one bed there lying somewhere not made up; so we spread the cloaks which we were wearing over it, and begged him to lie down on it and take his ease, while all the rest of us slept on the floor. But when he lay down he was troubled by the bugs; and as they became more and more troublesome to him, and it was already midnight, he said to them in the hearing of us all, "I tell you, you bugs, to behave yourselves, one and all; you must leave your home for tonight and be quiet in one place and keep your distance from the servants of God." And while we laughed and went on talking, John went to sleep; but we talked quietly and thanks to him were not disturbed (or "without disturbing him"—Translator).

61. Now as the day was *breaking* I got up first, and Verus and Andronicus with me; and we saw by the door of the room which we had taken a mass of bugs collected; and as we were astounded at the great number of them, and all the brethren had woken up because of them, John went on sleeping. And when he woke up we explained *to him* what we had seen. And he sat up (in) bed and looked at them and said, "Since you have behaved yourselves and listened to my correction, go (back) to your own place." And when he had said this and had got up from the bed, the bugs came running from the door towards the bed and climbed up its legs and disappeared into the joints. Then John said again, "This creature listened to a man's voice and kept to itself and was quiet and obedient; but we who hear the voice of God disobey his commandments and are irresponsible; how long will this go on?"

Second Stay in Ephesus (cc. 62–115)
Arrival in Ephesus

62. After this we came to Ephesus; and the brethren in that place, learning that John had arrived after all this time, came running to the house of Andronicus, where he was staying, and grasped his feet and laid his hands on their faces and kissed them. [*Ps.-Abdias has*, And many were glad even to touch his garments, and were healed by touching the clothes of the holy Apostle.]

Drusiana and Callimachus

63. And while great love and perfect joy prevailed among the brethren, a man prompted by Satan fell in love with Drusiana, although he saw and realized that she was the wife of Andronicus. And several people said to him, "It is impossible for you to get this woman, for she has long ago separated even from her husband for the sake of piety. Are you the only one who does not know that Andronicus, who formerly was not the god-fearing man he is now, shut her into a sepulchre, saying 'Either I must have you as the wife whom I had before, or you must die!' And she chose to die rather than commit that abominable act; so that if out of piety she would not consent to union with her lord and husband, but persuaded him to agree with her, do you think she will consent to your adultery? Leave off (this) madness, which has no rest in you! Leave off (this) project which you cannot fulfil!"

64. But his intimate friends could not persuade him with these words, but he had the *effrontery* to send to her; and when *she* learned of this disgrace and licence of *his, she* spent *her* days in melancholy. And after two days Drusiana became feverish from her melancholy and took to her bed, saying, "I wish I had never come to my native land, (now) that I have become a temptation to a man who is uninstructed in religion! If a man were *filled* with ⟨God's⟩ *word, he* would not have *come* to such a pitch of madness. So, Lord, since I have been partly to blame for the wounding of an ignorant soul, release me from this bondage and remove me to thee at once!" And while John was present, though no one knew (the truth of) the matter, Drusiana departed this life, having no joy at all but rather distress because of the spiritual hurt of that man.

65. But Andronicus, troubled with secret sorrow, grieved in his heart and also lamented openly, so that John often quietened him and said to him, "Drusiana has gone to a better hope out of this unjust life." And Andronicus answered him, "Yes, I am convinced (of it), John, and have no doubt about faith in my God; and I trust in this above all, that she departed this life in purity."

66. And when she was brought out (for burying), John took hold of Andronicus; and now that he knew the reason, he grieved

more than Andronicus; and he kept quiet, reflecting on the malice of the adversary, and sat (still) for a little. Then, when the brothers had collected to hear what speech he would make about the departed, he began to say,

67. "When the pilot in his voyage, together with the sailors and the ship herself, arrives in a calm and sheltered haven, then he may say that he is safe. And the farmer who has laid the seed in the earth and has laboured long to cultivate and guard it, *may rest* from his labours only when he lays up the seed increased many times in his storehouses. The man who enters for a race in the arena should triumph only when he brings back the prize. The man who puts in for a boxing-match should boast only when he gets his crowns. And (so are) all such contests and skills (acknowledged) when they do not fail in the end, but prove to be *equal* to what they promised(?).

68. The same I think is the case with the faith which each one of us practises; its truth is decided when it persists unaltered even to the end of life. For many hindrances assail and cause disturbances to the thoughts of men: anxiety, children, parents, reputation, poverty, flattery, youth, beauty, vanity, desire, wealth, (or, desire *of wealth*?), anger, presumption, indolence, envy, *passion*, jealousy, negligence, violence, lust, deceit (or, with ps.-Abdias, *slaves*) money, pretence, and all such other hindrances as there are in this life; just as the pilot sailing on a calm passage is opposed by the onset of contrary winds and a great storm and surge (that comes) out of the calm, and the farmer by untimely cold and mildew and the (pests) that creep out of the earth, and athletes by narrowly failing(?) and craftsmen by the (difficulties) of their crafts.

69. But the man of faith before all else must take thought for his ending and learn how it is to meet him, whether vigorous and sober and unhindered, or disturbed and courting worldly things and held fast by desires. So again one can praise the grace of a body (only) when it is wholly stripped and the greatness of a general (only) when he fulfils the whole promise of the war, and the excellence of a doctor (only) when he was succeeded in every cure, and the *faith* of a soul and its *worth* before God (only) when it has performed what agrees with (its) promise; one cannot

(praise the soul) which began (well) but *slipped down* into all the things of this life and fell away; nor the sluggish soul, which made an effort to follow better (examples), but then was reduced to transitory (pursuits); nor that which desired temporal things rather than the eternal, nor that which exchanged ⟨the enduring for⟩ the impermanent, nor that which respected what deserves no respect, ⟨nor that which loved⟩[1] the deeds of dishonour, nor that which takes pledges from Satan, nor that which received the serpent into its house, nor that which suffers reproach for God's sake and then is (*) ashamed, nor that which consents with its lips but does not *show itself* (consenting) in practice. But (we must praise the soul) which has had the constancy not to be *set on fire* by filthy pleasure, not to yield to indolence, not to be ensnared by love of money, not to be betrayed by the vigour of the body and by anger."

70. And while John was continuing his instructions to the brethren, that they should despise transitory things for the sake of ⟨the eternal⟩, Drusiana's lover, inflamed by the fiercest lust and by the influence of the many-formed Satan, bribed the steward of Andronicus, an acquisitive man, with a great sum of money; and he opened Drusiana's grave and gave (him) leave to perform the forbidden thing upon (her) dead body. *Having not succeeded* with her while she was alive, he still persisted with her body after her death, and said, "If you would not *consent* to union with me when alive, I will dishonour your corpse now you are dead." With this design, when he had arranged for his wicked deed through the abominable steward, he burst into the tomb with him; and when they had opened the door they began to strip the grave-clothes from the corpse, saying, "Miserable Drusiana, what have you gained? Could you not have done this while you were alive? It need not have distressed you, if you had done it willingly."

71. And while they were saying this, and only her usual *vest* was left upon her body, a strange spectacle was seen, such as those who do *such things* deserve to meet: a serpent appeared from somewhere and despatched the steward with a single bite; so it killed him; but it did not bite the young man, but wound

---

[1] Words supplied from ps.-Abdias.

itself round his feet, hissing terribly; and when he fell, the serpent mounted (his body) and sat upon him.

72. Now on the next day John came with Andronicus and the brethren to the sepulchre at dawn, it being now the third day (from) Drusiana's (death), so that we might break bread there. And at first when we came the keys could not be found when they were looked for; and John said to Andronicus, "It is right that they should be lost; for Drusiana is not in the sepulchre. Still, let us go on, that you may not be neglectful, and the doors will open of themselves, just as the Lord has granted us many other things."

73. And when we came to the place, at our master's command the doors came open, and *we saw* by the grave of Drusiana a handsome young man who was smiling. And when he saw him John cried out and said, "Have you come before us here also, beautiful one? And for what reason?" And he heard a voice saying to him, "For the sake of Drusiana, whom you are to raise up—for I nearly *found her dishonoured*—and for the sake *of the man who has expired* by her grave." And when the beautiful one had said this to John he went up to heaven in the sight of us all.

But when John turned to the other side of the sepulchre he saw a young man, a prominent citizen of Ephesus, Callimachus— for *that* was his name—and a huge serpent lying asleep upon him, and Andronicus' steward, who was called Fortunatus, (lying) dead. And when he saw them both he was perplexed, and he stood still and said to the brethren, "What is the meaning of this sight? Or why did not the Lord reveal to me what happened here, for *he has never neglected me*?"

74. And when Andronicus saw them (lying) dead he sprang up and went to Drusiana's grave; and seeing her only in her vest, he said to John, "I understand what has happened, John, blessed servant of God; this Callimachus was in love with my sister; and since he never gained her, though he often ventured upon it, he bribed this accursed steward of mine with a great sum of money, intending perhaps, as now we can see, to *execute* by means of him the tragedy which he had plotted; for indeed Callimachus avowed this to many and said, 'Even if she will not consort with me when living, she shall be violated when she is dead!' And

perhaps, master, the beautiful one knew (this) and did not allow her (mortal) remains to be dishonoured, and this is why the men who ventured on this are (lying) dead. And may it not be that the voice which said to you, 'Raise up Drusiana' was foretelling this? For she departed this life in distress (of mind). But I believe him who said that this is one of the men who were led astray; for you have been bidden to raise him up; as for the other, I know that he is unworthy of salvation. But I make you this one request: raise up Callimachus first, and he will confess to us what has happened."

75. So John looked at the dead body and said to the venomous beast, "Remove from him who shall be a servant of Jesus Christ!" Then he stood up and made this prayer: "O God, whose name is rightly glorified by us; God, who subduest every harmful influence; God, whose will is performed and who *hearest* us always; may thy bounty be performed on this young man; and if any dispensation is to be made through him, declare it to us when he is raised up." And at once the young man arose; and for a whole hour he kept silence.

76. But when he came to his senses, John asked him the meaning of his entry into the sepulchre; and when he heard from him what Andronicus had told him, that he had been in love with Drusiana, John asked him again whether he had *succeeded* with his abominable (design) of dishonouring *a body* full of holiness. And he answered him, "How could I then accomplish this, when this dreadful creature struck down Fortunatus with one bite before my eyes?—and rightly so, for he encouraged me in this (act of) madness after that untimely and dreadful madness had ceased—and it checked me with fright, and put me in the state in which you saw me *before* I arose. And I will tell you something else yet more marvellous, which undid me even more and nearly made me a corpse; when my soul *gave way to madness* and the uncontrollable sickness was troubling me, and I had already stripped off the grave-clothes in which she was clothed, and then had come out of the grave and laid them down as you see, I returned to my detestable work; and I saw a handsome young man covering her with his cloak. And from his face rays of light shone out on to her face. And he also spoke to me

and said 'Callimachus, you must die in order to live'. Now who he was I did not know, servant of God; but now that you have come, I know for certain that he is an angel of God; and I understand this in truth, that the true God is proclaimed by you, and of this I am convinced. But I beg you, do not be slow to deliver me from this calamity and dreadful crime, and present me to your God as a man who was deceived with a shameful and foul deceit. I need your help, and thus I grasp your feet. I will become one of those who set their hopes on Christ, so that the voice may prove true that said to me here, 'You must die in order to live!' That voice has indeed accomplished its effect; for that man is dead, that faithless, lawless, godless man; and I have been raised at your hands, and will be faithful and Godfearing, knowing the *truth, which* I beg you may be shown me by you."

77. And John seized with great gladness and contemplating the whole spectacle of man's salvation said, "Ah, what is thy power, Lord Jesu Christ, I know not, for I am amazed at thy great compassion and infinite forbearance. O, what greatness came down into bondage! What inexpressible freedom is put in bondage by us! What unthinkable glory is ours! Thou hast kept even the lifeless frame from dishonour, (thou) redeemer (even) of the man who stained himself with blood, correcting ⟨the soul⟩ of him that ⟨defiled⟩ corruptible bodies; Father that hast had pity and compassion on heedless men. We glorify thee and praise and bless and give thanks for thy great goodness and forbearance, holy Jesu; for thou alone art God and no other, the power beyond all conspiracy, now and for all eternity. Amen."

78. So saying John took Callimachus and kissed him and said, "Glory be to our God, my son, who has pitied you and entitled me to glorify his power, and has entitled you also by a (wise) arrangement to desist from that madness and frenzy that you *had*,[1] and has summoned you to your own (true) rest and renewal of life."

79. But when Andronicus saw that the dead Callimachus was raised up, he and all the brethren entreated John to raise up Drusiana also, and said, "John, let Drusiana rise up and spend

---

[1] Cod. R: τῆς παρὰ σοῦ ἐκείνης σου μανίας (Cod. M abbreviates the whole sentence); Rostalski, p. 21, emends to τῆς παρακειμένης σου μανίας.

happily that short space ⟨of life⟩ which she gave up through
distress about Callimachus, when she thought she had become
a temptation *to him*; and when the Lord wills he shall take her
to himself." And John made no delay, but went to her grave and
took her hand and said, "I call upon thee who art God alone, the
exceeding great, the unutterable, the incomprehensible; to whom
every power of principalities is subject; to whom every authority
bows; before whom every vanity falls down and keeps silence;
whom the demons hear and tremble;[1] whom all creation per-
ceives and keeps its bounds: let thy name be glorified by us, and
raise up Drusiana, that Callimachus may be further strengthened
⟨in thee⟩, who providest what to men is unattainable and
impossible, and to thee alone is possible, even salvation and
resurrection; and that Drusiana may *now come forth* in peace,
since now that the young man is converted she has no more
with her the least hindrance *in her hastening* towards thee."

80. And after these words John said to Drusiana, "Drusiana,
arise". And she arose and came out of the grave; and seeing
herself clad only in her vest, she was perplexed about what had
happened; but when she had learnt the whole truth from
Andronicus, while John lay upon his face and Callimachus with
(uplifted) voice and with tears gave praise to God, she also
rejoiced and gave praise in like manner.

81. Now when she had dressed herself she turned and saw
Fortunatus lying, (and) said to John, "Father, let this man arise
also, for all that he strove to become my betrayer". And when
Callimachus heard her say this, he said, "No, Drusiana, I beg
you; for the voice which I heard took no thought of him, but
made mention only of you; and I saw and believed. For if he
had been good, no doubt God would have pitied him and raised
him up through the blessed John. He knew(?) then that the man
had come to a bad end. [*Ps.-Abdias*: He judged him worthy of
death, whom he did not proclaim worthy of resurrection.]" And
John said to him "My son, we have not learned to return evil
for evil.[2] For God also, though *we* have done much ill and
nothing well towards him, has given us not retribution but
repentance; and although we knew not his name, he did not

[1] Cf. Jas. 2:19.   [2] Cf. Rom. 12:17; 1 Thess. 5:15; 1 Pet. 3:9.

forsake but forgave us; and though we blasphemed, he did not punish but pitied us; and though we disbelieved, he bore no grudge; and though we persecuted his brethren, he made no (such) return, but moved us to repentance and restraint of wickedness and so called us to himself, as (he has called) you too, my son Callimachus, and without insisting on your former misdeeds *he has made* you his servant through his *vigilant* mercy. If then you will not have ⟨me⟩ *raise up* Fortunatus, it is a task for Drusiana.''

82. And she made no delay, but rejoicing in spirit and soul she went up to the body of Fortunatus and said, "O God of (all) ages, Jesus Christ, God of truth, who sufferedst me to see wonders and signs and didst grant me to become partaker of thy name, who didst *reveal*[1] thyself to me with thy many-formed countenance and hadst mercy on me in every way; who by thy great goodness didst protect me when I suffered violence from my former consort Andronicus; who gavest me thy servant Andronicus as my brother; who hadst kept me, thine handmaid, pure until this day; who has raised me up *from death* through thy servant John, and when *I was raised* hast shown me the man who fell (as now) unfallen; who hast given me perfect rest in thee, and relieved me of the secret madness; whom I have loved and embraced; I entreat thee, O Christ, do not refuse thy Drusiana's petition that thou *raise up* Fortunatus, for all that he strove to become my betrayer.''

83. And she grasped the dead man's hand, and said, "Rise up, Fortunatus, in the name of our Lord Jesus Christ". And Fortunatus rose up, and saw John in the sepulchre and Andronicus and Drusiana, now raised from the dead, and Callimachus, *now a believer*, and the rest of the brethren glorifying God; and he said, "O, what end is there to the powers of these terrible men! I did not want to be resurrected, but would rather be dead, so as not to see them." And with these words he ran away and left the sepulchre.

84. And John seeing the unbending spirit (*lit.* soul) of Fortunatus said, "Ah, (what a) nature *unchanged* for the better! What

---

[1] 'Εμφανίσας, conjectured by Zahn (*Neue Kirchl. Ztschr.* 10, 1899, p. 201 n. 1) is preferable to ἐμφυσήσας (who didst inspire) read by Cod. R, and is also recommended by Hennecke (*Handb.*, p. 518).

a spring of the soul that persists in defilement! What essence of
corruption full of darkness! What a death, dancing among those
that are yours! What a barren tree that is full of fire! What a
branch (*lit.* wood) that *bears* coals of fire for fruit! What
matter, consorting with the madness of matter and neighbour to
unbelief![1] You have convinced (us) who you are; you are convicted for ever with your children. The power of praising better
things you do not know; for you do not possess it. Therefore as
your way (*or* *fruit*(?)) is, so is your root and nature. Be removed
then, from those who hope in the Lord; from their thoughts, from
their mind, from their souls, from their bodies, from their action,
their life, their behaviour, their *business*, their practice, their
counsel, from their resurrection to God, from their fragrance
which you wish to share, from their fastings, from their prayers,
from their holy bath, from their Eucharist, from the nourishment
of their flesh, from their drink, from their clothing, from their
love-feast (ἀγάπη), from their *burial*, from their continence,
from their justice; from all these, most wicked Satan, enemy of
God, shall Jesus Christ remove you, who is our God and ⟨the
judge⟩ of those who are like you and follow your ways."

85. And when he had said this John prayed; and he took
bread,[2] and brought it into the sepulchre to break it, and he said,
"We glorify thy name that converteth us from error and pitiless
deceit; we glorify thee who hast shown before our eyes what we
have seen; we testify to thy goodness, *in various ways appearing*; we praise thy gracious name, O Lord; ⟨we thank thee⟩
who hast convicted those that are convicted by thee; we thank
thee, Lord Jesus Christ, that we confide ⟨in thy grace⟩, which
is unchanging; we thank *thee* who hadst need (*) of (our)
nature that is being saved; we thank thee that hast given us this
unwavering ⟨faith⟩ that thou alone art ⟨God⟩ both now and
for ever; we thy servants, that are assembled and gathered (?)
with ⟨good⟩ cause, give thanks to thee, O holy one."

---

[1] ὦ ὕλη ὑλομανίας σύνοικε καὶ ἀπιστίας γεῖτον. Schimmelpfeng (*Apokr.* 1, p. 450,
13f.) translates "O wood of trees full of unwholesome shoots, neighbour to unbelief!"
Although ὑλομανία is lexically attested only in the sense of "luxuriant sprouting"
(Stephanus, Thesaurus s.v.), ὕλη in this context is better understood as "matter";
so James, p. 249: "O matter, that dwellest with the madness of matter and neighbour
of unbelief."

[2] Or perhaps: When John had said this in imprecation, he took bread . . .

86. And when he had made this prayer and glorified (God) he gave to all the brethren the Lord's Eucharist, and went out of the sepulchre. And he came to the house of Andronicus, and said to the brethren, "My brethren, some spirit within me has foretold that Fortunatus *must* shortly turn black and die from the bite of the serpent; but let someone go quickly and learn if this be true." Then one of the young men ran and *found* him now dead and the blackness spreading and *reaching* his heart. And he came and told John that he had been dead three hours. And John said, "Devil, *thou hast* thy son."

[For cc. 87–105 in Bonnet's numeration, see above, pp. 224ff.]

The Departure (cc. 106–115)

John's Last Act of Worship

106. John therefore kept company with the brethren rejoicing in the Lord. And on the next day, as it was a Sunday and all the brethren were assembled, he began to say to them, "My brethren and fellow-servants, joint-heirs and partners with me in the kingdom of God, you know the Lord, how many great works he has granted you through me, how many wonders, how many healings, how many signs, what gifts of grace, (what) teachings, directions, refreshments, services, enlightenments, glories, graces, gifts, and acts of faith and fellowship, which you have seen with your eyes are given you by him, (though) they are not seen with these eyes nor heard with these ears. Therefore be firmly settled in him, remembering him in all you do, understanding the mystery of (God's) providence that has been accomplished for men, why the Lord has performed it. He entreats you through me, my brethren, and makes request, desiring to continue free from distress, free from insult, and from disloyalty, and from injury; for he knows the insult that comes from you, he knows that dishonour, he knows that disloyalty, he knows even injury from those who do not listen to his commandments.

107. So let not our gracious God be grieved, the compassionate, the merciful, the holy, the pure, the undefiled, the immaterial, the only, the one, the unchanging, the simple, the guileless, the patient, the one that is higher and loftier than every name we can

utter or conceive, our God Jesus Christ. Let him rejoice with us because we behave honourably, let him be glad because we live purely, let him be refreshed because our ways are sober, let him be easy because we live strictly, let him be pleased at our fellowship, let him smile because we are chaste, let him be merry because we love him. I give you this charge, my brethren, because I am now hastening towards the task that is prepared for me, which is already being perfected by the Lord. For what else could I have to say to you? You have the pledges of our God, you have the securities of his goodness, you have his presence that is inescapable. If, then, you sin no longer, he forgives you what you did in ignorance; but if when you have known him and found mercy with him you resort again to such (deeds), then both your former (sins) will be laid to your charge, and you shall have no part nor mercy in his presence."

108. And after speaking these words to them he made this prayer: "O Jesus, who hast woven this crown with thy weaving, who has united these many flowers into the unfading flower of thy countenance, who hast sown these words in ⟨my⟩ (?) (heart); thou only protector of thy servants, and physician who healest for nought; only doer of good and despiser of none, only merciful and lover of men, only saviour and righteous one; who ever seest the (deeds) of all and dwellest in all (*or* "in all things") and art everywhere present, encompassing all things and filling all things; Christ Jesu, God, Lord, that with thy gifts and thy mercy protectest those that hope in thee, who exactly knowest all the devices and the malice of him that is everywhere our adversary, which he contriveth against us; do thou only, O Lord, assist thy servants by thy visitation. Even so, Lord!"

109. And he asked for bread, and gave thanks with these words: "What praise or what offering or what thanksgiving shall we name as we break this bread, but thee alone, Lord Jesu? We glorify thy name that was spoken by the Father; we glorify thy name that was spoken through the Son.[1] We glorify thine entering of the Door;[2] we glorify thy Resurrection[3] that is shown us through thee; we glorify thy Way;[4] we glorify thy Seed,[5] thy

---

[1] *Or:* "We glorify thy name of 'Father' that was spoken by ⟨thee⟩; we glorify thy name of 'Son' that was spoken through ⟨thee⟩."
[2] Cf. Jn. 10:9.   [3] Cf. Jn. 11:25.   [4] Cf. Jn. 14:6.   [5] Cf. Mk. 4:26 and pars.

Word,[1] thy Grace, thy Faith, thy Salt,[2] thine inexpressible Pearl,[3] thy Treasure,[4] thy Plough,[5] thy Net,[6] thy Greatness, thy Diadem, him that for us was called the Son of Man, that granted us the truth, repose, knowledge, power, commandment, confidence, hope, love, liberty and refuge in thee. For thou alone, O Lord, art the root of immortality and the fount of incorruption and the seat of the ages, who now art called all these things on our account, that calling on thee through them we may know thy greatness, which at the present is invisible to us, but visible only to the pure as it is portrayed in thy manhood only."

110. And he broke the bread and gave to all of us, praying over each of the brethren that he would be worthy of the Lord's grace and of the most holy Eucharist. And he partook of it himself and said, "May there be for me also a part with you", and, "Peace be with you, my beloved."

The Death of John

111. After this he said to Verus, "Take some men with you, with two baskets and shovels, and follow me." And Verus without delay did what was ordered by John the servant of God. So the blessed John came out of the house and walked outside the gates, having told the greater number that they should leave him; and when he came to a tomb of a brother of ours, he said to the young men, "Dig, my sons". And they dug. And he was more insistent with them, and said, "The digging must go deeper". And while they were digging he spoke to them the word of God and encouraged those that had come from the house with him, edifying them and preparing them for the greatness of God and praying for each one of us.

And when the young men had finished the trench as he desired, while we knew nothing (of his intention) he took off the outer clothes which he had on and laid them like a mattress in the bottom of the trench; and standing in his vest only he lifted up his hands and prayed, saying, 112. "O thou that didst choose us for the apostolate among the Gentiles;[7] O God who has sent us into (all) the world; who hast shown thyself through the law

---

[1] Cf. Jn. 1:1.   [2] Cf. Mt. 5:13.   [3] Cf. Mt. 13:46.   [4] Cf. Mt. 13:44.
[5] Cf. Lk. 9:62.   [6] Cf. Mt. 13:47.   [7] Cf. Rom. 1:5.

and the prophets; who hast never rested, but from the foundation of the world dost always save those who can be saved; who hast revealed thyself through all nature; who hast proclaimed thyself even among beasts; who hast made even the lonely and embittered soul (grow) tame and quiet; who hast given thyself to it when it thirsted for thy words; who hast speedily appeared to it when it was dying; who hast shown thyself to it as a law when sunk into lawlessness; who has revealed thyself to it when overcome by Satan; who hast overcome its adversary when it took refuge with thee; who hast given to it thine hand and aroused it from the works of Hades; who hast not suffered it to conform to the body; who hast shown it its own enemy; who hast made for it a pure knowledge of thee, O God Jesu; Father of beings beyond the heavens, Lord of those that are in the heavens, Law of the ethereal beings and Path of those in the air; Guardian of beings upon earth, and Terror of those beneath the earth, and Grace of those that are thine; receive also the soul of thy John which, it may be, is approved by thee.

113. "Thou who hast kept me also till this present hour pure for thyself and untouched by union with a woman; who when I wished to marry in my youth didst appear to me and say to me, 'John, I need thee'; who didst prepare for me also an infirmity of the body; who on the third occasion when I wished to marry didst prevent me at once, and then at the third hour of the day didst say to me upon the sea, 'John, if thou wert not mine, I should have allowed thee to marry;' who didst blind me for two years, letting me be grieved and entreat thee; who in the third year didst open the eyes of my understanding and didst give me (back) my eyes that are seen; who when I regained my sight didst disclose to me the repugnance even of looking closely at a woman; who hast saved me from the illusion of the present and guided me into that ⟨life⟩ which endureth for ever; who hast rid me of the foul madness that is in the flesh; who hast snatched me from a bitter death and presented me only to thee; who hast silenced the secret disease of my soul and cut off the open deed; who hast weakened and expelled the rebellious (enemy) within me; who hast made my love for thee unsullied; who hast ruled my course to thee unbroken; who hast given me faith in thee undoubting;

who hast instructed my knowledge of thee with purity; who givest to each man's works their due reward; who hast inspired my soul to have no possession but thee alone—for what is more precious than thee? So, Lord, now that I have fulfilled the charge which I was entrusted by thee[1] count me worthy of thy rest and grant me my end in thee, which is inexpressible and unutterable salvation.

114. "And as I come to thee let the fire retreat and the darkness yield, let chaos be enfeebled, the furnace grow dim and Gehenna be quenched; let angels follow and demons be afraid, let the rulers be shattered and the powers fall; let the places on the right hand stand fast and those on the left be removed; let the devil be silenced, let Satan be derided, let his wrath be burned out, let his madness be calmed, let his vengeance be disgraced, let his assault be distressed, let his children be wounded and all his root be *uprooted*. And grant me to finish my way to thee preserved from violence and insult, receiving what thou hast promised to them that live purely and love thee alone."

115. And having sealed himself in every part, standing thus, he said "(Be) thou with me, Lord Jesus Christ"; and he lay down in the trench where he had spread out his clothes; and he said to us, "Peace (be) with you, my brethren", and gave up his spirit rejoicing.

The Departure was subsequently expanded. According to Cod. R and V (with a similar treatment in ps.-Prochorus: Zahn, p. 164, 12f.) the Apostle's body could not be found on the next day (R) or after three days (V; while ps.-Prochorus evidently means, on the same day); "for," adds R, "it was removed through the power of our Lord Jesus Christ". The expansion in Γ and U is more elaborate; the Apostle dismisses the brethren, and when they return on the next day they find only his sandals and see the earth pouring out, on which remembering the words of Jesus in Jn. 21:22 they return giving praise. This conclusion, which is also presupposed by Ephraim of Antioch (above p. 192) combines two mutually conflicting traditions, both derived from Jn. 21:22; one of these has it that John had not died but been transported, while according to the other, which is explicitly reported by Augustine (in *Joh. tract.* 124, 2; Willems, CCh. 26, pp. 681f., ll. 28–37) he is indeed lying in the grave, but is not dead but asleep, so that the earth is shaken

---

[1] Cf. 1 Cor. 9:17.

by his breathing and dust pours out. The Latin version of ps.-Abdias makes the empty tomb produce manna, and Ephraim of Antioch also takes the dust that pours out to be a holy substance.[1]

2. THE ACTS OF PETER

(W. Schneemelcher)

INTRODUCTION.—FOREWORD: In this Introduction to the ancient Acts of Peter we cannot undertake to discuss the whole literature of the early Church concerned with Peter, and its interrelations, but must restrict ourselves to the problems of this one particular work, namely the ancient Πράξεις Πέτρου. Accordingly we shall not discuss the pseudo-Clementines (for which see pp. 532ff.).

1. BIBLIOGRAPHY: *Texts:* Lipsius, *Aa* I, pp. 45–103; L. Vouaux, *Les Actes de Pierre. Introduction, Textes, Traduction et Commentaire*, Paris 1922; C. Schmidt, *Die alten Petrusakten* (*TU* 24. 1) 1903, pp. 3–7 (Coptic text); on the oriental versions of the Martyrdom cf. Vouaux, *op. cit.*, pp. 19–22. Translations: German; G. Ficker, *Apokr.* 1, pp. 383–423; *Apokr.* 2, pp. 226–249; W. Michaelis, pp. 317–379. French; Vouaux, pp. 221ff. English; James, pp. 300–336.

Studies: For earlier literature see Lipsius, *Apostelgeschichten* II. 1 (1887) and supplementary volume (1890), also Harnack, *Gesch. der altchristl. Lit.* I. 1, pp. 131–136.—G. Ficker in *Handb.*, pp. 395–491; C. Schmidt, *Die alten Petrusakten* (see above), 1903; G. Ficker, *Die Petrusakten. Beiträge zu ihrem Verständnis*, 1903; Th. Nissen, "Die Petrusakten und ein bardesanitischer Dialog in der Aberkiosvita", *ZNW* 9, 1908, pp. 190–203; J. Flamion, " Les Actes apocryphes de Pierre", *RHE* IX, 1908, pp. 233–254 and 465–490; X, 1909, pp. 5–29 and 215–277; XI, 1910, pp. 5–28, 223–256, 447–470 and 675–692; XII, 1911, pp. 209–230 and 437–450; C. Schmidt, "Studien zu den alten Petrusakten", *ZKG* 43, 1924, pp. 321–348 (=Studien I); *ZKG* 45, 1927, pp. 481–513 (=Studien II); C. Schmidt, "Zur Datierung der alten Petrusakten", *ZNW* 29, 1930, pp. 150–155; C. H. Turner, "The Latin Acts of Peter", *JTS* 32, 1931, pp. 119–133; C. L. Sturhahn, *Die Christologie der ältesten apokryphen Apostelakten* (Theol. Diss. Heidelberg, 1951, duplicated).

2. ATTESTATION: The earliest certainly direct evidence for the existence of the Acts of Peter is the notice in Eusebius (*HE* III. 3. 2; for the text see Vol. I, p. 58). Eusebius speaks of the ἐπικεκλημέναι αὐτοῦ (sc. Πέτρου) Πράξεις, which means that he knows a work entitled Πράξεις Πέτρου and rejects this work as

---

[1] On the later history of the Departure-legend see M. Jugie, *La mort et l'assomption de la sainte Vierge* (*Studi e Testi* 114), 1944, pp. 710ff. (=Excursus D: "La mort et l'assomption de saint Jean l'Évangéliste"). With the narrative of John's self-burial cf. also the reference to the self-burial of Simon Magus in Hippolytus, *Ref.* VI. 20. 3 (Wendland, *GCS* 26, p. 148, 14–18).

uncanonical, just as he also rejects the Gospel of Peter, the Preaching of Peter and the Revelation of Peter. However Eusebius tells us nothing about the extent and contents of the Acts of Peter. Various attempts have indeed been made to establish earlier evidence for the Acts of Peter. The Muratorian Canon (see Vol. I, pp. 42ff. for the text) does not list the Acts of Peter, but many scholars (e.g. Schmidt, *Petrusakten* p. 105; cp. also Vouaux, pp. 110ff.) think there is a reference to the Acts in the passage: "For the 'most excellent Theophilus' Luke summarizes the several things that in his own presence have come to pass, as also by the omission of the Passion of Peter he makes quite clear, and equally by (the omission of) the journey of Paul, who from the city (of Rome) proceeded to Spain." According to Schmidt (*Petrusakten*, p. 105; cf. also Studien II, p. 495) this is intended to express the view which the author of this table of canonical books takes of events not recorded in the Lucan Acts of the Apostles, namely Peter's death and Paul's journey to Spain: "he knows them as actual occurrences, and not only on the basis of oral tradition, but of a written work which he has read with interest". But such an interpretation probably reads too much out of this brief comment. The author of the Canon gives no indication that he had before him any written account of the death of Peter or Paul's journey to Spain. His words must rather be taken to indicate that he did indeed know of these two events, but had not found them in the Lucan Acts because, in his opinion, Luke was not an eye-witness of these events. The source of his information cannot be discovered from his comment. This precludes the possibility of using the Muratorian Canon as a witness to the Acts of Peter or even for its date. The brief details there given cannot determine whether common traditions are to be assumed for the Muratorian Canon and the Acts of Peter, or what form they took.

Two passages found in Clement of Alexandria have been connected with the Acts of Peter. In *Strom*. III. 6. 52 Clement observes that Peter and Philip produced children, a remark which in no way helps to settle the problem of the Acts of Peter. In *Strom*. VII. 11. 63 he relates that Peter encouraged his wife on the way to her martyrdom. This statement also has nothing to do with the Acts of Peter, but belongs rather to the oral traditions known to Clement.

The same judgment applies to a passage in Hippolytus. In *Ref.* VI. 20 he describes the arrival of Simon at Rome: "This Simon, who perverted many in Samaria by magical arts, was convicted by the apostles and denounced, as is recorded in Acts; but afterwards in desperation he resumed the same practices, and on coming to Rome he (again) came into conflict with the

apostles; and as he perverted many by his magical arts Peter
continually opposed him. And nearing his end ⟨. . .⟩ he used to
sit beneath a plane-tree and teach. And now, being almost discredited, in order to gain time he said that if he were buried alive
he would rise again on the third day. And ordering a grave to be
dug by his disciples, he made them bury him. So they did as he
instructed them, but he has remained (buried) to this day; for
he was not the Christ." (Hipp. *Ref.* VI. 20. 2f.; Wendland,
GCS 26, p. 148, 8–18). C. Schmidt says of this passage "Hippolytus' narrative therefore already has this scene from the Acts of
Peter as its basis" (*Petrusakten* p. 104). But this assertion is quite
groundless. Hippolytus relies primarily on the account given in
the canonical Acts, and then gives a tradition of Simon's death
which has nothing to do with the Acts of Peter as we have them
(cf. Act. Verc. c. 32 = Mart. Petr. c. 3). Hippolytus therefore is
not a witness for the Acts of Peter.

Origen in the third book of his Commentary on Genesis
(according to Eusebius, *HE* III. 1. 2) relates that Peter was in
Rome towards the end of his life: "He was crucified head-
downwards; for he requested that he might suffer thus." This
statement agrees in substance with the account given in the
extant Acts of Peter (Act. Verc. c. 37 = Mart. Petr. c. 8), but is
not a literal citation. It can therefore be only a supposition that
Origen, who certainly knew some part of the apocryphal literature, had also read the Acts of Peter; this point cannot be certainly established. Certainly this statement gives no indication
whatever of the form and content of the Acts of Peter which
Origen possibly knew. If he did have the work before him, this
would establish the *terminus ad quem*, since the Commentary on
Genesis was compiled before 231 (Eusebius, *HE* VI. 24. 2).

Great importance has often been attached to some lines from
the *Carmen apologeticum* of Commodian, which mention the dog
who speaks to Simon (v. 626 = Act. Verc. cc. 9, 11, 12) and the
talking infant (v. 629f. = Act. Verc. c. 15). But even if Commodian's date were accurately known (on this question see most
recently K. Thraede, "Beiträge zur Datierung Commodians",
Jahrb. f. Antike und Christentum 2, 1959, pp. 90–114: middle of the
3rd century) these lines again would signify nothing more than
that Commodian knew the legends of the speaking animals as
they appear in the Acts of Peter and the Acts of Paul. They do
not prove knowledge of the Acts of Peter as a whole, and hardly
give grounds for more precise inferences about the currency of
the Acts of Peter in the West in the 3rd century.

On the other hand the author of the Didascalia (probably
first half of the 3rd century) seems actually to have used the

Acts of Peter. In VI, 7–9 he gives an account of the beginnings of heresy and makes Peter describe his encounters with Simon in Jerusalem and Rome. C. Schmidt has collected the various points which indicate that the Acts of Peter were the basis for the Didascalia (*Petrusakten*, p. 147; cf. also Vouaux, p. 119f. and Schmidt, Studien II, p. 507). Here the most important point is the fact that Simon's first meeting with the Apostles takes place in Jerusalem, which disagrees with Acts 8:14ff. We cannot in all points arrive at the certainty which Schmidt displays;[1] but there is plenty of evidence for the truth of the contention that the author of the Didascalia used the Acts of Peter. Following Harnack's suggestion Schmidt has also attempted to show that Porphyry knew the Acts of Peter (Schmidt, *Petrusakten*, pp. 167ff.). Two passages preserved by Macarius Magnes (II. 22 and IV. 4)[2] are taken as evidence of this knowledge. The point depends especially on the fact that according to Porphyry—and contrary to the official Roman tradition—Peter was in Rome for only a short time before his death there by crucifixion. But it is hardly possible to prove conclusively that Porphyry derived this assertion from the Acts of Peter.

Accordingly not much remains of the numerous so-called testimonies to the Acts of Peter for the period before Eusebius. Only Origen and the Didascalia can be used as witnesses to its existence; and they give no reliable information about the extent and contents of the work. However we have so far left out of account both the pseudo-Clementines and the Acts of John and the Acts of Paul.

In the Second Edition of this book, in the section on the Acts of Peter, H. Waitz cited extracts from the pseudo-Clementines (*Apokr.* 2, pp. 212–226). Here Waitz relied on his source-critical theories, which he claimed as an "assured result", and attempted to reconstruct from the "Clementine" Homilies and Recognitions the Πράξεις Πέτρου which he assumed. Waitz further defined the relationship of his Πράξεις Πέτρου to the rest of the Acts of Peter (i.e. the Vercelli Acts and the Coptic fragment) on the principle that both "derive from a common tradition, which has survived in its original form in the pseudo-Clementine Πράξεις Πέτρου" (*Apokr.* 2, p. 213). This contribution of Waitz's led C. Schmidt to a thorough investigation of the pseudo-Clementines, including a thorough discussion of the relationship

---

[1] Schmidt relies here mainly on the Coptic fragment, assigning the events it describes to Jerusalem. The place of action is not mentioned in the text, but may be inferred. As regards the Didascalia, however, we cannot say "but this derives simply and solely from the Acts of Peter" (Schmidt, *Petrusakten*, p. 147).

[2] On the problem of Macarius' use of Porphyry cf. Quasten III, pp. 486–488; and works there mentioned.

of these writings and their source-document to the Acts of Peter (C. Schmidt, *Studien zu den Ps.-Clementinen*, *TU* 46. 1, 1929, esp. pp. 1–46). Schmidt rightly criticizes Waitz for giving insufficient attention to the problem of the apocryphal Acts of Apostles and for numerous errors that result. Schmidt himself sought to show that the author of the source-document underlying the pseudo-Clementines used the ancient Acts of Peter. Since this document and the Didascalia, which certainly did use the Acts of Peter (see above) belong to the same region and period, this contention of Schmidt's is not improbable.

This is not the place to describe the more recent work on the pseudo-Clementines (cf. the survey of research in G. Strecker, *Das Judenchristentum in den Pseudo-klementinen*, *TU* 70, 1958, pp. 1–34; further details in Strecker, above, pp. 102ff. and Irmscher, below, pp. 532ff.). We need only remark that the question of their relationship to the Acts of Peter has been largely displaced by other problems in research on the pseudo-Clementines.[1] Strecker (*op. cit.*, p. 255) has rightly emphasized that Schmidt cannot command immediate agreement "if he sees the Πράξεις-Πέτρου-passages in the source-document as immediately derived from the ancient Acts of Peter". In particular it seems to me doubtful whether the different localities in which the encounters between Simon and Peter take place in the source-document of the pseudo-Clementines and in the Acts of Peter allow of such a simple explanation as Schmidt's (*op. cit.*, pp. 31ff.). We must therefore begin by regarding the relationships between the Acts of Peter and the pseudo-Clementines as an unsolved problem. The only fixed point is that the source-document of the pseudo-Clementines, which Strecker has good grounds for dating *c.* 260, is later than the Acts of Peter (on the date of which see below, p. 275); and further that there is a good deal to be said for the supposition that the author of the source-document knew at least the material which is used in the Acts of Peter. Whether this material reached him in the form of the Acts of Peter, of which only parts have come down to us, or in another form, cannot be determined.

The problem of the relationship of the Acts of Peter to the Acts of John is extremely difficult and obscure. While Th. Zahn (e.g. *Gesch. d. ntl. Kanons* II, p. 860) declared for identity of authorship, C. Schmidt endeavoured to prove that the author of the Acts of Peter used the Acts of John (*Petrusakten*, pp. 77–79). Vouaux also

---

[1] The question of supposedly Ebionite Acts of Apostles, thoroughly discussed by H. J. Schoeps, cannot and need not be pursued here; cf. H. J. Schoeps, *Theologie und Geschichte des Judenchristentums*, 1949, pp. 381–456, and W. Schneemelcher, "Das Problem des Judenchristentums": *Verkündigung und Forschung* 1951/52, pp. 229ff.

considers the Acts of John to be among the sources edited by the author of the Acts of Peter (pp. 49–52). All this presupposes that the Acts of John really are the earliest of the apocryphal apostolic Acts. "Leucius has really the honour of having composed the earliest romance about the Apostles; in so doing, and probably contrary to his own expectation, he paved the way to an entire new genre of early Christian literature; for his example was soon followed by the author of the Acts of Paul, who also came from Asia Minor, and pseudo-Peter stood on the shoulders of both of them in writing his romance" (C. Schmidt, *Petrusakten*, p. 99). This chronological pattern depended in the main on the detection of definite agreements and similarities in christological ideas, but partly also on other presuppositions, which then provided the basis for the explanation of these similarities. Meanwhile as far as the Acts of Paul are concerned C. Schmidt himself has proved this chronology untenable (see below, pp. 266ff.); and for the Acts of John Schäferdiek (above, pp. 189ff.) has shown that the attestation before Eusebius is so uncertain that the early dating can hardly be sustained. But the problem has to be more closely considered, since the question remains, whether the agreements and similarities can perhaps be explained by the Acts of Peter having served as the model for the Acts of John?

In the "Preaching of the Gospel" (Acts of John cc. 87ff.) John also comes to speak about the earthly appearance of Christ, and describes at the outset how he and his brother James were called by Jesus, when James saw the Lord as a boy, while John saw him standing by in the form of a handsome, good-looking man (cc. 88f.). There follows the account of the Transfiguration, a remarkable new version of the story (c. 90; on the interpretation cf. Sturhahn, pp. 32f.), and here too the theme of the Saviour's distinct forms plays an important part. Now in the Acts of Peter, c. 20, Peter likewise tells the congregation assembled to hear the Gospel that Christ was seen by the disciples in the form that each one could comprehend. Here too the story of the Transfiguration is given as an example, but without doubt the author keeps closer to the biblical narrative. Moreover the story in c. 21 about the widows whose sight is restored and who are then made to describe what they have seen is also characterized by the theme of polymorphy: some saw him as an old man, others as a youth, etc. The chapter concludes with Peter's saying "Certainly God is greater than our thoughts, as we have learned from the aged widows, how they saw the Lord in a variety of forms". This explanatory conclusion shows that the author of the Acts of Peter adopted the idea of polymorphy from other motives than those of the author of the Acts of John. But even apart from the intention which appears in this explanation, it must now be stated that a resemblance between the two passages in respect of an idea which we encounter elsewhere is all that can be shown; we can hardly speak of literary dependence (cf. Sturhahn, pp. 30ff. and 184ff.). Similar caution is needed in respect of the other passages which have been cited to prove dependence. Thus in the Acts of John, c. 98, there is a catalogue of various names given to the Cross of Light, so that a series of christological predicates is assembled; and in the Acts of Peter, c. 20, we find a similar catalogue of names given to Jesus: in *John*, it is *Logos*, Mind (νοῦς), Jesus, Christ, *Door, Way, Bread, Seed, Resurrection*, Son, Father, Spirit, *Life*, Truth, *Faith, Grace:* in *Peter* it is *Door*, Light, *Way, Bread*, Water, *Life, Resurrection*, Refreshment, Pearl, Treasure, *Seed*, Abundance, Mustard-seed, Vine, Plough, *Grace, Faith, Word.*

Is this a case of literary dependence? Once again we must disregard the intentions connected with these catalogues (on which cf. Sturhahn, pp. 33f. and 190f.). There is without doubt a certain affinity, but it is confined to individual conceptions, which in any case circulated freely as christological predicates drawn from the common Christian tradition. Furthermore these lists do not present a form which is peculiar to these two apocryphal Books of Acts. Justin (*Dial.* 100, 4) and the Letter to Diognetus (9, 6) are evidence for the fact that such catalogues occur in other connections as well. Here too, then, the question of literary dependence should be treated with the greatest circumspection.

Finally, C. Schmidt (*Petrusakten*, pp. 97ff.) sought to establish that the Acts of Peter c. 39 (10) are indebted to the Acts of John cc. 99ff. But this passage likewise does not admit a conclusive proof of dependence (cf. Sturhahn's interpretation, pp. 157ff., which also gives parallels in the Acts of Thomas). To sum up, the ostensible cases where *Peter* borrowed from *John*, which on the new chronology may and indeed must be seen as *John's* borrowings from *Peter*, are something quite different from demonstrable literary plagiarisms. They are in the main to be explained in that the ideas they contain have similar origins, from the historian of religion's point of view, despite their very different theological intention and application.[1] So, as far as we can see today, the Acts of John must be set aside in considering the attestation, date and sources of the Acts of Peter.

The case is different with the Acts of Paul. Here we can put

[1] Sturhahn's work is of prime importance for these problems, even though his interpretation cannot always be followed. For the historian of religion's estimate of the relationships we may refer to H. Schlier, *Religionsgeschichtliche Untersuchungen zu den Ignatiusbriefen*, Beih. zur ZNW 8, 1929. Schlier takes account of both the Acts of John and those of Peter.

the case more briefly, since C. Schmidt has probably said all that is necessary. Whereas formerly Schmidt strongly upheld the dependence of the Acts of Peter, he abandoned this view in consequence of the discovery of the Hamburg Papyrus of the Acts of Paul (cf. pp. 345f. below). In this papyrus there occurs a variant of the famous "Quo vadis" scene (Acts of Peter c. 35 = Mart. c. 6), which does not really fit its context. From this and other sections (especially the story of Theon, Acts of Peter c. 5) Schmidt has rightly concluded that the author of the Acts of Paul used and transcribed the Acts of Peter.[1] The significance of this for dating the Acts of Peter remains to be discussed (cf. p. 275). Here we need only report the Acts of Paul as being among the few witnesses for the existence of the Acts of Peter before Eusebius' time.

In the 4th century the sources mentioning the Acts of Peter become rather more plentiful. This has been pointed out often enough in the relevant literature (especially by C. Schmidt, Vouaux and Flamion) and need not be repeated here. Two facts stand out:

1. The *Manichaean Psalm-book* clearly uses the Acts of Peter among other apocryphal books of Acts (cf. above pp. 179f.).

2. The polemic against the apocryphal Acts of Apostles, known to us principally from numerous references in Augustine, led to an almost total disappearance of these Acts, including the Acts of Peter.[2]

One of the statements in Augustine is especially important as proving that the Coptic fragment (below, pp. 269f.) belongs to the Acts of Peter. Augustine in his treatise against Adimantus attacks the Manichaeans' rejection of the canonical Acts, in which they rely principally on Acts 5:1ff., and says, "They show great blindness in condemning this since, among the apocrypha, they read and treat as an important work the one which I have mentioned about the Apostle Thomas and about the daughter of Peter himself who became paralysed through the prayers of her father, and about the gardener's daughter who died at the prayer of the

[1] Cf. especially C. Schmidt, ΠΡΑΞΕΙΣ ΠΑΥΛΟΥ, Acta Pauli, 1936, pp. 127ff. Schmidt's view has been contested by W. Michaelis, pp. 377ff. In particular the Lord's words in the "Quo vadis" scene (Acts of Peter: πάλιν σταυροῦμαι; Acts of Paul: ἄνωθεν μέλλω σταυροῦσθαι) are thought by Michaelis to prove the dependence of the Acts of Peter on the Acts of Paul, or on a corresponding tradition. However I believe that Schmidt is to be followed: the Lord's saying does not fit its context in the Acts of Paul, whereas in the Acts of Peter it seems appropriate.

[2] We may remark in passing that this controversy and its results led 19th-century scholars, especially Lipsius, on the clearly false trail of "gnostic" as opposed to "catholic" books of Acts. It is to Schmidt's credit to have restored the position in some degree, though he also often speaks too exclusively of "popular-catholic" tendencies. Sturhahn's work shows that in the apocryphal Acts above all we have to do with a mixture of various elements; cf. also pp. 272ff. below.

said Peter; and they reply that this was expedient for them, that
the one should be crippled with paralysis and the other die; nevertheless they do not deny that this was done at the prayers of the
Apostle" (Augustine, *c. Adimantum Man. disc.* XVII; ed. Zycha,
CSEL XXV 1, p. 170, 9–16). Even if Augustine does not mention
the Acts of Peter directly, it is clear that he knows an apocryphal
work, translated into Latin, which contained the story of Peter's
daughter. But in fact it can only have been the Acts of Peter, to
which the Coptic fragment belonged.

Finally we may note that the scanty attestation of the Acts of
Peter even after Eusebius' time (until Photius, cod. 114, on which
see Schäferdiek, above pp. 178ff.) is supplemented through the
use of the Acts of Peter in later Acts of Apostles. The texts
which are to be mentioned in this connection include some which
are important for the textual tradition. In the *Vita Abercii* (4th
century; ed. Th. Nissen, 1912) the following passages are taken
verbatim from the Acts of Peter:

Act. Verc. c. 2 (Lipsius p. 46, = Vit. Ab. c. 13 (Nissen, p. 11,
    31–47, 11)   12–12, 9)
Act. Verc. c. 20 (p. 67, 3–8)   = Vit. Ab. c. 15 (p. 13, 7–11)
Act. Verc. c. 20 (p. 67, 26–68, = Vit. Ab. c. 15 (p. 13, 16–15, 2)
    15)
Act. Verc. c. 7 (p. 53, 20–29)   = Vit. Ab. c. 24 (p. 19, 9–20, 2)
Act. Verc. c. 21 (p. 68, 17–69, 2) = Vit. Ab. c. 26 (p. 20, 11–23, 1).

These passages, of which full use is made in the translation
presented below, are of special interest in that they put us in a
position to evaluate the Latin translation of the Acts of Peter
given in the Vercelli MS. The Latin translator has obviously
followed the Greek text practically word for word. Another
instructive feature is that these borrowed sections all consist of
speeches; clearly the imagination of the author of the *Vita Abercii*
was not quite equal to composing such occasional speeches and
he therefore borrowed from the Acts of Peter.

Less obvious is the use made of the Acts of Peter by the Acts of
Philip (late 4th–early 5th century; cf. below p. 577). According
to C. Schmidt (Studien I, pp. 329ff.) there are three passages in
the *Acta Philippi* which exhibit the knowledge and use of the Acts
of Peter:

Act. Phil. 142 (Bonnet p. 81)   = Coptic fragment (Peter's
                                 daughter)
Act. Phil. 140 (p. 74)   = Act. Verc. 38 (Mart. c. 9)
Act. Phil. c. 80–85 (p. 32f.)   = Act. Verc. 28.

It cannot indeed be conclusively proved that the author of the

Acts of Philip actually transcribed the Acts of Peter. But the agreements are so strong that literary dependence has to be suspected. Again, the *Acta Xanthippae et Polyxenae* (ed. M. R. James, *Apocrypha anecdota*, Texts and Studies II. 3, 1893, pp. 43–85) seem to have used the Acts of Peter. Thus following C. Schmidt (Studien II, pp. 494f.) we can see in c. 24 an excerpt from the beginning of the Vercelli Acts. Further details, especially the name Xanthippa, indicate a literary connection; indeed the author of these late Acts (probably 6th century) seems in general to have borrowed freely from other apocryphal books of Acts.[1]

In the *Acta SS. Nerei et Achillei* (5th–6th century; edited by H. Achelis, *TU* XI. 2, 1893) at least c. 15 can hardly be thought of without its prototype in the Acts of Peter, which, it is important to note, is the Coptic narrative of Peter's daughter. All sorts of developments must certainly be noted, but the prototype is clearly discernible (cf. Schmidt, Studien I, pp. 342f.; also Vouaux, pp. 155ff.). Finally it should be mentioned that the later Petrine texts (the so-called Linus- and Marcellus-texts) are derived from the ancient Acts of Peter (cf. Vouaux, pp. 129ff.; 160ff.; Lipsius, *Apostelgeschichten* II; further details below, p. 572), though probably not directly taken from the surviving Latin Vercelli Acts.

This later use of the Acts of Peter demonstrates, what C. Schmidt in particular has repeatedly emphasized, that the Acts of Peter long continued in use in catholic circles. They "originated in catholic circles and originally were read with great respect as products of the Great Church"; they fell into disfavour in the time after Nicaea, but nevertheless "persisted for a long time as favourite reading in good catholic circles, until a substitute had been devised for them in the form of supposedly orthodox revisions" (Schmidt, *Petrusakten*, p. 151). The history of the Acts of Peter in the early Church allows these facts to be acknowledged, even though much else remains obscure, and also reflects the history and development of the Church's doctrine and spirituality.

3. SURVIVING CONTENTS: The following passages of the ancient Acts of Peter are preserved:

(*a*) The so-called *Actus Vercellenses*, named after the single Latin MS. in which the text has come down to us, a codex at Vercelli (cod. Verc. CLVIII, 6th–7th century). The translation it presents originated according to Turner (*JTS* 32, 1931, pp. 119f.) not later than the 3rd or 4th century. Its contents are not quite correctly represented by the title inferred by Lipsius, "Actus Petri cum Simone" (cf. *Aa* I, p. 45). It is better to assume with

[1] Cf. the catalogue in James, *op. cit.*, pp. 47ff.; for the Acts of Peter we may refer also to Vouaux's commentary (cf. his index s.v. Actes de Xanthippe).

C. Schmidt (Studien II, p. 510) that the title read, actus Petri apostoli = Πράξεις Πέτρου τοῦ ἀποστόλου, which indeed would be the title which accords with the contents.

After a short account of the departure of Paul for Spain (cc. 1–3) we read of the arrival of Simon in Rome and of Peter's journey thither prompted by divine instructions (cc. 4–6). There follow the accounts of the recovery of the Roman congregation by Peter, of his controversy with Simon, which reaches its climax in the contest in the forum (cc. 7–29) and finally Peter's martyrdom (cc. 30–41), of which there are also two Greek MSS. (cod. Patm. 48, 9th century, = P; cod. Vatopedi 79, 10th–11th century, = A). The fact that the account of Peter's martyrdom belonged to the Acts of Peter from the first is shown by the two Greek MSS. beginning at different points: A begins at Act. Verc. 30, and so contains the narrative about Chryse, etc., before the martyrdom proper, whereas P does not begin until c. 33. Besides the two Greek MSS. of the Martyrdom there is further attestation of the original Greek text of the Acts of Peter for the end of c. 25 and the beginning of c. 26 in a papyrus fragment: Pap. Oxyrhynchos 849 (ed. Grenfell and Hunt, Ox. Pap. VI, 1908, pp. 6–12; text also given by Vouaux, pp. 374ff., in his apparatus). Lastly we must recall the passages of the *Vita Abercii* cited above (p. 267) which, in spite of the slight revision they disclose, agree with the two Greek MSS. of the Martyrdom and with the papyrus in showing that the Latin translation given in the cod. Verc. "is generally reliable, even though it is not free from misunderstandings, eccentricities and inexactitudes. We are also justified in observing that the Latin translator sometimes tries to make the sense clear by adding a few words, but seems nevertheless more anxious to abbreviate than to amplify" (Ficker, *Apokr.* 2, pp. 226f.).

As the Greek MSS. already prove, the Martyrdom was soon separated from the Acts of Peter. The oriental versions show how widely this extract circulated. We have Coptic, Syriac, Armenian, Arabic, Ethiopic and Slavonic texts of the Martyrdom, some beginning with Mart. c. 4 = Act. Verc. c. 33. A conspectus of these witnesses, which were not fully used by Lipsius in his edition, is given by Vouaux, pp. 19–22. The fact that the Vercelli Acts do not present the complete text of the Acts of Peter is shown by the Stichometry of Nicephorus (cf. Vol. I, pp. 49ff.), which makes the Acts of Peter consist of 2,750 lines, that is rather more than St. Luke's Gospel (2,600 lines). Accordingly Zahn calculated (*Gesch. d. ntl. Kanons* II, p. 841 n. 3) that about a third of the Acts of Peter is missing. Not much of this missing material has yet been discovered.

(*b*) The Story of Peter's daughter, preserved in the Coptic papyrus Berlin 8502.[1] This papyrus, discovered and edited by C. Schmidt (*Petrusakten*, 1903) contains on pp. 128–132 and 135–141 this story, which Schmidt claimed as belonging to the Acts of Peter; and after Ficker had contested it, Schmidt finally established his view (cf. esp. Schmidt, Studien I). The reasons adduced by Schmidt are of varying cogency, but are so convincing as a whole that it can no longer be doubted that we have here a fragment of the first part of the Acts of Peter, which is otherwise lost.

The contents of the story are not especially noteworthy. Peter demonstrates in the case of his daughter that outward suffering can be a gift from God if it has the effect of preserving virginity. This, then, is a miracle-story coloured by encratite sympathies such as we often find in the Vercelli Acts. The scene of the story is not directly indicated; but since it mentions Peter's going to his house, and since Peter's daughter lives with her father, one must assume that the setting is Peter's home; but this, according to Act. Verc. c. 5, is to be looked for in Jerusalem. But since this story must have belonged to the first section of the Acts of Peter, which has disappeared, one must suppose that it is in Jerusalem that the events of this section take place. It may be supposed that this first section already described a contest between Peter and Simon; since the fact that Peter when in Rome repeatedly speaks of this earlier contest with the magician is no argument against it (cf. the different accounts of Paul's conversion in Acts 9, 22 and 26). Apart from this, hardly anything can be said about the extent and further contents of this first section. We know of only one other narrative that must have belonged to it.

(c) In the apocryphal Epistle of Titus (above, pp. 141ff.) there is found a narrative of a gardener's daughter, who falls down dead at the prayer of Peter, is then restored to life on her father's petition, but a few days later is seduced and abducted. This story, which is hardly misinterpreted by the author of ps.-Titus, has the same (encratite) sympathies as the narrative of Peter's daughter (above): it is better for a man to be dead than to be polluted by sexual intercourse. That this narrative taken from ps.-Titus belongs to the Acts of Peter is shown by the reference in Augustine (*c. Adimant.* XVII, above, pp. 266f.) where the two events are put side by side, so that they were probably quoted from the same apocryphal work. Certainly we have here a case of parallel narratives. But the Vercelli Acts themselves and other apocryphal Acts present us with similar parallel narratives, which soon become tedious to the modern reader.

---

[1] A description of the MS. is given by W. Till, *Die gnostischen Schriften des kopt. Papyrus Berol.* 8502, *TU* 60, 1955, pp. 6–8.

It is questionable whether the fragment of a speech of Peter edited by de Bruyne belongs to the Acts of Peter (de Bruyne in *Revue Bénédictine* XXV, 1908, pp. 152f., presenting a fragment of a biblical concordance, Cod. Cambrai 254, 13th century). C. Schmidt connects these words with the narrative of the gardener's daughter: "It is highly probable that we have here the words spoken by the Apostle to the distracted father" (Studien I, p. 336). But this surely says more than can be proved; nothing more than a possibility can be established.

4. STRUCTURE, PURPOSE AND THEOLOGICAL ORIENTATION OF THE ACTS OF PETER: After our review of the surviving portions of the Acts of Peter, little remains to be said about the structure of this apocryphal history of the Apostle. As already mentioned, it may be inferred from the Act. Verc. that the first section, which apart from a few remnants has disappeared, took place in Jerusalem (cf. Schmidt, Studien II, pp. 497ff.). Here too there evidently occurred the first collision between Peter and Simon, together with the events which we learn from the Coptic account of Peter's daughter and from the fragment of ps.-Titus. It should be noted that the author of the Acts of Peter, who transferred the first controversy between Peter and Simon to Jerusalem, clearly did so because he was bound by the tradition of Peter's twelve-year stay in Jerusalem (cf. Act. Verc. c. 5; on the twelve years cf. W. Bauer, above, pp. 44f.). On the other hand he knew of Paul's activity in Rome, and of Peter's martyrdom at Rome, and presumably had information of some kind about operations of Simon in Rome. We cannot say whether he knew Justin's account (Apol. 26, 2) of the statue of Simon at Rome (cf. Act. Verc. c. 10: Marcellus reports that Simon had persuaded him to set up a statue to him).

The composition of the work was determined by these traditions which the author inherited. First the two scenes of action, Jerusalem and Rome, were determined. Next it had to be explained how the Roman congregation could come into being before Peter's arrival. For this purpose the author inserted the episode concerned with Paul in Act. Verc. c. 1–3. We cannot say with certainty whether, or in what way, the first section of the Acts of Peter dealt with Paul. But from Peter's observation in Act. Verc. 23 we may assume that Paul was present at his first meeting with Simon. For Peter describes how Simon tried to persuade, not John and himself, as in Acts 8:18ff., but Paul and himself, to sell him the power of working miracles, i.e. the Holy Ghost. It is probable that this fact, which Peter mentions in c. 23, was previously recounted in greater detail in the first section, thus

271

preparing the way for Paul's activity in Rome. On the other hand the corruption of the Roman congregation by Simon can only have gone on in the absence of an Apostle; Paul therefore had to leave Rome for Spain. No doubt the author took this journey of Paul's to Spain from his Epistle to the Romans, as he did with a number of names.

While Paul is already at work in Rome but Peter is still bound to Jerusalem by the Lord's command, there intervenes the story of Eubula, which Peter several times afterwards recalls (cf. Schmidt, Studien II, pp. 502ff.). This narrative must have been of some significance to the author, since he so often refers back to it. It is in fact important for him since it is through this event that Simon is exposed as a magician and a villain, and Peter can refer to this exposure.

The contest with Simon, which is indeed the real theme of the story of Eubula, is in every way an especially important element in the whole composition. This clearly appears in the Vercelli Acts; the controversy with the magician Simon is to some extent the predominant theme to which the other narratives, and also the Martyrdom, are attached and which they supplement. At the same time the Martyrdom is certainly assimilated to definite prototypes which were already known to the author (cf. inter alia H. von Campenhausen, Die Idee des Martyriums in der alten Kirche, 1936, especially pp. 144ff.). But he has set the narrative of Peter's ending in close connection with the contest against Simon. The controversy between the two fought out in public in the forum certainly goes in Peter's favour, but has no appropriate ending. The author has reserved his account of Simon's ending in order to use it as the introduction to Peter's martyrdom (Act. Verc. cc. 30–32): Simon attempts to ascend into heaven, but falls, breaks his limbs and comes to a miserable end. This is the beginning of the Martyrdom-story, which however displays no further connection with the story of Simon. Probably the author has here adapted well-defined traditions which he found ready to hand.

Although the contest with Simon is an essential theme of the Acts of Peter, this does not imply that the work was written as a polemical tract against Simonian gnosis. A cursory reading is enough to show how little the author could relate of Simon's teaching. Again, very little about the career of this character is conveyed to the reader. "In general the picture of Simon's personality given in the Actus is a remarkably meagre portrayal" (Sturhahn, p. 168). The whole emphasis of this picture rests on the constantly reiterated fact that Simon is nothing but a magician, an evil wizard. But here it is expressed in the phrase that he is an "expositor of Satan" (Sturhahn p. 170), the ἄγγελος τοῦ διαβόλου (Mart. c. 3). The Acts of Peter obviously do not intend to conduct a heresy-hunt; their purpose is to demonstrate, in the persons of Simon and his constantly victorious adversary, that God is stronger than Satan, whose service Simon has entered. Hence Peter can ascribe what is almost redemptive significance to this contest (Act. Verc. c. 6). We are dealing, not with the doctrines of Simonian Gnosticism, but with the contest between God and the devil. It is the merit of Sturhahn's work (cf. esp. pp. 168ff.) to have thrown light on these problems, even though in my opinion too little attention has been paid to the literary character and purpose of the Acts of Peter. The picture of Simon given in the Acts of Peter cannot be discussed without regard to the purpose of this work. The Acts of Peter belongs to the class of apocryphal Acts, and is therefore subject to the judgment already given about this literature in general (cf. pp. 168ff. above): the apocryphal Acts are designed for entertainment, instruction and edification. They are not simply an adaptation of the literary form of the Greek novel, nor are they a development of the ancient aretalogies; similarly the pattern of the Lucan Acts is not the determining factor. The literary activity of the authors of the apocryphal Acts was primarily the collection and arrangement of various traditions that circulated by word of mouth.

Applied to the Acts of Peter, this entails that this work also is governed by the purposes of edification, instruction and also entertainment. The picture of Simon given in the Acts of Peter clearly illustrates its difference from the anti-heretical literature. The doctrine of this arch-heretic is suppressed, and instead of it anti-christian objections of a general character are attributed to him.[1] In refuting these objections Peter does indeed make use of scriptural evidence (Act. Verc. c. 24), but achieves decisive success through his miracles, and through his frustrating or out-doing Simon's miracles, whose reality the author in no way denies. The popular character of the Acts of Peter, as of all the apocryphal Acts, is also shown in the fact that it is not extensive theological discussions that occupy the central place, but miracu-lous acts: marvels of all kinds, resurrections, apparitions, etc. Peter's speeches in Mart. cc. 8–10 constitute something of an exception, and in their theological content also they take up a position of their own (cf. Sturhahn, pp. 153ff.). But here the author may probably have modelled himself on an earlier writing of homiletic character. There is nothing here which alters our

---

[1] See for instance Act. Verc. 23: "Men of Rome, is God born? Is He crucified? He who owns a Lord is no God!" Cf. Sturhahn, pp. 176ff., including further examples from early Christian literature.

SECOND AND THIRD CENTURY ACTS

overall estimate of the character of the work; it only makes clear that the unity of the Acts of Peter does not depend on a formulated theological programme, but on its purpose of edification and entertainment together with certain moral inclinations.

It is no doubt difficult, and would overstep the limits of this introduction, to attempt to indicate in detail how far the author made use of orally transmitted legendary material of various kinds. There are some points at which this combination of traditions becomes evident. We need only recall the Martyrdom; but the legend of Simon also circulated without doubt in the form of single episodes before attaining a fixed form in the Acts of Peter. The miracle-stories in particular, which indeed are for the most part typical legends, were not previously combined with the legends about Simon, but arose and were passed on individually. The author of the Acts of Peter has collected this material and made of it a comparatively well-knit whole.

In so doing, was he aiming at a continuation of the canonical Acts, or was his work intended as an alternative account? This question is not quite correctly posed. Obviously the brief narrative of Acts 8:9ff. gave the impetus for the formation of legends centring on the figure of Simon. But it becomes very clear in the Acts of Peter that this narrative given in Acts is completely recast. But above all the theological intention, as well as the material which the Acts of Peter refashions, are different in character from those of the canonical Acts. Thus "alternative account" and "continuation" are equally unsuitable descriptions: the Acts of Peter is rather to be described as an attempt to supplement the canonical Acts with regard to the personal history of Peter. Here as in the other apocryphal Acts it is the interest in individual personalities, about whom the canonical Acts tells us little—and in Peter's case this corresponds with his later destiny—which has given the impetus to this literature.

There remains the question whether we can speak of a consistent theological orientation. The earlier alternative, Gnostic or catholic, has been already characterized as questionable (above, p. 266 n. 2). Obviously the Acts of Peter is not a Gnostic work. It is also no less clear that individual passages (esp. Mart. cc. 8–10) are heavily affected by Gnostic elements. In several sections of the Acts of Peter, again, a certain docetism is unmistakable (e.g. Act. Verc. c. 20), although the catch-word "docetism" does not suffice to describe the theology of the Acts of Peter. "There results . . . the . . . . situation that a popular Christian writing, whose non-Gnostic character may on other grounds be taken as proved, sees itself driven to answer the question, how we should understand the Saviour's entry into this world, in a docetic sense,

274

and in so doing concerns itself with traditions which in structure
are closely related to the Gnostic myth of the Redeemer . . .
while at the same time the Kerygma of the Virgin Birth lends
the docetic solution the appearance of legitimacy" (Sturhahn,
pp. 182f.). This characterization shows that it is not easy to sum
up the theology of the Acts of Peter in a single formula. Sturhahn
has tried to define the place occupied by the Acts of Peter in the
history of doctrine as popular modalistic monarchianism, but has
not been able to offer effective proof of this view. We must be
content with this: as well as docetic elements there are in fact
monarchian pronouncements (cf. earlier notice by C. Schmidt,
Petrusakten, p. 24). But the Acts of Peter are not a theological
treatise but popular literature, and so are more concerned with
edification and moral effect than with theological clarity.

The moral suggestions certainly embody certain encratite
trends. These are soon disclosed in Act. Verc. c. 2, in the eucharist
with bread and water. A more important point is the strong
emphasis placed on sexual continence as a condition of salvation
(cf. Mart. cc. 4f.). In the Coptic fragment, as in Peter's later
preaching at Rome, this motif plays a dominant part.

It may probably be said that the circles in which the Acts of
Peter originated were especially interested in precisely this point.
It is well known that encratite ethics and docetic christology often
go together. But the combination of docetic pronouncements and
encratite trends is not enough to prove the Gnostic character of
the Acts of Peter. It is rather the popular piety of the 2nd and
3rd century that here presents itself. Here, as in every age,
disparate elements are brought together which the theologians
tend to keep carefully apart.

5. DATE AND PLACE OF WRITING: The original Greek version of
the Acts of Peter was used by the author of the Acts of Paul, as
shown above, p. 266. The date of his work is fixed by a reference
in Tertullian as the end of the 2nd century (cf. p. 351 below).
We have here an indication for the Acts of Peter; they must have
originated before *c.* 190, perhaps in the decade 180–190. The
contents and theological trend agree with this.

The place of origin cannot be certainly determined. Rome and
Asia Minor have been proposed. Asia Minor is suggested by the
connection with the Acts of Paul, since Tertullian informs us
that the latter originated there. But on this point we cannot do
more than conjecture.

THE ACTS OF PETER*

1. FRAGMENTS OF THE FIRST SECTION

(a) Peter's Daughter

(Berlin Coptic Papyrus 8502, pp. 128–132 and 135–141; ed. C. Schmidt pp. 3–7).

(p. 128). But on the first day of the week, which is the Lord's day, a crowd collected, and they brought many sick people to Peter for him to heal them.[1] But one of the crowd ventured to say to Peter, "Look, Peter, before our eyes you have made many (who were) blind to see, and the deaf to hear and the lame to walk, and you have helped the weak and given them strength.[2] Why have you not helped your virgin daughter, who has grown up beautiful and (p. 129) has believed on the name of God? For she is quite paralysed on one side, and she lies there stretched out in the corner helpless. We see the people you have healed; but your own daughter you have neglected."

But Peter smiled and said to him "My son, it is evident to God alone why her body is not well. You must know, then, that God is not weak or powerless to grant his gift to my daughter. But to convince your soul and increase the faith of those who are here"—(p. 130) he looked then towards his daughter, and spoke to her: "Rise up from your place without any man's help but Jesus' alone and walk naturally before them all and come to me." And she rose up and went to him; but the crowd rejoiced at what had happened.[3] Then Peter said to them, "Look, your heart is convinced that God is not powerless in all the things which we ask of him." Then they rejoiced even more and praised God.

---

* For the translation the previous works of C. Schmidt, Ficker, Vouaux and Michaelis have been used. Reference has been made to notes on the translation by E. Hennecke and A. Kurfess found in Hennecke's papers. Conjectures based on the Latin text of the Cod. Verc. by Lipsius and Turner (*JTS* 32, 1931, pp. 119ff.) are sometimes noted, sometimes adopted without note. Titles of individual sections, apart from the Martyrdom, are not derived from the tradition. Biblical quotations and allusions are noted, without claiming completeness. Peter's speeches especially are pervaded by biblical expressions and trains of thought; for further information consult Ficker, Vouaux and Michaelis. VA=Vita Abercii (above, p. 267); Pap. Ox=Papyrus Oxyrhychos 849 (above, p. 269); ( )=explanatory additions by the translator; ⟨ ⟩=words restored.

[1] Cf. Mk. 6:55; Mt. 4:24; Acts 5:16, etc. [2] Cf. Mt. 11:5.
[3] On the whole scene cf. Mk. 2:1–12 and pars.

(Then) said (p. 131) Peter to his daughter, "Go to your place, lie down and return to your infirmity, for this is profitable for you and for me." And the girl went back, lay down in her place and became as she was before. The whole crowd lamented and entreated Peter to make her well.

Peter said to them: "As the Lord liveth, this is profitable for her and for me. For on the day when she was born to me I saw a vision, and the Lord said to me, 'Peter, today there is born for you a great (132) trial; for this (daughter) will do harm to many souls if her body remains healthy.' But I thought that the vision mocked me.

When the girl was ten years old she became a temptation to many. And a rich man named Ptolemaeus, who had seen the girl with her mother bathing, sent for her to take her as his wife; (but) her mother would not agree. He sent many times for her, he could not wait. . . .

(pp. 133 and 134 are missing).

(The servants of) Ptolemaeus brought the girl and laid her down before the door of the house and went away. But when I and her mother perceived (it), we went down and found the girl, (and) that all one side of her body from her toes to her head was paralysed and wasted; and we carried her away, praising the Lord who had preserved his servant from uncleanness and shame and. . . . This is the cause of the matter, why the girl (continues) in this state until this day.

Now then it is right that you should know the fate of (p. 136) Ptolemaeus. He went home and grieved night and day over what had happened to him; and because of the many tears which he shed, he became blind; and he resolved to go up and hang himself. And lo, about the ninth hour of that day, when he was alone in his bedroom, he saw a great light which lit up the whole house, and heard a voice which said to him: (p. 137) 'Ptolemaeus, God has not given the vessels for corruption and shame; nor is it right for you, a believer in me, to defile my virgin, one whom you are to know as your sister, as if I were for both of you one spirit. But get up and go quickly to the house of the Apostle Peter, and you shall behold my glory; he will explain this matter to you.' But Ptolemaeus made no delay, and told his servants (138) to show him the way and bring him to me. And coming to me he told (me) all that had happened to him in the power of our Lord Jesus Christ. Then he did see with the eyes of his flesh and with the eyes of his soul, and many people set their hopes on Christ. He did good to them and gave them the gift of God.

After this Ptolemaeus died; he departed (this) life and went to his Lord. (p. 139) And when he ⟨made⟩ his will, he bequeathed a piece of land in the name of my daughter, because (it was) through her (that) he had believed in God and had been made whole. But I being given this trust, executed it with care. I sold the land, and God alone knows—neither I nor my daughter (received the price)[1]—I sold the land, and kept back none of the price of the land but gave all the money to the poor.[2]

Know then, O servant of Jesus Christ, that God (p. 140) cares for his own and prepares good for every one of them, although we think that God has forgotten us. But now, brethren, let us be sorrowful and watch and pray, and God's goodness shall look upon us, and we wait for it." And Peter continued speaking before them all, and praising the name (p. 141) of the Lord Christ, he gave of the bread to them all; (and) when he had distributed it he rose up and went to his house.

The Act of Peter.

(b) The Gardener's Daughter

(Ps.-Titus, De dispositione sanctimonii, pp. 83ff.)

Consider and take note of the happening about which the following account informs us:

A peasant had a girl who was a virgin. She was also his only daughter, and therefore he besought Peter to offer a prayer for her. After he had prayed, the apostle said to the father that the Lord would bestow upon her what was expedient for her soul. Immediately the girl fell down dead.

O reward worthy and ever pleasing to God, to escape the shamelessness of the flesh and to break the pride of the blood!

But this distrustful old man, failing to recognize the worth of the heavenly grace, i.e. the divine blessing, besought Peter again

[1] Words supplied by James.   [2] Cf. Acts 5:1–11.

that his only daughter be raised from the dead. And some days later, after she had been raised, a man who passed himself off as a believer came into the house of the old man to stay with him, and seduced the girl, and the two of them never appeared again.

(c) Fragment of a speech of Peter's

(Cod. Cambrai 254, ed. de Bruyne, *Rev. Bénédictine* XXV, 1908, p. 153.)

Peter, speaking to a (man) who bitterly complained at the death of his daughter, said "So many assaults of the devil, so many struggles with the body, so many disasters of the world she has escaped; and you shed tears, as if you did not know what you yourself have undergone (i.e. what you have gained)."

II. ACTUS VERCELLENSES
(Peter's dealings with Simon)
(*Aa* 1, pp. 45–103)

1
(Paul's Departure from Rome)

1. While Paul was spending some time in Rome and strengthening many in the faith, it happened that a woman by name Candida, the wife of Quartus, a prison officer, heard Paul speak and paid attention to his words and believed. And when she had instructed her husband also and he believed, Quartus[1] gave leave[2] to Paul to leave the city (and go) where he wished. But Paul said to him, "If it is God's will, He himself will reveal it to me." And when he had fasted for three days and asked of the Lord what was right for him, Paul then saw a vision, the Lord saying to him, "Paul, arise and be a physician to those who are[3] in Spain." So when he had related to the brethren what God had enjoined, without doubting he prepared to leave the city. But when Paul was about to leave, great lamentation arose among all the brotherhood because they believed that they would not see Paul again,[4] so that they even rent their clothes. Besides, they had in view that Paul had often contended with the Jewish teachers and had confuted them, (saying) "It is Christ[5] on whom your

[1] Cf. Rom. 16:23.   [2] Turner: permisit.   [3] Turner: constituti.
[4] Cf. Acts 20:25, 38.   [5] Turner: Christum esse eum.

fathers laid hands. He abolished their sabbath and fasts and festivals and circumcision and he abolished the (p. 46) doctrines of men and the other traditions."[1] But the brethren besought[2] Paul by the coming of our Lord Jesus Christ that he should not stay away longer than a year; and they said, "We know your love for your brethren; do not forget us when you arrive there (in Spain), or begin to desert us like little children without their mother." And while they continued entreating him with tears, there came a sound from heaven and a great voice which said, "Paul the servant of God is chosen for (this) service for the time of his life; but at the hands of Nero, that godless and wicked man, he shall be perfected before your eyes." And great fear fell upon the brethren yet more because of the voice that had come from heaven; and they were much more confirmed (in the faith).

2. And they brought bread and water[3] to Paul for the sacrifice so that after the prayer he should distribute to everyone. Among them as it proved there was a woman named Rufina who indeed[4] wished that even she should receive the eucharist at Paul's hands. But as she approached, Paul, filled with the Spirit of God said to her, "Rufina, you are not coming to the altar of God like a true (worshipper), rising from beside (one who is) not your husband but an adulterer, yet you seek to receive God's eucharist. For behold Satan shall break your body[5] and cast you down in the sight of all that believe in the Lord, so that they may see and believe, and know that it is the living God, who examines (men's) hearts,[6] in whom they have believed. But if you repent of your action, he is faithful,[7] so that he can wipe away your sins (and) deliver you from this sin. But if you do not repent while you are still in the body, the consuming fire and the outer darkness[8] shall receive you for ever." And at once Rufina fell down, being paralysed on the left side from her head to her toe-nails. And she had no power to speak, for her tongue was tied.[9] And when the believers in the faith and the newly-converted saw this, they beat their breast remembering their own former sins, lamenting

---

[1] Cf. Col. 2:8, 16, 22.   [2] Lipsius: urgebant.
[3] On the eucharist with bread and water cf. Acts of Paul, below p. 372.
[4] Turner: utique.   [5] Turner: corpore.   [6] Cf. Acts 1:24, 15:8.
[7] Cf. 1 Jn. 1:9.   [8] Cf. Mt. 25:30.
[9] The story of Rufina is mentioned also in ps.-Titus, see above p. 145.

and saying, "We do not know whether God will forgive us the former sins which we have committed."

Then Paul called for silence and said, "Men and brethren, who have now begun to believe in Christ,[1] if you do not continue in (p. 47) your former works, those of the tradition of your fathers, but keep yourselves from all deceit and anger and cruelty and adultery and impurity, and from pride and envy and contempt and hostility, then Jesus the living God will forgive you what you have done in ignorance.[2] Therefore arm yourselves, you servants of God, each one of you in your inner man, with peace, composure, gentleness, faith, love, knowledge, wisdom, fraternal affection, hospitality, compassion, abstinence, purity, kindness, justice; then you shall have as your guide for ever the first-born of all creation[3] and have strength in peace with our Lord."[4] And when they heard Paul say this, they asked him to pray for them. But Paul lifted up his voice and said, "O God eternal, God of the heavens, God of unutterable majesty, who hast established all things by thy word, who hast ⟨broken⟩ the chain set fast ⟨upon man,⟩ who hast brought ⟨the light[5]⟩ of thy grace to all the world, Father of thine holy Son Jesus Christ, we entreat thee together through thy Son Jesus Christ to strengthen the souls which once were unbelieving but now have faith. I was once a blasphemer,[6] but now I am blasphemed; I was once a persecutor, but now I suffer persecution from others; once an enemy of Christ, but now I pray to be his friend. For I trust in his promise and his mercy; for I think that I am faithful and have received forgiveness for my former misdeeds. Therefore I exhort you also, brethren, to believe in the Lord, the Father almighty, and to put all your trust in our Lord Jesus Christ his Son. If you believe in him, no one will be able to uproot you from his promise. Likewise you must bend your knees and commend me to the Lord, as I am

[1] V.A.: You men, who have now come to believe and wish to do Christ's (war-) service.
[2] V.A.: Then God through his holy Son, on whom you now believe, will forgive you what you did in ignorance before you knew him. Cf. Acts 3:17, 17:30.
[3] Cf. Col. 1:15.
[4] V.A.: Then you shall find grace and mercy with God who is loving towards men, and with our commander, the first-born of all creation and power, our Lord Jesus Christ.
[5] Turner: qui vinculum inligatum ⟨homini confregisti, qui lumen⟩ omni saeculo.
[6] Cf. 1 Tim. 1:13.

about to set forth to another nation, that his grace may go before me and dispose my journey aright and may be able to gather in his holy vessels, even those that believe, and that they may give thanks to me for my preaching the Lord's word, and be well established (in the faith)". But the brethren continued weeping and entreated the Lord with Paul and said, "Lord Jesus Christ, be thou with Paul, and restore him to us unharmed; for we know our weakness which is still with us."

3. And a great crowd of women knelt down and fervently (p. 48) entreated the blessed Paul, and they kissed his feet and escorted him to the harbour, and with them[1] Dionysius and Balbus from Asia, who were Roman knights and illustrious men. And a senator by name Demetrius kept close to Paul on his right hand and said, "Paul, I could wish to leave the city, if I were not a magistrate, so as not to leave you." And (so said) some from Caesar's household,[2] Cleobius and Iphitus and Lysimachus and Aristaeus and two matrons, Berenice and Philostrate, with the presbyter Narcissus, after they had conducted him to the harbour. But as a storm at sea was threatening, he (Paul) sent the brethren back to Rome, so that if anyone wished he could come down and listen to Paul till he set sail. The brethren heard this (suggestion) and went up to the city. When they told the brethren that had remained in the city, the word went round at once; and they came to the harbour, some riding, some on foot and others by way of the Tiber; and they were greatly strengthened in the faith during three days, and on the fourth day until the fifth hour; and they prayed together with Paul and brought him gifts and put on the ship whatever he needed; and they delivered to him two young men who were believers to sail with him, and bade him farewell in the Lord and returned to Rome.

2

(Simon's arrival in Rome and his initial success;
Peter's journey to Rome)

4. But after some days there arose a great commotion in the church, for (some) said that they had seen miracles done by a

---

[1] Turner: sed ⟨et⟩.   [2] Cf. Phil. 4:22.

man whose name was Simon, and that he was at Aricia. They
added further,[1] "He says that he is the great power of God,[2] and
that without God he does nothing. Is he then himself the Christ?
But we believe in him whom Paul preached to us; for through
him we have seen the dead raised up and (men) delivered from
various infirmities. But what this contention is, we do not know;[3]
For it is no small excitement that has come upon us. Perhaps he
will now enter into Rome; for yesterday he was invited with great
acclamations, and they said to him, 'Thou art God in Italy,
thou art saviour of the Romans: make haste and go quickly to
Rome.' But he spoke to the people with a tuneful voice, saying,
'Tomorrow you shall see me about the seventh hour flying over
the city gate in the form in which you now see me speaking with
you.' So, brethren, if you agree, let us go (p. 49) and carefully
await the outcome of (this) matter." So they all ran together and
came to the gate. And when the seventh hour had come, behold
suddenly in the distance a cloud of dust was seen in the sky, like
a smoke shining from far away with (fiery) rays. And when it
approached the gate it suddenly vanished; and then he appeared
standing among the people, while they all worshipped him and
realized that it was he who had been seen by them the day before.
And the brethren were seriously disaffected among themselves,
especially because Paul was not at Rome, nor were Timothy or
Barnabas, since they had been sent by Paul to Macedonia;[4] and
there was no one to encourage us, especially those who were but
recently instructed. And Simon's reputation continually increased
with those among whom he worked, and some of them in their
daily conversations called Paul a sorcerer, others a deceiver; so
that out of so great a number that were established in the faith,
they all fell away except the presbyter Narcissus and two women
in the lodging-house of the Bithynians and four who could no
longer go out of their house; and being thus confined they
devoted themselves to prayer day and night, and entreated the
Lord that Paul might quickly return, or some other who could

[1] Lipsius proposes: adiecerunt quia. Since *quia* could render ὅτι, the direct speech
would begin here.
[2] Cf. Acts 8:10 and Haenchen, *Apostelgeschichte*[13] 1961, pp. 250ff.
[3] Cod. Verc.: But this woman (or this man, hic?) seeks for contention, we know.
The translation given above uses Bonnet's conjecture: quae sit dimicatio nescimus.
[4] Cf. Acts 19:22, Phil. 2:19ff.

care for his servants, since the devil in his wickedness had made them unfaithful.

5. But as they mourned and fasted, God was already preparing Peter for what was to come, now that the twelve years in Jerusalem which the Lord Christ had enjoined on him[1] were completed.[2] He showed him a vision of this kind, and said to him "Peter, the man Simon whom you expelled from Judaea, proving him a sorcerer, has again forestalled you (pl.) at Rome. In short you must know that Satan by his cunning and his power has perverted all those who believed in me; and (in this way Simon) proves himself his agent. But do not delay; set out tomorrow (for Caesarea), and there you will find a ship ready which is sailing to Italy. And in a few days I will show you my grace which has no bounds."[3] Peter then, instructed by this vision, related it to the brethren without delay and said, "I must go up to Rome to overthrow the opponent and enemy of the Lord and (p. 50) of our brethren."

And he went down to Caesarea and at once boarded the ship, when the gangway was already removed and without embarking any provisions. But the captain, whose name was Theon, looked at Peter and said, "All that we have here is yours. For what merit is it of ours, if we take on board a man like ourselves who takes his chance, and do not share with you all that we have? Only let us have a prosperous voyage." And Peter thanked him for his offer, but he himself fasted while aboard the ship, being grieved in mind yet comforting himself again because God had accounted him a worthy servant in his service.

But after a few days the captain rose up at the hour of his dinner, and asked Peter to eat with him, saying to him, "Sir, (*lit.* O) whoever you are, I hardly know you, whether you are God or man; but in my opinion, I take you for a servant of God. For in the middle of the night while I was steering the ship and had fallen asleep, it seemed that a man's voice said to me from heaven, 'Theon, Theon!' It called me twice by my name and said to me, 'Of all those who sail with you let Peter be highest in your esteem; for through him both you and the others shall escape

---

[1] Cf. Kerygma Petri, Fragm. 3, above, p. 101, and W. Bauer, above, pp. 44f.
[2] Turner's punctuation.   [3] Cf. Wis. 7:13: lit. "grudging".

uninjured from an unexpected (mis)chance.' "[1] Now Peter thought
that God wished to show his providence upon the sea to those
who were in the ship; so Peter began to relate to Theon the
wonderful works[2] of God, and how God had chosen him among
the apostles, and for what business he was sailing to Italy. And
day by day he imparted to him the words of God. And he considered him and found by conversing with him that he was like-
minded in the faith and worthy of (God's) service.[3]

But when the ship met with a calm in the Adriatic, Theon
remarked on the calm to Peter and said to him, "If you will
count me worthy to be baptized with the sign of the Lord, you
have the opportunity." For all those aboard the ship were drunk
and had fallen asleep. And Peter went down by a rope and baptized Theon in the name of the Father and of the Son and of the
Holy Ghost. And he came up out of the water rejoicing with great
joy, and Peter also was more cheerful because God had accounted
Theon worthy of his name. And it came to pass (p. 51) that at
the same place where Theon was baptized, there appeared a
young man shining with splendour, saying to them "Peace (be)
with you."[4] And straightway Peter and Theon went up and
entered the cabin; and Peter took bread and gave thanks to the
Lord, who had accounted him worthy of his holy service, and
because the young man had appeared to them saying "Peace
(be) with you." (And he said), "Most excellent, the only holy one,
it is thou that hast appeared to us, thou God Jesus Christ; in thy
name hath this man been washed[5] and signed with thy holy sign.
Therefore in thy name I impart to him thine eucharist, that he
may be thy perfect servant without blame for ever."

And as they feasted and rejoiced in the Lord, suddenly (there
came) a wind, not violent but temperate, on the ship's bow and
did not slacken for six days and as many nights, until they came
to Puteoli.

6. And when they had brought up at Puteoli, Theon sprang
down from the ship and came to the lodging-house where he used
to stay, to prepare it to receive Peter. Now the man with whom
he stayed was called Ariston; this man had always feared the

---

[1] Turner: ex insperato casu.   [2] Cf. Acts 2:11.
[3] Turner: diaconii; James's punctuation.
[4] Cf. Jn. 20:19, 21, 26.   [5] Lipsius: lotus.

Lord, and Theon entrusted himself to him on account of the Name. When he had come to the lodging-house and seen Ariston, Theon said to him, "God, who counted you worthy to serve him, has imparted his grace to me also through his holy servant Peter, who has just sailed with me from Judaea, being commanded by our Lord to come to Italy." And when Ariston heard this, he fell on Theon's neck and embraced him and asked him to take him to the ship and show him Peter; for Ariston said that since Paul had set out for Spain, there was no one of the brethren with whom he could refresh himself; and moreover that a certain Jew named Simon had invaded the city—"and he by incantation and by his wickedness has altogether perverted the entire brotherhood, so that I also fled from Rome, hoping that Peter would come. For Paul had told (us) of him, and I have seen many things in a vision. Now therefore I believe in my Lord that he is rebuilding his ministry, for all deception shall be uprooted from among his servants. For our Lord Jesus Christ is faithful, who can restore (p. 52) our minds."

Now when Theon heard this from Ariston, who was weeping, his spirit was restored and he was the more strengthened, because he knew that he had believed on the living God.

But when they came together to the ship, Peter looked at them, and being filled with the spirit he smiled; so that Ariston fell on his face at Peter's feet and said, "Brother and Lord, partaker of the holy mysteries and teacher of the right way which is in Jesus Christ our God; he has openly shown us of your coming;[1] for we have lost all those whom Paul entrusted to us, through the power of Satan. But now I hope in the Lord, who sent his messenger (i.e. angel) and told you to come (quickly) to us, since he has counted us worthy to see his great and wonderful works done at your hands. I beg you, therefore, to go quickly to the city; for I left the brethren who were causing distress, whom I saw falling into the temptation of the devil, and retired to this place and I said to them, 'Brethren, stand fast in the faith;[2] for it must be that within two months from now the mercy of our Lord will bring his servant to you.' For I had seen a vision of Paul saying to me, 'Ariston, retire from the city.' When I heard that I believed

[1] Turner: qui aperte adventum tuum.   [2] 1 Cor. 16:13.

286

without delay and departed in the Lord, although I bear great infirmity of the flesh, and I arrived at this place; and day by day I stood by the sea-shore and asked the sailors 'Has Peter sailed with you?' But now that the Lord's grace abounds (towards us), I beg you that we may go up to Rome without delay, or the teaching of this most wicked man may prevail yet further." And as Ariston said this with tears, Peter gave him his hand and raised him up from the ground, and Peter also groaning said with tears, "He has forestalled us, he who tempts the whole world by his angels;[1] but (God) shall quench his deceits and subdue him beneath the feet[2] of those who have believed in Christ whom we preach, who has power to deliver his servants from all temptation." And as they went in at the gate, Theon entreated Peter and said, "You did not refresh yourself on board on any day in all that long sea (voyage); and now will you set out straight from the ship over such a rough road? No, (p. 53) stay and refresh yourself, and then you shall set out. It is a flinty road from here to Rome, and I am afraid you may take some harm from the shaking." But Peter answered them saying, "Suppose it should be my fate, like the enemy of our Lord, to have a millstone hung about me, as my Lord said to us, if one should offend (any) of the brethren, and be drowned in the sea?[3] But it might be not only a millstone, but what is worse, it would be far away from those who have believed on the Lord Jesus Christ, that the opponent of this persecutor of his servants would find his end."[4] And Theon could not induce him by any persuasion to remain there even for a single day. But Theon for his part handed over all his ship's cargo to be sold for its fair price (German: to those who came as buyers) and followed Peter to Rome; and Ariston brought (them) to the house of the presbyter Narcissus.[5]

---

[1] Cf. Rev. 12:9.   [2] Cf. Rom. 16:20.   [3] Cf. Mk. 9:42 and pars.
[4] The text is corrupt. The sense is: Peter could not, like Simon, cause temptation, but again he could not meet his end far away from the Roman church (sc.—presumably—until he had convicted Simon).
[5] Cp. Rom. 16:11.

3
(Peter's first preaching at Rome)

7. Now the rumour flew about the city to the brethren who were scattered that Peter at the Lord's command[1] had come because of Simon, in order to show that he was a deceiver and a persecutor of good men. So the whole multitude collected to see the Lord's apostle establishing (the Church) in Christ. And on the first day of the week, when the multitude came together to see Peter, he began to say with a loud voice, "You men who are present here, who hope in Christ, you who have suffered temptation for a little, attend! Why did God send his Son into the world,[2] or why did he reveal him through the Virgin Mary,[3] if it were not to effect some grace or means of salvation?[4] For he wished to remove[5] all offence and all ignorance and all activity of the devil, frustrating his designs and his powers through which he formerly prevailed, before our God shone forth in the world.[6] Because (mankind) through ignorance fell into death in their many and varied weaknesses,[7] almighty God, moved with compassion, sent his Son into the world; and I was with him. And I walked on the water[8], and myself survive as a witness of it;[9] I confess that I was there when formerly in the world (p. 54) he was at work with the signs and all the miracles which he performed. Dearest brethren, I denied our Lord Jesus Christ, and not once only, but three times.[10] For there were wicked dogs who came about me, as said the prophet of the Lord.[11] But the Lord did not lay it to my charge; he turned to me and had compassion on the weakness of my flesh, so that afterwards I wept bitterly and lamented the weakness of my faith, because I was made senseless by the devil and did not keep my Lord's word in mind. And now I tell you, men and brethren, who have come

[1] Turner reads *discentem domini*, but translates, "the disciple of the Lord"; the German version reproduced above follows Turner's text only.—G.C.S.
[2] Cf. Jn. 3:17.
[3] V.A.: You men, who have put your hope in Christ, learn why God revealed his Son through the holy Virgin Mary and sent him into the world.
[4] Vouaux: Procuratio = οἰκονομία. [5] Turner: volens ⟨tollere⟩.
[6] V.A.: before our Lord Jesus shone out in his world.
[7] V.A. omits: Because . . . weaknesses.
[8] Turner: ambulavi is correct, not ambulavit, as altered by Lipsius.
[9] Cf. Mt. 14:22ff. [10] Cf. Mk. 14:66ff. and pars.
[11] Turner: sicut ait prophetes; cf. Ps. 21:17 (LXX).

together in the name of Jesus Christ: Satan the deceiver points his arrows at you too, that you may depart from the way. But do not be disloyal, brethren, nor let your spirit fall, but be strong and stand fast and do not doubt. For if Satan overthrew me, whom the Lord held in such great honour, so that I denied the light of my hope; if he subdued me and persuaded me to flee, as if I had put my trust in a man, what do you expect, you who are new to the faith? Did you expect that he would not subvert you, to make you enemies of the Kingdom of God and plunge you into perdition by the lowest deceit? For whoever he has dislodged from hope in our Lord Jesus Christ, that man is a son of perdition[1] for ever. Change your hearts, therefore, brethren beloved of the Lord, and be strong in the Lord Almighty, the Father of our Lord Jesus Christ, whom no man has ever seen, nor can see, save him who has believed on him.[2] And you must understand whence this temptation has come to you. For this is not only to convince you with words that it is the Christ that I am preaching, but also by deeds and marvellous powers I urge you through the faith in Jesus Christ, that none of you should expect another (saviour) than him who was despised and mocked by the Jews, this Nazarene who was crucified and died and rose again the third day."

4

(Marcellus. Recovery of the Church of Rome)

8. But the brethren repented and entreated Peter to overthrow Simon, who said that he was the power of God; now he was staying at the house of the Senator Marcellus, who was persuaded by his charms. And they said, "Believe us, brother Peter; no one was so wise (p. 55) among men as this Marcellus. All the widows who hoped in Christ found refuge with him; all the orphans were fed by him. And what more, brother? All the poor called Marcellus their patron, and his house was called (the house) of pilgrims and of the poor. The emperor said to him, 'I am keeping you out of every office, or you will plunder the provinces to benefit the Christians'; and Marcellus replied, 'All my goods are yours'; but Caesar said to him, 'They would be mine, if you

---

[1] Cf. Jn. 17:12; 2 Thess. 2:3.
[2] Cf. Jn. 1:18, 6:46; but there it is the Son, here the believers, who can see God.

kept them for me; but now they are not mine, because you give them to whom you will[1] and to I know not what wretches.' We have this in view, brother Peter, and warn you that all that man's great charity has turned to blasphemy; for if he had not been won over, we in turn should not have deserted the holy faith in our Lord God. This Marcellus is now enraged and repents of his good deeds, and says, 'All this wealth I have spent in all this time, vainly believing that I paid it for the knowledge of God.' So much so, that if one of the strangers comes to his house door, he strikes him with his staff and orders him to be driven away, saying, 'If only I had not spent so much money on these impostors!'—and yet more blasphemous words. But if there remains in you any of our Lord's mercy or of the goodness of his commandments, give help to this man's error who has so abundantly given alms to the servants of God."

But Peter perceiving this was struck with sorrow and uttered this reproach:[2] "O what manifold arts and temptations of the devil! O what contrivances and inventions of evil! He prepares for himself a great fire in the day of wrath[3], the destruction of simple men, the ravening wolf[4], the devourer and waster of eternal life! Thou hast ensnared the first man in lustful desire and bound him by thine ancient wickedness and with the chain of the body; thou art the fruit of the tree of bitterness, which is all most bitter, inducing lusts of every kind. Thou hast made Judas, who was a disciple and apostle together with me, do wickedly and betray our Lord Jesus Christ, who (p. 56) must punish thee. Thou didst harden the heart of Herod and provoke Pharaoh, making him fight against Moses, the holy servant of God; thou didst give Caiaphas the boldness to hand over our Lord Jesus Christ to the cruel throng,[5] and even now thou dost shoot at innocent souls with thy poisoned arrows. Thou wicked enemy of all, accursed shalt thou be from the Church[6] of the Son of holy and almighty God, and like a firebrand thrust out from the hearth thou shalt be quenched by the servants of our Lord

---

[1] Turner (following Lipsius): non sunt mea, quia cui vis ea donas.
[2] Turner: maledixit = ὠνείδισεν. [3] Cf. inter alia Rom. 2:5.
[4] Cf. Mt. 7:15; Acts 20:29.
[5] Cf. Mt. 27:2, etc., noting however the different account given; Jesus is handed over not to Pilate, but to the "throng", i.e. the Jews.
[6] Turner: eris ab ecclesia.

Jesus Christ. Upon thee may thy blackness be turned and upon
thy sons, that most wicked seed; upon thee be turned thy misdeeds, upon thee thy threats, and upon thee and thine angels be
thy temptations, thou source of wickedness and abyss of darkness!
May thy darkness which thou hast be with thee and with thy
vessels whom thou dost possess. Depart therefore from these who
shall believe in God, depart from the servants of Christ and from
them who would fight for him. Keep for thyself thy gates[1] of
darkness; in vain thou dost knock at the doors of others, which
belong not to thee but to Christ Jesus who keeps them. For
thou, devouring wolf, wouldst carry off sheep[2] which are not
thine, but belong to Christ Jesus, who keeps them with the most
careful care."

9. While Peter said this in great distress of mind, many more
were added[3] as believers in the Lord. And the brethren entreated
Peter to join battle with Simon and not allow him to vex the
people any longer. And without delay Peter left the assembly and
went to the house of Marcellus, where Simon was staying; and
great crowds followed him. And when he came to the door, he
called the doorkeeper and said to him, "Go and tell Simon:
'Peter, on whose account you fled from Judaea, is waiting for
you at the door'." The doorkeeper answered Peter, "I do not
know, Sir, whether you are Peter; but I have an order; for he
(i.e. Simon) found out that you came into the city yesterday,
and he said to me, 'Whether it be by day or by night, at whatever
time[4] he comes, tell him that I am not in (the house)'." But
Peter said to the young man, "You were right to say this, and
explain what he made you say"; and Peter turned to the people
who followed him, and said, "You shall see a great and marvellous
wonder." And Peter, seeing a great dog (p. 57) tied fast with a
massive chain, went up to him and let him loose. And when the
dog was let loose he acquired a human voice and said to Peter,
"What do you bid me do, you servant of the ineffable living
God?" And Peter said to him, "Go in and tell Simon in the
presence of his company, 'Peter says to you, Come out in public;
for on your account I have come to Rome, you wicked man and

---

[1] Turner: ianuas (for tunicas).   [2] Cf. Jn. 10:12.
[3] Cf. Acts 2:47.   [4] Turner: quacumque.

troubler of simple souls'." And immediately[1] the dog ran and went in and rushed into the middle of Simon's companions and lifting his fore-feet called out with a loud voice, "(I tell) you Simon, Peter the servant of Christ is standing at the door, and says to you, 'Come out in public; for on your account I have come to Rome, you most wicked deceiver of simple souls'." And when Simon heard it and saw the incredible sight, he lost the words with which he was deceiving those who stood by, and all were amazed.

10. But when Marcellus saw it he went to the door and threw himself down at Peter's feet and said, "Peter, I clasp your feet, you holy servant of the holy God; I have sinned greatly; but do not punish my sins, if you have any true faith in the Christ whom you preach, if you remember his commandments, not to hate anyone, not to be angry with anyone,[2] as I have learnt from Paul, your fellow-apostle. Do not consider my faults, but pray for me to the Lord, the holy Son of God, whom I provoked to anger by persecuting his servants. Pray therefore for me like a good steward of God, that I be not consigned—with the sins of Simon—to eternal fire; for he even persuaded me to set up a statue to him with this inscription, 'To Simon the young God'.[3] If I knew, Peter, that you could be won over with money, I would give my whole fortune; I would have given it to you and despised it, in order to regain my soul.[4] If I had sons, I would have thought nothing of them, if only I could believe in the living God. But I protest that he would not have deceived me except by saying that he was the power of God. Yet I will tell you, dearest Peter; I was not worthy to hear you, servant of God, nor was I firmly grounded in the faith of God which is in Christ; and for this reason I was overthrown. So I beg you, do not resent what I am about to say: that Christ (p. 58) our Lord, whom you preach in truth, said to your fellow-apostles in your presence, 'If you have faith like a grain of mustard-seed, you shall say to this mountain, Remove yourself, and at once it will remove.'[5] But, Peter, this Simon called you an unbeliever, since you lost faith when upon the water;[6] indeed I heard that he also had said, 'Those who are

[1] Turner: ilico. [2] Cf. Mt. 5:44
[3] Cf. Justin, Apol. 26:2. ("Young", *iuveni*, no doubt represents νέῳ, "new".—G.C.S.)
[4] Cf. Mk. 8:36 and pars. [5] Cf. Mt. 17:20. [6] Cf. Mt. 14:30f.

with me have not understood me.'[1] Therefore if you (pl.) lost faith, you on whom he laid his hands, whom he also chose, and with whom he worked miracles, then since I have this assurance, I repent and resort to your (sing.) prayers. Receive my soul, though I have fallen away from our Lord and from his promise. But I believe that he will have mercy on me, since I repent. For the Almighty is faithful to forgive me my sins."

But Peter said with a loud voice, "To thee, our Lord, be glory and splendour, almighty God, Father of our Lord Jesus Christ. To thee be praise and glory and honour, for ever and ever, Amen. As thou hast fully encouraged and established us now in thee in the sight of all beholders, holy Lord, so strengthen Marcellus and send thy peace to him and his house today; but whatever is lost or astray thou alone canst restore.[2] We all beseech thee, O Lord, the shepherd of sheep that once were scattered, but now shall be gathered in one through thee[3]: receive Marcellus again as one of thy lambs and suffer him no longer to riot in error or in ignorance; but accept him among the number of thy sheep. Even so, Lord, receive him, that with sorrow and tears doth entreat thee."

11. So saying, Peter embraced Marcellus. Then Peter turned to the crowd who stood by him, and saw in the crowd a man half laughing, in whom was a most wicked demon. And Peter said to him, "Whoever you are, that laughed, show yourself openly to all who stand by." And hearing this the young man ran into the courtyard of the house, and he shouted aloud and threw himself against the wall and said, "Peter, there is a huge contest between (p. 59) Simon and the dog which you sent; for Simon says to the dog, 'Say that I am not here'—but the dog says more to him than the message you gave; and when he has finished the mysterious work which you gave him, he shall die at your feet." But Peter said, "You too, then, whatever demon you may be, in the name of our Lord Jesus Christ, come out of the young man and do him no harm; (and) show yourself to all who stand by!" And hearing this he left the young man;[4] and he caught hold of a great marble statue, which stood in the courtyard of the house,

---

[1] Cf. Vol. I, p. 175. [2] Turner's punctuation. [3] Cf. Jn. 10:11ff.
[4] Turner: hoc audito iuveni expulit se; the demon is the subject.

and kicked it to pieces. Now it was a statue of Caesar. And when Marcellus saw that he beat his forehead and said to Peter, "A great crime has been committed; if Caesar hears of this through some busybody, he will punish us severely." But Peter answered him, "I see you are not the man you were just now; for you said you were ready to spend your whole fortune to save your soul. But if you are truly repentant and believe in Christ with all your heart, take (some) running water in your hands and pray to the Lord; then sprinkle it in his name over the broken pieces of the statue, and it will be restored as before." And Marcellus did not doubt, but believed with his whole heart, and before taking the water in his hands he looked upwards and said, "I believe in thee, Lord Jesus Christ, for I am being tested by thine apostle Peter whether I truly believe in thy holy name. Therefore I take water in my hands, and in thy name I sprinkle those stones, that the statue may be restored as it was before. So, Lord, if it be thy will that I remain in the body and suffer nothing at Caesar's hand, let this stone be restored as it was before." And he sprinkled the water upon the stones, and the statue was restored.[1] So Peter exulted because he had not doubted when he prayed to the Lord, and Marcellus also was uplifted in spirit, because this first miracle was done by his hands; and he therefore believed with his whole heart in the name of Jesus Christ the Son of God, through whom all things impossible are (made) possible.[2]

5

(Peter's miracles and first attacks on Simon)

12. But Simon (was) in (the house, and) said to the dog, "Tell Peter that I am not in (the house)." And the dog answered him in the presence of Marcellus, (p. 60) "You most wicked and shameless (man), you enemy of all that live and believe in Christ Jesus, (here is) a dumb animal sent to you and taking a human voice[3] to convict you and prove you a cheat and a deceiver. Have you thought for all these hours, (only) to say, 'Say that I am not here'? Were you not ashamed to raise your feeble and useless voice against Peter, the servant and apostle of Christ, as if you

[1] Cf. Philostratus, Vita Apoll. IV, 20.
[2] Cf. Mk. 10:27 and pars. [3] Cf. 2 Pet. 2:16.

could hide from him who commanded me to speak against (you to) your face? And this is not for your sake, but for those whom you were perverting and sending to destruction. Cursed therefore you shall be, you enemy and corruptor of the way to the truth of Christ, who shall prove your iniquities which you have done with undying fire, and you shall be in outer darkness."[1] Having said these words the dog ran off; and the people followed, leaving Simon alone. (So) the dog came to Peter, who was sitting with the crowd (who had come) to see the face of Peter; and the dog reported his dealings with Simon. So the dog said, "Messenger and apostle of the true God, Peter,[2] you shall have a great contest with Simon, the enemy of Christ, and with his servants; and you shall convert many to the faith that were deceived by him. Therefore you shall receive from God a reward for your work." And when the dog had said this, he fell down at the apostle Peter's feet and gave up his spirit. And when the crowd with great amazement saw the dog speaking, some began to throw themselves down at Peter's feet, but others said, "Show us another sign, that we may believe in you as the servant of the living God; (for) Simon too did many signs in our presence, and therefore we followed him."

13. But Peter turned round and saw a smoked tunny-fish hanging in a window; and he took it and said to the people, "If you now see this swimming in the water like a fish, will you be able to believe in him whom I preach?" And they all said with one accord, "Indeed we will believe you!" Now there was a fish-pond near by; so he said, "In thy name, Jesus Christ, in which they still fail to believe" (he said to the tunny) "in the presence of all these be alive and swim like a fish!" And he threw (p. 61) the tunny into the pond, and it came alive and began to swim. And the people saw the fish swimming; and he made it do so not merely for that hour, or it might have been called a delusion, but he made it go on swimming, so that it attracted crowds from all sides and showed that the tunny had become a (live) fish; so much so that some of the people threw in bread for it, and it ate it all up.[3] And when they saw this, a great number followed him

[1] Cf. Mt. 8:12.
[2] Turner's punctuation and reading: angele et apostole dei veri, Petre.
[3] Turner: totum comedebat.

and believed in the Lord, and they assembled by day and by night in the house of Narcissus the presbyter. And Peter expounded to them the writings of the prophets and what our Lord Jesus Christ had enacted both in word and in deeds.

14. Now Marcellus was being day by day (more) firmly established through the signs which he saw performed through Peter through the grace of Jesus Christ which he had granted him. And Marcellus ran in on Simon as he sat in his house in the dining-room, and he cursed him, saying: "Most hateful and foulest of men, corrupter of my soul and of my house, who would have had me abandon Christ, my Lord and Saviour!" And he laid hands on him and ordered him to be driven from the house. And now the slaves had (him in their) power, and rained insults upon him, some boxing his face, some (using) the stick and some the stone, while others emptied pots full of filth over his head, those who had offended[1] their master on his account and had long been in chains; and other fellow-slaves (of theirs) whom he had maligned before their master abused him and said to him: "Now we are repaying you a just reward, through the will of God, who has had mercy on us and on our master." So Simon was soundly beaten and thrown out of the house; and he ran to the house where Peter was staying; and he stood at the door of the house of Narcissus the presbyter and called out, "Here am I, Simon; so come down, Peter, and I will convict you of having believed in a (mere) man, a Jew and the son of a carpenter."[2]

15. Now Peter was told that Simon had said this; (and) Peter sent to him a woman who had a child at the breast, saying to her, "Go down quickly, and you will see someone looking for me. And you are not to answer him; but keep silent and hear what the child you are holding will say to him." So the woman went down. Now the child whom she suckled was seven months old; and it took the voice of a man and said to Simon (p. 62): "You abomination of God and men, you destruction of the truth and most wicked seed of corruption, you fruitless one of nature's fruits! But you appear but briefly and for a minute, and after this everlasting punishment awaits you. Son of a shameless father, striking no roots for good but only for poison, unfaithful creature,

---

[1] Turner: offenderant.   [2] Cf. Mt. 13:55.

devoid of any hope! A dog reproved you, yet you were not shaken; now I, an infant, am compelled by God to speak, and yet you do not blush for shame! But even though you refuse, on the coming sabbath another shall bring you to the forum of Julius[1] to prove what kind of man you are. So get away from the door which the feet (*lit.* footsteps) of the saints are using; for no longer shall you corrupt the innocent souls which you used to pervert and made them offended at Christ. So now your most evil nature shall be exposed and your contrivance destroyed. This last word I am telling you now: Jesus Christ says to you 'Be struck dumb by the power of my name, and depart from Rome until the coming sabbath'." And immediately he became dumb and could not resist, but left Rome until the sabbath and lodged in a stable. The woman went back with her child to Peter, and told him and the other brethren what the child had said to Simon; and they glorified the Lord who had shown these things to men.

6
(Peter's vision and narrative about Simon)

16. But when night came on Peter saw Jesus clothed in a robe of splendour, smiling and saying to him while he was still awake, "Already the great mass of the brethren have turned back to me through you and through the signs which[2] you have done in my name. But you shall have a trial of faith on the coming sabbath, and many more of the Gentiles and of the Jews shall be converted in my name to me, who was insulted, mocked and spat upon. For I will show myself to you when you ask for signs and miracles, and you shall convert many; but you will have Simon opposing you with the works of his father.[3] But all his (actions) shall be exposed as charms and illusions of magic. But now do not delay, and you shall establish in my name all those whom I send you." And when it was light he told the brethren that the Lord had appeared to him and what he had commanded.[4]

17. "But believe me, men and brethren, I drove this Simon (p. 63) out of Judaea, where he did much harm by his incantations.

---

[1] Cf. Jn. 21:18(?).　　[2] Turner: reversa est per te ad me et per quae signa.
[3] Cf. Jn. 8:44.
[4] No break must be assumed between cc. 16 and 17, *pace* Ficker.

He stayed in Judaea with a woman named Eubula, a woman of some distinction in this world, who possessed much gold and pearls of no little value. Simon stole into her house with two others like himself; though none of the household saw these two, but only Simon; and by means of a spell they took away all the woman's gold and disappeared. But Eubula discovering this crime began to torture her household, saying, 'You took advantage of (the visit of) this godly man and have robbed me, because you saw him coming in to me to do honour to a simple woman; but his name is 'the power of the Lord.'[1]

"Now as I fasted for three days and prayed that this crime should come to light, I saw in a vision Italicus and Antulus, whom I had instructed in the name of the Lord, and a boy who was naked and bound, who gave me a wheaten loaf and said to me, 'Peter, hold out for two days and you shall see the wonderful works of God.[2] For the things which are lost from Eubula's house were stolen by Simon and two others, using magical arts and creating a delusion. And you shall see them on the third day at the ninth hour by the gate which leads towards Naples, selling to a goldsmith named Agrippinus a young satyr made of gold, of two pounds weight, and having a precious stone set in it. Now you are not to touch it, to avoid pollution; but have with you some of the lady's servants; then show them the goldsmith's shop and leave them. For this event will cause many to believe in the name of the Lord. For the things which they have constantly stolen by their cunning and wickedness shall be brought to light.' When I heard this I came to Eubula and found her sitting and lamenting with her clothes torn and her hair in disorder; and I said to her, 'Eubula, rise up from your bed[3] and compose your face, put up your hair and put on a dress that becomes you, and pray to the Lord Jesus Christ who judges every soul. For he is the Son of the invisible God; in him you must be saved, if indeed you repent with all your heart of your former sins. And receive power from him; for now the Lord says to you through me, 'All that you have lost (p. 64) you shall find.' And when you have received them, be sure that you find yourself,[4] so as to renounce

---

[1] Turner: cui nomen est autem 'numen domini' (= δύναμις θεοῦ, cf. Acts 8:10).
[2] Cf. Acts 2:11.   [3] Turner: lecto.   [4] Turner: invenias.

this present world and seek for everlasting refreshment. Listen then to this: let some of your people keep watch by the gate that leads towards Naples. On the day after tomorrow, about the ninth hour, they will see two young men with[1] a young satyr in gold of two pounds weight set with stones, as a vision has shown me, and they will offer it for sale to a certain Agrippinus, who is familiar with the godly life and the faith in our Lord Jesus Christ. And through him (i.e. Christ) it will be shown you that you must believe in the living God and not in Simon the sorcerer, that inconstant demon, who would have you remain in mourning and your innocent household be tortured, who with his soothing eloquence perverted you with (empty) words and spoke of devotion to God with his lips alone, while he himself is wholly filled with wickedness. For when you meant to celebrate a festival and put up your idol and veiled it and put out all the ornaments upon a stand, he had brought in two young men whom none of you saw; and they made an incantation and stole your ornaments and disappeared. But his plan miscarried; for my God disclosed (it) to me, so that you should not be deceived nor perish in hell, whatever wickedness and perversity you have shown towards God, who is full of all truth and a just judge of the living and the dead. And there is no other hope of life for man, except through him, through whom your lost (possessions) are preserved for you. And now you must regain your own soul!' But she threw herself at my feet, saying, 'Sir, who you are I do not know; but I received him as a servant of God, and I gave by his hands whatever he asked of me for the care of the poor, a great deal, and made him large presents besides. What harm has he suffered from me, that he should cause such trouble to my house?' Peter answered her, 'We must put no faith in words, but in actions and deeds. So we must go on with what we have begun.'

"So I left her and went with two stewards of Eubula, and came to Agrippinus and said to him, 'Make sure that you take note of these men. For tomorrow two young men will come to you, wishing to sell you a young satyr in gold set with stones, which belongs to these men's mistress. So you are to take it (p. 65) as if to inspect it and to admire its workmanship. Afterwards these

[1] Turner: habentes.

men will come in; (then) God shall bring the rest to the proof.'
And on the next day the lady's stewards came about the ninth
hour, and also those young men, wishing to sell Agrippinus the
golden satyr; and at once they were seized, and word was sent
to the lady. But she in great distress of mind went to the magistrate, and loudly declared what had happened to her. And when
the magistrate Pompeius saw her so distressed, whereas she had
never (before) come out in public, he immediately rose up from
the bench and went to the guardroom and ordered them to be
produced and examined. And they under torture confessed that
they were acting as Simon's agents—'who gave us money (to
do it)'. And when tortured further they confessed that all that
Eubula had lost had been put underground in a cave outside
the gate, and more besides. When Pompeius heard this, he got
up to go to the gate, having those two men bound with two
chains each. And there!—Simon came in at the gate, looking
for them because they had been so long; and he saw a great
crowd coming, and those men held fast in chains. At once he
realized (what had happened) and took to flight, and has not
been seen in Judaea until this day. But Eubula having recovered
all her property gave it for the care of the poor; she believed in
the Lord Jesus Christ and was strengthened (in the faith); and
despising and renouncing this world she gave (alms) to the
widows and orphans and clothed the poor; and after[1] a long
time she gained her repose. Now these things, my dearest brethren,
were done in Judaea; and so he came to be expelled from there,
who is called the messenger of Satan.[2]

18. "Brethren most dear and beloved, let us fast together and
pray to the Lord. He who expelled him from there is able to
uproot him from this place also. May he give us power to resist
him and his incantations and to expose him as the messenger of
Satan. For on the sabbath our Lord shall bring him, even if[3] he
refuses to come, to the forum of Julius. So let us bow our knees
to Christ, who hears us even if we have not called upon him; it is
he who sees us, even if he is not seen with these eyes, but is within
us; if we are willing (p. 66) he will not forsake us. Let us therefore

---

[1] Gundermann: post (for per).   [2] Cf. 2 Cor. 12:7. *Lit.* "angel".
[3] Turner: et quidem.

cleanse our souls of every wicked temptation, and God will not depart from us; and if we only wink with our eyes, he is present with us."

7

(Peter's miracles)

19. When Peter had just said this, Marcellus came in and said, "Peter, I have cleansed my house for you of (all) traces of Simon and removed (all traces) of his wicked dust. For I took water and calling on the holy name of Jesus Christ, with other servants of mine who belong to him, I sprinkled all my house and all the dining-rooms and all the colonnades right out to the doorway; and I said, 'I know that thou, Lord Jesus Christ, art pure and untouched by any impurity; so that my opponent and enemy is driven away from before thy face.' And now, most blessed man, I have told the widows and the aged to meet you in my house which is cleansed, that they may pray with us. And each of them shall be given a piece of gold on account of their service, so that they may truly be called Christ's servants. And everything else is ready for the service; I beg you therefore, most blessed Peter, to endorse their request, so that you also may grace their prayers for me. Let us go, then, and let us also take Narcissus and all the brethren who are here." So Peter assented to his simplicity and went with him and the other brethren to do as he desired.

20. So Peter went in and saw one of the old people, a widow that was blind, and her daughter giving her a hand and leading her to Marcellus' house. And Peter said to her, "Mother, come here; from this day onward Jesus gives you his right hand, through whom we have light unapproachable[1] which no darkness hides; and he says to you through me, 'Open your eyes and see, and walk on your own'." And at once the widow saw Peter laying his hand on her.

And Peter went into the dining-room and saw that the gospel was being read. So he rolled up (the book) and said, "You men who believe and hope in Christ (p. 67), you must know how the

---

[1] Cf. i Tim. 6:16.

holy scriptures of our Lord should be declared. What we have
written by his grace, so far as we were able, although it seems
weak to you as yet, yet (we have written) according to our powers,[1]
so far as it is endurable to be implanted in human flesh.[2] We
should therefore first learn to know the will of God, or (his)
goodness;[3] for when error was in full flood and many thousands
of men were plunging to destruction, the Lord in his mercy was
moved to show himself in another shape and to be seen in the
form of a man, on whom neither the Jews nor we were worthy
to be enlightened. For each one of us saw (him) as he was able, as
he had power to see. And now I will explain to you what has just
been read to you. Our Lord wished me to see his majesty on the
holy mountain;[4] but when I with the sons of Zebedee saw the
brilliance of his light, I fell as one dead, and closed my eyes and
heard his voice, such as I cannot describe, and thought that I
had been blinded by his radiance. And recovering my breath a
little I said to myself, 'Perhaps my Lord willed to bring me here
to deprive me of my sight.' And I said, 'If this be thy will, Lord,
I do not gainsay it.' And he gave me his hand and lifted me up.
And when I stood up I saw him in such a form as I was able to
take in. So, my dearest brethren, as God is merciful, he has borne
our weaknesses and carried our sins, as the prophet says, 'He
beareth our sins and is afflicted for us; yet we thought him to be
afflicted and stricken with wounds.'[5] For 'he is in the Father and
the Father in him';[6] he also is himself the fullness of all majesty,
who has shown us all his goodness. He ate and drank for our
sakes, though himself without hunger or thirst, he bore and
suffered reproaches for our sakes, he died and rose again because
of us. He who defended me also when I sinned (p. 68) and
strengthened me with his greatness,[7] will also comfort you that
you may love him, this (God) who is both great and little,
beautiful and ugly, young and old, appearing in time and yet in
eternity wholly invisible; whom no human hand has grasped, yet
is held by his servants, whom no flesh has seen, yet now he is

---

[1] Cf. Isidore of Pelusium II. 99 (*PG* 78, 544): ἃ ἐχωρήσαμεν ἐγράψαμεν.
[2] Vouaux: inferri.   [3] V.A.: God's mercy and kindness to men.
[4] Cf. Mk. 9:2ff. and pars.; 2 Pet. 1:18.   [5] Is. 53:4.   [6] Jn. 10:38.
[7] V.A.: He ate and drank for our sakes, (and) for our sakes endured all things,
because he is kind towards men and good, who also strengthens me, who desire and
require him in all things for his greatness and for the knowledge of him.

seen;[1] whom no hearing has found yet now he is known as the
word that is heard; whom no suffering can reach, yet now is
(chastened) as we are;[2] who was never chastened, yet now is
chastened; who is before the world, yet now is comprehended in
time; the beginning greater than all princedom, yet now delivered
to the princes; beauteous, yet appearing among us as poor and
ugly, yet foreseeing; this Jesus you have, brethren, the door,[3] the
light, the way, the bread, the water, the life, the resurrection,[4]
the refreshment, the pearl, the treasure, the seed, the abundance,
the mustard-seed, the vine, the plough, the grace, the faith,
the word:[5] He is all things, and there is no other greater than he.
To him be praise for ever and ever. Amen."

21. And when the ninth hour was fully come they stood up to
pray. And now suddenly some of the old blind widows, who still
sat there unknown to Peter and had not stood up,[6] called out and
said to Peter, "We sit here together, Peter, hoping in Christ
Jesus and believing (in him). So as you have now made one of us
to see, we beg you, sir Peter, let us also share his mercy and
goodness."[7] And Peter said to them, "If there is in you the faith
which is in Christ, if it is established in you, then see with your
mind what you do not see with your eyes; and (though) your
ears be closed, yet let them open in your mind within you. These
eyes shall again be closed, that see nothing but men and cattle
and dumb animals and stones and sticks; but only the inner[8] eyes

---

[1] Turner: videtur.   [2] Turner: passionum exterum et nunc est tamquam nos.
[3] V.A. (continuing from 'knowledge of him', p. 302 n. 7): He likewise encourages
you also, that you may know him and love and fear him, who is little to those who
are ignorant, but great to those who know him, who is beautiful to those who understand but (appears) ugly to the ignorant, who is both old and young, who appears in
time and exists for ever, who is everywhere, yet is in nothing that is unworthy of
him; whom no human hand has held, yet himself holds all things, whom the flesh
has not seen to this day, yet is seen with the eyes of the soul by those who are worthy
of him, the Word that was proclaimed by the prophets and has now been shown
forth, who is untouched by sins yet was handed over to powers and authorities, who
always takes thought for us and for all who love him. This Jesus we call the door,
etc.
[4] V.A. (instead of 'the resurrection . . . Amen'): Him we also call the repose
(ἀνάπαυσις), the vine, the grace, the Word (Logos) of the Father; he has indeed
many names, but is in truth the one only-begotten Son of God.
[5] On the individual titles cf. Jn. 10:7, 9; 3:19; 8:12; 14:6; 6:35; 4:10; 7:38; 14:6;
11:25; Mt. 11:28; 13:46, 44, 24; 13:31; Jn. 15:1; Lk. 9:62; Jn. 1:1, 14.
[6] Turner: surgentes (for credentes).
[7] V.A.: We too entreat our Master and Lord Jesus Christ to show through you his
merciful kindness to us also.
[8] Turner: interiores (for non omnes).

see Jesus Christ.[1] Yet now, Lord, let thy sweet and holy name assist these women; do thou touch their eyes, for thou art able, that they may see with their own eyesight."

And when prayer was made by all, the room in which they were shone as if with lightning, such as shines in the clouds. Yet it was not such light as (p. 69) (is seen) by day, (but) ineffable, invisible, such as no man could describe, a light that shone on us so (brightly) that we were senseless with bewilderment, and called upon the Lord and said, "Have mercy on us thy servants, Lord. Let thy gift to us, Lord, be such as we can endure; for this we can neither see nor endure." And as we lay there, there stood there only those widows, which were blind. But the bright light which appeared to us entered into their eyes and made them see.

Then Peter said to them, "Tell (us) what you saw." And they said, "We saw an old man, who had such a presence as we cannot describe to you"; but others (said), "We saw a growing lad"; and others said, "We saw a boy who gently touched our eyes, and so our eyes were opened."[2] So Peter praised the Lord, saying, "Thou alone art God the Lord, to whom praise is due. How many lips should we need to give thanks to thee in accordance with thy mercy? So, brethren, as I told you a little while ago, God is greater[3] than our thoughts, as we have learnt from the aged widows, how they have seen the Lord in a variety of forms."

22. And he exhorted them all to understand the Lord with all their heart; then he and Marcellus and the other brethren began to attend to the virgins of the Lord and to rest until morning. Marcellus said to them, "You holy and inviolate virgins of the Lord, give ear; you have a place where you (may) stay. For the things that are called mine, to whom do they belong but you? Do not leave this place, but refresh yourselves; for on the sabbath which comes tomorrow Simon holds a contest with Peter, the

---

[1] V.A.: If your faith is as you say, established in him, then see him with the eyes of your heart, and if these your outward eyes be satisfied, then those of your soul shall be opened. And if now those eyes of yours are opened, they shall be closed again, and recovering their sight they shall see nothing but outward things, that is men and cattle and other animals and stones and sticks; but Jesus, who is truly God, these eyes were not designed to see.

[2] In V.A. only one widow returns each answer; but the answers largely correspond with the text of the Act. Verc.

[3] Turner: constat.

holy one of God. For as the Lord has always been with him, so may Christ the Lord stand for him now as his apostle! For Peter has continued tasting nothing but adding (to his austerities)[1] that he may overcome the wicked enemy and persecutor of the Lord's truth. For here are my young men who have come with the news that they have seen stands being set up in the forum, and the crowd saying 'Tomorrow (p. 70) at dawn two Jews will contend in this place concerning the worship of God.'[2] Now therefore let us watch till morning, praying and entreating our Lord Jesus Christ to hear our prayers on behalf of Peter."

And Marcellus went to sleep for a short time; and when he awoke he said to Peter, "Peter, apostle of Christ, let us boldly set about our task. For just now as I slept for a little I saw you sitting on a high place, and before you a great assembly; and a most evil-looking woman, who looked like an Ethiopian, not an Egyptian, but was all black, clothed in filthy[3] rags, (was) dancing, with an iron collar about her neck and chains on her hands and feet. When you saw her you said aloud to me, 'Marcellus, the whole power of Simon and of his god is this dancer; take off her head!' But I said to you 'Brother Peter, I am a senator of noble family, and I have never stained my hands, nor killed even a sparrow at any time.' And when you heard this you began to cry out even louder, 'Come, our true sword, Jesus Christ, and do not only cut off the head of this demon, but cut in pieces all her limbs in the sight of all these whom I have approved in thy service.' And immediately a (man who looked) like yourself, Peter, with sword in hand, cut her all to pieces, so that I gazed upon you both, both on you and on the one who was cutting up the demon, whose likeness caused me great amazement. And now I have awakened, and have told you these signs of Christ." And when Peter heard this he was the more encouraged, because Marcellus had seen these things; for the Lord is always careful for his own. So cheered and refreshed by these words he stood up to go to the forum.

---

[1] superponens: cf. Hermas, Sim. V. 3 (Bonnet). Later a technical term for special fasting, cf. Bingham, *Antiquities of the Christian Church* XXI. 1. 25 (*Works*, 1844, Vol. vii, pp. 227ff.); Bieler, *The Irish Penitentials*, 1963, index s.v.—R.M.W.
[2] Vouaux: conlocutio dei = προσηγορία θεοῦ.   [3] Bonnet: sordidis.

8

(The Contest with Simon in the Forum)

23. Now the brethren assembled and all those that were in Rome, taking their places and paying a piece of gold for each; and the senators, prefects and officers also collected together. Then Peter came in and took his place in the centre. They all cried out, "Show us, Peter, who is your god, or what is his greatness, which has given you such confidence. (p. 71) Do not be ungenerous to the Romans; they are lovers of the gods. We have had evidence from Simon, now let us have yours; convince us, both of you, whom we should truly believe." And while they said this, Simon also came in; and he stood in confusion at Peter's side and gazed at him closely.

After a long silence Peter said, "You men of Rome, you must be our true judges. Now I say that I have believed in the living and true God, and I promise you to give evidence of him, such as I have known already, as many among you bear witness. For you see that this man is completely silent, since he has been convicted and I drove him from Judaea because of the impostures which he practised on Eubula, an honourable and most simple woman, using his magic arts. Expelled from there by me, he has come to this place, believing he could hide himself among you; and there he stands face to face with me. Tell me now, Simon, did you not fall at my feet and Paul's in Jerusalem,[1] when you saw the healings which were done by our hands?—and you said, 'I beg you, take payment from me as much as you will, so that I can lay hands (on men) and work such benefits.' When we heard these words of yours we cursed you (saying) 'Do you think you can tempt us to wish for possession of money?' And now are you not afraid? My name is Peter, because the Lord Christ thought fit to call me 'prepared for all things'.[2] For I believe on the living God, through whom I shall destroy your sorceries. Now let him (Simon) do the marvellous things he used to do, here in your presence. And what I have just told you of him, will you not believe me?"

But Simon said, "You presume to talk of Jesus the Nazarene,

---

[1] Cf. Acts 8:18ff.   [2] Cf. Mt. 16:17-19(?).

the son of a carpenter and a carpenter himself,[1] whose family comes from Judaea. Listen, Peter, the Romans have sense; they are not fools." And he turned to the people and said, "You men of Rome, is God born? Is he crucified? He who owns a Lord is no God!" And as he said this, many answered, "Well said, Simon!"

24. But Peter said, "A curse on your words against Christ! Did you presume to speak in these terms, while the prophet says of him, 'His generation, who shall declare it?'[2] And another prophet says, 'And we saw (p. 72) him and he had no grace nor beauty.'[3] And: 'In the last times a boy is born of the Holy Spirit; his mother knows not a man, nor does anyone claim to be his father.'[4] And again he says, 'She has given birth and has not given birth.'[5] And again, 'Is it a small thing for you to make trouble. . .?'[6] (And again) 'Behold, a virgin shall conceive in the womb.'[7] And another prophet says in the Father's honour, 'We have neither heard her voice, nor is a midwife come in.'[8] Another prophet says, 'He was not born from the womb of a woman, but came down from a heavenly place';[9] and, 'A stone is cut out without hands and has broken all the kingdoms';[10] and, 'The stone which the builders rejected is become the head of the corner';[11] and he calls him a stone 'elect and precious'.[12] And again the prophet says of him, 'And behold I saw one coming upon a cloud like a son of man.'[13] And what more (need be said)? You men of Rome, if you were versed in the prophetic writings I would explain all (this) to you; for through them it had to be (told) in secret (*lit.* in a mystery) and the kingdom of God be fulfilled. But these things shall be disclosed to you hereafter.

Now as for you, Simon; do one of those things with which you used to deceive them, and I will undo it through my Lord Jesus Christ." Simon put on a bold front and said, "If the prefect permits."

[1] Cf. Mk. 6:3 and pars.   [2] Is. 53:8.
[3] Is. 53:2 ("form nor comeliness," *AV*).
[4] Unknown quotation.   [5] Cf. *Apokr.* 2, p. 388.
[6] Turner: part of the quotation from Isaiah 7:13 has been omitted.
[7] Is. 7:14.   [8] Ascension of Isaiah, 11:13f.
[9] Unknown; cf. Vouaux, p. 369.   [10] Dan. 2:34.
[11] Ps. 118:22; cf. Mk. 12:10 and pars.   [12] Is. 28:16.
[13] Dan. 7:13; cf. Mk. 13:26 and pars.

25. But the prefect wished to show impartiality towards both, so as not to appear to act unjustly. And the prefect put forward one of his young men, and said to Simon, "Take this man and put him to death." And he said to Peter, "And you, restore him to life." And the prefect addressed the people saying, "It is now for you to judge which of these men is acceptable to God, the one who kills or the one who gives life."

And immediately Simon spoke in the boy's ear, and made him speechless, and he died. And as a murmuring arose among the people, one of the (p. 73) widows who rested at Marcellus' house cried out from behind the crowd, "Peter, servant of God, my son is dead, the only one that I had."[1] And the people made room for her and led her to Peter. But she threw herself down at his feet and said, "I had only one son; he provided my food with his hands (*lit.* shoulders), he lifted me up, he carried me. Now he is dead, who will lend me a hand?" Peter said to her, "Take these men for witnesses and go[2] and bring your son, so that these may see, and be enabled to believe that by the power of God he is raised up." But when she heard this,[3] she fell down. Then Peter said to the young men, "Now we need some young men, who are also willing to believe." And immediately thirty young men stood up, who were ready to carry her or to bring her dead son. And when the widow had hardly recovered herself, the young men lifted her up. But she was crying out and saying, "Look, my son, the servant of Christ has sent for you," and tearing her hair and her face. Now the young men who came examined the boy's nostrils, (to see)[4] whether he were really dead. And seeing that he was dead they comforted his mother[5] and said, "If you truly believe in Peter's God,[6] we (will) lift him up and bring him to Peter, that he may revive him and restore him to you."

26. While the young men were saying these things the prefect in the forum looked at Peter and said, "What say you, Peter? See, the boy lies there dead[7]—of whom even the emperor thinks

---

[1] Cf. Lk. 7:11ff.　　[2] Vouaux: duc te = ὕπαγε.
[3] Turner: illa autem hoc audiens.
[4] Pap. Ox: inspected the boy's nostrils to see if . . .
[5] Pap. Ox: the old woman (in place of "his mother").
[6] Pap. Ox: Now if you are willing, mother, and have confidence in Peter's God.
[7] Pap. Ox: while they said these things, the prefect looking closely at Peter ⟨. . . , break⟩ "See, Peter, my servant lies dead."

kindly—and I have not spared him. Certainly I had many other young men, but I trusted in you, and in your Lord whom you preach, if indeed you are sure and truthful; therefore I allowed him to die."[1] Then Peter said, "God is not tested or weighed in the balance; but he is to be worshipped by those whom he loves[2] with (all) their heart, and he will listen to those who are worthy.[3] But now that God and my Lord Jesus Christ is tested among you, he is doing such signs and wonders through me for the conversion of his sinners. And now in the sight of them all, O Lord, in thy power raise up through my voice the man whom Simon killed with his touch!" And Peter said to the boy's master, "Come, take his right hand, and you shall have him alive and (able to) walk with you." And Agrippa the prefect ran and came to the boy and taking his hand restored him to life. And when the crowds saw it they all cried out, "There is but one God, the one God of Peter!"

27. (p. 74) Meanwhile the widow's son also was brought in on a stretcher by the young men; and the people made way for them and brought them to Peter. And Peter lifted up his eyes towards heaven and held out his hands and said, "Holy Father[4] of thy Son Jesus Christ, who hast given us thy power, that through thee we may ask and obtain, and despise all that is in this world, and follow thee alone; thou who art seen by few, and wouldst be known by many; shine thou about (us), Lord, give light, appear, and raise up the son of (this) aged widow who cannot help herself without her son. Now I take up the word of Christ my master, and say to thee, Young man, arise and walk[5] with thy mother, so long as thou art useful to her. But afterwards thou shalt offer thyself to me in a higher service, in the office of deacon and bishop." And immediately the dead man stood up, and the crowds were astonished at the sight, and the people shouted, "Thou art God the Saviour, thou, the God of Peter, the invisible God, the Saviour!" And they spoke among themselves, being truly astonished at the power of a man that called upon his

[1] Pap. Ox: but I wished to test you, and the God (who is preached) by you, whether you (pl.) are truthful.
[2] Turner: sed dilectis suis.
[3] Pap. Ox: God is not tested or proved, Agrippa; but being beloved and entreated he listens to those who are worthy.
[4] Cf. Jn. 17:11.   [5] Lk. 7:14.

Lord by his word; and they accepted it to their sanctification.

28. So while the news spread round the whole city, the mother of a senator approached and pressing through the middle of the crowd she threw herself at Peter's feet, saying, "I have heard from my household that you are a servant of the merciful God, bestowing his grace to all who desire this light. Bestow then this light on (my) son, for I have heard that you are not ungenerous towards anyone; if (even) a lady entreats you do not turn away!" Peter said to her, "Do you believe my God, by whom your son shall be restored to life?" But his mother cried aloud and said with tears, "I believe, Peter, I believe." The whole people shouted, "Grant the mother her son!" Then Peter said, "Let him be brought here before all these." And Peter turned to the people and said, "You men of Rome, seeing that I too am one of you, wearing human flesh, and a sinner, but have obtained mercy, (p. 75) do not look at me, as though by my own power I were doing what I do;[1] (the power is) my Lord Jesus Christ's, who is the judge of the living and of the dead. Believing in him and sent by him, I dare to entreat him to raise the dead. Go then, lady, let your son be brought here and restored to life."

Then the woman made her way through the crowd and went out into the street with haste and great joy, and believing in her heart she reached her house and made her young men carry him and came to the forum. And she told her young men to put their caps on their heads and walk in front of the bier, and all that was to be used for the body of her son (i.e. for the funeral) should be carried in front of the bier so that Peter should see it and have pity on the dead man and on herself. So with them all as mourners she came to the assembly; and a crowd of senators and ladies followed her to see the wonderful works of God. Now Nicostratus, the dead man, was much respected and liked among the senate; so they brought him in and laid him down before Peter. Then Peter called for silence and said with a loud voice, "Men of Rome, let there now be a just judgment between me and Simon, and consider which of us believes in the living God, he or I. Let him revive the body which lies here; then (you may) believe in him as an angel of God. But if he cannot, then I will

[1] Cf. Acts 3:12.

call upon my God; I will restore her son alive to his mother, and then you (shall) believe that this is a sorcerer and a cheat, this guest of yours!"

And they all heard this and accepted Peter's challenge as just; and they encouraged Simon, saying, "Now, if there is anything in you, bring it out! Spite him, or be spited! Why are you waiting? Go on, begin!" But Simon, seeing them all pressing him, stood there silent; (however), when he saw that the people had become silent and were looking at him, Simon raised his voice and said, "Men of Rome, if you see the dead man restored to life, will you throw Peter out of the city?" And all the people said, "We will not only throw him out, but that self-same hour we will burn him with fire."

Then Simon went to the dead man's head, and stooped down three times and stood up three times (p. 76), and showed the people that (the dead man) had raised his head and was moving, opening his eyes and bowing towards Simon.[1] And at once they began to look for wood and kindling, in order to burn Peter. But Peter gaining the strength of Christ raised his voice and said to the men who were shouting against him, "Now I see, people of Rome, that I must not call you foolish and empty-headed, so long as your eyes and ears and hearts are blinded. So long as your sense is darkened, you do not see that you are bewitched, since you believe that a dead man has been revived when he has not stood up. I would have been content, you men of Rome, to keep silent and die without a word and leave you among the illusions of this world. But I have before my eyes the punishment of unquenchable[2] fire. If you agree, then, let the dead man speak, let him get up if he is alive, let him free his jaw of its wrappings with his own hands, let him call for his mother, and when you call out, let him say, 'What is it you are calling?' Let him beckon to you with his hand. Now (if) you wish to see that he is dead and you are spell-bound, let this man withdraw from the bier— this man who has persuaded you to withdraw from Christ,—and

---

[1] Turner: inclinans se ter, ter erigens ostendit . . . aperientem et inclinantem se Simonem. illi . . . (?). The passage is still obscure. The essential point is that Simon has to use all kinds of techniques, whereas Peter performs similar actions by a single word of command (cf. Vouaux, pp. 386f. n. 3).
[2] Cf. Mk. 9:43.

you will see that the (young) man is (still) in the same state as (when) you saw him brought in."

But Agrippa the prefect could not contain himself, but got up and pushed Simon away with his own hands. And so the dead man lay there again as he was before. And the people were enraged and turned away from Simon's sorcery, and began to call out, "Hear (us), Caesar! If the dead man does not stand up, let Simon be burnt instead of Peter, for he has truly blinded us." But Peter held out his hand and said, "Men of Rome, have patience! I am not telling you that Simon should be burnt when the boy is restored; for if I tell you, you will do it." The people shouted "Even if you will not have it, Peter, we will do it!" Peter said to them, "If you are determined on this, the boy shall not return to life. For we have not learnt to repay evil with evil;[1] but (p. 77) we have learnt to love our enemies and pray for our persecutors.[2] For if even this man can repent, that is better; for God will not remember evil (deeds). So let him come into the light of Christ. But if he cannot, let him possess the inheritance of his father the devil; but your hands shall not be stained."

And when he had said this to the people, he went up to the boy, and before he revived him he said to his mother, "Those young men whom you set free in honour of your son, are they to do service to their master as free men, when he is alive? For I know that some will feel injured on seeing your son restored to life, because these men will become his slaves once again. But let them all keep their freedom and draw their provisions as they drew them before, for your son shall be raised up, and they must be with him." And Peter went on looking at her, to see what she thought. And the boy's mother said, "What else can I do? So I will declare in the presence of the prefect: all that I meant to lay out for my son's funeral shall be their property." And Peter said to her, "Let the remainder be distributed to the widows." But Peter rejoiced in his heart, and said in the spirit, "Lord who art merciful, Jesus Christ, appear to thy (servant) Peter who calls upon thee, as thou hast always shown mercy and goodness; in the presence of all these men, who have obtained their freedom

---

[1] Rom. 12:17; 1 Thess. 5:15.   [2] Cf. Mt. 5:44.

so as to do service, let Nicostratus now arise!" And Peter touched the boy's side and said, "Stand up." And the boy stood up and gathered up his clothes and sat down and untied his jaw and asked for other clothes; and he came down from the bier and said to Peter, "I beg you, sir, let us go to our Lord Jesus Christ whom I saw talking with you; who said to you, as he showed me to you, 'Bring him here to me, for he is mine'." When Peter heard this from the boy he was yet more strengthened in mind by the help of the Lord; and Peter said to the people, "Men of Rome, this is how the dead are restored to life, this is how they speak, this is how they walk when they are raised up, and live for so long as God wills. Now therefore, you people who have gathered to (see) the show, if (p. 78) you turn now[1] from these wicked ways of yours and from all your man-made gods and from every kind of uncleanness and lust, you shall receive the fellowship with Christ through faith, so that you may come to everlasting life."

29. From that same hour they venerated him as a god, and laid at his feet such sick people as they had at home, so that he might heal them. But the prefect seeing that such a great number (p. 79) were waiting upon Peter, made signs to Peter that he should withdraw. But Peter invited the people to come to Marcellus' house. But the boy's mother entreated Peter to set foot in her house.[2] But Peter had arranged to go to[3] Marcellus on the Lord's day, to see the widows as Marcellus had promised, so that they should be cared for by his own hands. So the boy who had returned to life said, "I will not leave Peter." And his mother went joyfully and gladly to her own house. And on the next day after the sabbath she came to Marcellus' house bringing Peter two thousand pieces of gold and saying to Peter, "Divide these among the virgins of Christ who serve him." But when the boy who had risen from the dead saw that he had given nothing to anyone, he went home and opened the chest and himself brought four thousand gold pieces, saying to Peter, "Look, I myself, who am restored to life, am bringing a double offering, and (present) myself as a speaking sacrifice[4] to God from this day on."

[1] Turner: nunc. [2] Cf. Acts 16:15.
[3] Turner: ire ad. [4] Cf. Rom. 12:1.

9

Martyrdom of the holy Apostle Peter

30 (1). Now on the Lord's day Peter was preaching to the brethren and encouraging[1] them to faith in Christ. Many of the senators were present and a number of knights and wealthy women ⟨and⟩ matrons, and they were strengthened in the faith. But there was present a very wealthy woman who bore the name of Chryse (the golden), because every utensil of hers was made of gold—for since her birth she had never used a silver or glass vessel, but only golden ones; she said to Peter, "Peter, servant of God, there came to me in a dream the one you say is God; and he said to me, 'Chryse, bring my servant Peter (p. 80) 10,000 pieces of gold; for you owe them to him.' So I have brought them, for fear lest I should suffer some harm from him who appeared to me, who has gone away into heaven." So saying, she laid down the money and departed. But Peter when he saw it gave praise to the Lord, because the afflicted could now be relieved. Now some of those who were present said to him, "Peter, you were wrong to accept this money from her; for she is notorious all over Rome for fornication and (they say) that she does not consort with one man only; indeed she even goes in to her own (house-) boys. So have no dealings with the 'golden' table (i.e. Chryse's table), but let her (money) be returned to her." But Peter, when he heard this, laughed and said to the brethren, "I do not know what this woman is as regards her usual way of life; but in taking this money I did not take it without reason; for she was bringing it as a debtor to Christ, and is giving it to Christ's servants; for he himself has provided for them."

31 (2). And they brought the sick people also to him on the sabbath, entreating him that they might be cured of their diseases. And many paralytics were healed, and many sufferers from dropsy and from two- and four-day fevers, and they were cured of every bodily disease, such as believed in the name of Jesus Christ, and very many were added every day to the grace of the Lord.[2]

But after a few days had elapsed Simon the magician promised the rabble that he would show Peter that he had not put his faith

---

[1] Turner: hortante.   [2] Cf. Acts 2:47.

in the true God but in a deception. Now while he performed many false miracles, he was laughed to scorn by those disciples who were already firm (in the faith). For in their living-rooms he caused certain spirits to be brought in to them, which were only appearances without real existence. And what more is there to say? Although he had often been convicted for his magic art,[1] he made the lame appear to be sound for a short time, and the blind likewise, and once he appeared to make many who were dead come alive and move, as he did with Nicostratus. But all the while Peter followed him and exposed him to the onlookers. And as he was now always out of favour and derided by the people of Rome and discredited, as not succeeding in what he promised to do, it came to such a point that he said to them, "Men of Rome, at present you think that Peter has mastered me, as having greater power, and you attend to him rather (than me). (But) you are deceived. For tomorrow I shall leave you, who are utterly profane and impious, and fly up to God, whose power I am, although enfeebled. If then you have fallen, behold I am He that Standeth.[2] And I am going up (p. 82) to my Father[3] and shall say to him, 'Even me, thy Son that Standeth, they desired to bring down; but I did not consent with them, and am returned to myself'."

32 (3). And by the following day a large crowd had assembled on the Sacred Way to see him fly. And Peter, having seen a vision, came to the place, in order to convict him again this time; for when (Simon) made his entry into Rome, he astonished the crowds by flying; but Peter, who exposed him, was not yet staying in Rome, (the city) which he so carried away by his deceptions that people lost their senses through him.

So this man stood on a high place, and seeing Peter, he began to say: "Peter, now of all times, when I am making my ascent before all these onlookers, I tell you: If your god has power enough—he whom the Jews destroyed, and they stoned you who were chosen by him[4]—let him show that faith in him is of God; let it be shown at this time whether it be worthy of God. For I

---

[1] The German reads, "After he had spoken at length about his magic art", which presupposes a grammatical slip in the Greek.—G.C.S.
[2] Cf. Clem. Alex., *Strom*. II. 11. 52; Hippolytus, Ref. VI. 17.
[3] Cf. Jn. 20:17.   [4] Cf. Mt. 23:37; Jn. 8:59; Acts 14:19.

by ascending will show to all this crowd what manner of being I am." And lo and behold, he was carried up into the air, and everyone saw him all over Rome, passing over its temples and its hills; while the faithful looked towards Peter. And Peter, seeing the incredible sight, cried out to the Lord Jesus Christ, "Let this man do what he undertook, and all who have believed on thee shall now be overthrown, and the signs and wonders which thou gavest them through me shall be disbelieved. Make haste, Lord, with thy grace; and let him fall down from (this) height, and be crippled, but not die; but let him be disabled and break his leg in three places!" And he fell down from that height and broke his leg in three places. Then they stoned him and went to their own homes; but from that time they all believed in Peter.

But one of Simon's friends named Gemellus, from whom Simon had received much (support), who was married to a Greek woman, came along the road shortly afterwards and seeing him with his leg broken said, (p. 84) "Simon, if the Power of God is broken, shall not the God himself, whose power you are, be proved an illusion?" So Gemellus also ran and followed Peter, saying to him, "I too desire to be one of those that believe in Christ." But Peter said, "Then what objection (can there be), my brother? Come and stay with us." But Simon in his misfortune found some (helpers) who carried him on a stretcher by night from Rome to Aricia; and after staying there he was taken to a man named Castor, who had been banished from Rome to Terracina on a charge of sorcery; and there he underwent an operation; and thus Simon, the angel of the devil,[1] ended his life.

33 (4). But Peter stayed in Rome and rejoiced with the brethren in the Lord and gave thanks night and day for the mass of people who were daily added to the holy name by the grace of the Lord.[2] And the concubines of the prefect Agrippa also came to Peter, being four in number, Agrippina and Nicaria and Euphemia and Doris. And hearing the preaching of purity and all the words of the Lord they were cut to the heart and agreed with each other to remain in purity (renouncing) intercourse with Agrippa; and they were molested by him. Now when Agrippa

---

[1] Cf. 2 Cor. 12:7.   [2] Cf. Acts 2:47.

was perplexed and distressed about them—for he loved them passionately—he made inquiries, and when he sent (to find out) where they had gone, he discovered that (they had gone) to Peter. And when they came (back) he said to them, "That Christian has taught you not to consort with me; I tell you, I will both destroy you and burn him alive." They therefore took courage to suffer every injury from Agrippa, (wishing) only to be vexed by passion no longer, being strengthened by the power of Jesus.

34 (5). (p. 86) But one woman who was especially beautiful, the wife of Albinus the friend of Caesar, Xanthippe by name, came with the other ladies to Peter, and she too separated from Albinus. He therefore, filled with fury and passionate love for Xanthippe, and amazed that she would not even sleep in the same bed with him, was raging like a wild beast and wished to do away with Peter; for he knew that he was responsible for her leaving his bed. And many other women besides fell in love with the doctrine of purity and separated from their husbands, and men too ceased to sleep with their own wives, since they wished to worship God in sobriety and purity. So there was the greatest disquiet in Rome; and Albinus put his case to Agrippa, and said to him, "Either you must get me satisfaction from Peter, who caused my wife's separation, or I shall do so myself"; and Agrippa said that he had been treated in the same way by him, by the separation of his concubines. And Albinus said to him, "Why then do you delay, Agrippa? Let us find him and execute him as a trouble-maker, so that we may recover our wives, and in order to give satisfaction to those who cannot execute him, who have themselves been deprived of their wives by him."

35 (6). But while they made these plans Xanthippe discovered her husband's conspiracy with Agrippa and sent and told Peter, so that he might withdraw from Rome. And the rest of the brethren together with Marcellus entreated him to withdraw, But Peter (p. 88) said to them "Shall we act like deserters, brethren?" But they said to him, "No, it is so that you can go on serving the Lord." So he assented to the brethren and withdrew by himself, saying, "Let none of you retire with me, but I shall retire by myself in disguise." And as he went out of the gate he saw the Lord entering Rome; and when he saw him he said,

"Lord, whither (goest thou) here?" And the Lord said to him, "I am coming to Rome to be crucified." And Peter said to him, "Lord, art thou being crucified again?" He said to him, "Yes, Peter, I am being crucified again." And Peter came to himself; and he saw the Lord ascending into heaven; then he returned to Rome rejoicing and giving praise to the Lord, because he said, "I am being crucified"; (since) this was to happen to Peter.

36 (7). So he returned to the brethren and told them what had been seen by him; and they were grieved at heart, and said with tears, "We entreat you, Peter, take thought for us that are young." And Peter said to them, "If it is the Lord's will, it is coming to pass even if we will not have it so. But the Lord is able to establish you in your faith in him, and he will lay your foundation on him and enlarge you in him, (you) whom he himself has planted, so that you may plant others through him. But as for me, so long as the Lord wills me to be in the flesh, I do not demur; again, if he will take me, I rejoice and am glad."

And while Peter was saying this and (p. 90) all the brethren were in tears, four soldiers arrested him and took him to Agrippa. And he in his distemper ordered that he be charged with irreligion and be crucified.

So the whole mass of the brethren came together, rich and poor, orphans and widows, capable and helpless, wishing to see Peter and to rescue him; and the people cried out irrepressibly with a single voice, "What harm has Peter done, Agrippa? How has he injured you? Answer the Romans!" And others said, "If this man dies, we must fear that the Lord will destroy us too."

And when Peter came to the place (of execution) he quietened the people and said, "You men, who are soldiers of Christ,[1] men who set their hopes on Christ, remember the signs and wonders which you saw through me, remember the compassion of God, how many healings he has performed for you. Wait for him that shall come and reward everyone according to his deeds.[2] And now do not be angry with Agrippa; for he is the servant of his father's influence; and this is to happen in any event, because the Lord has showed me what is coming. But why do I delay and not go to the cross?"

[1] Cf. 2 Tim. 2:4. [2] Cf. Mt. 16:27.

37 (8). Then when he had approached and stood by the cross he began to say, "O name of the cross, mystery that is concealed! O grace ineffable (p. 92) that is spoken in the name of the cross! O nature of man that cannot be parted from God! O love (Φιλία) unspeakable and inseparable, that cannot be disclosed through unclean lips! I seize thee now, being come to the end of my release from here. I will declare thee, what thou art; I will not conceal the mystery of the cross that has long been enclosed and hidden from my soul. You who hope in Christ, for you the cross must not be this thing that is visible; for this (passion), like the passion of Christ, is something other than this which is visible. And now above all, since you who can hear, can (hear it) from me, who am at the last closing hour of my life, give ear; withdraw your souls from every outward sense and from all that appears but is not truly real; close these eyes of yours, close your ears, withdraw from actions that are outwardly seen; and you shall know the facts about Christ and the whole secret of your salvation. Let so much be said to you who hear as though it were unspoken. But it is time for you, Peter, to surrender your body to those who are taking it. Take it, then, you whose duty this is. I request you therefore, executioners, to crucify me head-downwards—in this way and no other. And the reason, I will tell to those who hear."

38 (9). (p. 94) And when they had hanged him up in the way which he had requested, he began to speak again, saying "Men whose duty it is to hear, pay attention to what I shall tell you at this very moment that I am hanged up. You must know the mystery of all nature, and the beginning of all things, how it came about. For the first man, whose likeness I have in (my) appearance, in falling head-downwards showed a manner of birth that was not so before; for it was dead, having no movement. He therefore, being drawn down—he who also cast his first beginning down to the earth—established the whole of this cosmic system, being hung up as an image of the calling, in which he showed what is on the right hand as on the left, and those on the left as on the right, and changed all the signs of their nature, so as to consider fair those things that were not fair, and take those that were really evil to be good. Concerning this the Lord says in a mystery, 'Unless you make what is on the right hand as what

is on the left and what is on the left hand as what is on the right and what is above as what is below and what is behind as what is before, you will not recognize the Kingdom.'[1] This (p. 96) conception, then, I have declared to you, and the form in which you see me hanging is a representation of that man who first came to birth. You then, my beloved, both those who hear (me) now and those that shall hear in time, must leave your former error and turn back again; for you should come up to the cross of Christ, who is the Word stretched out, the one and only, of whom the Spirit says, 'For what else is Christ but the Word, the sound of God?'[2] So that the Word is this upright tree on which I am crucified; but the sound is the cross-piece, the nature of man; and the nail that holds the cross-piece to the upright in the middle is the conversion (or turning point) and repentance of man.

39 (10). Since then thou hast made known and revealed these things to me, O Word of life, which name I have just given to the tree,[3] I give thee thanks, not with these lips that are nailed fast, nor with the tongue, through which truth and falsehood issues forth, nor with this word that comes forth by the skill of physical nature; but I give thee thanks, O King, with that voice which is known in silence, which is not heard aloud, which does not come forth through the bodily organs, which does not enter the ears of the flesh, that is not heard by corruptible substance, that is not in the world or uttered upon earth, nor is written in books, nor belongs to one but not to another; but with this (voice), Jesu Christ (p. 98) I thank thee, with silence of the voice, with which the spirit within me, that loves thee and speaks to thee and sees thee, makes intercession. Thou art known to the spirit only. Thou art my Father, thou art my Mother, thou my Brother, thou art Friend, thou art Servant, thou art House-keeper; thou art the All, and the All is in thee; thou art Being, and there is nothing that is, except thou.

"With Him then do you also take refuge, brethren, and learning that in him alone is your real being, you shall obtain those things of which he says to you, 'What eye has not seen nor ear heard,

---

[1] Cf. Vol. I, p. 175.   [2] Quotation of unknown origin; cf. Vouaux, pp. 449f.
[3] Or, whom I have just called the tree.—Translator.

nor has it entered the heart of man.'[1] We ask then, for that which
thou hast promised to give us, O Jesus undefiled; we praise thee,
we give thanks to thee and confess thee, and being yet men without
strength we glorify thee; for thou art God alone and no other,
to whom be glory both now and for all eternity, Amen."

40 (11). But as the crowd that stood by shouted Amen with a
resounding cry, at that very Amen, Peter gave up his spirit to
the Lord.

But when Marcellus saw that the blessed Peter had given up
his spirit, without taking anyone's advice, since it was not allowed,
he took him down from the cross with his own hands (p. 100)
and washed him in milk and wine;[2] and he ground up seven
pounds of mastic, and also fifty pounds of myrrh and aloe and
spice and embalmed his body, and filled a trough of stone of
great value with Attic honey and laid it in his own burial-vault.[3]

But Peter visited Marcellus by night and said, "Marcellus, you
heard the Lord saying, 'Let the dead be buried by their own
dead'?[4]" And when Marcellus said, "Yes," Peter said to him,
"The things which you laid out for the dead, you have lost; for
you who are alive were like a dead man caring for the dead."
And Marcellus awoke and told the brethren of Peter's appearing;
and he remained with those whom Peter had strengthened in the
faith of Christ, gaining strength himself yet more until the coming
of Paul to Rome.

41 (12). But when Nero later discovered that Peter had departed
this life, he censured the prefect Agrippa because he had been
put to death without his knowledge; for he would have liked to
punish him more cruelly and with extra severity; for Peter had
made disciples of some of his servants and caused them to leave
him; so that he was greatly incensed and for some time would not
speak to Agrippa; for he sought to destroy all those brethren who
had been made disciples by Peter. (p. 102) And one night he saw
a figure scourging him and saying, "Nero, you cannot now persecute or destroy the servants of Christ. Keep your hands from
them!" And so Nero, being greatly alarmed because of this

[1] Cf. 1 Cor. 2:9; Gospel of Thomas, 17; see Vol. I, p. 300.
[2] Cf. Mk. 15:42ff. and pars.
[3] On this passage cp. Cullmann, Peter[2], p. 176 (ET 1962, p. 155).
[4] Cf. Mt. 8:22.

vision, kept away from the disciples from the time that Peter departed this life.

And thereafter the brethren kept together with one accord, rejoicing and exulting in the Lord,[1] and glorifying the God and Saviour of our Lord Jesus Christ with the Holy Spirit, to whom be the glory for ever and ever. Amen.

3. ACTS OF PAUL*
(W. Schneemelcher)

INTRODUCTION: 1. LITERATURE. Texts: Lipsius *Aa* 1, pp. 235-272, 104-117; W. Wright, *Apocryphal Acts of the Apostles*, 1871, I. pp. 128-169, II. pp. 116-145 (Syriac and English); F. Nau, La version syriaque des martyres de S. Pierre, S. Paul et S. Luc, *Revue de l'Orient chrétien* III, 1898, pp. 39-57; E. J. Goodspeed, The book of Thekla, *The American Journal of Semitic Languages and Literatures* XVII, 1901, pp. 65f. (Ethiopic); O. von Gebhardt, *Die lateinischen Übersetzungen der Acta Pauli et Theclae* (*TU NF* 7. 2) 1902.—Carl Schmidt, *Acta Pauli aus der Heidelberger koptischen Papyrushandschrift Nr.* 1 hrsg., 1904 (2nd enlarged ed. 1905; abbreviated: Schmidt, *AP*); L. Vouaux, *Les Actes de Paul et ses lettres apocryphes*, 1913.—Carl Schmidt, Πράξεις Παύλου, *Acta Pauli nach dem Papyrus der Hamburger Staats- und Universitätsbibliothek unter Mitarbeit von W. Schubart hrsg.*, 1936 (abbreviated: Schmidt, *ΠΠ*). —Small Fragments: W. E. Crum, *BJRL* V, 1920, pp. 497f.; H. A. Sanders, *HTR* 31, 1938, pp. 70-90; G. D. Kilpatrick and C. H. Roberts, *JTS* 47, 1946, pp. 196-199 (cf. W. D. McHardy, *Exp. Times* 58, 1947, p. 279); C. H. Roberts, *The Antinoopolis Papyri I*, 1950, pp. 26-28. Translations: German by E. Rolffs, *Apokr.* 1, pp. 357-383; *Apokr.* 2, pp. 192-212; W. Michaelis, pp. 268-317.—French by Vouaux, pp. 143ff.—English by James, pp. 270-299.

Studies: Older literature in Lipsius, *Apostelgeschichten* II. 1; bibliography to 1913 in Vouaux, pp. 135-140.—Rolffs, *Handb.* pp. 358-395.—Fundamental are the discussions of Schmidt, *AP* and *ΠΠ*.—K. Pink, Die pseudopaulinischen Briefe I, *Biblica* VI, 1925, pp. 68-91; F. Loofs, *Theophilus von Antiochien adv. Marcionem und die anderen theologischen Quellen bei Irenaeus* (*TU* 46. 2), 1930, pp. 148-157; F. J. Dölger, Der heidnische Glaube an die Kraft des Fürbittgebetes für

---

[1] Cf. Acts 2:46.

* In the work on the Acts of Paul I have had the benefit of the friendly assistance of M. Testuz and R. Kasser. To both the most cordial thanks are here extended.

Abbreviations: AP=Acta Pauli (Acts of Paul); AThe=Acta Pauli et Theclae (Acts of Paul and Thecla); MP=Martyrdom of Paul; 3 Cor. =Correspondence of Paul with the Corinthians; PH=Hamburg Papyrus; PB=Pap. Berlin 13893 and Pap. Michigan 1317; PO=Pap. Oxyrhynchus 1602 (=Pap. Ghent 62); PM= Papyrus Michigan 3788; PA=Pap. Antinoopolis; PHeid=Heidelberg Coptic Papyrus; Ry=Fragment in the John Rylands Library; PG=unpublished Coptic Papyrus of the Ephesus episode. For further particulars of these witnesses, see below, pp. 325ff. The manuscripts of AThe and MP are abbreviated as in Lipsius, those of 3 Cor. as in Testuz.

die vorzeitig Gestorbenen nach den Theklaakten, *Antike und Christentum* 2, 1930, pp. 13–16; W. Bauer, *Rechtgläubigkeit und Ketzerei im ältesten Christentum*, 1934, pp. 45–48 *et al.*; A. Kurfess, Zu dem Hamburger Papyrus der Πράξεις Παύλου, *ZNW* 38, 1939, pp. 164–170; E. Peterson, Die Acta Xanthippae et Polyxenae und die Paulusakten, *Anal. Bollandiana* 65, 1947, pp. 57–60; *id.*, Einige Bemerkungen zum Hamburger Papyrusfragment der Acta Pauli, *Vig. Chr.* 3, 1949, pp. 142–162 (now also in: *Frühkirche, Judentum und Gnosis*, 1959, pp. 183–208); P. Devos, Actes de Thomas et Actes de Paul, *Anal. Boll.* 69, 1951, pp. 119–130 (against Peterson); R. Kasser, Acta Pauli 1959, *RHPR* 40, 1960, pp. 45–57.

2. ATTESTATION. The attestation of the AP is both early and good. Tertullian writes in De baptismo 17 (date uncertain; Quasten II, p. 280: *c.* 198–200): "If those who read the writings that falsely bear the name of Paul adduce the example of Thecla to maintain the right of women to teach and to baptize, let them know that the presbyter in Asia who produced this document, as if he could of himself add anything to the prestige of Paul, was removed from his office after he had been convicted and had confessed that he did it out of love for Paul" (*CSEL* XX, p. 215). Here Tertullian manifestly has in view the Thecla story, which indeed is proved to be part of the AP. He probably did not yet know it, however, as an independent work, detached from the AP, for his testimony would scarcely fit the AThe alone (they would add but little to the prestige of Paul!). On the other hand the testimony fits the AP as a whole. A certain light is also shed upon the question of the title. In the Coptic PHeid the work is described in the colophon as "The Πράξεις of Paul ⟨according to⟩ the Apostle" (Schmidt, AP, p. 50* and p. 90). Now only one letter of the K⟨ατά⟩ (= according to) remains, but the restoration is probably correct and elucidates Tertullian's statement: the author of AP not only described his work as "Acts of Paul", but also probably sent it into the world as an apostolic pseudepigraphon.

While Tertullian rejects the AP on theological grounds (disapproving of the participation of women in teaching and the administration of the Sacraments), but does not attack it as heretical, his contemporary Hippolytus evidently used the work without hesitation. In his commentary on Daniel, composed probably *c.* 204, he writes: "If we believe that when Paul was condemned to the circus the lion which was set upon him lay down at his feet and licked him, why should we not also believe what happened in the case of Daniel?" (III. 29; *Sources chrét.* 14, 1947, p. 254). This passage might refer to AThe c. 28 and c. 33, but only becomes properly intelligible if Hippolytus had also read the scene of Paul's combat with the lions. We may thus conjecture that Hippolytus knew the whole AP and did not repudiate it, even if he does not name the source for his statement. Origen on the other hand twice mentions the AP. In his work De principiis he quotes a saying from the Acta Pauli (so in Rufinus' Latin translation): "This is the Word, a living Being" (De princ. I. 2. 3; Koetschau, p. 30). It is clear from the context that Origen is here quoting a work under the title Acta Pauli (Πράξεις Παύλου); for he compares the statement quoted with the Prologue of the Gospel of John. The quotation however has not yet come to light in any known text of the AP. C. Schmidt conjectured (ΠΠ, p. 128) that the author of the AP borrowed this saying as well as the Quo Vadis scene from the APt, and indeed from Peter's prayer on the cross (APt c. 38, cf. above, p. 320; cf. Rolffs, Handb. p. 366f.). But this remains pure conjecture. On the other hand we can now verify Origen's other quotation from the AP. In his commentary on John he says: "If anyone cares to accept what is written in the 'Acts of Paul', where the Lord says: 'I am on the point of being crucified afresh' . . ." (Com. in Jn. XX. 12; Preuschen, p. 342). As PH p. 7. 39 shows, this is a literal quotation from the AP. Origen thus knew this work, and probably valued it; at least he did not reject it as heretical.

The mention of the lion speaking to the people in Commodian (Carmen apol. v. 627f.) is not of great importance (on this see above, p. 261).

In Eusebius on the other hand we can see how the attitude to the AP has changed, without the document being yet entirely rejected. In his discussion of the writings of Peter and Paul Eusebius affirms that the Πράξεις (Παύλου) do not belong to the undisputed books (HE III. 3. 5; trans. in Vol. I, p. 58). In the summing up of his statement on the Canon Eusebius reckons the AP among the spurious writings, and sets them on the same level as the Shepherd of Hermas, the Apocalypse of Peter, etc. (HE III. 25; trans. in Vol. I, p. 57). Here also it is clear that the AP do not indeed possess any canonical dignity, but that they are distinguished from the inferior heretical works.

The same attitude seems to be reflected in the catalogue of the Codex Claromontanus (4th cent.; trans. in Vol. I, p. 46), where the AP stand between Hermas and the Apocalypse of Peter. The note of the number of lines, i.e. of its compass, shows that the AP still lay before the author as part of (or an appendix to?) a biblical manuscript.

On the other hand Jerome reckons the "Περίοδοι Pauli et Theclae and the whole fable of the baptized lion" among the apocryphal writings, and quotes Tertullian on this point (de vir.

ill. 7). But since in Tertullian nothing is said about a baptized lion, we may assume that Jerome knew the AP and rejected it as apocryphal. The period following shows that the Church gradually came to the same judgment as Jerome, even if as late as the 14th century Nicephorus Callistus in his Church History presents a long report about the Ephesian episode in the AP (*HE* II. 25; MPG 145, col. 822). Evidence for the further history of the AP in the Church in Vouaux, pp. 24–69; Schmidt, AP pp. 108–116 and at other points in this work.

That the AP then through their reception by the Manichees fell completely into disrepute in the Church is not surprising (on the use of the AP by the Manichees cf. the *Manichaean Psalm-book* II, ed. Allberry, p. 143, 4ff.). Thus they are rejected as apocryphal in the Decretum Gelasianum (twice: 1. All books which Leucius the disciple of the devil has made; 2. the Book which is called the Acts of Thecla and of Paul), in the Stichometry of Nicephorus, and in the Catalogue of the 60 canonical books (cf. the texts in Vol. I, pp. 46–52).

3. EXTANT REMAINS. In the last 60 years our knowledge of the AP, a work frequently attested but as a whole lost, has steadily grown. Above all the discovery of the Coptic PHeid in 1894 considerably increased our knowledge of this apocryphon, since thereby the Acta Pauli et Theclae, the Martyrdom of Paul and the apocryphal correspondence between Paul and the Corinthians were proved to be parts of the old AP. Since then many other finds have been added, in particular the great Hamburg Papyrus (*PH*). We must here content ourselves with a brief enumeration of the material.

The following, all unfortunately preserved only in a fragmentary condition, may be regarded as witnesses to the entire AP:

(*a*) The Greek Papyrus of the Hamburg Staats- und Universitäts-bibliothek (PH), 10 leaves of a papyrus book from the period about 300 (description of the manuscript in Schmidt-Schubart, *ПП* pp. 4–14). This manuscript contains a large part of the Ephesus episode (pp. 1–5), Paul's sojourn in Corinth (pp. 6–7), the journey from Corinth to Italy (pp. 7–8) and a part of the MP (pp. 9–11).

It is supplemented by various fragments: Papyrus Berlin 13893 and Papyrus Michigan 1317 belong together (PB), and present the text contained in PH p. 8. 3–26, 30–36 and a few lines more (text and commentary in H. A. Sanders, HTR 31, 1938, pp. 70–90). Papyrus Oxyrhynchus 1602 (=Pap. Ghent 62), not a papyrus leaf but one from a parchment codex of the 4th or 5th centuries (PO), contains the text PH p. 8. 17–26 (printed in

Sanders, *loc. cit.*). Papyrus Michigan 3788 (PM) presents the text PH p. 8. 23–29, and on the back probably a further part of Paul's sermon in Puteoli (cf. below, pp. 382f.; text in Kilpatrick and Roberts, *JTS* 47, 1946, pp. 196-199).

(*b*) The Coptic Papyrus No. 1 in Heidelberg (PHeid) contains extensive fragments of the whole AP (description of the manuscript, probably written in the 6th century, in Schmidt, AP pp. 3–20).

The fragment of a Coptic parchment of the 4th century in the John Rylands Library Suppl. 44 (Ry), so far not yet published, presents some lines from the beginning of the AP (cf. Schmidt, *ПП*, pp. 117f.).

On the Coptic papyrus, likewise not yet published, which contains the Ephesus episode complete (PG), cf. R. Kasser, below, pp. 387ff.

The three sections which were early detached from the AP have each a separate tradition, which supplements the above-named witnesses to the AP as a whole, but at the same time also makes possible at some points a reciprocal control.

(*c*) The Acta Pauli et Theclae were edited by Lipsius (*Aa* 1, pp. 235–269) on the basis of 11 Greek manuscripts as well as Latin, Syriac, Slavic and Arabic versions (cf. his Introduction, *Aa* 1, pp. XCIV–CVI). To these may be added a small Greek fragment POx. No. 6 (Grenfell-Hunt I, pp. 9f.) and another fragment from Antinoopolis (Roberts No. 13, pp. 26–28). Important are the Latin translations, of which according to O. von Gebhart (*TU NF* 7. 2, 1902) there were at least four, independent of one another. Further information on the tradition in Vouaux, pp. 12–19.—The relation of the witnesses to one another and the value of the individual versions probably requires a fresh investigation. Lipsius' text is frequently in need of correction. In this respect a special significance attaches to the Coptic version (see above under *b*), even if it is not of itself decisive.

(*d*) The correspondence between the Corinthians and Paul (3 Cor.) is shown by PHeid to be part of the AP. Even before the discovery of the Heidelberg papyrus it was known through its appearance in the Armenian Bible and through Ephraem's commentary. In addition five Latin manuscripts in which it is contained, in part however very fragmentarily, have so far been discovered: Cod. Ambros. E 53 inf. saec. X (M); Cod. Laon 45 saec. XIII (L); Cod. Paris. lat. 5288 saec. X/XI (P); Cod. Zürich Car. C 14 saec. X (Z); Cod. Berlin Ham. 84 saec. XIII (B). Finally, a few years ago a witness for the Greek text of 3 Cor. was brought to light for the first time in Papyrus Bodmer X (3rd cent.).

The texts of the different witnesses vary considerably, so that a reconstitution of the text is extremely difficult, if not indeed impossible. Further information in Testuz, *Papyrus Bodmer X–XII*, 1959.

(*e*) The Martyrium Pauli was edited by Lipsius according to two Greek manuscripts (Cod. Patmiacus 48 (9th cent.) = P; Cod. Athous Vatoped. 79 (10th/11th cent.) = A), as well as a Coptic, a Slavic and an Ethiopic version. Appended is the fragmentary Latin version according to three Munich manuscripts (Lipsius, *Aa* I, pp. 104–117; cf. pp. LII–LVII). To these may be added a Syriac version, which Lipsius did not take into account, and above all PH pp. 9–11. Lipsius' text must at many points be corrected on the basis of PH and PHeid.

4. RECONSTRUCTION AND COMPOSITION: RELATION TO THE LUCAN ACTS.

1. From Damascus to Jerusalem.—The beginning of the AP has not survived, but C. Schmidt has made the first episode available from some fragments. A small Coptic fragment (Ry) contains some lines of a narrative from the life of Paul. Evidently the appearance of Christ on the way to Damascus was previously reported. In the extant text Paul receives the command to go to Damascus, and from there to Jerusalem; he comes to Damascus to the community there assembled (and fasting!).[1] He seems then to have delivered a sermon in the presence of the Jews.[2] Presumably it was then reported, referring to Acts 9:26, that Paul journeyed from Damascus to Jerusalem.

Now in a later section of the AP Paul himself speaks of his passage from persecutor of Christians to preacher of Christ (cf. below, p. 388). In this address in Ephesus he recounts that he came to the community in Damascus (Judas, the brother of the Lord, plays a part here), that he was there instructed in the Christian faith and was then himself found worthy to preach the Gospel. The technique of the author of the Acts makes it seem possible that this short and indirect account relates to a preceding longer narrative (cf. for example the Eubula story in the APt; see above, p. 272). We may thus assume that in the context of Paul's sojourn in Damascus a sermon actually was recorded. Paul further relates in Ephesus that he departed from Damascus—the reasons are not stated, but his departure took place by night, cf. Acts 9:25—and marched in the direction of Jericho. He thus set

---

[1] Fasting is manifestly of special importance to the author: at any rate it continually recurs in the AP.

[2] The statement in the Acts of Titus c. 3 (Halkin, p. 245) that Paul "first proclaimed the Word of Christ in Damascus" need not go back to the AP, even if the following sentence derives therefrom. On the Acts of Titus cf. below, p. 329.

himself, in conformity with the Lord's injunction (cf. Ry), on the way to Jerusalem. On this road, according to the Apostle's later speech, took place the baptism of the lion (see below, p. 389), which presumably will have been narrated in detail at this point.

For Jerusalem we have no further reports. C. Schmidt however regarded two leaves of PHeid as parts of this episode. These are the pages 60/59 and 61/62, which however are so badly damaged that we can voice little more than a conjecture about their position in the AP as a whole. If on p. 61 it is said: "Thou findest thyself in sight of Jerusalem", that is no sure indication that the scene took place in Jerusalem. The mention of Peter on p. 59 is also not of much consequence, especially since we do not know who is really speaking at p. 59 lines 8ff. Hence we cannot by any means form so confident a judgment of these pages as Schmidt did (*ПП*, p. 118). Despite this it remains probable that a certain space in the AP was devoted to Paul's stay in Jerusalem.

2. Paul in Antioch.—In PHeid pp. 1–6 are preserved the remains of the description of Paul's activity in Antioch. These pages also however have so many gaps that we can only approximately reconstruct the course of the action. In particular it is not clear how Paul's passage from Jerusalem to Antioch was described in the AP, nor can we determine from the extant fragments whether the author of the AP adhered to the route of the canonical Acts.[1] Again it is not clear which Antioch is meant in PHeid pp. 1–6, the Syrian or the Pisidian. Since reference is made on p. 6 to Paul's flight from Antioch to Iconium, it has been assumed that it is the Pisidian Antioch that is in view (cf. the particulars in Schmidt, *ПП*, pp. 115ff.). On the other hand it is reported in AThe c. 26 that Paul came to Antioch with Thecla, and Thecla was there embraced by a man Alexander on the open street (see below, p. 360). Now this Alexander is characterized in the greater part of the Greek manuscripts as a Syrian, while one manuscript, which Tischendorf and Lipsius followed, describes him as συριάρχης. Even if this reading were correct,[2] which however can scarcely be the case, we cannot assume that here the Syrian Antioch was meant, but must rather assume the Pisidian.

C. Schmidt has repeatedly emphasized that "the AP, so far as the extant remains allow us to judge, never make Paul appear twice at one and the same place" (*ПП*, p. 118). Against this we must take into consideration the fact that our material is too

---

[1] Acts 9:30, Jerusalem-Tarsus; 11:25f. Tarsus-Syrian Antioch; 11:27ff.: Paul's journey with Barnabas to Jerusalem; 12:24f. return; 13: Antioch-Seleucia-Cyprus-Perga-Pisidian Antioch-Iconium.

[2] Cf. the variants in this passage in Lipsius, *Aa* 1, p. 253, and in Gebhardt, *Die lateinischen Übersetzungen*, p. XCVIII.

fragmentary to enable us to establish so far-reaching a contention; in any case it cannot for the present be proved.[1] In addition there are two other points of view to be considered here:

(a) In the Greek Acts of Titus[2] the AP have undoubtedly been used. Now it is said there in c. 4 (Halkin, p. 246): "When they reached Antioch, they found Barnabas, the son of Panchares, whom Paul had raised up. . . . Thereafter they journeyed to Seleucia and Cyprus, Salamis and Paphos, and from there to Perga in Pamphylia and *again* to Antioch in Pisidia and to Iconium, to the house of Onesiphorus, to whom Titus had previously related the matter concerning Paul". Part of this account probably goes back to the canonical Acts, but the name Panchares, the father of Barnabas, takes us beyond Acts. This name and the raising from the dead referred to appear in PHeid pp. 1–6, although admittedly the son is not there called by the name of Barnabas.[3] It is thus fairly clear that the author of the Acts of Titus borrowed from the AP .The Onesiphorus in Iconium and the role of Titus also derive from the AP (cf. AThe c. 2).[4] Now it is said in the Acts of Titus that Paul journeyed again (πάλιν) to Antioch in Pisidia. This can only be understood thus: that the author of the Acts of Titus assumed that the raising of Barnabas took place in Pisidian Antioch, and that Paul after his activity in Cyprus returned thither by way of Perga, and thence came to Iconium. It remains however obscure whether in this interpretation of the Antioch in the Panchares episode as the Pisidian the author of the Acts of Titus could really appeal to the AP, or whether he hit upon exactly the same conclusion as modern scholars.

(b) It must further be observed that we are probably ascribing rather too high an intellectual level to the author of the AP when we expect him to have elaborated all the details of his work consistently and harmonized them one with another, and at the same time also to have sought after the closest possible correspondence with the canonical Acts. Rather is the author of this apocryphal work to a great extent a compiler. He gave a fixed written form to legends which were current and inserted them into a larger composition; many a section he probably invented himself. In the process obscurities, gaps and contradictions have

[1] Michaelis likewise doubts Schmidt's thesis, but on grounds which are not convincing; cf. below, p. 345.
[2] Ed. M. R. James, *JTS* VI, 1905, pp. 549–556; cf. Schmidt, *ΠΠ*, pp. 113ff. James' edition is superseded by F. Halkin, La légende crétoise de saint Tite, *Anal. Boll.* 79, 1961, pp. 241–256; I quote here according to Halkin.
[3] The name Panchares is rendered in the Coptic as Anchares, i.e. the Coptic translator regarded the P at the beginning as the article; cf. Schmidt, *ΠΠ*, p. 115.
[4] τὰ κατὰ τὸν Παῦλον in the Acts of Titus is probably a condensation of ποταπός ἐστιν τῇ εἰδέᾳ ὁ Παῦλος in AThe.

remained. Further it must be emphasized that the dominating factor in the production of the AP was neither a geographical nor a historical interest. The author's purpose is the edification and upbuilding of the community, perhaps also the propagation of a particular "image" of Paul. We may therefore conjecture that he did not set particular store upon the distinction of the two Antiochs. Naturally he has a definite itinerary for the Apostle in view, and sought to present it. So too the model of the canonical Acts may in a certain fashion have influenced him and his work. But how strong this influence was, and whether it determined the itinerary, we do not know. The material is too fragmentary for us to decide with certainty whether Paul in fact appears only once in each place (this is uncertain for Corinth, see below, pp. 343f.). Thus the question which Antioch is here meant does not admit of a definite answer. The Acts of Titus speak for the Pisidian Antioch as the scene for all the events.[1] Against this is the fact that in PHeid only 8 pages of text could have preceded, if Schmidt's reconstruction is correct. On these 8 pages, then, room must have been found for the events in Damascus, Jerusalem and Antioch in Syria, which is scarcely possible. However that may be: even if the Panchares episode took place in Pisidian Antioch, this does not mean that in the AP there was no reference to Syrian Antioch at all. In particular, we cannot affirm with any certainty that PHeid contained the complete text of the AP. There is indeed much in favour of this view, but we cannot prove it.[2] It is quite possible that the lacuna before the Panchares episode (in Pisidian Antioch?) was greater than has been assumed on the basis of the Coptic manuscript. But this also remains conjecture.

From the fragmentary pages of PHeid 1–6 we can deduce at least in outline what Paul did in Antioch (see below, pp. 352f.).

3. Acts of Paul and Thecla (Iconium, Antioch, Myra, Iconium, Seleucia).—The next episode is particularly well known through the fact that it was transmitted as an independent piece (see above, p. 326). In PHeid it is directly attached to the events in Antioch, and is thus guaranteed by this manuscript as part of the AP. Paul's stay in Myra and Thecla's meeting with him there (AThe c. 40) also link the AThe with the AP.

Since the content of this piece is guaranteed by a wide textual tradition, the reconstruction offers no problem. The composition of the narrative is also clear: Paul comes to Iconium, preaches

[1] Kasser, op. cit., pp. 48f., assumes that first of all the Pisidian Antioch is in view and then the Syrian.
[2] It may be recalled that between PH p. 5 and p. 6 a whole episode has evidently been omitted, cf. below, p. 340. PH however bears in the colophon the designation Πράξεις Παύλου, and thus is probably not intended to be an extract.

there (the sermon is summarized, cc. 5f., in the form of blessings), and through this sermon converts Thecla. The consequences correspond to the pattern which occurs also in other apocryphal Acts: the husband (here it is the fiancé), who through the woman's continence has been deprived of her, stirs up the people or the authorities against the Apostle. Here Paul is now imprisoned. Thecla visits him by night, but this is discovered and in consequence, after Paul has been expelled from the town, she is condemned to death at the stake. Rain and hail however prevent the execution and Thecla, now set free again, is able to follow Paul, who is staying meanwhile with Onesiphorus and his family in a burial vault on the road to Daphne. Despite serious scruples Paul takes Thecla with him to Antioch (which?), where at once a fresh misfortune comes upon her. A Syrian Alexander (cf. above, p. 328) falls in love with Thecla, but naturally is rebuffed and takes his revenge by having her condemned by the governor to the arena. A woman named Tryphaena, who is later described as a queen and a kinswoman of the emperor, takes her under her protection. This Tryphaena has lost her daughter Falconilla, and begs Thecla to intercede for the deceased. We now come to the fight with the beasts, in the course of which Thecla baptizes herself. As many beasts are set loose against her, she throws herself into a large pit full of water. The seals in it are killed as by a flash of lightning. Since the other animals also do nothing to Thecla, but Tryphaena falls in a swoon and it is feared that she is dead, Thecla is set free. It is characteristic for the entire AP that the detailed description of the fight with the beasts, which owing to the help of a lioness and some marvellous events does not lead to Thecla's death, concludes with the conversion of Tryphaena and part of her household: "Now I believe that the dead are raised up! Now I believe that my child lives!" (c. 39). The miracles here as always are the proof of the truth of the Christian proclamation.

After Thecla has rested eight days in the house of Tryphaena and has there proclaimed the Word of God, she yearns after Paul. She learns that he is in Myra, and goes after him. After a short time together she goes back to Iconium with the commission to teach the Word of God, finds her fiancé no longer alive, attempts to convert her mother (nothing is reported of any outcome), and then proceeds to Seleucia. There she enlightens many through the Word of God and dies a peaceful death.[1]

This brief account of the contents shows that we have to do

---

[1] In later legends this conclusion is greatly altered or extended; cf. for example Lipsius, *Aa* 1, pp. 271f.; further information in *Bibliotheca hagiographica graeca*[3] II, pp. 267f.

with a homogeneous composition. Some questions remain, which are important from the point of view of the general composition of the AP. In the whole section it is not so much Paul as Thecla who stands in the foreground. Certainly there are also reports about Paul: his sermon in Iconium, his defence before the governor, his meetings with Thecla outside Iconium and in Myra. But this in no way alters the fact that here it is more a question of "Acts of Thecla" than of "Acts of Paul". Thus it is striking that Paul, who is the really guilty party, is according to c. 21 expelled from Iconium, but Thecla must suffer death by fire. The Apostle is indeed asked by Alexander in c. 26 to help him to win Thecla, but disappears from the ensuing narrative. When Thecla has successfully endured the combat with the beasts, she has to seek after Paul; he thus appears to have set out from Antioch for Myra without leaving any message. All this points to the view that the author of the AP has here absorbed independent Thecla-traditions into his book and worked them up.[1] It will be difficult to disentangle these traditions, which are probably connected with the worship of Thecla in Seleucia (or Iconium), since the linguistic form of the text today before us is the work of the author of the AP.[2] This means that the author has given a stamp of his own to the traditional material which came down to him. Whether the striking double narration of Thecla's deliverance in Iconium and Antioch belonged thereto, or whether here two different and in some respects competing traditions have been used, can scarcely be determined. Nevertheless we may here apply the general observation that the authors of the apocryphal Acts are fond of repetitions of motifs and scenes which to them were especially valuable—in this again a true reflection of popular tradition. This also, in my opinion, clears up a further question, which was keenly debated in earlier times, namely the problem of the historical reminiscences in the Thecla legend. W. M. Ramsay in particular (*The Church in the Roman Empire*, 1893, pp. 375ff.) wished to distinguish a primitive form of the AP (composed *c.* 50–70, thus shortly after the activity of Paul) which contained a historically reliable kernel. In this the author's knowledge of the roads and 'Queen' Tryphaena played an essential part. The theory of a primitive form of the AP is today probably no longer upheld by anyone (cf. already Harnack, *Lit.-gesch.* II. 1, pp. 503ff. and Rolffs, *Apokr.* 2, p. 194). Again, the homily of Ps.-Chrysostom cited by Rolffs (German trans. in *Handb.* pp. 376f.) hardly tells in favour of the view that here we

[1] Kasser, *op. cit.*, p. 57, raises for discussion the question whether such sections as the AThe were not originally published independently, and only later joined together with other pieces to make the AP. This however is improbable; cf. below pp. 348f.

[2] Cf. Schubart's demonstration, *ПII*, pp. 120ff.

have an older tradition than the legend fixed in writing in the AThe.[1] The author's local knowledge and knowledge of the roads are moreover—despite Ramsay—not beyond all doubt; and besides they are of no consequence, since such knowledge could easily be gained even later. And 'Queen' Tryphaena, who actually did exist (cf. Rolffs, *Handb.* pp. 377f., where there is also a family tree), likewise proves nothing. She may early have been brought into contact in local legend with Thecla 'the protomartyr like unto the Apostles'. That finally the personal description of Paul in c. 3 cannot raise any claim to historical reliability need scarcely be said. "It is rather a question of the typical portrait of a Jew, admittedly adapted to the eminence of the Apostle" (Michaelis, p. 313).

So even today we may broadly assent to Harnack's judgment: "The hypothesis is completely adequate that the author did not freely invent everything, but rather relies upon an oral tradition which dragged on throughout a century and also preserved a few small characteristic touches. How far the actual events extend, how far the legendary traditions which the author lit upon, how far finally his own additions—to determine this all means are lacking" (*Lit.-gesch.* II. 1, p. 505). Perhaps we ought to be even more sceptical in regard to the actual events. That the formation of the legend was influenced in a quite decisive manner by the local cult of the saintly Thecla, which spread very quickly from Seleucia to both East and West, seems to me well established.[2]

4. Paul in Myra.—Already in c. 40 of the AThe it was reported that Paul was in Myra (on the south coast of Lycia). Now on p. 28 of PHeid a new section is attached directly to the conclusion of the AThe. Its superscription was reconstructed by Schmidt (AP, p. 52): "⟨When he was departed from⟩ Antioch ⟨and taught in My⟩ra". This supplement to the seven extant letters may be correct. At any rate the following scene takes place in Myra. Unfortunately the Coptic papyrus has many lacunae, and in particular at least one leaf of the text is missing (cf. Schmidt, AP, p. 9). In spite of this the train of thought can be clearly recognized. During his activity in Myra Paul heals a man suffering from dropsy, named Hermocrates. This man's son Hermippus is but little pleased by the healing, since he had already been counting on the inheritance, while another son, Dion, "heard

[1] Kasser, *op. cit.*, p. 49 n. 44, conjectures that the conclusion of the narrative in Ps.-Chrysostom reflects the original version of the legend. But this naturally can scarcely be proved.

[2] The cult of Thecla cannot be dealt with here. Cf. already the Peregrinatio Aetheriae 22f. (*CSEL* 39, p. 69f.); *Bibl. hagiogr. graec.*[3] II, pp. 267–269 (lists all the relevant texts). Further literature: Leclerq, *Dict. d'Archéol. et Lit. chrét.* XV. 2, cols. 2225ff.; Rolffs, *Handb.* pp. 370ff.; C. Holzhey, *Lexicon für Theol. und Kirche* X, 1938, 28–30 (literature).

Paul gladly". Unfortunately the following text is not very clear. Dion appears to lose his life through a fall. His father mourns indeed at first, but during Paul's sermon forgets his sorrow, while his mother comes to Paul with her clothes rent, i.e. as one in mourning, and Paul sends young men to bring the dead Dion— probably with the intention of raising him again to life. Unfortunately the text here breaks off; a leaf is missing, on which probably reference was made to the resurrection of Dion. Further there will have been an account of Hermippus' preparations for revenge on Paul. P. 31 at any rate begins with a dream of Paul's, in which he is warned against a great danger. Hermippus comes against Paul with a crowd with a sword and staves, and Paul meets this attack as Christ did in the Garden of Gethsemane. As Hermippus sets upon Paul, he becomes blind and now not only repents of his hostility against Paul but also recognizes the vanity of this world's goods. Paul is shaken at the hearing of his prayer and the humbling of the proud Hermippus, but seems to have no intention of helping the blind man. If there is no leaf missing between pages 32 and 33, we must take the sequel to be that Paul goes into the house of Hermocrates, but the young men lay Hermippus down before the door. This however is not a very meaningful sequence of events, since after the preceding text the action of the young men is superfluous. It seems more natural to assume a lengthy lacuna, probably a whole leaf. On the following leaf we are told how Hermippus lies before the door, and how his parents on the other hand first distribute money and grain, but are then troubled over their blinded son. They pray with Paul, and Hermippus recovers his sight. He relates that Paul laid his hand upon him, which however according to the narrative cannot have been possible; the Lord himself healed him, in the form of Paul. The end of the story cannot be reconstructed, since not only are there lacunae on the extant pages but also there is probably a leaf missing between pages 34 and 35.

We can thus trace at least in outline a large part of this section of Paul's journey. Whether the author of the AP contented himself with a resurrection from the dead and the healing of a blind man, or whether a lengthy sermon by Paul also stood here, we cannot say. The material before us is sufficient only to enable us to recognize various motifs and scenes which are typical for the AP and the other apocryphal Acts. Here it must be said that this section has no detailed reference to the continence which elsewhere is so strongly emphasized; at most one might mention in this connection Hermippus' renunciation of the goods of this world, or the distribution of money and grain to the widows by his parents. But the sexual continence which in other parts of the

AP plays so prominent a role is lacking in the extant fragments
of this episode. It might in some way have been of importance
in the lost sections. We may however also assume that the author
wished in this case to display by means of an example the other
side of Paul's preaching, the resurrection. But even this is by no
means clearly said. However that may be, these considerations
lead to the conclusion that here also the author has worked into
his composition a tradition which had come down to him.

Here comparison with the canonical Acts is interesting. According to Acts 27:5f., Paul on his journey to Rome only changed
ships in Myra. In the AP he works there as a missionary, as always
not by word only but also through his acts. We may conjecture
that some local legends provided the author with the inspiration
and the pattern for this section.

5. Paul in Sidon.—Paul's activity in Myra is followed in
PHeid pp. 35–39, according to Schmidt's reconstruction, by the
unfortunately very fragmentary account of his stay in Sidon. This
reconstruction, to be sure, is only partially certain. In the first
place, it is probably correct that Sidon follows Myra, even if the
lemma on p. 35 is not preserved in full: "When he was departed
from Myra and ⟨wished to go to Sidon⟩". What now follows
however has to a great extent been very uncertainly restored or
interpreted by Schmidt (cf. his account of the contents, AP
pp. 95ff.). On pp. 35/36 we have first of all a report of Paul's
journey to Sidon. Paul is accompanied by a number of brethren
from Perga. On the way he appears to have entered into a discussion at a pagan altar with an old man, who quotes examples
of the punishment meted out by the gods to those who forsake
them. Here already, however, much remains obscure. There
follows a gap of at least 2 leaves. This figure was suggested by
Schmidt "since on p. 37 we are in the middle of the narrative of
the events in Sidon". On this line of argument it might naturally
have been 4 leaves. What was contained in these leaves we do
not know. On p. 37 we have first the end of an address by Paul
(we may probably assume that it is he who is speaking), in which
he seeks to restrain his hearers from some course of action by
referring to Sodom and Gomorrah. The consequence is however
that Paul, with the brethren Thrasymachus and Cleon (cf. p.
38. 5), is cast into the temple of Apollo where, surprisingly, the
people seek to fatten them up with good food (in preparation for
sacrifice?). Paul fasts and prays, and at his prayer the half of the
temple collapses (probably the part in which the prisoners were
not shut up). This occasions considerable alarm, and on the
insistence of the people Paul and his companions are brought
into the theatre. Here the text breaks off again. Whether here

SECOND AND THIRD CENTURY ACTS

again 2 leaves only are missing or more, we cannot say. On p. 39 we find the conclusion of the Sidon episode, of which unfortunately only a little is coherently preserved. We can recognize that Paul delivered an address, which possibly won the people over. A certain Theudas appears to have begged for baptism. The page ends with the departure from Sidon for Tyre.

It is thus scarcely possible to give an accurate account of the contents of this section. Many lacunae, obscurities and uncertainties remain. The brief notice in the Acts of Titus c. 3 does not help us very far. After briefly reporting that Paul first preached the word of Christ in Damascus (this may derive from Acts 9:22), the author continues: "And Apphia, the wife of Chrysippus, who was possessed by a demon, was healed by Paul; and after he had fasted seven days he overcame the idol of Apollo". Now the names Amphion and Chrysippus appear in PHeid p. 40 (Tyre, see below, p. 369). From this Schmidt (*ΠΠ* p. 114) concluded that the author of the Acts of Titus has condensed the episode at Tyre, the name Amphion in the Coptic being only a corruption of Apphia.[1] The note about the overcoming of the idol of Apollo in the Acts of Titus would then go back to the Sidon section of the AP. Against this it can hardly be objected that in the Acts of Titus the sequence Sidon-Tyre in the AP is reversed; in so summary a report this can readily be understood. It is more difficult to reconcile the overcoming of the idol with the collapse of the temple (according to Schmidt's reconstruction, p. 98). Even this however would be possible, only it would then have to be assumed that reference was made to it also in the narrative, and not only to the collapse of the temple. In favour of this view is the fact that p. 38. 19f. says: "The god of the Sidonians, Apollo, is fallen, and the half of his temple". All this shows however that here we can work only with cautious conjectures.

It may be further noted that the evidently quite detailed portrayal of Paul's experiences in Sidon does not tally very well with the brief mention of this town in Acts 27:3. According to Acts, Paul is brought from Caesarea to Sidon, and there by permission of the 'philanthropic' centurion Julius he is allowed to visit 'his friends', i.e. the Christian community in Sidon, which was either known to Luke or imagined by him. That the narrative of the AP cannot have originated out of this note needs no further proof. Again, the route of the journey does not agree with Acts. Whether this part of the AP goes back to a local legend of the Church in Sidon cannot be said, owing to the fragmentary state of the tradition.

[1] Kasser, *op. cit.*, p. 54 n. 87, asks whether Apphia may not be connected with Ammia in PG; but this to me is improbable.

ACTS OF PAUL

6. Paul in Tyre.—Still more difficult is the reconstruction of the part of the AP in which Paul's sojourn in Tyre is depicted. The lemma on p. 39 of PHeid is well preserved: "When he was departed from Sidon and wished to go to Tyre". This makes it certain that, contrary to the account in Acts, Paul travelled from Sidon to Tyre. There, according to PHeid p. 40, he had to deal with Jews. The Apphia and Chrysippus known from the Acts of Titus (cf. above, p. 336) make their appearance, and ultimately Paul appears to be active as an exorciser of demons. Schmidt by way of experiment attached some fragments from PHeid here, but it remains questionable whether these (pp. 64, 63, 70, 69, 68, 67, 66, 65) have anything to do with the episode at Tyre, or whether they belong to some other point on the route. It may be correct that a part of these fragments derives from a speech by Paul or from a disputation, but more we cannot say.[1] On pp. 60/59 and 61/62, which Schmidt originally wanted to accom-modate here as well, cf. above, p. 328.

We must thus content ourselves with the observation that only PHeid p. 40 belongs to the episode at Tyre, and that here the thread of the narrative breaks off. This is all the more regrettable in that the gap which here opens is very large, and cannot be removed by any kind of conjecture as to what may have stood in the lacuna. For this reason we must also reject Schmidt's state-ment (ΠΠ, p. 119) that Jerusalem could not appear here, since the author of the AP presumably reported on Paul's stay there at the beginning of his work (after Damascus). This statement, which rests upon the hypothesis that Paul according to the AP never makes his appearance in the same place twice, is incapable of proof and indeed, if what was said above (pp. 328ff.) about Antioch is correct, is false. So whether Paul went from Tyre to Caesarea[2] or Jerusalem or Crete or Cyprus (Schmidt ΠΠ, p. 119) remains unknown, pending the discovery of new material. That Ephesus was not the only scene of operations in Asia Minor Schmidt (loc. cit.) had already conjectured. But here, as we now see, it is a question not of Miletus but of Smyrna. This is shown by the beginning of the as yet unpublished PG (cf. Kasser, RHPR

---

[1] The fragment p. 68c (Schmidt AP p. 65) is interesting: "that man is ⟨not justified through the law⟩, but that he is justified ⟨through the⟩ works of righteousness". This shows clearly how far removed the author is from the historical Paul.

[2] On Caesarea cf. Kasser, op. cit., p. 50 n. 46 and p. 51 n. 61. For this question the "Letter of Pelagia", preserved in Ethiopic, has a certain significance, but into this I cannot enter here. It need only be remarked that this apocryphon, which unfortunately can neither be dated nor localized, made use of the AP. When the meeting between Paul and the lion is there transferred to the region of Caesarea, this probably goes back to the compiler; conclusions as to the composition of the AP cannot be drawn from this. Cf. E. J. Goodspeed, American Journal of Semitic Languages and Litera-tures XX, 1904, p. 95ff.; English translation also in Schmidt AP, 2nd ed., pp. XXI–XXV; G. Krüger, ZNW 1904, pp. 261ff.; Schmidt ΠΠ, pp. 87ff.

337

40, 1960, pp. 45–57, and below, p. 387). But what Paul did in Smyrna, and what stopping-places lay before it, remains uncertain.
7. Paul in Ephesus.—For Paul's stay in Ephesus we have, in addition to the unpublished PG (see below, pp. 387ff.), the Hamburg Papyrus, which presents this episode on pp. 1–5. This makes it possible to survey the structure of the whole section. Paul comes from Smyrna to Ephesus and there puts up at the house of Aquila and Priscilla. After a vision with the intimation of sorrows to come, Paul delivers a sermon, in the course of which he gives an account of his conversion and of the baptism of the lion. This sermon has the usual result: Paul is brought before the proconsul Hieronymus (PH p. 1. 30), and is required to give an account of himself (here PH p. 1 begins). The speech in which he does so is shot through with apologetic motifs. This is all the more striking in that previously there has not been—as Schmidt still conjectured (ΠΠ, p. 87)—any detailed account of an attack by Paul on the statuettes of Artemis. Only in a single sentence is the criticism of idol-worship suggested. We may ask whether the author of the AP did not wish so far as possible to avoid a doublet to Acts 19:23ff. But allusions have not entirely been renounced: in PH 1. 28 the χρυσοχόοι, the goldsmiths, appear as the agitators who wish to see Paul condemned. The pro-consul finds nothing at all wrong in Paul's speech, but bows before the determination of the people, who demand that Paul be thrown to the beasts. After six days there follows the procession of the animals, among whom a lion especially attracts attention. His roaring startles even Paul, who in his prison is deep in prayer. Here is inserted a story about the conversion and baptism of Artemilla, the wife of Hieronymus. Artemilla is informed of Paul's preaching and activity through Eubula, the wife of Diophantes, a freedman of the proconsul, and wishes to make the Apostle's acquaintance herself. A short address by Paul, in which he urges flight from and contempt for the world, brings about her desire for baptism, which takes place amid all kinds of wonderful phenomena and with the assistance of Christ himself. After the celebration of the eucharist with bread and water, Artemilla goes back to her house and Paul in prison returns to his prayers.[1] In the whole story Eubula plays no further part. It is a conversion-story, in which a prominent lady comes to the Christian faith. Difficulties are created only by the lines on PH p. 3. 1–4, according to which Diophantes informs the proconsul that the women are sitting day and night with Paul. Hieronymus thereupon interrupts his meal in order to hasten on the fight with the beasts. These lines

---

[1] PH p. 4. 2ff. remains obscure: Artemilla goes into the house (which? Her house or the prison?). But the eucharist probably takes place in the prison.

not only break the connection, but do not at all fit what has gone before. The whole story is played out in one night (Saturday to Sunday), while in these lines it is said of the two women that they stayed a longer time with Paul. It is thus possible to take these lines as a secondary insertion, but a better assumption is that the contradiction has arisen from the fact that the author has here worked together two different traditions, but has not quite succeeded. On the one hand he had before him, perhaps in the setting of the Ephesus episode, a story about the occasion for the persecution of the Apostle, i.e. about the jealousy of Diophantes (a favourite motif in all apocryphal Acts), on the other he may have lit upon a conversion story linked with the name of Artemilla. At all events I see here again an indication of the author's methods of working, making use in his composition of older traditions. This is to a certain extent confirmed by some observations on the following text. Next morning we come to the fight with the beasts, and here Paul meets the lion he had baptized. Since the lion does nothing to harm the Apostle, other animals are released. But a violent hailstorm brings to nothing all efforts to make away with Paul. Paul takes leave of the lion, who goes back to the mountains while the Apostle mingles with those who are fleeing in terror of the fall of the city, and embarks on a ship for Macedonia. Now in this story notes about Hieronymus and Diophantes, or about Artemilla and Eubula, are interspersed (PH p. 4, 8–11; 4, 14–18), and after Paul's departure we are told how Artemilla and Eubula were in sorrow and mourning for him, but were comforted by an angel (PH p. 5. 19ff.). Unfortunately the end of PH p. 5 has come down to us in very bad condition. But it seems to describe how Hieronymus called upon the God of Paul for help for his ear, injured in the hailstorm, and how the ear was then healed. Schmidt has described these last notices as a brief "Epilogue, concerned with the other leading figures in the Ephesus story" (ΠΠ, p. 94). This is certainly correct if we look at the composition as a whole. The question however remains, whether the author has not here also laid hold of a tradition which he himself was the first to bring into connection with the fight with the beasts in Ephesus. At any rate this conjecture has much in its favour.

The structure of this section is thus clear, but the problem of the use of tradition in its composition is also evident. The inspiration for the formation of this story of Paul's fight with the beasts may be sought in various NT passages: 1 Cor. 15:32; 2 Tim. 4:17, and above all Acts 19:23ff., but in these passages we can see no more than the initial impulse for this episode. The decisive motives were certainly different.

339

It may also be observed that this particular story evidently made a special impression. The baptized lion enjoyed a singular popularity, but also gave particular offence.[1]

8. Paul in Philippi.—From Ephesus Paul set out by ship for Macedonia, i.e. probably for Philippi (PH p. 5. 15ff.), but curiously we are not told anything about this period in PH. On the contrary the next episode is directly attached on p. 6 of PH, i.e. on the back of p. 5: "From Philippi to Corinth". A whole episode has thus been omitted in the manuscript. This situation can be explained in different ways. Either the writer of PH (or his *Vorlage*) wished only to produce an extract from the AP, in which case according to circumstances purely external reasons (e.g. the size of the book) might have been decisive. Or the passage omitted had already, before the compiling of the manuscript (or its *Vorlage*), been detached from the AP to circulate independently, and was therefore not copied by the scribe. Or offence was taken at particular views or expressions in the passage. In favour of the last possibility is the fact that according to PHeid Paul's apocryphal correspondence with the Corinthians (3 Cor.) stood in this section. At the beginning of the episode in PHeid (p. 44) the vital name is not indeed preserved; but from 3 Cor. 2:1 it is clear beyond mistake that the letter from Corinth was brought to Paul in Philippi.

Unfortunately it is not clear what has previously taken place in Philippi. The beginning of PHeid p. 45 is so fragmentary as to prohibit any conclusion. We learn from the introductory narrative only that in Corinth people were very anxious about Paul, even though his deliverance had been announced through a special revelation, and that on the other hand there was an urgent need for the Apostle's presence to head the resistance to Gnostic teachers. Accordingly a letter was written to Paul and brought by Threptus and Eutychus to Philippi, where Paul was a prisoner "because of Stratonice, the wife of Apollophanes" (3 Cor. 2:2). Evidently events thus took the same course at Philippi as at many other places: the preaching of continence met with success among the women, but aroused the men against the Apostle. According to PH p. 6. 5, Paul relates in Corinth what befell him in the ἐργαστρον in Philippi; he was thus probably condemned to penal servitude. Paul now answers the Corinthians and attempts to refute the heresy, largely, it must be said, in summary and apodeictic fashion and only in his argument on the question of the resurrection in a rather more judicious and lively way.

[1] Hippol. Dan. III. 29 (Bonwetsch, pp. 176f.); Commodian, Carmen apol. 627f.; Jerome, vir. ill. 7; Acta Titi c. 6; Letter of Pelagia; Nicephorus Callistus, *HE* II. 25 (PG 145, 822). Cf. also the collection in Schmidt, *ΠΠ*, pp. 85ff.—Bruce M. Metzger, St. Paul and the baptized lion, *Princeton Seminary Bulletin* XXXIX, 1945, pp. 11–21.

With the end of 3 Cor. the tradition regrettably once more breaks off, so that we hear nothing of the delivery of the letter and its outcome. The conclusion of the Philippi episode is however extant: PHeid pp. 41/42 and 44. Admittedly these pages also are not preserved complete, but the course of events appears to be as follows. Paul is working in the mines (?), but has apparently still found time to preach. At any rate reference is made to one Frontina who with Paul is to be put to death by her father Longinus, presumably because she has allowed herself to be converted by Paul's preaching. We then come to the execution, which Paul somehow or other escapes, while Frontina dies. In response to Paul's prayer (and that of her mother Firmilla?) Frontina is restored to life again, which occasions great alarm among the inhabitants. Paul leads Frontina to her father's house amid the acclamation of the crowd. In Longinus' house a celebration of the eucharist seems then to have taken place, and thereafter Paul departs for Corinth.

We can thus reconstruct this section to some extent, in analogy with the other episodes of the AP, but must in so doing emphasize that the details remain to a great degree unknown. The Philippi section however now presents, through 3 Cor., a difficulty of its own. As has already been shown (see above, pp. 326f.), this apocryphon was also transmitted as an independent piece, and indeed it belonged for a time to the Canon of the (Syrian and) Armenian Church. Of the witnesses which have handed down these letters by themselves, only a part contain the intervening material; the introduction is preserved only in PHeid. From this and other indications Testuz has drawn the conclusion that 3 Cor. came into being independently, and indeed before the AP (Testuz *op. cit.*, pp. 23–25). The author of the AP then united 3 Cor. with his own work by a few sentences. Despite this incorporation in the AP, 3 Cor. was still separately transmitted, as—according to Testuz—PBodm and the manuscripts M, L, P and B as well as its acceptance in the Syrian and Armenian Canon all show. The manuscript Z on the other hand is a fragment of the AP. Now we cannot deal in detail here with the problem of 3 Cor.[1] Yet the fact that in PBodm 3 Cor. appears after the Protevangelium Jacobi probably should not be taken as proof that it

---

[1] Testuz' theory probably rests to a considerable degree upon an over-estimate of PBodm, which is noticeable also in his assessment of textual questions. Naturally PBodm is a particularly important discovery, the only Greek witness for 3 Cor. and one which through its great age (3rd or 4th centuries) may lodge a claim to serious consideration. But this witness is not infallible, and there are passages in which the Latin MSS. of the 10th to 13th centuries have preserved the correct text against PBodm.—A. F. J. Klijn's article "The Apocryphal Correspondence between Paul and the Corinthians", *Vig. Chr.* XVII, 1963, pp. 2–23, appeared while this was in the press.

originated as an independent narrative and was later embodied in the AP. The Latin tradition in manuscripts of the Bible (apart from Z?) is surely to be explained thus: that this apocryphon was imported from Syria and was at some places accepted as material for public reading.[1] But above all the tradition in PHeid suggests the acceptance of the AP as the original locus of 3 Cor. In favour of this we may note further the agreements in conception and ideas to which Harnack already has referred.[2] To my mind two factors are decisive: (a) the letters are united with the AP by two stout brackets, namely the introduction in the Coptic text, which refers to 3 Cor. 1, and the intervening historical material, which appears also in Z, E and A. This means that the Syrian Church took the section from the AP, and that at the time of the translation into Coptic this correspondence was still a part of the AP. PBodm does not have the intervening material, and therefore surely represents a later stage of the tradition, which is represented also by the other Latin witnesses. (b) The kinship in spirit and in tendency between the letters and other parts of the AP is not to be overlooked; both 3 Cor. and the other sections are pronouncedly anti-Gnostic, a point which comes to expression above all in the realism of the belief in resurrection. These arguments are not deprived of their force by the fact that Testuz notes the absence in 3 Cor. of ascetic tendencies, which are undoubtedly characteristic of the AP. In the first place, they are not entirely lacking (cf. 3 Cor. 3:11ff.), and on the other hand it is not the case that the author of the AP does not have a certain capacity for variation at his disposal (cf. for example the absence of the ascetic tendency in the Myra episode also, above, pp. 334f.).

It must therefore be taken as certain that 3 Cor. was an original constituent of the AP, and indeed of the part which told of Paul's stay in Philippi. What happened in Philippi earlier remains unknown to us. Again, the question whether Paul had already been in Corinth previously cannot be answered from this section of the text. From 3 Cor. 1:4 ("For never have we heard such words, either from thee or from the other Apostles") it must probably be assumed that such a visit by Paul to Corinth has at some point already been reported. But whether, when and where it was referred to in the AP we cannot say. This question is important, because with it is connected the further question, whether the author intended to supplement or to supersede the canonical Acts. We shall have to go into this point when we have dealt with the Corinthian episode.

[1] A part of the Latin manuscripts probably derives from North Italy.
[2] A. Harnack, Untersuchungen über den apokryphen Briefwechsel der Korinther und des Apostels Paulus, Sitzungsber. Pr. Akad. 1905, I, pp. 3–35; cf. also Schubart, ΠΠ, pp. 122f.

9. Paul in Corinth.—According to PHeid p. 44 Paul's stay in Corinth follows immediately on the episode at Philippi. That this is correct is evident from the rubric in PH p. 6: "From Philippi to Corinth". Although imperfect, the text of the section is well enough preserved for the march of events to be clear: Paul comes in Corinth to the house of Epiphanius, preaches there, and then prepares for his departure for Rome. The community is dismayed at the prospect of this journey to Rome, but is comforted by a Spirit-inspired address by one Cleobius. In the course of a celebration of the eucharist something happens, which is interpreted by a certain Myrta.[1] Thereafter the meal proceeds. On the Day of Preparation Paul sets out and indeed—in contrast to the canonical Acts—as a free man.

This section is striking in the first place through its brevity and also through the absence of any miraculous acts by Paul. Although the Apostle stays 40 days with the brethren, we are told only of his sermons which, curious to relate, do not appear to enter at all upon the difficulties with the Gnostic heretics to which reference was made in 3 Cor., but are dedicated above all to Paul's experiences and to the divine benevolence shown in these experiences. "The theme of his preaching is perseverance (ὑπομονή)" (Schmidt, *ΠΠ*, p. 101), but over and above that also the providence of God, who is carrying through His οἰκονομία, i.e. His plan of salvation (PH p. 6. 26 and already PH p. 5. 27).

The reason for the brevity and also for the peculiarity of this section can only be conjectured: the author perhaps takes knowledge both of Acts and of Paul's letters for granted. Now according to Acts 18:11 Paul was eighteen months in Corinth; Acts 20:2 speaks of a further journey to Greece, in which Corinth is probably included; the two Corinthian letters show what a close connection Paul had with this community. All this may have moved the author not to recount too much of this period. Moreover he perhaps did not have for this section any legendary material which he could usefully employ. Since the work originated in Asia Minor the situation in this respect was in any case more difficult for the author where the communities outside his own country were concerned. Finally it must be borne in mind that he manifestly saw in this episode only a transition to the conclusion of his work, the martyrdom in Rome. The whole Corinthian section of the AP already bears the impress of this martyrdom upon it.

Whatever may have been the reason for the peculiarity of the Corinthian episode, one thing seems to me clear: the author does

---

[1] Kasser, *op. cit.*, p. 52 n. 68: "A prophecy is delivered by a branch of myrtle." This however does not seem to be correct.

not make Paul come to Corinth for the first time at this point in his work. Whether in so doing he simply presupposed the NT accounts, however, or whether he himself described a first visit by Paul to Corinth in an earlier section, we cannot say. One is inclined to accept the first explanation. But then we may draw the further conclusion that the author did not adhere to the stages of the canonical Acts, but arranged his material quite independently. From this it follows, in my opinion, that the dominant factor in the composition was not an endeavour to replace the canonical Acts, or to supplement it by the addition of the missing stages. We may speak of a supplementing of Acts at most in this sense, that for the author the figure of the Apostle does not stand out in Acts in the way that he in the situation of his time held to be correct. The author did not however derive from Acts the final incentive for his work; he wanted to edify and entertain, and to fortify the piety of the Church of his time by making Paul its herald. This is why he can proceed so independently and in large measure take no account of Acts.

10. From Corinth to Italy.—The journey from Corinth to Italy is preserved in PH pp. 7–8, to which we may add some fragments in PHeid pp. 72–74. Paul travels to Italy on a ship whose captain Artemon has been baptized by Peter. On the way the Lord appears to him, and his sombre countenance startles Paul. To his question as to the reason, the Lord answers: "I am on the point of being crucified afresh" (ἄνωθεν μέλλω σταυροῦσθαι). Without touching upon Paul's protest, Christ gives to the Apostle the injunction to exhort the brethren, and escorts the ship to Italy. The place of landing is not stated; presumably the author himself did not know, or else he assumed Puteoli as a matter of course (cf. Acts 28:13). On landing Artemon is awaited by a man named Claudius, introduces Paul to him, and the two carry the Apostle's baggage ashore. In Claudius' house Paul teaches "the word of truth". The sermon here presented contains first of all an Old Testament section, in which God's dealing with Israel is depicted as exemplary of God's faithfulness, while in the second part Christ is spoken of. Unfortunately the text in PH breaks off in the middle of the sermon. In PB 23 fragmentary lines follow, but they can scarcely be restored in a meaningful way. On the verso of PM some lines can be read, which probably join on to PB after a short lacuna. As McHardy has recognized (*Exp. Times* 58, 1947, p. 279), these fragmentary lines belong to the text which Schmidt declared to be part of an apocryphal gospel (AP pp. 236ff.) A certain difficulty is presented by the fact that in this text Jesus himself appears as one of the speakers, and that Peter and Philip speak directly to Jesus in conversation. But

these objections against the inclusion of the two pages are not insurmountable, for in PH p. 8. 31ff. already the author allows Jesus to speak directly. This is not surprising if we take note of the narrative technique of the apocryphal Acts. Again, the appearance of Peter and Philip is not a cogent argument against the assumption that these pages belong to Paul's speech in Puteoli. The author might here have taken over narrative portions from another context. This explanation is also suggested by the fact that in this section the author has in any case bedecked his work with borrowed plumage (see below). At any rate the text of PM or PHeid pp. 79/80 makes a good connection with PH p. 8 in point of subject-matter.

If however this is a part of the AP, and indeed of Paul's speech in Puteoli, then we should have to examine afresh the calculation undertaken by Kilpatrick and Roberts (*JTS* 47, 1946, pp. 196–199). The lacuna of 2–2½ pages there established, between the end of PM and the beginning of the Martyrdom, is for the most part already filled by the passage containing the speech, so that there would be no room left for further narrative reports. It is however entirely possible that the author, before passing to the Martyrdom proper, included a comprehensive speech by Paul as the crown and culmination, and at the same time as the transition to the final scene, thus renouncing any thought of including further material. Paul's farewell speech in Miletus in Acts 20:17–38 might have been the inspiration and the pattern for this composition.

Michaelis admittedly (pp. 273ff.) has denied that the presupposition underlying this calculation is correct, i.e. the assumption that between pages 8 and 9 of PH only four pages are missing. His argument however is built upon hypotheses about the course of Paul's life (second imprisonment, authenticity of the Pastorals, etc.) which are false. We must therefore rather incline to follow the exposition given by Schmidt, Kilpatrick and Roberts: Paul's speech leads on to his journey from the port to Rome, and there is no report of any further activity before his entrance into the city.

The short report of Paul's journey to Italy also presents a problem of its own, in that here we find a doublet to the famous Quo Vadis scene in the Acts of Peter (Mart. Petr. c. 6). With this scene we shall not here deal in detail. In regard to the problem of the composition, however, we must note the following points: The description in the AP shows clearly that it is secondary as compared with the APt. Above all, the reference to the crucifixion is in place in the APt, since Peter too was crucified, but not in the AP, since Paul was beheaded. In addition this scene fits in well in the APt, while in the AP it seems to be a foreign body. We ought not, as Michaelis does (pp. 327ff.), to argue against this that the APt has πάλιν while the AP reads ἄνωθεν.¹ At all events the author of the AP has borrowed from the APt. It is therefore not improbable that Schmidt's conjecture is correct, that the captain Artemon is the Theon of the APt (Schmidt, ΠΠ, pp. 128f.).

11. The Martyrdom of Paul.—This part of the AP was probably separated from the work as a whole at an early date, since it was used for reading on the day of commemoration of the Apostle. The tradition and also the further use and elaboration (cf. for example Schmidt, AP pp. 118ff.; ΠΠ, pp. 124f.) show the Martyrdom becoming an independent work. The text early ran wild, and this makes reconstitution difficult. That it originally belonged to the AP is certain from PHeid and PH, although in both witnesses the beginning is unfortunately missing and Paul's progress from Puteoli (?) to Rome has thus not been preserved.

In Rome Paul is awaited by Luke and Titus (in the Acts of Titus c. 6, where again the AP has been used, Timothy also is named). Paul rents a barn and there teaches "the word of truth" with great success. This introduction was probably shaped with Acts 28:30f. in mind. Then follows the story of the death of Patroclus, an imperial cup-bearer, and his revival. Since Patroclus confesses his Christianity before Nero, persecution breaks out. In the course of it Paul too is brought to trial, and as ringleader is condemned to death by the sword while the other Christians are to suffer death by fire. This is not quite logical, since surely death by decapitation was thought of as the less severe penalty. It was however in the tradition before the author that Paul was beheaded. Nero's fury against the Christians is brought to a check by the protests of the people, but the judgment against Paul is allowed to stand. In prison Paul preaches to the Prefect Longus and the centurion Cestus (in particular about the resurrection), and promises them that they will receive baptism at his grave. After a long prayer by Paul his execution follows, and in the course of it milk spurts on to the soldiers' clothes. Soon thereafter Paul appears to Nero, who in consternation sets the prisoners free. The narrative ends with the scene at Paul's grave: Longus and Cestus go there and meet Titus and Luke, who take to flight but are re-assured and then administer baptism to the other two.

By and large, the MP gives the impression of being a uniform work, complete in itself. Some passages admittedly are thoroughly clumsy, and one might conjecture that different traditions which originally had nothing to do with one another have here been

---

¹ On the meaning of the word ἄνωθεν (often the same as πάλιν) cf. for example W. Bauer, *Wörterbuch* s.v. (ET Arndt-Gingrich).

brought together (the story of Patroclus, the conversion of Longus and Cestus, the martyrdom of Paul). But whether this was done by the author of the AP or had already been achieved before him we cannot say. The composition of the whole scene probably derives from the author (cf. Schubart, *ΠΠ*, p. 123), but it must be said that here at the conclusion of his work he has not accomplished any masterly performance. The question how far he was able to rely on local Roman tradition cannot be confidently answered.

Like the author of the APt in his account of Peter's end (cf. above, p. 272), the author of the AP also could in the MP make use of certain models for guidance (Martyrdom of Polycarp, Martyrdom of Peter). Only he did not link the end of his hero so closely with other motifs as is done in the APt. Here also we can see how much the author is indebted to the popular narrative style, in which the stress is laid upon the individual episode.

In summary conclusion reference may be made to five points which result from the detailed discussion of the composition, and from the attempt at a reconstruction:

1. Our knowledge of the composition of the AP as a whole is still, despite all the discoveries, extremely imperfect. We can reconstruct certain sections, and also link together several stages of the journey, but for all that considerable gaps remain.[1] Here it must be observed that the AP was probably abridged already in ancient times (PH!), so that even when the connection is apparently clear we must in certain circumstances assume the existence of considerable lacunae. How much has actually been lost we can hardly say. According to the Stichometry of Nicephorus this work had a compass of 3,600 lines, the canonical Acts on the other hand only 2,800. This means that an appreciable portion is still missing.

2. From the material before us the route of Paul's journey is as follows: Damascus–Jerusalem–Antioch–Iconium–Antioch–Myra–Sidon–Tyre. Here there is a large gap. Then follow Smyrna–Ephesus–Philippi–Corinth–Italy–Rome. Now it is interesting that in this route the author, in contrast to the canonical Acts, was clearly concerned to describe *one* major journey by Paul. At any rate the material so far known does not allow us to discern that Paul had any one fixed base of operations (like Antioch for a time in Acts), to which he again and again returned. Rather does Paul after his conversion journey from place to place; he conducts his mission there according to a fixed pattern,

---

[1] Kasser, *op. cit.*, p. 48 n. 29, rightly warns against the hasty drawing of conclusions as to the position of fragments in the AP as a whole, from the appearance of names or of NT allusions.

is expelled, and travels farther.[1] In this a peculiarity of the apocryphal Acts undoubtedly finds expression: their interest centres in the individual narrative, and these isolated sections are held together by quite definite tendencies.

3. It is very natural to compare the AP with Luke's work, and such comparisons are to be found again and again in the literature. Now it is clear at the first glance that such a comparison produces only meagre results if we enquire about agreement in the itinerary or in other details. The author of the AP adhered to Acts neither in the matter of the route nor in respect of other facts. He collected and arranged his material independently. In so doing he certainly to a great extent followed a current legendary tradition, but he so handled the materials which lay before him that the analysis of tradition and composition is not simple. The author's language is uniform, and to a large extent that of the NT. In particular the Pastorals and Acts have been used, but so also have the Gospels and Paul's letters. Here however it is scarcely a question of exact quotations, but rather of linguistic and conceptual agreement on the basis of a knowledge of the NT literature.[2]

4. The fact that the author uses devotional language of a New Testament stamp indicates that he wanted his work to have an edifying and instructive effect. Certainly he had also theological intentions (see below), but these recede behind his primary aim. It is on this basis that we must answer the question whether the AP are intended to supersede or supplement the canonical Acts. The author scarcely thought of a substitute for Acts. Rather did he wish "out of love for Paul" to edify the Church of his time with his book, and to that extent we may speak of a certain intention to supplement.

5. If however the composition of the AP was so uniform, and if it was the author's intention to give expression to the "image" of Paul current in his time in the form of an edifying description of the Apostle's missionary journey, then it is improbable that the AP was published piecemeal and, so to speak, as a serialized novel. This hypothesis of Kasser's (op. cit., p. 57) may indeed find apparent support in the fact that some parts (AThe, MP and 3 Cor.) circulated independently, but on the other hand these sections are firmly anchored in the structure of the work as a

---

[1] Kasser, op. cit., p. 48 n. 31, has with reason pointed to a certain schematization: journey-preaching-persecution-miracle. But whether we are to link with this the other assumption, that Paul never returned to the same place, remains questionable.

[2] Cf. C. Schlau, Die Akten des Paulus und der Thekla, 1877, pp. 79ff.; Harnack, Lit.-gesch. II. 1, pp. 498f.—Schmidt (AP pp. 199ff.) has dealt in detail with the personages in the AP. His conclusion is that the 65 persons who appear have nothing to do with NT characters.

whole. That the author's creative power decreases towards the
end of his work need not be evidence of a temporal sequence for
the separate parts. Rather does the whole work seem all of a
piece, although the author has certainly built many older traditions into his production, and has not always succeeded in con-
cealing the seams.

5. THEOLOGICAL TENDENCY. The AP is not a theological treatise,
but a religious tract. The author certainly binds up with it certain
definite ecclesiastical and theological purposes, and it is based
upon a certain theological knowledge, but it was intended in the
first instance for the edifying and entertainment of the community
and not for theological discussion. This means that we do the
author an injustice, and put the wrong questions to him, when
we seek to extract a theological system from his work. Thus the
attempt by Loofs in his posthumous work (*Theophilus von Antiochien adversus Marcionem*, 1930) to claim the AP also as a source
for his theory of a Spirit-Christology is extremely questionable.
Much that Loofs adduces from the AP is capable of another
interpretation if we renounce the attempt to systematize the
statements in the book so forcibly as Loofs does, although he
himself observed the presence side by side of disparate elements.
Beside the statement that God is the one and only God (AThe 9)
stands the other, that Christ is Lord and God (AThe 31). But this
is surprising only if we mistake the literary character of the AP.
The categories which Loofs applies in his examination of the
text, quite apart from their questionable nature in other respects,
are inappropriate in the case of a popular religious tract. Again,
Peterson's attempt to determine the place of the AP in the history
of theology seems to me mistaken (Einige Bemerkungen . . . . in
Frühkirche, Judentum und Gnosis, 1959, pp. 183–208). Peterson holds
that the AP, just as the other apocryphal Acts, belongs to the
domain of Encratism which is associated with the name of Tatian.
Here however he has not only committed an error of method—as
Devos has convincingly shown (*Anal. Boll.* 69, 1951, pp. 119–
130)—but has also attributed to the AP a theological significance
that is much too great. Many traits which are interpreted by
Peterson as esoteric "symbolism" admit of a much simpler
explanation, namely as the graphic style of popular narrative
(e.g. Artemilla's change of clothing, PH p. 2. 16; cf. Peterson
op. cit. pp. 183f.). Moreover, that the heretics whom the author
has in view were not Jewish Christians or Encratites seems to me
to be clearly shown by 3 Cor. and other passages.

We must therefore, in conformity with the literary peculiarity
of the AP, renounce any attempt at illegitimate systematization,

and content ourselves with the indication of certain theological tendencies, which often indeed appear to contradict one another (much material is collected in Schmidt, AP pp. 183ff.).

Christian preaching for the author of the AP is preaching of continence and of the resurrection (AThe 5). In practically every episode the motif of sexual continence plays a dominant role. This demand, and the Apostle's success in preaching it, are often the occasion for persecution. The basis of this attitude is the conviction that the goods of this world are worthless and unprofitable, that salvation lies in the world to come, and that all depends on the securing of this other-worldly salvation (which in part appears to be envisaged as the survival of the immortal soul). From the blessings in AThe 5f. it is clear how the hope of glory with God is combined with the injunction to sexual purity. The resurrection is held out as the goal and the reward for those who keep themselves pure and set their hope on God and on Christ.

Here naturally we can show by a comparison with the authentic Paul how far this Christianity of the closing second century has departed from the Apostle. This however would not be a legitimate procedure, since it would presuppose that the communities from which the AP derives originally thought in purely Pauline fashion, which perhaps was not the case. It is much more important that we can see how the author makes the Apostle the herald of a very simple faith, which can be reduced to a few formulae and presents very clear positions against Gnostic speculation, rejection of the OT, denial of the resurrection and relaxation of ethical standards. How in the process Docetism is clearly rejected is shown not only by 3 Cor. but also by Paul's speech in PH p. 8. 9ff., in which it is also clear that the "Jesus of history" has by no means so completely vanished as has often been supposed.

The Christology of the AP can scarcely be set out unambiguously in terms of the later dogmatic decisions. The most important statement for the author is that Christ is Lord, not only the Lord of his Church, but also of the world, of life and death. If these christological statements frequently appear to be in conflict with monotheism, this is not a peculiarity of the AP but belongs to the problem presented by early Christian Christology as a whole. Of a well-marked Logos Christology there is in the AP hardly a trace.

Schmidt has justly noted (ΠΠ, pp. 104ff.) that the speeches of Paul in the AP are of special importance. In point of substance they are very varied, but their language and style show their homogeneous character, and in them the author gives his purpose the fullest rein. These speeches were probably shaped in close connection with the preaching of the period, and a careful interpretation of them shows what the Christians of the 2nd century believed and how they talked about God and Christ, sin and grace, salvation and judgment. Over against a speculative Gnosis they withdrew to a moralism rooted in the OT and to the triumphant hope of the future salvation (on the anti-Gnostic attitude of the AP cf. Bauer, *Rechtgläubigkeit und Ketzerei*, index s.v.). Many sides of the primitive Christian and in particular the Pauline preaching are no longer effective, but with this much-diminished armament the Churches of the 2nd century weathered the struggle with Gnosticism.

6. AUTHOR, DATE AND PLACE OF ORIGIN. According to the testimony of Tertullian (see above, p. 323) the author of the AP was a presbyter in Asia Minor, who was rewarded for his work by deposition from his office but not apparently by expulsion from the Church. This we can understand if we bear in mind the theological tendencies—which are really not heretical—but on the other hand observe what offence must have been occasioned on a more rigorous examination by certain particular traits in the AP. We need recall only Thecla's baptism of herself, the baptized lion, and 3 Cor. In particular 3 Cor. was a "forgery" which must have been a thorn in the flesh to the Church in its dealings with the heretics (cf. Rolffs, *Apokr.* 2, p. 196). In addition, comparison with the canonical Acts was very natural, and from this the AP must have come out rather badly. Certainly the author acted in all good faith when "out of love for Paul" he gathered up whatever legends were in circulation, set them in order, and also surely elaborated and expanded them. For in so doing he wished to help his Church in the struggle against the heretics, and to confirm the several communities in the Christian faith.

Of the person of the author nothing more can be said. His native land was Asia Minor. This is not only stated by Tertullian, but may also be seen from the work itself. So far as we can see, it is the places visited in Asia Minor about which the author has most to tell, whereas for Corinth he has less to offer and hence in part makes use of the APt. A more precise location is scarcely possible, even though we may be inclined, with Rolffs, to think of Iconium or Seleucia. But this remains conjecture.

The date likewise cannot be precisely determined. We can only say that the AP must have been written before 200, the approximate date of Tertullian's De baptismo. Since on the other hand it is dependent on the APt, the period between 185 and 195 may be regarded as a possible estimate.

351

THE ACTS OF PAUL*

1
(From Damascus to Jerusalem)
(Ry; PHeid pp. 60/59 and 61/62; cf. PG, p. 388 below)

After his conversion outside Damascus Paul receives the command (from whom?) to go to Damascus and later to Jerusalem. "With great joy" he enters Damascus, and finds the community in the (observance?) of fasting. Here probably a sermon before the Jews was included.

On Paul's journey from Damascus to Jericho (i.e. probably to Jerusalem) the baptism of the lion took place, according to Paul's later account in Ephesus. Whether the fragments PHeid pp. 60/59 and 61/62 contain remnants of the description of Paul's stay and activity in Jerusalem remains uncertain.

2
(Paul in Antioch)
(PHeid pp. 1–6)

In Antioch (Syrian or Pisidian?) Paul raises up a dead boy. The son of Anchares (Greek Acts of Titus: Panchares) and Phila has died, and Paul has evidently betaken himself to the house of the parents in order to assist, but is prevented by the woman (so Schmidt, AP p. 92). Anchares fasts and prays until the crowd comes to carry out his son (who according to the Acts of Titus was called Barnabas). Then Paul comes in and—the sequel is unfortunately lost—appears to have raised up the boy. How the story proceeded we cannot say. Possibly there was some discussion over the miracle. When at PHeid p. 4. 19f. it is said:

"⟨We⟩ believe, Anchares . . . , but save the city"

this points to occurrences of some kind which alarm the people. Perhaps Paul has already left the city, and is now to be brought back. At any rate, according to PHeid p. 5, the narrative probably led to a confession by Anchares, which is now followed by the persecution of Paul by the Jews:

---

* The translation of the text cannot be any substitute for a critical edition. Hence variants could not be completely taken into consideration or noted. Again, the lacunae in the parts extant on papyrus have not been quite exactly indicated. Allusions to NT passages and ideas are given only in selection. The language of the AP bears a NT impress throughout, but is largely formal devotional language. This has not been indicated in detail in the notes.
On the abbreviations see above, p. 322.

"and I ⟨also believe⟩, my ⟨brethren⟩, ⟨that⟩ there is no
other God save ⟨Jesus⟩ Christ, the son ⟨of the⟩ Blessed, unto
whom is the glory ⟨for ever.⟩ Amen." But when they ⟨observed⟩
that he would not turn to them, they pursued Paul, laid hold of
him, and brought him back ⟨into⟩ the city, ill-using (?) him,
(and) they cast stones at him, (and) thrust him out of their city
and out of their country.[1] But Anchares was not able to requite
evil with evil.[2]

What follows is so fragmentary that hardly anything can be
said about its content. The only thing certain is that immediately
after this scene there followed that part of the AP which was
independently transmitted as the Acta Pauli et Theclae.

3

Acts of Paul and Thecla[3]

(*Aa* 1, pp. 235–269; PHeid pp. 6–28)

1. As Paul went up to Iconium after his flight from Antioch,
his travelling companions were Demas and Hermogenes the
copper-smith,[4] who were full of hypocrisy and flattered Paul as
if they loved him. But Paul, who had eyes only for the goodness
of Christ, did them no evil,[5] but loved (p. 236) them greatly, so
that he sought to make sweet to them all the words of the Lord,
of the doctrine and of the interpretation of the Gospel, both of
the birth and of the resurrection of the Beloved, and he related to
them word for word the great acts of Christ[6] as they had been
revealed to him.

2. And a man named Onesiphorus,[7] who had heard that Paul
was come to Iconium,[8] went out with his children Simmias and
Zeno and his wife Lectra[9] to meet Paul (p. 237), that he might
receive him to his house. For Titus had told him what Paul looked
like. For (hitherto) he had not seen him in the flesh, but only in
the spirit. 3. And he went along the royal road which leads to
Lystra, and stood there waiting for him, and looked at (all) who

---

[1] Cf. Acts 14:19.   [2] Cf. Rom. 12:17.
[3] In other MSS.: Martyrdom of the holy proto-martyr Thecla (or something
similar).
[4] Cf. 2 Tim. 4:10; 1:15; 4:14 (?).   [5] Lat.: expected no evil from them.
[6] Cf. Acts 2:11.   [7] Cf. 2 Tim. 1:16; 4:19.
[8] For the following lines cf. Pap. Antinoopolis (PA).
[9] PA: with his children and Zeno and his wife.

came, according to Titus' description. And he saw Paul coming, a man small of stature, with a bald head and crooked legs, in a good state of body, with eyebrows meeting and nose somewhat hooked, full of friendliness; for now he appeared like a man, and now he had the face of an angel.[1] (p. 328)

4. And when Paul saw Onesiphorus he smiled; and Onesiphorus said: "Greeting, thou servant of the blessed God!" And he replied: "Grace be with thee and thy house!" But Demas and Hermogenes grew jealous, and went even further in their hypocrisy; so that Demas said: "Are we then not (servants) of the Blessed, that thou didst not greet us thus?" And Onesiphorus said: "I do not see in you any fruit of righteousness; but if ye are anything, come ye also into my house and rest yourselves!" 5. And when Paul was entered into the house of Onesiphorus there was great joy, and bowing of knees and breaking of bread, and the word of God concerning continence and the resurrection, as Paul said:

"Blessed are the pure in heart, for they shall see God.[2]

Blessed are they who have kept the flesh pure, for they shall become a temple of God.[3]

Blessed are the continent, for to them will God speak.

Blessed are they who have renounced this world, for they shall be well pleasing unto God.

Blessed are they who have wives as if (p. 239) they had them not, for they shall inherit God.[4]

Blessed are they who have fear of God, for they shall become angels of God.

6. Blessed are they who tremble at the words of God, for they shall be comforted.[5]

Blessed are they who have received (the) wisdom of Jesus Christ, for they shall be called sons of the Most High.[6]

Blessed are they who have kept their baptism secure,[7] for they shall rest with the Father and the Son.

Blessed are they who have laid hold upon the understanding of Jesus Christ, for they shall be in light.

Blessed are they who through love of God have departed from

---

[1] Cf. Acts 6:15.　　[2] Mt. 5:8.　　[3] Cf. 2 Clem. 8:6; 2 Cor. 6:16.
[4] Cf. 1 Cor. 7:29; Rom. 8:17.　　[5] Cf. Mt. 5:4.　　[6] Cf. Mt. 5:9.
[7] Cf. 2 Clem. 6:9.

354

the form of this world, for they shall judge angels[1] and at the right hand of the Father they shall be blessed.

Blessed are the merciful, for (p. 240) they shall obtain mercy,[2] and shall not see the bitter day of judgment.

Blessed are the bodies of the virgins, for they shall be well pleasing to God, and shall not lose the reward of their purity.[3] For the word of the Father shall be for them a work of salvation in the day of his Son, and they shall have rest[4] for ever and ever."

7. And while Paul was thus speaking in the midst of the assembly in the house of Onesiphorus, a virgin (named) Thecla—her mother was Theocleia,—who was betrothed to a man (named) Thamyris, sat at a near-by window and listened night and day to the word of the virgin life as it was spoken by Paul; and she did not turn away from the window (p. 241), but pressed on in the faith rejoicing exceedingly. Moreover, when she saw many women and virgins going in to Paul she desired to be counted worthy herself to stand in Paul's presence[5] and hear the word of Christ; for she had not yet seen Paul in person, but only heard his word. 8. Since however she did not move from the window, her mother sent to Thamyris. He came in great joy as if he were already taking her in marriage. So Thamyris said to Theocleia "Where is my Thecla, that I may see her?"[6] And[7] Theocleia said: "I have a new tale to tell thee, Thamyris. For indeed for three days and three nights Thecla has not risen from the window either to eat or to drink, but gazing steadily as if on some joyful spectacle she so devotes herself to a strange man who teaches deceptive and subtle words that I wonder how a maiden of such modesty as she is can be so sorely troubled. (p. 242) 9. Thamyris, this man is upsetting the city of the Iconians, and thy Thecla in addition; for all the women and young people go in to him, and are taught by him. 'You must' he says, 'fear one single God only, and live chastely.' And my daughter also, like a spider at the window bound by his words, is dominated by a new desire and a fearful passion; for the maiden hangs upon the things he says, and is

---

[1]. Cf. 1 Cor. 6:3. [2] Mt. 5:7; this beatitude is lacking in PHeid.
[3] Cf. Mt. 10:42. [4] Cf. Mt. 11:29. [5] So the Greek MSS.
[6] In the Greek MSS. "that I may see her" is lacking.
[7] The following lines in PO. 6.

taken captive. But go thou to her and speak to her, for she is betrothed to thee." 10. And Thamyris went to her, at one and the same time loving her and yet afraid of her distraction, and said: "Thecla, my betrothed, why dost thou sit thus? And what is this passion that holds thee distracted? Turn to thy Thamyris and be ashamed." And her mother also said the same: "Child, why dost thou sit thus (p. 243) looking down and making no answer, but like one stricken?" And those who were in the house wept bitterly, Thamyris for the loss of a wife, Theocleia for that of a daughter, the maidservants for that of a mistress. So there was a great confusion of mourning in the house. And while this was going on (all around her) Thecla did not turn away, but gave her whole attention to Paul's word.

11. But Thamyris sprang up and went out into the street, and closely watched all who went in to Paul and came out. And he saw two men quarrelling bitterly with one another, and said to them: "You men, who are you, tell me, and who is he that is inside with you, the false teacher who deceives the souls of young men and maidens, that they should not marry but remain as they are? I promise now to give you much money if you will tell me about him; for I am the first man of this city." 12. (p. 244) And Demas and Hermogenes said to him: "Who this man is, we do not know. But he deprives young men of wives and maidens of husbands, saying: 'Otherwise there is no resurrection for you, except ye remain chaste and do not defile the flesh,[1] but keep it pure'." 13. And Thamyris said to them: "Come into my house, you men, and rest with me." And they went off to a sumptuous banquet, with much wine, great wealth and a splendid table. And Thamyris gave them to drink, for he loved Thecla and wished to have her for his wife. And during the dinner Thamyris said: "Tell me, you men, what is his teaching, that I also may know it; for I am greatly distressed about Thecla because she so loves the stranger, and I am deprived of my marriage." (p. 245) 14. But Demas and Hermogenes said: "Bring him before the governor Castellius, on the ground that he is seducing the crowds to the new doctrine of the Christians, and so he will have him executed and thou shalt have thy wife Thecla. And we shall

---

[1] Cf. Rev. 14:4.

356

teach thee concerning the resurrection which he says is to come, that it has already taken place in the children whom we have,[1] and that we are risen again in that we have come to know the true God."[2]

15. When Thamyris had heard this from them, he rose up early in the morning full of jealousy and wrath and went to the house of Onesiphorus with the rulers and officers and a great crowd with cudgels, and said to Paul: "Thou hast destroyed the city of the Iconians, and my betrothed, so that she will not have me. Let us go to the governor Castellius!" And the whole crowd shouted: "Away with the sorcerer! For he has corrupted all our wives." And the multitude let themselves be persuaded. (p. 246) 16. And Thamyris stood before the judgment-seat and cried aloud: "Proconsul, this man—we know not whence he is—who does not allow maidens to marry, let him declare before thee for what cause he teaches these things." And Demas and Hermogenes said to Thamyris: "Say that he is a Christian, and so thou wilt destroy him." But the governor was not easily to be swayed, and he called Paul, saying to him: "Who art thou, and what dost thou teach? For it is no light accusation that they bring against thee."[3] 17. And Paul lifted up his voice and said: "If I today am examined as to what I teach, then listen, Proconsul. The living God,[4] the God of vengeance,[5] the jealous God,[6] the God who has need of nothing, has sent me since he desires the salvation of men, that I may draw them away from corruption and impurity, all pleasure and death, that they may sin no more. For this cause God sent His own Son, whom I preach and teach that in him men (p. 247) have hope, who alone had compassion upon a world in error; that men may no longer be under judgment but have faith, and fear of God, and knowledge of propriety, and love of truth. If then I teach the things revealed to me by God, what wrong do I do, Proconsul?" When the governor heard this, he commanded Paul to be bound and led off to prison until he should find leisure to give him a more attentive hearing.[7] 18. But Thecla in the night took off her bracelets and gave them

---

[1] Cf. 2 Tim. 2:18.
[2] So with PHeid against Lipsius, to be regarded as original.
[3] Cf. Mk. 15:4.   [4] Cf. Acts 14:15 *et al.*   [5] Cf. Ps. 94:1.
[6] Cf. Exod. 20:5.   [7] Cf. Acts 24:25.

to the door-keeper, and when the door was opened for her she went off to the prison. To the gaoler she gave a silver mirror, and so went in to Paul and sat at his feet and heard (him proclaim) the mighty acts of God.[1] And Paul feared nothing, but comported himself with full confidence in God; and her faith also was increased, as she kissed his fetters. (p. 248) 19. But when Thecla was sought for by her own people and by Thamyris, they hunted her through the streets as one lost; and one of the door-keeper's fellow slaves betrayed that she had gone out by night. And they questioned the door-keeper, and he told them: "She has gone to the stranger in the prison." And they went as he had told them and found her, so to speak, bound with him in affection. And they went out thence, rallied the crowd about them, and disclosed to the governor what had happened.[2]

20. He commanded Paul to be brought to the judgment-seat; but Thecla rolled herself upon the place where Paul taught as he sat in the prison. The governor commanded her also to be brought to the judgment seat, and she went off with joy exulting. (p. 249) But when Paul was brought forward again, the crowd shouted out even louder: "He is a sorcerer! Away with him!"[3] But the governor heard Paul gladly concerning the holy works of Christ; and when he had taken counsel he called Thecla and said: "Why dost thou not marry Thamyris according to the law of the Iconians?" But she stood there looking steadily at Paul. And when she did not answer, Theocleia her mother cried out, saying: "Burn the lawless one! Burn her that is no bride in the midst of the theatre, that all the women who have been taught by this man may be afraid!" 21. And the governor was greatly affected. He had Paul scourged and drove him out of the city,[4] but Thecla he condemned to be burned. And forthwith the governor arose and went off to the theatre, and all the crowd went out to the unavoidable spectacle. But Thecla sought for Paul, as a lamb in the wilderness looks about for the shepherd. (p. 250) And when she looked upon the crowd, she saw the Lord sitting in the form of Paul and said: "As if I were not able to endure, Paul has come to look after me." And she looked steadily at him; but he departed

---

[1] Cf. Lk. 10:39; Acts 2:11. [2] So EFG Lat. Syr. PHeid.
[3] Cf. Lk. 23:18. [4] Cf. Acts 13:50; 14:19.

into the heavens. 22. Now the young men and maidens brought wood and straw that Thecla might be burned. And as she was brought in naked, the governor wept and marvelled at the power that was in her. The executioners laid out the wood and bade her mount the pyre; and making the sign of the Cross (i.e. stretching out her arms) she climbed up on the wood. They kindled it, and although a great fire blazed up[1] the fire did not touch her. For God in compassion caused a noise beneath the earth and a cloud above, full of rain and hail, overshadowed (the theatre) and its whole content (p. 251) poured out, so that many were in danger and died, and the fire was quenched and Thecla saved. 23. But Paul was fasting with Onesiphorus and his wife and the children in an open tomb on the way by which they go from Iconium to Daphne. And when many days were past, as they were fasting the boys said to Paul: "We are hungry." And they had nothing with which to buy bread, for Onesiphorus had left the things of the world and followed Paul with all his house. But Paul took off his outer garment and said: "Go, my child, ⟨sell this and⟩[2] buy several loaves and bring them here." But while the boy was buying he saw his neighbour Thecla, and was astonished and said: "Thecla, where art thou going?" And she said: "I am seeking after Paul, for I was saved from the fire." And (p. 252) the boy said: "Come, I will take thee to him, for he has been mourning for thee and praying and fasting six days already." 24. But when she came to the tomb Paul had bent his knees and was praying and saying: "Father of Christ, let not the fire touch Thecla, but be merciful to her, for she is thine!" But she standing behind him cried out: "Father, who didst make heaven and earth,[3] the Father of thy beloved Son ⟨Jesus Christ⟩,[4] I praise thee that thou didst save me from the fire, that I might see Paul!" And as Paul arose he saw her and said: "O God the knower of hearts,[5] Father of our Lord Jesus Christ, I praise thee that thou hast so speedily ⟨accomplished⟩ what I asked, and hast hearkened unto me." 25. And within in the tomb there was much love, Paul (p. 253) rejoicing, and Onesiphorus and all of them. But they had five loaves, and vegetables, and water, and they were joyful over the

[1] Cf. Mart. Polyc. 15. 1.   [2] Only in part of the tradition.
[3] Cf. Acts 4:24; 14:15.
[4] Only in part of the tradition; lacking in PHeid.   [5] Cf. Acts 1:24; 15:8.

holy works of Christ. And Thecla said to Paul: "I will cut my hair short and follow thee wherever thou goest."[1] But he said: "The season is unfavourable, and thou art comely. May no other temptation come upon thee, worse than the first, and thou endure not and play the coward!" And Thecla said: "Only give me the seal in Christ, and temptation shall not touch me." And Paul said: "Have patience, Thecla, and thou shalt receive the water."

26. And Paul sent away Onesiphorus with all his family to Iconium, and so taking Thecla came into Antioch. But immediately as they entered a Syrian[2] by the name of Alexander, one of the first of the Antiochenes, seeing Thecla fell in love with her, and sought to win over Paul with money and gifts. But Paul said: "I do not know the woman (p. 254) of whom thou dost speak, nor is she mine." But he, being a powerful man, embraced her on the open street; she however would not endure it, but looked about for Paul and cried out bitterly, saying: "Force not the stranger, force not the handmaid of God! Among the Iconians I am one of the first, and because I did not wish to marry Thamyris I have been cast out of the city." And taking hold of Alexander she ripped his cloak, took off the crown from his head, and made him a laughing-stock. 27. But he, partly out of love for her and partly in shame at what had befallen him, brought her before the governor; and when she confessed that she had done these things, he condemned her to the beasts, ⟨since Alexander was arranging games⟩.[3] But the women were panic-stricken, and cried out before the judgment-seat: "An evil (p. 255) judgment! A godless judgment!" But Thecla asked of the governor that she might remain pure until she was to fight with the beasts. And a rich woman named Tryphaena, whose daughter had died, took her under her protection and found comfort in her. 28. When the beasts were led in procession, they bound her to a fierce lioness, and the queen Tryphaena followed her. And as Thecla sat upon her back, the lioness licked her feet, and all the crowd was amazed. Now the charge upon her superscription[4] was:

[1] Cf. Mt. 8:19.
[2] Cf. Gebhardt p. XCVIII; PHeid: "A Syrian by the name of Alexander, ⟨who⟩ was the great man in Antioch and did much in the city among all the rulers." On this passage cf. above, p. 328.
[3] Omitted in the Greek tradition, cf. Gebhardt pp. XCIX f. and PHeid.
[4] Cf. Mk. 15:26.

Guilty of Sacrilege. But the women with their children cried out from above, saying: "O God, an impious judgment[1] is come to pass in this city!" And after the procession Tryphaena took her again; for (p. 256) her daughter[2] who was dead had spoken to her in a dream: "Mother, thou shalt have in my place the stranger, the desolate Thecla, that she may pray for me and I be translated to the place of the just."[3] 29. So when Tryphaena received her back from the procession she was at once sorrowful, because she was to fight with the beasts on the following day, but at the same time loved her dearly like her own daughter Falconilla; and she said: "Thecla, my second child, come and pray for my child, that she may live; for this I saw in my dream." And she without delay lifted up her voice and said: "Thou God of heaven, Son of the Most High,[4] grant to her according to her wish, that her daughter Falconilla may live for ever!" (p. 257) And when Thecla said this, Tryphaena mourned,[5] considering that such beauty was to be thrown to the beasts. 30. And when it was dawn, Alexander came to take her away—for he himself was arranging the games—and he said: "The governor has taken his place, and the crowd is clamouring for us. Give me her that is to fight the beasts, that I may take her away." But Tryphaena cried out so that he fled, saying: "A second mourning for my Falconilla is come upon my house, and there is none to help; neither child, for she is dead, nor kinsman, for I am a widow. O God of Thecla my child, help thou Thecla." 31. And the governor sent soldiers to fetch Thecla. Tryphaena however did not stand aloof, but taking her hand herself led her up, saying: "My daughter Falconilla I (p. 258) brought to the tomb; but thee, Thecla, I bring to fight the beasts." And Thecla wept bitterly and sighed to the Lord, saying: "Lord God, in whom I trust, with whom I have taken refuge, who didst deliver me from the fire, reward thou Tryphaena, who had compassion upon thy handmaid, and because she preserved me pure." 32. Then there was a tumult,[6] and roaring of the beasts, and a shouting of the people and of the

---

[1] "Judgment" is perhaps secondary, cf. Gebhardt pp. C f.
[2] Lipsius with MS. A: "daughter Falconilla".
[3] Cf. on the other hand 2 Clem. 8. 3.   [4] So according to Gebhardt, pp. CI f.
[5] Gebhardt (p. CI) would assume as original: "And when Tryphaena heard this, she mourned."
[6] Cf. Mart. Polyc. 8. 3.

women who sat together, some saying: "Bring in the sacrilegious
one!" but the women saying: "May the city perish for this lawlessness! Slay us all, Proconsul! A bitter sight, an evil judgment!" 33. But Thecla was taken out of Tryphaena's hands and
stripped, and (p. 259) was given a girdle and flung into the
stadium. And lions and bears were set upon her, and a fierce
lioness ran to her and lay down at her feet. And the crowd of the
women raised a great shout. And a bear ran upon her, but the
lioness ran and met it, and tore the bear asunder. And again a
lion trained against men, which belonged to Alexander, ran
upon her; and the lioness grappled with the lion, and perished
with it. (p. 260) And the women mourned the more, since the
lioness which helped her was dead. 34. Then they sent in many
beasts, while she stood and stretched out her hands and prayed.
And when she had finished her prayer, she turned and saw a great
pit full of water, and said: "Now is the time for me to wash."
And she threw herself in, saying: "In the name of Jesus Christ
I baptize myself on the last day!" And when they saw it, the
women and all the people wept, saying: "Cast not thyself into
the water!"; so that even the governor wept that such beauty
should be devoured by seals. So, then, she threw herself (p. 261)
into the water in the name of Jesus Christ; but the seals, seeing
the light of a lightning-flash, floated dead on the surface. And
there was about her a cloud of fire, so that neither could the
beasts touch her nor could she be seen naked. 35. But as other
more terrible beasts were let loose, the women cried aloud, and
some threw petals, others nard, others cassia, others amomum,
so that there was an abundance of perfumes. And all the beasts
let loose were overpowered as if by sleep, and did not touch her.
So Alexander said to the governor: "I have some very fearsome
bulls—let us tie her to them." The governor frowning (p. 262)
gave his consent, saying: "Do what thou wilt." And they bound
her by the feet between the bulls, and set red-hot irons beneath
their bellies that being the more enraged they might kill her.
The bulls indeed leaped forward, but the flame that blazed around
her burned through the ropes, and she was as if she were not
bound. 36. But Tryphaena fainted as she stood beside the arena,
so that her handmaids said: "The queen Tryphaena is dead!"

And the governor took note of it, and the whole city was alarmed. And Alexander fell down at the governor's feet and said: (p. 263) "Have mercy upon me, and on the city, and set the prisoner free, lest the city also perish with her. For if Caesar should hear this he will probably destroy both us and the city as well, because his kinswoman Tryphaena[1] has died at the circus gates."

37. And the governor summoned Thecla from among the beasts, and said to her: "Who art thou? And what hast thou about thee, that not one of the beasts touched thee?" She answered: "I am a handmaid of the living God. As to what I have about me, I have believed in him in whom God is well pleased, His Son.[2] For his sake not one of the beasts touched me. For he (p. 264) alone is the goal of salvation and the foundation of immortal life. To the storm-tossed he is a refuge, to the oppressed relief,[3] to the despairing shelter; in a word, whoever does not believe in him shall not live, but die for ever." 38. When the governor heard this, he commanded garments to be brought, and said: "Put on these garments." But she said: "He who clothed me when I was naked among the beasts shall clothe me with salvation in the day of judgment." And taking the garments she put them on.

And straightway the governor issued a decree, saying: "I release to you Thecla, the pious handmaid of God." But all the women cried out with a loud voice, and as with one mouth gave praise to God, saying: "One is God, who has delivered Thecla!", so that all the city was shaken by the sound. (p. 265) 39. And Tryphaena when she was told the good news came to meet her with a crowd, and embraced Thecla and said: "Now I believe that the dead are raised up! Now I believe that my child lives! Come inside, and I will assign to thee all that is mine." So Thecla went in with her and rested in her house for eight days, instructing her in the word of God, so that the majority of the maidservants also believed; and there was great joy in the house.

(p. 266) 40. But Thecla yearned for Paul and sought after him, sending in every direction. And it was reported to her that he was in Myra. So she took young men and maidservants and girded

---

[1] Lipsius: Tryphaena, the queen. But this is probably a secondary addition, cf. Gebhardt p. CIV.
[2] Cf. Mk. 1:11 par.   [3] Cf. 2 Thess. 1:7.

herself, and sewed her mantle into a cloak after the fashion of men, and went off to Myra, and found Paul speaking the word of God and went to him. But he was astonished when he saw her and the crowd that was with her, pondering whether another temptation was not upon her. But observing this she said to him: "I have taken the bath, Paul; for he who worked with thee for the Gospel has also worked with me for my baptism." (p. 267) 41. And taking her by the hand Paul led her into the house of Hermias, and heard from her everything (that had happened), so that Paul marvelled greatly and the hearers were confirmed and prayed for Tryphaena. And Thecla arose and said to Paul: "I am going to Iconium." But Paul said: "Go and teach the word of God!" Now Tryphaena sent her much clothing and gold, so that she could leave (some of it) for the service of the poor. (p. 268) 42. But she herself went away to Iconium and went into the house of Onesiphorus, and threw herself down on the floor where Paul had sat and taught the oracles of God, and wept, saying: "My God, and God of this house where the light shone upon me, Christ Jesus the Son of God, my helper in prison, my helper before governors, my helper in the fire, my helper among the beasts, thou art God, and to thee be the glory for ever. Amen." (p. 269) 43. And she found Thamyris dead, but her mother still alive; and calling her mother to her she said to her: "Theocleia my mother, canst thou believe that the Lord lives in heaven? For whether thou dost desire money, the Lord will give it thee through me; or thy child, see, I stand beside thee."

And when she had borne this witness she went away to Seleucia; and after enlightening many with the word of God she slept with a noble sleep.

4

(Paul in Myra)
(PHeid pp. 28–35)
⟨When he was departed from⟩ Antioch
⟨and taught in⟩ Myra

(p. 28) When Paul was ⟨teaching⟩ the word of God in Myra, there ⟨was⟩ a man there named Hermocrates, who had the dropsy. He took his stand before the eyes of all, and said to Paul:

"Nothing is impossible with God,[1] but especially with him whom thou dost preach; for when he came he healed many,[2] he whose servant thou art. Lo, I and my wife ⟨and⟩ my children, (p. 29) we cast ourselves at ⟨thy⟩ feet, ⟨. . . . .⟩ that I also may believe ⟨as⟩ thou hast believed in the living God."[3] ⟨Paul⟩ said to him: "I will give thee ⟨. . . . .⟩ without reward, but ⟨through the⟩ name of Jesus Christ shalt thou become ⟨whole in the presence⟩ of all these."[4]

The following sentences are badly preserved, but probably the healing is described. The man loses a great deal of water, and falls as one dead.

. . . so that some said: "⟨It is⟩ better for him to die, that he may ⟨not⟩ be in pain." But when Paul had quietened the crowd he ⟨took⟩ his hand, raised him up and asked him, saying: "Hermocrates, ⟨. . . . .⟩ what thou wilt." But he said: "I wish to eat."[5] (And) he took a loaf and gave him to eat. He became whole in that hour, and received the grace of the seal in the Lord, he and his wife.

But Hermippus his son was angry ⟨with⟩ Paul, and sought for an appointed time (a good opportunity?) that he might rise up with those of his own age and destroy him. For he wished that his father should not be healed, but (p. 30) die, that he might quickly be master of his property. But Dion, his younger son, heard Paul gladly.

What follows is badly preserved. The content is probably: the friends of Hermippus take counsel as to how to put an end to Paul. Dion has a fall, and dies. Hermocrates mourns deeply but, listening to Paul's sermon, forgets that Dion is dead.

But when Dion was dead, his mother Nympha rent ⟨her⟩ clothing (and) went to Paul, and set herself before her husband Hermocrates and Paul. But when Paul saw her, he was startled and said: "Why (art thou doing) this, Nympha?" But she said to him: "Dion is dead." And the whole crowd wept as they looked upon her. And Paul looked upon the mourning crowd; he sent young men and said to them: "Go and bring him here to

[1] Cf. Mk. 10:27 par.　　[2] Cf. e.g. Mt. 15:29–31.
[3] Cf. 1 Thess. 1:9; Acts 14:15, etc.　　[4] Cf. Acts 3:6.　　[5] Cf. Mk. 5:43.

me." So they went, but Hermippus ⟨caught hold of⟩ the body in the street and cried out . . .

(A leaf missing)

(p. 31) . . . But an angel ⟨of the⟩ Lord had said to him in the night:[1] "Paul, ⟨there is before thee⟩ today a great conflict ⟨against⟩ thy body (?), but God, ⟨the Father⟩ of his Son Jesus Christ, will ⟨. . . . .⟩ thee." When ⟨Paul⟩ had arisen, ⟨he⟩ went to his brethren and remained ⟨. . . . .⟩, saying: "What means this vision?" But while Paul thought on this, he saw Hermippus coming with a drawn sword in his hand, and with him many other young men with their cudgels. Paul ⟨said to them⟩: "I am ⟨not⟩ a robber, nor am I ⟨a⟩ murderer.[2] The God of all things, ⟨the Father⟩ of Christ, will turn ⟨your hands⟩ backwards, and your ⟨sword⟩ into its sheath, and ⟨will transform⟩ your strength into weakness. For I am a servant of God, and I am alone, a stranger, small and of no significance among the heathen. But thou, O God, look down upon ⟨their⟩ plotting (?) and let me not be brought to nought by them." (p. 32) As Hermippus ⟨. . . . .⟩ his sword ⟨. . . . .⟩ against Paul, ⟨. . . . .⟩ he ceased to see, so that ⟨he⟩ cried aloud, saying: "⟨. . .⟩ comrades, forget not ⟨. . .⟩ Hermippus. For I have ⟨. . .⟩, Paul, I have pursued after ⟨. . .⟩ blood. ⟨Learn⟩, ye foolish and ye of understanding, ⟨this⟩ world is nothing, gold is ⟨nothing⟩, all possessions are nothing. I who glutted myself with all that is good am ⟨now⟩ a beggar, ⟨and⟩ entreat you all: Hearken, all ye my companions, and every one who dwells in Myra. ⟨I have⟩ mocked a man ⟨who saved⟩ my father, I have ⟨mocked . . .⟩ raised up my brother ⟨. . .⟩

Lines badly preserved, which are restored by Schmidt: ⟨I have mocked⟩ a man who ⟨has . . . without⟩ doing me any ⟨evil⟩ (?).

But entreat ye him; for look, ⟨since?⟩ he saved my father and raised up my brother, it is possible for him also to deliver me." But Paul stood there weeping, on the one hand before God (with God in mind), beause he had heard him (so) quickly, but on the other also before men (with men in mind), because the proud was brought low. He turned and went up . . .

[1] Cf. Acts 18:9.   [2] Cf. Mk. 14:48 par.

Probably a leaf is missing.

The upper part of p. 33 is preserved so fragmentarily that while we can indeed reproduce its contents with the help of Schmidt's restorations, a translation is not possible. On the contents cf. above, p. 334.

And they saw Hermippus ⟨their⟩ son in the form of ⟨. . . . .⟩, and how he touched the feet of each one, and also the feet of his parents, praying them like one of the strangers that he might be healed. And his parents were troubled and lamented to every one who went in, so that ⟨some⟩ said: "Why do they weep? For ⟨Dion is⟩ risen". But Hermocrates ⟨sold . . . . .⟩ and brought the price to the ⟨widows⟩, and took it and divided it . . . . .

The following lines are again badly damaged.

But they and Paul ⟨prayed⟩ to God. And when Hermippus recovered his sight, he turned to his mother Nympha, saying to her: "Paul came and laid his hand upon me while I wept. And in that hour I saw all things clearly". And she took his hand and brought ⟨him⟩ in to the widows and Paul.

The last lines of p. 34 are badly damaged. Between pages 34 and 35 a leaf is possibly missing. The end of a speech by Paul appears to have stood on p. 35. The last sentence before the lemma is restored by Schmidt:

⟨And when⟩ Paul ⟨had confirmed⟩ the brethren who ⟨were in⟩ Myra, he departed for ⟨Sidon⟩.

5

(Paul in Sidon)
(PHeid pp. 35–39)

When he was departed from Myra
and ⟨would go to Sidon⟩.

(p. 35) But ⟨when Paul was departed from Myra and wished to go⟩ up to Si⟨don⟩, there was great sorrow among the brethren who were in ⟨Pisidia⟩ and Pamphylia, since they yearned ⟨after⟩ his word and his holy presence; so that some from Perga[1] followed Paul, namely Thrasymachus and Cleon with their wives Aline (?) and Chrysa, the wife of Cleon.

---

[1] Cf. Acts 13:13ff.

The following section is preserved only fragmentarily. On its contents cf. above, pp. 335f. Then at least two leaves are missing, and possibly more (see above, p. 335). Page 37 begins with a speech by Paul in Sidon.

(p. 37) ". . . ⟨after⟩ the manner of strange men. Why do you presume to do things that are not seemly? Have you not heard of that which happened, which God brought upon Sodom and Gomorrah,[1] because they robbed . . ."

The remainder of the speech is severely damaged.

⟨But they⟩ did not listen to him, but ⟨laid hold of⟩ them and flung them into ⟨the temple of Apol⟩lo to keep them secure until ⟨the morning⟩, in order that they might assemble the city ⟨. . .⟩ Abundant and costly was the food they gave them, but Paul, who was fasting for the third day, testified all night long, sad at heart and smiting his brow and saying: "O God, look down upon their threats[2] and suffer us not to fall, and let not our adversary strike us down (?), (p. 38) but ⟨deliver⟩ us by speedily bringing down thy righteousness upon us."

The following lines are badly damaged. Probably at Paul's prayer a part of the temple collapses, which creates a considerable stir.

They (i.e. those who had seen the fallen temple) went away (and) proclaimed in the city: "Apollo the god of the Sidonians is fallen, with the half of his temple." And all the inhabitants of the city ran to the temple (and) saw Paul and those that were with him weeping at this tribulation, that they were to become a spectacle for everyone. But the crowd cried out: "Bring them to the theatre!" The magistrates came to fetch them; and they groaned bitterly in their soul . . .

Here at least two leaves are missing. On p. 39, which presents the end of the Sidon episode, only a little can be read. Apparently Paul makes a speech, which brings the crowd round. Schmidt restores the conclusion thus:

⟨But he⟩ commanded ⟨them⟩ to go to Tyre . . . ⟨in⟩ safety (?), and they put Paul ⟨aboard a ship?⟩ and went with him.

[1] Cf. Gen. 19.   [2] Cf. Acts 4:29.

6

(Paul in Tyre)

(PHeid p. 40)

When he was departed from Sidon
and would go to Tyre.

(p. 40) But when ⟨Paul⟩ had entered ⟨into Tyre⟩ there
⟨came a⟩ crowd of Jews . . . in to him.

The following lines are damaged. Paul probably preaches and also
drives out demons. The names Amphion and Chrysippus can be recognized.

But immediately the demons ⟨fled⟩. But when the crowd saw
⟨these things in the power⟩ of God, they praised him who
⟨. . . . .⟩ to Paul. Now there was one named ⟨. . .⟩rimos, who
had a ⟨son⟩ who had been born dumb . . .

Here the episode at Tyre breaks off; cf. above, p. 337.

7

(Paul in Ephesus)

(PH pp. 1–5)

This was preceded by a stay in Smyrna and the arrival in Ephesus,
where Paul preaches in the house of Aquila and Priscilla (cf. PG, below, p. 387). PH begins with the scene before the governor.

(p. 1) But Paul said to him: "⟨. . .⟩ For thou hast no power
⟨over me except over⟩ my body; but my soul thou ⟨canst⟩ not
⟨slay⟩.[1] But ⟨hear⟩ in what manner thou must be saved. And
taking all ⟨my words⟩ to heart ⟨. . .⟩ and the earth and stars
and dominions and ⟨. . .⟩ and all the good things in the world
for the sake of ⟨. . .⟩ moulded ⟨. . .⟩ of men ⟨. . .⟩ led astray
and enslaved ⟨. . .⟩ by gold ⟨. . .⟩ silver and precious stones
⟨. . .⟩ and adultery and drunkenness. ⟨. . .⟩, which lead to
deception through the afore-mentioned ⟨. . .⟩ went and were
slain.[2] Now then, since the Lord wishes us to live in God because
of the error in the world, ⟨and not⟩ die in sins, he saves through
the ⟨. . .⟩ who preach, that ye may repent and believe ⟨. . .⟩[3]

[1] Cf. Mt. 10:28.   [2] Cf. Rom. 13:13; Gal. 5:20f.; 1 Clem. 30:1.
[3] Probably to be restored: that there is only one God; cf. 1 Cor. 8:4ff.; Eph. 4:5, 6;
1 Tim. 2:5; James 2:19; cf. also PHeid p. 5. 11 (above, p. 353): There is no other
God save Jesus Christ, the Son of the Blessed.

and one Christ Jesus and no other exists. For your gods are of
⟨. . .⟩ and stone and wood, and can neither take food nor see
nor hear, nor even stand. Form a good resolve, and be ye saved,
lest God be wroth and burn you with unquenchable fire,[1] and
the memory of you perish."[2] And when the governor heard this
⟨. . .⟩ in the theatre with the people, he said: "Ye men of
Ephesus, that this man has spoken well I know, but also that
⟨. . .⟩ is no time for you to learn these things. Decide now what
you wish!" Some said he should be burned ⟨. . . . .⟩, but the
goldsmiths[3] said: "To the beasts with the man!" And since a
great ⟨tumult⟩ broke out Hieronymus condemned him to the
beasts, after having him scourged. Now the brethren, since it was
Pentecost, did not mourn or bow their knees, but rejoiced and
prayed ⟨standing⟩. But after six days Hieronymus made ⟨. . .⟩[4]
all who saw it were astonished at the size ⟨. . .⟩[5]

(p. 2) The first lines are imperfect. Paul sits a prisoner, and hears
the preparations for the fight with the beasts.

And ⟨when the lion⟩ came to the side door of the stadium,
⟨where Paul⟩ was imprisoned, it roared loudly, so that all ⟨. . .⟩
cried out: "The lion!" For it roared fiercely and angrily, ⟨so that
even Paul⟩ broke off his prayer in terror. There was ⟨. . .⟩
Diophantes, a freedman of Hieronymus, whose wife was a
disciple of Paul and sat beside him night and day, ⟨so that⟩
Diophantes became jealous and hastened on the conflict. ⟨And⟩
Artemilla, the wife of Hieronymus, wished to hear Paul ⟨praying⟩,
and said to Eubula, the wife of Diophantes: "⟨. . .⟩ to hear the
beast-fighter's prayer." And she went and told Paul, and Paul
full of joy said: "Bring her." She put on darker clothes, and came
to him with Eubula. But when Paul saw her, he groaned and
said: "Woman, ruler of this world, mistress of much gold, citizen
of great luxury, splendid in thy raiment, sit down on the floor
and forget thy riches and thy beauty and thy finery. For these
will profit thee nothing if thou pray not to God who regards as
dross all that here is imposing, but graciously bestows what

[1] Cf. Mt. 3:12 par.
[2] On Paul's sermon cf. the parallel tradition in PG; French translation in Kasser,
RHPR 40, 1960, pp. 55f.
[3] Cf. Acts 19:24ff.   [4] Restore: the display of animals.
[5] Restore: of the beasts.

there is wonderful. Gold perishes, riches are consumed, clothes
become worn out. Beauty grows old, and great cities are changed,
and the world will be destroyed in fire[1] because of the lawlessness
of men. God alone abides, and the sonship[2] that is given through
him in whom men must be saved.[3] And now, Artemilla, hope in
God and he will deliver thee, hope in Christ and he will give thee
forgiveness of sins and will bestow upon thee a crown of freedom,
that thou mayest no longer serve idols and the steam of sacrifice
but the living God[4] and Father of Christ, whose is the glory for
ever and ever. Amen."[5] And when Artemilla heard this she with
Eubula besought Paul that he would ⟨forthwith?⟩ baptize her in
God. And the fight with the beasts was (arranged) for the next day.

(p. 3) And Hieronymus heard from Diophantes that the women
sat night and day with Paul, and he was not a little wroth with
Artemilla and the freedwoman Eubula. And when he had dined
Hieronymus withdrew early, that he might quickly carry through
the beast-hunt. But the women said to Paul: "Dost thou wish us
to bring a smith, that thou mayest baptize us in the sea as a free
man?" And Paul said: "I do not wish it, for I have faith in God,
who delivered the whole world from (its) bonds." And Paul
cried out to God on the Sabbath as the Lord's day drew near, the
day on which Paul was to fight with the beasts, and he said: "My
God, Jesus Christ, who didst redeem me from so many evils,[6]
grant me that before the eyes of Artemilla and Eubula, who are
thine, the fetters may be broken from my hands." And as Paul
thus testified (or: adjured God),[7] there came in a youth very
comely in grace and loosed Paul's bonds, the youth smiling as
he did so. And straightway he departed. But because of the vision
which was granted to Paul, and the eminent sign relating to his
fetters, his grief over the fight with the beasts departed, and
rejoicing he leaped as if in paradise. And taking Artemilla he
went out from the narrow and ⟨dark place where the⟩ prisoners
were kept.

[1] Cf. 1 Cor. 3:13; 2 Pet. 3:7.   [2] Cf. Rom. 8:15, 23; 9:4; Gal. 4:5; Eph. 1:5.
[3] Cf. Acts 4:12.   [4] Cf. Acts 14:15, etc.
[5] On the speech cf. Acts of Thomas c. 88, and further Peterson and Devos (above,
p. 349).
[6] Cf. 2 Tim. 3:11.
[7] Schmidt ΠΗ, p. 33, ad loc.: "διαμαρτύρεσθαι strictly 'adjure', cf. 1 Tim. 5:21;
2 Tim. 2:14; 4:1—perhaps 'as Paul thus testified', see Acts 20:21, 23, 24; 23:11, etc.
AThe 269. 5 (Coptic text p. 37. 23) or generally 'pray in adjuration'."

In the following there are considerable gaps, which Schmidt has meaningfully restored. The subject is Artemilla's baptism at the sea. As Artemilla swoons at the sight of the surging sea, Paul prays:

"O thou who dost give light and shine, ⟨help, that⟩ the heathen may ⟨not⟩ say (p. 4) that Paul the prisoner fled after killing Artemilla." And again the youth smiled, and the matron (Artemilla) breathed again, and she went into the house as dawn was already breaking. But as he (Paul?) went in, the guards being asleep, he broke bread and brought water, gave her to drink of the word, and dismissed her to her husband Hieronymus. But he himself prayed.

At dawn there was a cry from the citizens: 'Let us go to the spectacle! Come, let us see the man who possesses God fighting with the beasts!" Hieronymus himself joined them, partly because of his suspicion against his wife, partly because he (Paul) had not fled; he commanded Diophantes and the other slaves to bring Paul into the stadium. He (Paul) was dragged in, saying nothing but bowed down and groaning because he was led in triumph by the city. And when he was brought out he was immediately flung into the stadium, so that all were vexed at Paul's dignity. But since Artemilla and Eubula fell into a sickness and were in extreme danger because of Paul's (impending) destruction, Hieronymus was not a little grieved over (his) wife, but also because the rumour was already abroad in the city and he did not have his wife with him. So when he had taken his place the ⟨. . .⟩ ordered a very fierce lion, which had but recently been captured, to be set loose against him.

The following text is very imperfect. It deals with the lion's prayer and its conversation with Paul. The people thereupon cry out:

"Away with the sorcerer![1] Away with the ⟨poisoner!" But the lion⟩ looked at Paul and Paul ⟨at the lion. Then⟩ Paul recognized that this ⟨was the⟩ lion (p. 5) which had come ⟨and⟩ been baptized. ⟨And⟩ borne along by faith[2] Paul said: "Lion, was it thou whom I baptized?" And the lion in answer said to Paul: "Yes." Paul spoke to it again and said: "And how wast thou captured?" The lion said with one (?) voice:[3] "Even as thou,

---

[1] Cf. AThe c. 20; known also elsewhere in descriptions of the baiting of Christians.
[2] Cf. 2 Pet. 1:21.   [3] Schmidt: μιᾷ φωνῇ corrupted from θίᾳ = θείᾳ φωνῇ.

Paul." As Hieronymus sent many beasts, that Paul might be slain, and against the lion archers, that it too might be killed, a violent and exceedingly heavy hail-storm fell from heaven, although the sky was clear, so that many died and all the rest took to flight. But it did not touch Paul or the lion, although the other beasts perished under the weight of the hail, (which was so severe) that Hieronymus' ear was smitten and torn off, and the people cried out as they fled: "Save us, O God, save us, O God of the man who fought with the beasts!" And Paul took leave of the lion, without his (i.e. the lion?) saying anything more, and went out of the stadium and down to the harbour and embarked on the ship which was sailing for Macedonia; for there were many who were sailing, as if the city were about to perish. So he embarked too like one of the fugitives, but the lion went away into the mountains as was cust.·mary for it.

Now Artemilla and Eubula mourned not a little, fasting and in ⟨. . .⟩¹ as to what had befallen Paul. But when it was night there came ⟨. . .⟩² visibly into the bedroom, where ⟨. . .⟩ Hieronymus was discharging at the ear.

The following lacunae have been so restored by Schmidt that their content becomes clear: the women are comforted as to Paul's fate. Hieronymus prays to Paul's God for help for his ear.

"Through the will of Christ Jesus ⟨heal⟩ the ear!" And it became whole, as ⟨the youth⟩ had commanded him: "Treat ⟨the ear?⟩ with honey."

8

(Paul in Philippi)
(PHeid pp. 45–50; 41, 42 and 44; for 3 Cor. see above, pp. 341f.)

The beginning of the Philippi episode is missing. The first lines of PHeid p. 45 are so fragmentary that no conclusions can be drawn from them.

⟨For⟩ the Corinthians were in ⟨great⟩ distress ⟨over⟩ Paul, because he was going out of the world before it was time. For men were come to Corinth, Simon and Cleobius, who said that there was no resurrection of the flesh but (only) of the spirit,

¹ Not to be restored; perhaps 'in anguish'.
² Schmidt restores: 'a comely youth'.

and that the body of man is not the creation of God; and of the
world (they said) that God did not create it, and that God does
not know the world; and that Jesus Christ was not crucified, but
was only a semblance, and that he was not born of Mary, or of
the seed of David.[1] In a word, many were the things which they
⟨taught?⟩ in Corinth, deceiving ⟨many others . . . and⟩ themselves. ⟨Because of this⟩, when ⟨the Corinthians⟩ heard ⟨that
Paul was in Philippi⟩ they sent a ⟨letter to Paul⟩ in Macedonia
⟨by⟩ Threptus ⟨and⟩ Eutychus ⟨the deacons⟩. And the letter
was ⟨in this form⟩.

(Letter of the Corinthians to Paul)[2]

1. 1. Stephanus and the presbyters who are with him, Daphnus,
Eubulus, Theophilus and Xenon, to Paul ⟨their brother⟩ in the
Lord, greeting.

2. Two men are come to Corinth, named Simon and Cleobius,
who pervert the faith of many through pernicious words, 3. which
thou shalt put to the test. 4. For never have we heard such words,
either from thee or from the other apostles; 5. but what we have
received from thee and from them, that we hold fast. 6. Since now
the Lord has shown mercy to us, that while thou art still in the
flesh we may hear such things again from thee, 7. do thou write
to us or come to us. 8. For we believe, as it has been revealed to
Theonoe, that the Lord has delivered thee out of the hand of the
lawless one. 9. What they say and teach is as follows: 10. We must
not, they say, appeal to the prophets, 11. and that God is not
almighty, 12. and that there is no resurrection of the flesh, 13. and
that the creation of man is not God's (work), 14. and that the
Lord is not come in the flesh, nor was he born of Mary, 15. and
that the world is not of God, but of the angels. 16. Wherefore,

---

[1] It is improbable that this sentence is intended to be direct speech (introduced in
the original Greek text by ὅτι?); the Coptic text of 3 Cor. 1:11ff. suggests the contrary.
[2] The superscriptions are very varied in the tradition. The notes to 3 Cor. 1–3
relate to the verses.
1. 1. cf. 1 Cor. 1:16; 16:15–17; 2 Tim. 4:21; Lk. 1:3; Acts 1:1. MBZAE: the brother;
PBodm: τῷ ἐν κυρίῳ.
2. cf. 2 Tim. 2:18.
4. PBodm: heard from the others; but probably a secondary abbreviation.
5. cf. 1 Cor. 11:2.
6. PBodm. omits: such. Cf. Phil. 1:24.
7. and 8. show many variants in the tradition.
16. cf. 2 Tim. 4:9.

brother, make all speed to come hither, that the church of the Corinthians may remain without offence, and the foolishness of these men be made manifest. Fare thee well in the Lord!

2. 1. The deacons Threptus and Eutychus brought the letter to Philippi, 2. and delivered it to Paul, who was in prison because of Stratonice, the wife of Apollophanes; and he began to shed many tears and to mourn, and cried out: 3. "Better were it for me to die and be with the Lord, than to be in the flesh and hear such things, so that sorrow after sorrow comes upon me, 4. and suffering such things to be bound and (have to see how) the tools (intrigues?) of the evil one run their course!" 5. And so Paul in affliction wrote the (following) letter.

(Letter of Paul to the Corinthians)

3. 1. Paul, the prisoner of Jesus Christ, to the brethren in Corinth—greeting! 2. Since I am in many tribulations, I do not wonder that the teachings of the evil one are so quickly gaining ground. 3. For ⟨my⟩ Lord Jesus Christ will quickly come, since he is rejected by those who falsify his words. 4. For I delivered to you in the beginning what I received from the apostles who were before me, who at all times were together with the Lord Jesus Christ, 5. that our Lord Jesus Christ was born of Mary of the seed of David, when the Holy Spirit was sent from heaven by the Father into her, 6. that he might come into this world and redeem all flesh through his own flesh, and that he might raise up from the dead us who are fleshly, even as he has shown himself as our example. 7. And since man was moulded by his Father, 8. for this reason was he sought when he was lost, that he might be quickened by adoption into sonship. 9. For the almighty God, who made heaven and earth, first sent the prophets to the Jews, that they might be drawn away from their sins; 10. for he had determined to save the house of Israel, therefore he sent a portion

2. 3. cf. Phil. 1:23; 2:27.
   5. cf. 2 Cor. 2:4.
3. 1. cf. Eph. 3:1; Phm. 9.
   2. cf. 2 Cor. 2:4; Gal. 1:6.
   3. PBodm omits: my.
   4. cf. 1 Cor. 15:3; Gal. 1:17; Acts 1:21f.
   5. cf. Rom. 1:3.
   6. cf. 1 Tim. 1:15.
   8. cf. Rom. 8:15, 23; 9:4; Gal. 4:5; Eph. 1:5.—After v. 8 in M & P a longer addition, which agrees with v. 15/16.

of the Spirit of Christ into the prophets, who at many times proclaimed the faultless worship of God. 11. But since the prince who was unrighteous wished himself to be God, he laid hands upon them and slew them, and so fettered all flesh of men to the passions ⟨to his will, and the end of the world drew nigh to judgment⟩. 12. But God, the almighty, who is righteous and would not repudiate his own creation, 13. sent the ⟨Holy⟩ Spirit ⟨through fire⟩ into Mary the Galilean, 14. who believed with all her heart, and she received the Holy Spirit in her womb that Jesus might enter into the world, 15. in order that the evil one might be conquered through the same flesh by which he held sway, and convinced that he was not God. 16. For by his own body Jesus Christ saved all flesh ⟨and brought it to eternal life through faith⟩, 17. that he might present a temple of righteousness in his body, 18. through whom we are redeemed. 19. They are thus not children of righteousness but children of wrath, who reject the providence of God, saying ⟨far from faith⟩ that heaven and earth and all that in them is are not works of the Father. 20. They are themselves therefore children of wrath, for they have the accursed faith of the serpent. 21. From them turn ye away, and flee from their teaching! ⟨22. For ye are not sons of disobedience but of the Church most dearly beloved. 23. Wherefore the time of the resurrection is proclaimed⟩.

24. As for those who tell you that there is no resurrection of the flesh, for them there is no resurrection, 25. who do not believe in him who is thus risen. 26. For indeed, ye men of Corinth, they do not know about the sowing of wheat or the other seeds, that they are cast naked into the ground and when they have perished below are raised again by the will of God in a body and clothed. 27. And not only is the body which was cast (into the earth) raised up, but also abundantly blessed. 28. And if we must not derive the

---

11. cf. 2 Thess. 2:4.—The conclusion of the verse is a secondary addition in MBPA.
13. MPA.: holy, but probably a secondary addition. PBodm: through fire.
14. cf. Lk. 1:45. v. 14 only in MPBA.
16. The conclusion is an addition in PA, similarly in B.
19. cf. Eph. 2:3.—M: far from faith.
22. cf. Eph. 2:2.—v. 22/23 only in MPBA.
26. cf. 1 Cor. 15:37; John 12:24f.
27. Translated according to PBodm.
28. Conclusion in MPBA.

similitude from the seeds alone, ⟨but from nobler bodies⟩,
29. you know that Jonah the son of Amathios, when he would not
preach in Nineveh ⟨but fled⟩, was swallowed by a whale, 30. and
after three days and three nights God heard Jonah's prayer out
of deepest hell, and no part of him was corrupted, not even a
hair or an eyelid. 31. How much more, O ye of little faith, will he
raise up you who have believed in Christ Jesus, as he himself
rose up? 32. And if, when a corpse was thrown by the children of
Israel upon the bones of the prophet Elisha, the man's body rose
up, so you also who have been cast upon the body and bones and
Spirit of the Lord shall rise up on that day with your flesh whole.

34. But if you receive anything else, do not cause me trouble;
35. for I have these fetters on my hands that I may gain Christ,
and his marks in my body that I may attain to the resurrection
from the dead. 36. And whoever abides by the rule which he
received through the blessed prophets and the holy Gospel, he
shall receive a reward ⟨and when he is risen from the dead shall
obtain eternal life⟩. 37. But he who turns aside therefrom—there
is fire with him and with those who go before him in the way,
38. since they are men without God, a generation of vipers;
39. from these turn ye away in the power of the Lord, 40. and
peace, ⟨grace and love⟩ be with you. Amen.

Between 3 Cor and the conclusion of the Philippi episode there is
a lacuna, the length of which cannot be determined. Of the first lines
on page 41 of PHeid only the names Longinus and Paul can be read.
Evidently Longinus, the father of Frontina, is speaking.

(p. 41) . . . nothing good has ⟨befallen⟩ my house." ⟨And⟩ he
advised that ⟨. . .⟩ who ⟨were to throw⟩ down Frontina ⟨his⟩
daughter should ⟨also⟩ throw down Paul alive ⟨with⟩ her. Now
Paul knew of the ⟨matter⟩, but he laboured and fasted in great
cheerfulness for two ⟨days⟩ with the prisoners. They ⟨commanded
that⟩ on the third day ⟨. . .⟩ bring out Frontina. But the ⟨. . .⟩
followed her. And Firmilla and Longinus and the soldiers

29. MP: but fled.—v. 29/30 cf. Mt. 12:40 par.
31. cf. Mt. 6:30 par.; Rom. 6:4.
32. cf. 2 Kings 13:21ff.—After v. 32 in MPA a longer addition (=v. 33).
34. cf. Gal. 6:17.
35. cf. Phil. 3:8; Gal. 6:17; Phil. 3:11.
36. cf. Gal. 6:16; 1 Cor. 3:14.—Conclusion of verse an addition in MPBA.
38. cf. Mt. 3:7, etc.
40. MP: grace and love.

⟨lamented⟩. But the prisoners carried the bier. And when Paul saw a great mourning . . .

Lacuna of about 8 lines

(p. 42) . . . Paul alive ⟨with the⟩ daughter. But when Paul ⟨had taken⟩ the daughter in ⟨his⟩ arms, he groaned to the Lord Jesus Christ because of Firmilla's sorrow; he threw himself on his knees in the mire ⟨. . .⟩ and prayed for Frontina and ⟨her⟩ in one prayer. In ⟨that⟩ hour Frontina ⟨rose up⟩. And all the ⟨crowd⟩ was afraid and fled. Paul ⟨took⟩ the daughter's hand and ⟨. . .⟩ through the city to the house ⟨of⟩ Longinus. But the whole ⟨crowd⟩ cried with one voice: "One is God, who has made heaven and earth, who has given life to the daughter ⟨. . . . .⟩ of Paul."

A few more lines follow on pages 42 and 44, but of these only a few letters or words can be recognized. On the content cf. above, p. 341. A new section begins in the middle of page 44 of PHeid. Of the lemma not much is preserved. In accordance with PH it may be restored:

⟨When he was departed from Philippi⟩
and would go ⟨to Corinth⟩.

9

(Paul in Corinth)
(PH pp. 6–7; PHeid pp. 44/43; 51/52)
From Philippi to Corinth

(p. 6) When Paul came from Philippi to Corinth, to the house of Epiphanius, there was joy,[1] so that all our people rejoiced but at the same time wept as Paul related what he had suffered in Philippi in the workhouse[2] and everywhere, what had befallen him, so that further his tears became ⟨. . .⟩[3] and continuous prayer was offered by all for Paul, and he counted himself blessed that so single-heartedly every day they guided his affairs in prayer to the Lord. Unrivalled therefore was the greatness of the joy, and Paul's soul was uplifted because of the goodwill of the brethren, so that for forty days he preached the word of persever-

---

[1] PHeid: great joy.
[2] ἐργαστρον according to Schmidt = workhouse, i.e. *ergastulum;* cf. Halkin, *op. cit.* p. 246 n. 7.
[3] Schmidt restores ἄνεσις; cf. 2 Cor. 7:5.

ance,[1] (relating) in what place anything had befallen him and what great deeds had been granted to him. So in every account he praised almighty God and Christ Jesus who in every place had been well pleased with Paul. ⟨But when⟩ the days were ended (and the time drew near) for Paul to depart for Rome, grief came upon the brethren as to when they should see him again. And Paul, full of the Holy Spirit, said: "Brethren, be zealous about ⟨fasting?⟩[2] and love. For behold, I go away to a furnace of fire ⟨. . .⟩[3] and I am not strong except the Lord ⟨grant⟩ me power. For indeed David accompanied Saul[4] ⟨. . .⟩,[5] for Christ Jesus was with him ⟨. . .⟩. ⟨The grace of⟩ the Lord will go with me, that I may ⟨fulfil⟩ the ⟨. . .⟩ dispensation with steadfastness." But they were distressed and fasted. Then Cleobius was filled with the Spirit and said: "Brethren, now must Paul fulfil all his assignment, and go up to the ⟨. . .⟩[6] of death ⟨. . .⟩ in great instruction and knowledge and sowing of the word, and (must) suffer envy[7] and depart out of this world." But when the brethren and Paul heard ⟨this⟩, they lifted up their voice and said: "O God, ⟨. . .⟩ Father of Christ, help thou Paul thy servant, that he may yet abide with us because of our weakness." But since Paul was cut (to the heart) and no longer fasted with them, when an offering (i.e. Eucharist) was celebrated by Paul . . .

(PH p. 7) The beginning of the page is very imperfect, nor does it admit of any meaningful restoration from PHeid p. 52.

But the Spirit came upon Myrta, so that she said: "Brethren, why ⟨are you alarmed at the sight of this sign?⟩[8] Paul the servant of the Lord will save many in Rome, and will nourish many with the word, so that there is no number (to count them), and he (?)

[1] Schmidt (*ΠΠ*, p. 45 n. 11) gathers together the expressions used to describe Paul's preaching.
[2] Schmidt restores νεότητα, which however does not make sense. In his apparatus he suggests νηστεία, but this does not fit the traces which remain.
[3] Restore with Schmidt: I mean to Rome. On the furnace of fire cf. Mt. 13:42, 50; Dan. 3.
[4] Cf. 1 Sam. 24.
[5] In the lacuna reference is made to Nabal, cf. 1 Sam. 24. On this cf. Schmidt *ΠΠ*, p. 47: "In both cases David thus overcame his adversary without any action of his own, since God was with him. So Paul too hopes to master the destiny which threatens him through the power bestowed upon him by the Lord."
[6] Lacuna in PH and PHeid; possibly: into the city of death.
[7] On ξηλωθέντα cf. 1 Clem. 3ff.; MP 1 (below, p. 383).
[8] Restoration after Schmidt.

will become manifest above all the faithful,[1] and greatly will the glory ⟨. . . come⟩ upon him, so that there will be great grace in Rome." And immediately, when the Spirit that was in Myrta was at peace, each one took of the bread and feasted according to custom ⟨. . .⟩[2] amid the singing of psalms of David and of hymns. And Paul too enjoyed himself. On the following day, after they had spent the whole night according to the will of God, Paul said: "Brethren, I shall set out on the day of preparation and sail for Rome, that I may not delay what is ordained and laid upon me, for to this I was appointed." They were greatly distressed when they heard this, and all the brethren contributed according to their ability so that Paul might not be troubled, except that he was going away from the brethren.

10

(From Corinth to Italy)
(PH pp. 7–8; PB; PO; PM)

(p. 7) As he embarked on the ship, while they all prayed, Artemon[3] the captain of the ship was there. He had been baptized by Peter, and ⟨. . . . .⟩ Paul, that so much was entrusted to him ⟨. . . . .⟩[4] the Lord was embarking. But when the ship had set sail, Artemon held fellowship with Paul to glorify the Lord Jesus Christ in the grace of God, since he had fore-ordained his plan for Paul.[5] When they were on the open sea and it was quiet, Paul fell asleep, fatigued by the fastings and the night watches with the brethren. And the Lord came to him, walking upon the sea, and he nudged Paul and said: "Stand up and see!" And he awakening said: "Thou art my Lord Jesus Christ, the king ⟨. . . . .⟩, But why so gloomy and downcast, Lord? And if thou ⟨. . . . .⟩ Lord, for I am not a little distressed that thou art so." ⟨And

---

[1] i.e. he will surpass all the faithful.

[2] Schmidt restores PH according to PHeid: according to the custom of fasting. This however would not fill the lacuna, and the expression remains obscure. Probably what is meant is that after the preparation by fasting the Eucharist is celebrated, and to this an Agape is appended.

[3] Whether the name Artemon is taken from Acts 27:40 remains questionable. The word, which in Acts indicates the foresail, also frequently occurs as a name.

[4] The meaning is probably: Artemon welcomes Paul, and esteems him as if the Lord himself had embarked on the ship.

[5] προοικονομοῦντα is to be understood from p. 7. 14f.: Paul's path, as part of the plan of salvation (οἰκονομία), is predetermined. Cf. 1 Tim. 2:7; 2 Tim. 1:11.

the⟩ Lord said: "Paul, I am about to be crucified afresh."[1]
And Paul said: "God forbid, Lord, that I should see this!" But
the Lord said to Paul: "Paul, get thee up, go to Rome and
admonish the brethren, that they abide in the calling to the
Father". And ⟨. . . . .⟩ walking on the sea, he went before them
⟨. . . . .⟩ showed (the way). But when the voyage was ended
⟨. . .⟩ Paul went ⟨. . . . .⟩ with great sadness, and ⟨he saw⟩ a
man standing ⟨on⟩ the harbour, who was waiting for Artemon
the captain, and seeing him greeted him ⟨. . . (p. 8) . . .⟩ and
he said to him: "Claudius, ⟨see here Paul⟩ the beloved of the
Lord, who is with me." ⟨. . .⟩ Claudius embraced[2] Paul and
greeted him. And without delay he with Artemon carried the
(baggage) from the ship to his house. And he rejoiced greatly and
informed the brethren about him, so that at once Claudius'
house was filled with joy and thanksgiving. For they saw how
Paul laid aside his mood of sadness and taught the word of
truth[3] and said: "Brethren and soldiers of Christ,[4] listen! How
often did God deliver Israel out of the hand of the lawless! And
so long as they kept the things of God[5] he did not forsake them.
For he saved them out of the hand of Pharaoh the lawless, and
of Og the still more ungodly king,[6] and of Adar[7] and the foreign
people. And so long as they kept the things of God he gave them
of the fruit of the loins,[8] after he had promised them the land of
the Canaanites, and he made the foreign people subject to them.
And after all that he provided for them in the desert and in the
waterless (country), he sent them in addition prophets to proclaim our Lord Jesus Christ;[9] and these in succession received
share and portion of the Spirit of Christ,[10] and having suffered
much were slain by the people. Having thus forsaken the living
God according to their own desires, they forfeited the eternal
inheritance. And now, brethren, a great temptation lies before
us. If we endure, we shall have access to the Lord, and shall

---

[1] ἄνωθεν here = afresh; cf. above, p. 346.   [2] Here PB begins.
[3] Cf. 2 Cor. 6:7; 2 Tim. 2:15.   [4] Cf. 2 Tim. 2:3.
[5] i.e. God's commandments.   [6] Cf. Num. 21:33.   [7] Cf. Num. 21:1-3.
[8] PO: of the fruit of the power. On "fruit of the loins" = posterity, cf. Acts 2:30
(Ps. 132:11). For the author of the AP the expression was probably only a pious
phrase.
[9] Cf. Acts 7:52.
[10] On the whole section cf. 3 Cor. Schmidt (ΠΠ, pp. 57ff.) has indicated the parallels.

receive as the refuge and shield of his good pleasure[1] Jesus Christ, who gave himself for us, if at least ye receive the word so as it is.[2] For in these last times God for our sakes has sent down a spirit of power into the flesh, that is, into Mary the Galilean, according to the prophetic word; who[3] was conceived and borne by her as the fruit of her womb until she was delivered and gave birth to ⟨Jesus⟩ the Christ, our King,[4] of Bethlehem in Judaea, brought up in Nazareth, who went to Jerusalem and taught all Judaea: 'The kingdom of heaven is at hand! Forsake the darkness, receive the light, you who live in the darkness of death![5] A light has arisen for you!' And he did great and wonderful works, so that he chose from the tribes twelve men whom he had with him in understanding and faith, as he raised the dead, healed diseases, cleansed lepers, healed the blind,[6] made cripples whole, raised up paralytics, cleansed those possessed by demons . . .

In PB there follow the fragments of 23 further lines, which however can scarcely be restored to make sense. Probably the text of PHeid pp. 79/80 and PM was attached here (see above, p. 326):

(p. 79) . . . wondered ⟨greatly and deliberated⟩ in their hearts. ⟨He said to them⟩: "Why are you amazed ⟨that I raise up⟩ the dead, or that ⟨I make the lame⟩ walk, or that I cleanse ⟨the lepers⟩, or that I raise up the ⟨sick, or that I have⟩ healed the paralytic and those possessed by demons, or that I have divided a little bread and satisfied many, or that I have walked upon the sea, or that I have commanded the winds?[7] If you believe this and ⟨are convinced⟩, then are you great. For truly ⟨I say⟩ to you: If you say to ⟨this mountain⟩, Be thou removed and cast ⟨into the sea⟩, and are not doubtful ⟨in your heart⟩, it will come to pass for you."[8] ⟨. . .⟩ when ⟨one of⟩ them was convinced, whose name was Simon and who said: "Lord, truly great are the

---

[1] Here begins PM, which however contains only 9 lines.
[2] The translation follows PB and Sanders. The sense is not quite clear.
[3] ὅς is related (wrongly) to the prophetic word, as if here the Logos (= Christ) was meant (cf. Schmidt *IIII*, p. 52). On the prophetic word cf. 2 Pet. 1 :19; κυοφορεῖσθαι occurs also in Ign. Eph. 18. 2.
[4] "King" restored after PM, where a β can be read.
[5] Translation after Sanders; cf. Mt. 4:16, Is. 9:2.
[6] Here PH p. 8 ends; the following words are from PB. On the enumeration of the miracles cf. Mt. 4:24; 10:8; 11:5, etc.
[7] The enumeration of the miracles follows the Synoptics.
[8] Cf. Mk. 11:22f. par.

works which thou dost do. For we have never heard, nor have ⟨we ever⟩ seen (p. 80) ⟨a man who⟩ has raised ⟨the dead⟩, except for ⟨thee." The Lord said to him:⟩ "You ⟨will pray for the works⟩ which I myself will ⟨do . . . . .⟩ But the other works ⟨I⟩ will do at once. For these I do ⟨for the sake of?⟩ a temporary deliverance in the time during which they are in these places, that they may believe in him who sent me." Simon said to him: "Lord, command me to speak." He said to him: "Speak, Peter!" For from that day he ⟨called⟩ them by name. He said: ⟨"What then is⟩ the work that is greater than these ⟨. . . . . apart from⟩ raising of the dead and ⟨the feeding⟩ of such a crowd?" The Lord said to him: "There is something that is ⟨greater than this⟩, and blessed are they who have believed with all their heart." But Philip lifted up his voice in wrath, saying: "What manner of thing is this that thou wouldst teach us?" But he said to him: "Thou . . .

On the lacuna between this speech by Paul and the beginning of the Martyrdom, which is probably not very great, cf. above, p. 345.

11

Martyrdom of the Holy Apostle Paul

(Aa 1, pp. 104–117; PH pp. 9–11; PHeid pp. 53–58)

1. There were awaiting Paul at Rome Luke from Gaul and Titus from Dalmatia.[1] When Paul saw them he was glad, so that he hired a barn outside Rome, where with the brethren he taught the word of truth. The news was spread abroad, and many souls were added to the Lord,[2] so that there was a rumour throughout Rome, and a great number of believers came to him from the house of Caesar,[3] and there was great joy.

But a certain Patroclus, Caesar's cup-bearer, came late to the barn and, (p. 106) being unable because of the crowd to go in to Paul, sat at a high window and listened to him teaching the word of God. But since the wicked devil was envious of the love of the brethren, Patroclus fell from the window and died,[4] and the news was quickly brought to Nero. But Paul, perceiving it in the spirit, said: "Brethren, the evil one has gained an opportunity to tempt you. Go out, and you will find a youth fallen from a height and

[1] Cf. 2 Tim. 4:10.   [2] Cf. Acts 2:41.   [3] Cf. Phil. 4:22.   [4] Cf. Acts 20:9ff.

already on the point of death. Lift him up, and bring him here to me!" So they went out and brought him. And when the crowd saw (him), they were troubled. Paul said to them: "Now, brethren, let your faith be manifest. Come, all of you, let us mourn to our Lord Jesus Christ, that this youth may live and we remain unmolested." But as they all lamented the youth drew breath again, and setting him upon a beast they sent him back alive with the others who were of Caesar's house. 2. When Nero heard of Patroclus' death, he was greatly distressed, and when he came out from the bath he commanded that another be appointed for the wine. But his servants told him the news, saying: "Caesar, Patroclus is alive and standing at the (p. 108) table." And when Caesar heard that Patroclus was alive he was afraid, and did not want to go in. But when he had entered he saw Patroclus and, beside himself, cried out: "Patroclus, art thou alive?" And he said: "I am alive, Caesar." But he said: "Who is he who made thee to live?" And the youth, borne by the conviction of faith, said: "Christ Jesus, the king of the ages."[1] But Caesar in perplexity said: "So he is to be king of the ages, and destroy all the kingdoms?" Patroclus said to him: "Yes, all the kingdoms under heaven he destroys, and he alone shall be for ever, and there shall be no kingdom which shall escape him." But he struck him on the face and said: "Patroclus, dost thou also serve in that king's army?" And he said: "Yes, lord Caesar, for indeed he raised me up when I was dead." And Barsabas Justus of the flat feet, and Urion the Cappadocian, and Festus the Galatian, Nero's chief men, (p. 110) said: "We also are in the army[2] of that king of the ages." But he shut them up in prison, after torturing dreadfully men whom he greatly loved, and commanded that the soldiers of the great king be sought out, and he issued a decree to this effect, that all who were found to be Christians and soldiers of Christ[3] should be put to death.

3. And among the many Paul also was brought bound; to him all his fellow-prisoners gave heed, so that Caesar observed that he was the man in command. And he said to him: "Man of the great king, but (now) my prisoner, why did it seem good to thee to come secretly into the empire of the Romans and enlist soldiers

[1] Cf. 1 Tim. 1:17.   [2] Cf. 1 Tim. 1:18; 2 Tim. 2:4.   [3] Cf. 2 Tim. 2:3.

from my province?" But Paul, filled with the Holy Spirit,[1] said before them all: "Caesar, not only from thy province do we enlist soldiers, but from the whole world. For this charge has been laid upon us, that no man be excluded who wishes to serve my king. If thou also think it good, do him service! for neither riches nor the splendour of this present life will save thee, but if thou submit and entreat him, then shalt thou be saved. For in one day he will (p. 112) destroy the world with fire."

When Caesar heard this, he commanded all the prisoners to be burned with fire, but Paul to be beheaded according to the law of the Romans. But Paul did not keep silence concerning the word, but communicated it to the prefect Longus and the centurion Cestus.

In Rome, then, Nero was (raging) at the instigation of the evil one, many Christians being put to death without trial, so that the Romans took their stand at the palace and cried: "It is enough, Caesar! For these men are ours. Thou dost destroy the power of the Romans!" Then he made an end (of the persecution), whereupon none of the Christians was to be touched until he had himself investigated his case. 4. Then Paul was brought before him in accordance with the decree, and he adhered to the decision that he should be beheaded. But Paul said: "Caesar, it is not for a short time that I live for my king. And if thou behead me, this will I do: I will arise and appear to thee (in proof) that I am not dead, but alive to my Lord Christ Jesus,[2] (p. 114) who is coming to judge the world."[3]

But Longus and Cestus said to Paul: "Whence have you this king, that you believe in him without change of heart, even unto death?" Paul communicated the word to them and said: "Ye men who are in this ignorance and error, change your mind and be saved from the fire that is coming upon the whole world. For we do not march, as you suppose, with a king who comes from earth,[4] but one from heaven, the living God, who comes as judge because of the lawless deeds that are done in this world. And blessed is that man who shall believe in him, and live for ever,[5] when he comes to burn the world till it is pure." So they besought

[1] Cf. Acts 4:8. [2] Cf. Rom. 14:8. [3] Cf. Acts 17:31.
[4] Cf. Jn. 18:36. [5] Cf. Jn. 11:25f.

him and said: "We entreat thee, help us and we will let thee go."
But he answered and said: "I am no deserter from Christ, but a
lawful soldier of the living God. Had I known that I was to die,
I would have done it, Longus and Cestus. But since I live to God
and love myself, I go to the Lord that I may come (again) with
him (p. 115) in the glory of his Father." They said to him: "How
then shall we live, when thou art beheaded?" 5. While they were
still saying this, Nero sent a certain Parthenius and Pheretas to
see if Paul had already been beheaded; and they found him still
alive. But he called them to him and said: "Believe in the living
God, who raises up from the dead both me and all who believe in
him!" But they said: "We are going now to Nero; but when thou
dost die and rise again, then will we believe in thy God." But
when Longus and Cestus questioned him further about salvation,
he said to them: "Come quickly here to my grave at dawn, and
you will find two men praying, Titus and Luke. They will give
you the seal in the Lord."

Then Paul stood with his face to the east, and lifting up his
hands to heaven prayed at length; and after communing in
prayer in Hebrew with the fathers he stretched out his neck
without speaking further. But when the executioner struck off
his head, milk spurted upon the soldier's clothing. And when they
saw it, the soldier and all who stood by were amazed, and glorified
God who had given Paul (p. 116) such glory. And they went off
and reported to Caesar what had happened.

6. When he heard it, he marvelled greatly and was at a loss.
Then Paul came about the ninth hour, when many philosophers
and the centurion were standing with Caesar, and he stood before
them all and said: "Caesar, here I am—Paul, God's soldier. I
am not dead, but alive in my God. But for thee, unhappy man,
there shall be many evils and great punishment, because thou
didst unjustly shed the blood of the righteous, and that not many
days hence!"[1] And when he had said this Paul departed from
him. But when Nero heard (it) he was greatly troubled, and
commanded the prisoners to be set free, including Patroclus and
Barsabas and his companions.

7. As Paul directed, Longus and Cestus went at dawn and with

---

[1] Acts 1:5.

fear approached Paul's tomb. But as they drew near they saw two men praying, and Paul between them, so that at the sight of this unexpected wonder they were astounded, while Titus and Luke were seized with human fear when they saw Longus and Cestus coming towards them, and turned to flight. (p. 117) But they followed after them, saying: "We are not pursuing you to kill you, as you imagine, ye blessed men of God, but for life, that you may give it to us as Paul promised us, whom we saw but now standing between you and praying." And when Titus and Luke heard this from them, with great joy they gave them the seal in the Lord, glorifying the God and Father of our Lord Jesus Christ, unto whom be the glory for ever and ever.[1] Amen.

Appendix

THE BEGINNING OF THE STAY IN EPHESUS

(From a Coptic Papyrus not yet published)[2]

(R. Kasser)

When Paul had said this, he departed from Smyrna to go to Ephesus. And he went into the house of Aquila and Priscilla, rejoicing to see the brethren whom he, Paul, loved. They also rejoiced, and prayed that they might be found worthy for Paul to set foot in their house (?). And there was joy and great gladness. And they spent the night watching in prayer, examining[3] ⟨the will of God⟩ to strengthen ⟨their⟩ hearts and praying with one accord in the same form.

The angel of the Lord came into the house of Aquila, and stood before them all. He spoke with Paul, so that all were troubled: for ⟨this angel⟩ who stood there was indeed visible (*lit.* revealed), but the words which he was speaking to Paul they (the bystanders) did not hear. But after he had stopped speaking with

---

[1] Cf. 1 Tim. 1:17, etc.

[2] Cf. *RHPR* 1960, pp. 45ff. The papyrus is in a very poor condition and we can give only extracts. In addition the translation here presented must be considered provisional. The text so far as it is legible, complete and with a more accurate translation, will be supplied in the Editio princeps. (M. Kasser has kindly checked the English translation against the Coptic text, and has included some further revisions; most of these must be considered not as improvements on the German version but as alternative renderings which equally deserve to be taken into consideration.—R.M.W.)

[3] Coptic: ἀνακρίνεσθαι.

Paul in tongues, they fell into fear and confusion, and were silent. But Paul looked at the brethren and said:

"Men (and) brethren, the angel of the Lord has come to me, as you all have seen, and has told me: There is a great tumult coming upon thee at Pentecost . . ."[1]

But Paul could not be sorrowful (?) because of Pentecost, for it was a kind of festival for (?) those who believe in Christ, the catechumens as well as the believers; but there was great joy and abundance of love, with psalms and praises to Christ, to the confirmation of those who heard. Paul said:

"Men (and) brethren, hearken to what befell me when I was in Damascus, at the time when I persecuted the faith in God. The Spirit which fell ⟨upon me⟩ from the Father, he it is who preached to me the Gospel[2] of his Son, that I might live in him. Indeed, there is no life except the life which is in Christ. I entered into a great church[3] with the blessed Judas, the brother of the Lord, who from the beginning gave me the exalted love of faith.

"I comported myself[4] in grace with the blessed prophet, and ⟨applied myself to⟩ the revelation of Christ who was begotten before ⟨all⟩ ages. While they preached him, I was rejoicing in the Lord, nourished by his words. But when I was able, I was found worthy to speak. I spoke with the brethren—Judas it was who urged[5] me—so that I became beloved of those who heard me.

"But when evening came I went out from the *agape* which Lemma the widow and her daughter Ammia were holding (?). I was walking in the night, meaning to go to Jericho in Phoenicia,[6] and we covered great distances.[7] But when morning came, Lemma and Ammia were behind me, they who gave the *agape*, for I (?) was dear ⟨to their hearts (?)⟩, so that they were not far from me (?). There came a great and terrible lion out of the valley of the burying-ground. But we were praying, so that through the prayer Lemma and Ammia did not come upon the beast (?).[8] But when I finished praying, the beast had cast himself at my feet. I was filled with the Spirit (and) looked upon him, (and)

---

[1] This section is scarcely legible. The substance is: "Put thy trust in God and Christ; they will support thee in this trial."
[2] Coptic: εὐαγγελίζειν.   [3] Coptic: ἐκκλησία.   [4] Coptic: πολιτεύεσθαι.
[5] Coptic: προτρέπειν.   [6] Confusion of "Phoenicia" and "palms".
[7] Lit. marches.   [8] An obscure passage: "fell upon"?

said to him: 'Lion, what wilt thou?' But he said: 'I wish to be baptized.'

"I glorified God, who had given speech to the beast and salvation to his servant. Now there was a great river in that place, (and) I went down into it . . .[1] ⟨Then⟩, men (and) brethren, I cried out, saying: 'Thou who dost dwell in the heights, who didst look upon the humble, who didst give rest to the afflicted, who with Daniel didst shut the mouths of the lions, who didst send to me (?) our Lord Jesus Christ, grant . . . befall the beast, and accomplish thy plan[2] which thou hast ⟨appointed⟩ for me.' When I had prayed thus, I took ⟨the lion⟩ by his mane (and) in the name of Jesus Christ immersed him three times. But when he came up out of the water he shook out his mane and said to me: 'Grace be with thee!' And I said to him: 'And likewise with thee.'

"The lion ran off to the country rejoicing (for this was revealed to me in my heart). A lioness met him, and he did not yield himself to her but . . . ran off . . .

"You also, Aquila and Priscilla, who have believed in the living God and heard . . . preach . . ."

But as Paul said this a great crowd was added to the faith, so that there was jealousy among the rulers[3] and ⟨all the house⟩ of Ammia turned against Paul, that he might die. For there was a woman in the city who did many ⟨good⟩ works for the Ephesians. Her name was Procla. He baptized her with all her household. And there was a fame of the grace and much blessing between . . . and Pentecost. The crown of Christ was multiplied, so that there was brightness(?), with a great report in the city that "This man destroys the gods, saying: Ye shall see them all burned with fire!"

But when Paul went out the people belonging to the city (?) seized him outside the prytaneum (?), brought him to the theatre, and called upon the governor[4] to come. But when he came he questioned Paul, saying: "Why dost thou say these things, teaching what the kings condemn? And the world . . .[5]

[1] Text damaged. The author here apparently described the supernatural accompaniments of this baptism, e.g. tongues (of fire?) strike terror into the demons, etc.
[2] Coptic: οἰκονομία. [3] Coptic: ἄρχων. [4] Coptic: ἡγεμών.
[5] Passage corrupt; the governor seems to tax the apostle with his teaching, which is incompatible with the ideas of a law-abiding Roman.

they have destroyed the ⟨gods⟩ of the Romans and of the ⟨people here⟩. Repeat[1] ⟨now⟩ what thou hast said, when thou didst persuade the crowd!"

But Paul said: "Proconsul, do what thou wilt. . . ." etc.[2]

4. ACTS OF ANDREW

(M. Hornschuh)

INTRODUCTION: I. LITERATURE. M. Blumenthal, *Formen und Motive in den apokryphen Apostelgeschichten*, *TU* 48. 1, 1933, pp. 38–57; F. Dvornik, *The Idea of Apostolicity in Byzantium and the Legend of the Apostle Andrew* (Dumbarton Oaks Studies IV), Cambridge, Mass., 1958; J. Flamion, *Les actes d'André et les textes apparantés, Recueil de travaux d'histoire et de philologie*, 33, Louvain, 1911; *Apokr.* 2, pp. 249–256; E. Hennecke, 'Zur christlichen Apokryphenliteratur', *ZKG* 45, 1926, pp. 309–315; R. A. Lipsius, *Die apokryphen Apostelgeschichten und Apostellegenden*, Vol. I, 1883; P. M. Peterson, *Andrew, Brother of Simon Peter, His History and His Legends* (Supplements to *Novum Testamentum*, I), Leiden, 1958; B. Pick, *The Apocryphal Acts of Paul, Peter, John, Andrew and Thomas*, Chicago, 1909; G. Quispel, 'An Unknown Fragment of the Acts of Andrew (Pap. Copt. Utrecht 1)', *Vig. Chr.* 10, 1956, pp. 129–148.

2. TRANSMISSION AND ATTESTATION. A. In comparison with the other major Acts least has been preserved of *AA*. There is indeed a long series of texts which relate the fate of the Apostle and certainly imply the lost Acts. These texts, deriving largely from Byzantine times, mostly present the material in a very much altered form; the result is that the theological peculiarity of the original *AA* can scarcely be recognized because they have been revised in the spirit of later ecclesiastical theology. The following texts should be mentioned: 1. the *Martyrium Andreae prius* (Cod. Vatic. graec. 807)[3] which is of great value for the reconstruction of the martyrdom; 2. the *Martyrium Andreae alterum*,[4] which exists in two versions in places diverging very much from one another (Codd. Paris. graec. 770 and Paris. graec. 1539); 3. *Martyrium sancti Apostoli Andreae*,[5] generally cited as 'Narratio'; 4. the *Vita Andreae* of Epiphanius Monachus;[6] 5. the *Acta Andreae Apostoli cum Laudatione contexta*,[7] generally cited as 'Laudatio'. Of particular value are 6. the *Cod. Vatic. graec.* 808,[8] which reproduces accurately a genuine part of the original Acts;[9] and 7. the fragment *Pap.*

[1] Lit.: "Say".
[2] The sequel is supplied by the Greek text of the Hamburg Papyrus; cf. also *RHPR* 1960, pp. 55ff.
[3] Bonnet, *Aa* II. 1, pp. 46–57.   [4] Bonnet, pp. 58–64.
[5] Ed. Bonnet, *Anal. Boll.* 13, 1894, pp. 353–372.
[6] Migne *PG* 120, cols. 218–260.
[7] Ed. Bonnet, *Anal. Boll.* 13, 1894, pp. 311–352.
[8] Bonnet, *Aa* II. 1, pp. 38–45.   [9] Cf. *Handb.*, pp. 551ff.

Copt. Utrecht 1, which similarly contains a part of the text of the original account though in Coptic translation.[1] In addition there are some Western texts, viz., 8. the Latin *Passio sancti Andreae Apostoli*,[2] in the form of a letter of the priests and deacons of Achaea; in addition to the Latin account it is transmitted also in two Greek versions,[3] of which the first is a word-for-word translation of the Latin while the second (designated by Flamion as *Épître grecque*) exhibits interpolations from the original text of the *AA*; 9. a further *Passio sancti Andreae Apostoli*,[4] usually cited according to its introductory words as '*Conversante et docente*'; and finally, 10. the *Liber de Miracuiis Beati Andreae Apostoli* of Gregory of Tours.[5] In addition 11. some fragments in Latin from the *AA* have been transmitted by Evodius of Uzala.[6]

J. Flamion has produced a careful investigation of all the Greek and Latin Andrew-martyrologies, attempting with great trouble to distinguish the original from the secondary in the various sources. If much remains hypothesis, yet the attempt as a whole deserves approval. In any case he has provided the assumptions on which the text can be reconstructed. The text offered by James (pp. 358–363) rests, like our text (*infra* pp. 416–423), on the work of Flamion and is a mosaic composed out of elements from *Martyrium* I and II, *Laudatio*, *Narratio*, *Conversante et docente* and *Épître grecque*.

B. Eusebius of Caesarea is the first to mention the *AA* by name (*HE* III. 25. 6).[7] He classes the 'Acts (πράξεις) of Andrew and John and the other apostles' among 'the writings which are put forward by heretics'. The next source from the 4th century which shows knowledge of the *AA* is the *Manichaean Psalm-book*[8] which mentions by name not only Andrew but also the women Maximilla and Iphidamia known to us from the *AA*.[9]

In the further course of the 4th century we find the *AA* mentioned

---

[1] The text in an English translation with comments has been published for the first time by G. Quispel in *Vig. Chr.* 10, 1956, pp. 129ff. The Coptic text has not yet been published.   [2] Bonnet, pp. 1–37.   [3] Bonnet, *ibid.*, under the Latin text.

[4] Ed. Bonnet, *Anal. Boll.*, 13, 1894, pp. 374-378.

[5] Ed. Bonnet in *Monumenta Germaniae Historica. Scriptorum Rerum Merovingicarum*, Vol. I, part II, 1885.

[6] *De fide contra Manichaeos* c. 38, CSEL 25. 2 (Zycha), pp. 968. 24–31, and 968. 31–969. 6.

[7] The statement of Eusebius (*HE* III. 1) according to which Andrew obtained Scythia by lot as his missionary sphere cannot rest on knowledge of the *AA* because the latter does not report anything about the work of the Apostle in Scythia.

[8] C. R. C. Allberry, *A Manichaean Psalm-book*, Manichaean Manuscripts in the Chester Beatty Collection 2, Stuttgart, 1938. The origin of this collection is dated by Allberry around 340.

[9] There can be no certainty that the *Manichaean Psalm-book* knew the *AA* in its original form. The few references and allusions to the history of Andrew diverge considerably from the course of the story as we know it from the sources mentioned above. Thus p. 142. 20f. says (Allberry's translation): 'Andrew the Apostle,—they set fire to the house beneath him. He and his disciples (μαθητής)—all hail to them,

by Philastrius of Brescia who came upon them in the possession of the Manichaeans: 'Nam Manichei apocrypha beati Andreae apostoli, id est Actus quos fecit veniens de Ponto in Graeciam quos conscripserunt tunc discipuli sequentes beatum apostolum, unde et habent Manichei et alii tales Andreae beati . . . Actus . . .'[1]

Epiphanius knew that the Encratites,[2] the Apotactites (61. 1; p. 381 Holl) and the so-called Origenists of the First Order (63. 2; p. 399 Holl) possessed the *AA*.

For later testimonies and references to the *AA* see Dvornik, pp. 188ff. and P. M. Peterson, pp. 9ff.[3]

3. CHARACTER. To determine the religious-historical nature of the *AA* we have to proceed from the fragments *Cod. Vat.* 808 and *Pap. Copt. Utrecht* 1. This is not to dispute the claim for a cautious widening of the base by the inclusion of those elements out of the *Laudatio, Narratio, Martyrium* I, II, etc., in which we recognize genuine parts of the original *AA*. In opposition to R. A. Lipsius (I, pp. 594ff.) who attributed a Gnostic character to the *AA*, J. Flamion (pp. 145ff.) viewed the author as an orthodox Christian, whose thinking however had been strongly influenced by Neopythagorean and Neoplatonic ideas. E. Hennecke (*Apokr.* 2, p. 250) rightly objected that the contacts which were indicated were not sufficient to make a Neoplatonic influence probable. More recently G. Quispel (pp. 142ff.) has again attempted to demonstrate over against Flamion a Gnostic imprint on the text. As becomes clear from the *Coptic Papyrus*, the *Vatican Fragment* (p. 44. 14) and the *Laudatio* (p. 384. 7–14), the author taught a Gnostic anthropology. He espoused a *praedestinatio physica*, such as was characteristic of the Gnosis of the 2nd century; for he distinguishes between the φύσει συγγενεῖς τοῦ οὐρανοῦ and the φύσει συγγενεῖς τοῦ σώματος. Quispel himself nevertheless concedes that an author belonging to the Church in the 2nd century could have gone as far in the acceptance of foreign thought as the author of our Acts has done without thereby stepping beyond the bounds of what was still possible within the catholic Church. In view of the absence of more important and more characteristic

they were crucified (σταυροῦν)'. While Gregory of Tours testifies (see below) to the episode about incendiarism, and so it must have been related in the *AA*, none of our sources knows anything of the disciples of Andrew as sharing his fate. According to the *Manichaean Psalm-book* the women also appear to have been sacrifices to the justice of Aegeates; cf. p. 143. 13f., 'Maximilla and Aristobula—on them was great torture inflicted. What need (χρειά) for them to suffer these things? It is purity for which they fight.' Cf. p. 192. 26f., where the text is indeed not quite certain: 'A shamer of the serpent is Maximilla the faithful (πιστός). A receiver of good news is Iphidama, her sister also, imprisoned (?) in the prisons.'

[1] *Diversarum hereseon liber* 61, *CSEL* 38 (Marx) 1898, p. 48.
[2] *Pan. haer.* 47.1.5 (*GCS* 31, ed. K. Holl, 1922, p. 216).
[3] On the question of the Manichaean corpus of the Acts, cf. *supra* pp. 178ff.

traits of Gnosticism, e.g. cosmic dualism, and an interest in the Pleroma with its Aeons, the thesis of the Gnostic character of the *AA* can only be defended with qualifications. More exactly examined, it turns out in the long run that even the Gnostic imprint on the anthropology is highly questionable. For there can be no question of a *praedestinatio physica*. To be sure the operation of the Apostle's words has its ground in the true φύσις or διανοητικὸν μέρος (Bonnet, p. 42. 13) of the hearer: in the acceptance of the proclamation of salvation man realizes his proper being, i.e. his true spiritual nature. Yet parallels can be cited to this conception from contemporary Hellenistic philosophy as well as from Gnosticism. There is no mention of the so-called Hyliki[1] who are incapable of accepting knowledge because of their nature. The Christians indeed do form a special γένος[2] in comparison with those who reject, or have not yet heard, the proclamation. But this distinction is not based on a dualism of natures. Correspondingly the frequent usage of the concepts συγγενής and ἀλλότριος should not be explained gnostically. The Christians are συγγενεῖς τοῦ ἀγεννήτου (Bonnet, p. 40. 32) because they now show themselves as belonging to God by their conversion and by their conduct with which God is pleased: Aegeates on the other hand is a συγγενὴς τοῦ σώματος (Bonnet, p. 41. 18), because he has not given up the desires of the flesh. Whoever persists in godlessness is considered a 'kinsman of (akin to) the serpent' (Bonnet, p. 42. 27) because he confesses to it by his actual behaviour. Everything which is foreign and hostile to God, and to true human nature akin to God, is considered as ἀλλότριον.[3] The chief theme of *AA* is the turning away from the world whose characteristics are transitoriness and illusion,[4] multiplicity[5] and movement,[6] and the realization of

---

[1] Cf. Quispel (p. 143) who for comparison quotes the Gnostic 'Treatise on the Three Natures'.

[2] P. 38. 5 (Bonnet). The Stoics also divided men into two groups; cf. Zeno (in Arnim, *Stoic. vet fragm.* I, p. 216): δύο γένη. . ., τὸ μὲν τῶν σπουδαίων, τὸ δὲ τῶν φαύλων. Thus the conception is not confined to Gnosticism.

[3] Pp. 41. 25; 42. 23; 43. 25; 45. 2, 17, 22 (Bonnet). The idea originated in philosophy. It denoted among the Stoics everything which is opposed to and not in accordance with the Logos, i.e. everything inimical and foreign to which man can be exposed.

[4] It is said of men that they ἐν κακοῖς τοῖς προσκαίροις διάγουσι, τερπόμενοι τοῖς ἐπιβλάβεσιν αὐτῶν φαντασίαις (p. 44. 7f.). It is also the conviction of the Stoics that evil is rooted in false ideas; e.g. Diog. Laert. (*Stoic. vet. frag.* II. 130 Arnim): ὥστε εἰς ἀκοσμίαν καὶ εἰκαιότητα τρέπεσθαι τοὺς ἀγυμνάστους ἔχοντας τὰς φαντασίας.

[5] P. 38. 16: τὰ πολλὰ ἀπεστράμμεθα. The Christians are τοῦ ἑνός. The pair of concepts τὰ πολλά—τὸ ἕν comes from philosophical language. Since the time of Parmenides the multiplicity and diversity of the material world were opposed to the unity and uniqueness of true being.

[6] The converted are now able to confess: οὐκ ἐσμὲν κινήσεως τέχνη (p. 38. 8f.) The world on its part presents the picture of a continual becoming and passing away. According also to the current philosophical view of the world it was subject to change and movement. The nature of true being on the contrary is permanence.

true being in the return to the One, i.e. to God. These conceptions correspond exactly to the aim of Platonism of the middle
period, to which of all the philosophical movements of the time
the author is nearest. The encratite tendency of the *AA* should
also be understood from the assumptions of this philosophy.
Philosophy, according to the definition of the Platonist Albinus,
is λύσις καὶ περιαγωγὴ ψυχῆς ἀπὸ σώματος (*didasc*. 1, ed. Hermann, Plat. *dial*. VI, p. 152). From the Platonic school of
philosophy we also receive light on the peculiar speculations
about the cross (Mart. I. 14). The idea of the cross as the symbol
of the logos goes back ultimately to the Platonic idea of the *chi* of
the world-soul;[1] cf. Plato (Tim. VIII, p. 36b): ταύτην οὖν τὴν
ξύστασιν πᾶσαν διπλῆν κατὰ μῆκος σχίσας (sc. the Demiurge) μέσην
πρὸς μέσην ἑκατέραν ἀλλήλαις οἷον χῖ προσβαλὼν κατέκαμψεν. To
the cross, symbolizing in the *AA* the 'heavenly Logos' (*Laud*.
p. 346. 19), the function is attributed to a principle giving an all-
embracing unity to the whole cosmos. It extends through the
whole cosmos to 'establish the unstable' (p. 54. 23f., Bonnet); it
'gathers the world into one' (p. 55. 2) and 'it binds the cosmos in its
circumference' (p. 55. 7f.). These are ideas which originated in the
Stoic teaching of the Logos but which, we may assume, were known
to the author through the medium of the Platonists who carried
over the characteristics of the Stoic logos to the world-soul. Cf. the
explanations of Albinus, *didasc*. 14 (Hermann, p. 170):
τῆς δὲ ψυχῆς ταθείσης ἐκ τοῦ μέσου ἐπὶ τὰ πέρατα, συνέβη αὐτὴν
τὸ σῶμα τοῦ κόσμου κύκλῳ διὰ παντὸς περιέχειν καὶ περικαλύψαι,
ὥστε ὅλῳ τῷ κόσμῳ αὐτὴν παρεκτείναι καὶ τούτῳ τῷ τρόπῳ αὐτὸν
συνδεῖν τε καὶ συνέχειν.

According to Euseb., *praep. ev*. XV. 12. 3 (Mras, *GCS* 43. 2,
p. 375. 18) Atticus expresses himself similarly about the world-
soul: It is διήκουσα διὰ τοῦ παντὸς καὶ πάντα συνδοῦσα καὶ
συνέχουσα. The union of Platonic and Stoic thought, which
appears here and is characteristic of Platonism of the middle
period, is also distinctive of the *AA*.

That we do not need to understand the dualism of the *AA*
gnostically follows with reasonable certainty from the quotation
in Augustine, *De Actis cum Felice manichaeo* II. 6 (*CSEL* 25. 2
Zycha, p. 833. 13–17):[2] *Etenim speciosa figmenta et ostentatio simulata
et coactio visibilium nec quidem ex propria natura procedunt, sed ex eo
homine, qui per se ipsum deterior effectus est, per seductionem*.[3]

[1] Cf. W. Bousset, 'Platons Weltseele und das Kreuz Christi', *ZNW* 14, 1913, p. 280f.
[2] The fragment, which Augustine found '*in actibus scriptis a Leucio*' and which
Evodius also cites with unimportant variations (*De Fide contra Manichaeos*, c. 5), should
probably be attributed to the *AA*.
[3] Similarly Tatian, who has been long misunderstood as a Gnostic; cf. *Oratio ad
Graec*. 11. 6 (ed. Schwartz, *TU* 4. 1, p. 12. 15f.): οὐδὲν φαῦλον ὑπὸ τοῦ θεοῦ πεποίηται,
τὴν πονηρίαν ἡμεῖς ἀνεδείξαμεν.

E. Peterson has drawn attention to close contacts with the theology of Tatian.[1] These appear in the phrase τὸ τοῦ λόγου φῶς ἐδείχθη,[2] and also in the epiphany of Christ as *puerulus speciosus*.[3] The theme of the Christ becoming manifest as child or youth and as brightness,[4] which the *AA* shares with the Acts of Paul and the Acts of Thomas, is explained, as E. Peterson has shown (*op. cit.*, passim), by a comparison with the related thought of Tatian. When Jesus appears as child, he appears as the Adam who lived in perfect innocence and purity before the fall in Paradise.[5] Redemption consequently consists in the restoration of the state proper to Paradise lost in the Fall. In the *Oratio ad Graecos*[6] Tatian is concerned with the same theme, i.e. the restoration of the pre-fall state. For Tatian[7] as for the *AA* the Fall is an event which follows the Creation and has no cosmological significance. For both, salvation takes place in self-knowledge,[8] in renunciation of the material[9] and in a struggle against the demonic.[10] Both represent a rigorous encratism which is not derived from Gnostic assumptions.[11]

The religious and theological character of the *AA*, despite certain contacts with Gnostic forms of expression, has been decisively formed by the ideas of Hellenistic philosophy and not by Gnosticism.[12] The contacts with Tatian's theology are especially close.

[1] *Frühkirche, Judentum und Gnosis*, 1959, pp. 202ff. (in the article 'Bemerkungen zum Hamburger Papyrus-Fragment der Acta Pauli', pp. 183ff.). Peterson's observation relates to the five major Acts together but is of interest to us in this connection only in reference to the *AA*.

[2] P. 45. 15 (Bonnet); cf. E. Peterson, *op. cit.*, p. 206 n. 86. According to Tatian (*Or. ad Graec.* 13. 3 (Schwartz, p. 14. 20)) the λόγος works in the darkness of the soul as τὸ τοῦ θεοῦ φῶς.

[3] According to Evodius, *De Fide* 38 (Zycha, p. 969. 1).

[4] *Speciosus* can have the meaning 'shining'. Corresponding to the *puerulus speciosus* of the *AA* is the νεανίσκος . . . φαίνων of the Acts of Paul according to the Hamburg Fragment (C. Schmidt, Πράξεις Παύλου, *Acta Pauli. Nach dem Papyrus der Hamburger Staats- und Universitätsbibliothek*, 1936, p. 34. 28). On Jesus as 'Brightness' cf. E. Peterson, *op. cit.*, pp. 193ff.

[5] Cf. E. Peterson, pp. 195f.

[6] Cf. M. Elze, *Die Theologie Tatians*, 1960 (Forschungen zur Kirchen- und Dogmengesch. 9), p. 85.

[7] Cf. Elze, p. 85.

[8] For the *AA* cf. p. 42. 3; 44. 15f. (Bonnet); on Tatian cf. Elze, p. 96.

[9] For the *AA* cf. p. 43. 30f. (Bonnet); on Tatian, cf. Elze, *ibid.*

[10] In the *AA* the power of the demonic, against which the believers have to wage an unceasing struggle, is concentrated in the figure of the devil; on this point cf. Flamion, pp. 150ff.; on Tatian, cf. Elze, *ibid.*

[11] The investigation of Elze, to which reference has been made above, has proved that the theology of Tatian in its basic conceptions is founded on the application of Platonic ideas of the middle period to Christianity.

[12] Cf. Flamion, p. 157: "What appears clearly evident is the profound influence which it (sc. the teaching of *AA*) has undergone from the philosophy which was dominant at the beginning of the empire."

4. TIME AND PLACE OF ORIGIN. No agreement on the question of date has yet been achieved. On the basis of the alleged contacts which he has pointed out with Neoplatonism, J. Flamion (p. 268) regards the *AA* as originating in the second half of the 3rd century. While James (p. 337) and Dvornik[1] agree with this thesis, Quispel correctly dates the book before A.D. 200.[2] Erik Peterson assumes a common encratite milieu for the Acts of Andrew, John and Thomas[3] and believes that they 'came into being in the period when the sect of the Encratites sprang up or was known, viz., under Hadrian 117–138'.[4] In any case the mutual agreement in religious symbolism, the in part very far-reaching similarity of ideas and of linguistic expression and certain obvious analogies of circumstances and situations[5] enforce the conclusion that there are close links with the other Acts and render it impractical to separate the *AA* very far from them in regard to date. To fix it in the time of Hadrian would be at present too hazardous. The approximate *terminus a quo* of the writing should rather be set in this period. As *terminus ad quem* we can presumably take the date of origin of the Acts of Paul—assuming that the close contacts between the *AA* and the Acts of Paul indicated by Quispel (pp. 145ff.) are to be explained as a dependence of the latter on the former. That the author of the Acts of Paul used older Apostolic histories has been demonstrated in the case of the Acts of Peter by C. Schmidt,[6] and at least shown as very probable in the case of the Acts of Thomas by E. Peterson (*op. cit.*, pp. 199f.). Thus we may undoubtedly trace back with confidence the connection between the *AA* and the Acts of Paul to the use of the former by the author of the latter. The composition of the Acts of Paul is dated by C. Schmidt (*op. cit.*, p. 107) to 190–200. This period consequently forms the *terminus ad quem*—admittedly inexact—for the composition of our Acts, which must accordingly have arisen in the interval between *c.* 120 and *c.* 200. It is however certainly advisable not to set the composition too early in this period, particularly because we are hardly justified

[1] P. 193. In favour of this dating Dvornik (pp. 212ff.) asserts that according to the information of the Monarchian prologue to the Gospel of Luke Achaea was the missionary sphere of Luke. This report is confirmed by Jerome (Migne, *PL* 26, col. 18). In the oldest tradition relative to Achaea there is no mention of Andrew. According to Dvornik this fact proves that the *AA*, which brought about the rise of the later tradition about Andrew's activity in Achaea, could have appeared only after Origen, who did not know this tradition, and indeed towards the end of the 3rd century. The proof is scarcely satisfactory.   [2] P. 142.

[3] Epiphanius, *Pan. haer.* 47. 1. 5 (Holl II, *GCS* 31, p. 216) informs us that these three Acts were in use among the Encratites.

[4] *Op. cit.*, p. 211 (in the article 'Beobachtungen zu den Anfängen der christlichen Askese', pp. 209–220).

[5] Cf. the article of E. Peterson mentioned above, 'Bemerkungen zum Hamburger Papyrus-Fragment der Acta Pauli', pp. 183ff.

[6] C. Schmidt, Πράξεις Παύλου, *Acta Pauli*, pp. 127–130.

in pushing the *AA* back by several decades from the Acts of Peter, dated by C. Schmidt (*op. cit.*, p. 130) around 180–190. The close material and stylistic relationship between the *AA* and the Acts of Peter demands rather a date for the origin of the *AA* in the second half of the century, but not after 190.

According to Flamion (pp. 266f.) the place of writing was Achaea. In favour of that is the almost exclusive use of Greek names by the author. Yet we do not therefore need to conclude that Greece was the place of origin. It does not seem to be at present possible to say where the author lived and worked.[1]

5. CONTENT AND COMPASS. The *AA*, which in their original version were certainly the most voluminous of the major acts, consist of two chief parts: the account of a journey[2] and the martyrdom.[3] Since Flamion (pp. 310ff.) it has been undisputed that the "Acts of Andrew and Matthias" as well as the "Acts of Peter and Andrew" do not belong to the *AA* but are of later date. In the restoration of the thread of the narrative Flamion ascribed most value to the *Liber de Miraculis Beati Andreae Apostoli* of Gregory of Tours. As Gregory informs us in his introduction, he used as source a book, *De virtutibus S. Andreae*, which many considered aprocryphal because of its prolixity.[4] Gregory's own book is an epitome which he constructed by the elimination of all heretical elements and by restricting himself to a selection of miracles.[5] In ch. 3 Gregory tells about a journey of the Apostle from Pontus to Achaea. This journey gave the Apostle an opportunity to perform many miracles. It led through the cities of Amasea, Sinope, Nicaea and Nicomedia, over to Byzantium, across Thracia to Perinthus (on the coast of Thracia), on to Macedonia

---

[1] Nothing also can be said as to the person of the author. On the question of Leucius, cf. Schäferdiek, *supra*, pp. 182ff. Innocent I (402–417) in a letter to the bishop of Toulouse mentions the Acts drawn up 'sub nomine Andreae . . . quae a Xenocharide et Leonida philosophis . . .' (in H. Wurm, *Apollinaris* 12, 1939, p. 77). The statement is valueless, cf. R. A. Lipsius, 2. 2, p. 430; *Handb.* p. 546; Flamion, p. 163 n. 1; Dvornik, p. 188 n. 24. Dvornik considers it possible that the names refer to two people mentioned in the original form of the Acts who had been heathen converted by Andrew and were later regarded in certain circles as the authors of the Acts.

[2] The attempt of Blumenthal, pp. 46f., to assign to the *AA* notices in relation to the time of Jesus in the *Narratio* and the *Laudatio* founders on Gregory, whose source began with the departure from Pontus to Greece.

[3] Gregory (ch. 36f.) only hints at the action of the martyrdom. He refers in addition to a Passion which must have circulated in Gaul in his time and is undoubtedly identical with the *Martyrium Conversante et docente* (Flamion, pp. 44, 53f.; James, p. 349; Dvornik, pp. 192f.). Cf. ch. 36, p. 845: ". . . quc*s* lectio passionis eius plenissime declarat"; ch. 37, p. 846: "Passionis quoque eius ita ordinem prosecuti non sumus, quia valde utiliter et eleganter a quodam repperimus fuisse conscriptum." Gregory was able to confine himself to the account of the journey because in this text a Latin report of the Passion was already in circulation (cf. Dvornik, pp. 192f.).

[4] "quia propter nimiam verbositatem a nonnullis apocrifus dicebatur" (p. 827).

[5] "retractis (retractatis?) enucleatisque tantum virtutibus, praetermissis his quae fastidium generabant" (*ibid.*).

397

(Philippi and Thessalonica) and finally to Patrae in Achaea, which was the journey's goal. There is no reason to doubt that it actually was the ancient *AA*, whether revised or in their original form, which served the Gallic bishop as source; for Philastrius (see above) corroborates that the miracles which Andrew performed on the journey from Pontus to Greece constituted the content of the *AA*.

In the first instance we obtain from the epitome of Gregory of Tours nothing more than a framework. If we were to claim that in this form it was a component of the original *AA* we should give a false picture. Certainly "nothing much is learned from the meagre accounts of miracles by the Gallic bishop of the characteristic tenor of the original Acts as we know them from the *Cod. Vatic.* 808".[1] The encratite views of the *AA* known to us from that text as well as from *Pap. Copt. Utrecht* 1 are not only contradicted in Gregory but perverted into their opposites when it is said that the apostle did not forbid marriage and that on the contrary the marriage state is a divine institution.[2] From that we see that Gregory subjected the material to a considerable transformation.[3] We can attribute only the external frame to the *AA* with any certainty; further material on the other hand can only be assigned in so far as it can be verified through parallels in eastern texts to be part of the content of the *AA*, or established as genuine by new discoveries. A comparison of the fragment *Pap. Copt. Utrecht* 1 with the parallel episode in Gregory of Tours (ch. 18) warns us to be cautious with Gregory, for it shows only how much the content and trend of the *AA* was varied by Gregory.[4] That leads to the foregone conclusion that we must not attempt a reproduction of the full text of the Epitome.

The arson episode, which Gregory recounts in ch. 12, at least in its nucleus, appears to have been a component part of the original Acts. The *Manichaean Psalm-book* also refers to this incident (p. 142. 20).

> Andrew the Apostle,—they set fire to the
> house beneath him.

The story as reported by Gregory ran as follows: Andrew is staying in Philippi and a young man called Exuos from Thessalonica comes to him. This young man, of a noble and rich family, who has come unknown to his parents, asks the Apostle for instruction in Christianity. He is taught by A. and converted and

---

[1] E. Hennecke, *ThLZ* 38, 1913, col. 74.
[2] "Non nos nuptias aut avertimus aut vitamus, cum ab initio Deus masculum iungi praecipisset et feminam, sed potius incesta damnamus" (ch. 11, p. 832).
[3] Cf. Quispel, pp. 137–141, 148.   [4] Cf. Quispel, *loc. cit.*

remains with him, concerned no more about worldly wealth. His parents follow him and vainly try to induce him to leave A. His own endeavours and those of the Apostle likewise fail to win the parents to Christianity. The latter gather a band and set on fire the house in which are the Apostle and Exuos.[1] Calling on the name of Jesus Christ Exuos extinguishes the fire with water from a flask. It is impossible to decide whether the story stood in the *AA* with all the details as Gregory relates them.—The episode of the exorcism in Nicaea (ch. 6, p. 830) can be certainly ascribed to the *AA*, although in this case again we are not in a position to reconstruct the report in accordance with its text. We learn that the story in some form was a part of the *AA* because it is mentioned also by two of the eastern texts, the *Narratio* (ch. 4; p. 356) and *Laudatio* (ch. 18; p. 325f.). It is told by the three sources in very divergent forms. *Gregory:* seven demons who live among tombs close beside a road throw stones at passers-by and have already killed many. The whole population comes out to meet the approaching Apostle waving olive branches and crying "Our salvation is in thy hand, O man of God" (Encounter and Acclamation). To the inhabitants who have told him about the situation A. replies along the lines of later ecclesiastical thought, that faith "in the Lord Jesus Christ, the son of Almighty God, who with the Holy Spirit is one God" is necessary for deliverance. A. commands the demons to appear before the whole population, who are ready to accept the faith. After a public confession of Christ by the crowd A. expels the demons who have appeared in the form of dogs; they retreat to barren and lonely areas. The inhabitants are baptized and receive a bishop.—*Laudatio:* A large crowd of demons live on a rock on which there is an image of Artemis. The spirits, who desire sacrifices, make the road leading past impassable at certain times of the day and at night. Although no one dares to come any more to the place A. by his mere presence drives away the spirits. They fly away in the form of ravens, crying, "O power from Thee, Jesus, Galilean, Nazarene, for thy disciples persecute us everywhere". A. purifies the place by overturning the statue and erecting a cross in its place.— *Narratio:* The east gate of the city is in the possession of evil spirits. Informed of it, A. goes and drives away the demons "by calling on Christ, our god". So A. purifies the place and makes the gate again passable.—We can confidently ascribe to the *AA* only what all three sources have in common: A. has made

---

[1] According to Gregory A. was on the third storey, cf. p. 832. 39: "apostolus descendit de tristicio"; cf. p. 832. 9. This remark, which may well have been taken from the *AA*, renders intelligible the statement of the Manichaean Psalmist that the house was set on fire "below him" (*haraf*).

usable by an act of exorcism a place[1] in Nicaea rendered impassable through demons. Probably before the action he talked with
the inhabitants (ch. 21f.; p. 838). Probably the Acts also related
a dialogue between Andrew and the demons. If that was so then
Gregory and *Laudatio* have preserved its memory, though we are
not in a position to detect word for word the elements of this
conversation.

By a comparison of Gregory and *Laudatio* we can reconstruct
in broad outline the events in Patrae, which precede the incidents
described in *Vatic.* 808. The two sources vary considerably from
one another in details and we are unable to decide with certainty
which lies nearer the original writing. Gregory (ch. 21f.; p. 838)
and *Laudatio* (ch. 33f.; p. 335) agree in their account of the first
events in the city: Lesbius the proconsul behaves at the beginning
in a hostile way towards A., is punished by a supernatural power,
summons A. and is converted. After that A. preaches in the city
with great success.

Gregory: Arriving, A. goes first to an inn. Before his arrival
Lesbius had already heard of his activity and in his hatred made
an abortive attempt to lay hold of A's person while he was in
Macedonia. The proconsul does not give up his hostile attitude
and at night two "Ethiopians" (demons) appear to him, intending
to give the proconsul a scourging to demonstrate their power for
the last time before being driven away. Bidden in a vision,
Lesbius has the Apostle summoned to him. The latter finds the
proconsul in a very sick condition and heals him. After that A.
preaches with great success in the city.—*Laudatio:* Immediately
after his arrival A. heals two sick people. The news spreads in the
city; however Lesbius, who was a victim of the ἑλληνικὴ πλάνη,
believes the Apostle is a magician and wishes to seize him and kill
him. In the night an angel appears who refutes and punishes
him. He passes several hours in a helpless condition, but comes
to himself, has A. summoned, is converted and is healed by
prayer. Further healings follow and the whole city accepts
Christianity. The succeeding account tells of the supersession of
Lesbius by Aegeates. A new situation arises through this change,
which must have happened during a temporary absence of the
Apostle from Patrae. After his return A. soon encounters the new
proconsul. Maximilla, the sick wife of Aegeates, as both sources

[1] Blumenthal, p. 45, is correct in saying that the image of Artemis should be set
to the account of the writer of the *Laudatio*, "not only because later times liked to
associate demons and idols, but because they had a particular interest in the destruction of images." On the contrary, Blumenthal says, the rock will be original because
the author of the *Laudatio* could have had no interest in it. We could ask with equal
correctness what interest Gregory could have had in tombs or the author of the
Narratio in city gates.

agree in reporting, begs the Apostle through Iphidamia[1] to come
to her. Both sources again report that Aegeates stands with drawn
sword alongside his wife, intending to take his own life in the
event of her death. In the words which A. speaks to the proconsul
the two witnesses have in common only the command, "Put thy
sword in its place". A. heals Maximilla[2] but refuses the reward
offered by Aegeates.[3]

The following incident (Gregory, ch. 31, p. 844; *Laud.* ch. 40,
p. 339) is linked by both witnesses to the preceding by corresponding phrases.[4] After A. has left the house of Aegeates he sees a
paralysed man lying in the mud. He heals him with words of
miraculous power.[5] Both witnesses report that the healed man
"at once" rose and praised God.

A further miracle is added here by both witnesses (Gregory,
ch. 32, p. 844; *Laud.* ch. 40, p. 339). It took place, as both
emphasize, in another place. There A. meets a blind man. With
him are his wife and son who are likewise blind. The two reports
about the procedure of healing differ.[6] They agree in testifying
that the healed man kissed the feet of the Apostle. It is probable
also that the *AA* reported the healed man's words of thanks or
confession.[7]

The following story of healing also is narrated in essential
agreement by Gregory (ch. 33, p. 844) and the *Laudatio* (ch. 41,
p. 339f.). A. is begged to come to the sea-shore;[8] there he would
meet a leper,[9] the son of a sailor.[10] No doctor has been able to
help him. Hearing this A. goes to the place. Both sources testify
to a dialogue between A. and the sick man. It is therefore probable

[1] *Laud.* ch. 38, p. 338. 11f.; Gregory, ch. 30, p. 844. 5. Iphidamia is termed the
intimate friend of Maximilla by the author of the *Laudatio*, but her sister according
to the *Manichaean Psalm-book*, p. 192. 27; according to Gregory she had been converted
by a certain Sosias, a disciple of A. The author of the *Laudatio* wastes no words on this
conversion; however he does relate that Iphidamia, sent by Maximilla, attended
personally on the apostle, who was teaching in the house of a certain Sossios, one of
his disciples. What role Sosias or Sossios actually played in the *AA* cannot now be
ascertained.
[2] According to Gregory, by taking her hand; according to the *Laudatio*, by the
laying on of hands. We omit agreements on further trivial details.
[3] Gregory: 100 silver pieces; *Laud.* 1,000 gold pieces.
[4] Gregory: Inde discedens . . . (p. 844. 18); *Laud.*: Ἐκεῖθεν δὲ κατελθών . . .
(Cod. Coisl.: ἐξελθών).
[5] Gregory: 'In the name of Jesus Christ, stand up healed!' *Laud.*: "Stand up!
Jesus, the Christ, heals thee through me. . . ."
[6] Gregory: Healing by the laying on of hands. *Laud.*: By touching the eyes. In
Gregory a longer explanation of miraculous power comes first.
[7] Whilst the *Laudatio* only knows that the healed "put up prayers of thanksgiving
to God", we find in Gregory an actual confession to the God whom A. serves.
[8] *Laudatio:* Harbour.
[9] Thus the *Laudatio*. Gregory mentions ulcers and worms, which are also certainly
referred to by the author of the *Laudatio* (cf. 340. 12), and moreover describes the sick
man as lame.
[10] According to *Laudatio* he is the son of a famous admiral.

that at this point in the original form of the Acts there was also a dialogue. We can however say nothing as to its contents because it has been transmitted by Gregory and the author of the Laudatio in very different forms. After the Apostle's order to stand up, the sick man arises, takes off his rotten and loathsome rags and goes with the Apostle to the sea, where the healing by immersion follows. The action of the miracle is perfect; no trace of suffering remains. The healed man is filled with so great a joy that he forgets to clothe himself and runs naked through the streets praising God. Everyone is amazed at what has happened.

To the next section in Gregory (ch. 34, p. 845) the corresponding section in Laudatio is found first at ch. 43, pp. 342ff. Both sources tell of the arrival from Italy of Stratocles, a brother of the proconsul. Stratocles has a very dear slave. This slave, Alcman, is possessed by a devil and lies on the ground foaming at the mouth. Stratocles is freed from his great worry by Maximilla and Iphidamia, who point him to A. Summoned, the Apostle appears at the house and heals the slave.[1] Stratocles is converted, and is thereafter continually with the Apostle to hear the word of God.

Maximilla also loses no opportunity of visiting the Apostle to hear the Word of God (Gregory, ch. 35, p. 845). The material from Evodius of Uzala, De Fide contra Manichaeos, ch. 38 (Zycha, p. 968. 24–31) belongs here: "In the Acts of Leucius, which he composed in the names of the apostles, consider what kind of things you accept in regard to Maximilla the wife of Egetes. When she refused to pay the due proper to her husband . . . , and foisted on him her maid Euclia, supplying her, as is written there, with enticements and cosmetics; she substituted her in the night for herself, so that he slept with her as if she were his wife, without knowing it." In the same place the AA appears again (Zycha, pp. 968. 31–969. 6): "Here it is also written that when Maximilla and Iphidamia went away together to hear the Apostle Andrew a handsome little boy,[2] whom Leucius took to be either God or at least an angel, handed them over[3] to the Apostle Andrew; and he departed to the Praetorium of Egetes,

---

[1] Alcman "arose" as A. took him by the hand. In the very verbose account of the Laudatio we are told among other things about the magicians and quacks, etc., who were present but could not help because they were the συγγενεῖς of the demon (p. 343. 15, 20). This also seems to have been in the AA; the frequent usage of συγγενής is characteristic of it. Original also in the report of the Laudatio will be the reference to Stratocles as converted to an ascetic life: ἐπιμελεῖσθαί τε ψυχῆς ὡς ἀθανάτου, σώματος δὲ καταφρονεῖν ὡς φθείρεσθαι μέλλοντος, ἐγκρατεύεσθαί τε καὶ ἀγνεύειν (344. 5–7). In this we see the dualistic and ascetic tendency of the AA.

[2] The puerulus speciosus is Christ, cf. supra.

[3] Commendare = παραδιδόναι; see Act. Thom. ch. 155 (Bonnet, p. 264. 6, 11); cf. E. Peterson, op. cit., p. 194 n. 48.

went into the bedroom and imitated a woman's voice, as if Maximilla were complaining about the suffering of the female sex and Iphidamia were answering her. When Egetes heard this conversation he believed that they were within and went away."[1]

The stubborn refusal of Maximilla to perform her marital duties made the proconsul throw A. into prison (Gregory, ch. 36, p. 845; *Laud.* ch. 44, p. 344).

As the witnesses report (*Laud.* ch. 45, p. 345f.; *Narr.* ch. 11ff.; pp. 359ff.; *Conversante* ch. 2f.; pp. 374f., etc.), A. was able to continue his activity from the prison, before which a large crowd appeared, among them Maximilla and Stratocles. This situation is assumed in the large fragment *Vatic.* 808.

TEXTS

A. PAP. COPT. UTRECHT 1

(Translation of the as yet unedited Coptic text by
G. Quispel and J. Zandee*)

Page 9.

the apostle. But when Andrew

the apostle of Christ heard

that they had arrested those from the city on his account,

he arose and went out into the middle

5. of the street and said unto the brethren

that there was no reason to pretend anything (ὑποκρίνειν).

And while the apostle was yet speaking these

words, a young man was there,

(one) of the four soldiers, in

10. whose body was hidden a demon. When

that young man had come into

the presence of the apostle, the demon

cried out, saying: O Varianus,

what have I done to you that you should send (me)

15. to this god-fearing man?

When the young man had said this,

the demon cast him down, and made

him foam (at the mouth). His fellow-soldiers

however seized him and persisted

[1] Cf. James, p. 350, "We do not wonder that such narratives as that which Evodius quotes have been expunged, either by Gregory or his source, from the text". The same is true of the Greek martyrdoms of Andrew.

* Prof. Quispel and Dr. Zandee have kindly revised and corrected the English translation from the Coptic text.

20. in holding him up. But Andrew
pitied the young man and said
to his fellow-soldiers: "Are you
ashamed, because you see your nature (φύσις)
convicting you? Why
25. do you take away the price so that
he does not appeal to his king, to receive
help so as to be able to fight
against the demon who is hidden in his
limbs? Not only (that) he is appealing
30. for this, but he is speaking in
the language of the palace (παλάτιον), so that his
king will soon hear him. For I
hear him say: [O]
Varianus, what [have I done to you]
35. that you should [send me to this god-]
fearing [man . . . . An-]
drew [. . . . .]

Page 10.
against me. For this thing which I have done,
I have not done it of myself, but
I have been compelled (to do it). I will tell you, then,
the whole meaning of this matter. This
5. young man who is tormented in his body,
has a sister, a virgin,
who is a great ascetic
and champion. Truly, I say,
she is near to God because of
10. her purity and her prayers and
her alms. Now, to relate it
briefly, there was
somebody near her house, who was a great
magician. It happened
15. one day thus: at the time of evening
the virgin went up on
her roof to pray, the young
magician saw her praying,
Semmath entered into him to

404

20. fight against this great champion.
The young magician said within
himself: "If I have spent twenty years
under the instruction of my master until I was taught
this skill, behold! now
25. this is the beginning of my skill; if I do not
prevail upon this virgin, I shall not
be able to do any work."
And the young magician conjured up some
great powers upon the virgin
30. and sent them after her. And when
the demons went to tempt
her or to persuade her,
they acted like her brother and knocked
at the door. She arose and went down
35. to open the door, thinking that
it was her brother. But first she prayed
much, so that the demons became like (?) . . .
    [flames of fire? *or* as the . . . and fell]?
. . . . and fled away
. . . . little

Page 13.
The virgin wept
with Erucia. Erucia however
said to the virgin: "Why
do you weep? I did not know that you
5. were to come here [. . . . .] to weep [. . . . . .]
[. . . . .] now
these powers come after you,
in order to tempt you (? *or*: in order to take you?)
                              [. . . . .] you weep,
while the sorrow [. . . . .]
10. Now however, if you weep over your brother
because a God(?) [. . . . .] with
him,
to-morrow I shall send him to the
apostle Andrew, that he may
heal him. Not only, however, that I shall

15. heal him, but I shall make him enter into the (military) service
(*lit.* gird himself) of the palace."
When the demon had said this, the apostle said
to him: "How did you acquire knowledge
concerning the hidden mysteries of
20. the height? A soldier, when
cast out of the palace, is not at all
allowed to learn the
mysteries of the palace; and how
will he learn the hidden mysteries
25. of the height?" The demon
said to him: [. . . . .] come down
into this night [. . . . .] this
young man, while a power out of
the height entered into [. . . . .]
30. [. . . . .] virgin
in him out [. . . . .] goes, while she
will go away [. . . . .] this
her friend [. . . . .] said
[. . . . .] sorrow (?)
35. befalls me [. . . . .]
the great power came out
of the height in this night [. . . . .]
[. . . . .]

Page 14. (The apostle is speaking)
"why then should you not tremble, since you speak (of)
the mysteries of the height.
I tremble completely in all my limbs
and I glorify the receiver (παραλήμπτωρ)
5. who will come for the souls
of the saints. O champions
of virtue, not in vain
have you fought. Behold! the judge of the contest
prepares for you the crown
10. unfading. O fighters,
not in vain have you put on
weapons and
shields, and not in vain have you

endured wars:

15. the king has prepared for you the
palace. O virgins,
not in vain have you guarded the
purity and not in vain have you
persevered in prayers,
20. your lamps burning at
midnight, until this
call reached you: "Arise,
go ye out to meet the
bridegroom". When the apostle
25. had said this, he turned
to the demon and said [to him]:
"Now indeed it is already time for you to come
out from this young man,
so that he may enter on (military) service (*lit.* gird himself)

at the

30. heavenly palace". The demon said
to the apostle:
"Truly, O man of God,
I have never destroyed a limb of his
because of the holy hands
35. of his sister. Now, however,
I shall go out from this
young man, while I have done no harm
at all to his limbs".
And when the demon had said this
40. he went out of [the young man]
When he had [gone out from]
the young [man]
[he put off his uniform]

Page 15.
of soldiery and [cast it]
before the feet of the apostle,
saying: "O man
of God, I have spent
5. twenty pieces of money to
acquire this

temporal garment; but now
I desire to spend all that I have
to acquire this garment
10. of your God". His
fellow-soldiers said to him:
"Poor youth, if you
deny the garment of the king,
you will be punished". Said
15. the young man to them: "Indeed
I am a miserable fellow because of my
earlier sins; would that
my punishment were only because of this (*lit.* this)
that I denied the garment of the
20. king and not that I am punished
because I have despised the garment
of the immortal King of the Ages.
O ignorant ones, do you not see
what kind of man this is?
25. For he has no sword in his hand nor
any weapon of war and (yet)
these great miracles are performed
by him."

The Act of Andrew

B. CODEX VATICANUS 808

"... is there in you only feebleness? Have you not yet convinced yourselves that you do not yet bear his goodness? Let us reverently rejoice among ourselves in our abundant fellowship with him. Let us say to one another: Happy is our race! by whom has it been loved? Happy is our existence! from whom has it received mercy? We are not cast to the ground, we who have been recognized by such a height. We do not belong to time in order that we may be then dissolved by time. We are not the product (handiwork) of movement, which is again destroyed by itself, (we are) not of (earthly) birth in order to die (again) therein. We are rather those who pursue greatness. We belong ⟨to it⟩ and to him who has mercy on us. We belong to the better; therefore we flee the worse. We belong to the noble, through whom we drive

408

away the mean; to the righteous, through whom we cast away unrighteousness; to the merciful, through whom we reject the unmerciful; to the Saviour, through whom we recognized the destroyer; to the light, through whom we banished the darkness; to the One, through whom we have turned away from the many; to the heavenly, through whom we understood the earthly; to the abiding, through whom we perceived the transitory. If we intend fitly to thank the God who has mercy on us or to acknowledge to him our confidence or to offer him a song of praise or to glorify him, ⟨we can do it on no other basis⟩ than that we have been recognized by him.''

2. When he had thus addressed the brethren he sent them away, each to his own home, saying to them: "Neither are you ever forsaken by me, you who are servants of Christ on account of the love that is in him, nor again shall I myself be forsaken by you on account of his mediation." And each went away to his own house. And there was such joy among them for many days during which Aegeates had no thought of pursuing the charge against the apostle. So they were then each confirmed in hope toward the Lord; and they gathered fearlessly with Maximilla, Iphidamia and the others into the prison, protected by the guardianship and grace of the Lord.

3. One day when Aegeates was acting as judge he remembered the affair of Andrew. And just as if he had become mad he left the case with which he was dealing and rising from the bench went at the run into the praetorium and embraced and flattered Maximilla. She, coming from the prison, had entered the house before him; and when he had come in he said to her:

4. "Thy parents, Maximilla, considered me worthy of marriage with you, and gave you to me as wife, looking neither to wealth nor family nor renown, but perhaps (only) to the good character of my soul. And intending to pass over much with which I wished to reproach you, both things which I have enjoyed from your parents and things which you (enjoyed) from me during all our life together, I have come from the court to learn this alone from you; answer me reasonably: if you were the person you used to be, living with me in the way we know, sleeping with me, keeping up marital intercourse with me, bearing my children, then I would

treat you well in everything; even more, I would release the stranger whom I have in prison. But if you are not willing, I would not do you any harm, indeed I could not; but the one whom you love more than me, I will torture him so much the more. Consider then, Maximilla, which you wish and answer me tomorrow; for I am completely prepared for it."

5. And when he had said this he went out. But Maximilla went again at the usual time with Iphidamia to Andrew; and laying his hands on her face she kissed them and began to tell him in full of the demand of Aegeates. And Andrew answered her: "I know, Maximilla my child, that you are moved to resist the whole allurement of sexual intercourse, because you wish to be separated from a polluted and foul way of life. And this (attitude) has governed my mind for a long time; and now you wish me to declare my opinion. I earnestly beseech you not to do this; do not give way to the threat of Aegeates; do not be overcome through association with him; do not fear his shameful intention; do not be overcome by his clever flattery; do not consent to give yourself up to his impure spells; but endure all his torments, looking unto us for a short time; and you will see him wholly paralysed and wasting away both from you yourself and from those who are akin (by nature) to you. For what I really ought to say to you—for I do not rest in accomplishing the matter seen through you and coming to pass through you—has eluded me (until now). And I rightly see in you Eve repenting and in myself Adam being converted: for what she suffered in ignorance you are now bringing to a happy conclusion because you are converted: and what the mind suffered which was brought down with her and was estranged from itself, I put right with you who know that you yourself are being drawn up. For you yourself who did not suffer the same things have healed her affliction; and I by taking refuge with God have perfected his (Adam's) imperfection: and where she disobeyed, you have been obedient; and where he acquiesced, there I flee; and where they were made to sin, there we have known. For it is ordained that everyone should correct his own fall.

6. I then said these things as I have said them; and I would also say the following:

Well done, O nature, you who are saved despite your weakness and though you did not hide yourself.

Well done, O soul, you who have cried aloud what you have suffered and are returning to yourself.

Well done, O man, you who are learning what is not yours and desiring what is yours.

Well done, you who hear what is being said. For I know that you are more powerful than those who seem to overpower you, more glorious than those who are casting you down in shame, than those who are leading you away to imprisonment. If, O man, you understand all these things in yourself, namely that you are immaterial, holy, light, akin to the unbegotten, intellectual, heavenly, translucent, pure, superior to the flesh, superior to the world, superior to powers, superior to authorities, over whom you really are, if you perceive yourself in your condition, then take knowledge in what you are superior. And you, when you have looked at your face in your own being and broken every bond,—I mean not only those about birth, but those beyond birth whose exceeding great names we have set out for you—desire to see him who has appeared to you, whom you alone will soon recognize with confidence.

7. I have said these things in reference to you, Maximilla, for what has been said in its meaning concerns even you. As Adam died in Eve because of the harmony of their relationship, so even now I live in you who keep the command of the Lord and who give yourself over to the state (dignity) of your (true) being. But scorn the threats of Aegeates, Maximilla, for you know that we have a God who is merciful to us. And do not let his empty talk move you, but remain chaste; and let him not only punish me with tortures and bonds, but let him even throw me to the beasts or burn me with fire or hurl me from a cliff—what does it matter? Let him ill-treat this body as he wishes, it is only one; it is akin (in nature) to his own.

8. My words are intended again for you, Maximilla. I say to you, Do not give yourself over to Aegeates; stand out against his snares, especially since I have seen the Lord (in a vision) who said to me: 'Andrew, Aegeates' father, the devil, will release you from this prison.' For you, then, keep yourself henceforward

chaste and pure, holy, undefiled, sincere, free from adultery, unwilling for relationship with him who is a stranger to you, unbent, unbroken, tearless, unhurt, immovable in storms, undivided, free from offence, and without sympathy for the works of Cain.[1] For if you do not give yourself over, Maximilla, to the things that are the opposites of these, I shall rest, being thus compelled to give up this life for your sake, that is for my own sake. But if I, who am perhaps even able to help other (souls) akin to you through you, am driven away from here and if you are persuaded by your relationship with Aegeates and by the flatteries of his father, the serpent, to return to your earlier ways, know that I shall be punished on your account until you would understand that I had spurned life for the sake of a soul that was unworthy.

9. I beg you, then, the wise man (*sic!*), that your noble mind continue steadfast; I beg you, the invisible mind, that you may be preserved yourself; I exhort you, love Jesus and do not submit to the worse; help me, you, on whose aid as man I call, that I may be perfect; help me, that you may know your own true nature; suffer with my suffering, that you may know what I suffer and you will escape suffering. See what I see and what you see will blind you; see what you ought to see and you will not see what you ought not; hear what I say and what you have not heard reject.

10. I have said these things to you and to everyone who will listen, if indeed he will listen. But you, Stratocles," he said, looking at him, "why are you so distressed with many tears and why do you sigh so audibly? Why your despondency? Why your great pain and great grief? You know what has been said, and why then do I beseech you as (my) child to be in control of yourself? Do you understand to whom the words that are said are addressed? Has each gripped your mind? Has it made contact with you in your intellectual part? Have I you as one who hears me? Do I find myself in you? Is there in you someone who speaks to you, whom I see as belonging to myself? Does he love the one who speaks in me and does he desire to have fellowship with him? Will he be made one with him? Does he find in him

[1] Cf. 1 Jn. 3:12.

any peace? Does he have where he may lay his head?[1] Is there nothing there which is opposed to him, which behaves unfriendly, which resists him, which hates him, which flees (from him), which is savage, which withdraws, which has turned away, which rushes away, which is burdened, which fights, which associates with others, which is flattered by others, which combines with others? Are there other things which trouble him? Is there someone within me who is foreign to me? An adversary? a destroyer? an enemy? a cheat? a sorcerer? a corrupted? a man of furtive character? a deceitful man? a misanthrope? a hater of the word? one like a tyrant? a boaster? an arrogant man? a madman? a kinsman of the serpent? a weapon of the devil? a champion of the fire? a friend of darkness? Is there in you, Stratocles, someone who will not endure me speaking like this? Who is it? Answer! Am I speaking in vain, have I spoken in vain? No, says the man in you, Stratocles, who is again weeping."

11. And Andrew took the hand of Stratocles and said: "I have him whom I loved. I will rest on him for whom I waited; your present groans and incessant weeping have become a sign to me that I have already enjoyed rest, that I have not addressed in vain to you these words which are akin to my own nature."

12. And Stratocles answered him: "Do not think, most blessed Andrew, that there is anything other than yourself which troubles me: for the words which come forth from you are like fiery arrows piercing into me; each of them touches me and truly sets me on fire. That part of my soul which inclines to the things I hear is being punished because it has a presentiment of the distress that comes after this. For you yourself go away and I know well that you will do it nobly. Where and in whom shall I seek and find hereafter your care and love? When you were the sower I received the seeds of the words of salvation. And for these to sprout and grow up there is need of no other than yourself, most blessed Andrew. And what else have I to say to you than this? I need the great mercy and help that comes from you, to be able to be worthy of the seed I have from you, which will only grow permanently and emerge into the light if you wish it and pray for it and for my whole self."

[1] Cf. Mt. 8:20.

13. And Andrew answered him: "That, my son, was what I myself also saw in you. And I praise my Lord that my opinion of you was not wrong but knows (rather) what it says. And so that you may know: Aegeates will to-morrow hand me over to be crucified. For the servant of the Lord, Maximilla, will enrage the enemy in him, the enemy to whom he belongs, when she refuses to take part with him in those things which are alien to her (to her true nature). And by turning on me he will think to console himself."

14. While the Apostle was so speaking Maximilla was absent. For when she had heard what he answered her and had been in some way impressed by it and had become what the words signified, she had gone out, neither rashly nor without set purpose, and had gone to the praetorium. And she had said farewell to her whole life in (with) the flesh and when Aegeates brought up the same matter which he had told her to consider, i.e. whether she was willing to sleep with him, she rejected it; from then on he turned his mind to the murder of Andrew and considered in what way he might kill him. And when crucifixion alone of all deaths mastered him he went away with some of his friends and dined. But Maximilla, the Lord going before her in the form of Andrew, went with Iphidamia to the prison. And there she came on him with a great crowd of the brethren discoursing as follows:

15. "Brethren, I was sent as an apostle by the Lord into these parts, of which my Lord thought me worthy, not indeed to teach anyone, but to remind everyone who is akin to these words that they live in transient evils while they enjoy their harmful delusions. From which things I always exhorted you to keep clear and to press towards the things that are permanent and to take flight from all that is transient. For you see that no one of you stands firm, but everything, even to the ways of men, is changeable. And this is the case because the soul is untrained and has gone astray in 'nature' and retains pledges corresponding to its error. I therefore hold blessed those who obey the words preached to them and who through them see as in a mirror the mysteries of their own nature, for the sake of which all things were built.

16. I therefore command you, beloved children, to build firmly

on the foundation[1] which has been laid for you, for it is un-shakeable and no evil person can assail it. Be rooted on this foundation. Stand fast remembering what ⟨you saw?⟩ and what happened while I was living among you all. You have seen works take place through me which you have not the power to dis-believe, and signs such that dumb nature would perhaps have cried them out.[2] I have communicated to you words which, I pray, have been received by you in the way the words themselves would wish. Stand fast then, beloved, in everything which you have seen and heard and shared in. And God, whom you have trusted, will have mercy on you and present you acceptable to himself, to have rest for all eternity.

17. Do not be troubled by what is about to happen to me as if it were some strange marvel; for the servant of God, to whom God himself has granted much through works and words, will be forcibly expelled from this temporal life by an evil man. For such will happen not only to myself but to all who have been loving him, trusting him and who confess him. The devil, who is utterly shameless, will arm his own children against them, so that they may be his adherents. But he will not obtain what he desires. And I will tell you why he attempts these things: From the beginning of all things, and, if I may so put it, from the time when he who is without beginning came down to be subject to his 'rule', the enemy, an opponent of peace, drives away (from God) whoever does not belong to him but is only one of the weaker and has not attained to full brightness and cannot yet be recognized. And because he did not even know him (the devil), he must for that reason be locked in combat with him. For since he (the devil) thinks that he possesses him and will always rule him, he fights against him so much that their enmity becomes a kind of friendship. In order to subject him he often sketched his own pleasure-seeking and deceitful nature, by which means he thought to dominate him completely. He did not therefore show himself openly as an enemy but he pretended a friendship worthy of himself.

18. And he carried on this work for so long that man forgot to recognize it, whereas he (the devil) knew: that is, on account of

1 Cf. Eph. 2:20.   2 Cf. Lk. 19:40.

his gifts he ⟨was not seen to be an enemy⟩.[1] But when the mystery of grace was lighted up, and the counsel of (eternal) rest was made known and the light of the word appeared and it was proved that the redeemed race had to struggle against many pleasures, the enemy himself was scorned, and, because of the goodness of Him who is merciful was mocked in respect of his own gifts by which he appeared to triumph over him (man), then he began to plot against us with hatred and enmity and arrogance. And this he practises: not to leave us alone until he thinks to separate us (from God). For then indeed our adversary was without care; and he pretended to offer us a friendship such as was worthy of him. And he had no fear that we whom he had led astray should revolt from him. However the possession of the plan of salvation, which enlightened us (like a light), has ⟨made his enmity⟩ not stronger ⟨but clearer⟩.[2] For the hidden part of his nature and what appeared concealed he has exposed and prepared it to confess what it (really) is. Since therefore, brethren, we know the future, let us awake from sleep, not being discontented, nor cutting a fine figure, nor bearing in our souls his marks which are not our own, but being lifted up wholly in the whole word, let us all await with joy the end and take flight from him, that henceforth he may be seen as he is, the one who our nature against our . . .

C. RECONSTRUCTED TEXT OF THE MARTYRDOM

Narr. 22

And he (Andrew) conversed all night with the brethren and prayed with them and committed them to the Lord; afterwards early in the morning the proconsul Aegeates had the prisoner Andrew brought to him and said to him:

Mart. II. 1

"The end of the proceedings against you has come, you stranger, opponent of this present life, and enemy of all my house. For why did you think it good to force your way into places which were no concern of yours and to corrupt a wife who

---

[1] Text corrupt. Restored in conformity with E. Hennecke, *Apokr.*, 2, p. 254. Similarly James, p. 356.
[2] Conj. Bonnet.

prior to that satisfied me? Why have you done this to me and all Achaea? Therefore receive gifts from me as retaliation for what you have done to me."

And he gave orders for him to be beaten with seven scourges. After that he ordered he was to be crucified. And he instructed the executioners not to break his legs, intending in that way to make his punishment more severe.

Narr. 23; Mart. II. 1

The news now spread abroad throughout all Patrae that the stranger, the righteous man, the slave of Christ, whom Aegeates held prisoner, was being crucified, although he had done nothing wrong; and with one accord they all ran together to the spectacle, angered by the proconsul's impious judgment.

Narr. 23; Mart. II. 2

And as the executioners led him to the spot and wished to carry out what they had been ordered, Stratocles, who had learnt what was happening, came running and saw the blessed Andrew being dragged along by the executioners like a criminal. And he did not spare them but beat every one of them soundly, ripping their coats from top to bottom, and he tore Andrew from them, crying to them: "You may thank this blessed man that he trained me and taught me to restrain the strength of my anger. Otherwise I would have shown you of what Stratocles and the foul Aegeates are capable. For we have learnt to endure what others inflict on us." And taking the apostle by the hand he went with him to the place beside the sea where he was to be crucified.

Narr. 24; Mart. II. 3

But the soldiers to whom the pro-consul had handed him over left him with Stratocles and returning reported to Aegeates: "As we were marching along with Andrew, Stratocles sprang on us, ripped our coats, seized him from us and took him with him; and now as you see here we are." And Aegeates answered them: "Put on other clothes and go and do and carry out what I have commanded you in regard to Andrew who has been condemned. Do not let Stratocles see you and do not gainsay him if he should ask anything from you. For I know his rash nature. He would not even spare me if he were provoked to anger."

Mart. II. 3

And these did just as Aegeates had told them. Stratocles however came with the Apostle to the predetermined place. When he (Andrew) now noticed that he (Stratocles) was embittered against Aegeates and was reviling him in a low voice, he said to him: "My child Stratocles, I wish that for the future you would possess your soul unmoved and would reject such a thing so that you neither inwardly respond to the wicked intentions (of men) nor outwardly be inflamed. For it is becoming that the slave of Jesus should be worthy of Jesus. And there is another thing that I would say to you and the brethren walking with me: Whenever the enemy dares something and finds no one who agrees with him, then he is struck and beaten and completely brought to death because he did not accomplish what he set out to do. Let us, little children, therefore, always hold him before our eyes so that we do not fall asleep and our adversary slay us."

Narr. 26; Mart. II. 4

He said these and many other things to Stratocles and to those who were going along with them. Then he came to the place where he was to be crucified. And when he saw the cross set in the sand at the sea-shore he left them all and went to the cross and with a strong voice addressed it as if it were a living creature:

Laud. 46; Mart. I. 14; Ep. Gr. 10

Hail, O cross; indeed may you rejoice. I know well that you will rest in the future because for a long time you have been weary set up awaiting me. I am come to you whom I recognize as mine own; I am come to you, who long for me. I know the mystery for which you have indeed been set up. For you are set up in the cosmos to establish the unstable. And one part of you stretches up to heaven so that you may point out the heavenly Logos,[1] the head of all things. Another part of you is stretched out to right and left that you may put to flight the fearful and inimical power

---

[1] Mart. I. 14, p. 54. 25; conj. Bonnet: the Logos above.

and draw the cosmos into unity. And another part of you is set on
the earth, rooted in the depths, that you may bring what is on
earth and under the earth into contact with what is in heaven.
O Cross, tool of salvation of the Most High! O Cross, trophy of
the victory of Christ over his enemies! O Cross, planted on earth
and bearing your fruit in heaven! O name of the Cross, filled with
all things! Well done, O Cross, that you have bound the circumference of the world! Well done, form of understanding, that you
have given a form to your own formlessness! Well done, invisible
discipline, that you discipline severely the substance of the knowledge of many gods and drive out from humanity its discoverer!
Well done, O Cross, that you have clothed yourself with the Lord,
and borne as fruit the robber, and called the apostle to repentance,
and not thought it beneath you to receive us! But for how long
shall I say these things and not be embraced by the cross, that in
the cross I may be made to live and through the cross I may go
out of this life into the common (to all) death? Approach,
ministers of my joy and servants of Aegeates, and fulfil the desire
we both have and bind the lamb to the suffering, the man to the
Creator, the soul to the Saviour.

Narr. 28; Ep. Gr. 10

The blessed Andrew said this standing on the ground and
staring steadfastly towards the cross. Then he besought the
brethren that the executioners should come and carry out what
they had been commanded. For they were standing at a distance.

Laud. 47; Mart. I. 15; Ep. Gr. 10; Narr. 28

And they came and bound his hands and his feet and did not
nail him; for they had been so instructed by Aegeates. He wished
in this way to torture him as he hung in that he would be eaten
alive by dogs. And they left him hanging and departed from him.

Narr. 29; Ep. Gr. 11; Mart. II. 5

And when the crowds that stood around who had been made
disciples in Christ by him saw that they did none of these things
which were usual in the case of crucifixions, they hoped to hear
again something from him. For as he hung he moved his head and

smiled. And Stratocles asked him: "Why do you smile, slave of God? Your laughter makes us mourn and weep because we are being deprived of you." And the blessed Andrew answered him: "Shall I not laugh, my child Stratocles, at the vain plot of Aegeates by which he intends to avenge himself on us? We are strangers to him and his designs. He is not capable of hearing. For if he had been capable he would have heard that a man who belongs to Jesus, because he is known to him, is immune from revenge for the future."

Ep. Gr. 11; Mart. II. 6; Narr. 30

Then he spoke a word to them all together—for even the heathen had come running up to join them, complaining about the iniquitous judgment of Aegeates: "You men who are present, and women and children and old people, slaves and free, and all who wish to hear, pay no heed to the vain illusion of this temporal life. Rather pay heed to us who hang (here) for the Lord's sake and soon forsake this body; renounce every worldly desire, and scorn (*lit.* spit on, *or,* up) the cult of abominable idols; hasten to the true worship of our God who does not lie, and make of yourselves a holy temple ready for the reception of the word."

Ep. Gr. 12; Narr. 31; Mart. II. 6; Conv. 5

And the crowds who heard his words did not leave the spot; and Andrew continued speaking further to them for a day and a night. And when on the following day they saw his constancy and steadfastness of soul, his wisdom of spirit and strength of mind, they burned with indignation and rushed with one accord to the judgment seat of Aegeates and cried out: "What, O proconsul, is this judgment of yours? You have condemned wrongly! You have judged unjustly! What wrong has this man done? What transgression has he committed? The whole city is in uproar! You wrong us all! Do not destroy Caesar's city! Hand over to us the righteous man! Give us the holy man! Do not kill a man who is dear to God! Do not destroy a man (so) gentle and pious! He has hung there for two days and he is still alive. He has eaten nothing but has nourished all of us with his words. And behold, we believe in the God whom he preaches. Take down the righteous man and we will all become philosophers. Set free the ascetic (*lit.* chaste man) and all of Patrae will have peace. Release the wise man and all Achaea will be freed through him."

Ep. Gr. 13; Narr. 32; Mart. II. 7; Conv. 5

When Aegeates at first would not listen and with a wave of his hand commanded the crowd to go away, they were filled with anger and determined to take some action against him. They were about two thousand in number.[1]

When the proconsul saw that they were in some way maddened he was afraid that he would suffer some terrible misfortune and he got up from the judge's bench and went with them, promising to set Andrew free. Some ran on ahead and told the apostle and the rest of the crowd with him why the proconsul was coming. And the crowd of disciples, among whom were Maximilla, Iphidamia and Stratocles, rejoiced.

Narr. 33

But when Andrew heard it he began to speak: "O the dullness and unbelief and simplicity of those whom I have instructed! How much have we said up to now and (yet) we have not persuaded our own to flee from the love of earthly things! But they are still bound to them and abide in them and do not wish to leave them. What kind of a friendship and love and habituation to the flesh is this? How long will you be taken up with earthly and temporal things? How long will you fail to understand what is higher than yourselves and not press forward to lay hold of what is there? Leave me now to be put to death in the manner you see, and let no one release me in any way from these bonds. For there has been allotted me this destiny: to depart out of the body and to live with the Lord, with whom I am even being crucified."

Narr. 34f; Laud. 48; Ep. Gr. 13f.

And Andrew turned to Aegeates and said to him: "Why have you come, Aegeates, to him who is (by nature) alien to you? What do you wish again to dare, to contrive, to fetch? What do you want to say (to us)? That you are come as a penitent to set

---

[1] Thus *Narr.*; in *Ep. Gr.* and *Mart.* II, 20,000.

us free? Even if you were truly repentant I would not come to terms with you. Even if you were to promise me all your possessions I would not stand aloof from myself. Even if you were to say that you yourself were mine (my disciple) I would not trust you. Do you set free him that is bound? (Or) do you rather not set free him that has been set free? Do you (not) set free him who was known by him (i.e. God) who is (in nature) akin to him? Who has received mercy from him and been loved by him? Who is an alien and a stranger to thee? Who appeared only to thee? I have him with whom I shall be for ever. I have him with whom I shall converse through countless ages. To him I depart; to him I hasten, even to him who caused me to recognize you, who said to me: 'Understand Aegeates and his gifts. Do not let that fearful man terrify you, nor let him think that he can get into his power you who belong to me. He is your enemy: a corrupter, deceiver, destroyer, a madman, a magician, a cheat, a murderer, wrathful, without compassion.' Leave me now, you worker of all iniquity. I, however, and those who are akin (in nature) to me, hasten towards what is ours, and we leave you to be what you were, although you do not know what you are."

And the proconsul stood there speechless and as it were out of his mind. When now the whole city noisily demanded that he free Andrew, and he ventured to approach the cross to unloose him and take him down, Andrew cried out loudly: "Do not permit, Lord, that Andrew who has been bound to thy cross, should be set free. Do not give me up, who am on thy mystery (Narr.: hang on thy mystery),[1] to the shameless devil. O Jesus Christ, let not thy adversary loose me who hang on thy grace. Father, let this little one no longer humiliate him who has known thy greatness. Jesus Christ, whom I have seen, whom I have, whom I love, in whom I am and will be, receive me in peace into thy eternal tabernacles,[2] that through my exodus the many who are akin (in nature) to me may enter to thee and may rest in thy majesty."

And when he had said these things and had glorified the Lord even more, he gave up the ghost, while all wept and lamented at his departure.

---

[1] 'Mystei ' = 'Cross'; so also 'grace' in the next sentence.   [2] Cf. Lk. 16:9 (?).

Narr. 36; Mart. II. 10; Ep. Gr. 15

And after the death of the blessed Andrew, Maximilla came with Stratocles without a thought of those who were standing around and took down the body of Andrew. And when the evening came she buried him, after she had given the body the customary attention. And she lived apart from Aegeates because of his savage nature and his wicked manner of life; she chose a holy and retired life which she, full of the love of Christ, spent among the brethren. Aegeates urged her strongly, promising her that she would have control over his affairs, but he was not able to persuade her. Then he got up one night exceptionally early and without any of his household knowing it threw himself down from a great height and died.

Narr. 37; Conv. 7; Mart. II. 10

But Stratocles, his brother according to the flesh, was not willing to touch any of his belongings—for the wretched man had died childless—but he said: "May your possessions go with you, Aegeates. For I am satisfied with the Lord Jesus whom I have known through his servant Andrew." And so the riot of the crowd came to an end, because they rejoiced at the extraordinary and untimely and sudden fall of the impious and lawless Aegeates.

D. A COPTIC FRAGMENT

J. W. B. Barns has edited with translation and commentary (in *JTS* N.S. 11, 1960, pp. 70–76, "A Coptic Apocryphal Fragment in the Bodleian Library") a hitherto unpublished Coptic text, which possibly ought to be ascribed to the *AA*. This page of parchment (Bodleian MS. Copt. f 103 (P)), which is badly preserved and in part completely illegible, reproduces an extract from a, probably longer, conversation between Andrew and the Saviour. It is certain that the text is part of an ancient apocryphon. Because of the role which Andrew plays in it the editor conjectures that it formed a part of the *AA*. He believes that when Andrew refers to the fact that he has left not only his parents but also his wife and children (II recto 24f.) this fits the encratitic tendency of the *AA*. But it must be said that it is difficult to prove an encratitic tendency in these words; so far as the fragmentary condition of the text allows us to judge, it is more probable that it is nothing more than a question of a practical parallel to the

thought of Mk. 10:24 and parallels.[1] The impartial reader's first
impression is of an incident from the life of Jesus. Yet we cannot
exclude the possibility that we have before us an extract from
teaching given to the disciples between Easter and Ascension after
the style of the apocryphal Epistle of James (Vol. I, pp. 333ff.)
and of the Epistula Apostolorum (*ibid.* pp. 189ff.). In neither
case would it be permissible to ascribe the piece to the *AA*, for
the latter's action began with the departure of the Apostle from
Pontus. A third possibility indeed exists, viz., that the dialogue
between Jesus and Andrew presupposes an appearance of the
risen Lord granted to Andrew somewhere on his journey. Because
this possibility cannot be rejected *a priori* and because the assignment of the fragment to the *AA* is always worth consideration, we
give a translation of the text, although we do not wish to commit
ourselves thereby to the thesis of the editor.*

Text of the Coptic Fragment

I recto

. . . man . . . to behold me[2]
Then (τότε) said Jesus to
Andrew, "Come nigh unto
Me, Andrew; thy name
5. is the fire; blessed art thou (?)[3]
among men." Answered
Andrew [answered][4]
and said unto the Saviour (σωτήρ) (?),
"Suffer me to speak."
10. Then (τότε) said He (?) unto him (?),
"Speak, Andrew, thou
firmly stablished pillar (στῦλος) (?)."
Andrew answered and said,
"As God (?) liveth
15. Who is (?) Thy Father (?),

---

[1] The considerations which Barns connects to II verso 51f. to prove the encratitic
character of the text are also not convincing. The fragmentary condition of the text
obliges us to leave the question of Encratism open.
[2] A second hand adds: 'in . . . member (μέλος) which is . . .'
[3] The question-marks have been inserted by Hornschuh,   [4] Dittography.

* The translation is reproduced from the *Journal of Theological Studies*, by permission
of Dr. Barns and the editors.

I verso

I (?) came out from (?)
the house of my father and
my mother; and as
my soul (ψυχή) liveth (?), I have not (?)
20. again gone
into it, and
I have not (?) beheld (?) the faces (?) of my (?) father (?)
and my mother, neither (οὐδέ) (?) have (?)
I (?) beheld the faces (?) of my (?) children (?)
25. and my wife (?), but (ἀλλά)
I bore my cross (σταυρός)[1]
every day, following after Thee
from morning till night
(and I have not?[2]) laid it down."[3]
30. Jesus answered and
said, "I know Andrew?[2] . . ."

II verso

. . .
a lesser (?) than one of (?)
50. us (?) who bear (?)[2] Thy Name (?).[4]
Two (?) coats (?) I have not desired (ἐπιθυμεῖν)
for myself (?); even this
coat (?) which is upon me . . ."

5. THE ACTS OF THOMAS
(G. Bornkamm)

INTRODUCTION: I. LITERATURE.[5] Of the older literature the following
deserve special mention: C. Thilo, *Acta S. Thomae Apostoli*, 1823 (an
obsolete edition of the text, which is however distinguished by a
discerning commentary, valuable even today); R. A. Lipsius, *Die
apokryphen Apostelgeschichten und Apostellegenden*, 1883, I, pp. 225ff.; W.
Bousset, *Hauptprobleme der Gnosis*, *FRLANT* 10, 1907; *id.*, Manichäisches

---

[1] Probably we should read with Barns: *ĕneïfi 'mpastauros.*
[2] These question-marks are in Barns' translation.
[3] Probably we should read with Barns: *ĕ'mpikaaf ĕpĕsēt.*
[4] Literally: "we who are under thy name", if the correct reading is: *anŏn ĕtha pĕkran.*
[5] In the following pages *ATh* = Acts of Thomas, and *Ev.Th.* = Gospel of Thomas.

in den Thomasakten, *ZNW* 18, 1917/18, pp. 30ff. R. Reitzenstein, *Das iranische Erlösungsmysterium*, 1921; *Id., Die hellenistischen Mysterienreligionen*, ³1927. Further abundant information on the older literature together with their own introductions to and explanations of the *ATh* in the first (pp. 473ff.: *Handb.* pp. 562ff.: R. Raabe and E. Preuschen) and second (pp. 256ff.: W. Bauer) editions of this book.—R. Söder, *Die apokryphen Apostelgeschichten und die romanhafte Literatur der Antike*, Würzburger Studien zur Altertumswissenschaft 3, 1932; G. Bornkamm, *Mythos und Legende in den apokryphen Thomasakten. Beiträge zur Geschichte der Gnosis und zur Vorgeschichte des Manichäismus*, FRLANT NF 31, 1933; *Id.*, art. Thomas, in: A. Pauly-G. Wissowa, *Realenc. d. Klass. Altertumswiss.* 2 R., Bd. VI, cols. 316ff.; G. Widengren, *The Great Vohu Manah and the Apostle of God. Studies in Iranian and Manichaean Religion*, Upps. Univ. Arsskr. 5, 1945; *Id., Mesopotamian Elementsin Manichaeism, ib.* 3, 1946; *Id., The Ascension of the Apostle and the Heavenly Book, ib.* 7, 1950; *Id.*, Der iranische Hintergrund der Gnosis, *ZRGG* 4, 1952, pp. 97ff; *Id.*, Stand und Aufgabe der iranischen Religionsgeschichte, *Numen* 1, 1954, pp. 16ff.; 2, 1955, pp. 1ff; *Id., Muhammed, the Apostle of God, and His Ascension*, Upps. Univ. Arsskr. 1, 1955; H. C. Puech, *Le manichéisme, son fondateur, sa doctrine*, 1949; H. Jonas, *Gnosis und spätantiker Geist I, Die mythologische Gnosis*, FRLANT NF 33, ²1954; A. Adam, *Die Psalmen des Thomas und das Perlenlied als Zeugnisse vorchristlicher Gnosis*, BZNW 24, 1959. Cf. also H. C. Puech in Vol. I of this book, pp. 278ff. and 307f.

For editions of the text of the *ATh* as a whole, see p. 428. Translations of the text, apart from those in the first and second editions of this book, in W. Wright, *Apocryphal Acts of the Apostles* II (English trans. from the Syriac), 1871; M. R. James, *The Apocryphal New Testament*, ⁶1955; A. F. J. Klijn, *The Acts of Thomas. Introduction, Text and Commentary*, 1962; W. Michaelis, *Die apokryphen Schriften zum NT* ²1958 (selection, with explanations).[1] On the special tradition of the Hymn of the Pearl and translations thereof, see p. 433 n. 2.

2. THE APOSTLE THOMAS (cf. Vol. I, pp. 286f.), called Judas Thomas among the Syrians and so also in the apocryphal Acts of Thomas (also Ἰούδας or Θωμᾶς, Ἰούδας ὁ καὶ Θωμᾶς or Ἰούδας Θωμᾶς ὁ καὶ Δίδυμος), ranks in the *ATh* as a twin brother of Jesus, like him both in appearance (c. 11) and also in his destiny and redeeming work (cc. 31, 39). As in other Gnostic literature (Epist. Apost. 42f.; Pistis Sophia 42f.; Introduction and Logion 13 of the new-found Gospel of Thomas, see Puech, Vol. I, p. 287), Thomas appears in the *ATh* also as the recipient and mediator of special secret revelations (c. 39: ὁ δίδυμος τοῦ Χριστοῦ, ὁ ἀπόστολος τοῦ ὑψίστου καὶ συμμύστης τοῦ λόγου τοῦ Χριστοῦ τοῦ ἀποκρύφου, ὁ δεχόμενος αὐτοῦ τὰ ἀπόκρυφα λόγια),

---

[1] In the following text Raabe's complete translation and the abbreviated one by W. Bauer have been used as the basis, checked and in part corrected. (The English translation at some points adheres more closely to the Greek text printed by Bonnet. Where the German version clearly renders a variant reading in Bonnet's apparatus, it has of course been followed.—R.M.W.)

but the interpretation of the name "twin" in the sense of the Gnostic fusion of Redeemer and Apostle is first complete in the *A Th* (cf. cc. 10, 47, 78 *et al.*). In the Gospel of Thomas the Apostle himself still does not by any means have the function of the Redeemer. Nevertheless the homeland of the *Ev.Th.* may be Syria, like that of the *A Th* (cf. W. C. van Unnik, *Evangelien aus dem Nilsand*, 1960, p. 60; ET *Newly Discovered Gnostic Writings*, 1960, p. 49). Other connections between the two documents in matters of content are not wholly lacking. However, these relate to particular motifs (cf. Vol. I, p. 287), which in the *A Th* are in any case more richly developed in the interest of Gnostic views, but do not certainly prove any literary dependence (cf. log. 2 and *A Th* c. 136; log. 13 and *A Th* cc. 37, 39, 47, 147; log. 22 and *A Th* cc. 92, 147; log. 37 and *A Th* c. 14). The Catholic Abgar-legend (on its historical value see most recently W. Bauer, *Rechtgläubigkeit und Ketzerei*, 1934, pp. 6ff.) traces back to Thomas the evangelizing of Edessa, where his bones have been preserved since the 4th century. A tradition supported already by Origen (in Euseb. *HE* III. 1. 1) and the pseudo-Clementines (R. IX. 29) designates Thomas as the Apostle of Parthia. As Apostle of India he appears for the first time in the *A Th*, in a legendary tradition which indeed makes skilful use for the colouring of the narrative of historical figures like King Gundaphorus (according to the evidence of coins which have been found, his reign fell in the first Christian century, cf. v. Gutschmid, *Kl. Schriften* II, pp. 332ff.) and the lively cultural and commercial relationships between North India and Syria, but has no claim to historicity. The Acts are also the oldest witness for the legend of Thomas' martyr death and the transference of his bones to Edessa.

3. THE TRANSMISSION OF THE ACTS OF THOMAS. The *A Th* belong to the collection of apocryphal Acts whose author is said, from the 5th century on, to have been Leucius Charinus; a tradition which seems to be of Manichaean origin, and may indeed hold good not for the composition but for the collecting together of these Acts (cf. above, pp. 182ff.). The use of the *A Th* in Gnostic sects is attested by Epiphanius (*Haer.* 47. 1; 61. 1); among the Manichees by Augustine (c. Faust. 22. 79; c. Adimant. 17. 2. 5; *de sermone domini in monte* I. 20. 65); Turribius of Astorga (*Epist. ad Idac. et Ceston.* 5, Manichees and Priscillianists). Yet they also enjoyed great favour in orthodox circles as Christian literature for edification and entertainment, as is shown by their manifold textual history and in particular by the tendency recognizable in it towards the expunging of Gnostic elements and assimilation to Catholic doctrine (later adaptations also in Latin, Ethiopic and Armenian). The *A Th* are extant in Greek and

427

Syriac, the Greek text (G) edited on the basis of 21 MSS.[1] by Bonnet, *Acta Apostolorum Apocrypha* II. 2 (1903), pp. 99–288; the Syriac text (S) edited and translated on the basis of a London MS. by W. Wright, *Apocryphal Acts of the Apostles* (1871) I, pp. 171ff. (Syr.), II, pp. 146ff. (English). Minor variations of the Syriac text (on the basis of a Berlin MS.) in a new edition by Bedjan, *Acta martyrum et sanctorum* III (1892) pp. 3ff. Older fragments in A. S. Lewis, *Mythological Acts of the Apostles* (Horae Semiticae IV, 1904); cf. also Burkitt in *Studia Sinaitica* IX (1900) app. VII, pp. 23ff.

As is today scarcely disputed, the *ATh* were originally composed in Syriac. Yet, taking it as a whole, preference is to be given to the Greek text over against the Syriac S available to us today, since the latter displays numerous catholicizing revisions. This does not exclude the possibility that S in many particular cases has preserved material certainly older. G and S may therefore go back to a common Syriac text, now lost.[2]

4. THE LITERARY CHARACTER OF THE ATh. The *ATh* are a Christian-Gnostic variety of the Hellenistic-Oriental romance. The elements and motifs abundantly employed in this literature may be recognized in a body in the *ATh*, although frequently in a popular and coarser form: the journey of a hero into a foreign wonderland, the linking of his story with that of historical figures, the description of fantastic works of power by the hero and of astonishing prodigies, the partiality for erotic scenes and the developed inclination towards the tendentious, and in addition the stylistic methods of the novel and of the narrative art of fiction (cf. R. Söder, *op. cit.*, and R. Helm, *Der antike Roman*, 1948, pp. 53–56, and above, pp. 174ff.). Just as clear in the Acts, of course, is the connection with Biblical material and narrative motifs. In thirteen Praxeis, whose centre of interest is the Apostle Thomas, the book relates his works of wonder, the stories of the conversion of numerous individuals, and finally the Apostle's sufferings down to his martyrdom. In the first six Praxeis the individual narratives are loosely strung together, but in the second part (Praxeis 7–13) on the other hand, as the motif of miracle recedes and that of conversion stands out more strongly, they are more artistically composed. The characters here are more individually drawn, the scenes carefully linked together. The single scene of action in the second part is the court of king Misdaeus, and there is no further

[1] Especially important are a Roman codex (*Vallicellanus B* 35) from the 11th century, in Bonnet under the siglum U, the most complete manuscript of the *ATh*, and a Paris codex (*B.N. graec.* 1510) from the 11th or 12th century, in Bonnet under the siglum P.

[2] On the special tradition of the Hymn of the Pearl cf. p. 433, on that of the Martyrdom cf. the text.

reference here to the scenes, the characters or the events of the first section. Despite this difference in the two parts, the Acts are of a uniform character. All the narratives are interspersed with numerous liturgical pieces, sermons, prayers and hymns, which are indeed introduced by the author in a meaningful way yet frequently stand in only loose connection with the narratives, and often by this very fact betray their independent origin. Here above all belong the two famous hymns, the song of the Bride in the first Praxis and the song of the Pearl in the ninth.

The speeches, prayers and hymns in the Acts allow us to recognize beyond mistake how the narratives were intended by the author: as legendary clothing for the mystery of redemption. They are thus usually marked by an ambiguity concerning which the Acts themselves express an unmistakable opinion, e.g. in cc. 36 and 78.

5. THE GNOSTIC CHARACTER OF THE PRAXEIS. The view of redemption which lies behind the Acts is that of Gnosticism. This becomes immediately clear when we assemble together into a uniform picture the most important traits of the Gnostic Redeemer-myth, which are scattered over the Acts as a whole: the Redeemer sent from heaven lays aside his heavenly glory; disguised in an earthly human form he appears to the powers, who do not recognize him and only hear his voice; he pursues them, fights with them, and conquers them (cc. 10, 45, 48, 80, 122, 152, 156 et al.). The faithful, who are strangers on earth but the intimate associates of the heavenly Redeemer or of his *alter ego* the Apostle (cc. 32, 34, 39, 48, 61, 81 et al.) are set free by the Redeemer from Hades, i.e. at the same time from the realm of the material body (c. 10, 21, 67, 156 et al.). The Redeemer prepares the way for them and is their guide (cc. 10, 80, 156 et al.), physician, bringer of life, a figure of light, a planter (c. 10, 15, 25, 34 et al.), the support of the faithful (cc. 19, 37, 39 and often), their shepherd (cc. 25, 39), spring and source (c. 39), the refuge, haven and rest of his own (cc. 10, 27, 37 et al.). He reveals to the faithful the heavenly mysteries (cc. 10, 47, cf. c. 27, 50), enables them to recognize himself, and thereby teaches them to recognize themselves (cc. 15, 34, 112, 144). Thus he aids them to secure an unimpeded heavenly journey through the kingdom of the powers (cc. 142, 144ff., 167).

All these motifs are known from Gnosticism, and could easily be multiplied. They are in harmony with the Gnostic views of the hymns (cc. 6ff., 108) and consecration prayers (cc. 27, 50), and are intended to be understood as clues to the interpretation of the separate narratives. At the outset, the sale of the Apostle as a slave, narrated in the first Praxis, signifies that he like the

Redeemer is humiliated (cc. 19, cf. c. 145, 167), just as the enumeration of his abilities as a craftsman to the merchant Abban and to king Gundaphorus (cc. 3, 17) is not without a mystical secondary meaning. This is matched by the motif of the second Praxis, the building of a heavenly palace out of the alms for which the Apostle employs the money sent him by the king. (This motif also appears in the legend of Barlaam and Josaphat, as a comic fairy-tale motif in the German Eulenspiegel saga, and with more profound intent in Andersen's tale of the emperor's new clothes.)

The frequent stories about demons in the *A Th* are also made to serve the Gnostic doctrine of redemption, as in the third Praxis the revival of the handsome youth slain by a dragon; the latter expressly introduces himself as the representative of the satanic power which rules the world (c. 32 with allusions, in part obscure, to Gnostic speculations). The story clearly reflects the mythical conflict of Ormuzd and Ahriman, and shows through its liturgical conclusion that it is intended to be a legendary dressing-up of the mystery of redemption. A similar conclusion holds for the long-drawn-out demon stories of the fifth, seventh and eighth Praxeis. If in the fifth a beautiful woman, in the seventh and eighth the wife and daughter of one of king Misdaeus' captains are set free from the power of lascivious demons and brought to the heavenly Redeemer, here also the speeches, the formulae of exorcism, the prayers and cultic actions all make it plain that the demons represent the power of darkness, for the conquest of which the Redeemer has descended, to snatch away from the darkness the stolen "light-souls" and even now to bring into effect the definitive separation of the "natures" of light and darkness (cc. 43, 75, 76). It is not difficult to recognize in the legends the familiar Gnostic myth of Sophia, who aroused the desire of the archons of this world and was prevented by them from ascending into the kingdom of light. Our narratives are accordingly legendary modifications of the Simon-Helena story, which has also found entry into the Manichaean legend (cf. F. C. Baur, *Das manichäische Religionssystem*, pp. 467ff.). Clear traces are also to be found especially in the introduction to the sixth Praxis.

Behind the fourth and eighth Praxeis lies the Gnostic motif of the heavenly journey of the soul. This is shown by the story (cc. 69ff.), again interspersed with speeches and prayers, of the talking ass's colt which offers itself to the Apostle as a mount and bears him to the (heavenly) "rest", but collapses dead before the gates of the city; an incident of mystic import which in the first place employs the widespread motif of the heavenly ride and finally makes use of the animal ridden as a symbol for the body. The latter "carries" the soul, but cannot be redeemed with it and therefore is not aroused again from the dead by the Apostle (c. 41; cf. c. 147; note the contrast to the Christian doctrine of the resurrection of the body). A similar function to that of the colt is served by the four wild asses (cc. 70ff.) which are yoked to the Apostle's travelling wagon, and bring him and the captain accompanying him to the city. Here also the speech (c. 68) expressly recalls the heavenly journey. That there are four animals, one of which then itself goes into action as an exorcist and mystagogue (cc. 73ff.), may have some connection with the number of the four heavenly beings named already in c. 32, in the obscure reference to the "four standing brethren".

The motif of the soul's descent into Hell with its description of the places of punishment is known from Greek Orphism, from mystery texts, and above all from the Apocalypse of Peter (cf. below, pp. 663ff.). This motif, broadly developed, is presented by the sixth Praxis—of special interest, since the description of the spheres of Hell clearly reproduces the five Manichaean elements of the world of darkness. This Act also ends with the redemption of the maiden, who under the guidance of a heavenly companion has accomplished the journey to Hell (cc. 57, 59ff.). The journey to Hell thus becomes at the same time a journey to Heaven, and the whole description becomes the presentation of a mystery such as we find in Apuleius (Met. XI. 23) but also in Gnostic and Manichaean texts.

A mythological background can also be shown for the droll scene (cc. 91f.) in which Charisius, a relative of king Misdaeus, recounts to his wife Mygdonia, whom the Apostle has already converted to sexual continence, a dream about an eagle which swooped down while the king was at table, carried off two partridges, a pigeon and a turtle dove, and flew away unharmed with his booty although the king's arrow struck him. The symbolic meaning of the dream is clear from the context: the stolen birds are the two women Mygdonia and Tertia, the young prince Vazan, and his young wife, who have been won by the Apostle for Christ and for a continent life. The image of the eagle is frequently used in Gnosticism for the Redeemer, but over and above this the whole scene is an exact reproduction of the Indian myth of the stealing of the food of immortality by the heavenly eagle Garuda, the sacred bird of Vishnu. Here also Indra shoots at him and hits him, but is unable to harm him. In the Acts the dream is linked with Charisius' misadventure on the following morning, when on rising he substitutes his left shoe for the right one; which is immediately interpreted, again in the light of a conception current also in Gnosticism, as the transformation of evil into good.

The final goal of redemption is the liberation of the soul from its entanglement in earthly appetites, and its union with the heavenly Redeemer. As in Gnosticism, so also in the *ATh* this is often presented under the image of the "sacred marriage". This is clearly shown by the first Praxis, the narrative of the wedding of the king's daughter in Andrapolis, with a two-fold legendary embroidery. For the Apostle, who shares the festivities but with ascetic renunciation of earthly food and drink, the earthly wedding is the occasion for the singing of a hymn about the heavenly marriage which is understood only by the Hebrew flute-girl, who like him is an "alien" and hence a kindred spirit. Between these two, the Apostle transformed in ecstasy and become a mystagogue, and the flute-girl who understands him, loves him and "gazes" steadily at him (this contemplation of the divine is in Gnosticism frequently a term for the completion of the initiation), the mystery of the *hieros gamos* with the Redeemer is already taking place, the latter being represented by his "twin brother". What is here mysteriously hinted is immediately the manifest meaning of the following scene in the bridal chamber: the bride and groom renounce conjugal intercourse and unite in a spiritual marriage (the same ascetic ideal also in the introduction to the sixth Praxis); the souls redeemed from shame and terror to "another marriage" and to love of the "true Man" have become in joy and peace partakers of the immortal, and in him have recognized their origin, their fall, and their destiny (cc. 14f.). In the second part of the Acts the same ideas dominate the broadly depicted stories of the conversion of Mygdonia (9th and 10th Praxeis), the queen Tertia (11th Praxis), and Prince Vazan and his wife. Cf. especially the speeches in cc. 88, 93, 98, 117, 135, and as a most important passage c. 124, where in a long series of antitheses the earthly and the heavenly marriage are set over against each other.

6. THE HYMNS IN THE ACTS OF THOMAS. Among the most valuable elements in the Acts are two Gnostic hymns, which are meaning-fully inserted into the course of the narrative.

(*a*) The first is the Wedding Hymn in the first Praxis (c. 6f.). It sings in luxuriant imagery of the marriage of the virgin of light and the heavenly bridegroom: the splendour of the bride, the bright bridal chamber, fragrant with sweet odours, and the bride's attendants. The images pass curiously one into another. The "king" and the "daughter of light" are related to one another as head and members. The bridegroom rests "upon her head", and the bride's body with its members encompasses in itself the Pleroma of the aeons. With the image of the body is combined the idea of the heavenly building and the heavenly city, and the marriage becomes a feast in which the faithful are united with the royal bridegroom, and receive from him light and the food of immortality. So the seven groomsmen and brides-maids and the twelve attendants enter immediately into the place of the virgin of light, to whom they belong (cf. c. 12 end: "and ye shall enter in as groomsmen into that bridal chamber which is full of immortality and light"). It is clear that here the redemption of Sophia is presented under the imagery of the sacred marriage, as in Valentinian, Marcosian and Ophite Gnosticism, and in this the "elect", the "high-born", have a share. The closest parallels to our wedding hymn are supplied by fragments from Bardesanian Gnosticism which Ephraim has preserved (*Against the Heretics*, Hymn 55. 5, 7): "When at last do we behold thy banquet, and see the maid, the daughter, whom thou hast set upon thy knee and dost lull to sleep?" "O origin of bliss, whose gates open on command before the mother" (Translation after A. Rücker, Bibliothek der Kirchenväter 61, Munich 1928, p. 186f.).

The motif of the heavenly bridal chamber occurs frequently in Manichaean prayers to Christ the Redeemer: "I would dwell in thine aeons, thy bridal chambers of light" (MPsB II. 197. 5;[1] further examples in Widengren, *Mesopotamian Elements*, pp. 109ff.). The description of those who share in the celebration as "megis-tanes" (princes) is common in the Manichaean Psalms (cf. index).

The Syriac text of the Wedding Hymn betrays a thorough catholicizing (instead of "the maiden", "my Church"; instead of the 32 who sing praises, the twelve and the 72 apostles; the double number seven for the bridal suite is deleted). The Wedding Hymn, related to the Bardesanian school as to the Manichaean and perhaps indeed deriving from the former, closes with a benediction which, as Bousset recognized (*Manichäisches* pp. 10f., 22f.), is a Manichaean addition. It names the three deities, the Father of Truth, the Mother of Wisdom and the living Spirit (in S modified into a Christian Trinitarian formula).

(*b*) The Hymn of the Pearl is among the most beautiful docu-ments of Gnosticism which have come down to us.[2] Clothed in a

---

[1] The Manichaean texts are cited according to: *Manichäische Handschriften der Samm-lung A. Chester Beatty, Band I Manichäische Homilien* (ed. H. J. Polotsky) 1934 (=MH); *Band II A Manichaean Psalm-book* (ed. C. R. C. Allberry) 1938 (=MPsB); *Manichäische Handschriften der Staatlichen Museen Berlin, Band I, Kephalaia*, I. Hälfte 1940 (=Keph.).

[2] Recent research is agreed that in contrast to the Wedding Hymn the Syriac version should here be given the preference; it is also the basis of the following translation, while that of Raabe in the first and second editions reproduced the Greek text extant only in the MS. U (and a paraphrase of Nicetas of Thessalonica), with occasional references to the Syriac. I have to thank Prof. Gustav Hölscher (†) for manifold advice in points of detail. The Syriac text, handed down in several MSS. but unfortunately often corrupt, is printed (in addition to Wright) in P. Bedjan, *Acta Martyrum et Sanctorum* III, 1892, pp. 110–115 (vocalized); A. A. Bevan, *The Hymn of the Soul*, *contained in the Syriac Acts of St. Thomas, re-edited with an English translation*, Texts and

fabulous narrative, the Gnostic Redeemer-myth unfolds in the poem in singular purity and completeness, never confused by cosmic speculations; here nothing points to a Christian origin. We can but assemble the most important motifs together, and add the most essential explanations; it is not possible here to adduce the abundant parallels in detail: the sending of the king's son as a little child (the heavenly messenger), the removal of the garment of light, the charge to bring back the pearl (the pearl = the original soul, Egypt frequently stands for the world or the body, the sea and the dragon for the realm of darkness and its ruler); the provision of food and money for the journey (the former frequently for "Gnosis" or the sacramental food which the soul needs for its heavenly journey, the latter to be thought of as money for the tolls which must be paid at the toll-house of the archons); then the departure with two companions (in the Syriac still the Iranian term *parwankin*, also found in Mandean and Manichaean texts), the "foreign-ness" of the emissary and his disguising, his deception through the magic food of the evil powers, his sleep and his forgetting of his origin and commission. Then comes the council in heaven, the sending of the heavenly letter which flies down like an eagle (the eagle is originally the bird of the sun, and in Mandean and Christian texts frequently stands for the Redeemer), delivers the redeeming message as a "call", summons the sleeper to awake and rise up, to recognize his origin and his present misery, and reminds him of his neglected commission, of his heavenly robe and the glory which awaits him. Finally we have the overcoming of the powers, the carrying off of the pearl, the laying aside of the filthy earthly garments, the journey home under the guidance of the "letter" which has itself become a messenger of light, the meeting with the robe of light, brought to meet him by two treasurers (the movements of Gnosis quiver upon it, the image of the King of Kings is embroidered on it), and in it the king's son recognizes as in a mirror his heavenly image; he is united with his image and finally returns to his father's palace.

The poem may with equal justice be described as a song of the

Studies V. 3, 1897; G. Hoffman, Zwei Hymnen der Thomasakten, *ZNW* 4, 1903, pp. 293f. (specially important for the reconstruction of the text); E. Preuschen, *Zwei gnostische Hymnen*, 1904; J. Halévy, Cantique syriaque sur Saint Thomas, *Revue sémitique* 16, 1908, pp. 85–94, 168–175 (with general use of Hoffmann's reconstruction).

On more recent translations in English, French and German, cf. A. Adam, *Die Psalmen des Thomas und das Perlenlied*, p. 49. Adam gives a translation of his own and important contributions for the division of lines and strophes, with conjectures and explanations of particular passages, some of which have been taken into account after a critical examination. Of other translations apart from Hoffmann's, that of M. R. James (*The Apocryphal New Testament*, pp. 411ff.) has in particular been consulted. On the problem of the Hymn of the Pearl cf. also A. F. J. Klijn, The so-called Hymn of the Pearl (Acts of Thomas, ch. 108–113), *Vig. Chr.* 14, 1960, pp. 154–164.

redeeming of the Redeemer or as a song of the deliverance of the soul. That both Redeemer and soul have one origin, one destiny and one essence, is one of the fundamental ideas of Gnostic doctrine. It finds expression in the hymn in various ways: in the duplication of what happens (awakening and return of the king's son, the recovery of the pearl) and in the kinship and "twin" motifs, in the union of the redeemed with his heavenly image. Despite the fabulous traits the religious character of the hymn is beyond doubt. For the general attitude as well as for the symbolic figures, imagery and particular ideas, Mandean texts above all supply parallels in such abundance that we may with confidence designate the pre-Manichaean Gnosis of East Syria and Mesopotamia, which they represent, as the place of origin of our poem from the point of view of the history of religions. In Mandean texts the young lad Hibil-Ziwa, the second son, is sent from the House of Life. Here also we find the same imagery of the "food for the journey" (=Gnosis), the "attendants" of the soul (described indeed by the same Persian word *parwanqua*), the "treasurers" as guardians of the heavenly robe, who clothe the soul in its ascent, the soul as a "pure pearl", "Egypt" as the land of darkness, the "heavenly letter", and the soul's return to its primal home (cf. Reitzenstein, *Iranisches Erlösungsmysterium*, pp. 70ff.; Widengren, *The Great Vohu Mana*, pp. 76ff.; *id., Mesopotamian Elements*, pp. 52ff., 74ff.; Adam, *Die Psalmen des Thomas*, pp. 68f.). From this pre-Manichaean early Mandean Gnosis may also derive the Psalms of Thomas, which have been added to the *Manichaean Psalm-book* by way of appendix. They also present numerous parallels, even to details, with the Hymn of the Pearl. Cf. W. E. Crum, Coptic Analecta, *JTS* 44, 1943, p. 181 n. 9, and Adam, *op. cit.*, who however in his early dating of the Psalms of Thomas (Ps. 1 is dated to the 1st century B.C.!) and of the Hymn of the Pearl (1st century A.D.!) may go considerably too far. The origin and date of the Hymn of the Pearl, as Widengren has shown (*ZRGG* 4, 1952, pp. 97–114), may be more exactly determined on the basis of geographical, political and philological indications, as well as those supplied by cultural history. The geographical horizon itself (Parthia, the mountain country of Warkan = Hyrcania, Garzak, India, Cushan, Mesene), the Arsacid titles of the king (the father is called "King of Kings"), the mention of the "great ones" of the kingdom who have joined in signing the letter (written on Chinese silk with red sulphur), the description of the nobility graded according to degrees of rank, of the royal servants as "girdled" and the prince's retainers as *parwanqe*, the description of the robe, ornamented with precious stones and adorned with the portrait of the Great King, which hastens to meet the king's son, and finally the use of Iranian words in the Syriac text—all this allows us to conclude that the poem originated before the fall of the Parthian dynasty and the rise of the Sassanids (A.D. 226), i.e. in the Arsacid period (Mani was born in 217). That the Manichees knew the Hymn of the Pearl (against Adam, *op. cit.*, p. 70) seems to me to be proved by some texts among the new-found Coptic Manichaica, in particular the fragment of a Psalm to Christ (MPsB II, p. 116. 24ff.): "Christ, lead me; my Redeemer, forget me not . . . I am a prince (megistanos), bearing a crown with the kings. I knew not how I should fight, for I spring from the city of the gods . . . I left my parents, I went out, I gave myself up to death for them. . . ." (Then follows the description of the equipment, the charge to conquer the evil powers and the promise of the crown of victory, the forgetting of his divine origin, the drinking of the magic potion and his defeat by the powers.) At another point we read: "He drew the Urmensch up from the fight like a pearl which is drawn up from the sea" (Keph. p. 85. 24f.). Also instructive are the badly damaged texts in which the role of the Redeemer is transferred to Mani, the great ambassador of the great Babylon (MH, p. 54. 12ff.): ". . . the Apostle of Light . . . the pearl of light, which . . . out of the restless sea . . ." (*ib.*, p. 55. 17ff.). The close connections of the Hymn of the Pearl and the new Manichaean texts help in my view towards the clarification of a question, hitherto debated, which is posed by the geographical statements in the hymn. On the basis of these Hilgenfeld (*Berliner philolog. Wochenschr.* 1898, p. 13) and Bousset (*ZNW* 18, 1917/18, pp. 23ff.) maintained that the king's son was Mani. In favour of this were the facts that Mani derived from the high Parthian nobility, that Mesene was probably the land of his birth and Babylon certainly that of his activity, and also where he died a martyr's death. Again, the *Sarbūg* three times mentioned in the Syriac text but difficult to identify, which is translated in the Greek by Λαβύρινθος, may well be intended to denote the inner city of Babylon (cf. Adam, *op. cit.*, p. 64), according to an illuminating conjecture by W. E. Crum (*JTS* 44, 1943, p. 123; 181), who recalls the Arabic word *sarbūka* = labyrinth. Since however on grounds already mentioned the hymn cannot originally have been conceived with Mani in view, and also Mesene lies aside from the direct route to Egypt, while Babylon (Sarbūg?) vies with Egypt as the city of the demons, we may assume that the Hymn of the Pearl which was already in existence was soon transferred to Mani and furnished with a few details from the story of his life. It is in keeping with this that he certainly understood himself as an emissary of light and became a Redeemer-figure (in the

Turfan fragments he calls himself the "child of princes" who "from high sovereignty has become a stranger"; cf. F. W. K. Müller, Handschriftenreste aus Turfan II, *Abh. d. Berl. Akad.* 1904, 20, p. 29, 108). Possibly this is also the explanation of the surprising conclusion of the poem, which after the son's arrival in his father's house goes on to announce his appearance together with his father before the "King of Kings", although in *c.* 110 the prince's father himself already bears this title of the Parthian kings. This inconsistency also can be explained on the assumption of a biographical fiction, intended for Mani, which has subsequently been imposed upon the whole. That this myth of the messenger who journeys to a strange land and on the way must face the snares of the enemy, pretends in their presence to be a "stranger" and then forgets his native land, found its way into Manichaean legend, can also be seen from the anti-Manichaean history of heresy in the Acta Archelai c. 4 (cf. G. Bornkamm, *Mythos und Legende*, pp. 119f.). If the assumption is correct that the features mentioned are intended to prove that Mani is the king's son, then we may assume that his conflict with the authorities in Babylon and his death are here already presupposed. Of the favour which the redemption-myth of this hymn enjoyed, and precisely among the Manichees, there is at any rate no doubt. It engrossed the attention of Manichaean poetry and doctrine for a long time to come (H. Söderberg, *La Religion des Cathares*, 1949, *passim*). The possibility that the myth related in this hymn in the *ATh* later exercised an influence upon the poetry of the Middle Ages is not out of the question, and has occasionally been asserted, but as yet it does not admit of conclusive proof.

7. SACRAMENTS AND CONSECRATION PRAYERS. With a few exceptions all the stories of conversion in the *ATh* conclude with a ceremony of initiation, the ritual of which is composed of several sacramental acts (cf. c. 26f., 49f., 121, 133, 157). What is clear at all points is the combination of the sealing of the new converts with oil and a Eucharist associated with it. Both sacraments are administered by the Apostle. The sealing is effected 1. by the pouring of consecrated oil upon the head of the neophyte, and 2. by the anointing of the unclothed body (cc. 27, 157); the person sealed is thus marked as the slave or handmaid of God, and becomes partaker of the power of the deity and a member of his flock. What is not quite clear is the relation of the unction to water-baptism. That the sealing is not simply a constituent of water-baptism is apparent from the fact that at some points the latter is expressly added (cc. 120f., 132, 157), and the ritual is different. Since in cc. 26f. and 49f. water-baptism has no place in the ritual described, and the brief and occasional mention of it

is markedly different from the detailed description of the unction and the prayers adjoined to it, we must regard it as probable that water-baptism was first introduced into the text through Catholic interpretation (the tendency to understand the sealing as baptism, or expressly to mention the baptismal act, is at any rate quite clear in the Catholicizing Syriac version). The liturgical portions thus clearly point to a Gnostic sect which knew only the unction as a sacrament of initiation (Bousset, *Hauptprobleme* p. 300; *Manichäisches* p. 16). Such a rejection of Christian water-baptism is to be found both in Gnostic sects and in Manichaeism, whereas among the Mandeans in particular water-baptism and unction belong together, both as in the *ATh* closely connected with the sacramental meal. The Eucharist which is celebrated in the *ATh* is a communion in the bread alone (cc. 27, 29, 49f., 133), and the cup associated with it a cup of water (c. 120). Only in c. 49 and 158 is there any reference in the appended prayers to partaking of the body and blood of Christ, but these also stand apart as clear Catholic interpolations, just as the Syriac version has consistently deleted the traces of a Eucharist with water and inserted the wine (Bousset, *Hauptprobleme* p. 307; Lietzmann, *Messe und Herrenmahl* pp. 243ff.). Once again this form of the Eucharist has its parallels elsewhere precisely in Gnostic mysteries. In c. 152 oil, water and bread are designated by king Misdaeus as the Apostle's magical agencies.

The character of the celebration of the sacraments as a mystery transaction is especially clear from c. 26f., where the new converts at the beginning of the sealing are aware only of the voice of Jesus, but thereafter behold him in person in the form of a youth with a blazing torch. After this celebration by night the Eucharist according to c. 27 follows on the next morning.

Unmistakably Gnostic are the two epicleses addressed to the "Mother", the first of which (c. 27) is adjoined to the unction and the second (c. 50) to the communion, the latter in contrast to the first epiclesis without the traces of Christianization through which the heavenly "Mother of Life" (on her origin in ancient oriental religion see Widengren, *Mesopot. Elem.* pp. 16ff.) was in Christian Gnosticism equated with the Name of Christ and with the Holy Spirit (in Semitic languages feminine). Her epithets of "Mother", "perfect compassion", "rest" or "revealer of the hidden secrets" allow us to recognize in her the *Mētēr, Charis, Sige, Aletheia,* the heavenly Sophia, without however reproducing the succession of the heavenly aeons about which Gnosis elsewhere speculates. She is called "consort (?) of the male" probably as the associate of the heavenly Primal Father (other titles like "holy dove, thou who givest birth to the twin boys" cannot be explained with any confidence). At all events it is clear that the goddess addressed is not the fallen Sophia of numerous Gnostic systems, any more than is the virgin of light of the Wedding Hymn (see above), who is undoubtedly identical with the "Mother"; rather is she the Mother and heavenly "companion in arms" of the Redeemer on earth, and thus herself a revealer and a redeemer of souls. To the individual titles of these two epicleses parallels may be found in the most varied fields of Gnosis. The closest are again the fragments of Bardesanian Gnosticism, in which the "Mother" belongs to the heavenly Pleroma, and then the epicleses and cultic formulae of the Marcosians which Irenaeus has handed down (I. 13 and 21): here also the Father and Truth, the Mother of all things, appear as the highest deities in heaven (I. 21. 3), the latter identical with Achamoth (Sophia), the assessor of God and mysterious eternal Sige (I. 13. 6), in the *ATh* the "Name" which Jesus assumed at his baptism. In her name the Marcosian sacrament of the Apolutrosis is celebrated, just as in the *ATh* an unction, which as Irenaeus notes was performed by some as a final sacrament beside water-baptism in order to secure for the initiate an unimpeded ascent into the kingdom of light. The sealing with oil in the *ATh* has the same significance; cf. the prayer over the oil in c. 157. If we bear in mind the exactly corresponding roles of Marcus and of Thomas in the celebration of the sacrament, and the conception of the consecration as the mystery of the "bridal chamber" which is characteristic both for the Marcosians and for the *ATh*, then the connection is evident, just as indeed the use of Syrian consecration formulae among the Marcosians indicates that this Gnosis belongs to the same geographical area. This does not exclude the possibility that other Gnostic sects also may be related to these two. The Gnosis which has here become visible is however at the same time the direct antecedent from the religio-historical point of view of Manichaeism, in which likewise the "Mother of Life" plays a specially important role as a redeemer-god, just as the anointing of the head with oil for the confirmation of the faith (performed on the *Electi*) is customary among them (Acta Archelai 16. 10ff.); probably also a sacramental meal (the latter is disputed, cf. C. R. C. Allberry, Das manichäische Bema-Fest, *ZNW* 37, 1938, pp. 6ff.). The epicleses also were for Manichaeans perfectly comprehensible and serviceable. Indeed the address: "Come, thou emissary of the five members, of understanding, thought, insight, deliberation, judgment" (in S only "emissary of reconciliation") was rightly recognized by Bousset (*Manichäisches* pp. 1ff.) as a Manichaean addition; it applies to the third emissary, who incorporates in himself the elements of the world of light. If finally we raise the question how the Gnostic epicleses could remain tolerable for a Christian community (the Syriac here also has indeed catholicized in details, but has still left Gnostic elements enough), then we must answer that on the one hand the strongly gnosticizing conception of the Spirit in the Syrian Church, which was only late catholicized, and on the other hand its Mariology, which was no less adaptable to Gnostic motifs, both provided the opportunity. The latter, as it appears, was also taken over by Manichaeism, as is shown by the numerous hymns in the new-found *Psalm-book* which end in stereotyped fashion with praise to the "soul of the blessed Mary" (hardly the name of a martyr).

8. THE POSITION OF THE ATh IN THE HISTORY OF RELIGIONS can be fixed, as the analysis has shown, with some confidence. The book represents the Gnostic Christianity of Syria in the third century, which was domiciled in the region of Mesopotamia (somewhere between Edessa and Mesene) and was only catholicized at a relatively late date (in the 4th and 5th centuries; cf. Bauer, *Rechtgläubigkeit und Ketzerei*, pp. 6ff.). Close connections with the Bardesanian Gnosis can be seen in the Wedding Hymn of Sophia and in the "Mother" epicleses, but there is in addition a long free quotation from the Bardesanian "Book of the Laws of the Lands" in the speech in c. 91 (Bornkamm, *Mythos und Legende*, pp. 85ff.). That the Bardesanites composed apocryphal Acts and put their doctrines into the mouth of the Apostles is moreover expressly stated by Ephraem Syrus (cf. Bauer, *op. cit.*, pp. 46f.). All the same, the *ATh* give the impression of a "vulgar" Gnosticism (Lipsius I. 345), and are distinguished from Bardesanes himself (not from his school, cf. H. H. Schaeder, Bardesanes von Edessa, *ZKG* 51, 1932, pp. 21ff.) by their radical dualism and their severely Encratite tendency. The latter links them all the more closely with Manichaeism, which itself took its origin from the Bardesanian Gnosis and made its appearance in the latter's sphere of influence in the century in which the *ATh* came into being.

This is shown also by the canon of ascetic ethics which is expressly formulated at several points in the *ATh* (cc. 28, 126)—rejection of the pleasures of the table, of avarice and of sexual intercourse—and which was adopted by the Manichees in their precepts for the *Electi* (*tria signacula*). This ascetic canon is certainly pre-Manichaean. The same holds for numerous particular ideas and conceptions, which have their exact parallels indeed in Manichaeism but derive in fact from the older Gnosticism. From this point of view we can understand the diffusion and appreciation of these Acts among the Manichees, and the fact that traces of Manichaean redaction are almost certainly to be found in the doxology to the Wedding Hymn (c. 7), in the epiclesis (c. 27) and in the Hymn of the Pearl. The Acts as a whole however prove to be a connecting-link between the older Gnosticism and Manichaeism. They allow us to recognize a pre-Manichaean Syrian Gnosticism, out of whose elements Mani shaped his own doctrine. Possibly, as Schaeder has conjectured (*Gnomon* 1933, pp. 351f.), the very figure of Thomas, the Apostle of Syria, played an extremely important role for Mani. According to the Arabian Fihrist he was called by an angel "*at-taum*". This angelic name is only the transposition of the Aramaic "*toma*", which at one and the same time is the proper name and signifies "twin". This call is now confirmed by Mani's own account (Keph. 14f.), where in the place of that angel there appears the "living Paraclete", whom Mani must have identified with him. The exact counterpart to the "twin" of the *ATh* is formed by the term "bosom friend", frequent in the Coptic texts (Widengren, *The Great Vohu Mana*, pp. 25ff.). The new Manichaean texts also show that the Thomas legend, as presented in the *ATh*, was well known in Manichaeism. Thomas is the Apostle of India (MPsB 194. 13 *et al.*), who met his death at the hands of four soldiers who thrust him through with lances (*ib.* 142. 17ff.; cf. *ATh* 165, 168). The Gnostically interpreted figure of the Apostle Thomas may thus have been of considerable importance for Mani's understanding of himself. It mediated to him the apostolic connection with Jesus, and appeared in his eyes indeed his *alter ego*, just as Mani's missionary journey to India before his appearance in Babylon corresponds to that of the Apostle.

The Gnosticism documented in the *ATh* evidently provided the Manichaeism which was soon thereafter systematically developed with a considerable portion of its mythological material, and the "vulgar" form probably with its essential content. That in Catholic circles also these Acts could be widely read and valued, without concern, is not surprising, since the translation of the Gnostic myths into legend seems to have made the heretical poison largely ineffective for uncritical readers. The period of origin of the *ATh* is settled by their place in the history of religions between Bardesanes and Mani; they will have been composed in the first half of the 3rd century.

Postscript: Only after the manuscript had gone to press there appeared a detailed commentary on the *ATh* by A. F. J. Klijn, *The Acts of Thomas*, Suppl. Nov. Test. V, 1962. In contrast to the text printed below, the author made the extant Syriac version the basis of his English translation, founded on that of Wright.

Yet the author himself admits that the Greek text stands nearer to the lost Syriac text and its tradition than does the extant Syriac, which has many very puristic passages and allows us to recognize a growing orthodoxy. Certainly the author is correct in holding that in the *ATh* there is reflected the highly complex image of Syrian Christianity at the beginning of the 3rd century. The extensive collection of parallels is the real merit of Klijn's work. But the various streams of this early Syrian Christianity may be more precisely distinguished than appears in Klijn, and his denial of the Gnostic character of the Acts is not justified. This Gnostic character is confirmed also by the close relation between the *ATh* and Manicheism. As W. Bauer has shown (*Rechtgläubigkeit und Ketzerei*, 1934; scarcely noticed in Klijn), orthodoxy in Syria stands at the end, whereas at the beginning powerful Gnostic currents held sway. The process is shown in the clearest possible manner by the *ATh* itself in its nonchalant acceptance of Gnostic myths and conceptions in hymns, liturgical passages and narrative, its disguising of myths and legends, but also in its revision in the interest of orthodoxy, in which the passages later considered heretical were altered or suppressed (see textual history). The process can be demonstrated only by an analysis which, otherwise than is done in Klijn, unites more widely extended religio-historical, literary and form-critical investigations and combines them with the textual history (*Dieter Georgi*).

THE ACTS OF THE HOLY APOSTLE THOMAS

(*Aa* II. 2, pp. 99–287)

⟨First Act of the Apostle Judas Thomas

How the Lord sold him to the merchant Abban, that he might go down and c⟨n⟩vert India S⟩*

1. At that time we apostles[1] were all in Jerusalem, Simon called Peter and Andrew his brother, James the son of Zebedee and John his brother, Philip and Bartholomew, Thomas and Matthew the publican, James (the son) of Alphaeus and Simon the

---

* Brackets are used as follows:
    (   ) explanatory additions by the translator.
    ⟨   ⟩ conjecture or emendation.
    ⟨ S⟩ correction or restoration on the basis of the Syriac text.
    ⟨ G⟩ correction or restoration on the basis of the Greek text (in the Hymn of the Pearl).
    ⟨ . . . . ⟩ deletion.
The bracketed page numbers refer to Bonnet's edition.
[1] Cf. Mk. 3:16–19; Mt. 10:2–4; Lk. 6:14–16; Acts 1:13.

Cananaean, (p. 100) and Judas (the brother) of James; and we divided the regions of the world, that each one of us might go to the region which fell to his lot, and to the nation to which the Lord sent him. According to lot, India fell to Judas Thomas, who is also (called) Didymus; but he did not wish to go, saying that through weakness of the flesh he could not travel, and: "How can I, who am a Hebrew, go and preach the truth among the Indians?" And as he considered and said this, the Saviour appeared to him by night[1] and said to him: "Fear not, Thomas, go to India and preach the word there, for my grace is with thee." But he would not obey (p. 101) and said: "Send me where thou wilt—but somewhere else! For I am not going to the Indians." 2. And as he thus spoke and thought, it happened that a certain merchant was there who had come from India. His name was Abban and he had been sent by king Gundaphorus, and had received orders from him to buy a carpenter and bring him back to him. Now the Lord saw him walking in the market-place at noon, and said to him: "Dost thou wish to buy a carpenter?" He said to him: "Yes." And the Lord said to him: "I have a slave who is a carpenter, and wish to sell him." And when he had said this he showed him Thomas from a distance, and agreed (p. 102) with him for three pounds of uncoined (silver), and wrote a ⟨deed of S⟩ sale saying: I Jesus the son of Joseph the carpenter confirm that I have sold my slave, Judas by name, to thee Abban, a merchant of Gundaphorus the king of the Indians. And when the ⟨deed of S⟩ sale was completed the Saviour took Judas, who is also (called) Thomas, and led him to the merchant Abban. And when Abban saw him, he said to him: "Is this thy master?" And the apostle in answer said: "Yes, he is my Lord." But he said: "I have bought thee from him." And the apostle was silent. 3. On the following morning the apostle prayed and besought the Lord, and said: "I go whither thou wilt, Lord Jesus; (p. 103) *thy will be done!*"[2] And he went off to Abban the merchant, carrying with him nothing at all, save only his price. For the Lord had given it to him, saying: "Let thy price also be with thee, with my grace, whithersoever thou goest!" But the apostle found Abban ⟨.⟩ carrying his

_____
[1] Cf. Acts 18:9; 23:11.   [2] Mt. 6:10; Lk. 22:42.

baggage aboard the ship, and he too began to carry it with him. And when they had embarked on the ship and sat down, Abban questioned the apostle, saying: "What manner of trade dost thou know?" And he said: "In wood (I can make) ploughs and yokes and balances ⟨goads⟩ and ships and oars for ships and masts and pulleys; and in stone, pillars and temples and royal (p. 104) palaces." And Abban the merchant said to him: "(It is good), for of such a craftsman are we in need." So they began their voyage. They had a favourable wind, and sailed prosperously until they arrived at Andrapolis, a royal city. 4. Leaving the ship, they went into the city. And lo, sounds of ⟨flutes⟩ and water-organs and trumpets echoed round about them; and the apostle inquired, saying: "What is this feast which (is being celebrated) in this city?" The people there said to him: (p. 105) "Thee too have the gods brought to keep festival in this city. For the king has an only daughter, and now he is giving her to a man in marriage. So it is for the wedding, this rejoicing and this assembly for the feast today which thou hast seen. And the king has sent out heralds to proclaim everywhere that all should come to the wedding,[1] rich and poor, bond and free, strangers and citizens; but if any man refuse, and come not to the marriage, he shall be accountable to the king." When Abban heard it, he said to the apostle: "Let us also go, then, that we may not give offence to the king, especially since we are strangers." And he said: "Let us go." And after taking quarters at the inn and resting a little they went to the wedding. (p. 106) And the apostle, seeing them all reclining, himself lay down in the midst; and they all looked at him, as at a stranger and one come from a foreign land. But Abban the merchant, as being the master, lay down at another place. 5. But while they dined and drank, the apostle tasted nothing; so those who were round about him said: "Why didst thou come here neither eating nor drinking?" But he answered and said to them: "For something greater than food or drink am I come hither, ⟨for the king's rest S⟩ and that I may accomplish the king's will. For the heralds proclaim the king's (commands) and (p. 107) whoever does not listen to the heralds shall be liable to the king's judgment." And when they had dined and drunk, and

---

[1] Cf. Mt. 22:3–14.

crowns and scented oils were brought, each one took of the oil,
and one anointed his face, another his chin (his beard), another
again other parts of his body; but the apostle anointed the crown
of his head and smeared a little upon his nostrils, dropped some
also into his ears, touched his teeth with it, and carefully anointed
the parts about his heart; and the crown that was brought to him,
woven of myrtle and other flowers, he took and set upon his head;
and he took a branch of a reed (p. 108) in his hand and held it.
Now the flute-girl, holding her flute in her hand, was going round
all the company and playing; but when she came to the place
where the apostle was, she stood over him and played at his head
for a long time. Now that flute-girl was by race a Hebrew. 6. While
the apostle was looking at the ground, one of the cup-bearers
stretched out his hand and slapped him. But the apostle lifted up
his eyes, directed his gaze at the man who had struck him, and
said: "My God will forgive thee this injury in the world to come,
but in this world he will show forth his wonders, and I shall even
now see that hand that smote me dragged by dogs." And when
he had said this he began to sing this song and to say:

(p. 109) The maiden is the daughter of light,
Upon her stands and rests the majestic effulgence of kings,
Delightful is the sight of her,
Radiant with shining beauty.
Her garments are like spring flowers,
And a scent of sweet fragrance is diffused from them.
In the crown of her head the king is established,
Feeding with his own ambrosia those who are set ⟨under⟩ him.
Truth rests upon her head,
By (the movement of) her feet she shows forth joy.
Her mouth is open, and that becomingly,
⟨For (with it) she sings loud songs of praise. S⟩
Thirty and two are they that sing her praises.
Her tongue is like the curtain of the door,
Which is flung back for those who enter in.
⟨Like steps her neck mounts up S⟩,
Which the first craftsman wrought.
Her two hands make signs and secret patterns, proclaiming
　　　　　　　　　　　　the dance of the blessed aeons,

445

Her fingers ⟨open S⟩ the gates of the city.
Her chamber is full of light,
Breathing a scent of balsam and all sweet herbs,
(p. 110) And giving out a sweet smell of myrrh and (aromatic)
                                                              leaves.
Within are strewn myrtle branches and ⟨all manner of
                                              sweet-smelling flowers⟩,
And the ⟨portals⟩ are adorned with reeds.
7. Her ⟨groomsmen⟩ keep her compassed about, whose number
                                                        is seven,
Whom she herself has chosen;
And her bridesmaids are seven,
Who dance before her.
Twelve are they in number who serve before her
And are subject to her,
Having their gaze and look toward the bridegroom,
That by the sight of him they may be enlightened;
And for ever shall they be with him in that eternal joy,
And they shall be at that marriage
For which the princes assemble together,
And shall linger over the feasting
Of which the eternal ones are accounted worthy,
And they shall put on royal robes
And be arrayed in splendid raiment,
And both shall be in joy and exultation
And they shall glorify the Father of all,
Whose proud light they received
And were enlightened by the vision of their Lord,
Whose ambrosial food they received,
Which has no deficiency at all,
And they drank too of his wine
Which gives them neither thirst nor desire;
And they glorified and praised, with the living Spirit,
The Father of Truth and the Mother of Wisdom.

8. (p. 111) And when he had sung and ended this song, all who were present gazed upon him; and he was silent. They saw also his appearance changed, but they did not understand what he said, since he was a Hebrew and what he said was spoken in

446

the Hebrew tongue. The flute-girl alone heard it all, for she was
a Hebrew by race; and moving away from him she played to the
others, but often looked back and gazed on him. For she loved
him greatly, as a man of her own race; moreover in appearance
he was comely above all that were present. And when the flute-
girl had ⟨quite⟩ finished ⟨her playing⟩, she sat down opposite
him and looked steadily at him. But he looked at no-one at all,
nor did he pay attention to anyone, but kept his eyes only on the
ground, waiting for the time when (p. 112) he might take his
departure. But the cup-bearer who had slapped him went down
to the well to draw water. And it happened that there was a lion
there, and it slew him and left him to lie on the spot, after tearing
his limbs to pieces. And immediately dogs seized his limbs, and
among them a black dog grasped his right hand in its mouth and
carried it into the place where the feast was. 9. But when they
saw it, they were all amazed and inquired which of them was
absent. But when it became evident that it was the hand of the
cup-bearer who had struck the apostle, (p. 113) the flute-girl
smashed her flute and threw it away, and went to the apostle's
feet and sat down, saying: "This man is either a god or an apostle
of God; for I heard him say to the cup-bearer in Hebrew: 'Even
now shall I see the hand that smote me dragged by dogs'—which
you also have now seen; for as he said, so did it come to pass."
And some believed her, but some did not. But when the king
heard it, he came and said to the apostle: "Arise and come with
me, and pray for my daughter! For she is my only child, and
today I give her in marriage." But the apostle would not (p. 114)
go with him, for the Lord was not yet revealed to him there.
But the king led him away against his will into the bridal chamber,
that he might pray for them (the bridal pair). 10. And the apostle
standing began to pray and to speak thus: "*My Lord and my
God*,[1] the companion of his servants, who doth guide and direct
those who believe in him, the refuge and rest of the oppressed,
the hope of the poor and redeemer of the captives, the physician
of the souls laid low in sickness and saviour of all creation, who
dost quicken the world to life and strengthen the souls, thou dost
know what is to be, who also dost accomplish it through us;

[1] Jn. 20:28.

447

thou, Lord, who dost reveal hidden mysteries and make manifest words that are secret; thou, Lord, art the planter of the good tree, and by thy hands are all good works engendered; thou, Lord, art he who is in all and passes through all and dwells in all thy works, and manifest in the working of them all*; Jesus Christ, Son of compassion and (p. 115) perfect Saviour; Christ, *Son of the living God*,[1] the undaunted power which overthrew the enemy, the voice that was heard by the archons, which shook all their powers; ambassador sent from the height who didst descend even to Hell, who having opened the doors didst bring up thence those who for many ages had been shut up in the treasury of darkness, and show them the way that leads up to the height; I pray thee, Lord Jesus, as I bring to thee my supplication for these young people, that thou do for them the things that help and are useful and profitable." And after laying his hands upon them and saying: "The Lord shall be with you", he left them in that place and departed. 11. The king required the attendants to go out of the bridal chamber. And when all had gone out and the doors were shut, the bridegroom lifted up the veil of the bridal chamber, (p. 116) that he might bring the bride to himself. And he saw the Lord Jesus in the likeness of the apostle Judas Thomas, who shortly before had blessed them and departed from them, conversing with the bride, and he said to him: "Didst thou not go out before them all? How art thou now found here?" But the Lord said to him: "I am not Judas who is also Thomas, I am his brother." And the Lord sat down upon the bed and bade them also to sit on the chairs, and began to say to them: 12. "Remember, my children, what my brother said to you, and to whom he

---

* Here the Syriac has: Thou art the beginning, and didst put on the first man. Thou art the power and wisdom, understanding, will and rest of thy Father, through whom thou art hidden in glory and through whom thou art revealed in thy doings. And ye are one in two names. And thou didst appear as one that was weak, and those who saw thee thought of thee that thou wast a man who had need of help, and thou didst show the glory of thy godhead through the forbearance of thy Spirit with our humanity, in that thou didst cast down the evil one from his power and call with thy voice upon the dead, that they might live, and didst promise to those who live and hope in thee an inheritance in thy kingdom. Thou didst become an ambassador and wast sent from the heights above, since thou canst do the living and perfect will of him who sent thee. Blessed be thou, Lord, in thy might, and thy government works with renewing power in all thy creatures and in all the works which thy godhead has accomplished, and no other can make the will of thy majesty of none effect and stand up against the nature of thine eminence, as thou art. Thou didst descend to Hell. . . .

[1] Mt. 16:16,

commended you; and know this, that if you (p. 117) abandon this filthy intercourse you become holy temples, pure and free from afflictions and pains both manifest and hidden, and you will not be girt about with cares for life and for children, *the end of which is destruction.*[1] But if you get many children, then for their sakes you become robbers and avaricious, (people who) flay orphans and defraud widows, and by so doing you subject yourselves to the most grievous punishments. For the majority of children become unprofitable, possessed by demons, some openly and some in secret; for they become either lunatic or half-withered (consumptive) or crippled or deaf or dumb or paralytic or stupid. Even if they are healthy, again will they be unserviceable, performing useless (p. 118) and abominable deeds; for they are caught either in adultery or in murder or in theft or in unchastity, and by all these you will be afflicted. But if you obey, and keep your souls pure unto God, you shall have living children whom these hurts do not touch, and shall be without care, leading an undisturbed life without grief or anxiety, waiting to receive that incorruptible and true marriage (as befitting for you), and in it you shall be groomsmen entering into that bridal chamber ⟨which is full of⟩ immortality and light." 13. But when the young people heard this, they believed the Lord and gave themselves entirely to him, and refrained (p. 119) from the filthy passion, and so remained throughout the night in that place. And the Lord departed from them, saying: "*The grace of the Lord shall be with you!*"[2] When morning broke, the king came to meet them, and after furnishing the table brought it in before the bridegroom and the bride; and he found them sitting opposite one another, the bride with her face unveiled and the bridegroom very cheerful. But her mother came in and said to the bride: "Why dost thou sit thus, child, and art not ashamed, but dost behave as if thou hadst lived a long time with thine own husband?" And her father said: "Because of thy great love for thy husband dost thou not even veil thyself?" 14. The bride in answer said: "Truly, father, I am in great love, and I pray to my Lord that the love (p. 120) which I experienced this night may remain with me, and I will ask for the husband of whom I have learned today.

[1] Cf. Phil. 3:19.   [2] 1 Cor. 16:23.

449

⟨But that I do not veil myself S⟩ (is) because the mirror ⟨veil S⟩ of shame is taken from me;[1] and I am no longer ashamed or abashed, because the work of shame and bashfulness has been removed far from me. And that I am not alarmed, (is) because alarm did not remain with me. And that I am in cheerfulness and joy (is) because the day of joy was not disturbed. And that I have set at naught this man, and this marriage which passes away from before my eyes, (is) because I am bound in another marriage. And that I have had no intercourse with a short-lived husband, the end of which is ⟨remorse and bitterness⟩ of soul, (is) because I am yoked with ⟨the⟩ true man."

15. And while the bride was saying yet more than this, the bridegroom answered and said: "I thank thee, Lord, who through the (p. 121) stranger wast proclaimed and found in us; who hast removed me from corruption and sown in me life; who didst free me from this sickness, hard to heal and hard to cure and abiding for ever, and didst implant in me sober health; who didst show thyself to me and reveal to me all my condition in which I am; who didst redeem me from the fall and lead me to the better, and free me from things transitory but count me worthy of those that are immortal and everlasting; who didst humble thyself to me and my smallness, that setting me beside thy greatness thou mightest unite me with thyself; who didst not withhold thy mercy from me that was ready to perish, but didst show me to seek myself and to recognize who I was and who and how I now am, that I may become again what I was; whom I did not know, but thou thyself didst seek me out; of whom I was unaware, but thou thyself didst take me to thee; whom I have perceived, and now cannot (p. 122) forget; whose love ferments within me, and of whom I cannot speak as I ought, but what I can say about him is short and very little and does not correspond to his glory; but he does not blame me when I make bold to say to him even what I do not know; for it is for love of him that I say this."

16. But when the king heard this from the bridegroom and the bride he rent his garments and said to those who stood near him: "Go out quickly and go through all the city, and seize and bring to me that man, the sorcerer who by an evil chance is in this

---

[1] Cf. the Gospel of Thomas, log. 37 (Vol. I, p. 298).

city. For I brought him with my own hands into my house, and told him to pray over my most unfortunate daughter. And whosoever finds and brings him to me, to him do I give ⟨all that he may ask of me⟩." (p. 123) So they departed and went about in search of him, and did not find him; for he had set sail. They went also into the inn where he had lodged, and there they found the flute-girl weeping and distressed, because he had not taken her with him. But when they told her what had happened in the case of the young people, she was very glad when she heard it, and setting aside her grief she said: "Now have I too found rest here!" And rising up she went to them, and stayed with them a long time, until they had taught the king also. And many of the brethren also gathered there, until they heard a report (p. 124) about the apostle, that he had landed in the cities of India and was teaching there. And they went off and joined themselves with him.

Second Act of the Apostle Thomas
Concerning his coming to King Gundaphorus

17. But when the apostle came to the cities of India with Abban the merchant, Abban went off to salute King Gundaphorus, and reported to him concerning the carpenter whom he had brought with him. The king was glad, and commanded that he should come to him. So when (p. 125) he came the king said to him: "What kind of trade dost thou understand?" The apostle said to him: "Carpentry and building." The king said to him: "What craftsmanship, then, dost thou know in wood, and what in stone?" The apostle said: "In wood, ploughs, yokes, balances, pulleys, and ships and oars and masts; and in stone, pillars, temples and royal palaces." And the king said: "Wilt thou build me a palace?" And he answered: "Yes, I will build and finish it; for this is why I came, to build and work as a carpenter." 18. And the king took him and went out of the gates of the city, and began to discuss with him on the way (p. 126) the building of the palace and how the foundations should be laid, until they came to the place where he wanted the building to be. And he said: "I wish the building to be here." And the apostle said: "Yes, for this place is suitable for the building."

But the place was wooded, and there was much water there. So the king said: "Begin to build." But he said: "I cannot begin to build now at this season." And the king said: "When canst thou?" And he said: "I will begin in November and finish (p. 127) in April." But the king said in astonishment: "Every building is built in summer, but thou canst build and establish a palace even in winter?" And the apostle said: "So it ought to be, and there is no other way." And the king said: "Well then, if this is thy resolve, draw me a plan how the work is to be, since I shall come back here (only) after some time." And the apostle took a reed and drew, measuring the place; and the doors he set toward the east, to face the light, and the windows to the west towards the winds, and the bakehouse he made to be to the south, and the aqueduct for the service to the north. But when the king saw it, he said to the apostle: "Truly thou art a craftsman, and it is fitting (p. 128) for thee to serve kings." And leaving much money with him he departed from him. 19. And at appointed times he used to send him money and what was necessary both for his own sustenance and for that of the other workmen. But he took it all and dispensed it, going about the towns and the villages round about, distributing it and bestowing alms on the poor and afflicted, and he gave them relief, saying: "The king knows that he will receive a royal recompense, but the poor must for the present be refreshed." After this the king sent (p. 129) an ambassador to the apostle, writing to him thus: "Show me what thou hast done, or what I should send thee, or what thou dost require." The apostle sent to him, saying: "The palace is built, and only the roof remains." When the king heard this, he sent him again gold and uncoined silver, writing: "If the palace is built, let it be roofed!" But the apostle said to the Lord: "I thank thee, Lord, in every respect, that thou for a short time didst die that I might live eternally in thee, and that thou didst sell me in order to deliver many through me." And he did not cease from teaching and refreshing the afflicted, (p. 130) saying: "The Lord has dispensed this to you, and himself provides to each his food. For he is the nourisher of the orphans and supporter of the widows, and to all that are afflicted he is relief and rest." 20. But when the king came to the city he inquired of his friends concerning the palace which Judas who is also Thomas was building for him. But they said to him: "Neither has he built a palace, nor has he done anything else of what he promised to do, but he goes about the towns and villages, and if he has anything he gives it all to the poor, and he teaches a new God ⟨.⟩ and heals (p. 131) the sick and drives out demons and does many other wonderful things; and we think he is a magician. But his works of compassion, and the healings which are wrought by him without reward, and moreover his simplicity and kindness and the quality of his faith, show that he is righteous or an apostle of the new God whom he preaches. For continually he fasts and prays, and eats only bread with salt, and his drink is water, and he wears one garment whether in fine weather or in foul (winter), and takes nothing from anyone, and what he has he gives to others." When he heard this, (p. 132) the king smote his face with his hands, shaking his head for a long time. 21. And he sent for the merchant who had brought him, and for the apostle, and said to him: "Hast thou built me the palace?" And he said: "Yes, I have built it." The king said: "Then when shall we go and see it?" But he answered him and said: "Now thou canst not see it, but when thou dost depart this life thou shalt see it." But the king in great wrath commanded (p. 133) both the merchant and Judas who is also Thomas to be put in bonds and cast into prison until he should investigate and learn to whom the king's money had been given, and so destroy him together with the merchant. But the apostle went rejoicing into the prison, and said to the merchant: "*Fear nothing*, but *only believe*[1] in the God who is preached by me, and thou shalt be freed from this world but from the age to come shalt obtain life." Now the king was considering with what manner of death (p. 134) he should destroy them. But when he had resolved to flay them alive and then burn them with fire, in the same night Gad the king's brother fell sick, and because of the pain and disappointment which the king had suffered he was greatly depressed. And he sent for the king and said to him: "My brother the king, my house and my children I commend to thee. For I have been grieved on account of the despiteful usage that has befallen thee and behold, I am dying, and if thou do not come down with

[1] Mk. 5:36.

vengeance upon the head of that magician, thou wilt give my soul no rest in Hades." But the king said to his brother: "The whole night through I was considering how I should put him to death; and this have I resolved, to flay him alive and then burn him with fire, both him and with him the merchant who brought him." (p. 135) 22. And as they conversed the soul of Gad his brother departed. The king mourned Gad deeply, for he loved him greatly, and commanded him to be buried in royal and costly apparel. But when this happened, angels took the soul of Gad the king's brother and carried it up into heaven, showing him the places there and the dwellings and asking him: "In what kind of place wouldst thou live?" But when they drew near to the building of Thomas the apostle, which he built for the king, Gad when he saw it said to the angels: "I pray you, sirs, allow me to live in one of these lower apartments." But they said to him: (p. 136) "Thou canst not live in this building." And he said: "Why?" They said to him: "This palace is the one which that Christian built for thy brother." But he said: "I pray you, sirs, allow me to go to my brother, that I may buy this palace from him. For my brother does not know of what kind it is, and will sell it to me." 23. Then the angels let Gad's soul go. And while they were putting the grave clothes on him, his soul entered into him; and he said to those who stood around him: "Call to me my brother, that I may ask of him one request." So at once they brought the good news to the king, (p. 137) saying: "Thy brother is alive again!" The king sprang up and came with a great crowd to his brother, and going in he stood by his bed as if stupefied, unable to speak to him. But his brother said: "I know and am persuaded, brother, that if anyone asked of thee the half of thy kingdom, thou wouldst have given it for my sake. Wherefore I beseech thee to grant me one favour which I ask of thee, that thou sell me what I ask from thee." But the king said in answer: "And what is it that thou dost ask me to sell thee?" But he said: "Convince me by an oath that thou wilt grant it me." And the king swore to him: "⟨Whatever of my possessions thou dost ask for thyself⟩, (p. 138) I give it thee." And he said to him: "Sell me that palace which thou hast in heaven." And the king said: "Whence should I have a palace in heaven?" But he said: "The one that Christian built for thee, who is now in prison—the man the merchant brought thee after buying him from one Jesus. I mean that Hebrew slave whom thou didst wish to punish, as having suffered some deception at his hand—against whom I too was vexed, and died, and now I am alive again." 24. Then the king, considering the matter, understood (his words) concerning the eternal goods which were more excellent for him and which he was to receive, and said: "That palace I cannot sell to thee, but I pray that I may enter it and live in it, and be counted worthy ⟨to belong to⟩ its inhabitants. But if thou dost truly wish to buy such a palace, behold the man is alive, and will build thee one better than that." (p. 139) And immediately he sent and brought the apostle out of the prison, and the merchant who had been shut up with him, saying: "I entreat thee, as a man entreating the servant of God, to pray for me and beseech him whose servant thou art, that he forgive me and overlook the things that I have done against thee, or thought to do, and that I may become a worthy inhabitant of that dwelling for which I did not labour at all, but thou didst build it for me labouring alone, the grace of thy God working with thee, and that I too may become a servant, and serve this God whom thou dost proclaim." And his brother also fell down at the apostle's feet and said: "I pray thee and implore before thy God, that I may become worthy of this ministry and service, and that it may be my lot to be worthy of the things ⟨shown to me by his angels⟩." (p. 140) 25. But the apostle, possessed ⟨with⟩ joy, said: "I praise thee, Lord Jesus, that thou hast revealed thy truth in these men. For thou alone art the God of truth, and no other; and thou art he who knows all that is unknown to the many; thou, Lord, art he who in all things shows ⟨mercy and forbearance to men⟩. For men because of the error that is in them forsook thee, but thou didst not forsake them. And now as I beseech and supplicate thee, receive the king and his brother and unite them with thy flock, cleansing them with thy washing and anointing them with thy oil from the error which surrounds them. Preserve them also from the wolves, leading them in thy pastures. Give them to drink from thine ambrosial spring which neither is turbid nor dries up. For they pray thee and implore and desire to become thy ministers and servants, and

455

for this cause they are content even to be persecuted by thine enemies, (p. 141) and for thy sake to be hated by them and be despitefully used and put to death, even as thou for our sakes didst suffer all these things that thou mightest preserve us, who art Lord and truly a *good shepherd*.[1] But do thou grant to them that they may have confidence in thee alone, and ⟨obtain⟩ the help which cometh from thee and hope of their salvation, which they expect from thee alone, and that they may be established in thy mysteries and receive of thy graces and gifts the perfect good, and may flourish in thy service, and bring forth fruit to perfection in thy Father." 26. Being now well disposed to the apostle, King Gundaphorus and his brother Gad followed him, departing from him not at all and themselves supplying those who were in need, giving to all and refreshing all. And they besought him that they also might now receive the seal of the word, saying to him: "Since our souls are at leisure and we are zealous for God, give us the seal! For we have heard thee say that the God whom thou dost preach knows his own sheep by his seal." But the apostle said to them: "I also rejoice and pray you to receive this seal, and to share with me in this eucharist (p. 142) and (feast of) blessing of the Lord, and be made perfect in it. For this is the Lord and God of all, Jesus Christ whom I preach, and he is the Father of truth in whom I have taught you to believe." And he commanded them to bring oil, that through the oil they might receive the seal. So they brought the oil, and lit many lamps; for it was night. 27. And the apostle rose up and sealed them. But the Lord was revealed to them by a voice, saying: "*Peace be with you*,[2] brethren!" But they only heard his voice, but his form they did not see; for they had not yet received the additional sealing of the seal. And the apostle took the oil and pouring it on their heads anointed and chrismed them, and began to say:

Come, holy name of Christ *that is above every name*;[3]
Come, power of the Most High and perfect compassion;
Come, thou highest gift;
Come, compassionate mother;
Come, fellowship of the male;
Come, thou (fem.) that dost reveal the hidden mysteries;

---

[1] Cf. Jn. 10:12, 14.   [2] Jn. 20:19, 21, 26.   [3] Phil. 2:9.

Come, mother of the seven houses, that thy rest may be in the
  eighth house;
Come, elder ⟨messenger S⟩ of the five members, understanding,
  thought, prudence, (p. 143) consideration, reasoning,
Communicate with these young men!
Come, Holy Spirit, and purify their reins and their heart
And give them the added seal in the name of Father and Son
  and Holy Spirit.

And when they had been sealed there appeared to them a
young man carrying a blazing torch, so that the very lamps were
darkened at the onset of its light. And going out he vanished from
their sight. But the apostle said to the Lord: "Beyond our comprehension, Lord, is thy light, and we are not able to bear it; for it
is greater than our sight." But when dawn came and it was light,
he broke bread and made them partakers in the eucharist of
Christ. And they rejoiced and were glad. And many others also,
believing, were added (to the faithful) and came into the refuge
of the Saviour. 28. But the apostle did not cease preaching and
saying (p. 144) to them: "Men and women, boys and girls,
youths and maids, vigorous and aged, whether you are slaves or
free, abstain from fornication and avarice and the service of the
belly; for in these three heads all lawlessness is comprised. For
fornication blinds the mind and darkens the eyes of the soul, and
is a hindrance to the right ordering of the body, turning the whole
man to weakness and throwing the whole body into sickness.
Insatiate desire brings the soul into fear and shame, since it is
within the body and plunders the goods of others, and harbours
this suspicion, ⟨that if it restore⟩ the goods of others to the
owners ⟨it will be put to shame⟩. And the service of the belly
plunges the soul into cares and anxieties and sorrows, ⟨since it
becomes anxious lest it come to be in want, and reaches out for
what is far from it⟩. If then you escape from these, you become
free from care and sorrow and fear, and there remains with you
that which was said by the Saviour: *Be not anxious for the morrow,
for the morrow will take care of itself.*[1] Remember also that word
which was spoken before: Look at *the ravens* and (p. 145) consider *the birds of the heaven, that they neither sow nor reap nor gather*

---

[1] Mt. 6:34.

into barns, and God provides for them. How much more for you,[1] *O ye of little faith?*[2] But do you wait for his coming, and set your hope in him, and believe in his name. For he is *the judge of living and dead*,[3] and he *gives to each one according to his works*.[4] And at his coming and later appearance no man has any word of excuse[5] when he is about to be judged by him, as if he had not heard. For his heralds are proclaiming to the four regions of the world. Repent, then, and believe the gospel, and receive a yoke of meekness and a light burden,[6] that you may live and not die! These things obtain, these do ye keep. Come out from the darkness, that the light may receive you! Come to him who is truly good, that you may receive grace from him and lay up his sign in your souls." 29. When he had said this, some of the by-standers said to him: "It is time for the creditor to receive the debt." But he said to them: "The creditor always wishes to receive more than enough, (p. 146) but let us give him what is needful." And when he had blessed them he took bread and oil and herbs and salt, and blessed and gave to them; but he himself continued in his fasting, for the Lord's day was about to dawn. As he slept in the following night, the Lord came and stood at his head and said: "Thomas, rise up early and bless them all, and after the prayer and service go down the eastern road two miles, and there I will show in thee my glory. For because of thy going many will take refuge in me, and thou shalt demonstrate the nature and power of the enemy." And rising up from sleep he said to the brethren who were with him: "Children and brethren, the Lord wishes to accomplish something through me today. But let us pray and entreat him, that nothing may become a hindrance for us towards him, but that as at all times so now it may come to pass through us according to his will and desire." And when he had said this he laid his hands upon them and blessed them. And breaking the bread of the eucharist he gave it to them, saying: "This eucharist shall be to you for compassion and mercy, and not for judgment and requital." And they said: "Amen."

---

[1] Mt. 6:26; cf. Lk. 12:24.   [2] Mt. 6:30 par.   [3] Acts 10:42.   [4] Mt. 16:27.
[5] Cf. the Kerygma Petrou f. 4, above p. 101.   [6] Cf. Mt. 11:30.

(p. 147)   Third Act
Concerning the Serpent

30. And the apostle went out to go whither the Lord had commanded him; and when he was near the second mile(stone) and had turned aside a little from the road he saw lying there the body of a comely youth, and said: "Lord, was it for this that thou didst bring me out here, that I might see this temptation? Thy will be done, then, as thou wilt." And he began to pray and say: "O Lord, *judge of living and dead*,[1] of the living who stand by and the dead who lie (here), thou Lord of all and Father—but Father not of the souls that are in bodies, but of those that are gone out; for of the souls that are in pollutions thou art Lord and judge—come in this hour in which I call upon thee, and show thy glory toward this man who lies here." And turning to those who followed him he said: "This thing has not happened to no purpose, but the enemy has been at work, and has wrought this that he may make an attack thereby; and you see that he has made use of no other form and wrought through no other creature than that which is his subject." 31. And when he had said this a great serpent came out of a hole, darting his head and lashing his tail on the ground, and said with a loud voice to (p. 148) the apostle: "I will say before thee for what reason I slew him, for to this end art thou come, to put my works to shame." And the apostle said: "Yes, speak on." And the serpent: "There is a certain beautiful woman in this village over against us. And as she once ⟨passed by my place⟩ I saw her and fell in love with her, and following her I kept watch on her. And I found this young man kissing her, and he had intercourse with her and did other shameful things with her. Now it would be easy for me to disclose them before thee, ⟨but I dare not do it S⟩. For I know that thou art the twin brother of Christ, and dost ever abolish our nature. But not wishing to disquiet her I did not kill him in that very hour, but watched for him, and as he came by in the evening I smote and slew him, the more especially since he dared to do this on the Lord's day." But the apostle questioned him, saying: "Tell me of what seed and what race thou art." 32. And

---

[1] Acts 10:42.

he said to him: "I am a reptile of reptile nature, the baleful son of a baleful father; I am son of him who hurt and smote the four standing brothers; I am son of him who sits upon the throne ⟨and has power over the creation S⟩ which is under heaven, who takes his own (p. 149) from those who borrow; I am son of him who girds the sphere about; and I am a kinsman of him who is outside the ocean, whose tail is set in his own mouth; I am he who entered through the fence into Paradise and said to Eve all the things my father charged me to say to her;[1] I am he who kindled and inflamed Cain to slay his own brother,[2] and because of me thorns and thistles sprang up on the earth;[3] I am he who hurled the angels down from above, and bound them in lusts for women, that earth-born children might come from them[4] and I fulfil my will in them; I am he who hardened Pharaoh's heart, that he might slay the children of Israel and enslave them in a yoke of cruelty;[5] I am he who led the multitude astray in the wilderness, when they made the calf;[6] I am he who inflamed Herod[7] and kindled Caiaphas to the false accusation of the lie before Pilate;[8] for this was fitting for me; I am he who kindled Judas and bribed him to betray Christ to death;[9] I am he who inhabits and possesses the abyss of Tartarus,[10] but the Son of God did me wrong against my will, and chose out his own from me; I am a kinsman of him who is to come from the east, to whom also is given power to do what he will on the earth." 33. When the serpent had said this, in the hearing of all the crowd,* the apostle lifted up his voice on high and said: "Cease now, most shameless one, and be thou put to shame and (p. 150) entirely done to death! For thine end, destruction, is come. And do not dare to say what thou hast wrought through those who have become subject to thee. I command thee in the name of that Jesus who contends with you until now for the men who are his own, that thou suck out thy poison which thou didst put into this man, and draw it

---

[1] Cf. Gen. 3:1ff.   [2] Cf. Gen. 4:5ff.   [3] Cf. Gen. 3:18.
[4] Cf. Gen. 6:1–4.   [5] Cf. Exod. 1ff.   [6] Cf. Exod. 32.
[7] Cf. Mt. 2; Lk. 23:6–16.   [8] Cf. Mt. 26:3ff.; 27:11ff.; Jn. 18:28ff.
[9] Cf. Mt. 26:14–16.   [10] Rev. 9:11.
* Here according to the Syriac the crowd says: "One is (God), the God of this man, who has taught us about his God and through his word has commanded this fearful beast to reveal its nature to us." Then the narrative continues: And they prayed him that, as he by his word had commanded it to speak like a man, he would also kill it by his word.

460

out and take it from him." But the serpent said: "Not yet is the time of our end come, as thou hast said. Why dost thou compel me to take what I have put into this man and die before the time? For indeed if my father draw forth and suck out what he cast into the creation, then is his end." But the apostle said to him: "Show now the nature of thy father!" And the serpent came forward and set his mouth against the young man's wound and sucked the gall out of it. And little by little the young man's colour, which was as purple, became white, but the serpent swelled up. But when the serpent had drawn up all the gall into himself, the young man sprang up and stood, then ran and fell at the apostle's feet. But the serpent, being swollen, burst and died, and his poison and gall poured out; and in the place where his poison poured out there came a great chasm, and that serpent was swallowed up. And the apostle said to the king and his brother: "Send workmen and fill up that place, and lay foundations and build houses on top, that it may become a dwelling-place for the strangers." 34. But the young man said to the apostle, with many tears: "Wherein have I sinned against thee? For thou art a man that has two forms, (p. 151) and wherever thou wilt, there thou art found, and thou art restrained by no man, as I see. For I saw how that man stood beside thee, and said to thee: 'I have many wonders to show through thee, and I have great works to accomplish through thee, for which you shalt receive a reward; and thou shalt make many live, and they shall be in rest in eternal light as children of God. Do thou, then,' he said, speaking to thee of me, 'revive this young man stricken by the enemy, and become at all times his guardian.' Thou hast done well to come here, and again thou shalt do well to depart to him, for indeed he never leaves thee at all. But I have become free from care and reproach, and the light shone upon me (so that I am free) from the care of the night, and I am at rest from the toil of the day; but I am free also from him who urged me to do these things. I sinned against him who taught me the opposite, and I have lost that kinsman of the night who compelled me to sin by his own deeds; but I found that figure of light to be my kinsman. I have lost him who darkens and blinds his subjects, that they may not know what they are doing and, being ashamed at their works, depart from them and their deeds come to an end; but I found him whose works are light and his deeds truth, of which if a man does them he does not repent. I have been freed (p. 152) from him whose lie is persistent, before whom darkness goes as a veil and behind whom follows shame, shameless in inactivity; but I found him who revealed to me beautiful things that I might take hold of them, the Son of Truth, who is kinsman of concord, who driving away the mist enlightens his own creation, and healing its wounds overthrows its enemies. But I pray thee, man of God, make me to look upon him again, and to see him who is now become hidden from me, that I may also hear his voice, the wonder of which I cannot express; for it is not of the nature of this bodily organ." 35. But the apostle answered and said to him: "If thou art freed from those things of which thou hast received knowledge, as thou hast said, and dost know who it is that has wrought this in thee, and dost learn and become a hearer of him whom now in thy fervent love thou seekest, thou shalt both see him and be with him for ever, and in his rest shalt thou rest, and thou shalt be in his joy. But if thou be lightly disposed towards him, and turn again to thy former doings, and let go the beauty and that radiant countenance which now was shown to thee, and the effulgence of his light which now thou dost desire ⟨be wholly hidden from thee⟩, not only of this life shalt thou be deprived but also of that which (p. 153) is to come, and thou shalt depart to him whom thou didst say thou hadst lost, and no longer look on him whom thou didst say thou hadst found." 36. And when the apostle had said this, he went into the city holding fast that young man's hand and saying to him: "These things which thou hast seen, child, are but a few of the many which God has; for it is not about these visible things that he brings good news to us, but greater things than these he promises us. But so long as we are in the body we cannot speak and declare what he is to give to our souls. If we say that he gives us light, this is ⟨something⟩ visible, and we possess it; and if (we say that he gives us) wealth, ⟨this⟩ both exists and is visible in this world, and we name it, and do not require it, for it has been said: *Hardly shall a rich man enter into the kingdom of heaven.*[1] And if

---

[1] Mt. 19:23.

we speak of the mantle of clothing which the luxurious in this life put on, it is named and it has been said: *They who wear soft raiment are in kings' houses.*[1] And if (we speak of) costly banquets, concerning these we have received a commandment to *beware* of them (and) *not to be weighed down in intemperance and drunkenness and the cares of this life*[2] (. . .), and it is said: *Be not anxious for your life, what ye shall eat or what ye shall drink, neither for your body, what ye shall put on, for the life is more than meat, and the body than raiment.*[3] And if we speak of this rest which is temporal, judgment is appointed for this also. But we speak about the world above, (p. 154) about God and angels, about watchers and saints, about the ambrosial food and the drink of the true vine, about clothing that endures and does not grow old, about things *which eye has not seen nor ear heard, neither have they entered into the heart of* sinful *men, which God has prepared for those who love him.*[4] These things we discuss, and about these we bring good tidings. Do thou also, therefore, believe in him, that thou mayest live, and set in him thy trust, and thou shalt not die. For he is not persuaded by gifts, that thou shouldest offer to him, nor does he need sacrifice, that thou shouldest sacrifice to him. But look thou to him, and he will not disregard thee; and turn to him, and he will not forsake thee. For his comeliness and beauty will make thee very eager to love him, but also it does not allow thee to turn thyself away ⟨from him⟩." 37. And when the apostle said this, a large crowd joined that young man (gathered round him). But as he looked the apostle saw them lifting themselves up that they might see him, and they were going up on high places. And the apostle said to them: "Ye men who have come to the assembly of Christ and wish to believe in Jesus, take an example (a lesson) from this and see that unless you are lifted up you cannot see me who am small, and though I am like you you cannot observe me. If then you cannot see me, who am like you, unless you raise yourselves (p. 155) a little from the earth, how can you see him who dwells in the height and now is found in the depth, unless you first raise yourselves out of your former condition and your unprofitable deeds, and the desires that do not abide, and the wealth which is left here, and the possession which ⟨comes⟩ of the earth ⟨and⟩

[1] Mt. 11:8. [2] Lk. 21:34. [3] Mt. 6:25. [4] 1 Cor. 2:9; cf. Vol. I, p. 300.

grows old, and the clothing which deteriorates, and the beauty which grows old and vanishes, and indeed the whole body in which all these are stored and which growing old becomes dust, returning to its own nature? For all these things support the body itself. But believe rather in our Lord Jesus Christ, whom we preach, that your hope may be in him and that in him you may have life for ever and ever, that he may become for you a fellow-traveller in this land of error, and may be a haven for you in this turbulent sea. And he shall be for you a spring gushing forth in this thirsty land,[1] and a ⟨house⟩ full of food in the place of the hungry, and a rest for your souls, and also a physician of your bodies." 38. Then the crowd of those who had gathered together, when they heard this, wept and said to the apostle: "Man of God, we dare not say that we belong to that God whom thou dost preach, because our works which we have done are alien to him and not pleasing to him. But if he has compassion on us and pities us and saves us, overlooking our former deeds, and (p. 156) frees us from the evils which we wrought when we were in error, and does not reckon them to our account nor make mention of our former sins, we shall become his servants and shall carry out his will to the end." But the apostle answered them saying: "He does not condemn you, nor does he count against you the sins which you wrought while you were in error, but overlooks your transgressions which you have done in ignorance."

Fourth Act
Concerning the Colt

39. While the apostle was still standing in the highway and speaking with the crowd, an ass's colt came and stood before him, opened its mouth and said: "Twin brother of Christ, apostle of the Most High and fellow-initiate into the hidden word of Christ, who dost receive his secret sayings, fellow-worker of the Son of God, who being free didst become a slave and being sold didst lead many to freedom; thou kinsman of the great race which condemned the enemy and redeemed his own, who hast become a cause of life for many in the land of the Indians—for thou didst come to the men who erred, and through thine appearance and

---

[1] Cf. Gospel of Thomas log. 13, Vol. I, p. 287.

thy divine words they are now turning to the God of truth who sent thee—mount and sit upon me and rest until thou enter the city." And in answer the apostle said: "O Jesus Christ, ⟨son⟩ (p. 157) of the perfect compassion! O peace and quiet, who art now spoken of even among unreasoning beasts! O hidden rest, and revealed by thy working as our Saviour and nourisher, preserving us and giving us rest in alien bodies, the Saviour of our souls, the spring that is sweet and unfailing, the fountain that is secure and pure and never defiled,[1] the defender and helper of thine own servants in the fight, who dost turn aside the enemy and drive him away from us, who in many battles dost fight for us, and make us conquer in them all, our true and invincible champion, our holy and victorious commander, the glorious, and providing for thine own a joy that does not pass away and a relief that contains no affliction at all, the good shepherd who didst give thyself for thine own sheep, and conquer the wolf and redeem thine own lambs[2] and lead them into good pasture; we glorify and praise thee and thine invisible Father and thy Holy Spirit and the Mother of all creation." 40. When the apostle said this, all the crowd that was present looked at him, expecting to hear what he would answer to the colt. But after the apostle had stood for a long time ⟨as if in a trance⟩, and had looked up to heaven, he said to the colt: "⟨Who art thou⟩, and to whom dost thou belong? For astonishing are the things (p. 158) shown forth by thy mouth, and beyond expectation, such as are hidden from the many." And the colt in answer said: "I am of that race that served Balaam,[3] and thy Lord and teacher also sat upon one that belonged to me by race. And[4] now am I sent to give thee rest as thou dost sit upon me, and ⟨that these may receive faith⟩ and that to me may be given that portion which I am now to obtain through the service which ⟨I render to thee⟩, and which if I serve thee ⟨not⟩ is taken from me." But the apostle said to it: "He who has bestowed on thee this gift (of speech) is able to cause it to be fulfilled to the end in thee and in those who belong to thee by race; for as to this mystery I am weak and feeble." And he would not sit upon it. But the colt prayed and entreated

---

[1] Cf. Gospel of Thomas, log. 13, Vol. I, p. 287.   [2] Cf. Jn. 10:11f.
[3] Cf. Num. 22:21ff.   [4] Cf. Mk. 11:1ff. pars.

that he would bless it ⟨by riding upon it⟩. Then the apostle mounted and sat, and they followed with him, some going before and some following after. And they all ran, wishing to see the end and how he would dismiss the colt. 41. But when he came near to the gates of the city, he dismounted from it, saying: "Go, and be thou kept safe where thou wert." But immediately the colt fell down on the ground at the apostle's feet and died. All those who were present were sorrowful, and said to the apostle: "Bring it to life and raise it up!" But he (p. 159) said in reply: "I could indeed raise it up through the name of Jesus Christ. But this is ⟨not⟩ expedient at all. For he who gave it speech that it might speak was able also to make it not die. But I do not raise it up, not because I am not able but because this is what is useful and helpful for it." And he instructed those who were present to dig a pit and bury its body; and they did as he commanded.

Fifth Act
Concerning the demon that dwelt in the woman

42. The apostle went into the city, all the people following him; and he was thinking of going to the parents of the young man whom he had made alive after he had been killed by the serpent, for they earnestly besought him to come to them and enter into their house. But a very beautiful woman suddenly uttered a piercing cry, saying: "Apostle of the new God, who art come to India, and servant of that holy and only good God—for by thee is he preached as Saviour of the souls of those who come to him, and by thee are healed the bodies of those who are scourged by the enemy, and thou art he who is become an occasion of life for all who turn to him—command me to be brought before thee, that I may relate to thee what has befallen me, and perhaps from thee there may be hope for me, and these who stand beside thee (p. 160) may become more confident in the God whom thou dost preach. For I am no little tormented by the adversary these five years past. As a woman I formerly sat in quiet, and peace encompassed me on every side, and I had no anxiety over anything, for indeed I took no thought for any other. 43. But it happened one day, as I came out of the bath, there met me ⟨a man like one⟩ troubled and disturbed. His voice and his answer

seemed to me to be very faint and weak. And standing in front of me he said: 'I and thou shall be in one love, and we shall associate with one another as a man unites with his wife.' And I answered saying to him: 'With my betrothed I never united, since I declined to marry, and how shall I give myself up to thee, who dost wish to associate with me as in adultery?' And when I had said this I passed on; but I said to the handmaid who was with me: 'Didst thou see the youth and his shamelessness, how without shame he spoke with me openly?' But she said to me: 'I saw an old man conversing with thee.' But when I was in my house and had dined, my soul suggested ⟨.⟩ a certain suspicion to me, and especially since he appeared to me in two forms. And having this in my mind I fell asleep. (p. 161) In that night, then, he came and united with me in his foul intercourse. I saw him also when it was day, and fled from him; but in the night that is akin to him he came and misused me. And now as thou dost see me I have been troubled by him five years, and he has not departed from me. But I know and am persuaded that demons and spirits and avengers are subject to thee, and become all a-tremble at thy prayer. Pray therefore for me, and drive out from me the demon that continually vexes me, ⟨that⟩ I too may be free and may be gathered together into my original nature, and receive the gift that has been given to my kindred." 44. The apostle said: "O evil not to be restrained! O shamelessness of the enemy! O envious one, never at rest! O hideous one that dost subdue the comely! O thou of many forms—he appears as he may wish, but his essence cannot be altered. O thou from the crafty and faithless one! O bitter tree, whose fruits are like him! O thou from the devil that fights for the aliens! O thou from the deceit that uses shamelessness! O thou from the wickedness that creeps like a snake and ⟨is akin to it⟩!" (p. 162) And when the apostle had said this, the enemy came and stood before him, no one seeing him except the woman and the apostle, and with a very loud voice said in the hearing of all: 45. *"What have we to do with thee,* apostle *of the Most High?*[1] What have we to do with thee, servant of Jesus Christ? What have we to do with thee, counsellor of the holy Son of God? Why dost thou wish to destroy

---

[1] Mk. 5:7.

us, when our time is not yet come? Why dost thou wish to take our authority? For until this present hour we had hope and time remaining. What have we to do with thee? Thou hast authority in thine own (sphere) and we in ours. Why dost thou wish to exercise despotic rule against us, especially since thou thyself dost teach others not to act despotically? Why dost thou crave what belongs to others, as one not satisfied with his own? Why art thou made like to the Son of God who wronged us? For thou art altogether like him, as if begotten of him.* For we thought to bring him also under the yoke, even as the rest, but he turned and held us in subjection. For we knew him not; but he deceived us by his form most unsightly and by his poverty and need. For as we beheld him, such as he was, we thought that he was a man bearing flesh, not knowing that it is he who gives life to men. But he gave us authority in our own (sphere), and that in our time we should not abandon our own, but live in them; but thou dost wish to obtain above what is due, and what was given thee, and do us violence!" 46. And when the demon had said this, he wept, saying: "I leave (p. 163) thee, my fairest consort, whom I found ⟨a long time ago⟩ and with whom I rested. I forsake thee, my steadfast sister, my beloved in whom I was well pleased. What I shall do I know not, nor on whom I shall call that he may hear and help me. I know what I shall do: I shall go to places where the fame of this man has not been heard, and for thee, my beloved, I shall perhaps find one with another name." And lifting up his voice he said: "Abide in peace, since thou hast taken refuge in one greater than I; but I will depart and seek one like thee, and if I find her not I return to thee again. For I know that while thou art near to this man thou hast thy refuge in him, but when he is gone thou shalt be as thou wert before he appeared, and him shalt thou forget, but for me there shall be opportunity and confidence; but now I fear the name of him who hath saved thee." And when he had said this, the demon vanished; only as he departed fire and smoke were seen there, and all who stood by there were astounded. 47. When the apostle saw it, he said to them: "That demon showed nothing strange or alien, but his own

---

* Here the Syriac has: Why art thou like God thy Lord, who hid his majesty and appeared in a body (flesh)? And we thought regarding him that he was mortal. But he turned and did us violence; art thou, then, born of him?

nature, in which also he shall be burned up. For indeed the fire shall consume him utterly, and the smoke of him shall be scattered abroad." And he began to say: "Jesus, the hidden mystery that has been (p. 164) revealed to us, thou art he who has made known to us many mysteries; who did set me apart from all my companions and speak to me three words,[1] wherewith I am inflamed, and tell them to others I cannot; Jesus, man, slain, corpse, buried; Jesus, God of God, Saviour who dost quicken the dead and heal the sick; Jesus, who wert in need like ⟨a poor man S⟩, and dost save as one who has no need; thou who didst catch the fish for the breakfast and the dinner,[2] and didst make all satisfied with a little bread;[3] Jesus, who didst rest from the weariness of the journey like a man,[4] and walk upon the waves like a God;[5] 48. Jesus most high, voice arising (like the sun) from the perfect mercy, Saviour of all, right hand of the light which overthrows the evil one by his own nature, thou who dost gather all his nature into one place; thou of many forms, who art only-begotten, the *first-born of many brethren;*[6] God from God Most High, man despised until now;* Jesus Christ, who dost not neglect us when we call upon thee; who art become ⟨an occasion of life to all mankind⟩; who for our sakes wast judged and shut up in prison, and dost set free all that are in bonds; who wast called a *deceiver,*[7] and dost deliver thine own from deception; I pray thee for these (p. 165) who stand (here) and believe in thee. For they crave to obtain thy gifts, having good hope in thy help, and having ⟨their⟩ refuge in thy greatness. They have their ears open to hear from us the words which are spoken to them. Let thy peace come and dwell in them, and let it renew them from their former deeds, and let them *put off the old man with his deeds and put on the new*[8] who is now proclaimed to them by me." 49. And laying his hands upon them he blessed them, saying: "*The grace of our Lord Jesus*

---

[1] Cf. the Gospel of Thomas log. 13, Vol. I, p. 287.   [2] Cf. Jn. 21:6, 11f.
[3] Cf. Mk. 6:34ff. pars.   [4] Cf. Jn. 4:6.   [5] Cf. Mk. 6:45ff. pars.
[6] Rom. 8:29.   [7] Mt. 27:63.   [8] Col. 3:9f.
* Here the Syriac has: Jesus, right hand of the Father, who hast hurled down the evil one under his nature (other MSS: to the lowest limit) and hast gathered his possessions into a blessed place of assembly; Jesus, king over all, who dost subdue all; Jesus, who art in the Father and the Father in thee; and ye are one in power, will, glory and essence, and for our sakes thou wast named by name and art the Son and didst put on a body; Jesus, who didst become a Nazirite, and thy grace provides for all like God; Son of the Most High God, who didst become a despised man . . .

Christ be upon you for ever!"[1] And they said: "Amen." But the
woman besought him, saying: "Apostle of the Most High, give
me the seal, that that enemy may not return to me again!" Then
he made her come near to him, and laying his hands upon her
sealed her in the name of the Father and of the Son and of the
Holy Spirit. And many others also were sealed with her. And the
apostle commanded his servant (deacon) to set a table before
them; and he set out a stool which they found there, (p. 166)
and spreading a linen cloth upon it set on the bread of blessing.
And the apostle stood beside it and said: "Jesus, who hast made
us worthy to partake of the Eucharist of thy holy body and blood,
behold we make bold to approach thy Eucharist, and to call
upon thy holy name; come thou and have fellowship with us!"
50. And he began to say:

〈Come, gift of the Most High; S〉
Come, perfect compassion;
Come, fellowship of the male;
〈Come, Holy Spirit; S〉
Come, thou that dost know the mysteries of the Chosen;
Come, thou that hast part in all the combats of the noble
             Athlete;
〈Come, treasure of glory; S〉
〈Come, darling of the compassion of the Most High; S〉
Come, silence
That dost reveal the great deeds of the whole greatness;
Come, thou that dost show forth the hidden things
And make the ineffable manifest;
Holy Dove
That bearest the twin young;
Come, hidden Mother;
Come, thou that art manifest in thy deeds and dost furnish joy
And rest for all that are joined with thee;
Come and partake with us in this Eucharist
Which we celebrate in thy name,
And in the love-feast
In which we are gathered together at thy call.

[1] Rom. 16:20.

470

And when he had said this, he marked the Cross upon the bread and broke it, and began to distribute it. And first he gave to the woman, saying: "Let this be to thee for forgiveness of sins and eternal transgressions!" And (p. 167) after her he gave also to all the others who had received the seal.

Sixth Act
Concerning the youth who had murdered the maiden

51. Now there was a certain young man who had wrought a lawless deed. As he came forward and took the Eucharist with his mouth, his two hands withered up, so that he could no longer put them to his mouth. When those who were present saw him, they informed the apostle of what had happened, and calling him the apostle said to him: "Tell me, child, and be not ashamed: what (was it) that thou didst and camest here? For the Lord's Eucharist has convicted thee (of an evil deed). For this gift, passing into many, brings healing, especially to those who approach in faith and love, but thee it has withered away, and what has happened has not taken place without some action (on thy part)". But the young man, convicted by the Lord's Eucharist, came and fell at the apostle's feet and besought him, saying: "An evil deed has been wrought by me, ⟨although⟩ I thought to do something good. I loved a woman who lives outside the city in an inn, and she also loved me. But when I heard (the sermon) from thee (p. 168) and believed that thou dost proclaim (the) living God, I came forward and received the seal from thee with the others. But thou didst say: Whoever shall unite in the impure union, and especially in adultery, he shall not have life with the God whom I preach. Since, then, I loved her greatly, I besought her and tried to persuade her to become my consort in chastity and pure conduct, which thou thyself dost teach; but she would not. Since she was unwilling, then, I took a sword and slew her; for I could not see her commit adultery with another." 52. When the apostle heard this, he said: "O insensate union, how dost thou run to shamelessness! O desire not to be checked, how didst thou move this man to do this! O work of the serpent, how dost thou rage in thine own!" But the apostle commanded water to be brought to him in a basin. And when the water was brought, he said:

"Come, waters from the living waters, the existent from the existent and sent to us; rest that was sent to us from the Rest; power of salvation that cometh from that power which conquers all things and subjects them to its own will—come and dwell in these waters, that the gift of the Holy Spirit may be perfectly fulfilled in them!" And he said to the young man: "Go, wash thy hands in these waters!" And when he had washed (p. 169) they were restored, and the apostle said to him: "Dost thou believe in our Lord Jesus, that he is able to do all things?" And he said: "Though I be but the least, I believe. But I wrought this deed thinking to do something good; for I besought her, as I told thee, but she would not obey me, to keep herself chaste." 53. But the apostle said to him: "Come, let us go to the inn where thou didst commit this deed, and let us see what has come to pass!" And the young man went before the apostle on the way; and when they arrived in the inn they found her lying. And seeing her the apostle was despondent, for she was a comely girl. And he commanded her to be brought into the middle of the inn. And they laid her on a bed, carried her out, and laid her in the middle of the court of the inn. And the apostle laid his hand upon her, and began to say: "Jesus, who dost appear to us at all times—for this is thy will, that we should ever seek thee, and thou thyself hast given us this right to ask and to receive, and not only didst thou grant this, but also thou didst teach us to pray,[1]—thou who art not seen with our bodily eyes, but art never hidden at all from those of our soul, and in thy form indeed art hidden, but in thy works (p. 170) art manifest to us; and by thy many works we have come to know thee, as we are able, but thou thyself hast given to us thy gifts without measure, saying: *Ask, and it shall be given you, seek and ye shall find, knock and it shall be opened unto you.*[2] We pray now, since we have a fear because of our sins. But we ask thee not for wealth, neither gold nor silver nor possessions nor any other of the things which come of the earth and return again to the earth, but this we beseech of thee and entreat, that in thy holy name thou raise up her who lies here by thy power, to (thy) glory and (the confirmation of) the faith of them that stand by." 54. And he said to the young man, after sealing him: "Go, take

---

[1] Cf. Mt. 6:5ff.; Lk. 11:1ff.   [2] Mt. 7:7.

her hand and say to her: I with my hands did slay thee with iron, and with my hands by faith in Jesus I raise thee up." So the young man went and stood beside her, saying: "I have believed in thee, Christ Jesus." And looking at Judas Thomas the apostle, he said to him: "Pray ⟨for me⟩, that my Lord, upon whom I call, may come to my help." And laying his hand upon her hand he said: (p. 171) "Come, Lord Jesus Christ; unto her grant life, and to me the earnest of thy faith!" And immediately when he drew on her hand she sprang up and sat, looking on the great crowd that stood by. She saw also the apostle standing opposite her, and leaving the bed and springing up she fell at his feet and caught hold of his garments, saying: "I pray thee, my Lord, where is that other who was with thee, who did not leave me to remain in that dreadful and cruel place, but delivered me to thee, saying: Take thou this woman, that she may be made perfect, and hereafter be gathered to her place?" 55. But the apostle said to her: "Relate to us where thou hast been." And she answered: "Thou who wast with me, to whom also I was delivered, dost thou wish to hear?" And she began to say: "A man received me, hateful of countenance, entirely black, and his clothing exceedingly dirty. And he led me to a place[1] in which there were many chasms, and much ill odour and a hateful vapour was given off thence. And he made me look down into each chasm, and I saw in the (first) chasm a flaming fire, and wheels of fire were running ⟨hither and⟩ thither, and souls were hung upon those wheels, dashed against each other. And there was a cry there and a very great lamentation, but there was none to deliver. And that man said to me: These souls are kindred to thee, (p. 172) and in the days of reckoning they were delivered for punishment and destruction. And then (when the chastisement of each is ended) others are brought in their stead, and likewise these again to another (chasm). These are they who perverted the intercourse of man and woman. And when I looked, I saw (new-born) infants heaped one upon another and struggling with one another as they lay upon them. And he answered and said to me: These are their children, and therefore are they set here for a testimony against them. 56. And he led me to another

[1] Cf. Apoc. Petri, below pp. 672ff.

473

chasm, and looking in I saw mire, and worms welling up, and souls wallowing there, and (heard) a great gnashing break out thence from among them. And that man said to me: These are the souls of women who forsook their husbands (and men who left their wives) and committed adultery with others, and have been brought to this torment. Another chasm he showed me, and when I looked into it I saw souls, some hanging by the tongue, some by the hair, some by the hands, some by the feet head downwards, and (all) reeking with smoke and brimstone. Concerning these that man who was with me answered me: These souls which are hung by the tongue are slanderers, and such as utter lying and infamous words and are not ashamed. And those that are hung by the hair are the shameless who have no modesty at all (p. 173) and go about in the world bare-headed. And those which are hung by the hands, these are they who took away and stole the goods of others, and never gave anything to the needy or gave help to the afflicted, ⟨and⟩ did this because they wished to take everything, and paid no heed whatever to justice and to the law. And those who hang upside down by the feet, these are they who lightly and eagerly run ⟨upon⟩ evil ways and disorderly paths, not visiting the sick and not escorting them that depart this life. And for this cause each several soul receives what was done by it. 57. Leading me away again he showed me a cave, very dark (and) breathing out a great stench, and many souls looked out thence, wishing to get something of the air; but their guards did not allow them to look out. And he who was with me said: This is the prison of those souls which thou didst see. For when they have fulfilled their punishments for what each one did, others later succeed them. And some are entirely consumed, and ⟨some⟩ are handed over to other punishments. Now those who guarded the souls that were in the dark cave said to the man who had received me: Give her to us that we may take her in to the others until (p. 174) the time comes for her to be handed over for punishment. But he answered them: I do not give her to you, for I fear him who delivered her to me; for I was not commanded to leave her here. I am taking her back with me until I receive an order concerning her. And he took me and led me to another place, in which were men who were being tortured cruelly. But he who is like thee took and delivered me to thee, saying to thee: Take her, for she is one of the sheep that have gone astray. And received by thee I am now before thee. I beseech thee, therefore, and entreat that I may not depart into those places of punishment which I saw." 58. But the apostle said: "You have heard what this woman related. But there are not only these punishments, but also others worse than these. And you also, if you do not turn to this God whom I preach, and desist from your former works and from the deeds which you wrought without knowledge, shall have your end in these punishments. Believe therefore in Christ Jesus, and he forgives you the sins committed before this and will cleanse you from (p. 175) all your bodily desires which remain on the earth, and will heal you from the trespasses which follow you and depart with you and are found before you. Each one of you, therefore, put off the old man and put on the new,[1] and abandon your first way of life and conduct. And let them that steal steal no more, but live by labouring and working.[2] Let the adulterers no longer practise lechery, that they may not utterly deliver themselves to eternal punishment; for with God adultery is exceeding wicked, above the other evils. Put away also avarice and falsehood and drunkenness and slander, and do not return evil for evil.[3] For all these things are strange and alien to the God who is preached by me. But walk ye rather in faith and meekness and holiness and hope, in which God delights, that ye may become his kinsmen, expecting from him the gifts which only some few receive." 59. So all the people believed, and yielded their souls obedient to the living God and to Christ Jesus, rejoicing in the blessed works (p. 176) of the Most High and in his holy service. And they brought much money for the service of the widows; for he had them gathered together in the cities, and to them all he sent what was necessary by his deacons, both clothing and provision for their nourishment. But he himself did not cease preaching and speaking to them and showing that this is Jesus the Christ whom the Scriptures proclaimed, who came and was crucified and after three days was raised from the dead. And secondly he showed them and explained, beginning from the prophets, the things concerning

[1] Cf. Col. 3:9.   [2] Cf. Eph. 4:28.   [3] 1 Pet. 3:9.

Christ, that he must come and that in him all that had been prophesied concerning him must be fulfilled.[1] And the fame of him spread into all the towns and villages, and all who had sick or such as were troubled by unclean spirits brought them, and laid them on the road by which he was to pass, and he healed them all in the power of the Lord. Then all who were healed by him said with one accord with one voice: "Glory be to thee, Jesus, who (to all) alike hast granted healing through thy servant (p. 177) and apostle Thomas! And being in health and rejoicing we beseech thee that we may become (members) of thy flock and be numbered among thy sheep. Receive us therefore, Lord, and do not reckon unto us our transgressions and our ⟨former⟩ errors which we committed while we were in ignorance." 60. And the apostle said: "Glory be to *the only-begotten of the Father*,[2] glory to *the first-born of many brethren*,[3] glory to thee, the defender and helper of those who come to thy refuge, the sleepless and the one who awakens those in sleep, who lives and gives life to those who are in death, O God Jesus Christ, Son of the living God, redeemer and helper, refuge and rest of all who labour in thy work, giver of healing to those who for thy name's sake endure *the burden and the heat of the day*[4]: we thank thee for the gifts given to us from thee, and the help bestowed upon us by thee, and thy provision that cometh to us from thee. 61. Perfect these things therefore unto us even to the end, that we may have the confidence that is in thee. Look upon us, because for thy sake we have left our homes and our fathers' goods,[5] and for thy sake have gladly and willingly become strangers. Look upon us, Lord, (p. 178) because we have left our own possessions for thy sake, that we may obtain thee, the possession that cannot be taken away. Look upon us, Lord, because we have left those who belong to us by race, that we may be united with thy kindred. Look upon us, Lord, who have left our fathers and mothers and fosterers, that we may behold thy Father and be satisfied with his divine nourishment. Look upon us, Lord, for for thy sake we have left our bodily consorts and our earthly fruits, that we may share in that abiding and true fellowship and bring forth true fruits, whose

[1] Cf. Lk. 24:27. [2] Jn. 1:14. [3] Rom. 8:29.
[4] Mt. 20:12. [5] Cf. Mt. 19:27, 29.

nature is from above, which none can take away from us, with whom we abide and they abide in us."

Seventh Act
Concerning the Captain

62. While the apostle Thomas was proclaiming the word of God in all India, a certain captain of king Misdaeus (Mazdai S) came to him and said to him: "I have heard concerning thee that thou dost not take reward of any man, but whatever thou hast thou dost give to the needy. For if thou didst take rewards, I would have sent much money and would not have come hither myself, for the king takes no action without me. For I have many possessions and am rich, one of the (p. 179) wealthy in India. And I never wronged anyone at all; but the contrary has befallen me. I have a wife, and of her I had a daughter, and I am wholly devoted to her, as indeed nature requires, and have not made trial of another wife. Now it happened that there was a wedding in our city, and those who made the marriage were my very close friends. So they came and bade me (to it), inviting also her (my wife) and her daughter. Since they were my good friends, I could not refuse. So I sent her, although she did not wish to go, and with them I sent many servants also. So off they went, dressed in great finery, she and her daughter. 63. But when evening came and it ⟨was⟩ time to come away from the wedding, I sent lamps and torches to meet them. And I stood in the street watching when she should come and I see her with my daughter. And as I stood I heard a sound of wailing. Woe for her! was heard from every mouth. And the servants came to me with their clothes torn and told me what had happened. We saw, they said, a man and a boy with him. And the man laid his hand upon thy wife and (p. 180) the boy upon thy daughter, but they fled from them. We wounded them with our swords, but our swords fell to the ground. And in the same hour they (the women) fell down, gnashing their teeth and dashing their heads on the ground; and when we saw this we came to tell thee. And when I heard this from the servants I rent my clothes and struck my face with my hands, and ran down the street like one gone mad; and when I came I

found them prostrate in the market place. And I took them and brought them to my house, and after a long time they came to themselves, and when they were calmed they sat down. 64. So I began to question my wife: What has happened to thee? And she said to me: Dost thou not know what thou hast done to me? For I prayed thee that I might not go to the wedding, since I was not in a good state of body. And as I went along the street and drew near the channel in which the water was flowing, I saw a black man standing opposite me, ⟨nodding his head at me S⟩, and a boy like him standing beside him. And I said to my daughter: Look at these two ugly men, whose teeth are like milk but their lips like soot. And we left them by the aqueduct and went on. But when the sun had set and ⟨we came away⟩ from the wedding (p. 181) ⟨and⟩ were going through (the town) with the young men, ⟨and⟩ had come very near the aqueduct, my daughter saw them first and stealthily took refuge with me. And after her I too saw them coming against us, and we fled from them; and the servants who were with us ⟨fled likewise⟩. ⟨But they (the two men)⟩ struck us and threw us down, me and my daughter. And when she had told me this, the demons came upon them again and threw them down. And from that hour they cannot go outside, but are shut up in one room or another. And on their account I suffer much and am distressed. For they throw them down wherever they find them, and strip them naked. I pray thee and entreat before God: help me and have pity on me. For it is three years now since a table was set in my house, and my wife and daughter have not sat at table. And especially (I pray thee) for my unhappy daughter, who has seen no good at all in this world." 65. And when the apostle heard this from the captain (p. 182) he was greatly grieved for him; and he said to him: "Dost thou believe that Jesus will heal them?" And the captain said: "Yes." And the apostle: "Commit thyself then to Jesus, and he will heal them and bring them help." But the captain said: "Show me him, that I may entreat him and believe in him." But the apostle said: "⟨Stretch thy mind upward as much as thou canst, for S⟩ he does not appear to these bodily eyes, but with the eyes of the mind is he found." So the captain lifted up his voice and said: "I believe in thee, Jesus, and I pray thee and entreat: help thou my little faith[1] which I have in thee." But the apostle commanded Xenophon the deacon to assemble all at one place, and when the whole crowd was gathered the apostle stood in the midst and said: 66. "My children and brethren who have believed in the Lord, abide in this faith, preaching Jesus who was proclaimed to you by me and having your hopes in him. And ⟨do not forsake him⟩, and he will not forsake you. While you lie asleep in this slumber that weighs down the sleepers, (p. 183) he being sleepless keeps watch; and when you sail on the sea and are in danger, and none can help, he walking upon the waters[2] rights ⟨your ship S⟩ by his help. For I am now going from you, and it is uncertain whether I shall see you again according to the flesh. Be ye not, therefore, like the people of Israel, who ⟨when their shepherd departed from them⟩ for a short time stumbled.[3] But I leave with you Xenophon the deacon in my place, for he also preaches Jesus, even as I do. For neither am I anything, nor is he, but Jesus. For indeed I too am a man clothed with a body, a son of man like one of you. Neither have I riches such as are found with some, which convict their possessors since they are utterly useless, and are abandoned upon the earth from which they came. But the transgressions which come upon men because of them, and the stains of sins, ⟨they carry away⟩ with them. But seldom are rich men found in acts of mercy; but the merciful (p. 184) and the lowly in heart, they shall inherit the kingdom of God.[4] For it is not beauty that is enduring with men; for those who rely upon it, when old age takes hold of them, shall be suddenly put to shame. All things have their season; so at one time there is loving and at another hating.[5] Let your hope therefore be in Jesus Christ the Son of God, who is ever loved and ever desired. And remember us, as we do you. For we ⟨ourselves⟩, if we do not ⟨bear⟩ the burden of the commandments, are not worthy to be preachers of this name, and shall later suffer punishment there." 67. And when he had prayed with them, remaining a long time in prayer and supplication, he commended them to the Lord and said: "Lord, who rulest over every soul that is in a body; Lord, Father of the souls that have their hope in thee and

---

[1] Cf. Mk. 9:24.   [2] Cf. Mk. 6:45ff. par.   [3] Cf. Exod. 32.
[4] Cf. Mt. 5:7; 11:29.   [5] Cf. Eccles. 3:1–8.

await thy mercies, thou who dost deliver thine own men from error and set free from slavery and corruption those who are subject and come to thy refuge; be thou with Xenophon's flock, anoint it with holy oil, heal it from the wounds and preserve (p. 185) it from the ravening wolves." And laying his hand upon them he said: "The peace of the Lord be upon you and go with us."

Eighth Act
Concerning the Wild Asses

68. So the apostle went out to depart on his way. And they all escorted him, weeping and adjuring him to remember them in his prayers and not ⟨forget⟩ them. When he had mounted and taken his seat on the wagon, and all the brethren were left behind, the captain came and roused the driver, saying: "I pray and entreat that I may become worthy to sit beneath his feet, and I shall become his driver along this road, that he may become my guide to that road by which few travel." 69. Now when they had journeyed about two miles, the apostle begged of the captain and made him rise and sit with him, allowing the driver to sit in his own place. But when they went off along the road, it befell that the beasts became weary with the great heat, and ⟨could⟩ not move at all. The captain was vexed and altogether in despair, and thought of going on his own feet (p. 186) and bringing other animals for the wagon. But the apostle said: "Let not thy heart be troubled or afraid,[1] but believe in Jesus Christ whom I declared to thee, and thou shalt see great wonders." And looking about he saw a herd of wild asses grazing beside the road. And he said to the captain: "If thou ⟨dost believe⟩ in Jesus Christ, go to that herd of wild asses and say: Judas Thomas, the apostle of Christ the new God, says to you, Let four of you come, of whom we have need." 70. And the captain went, although he was afraid; for they were many. And as he went, they came to meet him. And when they drew near he said to them: "Judas Thomas, the apostle of the new God, commands you: Let four of you come, of whom I have need." When the wild asses heard this, they came to him with one accord at a run, and having come they did him

---

[1] Cf. Jn. 14:27.

reverence.* But the apostle said to them: "Peace be with you! Yoke four (of you) in place of these beasts that have come to a stand." And every one of them came and pressed to be yoked. Now there were four there, stronger ⟨than the rest⟩, and these were yoked. (p. 187) As to the others, some went before and some followed. But when they had travelled a short distance he dismissed ⟨them⟩, saying: "To you dwellers in the wilderness I say, Go to your pastures! For if I needed all, you would all come with me. But now go to your place in which you ⟨were dwelling⟩." But they went off quietly until they were out of sight. 71. Now as the apostle, the captain and the driver ⟨took their seats S⟩, the wild asses pulled the wagon quietly and evenly, that they might not disturb the apostle of God. And when they came near the gate of the city they turned aside and stood before the doors of the captain's house. And the captain said: "It is not possible for me to relate what has happened, but when I see the end then I will speak." So the whole city came, when they saw the wild asses yoked; moreover they heard the report about the apostle, that he was to stay there. But the apostle asked the captain: "Where is thy dwelling, and whither art thou taking us?" And he said to him: "Thou thyself dost know that we stand before the doors, and these that are come with thee by thy command know it better than I." 72. Saying this, he dismounted from the wagon. So the apostle began to say: "Jesus Christ, ⟨the knowledge of whom is blasphemed in this land S⟩, Jesus Christ, whose fame is strange in this city, Jesus who dost receive all (p. 188)

---

* Here the Syriac has the following hymn from the apostle: Blessed be thou, God of truth and Lord of all being, that thou didst will with thy will and make all thy works and finish all thy creations and bring them to the rule of their nature and lay thy fear upon them all, that they might be subject to thy command. And thy will trod the way from thy secrecy to revelation, and cared for every soul which thou didst make. And he was proclaimed by the mouth of all the prophets in all visions, sounds and voices. But Israel did not obey because of their evil inclination. And since thou art Lord of all, thou dost take care of all thy creatures, so that thou dost spread out thy mercy upon us in him who came by thy will and put on the body, thy creature; whom thou didst will and form in thy blessed wisdom; whom thou didst appoint in thy secrecy and establish in thy revelation; to whom thou didst give the name of Son; who is thy will and the power of thy thought; so that ye are in various names, Father, Son and Spirit, because of the government of thy creatures, for the nourishing of all natures, while ye are one in glory, power and will. And ye are divided without being separated, and one although divided; and all subsists in thee and is subject to thee, since all is thine. And I trust in thee, Lord, and through thy command have I subjected these dumb beasts, that thou mightest rule us and them, because it is necessary (one MS. that thou mightest minister to us and them with what is needful), and that thy name might be glorified in us and the dumb beasts.

the apostles in every land and in every city, and all who are worthy
of thee are glorified in thee; Jesus, who didst take shape and
become as a man, and didst appear to us all, that thou mightest
not separate us from thine own love; thou, Lord, art he who gave
himself for us and by thy blood bought us and gained us as a
precious possession. But what have we to give thee, Lord, in
exchange for thy life[1] which thou didst give for us? ⟨For what
we have is thy gift.⟩ ⟨And thou dost ask of us nothing S⟩ but
this, that we entreat of thee and (thereby) live." 73. And when
he said this, many gathered together from all sides to see the
apostle of the new God. But the apostle said again: "Why stand
we idle? Lord Jesus, the hour is come. What dost thou require
to be done? Command therefore that that be fulfilled which must
come to pass." . . . And the apostle said to one of the wild asses
that were yoked on the right side: "Go into the court and stand
there, call the demons and say to them: Judas Thomas, the
apostle and disciple of Jesus Christ, says to you: Come out here!
(p. 189) For because of you was I sent, and against those who
belong to you by race, to destroy you and pursue you to your
place, until the time of fulfilment comes and you go down to
your depth of darkness." 74. And that wild ass went in, a great
crowd accompanying him, and said: "To you I speak, the
enemies of Jesus who is called Christ; to you I speak, who shut
your eyes that you may not see the light—for the nature most
evil cannot be transformed to the good; to you I speak, the
children of Gehenna and of destruction, of him who does not
cease from evil until now, who ever renews his workings and the
things that fit his substance; to you I speak, the most shameless,
who are being destroyed by yourselves; but what I shall say of
your destruction and end, and what I shall advise, I know not.
For there are many things and innumerable for the hearing. But
greater are your deeds than the punishment that is reserved for
you. But to thee I speak, thou demon, and to thy son who follows
with thee, for now am I sent against you—but why do I make a
long story of your nature and root, which you yourselves know
and are unashamed? But Judas Thomas says to you, the apostle
of Christ Jesus who out of great love and good will has been sent

---

[1] Cf. Mk. 8:37 pars.; 2 Clem. 1.

here: (p. 190) Before all the crowd that stands here come out and tell me of what race you are." 75. And immediately the woman came out with her daughter, ⟨like⟩ people dead and dishonoured. And when the apostle saw them he was grieved, especially for the girl, and said to the demons: "God forbid that there be propitiation or sparing for you, for you know not sparing or compassion. In the name of Jesus, depart from them and stand by their side." When the apostle said this, the women fell down and died; for they neither had breath nor uttered a sound. But the demon in answer said with a loud voice: "Art thou come hither again, thou that mockest our nature and race? Art thou come again, thou that dost blot out our crafty devices ⟨traces S⟩? And as I think, thou dost not consent to our being on earth at all. But this thou canst not do now at this time." But the apostle recognized that this was the demon who had been driven out of that woman. 76. But the demon said: "I pray thee, give me leave to go and dwell where thou wilt, and to receive commandment from thee, and I fear not the mighty one who has authority over me. For even as thou didst come to preach the Gospel, so did I come to destroy. And even as, if thou fulfil not (p. 191) the will of him who sent thee, he brings punishment upon thy head, so I also, if I do not do the will of him who sent me, am sent back before the time and appointed season to my nature. And as thy Christ helps thee in what thou dost perform, so my father helps me in what I perform. And as he prepares for thee vessels worthy of thy habitation, so also he (my father) seeks out for me vessels through which I may accomplish his deeds. And as he nourishes and provides for his subjects, so for me also he (my father) pre-pares punishments and tortures with those who have become my dwellings. And as to thee he gives eternal life as reward for thy working, so for me he (my father) provides in requital for my works eternal destruction. And as thou art refreshed by thy prayer and good works and spiritual hymns, so am I refreshed by murders and adulteries and sacrifices wrought with wine at the altars. And as thou dost convert men to eternal life, so do I pervert those who obey me to destruction and eternal punishment. And thou dost receive thine own ⟨reward⟩, and I mine." 77. When the demon had said this and much more (p. 192), the apostle

483

said: "Jesus commands thee and thy son through me to enter no more into the habitation of man, but go out and depart and live wholly outside the dwelling of men." But the demons said to him: "A hard command hast thou given us. But what wilt thou do against those who are now hidden from thee? For those who have wrought ⟨. . .⟩ the images rejoice in them more than thee, and the many worship them ⟨. . .⟩ and do their will, sacrificing to them and bringing food in libations ⟨of⟩ wine and water and ⟨offering oblations⟩." And the apostle said: "They also shall now be abolished, together with their works." And suddenly the demons became invisible; but the women lay prostrate on the ground like dead people, without a sound. 78. And the wild asses stood together and did not separate one from another; but while all were silent and watched to see what they would do, that wild ass to whom speech was given by the power of the Lord (p. 193) said to the apostle: "Why dost thou stand idle, apostle of Christ the Most High, who looks for thee to ask of him the fairest learning? Why then dost thou delay? For thy teacher wishes to show his mighty works by thy hands. Why dost thou stand, herald of the hidden one? For thy master wishes to make known the ineffable things through thee, preserving them for those who are worthy to hear them from him. Why dost thou rest, thou who dost perform mighty works in the name of the Lord? For thy Lord urges thee on, engendering boldness in thee. Fear not, therefore; for he will not forsake the soul that belongeth to thee by race. Begin then to call upon him, and he will readily hear thee. Why dost thou stand wondering at all his deeds and workings? For these things are small which he has shown through ⟨thee⟩. And what wilt thou tell concerning his great gifts? For thou wilt not be sufficient to declare them. And why dost thou wonder at his bodily healings, ⟨which come to nought S⟩, especially when thou dost know that sure and abiding healing of his which he offers to ⟨his own possession⟩? And why dost thou look to this temporal life, and take no thought of the eternal? 79. (p. 194) But to you crowds who stand by and expect those that are cast down to be raised up I say: Believe the apostle of Jesus Christ! Believe the teacher of truth! Believe him who shows you the truth! Believe in Jesus! Believe in Christ, who was born that the born might live through his life, who ⟨became a child and was raised up⟩ that ⟨the perfect manhood⟩ might become manifest ⟨through him⟩. He taught his own ⟨teacher⟩,[1] for he is the teacher of truth and the wisest of the wise, who also offered the gift in the temple[2] to show that all offering is sanctified ⟨through him⟩. This man is his apostle, the revealer of truth. This is he who performs the will of him who sent him. But there shall come false apostles and prophets of lawlessness, whose end shall be according to their deeds,[3] who preach indeed and ordain that men should flee from impieties but are themselves at all times found in sins; *clothed* indeed *with sheep's clothing, but inwardly ravening wolves*.[4] Not satisfied with one wife, they corrupt many women; saying they despise children, they ⟨ruin⟩ many children, (p. 195) for which they pay the penalty; who are not ⟨content⟩ with their own possession but wish that everything ⟨useful⟩ should minister to them alone, and yet profess themselves as his (Christ's) disciples. And with their mouth they utter one thing, but in their heart they think another; they exhort others to secure themselves from evil, but they themselves accomplish nothing good; who are thought to be temperate, and exhort others to abstain from fornication, theft and avarice, but ⟨secretly practise all these things themselves⟩, although they teach others not to do them." 80. As the wild ass ⟨said⟩ this, they all looked at him. And when he fell silent the apostle said: "What I am to think about thy beauty, Jesus, and what I am to tell about thee, I do not know. Or rather, I am not able. For I have no power to declare it, O Christ who art at rest and only wise, who alone knowest what is in the heart and understandest the content of the thought—to thee be glory, merciful and tranquil; to thee be glory, wise word;* glory to thy compassion that was poured out upon us; glory to thy pity that was spread out over us; glory to thy majesty which for our sakes was made small; glory to thy most exalted kingship which (p. 196) for our sakes was humbled;

---

[1] Cf. Infancy Gospel of Thomas 6–8; 14 and 15; 19; Vol. I, pp. 394–398.
[2] Cf. Mt. 17:27.   [3] Mt. 7:15; 24:11 parr.; 2 Pet. 2:1; 2 Cor. 11:13, 15.
[4] Mt. 7:15.
* Here the Syriac has: How I am to name thee, I know not. O noble one, silent, tranquil and speaking, seer who art in the heart, seeker who art in the understanding. Glory to thee, the gracious; glory to thee, the living word; glory to thee, who hast many forms; glory to thy compassion. . . .

glory to thy strength which for our sakes was made weak; glory to thy Godhead which for our sakes was seen in the likeness of men; glory to thy manhood which for our sakes died that it might make us live; glory to thy resurrection from the dead, for through it rising and rest come to our souls; glory and honour to thine ascent into the heavens, for through it thou hast shown us the ascent to the height, having promised us that we shall *sit* on thy right hand *and* with thee *judge the twelve tribes of Israel*.[1] Thou art the heavenly word of the Father, thou art the hidden light of the understanding, he who shows the way of truth, pursuer of the darkness and obliterator of error." 81. When he had said this, the apostle stood over the women, saying: "My Lord and my God, I doubt not concerning thee, nor in unbelief do I call upon thee, who art ever our helper and defender and restorer, who dost breathe thine own power into us and encourage us and furnish boldness in love to thine own servants; I pray thee, let these souls rise healed, and become as they were before they were smitten by the demons." And when he said this, the women turned (p. 197) and sat up. And the apostle charged the captain that his servants should take them and lead them inside. But when they had gone in, the apostle said to the wild asses: "Follow me." And ⟨they followed him S⟩ until they were outside the gates. And when they came out he said: "Depart in peace to your pastures." So the wild asses went off readily. But the apostle stood and watched over them, that they might not be harmed by anyone, until they were far off and out of sight. And the apostle returned with the crowd to the captain's house.

Ninth Act
Concerning the wife of Charisius

82. Now it happened that a certain woman whose name was Mygdonia, the wife of Charisius, the close kinsman of the king, came to see and behold ⟨the new phenomenon of the new God who was being proclaimed⟩, and the new apostle who had come to stay in their land. She was carried by her own slaves, and because of the great crowd and the narrow space they were not able to bring her to him. But she sent to her husband, that he

[1] Mt. 19:28; cf. 20:23.

might send her more of their servants; and they came and ⟨went ahead of her⟩, pressing upon the people (p. 198) and cuffing them. But when the apostle saw it, he said to them: "Why do you trample on those who come to hear the word, and are eager for it? But you wish to be beside me, when you are yet far off—as it was said of the crowd that came to the Lord: *Having eyes, you see not, and having ears, you do not hear.*"[1] And he said to the crowds: "*He that hath ears to hear, let him hear!*[2] And: *Come unto me, all ye that labour and are heavy-laden, and I will give you rest!*"[3] 83. And looking on those who carried her, he said to them: "This blessing and this admonition[4] which was promised to them is now for you who are heavy laden. You are they who bear burdens grievous to be borne, you who ⟨are driven forward⟩ at her command. And though you are men they lay burdens on you, as on unreasoning beasts, while (p. 199) those who have authority over you think that you are not men such as they are. ⟨And they know not that all men are alike before God S⟩, be they slaves or free. ⟨And righteous is the judgment of God which comes upon all souls on earth, and no man escapes it S⟩. For neither will possession at all profit the rich, nor poverty deliver the poor from the judgment. ⟨For⟩ we have not received a command which we cannot fulfil, nor has he laid upon us burdens grievous to be borne, which we cannot carry. Nor has he ⟨imposed upon us⟩ such a building as men build, nor to hew stones and prepare houses as your craftsmen do by their knowledge; but we have received this commandment from the Lord, that what does not please us when it is done by another, this we should not do to any other man.[5] 84. Abstain then first from adultery, for of all evils this is the beginning, ⟨and from murder, because of which the curse came upon Cain[6] S⟩, (p. 200) then also from theft, which ensnared Judas Iscariot and brought him to hanging,[7] ⟨and from intemperance, which cost Esau his birthright,[8] and from avarice S⟩, for those who ⟨yield themselves to avarice⟩ do not see what is done by them; and from ostentation ⟨and from slander S⟩ and from all disgraceful deeds, especially those of the body, ⟨and from the horrid intercourse

[1] Mk. 8:18 (Jer. 5:21; Ezek. 12:2).   [2] Mt. 11:15 par.   [3] Mt. 11:28.
[4] The following is according to the Rome MS. U, here however very corrupt. The Paris MS. P is very much shorter.
[5] Cf. Did. 1. 2; Tob. 4. 15; Mt. 7:12.   [6] Cf. Gen. 4:11f.
[7] Cf. Jn. 12:6; Mt. 27:5; Acts 1:18.   [8] Cf. Gen. 25:29–34.

and couch of uncleanness S⟩, whose outcome is eternal con-demnation. For this (impurity) is the mother-city of all evils. And likewise it leads those who walk proudly into slavery, dragging them down to the depth and subduing them under its hands that they may not see what they do; wherefore their deeds are unknown to them. 85. But do you ⟨walk in holiness, for this is choice before God, more than any other good S⟩, and become thereby pleasing to God; ⟨and in sobriety, for this shows com-merce with God S⟩, and gives eternal life and sets death at nought. And (walk) in friendliness, ⟨. . . .⟩ for this conquers the enemies and alone receives the crown of victory. And in ⟨good-ness⟩ and (p. 201) ⟨in stretching out of the hand to the poor and supplying⟩ the want of the needy, bringing to them (of your goods) and distributing to the needy, especially those who walk in holiness. For this is choice before God, and leads to eternal life. For this before God is the mother-city of all good. For those who do not contend in Christ's stadium shall not attain holiness. And holiness appeared from God, abolishing fornication, over-throwing the enemy, well pleasing to God. For she is an invincible athlete, standing in honour with God and glorified by many. She is an ambassador of peace, proclaiming peace. ⟨But temper-ance—⟩ if anyone gains it, he remains without care, pleasing the Lord, awaiting the time of redemption. For it does nothing unseemly, and gives life and rest and joy to all who gain it. 86. But meekness has overcome death, bringing it under authority. Meekness (p. 202) has enslaved the enemy.[1] Meekness is a good yoke. Meekness fears no man and does not offer ⟨. . .⟩ resistance. Meekness is peace and joy and exultation of rest. Abide therefore in holiness, and receive freedom from care, and be near to meekness; for in these three heads is portrayed the Christ whom I proclaim to you. Holiness is a temple of Christ, and he who dwells in it receives it as a habitation. ⟨And temperance is the refreshing of God S⟩; for forty days and forty nights he fasted, tasting nothing.[2] And he who observes it (temperance) shall dwell in it as in a mountain. But meekness is his boast, for he said to Peter our fellow-apostle: *Turn* back *thy sword and restore it* again *to its sheath*! For if I wanted to do this, *could I not have brought more*

---

[1] From this point again according to the two MSS. P and U.   [2] Cf. Mt. 4:2.

than twelve legions of angels from *my Father?*"[1] 87. When the apostle
said this in the hearing of all the crowd, they pressed and trampled
one another. But the wife of Charisius the king's kinsman sprang
from the litter and threw herself on the ground before the apostle,
and catching his feet she said in entreaty: "Disciple of the living
God, thou art come into a desert country. For we live in a desert,
like unreasoning beasts in our conduct; but now by thy hands
shall we be saved. I pray thee, then, take thought for me and
pray for me, that the compassion of the God whom thou dost
preach may come upon me, and that I may become (p. 203) his
dwelling-place and ⟨have part with you⟩ in the prayer and hope
and faith in him, and that I too may receive the seal and become
a holy temple, and he dwell in me." 88. And the apostle said:
"I pray and entreat for you all, brethren, who believe on the
Lord, and for you sisters who hope in Christ, that the word of
God may settle upon all and tabernacle in you; for we have no
power over you." And he began to say to the woman Mygdonia:
"Rise up from the ground and compose thyself. For this added
adornment shall profit thee nothing, nor the beauty of thy body,
nor thy garments. But neither the fame of the honour that
surrounds thee, nor the power of this world, nor this sordid communion with thy husband shall avail thee if thou be deprived of
the true communion. For the pomp of adornment comes to
nothing, and the body grows old and changes, and garments
become worn out, and authority and lordship pass away, accompanied by punishment for the manner in which each has conducted himself in it (lordship). And the fellowship of procreation
also passes away, as being indeed matter of condemnation. Jesus
alone abides for ever, and they who hope in him." Having thus
spoken he said to the woman: (p. 204) "Depart in peace,[2] and
the Lord will make thee worthy of his own mysteries." But she
said: "I fear to depart, lest thou forsake me and go to another
nation." But the apostle said to her: "Even if I go, I will not leave
thee alone, but Jesus because of his compassion will be with thee."
And she falling down did him obeisance and departed to her
house. 89. But Charisius the kinsman of king Misdaeus came back
after bathing and sat down to dine. And he asked concerning his

[1] Mt. 26:52f.   [2] Cf. Lk. 7:50.

wife, where she was; for she had not come from her own chamber to meet him as she was wont. Her handmaids said to him: "She is not well." And he sprang up and went into the chamber, and found her lying on the bed and veiled; and unveiling her he kissed her, saying: "Why art thou sorrowful today?" And she said: "I am not well." And he said to her: "Why didst thou not have regard to thy position as a free woman and remain in thy house, but go out and listen to vain words and look upon magic works? But rise up and dine with me, for without thee I cannot dine." But she said to him: "I pray thee, today excuse me; for I am sore afraid." 90. When Charisius heard this from Mygdonia, he did not want to go out to dinner, but commanded his servants to bring her to dine with him. (p. 205) So when they brought her he asked her to dine with him, but she excused herself. Since she was unwilling, he dined alone, saying to her: "For thy sake I declined to dine with king Misdaeus, and wert thou unwilling to dine with me?" But she said: "Because I am not well." When he rose, Charisius wanted as usual to sleep with her, but she said: "Did I not tell thee that for today I have declined?" 91. When he heard this, he went and slept in another bed. But when he awoke from sleep he said: "My lady Mygdonia, listen to the dream which I have seen. I saw myself reclining near king Misdaeus, and a full-laid table was set beside us. And I saw an eagle coming down from heaven and carrying off from before me and the king two partridges, which he bore off to his ⟨nest⟩. And again he came upon us, flying round above us; but the king commanded a bow ⟨to be brought⟩ to him. And the eagle again snatched from before us a pigeon and a dove. But the king shot an arrow at him, and it passed through him from one side to the other, and did him no harm; and he rose up quite unscathed to his nest. And now that I am awake I am afraid and sore troubled, because I had tasted of the partridge, and he did not allow me to put it to my mouth again." But Mygdonia said to him: "Thy dream is good, for thou dost eat partridges daily, but this eagle had not tasted of a partridge until now." 92. (p. 206) But when morning came, Charisius went off and dressed, and he bound his left sandal on his right foot.[1] And pausing, he said to Mygdonia:

---

[1] Cf. Gospel of Thomas log. 22, Vol. I, p. 298.

"Now what is the meaning of this? For see—the dream and ⟨this business⟩!" But Mygdonia said to him: "This too is nothing bad, but seems to me very good; for from a bad business it will come to the better." But he after washing his hands went away to salute king Misdaeus. 93. And likewise Mygdonia also rose up early and went to salute Judas Thomas the apostle. And she found him conversing with the captain and all the crowd; and he was exhorting them, speaking about the woman who had received the Lord in her soul (and asking)[1] whose wife she was. ⟨The captain said⟩: "She is the wife of Charisius, the kinsman of king Misdaeus," and "Her husband is a very hard man, and in all that he says to the king he obeys him.[2] And he will not allow her to continue in this opinion which she has avowed. For indeed he has often praised her before the king, saying that there is no other like her for love. So all that thou dost discuss with her is strange to her." But the apostle said: "If the Lord has truly and surely risen in her soul, and she has received the seed sown, she will neither take thought (p. 207) for this transient life nor fear death, nor will Charisius be able in any way to harm her. For greater is he whom she has received into her soul, if she has truly received him." 94. When Mygdonia heard this, she said to the apostle: "Truly, my lord, I have received the seed of thy words, and will bring forth fruit like to such seed." The apostle said: "⟨These souls which are thy possession⟩ praise and thank thee, Lord; the bodies thank thee, which thou hast held worthy to become dwelling-places of thy heavenly gift." And he said also to all those who stood by: "Blessed are the holy, whose souls have never condemned them; for having gained these (souls) they are not divided against themselves. Blessed are the spirits of the holy, and those who have received the heavenly crown intact from the aeon appointed for them. Blessed are the bodies of the holy, because they have been counted worthy to become temples of God, that Christ may dwell in them. Blessed are ye, because you have power to forgive sins.[3] Blessed are ye if you lose not what is committed to you, but with joy ⟨and gladness⟩ bring it with you. Blessed are you holy, for to you it is given to ask and to receive. *Blessed*

[1] The following according to U. P differs.
[2] From this point again according to the two great MSS.
[3] Cf. Jn. 20:23; Mt. 16:19; 18:18.

are you *meek*,[1] because God has counted you worthy to become *heirs* of the heavenly kingdom. *Blessed are* you *meek*, for you are (p. 208) they who have conquered the enemy. *Blessed are* you *meek*, because you *shall see* the face of the Lord.[2] *Blessed are* you who *hunger*[3] for the Lord's sake, because for you is rest preserved and now on your souls rejoice. Blessed are you quiet, (because you have been counted worthy) to be freed from sin ⟨. . . . . .⟩." When the apostle had said this in the hearing of all the crowd, Mygdonia was the more confirmed in the faith, and in the glory and majesty of Christ. 95. But Charisius the king's kinsman and friend came to breakfast, and did not find his wife in the house. And he inquired of all in the house: "Where did your mistress go?" And one of them said in reply: "She is gone to that stranger." But when he heard this from his slave he was angry with his other servants, because they did not at once report to him what had happened; and he sat down and waited for her. And when it was evening and she came into the house, he said to her: "Where wert thou?" And she said in answer: "At the doctor." But he said: "Is that stranger a doctor?" And she said: "Yes, a physician of souls. For most doctors heal bodies which are dissolved, but he souls which are not destroyed." When Charisius heard this, he was very angry at heart against Mygdonia because of the apostle, but he made her no answer, for he was afraid; for she was better than he both in wealth and in understanding. But he went off (p. 209) to dinner, and she went into her chamber. And he said to the servants: "Call her to dinner!" But she would not come. 96. When he heard that she would not come out of her chamber, he went in and said to her: "Why wilt thou not dine with me, and perhaps not sleep with me as usual? And on this point I have the greater suspicion, for I have heard that that magician and deceiver teaches that a man should not live with his own wife, and what nature requires and the deity has ordained he overthrows." When Charisius said this, Mygdonia remained silent. He said to her again: "My lady and consort Mygdonia, be not led astray by deceitful and vain words, nor by the works of magic which I have heard this man performs in the name of Father, Son and Holy Spirit. For never was it heard in

---

[1] Mt. 5:5.   [2] Mt. 5:8; cf. Rev. 22:4.   [3] Mt. 5:6.

this world that anyone raised a dead man; but as I hear, ⟨it is rumoured of him⟩ that he raises the dead. And that he neither eats not drinks, do not think that it is for righteousness' sake that he neither eats not drinks; but this he does because he possesses nothing. For what should he do, who does not even have his daily bread? And he has one garment because he is poor. As for not taking anything from anyone, (p. 210) (he does that) because he knows ⟨that no-one is really healed by him.⟩" 97. But when Charisius said this, Mygdonia was silent like a stone; but she prayed that when it was day she might go to the apostle of Christ. And he departed from her, and went off to dinner despondent; for he was anxious to sleep with her as usual. But when he had gone, she bowed her knees and prayed, saying: "Lord God, Master, merciful Father, Saviour Christ, do thou give me strength that I may overcome Charisius' shamelessness, and grant me to keep the holiness in which thou dost delight, that I too through it may find eternal life." And when she had so prayed she laid herself veiled on the bed. 98. But Charisius when he had dined came upon her, and she cried out, saying: "Henceforth thou hast no place with me, for my Lord Jesus who is with me and rests in me is greater than thou." But he laughed and said: "Well dost thou mock, saying these things about that sorcerer, and well dost thou deride him when he says: Ye have no life with God unless ye sanctify yourselves." And when he had said this he attempted to sleep with her; and she did not endure it, but crying out bitterly said: "I call upon thee, Lord Jesus, forsake me not! For with thee I have made my refuge. For as I learned that thou art he who seeks out those imprisoned in ignorance, and delivers those held fast in error, so now I pray thee whose fame (p. 211) I have heard and believed: Come thou to my help and deliver me from Charisius' shamelessness, ⟨that⟩ his foulness may not gain the mastery over me!" And striking her hands ⟨against her face⟩ she fled from him naked; and as she went out she tore down the curtain of the chamber, and throwing it about her went away to her nurse and slept there with her. 99. But Charisius all through the night was in despair, beating his hands against his face. And he wanted to go off in that very hour and bring the king the news of the violence that had come upon him; but he reflected, saying to himself: "If the great despair that is about me should compel me to go now to the king, who will bring me in to him? For I know[1] that an evil report has overthrown me from my proud bearing and vainglory and grandeur, and cast me down to this pettiness, and separated my sister Mygdonia from me.[2] Even if the king himself stood before the doors in this hour, I could not have gone out and given him answer. But I will wait until it is day; and I know that whatever I ask of the king he grants me. I will tell of the madness of that stranger, which tyrannously casts down the great (p. 212) and notable into the depth. For it is not this that grieves me, that I am deprived of her company, but I am grieved for her, because her great soul is humbled. Noble lady as she is, whom none of her house ever charged ⟨with impropriety S⟩, she has fled naked from her chamber and run outside, and I know not where she has gone. And perhaps, maddened by that sorcerer, she has in her frenzy gone into the market-place in search of him. For indeed nothing seems lovable to her but that man and the things said by him."

100. When he had said this he began, lamenting, to say: "Woe to me, my consort, and to thee also! For I have been too quickly deprived of thee. Woe is me, most beloved, for thou art better than all my race! Neither son nor daughter have I of thee, that I might rest upon them; nor didst thou live with me ⟨a full⟩ year,[3] but an evil eye has snatched thee from me. ⟨.⟩ Would that the violence of death had taken thee, and I should have ⟨reckoned myself⟩ among kings and chieftains! But that I should suffer such a thing at the hands of a stranger! And perhaps he is a slave who has run away, to my hurt and that of my most unhappy soul. (p. 213) May there be for me no hindrance until I destroy him and avenge this night; and may I not be well-pleasing before king Misdaeus if he does not give me satisfaction with the head of the stranger, and in the matter of Siphor the captain, who was the cause ⟨of her loss S⟩. For through him did he appear here, and with him he lodges; and many are they who go in and come out, whom he teaches a new doctrine, saying that none can live except he give over all his possessions and become a renouncer

---

[1] The following according to U. P differs.
[2] From this point again according to the two great MSS.
[3] The following according to U. P differs and is very much shorter.

like himself; and he is zealous to make many partners with himself."[1] 101. While Charisius thought on these things, day dawned. And having watched all night he put on mean clothing, bound on his sandals, and went gloomy and despondent to salute the king. But when the king saw him, he said: "Why art thou sorrowful, and come in such attire? And I see that thy face too is changed." But Charisius said to the king: "I have a new thing to tell thee, and a new desolation, which Siphor (p. 214) has brought into India: a Hebrew man, a sorcerer, whom he has sitting in his house and who does not depart from him; and many are they who go in to him, whom he teaches a new God, and lays on them new laws which were never yet heard, saying: It is impossible for you to enter into the eternal life which I proclaim to you, except you rid yourselves of your wives, and likewise the women of their husbands. But it happened that my ill-fated wife also went to him, and became a hearer of his words; which she believed, and leaving me in the night she ran to the stranger. But send both for Siphor and for that stranger who is hidden with him, and visit them with death, that all who are of our race may not perish." 102. When his friend Misdaeus heard this, he said to him: "Be not grieved or disheartened, for I will send for him and avenge thee, and thou shalt have thy wife again. ⟨For if I avenge others S⟩ who cannot avenge ⟨themselves⟩, ⟨thee above all S⟩ will I avenge." And going out the king sat down on the judgment seat; and when he was set he commanded Siphor the captain to be called. So they went to his house, and found him sitting (p. 215) at the apostle's right hand, and Mygdonia at his feet listening to him with all the crowd. And those who were sent from the king came up to Siphor and said: "Dost thou sit here listening to vain words, and king Misdaeus in his wrath is thinking to destroy thee because of this magician and deceiver whom thou hast brought into thy house?" When Siphor heard this he was dejected, not because of the king's threat against him but because of the apostle, because the king had pronounced adversely concerning him. And he said to the apostle: "I am distressed about thee. For I told thee from the beginning that that woman is the wife of Charisius, the king's kinsman and friend, and he does not allow

[1] From this point again according to the two great MSS.

her to do what she promises, and all he asks of the king he grants him." But the apostle said to Siphor: "Fear nothing, but believe in Jesus, who plays the advocate for us all. For to his refuge are we gathered together." When Siphor heard this, he flung his cloak about him and went off to king Misdaeus. 103. But the apostle inquired of Mygdonia: "What was the reason that thy husband was angry and devised this against us?" And she said: "Because I did not give myself to his destruction. For last night he wanted to subdue me, and subject me to that passion which he serves; and he to whom I (p. 216) have committed my soul delivered me out of his hands. And I fled from him naked and slept with my nurse. But what has come upon him that he has contrived this, I do not know." The apostle said: "These things will not harm us; but believe in Jesus, and he will overthrow Charisius' anger and his madness and his passion. And he shall be a companion for thee in the fearful way, and himself shall guide thee into his kingdom. And he shall bring thee into eternal life, granting thee the confidence which neither passes away nor changes." 104. But Siphor stood before the king, and he questioned him: "Who is he and whence, and what does he teach, that magician whom thou hast lurking in thy house?" And Siphor answered the king: "Thou art not ignorant, O king, what trouble and grief I had, with my friends, concerning my wife, whom thou also dost know and many others remember; and concerning my daughter, whom I value above all my property, what a time and trial I have suffered. For I became a laughing-stock and a curse to all our country. But I heard the report of this man, went to him and besought him, and took him and brought him here. And as I came along the road (p. 217) I saw wonderful and astonishing things, and here many heard the wild ass, and about the demon whom he drove out; and he healed my wife and daughter, and now they are whole. And he did not ask for reward, but demands faith and holiness, that (men) may become partakers with him in what he does. This he teaches, to worship and fear one God, the Lord of all, and Jesus Christ his Son, that they may have eternal life. What he eats is bread and salt, and his drink is water from evening to evening, ⟨and⟩ he makes many prayers; and whatever he asks of his God, he gives him. And he teaches that this God is holy and powerful, and that Christ is life and giver of life. Therefore he charges those who are with him to approach him (God) in holiness and purity and love and faith." 105. When king Misdaeus heard this from Siphor, he sent many soldiers to the house of Siphor the captain to bring Thomas the apostle and all who were found there. And when those who were sent went in, they found him teaching a great number; and Mygdonia was sitting at his feet. But when they saw the great crowd around him, they were afraid and went back to their king and said: "We did not dare to say anything to him, for there was a great crowd (p. 218) around him; and Mygdonia, sitting at his feet, was listening to what was said by him." When king Misdaeus and Charisius heard this, Charisius sprang up from the king's presence and taking a large crowd with him said: "I will bring him, O king, and Mygdonia, whose understanding he has taken away." And he went to the house of Siphor the captain, greatly perplexed. And he found him teaching; but Mygdonia he did not catch, for she had returned to her house, having learned that it had been reported to her husband that she was there. 106. But Charisius said to the apostle: "Stand up, thou wicked man and destroyer and enemy of my house! For me thy magic does not harm; for I will visit thy magic upon thy head!" But when he said this, the apostle looked at him and said to him: "Thy threats shall return against thee, for me thou wilt not harm in any way. For greater than thou and thy king and all your army is the Lord Jesus Christ in whom I have my hopes." But Charisius took a kerchief of one of his slaves and threw it round the apostle's neck, saying: "Hale him off and take him away! Let me see if his God can deliver him out of my hands." And they dragged him off and brought him to king Misdaeus. ⟨But when the apostle stood⟩ before the king, the king said to him: "Tell me who thou art, and *by what power*[1] thou dost perform these things." But the apostle remained silent. And the king commanded his subjects that he should be scourged with a hundred and twenty-eight lashes and flung in bonds (p. 219) into the prison. And they put him in chains and led him away. But the king and Charisius considered how they might put him to death. But the crowd worshipped him as a

---

[1] Acts 4:7.

497

god. And they had it in mind to say: The stranger insulted the king, and is a deceiver. 107. And as the apostle went away to the prison he said, rejoicing and exulting: "I praise thee, Jesus, that thou hast made me worthy not only of faith in thee, but also of suffering much for thy sake. I thank thee therefore, Lord, that thou hast taken thought for me, and given me patience. I thank thee, Lord, that for thy sake I have been called a sorcerer and a magician. ⟨May I⟩ therefore ⟨receive⟩ of the blessing of the humble, and of the rest of the weary, and of the blessings of those whom men hate and *persecute* and *revile*, speaking evil words of them.[1] For lo, for thy sake am I hated; lo, for thy sake am I cut off from the many, and for thy sake they call me such as I am not." 108. And as he prayed all the prisoners looked at him, and besought him to pray for them. And when he had prayed and sat down, he began to utter a psalm in this fashion:[2]

1 When I was a little child
  And dwelt in my kingdom, the house of my father,
2 And enjoyed the wealth and the ⟨luxuries⟩
  Of those who brought me up,
3 From the East, our homeland,
  My parents provisioned and sent me;
4 And from the wealth of our treasury
  They had already bound up for me a load.
5 Great it was, but (so) light
  That I could carry it alone:
6 Gold from Beth 'Ellaye
  And silver from great (p. 220) Gazak
7 And chalcedonies of India
  And opals of the realm of Kushan.
8 And they girded me with adamant,
  Which crushes iron.
9 And they took off from me the splendid robe
  Which in their love they had wrought for me,
10 And the purple toga,
  Which was woven to the measure of my stature,

[1] Cf. Mt. 5:11.
[2] Prof. M. Black has kindly checked the English translation of the following hymn against the Syriac text.

11 And they made with me a covenant
   And wrote it in my heart, that I might not forget:

12 "If thou go down to Egypt
   And bring the one pearl

13 Which is in the midst of the sea,
   In the abode of the loud-breathing serpent,

14 Thou shalt put on (again) thy splendid robe
   And thy toga which lies over it,

15 And with thy brother, our next in rank,
   Thou ⟨shalt be heir⟩ in our kingdom."

109. 16 I quitted the East and went down,
       Led by two couriers,

17 For the way was dangerous and difficult
   And I was very young to travel it.

18 I passed over the borders of Maišân (Mesene),
   The meeting-place of the merchants of the East,

19 And reached the land of Babel,
   And entered in to the walls of Sarbûg.

20 I went down into Egypt,
   And my companions parted from me.

21 I went straight to the serpent,
   Near by his abode I stayed,

22 Until he should slumber and sleep,
   That I might take my pearl from him.

23 And since I was all alone
   I was a stranger to my companions of my hostelry.

24 ⟨But⟩ one of my race I saw there,
   A nobleman out of ⟨the East⟩,

25 A youth fair and lovable,

26 An ⟨anointed one⟩,
   And he came and attached himself to me (p. 221)

27 And I made him my intimate friend,
   My companion to whom I communicated my business.

28 I (He?) warned him (me?) against the Egyptians
   And against consorting with the unclean.

29 But I clothed myself in garments like theirs,
   That ⟨they might⟩ not ⟨suspect⟩ that I was come from
                                                    without

499

30 To take the pearl,
   And so might waken the serpent against me.

31 But from some cause or other
   They perceived that I was not their countryman,

32 And they dealt with me treacherously
   And gave me to eat of their food.

33 And I forgot that I was a king's son
   And served their king.

34 And I forgot the pearl
   For which my parents had sent me.

35 And because of the heaviness of their ⟨food⟩
   I fell into a deep sleep.

110. 36 ⟨And all this⟩ that befell me
   My parents observed and were grieved for me.

37 And a proclamation was published in our kingdom
   That all should come to our gate,

38 The kings and chieftains of Parthia
   And all the great ones of the East.

39 They made a resolve concerning me,
   That I should not be left in Egypt,

40 And they wrote to me a letter
   And every ⟨noble⟩ set his name thereto:

41 "From thy father, the king of kings,
   And thy mother, the mistress of the East,

42 And from thy brother, our other son,
   To thee, our son in Egypt, greeting!

43 ⟨Awake⟩ and rise up from thy sleep,
   And hearken to the words of our letter.

44 Remember that thou art a son of kings.
   See the slavery—him whom thou dost serve!

45 (p. 222) Remember the pearl
   For which thou didst journey into Egypt.

46 Remember thy splendid robe,
   And think of thy glorious toga,

47 That thou mayest put them on and ⟨deck thyself
                                          therewith⟩,
   ⟨That⟩ thy name may be read in the book of the heroes

48 And thou with thy brother, our crown prince,
⟨Be heir⟩ in our kingdom."

III. 49 And the letter was a letter
Which the king ⟨had sealed⟩ with his right hand

50 Against the wicked, the people of Babel
And the ⟨rebellious⟩ demons of Sarbûg.

51 It flew in the form of an eagle,
The king of ⟨all⟩ birds,

52 It flew and alighted beside me
And became all speech.

53 At its voice and the sound ⟨of its rustling⟩
I awoke and stood up from my sleep,

54 I took it and kissed it,
Broke ⟨its seal⟩ and read.

55 And even as it was engraven in my heart
Were the words of my letter written.

56 I remembered that I was a son of kings
And my noble birth asserted itself.

57 I remembered the pearl
For which I was sent to Egypt,

58 And I began to cast a spell
On the terrible loud-breathing serpent.

59 I brought him to slumber and sleep
By naming my father's name over him,

60 And the name of our next in rank
And of my mother, the queen of the East.

61 And I snatched away the pearl
And turned about, to go to my father's house.

62 And their dirty and unclean garment
I took off and left in their land,

63 And directed my way ⟨that I might come⟩
To the light of our homeland, the East.

64 And my letter, my awakener,
I found before me on the way;

65 As with its voice (p. 223) it had awakened ⟨me⟩,
(So) it led me further with its light,

66 (Written) on Chinese tissue with ruddle,
Gleaming before me with its aspect

67 And with its voice and its guidance
  Encouraging me to speed,

68 And ⟨drawing⟩ me with its love.

69 I went forth, passed through Sarbûg,
  Left Babel on my left hand

70 And came to the great (city) Maišân (Mesene),
  The haven of the merchants,

71 ⟨Which lies⟩ on the shore of the sea.

72 And my splendid robe which I had taken off,
  And my toga with which it was wrapped about,

73 From the heights ⟨of⟩ Warkan (Hyrcania)
  My parents sent thither

74 By the hand of their treasurers,
  Who for their faithfulness were trusted therewith.

112. 75 Indeed I remembered no more its dignity,
  For I had left it in my childhood in my father's house,

76 But suddenly, when I saw it over against me,
  The ⟨splendid robe⟩ became like me, as my reflection
  in a mirror;

77 I saw it ⟨wholly⟩ in me,
  And in it I saw myself ⟨quite⟩ apart ⟨from myself⟩,

78 So that we were two in distinction
  And again one in a single form.

79 And the treasurers too
  Who had brought it to me, I saw in like manner,

80 That they were two of a single form,
  For one sign of the king was impressed upon them,

81 (His) who restored to me through them
  ⟨The honour G⟩, my pledge and my riches,

82 My splendid robe adorned
  ⟨Gleaming⟩ in glorious colours,

83 With gold and beryls,
  Chalcedonies and ⟨opals⟩,

84 And ⟨sardonyxes⟩ of varied ⟨colour⟩,
  This also made ready in its grandeur,

85 And with stones of adamant
  (Were) all its seams fastened.

86 And the likeness of the king of kings
    Was ⟨completely⟩ embroidered all over it

87 ⟨And like⟩ stones of sapphire again in its
    Grandeur resplendent with manifold hues.

113.   88 (p. 224) And again I saw that all over it
    The motions of ⟨knowledge⟩ were stirring.

89 And I saw too
    That it was preparing as for speech.

90 I heard the sound of its songs
    Which it whispered ⟨at its descent⟩:

91 "I belong to the most valiant servant,
    For whom they reared me before my father,

92 And I ⟨perceived⟩ also in myself
    That my stature grew according to his labours."

93 And with its royal movements
    It poured itself entirely toward me,

94 And in the hands of its bringers
    It hastened, that I might take it;

95 And my love also spurred me
    To run to meet it and receive it,

96 And I stretched out and took it.
    With the beauty of its colours I adorned myself.

97 And my toga of brilliant colours
    I drew ⟨completely⟩ over myself.

98 I clothed myself with it and mounted up
    To the gate of greeting and homage.

99 I bowed my head and worshipped
    The splendour of the father ⟨who⟩ had sent it (the
                                                robe) to me,

100 Whose commands I had accomplished,
    As he also had done what he promised.

101 And at the gate of his satraps
    I mingled among his great ones.

102 For he rejoiced over me and received me,
    And I was with him in his kingdom.

103 And with the sound ⟨of the organ⟩
    All his servants praise him.

SECOND AND THIRD CENTURY ACTS

104 And he promised me that to the gate
      Of the king of kings I should journey with him again
105 And with my gift and my pearl
      With him appear before our king.

114. Charisius went off home rejoicing, thinking that his wife would be with him again and that she ⟨would be S⟩ as (p. 225) of old, before she heard the divine word and believed in Jesus. But when he went, he found her with ⟨her hair shorn S⟩ and her garments rent. And seeing this he said to her: "My lady Mygdonia, why does this cruel sickness hold thee fast? And why hast thou done these things? I am thy husband from thy virginity, and both the gods and the laws give me (the right) to rule over thee. What is this great madness of thine, that thou art become a laughing-stock in all our nation? But put away the care that comes from that sorcerer; and I will take away the sight of him from our midst, that thou mayest see him no more." 115. But when Mygdonia heard this, she gave ⟨herself⟩ up to her grief, groaning and lamenting. And Charisius said again: "Have I then so much wronged the gods, that they have compassed me about with such a sickness? What offence have I committed so great that they have flung me into such a humiliation? I pray thee, Mygdonia, do not torment my soul at the pitiful sight of thee, and thy mean appearance, and do not burden my heart with care over thee! I am Charisius thy ⟨husband⟩, whom all the nation honours and fears. What must I do? I know not how to ⟨conduct⟩ myself. And what am I to think? Shall I keep silent and endure? And who will bear it when people take his treasure? But who would endure ⟨to be robbed⟩ of thy sweet ways? ⟨. . .⟩ Thy fragrance is in my nostrils, and thy radiant face is fixed in my eyes. They are taking away (p. 226) my soul, and the beautiful body in which I rejoiced when I saw it they are destroying; the sharpest of eyes they are blinding, and they are cutting off my right hand. My joy is turned to grief and my life to death, and the light ⟨is plunged⟩ in darkness. ⟨Let⟩ none of my kinsmen look on me henceforth, they from whom no help has come to me, nor will I worship henceforth the gods of the East, who have compassed me about with such evils. In truth, I will neither pray to

them any more nor sacrifice to them, if I am robbed of my spouse. But what else should I ask of them? For all my glory is taken away. I am a prince, second to the king in authority. But all this Mygdonia ⟨by rejecting me⟩ has taken away. ⟨Would that someone would strike out my eyes, if thou wouldst turn thine eyes upon me as of old!⟩" 116. While Charisius said this with tears, Mygdonia sat silent and looking on the ground. But he came to her again and said: "My lady, most beloved Mygdonia, remember that out of all the women in India I chose thee as the fairest and took thee, when I could have joined to myself in marriage others far more beautiful than thee. But rather do I lie, Mygdonia. For by the gods it ⟨is⟩ not possible that another like thee should be found in the land of the Indians. But woe is me for ever more, that thou wilt not (p. 227) answer me at all. Revile me if thou please, that I may but be granted a word from thee! Look upon me, for I am ⟨far better and more handsome S⟩ than that sorcerer! ⟨I have riches and honour, and all recognize that none has such a lineage as I. But thou art my riches and my honour⟩, thou art my family and kinship—and lo, he is taking thee away from me!" 117. When Charisius said this, Mygdonia said to him: "He whom I love is better than thee and thy possessions. For thy possession is of the earth and returns to earth; but he whom I love is heavenly, and will take me with him into heaven. Thy wealth shall pass away, and thy beauty shall vanish, and thy robes and thy many works; but thou (shalt remain) alone with thy transgressions ⟨. . .⟩ Remind me not of thy deeds towards me; for I pray the Lord that thou mayest forget, so as to remember no more the former pleasures and the bodily intimacy, which will pass away like a shadow; but Jesus alone abides for ever, and the souls which hope in him. Jesus himself will set me free from the shameful deeds which I did with thee." And when Charisius heard this (p. 228) he turned broken-hearted to sleep, saying to her: "Consider this by thyself all through this night! If thou wilt be with me, such as thou wast before thou didst see that sorcerer, I will do all thy desires, and if because of thy friendship for him thou shouldst wish it, I will take him out of the prison and set him free, and he may go to another country. And I will not vex thee, for I know that thou art greatly attached to the stranger.

And it was not with thee first that this matter came about, but he has also deceived many other women along with thee. But they have come to their senses and returned to themselves. So do not set my words at nought, and make me a reproach among the Indians." 118. As Charisius was saying this he fell asleep. But she took ten denarii and went out secretly to give them to the gaolers, that she might go in to the apostle. ⟨But on the way Judas Thomas met her, coming to her⟩, and seeing him she was afraid; for she thought he was one of the rulers, for a great light went before him. And she said to herself as she fled: "I have destroyed thee, unhappy soul! For thou wilt not again see Judas, the apostle of the living ⟨God⟩, and as yet (p. 229) thou hast not received the holy seal." And as she fled she ran into a narrow place and there hid herself, saying: "It is better to be ⟨taken⟩ by the poorer, whom it is possible to persuade, than to fall in with this powerful prince, who despises gifts."

Tenth Act

How Mygdonia receives baptism

119. As Mygdonia was considering this by herself, Judas came and stood over her. And seeing him she was afraid, fell down in terror, and lay like one dead. But standing beside her and taking her hand he said to her: "Fear not, Mygdonia. Jesus will not desert thee, nor will thy Lord to whom thou hast committed thy soul overlook thee. His compassionate rest will not forsake thee. He who is kind will not forsake thee, because of his great kindness, and he that is good, because of his goodness. Rise up then from the earth, since thou art become wholly above it. See the light, for the Lord does not allow those who love him to walk in darkness. Look upon the fellow-traveller of his servants, for he is to them an ally in dangers." And Mygdonia stood up and looked at him, and said: "Where wert thou going, my Lord? And who is he who brought thee out of the prison to behold the sun?" Judas Thomas says to her: "My Lord Jesus is more powerful than all powers and kings and rulers." 120. And Mygdonia said: "Give me the seal of Jesus Christ, and I will receive a gift from thy hands (p. 230) before thou depart from life." And taking him with her she went into the court and wakened her nurse, saying

to her: "My mother and nurse Marcia (Narcia S), all the services and refreshments thou hast rendered me from childhood to my present age are vain, and for them I owe thee (only) temporal thanks. But do me now also a favour, that thou mayest for ever receive the recompense from him who bestows the great gifts." At these words Marcia said: "What dost thou wish, my daughter Mygdonia, and what is to be done for thy pleasure? The honours which thou didst promise me before, the stranger did not allow thee to bring to fulfilment, and thou hast made me a reproach in all the nation. And now what is the new thing which thou dost command me?" And Mygdonia said: "Become my partner in eternal life, that I may receive from thee a perfect nourishment. Take bread and bring it me, and a mixture of (wine and) water, and spare my freedom (have regard for my free birth)." And the nurse said: "I will bring many loaves, and instead of water gallons (*metretai*) of wine, and fulfil thy desire." But she says to the nurse: "Gallons I do not need, nor the many loaves, but bring this only: a mixture of (wine and) water, and one loaf, and oil." 121. And when Marcia had brought these things, Mygdonia stood before the apostle with her head bare; and he taking the oil poured it on her head, saying: "Holy oil given to us for sanctification, hidden mystery in which the Cross was shown to us, thou art the straightener of (p. 231) the ⟨crooked⟩ limbs; thou art the humbler of hard works; thou art he who shows the hidden treasures; thou art the shoot of goodness. Let thy power come; let it be established upon thy servant Mygdonia; and heal her through this ⟨unction⟩!" And when the oil had been poured out he bade the nurse unclothe her and gird a linen cloth about her. Now there was there a spring of water, and going to it the apostle baptized Mygdonia in the name of the Father and the Son and the Holy Spirit. And when she was baptized and clothed, he broke bread and took a cup of water, and made her partaker in the body of Christ and the cup of the Son of God, and said: "Thou hast received thy seal, and ⟨obtained⟩ for thyself eternal life." And straightway there was heard from above a voice saying: "Yea, Amen." And when Marcia heard this voice she was startled, and besought the apostle that she too might receive the seal. And giving it to her the apostle said: "The zeal of the Lord be about thee, as about the others." 122. When the apostle had done this he returned to the prison; but he found the doors open and the guards still asleep. And Thomas said: "Who is like thee, O God, who dost withhold from none thy tender love (p. 232) and zeal? Who is like thee ⟨in compassion⟩, who hast delivered thy ⟨creatures⟩ from evil? Life that has mastered death, rest that has ended toil! Glory be to the only-begotten of the Father,[1] glory to the compassionate who was sent from his heart!" And when he said this, the guards woke up and saw all the doors open, and the prisoners ⟨asleep S⟩. And they said among themselves: "Did we not secure the doors? And how are they now open, and the prisoners inside?" 123. But Charisius as soon as it was dawn went to Mygdonia, and he found them praying and saying: "New God, who through the stranger didst come to us here: God, who art hidden from the dwellers in India; God who hast shown thy glory through thine apostle Thomas; God whose fame we heard and believed in thee; God to whom we came to be saved; God who through love for men and through pity didst descend to our littleness; God who didst seek us out when we knew thee not; God who dost dwell in the heights and dost not remain hidden from the depths: turn thou away Charisius' madness from us!" But when Charisius heard this he said to Mygdonia: "Justly dost thou call me evil and mad and base! For if (p. 233) I had not borne thy disobedience and made thee a gift of freedom, thou wouldst not have invoked ⟨the witchcraft of that man S⟩ against me and made mention of my name before God. But believe me, Mygdonia, that with that sorcerer there is no profit, and what he promises he cannot perform. But I do for thee before thine eyes all that I promise, that thou mayest believe and bear with my words and become to me as thou wert before." 124. And drawing near he besought her again, saying: "If thou wilt listen to me, there will be no grief for me henceforth. Remember that day on which thou didst meet me first. Tell me the truth: was I more beautiful to thee at that time, or Jesus at this?" And Mygdonia said: "That time required its own, and this time also. That was the time of beginning, but this of the end. That was the time of a transitory

---

[1] Cf. Jn. 1:14.

life, but this of eternal. That was of a passing pleasure, but this of one that abides for ever; that, of day and night, but this of day without night. Thou hast seen that marriage, which passed away ⟨and remains here (on earth)⟩, but this marriage abides for ever. That fellowship was one of corruption, but this of life eternal. Those attendants are short-lived men and women, but these now remain to the end. ⟨That marriage was founded on earth, where there is a ceaseless pressure; but this on the fiery bridge, whereon grace is sprinkled. S⟩ That bridal chamber is taken down, but this remains for ever. That bed was spread with coverlets, but this with love and faith. Thou art a bridegroom who passes away and is destroyed, (p. 234) but Jesus is a true bridegroom, abiding immortal for ever. That bridal gift was money and robes that grow old, but this is living words which never pass away."

125. When Charisius heard this, he went away to the king and told him everything. And the king commanded Judas to be brought, that he might judge and destroy him. But Charisius said: "Have patience a little while, O king. First terrify the man with words and persuade him, that he may persuade Mygdonia to become to me as formerly." And Misdaeus sent for the apostle of Christ, and had him brought from the prison. But all the prisoners were grieved because the apostle was departing from them. For they yearned after him, saying: "Even this comfort which we had they have taken from us." 126. But Misdaeus said to the apostle: "Why dost thou teach this new doctrine, which both gods and men hate and ⟨in which there is no profit⟩?" And Judas said: "What evil do I teach?" And Misdaeus said: "Thou dost teach that ⟨it is not possible for men to have life with God, if they do not keep themselves pure⟩ for the God whom thou dost preach." Judas says: "Thou speakest truly, O king; thus do I teach. For tell me: art thou not vexed with thy soldiers if they escort thee in dirty garments? If thou then, who art an earthly king and dost return to earth, (p. 235) dost require that thy subjects be seemly ⟨in their appearance⟩, how canst thou be wrathful and say I teach ill when I say: Those who serve my king must be holy and pure and free from all grief and care for children and useless riches and from vain trouble? For indeed thou dost wish thy subjects to follow thy behaviour and thy ways, and thou

dost punish them if they scorn thy commands. How much more must those who believe in my God serve him with great holiness and purity and ⟨chastity⟩, free from all bodily pleasures, adultery and prodigality, theft and drunkenness and service of the belly and (other) shameful deeds?" 127. When Misdaeus heard this he said: "See, I set thee free. So go and persuade Mygdonia, the wife of Charisius, not to desire to part from him." Judas says to him: "Do not delay, if thou hast anything to do (against me). For if she has rightly received what she has learned, neither iron nor fire nor anything else stronger than these will be able to harm her or cut away him who is held in her soul." Misdaeus says to Judas: "Some drugs make other drugs ineffective, and an antidote makes an end of the viper's bites; and thou if thou wilt canst give release from those poisons, and bring peace and concord to this (p. 236) marriage. For by doing so thou dost spare thyself; for thou hast not yet thy fill of life. But know that if thou do not persuade her I will pluck thee out of this life ⟨that is desirable⟩ to all." And Judas said: "This life is given in usufruct, and this time changes; but that life which I teach is incorruptible. But the beauty and the youth which is seen shall soon be no more." The king says to him: "I have advised thee what is expedient, but thou knowest thine own affairs." 128. But as the apostle was departing from the king, Charisius came up and said to him in entreaty: "I pray thee, O man: never have I sinned at all, neither against thee or any other, nor against the gods. Why hast thou stirred up so great an evil against me? And why hast thou brought such confusion on my house? And what profit is there for thee from this? But if thou dost think to gain anything, tell me what kind of a gain it is, and I will procure it for thee without trouble. For what reason dost thou drive me out of my mind, and cast thyself into destruction? For if thou persuade her not, I will both slay thee and finally take myself out of life. And if, as thou sayest, after ⟨our release from life here⟩ there is yonder life and death, and also condemnation and victory and a tribunal, I too will go in there to be judged with thee. And if the God whom thou dost preach is just, and awards the punishments justly, I know that I shall obtain justice (p. 237) ⟨against thee⟩. For thou hast injured me, though thou hast suffered no wrong at my hands. For indeed here I am able to avenge myself ⟨for all that⟩ thou hast done against me. Therefore listen to me and come home with me, and persuade Mygdonia to become with me as formerly, before she saw thee!" But Judas says to him: "Believe me, child, if men loved God as much as (they love) each other, they would receive from him all they asked, without anyone constraining him." 129. As Thomas said this, they went into Charisius' house and found Mygdonia sitting, and Marcia standing beside her with her hand laid on Mygdonia⟨'s cheek⟩; and (Mygdonia) was saying: "May the remaining days of my life be cut short for me, mother, and may all the hours become as one hour, and may I depart from life, that I may go the more quickly and see that beautiful one whose fame I have heard, that living one and giver of life to those who believe in him, where there is neither day and night, nor light and darkness, nor good and evil, nor poor and rich, male and female, no free and slave, no proud that subdues the humble." As she said this, the apostle stood beside her; and at once she stood up and did him reverence. Then Charisius (p. 238) said to him: "Dost thou see how she fears and honours thee, and does willingly all that thou dost command?" 130. But as he said this, Judas says to Mygdonia: "My daughter Mygdonia, obey what brother Charisius says!" And Mygdonia said: "If thou couldst not ⟨name⟩ the deed in word, ⟨how⟩ dost thou compel me to endure the act? For I heard from thee that this life is ⟨. . .⟩ a loan, and this rest temporary, and these possessions transitory. And thou didst say again that he who renounces this life shall receive the eternal, and he who hates the light of day and night shall see a light that is not ⟨extinguished⟩, and that he who despises these goods shall find other, eternal goods. But now ⟨thou sayest this S⟩ because thou art afraid. But who that has done something and been praised for the work changes it? ⟨Who builds a tower S⟩ and again overthrows it from the foundations? Who when he has dug a well of water in a thirsty place fills it in again? Who finding a treasure did not make use of it?" But when Charisius heard this, he said: "I will not imitate you nor hasten to destroy you. ⟨But since it is in my power I will put ⟨thee⟩ in fetters, and will not allow thee to converse with this sorcerer. And if thou obey me ⟨not⟩, I know what I must do." 131. But Judas departed from Charisius' house and went away to the house of Siphor, and stayed there with him. And Siphor said: "I will prepare for Judas a room (triclinium) in which he ⟨may⟩ teach." (p. 239) And he did so; and Siphor said: "I and my wife and daughter will live henceforth in holiness, in purity, and in one disposition. I pray thee, that we may receive the seal from thee, that we may become servants to the true God, and be numbered among his sheep and lambs." But Judas says: "I am afraid to say what I think. But I know something, and what I know it is not possible for me to declare." 132. And he began to speak about baptism: "This baptism is forgiveness of sins.[1] It brings to new birth a light that is shed around. It brings to new birth the new man, ⟨renews the thoughts, mingles soul and body S⟩, raises up the new man in three-fold manner, and is partaker in forgiveness of sins. Glory be to thee, hidden power that is united with us in baptism! Glory be to thee, ineffable power that is in baptism! Glory be to thee, renewal through which are renewed the baptized who take hold of thee with affection!"[2] And when he had said this he poured oil upon their heads and said: "Glory be to thee, the love of compassion! Glory be to thee, (p. 240) name of Christ! Glory be to thee, the power established in Christ!" And he commanded a basin to be brought, and baptized them in the name of the Father and the Son and the Holy Spirit. 133. And when they were baptized and clothed, he set bread upon the table and blessed it and said: "Bread of life, those who eat of which remain incorruptible; bread which fills hungry souls with its blessing—thou art the one ⟨thought worthy⟩ to receive a gift, that thou mayest become for us forgiveness of sins, and they who eat thee become immortal. We name over thee the name of the mother of the ineffable mystery of the hidden dominions and powers, we name ⟨over thee the name of Jesus⟩." And he said: "Let the power of blessing come and ⟨settle upon the bread⟩, that all the souls which partake of it may be washed of their sins!" And breaking it he gave to Siphor and his wife and daughter.

[1] The following in the main according to U. P differs.
[2] From here on again according to both MSS.

Eleventh Act
Concerning the wife of Misdaeus

134. After king Misdaeus had set Judas free, he went off home
⟨to dine S⟩. And he told his wife what had befallen their kinsman
Charisius, saying: "See what has happened to that unhappy man!
But thou thyself dost know, my sister Tertia, that there is nothing
(p. 241) fairer to a man than his own wife, by whom he rests.
But it happened that his wife went away to that sorcerer, of whom
thou hast heard that he is come to the land of the Indians, and
fell a victim to his potions and was parted from her husband;
and he is at a loss what he should do. But when I wished to
destroy the malefactor, he would not have it. But do thou go
and advise her to incline to her husband, and to keep away
from the vain words of the sorcerer." 135. And Tertia at once
arose and went away to the house of Charisius her husband's
kinsman; and she found Mygdonia lying on the ground in abase-
ment. Ashes and sackcloth were spread under her, and she was
praying that the Lord might forgive her her former sins, and she
depart quickly from life. And Tertia said to her: "Mygdonia, my
dear sister and companion, ⟨. . . . .⟩ what is the sickness that has
taken hold of thee? And why dost thou do the deeds of madmen?
Know thyself, and return to thine own way! Come near to thy
many kinsfolk, and spare thy true husband Charisius, and do
not do what is alien to thy free birth!" Mygdonia says to her:
"O Tertia, thou hast not yet heard the preacher of life! Not yet
has (his message) fallen upon thine ears, (p. 242) not yet hast
thou tasted the medicine of life and been freed from corruptible
groaning. Thou standest in the transient life, the eternal life and
salvation thou knowest not; and perceiving not the incorruptible
fellowship ⟨thou art afflicted by a corruptible fellowship S⟩.
Thou standest clothed in robes that grow old, and dost not desire
the eternal; and thou art proud of this beauty that vanishes, but
takest no thought of the ugliness of the soul. And in a multitude of
servants thou art rich, ⟨but hast not freed thine own soul from
slavery S⟩; and thou dost plume thyself in the glory that comes
from many, but dost not redeem thyself from the condemnation
unto death." 136. When Tertia heard this from Mygdonia she

513

said: "I pray thee, sister, take me to that stranger who teaches these great things, that I too may go and hear him, and be taught to worship the God whom he preaches, and become a sharer of his prayers and a partaker in all the things of which thou hast told me." But Mygdonia says to her: "He is in the house of Siphor the captain. For indeed he is become an occasion ⟨of life⟩ for all who are saved in India." But when Tertia heard this, she went off in haste to Siphor's house, that she might see the new apostle who had come to the country. But when she went in Judas said to her: "What hast thou come to see? A strange man and poor and contemptible and beggarly, who has neither wealth nor possession? But one possession have I obtained which (p. 243) neither king nor rulers can take away, which neither perishes nor comes to an end, which is Jesus, the Saviour of all mankind, the Son of the living God, who has given life to all who believe in him and take refuge with him, and is known in the number of his servants." Tertia says to him: "May I become a partaker in this life which thou dost promise all shall receive who come together to God's hostelry!" And the apostle said: "The treasury of the holy king is open wide, and those who worthily partake of the goods there do rest, and resting reign.[1] ⟨.⟩ But no man comes to him who is unclean and vile; for he knows our inmost hearts and the depths of our thought, and none can escape his notice. Thou too, then, if thou dost truly believe in him, shalt be made worthy of his mysteries; and he shall magnify thee and enrich thee and make thee heir of his kingdom."[2] 137. When Tertia heard this, she went back home rejoicing; and she found her husband ⟨awaiting her⟩, without having broken his fast. And when he saw her Misdaeus said: "Whence is thy coming in today more beautiful? And why didst thou come on foot, which is not fitting for free-born women like thee?" And Tertia says to him: "I owe thee the greatest thanks that thou didst send me to Mygdonia. For when I went I heard of a new life, and I saw the apostle of the ⟨new⟩ God who gives life (p. 244) to those who believe in him and fulfil his commands. I ought therefore myself to requite thee for this favour and admonition with good advice.

---

[1] Cf. the Gospel of the Hebrews 4ab, Vol. I, p. 164. Cf. also next note.
[2] Cf. the Gospel of Thomas, log. 2, Vol. I, p. 297. Cf. also the previous note.

For thou shalt be a great king in heaven if thou obey me and fear the God who is preached by the stranger, and keep thyself holy to the living God. For this kingdom passes away, and thy comfort shall be turned into affliction. But go to that man, and believe him, and thou shalt live unto the end!" When Misdaeus heard this from his wife, he smote his face with his hands and rent his clothing, and said: "May the soul of Charisius find no rest, because he has hurt me to the soul; and may he have no hope, because he has taken my hope away." And he went out greatly troubled. 138. And he found Charisius his friend in the market-place and said: "Why hast thou thrown me ⟨as thy companion S⟩ into Hades? Why hast thou robbed and defrauded me to gain no profit? Why hast thou hurt me at no benefit to thyself? Why hast thou slain me, and thyself not lived? Why hast thou wronged me without thyself obtaining what is rightful? Why didst thou not consent to my destroying that sorcerer, before he ruined my house with his ⟨sorcery⟩?" And he ⟨was upbraiding Charisius S⟩. But Charisius said: "What has befallen thee?" Misdaeus said: "He has bewitched Tertia." (p. 245) And they both went away to the house of Siphor the captain, and found Judas sitting and teaching. Now all who were there stood up for the king, but he (Judas) did not rise. But Misdaeus recognized that he was the man, and taking hold of the chair overturned it, and lifting up the chair with both hands he struck him on the head so that he wounded him. And he handed him over to his soldiers, saying: "Take him away, and drag him roughly and without restraint, that his insolence may be manifest to all." And they dragged him off and brought him to a place where Misdaeus used to sit in judgment. And there he stood, held fast by Misdaeus' soldiers.

Twelfth Act

Concerning Vazan (Vîzan), the son of Misdaeus

139. But Vazan, the son of Misdaeus, went to the soldiers and said: "Give him to me, that I may converse with him until the king comes." And they gave him up, but he led him in where the king used to sit in judgment. And Vazan said: "Dost thou not know that I am the son of king Misdaeus, and that I am free to say to the king what I wish, and ⟨if I tell him⟩ he will let thee

live? Tell me, then, who is thy God, and (p. 246) to what power dost thou cling, and glory in it? For if it is a magic power and craft, tell it and teach me, and I will set thee free." Judas says to him: "Thou art the son of king Misdaeus, who is a king for a season; but I am the servant of Jesus Christ, ⟨the⟩ eternal king. Thou art free to speak to thy father to save whom thou wilt in this transient life, in which men do not continue, which thou and thy father give; but I pray my Lord and cry aloud on behalf of men, and he gives them a new life which is altogether ⟨enduring⟩. Thou dost boast of possessions and slaves and robes and luxury and beds impure; but I boast of poverty and love of wisdom ('philosophia') and humility and fasting and prayer and fellowship with the Holy Spirit and with my brethren who are worthy of God; and I boast of eternal life. And thou hast sought refuge with a man who is like thee, who cannot save his own soul from judgment and death; but I have sought refuge with the living God, the Saviour of kings and rulers, who is judge of all. And you are, perhaps, for today, but tomorrow no more; but I have taken refuge with him who abides for ever, who knows all our seasons and times. But if thou wilt become a servant of this God, thou shalt do so quickly. And that thou wilt be a servant worthy of him, ⟨thou shalt⟩ show by these tokens: first by holiness, which is the chief of all good things; then by fellowship with this God whom I preach, and by love of wisdom ('philosophia'), and by simplicity and love and faith, and by ⟨hope in him⟩, and by ⟨simplicity of pure living⟩." (p. 247) 140. But the young man, persuaded by the Lord, sought occasion how he might help Judas to escape. But while he was considering, the king ⟨arrived⟩, and the soldiers took Judas and led him out. And Vazan went out with him and stood beside him. And when the king was seated he commanded Judas to be brought in with his hands bound behind him. And he was brought into the midst and stood there. And the king said: "Tell me who thou art, and *by what power*[1] thou dost do these things." But Judas says to him: "I am a man like thee, and by the power of Jesus Christ I do these things." And Misdaeus says: "Tell me the truth before I destroy thee." And Judas says: "Thou hast no power against me,

[1] Acts 4:7.

516

as thou dost think, and thou wilt not hurt me at all." But the king, annoyed at these words, gave orders to heat (iron) plates and set him on them barefoot. And as the soldiers took off his shoes he said: "The wisdom of God is better than the wisdom of men. Do thou, Lord and King, resist his wrath!" And they brought the plates, which were like fire, and set the apostle upon them; and immediately water gushed abundantly from the ground, so that the plates were swallowed up. And those who held him let him go and fell back. 141. But when the king saw the abundance of water, he said to Judas: "Pray thy God that he deliver me from this death, that I may not perish in the flood." And the apostle prayed and said: "Thou who didst bind this nature and gather it (p. 248) into one place, and dost send it out to different countries; thou who out of disorder didst bring into order; thou who givest mighty works and great wonders by the hands of thy servant Judas; thou who hast compassion on my soul, that I may always receive thy light; who givest reward to those who have laboured; thou saviour of my soul, who dost restore it to its own nature, to associate no more with the hurtful; thou who art ever an occasion of life—restrain this element, that it may not rise up and destroy! For *there are some of those here standing who shall live*,[1] when they have believed in thee." But when he had prayed, the water was in a short time consumed, and the place became dry. And when Misdaeus saw it, he commanded him to be taken into the prison "until I consider how we must deal with him". 142. But as Judas was led away to the prison they all followed him, and Vazan the king's son walked at his right hand and Siphor on his left. And going into the prison he sat down, and Vazan and Siphor with him, and he (Siphor) persuaded his wife and daughter (also) to sit down; for they too had come to hear the word of life. For indeed they knew that Misdaeus would slay him because of the extremity of his anger. But Judas (p. 249) began to say: "Liberator of my soul from the bondage of the many, because I gave myself to be sold; behold, I rejoice and ⟨exult⟩, knowing that the times are fulfilled for me to enter in and receive ⟨thee S⟩. Behold, I am set free from the cares on earth. Behold, I fulfil my hope and receive truth. Behold, I am

[1] Cf. Mk. 9:1 pars.

517

set free from grief, and put on only joy. Behold, I become carefree and unpained, dwelling in rest. Behold, I am set free from slavery, and called to liberty. Behold, I have served times and seasons, and am lifted ⟨above⟩ times and seasons. Behold, I receive ⟨my reward S⟩ from the requiter who gives without reckoning, ⟨because his wealth is sufficient for his gifts⟩. ⟨Behold, I unclothe myself and clothe myself S⟩, and shall not again be unclothed. Behold, I sleep and awake, and shall not again fall asleep. Behold, I die and come to life again, and shall not again *taste of death*.[1] Behold, they await rejoicing, that I may come and be united with their kindred, and be set as a flower in their crown. Behold, I reign in the kingdom on which even here I have set my hope. ⟨Behold, the wicked shall be put to shame, who thought that they would subject me to their powers S⟩. Behold, the rebellious fall before me, because I have escaped them. Behold, peace has come, and all go to meet it." 143. As the apostle said this, all who were there listened, thinking that ⟨in that hour⟩ he ⟨would⟩ depart from life. And again he said: "Believe in the physician of all, both visible and invisible, and in the ⟨saviour⟩ of the souls that need his help. This is the free man, (scion) of kings. This is the physician of his ⟨creatures⟩. This is he (p. 250) who was reviled by his own servants. This is the Father of the height and Lord and Judge of nature. Most high is he become from the Greatest, the only-begotten son of Depth; and he was called son of Mary a virgin, and was termed son of Joseph a carpenter. He whose lowliness ⟨we beheld⟩ with the eyes of the body, but his greatness we received by faith, and saw it in his works; whose human body *we handled* even *with our hands*, and his appearance *we saw* transfigured *with our eyes*,[2] but his heavenly form we could not see upon the mount;[3] who baffled the rulers and overpowered death; he who is truth that does not lie, and paid tribute ⟨and S⟩ poll-tax for himself and his disciples;[4] ⟨he whom⟩ the Archon feared when he saw him, and the powers that were with him were confounded. And the Archon ⟨asked⟩ who and whence he was, and did not know the truth, for indeed he is alien to the truth.[5] He, though he has authority over the world and the

---

[1] Mk. 9:1.   [2] I Jn. 1:1.   [3] Cf. Mk. 9:2ff. pars.
[4] Cf. Mt. 17:24–27.   [5] Cf. Jn. 8:44.

pleasures in it, and the possessions and the indulgence, ⟨has rejected⟩ all these things, and incites his subjects to make no use of them." 144. And when he had finished this he stood up and prayed thus: "*Our Father who art in heaven, hallowed be thy name; thy kingdom come; thy will be done, as in heaven so on earth; ⟨give us the constant bread of the day S⟩; and forgive us our debts, as we also have forgiven our debtors; and lead us not into temptation, but deliver us from evil.*[1] (p. 251) *My Lord and my God,*[2] hope and confidence and teacher and ⟨my comforter S⟩, thou hast taught me to pray thus. Behold, I pray this prayer and fulfil thy command. Be thou with me unto the end. Thou art he who from childhood has sown life in me, and preserved me from corruption. Thou art he who brought me into the poverty of the world, and invited me to true riches. Thou art he who made himself known to me, and showed me that I am thine; and I withheld myself from woman, that what thou dost require might not be found in defilement. 145 (p. 252). My mouth does not suffice to render thanks unto thee, nor my understanding to ponder on ⟨thy zeal for me⟩, who when ⟨I wished⟩ to be rich and possess ⟨. . .⟩ didst show me that ⟨for many⟩ on earth riches are a loss. But I believed thy revelation and remained in the poverty of the world, until ⟨thou⟩, the true riches, didst appear and fill with riches both me and those worthy ⟨of thee⟩, and didst free us from want and care and avarice. Behold, therefore, I have fulfilled thy work and accomplished thy command; and I have become poor and needy and a stranger and a slave, despised and a prisoner and hungry and thirsty and naked and weary. Let not my trust, then, (p. 253) come short (of its fulfilment), and let not my hope in thee be put to shame! Let not my labours become vain! Let not my continual prayers and fastings perish, and let my works to thee-ward not be diminished! Let not the devil snatch away the seed of wheat ⟨from the⟩ land, and ⟨let not his tares be found upon it;[3] for thy land cannot receive his tares, neither can they be laid in

[1] Mt. 6:9ff. From this point the two MSS. U and P diverge considerably. P (with 3 and in part even 4 other MSS.) presents this long prayer (from *My Lord and my God* to c. 148) only in the Martyrdom (after c. 167) and with a very divergent text. S on the other hand agrees by and large with U. James (p. 364) considers the position and textual tradition of this chapter presented by P (and the parallel MSS.) the more original. (Cf. also what is said below on the Martyrdom.) The above text on the whole follows the substantially shorter form of U and its arrangement.
[2] Jn. 20:28.   [3] Cf. Mt. 13:25.

the barns of thy husbandmen." And again he said: 146. "Thy vine have I planted in the land S⟩; may it send its roots into the depth, and the spread of its branches up to heaven! And may its fruits be seen on the earth, and may they delight in it who are worthy of thee, and whom thou hast acquired! Behold, the money which thou hast given me I have laid (p. 254) on the table (of the money-changers);[1] demand it and return it to me with interest, as thou didst promise! With thy mina I have gained another ten;[2] may they be added to me (to my property) as thou didst ordain! I remitted the mina to the debtors;[3] may that not be demanded from me which I have remitted! When called to dinner I have come, released from field and wife; may I not, then, be cast out, but blamelessly taste of it![4] To the wedding have I been invited, and have put on white robes; may I be worthy of them and not go out, bound hand and foot, into outer darkness![5] ⟨My lamp shines with its light;[6] may its Lord preserve it (keep it burning) until he leaves the bridal house and I receive him; may I not see it (p. 255) extinguished for lack of oil!⟩ Let mine eyes behold thee and my heart rejoice, because I have fulfilled thy will and accomplished thy command! ⟨Let me be like the wise and God-fearing servant, who with careful diligence did not neglect his vigilance!⟩[7] Watching all the night I have wearied myself, to guard my house from the robbers, that they might not break in.[8] 147.[9] *My loins have I girded with truth*[10] and my shoes have I bound to my feet,[11] that I may not see their thongs loosened altogether. My hands have I put to the yoked plough, and have not turned away backward,[12] that the furrows may not be crooked. The field is become white and the harvest is at hand,[13] that I may receive my reward. My garment that grows old (p. 256) I have worn out, and the laborious toil that leads to rest I have accomplished. I have kept the first watch and the second and the third,[14] that I may behold thy face and worship thy holy radiance. I have pulled down the ⟨barns⟩ and left them desolate on earth, that

---

[1] Cf. Mt. 25:27.   [2] Cf. Lk. 19:13ff.   [3] Cf. Mt. 18:23ff.
[4] Cf. Lk. 14:16ff. par.   [5] Cf. Mt. 22:1ff.   [6] Cf. Mt. 25:1ff.
[7] Cf. Mt. 24:45ff.   [8] Cf. Mt. 24:43.
[9] C. 147 has been supplemented according to the tradition presented by P and S. U here has only two sentences.
[10] Cf. Eph. 6:14.   [11] Cf. Eph. 6:15.   [12] Cf. Lk. 9:62.
[13] Cf. Jn. 4:35.   [14] Cf. Lk. 12:38.

I may be filled from thy treasures.[1] The abundant spring within
me I have dried up, that I may find thy living spring.[2] The
prisoner whom thou didst commit to me I have slain, that the
freed man in me may not lose his trust. The inside I have made
outside, and the outside ⟨inside⟩,[3] and thy whole fullness has
been fulfilled in me. I have not turned back to what is behind,
but have advanced to what is before, that I may not become a
reproach. The dead man I have brought to life and the living I
have put to death, and what was lacking I have filled up, that
(p. 257) I may receive the crown of victory and the power of
Christ be perfected in me. Reproach have I received on earth,
but give me recompense and requital in heaven! 148. Let not the
powers and dominions perceive me, and let them form no plan
concerning me! Let not the tax-gatherers and the exactors busy
themselves with me! Let not the base and the wicked mock at
⟨me, the brave and kind⟩! And when I am borne upward, let
them not venture to stand before me, by thy power, Jesus, which
enwreathes me. For they flee and hide themselves; they cannot
look thee in the face. For suddenly do they fall upon their subjects,
and the portion of the sons of the evil one itself cries out and
convicts them. (p. 258) And none of them remains hidden, for
their nature is made known. The children of the evil one are
separated; ⟨the tree of their fruit is bitterness S⟩. Grant me now,
Lord, that in quietness I may pass by, and in joy and peace cross
over and stand before the judge. And let not the devil look upon
me; let his eyes be blinded by thy light which thou hast made to
dwell in me. Stop up his mouth, for he has nothing against me."
149.[4] And he said again to those who were about him: "⟨Believe,
my children, in this God whom I proclaim; believe in Jesus
Christ, whom I preach; believe in the giver of life and helper of
his servants S⟩; believe in the saviour of those who have grown
weary in his service! For my soul already rejoices, because my
time is near to receive him. For being beautiful he leads me to

[1] Some Greek MSS. have here: "All my goods have I sold, that I may gain thee, the pearl."
[2] Cf. Gospel of Thomas log. 13, Vol. I, p. 287.
[3] Cf. the Gospel of the Egyptians, Vol. I, p. 168 g; Gospel of Thomas log. 22, Vol. I, p. 298.
[4] U and S alone have c. 149. In chapters 150–158 the great Greek MSS. are in fairly close agreement.

speak ever of his beauty, of what manner it is, although I am neither able nor sufficient to speak of it worthily. Thou who art the light of my poverty and supplier of my deficiencies and nourisher of my need: be thou with me until I come and receive thee for ever more."

(p. 259)   Thirteenth Act
        How Vazan receives baptism with the others

150. But the youth Vazan besought the apostle, saying: "I pray thee, O man, ⟨holy man S⟩, apostle of God, allow me to go, and I will persuade the gaoler to permit thee to come home with me, that through thee I may receive the seal, and become thy servant and a keeper of the commandments of the God whom thou dost preach. For indeed formerly I walked in those things which thou dost teach, until my father constrained me and joined me to a wife named Mnesara; for although I am (only) twenty-one years old I have already been seven years married. But before I was joined in marriage I knew no other woman; and therefore was I reckoned useless in my father's eyes. Nor has either son or daughter ever been born to me of this wife: but indeed my wife has lived with me in chastity during this time, and today (p. 260) had she been in health and had listened to thee, I know that I should be at rest and she would receive eternal life. But she is in peril, and tried by much sickness. So I will persuade the guard, if thou promise to come with me, for I live alone by myself; and at the same time thou shalt heal that unhappy one." When Judas the apostle of the Most High heard this, he said to Vazan: "If thou dost believe, thou shalt see the wonders of God, and how he saves his servants." 151. But while they were dis-cussing these things, Tertia and Mygdonia and Marcia were standing at the door of the prison, and after giving the gaoler 363 staters of silver they went in to Judas. And they found Vazan and Siphor and his wife and daughter and all the prisoners sitting and hearing the word. And as they stood before him he said to them: "Who allowed you to come to us? And who opened the sealed door for you to come out?" Tertia says to him: "Didst thou not open the doors for us, bidding us go to the prison (p. 261) that we might meet our brethren who were there, and then the

Lord might show his glory in us? And when we were near the door, I know not how, thou didst separate from us, and hiding thyself didst come here before us, where indeed we heard the noise of the door as thou didst shut us out. So we gave money to the guards and came in: and lo, we are here, praying thee that thou wilt be persuaded and we help thee to escape until the king's wrath against thee shall abate." Judas said to her: "Tell us first how you were shut up." 152. And she said to him: "Thou wast with us, and didst never leave us for a single hour, and dost thou ask in what manner we were shut up? But if thou dost desire to hear, hear. King Misdaeus sent for me and said: Not yet has that sorcerer prevailed over thee, for as I hear he bewitches men with oil and water and bread, and thee he has not yet bewitched. But obey thou me, for otherwise I will shut thee up and crush thee, but him I will destroy. For I know that ⟨so long as⟩ he has not given thee oil and water and bread he has not gained the power to prevail over thee. (p. 262) But I said to him: Over my body thou hast authority; do to it all that thou wilt. But my soul I will not destroy with thee. But when he heard this he shut me up in a room. And Charisius also brought Mygdonia, and shut her in with me. And thou didst lead us out and bring us to those here (assembled). But give us the seal quickly, that the hopes of Misdaeus, who is plotting thus, may be cut off." 153. When the apostle heard this, he said: "Glory be to thee, Jesus of many forms, glory to thee who dost appear in the guise of our poor manhood! To thee be glory, who dost encourage us and strengthen us and give ⟨joy⟩ and comfort us, and stand by us in all our dangers and strengthen our weakness!" But as he was saying this the gaoler came and said: "Put away the lamps, lest anyone accuse ⟨us⟩ to the king." And then, extinguishing the lamps, they turned to sleep. But the apostle conversed with the Lord: "Now it is time, Jesus, for thee to make haste; for behold, the children of darkness ⟨make us to sit⟩ in their darkness. Do thou therefore enlighten us ⟨through the light of thy nature⟩!" And suddenly the whole prison was as bright as the day. But while all who were in the prison slept in a deep slumber, only those who had believed in the Lord were just then awake. 154 (p. 263) So Judas says to Vazan: "Go ahead and make ready for us the things we need." Vazan says: "And who will open the doors of the prison for me? For the gaolers have shut them and gone to sleep." And Judas said: "Believe in Jesus, and thou shalt find the doors open!" But as he went away to go out, all the others followed behind him. And since Vazan had gone ahead, his wife Mnesara met him, on her way to the prison. And recognizing him she said: "My brother Vazan, is it thou?" And he said: "Yes; and art thou Mnesara?" And she said: "Yes." Vazan said to her: "Whither goest thou, and especially at such an untimely hour? And how wast thou able to get up?" But she said: "This young man laid his hand upon me and raised me up, and I saw in a dream that I was to go where the stranger is sitting, and become perfectly healthy." Vazan said to her: "What young man is with thee?" And she said: "Dost thou not see the one on my right hand leading me?" 155. (p. 264) But while they were conversing thus, Judas with Siphor and his wife and daughter, and Tertia and Mygdonia and Marcia, came to Vazan's house. And when she saw (him), Mnesara the wife of Vazan made obeisance and said: "Art thou come, our Saviour from the troublesome disease? Thou art he whom I saw in the night delivering to me this young man to lead me to the prison. But thy goodness did not allow me to grow weary, but thou thyself didst come to me." And saying this, she turned about, and saw the young man no more; and since she did not find him she said to the apostle: "I cannot walk alone; for the young man is not here whom thou gavest me." And Judas said: "Jesus shall lead thee by the hand henceforth." And after this she went ⟨before them S⟩ at a run. But when they went into the house of Vazan the son of king Misdaeus, although it was still night, a great light shone, shed round about them. 156. And then Judas began to pray and to speak thus: "Companion and ally, hope of the weak and confidence of the poor, refuge and lodging of the weary, ⟨voice that came forth from the height⟩, comforter who (p. 265) dwellest in ⟨our⟩ midst, lodging and haven of those who pass through ⟨regions of darkness S⟩, physician (who healest) without payment, who among men wast crucified for many, who didst descend into Hades with great power, the sight of whom the princes of death did not endure, and thou didst ascend with great glory,

524

and gathering all those who took refuge in thee thou didst prepare a way, and in thy footsteps they all journeyed whom thou didst redeem, and thou didst bring them to thine own flock and unite them with thy sheep; son of compassion, the son sent to us out of love for men from the perfect fatherland above; Lord of possessions ⟨undefiled S⟩; thou who dost serve thy servants, that they may live; thou who hast filled creation with thy riches; the poor, who was in need and hungered forty days;[1] who dost satisfy thirsty souls with thine own good things; be thou with Vazan the son of Misdaeus, and Tertia, and Mnesara, and gather ⟨them⟩ into thy fold and (p. 266) unite them with thy number. Be thou their guide in a land of error; be thou their physician in a land of sickness; be thou their rest in a land of the weary; sanctify them in a land ⟨polluted⟩; be the physician of their bodies and souls; make them thy holy temples, and let thy Holy Spirit dwell in them!" 157. When the apostle had thus prayed for them, he said to Mygdonia: "Unclothe thy sisters!" And she unclothed them, girded them with girdles, and brought them. But Vazan had come forward before, and they came after him. And Judas took oil in a silver cup, and spoke thus over it: "O fruit fairer than the other fruits, with which no other can be compared at all; thou altogether merciful; fervent with the force of the word; power of the tree which if men put on they conquer their adversaries; thou that crownest the victors; symbol and joy of the weary; who hast brought to men glad tidings of their (p. 267) salvation; who dost show light to those in darkness; who in thy leaves art bitter, ⟨but in thy fruit most sweet⟩; who in appearance art rough, but soft to the taste; who seemest weak, but by the greatness of thy power dost carry the power that sees all things; ⟨. . .⟩ Jesus, let ⟨thy⟩ victorious power come, and ⟨let it settle⟩ in this oil as then it settled in the wood that is its kin ⟨. . .⟩ and they who crucified thee did not endure its word; let the gift also come by which, breathing upon ⟨thine⟩ enemies, thou didst make them draw back and fall headlong, and let it dwell in this oil, over which we name thy holy name!" And when the apostle had said this, he poured it first on Vazan's head, then on the heads of the women, saying: "In thy name, Jesus

---

[1] Cf. Mt. 4:2.

Christ, let it be to these souls for remission of sins, and for the turning back of the adversary, and for salvation of their souls!" And he commanded Mygdonia to anoint them (the women), but he himself anointed Vazan. And when he had anointed them he led them down to the water in the name of the Father and of the Son and of the Holy Spirit. (p. 268) 158. But when they had come up from the water he took bread and a cup, and blessed and said: "Thy holy body which was crucified for us we eat, and thy blood which was poured out for us for salvation we drink. Let thy body, then, become for us salvation, and thy blood for remission of sins! For the gall which thou didst drink for our sakes, let the gall of the devil be taken away from us; and for the vinegar which thou hast drunk for us,[1] let our weakness be made strong; for the spitting which thou didst receive for our sakes,[2] let us receive the dew of thy goodness; and for the reed with which they smote thee for our sakes,[3] let us receive the perfect house! Because thou didst receive a crown of thorns for our sakes,[4] let us who have loved thee put on a crown that does not fade away; and for the linen cloth in which thou wast wrapped,[5] let us be girt about with thine unconquerable power; and for the new grave[6] and burial let us receive renewal of soul and body! Because thou didst rise (p. 269) and come to life again, let us come to life again and live and stand before thee in righteous judgment!" And breaking (the bread of) the Eucharist he gave[7] to Vazan and Tertia and Mnesara and Siphor's wife and daughter, and said: "Let this Eucharist be to you for salvation and joy and health for your souls!" And they said: "Amen." And a voice was heard saying: "Amen. Fear not, but only believe."[8]

Martyrdom of the holy and esteemed apostle Thomas[9]

159. And after these things Judas went away to be imprisoned. And not only so, but Tertia and Mygdonia and Marcia too (p. 270) went away to be imprisoned. And Judas said to them:

---

[1] Cf. Mt. 27:34, 48   [2] Cf. Mt. 27:30.   [3] Cf. Mt. 27:30.
[4] Cf. Mt. 27:29.   [5] Cf. Mt. 27:59.   [6] Cf. Mt. 27:60.
[7] Cf. Mt. 26:26.   [8] Cf. Mk. 5:36 parr.
[9] In the tradition of the Martyrdom the great Greek MSS. U and P diverge considerably, even apart from the insertion in P of the great prayer (cf. on this p. 519 n. 1 above). There is much to be said for the view that the Martyrdom had a textual history of its own. Thus James (pp. 434ff.) prefers the text of P (and its parallel MSS.). Here again we present the text of U (like Rabbe, cf. also Bonnet).

"My daughters, handmaids of Jesus Christ, hear me in this my last day ⟨on which⟩ I shall accomplish my word among you, to speak no more (with you) in the body. For behold, I am taken up to my Lord Jesus who had mercy on me, who humbled himself even to my littleness and led me to a service of majesty, and counted me worthy to become his servant. But I rejoice that the time is near for my release from hence, that I may go and receive my reward (p. 271) in the end. For righteous is my requiter, he knows how recompense must be made. For he is not grudging, but he is lavish with his goods, since he is confident ⟨that his possessions are unfailing⟩. 160. I am not Jesus, but a servant of Jesus. I am not Christ, but I am a minister of Christ. I am not the Son of God, but I pray to be counted worthy with him. But abide in the faith of Jesus Christ! Wait for the hope of the Son of God! Do not shrink in afflictions, neither be ye doubtful when ye see me insulted and imprisoned and dying. For in these I fulfil what has been appointed for me by the Lord. For ⟨. .⟩ if I wished not to die, ⟨you know S⟩ that I am able. But this apparent death is not death, but deliverance and release from the body. (p. 272) And this I shall await gladly, that I may go and receive that fair one, the merciful. For I am altogether worn out in his service, and what I have done by his grace, and now he will certainly not forsake me. But do you see to it that that one come not upon you, who comes in by stealth and divides the thoughts (casts into doubt); for stronger is he whom you have received. Look then for his coming, that when he comes he may receive you; for ye shall see him when ye depart." 161. But when he had completed his word to them, he went into (the) dark house, and said: "My Saviour, who didst endure much for our sakes, let these doors become as they were, and ⟨let them be sealed⟩ with their seals!" And leaving the women he went away to be shut up. But they were grieved and wept, since they knew that king Misdaeus would destroy him. 162. But Judas, when he ⟨returned⟩, found the guards fighting and saying: "What sin have we committed against that sorcerer, that by magic art he opened the doors of the prison, and wishes all the prisoners to escape? But let us go and inform the king, and ⟨let us tell him also⟩ about his wife and son!" But while the gaolers were saying this, Judas

527

was listening in silence. And as soon as day broke they arose and went off (p. 274) to king Misdaeus, and said: "Lord, release that sorcerer, or command him to be kept in custody somewhere else. For ⟨twice⟩ has thy good fortune kept the prisoners together. Though we shut the doors at the proper time, yet when we awake we find them open. And moreover, thy wife and thy son, together with those others, do not stay away from the man." When he heard this, the king went to inspect the seals which he had set upon the doors; and he found the seals as they were (before). And he said to the gaolers: "Why do you lie? For indeed these seals are still intact. And how say you, that Tertia and Mygdonia went into the prison?" And the guards said: "We told thee the truth." 163. (p. 275) After this the king went into the ⟨judgment-hall S⟩ and sent for Judas. But ⟨when he came⟩, they stripped him and girded him with a girdle, and set him before the king. And Misdaeus said to him: "Art thou a slave or a free man?" And Judas said: "I am a slave, ⟨but thou hast no authority over me at all⟩." And Misdaeus said: "How didst thou come as a runaway to this country?" And Judas said: "I came here to save many, and that I (p. 276) might at thy hands depart from this body." Misdaeus says to him: "Who is thy master? And what his name? And of what country?" "My Lord," says Thomas, "is my master and thine, since he is Lord of heaven and earth." And Misdaeus said: "What is his name?" Judas said: "Thou canst not hear his true name at this time, ⟨. . .⟩ but the name which was bestowed upon him for a season is Jesus, the Christ." And Misdaeus said: "I have not hastened to destroy thee, but have restrained myself. But thou hast made addition to thy deeds, so that thy sorceries are reported (p. 277) in all the land. But now I will ⟨so⟩ deal with thee ⟨that⟩ thy sorceries may perish with thee, and our nation ⟨be cleansed⟩ from them." And Judas said: "These sorceries, as thou dost call them, ⟨. . . shall never depart from hence⟩." 164. During these words Misdaeus was considering in what manner he should put him to death; for he was afraid of the crowd which stood around, since many believed him, and even some of the leading people. And rising up he took Judas with him outside the city; and a few armed soldiers followed him. But the ⟨.⟩ crowds supposed that the king wished (p. 278) to learn something from him; and they stood and observed him. But when they had advanced three stadia, he handed him over to four soldiers and one of the officers, commanding them to take him to the mountain and despatch him with spears. And he himself returned to the city. 165. The bystanders ran to Judas, eager to snatch him away. But he was led away, the soldiers escorting him two on either side, holding their spears, and the officer (p. 279) holding his hand fast and leading ⟨him⟩. And as they went, Judas said: "O thy hidden mysteries, ⟨which⟩ even to life's end are fulfilled in us! O riches of thy grace, who dost not allow ⟨that we should feel the sufferings of the body⟩! For behold, how four have laid hold of me, since from the four elements I came into being! And one leads me, since I belong to one, to whom I depart ⟨. . .⟩ But now I learn that my Lord, since he was of one, to whom I depart and who is ever invisibly with me, was smitten by one;[1] but I, since I am of four, am smitten by four." 166. (p. 280) But when they came to the place where they were to slay him, Judas said to those who held him: "Listen to me now at least, because I stand at the point of departure from the body! And let not the eyes of your understanding be darkened, nor your ears stopped that they do not hear ⟨. . .⟩! Believe in the God whom I preach! Released from the arrogance of the heart, conduct yourselves in a manner of life befitting free men, and in esteem among men and in life with God!" 167. (p. 281) But to Vazan he said: "Son of the earthly king, but servant of Jesus Christ, give to those who attend on the command of king Misdaeus what is due, that I may be released by them and go and pray." And when Vazan had persuaded the soldiers, Judas turned to prayer; and it was this: *"My Lord and my God,*[2] and hope and redeemer and leader and guide in all the lands, be thou with all who serve thee, and lead me today, since I come to thee! Let none take my soul, which I have committed unto thee. Let not the tax-collectors see me, and let not the exactors lay false charge against me! Let not the serpent see me, and let not the children of the dragon hiss me! Behold, (p. 282) Lord, I have fulfilled thy work and accomplished thy command. I have become a slave; therefore today do I receive freedom. Do

[1] Cf. Jn. 19:34.   [2] Cf. Jn. 20:28.

thou now give it to me ⟨completely⟩! But this I say not as one doubting, but that they may hear who ought to hear." 168. And when he had prayed, he said to the soldiers: "Come and fulfil ⟨the command⟩ of him who sent you!" And at once the four smote him and slew him. But all the brethren wept. And wrapping him in fine robes and (p. 283) many fine linen cloths they laid him in the tomb in which the kings of old ⟨were buried⟩. 169. But Siphor and Vazan were unwilling to go down into the city, but after spending the whole day there they passed the night there also. And Judas appeared to them, and said: "I am not here. Why do you sit here and watch over me? For I have gone up and received what was hoped for. But arise and walk, and after no great time ye shall be gathered to me." But Misdaeus and Charisius brought great pressure to bear on Tertia and Mygdonia, but did not persuade them to depart from their belief. And Judas appeared and said to them: (p. 284) "Forget not the former things! For Jesus the holy and living will himself help you." And those about Misdaeus and Charisius, being unable to persuade them, allowed them to live according to their own will. And all the brethren there used to assemble together; for Judas on the mountain had made Siphor a presbyter and Vazan a deacon, when he was being led off to die. (p. 285) But the Lord helped them, and increased the faith through them.

170. But after a long time had passed it ⟨befell⟩ that one of Misdaeus' sons was possessed by a demon; and since the demon was stubborn, no-one was able to heal him. But Misdaeus pondered and said: "I will go and open the tomb, and take ⟨one of the bones of the apostle⟩ of God, and fasten it upon my son, and I know that he will be healed." And he went away to do what he had in mind. (p. 286) And Judas appeared to him and said: "Since thou didst not believe in the living, how dost thou wish to believe in the dead?[1] But fear not! Jesus the Christ, because of his great goodness, acts humanely towards thee." But Misdaeus did not find the bones; for one of the brethren had stolen them away, and carried them to the regions of the West. But taking dust from the place where the bones of the apostle had lain, (p. 287) he attached it to his son and said: "I believe in thee,

---

[1] Cf. Gospel of Thomas log. 52, Vol. I, p. 302.

Jesus, now when he has left me, who ever confuses men that they may not look upon thy rational light." And when his son was in this manner restored to health, he (Misdaeus) came together with the other brethren, becoming submissive to Siphor. And he besought all the brethren to pray for him, that he might find mercy from our Lord Jesus Christ.

The acts of Judas Thomas the apostle are completed, which he wrought in the land of the Indians, fulfilling the command of him who sent him; to whom be glory for ever and ever. Amen.

XIV

THE PSEUDO-CLEMENTINES

(*J. Irmscher*)

1. CONTENTS. The Pseudo-Clementines is the name given to a series of writings which deal with the life of St. Clement of Rome and name him as their author. In their principal traits their contents are everywhere cast in the same mould.

Clement is born of an aristocratic family belonging to the city of Rome. Great misfortune breaks in upon it because Clement's mother, as directed in a vision, leaves the city secretly along with the narrator's two older twin brothers. When all inquiries after her fail, the father himself finally goes in search of her. He likewise does not come back. Clement, who meanwhile has grown to be a young man, busies himself in a complete devotion to religious problems. To these the doctrines of the philosophers fail to give him any satisfactory answer. Accordingly, immediately on hearing of the appearance of the Son of God in Judaea, he proceeds on a journey. He makes contact with Peter, who makes known to him the word of God, which does away with his doubts. From this time onwards he attaches himself to the apostle as a disciple on missionary journeys which take him into the cities in the region of the Syrian coast. As a preacher, as a missionary and as an apologist, Peter is here able to display an abundant activity, of special significance being his contests with the Simon Magus known to us from the Acts of the Apostles (8:9–24), who appears with his magical arts as Peter's opponent and is finally refuted by him in word and deed. In the end also Clement's family is re-united; as becomes apparent, its several members have been far scattered, but all have continued to live. These recognitions (ἀναγνωρισμοί, ἀναγνώσεις, *recognitiones*) as also other motives of the story bring the Clementines into intimate connection with the profane romances in which precisely such developments are usual (W. Bousset, *ZNW* 5, 1904, pp. 18ff.; K. Kerényi *Die griechisch-orientalische Romanliteratur*, 1927, pp. 67ff.; R. Helm, *Der antike Roman*, 1948, p. 61; A. Salač, Listy filologické 7, *Eunomia* 3, 1959, pp. 45ff.).

But the mere telling of a story is only one concern of this literature, at least in its original state, there being side by side with it a purpose to communicate the Christian doctrine or certain outward forms of it apologetically and systematically. This sets the Clementines at a certain distance from the apocryphal

Acts, which aim first and foremost at being *acta*, πράξεις, accounts (O. Stählin, *Die altchristliche griechische Literatur*, S.A. 1924, pp. 1200f.), and through just this theological tendency the Clementines at the same time held out an incentive to remodellings and revisions of many sorts.

2. SOURCES AND HISTORY OF THE TEXT. The Clementines have not come to us as they were originally composed. Today the view is widely entertained that they go back to a basic writing (B. Rehm, *ZNW* 37, 1938, pp. 155f.); on the other hand, reserve is needed in regard to the theory advocated above all by H. Waitz (*Die Pseudoklementinen*, 1904, and finally *ZKG* 58, 1940, pp. 327ff.), according to which this basic writing rested upon two main source-writings, which in essentials can still be reconstructed, the Κηρύγματα Πέτρου and the Πράξεις Πέτρου. The basic writing has not been preserved, but in its general features it can be deduced from the recensions derived from it. The decisive components of the romance of Clement already belong to it. Its main attitude is the *rationalismus* of the age of the apologists. Just conduct on earth is the guarantee of a successful undergoing of the last judgment; *rationabiliter vivere* is the demand that results from such practical philosophy. Belief plays only a subordinate rôle; the death of Jesus has no religious significance; the Christological problem scarcely exists. The guarantor of the metaphysical notions is the true prophet, whose call has to be proved by the coming true of his predictions. The basic writing belongs to Syria, where it may have originated in the first half of the third century (Waitz, *op. cit.*, pp. 72ff.; Rehm, *op. cit.*, p. 156).

The basic writing, which certainly was not widely disseminated, underwent a first revision at the hands of a speculatively minded theologian, the Homilist. To a profound ethical interest he joined one that was metaphysical, which permitted him to develop a 'doctrinal system' (G. Uhlhorn, *Die Homilien und Recognitionen des Clemens Romanus*, 1854, pp. 153ff.) entirely his own, but this, it is true, he was not able to press home everywhere in an entirely consistent way upon the material that already lay before him. The doctrine of the syzygies, the opposite pairs, which the Homilist finds everywhere, even in the being of God, provides a foundation for that opposition of Peter to Simon which becomes the leading motif of the story. The critical position which the Homilist occupies in reference to the OT is noteworthy (Rehm, *op. cit.*, p. 159). His attitude to the Trinitarian question (XVI. 16; XX. 7) ties him down to the time before 381; also he must have written in the East.

It is extremely likely that this highly original writing was not widely disseminated and that it would perhaps have been lost altogether had the Ebionites not taken a liking to it. To them this exemplary pattern for their adherence to Jewish tradition came in the nick of time. By appropriate interpolations they further reinforced this tendency, and for the rest, by the addition of the *Epistula Petri* and the *Διαμαρτυρία*, converted the writing into a constituent part of a Petrine, anti-Pauline secret tradition.

It is possible that this heretical corruption of the Homilies gave occasion to the writing of the Recognitions, which presuppose the Homilies in addition to the basic writing and are more closely connected sometimes to the one and sometimes to the other. The Ebionitic presentation of Peter and James is carried still farther; but otherwise the author confines himself to eliminating what contradicts the dogma of the great church. The time of composition is earlier than that of the *Apostolic Constitutions*, which originated in Syria between 360 and 380 (E. Schwartz, *ZNW* 31, 1932, p. 178).

Nevertheless the Recognitions, like the Homilies, had the misfortune to be interpolated by heretics so as to authenticate their irregular teaching. In a way that is nothing short of ingenious a disciple of Eunomius knew how to make room there for his own conception of the Trinity (III. 2–11), with the result that the Recognitions also became suspect in the great church and gradually disappeared from it. Rufinus, Jerome's opponent, who translated the Recognitions into Latin, secured for them acceptation and circulation in the West, omitting in his rendering the portions that gave offence; and no difference was made to this by the fact that these portions were later brought back by another translator. Such is the history of the text so far as Bernard Rehm, *op. cit.*, pp. 77ff. has worked it out.

3. TRADITION. The Homilies (*Κλήμεντος τοῦ Πέτρου ἐπιδημιῶν κηρυγμάτων ἐπιτομή*) together with two epistles to James, one of Peter and one of Clement, as also the instructions for the right use of the book (*Διαμαρτυρία περὶ τῶν τοῦ βιβλίου λαμβανόντων*) are preserved in Greek in two codices, the *Parisinus Graecus* 930, which is incomplete from XIX. 14, and the *Vaticanus Ottobonianus* 443 discovered in 1838 by A. R. M. Dressel. The first complete edition comes from Dressel and appeared at Göttingen in 1853 (reproduced in Migne, *PG* 2, cols. 19ff.). Meanwhile it has been surpassed by the editions of de Lagarde, Leipzig 1865, and B. Rehm (*GCS* 42), Berlin 1953.

The Recognitions have come down to us only in the Latin rendering of Rufinus without the *Διαμαρτυρία* and the two epistles, of which the translator had published that of Clement separately (edited by O. F. Fritsche, *Universitäts-Programm Zürich* 1873). The book, which was preceded by a dedication to bishop Gaudentius, was widely disseminated in the West, as is proved by over a hundred manuscripts that have been preserved. They have all been drawn upon for the edition of B. Rehm in the *GCS*, which, one hopes, may be expected shortly, the latest available edition—that of E. G. Gersdorf, Leipzig 1838, reprinted in Migne *PG* 1, cols. 1201ff.—no longer satisfying present-day requirements.

Both the Homilies and the Recognitions were early translated into Syriac. A manuscript from Edessa (British Museum Add. 12150) of the year 411 contains a collection of texts from R I–IV. 1, 4 and H X–XIV. 12 from the pen of two different translators. Following Lagarde (Leipzig 1861) this text with a reconstruction of the Greek original has been edited by W. Frankenberg, *TU* 48. 3 (1937).

The interest taken in the narrative portion of the Clementines by a wide circle of readers gave occasion to the drawing up of summaries in which the dogmatic discussions were relegated to the background. We possess in Greek two such epitomes (edited by Dressel, 1859). Particularly the older of the two, which has been handed down in about thirty manuscripts, is of importance for the state of the text of the Homilies; on the other hand, the so-called Cotelierian epitome, which is entered in numerous codices, represents simply a paraphrase of the older summary. Finally, in addition to the Sinai-epitome composed in Arabic (ed. by M. Gibson, *Studia Sinaitica* 5, 1896), which presents a text of the Recognitions independent of Rufinus, we possess Clementine fragments in Ethiopic (Stählin, *op. cit.*, p. 1213).

4. LITERATURE. The numerous literary and theological problems which are connected with the Clementines have called forth a large number of essays and treatises. B. Rehm, *ZNW* 37, 1938, p. 77 n. 1, lists the older compilations and works down to 1937. The works that have appeared since then are given in G. Strecker, *Das Judenchristentum in den Pseudoklementinen*, *TU* 70, 1958, pp. 276ff. Strecker himself brings forward a view that differs from the one advocated here. Cf. also pp. 102ff. above. Besides the literature given there cf. also W. Frankenberg, *ZDMG* 91, 1937, pp. 577ff.; H. J. Schoeps, 'Iranisches in den Pseudoklementinen', *ZNW* 51, 1960, pp. 1–10; W. Ullmann, 'The Significance of the Epistula Clementis in the Pseudo-Clementines', *JThSt*, NS 11, 1960, pp. 295ff.

TEXTS*

Clement's Spiritual Development (H I)

1. 1. I Clement, a Roman citizen, was able even in my youth to pursue a circumspect line of conduct, whilst my pensiveness from childhood held down my desires and brought me much affliction and tribulation. 2. Again and again there came to me—whence I cannot tell—thoughts of death. After my departing this life, would I be no more and no one remember me, 3. seeing that time, which knows no limits, brings every thing, even every thing, into oblivion? I wondered too if I would be without existence and without knowledge of those to whom existence belongs . . . 4. Did the world begin at some time? I asked further. And what was then before its beginning? If it has always existed, then it will also continue to exist; if, however, it has come into being, then it must also pass away. 5. And what will be then after its dissolution but silence perhaps and oblivion? Or can there then be something which at the present time we cannot even conceive? 2. 1. With such and such-like thoughts I concerned myself continually—why I know not—and was so painfully distressed by them that I fell ill with anaemia and consumption. And the worst of it was that when at any time I sought to drive these thoughts away as futile, I had to suffer all the more severely. 2. That embittered me, for I did not yet know that in these thoughts I had good companions who would provide for me an introduction to immortality, 3. as later my experience in life showed me, and for that I have been thankful to God, the Lord of all things. For by these anxieties which at the beginning I felt as oppressive I was made to probe things to their foundation and to find this foundation; 4. then I pitied those whose happiness I in my ignorance formerly thought should be praised. 3. 1. As then onwards from childhood I occupied myself with such problems, I resorted to the lectures of the philosophers that I might learn something definite. Dogmas refuted and anew established fought and wrangled with one another; deductions that had been puzzled out were produced and new conclusions were devised; I was unable to catch a glimpse of anything else. 2. To

---

* A translation of the *Epistula Petri* and of the *Contestatio* above in Strecker, pp. 111ff.

give an instance, at one time it was said that the soul is immortal, at another time that it is mortal. When the view prevailed that it is immortal, then I was glad; when on the other hand it was said that it is mortal, then I was grieved on that account. 3. Still greater, I confess, was my despair over my inability to make my own either the one or the other opinion; rather I had the impression that the hypotheses put forward are regarded as false or correct according to the person who champions them and are not set forth as they actually are. 4. As soon, however, as I had once grasped the truth that conclusions are not drawn according to the measure of the facts that are advocated but that opinions usually gain ground according to the personality of their champions, my confusion regarding these questions increased still more. At this I groaned in the bottom of my heart. For neither was I able to come to a firm decision nor had I power to free myself altogether from these thoughts, although, as I have already said, I had a will thereto.

(R I 6)

6. 1. While a flood of such reflections laid hold of me, there got through to us in the reign of the emperor Tiberius a report which took its rise in the East; it spread everywhere and finally, like a good message from God, it filled the whole world, not willing to permit that the will of God should remain unproclaimed. 2. It reached the remotest corners, and this was its content: There is a Man in Judaea who since the beginning of spring has been proclaiming to the Jews the kingdom of God; those, he states, will attain it who keep the demands of his commandments and of his doctrine. 3. As proof that his speech is worthy of credit and is from the divine Spirit, he performs, so it is said, by his mere word many signs and singularly miraculous deeds, 4. so that, as it were in the power of God, he makes the deaf to hear and the blind to see, makes the infirm and lame to stand erect, expels every weakness and all demons from men, yea even raises dead persons who are brought before him, and besides brings healing to lepers whom he sees from a distance, and there is nothing at all that is impossible for him. 5. In the course of time we came to know such things no longer through the numerous rumours that were

537

in circulation; rather they were confirmed by the trustworthy reports of travellers who came from that quarter, and the truth of the story became clearer with every passing day. 7. 1. At length meetings took place here and there in Rome, there were discussions about these reports and interest manifested itself as to who this might be who had appeared there and what message he had delivered to men. 2. That went on until in the same year a man appeared in a very busy place in the city and addressed himself to the multitude in the following terms: 3. "Hear me, ye citizens of Rome! The Son of God has appeared in the land of Judaea and promises eternal life to everyone who will hear, provided that he fashions his doings according to the will of God the Father, by whom he has been sent. 4. Wherefore turn ye from evil things to good, from what is temporal to what is eternal! 5. Recognize that there is one God, who rules heaven and earth and in whose righteous sight ye unrighteous populate the world that belongs to him! 6. If ye repent you and act according to his will, ye will enter into a new era, will become immortal and participate in his unspeakably delightful treasures and gifts." 7. The man who thus spoke to the multitude came from the East, was a Hebrew by name Barnabas, and stated that he belonged to the circle of the disciples of that Son of God and had been sent to the end that he might proclaim this message to those who would hear it. 8. On learning that, I followed him with the rest of the people and heard further what he said. Then it was clear to me that in the case of this man words were not of a mere rhetorical finery, but that he made known simply and without circumlocution what he had heard from the Son of God or had seen of him. 9. For he supported his assertions not with plausible arguments, but brought forward, even from the circle of the bystanders, numerous witnesses of the sayings and marvels which he proclaimed. 8. 1. But while the simple people willingly assented to such sincere words, and welcomed his simple manner of speech, those who fancied themselves scholars and philosophers began to laugh at Barnabas and to scoff at him and to direct against him the snares of their syllogisms as their heaviest weapons. 2. But he did not allow himself to be confused by that, regarded their sophistry as foolery and deemed them not even worthy of an answer, but courageously pursued the way on which he had entered. 3. Once when he was speaking someone interrupted him with the question why the gnat, which is merely a tiny creature, is so made that it has six feet and wings besides, whereas the elephant, in spite of its extraordinary size, has no wings at all and only four feet; 4. to that, however, he paid no attention whatever, but with persistent attentiveness went on with his discourse which the inappropriate remark had interrupted, merely uttering the one admonition every time he was interrupted: 5. "We have the commission to proclaim to you the words and miraculous doings of him who has sent us and to confirm the trustworthiness of our proclamation not by ingenious arguments but by testimony from your own ranks. 6. For I see standing among you very many who, as I know, have heard along with us what we have heard and have seen along with us what we have seen. It lies with you to decide to accept or to repudiate our preaching. 7. We cannot hold back what, as we know, is profitable to you. For not to mention it would be hurt to us, and not to receive what we proclaim is destruction to you. 8. But as regards your absurd objection—I have in mind the difference between a gnat and the elephant—I could answer it without difficulty if you asked to learn the truth; but it would be foolish to speak to you now about creatures when you do not know the Creator and Founder of all things." 9. 1. Scarcely had he ended when all of a sudden, as with one consent, they all started an unrestrained laughter, by which they aimed at overawing him and putting him to silence, and called him a barbarian who was out of his senses. 2. As I had to witness all this, I was suddenly seized—I know not how—, holy indignation burned in me, I could no longer hold myself in check, but declared with all frankness: 3. "Very rightly has Almighty God hid his will from you, foreseeing your unworthiness to know him, an unworthiness that is too manifest to every discerning person from your present behaviour. 4. For whilst you see among you heralds of God's will whose manner of discourse gives no evidence of schooling in grammar, but who communicate to you the divine commands in simple, artless words so that all hearers can follow and understand what is said, 5. you deride the executors and bearers of your salvation, not knowing that to you, who fancy yourselves clever people and excellent speakers, it means sentence of condemnation that the truth is recognized by barbarous and uncivilized men. 6. For after it has come to you, it finds no hospitable reception although, had your rebellion and dissoluteness not stood against it, it would have been your beloved fellow-citizen. 7. In consequence it is made a reproach to you that you are not friends of truth and philosophy, but boasters and braggarts who think that the truth is to be found not in simple but only in subtilizing ingenious speech, and who chatter many thousands of words, which yet cannot compensate for a single true one. 8. What think ye then, all ye Greeks, what will happen to you if there takes place the judgment of God of which this man speaks? 9. Wherefore at once give up laughing at him to your own destruction, and let any one of you explain to us why by your bleating you seek to deafen the ears of those who desire to be saved, and why by your hubbub you entice to fall into unbelief minds that are ready to believe. 10. How can there be pardon for you if you deride and ill-treat the messenger of God who promises you the knowledge of God? 11. In any case, even if he had no sort of truth to bring to you, he ought, merely because of his good-will towards you, to be received and welcomed."

10. 1. Whilst I was expressing myself in these and such-like terms, violent discussions started among the bystanders. Some were moved with compassion on Barnabas, who after all was a visitor of theirs, and in consequence they regarded my speech as altogether justified. Others attempted in impudence and stupidity to wreak their anger upon me as much as upon Barnabas. 2. But as soon as evening drew on, I took Barnabas by the right hand and, paying no attention to his reluctance, brought him to my house and would not let him out any more lest some rowdy should lay violent hands upon him. 3. Thus we spent several days together; he succinctly expounded to me the word of truth, and at the same time I was his willing hearer. 4. Yet he hastened his departure since, as he said, he wished by all means to keep an approaching feast of his religion in Judaea; and there also he would remain with his own countrymen and brethren. Thereby he clearly indicated that he was grievously agitated by the wrong that he had suffered.

11. 1. At last I said to him, "Only expound to me the doctrine of the Man whose appearing you proclaim! I shall then introduce your words into my discourses and preach the kingdom and righteousness of Almighty God; and after that, if you wish it, I shall travel with you. 2. For I desire extremely to become acquainted with Judaea that, if possible, I may always remain with you." 3. To that Barnabas replied: "If you wish to see our fatherland and to learn what you desire to know, then sail right now with me! 4. If, however, something still keeps you here, I shall give you particulars that identify our dwelling, so that you may find it easily when you please to come. For tomorrow morning I shall set out on my way." 5. As it was clear to me that he would not reverse this decision, I accompanied him to the harbour and had him make quite clear to me the particulars of which he had spoken that would identify his dwelling. At the same time I said to him: 6. "Had I not to demand from debtors the payment of a sum of money, I would not delay for another moment, but I shall soon follow you." 7. When I had said that and had very warmly commended Barnabas to the ship-owners, I returned in sadness, for I had an intense longing for this esteemed guest and good friend.

12. 1. Having for the most part settled the question of the money that was owing to me—in this connection, that I might not be turned aside from my purpose, I overlooked a great deal in my haste—I set sail some days later direct for Judaea and after a voyage of fifteen days landed at Caesarea Stratonis, the largest city in Palestine. 2. On landing I made enquiries for a lodging and got to know from what was told me by the people that a certain Peter, a very highly approved disciple of the Man who had appeared in Judaea and wrought with divine power many signs and wonders among the people, was to hold a disputation on the following day with Simon a Samaritan from the village of Gittha. 3. On hearing this, I asked to be shown Peter's quarters. 4. When I had found them and was standing at the door, I told the door-keeper who I was and whence I came. 5. And, behold, Barnabas came out and, as soon as he saw me, fell into my arms with tears of joy. Then he took me by the hand and led me to Peter. 6. Having pointed him out to me from a distance, he said: "That is Peter,

of whom I have told you that he has penetrated most deeply into the divine wisdom. I told him about you without delay. 7. You can therefore face him as one well known to him. 8. For he has an accurate knowledge of all your good qualities and has attentively followed your purpose; on which account he very much wishes to get to know you. 9. And thus I present you to him today as a great gift." Then, presenting me, he said: "This, beloved Peter, is Clement!" 13. 1. When this good man Peter heard my name, he stepped towards me and remained standing for a little before me; then, having invited me to sit down, he said: 2. "You did well in receiving Barnabas, a herald of the truth, into your house, not fearing the fury of the raving mob. You will be blessed. 3. For as you received the messenger of truth, so will the truth itself receive you, a pilgrim and a stranger, and bestow upon you the citizen rights of her own city. You will greatly rejoice when, because now you show a small favour, you are appointed heir of good things that are eternal. 4. You need not now trouble yourself to provide me with an explanation of yourself. For Barnabas has truthfully told me everything about you and the qualities of your character, and almost every day without ceasing he has praised your doings."

Clement's Outward Fortunes (H XII)

8. 2. There are (related to me) many important men who belong to the emperor's family. Indeed the emperor gave a relative of his own as wife to my father because he had grown up with him. She bore three sons, the two other brothers before me. Moreover they were twins and were quite like one another, as my father himself told me. For I knew neither them nor my mother, but carry in me merely a dim, dream-like picture of them. 3. My mother was called Mattidia, my father Faustus, of my brothers the one Faustinus and the other Faustinianus. 4. Now after I was born as the third, my mother had on one occasion a dream—such at all events is the story told me by my father: unless, along with her twin sons, she immediately left the city of Rome for a period of ten years, she would, together with them, die a fearful death. 9. 1. Then my father, who very much loved his children, provided them amply with all essentials, put them

with male and female slaves on board a ship and sent them to Athens, where the sons would have an opportunity of being educated; me alone he retained as a single child to be a comfort to him. And I am very thankful that the dream had not ordered me also to leave Rome in company with my mother. 2. For when a year had passed, my father sent money for his sons to Athens and ordered that inquiries be made as to how things were going with them. But those who set out on the journey did not return. 3. In the third year my father in his despair sent other messengers also with money for their support, and in the fourth year they came back with the report that they had seen neither my mother nor my brothers, indeed that they had never reached Athens and that no trace could be found of those who had accompanied them. 10. 1. On hearing that, my father almost passed away in his great grief, for he no longer knew where he should turn and seek his own. Eventually he took me with him and went down with me to the harbour. There again and again he put the question, now to one person and now to another, whether he had seen or heard where there had been a shipwreck four years ago. To that he obtained many answers. He inquired further whether the dead bodies of a woman and her children had been seen washed up on the shore. 2. When those questioned answered that they had seen numerous dead bodies in different places, my father sighed at the information. Nevertheless, bewildered by his great heart-burnings, he raised the insane question of his attempting to search the sea, far as it might extend; and it must be put down to his credit that it was out of his love for those he missed that he entertained such vain hopes. Finally he placed me, at that time twelve years of age, under the care of tutors and thus left me behind in Rome, whilst he himself, weeping, went down to the harbour, boarded a ship, put to sea and set out on his quest. 3. And from that day until now I have never had a letter from him, nor do I know precisely whether he is alive or dead. 4. But I do regard it as more likely that in some way or other he also has perished; possibly anguish has overwhelmed him or he has fallen a victim in a shipwreck. For this conjecture there speaks the fact that twenty years have already gone past since I had any sure account of him.

The True Prophet (H I)

18. 1. (Peter says to Clement:) The will of God has fallen into oblivion for many sorts of reasons, 2. above all in consequence of inadequate instruction, careless upbringing, bad company, unseemly conversation and erroneous statements. 3. Thence there comes ignorance, and there come also dissoluteness, unbelief, unchastity, avarice, vanity and innumerable vices of this kind, which have occupied the world as it were a house which, like a cloud of smoke, they have filled; they have thus made muddy the eyes of those who dwell in the house and have prevented them from looking up and recognizing the Creator God from his works and inferring his will. 4. Therefore the friends of truth who are in the house must cry from the depth of their heart for help for their truth-seeking souls, that if someone is outside the smoke-filled house, he may come and open the door, so that the sunlight from outside may invade the house and that the smoke within may be dissipated. 19. 1. Now the man who can help here, I call the true prophet; he alone can enlighten the souls of men that with their own eyes they may be able to see the way to eternal salvation. 2. That is not possible in any other way, as indeed you yourself know; only just now you said 3. that every view has its friends and opponents and counts as true or false according to the qualification of its advocate, and in consequence different opinions do not come to light as what they are, but receive the semblance of worth or worthlessness from their advocates. 4. Wherefore the world needs the godly efforts of the true prophet that he may describe things to us as they actually are and tell us what we have to believe regarding everything. 5. First of all then we must examine the prophet with all seriousness and arrive at the certainty that he is a true prophet, 6. and then we should believe him in all matters and ought not to quibble at the least small particular in his teaching, but should accept all his words as valid, as it may appear in faith, yet actually on the ground of the sound examination that we have made. 7. For by proof at the outset and an extensive, meticulous examination everything is received with right deliberation. 8. Therefore it counts above all things to find the true prophet, for without him there cannot possibly be anything certain among men.

The Doctrine of the Pairs of Opposites or Syzygies (H II)

15. 1. (Peter:) Now that he might bring men to the true knowledge of all things, God, who himself is a single person, made a clear separation by way of pairs of opposites, in that he, who from the beginning was the one and only God, made heaven and earth, day and night, life and death. 2. Among these he has gifted free-will to men alone so that they may be just or unjust. For them he has also permuted the appearing of the pairs of opposites, in that he has set before their eyes first the small and then the great, first the world and then eternity, this world being transitory, but the one to come eternal; so also ignorance precedes knowledge. 3. In the same way he has ordered the bearers of the prophetic spirit. For since the present is womanly and like a mother gives birth to children, but the future, manly time on the other hand takes up its children in the manner of a father, 4. therefore there come first the prophets of this world (who prophesy falsely, and) those who have the knowledge of eternal things follow them because they are sons of the coming age. 5. Had the God-fearing known this secret, then they would never have been able to go wrong, and also they would even now have known that Simon, who now confounds all, is merely a helpmate of the feeble left hand (of God, i.e. the evil one). 16. 1. As regards the disposition of the prophetic mission the case is as follows. As God, who is one person, in the beginning made first the heaven and then the earth, as it were on the right hand and on the left, he has also in the course of time established all the pairs of opposites. But with men it is no longer so—rather does he invert the pairs. 2. For as with him the first is the stronger and the second the weaker, so with men we find the opposite, first the weaker and then the stronger. 3. Thus directly from Adam, who was made in the image of God, there issued as the first son the unrighteous Cain and as the second the righteous Abel. 4. And in the same way from the man who amongst you is called Deucalion two symbols of the Spirit, the unclean and the clean, were sent out, the black raven and after it the white dove. 5. And also from Abraham, the progenitor of our people, there issued two sons, the older Ishmael and then Isaac, who was blessed by God. 6. Again from this same Isaac there sprang two sons, the

godless Esau and the godly Jacob. 7. Likewise there came first, as first-born into the world, the high priest (Aaron) and then the law-giver (Moses). 17. 1. The syzygy associated with Elias, which ought to have come, willingly held off to another time, being resolved to take its place when the occasion arises. 2. Then in the same way there came first he who was *among them that are born of women*[1] and only after that did he who belongs to the sons of men appear as the second. 3. Following up this disposition it would be possible to recognize where Simon belongs, who as first and before me went to the Gentiles, and where I belong, I who came after him and followed him as the light follows darkness, knowledge ignorance and healing sickness. 4. Thus then, as the true prophet has said,[2] a false gospel must first come from an impostor and only then, after the destruction of the holy place, can a true gospel be sent forth for the correction of the sects that are to come. 5. And thereafter in the end Antichrist must first come again and only afterwards must Jesus, our actual Christ, appear and then, with the rising of eternal light, everything that belongs to darkness must disappear. 18. 1. Since now, as has been said, many do not know this conformity of the syzygies with law, they do not know who this Simon, my forerunner, is. For were it known, no one would believe him. But now, as he remains unknown, confidence is wrongly placed in him. 2. Thus he who does what haters do finds love; the enemy is received as a friend; men long for him who is death as a bringer of salvation; although he is fire, he is regarded as light; although he is a cheat, he obtains a hearing as a proclaimer of truth.

Simon's Former Life (H II)

22. 2. (Aquila [see p. 566] relates:) The father of this Simon is called Antonius, his mother Rachel. By nationality he is a Samaritan and comes from the village of Gittha, which is six miles distant from the capital. 3. During his stay in Egypt he acquired a large measure of Greek culture and attained to an extensive knowledge of magic and ability in it. He then came forward claiming to be accepted as a mighty power of the very God who has created the world. On occasion he sets himself up for the

[1] Mt. 11:11. [2] Cf. Mt. 24:24; 7:15.

Messiah and describes himself as the Standing One. 4. He uses this title since he is to exist for ever and his body cannot possibly fall a victim to the germs of corruption. 5. He also denies that the God who created the world is the highest, nor does he believe in the resurrection of the dead. Turning away from Jerusalem, he sets Mount Gerizim in its place. 6. In the place of our true Christ he shows himself (as the Christ). The content of the law he interprets according to personal arbitrariness. He speaks indeed of a future judgment, but he does not reckon with it in earnest; for were he convinced that God will call him to account, he would not have ventured in his wickedness to turn against God Himself. 7. Thus there are ruined not a few who do not know that Simon uses piety merely as pretence in order to steal secretly from men the fruits of truth, and who believe in him, as though he were himself pious, in his manifold promises and in the judgment promised by him.

23. 1. Simon's contact with the tenets of religion came about in the following way. There appeared a certain John the Baptist, who according to the disposition of the syzygies was at the same time the forerunner of our Lord Jesus. 2. And as the Lord had twelve apostles according to the number of the solar months, so also there gathered about John thirty eminent persons according to the reckoning of the lunar month. 3. Among these was a woman Helena by name, and herewith a significant disposition prevailed. For the woman, who makes up only the half of the man, left the number 30 incomplete, precisely as in the case of the moon, the revolution of which is not altogether a month in duration. 4. Of these thirty Simon counted with John as the first and most distinguished; and indeed he was prevented after the death of John from assuming the leading place for a reason which we shall hear directly. 24. 1. John was made away with at the very time when Simon had journeyed to Egypt to study magic; therefore a certain Dositheus, who aimed at becoming the head of the school, was able to spread abroad a false report that Simon was dead and to take over the leadership of the sect. 2. When now a little later Simon returned, he did not, on meeting Dositheus, demand of him his post, much as he desired it for himself, for he knew quite well that the man who had forestalled him in this office could not

be removed against his will. 3. For this reason he made a pretence of friendship and for a while rested content with the second place after Dositheus. 4. When, however, after a time he met his thirty fellow-disciples, he began to circulate slanders against Dositheus. This man, he asserted, hands down the doctrines incorrectly, and does so less because of an evil intent and more out of ignorance. 5. Dositheus observed that Simon's well-calculated slanders were shaking his own standing among the great multitude so that they no longer regarded him as the Standing One; then on one occasion when Simon arrived for the ordinary meeting, he struck out at him with indignation. The stick seemed to go through Simon's body as if it were smoke. 6. Affrighted at this, Dositheus shouted to him, 'If thou be the Standing One, I also shall pay homage to you'. 7. As Simon answered in the affirmative Dositheus, knowing that he himself was not the Standing One, fell down and did homage to Simon and, associating himself with the twenty-nine others, set him in his own place. Then Dositheus died a few days after Simon had attained to standing but he himself had suffered downfall. 25. 1. Simon then took Helena to himself, and since then he moves about with her and up to the present day, as you yourself see, he upsets the people. 2. Of Helena herself he asserts that he brought her down to the world from the highest heaven, of which she is the mistress as the mother of all being and Wisdom. Because of her, he says, there came about a conflict between the Greeks and the barbarians; although they clung only to an image of the reality, for the true Helena dwelt at that time with the supreme God. 3. Giving thus a new interpretation to other concoctions of the Greek saga, he deceives many in a plausible manner, and at the same time he performs numerous wonderful deeds, by which we would ourselves have been imposed on, had we not known that he works them only by sorcery. . . . 26. 1. He has also burdened himself with bloodguiltiness and has even related among his friends that he separated the soul of a boy from its body by means of secret magical invocations and keeps it in the interior of his house, where his bed is, to assist him in his performances, having in this connection drawn a likeness of the boy. 2. This boy, he asserts, he at one time fashioned out of air by a divine transformation and then, having put his appearance on record, he returned him again to air. 3. That came about in the following way. In his way of thinking the human spirit, which tends to what is warm, first imbibes the surrounding air in the manner of a cucumber and sucks it in; having infiltrated into the interior of the human spirit, this air then changes into water. 4. Since now the water in the human spirit cannot be drunk in consequence of its consistency, it has to undergo a transformation into blood. Let the blood coagulate and the flesh is fashioned. Then the flesh becomes solid, and so man comes into being not from the earth but out of air. 5. And so Simon persuaded himself that in such a way he had been able to fashion a new man; of him he asserted that he had returned him to air, having reversed the changes that had taken place.

Disputation between Simon and Peter in Caesarea (H II)

35. 1. Towards morning Zacchaeus came in with the following communication for Peter: 2. "Simon wishes the disputation postponed until tomorrow; 3. for today is his tenth-day Sabbath." 4. To that Peter answered: "Inform Simon that he may use his own discretion and be assured that we hold ourselves in readiness, when he pleases, to confront him in a way well-pleasing to God." 5. When Zacchaeus heard that, he went on his way to deliver the answer.

(H III)

29. 1. Zacchaeus returned and said: "Beloved Peter, now it is about time to go to the disputation. 2. For a great crowd has assembled in the courtyard and awaits you, and in its midst Simon stands like a commander, surrounded by the people as by his guardsmen." 3. When Peter heard that, he invited me, as I had not yet received the baptism that is necessary for salvation, to go aside for a little; for he desired to say his prayers. But to those who were already perfect (through baptism) he said: 4. "Let us rise to our feet and pray that God in his unending mercy may support me in my conflict for the deliverance of the men whom he has created." 5. Thereafter he prayed and betook himself to the great, open courtyard in which many were assembled out of curiosity, the impending decision having increased their wish to

listen to it. 30. 1. There then Peter entered; and when he had looked on the multitude, every eye in which was fixed upon him in breathless stillness, and on the magician Simon, who stood in the midst, he began to discourse as follows: 2. "Peace be with you all who are ready to commit yourselves to the truth of God, this his great and incomparable gift to our world! He who has sent us, the true prophet of good principle, has commissioned us, by way of salutation and before any instruction, to speak to you of this truth. 3. If then there be among you any son of peace, then by virtue of our instruction peace will enter into him. But if any one among you does not accept peace, then for a testimony thereto we *shall shake off from us the dust of the street* which through the hardships of the way we have carried on ourselves and brought to you for your salvation, and shall go into other houses and cities . . ."[1]

38. 1. When Peter had thus spoken, Simon at a distance from the multitude cried aloud: "Will you by your lies deceive the simple people who surround you, persuading them that one ought neither to believe nor to assert that there are gods, although the literature of the Jews mentions many gods? 2. For now in the presence of all I would argue with you from these very books that one must necessarily assume the existence of gods. It is in the first place a question of the God of whom you speak. With regard to him I prove that he cannot be the supreme and almighty power, being unable to foresee the future, and that he is imperfect, not without needs, not good, and is subject to innumerable dubious passions. 3. But once that is proved from Holy Scripture, then there remains, I assert, yet another god not mentioned in Scripture who foresees the future and is perfect, without needs, good and free from all dubious passions . . . 39. 1. Thus then forthwith Adam, who came into being after that image, is created blind and knows, as it is said, neither about good nor about evil, he proves himself disobedient, is expelled from Paradise and is punished with death. 2. In the same manner his Creator, being unable to see everywhere, says at the time of the fall of Sodom, *Come, let us go down and see whether or not they do according to their cry that comes before me, that I may know it,*[2] thus making his ignorance

---

[1] Cf. Mt. 10:12ff; Mk. 6:11; Lk. 10:5.   [2] Gen. 18:21.

notorious. 3. When it is said of Adam: *Let us send him forth lest perhaps he stretch out his hand, touch the tree of life, eat thereof and live for ever*,[1] the *perhaps* manifests his ignorance; moreover the phrase *lest he eat thereof and live for ever* manifests his jealousy. 4. And if it stands written: *It repented God that he had made man*,[2] then that points to a change of mind and to ignorance. For *he repented* signifies reflection through which one who does not know what he will do attempts to fix his purpose, or is characteristic of one penitent at something which has not gone as he has wished. 5. And if it stands written: '*And the Lord smelled a pleasing odour*',[3] that does not indicate freedom from need, and the fact that he enjoyed the smell of the flesh of the sacrifice is not exactly a proof of his goodness. His making trial—why, it is said: '*And the Lord tried Abraham*'[4]—allows a being to be inferred who is wicked and does not foresee the end of his patience."

40. 1. In such a way Simon produced from Holy Scripture seemingly manifold evidences that God is subject to all passions. To that Peter replied: "Is a scoundrel or malefactor ready to admit his offence to himself? Answer me that!"—"No," Simon replied, "he is not." 2. Peter proceeded: "How then can God be bad and wicked if the shameful actions ascribed to him are imputed to him with his consent in all publicity?"—Simon: "That is to assume that the charges against him were formulated by another power against his will." 3. Again Peter: "Let us first of all investigate that! If of his own will he has incriminated himself, then, as you have just allowed, he cannot be wicked; but if it has come about through the action of another power, then we need to ask and by all means to investigate whether someone has not subjected him, who alone is good, to all these evils." 41. 1. To that Simon: "Apparently you would ignore the charges which emerge from Holy Scripture against your God." Again Peter: "I believe that that is precisely what you do. For he who will not stick to the order of the discussion clearly does not wish a real investigation to take place. 2. If then I advance in file and wish first to consider the author, it is clear that I decide for the straight way." . . . 42. 2. Again Simon: "How can one know the truth when of the books of Scripture some describe God

[1] Gen. 3:22.　　[2] Gen. 6:6.　　[3] Gen. 8:21.　　[4] Gen. 22:1.

as wicked and others describe him as good?" 3. To that Peter: "Those statements of the Holy Scriptures which are in keeping with the creation wrought by God must be counted as genuine and those which contradict them as false." 4. Simon: "How can you prove that there is contradiction in Holy Scripture?" To that Peter: "Of Adam you assert that he was created blind, but that he was not. For to a blind man God would not have given the commandment: *Of the tree of the knowledge of good and evil thou shalt not eat.*"[1] 5. Simon: "He has described his mind as blind." Peter: "How could he be blind in mind who, before he ate of the fruit and with the approval of his Creator, gave appropriate names to all living things?" 6. Simon: "Why did Adam, if he could see into the future, not suspect beforehand the serpent's deception of his wife?" 7. Peter: "How could Adam, if he was not able to see into the future, give to his sons at the time of their birth names according to their future deeds? For he named his first son Cain, which means jealousy: for out of jealousy he slew his brother Abel, whose name means mourning, for his parents mourned for him, the first to be murdered. 43. 1. And now if Adam, who was yet a creature of God, was able to see into the future, by how much more then must God who created him be able to do so? 2. Also that is incorrect which stands written: *It repented God*[2] as if out of ignorance he had to reflect; likewise the statement: *The Lord tried Abraham*[3] in order to find out whether he would hold his ground . . . 3. All these passages . . . are shown to be false and are overturned by others which assert the opposite."

58. 2. This disputation lasted for three days. In the night before the fourth day dawned, Simon made off in the direction of Tyre.

The Appointment of Zacchaeus (H III)

59. 1. On the following night Peter called the multitude of his followers together. As soon as they had assembled, he said to them: 2. "Whilst I betake myself to the heathen, who say that there are many gods, to preach and proclaim the one only God, who made heaven and earth and all that is therein, that they may love him and be saved, wickedness has anticipated me according

[1] Gen. 2:17.   [2] Gen. 6:6.   [3] Gen. 22:1.

to the law of the syzygies, and has sent Simon ahead, 3. in order that those men who, rejecting the gods assumed to exist on the earth, speak no more of their great number, may believe that there are many gods in heaven. Thus would men be brought to dishonour the monarchy of God and to meet severe punishment and eternal perdition . . . 5. But I must hasten after him that his lying assertions may not find a footing and establish themselves everywhere. 60. 1. Since now some one must be appointed to fill my place, let us all with one accord pray God to make known the ablest among us who may set himself in the chair of Christ and lead his church in the spirit of godliness. 2. Who then is to be decided upon? By the decree of God that man is described as blessed whom his lord *will appoint* to serve his fellow-servants, *to give them their meat at the proper time,*[1] without thinking in himself: *My lord delays his coming*[2] . . . 61. 1. But should one of those present who is able to restrain the ignorance of his fellow-citizens withdraw from this duty simply out of a care for his own personal peace, then he must be prepared to hear the words: *Thou wicked, slothful servant, you ought to have deposited my money with the bankers, that on my return I might have had my gain; cast out the worthless servant into the uttermost darkness.*[3] 2. And that rightly. For it is your duty—he would say therewith—to bring my words as money to the bankers and to regard them as values that you possess. 3. The community of believers must be obedient to one particular person that their unity may be preserved. 4. For a finally emerging leadership through a single organ of government, in the likeness of the monarchy of God, brings those who yield themselves to it into the delights of peace, . . . 62. 1. And beyond that the things that are happening before our eyes should certainly instruct us that at the present time wars are constantly being waged because many kings reign in all the world; for each of them the lordship of another is reason enough for war. 2. But if there is one head of the whole, he has no occasion for war and therefore maintains perpetual peace. 3. For in the end, for those who are held to be worthy of eternal life, God appoints one king over all in this world that in consequence of this monarchy there may prevail a

---

[1] Mt. 24:45ff.; Lk. 12:42.   [2] Mt. 24:48; Lk. 12:45.
[3] Mt. 25:26f.; Lk. 19:23.

peace that is not to be disturbed. 4. In short, all must follow a single person as their leader, honouring him as the likeness of God; but the leader must know well the way that goes to the holy city.[1] 63. 1. But among those present whom else should I choose for this but Zacchaeus, in whose house even our Lord stayed and rested,[2] holding him worthy to be saved?" With these words he laid his hand upon Zacchaeus, who was standing before him, and invited him to be seated on his stool. 2. But Zacchaeus fell at Peter's feet and besought him to release him from ruling, declaring emphatically: "All that a ruler must do I shall attend to, only permit me to renounce this name! For I hesitate to adopt this designation; indeed it involves bitter envy and danger." 64. 1. Peter replied, "If you are apprehensive of that, then allow yourself to be designated not ruler but commissioner, a designation which the Lord himself coined when he said: *Blessed is the man whom the Lord will commission to serve his fellow-servants.*[3] 2. But if you absolutely refuse to be regarded as the holder of an administrative office, then you are apparently unaware that the recognized status of a president can contribute much towards keeping the multitude in check; for everyone obeys the office-bearer, since conscience very much constrains him to do so. 3. And is it not sufficiently clear to you that you have not to wield the sceptre as do the rulers of the nations, but as a servant who ministers to them as a father who cares for them, as a physician who visits them, as a shepherd who watches over them—in short as one who is concerned for their well-being in every respect? Can you possibly think that I do not know what a charge I impose upon you in requiring that you suffer yourself to be criticized by the rabble that no one can please? . . . 4. Wherefore I beseech you to undertake it confidently in God's name and in Christ's, for the salvation and blessing of the brethren and for your own benefit. 65. 1. Consider also this other point, that the more troublesome and the more dangerous it is to govern the church of Christ the greater is the reward, but the greater also is the punishment of him who is in a position to do so and refuses. 2. I desire then that you, of whom I know that you are more educated than the others present, make the most of the excellent attainments with which

---

[1] Cf. Rev. 3:12; 21:10. [2] Lk. 19:5, 9. [3] Cf. Mt. 24:45f.; 25:21; Lk. 12:42f.

God has entrusted you, that some day it may be said of you: *Well done, my good and faithful servant!*[1] and that you be not rebuked and declared liable to punishment as was the man who hid his talent.[2] 3. If, however, you do not wish to be a good shepherd of the church, then name another in your stead who is more learned and more trustworthy than you are! This indeed you cannot do, for you associated even with the Lord, saw his miraculous deeds and learned how to govern the church. 66. 1. Your work then is to command what needs to be done, that of the brethren to conform and not be disobedient. If they conform, then they will be saved; if they abide in disobedience, then they will be punished by Christ, for the place of Christ is entrusted to the president. 2. Therefore the honour or defamation of the president lights upon Christ and from Christ upon God. 3. This I have said that the brethren also may recognize the danger into which disobedience to you leads them. For he who disobeys your command resists Christ, and he who is disobedient to Christ makes God angry.[3]

67. 1. The church as *a city built on a hill*[4] must have an order pleasing to God and good administration. Above all the bishop as the authoritative leading spokesman must be heard. 2. The elders have to attend to the carrying through of his orders. The deacons should walk about, looking after the bodies and souls of the brethren, and report to the bishop. 3. All the rest of the brethren should be ready even to suffer wrong. But if they desire an inquiry into a wrong that has been done to them, then they should be reconciled in the presence of the elders, and the elders should submit the agreement to the bishop. 68. 1. They should urge on to marriage not only the young people but also those who are older, in order that lust may not flare up and infect the church with unchastity and adultery. 2. For God hates the committing of adultery more than any other sin because it destroys not only the sinner himself but also those who feast and keep friends with him; it is like canine madness for it has the capacity to spread farther its own frenzy. 3. For the sake of morality not only the elders but also all the other members of the church should encourage marriage; for the sin of the man who is lewd necessarily

[1] Mt. 25:21.   [2] Cf. Mt. 25:27, 30.   [3] Cf. Lk. 10:16.   [4] Mt. 5:14.

comes upon all the rest. 4. To urge the brethren to morality is love's highest service, for it is the saving of the soul, whereas the nourishing of the body is only refreshment. 69. 1. But if you love your brethren, take nothing of what is theirs, but rather give them of what you possess; for *you should feed the hungry, give drink to the thirsty, clothe the naked, visit the sick, do your best to help those in prison,*[1] receive strangers willingly into your dwellings and *hate no man.*[2] 2. How you have to manifest your piety, that, if you are sufficiently wise, your own intelligence should show you. Above all, if indeed I need to say it, you must assemble very frequently, where possible hourly, but by all means on the appointed days of assembly. 3. When you do that, you find yourselves within the walls of a place of refuge. For perdition begins in eccentric ways. 4. Therefore let no one keep himself away from the community out of a petty attitude of mind towards a brother. For if one of you abandons the community, then he will be counted in the number of those who scatter the church of Christ,[3] and he will find his punishment as a leader of the enemies of Christ. 5. He will be rejected together with the adulterers. For like an adulterer, through the spirit that dwells in him and on some pretext or other he has separated himself and has given place to the evil one against himself, to steal the sheep that he has found ostensibly outside the fold. 70. 1. Moreover, hear your bishop and do not become weary in showing him all honour; for you must know that, by showing it to him, it is carried over to Christ and from Christ to God; and to him who shows it, it is requited manifold. 2. Hold then the chair of Christ in honour, for you are also bidden to honour *the chair of Moses,*[4] although its occupants may have to be reckoned sinners. 3. Therewith I have perhaps said enough to you. On the other hand it is not necessary to say to Zacchaeus how he must live without stain, for he is a true disciple of him who taught me also. 71. 1. There are assuredly some things, beloved brethren, which you should not leave till they are said to you, but which you should recognize of yourselves. Zacchaeus alone is wholly absorbed in service for you. He also has his necessities of life, but no time for himself. How then can he procure the support he needs? 2. Is it not then the right thing that all of

[1] Cf. Mt. 25:35ff.   [2] *Didache* 2, 7.   [3] Cf. Mt. 12:30.   [4] Mt. 23:2f.

you should attend to his necessities without waiting for him to ask you to do so? For that means begging, and he would rather die of hunger than condescend to that. 3. And how can you not be culpable if you do not give a thought to this, that *the labourer is worthy of his hire?*[1] And let no one say: 'Then *the word that is freely received* is sold!'[2] That is not at all the case! 4. If one who possesses the means of living takes something, he sells the word; but he who possesses nothing and takes the necessities of life does no wrong. For the Lord also accepted at dinner-parties and among friends at a time when he, who later was to possess all things, possessed nothing. 5. And you ought to honour suitable elders, catechists, competent deacons, widows whose conduct is respectable, and orphans as children of the church. And when outlays become necessary for some purpose, you should contribute all of you together. 6. Be kind to one another and do not delay to undertake whatever conduces to your salvation."

72. 1. After these words he laid his hand upon Zacchaeus and said: "Ruler and Lord of all, Father and God, guard Thou the shepherd with the flock. 2. Thou art the cause, Thou art the power. We are that for which help is intended. Thou art the helper, the physician, the saviour, the wall, the life, the hope, the refuge, the joy, the expectation, the rest; in a word: Thou art everything. 3. Help, deliver and preserve us unto eternal salvation. Thou canst do all things. Thou art the Sovereign of sovereigns, the Lord of lords, the Ruler of kings. 4. Give Thou power to the president to loose what is to be loosed and to bind what is to be bound.[3] Through him as thine instrument preserve the church of thy Christ as a beautiful bride. For thine is eternal glory. 5. Praise to the Father and to the Son and to the Holy Spirit to all eternity. Amen."

The Appion Disputation (H IV)

1. 1. From Caesarea Stratonis I betook myself with Nicetas and Aquila to Tyre in Phoenicia, and, as instructed by Peter who had sent us forth, we lodged with Berenice, the daughter of Justa the Canaanitess, who received us very courteously. . . . 6. 2. But in the morning there came a relative of Berenice who told us that

[1] Lk. 10:7.   [2] Cf. Mt. 10:8.   [3] Cf. Mt. 16:19; 18:18.

Simon had set sail for Sidon, but had left behind him the following from the circle of his disciples: Appion Pleistonices of Alexandria, a grammarian by profession, in whom I recognized a friend on my father's side, Annubion of Diospolis, an astrologer, and Athenodorus of Athens, an Epicurean. 3. On learning this about Simon, we wrote it down in a letter which we despatched to Peter; after that we went for a walk.

7. 1. While we were doing so Appion met us. He was accompanied not only by the two above-mentioned companions but in addition by about thirty other men. 2. As soon as he caught sight of me, he saluted and kissed me. "This," he said, "is Clement of whose noble birth and superior culture I have told you much; he belongs to the family of the Emperor Tiberius and is well read in all the departments of Grecian learning, only he has allowed himself to be deceived by a barbarian named Peter with the result that he now thinks and acts after the manner of the Jews. 3. Therefore I beseech you to give me your help in my endeavour to correct him, and in your presence I ask him. Since he thinks that he has devoted himself to the culture of piety, let him tell me if he has not sinned exceedingly in forsaking the ancestral traditions and turning to the customs of the barbarians." 8. 1. To that I answered: "I acknowledge the kindly inclination toward me of which you give evidence, but I take exception to your ignorance." . . . 2. Appion said: "Does it seem to you to be ignorance to retain the ancestral customs and to accord with the Greek way of thinking?" 3. I answered: "The man who makes up his mind to be godly should never on principle cling to the ancestral customs, but must preserve them if they are pious and renounce them if they are impious. For it is quite conceivable that a man may be the son of an impious father but himself desire to be pious and therefore may not be prepared to follow his father in his principles." 4. To that Appion replied: "What? do you then impute to your father a bad course of life?" "It was not his course of life that was bad," I answered, "but his religious conviction." 5. Appion: "I would like to know then what it was that was so bad in his views." To that I replied: "That he believed in the false, bad myths of the Greeks." "What then," Appion asked, "are these false, bad myths of the Greeks?" "Their false

conception of God," I replied. . . . 11. 1. "Then, my beloved Greek friends, there is a great difference between truth and custom. For where truth is honestly sought for, there also it is found, but custom, be it true or false, maintains its ground undisputed, just as it was taken over, and he who takes it over has no joy in it if it is true, nor is he angry with it if it is false. . . . 2. And it is not easy to cast off the ancestral garment, even when it seems to the bearer of it to be worn out and ridiculous. 12. 1. Accordingly I assert outspokenly that Greek culture is in its entirety a most malicious concoction of the evil spirit. 2. For some Greeks have brought in many gods, gods that are evil and guilty in manifold respects, in order that he who wishes to do similar things himself may not need to be ashamed, as man naturally is, being able to plead as an example the bad, sinful conduct of the mythical gods. . . . 3. Others again have brought in fate . . . contrary to which no one can do or suffer anything. 4. Here the situation is the same as in the first case; for when a man believes that he can do nothing and suffer nothing contrary to his fate, it is easy for him to be ready to sin. . . .

13. 1. Others again believe in unforeseen chance and think that everything takes its course of itself without the supervision of a ruler. This view is . . . of all conceptions the worst. 2. For if there is no being who directs all things and cares for all things and duly assigns to every man his portion, then men, having nothing to fear, are quickly prepared for all possibilities. . . . 3. On the other hand, the doctrine of the barbarian Jews, as you call them, is the most godly. It accepts one Father and Creator of all things who in his nature is good and righteous, good in that he pardons those who repent of their sins, righteous in that he rewards every one who knows no repentance according to his deeds. . . . 15. 1. Nevertheless I return to the first view of the Greeks, which speaks of the existence of many gods who have become culpable in manifold respects. 2. Only I shall not spend much time on things that are known and tell the stories of the vicious doings of every one of these so-called gods . . .with which through your Greek education you are well acquainted; 16. 1. but I may well make a beginning with the very kingly Zeus. . . . 2. He put his own father in irons and imprisoned him in Tartarus and punishes

the other gods! For those who desire to practise unmentionable indecencies he swallowed Metis after he had begotten her. For Metis means seed, it being impossible to swallow a child. 3. As an excuse for sodomites he carried off Ganymede. As a help to adulterers he himself is often exposed as an adulterer. He has incited to incest with sisters by cohabiting with his own sisters Hera, Demeter and Aphrodite Urania. . . . 4. To those who wish to have sexual intercourse with their daughters he proves a bad mythical example in his cohabiting with Persephone. And in addition to that he has wrought impiously in manifold other ways. . . . 17. 1. That men of no learning do not worry much about such notions may well be understood, but what ought cultured men to say of them? Now many among them, who profess to be grammarians and sophists, assert that such doings are compatible with the dignity of the gods. 2. For they themselves live an uncontrolled life and readily lay hold on the myth as an excuse that they may be able to commit their iniquities without hesitation after the example of the higher powers. . . . 19. 3. We must then shun such myths of the Greeks, as also their theatres and their books, yea, if it be possible, their cities also. For their inhabitants are full of false doctrine and this they transmit as a plague. . . . 20. 1. Some among them who even pass themselves off as philosophers, represent these offences as indifferent and call those who are indignant at such doings blockheads. . . . 22. 1. Let us regard that as enough for the present! This much at all events we all know, that only too frequently men fly into uncontrolled passion about it and that on its account wars have broken out, houses have been overthrown, and cities taken possession of, and many other evils come about. 2. Therefore have I taken refuge with the holy God and the law of the Jews, having attained, after I had made positive examination, to the conviction that the law has been prescribed on the basis of the righteous judgment of God and that in all cases the soul receives some day what befits it according to its deeds."

Peter on his Mission Journeys (H VII)

1. 1. In Tyre not a few people from the neighbourhood and numerous inhabitants of the city came to Peter and cried to

him: "May God have mercy upon us through you, and may he through you bring us healing!" And Peter, having mounted a high rock that he might be seen of all, greeted them in a godly way and began as follows: 2. 1. "God, who has made heaven and the universe, is not wanting in power to save those who desire to be saved. . . . 4. 2. And what is pleasing to God is this, that we pray to him and ask from him as the one who dispenses everything according to a righteous law, that we keep away from the table of devils,[1] that we do not eat dead flesh, that we do not touch blood, that we wash ourselves clean from all defilement.[2] 3. Let the rest be said to you also in one word, as the God-fearing Jews heard it, while you show yourselves, many as you are, of one mind: 'What good a man wishes for himself, let him confer the same also on his neighbour!'[3] ". . .

5. 1. After they had thus been instructed for some days by Peter and had been healed, they were baptized. At the time of his other miraculous deeds the rest sat beside one another in the middle of the market-place in sackcloth and ashes and did penance for their former sins. 2. When the Sidonians heard this, they did likewise; and because they themselves were not able on account of their diseases to come to Peter, they sent a petition to him. 3. After he had stayed for some days in Tyre and had instructed all the inhabitants and freed them from numerous sufferings, Peter founded a church and appointed a bishop for them from the number of the elders who were accompanying him; then he set out for Sidon.

6. 1. When Peter entered Sidon, the people brought many sick folk in beds and set them down before him. 2. And he said to them: "Do not on any account believe that I, a mortal man, myself subject to many sufferings, can do anything to heal you! But I greatly desire to tell you in what way you can be delivered. . . . 7. 1. For I mention to you two ways,[4] showing you in the first place in what way men fall into misfortune and in the second place in what way under God's guidance they are delivered. 2. The way of those who perish is broad and very easy, but it leads straight away to misfortune; the way of those who

---

[1] Cf. 1 Cor. 10:21.   [2] Cf. Acts 15:20, 29; 21:25.
[3] Cf. Tobit 4, 15; Mt. 7:12; Lk. 6:31.   [4] Cf. Mt. 7:13f.

are delivered is narrow and rough, but in the end it leads to salvation those who have taken its burdens upon themselves. Before these two ways there stand belief and unbelief." . . .

8. 3. Such were the addresses that Peter gave in Sidon. There also within a few days many were converted and believed and were healed. So Peter founded a church there and enthroned as bishop one of the elders who were accompanying him. He then left Sidon.

9. 1. Immediately after the arrival of Peter in Berytus an earthquake took place; and people came to Peter saying: "Help, for we greatly fear that we shall all together perish!" 2. Then Simon dared, along with Appion, Annubion, Athenodorus and his other comrades, to turn against Peter in the presence of all the people: "Flee, ye people, from this man; 3. for he is a magician—you may believe me—and has himself occasioned this earthquake and has caused these diseases to frighten us, as if he himself was a god!" 4. And many other false charges of this sort did Simon and his followers bring against Peter, suggesting that he possessed superhuman power. 5. As soon as the multitude gave him a hearing, Peter with a smile and an impressive directness spoke the words: "Ye men, I admit that, God willing, I am capable of doing what these men here say and in addition am ready, if you will not hear my words, to turn your whole city upside down."

10. 1. Now when the multitude took alarm and readily promised to carry out his commands, Peter said: "Let no one of you associate with these magicians or in any way have intercourse with them." 2. Scarcely had the people heard this summons when without delay they laid hold of cudgels and pursued these fellows till they had driven them completely out of the city. . . .

12. 2. After he had stayed for several days with the inhabitants of Berytus, had made many conversant with the worship of the one God and had baptized them, Peter enthroned as bishop one of the elders who were accompanying him and then journeyed to Byblus. 3. On coming there he learned that Simon had not waited for him even for a single day, but had started at once for Tripolis. Accordingly Peter remained a few days with the people of Byblus, effected not a few healings and gave instruction in the Holy Scriptures. He then journeyed in the track of Simon to

Tripolis, being resolved to pursue him rather than to make room for him.

(H VIII)

1. 1. Along with Peter there entered into Tripolis people from Tyre, Sidon, Berytus, Byblus and neighbouring places, who were eager to learn, and in numbers that were not smaller people from the city itself crowded about him desiring to get to know him. . . . 4. 1. Astonished at this eagerness of the multitudes, Peter answered: "You see, beloved brethren, how the words of our Lord are manifestly fulfilled. For I remember how he said: *'Many will come from east and west, from north and south, and repose in the bosom of Abraham, Isaac and Jacob.'*[1] Nevertheless *many are called, but few are chosen.*[2] 2. In their coming in response to the call so much is fulfilled. 3. But since it rests not with them but with God who has called them and permitted them to come, on this account alone they have no reward. . . . 4. But if after being called they do what is good, and that rests with them themselves, for that they will receive their reward. 5. 1. For even the Hebrews who believe in Moses . . . are not saved unless they abide by what has been said to them. 2. For their believing in Moses lies not with a decision of their own will but with God, who said to Moses: *'Behold, I come to thee in a pillar of cloud that the people may hear me speaking to thee and believe for ever!'*[3] 3. Since then it is granted to the Hebrews and to them that are called from the Gentiles to believe the teachers of truth, whilst it is left to the personal decision of each individual whether he will perform good deeds, the reward rightly falls to those who do well. 4. For neither Moses nor Jesus would have needed to come if of themselves men had been willing to perceive the way of discretion. And there is no salvation in believing in teachers and calling them lords. 6. 1. Therefore is Jesus concealed from the Hebrews who have received Moses as their teacher, and Moses hidden from those who believe Jesus. 2. For since through both one and the same teaching becomes known, God accepts those who believe in one of them. 3. But belief in a teacher has as its aim the doing of what God has ordered. 4. That that is the case our Lord himself declares, saying:

[1] Mt. 8:11; Lk. 13:29.   [2] Mt. 22:14.   [3] Ex. 19:9.

563

'I confess to thee, Father of heaven and earth, that thou hast hidden this from the wise and elder, but hast revealed it to simpletons and infants.'[1] 5. Thus has God himself hidden the teacher from some since they know beforehand what they ought to do, and has revealed him to others since they know not what they have to do. 7. 1. Thus the Hebrews are not condemned because they did not know Jesus . . . provided only they act according to the instructions of Moses and do not injure him whom they did not know. 2. And again the offspring of the Gentiles are not judged, who . . . have not known Moses, provided only they act according to the words of Jesus and thus do not injure him whom they did not know. 3. Also it profits nothing if many describe their teachers as their lords, but do not do what it befits servants to do. 4. Therefore our Lord Jesus said to one who again and again called him Lord, but at the same time did not abide by any of his commands: *'Why sayest thou Lord to me and doest not what I say?'*[2] For it is not speaking that can profit any one, but doing. 5. In all circumstances good works are needed; but if a man has been considered worthy to know both teachers as heralds of a single doctrine, then that man is counted rich in God. . . ."

From the Recognition Scenes (H XII)

12. 1. One of us took courage and in the name of all directed a request to Peter that on the following day early in the morning we should set sail for the island Aradus which lay opposite to us. . . . 13. 1. Peter, who alone had not thought it necessary to take a view of the sights that were there, observed attentively a woman who sat outside before the doors and got her livelihood by begging. 2. "Dear woman," he said to her, "what limb fails you that you have submitted to such disgrace—I mean that of begging—and do not rather earn your livelihood by working with the hands that God has given you?" 3. She answered with a sign, "Had I only hands that could work! Now they have merely the appearance of hands and are actually dead. . . ." 4. To Peter's question, "For what reason do you suffer so grievous a misfortune?" 5. she answered, "Weakness in my soul and nothing else. For had I had the heart of a man, then there would have been a

---

[1] Mt. 11:25; Lk. 10:21.　　[2] Cf. Mt. 7:21; Lk. 6:46.

precipice, there would have been waves of the sea into which I would have cast myself and so have been able to make an end of my life."

19. 1. Whilst the woman related her life's story, it appeared as if Peter's thoughts drew him sometimes here and sometimes there. . . . 3. Finally he asked, "Dear woman, tell me your family, your native place and the names of your children!" . . . 4. But the woman stated that she came from Ephesus and that her husband was a Sicilian; and in the same way she changed the names of her three sons. 5. Being of opinion that she spoke the truth, Peter said, "What a pity! I thought, dear woman, that today I would be able to bring you great joy, supposing you to be a certain person whose life's story I know very well from hearsay." 6. Then she implored him with the words: "I beseech thee, tell me that I may know if among all women there is one more unfortunate than I!" 20. 1. And Peter, who could not lie, out of pity for her began to tell her the truth: "Among my companions there is a young man who willingly takes part in religious discussions, a Roman citizen, who, as he has told me, has besides his father two twin brothers, and on no one of these latter has he set eyes. 2. For according to his father's account his mother had a dream and thereupon left Rome for a time together with her twin sons lest she should die an evil death; but since she left the city with them, it has been impossible to find her. 3. Her husband, the father of the narrator, went in search of her, and since that time he has not been heard of."

21. 1. At these words of Peter the woman, who had listened attentively, started in amazement. Then Peter approached her, supported her, and called upon her to maintain her upright bearing, advising her to say openly what was going on in her. 2. And whilst her body was still stricken as with intoxication, she yet recovered consciousness and was able to estimate the greatness of the joy that was awaiting her. Rubbing her eyes, she asked, "Where is this young man?" 3. Then Peter, who saw through everything, answered, "First speak your mind, for otherwise you cannot see him." Then she made haste, saying: "I am the mother of the young man." Peter: "What is his name?" She: "Clement." 4. Thereupon Peter: "It is so." . . . 5. She: "I

am ready for anything, only let me see my only son! For in him
I shall again recognize my two children who died here."

(H XIII)

1. 3. The next day we reached Laodicea. And, think of it!
there met us before the gates Nicetas and Aquila, who greeted
us and brought us to the inn. 4. When Peter saw the large,
beautiful city, he said: "It is worth while to stay here for some
days." 5. And Nicetas and Aquila asked who the strange woman
was. I answered them, "My mother! God has granted to me
through my lord Peter to recognize her again." 2. 1. After I had
spoken these words, Peter told them the whole story in its main
features. . . . 3. 1. At that Nicetas and Aquila were startled and
cried out: 2. "O Lord and Ruler of all things, is this truth or a
dream?" Peter answered: "Provided we are not asleep, it is the
truth." 3. For a little the two of them paused to recover their
senses, and then they said: "We are Faustinus and Faustinianus."

7. 1. Thereupon Nicetas began the following account: "On that
night in which, as you know, the ship went to pieces, we were
sheltered by some men whom no inner restraints kept from being
pirates. They put us in a boat and . . . brought us to Caesarea
Stratonis. 2. As we wept because of hunger and fear and the
blows we received, they sold us, after changing our names that
we might not say all of a sudden something that was unacceptable
to them. 3. A very respectable woman, who had become a convert
to Judaism, Justa by name, bought us and adopted us and brought
us up very attentively in all the departments of Greek learning.
4. When we came to the age of discretion, we became fond of
worship, and found delight in study that through discussions with
other peoples we might be able to convince them of their error.
We also made ourselves thoroughly familiar with the doctrines
of the philosophers, especially with the most godless, those of
Epicurus and of Pyrrho, that we might be able all the better to
refute them. 8. 1. We were school-fellows of Simon the magician,
and through this friendship we ran the risk of becoming victims
to deceit."

566

(H XIV)

2. 1. Peter . . . related . . .: 2. "Whilst you were withdrawing, an old workman came on the scene, who kept himself curiously aloof in order that, ere he himself was seen, he might be able to make out what we would do. . . . 3. He then followed us farther that he might come upon a fitting opportunity to address me. 'For long,' he said, 'I have been following you and would have spoken to you, but I was afraid that you might be angry with me because of my curiosity. But now I say to you, if you will please hear it, what appears to me to be the truth.' . . . 3. 5. And I asked, 'What then is it that you have had to suffer?' 'That I do not need to say now,' he replied, 'perhaps you will get to know later who I am, whence I originate and into what circumstances I have fallen. For the present I would like it to be clear to you that everything depends on nativity.' 4. 1. Thereupon I said, 'If everything depends on nativity, and you are convinced that that is the case, then your present reflections are contrary to your basic conceptions. 2. For if it is not possible so much as to fashion a thought contrary to nativity, why do you trouble yourself in vain as to whether something can take place which yet cannot possibly take place? 3. Even if nativity has its significance, you do not need to go to any trouble at all to dissuade me from worshipping him who is even the Lord of the stars; if he wills that a thing should not take place, then its coming to pass is impossible. For of necessity the subordinate part must always obey the superior part.' . . . 6. 1. To that the old man answered, 'To a certain extent that sounds likely enough, but in its entirety my experience of life is opposed to your incomparable arguments. 2. For earlier I lived as an astrologer in Rome, came there into touch with a member of the emperor's house and obtained information about the nativity of this man and of his wife; and having seen that their fate turned out in actual agreement with their nativity, I can no more allow myself to be convinced by your exposition. 3. The constellation of the wife's nativity pointed to this, that she would commit adultery, love her own slaves and meet her death abroad in the sea. And that is precisely what came about. For she fell in love with her slave, fled with him, being unable to bear the reproach, went to a foreign land, cohabited

567

with him there and finally perished in the sea.' 7. 1. At that I asked, 'Whence do you know that after her flight she married the slave in the foreign land and after this marriage met her death?' To that the old man replied, 2. 'Naturally I do not know accurately about her marriage to him, indeed I knew nothing even of her falling in love with him; but after her departure the man's brother told me the whole story of her amour . . . and also that the wretched woman—for she cannot be blamed seeing that she was obliged to do and to suffer all this in consequence of her nativity—devised a dream, whether true or false I do not know. 3. According to his story she certainly asserted that in the dream a man appeared to her and ordered her to leave Rome immediately with her children. 4. Anxious for the well-being of his wife and children, the husband at once sent them in the company of their mother and several slaves to Athens for their education; only the third, the youngest, son he kept with him, the person who had appeared in the dream having granted that this son should remain with him. 5. Receiving in the course of a long time no word from his wife, although he himself had frequently sent to Athens, he called me to himself as the nearest of his friends and with me set out in search of her. 6. In this journey I willingly endured with him many hardships, remembering that earlier he had permitted me to share in all his prosperity, for he loved me more than all his other friends. 7. Leaving Rome, we came here to Syria. We landed at Seleucia; and after we had left the ship, it came about that after a few days my friend died of despair, whilst I came to this place, hired myself out, and up till this day have earned my bread by the work of my hands.'

8. 1. Whilst the old man told this story it became clear to me that the man of whom he said that he had died was himself, your father. But I did not wish to confront him with your lot until I had unbosomed myself to you."

The Installation of Clement (Epitome II)

144. Thus we, I Clement, Aquila and Nicetas, remained together with the apostle Peter and in the service of God proclaimed the word of truth in very many villages and cities. Peter, the apostle of Christ, attended many who were sick, healed those

who were possessed, and through the power of the Lord Jesus
Christ raised to life again numerous persons who were dead; he
led me through cities and villages and finally betook himself
even to Rome that there also he might proclaim the word of
truth. Arriving in the city, he taught the word of truth daily in
the synagogues and in private houses and through holy baptism
brought much people, important and unimportant, to Christ,
and finally also the influential among the women of rank, so that
in a short time almost all came to holy baptism and through the
teaching of the apostle believed in God.

145. . . . When the brethren were assembled, Peter suddenly
seized me by the hand, rose and said in presence of the church:
146. "Hear me, brethren and fellow-servants. Since I have been
taught by our Lord and Master Jesus Christ, who sent me, that
the time of my death is near, I appoint Clement to be your
bishop. To him I commit my teacher-ship; for from the beginning
to the end he has been my companion and has thus listened to
all my discourses. He has shared in all my temptations, and
always it was evident that he could hold his ground in the faith.
I have proved him to be more than all others god-fearing, sober-
minded, humane, good, learned, pure, upright, patient and
capable of tolerating calmly the bad conduct of some catechumens. Therefore I transfer to him the power to *bind* and to *loose*
in order that all he orders on earth may be decreed in heaven.[1]
He will bind what is to be bound, and loose what is to be loosed,
knowing the rule of the church. Hearken to him and be assured
that he who grieves the teacher of the truth sins against Christ
and provokes the anger of the Father of all things; therefore he
will not live. But the president himself must assume the place of a
physician and not show the nature of a savage beast."

147. During this discourse I fell at Peter's feet and besought
him earnestly to release me from the honour and power of the
bishop's office. But Peter answered: "Ask me not about this. It
is thus decreed, for this bishop's chair needs no thoughtless,
ambitious person but one who is distinctively trustworthy and
spiritually refined. Or give me one who is better than you are,
who has travelled more with me, who has heard more of my

[1] Cf. Mt. 16:19; 18:18.

discourses, and has learned more thoroughly how to lead the church, and I will not constrain you to do good against your will. . . . The sooner then you consent, the more will you ease my difficult situation." 158. After these words he laid his hands upon me in the sight of all and called me to take my place in his own chair.

XV

LATER ACTS OF APOSTLES
(*W. Schneemelcher and A. de Santos*)

The literary 'type' of the apocryphal Acts lingered on and proved effective beyond the 3rd century, and then it gradually merged into that of sacred legend. This transition is naturally connected with the origin and spread of the cult of the saints.

In the process the five early Acts of Apostles were influential in various ways, they were made use of and revised, perhaps they were also a model for later works. But it was not by them that the further development of this literature was determined. Rather there must be reckoned as equally powerful an aggravated hankering after wonders (and that means an intensified intruding into the church of the inheritance of pagan antiquity), theological tendencies of many sorts, and other factors. Certainly from the 4th century onwards there is an abundance of texts which could be designated as late apocryphal Acts of Apostles. It needs of course to be realized that it is difficult to define the boundaries of the hagiographic literature. Perhaps one may say that the theological intention which is native to the early apocryphal Acts recedes into the background. Likewise the impulse to entertain no longer comes so much to the front. Instead these late writings aim at being edifying in a sense other than do the earlier ones, frequently indeed—at least in the portion which treats of the martyrdom of the hero—they are designed for liturgical use. Here the relation to the canon is also of importance. Whilst it may be conjectured that in the case of the five early Acts there was an intention to supplement the canonical Acts of the Apostles, in the case of the later works this purpose has completely fallen away. The canon has long been a fixed entity, and in the newly produced works there is no intention to alter this situation in any way.

Here of course this extensive literature cannot be dealt with in detail. These writings are at any rate no longer New Testament apocrypha, if the concept is not to be completely devaluated. But a short survey may be given of their stock, their editions and the literature about them. The choice of the texts that should be enumerated is not easy, and certainly somewhat arbitrary. It proceeds from the point of view that examples should be given of material that has an important bearing on the development from the apocrypha to the literature about the saints. It remains a regrettable deficiency of this survey that the manifold oriental traditions cannot be sufficiently taken into consideration. That would burst the frame completely asunder. For them reference may be made to the literature in Vol. I, pp. 67f. For the later hagiography compare: F. Halkin, *Bibliotheca hagiographica graeca*, I–III, ³1957 (*BHG*). This work is not cited below in each particular case, but is presupposed. Cf. further H. G. Beck, *Kirche und theologische Literatur im byzantinischen Reich*, 1959, pp. 267–275.

A. The Continuation of the Early Acts of Apostles

1. PETER. (*a*) *Martyrium beati Petri Apostoli a Lino episcopo conscriptum* (text: *Aa* I, pp. 1–22; A. H. Salonius, *Martyrium b. Petri* . . . , Soc. Scient. Fennica, *Commentationes Humanorum Litterarum* I. 6, 1926). This text, which originated perhaps in the 6th century (?), is a Latin paraphrase and expansion of the Martyrium of the early *Acts of Peter* (see pp. 314ff. above, probably on the basis of the Greek text, but not arranged according to the Latin translation of the *Actus Vercellenses*. There is a summary of the contents in Lipsius, *Apostelgeschichten*, II. i, pp. 91–93; Lipsius also enumerates the manuscripts, but appraises the text wrongly. Cf. further Harnack, *Litgesch.*, I. i, p. 133.

(*b*) *Acts of Nereus and Achilleus* (text: H. Achelis, *TU* XI. 2, 1893). This account of the martyrdom of Domitilla and a series of other martyrs (especially of the time of Domitian and Trajan) is a combination of different accounts. In the first portion the *Acts of Peter* are the basis of the story. The account of the martyrs is connected with the Peter-Simon legend. The author also knew the portion of the *Acts of Peter* which is preserved only in the Coptic fragment (on this cf. pp. 269f. above; C. Schmidt, 'Studien zu den alten Petrusakten', *ZKG* 43, 1924, pp. 340ff.). It is difficult to decide whether he relied on the Greek or Latin version. He also used the Linus texts of the Passions of Peter and Paul. The time of composition of the Greek Acts is variously determined: 5th or 6th century; the Latin translation comes doubtless from the 7th century. In addition to Achelis cf. also Lipsius, *Apostelgeschichten*, II. i, pp. 106ff.

(*c*) *The Preaching of Simon Cephas in the City of Rome* (text: W. Cureton, *Ancient Syriac Documents*, 1864, pp. 35–41), composed 5th/6th century and handed down in Syriac, is connected only very loosely with the early *Acts of Peter*, but has borrowed certain traits from them and has been enlarged with many other traditions. The dogmatic statements in the work refer it to the time of the later Christological controversies. Cf. Lipsius, *Apostelgeschichten* II. i, pp. 206f.; A. Baumstark, *Die Petrus- und Paulusakten in der literarischen Überlieferung der syrischen Kirche*, 1902, pp. 38–40.

(*d*) A Syriac *History of Simon Cephas, the Chief of the Apostles* (text: P. Bedjan, *Acta martyrum et sanctorum* I, 1890, pp. 1–33) is based upon the *pseudo-Clementine Recognitions*, the *Preaching of Simon Cephas* mentioned above in (*c*), the statements of the canonical Acts and lastly the narrative of the *Acts of Peter*. Cf. Baumstark, *op. cit.*, pp. 40ff.; Harnack, *Litgesch.*, I. 2, p. 928.

(*e*) Slavic Accounts of Peter (*A. de Santos*). There are three Slavic church documents which treat of the life of Peter. Lipsius-Bonnet (*Aa* I, pp. LXXXIX–XC), M. N. Speranskij (Bibliografičeskie Materialy: Čtenija v Imp. obščestve istorii i drevnostej rossijskich pri moskovskom Universitete, Moscow 1889, pp. 1–52) and N. Bonwetsch (in Harnack, *Litgesch.*, I. 2, pp. 903–904) have given accounts of the Slavic 'Passio' and the 'Disputatio cum Simone Mago', which are connected with the *Acts of Peter*.

In addition there has come to hand a Slavic 'Vita Petri', a Greek original of which is not known. To the dissemination of this noteworthy document in the Slavic area evidence is given by the Slavic Apocrypha Index, which in twelve of its versions, totalling in all fifteen, mentions a 'Žitie blaženago apostola Petra' and attributes to it a heretical origin (cf. A. I. Jacimirskij, Bibliografičeskij obzor Apokrifov v juznoslavjanskoj i russkoj pis'mennosti. I, St. Petersburg 1921, pp. 44f. under no. 46). The Index just mentioned distinguishes two portions: (*a*) a 'Vita Petri' with a reference to noteworthy wonders related in it, and (*b*) a description of the 'childhood of Christ'. In the text that has come to hand the two parts are fused in a uniform narrative, which treats, it is true, of Peter's journey to Rome, but whose leading character is Christ himself in the form of a child.

This 'Vita' has nothing in common either with the literature on Peter hitherto known or with the apocryphal infancy narratives (and nothing with the later 'Evangelium Petri Infantiae' of Catulle Mendès (cf. James, p. 89)). When this text is considered from the linguistic angle, the conclusion is easily come to that this story derives from an early translation from the Greek. This opinion gains in interest and also in certainty when we reflect that, so far as the literature on Peter is concerned, we are frequently directed to versions.

As regards content, the Slavic 'Vita Petri' exhibits many traits (mostly of a Gnostic colouring) in common with the known Acts of Apostles. Some of these may be indicated. The embarkation of Peter (cf. Radčenko—see below—p. 200, line 25) takes place under similar circumstances as in the 'Acta Andreae et Matthiae' c. 5 (cf. *Aa* II. 1, pp. 69f.). The appearance of Christ in the form of a child in the wilderness (cf. Radčenko, p. 199, line 23) recalls a similar appearance in the Greek 'Martyrium Matthaei' c. 1 (cf. *Aa* II. 1, p. 217). Lastly the sale of Christ by Peter (cf.

573

Radčenko, p. 204, line 7) has its prototype in the 'Acta Thomae' (cf. *Aa* II. 2, pp. 101f.), where, however, conditions are reversed, Thomas (or Judas?) being sold by Christ. Of interest is also the reference to the writing entrusted by Christ to Peter, which recalls 'the Epistle of Christ that fell from Heaven (on the altar of Peter)' (cf. De Santos, *Los Ev. Ap.*, pp. 712–725, and in *Studia Patristica, TU* 78, pp. 290–296.

The slavic 'Vita Petri' is extant in two different redactions. The first is represented by the manuscript no. 111a. 10 of the Academy in Agram, fol. 45–49 (16th century). It is to be regarded as a later digest of the second redaction. This text was first published by V. N. Močul'skij (Apokrifič. Žitie apostola Petra: Trudy X-go Archeologičeskago S'êzda v Rigê, Moscow 1896).

Of the second redaction two texts have thus far been edited. The first comes from the omnibus codex no. 68 of the Public Library in Sofia (16th century) and is preserved only incompletely. It was published by A. S. Archangel'skij (K istorii junžoslavjanskoj i drevnerusskoj apokrifičeskoj literatury: Izvestija Otdelenija Russkago Jazyka i Slovesnosti Akademii Nauk IV, 1899, pp. 101–147). The expositions of I. Franko, 'Beiträge aus dem Kirchenslavischen zu den Apokryphen des NT, II: zu den gnostischen "περίοδοι Πέτρου"', *ZNW* 3, 1902, 315–335, are based only on this fragment.

The complete text of the second redaction is preserved in the omnibus codex no. 137 of the Imperial Library in Vienna fol. 169ᵛ–177 (14th century) and was edited by K. Th. Radčenko (Zametki o pergamennom Sbornikê XIV-go vêka Vênskoj Pridvornoj Biblioteki: Izvestija Otdelenija Russkago Jazyka i Slovesnosti Akademii Nauk, St. Petersburg VIII (1903), kn. 4, pp. 199–211. This is the oldest and best-preserved text of the Slavic 'Vita Petri'.

In conclusion reference may be made to other manuscripts. In an article (cf. 'Kievskaja Starina' 47, 1894, p. 431) Miron refers to an omnibus codex in the possession of Pop Jaremeckij. In this codex, under nos. 22 and 26, there may be two manuscripts of Ukrainian origin of our 'Vita'. Here also there may belong the manuscripts mentioned with question marks by Bonwetsch (*op. cit.*, p. 904) under the titles 'Wanderings' or 'Processions of the Apostle Paul through the Countries'. These are: Soloveck. Bibliothek no. 89 S. XVI. fol. 3–5 (now in Leningrad: Gosudarstvennaja Ord. Trud. Krasn. Znameni Publičnaja Biblioteka imeni M. E. Saltykova-Ščedrina) and Moskovsk. Sinodal'n. Bibl. no. 51 S. XVI/XVII fol. 311ᵛ (now in Moscow: Gosudarstvennyj Istoričeskij Muzej). The circumstance that our 'Vita' begins with a reference to the missionary activity of Paul among the Gentiles (whilst Peter, disappointed by the Jews, withdraws into the wilderness) may have deceived the reporter into thinking that these manuscripts belonged to the 'Periodoi Paulou'.

2. PAUL. (*a*) *Martyrium beati Pauli Apostoli a Lino episcopo con-scriptum* (text: *Aa* I, pp. 23–44). This Martyrium, in the title of which the words 'A Lino episcopo conscriptum' are omitted in a portion of the tradition, represents a later Latin working-up of the concluding portion of the *Acts of Paul* (see pp. 383ff. above). The time of composition can hardly be determined; only it is certain that this text is later than the shorter form of the Martyrium (against Lipsius). Cf. Bardenhewer, *Litgesch.*, I, pp. 559f.

(*b*) *The Syriac History of the Holy Apostle Paul* (text: Bedjan, *op. cit.*, I, pp. 33–34) does not seem to go back to the *Acts of Paul*, but to rest above all upon the canonical Acts of the Apostles. Cf. Harnack, *Litgesch.*, I. 2, p. 128; Baumstark, *op. cit.*, pp. 40ff.

3. PETER AND PAUL. The *Acts of Peter and Paul* are a later com-pilation of different traditions, among them certainly the early *Acts of Peter*, intended to delineate the activity together of the two apostles in Rome and their martyr death. There are three different versions of the work (also called the Marcellus text): (*a*) Πράξεις τῶν ἀγιῶν ἀποστόλων Πέτρου καὶ Παύλου (*Aa* I, pp. 178–222); (*b*) *Passio sanctorum apostolorum Petri et Pauli* (Greek and Latin *Aa* I, pp. 118–177); (*c*) *Passio apostolorum Petri et Pauli* (Latin compilation: *Aa* I, pp. 223–234). 'Over the origin of the *Acts of Peter and Paul* there rests a thick veil' (Bardenhewer, *Litgesch.*, I, p. 567). The hypotheses of Lipsius are certainly wrong. For the present the time of composition cannot be fixed accurately, except for the compilation named under (*c*), which doubtless belongs to the 6th or 7th century. Cf. Bardenhewer, *Litgesch.*, I, pp. 564–568; R. Söder, *op. cit.*, pp. 11ff.; A. van Lantschoot, 'Contribution aux Actes de S. Pierre et de S. Paul', *Muséon* 68, 1955, pp. 17–46 and 219–233 (Ethiopic).

4. JOHN. (*a*) *The Acts of John by Prochorus*, Πράξεις τοῦ ἁγίου ἀποστόλου καὶ εὐαγγελιστοῦ 'Ιωάννου τοῦ θεολόγου συγγράφοντος τοῦ αὐτοῦ μαθητοῦ Προχόρου (text: Th. Zahn, *Acta Joannis*, 1880, pp. 1–165). This text, supposedly composed by Prochorus (cf. Acts 6:5), which was translated into many languages, records the doings of John, above all in Patmos (there is a summary in Lipsius, *Apostelgeschichten* I, pp. 366–397). The author has used the early *Acts of John*, but has moulded the material very freely. The time of com-position is doubtless the 5th century. Cf. Lipsius, *op. cit.*; Zahn, *op. cit.*; Bardenhewer, *Litgesch.*, I, p. 578; Musikides, *Nea Sion* (Jerusalem), 1947, pp. 245f.; 1948, pp. 51–53; 121f.

(*b*) The *Virtutes Joannis* (text: J. A. Fabricius, *Codex apocryphus novi Testamenti*, 1703, ii, pp. 531–590), a part of the so-called

Abdias compilation (not before the end of the 6th century), have made a larger use of the *Acts of John*. Cf. Lipsius, *Apostelgeschichten*, pp. 408–431; Zahn, *op. cit.*, passim.

(c) A *Passio Joannis* under the name of Mellitus of Laodicea (= Melito of Sardis?) is merely a shorter and later redaction of the *Virtutes* mentioned under (b) (the text has frequently been edited, see Lipsius I, p. 408; the edition of G. Heine, *Bibliotheca anecdotorum* I, Leipzig 1848, pp. 108ff., is printed in Migne, *PG* V, cols. 1241ff.). Cf. Lipsius, *op. cit.*; Zahn, *op. cit.*; Bardenhewer, *Litgesch.* I, pp. 578f.

5. ANDREW. (a) *The Acts of Andrew and Matthias among the Cannibals*, Πράξεις Ἀνδρέου καὶ Ματθεία εἰς τὴν πόλιν τῶν ἀνθρωποφάγων (text: *Aa* II. 1, pp. 65–116), is an account (6th century?) of the fortunes of Matthias and Andrew which is extant in different translations (there is a summary in Lipsius, *Apostelgeschichten* I, pp. 550–553). In part it may well go back to the early *Acts of Andrew*. Cf. J. Flamion, *Les actes d'André et les textes apparentés*, 1911; Bardenhewer, *Litgesch.*, I, pp. 570ff.; F. Blatt, *Die lateinischen Bearbeitungen der Acta Andreae et Matthiae apud anthropophages mit sprachlichem Kommentar hrsg.* (supplement to *ZNW* 12), 1930.

(b) *The Acts of the Apostles Peter and Andrew*, Πράξεις τῶν ἁγίων ἀποστόλων Πέτρου καὶ Ἀνδρέα (text: *Aa* I. 2, pp. 117–127), preserved in Greek, Slavic and Ethiopic, a continuation of the *Acts of Andrew and Matthias* (there is a summary in Lipsius, *Apostelgeschichten*, I, pp. 553–557), are likewise a working-up of the material of the early *Acts of Andrew*. Cf. Flamion, *op. cit.*; Bardenhewer, *Litgesch.*, I, pp. 571f.

(c) *The Martyrdom of Andrew*. A series of versions of the Martyrium has already been detailed, see pp. 390f. above. Cf. further *BHG*³ I, pp. 29–33.

(d) *The Acts of Andrew and Paul*, a story preserved in Coptic (text: G. Zoëga, *Catalogus codicum copticorum*, 1810, pp. 230–235; partially also in G. Steindorff, *Kurzer Abriss der koptischen Grammatik*, 1921, pp. 34*–47*), record a journey of Paul in the nether world and his rescue by Andrew (there is a summary in James, pp. 472–474). The text seems to be connected with the *Acts of Paul* rather than with the *Acts of Andrew*. Cf. Lipsius, *Apostelgeschichten*, supplement, pp. 95f.; S. Morenz, 'Der Apostel Andreas als νέος Σάραπις', *ThLZ* 72, 1947, pp. 295–297.

6. THOMAS. There is a working-up in Greek of the *Acts of Thomas* with the title Πράξεις τοῦ ἁγίου ἀποστόλου Θωμᾶ (text: M. R. James, *Apocrypha anecdota* ii, 1897, pp. 28–45). The age of this text can however hardly be determined. Related to this writing is a medieval Ethiopic work: *The Contending of Thomas*

(text: E. A. W. Budge, *The Contendings of the Apostles*, 1899; English translation by S. C. Malan in James, *op. cit.*, pp. 46–63). Cf. Bardenhewer, *Litgesch.*, I, p. 584.

B. Later Acts of Other Apostles

1. ACTS OF PHILIP. The *Acts of Philip* have come down to us only fragmentarily in single acts (text: *Aa* II. 2, pp. 1–90; there is also a later digest: pp. 91–98). Philip, the hero of the story, is the 'apostle' (Mk. 3:18, parallels and elsewhere) and the 'deacon' (Acts 6:5; 21:8) in one person. The work is dependent on older legends and originated at the earliest at the end of the 4th century, and probably not until the 5th century. A Syriac version (text: W. Wright, *Apocryphal Acts of the Apostles*, 1871, I, 73–99; English translation: II, pp. 69–92) is a later revision. Cf. Bardenhewer, *Litgesch.*, I, pp. 584–588; Lipsius, *Apostelgeschichten* II. 2, pp. 1–53; E. Peterson, 'Die Haeretiker der Philippus-Akten', *ZNW* 31, 1932, pp. 97–111; *id.*, 'Zum Messalianismus der Philippus-Akten', *Oriens Christ.* 29, 1932, pp. 172–179; *id.*, 'Die Philippus-Akten im armenischen Synaxar', *Theol. Quartalschr.* 113, 1932, pp. 289–298; A. Kurfess, 'Zu den Philippusakten', *ZNW* 44, 1952/53, pp. 145–151.

2. ACTS OF MATTHEW. Of the *Acts of Matthew* there is preserved in a Greek and Latin version only the Martyrium with the story in which it is enframed (text: *Aa* II. 2, pp. 217–262). In spite of a certain dependence these Acts do not belong to the *Acts of Andrew and Matthias* (see A 5a above). The Coptic Acts (F. Wüstenfeld, *Synaxarium*, 1879, pp. 65ff.) are a shortened version. Cf. Lipsius, *Apostelgeschichten* II. 2, pp. 109–141; Bardenhewer, *Litgesch.*, I, pp. 588f.; R. Söder, *op. cit.*, pp. 17f.; T. Atenolfi, *I testi meridionali degli Atti di S. Matteo l'Evangelista*, 1958.

3. ACTS OF BARTHOLOMEW. An account of Bartholomew is given in a Martyrium (text: *Aa* II. 1, pp. 128–150) preserved in Greek and Latin which may well have originated in the 5th or 6th century. In addition there are later Ethiopic and Armenian texts. Cf. Lipsius, *Apostelgeschichten* II. 2, pp. 54–108; Supplement, p. 130 (Index s. v. Bartholomäusakten); R. Söder, *op. cit.*, p. 18.

4. ACTS OF SIMON AND JUDAS. A Latin *Passio Simonis et Judae* (text: Fabricius, *op. cit.*, ii, pp. 608ff.) is doubtless a portion of a larger compilation on the apostles and describes the activity in Babylonia and Persia of the two who have just been named. The work was composed at the earliest in the 6th century. Cf. Lipsius, *Apostelgeschichten* II. 2, pp. 164–178; R. Söder, *op. cit.*, p. 19.

5. ACTS OF THADDAEUS. The Greek *Acts of Thaddaeus* (text: *Aa* I, pp. 273–278 and 279–283) are closely connected with the Abgar saga. On it see Vol. I, pp. 437–444.

6. ACTS OF BARNABAS. Under the title Περίοδοι καὶ μαρτύριον τοῦ ἁγίου Βαρνάβα τοῦ ἀποστόλου (text: *Aa* II. 2, pp. 292–302) there is an account composed, it is alleged, by John Mark of the activity and the death of Barnabas in Cyprus. These Acts doubtless originated at the end of the 5th or in the beginning of the 6th century. Cf. Lipsius, *Apostelgeschichten* II. 2, pp. 270–320; Bardenhewer, *Litgesch.*, I, p. 116.

C. APOCALYPSES AND RELATED SUBJECTS

INTRODUCTION

(*P. Vielhauer*)

Christianity commenced its career as an eschatological and enthusiastic movement and gave expression to its faith largely in the language of *Apocalyptic* and of *Prophecy*. From the end of the 1st century to the beginning of the Middle Ages it produced an extensive apocalyptic literature, to which the Sibyllines also belong. Christian prophecy was not similarly productive of literature, but, in the combination "Apocalypses and Related Subjects", it must be taken into account by reason of its actual historical significance.

While the Gospels represent a literary genre created by primitive Christianity itself, and while the apocryphal Acts of Apostles—as distinct from the canonical Acts—belong within the tradition of the Hellenistic romance, Christianity took over the genre of the Apocalypse from Palestinian Judaism and that of the Sibyllines from Hellenistic Judaism. It was able to do this because the earliest community was influenced in the highest degree by apocalyptic ideas and expectations and repeated these in its mission; that this led ultimately to the composition of books of Apocalypses was only natural. In addition, early Christianity adopted Jewish apocalypses; it employed them as Holy Scripture (cf. for example, the apocryphal quotations in Jude 9 and 14) and, by reworking of various kinds, christianized them. Furthermore, it is due to this process of adoption that this Jewish literature (like almost the entire extant non-Rabbinic literature) was saved from destruction by the "orthodox" Judaism, i.e. by the party which asserted itself successfully after A.D. 70.

In view of these circumstances, Jewish Apocalyptic must be described in the following introduction in order that the affinities and differences between the Jewish and the Christian may become clear; consequently we begin with the literary phenomenon, not with general features of the period. Moreover, a description of Jewish and Christian prophecy is necessary in order that their relation to one another and to Apocalyptic may be made clear; in this case it is certainly not possible to begin with larger literary evidences, and we are left to testimonies concerning them and to inferences.

LITERATURE: R. H. Charles, *The Apocrypha and Pseudepigrapha of the Old Testament*, 2 vols., 1913; E. Kautzsch, *Die Apokryphen und Pseud-epigraphen des Alten Testamentes*, 2 vols., 1921; P. Riessler, *Altjüdisches*

Schrifttum ausserhalb der Bibel, 1928; W. Bousset/H. Gressmann, *Die Religion des Judentums im späthellenistischen Zeitalter*, ³1926; P. Volz, *Die Eschatologie der jüdischen Gemeinde im neutestamentlichen Zeitalter*, ²1934 (with details on the literary problems of the texts); H. H. Rowley, *The Relevance of Apocalyptic*, ²1955; M. Noth, Das Geschichtsverständnis der alttestamentlichen Apokalyptik, in *Gesammelte Studien zum AT*, 1957, pp. 248–273; *id.*, Die Heiligen des Höchsten, *ibid.*, pp. 274–290; O. Plöger, *Theokratie und Eschatologie*, 1959; D. Rössler, *Gesetz und Geschichte*, 1960.

1. APOCALYPTIC

(*a*) NAME AND IDEA. By means of the word "Apocalyptic" we designate first of all the literary genre of the Apocalypses, i.e. revelatory writings which disclose the secrets of the beyond and especially of the end of time, and then secondly, the realm of ideas from which this literature originates.

This name is obviously taken from the New Testament Apocalypse of John, for the contents of this book are characterized at 1. 1 as: Ἀποκάλυψις Ἰησοῦ Χριστοῦ, ἥν ἔδωκεν αὐτῷ ὁ θεός, δεῖξαι τοῖς δούλοις αὐτοῦ ἃ δεῖ γενέσθαι ἐν τάχει. Here the word ἀποκάλυψις is used for the first time with the meaning "revelation of that which must shortly take place". We meet it for the first time as the designation of a book in the title of the Johannine Apocalypse, Ἀποκάλυψις Ἰωάννου. Because of the significance of this Apocalypse the word ἀποκάλυψις became a literary title and the designation of related Christian books—about A.D. 200 the Muratori Canon mentions "apocalypse . . . johannis et petri" (lines 71f.)—and was then assigned to Jewish works of this type, and that by Christians. The word certainly appears also in the title of a Jewish Apocalypse, the Syriac Baruch: "Book of the Revelation of Baruch, son of Neria, translated from Greek into Syriac" (Kautzsch, *Pseudepigraphen*, p. 410; Charles, *Pseudepigrapha*, p. 481). This title, however, obviously does not belong to the original form of the Apocalypse; the book is translated from Greek, and perhaps goes back to a Hebrew or Aramaic original which must have come into being between A.D. 70 and 132 (Plöger, *RGG*³ 1, col. 902); consequently we may regard the influence of Christian usage on the title of the Syriac translation as possible or even probable. The same is true of the title of the Greek Baruch. At all events, the use of the term "Revelation" to designate this literary work is not proved to be pre-Christian. This literary genre does not appear originally to have had any common title.

(*b*) LITERARY CHARACTER. In most of the Jewish Apocalypses definite formal pecularities recur, and these we must regard as fixed features, as elements in the style of this literary genre.

1. Pseudonymity. The Apocalyptist does not write under his own name, but under that of one of the great personages of the past (e.g. Daniel, Elijah and Isaiah, Moses and Ezra, Enoch and Adam). He has not sufficient authority of his own, as the writing prophets had, but has to borrow it from these great men. Together with pseudonymity, a fictitious antiquity is found as an element in the style of the apocalyptic writer. In this case, it has to be made clear why the book has just recently become known and not a long time ago. This happens because of the sealing-up of the book, or because of the command for its secret preservation till the end of days (Dan. 12:9; 4 Esd. 12:35–38; 14:7f., and often).

2. Account of the Vision. The Apocalyptist receives his revelations mostly in visions, whereas they were granted to the prophets mostly through auditions. But just as the prophets had visions as well, so the Apocalyptists also occasionally have auditions, but the visions predominate so strongly that the Apocalypses are generally presented in the form of an account of a vision. The apocalyptic vision takes place in various ways; first, through a dream (Dan. 7:1ff., cf. also 2:1; 4:2; eth. Enoch 83f.; 85ff.; slav. Enoch 1:3ff.; 4 Esd. 11:1; 12:1; 13:1, 13, etc.), and then through visionary ecstasy. The visions of Dan. 10–12 will have been experienced by the seer in a waking state. Cf. syr. Bar. 13:1f., and particularly 22:1:

> And afterwards, the heavens opened, and I saw . . . and a voice was heard from the height, and it said unto me . . .

In the Johannine Apocalypse there are no dream-visions, only ecstatic visions (1:10; 4:2; cf. 17:3; 21:10). Bousset is of the opinion that Jewish Apocalyptic "tended more and more to move away from the simple dream-vision to ecstatic vision" (*Die Offenbarung Johannis*, 1906, p. 4). Eventually the apocalyptic vision takes place through visionary rapture. In his ecstasy the seer experiences changes of location and wanders through strange and mysterious regions on earth and in heaven. Rapture of this kind is found for the first time in Ezekiel, who, on the whole, has had a very strong influence on apocalyptic (Ez. 8:3ff.). The prophet Habakkuk (the dragon in Babylon) and Baruch (syr. Bar. 6:3ff.) were enraptured. Raptures into heaven were experienced by Enoch (eth. Enoch 70f.), by Paul (2 Cor. 12:3) and by John the Apocalyptist (4:1). The idea of the journey to heaven, originally only a means to an end, becomes the theme of a special literature in which cosmological, astrological and other-worldly secrets in general are disclosed (slav. Enoch).

The vision itself is a picture: either a picture which represents the occurrences themselves directly, or a picture which portrays them indirectly, in the form of symbols and allegories.

In the last-mentioned instance, an explanation is essential. This is given by a mediator of the revelation. Thus Daniel explains the dream of Nebuchadnezzar. Generally an interpreting angel, an *angelus interpres*, takes over this role, as, for example, in Dan. 7 where the seer experiences the vision and its interpretation in a dream. In eth. Enoch there is quite a number of these *angeli interpretes*. In 4 Esd. the interpreting angel plays only a minor role, and he is completely absent from syr. Bar., in which the seer communicates directly with God. Sometimes, as in the vision of Beasts in eth. Enoch, no explanation is given and the interpretation is left to the reader.

The imagery in the visions is, in the main, traditional, but often an image taken over ready coined resists a completely allegorical interpretation. Sometimes the seer adds to an image taken over a new and subordinate one which will restore the connection with the actual situation. According to Bousset, it is the small allegorical vision which is the germ-cell of the Apocalypse; in it either a number of individual features are woven into an allegorical pattern or a number of small and separate images are set side by side. Considering the traditional character of the imagery and the manner of its composition, the question arises how far the apocalyptic visions are true to experience. Apocalyptic is book-wisdom, a "literature", and in fact collected literature, but the ardour of the expectation and the strength of the hope are genuine. Moreover, it cannot be denied that the apocalyptists had visions, but it is quite another question how far these experiences have been deposited in the literature. Even with the aid of the psychology of religion and of type-psychology, the work of distinguishing neatly between actual experience and literary activity in the Apocalypses will scarcely be successful.

> There is in fact an apocalyptic culture which transmits to the ecstatics visions and experiences which are to a certain degree fixed, —however much it may appear as a psychological curiosity that someone gives frenzied expression to what someone else has previously communicated to him in a frenzied state, and that people are raptured, not independently, but in something like a process of borrowing, and according to a mechanical routine. Nevertheless this is the position. (Th. Mann, *Doctor Faustus*, p. 567.)

3. Surveys of History in Future-Form. Related to the fiction of antiquity is the fact that the apocalyptic writers frequently present the history of the past right up to their own present time in the form of prophecies. This is always followed by a prediction of the End, and on this the emphasis lies: the present of the actual

(not the fictional) author is always the last time. This imminent expectation can also be formulated from the standpoint of the fictional author: "The history of the world is divided into twelve parts; we have come to the tenth, to the middle of the tenth; but there remain two parts, in addition to the half of the tenth" (4 Esd. 14:11f.). The description naturally does not employ clear references (names of people, countries, etc.), but uses a code with images, symbols and allegories, and it generally has attached to it a comprehensive interpretation. "This method often permits the dating of apocalypses; the point at which the history loses precision and accuracy is the moment of writing" (C. K. Barrett, *The Background of the New Testament: Selected Documents*, 1957, p. 231).

We can distinguish two types of such historical description: first, that which takes in its view world-history as a whole, and secondly, that which begins from a definite point of time within history, generally the time of the imaginary author, and from that point traces the picture to the End. Occasionally both may be found in the same Apocalypse (Dan. and syr. Bar.). To the first type belong the picture of the four world-empires (Dan. 2 and 7) which represent in their number the whole of world-history; the Vision of Clouds (syr. Bar. 53–71) which depicts world-history from Adam till the appearance of the Messiah and his rule; and also the Vision of Beasts and the Apocalypse of Ten Weeks in Enoch (eth. Enoch 85–90; 93; and 91:12–17). To the second type belong the visions of Dan. 8–12 which begin with the Persian empire and the last of which (10:11–11:45) opens into a very precise description of contemporary events as being the eschatological period; also the so-called Vision of Cedars (syr. Bar. 35–40) which sketches the entire course of history from the time of the biblical Baruch, from the exile of Judah at the hands of the Babylonians, using in an entirely different manner the schema of the four kingdoms in Daniel; in addition, the apocalypse in the Testament of Levi 16–18 (commencing with Aaron), the Vision of Eagles at 4 Esd. 11f., which begins with the fourth kingdom of Daniel and reinterprets it with specific reference to Rome, Ass. Mos. 2–10 and Apoc. Abr. 27–30. Sometimes these outlines of history were divided into periods: the history of the world in four empires in Daniel, in ten weeks in Enoch (cf. Sib. 4:47ff.), in twelve parts in 4 Esd. and in the Vision of Clouds in syr. Bar; the history of Israel in seven Jubilees (Test. Levi 17); the division of Israel's internal history into periods, in terms of the seventy shepherds (eth. Enoch 89:59ff.), is not carried through clearly. Although these divisions into periods may often appear so multifarious and frivolous, they pursue the same aim as the historical surveys, that is, to express and to awaken the consciousness of the imminent end.

The apocalyptic writers employ this description of history in future form in order to arouse confidence in their own predictions of the future. If the imaginary author has so precisely predicted the past which can be checked from the standpoint of the reader, then the future also will come to pass as he predicts it. However, we must not fail to appreciate the fact that behind the *pia fraus* of this stylistic method there stands the religious conception of God's determining the course of the world.

This presentation of history as *vaticinium ex eventu* has only very remote OT parallels in the Blessing of Jacob (Gen. 49) and of Moses (Deut. 33), or in the Oracles of Balaam (Num. 23f.). These scarcely come into the question as models. It has been suggested that the Sibylline oracles of the Hellenistic-Roman period which, as prophecy, bring us to the actual present, have served as models for the apocalyptic descriptions of history. Moreover a Sibylline model has been assumed for the apocalyptic pseudonymity: the ancient Sibyl, active throughout the ages, has provided the stimulus for figures of salvation-history to be made in Apocalyptic the guarantors of these predictions (R. Meyer, *ThWtB* VI, p. 828).

4. Forms and Combinations of Forms. As has been said, there was in pre-Christian times no common title for the genre of the Apocalypse. In the eth. Enoch we meet several times the characterization *Symbolic Utterances* (1:2; 37:5; 38:1; 45:1; 58:1); sometimes this is parallel to *Vision* (1:2; 37:1) and *Blessings* (1:1), *Wisdom sayings* and *Sacred sayings* (37:2). The term *Symbolic Utterance* does not always designate the symbolic or allegorical character of the statements (eth. Enoch 1–6), but the report of the vision is generally given in symbolic form.

Not all Apocalypses are reports of visions. The Ass. Mos., for example, purports to be a speech of Moses, given shortly before his death to Joshua in order to install him as his successor and to teach him about Israel's future destiny. This apocalypse has the form of a farewell discourse and displays all the marks of this genre. Likewise the slav. Enoch is a farewell discourse which Enoch, on the day of his rapture, delivers to his son and in which he describes his journey into the beyond, undertaken on that very day. Slav. Enoch is therefore a report of a vision in the form of a farewell discourse. Similar features may be seen in many parts of eth. Enoch, except that there Enoch is not expressly characterized as being about to depart; but, since he refers there to visions long past, we may doubtless presume that he is recounting his revelations shortly before his rapture. He narrates to his son Methuselah the two dream-visions concerning the coming judgment by flood (83f.) and concerning the fate of Israel (the Vision of Beasts 85–90); likewise the paraenetic book (91–105) claims to be a speech of Enoch to his son; the astronomical book (72–82) is also composed for Methuselah (76:14), like the small final Warning (108). Here again, then, we have a combination of an account of a vision and a farewell discourse. Nevertheless, it is not the latter, but the former which is the real apocalyptic type. We must distinguish precisely between the two genres, even if in farewell discourses like the Test. XII Patr. eschatological texts and even small apocalypses are occasionally present (Test. Levi 18, cf. D. Rössler, *op. cit.*, p. 43).

Very frequently the apocalyptic writers include prayers in their books. It is not unusual for these to appear between a vision and its interpretation, and sometimes they rise to hymn-forms of great beauty (cf. Dan. 9:4–19; eth. Enoch 84:2–6; syr. Bar. 38; 48; 54, etc.). 4 Esd. is especially rich in prayers: before the first four visions the seer each time expounds his questions in prayer (3:4–36; 5:23–39; 6:38–59; 9:29–37) and receives an answer in a vision and interpretation: at times his book produces the impression of being a collection of prayers (8:6–19, 20–36; 13:14–20; 14:18–22).

Finally all Apocalypses include paraenesis, both exhortations to repentance and conversion in view of the imminent end and of judgment, and also paraenesis in the form-critical sense of the word, i.e. traditional ethical exhortations in the form of maxims and series of aphorisms which are sometimes arranged thematically. In eth. Enoch the paraenesis appears at the beginning and at the end (2–5; 91–105; 108), while in slav. Enoch it forms the last part of the book (43–65 Riessler). In 4 Esd. and syr. Bar. the paraenesis is inserted in the prophecies. Paraenesis may also be given in the form of a farewell discourse (eth. Enoch 91–105; slav. Enoch 43–65; syr. Bar. 44f.).

(*c*) THE WORLD OF IDEAS. The Apocalypses contain not only revelations on the Last Things (including the termination of history), but also on other *Secrets*, on the Beyond, Heaven and Hell and their inhabitants, on astronomy, meteorology and geography (especially eth. and slav. Enoch), as well as on the origin of sin and evil in the world (4 Esd. and syr. Bar.). The main interest, however, does not lie in problems of cosmology or theodicy, but in eschatology. We may therefore designate Apocalyptic as a special expression of the Jewish eschatology which existed alongside the national eschatology represented by the Rabbis. It is linked with the latter by many ideas, but is differentiated from it by a quite different understanding of God,

587

the world, and man. The world of ideas in Apocalyptic is very varied and anything but uniform; in the following discussion we must characterize only its most important common features.

1. The Doctrine of the Two Ages. The essential feature of Apocalyptic is its dualism which, in various expressions, dominates its thought-world. Above all, in the doctrine of the Two Ages, in the dualistic time-scheme of world eras (ὁ αἰὼν οὗτος and ὁ αἰὼν μέλλων), the entire course of the world is comprehended. *This Age* is definitely detached from the *Age to come*, and therefore the words *"this"* and *"to come"* are not simply time-divisions, but have a qualitative significance: *this Age* is temporary and perishable, the *Age to come* is imperishable and eternal. This idea first becomes explicit as a theory in the later Apocalyptic (4 Esd. and syr. Bar.), but it is in fact present already in the oldest Apocalypses. It finds symbolic expression as early as Daniel, in the contrast between the four kingdoms and the stone, or Son of man, who destroys the former and so brings in the eternal kingdom (Dan. 2 and 7). The national eschatology also is acquainted with the Two-Ages doctrine, but here, up to the 2nd century A.D., *the coming Olam* is the continuation within the world of *this Olam* in the glorious earthly kingdom of the Messiah (cf. Volz, *Eschatologie*, pp. 64ff., 71f., 166f.). According to the Apocalyptic conception, on the other hand, the new Age is of a transcendent kind: it breaks in from the beyond in supernatural fashion, through divine intervention and without human activity, and puts an end to this world-era. This thought finds expression, in a particularly impressive fashion, in the image of the stone which "broken off without the action of human hand, struck the iron and clay feet of the image and crushed them", and its interpretation, "The God of heaven shall set up a kingdom which shall remain for ever indestructible, and the dominion shall not be left to other people. It will crush and destroy all these kingdoms, but itself shall stand for ever" (Dan. 2:34, 44; cf. 7:11–14, 18). This end is extreme: it is judgment, a destruction of this world and the simultaneous appearance of a new one, a "new heaven and a new earth" (eth. Enoch 45:4f.; 91:16, etc.), a "new creation" (eth. Enoch 72:1; 4 Esd. 7:75; syr. Bar. 32:6, etc.). The dualism of the Two-Ages doctrine recognizes no continuity between the time of this world and of that which is to come: "For behold, the days are coming when everything that has come into being will be given over to destruction, and it will be as if it had never been" (syr. Bar. 31:5). Between the two Ages there is a qualitative difference, and this comes to its clearest expression in Dan. 7 with the contrast of the beasts rising from the sea and the "man" coming from heaven (cf. also 4 Esd. 7:52–61).

This eschatological dualism is the essential characteristic of Apocalyptic so far as its contents are concerned: it distinguishes it fundamentally even from those texts which possess a formal similarity to Apocalyptic and have enriched its language and imagery (e.g. Ezekiel). The old must first entirely pass away before the new, the holy, can be established as the final state. This dualism is not absolute or metaphysical, but temporal, and is thereby different from the dualism of Gnosis. God is Creator and Lord of both Ages (see under No. 4).

2. Pessimism and Hope of the Beyond. The other-worldly character of the coming Age implies an extreme devaluation of this Age, the so-called apocalyptic pessimism.

The real baseness and transitoriness of this world-era is symbolized mythologically by the idea of the dominion over it of Satan and evil powers, but it is conveyed also by the notion of its growing physical and moral *degeneration*. On the physical decline, see the image of the four metals in Dan. 2 or the statement of Esra:

> For the world has lost its youthfulness,
> The times draw near to old age.
> (4 Esd. 14:10; cf. 5:55; syr. Bar. 85:10).

The moral degeneration is represented for the Apocalyptic writers by a decay of all morality and the increase of godlessness, which culminates in an assembling of the hostile powers to struggle with the saints and with God himself in a final conflict (Dan. 7:19–25; eth. Enoch 93:9; 4 Esd. 13, and often). The Apocalyptic writers devote their special interest to the final evil time (the so-called *Messianic Woes*), which is their own present and immediate future, and elaborate it in various ways. The natural ageing of the world and the moral and religious decay of mankind culminate in a cosmic catastrophe in which *this Age* perishes in order to make way for the new:

> Then the world shall return to the silence of old for seven days, like as in the first beginning, so that no man shall remain. After the seven days, the Age which still sleeps shall awake and that which is transitory shall perish (4 Esd. 7:30f.).

In this pessimism the basic thought of apocalyptic dualism is clearly expressed: it indicates the radical discontinuity between *this Age* and *the Age to come*, and consequently the strict other-ness of the latter.

To the depreciation of this Age there corresponds an intensification of the desire for and speculation about the Beyond. The apocalyptic writers compensate for their sorrow at the affliction of *this world* by fantastic pictures of the after-life, the glory of the blessed and the torments of the impious. It is intended that knowledge concerning the other-ness of the divine world should be conveyed in this fantasy. As it is brought about in wonderful ways—in which resurrection and judgment form the chief acts (4 Esd. 7:32–38)—so it is itself wonderful and divine. We need only refer in passing to the various images of the *coming Age* (new creation, new heaven and new earth, heavenly Jerusalem, Paradise). Its characteristics are incorruptibility (4 Esd. 7:31) and eternity (Dan. 2:44; eth. Enoch 91:17; slav. Enoch 65:7f.; syr. Bar. 44:11f.).

3. Universalism and Individualism. With what has been said up to this point another feature of Apocalyptic has already become clear, namely, its universalism. Its temporal horizon is incomparably wider than that of the national eschatology, for it reaches from the creation to the dissolution of the world, and the sphere in which the events take place is not limited to the earth, with Palestine and Jerusalem as the focal points, but includes earth, heaven and the underworld (cosmological speculations, the idea of judgment on the angels). Within this cosmic-universal framework the Jewish people does not play the central and sustaining role it does in the national eschatology, not even when a strong Jewish national colouring can be traced in many Apocalypses. The trend in apocalyptic modes of thought is unmistakably universalistic. Daniel can symbolize the whole of world-history in a statue made of four metals or in four beasts, without even mentioning Israel; and even when Israel's history is narrated, it is done in a framework which is as universal as possible, through a kind of regression to the creation (Vision of Bulls, eth. Enoch 85–90; Apocalypse of Ten Weeks, eth. Enoch 93; 91. 12–17; Vision of Clouds, syr. Bar. 53–71). This universalistic trend explicitly influences the description of the eschatological events, for three of them—resurrection, world judgment, world dissolution—are on a cosmic scale. The apocalyptic writer sees the world and mankind as a unity and as a whole, and therefore as something over against God.

Just as the fate of all mankind is drawn into the apocalyptic drama, so man no longer stands as a member of the sacred Jewish race or of the heathen nations, but as an individual before God. From this stems the thought of individual resurrection and of individual judgment (Dan. 12:1ff., etc.). Hence there is a demand in this Age to observe the law and to practise righteousness, always as an individual (cf. the ethical exhortations in the Apocalypses). Man must prove his righteousness as an individual in order to stand firm in the judgment.

4. Determinism and Imminent Expectation. Alongside dualism,

the outstanding characteristic of the apocalyptic thought-world is determinism. God has fore-ordained everything: all that happens happens precisely according to the fixed plan of God, which human plans and actions can neither advance nor hinder.

> He said to me: In the beginning of the world,
> Before the portals of heaven stood,
> Before the blast of the wind blew,
> Before the peals of thunder sounded,
> Before the flashes of lightning shone,
> Before the foundations of Paradise were laid,
> Before the beauty of its flowers was seen,
> Before the powers of the earthquake were established,
> Before the innumerable hosts of angels were gathered,
> Before the heights of the air were lifted,
> Before the spaces of heaven were named,
> Before the footstool of Zion was established,
> Before the years of the present were reckoned,
> Before the designs of sin were repudiated,
> But those who gather the treasure of faith were sealed,—
> Then did I consider all this, and through me
> And none other it came into being:
> So also shall the End come through me and none other!
> (4 Esd. 6:1–6.)

God created both Ages ("The Most High created not one Age, but two", 4 Esd. 7:50; "The Most High created this world for many, but the future age for a few", 4 Esd. 8:1). In fact, he created all things at the same time, even the Eschata, the coming Age "which now sleeps" (4 Esd. 7:31), the sacred persons and the sacred joys of the Age to come; they are pre-existent and the seer can see them either in the world above or descending from it (Dan. 7:13; eth. Enoch 39: 3ff.; 48:3, 6; 49:2; 4 Esd. 13:36).

For everything God has set its *measure*, and everything proceeds without interference or recall:

> God has weighed the world in the balance,
> By measure has he measured the hours
> And by number has he numbered the times (seasons),
> He will not disturb nor stir them,
> Until the said measure be fulfilled. (4 Esd. 4:36ff.)

Since everything has its time precisely determined, the end of this Age can be calculated, either by reckoning its entire duration from the creation (in which case different conclusions may be arrived at; cf. Volz. *op. cit.*, pp. 143f.), or by reckoning from a point within history (in which case information is provided by the apocalyptic writers from Daniel on in complex and obscure tricks with numbers; cf. Volz, *op. cit.*, pp. 142f.), or by observing the *signs of the times*. But these calculations are always determined by the conviction that the End is very near at hand.

This conviction about the predetermined character of all that happens and about the nearness of the End also stands behind the division of history into periods (cf. p. 585 above). From the standpoint of the imminent End, the Apocalyptist sees history complete, just as it was seen by God in the very beginning, as a unity and as a whole, so much so indeed that all the movements of history are levelled out and become of no interest, and the division of history into periods lies in the free choice of the individual writer. Whether he takes history in his view by applying the Four-Ages doctrine of Hesiod or by using the Biblical accounts, whether he gives Israel prominence or not, whether he divides it into four, seven, ten or twelve periods, is of no importance. What matters is not history itself nor the activity of God within it—one knows, of course, that it proceeds according to his prehistoric plan—but solely the demonstration of its completedness and so of one's own historical position as immediately preceding the End. "Apocalyptic really was concerned only with the last generation of Israel which, according to its own conviction, was on the point of entering into the last things. Therefore it is comparatively unimportant whether the history of God's people is described at one time in detail, at another in concise terms" (G. von Rad, *Theologie des Alten Testaments*, II, 1960, p. 317).

This imminent expectation is expressed in the most varied ways: not only in surveys and divisions of history, in reflections on the world's duration, in observation of the *signs of the times* and calculations of the end, but also in the existence and publication of apocalypses; for these books by figures of past history were to be made public only at the End of Days (Dan. 12:4, 9; eth. Enoch 105:1; 4 Esd. 12:37f.; 14:7f. etc.). All this, however, does not mean that the imminent expectation had to be stimulated: it is in fact completely genuine. It is expressed with convincing directness in the passionate questions concerning the End which extend through all the Apocalypses (Dan. 8:13; 12:5ff.; 4 Esd. 6:59; syr. Bar. 26; 81:3, etc.) and often bear upon them the marks of eschatological impatience:

> And I answered and said: How long? When shall these things come to pass? Wherefore is our life so short and miserable? But he answered and said: Art thou not wanting to hasten more than the Most High? For thou desirest haste for thine own sake, but the Most High for the sake of many (4 Esd. 4:33f.; cf. eth. Enoch 97:3, 5; 104:3).

The distresses of the present (the Maccabean period, the destruction of Jerusalem, etc.) are reflected in this kind of impatience; but these, however, are only the occasion, not the cause, of the apocalyptic mood of the End, else the latter would have disappeared with the former; rather this mood is general (Dan. 2;7; 11:21–12:4; eth. Enoch 93:9f.; 4 Esd. 4:48–50; 5:55).

> For the youth of the world is past; the strength of the creation has long ago come to its end, and the approach of the times is (already) at hand and (indeed already) passed by. For the pitcher is near to the well, the ship to harbour, the caravan to the city, and life to its conclusion (syr. Bar. 85:10).

This cosmological statement makes it clear that the conviction concerning the nearness of the End is rooted in the deep levels of the apocalyptic understanding of the world.

G. von Rad raises the question "whether Apocalyptic has still, in general, an existential relation to the dimension of history" and "whether this conception is not the signal for a serious loss of history, whether, behind this gnosticizing understanding of the termination which people can measure and even calculate, there does not stand a fundamentally unhistorical type of thought, since it has eliminated even the phenomenon of contingency' (*op. cit.*, 317; 318f.). His question really implies its answer. He might even speak, like R. Bultmann (*Geschichte und Eschatologie*, 1958, p. 35) of a "complete de-historicizing of history through Apocalyptic".* In contrast to this, D. Rössler, in his pretentious little book (*Gesetz und Geschichte*), puts forward the curious thesis that the essential interest of Apocalyptic lies in history, and actually in the history of Israel. He can put forward this view only by ignoring, to a large extent, the eschatology and imminent expectation of Apocalyptic. He ignores other things too: for example, in spite of occasional mention, Daniel and Noth's essay on "Das Geschichtsverständnis der alttestamentlichen Apokalyptik", the dualism, and the doctrine of the Two Ages, to name only the most important. Consequently he misunderstands the function which the historical surveys have in the eschatologically oriented thought-world of Apocalyptic, and even his correct and often interesting observations do not find their fitting place in the apocalyptic system of co-ordinates. The entire presentation is so one-sided as to have no longer any value. Since the essential thing in Apocalyptic has been missed out, the book is scarcely a lasting contribution to the understanding of this religio-historical phenomenon.

* The earlier English edition of this work, *History and Eschatology*, 1957, does not contain this exact phrase; but for the idea of which it is a convenient summary, see there pp. 27–37, esp. 37.—Trans.

5. Lack of Uniformity. In view of what has been said, the fact that the world of ideas of Apocalyptic is uniform only in its basic structure, but lacks that uniformity and harmony in its expressions, will not cause any surprise. By way of addition, we need only refer to the variations in the conception of the Saviour-figure. The central figure of the national eschatology, the Davidic Messiah, is completely absent from many of the Apocalypses: in them it is God or an angel of God who brings in the salvation and judgment and replaces the old Age by the new (Dan. 2;7; 12:1–4; Apocalypse of Ten Weeks, eth. Enoch 93; 91; Ass. Mos.). Where world-judgment plays such an important role, the figure of the national, earthly Saviour-King is out of place. It is replaced occasionally by the pre-existent, transcendent Judge and Redeemer figure, the Son of Man (eth. Enoch 37–71; 4 Esd. 13) who draws to himself many of the titles and traits of the Davidic Messiah, without our being permitted to speak of a fusion of the two figures. Of course, the expectation of the Davidic Messiah is not allowed to disappear completely. He appears in the Vision of Bulls in eth. Enoch, completely without motive, suddenly and without his having anything to do, after the judgment of the world has already been consummated and the new world brought in (90. 37). In 4 Esd. 7 the national and transcendent expectations are combined in such a way that, at the end of this Age, a Messianic inter-regnum lasting 400 years is inserted; at the end of this period, the Messiah and all men die, whereupon this Age sinks back into the silence of the Beginning, the judgment of the world takes place and the new Age appears (7:26–31). Less successful combinations are found in syr. Bar. (for an analysis of which cf. Volz, *op. cit.*, pp. 40f.). Test. Levi 18 promises the figure of a priestly Messiah, and this has parallels in the Qumran texts but, in contrast, is of a transcendent kind (1 QS 9. 11; 1 QSa 2. 11–21; cf. M. Burrows, *More Light on the Dead Sea Scrolls*, 1958, pp. 308ff.; A. Dupont-Sommer, *The Essene Writings from Qumran*, 1961, p. 94 n. 3; pp. 108f.). How far this lack of uniformity in the conception of the Saviour is due to literary complexity or to the reworking of heterogeneous traditions would require detailed investigation. The same is true of the complexity of other apocalyptic themes, but that of the Saviour has been briefly summarized here because of its significance for Christian Apocalyptic.

(*d*) ORIGIN. The problem as to the origin or the rise of Apocalyptic and the "*Sitz im Leben*" of the Apocalypses is still unresolved and can be treated only briefly here.

Without doubt the influx of foreign ideas, especially the cosmological dualism of Iranian origin (the doctrine of the Two Ages, determinism), played an important role in the rise of Jewish

Apocalyptic. But the essential problem of how far an under-standing of God, the world and mankind so opposed to the basic convictions of the OT could have been taken over by Israel has not been answered, but only presented, especially since this influx must have taken place in post-exilic times (the Persian and Hellenistic periods) when "Israel" consolidated itself as a theo-cracy and sought to shield itself from all foreign influences. O. Plöger (*Theokratie und Eschatologie*, 1959) has investigated this problem and he concludes that it was eschatologically-stimulated circles in the post-exilic community (*c*. 400–200 B.C.), who stood in a certain opposition to the non-eschatological theocracy and who were therefore more and more forced into the role of sec-tarians, who were the "soft spots" on which the foreign ideas had influence. It is in these circles, to which he traces back, with good reason, the "anonymous additions" to the prophetic books (e.g. Is. 24–27; Zech. 12–14, etc.) that he thinks the beginnings of Apocalyptic are located; it then unfolded itself powerfully in the distresses of the Maccabean period.

While acknowledging foreign influence, other scholars have seen in Apocalyptic the continuation of prophecy (so most recently H. H. Rowley, *The Relevance of Apocalyptic*, [2]1955). On this point we must ask whether this was the intention of the Apocalyptic writers and whether it is actually the case. The first question should, in my opinion, be answered in the affirmative. The "anonymous additions" to the prophets should certainly be understood as continuing interpretation—though the fact that these additions were not characterized as such, but were "ascribed" to the prophets in the proper sense of the word, so that anonymity borders on pseudonymity, is a sign that the authors in question did not consider themselves prophets. The same is shown in the real, pseudonymous, Apocalyptic. When, for instance, Daniel interprets the seventy years mentioned in Jer. 25:11ff.; 29:10 as seventy weeks of years, and when the angel says to Daniel, "Seventy weeks of years are fixed for thy people . . . till vision and prophet are sealed" (Dan. 9:2, 20–27), the apoca-lyptic writer's understanding of himself is clear: he is not himself a prophet, but rather the authentic interpreter of prophecy, and as such is the legitimate successor to the prophets. That such a self-understanding is not the property of Daniel alone is shown by syr. Bar., in which a conscious reflection on the relation to prophecy is shown. Here we find the well-known sentence which can easily be interpreted as an admission of decadence ("But now . . . the prophets have lain down to sleep" 85:3), but this provides only a partial view; the rest is made clear by the book as a whole. Baruch conveys to Jeremiah God's command to leave

Jerusalem (2:1ff.; 5:5ff.), likewise, after the destruction, to remove to Babylon with the prisoners, while he himself (Baruch) remains in Jerusalem at the divine bidding.

> Say to Jeremiah that he go forth and take care of the prisoners of the people to Babylon. But do thou linger here in the ruins of the city and I will make known to thee after these days what will happen at the end of days (syr. Bar. 10. 2f.).

Baruch receives his comprehensive vision, acts as the messenger of God to the elders (44–46) and people (77), writes to the exiles, not only like Jeremiah to those in Babylon (Jer. 29) but also to those in Assyrian captivity (78–86), and is convinced that he knows and says better things than the prophets (10:3; 85:4f.). The self-awareness of the Apocalyptic writer might then be described as follows: the prophets have disappeared; the Apocalyptists have taken their place and continue their work in other, but better ways.

The other question, whether Apocalyptic is actually a continuation of OT prophecy, should in my opinion, with M. Buber (*Kampf um Israel*, 1933, pp. 50–67) and G. von Rad (*Theologie des AT* II, 1960, pp. 314–328), be answered in the negative. The dualism, determinism and pessimism of Apocalyptic form the gulf which separates it from prophecy.

> The prophetic belief in the End is in all essentials autochthonous, whereas the apocalyptic is really built up from elements of Iranian dualism. Accordingly, the former predicts a termination of creation, the latter its dissolution, its replacement by another and completely good world; the former allows the now aimless powers, "evil", to find their way to God and change to good, the latter sees good and evil finally separated at the end of days, the one redeemed, the other unredeemed for ever; the former believes in the sanctification of the earth, the latter despairs of it as hopelessly ruined; the former allows the original creative will of God to be fulfilled without remainder, the latter makes the faithless creation powerful over the Creator, in that it compels him to surrender Nature. . . .
>
> The Apocalyptic writers wish to assume an irrevocably fixed future event; therefore they are rooted in Iranian ideas which divided history into equal thousand-year cycles and fixed, with numerical accuracy, the end of the world, the final triumph of good over evil. It was otherwise with the prophets of Israel: they prophesied "to the converted", that is to say, they did not state something which would happen in any event, but something which would happen, if those summoned to conversion were not converted. (M. Buber, *op. cit.*, pp. 61–63.)

On the basis of a penetrating analysis of the prophetic tradition, von Rad comes to the same conclusion: he summarizes the irreconcilable difference in the pregnant formula of "the in-compatibility of the understanding of history in Apocalyptic with that in the prophets" (*op. cit.*, p. 316).

The earlier theories on the spiritual home of Apocalyptic—the Apocalypses are "folk-books" (W. Bousset, E. Stauffer) or the esoteric literature of the Rabbis (A. Schlatter, J. Jeremias)—would scarcely be advocated today. Attention may be given rather to the increasing tendency, under the influence of the discoveries from the Dead Sea, to establish an "Essene" origin for Apocalyptic. Among the texts found at Qumran are fragments of the Book of Enoch, the Testaments of the XII Patriarchs (Levi and Naphtali) and of Jubilees. In terminology and ideas there are points of connection: the characteristically broken dualism, which marks the apocalyptic doctrine of the Two Ages, also marks the Qumran teaching on the Two Spirits, and here and there a strong expectation of the imminent End is alive. But really the material, in my opinion, does not yet provide convincing conclusions. The fact that the Book of Enoch was read in Qumran does not prove that it originated there. The eschatological texts of the Qumran community differ, in form and content, from the Jewish Apoca-lypses. The relevant passages in the Manual of Discipline, the War Scroll, the commentaries on Habakkuk and Nahum, as well as the other fragmentary commentaries on the prophetic books, are not Apocalypses in the "form-historical" sense of the word, although it may be otherwise in the case of the "Pseudo-Daniel Apocalypse" from Cave IV (cf. Dupont-Sommer, *op. cit.*, pp. 320ff.). Differences in content may be shown with reference to the saving figures—the Teacher of Righteousness, the Prophet and the Two Messiahs are to be found in this combination in none of our Apocalypses,—and also with reference to the nature of the events of the End—in the Qumran texts, these are earthly; in Apocalyptic, and even in those parts of the Book of Enoch known in Qumran, they are transcendent. So some considerations resist the acceptance of the theory of an Essene origin of Apoca-lyptic.

Von Rad has vigorously tried to make probable the view that *Wisdom* (Hochmah) is "the real native-soil" of Apocalyptic (*op. cit.*, pp. 319ff.): Daniel, Enoch and Ezra are characterized as "wise" (Dan. 1:3ff.; 2:48; eth. Enoch 32:2–4; 4 Esd. 14:50; dream-interpretation is the domain of the wise, Dan. 2:30; 5:11; Gen. 41:8, 39); the genre of the figurative utterances is a "tradi-tional Sapiential form of teaching"; the material also is, to a large extent, of Wisdom character; the knowledge of the cosmos which eth. Enoch 8:72–79 in particular displays, and of history, i.e. more precisely the kind of "presentation which is empty of interest in salvation-history and only enumerates the events", of which Sir. 44–50 is the first example. We would scarcely wish to take away from the strength of von Rad's argument, but the fact that there is no eschatology and imminent expectation in the Wisdom literature corresponding to the presence of Wisdom-motifs in the Apocalypses forms an insurmountable objection to his thesis. The eschatological ideas and the expectation are doubtless primary and so fundamental that the Wisdom elements must be evaluated as colouring, and not as the basis. But the fact that connections with "Wisdom" exist—cf. also eth. Enoch 42[1]; 4 Esd. 5:9f.—is undeniable and this would make intelligible the association of Apocalyptic with Gnosis which von Rad has also stressed.

With all necessary reserve and with proper readiness to revise opinions, we may accept the view that the home of Apocalyptic is in those eschatologically-excited circles which were forced more and more by the theocracy into a kind of conventicle existence. In their eschatological expectation, dualistic ideas and esoteric thought these have a certain connection with the Qumran community; in their organization, materials and forms they have a certain connection with "Wisdom" circles. The origin and, in particular, the history of these circles are not yet clear.

The Apocalypses represent the literature of these conventicles. They were frequently written out of actual distresses and for the strengthening of the community in them (Dan., Ass. Mos., 4 Esd., syr. Bar), not for the instruction of an interested public in knowledge and prudence, as Wisd. Sol. and Sir. were, even though many Apocalypses include an "encyclopaedic erudition" (large parts of eth. Enoch, gk. Bar., slav. Enoch); their wisdom is a secret wisdom. This esotericism and the real concern with the strengthening and comforting of the particular community mark out these works as the literature of conventicles.

(*e*) CONTINUATION IN THE CHRISTIAN PERIOD. The thought-world and temper of Jewish Apocalyptic were shared, to a large extent, by the early Christian movement as well, especially the Palestinian and Hellenistic-Jewish Christian wing. In fact, as has already been said, it took over the literary documents of the former, the Apocalypses, and "christianized" them by means of a rewriting of varying kinds and intensity. It took over also the literary form and produced numerous works of its own in this genre. The Christian Apocalypses presented in Sections XVI–XVIII are the oldest and the most characteristic; but the stock is much greater. H. Weinel (*EYXAPIΣTHPION* Part 2, 1923,

---

[1] But this chapter is probably interpolated: cf. E. Sjöberg, *Der Menschensohn im Äthiopischen Henochbuch*, 1946, pp. 34f.

pp. 141–173) gives a survey of "The Later Christian Apocalyptic", and two of the Apocalypses mentioned by him, those of Paul and of Thomas, are to be found below in Section XVIII. Within the limits of this book no reference can be made to the others, but the reader is referred to Weinel's essay.

The number of Christian or Christian-Gnostic Apocalypses will probably be increased by the discoveries of Nag-Hammadi, but unfortunately the texts are still not available (Jan. 1962).[1] In the meantime we are referred to the thought-provoking and interesting survey by Jean Doresse, *The Secret Books of the Egyptian Gnostics* (ET), 1960, pp. 146–248. Here there are writings with the titles *Apocalypse of . . .* or *Revelation(s) of . . .*, but the contents of these appear to be extensively cosmological and soteriological, and not of an eschatological-apocalyptic nature. On the other hand, apocalyptic material appears in writings with other labels (Gospel; Letter) or without any such title (cf. Text No. 24 in Doresse, pp. 187f.). The "Sacred Book of the Invisible Great Spirit" concludes with the typical Apocalyptic secret formula:

> This Book, the Great Seth wrote it in the writings of a hundred and thirty years: he left it in the mountain called Charax so that in the last times and in the last instants, it might become manifest (Doresse, *op. cit.*, p. 180).

The title at the end of the work reads "The Gospel of the Egyptians, a book written from God, sacred and hidden . . .". It is a matter of Gnostic revelatory writings which belong to various literary genres. The designations of form (Gospel, Apocalypse) which these writings often carry in their titles should not be understood in the traditional sense as literary characterizations. Their significance is evidently more or less that of the *Revelation* or *Good News* of the redeeming Gnosis. The extent to which the "Apocalypses" and other texts from Nag Hammadi stand apart from Jewish-Christian Apocalyptic in form, style and content cannot be gauged on the basis of the present state of their editing (cf. also H. Ch. Puech, Vol. I, pp. 231–362).

Christian Apocalyptic, like the Jewish, is pseudepigraphical: only the author of the Johannine Apocalypse writes under his own name (so does Hermas, but his book is not a real Apocalypse). All the others are presented under the authority of great names: Jesus (e.g. the Synoptic Apocalypse, the Testamentum Domini), various Apostles (Peter, Paul, Thomas, John, Bartholomew, Philip, etc.), the mother of Jesus, Mary; even OT figures were

---

[1] Cf. now Böhlig-Labib, *Koptisch-gnostische Apokalypsen aus Codex V von Nag Hammadi* (Wiss. Zeitschr. der Martin-Luther-Universität, Halle-Wittenberg, Sonderband 1963). This contains an Apocalypse of Paul (not the one mentioned above), two Apocalypses of James, and an Apocalypse of Adam (R.M.W.).

used as authorities for Christian Apocalypses (Abraham, Ezra, Zephaniah and Elijah). Visions and raptures are the usual means of revelation.

So far as content is concerned, these Christian books took over, on the widest scale, Jewish material, whether it existed in "traditions" (fixed ideas, imagery and schemata) or in written documents. But through its concern with the Parousia of Christ there occurs a concentration on this one theme, which means a sharp reduction in the Jewish materials and devices. Above all, the surveys of history disappear; they pass over from Apocalyptic to Apologetic (e.g. Luke and Theophilus of Antioch) and exchange the eschatological function for that which is concerned with salvation-history. On the other hand, Christian Apocalyptic takes over much non-Jewish, heathen and Gnostic material, especially ideas concerning the Beyond (Ascens. Isaiah, Apocalypse of Peter).

The themes of Christian Apocalyptic became more limited the longer it continued. At first, the imminent expectation of the Parousia was the organizing principle, but then, with the delay of the return of Christ, interest moved to the Anti-Christ and things associated with him, and to the Beyond, to Heaven and its blessedness, to Hell and its miseries. The Anti-Christ and the After-life, which in the New Testament are only subsidiary themes of the Parousia expectation, are the two main themes around which Christian Apocalyptic revolves from the middle of the 2nd century.

2. THE SIBYLLINES

The Sibyllines represent the Apocalyptic of Hellenistic Diaspora Judaism (from which only one real Apocalypse is known, slav. Enoch, which goes back to a Greek original). In the second half of the 2nd century B.C. it seized on the Greek Sibylline literature as a means of literary propaganda. By that time the Greek Sibyllines had long since found their definitive form— hymns, in hexameters, which contained prophecies of disastrous content, and which were attributed to the ancient Sibyl who kept prophesying through the ages. In these prophecies it was a matter of *vaticinium ex eventu*, of "a kind of Greek history in future form" (J. Geffcken, *Apokr.* 2, p. 400). Diaspora Judaism adopted this literary genre in such a way that it inserted in the pagan texts prophecies for Israel and events of the actual recent past and present, also attacks on polytheism, propaganda for monotheism, even eschatological promises and threats, or it even created entirely new Sibyllines for this content. The Jewish Sibyllines are related in various respects to the Apocalypses: formally, in respect of pseudonymity, that is, by the attributing of the statements to an ancient sacred authority, and in respect of the description of history in the future; then, as far as content is concerned, in respect of the eschatological material. Reference has already been made to the suggestion that the two Apocalyptic features mentioned stem from the Sibyllines. There is, however, a basic difference in the function of the two genres. While the Apocalypses are fundamentally a conventicle-literature designed to strengthen a particular community, the Jewish Sibyllines originated as missionary propaganda writings which were turned, from the very beginning, towards those outside; their "Sitz im Leben" is originally the mission of Diaspora Judaism to the heathen.

In the second half of the 2nd century A.D. the Christians took over from Hellenistic Diaspora Judaism this literary genre, which seemed very suitable for the struggle to maintain and assert their faith in a pagan world. In their reception of the Jewish Sibyllines they proceeded in the same way as the Jews had done with the pagan. Details of the early history and development of Christian Sibyllines are found in XVII. 2 below.

3. PROPHECY

The prophecy of the period in question (*c.* 200 B.C.–A.D. 200) cannot be treated in the same way as Apocalyptic or the Sibyllines because, unlike these and unlike the writing prophets of the Old Testament, it has left behind no literary documents. Nevertheless, its significance in Judaism and certainly in early Christianity should not be underestimated. For knowledge concerning it we are dependent on reports about it, on literary-critical and form-historical analyses, and on sparse testimonies.

(*a*) JUDAISM in the Hellenistic-Roman period was by no means without prophets (as a popular theory maintains) but was in fact rich in prophetic figures (cf. R. Meyer, *ThWtb* VI, pp. 813–828). According to Josephus, they are to be found among almost all the groups of the Jewish people. Concerning the Essenes in particular, he reports that they possessed and cultivated the gift of prophecy (Bell. 2. 159), and he records the names of Essene prophets and the contents of many of their prophecies. Moreover he mentions prophetically-gifted Pharisees at the court of Herod (Ant. 17. 43ff.), tells of a Zealot "pseudo-prophet" in the last hours of the Temple (Bell. 6. 283–286), of a mass ecstasy of priests (*ibid.* 299) and of the peasant Jesus ben Chananiah who alarmed Jerusalem for years with his sinister prophesying of disaster (*ibid.* 300–309). Rabbinic sources ascribe to many scholars the gift of prophecy, as well as other wonderful abilities, and it is well known that R. Akiba appeared as a prophet of the Messiah Simon bar Cosiba.

In spite of the variety of the phenomena and in spite of the tendentious description in Josephus, we can recognize some types of prophecy (the vision of the future which many Rabbis were supposed to have had on their death-beds is here left out of consideration).

First, there is the spiritual and topical interpretation of the prophetic writings, as it was practised by the Essenes (Jos. Bell. 2. 159; an example is the Habakkuk "Commentary" from Qumran; particularly instructive for the spiritual understanding of what God actually wanted to say through the prophets is 1QpHab. 7:1–5; a similar phenomenon is found at Dan. 9:1–3, 20–27). The fact that this kind of interpretation was not purely academic and was not confined to the Essenes is shown by the following: in the time of the Jewish war "an ambiguous oracle which was found in Holy Scripture"—one readily thinks of Dan. 7:13f.—and which prophesied world-dominion "to one from this country" was openly and violently disputed, and people differed in their answers to the question whether it signified salvation or disaster for Israel (Jos. Bell. 6. 312f.). In both cases an eschatological occurrence is seen in the fulfilment of the prophecy.

Then there are the different kinds of active prophecy, the vision into the future. We may divide these into prophecy concerned with salvation and that concerned with catastrophe, but that brings us no nearer to its essence.

Professional prophesying, which a man may learn, is represented, alongside the first-mentioned, among the Essenes. The Essene Judas, who prophesied destruction to Antigonus, was accompanied "by his followers and confidants who stayed with him in order to learn how to predict the future" (Jos. Ant. 13. 311). Prophets like these announced their fate to individuals, and in particular to rulers (Menachem to the young Herod, Ant. 15. 373ff.), sometimes in the form of the interpretation of a dream (Ant. 17. 345ff.).

A special type is to be seen in the "messianic prophets" (R. Meyer) or the prophetic pretenders to messiahship, who promised to the people a startling authentication of their case and the arrival of the imminent salvation. To this type belong the Samaritan who promised to show to his followers the Temple-furniture which had been hidden by Moses on Gerizim (Jos. Ant. 18. 85ff.), Theudas, who promised to the people the repetition of Joshua's miracle in the cleaving of Jordan (Ant. 20. 97f.; Acts 5:36), the "false leaders", the "impostors" who again and again led the people into the wilderness (Bell. 2. 258ff., Ant. 20. 167f.) and the prophet from Egypt who held out the prospect of a repetition of the Jericho miracle at Jerusalem (Ant. 20. 169ff.; Acts 21:38). These prophets were convinced that the eschatological age of salvation would correspond to the early history of Israel (hence the wilderness and Moses typologies), that the age of salvation was imminent and that they were called as the second Moses or Joshua to bring things to a head. These messianic pretenders are exponents of the imminent expectation of the national eschatology.

Finally a type of prophet which seems to come closest to those in the Old Testament—men who, in a definite political situation, brought messages from God. The most impressive figure among these is that Jesus ben Chananiah who, on the Feast of Tabernacles in A.D. 62, four years before the outbreak of the war, appeared in Jerusalem and by his woeful pronouncements threw into panic a city which was completely at peace. Insensitive to cruelties and kindnesses alike, he continued his disastrous prophesying unflinchingly for seven years and five months till he fell, shortly before the taking of the city (Jos. Bell. 6. 300ff.). Rather similar is the Zealot who, a few hours before the burning of the Temple, urged 6000 men to their death; this was no "false prophet", but a prophet filled with the imminent eschatological expectation, who dragged the despairing masses along with him by means of an oracle of deliverance. How inextricably religious enthusiasm and national fanaticism were bound up in the Messianic hope of Judaism, especially in times of crisis, is shown by the figure of R. Akiba who allied himself, religiously and politically, to the rebellion against Hadrian, and who, with the pledge of his entire personal authority, advanced the cause of Simon ben Cosiba as Messiah.

There were certainly even more types of prophets, but the tendency of Josephus to give a Hellenized picture of Judaism and to conceal Jewish messianism as much as possible makes it difficult to find out the personal awareness of those figures who are called and characterized by him as false leaders, cheats and bandits. He presents with sympathetic understanding only the Essene and Pharisaic soothsayers and the prophets of disaster.

For this reason we are poorly informed concerning the form of prophetic statements. Josephus gives the prophecy mostly in indirect speech, and only twice, so far as I can see, in direct speech. The first is the oracle of Menachem to the young Herod, which is linked with a corroborating sign (Ant. 15. 374ff.). In this he predicts the elevation of Herod to kingship, refers to the inconstancy of fortune, exhorts him to righteousness, piety and gentleness, foretells his wickedness and threatens him with the wrath of God. In view of the Hellenistic terminology, it seems likely that Josephus is not citing the oracle verbatim, but has formulated it independently. On the other hand, he may have reproduced the calamitous cry of Jesus ben Chananiah in a literal translation:

> A voice from the sunrise,
> A voice from the sunset,
> A voice from the four winds:
>
> Woe to Jerusalem and the Temple!
> Woe to bridegroom and bride!
> Woe to the whole people! (Bell 6. 301.)

The rhythmical and metrical form of the two three-lined parts, the parallelismus membrorum and the Semitisms argue for its originality (cf. R. Meyer, *Der Prophet aus Galiläa*, 1940, pp. 46f.). This is a threatening message, without any word of rebuke at its base and without any call to repentance, which in the second strophe proclaims the unavoidability and the completeness of the destruction, and in the first asserts with uncanny impressiveness the divine origin of the oracle. The prophecies of the messianic pretenders and of the Zealot prophets of salvation can be reconstructed only roughly as far as content is concerned, but not in their formal structure. The prophetic propaganda of Akiba for Simon worked with the contemporary interpretation of the "Star of Jacob" (Num. 24:17) in terms of this leader, but even more significant than this interpretation of a traditional messianically understood prophecy in terms of a figure of the present is the statement of Akiba concerning Simon ben Cosiba, "This is the King, the Messiah!" (jer. Taan. 4. 8 (68d, 50) cited by R. Meyer, *ThWtb* VI, p. 825 and note 306). The sentence has the structure and the sense of an acclamation.

These observations may suffice to show how lively and many-sided prophecy was in Judaism at this time. These prophets believed that they were commissioned by God (as did the Essene soothsayers as well). In their messianic hopes they were religiously and politically active, but unlike the Apocalyptic writers they were not productive of literature. Their prophecy is entirely determined by the national eschatology and stands beside Apocalyptic as the expression, today difficult to grasp, but then at least as powerfully effective, of the eschatological expectation of Judaism.

John the Baptist occupies a unique position. He is a prophet, but he challenges the national hope of Judaism; he is not an Apocalyptist, although he proclaims the coming of a supernatural figure and the nearness of the end of the world; he unites radical eschatology with the old prophetic preaching of repentance and the sacramental penitence of baptism (cf. *RGG*³, III, cols. 804–808).

(*b*) THE EARLY CHRISTIAN PROPHETS (cf. *RGG*³, V, cols. 633f. and Fascher, *ibid.* cols. 634f.) are likewise charismatics but, in distinction to the Jewish prophets who were active sporadically, these form a definite "estate" in the local community which ranked in authority under the Apostles and above the teachers (1 Cor. 12:28; Eph. 2:20; 3:5; 4:11; Rev. 18:20; Acts 13:1), and they exercise their function chiefly in worship (1 Cor. 11:4; 14:23f., 29ff. and also Didache 10. 7; 11. 9). Itinerant prophets no longer belong to the New Testament period (Did. 11. 3; 13. 1: Luke traces this phenomenon back to the early period, Acts 11:27f.; 21:10). The statement of Did. 13. 1 that prophets—as distinct from the Apostles, Did. 11. 5—should remain for a rather long time in a community is probably a reflection of their original settledness. The rights which are accorded to them in Did. reflect their original significance in connection with the leading of the community, and this is borne out by Eph. which for its own area characterizes the prophets as great men of the past (Eph. 2:20; 3:5; 4:11). The early Christian prophetic movement has territorially a very varied history.

Paul gives a relatively clear picture of the function of the prophets in his churches. Prophecy is the highest charisma. The prophets possess knowledge of "mysteries" (1 Cor. 13:2) and impart it; they have the task of exhortation, of comforting, of testing and of "convicting" (1 Cor. 14:3, 24f.) but they are subject to control (1 Cor. 14:29–33, cf. Rom. 12:6; but see Did. 11. 7). We know very little, however, about the contents of this kind of prophecy; we may suppose that "mysteries" belonged to it similar to those which were revealed to Paul himself (Rom. 11:25f.; 1 Cor. 15:51f.), or other eschatological statements (like Gal. 5:21), as well as certain predictions of earthly events (like 1 Thess. 3:4; cf. Acts 11:27f.; 21:10ff.). Käsemann has made it likely that "statements of divine justice" in particular go back to the prophets, statements which lay down the eschatological *ius talionis* (1 Cor. 3:17; 14:38; 16:22); should this suggestion hold—in my opinion it is correct—it would then become understandable why the prophets possessed an authority in the Church similar to that of the Apostles.

From the Synoptic Gospels we can gain some information about Palestinian-Christian prophecy. Naturally these books, being accounts about Jesus, do not mention Christian prophets, but their emphatic warning on false prophets (Mk. 13:22 and par.) presupposes that the genuine prophet was a well-known and common figure. That Mk. 13:22 cannot mean only Jewish messianic pretenders (see above) is proved by 13:6. The polemic against Christian false prophets shows that in the region in which our oldest Gospel originated, Palestine and Syria, the problem of distinguishing between true and false prophets was a real one. Now form-critical analysis of the Synoptic tradition permits us to recognize the work of Christian prophets in the older strata of the tradition, that is, in earlier periods and in the Palestinian neighbourhood. It reveals that there are numerous "non-genuine" utterances of the Lord which cannot be considered as distortions of the original or as literary falsifications, or as emanating from discussions with the Jews or from controversies within the community, but which must be considered as utterances of men who spoke "in the name", that is, at the command and with the authority of the exalted Lord, and whose words were heard and honoured as words of the exalted Lord himself, and were repeated in the accounts of his earthly life as words of the earthly Lord. These are the people who are meant by the designation Palestinian-Christian prophets. For the understanding of their prophetic consciousness we might refer to the "heavenly letter" of Rev. 2 and 3, or to the well-known statement in Odes of Sol. 42. 6:

> And I have arisen and am among them,
> And I speak through their mouth.

Prophetic utterances which are placed on the lips of Jesus are found especially in that genre of dominical sayings which Bultmann calls "Prophetic and Apocalyptic Sayings", but also under "Legal Sayings and Christian Rules" (cf. Bultmann, *The History of the Synoptic Tradition*, ET 1963, pp. 108ff., 130ff.). It is impossible to enumerate here the words which go back to these prophets. In the prophetic utterances various forms may be distinguished; Bultmann distinguishes preaching of salvation, words of threat, words of exhortation, apocalyptic predictions, and Käsemann here also points out "statements of divine justice" (e.g. Lk. 12:8 and par.).

These observations compel us to conclude that Palestinian Christianity had a strongly pneumatic colouring and that the prophets must have had a considerable significance in the leading of the Palestinian church.

The Christian prophecy of Palestine stands in sharp contrast to the Jewish prophecy of the same period. It rejects the national eschatology and Messianology and pays homage, like the primitive church as a whole, to apocalyptic ideas. Here we find for the first time the union of prophecy and Apocalyptic, a union which finds expression again and most impressively in the author of the Apocalypse of John (see under XVI, Introduction). As far as their vocation is concerned, the prophets were not Apocalyptists, but charismatic leaders of the churches, and the seer John did not compose the Apocalypse in his capacity as prophet—for the other prophets mentioned by him wrote no such books—but at the direct command of the exalted Lord, and that means, with authentic prophetic consciousness; consequently he did not write under a pseudonym, but under his own name. Later Apocalyptic and prophecy again fall apart; all Christian apocalypses are pseudonymous.

By the end of the 1st century prophecy has lost its original significance; only in Asia Minor does it still appear to play a part, if the statements in the book of Revelation correspond to the historical situation and are not assumptions of the seer. It certainly remained alive, but it flourished more and more in the twilight of the discussion about true and false prophets (Did. 11. 7ff.; Herm. Mand. XI; Justin, Dial. 35. 3; 51. 2; 69. 1; 82. 1f.). In a church which was building more and more on the hierarchical offices and the normative tradition, it soon had no place; as such, it was suspected of being Gnostic, and about the middle of the 2nd century was forced into heresy by an orthodoxy which was in process of consolidating itself. It flourished occasionally on the edge of the church, in Elchasai at the beginning of the 2nd century and in Montanus at its end, and here also created a literary deposit. These are the only literary witnesses to early Christian prophecy that we possess.

XVI

APOCALYPTIC IN EARLY CHRISTIANITY

1. INTRODUCTION

(P. Vielhauer)

In what follows the Apocalyptic material and sketches in the early Christian literature, from the New Testament to the formation of the oldest Apocryphal Apocalypses, are described in order to make clear the background of this literature. In the survey a rather large amount of space is devoted to the texts which provide special problems, and so the presentation will be somewhat lacking in proper proportions.

1. JESUS. In the preaching of Jesus, in so far as it can still be recovered by critical methods from the Synoptic tradition, it is the concepts *Kingdom of God* and *Son of Man* which provide the strongest link with Apocalyptic. Even the authenticity of the Son of Man sayings is disputed in the critical investigations, and, in my opinion, the objections preponderate (cf. P. Vielhauer, Gottesreich und Menschensohn, Festschrift G. Dehn, 1957, pp. 51–79: for the contrary view, E. Schweizer, Der Menschensohn, *ZNW*, 50, 1959, pp. 185–209). *The sovereignty of God* is not a familiar apocalyptic concept, but it corresponds, in some measure, to the *Age to come*, the *New Creation*, the *new Heaven and the new Earth*, and expresses what these ideas intended. Jesus' preaching of the Kingdom and his vocation presuppose the apocalyptic dualism in so far as he understands the coming of God's rule not as an event within the world, but as a divine miracle which puts a definitive end to this world and to time and brings in the eternal world of God. Nonetheless, the differences from Jewish Apocalyptic are unmistakable. They are already revealed in the choice of the central concept of *the sovereignty of God*, in terms of which Jesus replaces the popular apocalyptic notions of the eschatological salvation by the thought that God is king and assumes Lordship over all things. The rigour and clarity of this concept puts an end to all descriptions of the *spectaculum mundi* and of the glory of the Beyond; only the image of a banquet as the symbol of community with God is retained. The imminent expectation also seems to link Jesus with Apocalyptic. But in addition to the statements concerning the nearness of the reign of God are those concerned with its contemporaneity, and this characteristic juxtaposition of future and present shatters the time-scheme of the Two-Ages doctrine. The question about the actual point in time

then drops out, for the meaning of the expectation consists "in the qualifying of the human situation in view of the coming of the Kingdom. Now one can no longer watch and ask about the terminal event, but only prepare oneself immediately for the Kingdom, i.e. repent" (Conzelmann, *RGG*[3], II, col. 667). Consequently surveys and divisions of history, numerical speculation and divination are absent from the preaching of Jesus. In the matter of form also, this preaching has nothing in common with Apocalyptic. Finally, the authority with which Jesus makes his appearance is not that of an Apocalyptist (an imaginary figure of the past) nor that of an Apocalyptic figure (an angel or the Son of Man); it is something too high to be rendered in categories suitable to eschatological expectation. Jesus claims that his proclamation of the reign of God and his actions, as signs of this Lordship, are the final summons of God, on the acceptance or rejection of which eternal salvation or damnation depends. To this extent, the preaching of Jesus "implies" a Christology, even if he did not make his person the object of faith (Bultmann).

2. APOCALYPTIC MATERIAL IN THE NEW TESTAMENT. (*a*) Point of departure. The primitive church could not reproduce the proclamation of Jesus without alteration, but had to include his death and resurrection in its preaching. They understood both as eschatological and soteriological events, which had taken place *according to the Scriptures* (1 Cor. 15:3ff.), i.e. as eschatological fulfilment of the prophecies of Scripture. While they first of all interpreted his death in cultic-juridical categories as an atoning sacrifice (1 Cor. 15:3; Rom. 3:25; 4:25, etc.) they interpreted his resurrection as an exaltation to God, an installation into the dignity of an eschatological Saviour. In place of the expectation of the reign of God there now appears the expectation of the Parousia of Christ, and at this point the momentous influx of apocalyptic ideas takes place. The conception of the Son of Man, now sojourning with God and coming at the end of time as Saviour and Judge from Heaven, was best suited to bring together the heavenly dignity of the Exalted One and the eschatological crisis-character of the earthly person. The national expectation of the Davidic Messiah could not, on account of Jesus' preaching and fate, be used for this purpose. The apocalyptic Son of Man ideas dominate and shape the early Christian expectation of the Parousia, even when the title *Son of Man* is replaced by other titles of dignity, for example, by *Son of God* (1 Thess. 1:10), *Kyrios* (1 Thess. 4:15ff.) or *Soter* (Phil. 3:20), which do not stem from Apocalyptic.

(*b*) The Bearers and the Forms of Apocalyptic Instruction. The oldest form of Apocalyptic communication is the saying of

Jesus. This is demonstrated not only by the numerous "non-genuine" words of Jesus with apocalyptic content which are found in the Synoptic tradition, but also by the "word of the Lord" cited by Paul in 1 Thess. 4:16f. In this fact we might discover an analogy with the pseudonymity of the Apocalypses. However, in these words it is evidently a matter of utterances of early Christian prophets which are understood as utterances of the Exalted Lord (see above, p. 606); the situation is different in the composition of such sayings and other material into an apocalyptic "address" of Jesus (on the Synoptic Apocalypse see below pp. 616ff.); here pseudonymity lies before us.

Instruction on the Parousia of Christ belonged to the main articles of the missionary preaching to the heathen (1 Thess. 1:9f.) and the bearers of this instruction were thus the apostles and missionaries. But they were clearly only transmitters, not elaborating the thought further. Paul, at any rate, speaks on this matter in his genuine epistles in a very reserved manner, bound by tradition and not at all thematically; thus, the description of the Parousia in 1 Thess. 4:15ff. is a citation which stands in association with comforting instruction on the destiny of deceased Christians; likewise, the picture of the Parousia in 1 Cor. 15:20–28 appears in the context of instruction on the resurrection of the body. In so far as we can judge from his letters Paul gave apocalyptic instruction to a large extent only in connection with the resurrection and the being "with Christ" (certainly with the help of Gnostic motifs). His reluctantly given report of the visionary experience of rapture into Paradise and into the third heaven (2 Cor. 12:1–4) had a literary sequel, the Apocalypse of Paul.

Only in the post-apostolic generation do "the Apostles of the Lord" become the bearers and the guarantors of apocalyptic tradition (Jud. 17); and so the fictitious apostolic letter is the form of their communication (2 Thess.; 2 Pet.), providing a parallel to the Apocalypses with apostolic names.

In the course of the long and by no means straight path from the simple form of the apocalyptic saying of Jesus to the developed Apocalypse there may be observed an increase in the subject-matter: first it was the Parousia and the events following it (resurrection and judgment), then it included the time immediately preceding the Parousia (with its "signs", apostasy and Anti-Christ), and finally a complete apocalyptic outline embracing the time from the present right to the End. The fact that the use of apocalyptic material and forms reflects very clearly the ups and downs of the early Christian expectation is self-evident.

(c) The Parousia. The apocalyptic utterances of Jesus on the coming Son of Man vary in their intention: statements of sacred justice (Mk. 8:38; Lk. 9:26; 12:8f.; Mt. 10:32f.), comfort (Mt. 10:23), warning (Mt. 24:26f.; Lk. 17:23f.) and threat (Mt. 24:37ff.; Lk. 17:26f.). The themes developed vary accordingly: the Parousia takes place suddenly and unequivocally, hence the challenge to constant preparedness (Mt. 24:37 and par.) and the warning against deception (Mt. 24:26f. and par.); the Son of Man is saviour of his people (Mt. 10:23) and the judge who judges according to the eschatological *ius talionis* (Mk. 8:38; Lk. 12:8 and par.). On the other hand, the word of the Lord, 1 Thess. 4:16f.—the original text of which cannot be reconstructed with certainty (cf. M. Dibelius, *Handb. z. NT*, ad loc.)—is a miniature Apocalypse which describes the event of the Parousia itself; it presents this in three acts, succeeded by the resurrection and the rapture of the faithful to meet the Lord. This, the oldest apocalyptic text in the New Testament, shows that the primitive Church had already, at a very early stage, pictured the Parousia with the aid of Apocalyptic material (examples in Dibelius, ad loc.).

The association of the Parousia and the resurrection of the dead is naturally very frequent, and this corresponds to the Jewish eschatology and the apocalyptic Son of Man ideas. It is understandable that the event of the Parousia was more and more richly endowed with apocalyptic colouring and requirements, and indeed was described by taking over Jewish texts. This is for example the case with Mk. 13:24–27 and par. (cosmic catastrophes, the appearing of the Son of Man, the gathering of the elect). Behind the description of the Parousia of Christ in the deutero-Pauline 2 Thess. (1:5–10) there lies, as Dibelius has suggested, the Jewish text of a judgment-theophany. Dibelius' reconstruction is as follows:

(This is) a sign of the righteous judgment of God: . . . for it is right in the sight of God to repay with affliction your oppressors and (to give) liberation to you who are oppressed, at the revelation of the Lord . . . from heaven with the angels of his might in flaming fire, who grants pardon to all who do not know God . . . They shall receive as punishment eternal destruction from the presence of God and from the glory of his might, when he comes . . . on that day to be glorified among his saints and to be extolled among all the faithful. (2 Thess. 1:5–10; cf. Dibelius, *op. cit.*, pp. 40–43.)

This text may be the first example of the literary expression of early Christian Apocalyptic.

(d) The Signs. While the NT authors exercise remarkable reserve in describing the events which follow on the Parousia, they have devoted all the greater attention to the time preceding it. Being an eschatological community, the early Church understood its present and its immediate future as the End-time, and the events which befell it as being in essential connection with the Christ who had come and would come again. The expression of this awareness in terms of the Mysteries and of Gnostic ideas may be left out of account here, since we are dealing only with Apocalyptic. The grievous experiences of the Church were connected with the theme, common to the entire Jewish eschatology, of a final evil period (the "Woes of the Messiah") before the appearance of the Saviour. This connection, which was equivalent to an extensive retention of traditional Jewish eschatology, was in itself natural, and moreover it was encouraged by the fact that the Church found certain features of Jewish eschatology corroborated in her own experiences (persecution; the appearance of political and religious seducers). Consequently the motifs of wars and famine, the ruin of families, the increase of tribulation to the point of excess, the appearance of the last great adversary, all find acceptance within the apocalyptic ideas of early Christianity. This linking of traditional Jewish elements with actual Christian experience has its literary deposit in the "words of the Lord", Mk. 13:5–23 and par.; Mt. 10:17–36, and—with various modifications—in the epistolary literature.

Even in the preaching of Jesus and of the Church in its earliest period (Paul), "the signs of the times" had played a part, certainly with the aim of providing knowledge of the time, but not of calculating it; that is to say, with the aim of making clear that the present is the period of decision with reference to the End, but not of outlining a picture of the future. Accordingly we find the exhortation to vigilance and constant preparedness for the reign of God in Jesus' teaching and for the Parousia of Christ in Paul (1 Thess. 5:1ff. and often).

The systematizing of this idea into an apocalyptic picture of the future presupposes that people do not believe any more that the End is immediately impending, even though a relatively imminent expectation may still exist (on the Synoptic and Johannine Apocalypses, see below pp. 616ff.; 620ff.).

The way in which such an outline, and in particular the corroboration of definite signs of the time, may even be turned against the imminent expectation is shown by the apocalypse in 2 Thess. 2:1–12. Because of its significance and its problems this passage will be treated here in a somewhat more detailed fashion. As against the opinion that the day of the Lord is immediately impending, the author claims that the great apostasy must come first and the Anti-Christ appear; only then will Christ come again. In fact, "the mystery of lawlessness" is already at work, but the appearing of the Anti-Christ is still delayed by a restraining power (τὸ κατέχον v. 6, ὁ κατέχων v. 7), and can follow only upon the elimination of the latter. All the features in this picture are traditional, but the stress, in the sense of a quenching of the imminent expectation, is new. For that reason, the restraining power becomes a matter of special interest.

The great apostasy is, along with the assault of the enemy on the people of God, a constant feature of Jewish (national and apocalyptic) eschatology (Dan. 11:31; Jubil. 23. 14–23; eth. Enoch 91. 7; Ass. Mos. 5; 4 Esd. 5:1f.; Damas. Doc. 1. 20; 5.21; 8. 19; 19. 5, 32; 1 QpHab. 2. 1–6, etc.).

The *Antichrist* represents a Christian variant on the eschatological opponent of God in Apocalyptic. This opponent must be of mythological origin, as Bousset, Gunkel and Dibelius have shown: he is a mythical monster, the adversary of God in the Creation, who, according to the ancient Eastern conception of the return of primordial time at the end of time, appears again at the End and takes up afresh his struggle against God, but is finally destroyed; in the conflict of primordial times, he was only defeated and bound. As the opponent of God, he appears in the End-time as Satan or a dragon, and in human form as well, as a tyrant or a prophet hostile to God. The experiences under pagan rulers, especially in the time of the Maccabees (Antiochus IV Epiphanes), caused the mythical monster to be identified in history with the representatives or envoys of the Devil. The figure does not appear in all Jewish Apocalypses. Whether it was developed into the figure of an anti-Messiah is questionable. Although a development of this kind has been suggested by some investigators, it is not proven. It is always a matter of an opponent of God, not of the Messiah or the Son of Man. It is therefore possible that the Antichrist is not a christianized Jewish anti-Messiah, but a Christian development of the human adversary of God found in Jewish Apocalyptic. The title "Antichrist" is found in the New Testament only in 1 Jn. 2:18, 22; 4:3; 2 Jn. 7., but the figure is present elsewhere, 2 Thess. 2:1–12, and also Mk. 13:14 and par. and Rev. 13 and 17, but with different features. 2 Thess. 2 characterizes this "adversary" of God and of all religion (v. 4a) as a tool of Satan (9a) and as an antitype of Christ: he executes deeds of power, signs and wonders, by which he wins over men (v. 9b, 10a); he takes his place in the Temple and proclaims himself to be God (v. 4b). The theme of Temple-profanation is found also in Mk. 13:14 (based on Dan. 12:11) and, in a spiritualized form, in Rev. 13:5f. The theme of self-deification occurs in Rev. 13:4, 8, 12 (cf. Ezek. 28:2) and the parallelism with Christ is extended in Rev. 13:3, 12 by the references to the mortal wound and recovery from death. In all three texts, Antichrist is a political figure, a powerful tyrant; his external authority and his power to tempt—features which 2 Thess. combines in the one figure—are assigned separately by Rev. 13 to Antichrist and to the false teachers. While the Antichrist of 2 Thess. is an individual figure, in Rev. 13, as the emperor, he represents the Imperium Romanum as well. The collective understanding of the original mythical and historical figure is shown in its application to a multiplicity of Antichrists (1 Jn. 2:18ff.), i.e. to false teachers.

The restraining factor—denoted once as neuter τὸ κατέχον and once as masc. ὁ κατέχων, both times without an object—is a present power which the Thessalonians know.

> And what is restraining him now so that he may be (first) revealed in his time, you know. For the mystery of transgression is already at work; only (there remains still a period) until he who restrains it for a time is eliminated, and then will the lawless one be revealed (2 Thess. 2:6ff. Trans. after Dibelius; on the reference of the νῦν see M. Dibelius, Hdb. z. NT and B. Rigaux, *Les Épîtres aux Thess.*, Études Bibliques, 1956, *ad loc.*).

The identity of the Katechon is uncertain. Although it has been dominant for a long time and goes back to the Apologists and their kingdom-ideology, the political explanation of κατέχον in terms of the Imperium Romanum and of κατέχων as the Roman emperor has scarcely an advocate today; it is not likely on Jewish presuppositions, for to apocalyptically and nationalistically inclined Jews the Roman state and emperor were the embodiments of opposition to God; nor is it likely on Christian presuppositions since, in spite of Rom. 13, the 1st-century Christians had no political philosophy, and since Antichrist according to Rev. 13 is embodied in the emperor and in 2 Thess. 2:4 also has political features. Today it is the interpretation in terms of salvation-history that is the most widespread. This view was ingeniously put forward by O. Cullmann (*RHPR* 16, 1936, pp. 210–245) and has been championed in particular by J. Munck (*Paul and the Salvation of Mankind* (ET), 1959, pp. 36–42). In this interpretation τὸ κατέχον is the Gospel which "first must be preached to all nations" (Mk. 13:10) before the End comes, and ὁ κατέχων is the Apostle of the Gentiles, Paul himself, whose death is the prelude to the appearing of the Antichrist. However, on the hypothesis of the authenticity of 2 Thess., Rigaux has raised weighty objections to this explanation (*op. cit.*, pp. 274–280).

> Either Paul, during his stay among the Thessalonians, did not content himself with teaching that two signs precede the Day of

the Lord, but had added the claim that the revelation of the Anti-christ would be delayed by the Apostolic preaching and his own activity. In this case we can no longer understand the fact that the Thessalonians could believe, some months after Paul's departure, that the Gospel had been propagated to the end of the earth, or that they had forgotten that the Parousia could not come so long as Paul was preaching. Or else in Thessalonica he had spoken only of apostasy and of the man of lawlessness, and only added by letter that the coming of the lawless one would be delayed by the Christian preaching and by his own. In this second case, the Thessalonians would have required an exegete to discover in the statements of Paul a prediction referring to the Christian preaching and to the activity of Paul himself. Against the view which identifies Paul with the κατέχων and makes his death the pre-condition for the outbreak of the eschatological struggle, we must advance the claim that, in this case, a flagrant contradiction would exist between our pericope and 1 Thess. 4:13–18 in which Paul expresses the hope that he would live to see the Parousia (pp. 276f.).

Especially if we assume the spuriousness of 2 Thess., this explana-tion of the Katechon is not likely. After the death of Paul the Antichrist did not come and the author believes that his appear-ance still lies in the distant future. The mythological interpreta-tion of the Katechon sees in him a divine or heavenly power who holds the mythical monster bound until the time fixed by God. Just as in an Egyptian prayer Horus is called ὁ κατέχων δράκοντα and in a Magical Papyrus Michael is called ὁ κατέχων, ὃν καλέσουσιν δράκοντα, so, in Rev. 20:1–10, it is an angel who holds the devil captive; analogously with this, 2 Thess. 2:6ff. lets the Antichrist, the devil in human form, be "bound". On this interpretation, the statement that the "restraining" heavenly power will be "eliminated" is difficult. It also remains obscure whom the author understands by him. On the assumption of the letter's genuineness, we see in 2 Thess. 2:6ff. a new piece of information, namely that an impediment still exists to the coming of the Antichrist, but we are not told in what it consists. On the assumption of spuriousness, we must go on to say that the change in gender is an intentional veiling, and thus an apocalyptic stylistic feature.

The date of the little Apocalypse is uncertain. The tendency to subdue the imminent expectation draws it into the post-Pauline period. The remaining features are not patent of one explanation: the theme of temple-profanation does not prove that the origin was before A.D. 70, for even after the destruction this was a common feature in the Apocalypses (cf. Dibelius, *op. cit.*, pp. 45f.): the self-deification does not unquestionably indicate the Flavian period—though the worship of the living Caesar first became

615

customary under the Flavians—for this feature may be a reflection of the Hellenistic ruler-cults or a recollection of Ezek. 28, and is obviously not yet topical. The letter belongs to a period in which the delay of the Parousia had become a problem and is directed against enthusiasts who, appealing to Paul, wanted to revive the imminent hope artificially.

(e) The Dogmatizing of Apocalyptic Ideas. The author of 2 Pet., the latest NT document, coming from the middle of the 2nd century, attacks Gnostics who jeer at the delay of the Parousia and impress part of the community with their arguments. He characterizes them as those whose appearance was predicted by the OT prophets and NT apostles.

> In the last days, scoffers will come with scoffing, who follow their own passions, saying, Where is the promise of his coming? For ever since the fathers fell asleep all things have continued as they were from the beginning of the world (3:3f.).

The author defends the traditional apocalyptic eschatology of early Christianity and lays particular emphasis on the sudden and spectacular dissolution of the world (3:10); he delineates the goal as "the victorious entry of the faithful into the eternal kingdom and the destruction of the godless" (Käsemann, Eine Apologie der urchristlichen Eschatologie, in *Exegetische Versuche und Besinnungen*, I, 1960, p. 157; cf. 1:11; 2:9; 3:7). He presents arguments for the imminent hope: (1) concepts of time are not adequate when referred to the action of God (3:8), (2) the matter in question is not delay, but forbearance (3:9) and (3) the faithful can and should hasten the coming of the Parousia by holy conduct (3:11f.). The apocalyptic eschatology is retained as *locus de novissimis* and the imminent hope is repeated artificially as dogma, without either having any living relationship to Christian existence; it belongs simply to the traditional picture of the future and as such is made into dogma (on 2 Pet. cf. particularly E. Käsemann, *op. cit.*, pp. 135–157).

3. THE SYNOPTIC APOCALYPSE. (a) The Synoptic Apocalypse at Mk. 13 presents a detailed summary of the events of the End. Mark represents this Apocalypse formally as esoteric teaching of Jesus to his four intimate friends who, after his prediction of the destruction of the Temple (v. 2), raised the question, "When will this happen? And what is the sign when these things are all to be accomplished?" (v. 4). In his answer Jesus first of all sketches a picture of the future: many false leaders will appear who will claim to be Christ; wars, earthquakes and famines will occur (v. 6–8); oppression of the disciples, persecution by Jewish and pagan courts, divisions in families, hatred for the sake of Jesus (vs. 9–13);

then the last great affliction: the profanation of the Temple, flight to the mountains (vs. 14–20) and the appearance of false prophets and Messiahs (vs. 21–23); finally the End, with the appearing of the Son of Man amid cosmic catastrophes, and the gathering of the elect (24–27). Then Jesus concludes his answer with a detailed exhortation on observing the signs and on constant preparedness, for the fixed time of the End is unknown, but is near (vs. 28–37).

This "address" is composed, as critical analysis has shown, of larger and smaller fragments of various origin and often of divergent purpose which the evangelist has furnished with his own additions and formed into a whole. Side by side with the pieces which reflect the situation of the Christian community (vs. 5f., 9, 11, 13, 21–23) stand those of a Jewish-apocalyptic kind which reveal nothing Christian (vs. 7f., 12, 14–20, 24–27); verse 10 (and perhaps v. 6 also) and many of the notes of time may go back to the evangelist. Especially controversial is the question whether he brought together the whole discourse from separate fragments, or whether in vs. 7f., 12, 14–20, 24–27 a connected Jewish Apocalypse or connected parts of one were available to him. G. Hölscher (*Theol. Blätter*, 12, 1933, pp. 193ff.) considers the verses mentioned to be an apocalyptic pamphlet from the year A.D. 40 when Caligula demanded that his statue be set up in the Temple at Jerusalem. But W. G. Kümmel objects that this "apocalypse" is too short and colourless (*Promise and Fulfilment* (ET), 1957, pp. 98ff.). Nevertheless the two fragments, vs. 14–20 and 24–27, are so coherent in themselves and with one another that we must see in them a literary prototype. The critical revisions which Mark applies in vs. 5–13 (see below) permit us to conclude that he is not here arranging collected material with complete independence, but that there was available to him in this complex a connected tradition which, if it was not in literary form, was yet already fixed. We may thus infer that there existed, even before Mark, a Christian Apocalypse which was assembled out of the Jewish fragments mentioned and Christian elements— that is, an Apocalypse which included not only the Parousia and the events immediately preceding it, but also events even earlier, reaching down to the time of the evangelist and his community. However, the extent of this Apocalypse cannot be reconstructed from Mk. 13 with certainty.

It is significant that the present text exhibits a temporal arrangement and an objective emphasis. It is widely recognized that the time-references are not all of equal value and only partially serve the chronology. Opinions diverge widely on particulars and especially on the question as to where the actual events of the

End begin in Mark's view, whether it is at v. 14 or at v. 24. Support for the first view is provided by the well-founded assumption that vs. 14–20 and 24–27 originally formed a connected text. E. Lohmeyer (Kommentar, ad loc.) and W. Marxsen (*Der Evangelist Markus*, 1956, pp. 112ff.) therefore claim that the real events of the End begin at v. 14. On the other hand, H. Conzelmann (Geschichte und Eschatologie nach Mc 13, *ZNW* 50, 1959, pp. 210ff.) stresses, on good grounds, the fact that Mark makes two definite incisions, one at v. 14 where he intervenes with the description of the last epoch of history, and then at v. 24 where he begins ("after that tribulation"!) with the description of the actual eschaton, which is no longer an historical, but a supernatural Parousia. Conzelmann affirms that Mark makes a fundamental distinction between the historical and the supernatural instead of that gradual transition into the future which is represented in Apocalyptic. "The essential *novum* in the Marcan description lies in this . . . that here (so far as we can see, for the first time) the future (!) events are consciously divided into two groups, certainly related to one another, but nevertheless basically different: there is a contrast between the final epoch of world-history, i.e. the great affliction which, for all its increase, . . . still remains fundamentally within the framework of the existing course of history, and the concluding, cosmic catastrophe which takes place in supernatural form. The latter is the real sign of the Parousia, but in such a way that both sign and in-breaking happen together" (p. 215).

If this is correct, we can understand the two preceding sections accordingly: vs. 5–8 present not so much the first phase as a "summary survey" describing the fundamental situation of the world, while vs. 9–13 characterize the present situation of the Church in this world. The comments, "But the end is not yet" (v. 7) and "this is the beginning of woes" (v. 8) may be notes by Mark himself which do not contribute to the temporal arrangement of the future but serve as a defence against the hasty explanation of events as events of the End: these events are "not yet the End", but just "the beginning of the woes". It is in this antithesis to traditional apocalyptic ideas, and to a large extent even early Christian ideas, that the reflection on the delay of the Parousia becomes noticeable. This is especially the case with the Marcan v. 10 which inserts, between the present and the Parousia, the period of the Christian world-mission as a divinely ordained epoch ($\delta\epsilon\hat{\imath}$).

Nevertheless, Mark does not wish to suppress the imminent hope, as the writer of 2 Thess. does, but really to maintain it (v. 30). He seeks "the balance between the two motifs which belong to the very substance of eschatology: the observing of the signs in which that which is to come is proclaimed, and the expectation of a sudden unsuspected invasion," (Conzelmann, *op. cit.*, p. 220). Accordingly, the apocalyptic teaching is not an end in itself; just as it is interspersed with warnings and exhortations and words of comfort, so it is followed by detailed instruction (vs. 28–37); its aim is to exhort to sobriety and constant preparedness.

As to the dating of Mark 13 as a literary unit, there is no definite clue in the chapter. Apart from the possible Caligula-Apocalypse, which might be dated to A.D. 40, the rest of the material, because of its traditional character, is not serviceable for chronology. Even the theme of Temple-profanation (v. 14) neither supports nor denies a date for composition before A.D. 70, for this theme emerges also in Apocalyptic texts even after the destruction of the Temple. We cannot even claim that the destruction would have left traces in the formulation of v. 14, and that since this is not the case Mark 13 must be placed before A.D. 70, for even in Matthew there are no traces at this point (24:15), although the Gospel of Matthew is dated after the fall of Jerusalem, and the destruction of the Temple was already quite clearly predicted at Mk. 13:2. The origin of Mark's Gospel and therefore also the present form of Mk. 13 may, in view of Mk. 12:9; 15:38, be placed in the period after the destruction of Jerusalem, rather than before that event.

(*b*) The Modification of the Synoptic Apocalypse in Matthew and Luke cannot be treated in detail here; only a few points may be raised. Both evangelists change the private teaching of Jesus into something open, Matthew into general instruction to disciples, and Luke into an address of Jesus to his customary public. Both concentrate their attention more strongly than Mark does on the delay of the Parousia, though they do so in different ways.

Matthew transposes Mk. 13:9–13 to the Mission-charge (Mt. 10:17–21) and replaces the Marcan passage by a series of general and "apocalyptically" related prophecies on external oppression and internal danger to the community (24:10–12). Otherwise he has taken over the outline from Mark and enlarged it with sayings from Q which give warnings on false identifications of the Son of Man and refer to the suddenness of his Parousia (24: 26–28, 37–41). He does not eliminate the imminent hope, but he stresses more strongly than Mark the interim period of the Church and the world-mission: the existence of these is a sign of the nearness of the reign of God (24:14) and thus an eschatological phenomenon (10:1–40; 13:36–43). He defines the interim period of the

Church differently from Mark, by the presence of the exalted Christ as Lord of the world in his Church (28:18–20; 18:20).

Luke alters the Marcan sketch by interventions which are insignificant but which go very deep (21:5–36). In particular, by the comment, "before all this" (v. 12), he advances the persecution of the Church to the beginning of the events which are described in Mk. 13: 5–8 = Lk. 21:8–11 and which he augments by cosmic catastrophes (11b), and therefore locates it long before the Parousia. By additions, he alters Mk. 13:14–20 in such a way that out of the final epoch of history comes the episode of the destruction of Jerusalem, out of an eschatological act comes an event of past history. So Lk. presents the following sequence: (1) persecution of the community, (2) political and (3) cosmic catastrophes. The tendency is to postpone the Parousia as far as possible and to prevent the eschatological explanation of temporal events. Luke inserts at the very beginning of the address an express rejection of the imminent hope (cf. v. 8 with Mk. 13:5f.) and describes its propagators as seducers just as much as the false Messiahs. The essential connection with 2 Thess. 2:1ff. is clear: a judgment is given, and it is in even sharper tones than there, and not with the authority of an apostle, but with that of Jesus himself. The interim period of the Church is not thought of as a phenomenon of the End, as in Mt., but as an independent period in the process of salvation-history (cf. H. Conzelmann, *The Theology of St. Luke* (ET), 1960).

4. THE JOHANNINE APOCALYPSE. The Revelation of John is the only Christian Apocalypse which has found acceptance as a separate book in the Canon of the New Testament. On the one hand it shows a close relationship to Jewish Apocalyptic in form and materials, but on the other it reveals the not inconsiderable influence of Christian features on the accepted tradition. Nevertheless, it is unique even among the Christian apocalypses.

(a) Form. The Apocalypse declares itself, through a meagre epistolary framework (Preface 1:4f., cf. v. 11; closing greeting, 22:21), as a circular letter sent "to the seven churches in Asia". The epistolary character is elsewhere prominent only in chs. 2 and 3, which contain a special message for each of the seven Asian churches. As a whole the Apocalypse, from 1:9 to 22:20, is the record of a vision, and the author repeatedly stresses his ecstatic state (1:10; 4:2; 17:3; 20:10). One Lord's Day on the isle of Patmos the seer John experienced a visionary call (1:9–20) in which the Exalted Lord commanded him to write what he saw in a βιβλίον and to send it to the seven churches; in this vision he also writes the seven letters (heavenly letters) at the dictate of the Exalted One. At 4:1 a new ecstasy appears to begin in which the seer, raptured to heaven, views what is described in 4:1 to 22:20. At the end of the vision even the writing down of the βιβλίον seems to be complete (22:10). We ought not to ask when he wrote it: this kind of thing belongs to the apocalyptic style (Dan. 12:6).

(b) Construction. The outline of the book is given in 1:19, "Write what thou hast seen and what is and what will be hereafter"; hence, the visionary call (1:9–20), the seven letters to the churches on their present state (2f.) and the revelation of future events (4:1–22:5). In the construction of Revelation the number seven plays an important role. The seven churches with their symbols (candlesticks and stars) represent, in the number seven, the totality of the Church. In the apocalyptic section there are 3 seven-fold visions: the vision of the seals (5:1–8:1), of the trumpets (8:2–9:21; 11:15–19) and of the vials (15f.), and even in ch. 14 we can count seven visions. At the same time other numbers come into prominence, three, four and twelve, but the number seven is the most important. Nevertheless it is not the key to the construction of the Apocalypse. More important for the elucidation of this is the understanding of the "book with the seven seals" (5:1) and the parallelism of certain parts in ch. 6–20 (on this see especially G. Bornkamm, Die Komposition der apokalyptischen Visionen in der Offenbarung Johannis, in *Studien zu Antike und Urchristentum*, 1959, pp. 204–222).

The "βιβλίον, written within and without and sealed with seven seals," is, according to Bornkamm's convincing explanation, "a document in two parts which, being written in two-fold fashion, comprises one legally valid text and a corresponding second text, unsealed and proffered for the inspection of everyman" (p. 205). The "outside" designates the unsealed part of the document, and the "inside" the sealed part. Consequently, the phenomena which accompany the opening of the seven seals (6:1 to 8:1) do not form the contents of the document, for these are first made accessible after the loosing of the last seal and so embrace rather what follows, the visions, 8:2 to 22:5.

The parallelism of the three seven-fold visions has always attracted attention. Bornkamm, however, has pointed out the parallelism of the texts following the visions of the trumpets and the vials (chs. 12–14 and 17–19) and, on the basis of a careful analysis, has drawn the conclusion that in 8:2–14:20 and 15:1–20:5 the same events of the End are being described, first in preparatory fashion and then in a final way, as were described in concise outline in the visions of the seals. Chap. 12–14 and 17–19 do not provide the chronological continuation of the events predicted in the visions of the trumpets and vials, but additional concrete supplements to what was systematically represented in the series of sevens.

The arrangement of the actual apocalyptic section of Rev. (4:1 to 22:6) is therefore governed by the fact that the same eschatological period is predicted three times: in summary form in the vision of the seven seals, 6:1–8:1; in a suggestive but fragmentary way in 8:2–14:20; and finally and completely in 15:1–22:5. The summary description in 6:1–8:1 is to be understood as the list, visible on the outside of the double document, of the contents of the sealed text on the inside, which will be set forth after the loosing of the seventh seal, in 8:2–22:5. The number seven in the visions of the seals, trumpets and vials means on each occasion the totality of time and events. That the author presents the descriptions in chs. 12–14 and 17–19 as additional material instead of working them into the system of sevens is due partly to the fact that his material resists such treatment. Moreover, the various tensions in the general apocalyptic picture are due largely to the traditional material with which the seer is working and also to the historical emphasis he lays upon it. On the whole, however, the Apocalypse is a work of strict arrangement and of magnificent inclusiveness.

(c) Sources. The complex question concerning sources and the hypotheses offered for its solution cannot be entered upon here, even by way of suggestion. On this we should consult the commentaries and the survey of research by E. Lohmeyer, *Theol. Rundschau*, NF 6, 1934, pp. 269–314; 7, 1935, pp. 28–62. The Fragment-theory of W. Bousset (*Die Offenbarung Johannis*, 1906) would seem—with modification in its details—most nearly to do justice to the facts of linguistic and stylistic unity and the effort to attain uniformity of construction on the one hand, and the various tensions of subject-matter on the other. Such fragments taken over are 7:1–8; 11:1–13; 12, or are found in 13f., 17f., 21f. In type and in origin they are very varied: while 11:1f. would seem to be a Jewish pamphlet from the time of the siege of Jerusalem, the vision of the queen of heaven, the child and the dragon derives from Eastern mythology (12), and in ch. 17 an older and a more recent version of the Nero redivivus tale seem to be merged. The writer has worked over these fragments with different degrees of intensity in some parts, but in other parts not at all. It is not always clear whether the fragments existed before in a state of written or oral fixity.

The Old Testament served the seer as his "source". The Apocalypse is full of OT allusions and images, and basic to it are the chariot vision of Ezek. 1 and the Son of Man chapter, Daniel 7. There are numerous parallels to Jewish Apocalyptic as well, but no direct quotations from which one could infer literary dependence; it is a case of general dependence on the same apocalyptic world of ideas.

(d) Special Character. In spite of this there are remarkable differences. The most noticeable, and one which distinguishes the Johannine Apocalypse from all Christian Apocalypses also, is the absence of pseudonymity and of fictitious antiquity. The author does not write under the disguise and with the borrowed authority of some hero of the past, but under his own name and in his own authority. He is a genuine prophet. His self-awareness is based on the fact that he knows he has been called by Christ to be a prophet (1:9–20) and it is revealed by the fact that he calls his writing λόγοι τῆς προφητείας (1:3; 22:7, 10, 18f.) and lays claim to "canonical" authority for it (22:18f.). All the traditional apocalyptic features associated with pseudonymity and antiquity are missing, e.g. the surveys of history in phases given in the form of predictions, and the sealing of the revelation with the obligation to secrecy (22:10; cf. for the contrary Dan. 8:26; 12:4). The author emphatically stresses his contemporaneity with his readers and, instead of a review of history, provides a description and critique of the present situation of the Church (ch. 2f.), and he takes care that his writing should be understood as an ecumenical letter, not as a secret document (1:4, 11, 19; 22:16, 21).

Corresponding to these peculiarities is the relative departure from the practice of making *vaticinia ex eventu* on events of the present or recent past. In spite of the system of sevens, all calculations of the End are absent, for the three and a half years, 42 months or 1260 days (11:2f.; 12:6, 14; 13:5) is a stereotyped apocalyptic number which does not serve a chronological interest. And despite the numerous cosmic phenomena which he describes, the seer's interest does not lie in cosmology.

Finally, amongst the peculiarities of the Johannine Apocalypse, we note the fact that the mode of revelation is not the dream, but visionary ecstasy—a sign of the advanced development of Apocalyptic—and secondly, that the mediator of the revelation is only rarely an *angelus interpres* (17:1ff.; 21:9; cf. 1:1; 22:6ff.), but elsewhere always Christ—an understandable Christian modification—and thirdly, that only rarely is an explanation of the vision given (e.g. ch. 17; otherwise only for details).

(e) Purpose. The Apocalypse most probably originated in Asia Minor at the beginning of the so-called Domitianic persecution (c. A.D. 95). Its aim is to strengthen Christians in this emergency to endure faithfully and to witness to their confession. But does this need such a great display as the composition of an entire Apocalypse? The contents of the book go far beyond its actual

aim. It is the codification and, in a certain fashion, the systematization of apocalyptic expectations such as were cherished in those
Jewish-Christian circles in Asia Minor which were eschatologically
stimulated. The author desires not only to strengthen and comfort, but also to enlist sympathy for these ideas. That in fact
appears to have been his chief aim. Consequently the apocalyptic
material outweighs the hortatory (2f.) and at 1:1 the author
mentions only the former as the content of his book.

Among his ideas—which are not treated in detail here—some
which were evidently specially important to the author may be
singled out. Like all apocalyptic writers he is interested, not in
the past, but only in the period of time from the present to the
End, and this period is very short. The entire Apocalypse is
characterized by a strong imminent expectation (1:1, 3; 3:11;
16:15; 22:7, 10, 17, 20), and it is more intense than in the
Synoptic Apocalypse of Mk. 13. That means, since traces of the
delay of the Parousia are present (e.g. 3:3), that the imminent
hope has been awakened afresh, and where it is no longer present
the author seeks to arouse it. To achieve this end, he employs, as
has been said, no reviews of history in the form of predictions, but
uses daring, yet, for the Christian reader of that time, fairly clear
allusions to great events and figures of the present and the recent
past. Thus in the *vaticinium ex eventu* in 17:3-11, v. 10 predicts,
that is, presupposes the short reign of the seventh king (Titus),
and v. 11 points to Domitian as the eighth king who is also one
of the earlier seven, i.e. it characterizes him as Nero redivivus.
Domitian is also referred to in the beast from the pit (11:7; 17:8)
or from the sea (13:1-10, 18). If the seer lets the beast's persecution of witnesses and Christians extend to the time of the sixth
trumpet (11:7; cf. 9:13; 11:15) and of the sixth vial (16:13ff.),
then it is clear that he believes the End to be immediately at hand.

He advocates apocalyptic determinism even more clearly than
the Apocalypse of Mark 13 par. and 2 Thess. do with their δεῖ.
The plan of God for history is unalterably laid down in the "book
with seven seals" and, after the opening of this, it is unfolded
without obstruction. But—and this is a Christian element—the
book is in the hands of the Lamb who alone is able to loose the
seal, which means that it is Christ who inaugurates the End.
This idea is not present in the other apocalyptic texts of the NT,
in which Christ first takes action right at the end of the events,
but it has a certain parallel in Paul (1 Cor. 15:24f.).

Moreover, the apocalyptic dualism is more strongly marked in
the Johannine Apocalypse than in the rest of the NT Apocalyptic.
It is expressed in the notion that heaven and earth, space and
time, must pass away to make room for the new heaven and the

new earth (20:11; 10:6f.; 21:1; cf. 2 Pet. 3:12f.). It is expressed
in the antagonism between the Christian Church and the pagan
world-power, which is but the foreground of the real struggle
between Christ and Satan (12–14). It finds expression also in the
fact that in the visions of the trumpets and vials numerous catastrophes in history are depicted as catastrophes of nature and their
actors are occasionally described as demonic beings; in other
words, the End-event is raised to cosmic dimensions (angels and
demons). The strict distinction between historical and supernatural event which is found in Mk. 13 is not found here.

In the apocalyptic section of his book the seer wishes to point
to two things: first, the End-events which concern the whole
world and which are described by him in the seven-fold visions
whose scheme makes clear the fixed irresistibility of events;
secondly, the events which concern the Church in particular and
which he describes in the supplements (12f., 17f.) where the
antithesis, Christ-Satan, shows the crisis-situation of the Church.
He unites the two groups of themes by inserting motifs from the
second in the seven-fold series (11:3–14; 16:13–16; cf. also 6:9–11)
and by merging both themes in the final act (world-dissolution
and the conquest of the Satanic powers, 16:17–21; 19:11–20:15).
So the stress shifts more and more to the second theme, and in
this the real interest of the author lies. For this reason he does
not include it in the seven-fold visions, but in the supplementary
additions.

The motifs of the second group of themes are to a large extent
familiar from Mk. 13 and par. and 2 Thess. 2, but they are
worked out in the Johannine Apocalypse more broadly and
clearly, in a mythological way but also with topical purposeful-
ness. Satan, who is not mentioned at all in Mk. 13 and only
briefly in 2 Thess 2:9, appears in the Apocalypse as the real
opponent of Christ and his Church (12–20). The Antichrist, who
is mentioned in veiled language in Mk. 13:14 and par. and
suggestively described in 2 Thess. 2, is characterized by the seer
as the exact image of Satan and the counterpart of the dead and
resurrected Christ, and as the representative of the world-
dominion of Rome. He identifies him for the first time with a
figure of the present, the Emperor Domitian, understood as Nero
redivivus (12:17–13:10, 18; 17:3–11). The false prophets whom
2 Thess. 2 omits but who are a sign of the End at Mk. 13:22ff.
appear at Rev. 13:11–17 in a single figure, the second beast, the
pseudo-prophet (16:13). Whether the seer meant a concrete
contemporary person or merely intended a personification cannot
be decided. In any case, he combines the Devil, Antichrist and
the false prophet into an extremely impressive "satanic trinity"

(12f., 16:13; cf. W. Bousset, *Der Antichrist*, 1895; H. Schlier, Vom Antichrist, in *Die Zeit der Kirche*, 1956, pp. 16–29). He makes the cult of Caesar (13:4ff; 12–17) the motive for the persecution of the church (cf. Mk. 13:9ff.; perhaps hinted at in 2 Thess. 2:4), describes it as the work of Satan (12:13–17) and he allows it to pass over into the great assault of the hostile powers (16:13–16; 17:12–14). Accordingly he describes the Parousia of Christ as a Messianic battle and conquest of these hostile powers, and this he does twice (14:14–20; 19:11–20:3). 2 Thess. also characterizes it as the conquest of Antichrist and therefore of Satan, and even at Mk. 13:26 the idea of the conquest is indicated.

With the Parousia the writer connects two other ideas which are unique in the NT but obviously important to him. One is the idea of the thousand-year reign. This is a Messianic reign of peace on this earth taking place between the Parousia and the dissolution of the world. During it the devil is bound, and after it, being loosed again, he leads the powers of the world (Gog and Magog) to the final struggle against the holy city; he is conquered and thrown, for eternity, into the lake of fire and brimstone (20:1–10). There follows then the end of the world, the judgment and the appearing of the new world. This idea of a Messianic interregnum originates in Jewish Apocalyptic (e.g. 4 Esd. 7:28ff.; syr. Bar. 29:3ff.) and is a combination of the national and transcendent eschatological expectations. Then there is the idea of the two resurrections, one before and one after the millennium (20:4–6, 12–15). This is a combination of two Jewish conceptions, the older one of the resurrection of the righteous only, and the later one of the general resurrection of all the dead. The splendidly coloured description of the new world (21:1–8) and of the new Jerusalem (21:9–22:5) is also unique in the New Testament. By means of this the seer offers to his persecuted companions in the faith a glimpse that is full of promise into their glorious future. He forgoes giving a corresponding picture of Hell; later Apocalyptists would make up for this.

When the actual cause of its existence was gone, the purpose of the Apocalypse was no longer understood. Detached from its concrete historical reference it really became a "book with seven seals" which for some was suspect and objectionable, but to others it became an inexhaustible arsenal of apocalyptic speculations.

5. THE FINAL CHAPTER OF THE DIDACHE.—Literature. Editions of the text: Th. Klauser, *Doctrina duodecim apostolorum. Barnabae epistula* (Florilegium Patristicum 1) 1940; K. Bihlmeyer–W. Schneemelcher, *Die Apostolischen Väter*, I, ²1956. Translation and Commentary: R. Knopf, Handb. z. NT, Suppl. Vol., 1923, 1–40; Hennecke, *Apokr.* 2,

1925, 555–565; J.-P. Audet, *La Didaché* (Études Bibliques), 1958 (Lit.). Specialized Studies: A. Adam, Erwägungen zur Herkunft der Didache, *ZKG*, 68 1957, 1–47; E. Peterson, Über einige Probleme der Didache-Überlieferung, in *Frühkirche, Judentum und Gnosis*, 1959, 146–182; E. Bammel, Schema und Vorlage von Didache 16, in *Studia Patristica* IV, (*TU* 79) 1961, 253–262. English translations: J. B. Lightfoot, *The Apostolic Fathers* (ed. J. R. Harmer) 1891; K. Lake, *The Apostolic Fathers* (Loeb Classical Library) 1912–13.

The Didache, a compilation of Church regulations, dated probably in the first decade of the 2nd century, has at its end a little Apocalypse (Did. 16):

1. Be ye watchful[1] for your life! Let not your lamps be extinguished nor your loins ungirded,[2] but be ye ready! For ye know not the hour in which your Lord cometh. 2. Assemble yourselves frequently, seeking what is fitting for your souls. For the whole time of your faith will not be profitable to you, if you are not made perfect in the last time.[3] 3. For in the last days the false prophets and corrupters will be multiplied and the sheep will be turned into wolves and love shall be changed into hate.[4] 4. For as lawlessness increases, they shall hate one another and shall persecute and betray,[5] and then the world-deceiver[6] shall appear as a son of God, and shall work signs and wonders, and the earth shall be delivered into his hands, and he shall commit crimes such as have never been seen since the world began.[7] 5. Then shall created mankind come to the fire of testing,[8] and many shall be offended[9] and perish, but those who have endured in the faith[10] shall be saved by the Curse (?Christ? Audet—from the grave). 6. And then shall the signs of the truth appear,[11] first, the sign of a rift in heaven, then the sign of the sound of a trumpet,[12] and thirdly, a resurrection of the dead,[13] 7. but not of all, but as it was said, "The Lord will come and all his saints with him."[14] 8. Then shall the world see the Lord coming on the clouds of heaven.[15]

The text commences with an exhortation to wakefulness and constant preparedness in view of the coming of the Lord (vs. 1f.) and to this is added an account, as concise as it is clear in construction, of the last things, the main acts of which are indicated from time to time in their historical sequence by a τότε (4b, 5, 6, 8): 1. The increase in "lawlessness", the appearance of false prophets and corrupters; the struggle of all against all (3, 4a); 2. The appearance of the "world-deceiver" (Antichrist) who

[1] Cf. on the whole verse Mt. 24:42, 44; 25:13.　[2] Cf. Lk. 12:35.
[3] Barn. 4:9.　　[4] Cf. Mt. 24:10–12; 7:15; 2 Pet. 3:3; 1 Tim. 4:1.
[5] Cf. Mt. 24:24.　　[6] Cf. 2 Jn. 7; Rev. 12:9.
[7] Cf. 2 Thess. 2:3f., 9f.; Rev. 13:1–10, 13f.　[8] Cf. Mt. 24:21f. and par.
[9] Cf. Mt. 24:10.　　[10] Cf. Mt. 24:13 and par.　[11] Cf. Mt. 24:30.
[12] Cf. Mt. 24:31; 1 Cor. 15:52; 1 Thess. 4:16.　[13] Cf. 1 Thess. 4:16.
[14] Zech. 14:5.　　[15] Cf. Mt. 24:30; 26:64.

performs signs and wonders, accomplishes unprecedented crimes and subjects the world to himself (4b); 3. The commencement of the final distress in which only those who endure in the faith shall be saved (5); 4. The appearance of "the signs of the truth", three apocalyptic acts (6f.); 5. The Parousia of the Lord on the clouds of heaven (8).

The scheme and the details of this Apocalypse are found in Mt. 24 and 2 Thess. 2. One feels however that the description of the Parousia in v. 8 is incomplete. The Georgian translation renders 16:8 as follows:

> Then will the world see our Lord Jesus Christ, the Son of Man who (at the same time) is Son of God, coming on the clouds with power and great glory, and in his holy righteousness to requite every man according to his works before the whole of mankind and before the angels, Amen. (Gr. Peradse, 'Die Lehre der zwölf Apostel' in der georgischen Überlieferung, *ZNW*, 31, 1932, 111–116; quotation from p. 116.)

The rendering in the Seventh Book of the Apostolic Constitutions gives a similar ending:

> . . . with the angels of his power, at the throne of his dominion to judge the world-deceiver, the devil, and to requite each according to his deeds (Audet, p. 73).

Palaeographical observations on the manuscript of the Bryennios text support the view that the present text of 16:8 is incomplete and should be supplemented by the sense of the two readings noticed above (Audet, p. 73f.; p. 473f.; Bammel, p. 259f.). Admittedly the missing judgment is already included in the statement of v. 7 (if this sentence is not a secondary addition, cf. Bammel, p. 261 n. 3), but still, something is missing in v. 8, if not the judgment, then the gathering of the elect (Mt. 24:31) or the union of the faithful with the Lord (1 Thess. 4:17).

The almost complete absence of specifically Christian features in vs. 3–8 is striking. If we disregard the enigmatic κατάθεμα in v. 5, only the description of the world-deceiver as ὡς υἱὸς θεοῦ points to Christian enlargement; however, without damaging the text, these words could be erased and then it would be purely Jewish. For there is nothing in the description of the distress in vs. 3–8 which suggests that the persecution is directed against Christians. Nevertheless we can hardly assume that we have here before us a Jewish text with Christian interpolations. As is generally the case with early Christian Apocalyptic the scheme and the material of this apocalypse are of Jewish origin. But the description in vs. 3–8 is so strongly indebted to New Testament phraseology, especially Mt. 24 but also 2 Thess. 2, that we should probably assume that these texts provided the *"Vorlage"*.

Unlike the Apocalyptic sections of the New Testament the Apocalypse at Did. 16. 3–8 has no reference to the period of the author himself. There is no imminent hope. This is not conveyed by the introductory exhortation to constant wakefulness and preparedness for the unknown hour of the Parousia (v. 1f.); for this exhortation is traditional and v. 2 shows clearly that "the last time", according to the author's interpretation, has not yet commenced. Did. 16 thus does not aim to exhort or comfort a community exposed to eschatclogical tension and distress, or even (like 2 Pet.) to awaken to a new eschatological hope a Church which has become languid. Did. 16 has also no speculative aim. The text pictures nothing; rather everything is schematized. The author's main concern is evidently to give a general outline of the last things with distinct conciseness and clear arrangement. This suggests that Did. 16 is a fragment of something like a catechism.

As such it fits well into Didache as a whole and possibly belonged to it from the start. Whether it originally formed the end of the Two-Ways catechism is questionable. More important than the question of sources and redaction from our point of view is the observation that an Apocalypse—without concrete reference to the present and without interest in the speculative arrangement of the last things—has become a component part of the "Teaching" and, as a *locus de novissimis*, has found a place in a manual of church order.

6. THE SHEPHERD OF HERMAS. (*a*) Literature. Editions: O. von Gebhardt—A. Harnack, Hermae Pastor graece addita versione latina recentiore e codice Palatino, *Patr. Apostol. Opera*, Fasc. III, 1877; F. X. Funk, *Opera Patr. Apostol.* I, ²1901; M. Whittaker, *Der Hirt des Hermas*, GCS 48, 1956.—Commentaries: M. Dibelius, *Der Hirt des Hermas*, Handb. z. NT, Suppl. Vol. 1923, pp. 415–644 (Lit.).— Studies: M. Dibelius, Der Offenbarungsträger im "Hirten" des Hermas (*Botschaft und Geschichte* II, 1956, pp. 80–93); R. van Deemter, *Der Hirt des Hermas, Apokalypse oder Allegorie?*, 1929; A. V. Ström, *Der Hirt des Hermas. Allegorie oder Wirklichkeit?* (Act. Sem. NT Ups. III), 1936; E. Peterson, Beiträge zur Interpretation der Visionen im "Pastor Hermae" (*Frühkirche, Judentum, und Gnosis*, 1959, pp. 254–270); *id.*, Kritische Analyse der fünften Vision des Hermas (*ibid.* pp. 271–284); *id.*, Die Begegnung mit dem Ungeheuer (*ibid.* pp. 285–309); E. Molland, *RGG³*, III, col. 242 (Lit.).

English translations: Lightfoot, Lake (above, p. 627).

(*b*) Textual Tradition. The Greek text of Pastor Hermae is not extant in its entirety. The most extensive text (Vis. I. 1–

Sim. IX. 30. 2) is provided by the MS. 96 from the Monastery of St. Gregory on Athos, which is now in part in Leipzig (14th or 15th cent.; siglum A=Athous, earlier G). Codex Sinaiticus (4th cent.; א) provides, after the NT and the letter of Barnabas, the text of Vis. I. 1–Mand. IV. 3. 6. In addition to these earlier known MSS. there appeared in 1936 Pap. 129 of the Papyrus collection of the University of Michigan (3rd cent.; siglum M) which contains Sim. II. 8–Sim. IX. 5. 1. The Greek text is also attested by a great number of papyrus and parchment fragments which include larger or smaller pieces from all sections of the book.

Of the translations, the two into Latin are the most important: the so-called Vulgata, an old-Latin translation which exists in a number of MSS. and which includes the end of the book, not extant in Greek (L¹); and the so-called Palatina, which exists in two MSS. of the 15th century (L²). Then there is an Ethiopic version (probably 6th cent.; E) and two Coptic versions, an Achmimic (C¹)and a Sahidic (C²), which are only fragments, and finally a fragmentary middle-Persian version (Mpers).

For textual criticism Ps. Athanasius, Praecepta ad Antiochum (ed. G. Dindorf, 1857) and Antiochus Monachus, Homiliae (PG 89, 1413ff.) are also drawn upon.

The attempt to bring the Greek witnesses and the versions into a relation of dependence and to draw up a stemma has not yet been successful. Nevertheless, the textual criticism of the Pastor Hermae has been greatly advanced by the discovery of the Michigan papyrus M. A critical edition of the Latin versions is expected.

The witnesses differ in the headings they use and in their numbering system. The latter is meaningless in the case of the Visions. The most recent edition, that by Whittaker, replaces the traditional division into 5 visions, 12 mandates and 10 similitudes, with their subdivisions into chapters and paragraphs, by a continuous numbering of the chapters which are arranged, for their part, in the traditional paragraphs. This new system of numbering is certainly shorter than the more laborious earlier system, but it is by no means more convenient or even clearer. Since it is not suitable for our purposes, we abide by the customary method of citation.

(c) Contents. The book is an Apocalypse in its form and style, but not in its contents, since it includes no disclosures of the eschatological future or of the world beyond. Two heavenly figures, an old lady and a shepherd, mediate to Hermas, in and around Rome, revelations on the possibility of Christian repentance. The book takes its name from the second bearer of revelation, the shepherd, to whom some four-fifths of the book go back.

Vision I comprises the early part of the story: Hermas sees his former mistress bathing in the Tiber and desires to have such a beautiful woman for his wife. Then follows the account of the actual vision. Some days later, Hermas, while journeying to Cumae, is raptured by the Spirit into a strange region, and he sees his former mistress as a heavenly figure who proceeds to tell him that his desire was a sin of thought. There then appears to him an old lady in gleaming raiment, with a book in her hand and sitting on a great white seat; she preaches repentance to Hermas and his house and reads to him a song of praise to God (2, 3); after that the angels carry away the chair and then the old lady departs (4).

Vision II takes place a year later at the same place. The aged lady gives to Hermas a heavenly letter, which he, without understanding it, copies; it then mysteriously vanishes (1). Only fifteen days later, after prayer and fasting, can Hermas read the letter; it contains the divine message that contemporary Christianity has still the possibility of a single repentance, and charges Hermas to impart this message to the leaders of the Church (2 and 3). There follow two additional visions: while sleeping, Hermas receives the revelation that the old lady is not the Sybil, as he had thought, but the Church; then the old lady appears in his house and gives him instructions for the circulation of the heavenly letter (4).

Vision III, concerning the building of the tower. After long prayer and fasting, Hermas is commanded by the old lady to go to his farm, and he finds there an ivory couch on which the old lady sits and appoints to him the place on her left hand. She shows him six young men building an enormous tower, raised upon the waters, using white stones which were being brought by thousands of men (1 and 2); she explains the building of the tower as an allegory of the Church (3–7). She then lets him see seven young women around the tower and interprets these as the virtues (8. 1–7) and she mediates to him exhortations for the Church (8:11–9:10). In a long addition, which still reports on the two visions, we learn that the old lady, in the three encounters up to the present, has appeared in successively rejuvenated form. Hermas receives an allegorical explanation of these three figures (10–13).

Vision IV, the vision of the Beast. Twenty days later, on his way to his farm, Hermas meets a gigantic sea-monster (1) and the old lady, who has changed into a young girl. She explains the monster to him in terms of the coming affliction (2:1–3:6) and then, in mysterious fashion, vanishes for ever.

Vision V. Introduction to the Mandates and Similitudes. The

new bearer of revelation, the Shepherd, appears to Hermas in his house and reveals his identity as he "to whom he was delivered," while Hermas recognizes him as "the angel of repentance". The Shepherd instructs Hermas to write down his commandments and parables.

Mand. I: Faith, Fear and Continence.
II: Purity.
III: Truth.
IV: Chastity, Divorce and Second Marriage (including at 2:1–3:7, Christian repentance).
V: Patience and Violent Anger.
VI: The two kinds of faith.
VII: The two kinds of fear.
VIII: The two kinds of continence.
IX: Doubt.
X: Sorrow.
XI: The false prophet: true and false prophecy.
XII: 1:1–3:1: Two-fold kinds of desire.
3:2–6:5: Epilogue to the Mandates.

Sim. I: The foreign and the home city.
II: Elm and Vine.
III: The wintry wood.
IV: The summer wood.
V: The faithful slave (1,2); application to works (3), to Christ (4–6) and the preservation of the flesh (7).
VI: The angel of revelry and the angel of punishment.
VII: The effect of the angel of punishment on Hermas.
VIII: Willow-tree; allegorical explanation.
IX: The twelve mountains in Arcadia (1); repetition of the vision of the tower (2–4); testing and cleansing of the tower (5–11); the meaning of the building (12–16) and of the mountains (17:1–31:3). Final exhortation (31:4–33:3).
X: Appearance of Christ to Hermas and the Shepherd; Concluding exhortation and promise.

(d) Construction. The division of the book into Visions, Mandates and Similitudes does not correspond to its arrangement in composition. The fifth Vision does not belong with the four preceding, but is the introduction to the following Mandates and Similitudes. The Shepherd appears in Vision V and acts as mediator of the commandments and parables, while the old lady is the bringer of revelation only in Visions I–IV. From this distinction in the mediators of revelation it is obvious that there is a caesura in the construction between Visions IV and V, but there does not

seem to be one between the Mandates and the Similitudes. There
is indeed a long Epilogue to the 12 Mandates (Mand. XII. 3.
2–6. 5), but the Shepherd plays the main part both before and
after. Sim. I brings no new declaration of situation, but begins
with the sequence-formula, "He saith to me", and the headings
("Parables which he spake to me" etc.) come not from the
author, but have grown up in the manuscript tradition (as the
Ethiopic version clearly reveals by placing a corresponding
heading at Mand. XII. 3. 4). Add to this the fact that the author
seems to have understood the commandments and the parables
as a unity: in the introductory vision (Vis. V. 5f.) he speaks of
them three times in such a way that they must be understood as
very closely related (the first time, the nouns ἐντολαί and
παραβολαί are linked by a personal pronoun used only once,
while the other two cases link them by the use of the article only
once); the same is true at Sim. IX. 1. 1. Furthermore, the first
Similitudes are closely associated with the Mandates (cf. Dibelius,
Kommentar, pp. 493f., p. 546, pp. 550f.) and Sim. VII. 7 speaks
of the παραβολαί as ἐντολαί. The difference between them is so
fluid that it cannot be evidence for the arrangement of the book.
Dibelius suggests, probably quite correctly, that the division into
Mandates and Similitudes was first produced in accordance with
the two-fold expression, and that the epilogue to Man. XII was
"joined on as an addition" (op. cit., p. 493). The book falls into
two parts of very different size: Visions I–IV on the one hand,
and the commandments and parables on the other. Obviously
the second part originally ended with Sim. VIII. Sim. IX. 1. 1
begins entirely afresh ("When I had written down the commandments and parables of the shepherd, the angel of repentance"—
Hermas has followed the instruction of the Shepherd at Vis.
V. 5—"he came to me and said to me, I wish to show thee all
things which the Holy Ghost, which spake with thee in the form
of the Church, has shown to thee"), and 1. 4–33. 3 provides an
excessively circumstantial and allegorized repetition of the vision
of the tower in Vis. III ("And yet must thou learn everything
more accurately from me" Sim. IX. 1. 3). This repetition is in
fact a supplement and is clearly recognizable as such. The
shepherd's statement in Vis. V. 5a ("For I was sent . . . to show
thee again all that thou didst see before, which is especially
important and profitable for you") is an addition which is meant
to prepare the way for this supplement (Dibelius, op. cit., p. 421,
p. 493, pp. 601f.).

These observations support the hypothesis advanced by Dibelius
and others that (i) the book of Visions (Vis. I–IV) and the book
of commands and parables (Vis. V–Sim. VIII) originated and

existed independently of one another, that (ii) the book of Visions is the older of the two, and that (iii) at the time when the two were combined, Sim. IX and X were added, Sim. IX to emphasize what the author considered particularly important and profitable, Sim. X to form the conclusion to the whole composition.

Both the books, as well as their linking together, are probably the work of the same author. At any rate the composition does not suggest more than one author; and the many discrepancies are resolved better, as Dibelius has shown, by tradition-criticism than by literary criticism. The epilogue alone, Mand XII. 3. 2–6. 5, may be an interpolation. Some of the headings, and particularly their numbering, have been added in the course of the manuscript tradition.

(e) Literary Character. The form of the book is apocalyptic in so far as *angeli interpretes* reveal and explain the entire contents to Hermas. The fixed outlines (visions and raptures), the 1st-person narrative throughout the whole and the many dialogues, all comply with this form.

But the two bearers of revelation are not anonymous, as they are in Jewish apocalypses and in the Johannine Apocalypse, nor are they even specially named angels who are absorbed in the task of interpreting, but, as Dibelius in particular has shown, figures with several layers. In Vis. II. 4. 1 and III. 3. 3 the old lady is identified with the Church; this is an entirely secondary feature which conflicts with the fact that the Church is the recipient of the message of repentance from the old lady and that its condition is dealt with by her in Vis. III.

The Sibyl has provided the model for this figure. Certain features clearly show that the old lady is really the Sibyl with whom Hermas at first identified her (great old age, the journey to Cumae, written communication of revelation, the seat; Peterson, p. 267, even refers the schema of the three stages of life to the Sibyl). An analogous situation obtains in the case of the Shepherd. He is designated as the angel of repentance, but he is also the one to whom Hermas "has been delivered," and he "who will live with him the rest of the days of his life", i.e. a protecting angel. The dress of the Shepherd is associated with this role and this points to a non-Jewish origin for the figure, to Hermes; and that is suggested also by the mention of Arcadia (Sim. IX. 1. 4; further evidence in Dibelius, *op. cit.*, pp. 495f., and *Botschaft und Geschichte* II, pp. 8off.). The appearing of the Shepherd in Vis. V displays the typical features of the epiphany of a divine being. Both figures are clearly of pagan origin: a Sibyl and a protecting angel; furthermore they take upon themselves the function of *angeli interpretes* and, in the end, become allegories of Christian realities, the Church and the angel of repentance. In both the main figures of the book one feature which is prominent, and which is remarkable throughout the entire work, is the artificial linking and allegorizing of different figures and motifs. The author is particularly concerned with allegory in order that, with its help, he may adapt his heterogeneous and diverging pictorial and conceptual material to his own purpose.

Hermas no doubt wishes to write an Apocalypse, but the apocalyptic framework embraces no apocalyptic picture. The Mandates include exhortation, traditional ethical sayings which the author arranges thematically, works out in an interpretative fashion and casts partly in the form of dialogue. Reference has been made in the survey of contents to the repetition, with commentary, of the three themes of Mand. I in Mand. VI–VIII. "The clothing of these rules in a heavenly revelation is not to be discovered in the content in general; for many an early Christian teacher could, and in fact did, speak like this angel of repentance" (Dibelius, Kommentar, 496). Only Mand. IX falls out of the paraenetic framework, but with its topical warning against false prophets it fits in with the ethical tendency of the Mandates.

The "parables" Sim. I–V are marked by strong allegorical tendencies and possess a "precept-character" (Dibelius), and are thus used likewise for exhortation. Even the christological passage at Sim. V. 4–6 is ethically oriented. Eschatological ideas are scarcely to be found: the Parousia is mentioned quite by the way and without emphasis in V. 5. 3, and occasionally the Shepherd promises eternal life to the righteous who follow his commandments. Sim. VI–IX are "visionary parables" (Dibelius), allegories in visionary form on the effect of repentance. The visionary form is at its clearest in Sim. IX (rapture) but it is unmistakable in Sim. VI and VIII as well (appearance of the angels: the elegant Shepherd = the angel of revelry; the dishevelled Shepherd = the angel of punishment, Sim. VI; the appearing of the angel of the Lord, Sim. VIII). Sim. X is not a parable, but an account of the epiphany of God's Son; it is actually an addition to the introductory vision, Vis. V.

The presence of paraenesis and allegory would not in itself argue against the apocalyptic character of the book, for both appear in Apocalypses. Allegory, in particular, is a stylistic feature in Apocalyptic, while every early Jewish and Christian Apocalypse has a paraenetic angle. But in that case, paraenesis and allegory are eschatologically determined, whereas this eschatological determination is absent from the Pastor Hermae.

The same is true also of the book of Visions (Vis. I–IV). In spite of Apocalyptic items, there are no revelations on the Eschaton or on the Beyond. The book belongs, if at all, only to a limited extent to the visionary literature (cf. the list in M. Buber, *Ekstatische Konfessionen*, 1921). All four visions (the preaching of penitence by the old lady, Vis. I; the heavenly letter on Christian repentance, Vis. II; the allegory of the building of the tower, Vis. III; the vision of the beast, Vis. IV) have no eschatological purpose, but rather a moral one. Vis. III and IV are intricate allegories, but not well harmonized; the author makes traditional material serve his own ends, which do not correspond to the original meaning (cf. Dibelius, *op. cit.*, pp. 454ff., 482ff.). This is particularly clear in Vis. IV, which is the only section of the book where Hermas works with apocalyptic material. For that reason we quote it here.

> The fourth vision which I beheld, brethren, twenty days after the former vision, a type of the impending tribulation. I was going into the country by the Campanian way. From the high road it is about ten stades away, and the place is easily reached. While I was walking alone, then, I entreated the Lord to accomplish the revelations and the visions which he showed me through his holy church, that he might strengthen me and grant repentance to his servants who have stumbled, that his great and glorious name might thus be extolled, for that he held me worthy to be shown his marvels. While I was giving praise and thanksgiving, a kind of voice came to me in answer, "Do not doubt, Hermas." I began to ponder within myself and to say, "What have I to doubt about, seeing that the Lord has established me on firm ground and has allowed me to behold glorious things?" And I went on a little farther, brethren, and behold I perceived a cloud of dust rising as it were to heaven and I began to ask myself, "Is it perhaps cattle coming which are raising the dust?" for it was just about a stade from me. As the cloud became greater and greater, I perceived that it was something supernatural. Then the sun broke through a moment, and behold, I saw a huge beast like some sea-monster, and from its mouth fiery locusts issued forth. It was about a hundred feet long and its head was like a barrel (?). And I began to weep and to entreat the Lord to rescue me from it, and I remembered the word which I had heard, "Hermas, do not doubt." So, brethren, I gained new faith in the Lord; I placed before my eyes the mighty things he had taught me and courageously went to meet the beast. But it was coming on with such a rush that it could have destroyed a city. As I came near to it, the huge monster stretched itself on the ground and did no more than put forth its tongue and did not stir at all till I had passed by. And the beast bore on its head four colours: black, red like fire and blood, gold and white. After I had passed by and had gone forward about thirty feet, there met me a virgin adorned like a bride going forth from a bride-chamber, all in white,

with white sandals, veiled up to her forehead and with a turban as her head-covering; and her hair was white. I recognized from the former visions that it was the church and so I became more cheerful. She greeted me, saying "Good day, my good man," and I replied, "Lady, good day." She asked me, "Did you meet nothing?" "Lady," I answered, "such a huge beast as might have destroyed whole peoples. But I escaped, thanks to the grace and power of the Lord." "Thou didst escape fortunately," said she, "for thou didst cast thy care upon God and hast opened thy heart to the Lord, certain in the faith that thou canst attain deliverance by no other means than by his great and glorious name. Therefore the Lord has sent his angel, to whom the beasts are subject—his name is Segri—and has shut its mouth that it should not hurt thee. Thou hast escaped a great tribulation because thou hast believed and at the sight of such a huge beast hast not doubted. Go therefore and declare to the elect of the Lord his mighty deeds and say to them that this beast is a type of the great tribulation which is to come. If ye therefore prepare yourselves and with your whole heart turn to the Lord in repentance, then shall ye be able to escape it, if your heart be pure and blameless and if, for the future days of your life, ye serve the Lord without blame. Cast your cares upon the Lord and he will bring them to a right end. Trust in the Lord, ye doubters, for he can do all things: he can turn away his wrath from you and can send his punishments on you who doubt. Woe to them who hear these words and ignore them! It were better for them that they had not been born." Then I asked her about the four colours which the beast wore on its head. She answered me, "Again thou art curious about such things." "Yes, lady," said I, " make known unto me what these things are." "Listen," said she, "the black is this world in which ye dwell; the fire and blood colour shows that this world must perish by blood and fire. The golden colour stands for you who have escaped from this world. For as the gold is tested by fire and becomes useful, so ye also who dwell in it are being tested. And all ye that endure and undergo the fiery trial in it will become pure. As the gold loses its dross, so shall ye also cast away all sorrow and anxiety and shall be pure and useful for the building of the tower. The white colour stands for the future world, in which the elect of God will dwell; for they will be blameless and pure whom God has chosen for eternal life. Therefore cease not thou to speak in the ears of the saints. Now ye know the symbol of the great tribulation to come. But if ye are willing, it shall be nothing. Remember the things pointed out beforehand." After these words she departed without my seeing in which direction she went. For there was a noise, and I turned back in fear because I thought that the beast was coming.

The most important results of the analysis carried out by Dibelius (pp. 482ff.) and Peterson (pp. 285ff.) may be briefly noted. The fact that the locusts are not explained and that the interpretation of the four colours is artificial—how could the wicked beast bear the colours of Christ and the World to come?—make it clear that Hermas did not form the picture by himself, but took it over from elsewhere. This picture and its figures are of apocalyptic origin. The sea-monster is the mythical demon who is fettered from Creation and will be released at the end of the world; the locusts are eschatological plagues and the four colours, originally cosmic colours, are characteristics of Apocalyptic figures (Rev. 6:1ff.). All these are fixed traits in the picture of the future End-time which threaten the whole of mankind. But in Vis. IV they are not used for apocalyptic description; they are "de-eschato-logized" and re-interpreted. Hermas "does not catch sight in advance, in a visionary way, of a fragment of the End-time but, on a walk in the neighbourhood of Rome, experiences in a vision phenomena of the End-time as personal menaces in the present ... The peculiar character of the Beast-vision is thus explained by the fact that the author has individualized apocalyptic terrors" (Dibelius, *op. cit.*, p. 485). In a modification of this kind a new understanding of existence seeks expression. "This process of individualization corresponds to an alteration in the Christian hope which was significant for that time: it is not the fate of mankind at the end of days, but the fate of the individual at the end of his life that is the centre of interest" (Dibelius, *op. cit.*, p. 486). The description of the heavenly journey of the individual takes on features of the final fate of the cosmos.

This example shows particularly clearly how Hermas gives a new interpretation to traditional material. As well as making apocalyptic material serve his own ends, he has done the same with the apocalyptic form. In his case, the literary form of the Apocalypse is no longer the sufficient expression of its declarations, as is the case still with the later Apocalypse of Paul. We should reckon the Pastor Hermae as falling in the genre of Apocalypse only in a non-literal sense, and must therefore designate it as a Pseudo-Apocalypse.

(*f*) Intention. The intention of the book is paraenetic through-out and directed towards repentance. This follows not only from the Mandates and from Sim. I–IV, which comprise in the main only exhortation, but from the remaining parts as well, for they are clearly oriented towards paraenesis and have as their aim repentance, whether they illustrate repentance itself (Sim. V) or its effects (Sim. VI–VIII) or its meaning for the church (Vis. III, Sim. IX). Vis. II proclaims this repentance by a heavenly letter and Vis. I introduces the general theme.

In the repentance propagated by Hermas it is a question of the possibility opened up by God that Christians, after repentance at their conversion and baptism, may still have a last chance to do penance, and this possibility is offered to them in the message of Hermas. He is commissioned by the letter from heaven to make known to the church this opportunity for repentance on the part of Christians.

> After thou hast made known unto them all these words which the Lord commanded me to reveal to thee, then all the sins they sinned aforetime are forgiven them; also to all the saints that have sinned up to this day, if they repent with their whole heart and banish doubt from their heart. For the Lord has sworn this oath by his own glory concerning the elect, that if, now that this day has been set as a limit, sin shall hereafter be committed, they shall have no more deliverance. For repentance for the righteous has an end: the days of repentance are accomplished for all the saints, whereas for the Gentiles repentance is open till the last day. (Vis. II. 2. 4f.)

With this programme Hermas is set apart from the earlier Christian conceptions which knew only of a repentance at conversion (Heb. 6:4ff.; 10:26–31; 12:16f.; 1 Jn. 3:6). The sins of Christians had not assumed the proportions of a theological problem—though the actual presence of sins in Christians made any theory of sinlessness impossible—and so neither had the repentance of Christians. This was a result of the eschatological expectation. With the weakening of this expectation which resulted from the continuing existence of the world, the sins and the repentance of Christians became a problem. Hermas is aware of the novelty of his solution to the problem, in which he diverges from the early Christian radicalism which he himself considered fundamentally correct:

> I said, "I have heard from certain teachers that there is no other repentance save that which took place when we went down into the water and obtained remission of our former sins." He (the Shepherd) answered me: "Thou hast heard rightly, for so it is. For whoever received remission of sins was pledged to sin no more, but to abide in purity. But since thou enquirest all things accurately, I will declare this also to thee, for I do not wish to mislead (into sin) those who in the future will believe or those who have already believed on the Lord. For they that have already believed, or will believe in the future, have no further chance to repent of their (future) sins, but have only remission of their former sins. But for all them that were called before these days the Lord has appointed repentance. For the Lord, the discerner of hearts, who knows all things beforehand, perceived the weakness of men and the craftiness of the devil, that he will be doing some mischief to the servants of God and will commit evil against them. The Lord then, being compassionate, had mercy upon his creation and appointed this repentance, and to me was transmitted the discharge of this repentance. But I say (now), saith he, If after this great and holy calling

anyone, being tempted by the devil, falls into sin, there shall be only one repentance for him. But if he sin over and again and repent, it is unprofitable for him: he will reach life with difficulty." I said to him: "I have come alive again since I have heard this so precisely from thee. For I know that, if I add no more to my sins, I shall be saved." "Thou shalt be saved," said he, "thou and all, if they do this." (Mand. IV. 3.)

In the fixing of a time for repentance we must see an echo of the eschatological expectation. God grants to his own "a final hour of grace" (Dibelius). Hermas bases the extension of time (Man. IV. 3. 5) on the merciful character of God, just as the almost contemporary 2 Pet. (3:9) bases it on his forbearance. But the eschatology is given a new interpretation in terms of the ethical (the "day" which originally designated the End is, for example, according to Vis. II. 2. 4f. the last opportunity for repentance in the message of Hermas).

Hermas is aware that he stands in opposition to the earlier eschatology just as much as he does to the earlier theory and practice of repentance. He intentionally allows the relation between the coming great tribulation and the End to remain unclear. Because his theory of repentance is a result of the non-appearance of the End of the world and the extension of time, he lengthens the period of repentance. The publication of the heavenly letter is delayed (Vis. II. 4. 2f.) and reference is expressly made to a "pause" in the building of the tower of the Church (Sim. IX. 5. 1; 14. 2). "For it is on your account that the building is interrupted, for unless ye hasten to do right, the tower will be completed and ye will be shut out" (Sim. X. 4. 4). How little life there is in this theoretically fixed expectation is shown by Vis. III. 8. 9f., a passage which rejects the question about the End as foolishness and directs the questioner to the "reminder" and to the "renewal of the spirit", to repentance:

> I asked her concerning the times, whether the End is even now. But she cried with a loud voice, "Foolish man, seest thou not that the tower is still being built? Whenever the tower is completed, then is the End: but it will soon be ready. Ask me no more questions. This reminder and the renewal of your spirit is enough for you and for the saints. But it was not revealed for thee alone, but that thou mightest make it known to all. . . ."

The position of Hermas is very clear here. The traditional motif of the imminent hope and the actual problem of the life of Christians in the continuing world, as well as of the Church as a *corpus permixtum*, conflict with one another. He escapes from this collision by means of his theory and message concerning a

Christian repentance which is limited to one occasion. The problem which occupies him is not the non-appearance of the end of the world, but the relation of the ideal and the empirical Church. The latter must be purified and in this way perfected—the interpretation of the parable of the weeds among the wheat (Mt. 13:36ff.) has a broadly casuistic continuation in the allegory of the building of the tower (Vis. III, Sim. IX). Cf. also the allegory of the willow tree, Sim. VIII. Only when the ideal and the empirical Church coincide, "only when the tower is completed, then comes the End" (Vis. III. 8. 9).

(g) The Significance of the Form. The significance of the form can be understood if we remember Hermas' position and programme and that he was aware of their opposition to the earlier rigorous ideas. "A breaking through of radical demands is . . . generally only possible if God himself gives the impetus" (Dibelius, *op. cit.*, p. 511). Consequently the opportunity of a single repentance after baptism is first proclaimed in the form of a letter from heaven and is then repeated in detail by the Shepherd, "the angel of repentance". Hence the apocalyptic form of the book as a whole: it lends to it the character of a revelation, that is, a divine authority for the claims put forward in it, an authority which the author could not lay claim to for himself.

(h) Author; Place and Time of Composition. The author is not an apocalyptist, for he presents no disclosures on the End of the world or the life to come. Moreover he is not a prophet, for the alleged adoption of the "old prophetic summons to repentance" does not mark him out as such (contra Weinel, *Apokr.* 2, pp. 327f.), and the early Christian prophets produced no apocalyptic literature (even if the Apocalyptist John counts himself among the prophets, see above, p. 623); compare also the descriptions of false and true prophecy (Man. XI). Hermas may have been a visionary and have received his illumination concerning the possibility of a single repentance for Christians in an ecstatic state. But he was well versed in the ideas of Apocalyptic and of the magical papyri, and probably in the related literature as well; in any case, he knew how to mould this material to suit his own ends. The evidence for this strongly traditional element in Hermas has been conclusively provided by Dibelius and Peterson. The attempt by R. van Deemter and A. V. Ström to prove that the author was a genuine apocalyptic visionary, and in addition one of a particular psychological type, has, against their will, only confirmed the former evidence.

It is a debated question whether and how far we can trust the numerous autobiographical details in Hermas concerning himself and his family. Discounting such of these details as may have been intended typologically (cf. Dibelius, *op. cit.*, pp. 419f. and passim), it seems that Hermas was a small business man in Rome. The *Muratori Canon* affirms that he was the brother of the then bishop of Rome (ll. 73ff.; cf. Vol. I, p. 45), so also the *Catalogus Liberianus* (A. Harnack, *Chronologie* I, p. 145) and the *Liber Pontificalis* (Dibelius, *op. cit.*). The truth of these assertions has been placed in doubt by the fact that the Muratori Canon impugns the canonicity of the "Shepherd" by giving to it an obviously tendentious late date (Hermas composed the book "quite lately in our time, when on the throne of the church of the city of Rome the bishop Pius, his brother, sat"). E. Peterson declares that this comment is "false ascription" and that it is "a fixed form of school-polemic" in the circles of the Roman "teachers" of the 3rd century against the apocalypses handed down in the Church. But only the dating is polemical; the late date of the "Shepherd" makes it unsuitable for use in worship: but the person of its author remains untouched. It has been demonstrated by Dibelius (*op. cit.*, pp. 421f.) that this particular dating of the book to Pius' tenure of office does not exclude the possibility of the relationship of the author to the Roman bishop or, more correctly, presbyter. We may therefore accept this statement. Peterson wants to dissociate the entire work from Rome and sees Hermas as a Palestinian-Jewish Christian and his "house" as a *chaburah* of Jewish-Christian ascetics. Against this and similar views, however, we must urge the methodological considerations which Dibeluis raised as far back as 1923: "There is no justification for explaining the strong connections of the book with Jewish tradition by postulating a Jewish-Christian origin for the author. Customary Semitisms based on Bible reading, Jewish cult-formulae and Jewish paraenesis were taken over as their inheritance by 2nd-century Christians in such measure that we cannot interpret every trustee of the inheritance as a relative of the testator" (*op. cit.*, p. 423).

On the basis of internal criteria, we may place the composition of the book in the third, or, at the outside, in the fourth decade of the 2nd century (Dibelius, *op. cit.*, p. 422; Weinel, *op. cit.*, p. 331; likewise Molland, *RGG³*, III, col. 242).

2. THE ASCENSION OF ISAIAH

(*J. Flemming—H. Duensing*)

INTRODUCTION: 1. CONSTRUCTION; DATE OF COMPOSITION. The following text falls into two parts which differ in their contents: chs. 1–5 which narrate the martyrdom of Isaiah, and chs. 6–11 which describe a heavenly journey or vision of the prophet. Neither section is a unity in itself: in the first section, 3. 13–5. 1 forms an extraneous unit as does 11. 2–22 in the second section. The view that the latter is a separate piece is made certain by the fact that the passage is absent from the Latin version first published in 1522 and from the three Slavonic versions as well. The division of the whole into two distinct parts is confirmed by the fact that in the versions mentioned only the vision is recorded. Within the first part, the first chapter is not a unified whole: vs. 2b–5a and the main part of v. 13, at least, are separate; otherwise we would have to regard the entire opening chapter as a later addition, as Dillmann and others did. The martyrdom narrated in the first section is a Jewish writing of uncertain date, the substance of which was known, according to Heb. 11:37, in the first Christian century. The vision which describes the ascension of Isaiah through the seven heavens and the revelation of the future redemption through Christ may have originated in the 2nd century A.D. The remaining parts distinguished above are also Christian productions. In opposition to this view of the composition of the whole, a view till then almost universally accepted, F. C. Burkitt (*Jewish and Christian Apocalypses*, 1914) and Vacher Burch (*JTS* 21, 1920, pp. 249ff.) argue for the unity of the text, with the exception of the interpolation in ch. 11.

2. TRADITION; EDITIONS. Various parts or fragments of the book are available in Greek, old Slavonic and Coptic, but the entire work has come down to us only in Ethiopic translation. Editions of the Ethiopic text were prepared by the English scholar R. Laurence 1819, A. Dillmann 1877 and R. H. Charles, *The Ascension of Isaiah*, London, 1900 (with many conjectures). The Latin text of the vision, chs. 6–11, was printed in Venice in 1522 and again by Gieseler in 1832; the fragments chs. 2. 14–3. 13 and 7. 1–19 were printed by A. Mai in 1828 from an old Latin version; these texts are also found in Dillmann, Charles and Tisserant. The passages 2. 14–3. 13 and 7. 1–19 are found in Latin in Migne PL 13, cols. 629 and 630. Three Slavonic versions of chs. 6–11 are available. Fragments of chs. 2. 3–6; 9–12 and of chs. 11. 24–31; 35–40 in Sahidic, as well as of chs. 7. 12–15; 8. 16f.; 9. 9–11; 10. 9–11 in the Achmimic dialect of Coptic, have been edited by Lefort in *Muséon* 1938 and 1939, and further fragments by Lacau, *ibid.*, 1946 pp. 453–467; these fragments are 1. 1–5; 3. 25–28; 5. 7–8; 6. 7–11; (7. 10 to 15); 7. 28–32; (8. 16f.; 9. 9–11); 9. 28–30; (10. 9–11); 10. 17; 11. 14–16; (11. 35–37). The passages in brackets had already been published by Lefort (see above). Grenfell and Hunt in 1900 published a Greek fragment, chs. 2. 4–4. 4, in *The Amherst Papyri* I, and O. Gebhardt published a Greek reworking of the entire Ascensio as a Christian "sacred legend"; this was published again by Charles and translated into French by Tisserant, *Ascension d'Isaie*, Paris, 1909. Pp. 42–61 and 79–83 of this work and Schürer 3, pp. 386–393 (ET Div. II, Vol. III, pp. 144ff.) give the more detailed literary references. Eng. trans. by Charles, *op. cit.*, and by G. H. Box, 1919 (cf. M. Dibelius, *ThLZ* 47, 1922, col. 544): a Danish translation of the Martyrdom of Isaiah by E. Hammershaimb is found in *De Gammeltestamentlige Pseudepigrafer*, Vol. 3, Copenhagen, Oslo and Lund, 1958, pp. 303–315.

For the connections between the Ascension of Isaiah and the Dead Sea Sect cf. D. Flusser, The Apocryphal Book of Ascensio Isaiae and the Dead Sea Sect, in *Israel Exploration Journal* (Jerusalem) 3, 1953, 30–47. (Previously published, in Hebrew, in *Bulletin of the Israel Exploration Society*, 1952, 28–46.)

The Ascension of the Prophet Isaiah

1. 1. It came to pass in the twenty-sixth (Coptic: sixteenth) year of the reign of Hezekiah, king of Judah, that he called Manasseh his son who was the only son he had. 2. And he called him into the presence of the prophet Isaiah, the son of Amoz, and into the presence of Jasub, the son of Isaiah, in order to deliver to him the words of righteousness (truth?) which he, the king, himself had seen,[1] 3. and the eternal judgments and the punishments of Hell and of the prince of this world, and of his angels, authorities and powers; 4. and the words of the faith concerning the Beloved which he himself had seen in the fifteenth year of his reign during his illness. 5. And he delivered to him the recorded words which Sebna, the scribe, had written and that which Isaiah the son of Amoz had given to him together with the prophets, that they might write down and store with him what he himself had seen in the king's house concerning the judgments of the angels and the destruction of this world, concerning the garments of the righteous, and concerning the going forth, the transformation, the persecution and ascension of the Beloved. 6. And in the twentieth year of the reign of Hezekiah, Isaiah had seen the words of this prophecy and had delivered them to his son Jasub. And whilst the former gave commands, with Jasub the son of Isaiah present, 7. Isaiah said to king Hezekiah, but not in the presence of Manasseh alone did he say it to him, "As truly as the Lord liveth, whose name has not been sent into this world, and as truly as the Beloved of my Lord liveth, and the spirit which speaketh in me liveth, all these commands and these words will have no value for thy son Manasseh, and by the outrage of his hands I shall depart amid the torture of my body. 8. And Sammael Malkira will serve Manasseh and execute all his desires, and he will be a follower of Beliar rather than of me. 9. And many in Jerusalem and in Judah will he cause to depart

---

[1] Is. 7:3.

from the true faith, and Beliar will dwell in Manasseh, and by his hand shall I be sawn asunder." 10. And when Hezekiah heard these words, he wept very bitterly, rent his clothes, cast dust upon his head and fell on his face. 11. And Isaiah said to him, "The design of Sammael against Manasseh is (already) settled: nothing will help thee." 12. On that day Hezekiah resolved within himself to kill his son. 13. But Isaiah said to Hezekiah, "The Beloved will make thy purpose fruitless and the thought of thy heart will not be accomplished, for with this calling have I been called, and I must have my portion with the inheritance of the Beloved."

2. 1. And after Hezekiah died and Manasseh became king, he remembered no more the commands of his father Hezekiah, but forgot them, and Sammael settled upon Manasseh and clung fast to him. 2. And Manasseh ceased from serving the God of his father and served Satan and his angels and powers. 3. And he caused the house of his father, which had been under the eye of Hezekiah, to depart ⟨from⟩ the words of wisdom and from the service of God. 4. And Manasseh altered his purpose and became a servant of Beliar, for the prince of unrighteousness who rules this world is Beliar, whose name is Matanbukus. Now this Beliar rejoiced in Jerusalem over Manasseh and strengthened him in his leading to apostasy and in the lawlessness which was spread abroad in Jerusalem. 5. Witchcraft and the practice of magic increased, and predictions from the flight of birds, divination, fornication, [adultery], the persecution of the righteous by Manasseh, [Belchira], Tobia the Canaanite, John of Anathoth and ⟨Zadok⟩ the overseer of works. 6. The rest of the narrative is recorded in the book of the kings of Judah and Israel.[1] 7. And when Isaiah the son of Amoz saw the evil which was taking place in Jerusalem, the worship of Satan and its wantonness, he withdrew from Jerusalem and settled in Bethlehem-Judah. 8. But there was much lawlessness there also; so he withdrew from Bethlehem and settled on a mountain in desert country. 9. And Micaiah the prophet and Ananias the aged, and Joel, Habakkuk and Jasub his son, and many of the faithful who believed in the ascension to heaven withdrew and settled on the mountain.

---

[1] 2 Kings 21:17; 2 Chron. 33:18.

10. And they all put on sackcloth and all were prophets; they had nothing with them, but were naked and they bitterly lamented the apostasy of Israel. 11. And they had nothing to eat except wild herbs which they gathered on the mountains, and after they had cooked them, they ate them in the company of the prophet Isaiah. And thus they spent two years on the mountains and hills. 12. And after this, while they were in the desert, a man appeared in Samaria named Belchira, of the family of Zedekiah, the son of Chenaan, a false prophet who had his dwelling place in Bethlehem; now Hezekiah, the son of Chanani, his father's brother, was in the days of Ahab king of Israel the teacher of the 400 prophets of Baal, and he (Zedekiah) smote and abused the prophet Micaiah, the son of Imlah. 13. And he, Micaiah, was (also) abused by Ahab and was thrown into prison. ⟨And he was⟩ with the ⟨false⟩ prophet Zedekiah; they were with Ahaziah the son of Ahab(?) in Samaria(?) . . . 14. But Elijah the prophet from Thisbe in Gilead rebuked Ahaziah and Samaria, and prophesied concerning Ahaziah that he would die on his bed of a sickness, and that Samaria would be delivered into the hand of Salmanasser, because he had slain the prophets of God. 15. And when the false prophets who were with Ahaziah, the son of Ahab, and their teacher Jallarias from Mount Joel (Israel?) heard—16. now he (i.e. Jallarias) [Belchira] was a brother of Zedekiah—when they heard, they prevailed upon Ahaziah, king of Gomorrah, and ⟨slew⟩ Micaiah.

3. 1. But Belchira found and saw the whereabouts of Isaiah and the prophets who were with him, for he lived in the region of Bethlehem and was an adherent of Manasseh. And he appeared as a false prophet in Jerusalem and many in Jerusalem joined with him, although he was from Samaria. 2. And it came to pass when Salmanasser, king of Assyria, came and captured Samaria and led the nine ⟨and a half⟩ tribes into captivity, and dragged them off to the mountains of the Medes and to the river Gozan, 3. this man, while still a youth, escaped and reached Jerusalem in the days of Hezekiah, king of Judah; but he walked not in the ways of his father of Samaria, for he feared Hezekiah. 4. And he was found in the days of Hezekiah delivering impious speeches in Jerusalem. 5. And the servants of Hezekiah accused him and

he fled to the region of Bethlehem, and they persuaded (*Sahidic and Ethiopic:* he persuaded). . . . 6. Now Belchira accused Isaiah and the prophets who were with him in these words, "Isaiah and his companions prophesy against Jerusalem and against the cities of Judah that they shall be laid waste, and ⟨against the children of Judah⟩ and Benjamin, that they shall go into captivity, and against thee also, O lord my king, that thou shalt go (bound) with hooks and iron chains;[1] 7. but they prophesy falsely concerning Israel and Judah. 8. And Isaiah himself has said, 'I see more than the prophet Moses.' 9. Now Moses said, 'There is no man who can see God and live,' but Isaiah has said, 'I have seen God and behold I live.'[2] 10. Know therefore, O king, that he is a liar. Moreover he has called Jerusalem Sodom and the princes of Judah and Jerusalem he has declared to be the people of Gomorrah."[3] And he brought many accusations against Isaiah and the prophets before Manasseh. 11. But Beliar abode in the heart of Manasseh and in the hearts of the princes of Judah and Benjamin, of the eunuchs and councillors of the king. 12. And the speech of Belchira pleased him [exceedingly] and he sent and seized Isaiah.

13. For Beliar harboured great wrath against Isaiah on account of the vision and of the exposure with which he had exposed Sammael, and because through him the coming forth of the Beloved from the seventh heaven had been revealed, and his transformation, his descent and the likeness into which he was to be transformed, namely, the likeness of a man, and the persecution which he was to suffer, and the tortures with which the children of Israel were to afflict him, and [the coming] of the twelve disciples [and the] instruction, [and that he should before the Sabbath be crucified on the tree] and that he was to be crucified together with criminals, and that he would be buried in a sepulchre, 14. and that the twelve who were with him would be offended because of him, and the watch of the guards of the grave, 15. and the descent of the angel of the church which is in the heavens, whom he will summon in the last days; 16. and that the angel of the Holy Spirit and Michael, the chief of the holy angels, would open his grave on the third day, 17. and that the

[1] Cf. 2 Chron. 33:11.   [2] Ex. 33:20; Is. 6:5.   [3] Is. 1:10.

Beloved, sitting on their shoulders, will come forth and send out his twelve disciples, 18. and that they will teach to all the nations and every tongue the resurrection of the Beloved, and that those who believe on his cross will be saved, and in his ascension to the seventh heaven, whence he came; 19. and that many who believe in him will speak in (the power of) the Holy Spirit, 20. and that many signs and wonders will take place in those days; 21. and afterwards, when he is at hand, his disciples will forsake the teaching of the twelve apostles and their faith, their love and their purity, 22. and there will arise much contention about [his coming and] his appearing. 23. And in those days there will be many who will love office though they are devoid of wisdom, 24. and many elders will be lawless and violent shepherds to their sheep and will become ravagers (of the sheep), since they have no holy shepherds. 25. And many will exchange the glory of the garment of the saints for the garment of the covetous, and respect for persons will be common in those days, and such as love the honour of this world. 26. And there will be much slandering and boasting at the approach of the Lord and the Holy Spirit will depart from many. 27. And in those days there will not be many prophets nor such as speak reliable words, except a few here and there, 28. on account of the spirit of error, of fornication, of boasting and of covetousness which shall be in those who yet will be called his servants and who receive him. 29. Great discord will arise among them, between shepherds and elders. 30. For great jealousy will prevail in the last days, for each will say what seems pleasing in his own eyes. 31. And they will set aside the prophecies of the prophets which were before me and also pay no attention to these my visions, in order to speak (forth from the) torrent of their heart.

4. 1. And now, Hezekiah and Jasub, my son, these are the days of the completion (?) of the world. 2. And after it has come to its consummation, Beliar, the great prince, the king of this world who has ruled it since it came into being, shall descend; he will come down from his firmament in the form of a man, a lawless king, a slayer of his mother, who himself (even) this king 3. will persecute the plant which the Twelve Apostles of the Beloved have planted; and one of the twelve will be delivered into his

hand.—4. This ruler will thus come in the likeness of that king and there will come with him all the powers of this world and they will hearken to him in all that he desires. 5. And at his word the sun will rise in the night and he will cause the moon to shine at the sixth hour. 6. All that he desires he will do in the world; he will act and speak in the name of the Beloved and say "I am God and before me there has been none else." 7. And all the people in the world will believe in him, 8. and will sacrifice to him and serve him saying, "This is God and beside him there is none other." 9. And the majority of those who have united to receive the Beloved will turn aside to him, 10. and the power of his miracles will be manifest in every city and region, 11. and he will set up his image before him in every city, 12. and he shall rule three years, seven months and twenty-seven days. 13. And many believers and saints, after they have seen him for whom they hoped, Jesus Christ the crucified—after I, Isaiah, have seen him who was crucified and ascended—who thus believed in him, of these (only) a few will remain as his servants, fleeing from desert to desert and awaiting his coming.[1] 14. And after ⟨one thousand⟩ three hundred and thirty-two days the Lord will come with his angels and with the hosts of the saints from the seventh heaven with the glory of the seventh heaven, and will drag Beliar with his hosts into Gehenna,[2] 15. and he will bring rest to the pious who shall be found alive in the body in this world [and the sun shall grow red with shame][3], 16. and to all who through faith in him have cursed Beliar and his kings. But the saints will come with the Lord in their garments which are stored on high in the seventh heaven; with the Lord they will come, whose spirits are clothed, they will descend and be present in the world, and those who are found in the body will be strengthened by the image of the saints in the garments of the saints, and the Lord will minister to those who were watchful in the world.[4] 17. And afterwards they will turn themselves upwards in their garments but their body will remain in the world. 18. Then the voice of the Beloved will in wrath rebuke this heaven and this dry place (= the earth) and the mountains and hills, the cities, the desert and the forests, the angels of the sun and of the moon and all things wherein

---

[1] Cf. 1 Cor. 1:7.   [2] Cf. 2 Thess. 1:7ff.   [3] Cf. Is. 24:23.   [4] Cf. Lk. 12:37.

Beliar manifests himself and acts openly in this world, and resurrection and judgment will take place in their midst in those days, and the Beloved will cause fire to go forth from himself, and it will consume all the impious and they will be as if they had not been created.

19. The remainder of the words of the vision is recorded in the vision concerning Babylon.[1] 20. And the rest of the vision of the Lord, behold, it is recorded in parables in my words which are written in the book which I openly proclaimed. 21. Moreover the descent of the Beloved into the realm of the dead is recorded in the section where the Lord says "Behold, my servant is prudent".[2] And behold, all these things are written [in the Psalms] in the poems of David, the son of Jesse, in the sayings of his son Solomon, in the words of Korah and Ethan, the Israelite, and in the words of Asaph and in the remaining Psalms which the angel of the spirit caused to be written by those whose name is not recorded, and in the words of Amoz, my father, and of the prophets Hosea and Micah, Joel, Nahum, Jonah, Obadiah, Habakkuk, Haggai, Zephaniah, Zechariah and Malachi, and in the words of Joseph the Just, and in the words of Daniel.

5. 1. On account of this vision, therefore, Beliar grew angry with Isaiah and he dwelt in the heart of Manasseh, and Isaiah was sawn asunder with a tree-saw. 2. And when Isaiah was being sawn asunder, Belchira his accuser and all the false prophets stood there, laughing and expressing their malicious joy over Isaiah. 3. And Belchira, at the instigation of Mekembukus, stood before Isaiah, mocking him. 4. And Belchira said to Isaiah: "Say 'In all that I have spoken, I have lied: the ways of Manasseh are good and right, 5. also the ways of Belchira and his companions are right'." 6. This he said to him when they were beginning to saw him asunder. 7. But Isaiah (was absorbed) in a vision of the Lord, and although his eyes were open, he did not see them. 8. And Belchira spoke thus to Isaiah, "Say what I say to thee and I will alter their purpose, and I will prevail upon Manasseh and the princes of Judah and the people and all Jerusalem to reverence thee (upon their knees)." 9. And Isaiah answered and said "So far as I am concerned, so to speak, damned and cursed be thou,

[1] Cf. Is. 13:1 (LXX).   [2] Is. 52:13 (LXX).

all thy powers and thy whole house, 10. for thou canst take no more than the skin of my flesh." 11. So they seized and sawed asunder Isaiah the son of Amoz, with a saw. 12. And Manasseh, Belchira, the false prophets and the princes and the people all stood and looked on. 13. And to the prophets who were with him he said before he was sawn asunder: "Go to the region of Tyre and Sidon; for me alone has God mingled the cup." 14. But while he was being sawn asunder Isaiah neither cried out nor wept, but his mouth conversed with the Holy Spirit until he had been sawn apart.

15. This did Beliar to Isaiah through Belchira and Manasseh, for Sammael cherished fierce anger against Isaiah from the days of Hezekiah king of Judah, on account of the things which he had seen concerning the Beloved, 16. and because of the destruction of Sammael, which he had seen through the Lord, while his father Hezekiah was still king. And he acted according to the will of Satan.

The Vision which Isaiah the son of Amoz saw.

6. 1. In the twentieth year of the reign of Hezekiah, king of Judah, Isaiah the son of Amoz and Jasub the son of Isaiah came from Gilgal to Jerusalem to Hezekiah. 2. And ⟨after he (Isaiah) had entered⟩ he sat down on the king's couch and (although) they brought him a chair, he refused to sit on it. 3. So Isaiah began to speak words of faith and righteousness with Hezekiah, while all the princes of Israel sat (around) with the eunuchs and the king's councillors. And there were there forty prophets and sons of the prophets who had come from the neighbouring districts, from the mountains and from the plains, when they heard that Isaiah had come from Gilgal to Hezekiah. 4. They had come to greet him and to hear his words, 5. and that he might lay his hands upon them and that they might prophesy and that he might hear their prophecy; and they were all before Isaiah. 6. When Isaiah was speaking to Hezekiah the words of truth and faith, they all heard [the door which someone had opened, and] the voice of the spirit. 7. Then the king called all the prophets and the entire people who were found there, and they came (in), and Micaiah and the aged Ananias, and Joel and Jasub sat on his

right hand ⟨and on his left⟩. 8. And it came to pass when they all heard the voice of the Holy Spirit they all fell upon their knees in worship and glorified the God of righteousness, the Most High in the highest world who as the Holy One has his seat on high and rests among his saints,[1] 9. and they gave honour to him who had granted ⟨such⟩ a door (*Slav:* excellence of words) in the alien world, and had granted it to a man. 10. And while he was speaking by the Holy Spirit in the hearing of all, he (suddenly) became silent and his consciousness was taken from him and he saw no (more) the men who were standing before him: 11. his eyes were open, but his mouth was silent and the consciousness in his body was taken from him; 12. but his breath was (still) in him, for he saw a vision. 13. And the angel who was sent to make him behold it belonged neither to this firmament nor to the angels of the glory of this world, but had come from the seventh heaven. 14. And the people who were standing around, with the exception of the circle of prophets, did ⟨not⟩ think that the holy Isaiah had been taken up. 15. And the vision which he saw was not of this world, but from the world which is hidden from ⟨all⟩ flesh. 16. And after Isaiah had beheld this vision, he imparted it to Hezekiah, his son Jasub, and the remaining prophets. 17. But the leaders, the eunuchs and the people did not hear, with the exception of Sebna the scribe, Joachim and Asaph the chronicler, for they were doers of righteousness and the sweet fragrance of the spirit was upon them. But the people did not hear, for Micaiah and Jasub his son had caused them to go forth, when the knowledge of this world was taken from him and he became as a dead man.

7. 1. Now the vision which he had seen Isaiah narrated to Hezekiah, his son Jasub, Micaiah and the rest of the prophets saying, 2. "In that moment when I was prophesying according to things heard by you, I saw a sublime angel and he was not like the glory of the angels which I was accustomed (already) to see, but he possessed great glory and honour, so that I cannot describe the glory of this angel. 3. And he took hold of me by my hand and then I saw (*Slav:* he led me on high); and I said to him, 'Who art thou, and what is thy name, and wherefore dost

[1] Cf. Is. 57:15 acc. to LXX.

thou lead me on high?', for strength was granted to me to speak with him. 4. And he said to me: 'When I have led thee on high by degrees and have shown thee the vision for which I have been sent to thee, then wilt thou know who I am, 5. but my name thou shalt not find out, since thou must return to this thy body. But whither I would raise thee on high, thou shalt see, since for this purpose I have been sent.' 6. And I rejoiced because he spoke amiably with me. 7. And he said to me: 'Dost thou rejoice because I have spoken amiably to thee?'; and he went on, 'Thou wilt see one who is greater than I, who will speak amiably and peaceably with thee; 8. and his Father also who is greater wilt thou see, because for this purpose have I been sent from the seventh heaven to explain all these things for thee.' 9. And we ascended to the firmament, I and he, and there I saw Sammael and his hosts, and a great struggle was taking place there, and the angels (so L¹) of Satan were envious of one another. 10. And as it is above, so is it also on the earth, for the likeness of that which is in the firmament is also on the earth. 11. And I said to the angel, '⟨What is this struggle⟩ and what is this envy?' 12. And he said to me, 'So it has been, since this world began until now, and this struggle (will continue) till he whom thou shalt see shall come and destroy him (Satan)'. 13. And after this he brought me up above the firmament, which is the ⟨first⟩ heaven. 14. And there I saw a throne in the midst, and on the right and on the left of it were angels. 15. But ⟨the angels on the left⟩ were not like the angels who stood on the right, for those on the right possessed a greater glory, and they all praised with one voice; and there was a throne in the midst; and likewise those on the left sang praises after them, but their voice was not such as the voice of those on the right, nor their praise like their praise. 16. And I asked the angel who led me and said unto him, 'To whom is this praise given?' 17. And he said to me, '(It is) for the praise ⟨of him who is in⟩ the seventh heaven, for him who rests ⟨in⟩ eternity among his saints, and for his Beloved, whence I have been sent unto thee. [Thither is it sent]'. 18. And again he caused me to ascend to the second heaven, and the height of that heaven is the same as from heaven to earth [and to the firmament]. 19. And ⟨I saw there as⟩ in the first heaven, angels on the right and on the left and a throne in the midst and the praise of the angels in the second heaven; and he who sat on the throne in the second heaven had a greater glory than all (the rest). 20. And there was much (more) glory in the second heaven, and their praise was not like the praise of those in the first heaven. 21. And I fell on my face to worship him, and the angel who conducted me did not allow me, but said to me, 'Worship neither angel nor throne which belongs to the six heavens—for this reason was I sent to conduct thee—till I tell thee in the seventh heaven. 22. For above all the heavens and their angels is thy throne set, and thy garments and thy crown which thou shalt see.' 23. And I rejoiced greatly that those who love the Most High and his Beloved will at their end ascend thither by the angel of the Holy Spirit. 24. And he brought me up to the third heaven, and in like manner I saw those on the right and on the left, and there stood there also a throne in the midst but the remembrance of this world is not known there. 25. And I said to the angel who was with me, for the glory of my countenance was being transformed as I ascended from heaven to heaven, 'Nothing of the vanity of that world is here named.' 26. And he answered and said to me, 'Nothing is named by reason of its weakness, and nothing is hidden here of what took place.' 27. And I desired to find out how it is known, but he answered and said to me, 'When I have brought thee to the seventh heaven whence I was sent, high above these, then shalt thou know that nothing is hidden from the thrones and from those who dwell in the heavens and from the angels.' And great were the praises they sang and the glory of him who sat on the throne, and the angels on the right and on the left possessed a greater glory than those in the heaven beneath them. 28. And again he carried me upwards to the fourth heaven, and the distance from the third heaven to the fourth is greater than that from earth to the firmament. 29. And there once more I saw those on the right and on the left, and he who sat on the throne was in the midst, and here also they sang their praises. 30. And the praise and glory of the angels on the right was greater than that of those on the left, 31. and again the glory of him who sat on the throne was greater than that of the angels on the right, and their glory was greater than that of those

who were below. 32. And he brought me up to the fifth heaven.
33. And again I saw those on the right and those on the left and
him who sat on the throne, possessing greater glory than those
in the fourth heaven. 34. And the glory of those on the right
surpassed that of those on the left. 35. And the glory of him who
sat on the throne was greater than the glory of the angels on the
right, 36. and their praises were more glorious than those in the
fourth heaven. 37. And I praised the unnamed one and the only
one, who dwells in the heavens, whose name is unfathomable for
all flesh, who has bestowed such a glory from heaven to heaven,
who makes great the glory of the angels and makes greater the
glory of him who sits on the throne.

8. 1. And again he raised me up into the air of the sixth heaven,
and I saw there a glory such as I had not seen in the fifth heaven,
2. as I ascended, namely, angels in greater glory; 3. and there was
a holy and wonderful song of praise there. 4. And I said to the
angel who conducted me 'What is this that I see, my Lord?'
5. And he said, 'I am not thy Lord, but thy companion.' 6. And
once more I asked him saying, 'Why are the angels not (any
longer) in two groups?' 7. And he said, 'From the sixth heaven
and upwards there are no longer any angels on the left, nor is
there a throne in the midst, but ⟨they receive their arrange-
ment⟩ from the power of the seventh heaven, where the unnamed
one dwells and his Elect one whose name is unfathomable and
cannot be known by the whole heaven, 8. for it is he alone to
whose voice all the heavens and thrones give answer. Thus I
have been empowered and sent to bring thee up here to see the
glory, 9. and to see the Lord of all those heavens and these thrones
10. being transformed till he comes to your image and likeness.
11. But I say to thee, Isaiah, that no one who has to return to a
body in this world has ascended or seen or perceived what thou
hast perceived and what thou shalt (yet) see; 12. for it is appointed
unto thee in the lot of the Lord [the lot of (the cross of) wood,]
to come hither [and from hence comes the power of the sixth
heaven and the air].' 13. And I extolled my Lord with praise
that I through his lot should come hither. 14. And he said, 'Hear
then this from thy companion: when thou by the will of God hast
ascended here from the body, then shalt thou receive the garment

which thou shalt see, and the other garments as well, numbered and stored up, thou shalt see; 15. and then shalt thou resemble the angels in the seventh heaven.' 16. And he brought me up into the sixth heaven and there was no one on the left and no throne in the midst, but all had one appearance and their song of praise was the same. 17. And (power) was given to me and I sang praise with them, and that angel also, and our praise was like theirs. 18. And there they all named the primal Father and his Beloved, Christ, and the Holy Spirit, all with one voice, 19. but it was not like the voice of the angels in the fifth heaven, 20. nor like their speech, but another voice resounded there, and there was much light there. 21. And then, when I was in the sixth heaven, I considered that light which I had seen in the five heavens as darkness. 22. And I rejoiced and praised him who has bestowed such light on those who wait for his promise. 23. And I besought the angel who conducted me that he would no more take me back to the world of the flesh. 24. I say to you, Hezekiah and Jasub my son and Micaiah, that there is much darkness here. 25. And the angel who conducted me perceived what I thought and said, 'If thou dost rejoice already in this light, how much wilt thou rejoice when, in the seventh heaven, thou seest that light where God and his Beloved are, whence I have been sent, [who in the world will be called "Son". 26. Not yet is he revealed who shall be in this corrupted world] and the garments, thrones and crowns which are laid up for the righteous, for those who believe in that Lord who shall descend in your form. For the light there is great and wonderful. 27. As far as thy wish not to return to the flesh is concerned, thy days are not yet fulfilled that thou mayest come here.' 28. When I heard that I was sad; but he said, 'Do not be sad.'

9. 1. And he conveyed me into the air of the seventh heaven and I heard again a voice saying, 'How far shall he ascend who dwells among aliens?' And I was afraid and began to tremble. 2. And when I trembled, behold, there came another voice, sent forth thence, and said, 'It is permitted to the holy Isaiah to ascend hither, for his garment is here.' 3. And I asked the angel who was with me and said, 'Who is he who forbade me, and who is this who has permitted me to ascend?' 4. And he said unto me,

'He who forbade thee is he who (is placed) over the praise of the sixth heaven, 5. and he who gave permission is thy Lord, God, the Lord Christ, who will be called Jesus on earth, but his name thou canst not hear till thou hast ascended out of thy body.' 6. And he caused me to ascend into the seventh heaven and I saw there a wonderful light and angels without number. 7. And there I saw all the righteous from Adam. 8. And I saw there the holy Abel and all the righteous. 9. And there I saw Enoch and all who were with him, stripped of the garment of the flesh, and I saw them in their higher garments, and they were like the angels who stand there in great glory. 10. But they did not sit on their thrones, nor were their crowns of glory on their heads. 11. And I asked the angel who was with me, 'How is it that they have received their garments, but are without their thrones and their crowns?' 12. And he said to me, 'Crowns and thrones of glory have they not yet received, (but) first the Beloved will descend in the form in which you will see him descend;—13. that is to say, in the last days the Lord, who will be called Christ, will descend into the world.—Nevertheless, they see the thrones and know to whom they shall belong and to whom the crowns shall belong after he has descended and become like you in appearance, and they will think that he is flesh and a man. 14. And the god of that world will stretch forth his hand against the Son, and they will lay hands on him and crucify him on a tree, without knowing who he is. 15. So his descent, as thou wilt see, is hidden from the heavens so that it remains unperceived who he is. 16. And when he has made spoil of the angel of death, he will arise on the third day and will remain in that world 545 days; 17. and then many of the righteous will ascend with him, whose spirits do not receive their garments till the Lord Christ ascends and they ascend with him. 18. Then indeed will they receive [their garments and] thrones and crowns when he shall have ascended into the seventh heaven.' 19. And I said unto him, 'As I asked thee in the third heaven, 20. show me (*Ethiop.:* and he said to me) how what happens in the world becomes known here.' 21. And while I was still talking with him, behold, (there came) one of the angels who stood by, more glorious than the glory of that angel who had brought me up from the world, 22. and he showed me books [but not like books of this world] and he opened them and the books were written, but not like books of this world. And he gave them to me and I read them and behold, the deeds of the children of Israel were recorded therein, and the deeds of those whom I know (*Eth.:* thou knowest) not (missing from Eth.), my son Jasub. 23. And I said, 'Truly there is nothing hidden in the seventh heaven of that which happens in the world.' 24. And I saw there many garments stored up, and many thrones and many crowns, 25. and I said to the angel who conducted me, 'To whom do these garments and thrones and crowns belong?' 26. And he said to me, 'These garments shall many from that world receive, if they believe on the words of that one who, as I have told thee, shall be named, and observe them and believe therein, and believe in his cross. For them are these laid up.' 27. And I saw one standing whose glory surpassed that of all, and his glory was great and wonderful. 28. And after I had beheld him, all the righteous whom I had seen and all the angels whom I had seen came unto him, and Adam, Abel and Seth and all the righteous approached first, worshipped him and praised him, all with one voice, and I also sang praise with them, and my song of praise was like theirs. 29. Then all the angels drew near and worshipped and sang praise. 30. And ⟨again⟩ I was transformed (*Eth.:* he was transformed) and became like an angel. 31. Then the angel who conducted me said to me, 'Worship this one;' so I worshipped and praised. 32. And the angel said to me, 'This is the Lord of all glory whom thou hast seen.' 33. And while he (the angel) was still speaking, I saw another glorious one, like to him, and the righteous drew near to him, worshipped and sang praise, and I too sang praise with them, but my glory was not transformed in accordance with their appearance. 34. And thereupon the angels approached and worshipped. 35. And I saw the Lord and the second angel, and they were standing; but the second one whom I saw was on the left of my Lord. 36. And I asked, 'Who is this?', and he said to me, 'Worship him, for this is the angel of the holy Spirit, who speaks (*Eth.:* has spoken) through thee and the rest of the righteous.' 37. And I beheld the great glory, for the eyes of my spirit were open, and I was not thereafter able to see, nor the angel who was with me, nor all the angels whom I had seen worshipping my Lord. 38. But I saw the righteous beholding with great power the glory of that One. 39. So my Lord drew near to me, and the angel of the Spirit, and said, 'Behold, now it is granted to thee to behold God, and on thy account is power given to the angel with thee.' 40. And I saw how my Lord worshipped, and the angel of the Holy Spirit, and how both together praised God. 41. Thereupon all the righteous drew near and worshipped, 42. and the angels approached and worshipped, and all the angels sang praise.

10. 1. And thereupon I heard the voices and the hymns of praise which I had heard ascending in each of the six heavens ⟨and they were audible⟩ here. 2. And they were all directed to the glorious One whose glory I could not see. 3. And I myself heard and saw the praise for him. 4. And the Lord and the angel of the spirit beheld all and heard all; 5. and all the praises, which are sent forth from the six heavens, are not only heard, but are seen also. 6. And I heard the angel who led me, how he said, 'This is the Most High of the High ones, who dwells in the holy world and rests with the holy ones, who will be called by the holy Spirit, through the mouth of the righteous, the Father of the Lord.' 7. And I heard the words of the Most High, the Father of my Lord, as he spoke to my Lord Christ who shall be called Jesus: 8. 'Go and descend through all the heavens; descend to the firmament and to that world, even to the angel in the realm of the dead; but to Hell thou shalt not go. 9. And thou shalt become like to the form of all who are in the five heavens; 10. and with carefulness thou shalt resemble the form of the angels of the firmament and the angels also who are in the realm of the dead. 11. And none of the angels of this world will know that thou, along with me, art the Lord of the seven heavens and of their angels. 12. And they will not know that thou art mine till with the voice of heaven I have summoned their angels and their lights, and the mighty voice be made to resound to the sixth heaven, that thou mayest judge and destroy the prince and his angels and the gods of this world and the world which is ruled by them, 13. for they have denied me and said "We alone are, and there is none beside us". 14. And afterwards thou wilt ascend from the angels of death to thy place, and thou wilt not be transformed

in each heaven, but in glory thou wilt ascend and sit on my right hand. 15. And the princes and powers of this world will worship thee.' 16. Thus I heard the great glory give command to my Lord. 17. Then I saw that my Lord went forth from the seventh heaven to the sixth heaven. 18. And the angel who conducted me [from this world was with me and] said, 'Attend, Isaiah, and behold, that thou mayest see the transformation of the Lord and his descent.' 19. And I beheld and when the angels who are in the sixth heaven saw him they praised and extolled him, for he had not yet been transformed into the form of the angels there, and they praised him, and I also praised with them. 20. And I saw how he descended into the fifth heaven, and in the fifth heaven took the appearance of the angels there, and they did not praise him, for his appearance was like theirs. 21. And immediately he descended into the fourth heaven and took the form of the angels there; 22. and when they saw him, they did not praise and laud him, for his appearance was as theirs. 23. And again I beheld when he descended into the third heaven and took the form of the angels of the third heaven. 24. And the guardians of the gate of this heaven demanded the pass-word and the Lord gave it to them in order that he should not be recognized, and when they saw him they did not praise and extol him, for his appearance was as theirs. 25. And again I beheld when he descended into the second heaven, and again he gave the pass-word there, for the door-keepers demanded it and the Lord gave it. 26. And I saw when he took the form of the angels in the second heaven; they saw him but did not praise him, since his form was like theirs. 27. And again I beheld when he descended into the first heaven and also gave the pass-word to the door-keepers there, and took the form of the angels who are on the left of that throne; and they did not praise or laud him, for his appearance was as theirs. 28. But no one asked me, on account of the angel who conducted me. 29. And again he descended into the firmament where the prince of this world dwells, and he gave the pass-word to those on the left, and his form was like theirs, and they did not praise him there, but struggled with one another in envy, for there the power of evil rules, and envying about trifles. 30. And I beheld, when he descended and became like the angels of the air and was like one of them. 31. And he gave no pass-word for they were plundering and doing violence to one another.

11. 1. And after this, I beheld, and the angel who talked with me and conducted me said to me, 'Attend, Isaiah, son of Amoz, because for this purpose have I been sent from God.' 2. And I saw of the family of David the prophet a *woman named Mary*, who was a *virgin, and betrothed to a man called Joseph*,[1] a carpenter, and he also was of the seed and family of the righteous David, of Bethlehem in Judah. 3. And he came to his portion. And *when she was betrothed, it was found that she was with child*, and *Joseph*, the carpenter, *wished to put her away*. 4. But the *angel* of the Spirit *appeared* in this world, and after that Joseph did not put Mary away, but kept her; but he did not reveal the matter to anyone.[2] 5. And he did not approach Mary, but kept her as a holy virgin, although she was with child. 6. And he did not (yet) live with her for two months. 7. And after two months, when Joseph was in his house, and his wife Mary, but both alone, 8. it came to pass, while they were alone, that Mary straightway beheld with her eyes and saw a small child, and she was amazed. 9. And when her amazement wore off, her womb was found as it was before she was with child. 10. And when her husband Joseph said to her, 'What made thee amazed?' his eyes were opened and he saw the child and praised God, that the Lord had come to his portion. 11. And a voice came to them: 'Tell this vision to no one.' 12. But the report concerning the child was noised abroad in Bethlehem. 13. Some said, 'The virgin Mary has given birth before she was married two months,'' 14. and many said 'She has not given birth: the midwife has not gone up (to her) and we have heard no cries of pain.' And they were all in the dark concerning him, and they all knew of him, but no one knew whence he was. 15. And they took him and came *to Nazareth* in *Galilee*.[3] 16. And I saw, O Hezekiah and Jasub my son, and declare before the other prophets who stand (here) that this was hidden from all the heavens and all the princes and every god of this world. 17. And I saw: in Nazareth he sucked the breast like a baby, as was customary, so that he would not be recognized. 18. And when he grew up he performed great signs and wonders in the land of Israel and in

---

[1] Lk. 1:27.   [2] Mt. 1:18–20.   [3] Mt. 2:23; Lk. 2:39.

Jerusalem. 19. And after this the adversary envied him and roused the children of Israel against him, not knowing who he was, and they delivered him to the king and crucified him, and he descended to the angel (of the underworld). 20. In Jerusalem indeed I saw how he was crucified on the tree, 21. and how he was raised after three days and remained (still many) days. 22. And the angel who conducted me said to me, 'Attend, Isaiah.' And I saw when he sent out his twelve apostles and ascended. 23. And I saw him and he was in the firmament, but he had not changed to their form, and all the angels of the firmament and the Satan saw him, and they worshipped him. 24. And great sorrow was occasioned there, while they said, 'How did our Lord descend in our midst and we perceived not the glory [which was upon him] which, as we see, was found on him from the sixth heaven?' 25. And he ascended into the second heaven and was not changed, but all the angels on the right and on the left and the throne in the midst 26. worshipped him and praised him saying 'How did our Lord remain hidden from us when he descended, and we perceived not?' 27. And in like manner he ascended to the third heaven and they sang praise and spoke in the same way. 28. And in the fourth and the fifth heavens they spoke exactly in the same manner; 29. there was rather one song of praise and (also) after that he was not changed. 30. And I saw when he ascended to the sixth heaven, and they worshipped him and praised him, 31. but in all the heavens the song of praise increased. 32. And I saw how he ascended into the seventh heaven, and all the righteous and all the angels praised him. And then I saw how he sat down on the right hand of that great glory, whose glory, as I told you, I was not able to behold. 33. And also I saw the angel of the holy Spirit sitting on the left. 34. And this angel said to me, 'Isaiah, son of Amoz, it is enough for thee, for these are great things; for thou hast seen what none born of flesh has yet seen, 35. and thou wilt return into thy garment till thy days are fulfilled: then thou wilt come hither.' This have I seen." 36. And Isaiah told it to all who stood before him, and they sang praise. And he spoke to king Hezekiah and said, "Such things have I spoken, 37. and the end of this world 38. and all this vision will be consummated in the last generation." 39. And Isaiah made him swear that he would not tell this to the people of Israel, nor permit any man to write down the words. 40. ⟨As far as ye understand from the king what is said in the prophets⟩, so far shall ye read. And ye shall be in the holy Spirit so that ye may receive your garments and the thrones and crowns of glory which are preserved in the seventh heaven.

41. On account of these visions and prophecies Sammael Satan sawed asunder the prophet Isaiah the son of Amoz, by the hand of Manasseh. 42. And all these things Hezekiah delivered to Manasseh in the twenty-sixth year. 43. But Manasseh did not remember them nor take them to heart, but after becoming the servant of Satan, he went to ruin.

Here endeth the vision of the prophet Isaiah with his ascension.

3. APOCALYPSE OF PETER

(Ch. Maurer; Translation of the Ethiopic Text by H. Duensing)

1. TEXTUAL TRADITION. The text of the Apocalypse of Peter has been known to us since 1887 in a *Greek fragment*, and since 1910 in an *Ethiopic translation*. The Greek text comes from the discovery at *Akhmim* (Upper Egypt) which brought to light, from the grave of a Christian monk, the Apocalypse of Peter, together with the fragment of the Gospel of Peter and the Greek Book of Enoch. The manuscript is in Cairo. The same hand worked on all three texts in the 8th–9th century. The text of the Apocalypse of Peter, which comprises not quite half of the original book, was divided by Harnack into 34 verses. Despite the lack of a heading the identity is firmly established: v. 26 agrees with a quotation which Clement of Alexandria (Ecl. 41. 2) gives from the Petrine Apocalypse.

A. Dillman (*NGA* 1858) and P. de Lagarde (*Mitteilungen* IV, 1891) had already referred to the extensive *Ethiopic* translation of the Corpus Clementinum, which as a whole is to be located in the 7th–8th century. E. Bratke (*ZwTh* 36, 1893, pp. 454–493) consciously sought the Apocalypse of Peter there, but without success. Sylvain Grébaut published in 1907–10, in the *Revue de l'Orient chrétien*, MS. No. 51 from the collection of A. d'Abadie, containing some tractates of this literature, and gave a French translation. Immediately the English scholar M. R. James recognized that the Apocalypse of Peter was contained in it; his essay, which deals with all the problems of the new discovery, is still instructive today (*JTS*, 1910–11). H. Duensing produced a German translation in *ZNW* 14, 1913, pp. 65ff. Depending on the divisions made in Grébaut's work H. Weinel, in *Apokr.* 2, divided the text into seventeen chapters.

Besides the Akhmim fragment and the Ethiopic translation there also exist two small *Greek fragments:* the one in the Bodleian, comprising vv. 33–34 in Greek, comes from the 5th century and was bought in

Egypt in 1894–95; the second is in the Rainer collection in Vienna and perhaps comes from the 3rd–4th century, and reproduces ch. 14. James (*JTS*, 1931, p. 278) thinks that the two fragments are parts of the same manuscript.

Among the citations in the Fathers the following may be mentioned: Theophilus of Antioch (ad Autolycum II. 19) alludes to the Apocalypse of Peter (Akhmim fragment, 15) around A.D. 180. Clement of Alexandria (d. before 215) quotes ch. 8 twice, Methodius of Olympus (d. 311) quotes ch. 8 once, and Macarius of Magnesia (*c*. 400) once each from ch. 4 and ch. 5. As a consecutive text we present below the translation of the Ethiopic made by H. Duensing (*ZNW* 1913, with improvements in his own hand); in the right-hand column there appears the translation of the Akhmim text. The quotations from the Fathers are in the notes.

The Gnostic Apocalypse of Peter should not be confused with our text. It was discovered in 1946 at Nag Hammadi, together with other Gnostic literature and is to be found in the Coptic Museum in Cairo (see p. 15). Likewise there is no point of contact with the so-called Apocalypse of Peter translated from the Arabic (A. Mingana, *The Apocalypse of Peter, edited and translated*, Woodbrooke Studies 3. 2, Cambridge, 1931; reviewed by M. R. James, *JTS* 33, 1932, pp. 311ff.).

2. PERIOD OF ORIGIN AND CIRCULATION. The fact that Clement of Alexandria mentions the Apocalypse as a writing of the Apostle Peter (Eus. *HE* VI. 14. 1) means that the period of origin must be fixed at least in the first half of the 2nd century. The *terminus a quo* is formed by 4 Esd., which belongs to *c*. A.D. 100 and which was probably used (cf. 4 Esd. 5:33 with ch. 3), together with the second letter of Peter, the priority of which has been demonstrated by F. Spitta. If the parable of the fig-tree in ch. 2 belongs to the original form and is to be referred to Bar Cochba, the Jewish enemy of the Christians (Weinel), then we come to the time around A.D. 135.

The undoubted recognition of the Apocalypse by Clement as well as the reference to the Egyptian reverence for animals in ch. 10 (in so far as this is not a later interpolation!) may point to Egypt as the place of origin.

Despite the mistrust which it occasioned in ecclesiastical circles, the Apocalypse of Peter found wide circulation in both the west and the east. In the east, Methodius still reckons it as being among the inspired writings, the Stichometry of Nicephorus considers that it belongs with the Antilegomena, while Macarius and Eusebius (*HE* III. 3. 25) relegate it to the non-genuine writings. Nevertheless it was widely read, especially perhaps in Egypt, whence it may have found its way into Arabic and Ethiopic, then also in Palestine, where Sozomen, even in the 5th century, mentions its regular public reading (*HE* VII. 19). In the west, it is listed by the Muratori Canon among the disputed writings. Moreover, it was used in a Latin sermon in the 4th century (cf. James, *JTS*, 1911, p. 383 on the MS. from Epinal). On further indirect testimony for the west, see Harnack, *TU* 13, 1895, pp. 71ff.

3. THE PROBLEM OF THE TWO TEXTS. Which text is nearer to the

original Apocalypse of Peter, the *Akhmim fragment* or that of the *Ethiopic translation*? In addition to some linguistic differences which can be accounted for by the fact that the Ethiopic gives a translation which is in parts faulty, the following variations may be noted. 1. The *extent* of the whole account in the Ethiopic is almost three times as great as that of the Akhmim text. 2. In the *content* of the parallel passages there is a considerable difference, more than has hitherto been noticed, between the description of Hell and that of Heaven. In the first the two forms are in substance in extensive agreement. The Akhmim fragment breaks off in the middle of the description and also leaves a piece missing in the middle of its text (chs. 8b and 11ff.). Great differences appear in the description of Paradise. Strictly speaking, the Ethiopic speaks of the place of the elect only in ch. 14. Ch. 15, on the other hand, narrates the story of the transfiguration, with the appearance of Moses and Elijah and the rest of the OT saints, to which Jesus adds that his disciples will attain to similar honour and glory. In the Akhim frag. there is no parallel to the Eth. ch. 14: on the contrary, the story of the transfiguration has become a real description of Paradise, in which the explicit request of the disciples for a glimpse of the departed saints and their world, as well as the detailed character of the corresponding description, are striking. 3. The *form* in which the account of the world of the righteous is presented is the same in both texts. Peter gives an account, in the past tense, of the vision which Jesus mediated on the holy mountain. The Greek version places the description of Hell within the same framework, but the Ethiopic translation gives this description as one of the Lord's predictions of the future. 4. The *sequence* of the descriptions is disordered in places. In association with the promise of Christ regarding his return, the resurrection of the dead and the Last Judgment, the Ethiopic takes first the description of Hell, and only in the second place gives the story of the transfiguration. The Akhmim fragment, on the other hand, has the opposite order.

Developing the suggestion made by Dieterich and Zahn, James comes to the conclusion that the Ethiopic corresponds tolerably well to the original Apocalypse of Peter, and that the Akhmim frag., on the other hand, represents a part of the Gospel of Peter. James agrees with Zahn that the original Apocalypse of Peter did not develop out of the Gospel of Peter (which was what Dieterich suggested) but was worked into it. The Akhmim fragment is then considered to be a recasting of the original Apocalypse to make an apocalyptic address of Jesus, in the manner of Mk. 13. On the other hand, Weinel finds in the Ethiopic later features and sees the story of Paradise actually as a further development of the older Akhmim text.

In the present discussion the following points may be taken as settled: (1.) The Eth. form approximately corresponds to the original length of the Apocalypse of Peter, for it exceeds only slightly the figures which are given by the Stichometry of Nicephorus (300 lines) and the Codex Claromontanus (270 lines). (2.) On the whole the Eth. presents the original contents of the Apocalypse. All the old citations

665

can be found in this and, in fact, are found distributed over chaps. 4, 5, 8, 10, 12 and 14. (3.) The fact that the Eth. has suffered severely from the translation is shown, with the utmost clarity, by the Rainer fragment. With its help Prümm shows how many details are simply to be traced back to the Ethiopic translator's deficient knowledge of Greek (*Biblica* X, 1929, pp. 77ff.). (4.) In the description of Hell priority is to be given to the Eth. by reason of its attestation from three quarters. The witness of Clement and the Bodleian fragment attest the promise-form of the Eth., and again Clement and Methodius bear witness to the fact that ch. 8b belongs to the original Apocalypse of Peter.

The only critical problems remaining are accordingly the content of the description of the transfiguration (or Paradise) and the sequence of the accounts concerning heaven and hell. It seems clear to me that the Akhmim fragment can be understood as a revision by someone who knew nothing more of the whole Apocalypse than the two sections, chs. 7–10 and 15–16a. On the basis of the "I" in chs. 15 and 16a, he could recognize the text as belonging to the Apocalypse of Peter; but, on account of the absence of 16b, he could not recognize that it was concerned with the transfiguration story, which in ch. 17 changes to an account of the heavenly journey; therefore he had to assume that he had before him the clear counterpart of the other fragment, i.e. the actual description of Paradise. He rounds off this new picture by means of the earlier-mentioned material additions (the request of the disciples to see the departed brethren and their world; the extensive description of the place of light and its inhabitants; the alteration of the OT "father" into the NT "high priest (brother?)"). He makes the opening words of ch. 15 the introduction to the whole, and as a result of this the change in the sequence is produced. We have a secondary witness to the original order in Sibyllines II, 238–338 (3rd century, see below, pp. 715ff.), in which the Apocalypse of Peter is used. The parallel passages in Akhmim fragment, vv. 17f. and 21 (angels of light or of punishment; bright or obscure air; the pregnant designation—which occurs only here—of heaven or hell as the "place") belong to the transitional work of the redactor; likewise vv. 1–3, which are drawn from 2 Pet. 2:1ff.

But what reasons could induce the finder of the fragment to make such an attempt at rounding it off? The answer is perhaps to be found in the suggestion of Dieterich, Zahn and James which, on the basis of the common place of discovery and the linguistic affinities, considers that the Akhmim text is a piece belonging to the Gospel of Peter. The suggestion is strengthened by the observation that, among other things, the two most important parallels are to be found only in the additional redactional work: the absolute form "the Lord" appears often in the Gospel of Peter (vv. 2, 3, 6, etc.) and in the Akhmim text at vv. 4, 6, 12, 15, 20, always as the special peculiarity of the Greek rendering against the Ethiopic, which never uses this expression. "We the twelve apostles" is found at v. 59 in the Gospel and at v. 5 in the Akhmim text, while the Ethiopic does not have the phrase. The old witnesses, however, always speak of the Gospel and the

Apocalypse as two separate writings. Consequently, we must assume, not that the author of the Gospel assimilated the Apocalypse (Zahn, James), but that it was a later finder of the two Greek fragments who first adapted the Apocalypse to the Gospel. Was it perhaps even the copyist of the Akhmim fragment in the 8th–9th century?

4. THE SIGNIFICANCE of the Apocalypse of Peter lies particularly in the realm of the history of religions. We have before us an outstanding and ancient example of that type of writing by means of which the pictorial ideas of Heaven and Hell were taken over into the Christian Church. In contrast to the Revelation of John which displays the final struggle and triumph of Jesus Christ, its interest no longer lies on the person of the Redeemer, but on the situation in the after-life, on the description of different classes of sinner, on the punishment of the evil and the salvation of the righteous. If the Apocalypse of Peter as a book lost its meaning in time, the ideas represented in it lived on in various ways (Sibyllines II; Apocalypse of Thomas 55–57; Apocalypse of Paul; apocalypsis seu visio Mariae virginis; right up to the full tide of description in Dante's Divina Commedia).

Dieterich sought the origin of this stock of ideas uniformly in the Orphic-Pythagorean mysteries. This may be, broadly speaking, true in the case of the description of Hell, but the ideas of the last judgment, the resurrection of the dead, of the destruction of the world by fire, etc., are to be traced back, through the medium of Jewish Apocalyptic (the Book of Enoch, the Apocalypse of Zephaniah, Wisdom of Solomon, etc.) to oriental origins.

5. LITERATURE. (a) Editions and Translations: *Akhmim text:* Editio princeps: U. Bouriant (*Mémoires publiées par les membres de la mission archéologique française au Caire*, Tom. IX, Paris, 1892).—With reproductions of the MS.: A. Lods, *ibid.*, 1893; O. von Gebhardt, 1893 (with German translation):—further, E. Preuschen: *Antilegomena*, ²1905 (with German translation); E. Klostermann, *KlT* 3, 1903; ²1908 and reprints; James, pp. 505–524 (English translation); *Apokr.* 2, pp. 314–327. *Ethiopic Text:* Sylvain Grébaut, *Revue de l'Orient chrétien*, Paris, 1907, pp. 139ff.; 1910, pp. 198ff.; 307ff.; 425ff. (with French translation). German translation: H. Duensing: Ein Stücke der urchristlichen Petrusapokalypse enthaltender Traktat der äthiopischen pseudoclementinischen Literatur, *ZNW* 14, 1913, pp. 65ff.; H. Weinel: *Apokr.* 2, pp. 318ff. (b) Investigations: on the basis of the Akhmim text: A. von Harnack: *Bruchstücke des Evangeliums und der Apokalypse des Petrus, TU* 9, 1893; id., *Die Petrusapokalypse in der abendländischen Kirche, TU* 13, 1895, pp. 71ff.; A. Dieterich: *Nekyia*, 1893, ²1913; F. Spitta; *Die Petrusapokalypse und der zweite Petrusbrief, ZNW* 12, 1911, pp. 237ff.; Th. Zahn: *Grundriss der Geschichte des nt.lichen Kanons*, ²1904, p. 24.

Since the appearance of the Ethiopic text: M. R. James: A new Text of the Apocalypse of Peter, *JTS* 1911, pp. 36ff.; 362ff.; 573ff.; id., The Recovery of the Apocalypse of Peter, *The Church Quarterly Review*, April 1915, pp. 1ff.; A. Bardenhewer, *Geschichte der altkirchlic²n Literatur*, Bd. 1, ²1913, pp. 610–615; K. Prümm: De genuino apocalypsis

Petri textu, examen testium iam notorum et novi fragmenti Raineriani, *Biblica* X, Rome, 1929, pp. 62ff.; J. R. Harris: The Odes of Solomon and the Apocalypse of Peter, *Exp. Times* 42, 1930, pp. 21f.; M. R. James: The Rainer Fragment of the Apocalypse of Peter, *JTS* 32, 1931, pp. 270–278; C. M. Edsmann: *Le baptême de feu*, Leipzig-Uppsala, 1940, pp. 57–63; J. Quasten, *Patrology*, Vol. 1, The Beginning of Patristic Literature, 1950, pp. 144–146 (with bibliography); G. Quispel and R. M. Grant: Note on the Petrine Apocrypha, *Vig. Chr.* 6, 1952, pp. 31–32; E. Peterson, Die Taufe im Acherusischen See, *Vig. Chr.* 9, 1955, pp. 1–20; W. Michaelis: *Die Apokryphen Schriften zum Neuen Testament, übersetzt und erklärt*, 1956, pp. 469–481 (with translation of the Akhmim text).

(Ethiopic)

1. *And when he was seated on the Mount of Olives*, his own *came unto him*,[1] and we entreated and implored him severally[2] and besought him, saying unto him, "Make known unto us what are *the signs of thy Parousia and of the end of the world*,[3] that we may perceive and mark the time of thy Parousia and instruct those who come after us, to whom we preach the word of thy Gospel and whom we install in thy Church, in order that they, when they hear it, may take heed to themselves that they mark the time of thy coming." And our Lord answered and said unto us, "*Take heed that men deceive you not*[4] and that ye do not become doubters and serve other gods. *Many will come in my name saying 'I am Christ'*.[5] *Believe them not and draw not near unto them*.[6] For *the coming of the Son of God will not be manifest, but like the lightning which shineth from the east to the west*,[7] so shall I *come on the clouds of heaven with a great host in* my *glory*;[8] with my cross going before my face[9] will I come in my glory, shining seven times as bright as the sun will I *come in my glory, with* all *my saints, my angels*,[10] when my Father will place a crown upon my head, that I may *judge the living and the dead*[11] and *recompense every man according to his work*.[12]

2. And ye, *receive ye the parable of the fig-tree* thereon: as soon as *its shoots* have gone forth and *its boughs* have *sprouted*, the end of the world will come."[13] And I, Peter, answered and said unto him, "Explain to me concerning the fig-tree, [and] how we shall

[1] Mt. 24:3 and par.
[2] Perhaps a wrong translation of κατ' ἰδίαν, Mt. 24:3 and par.　　[3] Mt. 24:3.
[4] Mt. 24:4 and par.　　[5] Mt. 24:5 and par.　　[6] Mt. 24:26; Lk. 17:23.
[7] Lk. 17:20; Mt. 24:27.　　[8] Mk. 13:26 and par.　　[9] Cf. Mt. 24:30.
[10] Lk. 9:26 and par.; Mt. 16:27.　　[11] 1 Pet. 4:5; 2 Tim. 4:1.
[12] Mt. 16:27; Ps. 62:12.　　[13] Mk. 13:28f. and par.

perceive it, for throughout all its days does the fig-tree sprout and every year it brings forth its fruit [and] for its master. What (then) meaneth the parable of the fig-tree? We know it not."— And the Master answered and said unto me, "Dost thou not understand that the fig-tree is the house of Israel? Even as a man *hath planted a fig-tree in his garden* and it brought forth no fruit, and he *sought its fruit for* many *years.* When he *found it not, he said to the keeper of his garden, 'Uproot the fig-tree* that *our land may* not be *unfruitful for us.'* And the gardener *said* to God, 'We thy servants (?) wish to clear it (of weeds) and to *dig*[1] the ground around it and to water it. *If it does not then bear fruit,* we will immediately *remove* its roots from the garden and plant another one in its place.' Hast thou not grasped that the fig-tree is the house of Israel? Verily, I say to you, when its boughs have sprouted at the end, then *shall deceiving Christs come,*[2] and awaken hope (with the words): '*I am the Christ,*[3] who am (now) come into the world.' And when they shall see the wickedness of their deeds (even of the false Christs), they shall turn away after them and deny him to whom our fathers gave praise (?), the first Christ whom they crucified and thereby sinned exceedingly. But this deceiver is not the Christ. And when they reject him, he will kill with the sword (dagger) and there shall be many martyrs. Then shall the boughs of the fig-tree, i.e. the house of Israel, sprout, and there shall be many martyrs by his hand: they shall be killed and become martyrs. Enoch and Elias will be sent to instruct them that *this is the deceiver who must come into the world*[4] *and do signs and wonders in order to deceive.*[5] And therefore shall they that are slain by his hand be martyrs and shall be reckoned among the good and righteous martyrs who have pleased God in their life."

3. And he showed me in his right hand the souls of all (men) and on the palm of his right hand the image of that which shall be fulfilled at the last day; and how the righteous and the sinners shall be separated and how those will do (?) who are upright in heart, and how the evil-doers will be rooted out for all eternity. We saw how the sinners wept in great distress and sorrow, until all who saw it with their eyes wept, whether righteous, or angels

---

[1] Lk. 13:6ff.   [2] Mk. 13:22 and par.   [3] Mt. 24:5.
[4] 2 Jn. 7; Rev. 12:9.   [5] Mk. 13:22 and par.

or himself also. And I asked him and said, "Lord, allow me to speak thy word concerning these sinners: '*It were better for them that they had not been created*'." And the Saviour answered and said "O Peter, why speakest thou thus, '*that not to have been created were better for them*'?[1] Thou resistest God. Thou wouldest not have more compassion than he for his image, for he has created them and has brought them forth when they were not (perhaps = and has brought them forth from not-being into being). And since thou hast seen the lamentation which sinners shall encounter in the last days, therefore thy heart is saddened; but I will show thee their works in which they have sinned against the Most High.

4. Behold now what they shall experience in the last days, when the day of God comes. On the day of the decision of the judgment of God, all the children of men from the east unto the west shall be gathered before my Father who ever liveth, and he will command *hell* to open its bars of steel and to *give up* all *that is in it*.[2] And the beasts and the fowls shall he command to give back all flesh that they have devoured, since he desires that men should appear (again); for nothing perishes for God, and nothing is impossible with him, since all things are his. For all things (come to pass) on the day of decision, on the day of judgment, at the word of God, and as all things came to pass when he created the world and commanded all that is therein, and it was all done[3]—so shall it be in the last days; for everything is possible with God and he says in the Scripture: 'Son of man, prophesy upon the several bones, and say to the bones—*bone unto bone* in joints, *sinews, nerves, flesh* and *skin* and hair thereon.' And *soul* and *spirit*[4] shall the great Uriel[5] give at the command of God. For him God has appointed over the resurrection of the dead on the day of judgment. Behold and consider the corns of wheat which are sown in the earth.[6] As something dry and without a soul does a man sow (them) in the earth; and they live again, bear fruit, and the earth gives (them) back again as a pledge entrusted to it. And this which dies, which is sown as seed in the earth and shall become alive and be restored to life, is man. How much more shall God

---

[1] Mk. 14:21 and par. [2] Rev. 20:13. [3] Cf. Gen. 1:3; Ps. 33:9.
[4] Cf. Ezek. 37:4ff. [5] Cf. Enoch 20:1. [6] Cf. 1 Cor. 15:36ff.

raise up on the day of decision those who believe in him and are chosen by him and for whom he made (the earth); and all this shall the earth give back on the day of decision, since it shall also be judged with them, and the heaven with it.[1]

5. And these things shall come to pass in the day of judgment of those who have fallen away from faith in God and have committed sin: cataracts of fire shall be let loose; and obscurity and darkness shall come up and cover and veil the entire world, and the waters shall be changed and transformed into coals of fire, and all that is in it (the earth?) shall burn and the sea shall become fire; under the heaven there shall be a fierce fire that shall not be put out and it flows for the judgment of wrath. And the stars shall be melted by flames of fire,[2] as if they had not been created, and the fastnesses of heaven shall pass away for want of water and become as though they had not been created. And the lightnings of heaven shall be no (?) more and, by their enchantment, they shall alarm the world (perhaps = the heaven will turn to lightning and the lightnings will alarm the world). And the spirits of the dead bodies shall be like to them and at the command of God will become fire. And as soon as the whole creation is dissolved, the men who are in the east shall flee to the west ⟨and those in the west⟩ to the east; those that are in the south shall flee to the north and those in the ⟨north to the⟩ south, and everywhere will the wrath of the fearful fire overtake them; and an unquenchable flame shall drive them and bring them to the judgment of wrath in the stream of unquenchable fire which flows, flaming with fire, and when its waves separate one from another, seething, there shall be much *gnashing of teeth*[3] among the children of men.

6. And all *will see how I come upon* an *eternal shining cloud, and the angels* of God who *will sit with me on the throne of my glory at the*

---

[1] Cf. Macarius Magnes, Apocritica IV. 6. 16: "By way of superfluity let this word also be quoted from the Apocalypse of Peter. He introduces the view that the heaven will be judged along with the earth in the following words, '*The earth will present before God on the day of judgment all men who are to be judged and itself also will be judged with the heaven that encompasses it*'."
[2] Cf. Macarius Magnes, Apocritica IV. 7: "And again he says (i.e. Peter in the Apocalypse) this statement which is full of impiety, saying '*And every power of heaven shall burn, and the heaven shall be rolled up like a book and all the stars shall fall like leaves from a vine and like the leaves from the fig-tree*'."—Probably the pagan writer whom Macarius opposes read not only the first part but also the continuation from Is. 34:4 (Heb.), "and the heaven shall be rolled up . . . fig-tree" in his text of the Apocalypse. Cf. 2 Pet. 3:10ff. [3] Mt. 8:12 etc.

right hand of my heavenly Father. He will set a crown upon my head. As soon as *the nations* see it, they *will weep,*[1] each nation for itself. And he shall command them to go into the *river of fire,*[2] while the deeds of each individual one of them stand before them. ⟨*Recompense shall be given*⟩ *to each according to his work.*[3] As for the elect who have done good, they will come to me and will not see (?) death by devouring fire. But the evil creatures, the sinners and the hypocrites will stand in the depths of the darkness that passes not away, and their punishment is the fire, and angels bring forward their sins and prepare for them a place wherein they shall be punished for ever, each according to his offence. The angel of God, Uriel, brings the souls of those sinners who perished in the flood, and of all who dwell in all idols, in every molten image, in every love and in paintings, and of them that dwell on all hills and in stones and by the wayside, (whom) men call gods: they shall be burned with them (i.e. the objects in which they lodge) in eternal fire. After all of them, with their dwelling places, have been destroyed, they will be punished eternally.

Ethiopic

Akhmim

21. But I saw also another place, opposite that one, very gloomy; and this was the place of punishment, and those who were punished there and the angels who punished had dark raiment, clothed according to the air of the place.

7. Then will men and women come to the place prepared for them. By their tongues with which they have blasphemed the way of righteousness will they be hung up. There is spread out for them unquenchable fire. . . .

22. And some there were there hanging by their tongues: these were those who had blasphemed the way of righteousness; and under them was laid fire, blazing and tormenting them. 23. And there was a great lake full of burning mire

[1] Mt. 26:64 and par.; Mt. 24:30 and par.; Mt. 16:27; Lk. 9:26 and par.
[2] Cf. Dan. 7:9f.   [3] Mt. 16:27; Ps. 62:12.

And behold again another place: this is a great pit filled, in which are those who have denied righteousness; and angels of punishment visit (them) and here do they kindle upon them the fire of their punishment. And again two women: they are hung up by their neck and by their hair and are cast into the pit. These are they who plaited their hair,[1] not to create beauty, but to turn to fornication, and that they might ensnare the souls of men to destruction. And the men who lay with them in fornication are hung by their thighs in that burning place, and they say to one another, "We did not know that we would come into everlasting torture."

And the murderers and those who have made common cause with them are cast into the fire, in a place full of venomous beasts, and they are tormented without rest, as they feel their pains, and their worms are as numerous as a dark cloud. And the angel Ezrael will bring forth the souls of them that have been killed and they shall see the torment ⟨of those who⟩ killed ⟨them⟩ and shall say to one another, "*Righteousness and justice is the*

in which were fixed certain men who had turned away from righteousness, and tormenting angels were placed over them.

24. And there were also others there: women hanging by their hair over that boiling mire. These were they who had adorned themselves for adultery. But those (men) who had united with them for the adulterous defilement ⟨were hanging⟩ by their feet ⟨and⟩ had their heads in the mire, and with ⟨loud voice⟩ cried out, "We did not believe that we would come to this place."

25. And I saw the murderers and their accessaries cast into a gorge full of venomous reptiles and tormented by those beasts, and thus writhing in that torture, and worms oppressed them like dark clouds. But the souls of those who had been murdered stood and watched the punishment of those murderers and said, "*O God, righteous is thy judgment.*"[2]

[1] Cf. 1 Pet. 3:3. [2] Ps. 19:9; Rev. 16:7; 19:2.

673

judgment of God."[1] For we have indeed heard, but did not believe that we would come to this place of eternal judgment."

8. And near this flame there is a great and very deep pit and into it there flow all kinds of things from everywhere: judgment(?), horrifying things and excretions. And the women (are) swallowed up (by this) up to their necks and are punished with great pain. These are they who have procured abortions and have ruined the work of God which he has created. Opposite them is another place where the children sit, but both alive, and they cry to God. And lightnings go forth from those children which pierce the eyes of those who, by fornication, have brought about their destruction.[2] Other men and women stand above them naked. And their children stand opposite to them in a place of delight. And they sigh and cry to God because of their parents, "These are they who neglected and cursed and transgressed thy commandment. They killed us and cursed the angel who created (us) and hung us up.

26. And near that place I saw another gorge in which the discharge and the excrement of the tortured ran down and became like a lake. And there sat women, and the discharge came up to their throats; and opposite them sat many children, who were born prematurely, weeping. And from them went forth rays of fire and smote the women on the eyes.[2] And these were those who produced children outside marriage and who procured abortions.

---

[1] Ps. 19:9; Rev. 16:7; 19:2.

[2] Cf. Clement of Alexandria, Ecl. 41: "The Scripture says that the children exposed by parents are *delivered to a protecting* (= *temelouchos*) *angel*, by whom they are brought up and nourished. And they shall be, it says, as the faithful of a hundred years old here (cf. Is. 65:20; Wisd. Sol. 4:16). Wherefore Peter also says in his Apocalypse, *"and a flash of fire, coming from their children and smiting the eyes of the women"*.

And they withheld from us the light which thou hast appointed for all." And the milk of the mothers flows from their breasts and congeals and smells foul, and from it come forth beasts that devour flesh, which turn and torture them for ever with their husbands, because they forsook the commandment of God and killed their children. And the children shall be given to the angel Temlakos.[1] And those who slew them will be tortured for ever, for God wills it to be so.

9. Ezrael, the angel of wrath, brings men and women with the half of their bodies burning and casts them into a place of darkness, the hell of men; and a spirit of wrath chastises them with all manner of chastisement, and a worm that never sleeps consumes their entrails. These are the persecutors and betrayers of my righteous ones.

27. And other ⟨men⟩ and women stood in flames up to the middle of their bodies and were cast into a dark place and were scourged by evil spirits and had their entrails consumed by worms which never wearied. These were those who persecuted the righteous and handed them over.

[1] Cf. besides:

(a) Clement of Alexandria, Ecl. 48f.: "For example Peter in the Apocalypse says *that the children born abortively* receive the better part. These *are delivered to a care-taking (temelouchos) angel*, so that after they have reached knowledge they may obtain the better abode, as if they had suffered what they would have suffered, had they attained to bodily life. But the others shall obtain salvation only as people who have suffered wrong and experienced mercy, and shall exist without torment, having received this as their reward. 49. *But the milk of the mothers which flows from their breasts and congeals,* says Peter in the Apocalypse, *shall beget tiny flesh-eating beasts and they shall run over them and devour them*—which teaches that the punishments will come to pass by reason of the sins."

(b) Methodius, Symposium II. 6: "Wherefore have we received it handed down in Scriptures inspired by God *that children who are born before their time, even if they be the offspring of adultery, are delivered to care-taking angels.* . . . *How could they* have confidently summoned *their parents* before the judgment seat of Christ *to bring a charge against them,* saying, 'Thou, O Lord, didst not grudgingly deny us this light that is common (to all), but these have exposed us to death, despising thy commandment' ".

675

And near to those who live thus were other men and women who chew their tongues, and they are tormented with red-hot irons and have their eyes burned. These are the slanderers and those who doubt my righteousness.

Other men and women—whose deeds (were done) in deception—have their lips cut off and fire enters into their mouths and into their entrails. ⟨These are those⟩ who slew the martyrs by their lying.

In another place situated near them, on the stone a pillar of fire (?), and the pillar is sharper than swords—men and women who are clad in rags and filthy garments, and they are cast upon it, to suffer the judgment of unceasing torture. These are they which trusted in their riches and despised widows and the woman (with) orphans . . . in the sight of God.

10. And into another place near by, saturated with filth, they throw men and women up to their knees. These are they who lent money and took usury.

And other men and women thrust themselves down from a high place and return again and run, and demons drive them.

28. And near to them again were men and women who bit through their lips and were in torment, with heated iron in their eyes. These were those who blasphemed the way of righteousness and slandered it.

29. And opposite these were still other men and women who bit through their tongues and had flaming fire in their mouths. These were the false witnesses.

30. And in another place were glowing pebbles, sharper than swords or any spit, and men and women, clad in filthy rags, rolled upon them in torment. These were they who were rich and trusted in their riches and had no mercy upon orphans and widows, but despised the commandment of God.

31. And in another great lake, full of discharge and blood and boiling mire, stood men and women up to their knees. These were those who lent money and demanded compound interest.

32. Other men and women who cast themselves down from a high slope came to the bottom and were driven by their tor-

These are the worshippers of idols, and they drive them to the end of their wits (slope?) and they plunge down from there. And this they do continually and are tormented for ever. These are they who have cut their flesh as apostles of a man, and the women who were with them ... and thus are the men who defiled themselves with one another in the fashion of women.

And beside them ... (an untranslatable word), and beneath them the angel Ezrael prepares a place of much fire, and all the golden and silver idols, all idols, the works of men's hands, and what resembles the images of cats and lions, of reptiles and wild beasts, and the men and women who manufactured the images, shall be in chains of fire; they shall be chastised because of their error before them (the images) and this is their judgment for ever. And near them other men and women who burn in the flame of the judgment, whose torture is for ever. These are they who have forsaken the commandment of God and followed ... (*unknown word*) of the devils.[1]

turers to go up the precipice and were then thrown down again, and had no rest from this torture. These were those who defiled their bodies, behaving like women. And the women with them, these were those who behaved with one another as men with a woman.

33. And near that precipice was a place filled with powerful fire. And there stood men who, with their own hands, had fashioned images in place of God.

And beside them were other men and women who had glowing rods and smote one another and had no rest from this torture.

34. And near to them still other men and women who were burned and turned (in the fire) and were baked. These were those who forsook the way of God.[1]

---

[1] Cf. the Bodleian Fragment (James, *JTS* 1911, pp. 367ff.): "⟨*Men and women*⟩ *who hold chains and scourge themselves before the deceitful images, and will ceaselessly experience the torment: and near to them other men and women* ... *these are they who have* ⟨*utterly*⟩ *forsaken the way of God* ...*"

11. And another very high place . . . (*some unintelligible words*), the men and women who make a false step go rolling down to where the fear is. And again, while the (fire) that is prepared floweth, they mount up and fall down again and continue their rolling. They shall be punished thus for ever. These are they who have not honoured their father and mother, and of their own accord withdrew themselves from them. Therefore shall they be punished eternally. Furthermore the angel Ezrael brings children and maidens to show to them those who are punished. They will be punished with pain, with hanging up (?) and with many wounds which flesh-eating birds inflict. These are they that have confidence in their sins, are not obedient to their parents, and do not follow the instruction of their fathers and do not honour those who are older than they. Beside them, maidens clad in darkness for raiment, and they shall be seriously punished and their flesh will be torn in pieces. These are they who retained not their virginity till they were given in marriage; they shall be punished with these tortures, while they feel them.

And again other men and women who ceaselessly chew their tongues and are tormented with eternal fire. These are the slaves who were not obedient to their masters. This then is their judgment for ever.

12. And near to this torment are blind and dumb men and women whose raiment is white. They are packed closely together and fall on coals of unquenchable fire. These are they who give alms and say, "We are righteous before God", while they yet have not striven for righteousness. The angel of God Ezrael allows them to come forth out of this fire and sets forth a judgment of decision (?). This then is their judgment. (And) a stream of fire flows and all judgment (=all those judged)[1] are drawn into the midst of the stream. And Uriel sets them down (there). And there are wheels of fire, and men and women hung thereon by the power of their whirling. Those in the pit burn. Now these are the sorcerers and sorceresses. These wheels (are) in all decision by fire without number (?).

[1] Cf. the sermon on the parable of the Ten Virgins in the Epinal MSS. from the 4th century (cited by James, *JTS* 1911, p. 383): "*The closed door is the river of fire by which the ungodly will be kept out of the kingdom of God, as it is written in Daniel* (Dan. 7:9f.) *and by Peter in his Apocalypse*", and " *That party of the foolish shall also rise and find the door shut, that is, the river of fire lying before them*".

13. The angels will bring my elect and righteous which are perfect in all righteousness, and shall bear them in their hands and clothe them with the garments of eternal life. *They shall see (their desire) on those who hated*[1] them, when he punishes them. Torment for every one (is) for ever according to his deeds. And all those who are in torment will say with one voice, "Have mercy upon us, for now we know the judgment of God, which he declared to us beforehand, and we did not believe." And the angel Tatirokos (= Tartarouchos) will come and chasten them with even greater torment and will say unto them, "Now do ye repent when there is no more time for repentance, and nothing of life remains." And all shall say, *"Righteous is the judgment of God:* for we have heard and perceived that *his judgment is good,*[2] since we are punished according to our deeds."

14. Then will I give to my elect and righteous the baptism and the salvation for which they have besought me, in the field Akrōsjā (= Acherusia) which is called Anēslaslejā (= Elysium). They shall adorn with flowers the portion of the righteous and I will go. . . . I will rejoice with them. I will cause the nations to enter into my eternal kingdom and show to them that eternal thing to which I have directed their hope, I and my heavenly Father. I have spoken it to thee, Peter, and make it known to thee. Go forth then and journey to the city in the west in the vineyard which I will tell thee of . . . by the hand of my Son who is without sin, that his work . . . of destruction may be sanctified. But thou art chosen in the hope which I have given to thee. Spread thou my gospel throughout the whole world in peace! For there will be rejoicing (?) at the source of my word, the hope of life, and suddenly the world will be carried off.[3]

[1] Ps. 54:7; 59:10.   [2] Ps. 19:9; Rev. 16:7; 19:2.
[3] Cf. the Rainer Fragment (*PO* XVII, 1924, pp. 482f.; K. Prümm, *Biblica* X, 1929, pp. 77ff.; M. R. James, *JTS* 1931, pp. 270ff.): *"Then will I grant to my called and chosen whomsoever they shall ask me for out of torment* (so James, who reads ὃν ἐὰν αἰτήσωνται instead of the difficult θεὸν ἐὰν στέσωνται = I shall grant to them God, if they call to me in the torment) *and I will give to them a precious baptism unto salvation from the Acherusian lake, which men say (is situated) in the Elysian field, the portion of the righteous with my holy ones. And I shall depart, I and my exulting chosen, with the patriarchs, into my eternal kingdom, and I will fulfil for them my promises which I have given to them, both I and my Father in heaven. Behold, I have manifested all unto thee, Peter, and expounded it. Go into the city which rules over the west* (so James, who reads δύσεως instead of ὁπύσεως = over fornication) *and drink the cup which I have promised thee* (cf. Mk. 10:39 and par.) *at the hands of the son of him who (is) in Hades, that his destruction* (cf. 2 Thess. 2:3, 8) *may begin and thou mayest be worthy of the promise (?) . . ."* The transference of men from the fiery torment to the Acherusian lake by means of the intercession of the blessed is found particularly in Or. Sib. II. 330–339.

Ethiopic

Akhmim

1. Many of them shall be false prophets and shall teach ways and diverse doctrines of perdition. 2. And they shall become sons of perdition.[1] 3. And then God will come to my faithful ones who hunger and thirst[2] and are afflicted and prove their souls in this life, and shall judge the sons of iniquity. 4. And the Lord continued and said, "Let us *go to the mountain and pray*."[3] 5. And we, the twelve disciples, went with him and entreated him to show to us one of our righteous brethren who had departed from the world that we might see in what form they are, and taking courage might encourage the men who should hear us.

15. And my Lord Jesus Christ, our King, said to me, "Let us *go into the holy mountain*." And his disciples went with him, *praying*.[3]

And behold, there were *two men*, and we could not look on their *faces*, for a light came from them which *shone more than the sun*, and their *raiment* also *was glistening*[4] and cannot be described, and there is nothing sufficient to be compared to them in this world. And its gentleness . . . that no mouth is able to express the beauty of their form. For their aspect was astonishing and wonderful. And the other, great, I say,

6. And as we prayed, suddenly there appeared *two men*, standing before the Lord, on whom we were not able to look. 7. For there went forth from their *countenance a ray, as of the sun*, and their *raiment was shining, such as* the eye of man never[4] ⟨saw. For⟩ no mouth can describe nor ⟨heart conceive⟩ the glory with which they were clad nor the beauty of their countenance. 8. And when we saw them we were

[1] Cf. 2 Pet. 2:1ff.; Jn. 17:12; 2 Thess. 2:3.   [2] Cf. Mt. 5:6.
[3] 2 Pet. 1:18; Mk. 9:2ff. and par.; Lk. 9:28.   [4] Cf. Mk. 9:2ff. and par.

shines in his appearance more than hail (crystal). Flowers of roses is the likeness of the colour of his appearance and his body . . . his head. And upon his shoulders and on their foreheads was a crown of nard, a work woven from beautiful flowers; like the rainbow in water was his hair. This was the comeliness of his countenance, and he was adorned with all kinds of ornament. And when we suddenly saw them, we marvelled.

16. And I approached God Jesus Christ and said to him, "My Lord who is this?" And he said to me, "These are *Moses and Elias*."[1] And I said to him, "(Where then are) Abraham, Isaac, Jacob and the other righteous fathers?"

And he showed us a great open *garden*. (It was) full of fair *trees* and blessed *fruits*,[2] full of the fragrance of perfume. Its fragrance was beautiful and that fragrance reached to us. And of it . . . I saw many fruits.

astonished, for their bodies were whiter than any snow and redder than any rose. 9. But the redness of them was mingled with the whiteness, and I simply cannot describe their beauty. 10. For their hair was curled and charmingly suited their faces and their shoulders like some garland woven of blossom of nard and various coloured flowers, or like a rainbow in the air; so beautifully formed was their appearance. 11. When we saw their beauty, we were astonished before them, for they had appeared suddenly.

12. And I approached the Lord and said, "Who are these?" 13. He said to me, "These are your righteous brethren whose form ye did desire to see." 14. And I said to him, "And where are all the righteous, and what is the nature of that world in which these are who possess such glory?" 15. And the Lord showed me a widely extensive place outside this world,[3] all gleaming with light, and the air there flooded by the rays of the sun, and the earth itself budding with flowers which fade not, and full of spices and plants which

---

[1] Mk. 9:4 and par.   [2] Gen. 1:8ff; Rev. 22:2.
[3] On the following cf. Theophilus of Antioch, Ad Autolycum II. 19, "God chose for Adam as paradise '*a place in the eastern region, marked out by light, illumined by shining air, with plants of wondrous beauty*' ".

681

blossom gloriously and fade not and bear blessed fruit. 16. So great was the fragrance of the flowers that it was borne thence even unto us. 17. The inhabitants of that place were clad with the shining raiment of angels and their raiment was suitable to their place of habitation. 18. Angels walked there amongst them. 19. All who dwell there had an equal glory, and with one voice they praised God the Lord, rejoicing in that place. 20. The Lord said unto us, "This is the place of your high-priests ⟨brothers?⟩, the righteous men."

And my Lord and God Jesus Christ said unto me, "Hast thou seen the companies of the fathers? As is their rest, so also is the honour and glory of those *who will be persecuted for my righteousness' sake.*"[1]

⟨And I was joyful and believed⟩ and understood that which is written in the book of my Lord Jesus Christ. And I said to him, " *My Lord, wilt thou that I make here three tabernacles, one for thee, one for Moses and one for Elias?*"[2] And he said to me in wrath, "*Satan* maketh war against thee, and has veiled *thine understanding,*[3] and the good things of this world conquer thee. Thine eyes must be opened and thine ears unstopped that . . . a tabernacle, which the hand of man has not made, but which my heavenly Father has made for me and for the elect." And we saw (it) full of joy.

17. And behold there came suddenly a *voice from heaven* saying, "*This is my Son, whom I love and in whom I have pleasure,*[4] and my commandments. . . . And there came a great and *exceeding white cloud* over our heads and *bore away our Lord*[5] and Moses and Elias. And I trembled and was afraid, and we looked up and the

---

[1] Mt. 5:10.   [2] Mt. 17:4 and par.   [3] Mt. 16:23 and par.
[4] Mt. 17:5 and par.; Mt. 3:17 and par.   [5] Mt. 17:5; Acts 1:9.

heavens opened and we saw men in the flesh, and they came and greeted our Lord and Moses and Elias, and went into the second heaven. And the word of Scripture was fulfilled: *This generation seeketh him and seeketh the face of the God of Jacob.*[1] And great fear and great amazement took place in heaven; the angels flocked together that the word of Scripture might be fulfilled which saith: *Open the gates, ye princes!*[2] After that the heaven was shut, that had been opened. And we prayed and *went down from the mountain, and we praised God*[3] who *hath written the names* of the righteous in heaven *in the book of life.*[4]

[1] Ps. 24:6.
[2] Ps. 24:7–9—E. Kähler, *Studien zum Te Deum und zur Geschichte des 24. Psalms in der alten Kirche*, 1958, pp. 53–55, finds in ch. 17 of the Apocalypse of Peter a description of the post-Easter triumphal ascension to heaven, in which the opposition of hostile powers is broken by the angels, and the righteous, in the train of the Redeemer, are led into the second, i.e. the real heaven.
[3] Mk. 9:9 and par.; Lk. 24:52f.   [4] Dan. 12:1; Rev. 17:8, etc.

XVII

APOCALYPTIC PROPHECY OF THE EARLY
CHURCH

INTRODUCTION

(W. Schneemelcher)

Judaism in the Hellenistic-Roman period was stirred by manifold hopes and expectations. These hopes found very varied expression in Apocalyptic, the Sibyllines and many kinds of Prophecy. Consequently, when we point out a contrast between national and universal eschatology, we characterize only one aspect of this variegated picture (on Jewish Apocalyptic, cf. above, pp. 582ff.).

In early Christianity, Apocalyptic, Sibyllines and Prophecy continued their existence, but they were purified of their national-Jewish elements. It is significant that the association of Apocalyptic and Prophecy is found in early Christianity (cf. above, pp. 605ff.), i.e. that the early Christian prophets, who were in fact above all charismatic leaders of the community, used Apocalyptic terminology and ideas. This association lasted only so long as the prophets played a definite role in the Christian church. From the time when the prophets were replaced by other functionaries, Apocalyptic also found another place in the Church: it became again what it had originally been, namely book-wisdom, in which much traditional material lived on, but which remained a marginal feature in a Church presided over by officials.

Only a few witnesses are extant for what may be called apocalyptic prophecy in the 2nd century; in fact, we might even ask whether the pieces treated together in the section (5 and 6 Ezra, the Sibyllines, and Elchasai) are rightly assembled under this collective title. They certainly do not represent any firm unity; in one, an Apocalyptist speaks as an OT prophet; then the "ancient seer", the Sibyl, gives forth her messages, which are stamped by Jewish and Christian apocalyptic; and finally the prophet Elchasai emerges and joins together visions and ethical exhortation and Jewish-apocalyptic prophesyings. Even in terms of the history of religion, these texts scarcely present a unity. However, it is characteristic of the prophets in the early Church that they represent no theological or dogmatic unity, and that, depending on their origin, they could give very different clothing to their preaching. The texts here presented can be taken together because in them prophets speak, i.e. men filled with the Spirit, and because they clothe their teaching in apocalyptic imagery and ideas.

We must be clear, however, that in the time of the early Church there was evidently an abundance of these prophetic figures in the most varied spheres. How very similar the phenomenon might be in Christianity, paganism and Judaism, is shown by the uncertainty which obtains in the interpretation of a report of Celsus, treating of such prophets:

> Many people and (indeed such) without names act as soothsayers with the greatest readiness, for some incidental cause, outside and inside temples; others go around begging in cities and camps. It is common practice and customary for each to say, "I am God or a child of God or a divine Spirit. But I have come: for already the world is passing away, and you, O men, go hence by reason of your iniquities. But I wish to save you, and you will see me coming again with heavenly power. Blessed is he who has worshipped me now, but upon all the rest will I inflict eternal fire, upon cities and country places. And those men who know not their penalties shall repent in vain and groan, but those who obey me will I preserve for ever." . . . Having uttered these sayings abroad, they even add unintelligible, half-crazy and utterly obscure words, the meaning of which no intelligent person can discover. (Origen, c. Celsum, VII. 9.)

It has been thought that in the figures caricatured by Celsus we may see Christian, Christian-Gnostic or Montanist prophets. But it is more probable that Celsus had in mind some pagan prophets from Phoenicia or Palestine.[1] In any case, there seem to have been many figures of this kind in all religions. But such prophets scarcely spent much time on the writing of books; at any rate, not much is known of any such literary deposit of their prophetic activity. We may assume that the authors of the texts collected below were probably figures like this, although we would not wish to burden them wholly and completely with all the features found in the prophets of Celsus.

Even the last great prophetic movement in the early Church, Montanism, left behind no books, though the opponents of the heresy report that Montanus himself, Priscilla (Prisca) and Maximilla composed numerous writings.[2] Unfortunately, there is nothing extant; we are dependent on the few prophetic utterances

---

[1] That it is not a matter of Montanist prophets has already been demonstrated by P. de Labriolle, *La crise montaniste*, 1913, pp. 99f.

[2] Hippolyt. Ref. VIII. 19. 1; Euseb. *HE* VI. 20. 3. Further details in K. Aland, Bemerkungen zum Montanismus: *Kirchengeschichtliche Entwürfe*, 1960, pp. 105f.; cf. there also the evidence for the later political legislation against Montanism, which is made responsible for the disappearance of the Montanist literature. But was there really such a literature?

handed down if we would attempt to answer the question whether Montanism—the Montanism of Asia Minor in the 2nd century, not that in Africa (Tertullian) in the 3rd century—falls within the terms of reference of apocalyptic prophecy or not. This question is the only one we can pursue in our discussion. All the other problems raised by Montanism cannot be opened up here.[1] First of all, we collect the prophetic sayings whose authenticity seems to be secure.[2]

1. (Montanus says:) I am the Father and I am the Son and I am the Paraclete. (Dialogue of a Montanist with an Orthodox: edited by G. Ficker, *ZKG* 26, 1905, p. 452. Cf. also Didymus, De Trin. III. 41. 1.)

2. (Montanus speaks:) I the Lord, the Almighty God, remain among men. (Epiphanius, *Haer.* 48. 11. 1.)

3. (Montanus says:) Neither angel, nor ambassador, but I, the Lord God the Father, am come.
(Epiphanius, *Haer.* 48. 11. 9.)

4. (Montanus says:) Behold, man is like a lyre and I rush thereon like a plectrum. Man sleeps and I awake. Behold, the Lord is he who arouses the hearts of men (throws them into ecstasy) and gives to men a new heart.
(Epiphanius, *Haer.* 48. 4. 1.)

5. (Montanus says:) Why dost thou call the super-man (?) saved? For the righteous man, he says, will shine a hundred times more strongly than the sun, but the little ones who are saved among you will shine a hundred times stronger than the moon. (Epiphanius, *Haer.* 48. 10. 3.)

6. (The Paraclete in the new prophets says:) The Church can forgive sins but I will not do it, lest they sin yet again.
(Tertullian, de pud. XXI. 7.)

7. (The Spirit says:) Thou wilt be publicly displayed: that is good for thee; for whosoever is not publicly displayed before men will be publicly displayed before God. Let it not perplex thee! Righteousness brings thee into the midst (of men). What perplexes thee about winning glory? Opportunity is given, when thou art seen by men.
(Tertullian, de Fuga IX. 4.)

[1] Cf. on Montanism in general, Aland, *op. cit.*, also the older literature there. On chronology: G. S. P. Freeman-Grenville, The date of the outbreak of Montanism, *Journal of Eccl. Hist.* 5, 1954, pp. 7–15.
[2] Details on the question of authenticity in Aland, *op. cit.*, pp. 111ff., and pp. 143ff.; the different enumerations of the Sayings in Hilgenfeld, Bonwetsch, Labriolle and Aland are here disregarded.

8. (The Spirit speaks:) Desire not to die in bed, nor in delivery of children, nor by enervating fevers, but in martyrdom, that He may be glorified who has suffered for you.
(Tertullian, de Fuga IX. 4; cf. Tertullian, de Anima LV. 5.)

9. (The Paraclete says through the prophetess Prisca:) They are flesh and (yet) they hate the flesh.
(Tertullian, de Resurr. Mort. XI. 2.)

10. (The holy prophetess Prisca proclaims:) A holy minister must understand how to minister holiness. For if the heart gives purification (?), says she, they will also see visions (visiones), and if they lower their faces, then they will perceive saving voices, as clear as they were obscure.
(Tertullian, de Exhort. Cast. X. 5.)

11. (Quintilla or Priscilla says:) In the form of a woman, says she, arrayed in shining garments, came Christ to me and set wisdom upon me and revealed to me that this place (=Pepuza) is holy and that Jerusalem will come down hither from heaven. (Epiphanius, *Haer.* 49. 1. 2–3.)

12. (Maximilla says:) After me, says she, there will be no more prophets, but (only) the consummation.
(Epiphanius, *Haer.* 48. 2. 4.)

13. (Maximilla says:) Listen not to me, but listen to Christ.
(Epiphanius, *Haer.* 48. 12. 4.)

14. (Maximilla says:) The Lord has sent me as adherent, preacher and interpreter of this affliction and this covenant and this promise; he has compelled me, willingly or unwillingly, to learn the knowledge of God.
(Epiphanius, *Haer.* 48. 13. 1.)

15. (The Spirit says through Maximilla:) I am chased like a wolf from (the flock of) sheep; I am not a wolf; I am word and spirit and power. (Euseb. *HE* V. 16. 17.)

A separate interpretation of each of these fifteen sayings, which probably stem from the early period of Montanism, cannot be provided here.[1] Can what Montanism really was be read off from these sayings? Naturally not without looking back at the accounts we have elsewhere. However, the self-awareness of Montanus and of his two prophetesses seems to me to come to light in these words. Three points concerning them should be emphasized.

[1] A form-historical investigation of the Sayings must also be put aside, though this would be valuable.

1. Montanus considers himself to be exclusively an instrument of God. Through him God, or the Spirit of God, speaks (Sayings 1–4). We should probably not argue from Saying 1 to some special Trinitarian teaching—Montanism, at the time of its beginning, was considered orthodox—but should understand it only as a testimony to the spirit-filled character of the prophet. Saying 11 (Priscilla's vision) and Saying 14 (Maximilla's testimony) should be explained in this direction too. It is quite clear from Saying 14 that the prophetess was impelled against her will. This means that Montanism, in its beginning, was a prophetic movement which stood in a not very closely demonstrable relationship to early Christian prophecy.

2. This prophetic movement does not appear to have been especially strongly influenced by apocalyptic thoughts; at any rate, specifically apocalyptic notions do not appear in the forefront in the Sayings. Only the imminent expectation of the End (S. 12) and the hope of the appearance of the heavenly Jerusalem in Pepuza (S. 11) allow us to conclude that in Montanism apocalyptic ideas were effective. Yet the Revelation of John would have suggested such ideas. On the whole, early Montanism seems to have been a prophetic, but not a strictly apocalyptic, movement.

3. Even if rigorist ethics first appeared in the forefront in the later stages of Montanism (Tertullian), some of these prophetic sayings (4, 5, 6) indicate that such a pressure for ethical renewal was not lacking in the early stages. Even the trouble taken by opponents to disparage the morality of the Montanists means that a part of Montanus' preaching did relate to ethical renewal and repentance. The Spirit produces not only ecstasy, but a new heart as well (Saying 4). This feature also belongs quite satisfactorily within the pattern of the prophetic movement, for the prophetic charisma is revealed in hortatory sayings as well. Apocalyptic too naturally did not lack paraenesis, but there it is not a specific feature and it is not strictly rigorist, in the Montanist sense. All in all, we must understand Montanism as a restoration of early Christian prophecy in which the Apocalyptic world of ideas falls into the background.

Attention must be given to one final question. Did the sayings of Montanus and his prophetesses, sayings which were evidently collected early and handed down, enjoy an authority which could be called canonical? The use which Tertullian made of these sayings might suggest some such idea, in so far as it shows the kind of authority which was attributed to these sayings. But they could scarcely be said to take the place of Scripture, in any case not in the second period of Montanism (post 200), but probably not even in the first period. This seems to provide evidence that the prophets of Montanism stand in continuity with the early Christian prophets but not with Apocalyptic.

1. THE FIFTH AND SIXTH BOOKS OF ESRA
(*H. Duensing*)

1. TRADITION. In the texts of the Latin Bible, the Fourth Book of Esra has two additional chapters at the beginning and at the end; these are missing in the Oriental translations. Chapters 1 and 2 are a Christian Apocalypse which is introduced in the MSS. before or after 4 Esra, and are known to some extent as the Fifth Book of Esra. Chapters 15 and 16 form an appendix: these chapters, in point of style, are prophecies filled with sayings of woe in the fashion of the OT, and, like the introductory chapters as a whole, they are available only in Latin. Linguistic observations point to a Greek original and this is confirmed for chs. 15–16 by the discovery of a small Greek fragment of ch. 15, vv. 57–59, among the Oxyrhynchus papyri. The manuscript tradition is divided into two groups: a Frankish, represented by S, the Codex Sangermanensis of the year 822, and the Codex A = Ambianensis, also from the 9th century; and a Spanish, represented by C = Complutensis from the 9th–10th century and M = Mazarinaeus, from the 11th–12th century, and in addition some other secondary witnesses among which the C. Legionensis = L has a sharply divergent text; according to Violet, this text is indebted to the modifying treatment by a writer of independent spirit. The group S A as a rule has a higher value than C M (NVL).

2. CONTENTS. The prophecy of the two introductory chapters falls into two parts. The first turns against the Jewish people, the second is concerned with the Christians who must take their place. It is possible that in the first section material from a Jewish text has been used and has been worked over by a Christian hand (see 1. 11; 1. 24; 1. 30 and especially 1. 35–40) to provide an invective against the Jewish people. On the other hand, the second part, 2. 10–48, which brings comforting promises to the Christians, is purely Christian, in spite of 2. 33, 42, etc., which are decoration. Chs. 15 and 16 comprise the Sixth Book of Esra and include descriptions of the dissolution of the world which comes to its fulfilment in terrible wars and natural events by which Babylon, Asia, Egypt and Syria in particular are threatened, but which will admonish, strengthen and comfort the people of God who will have suffered the afflictions of persecution.

3. TIME OF COMPOSITION. In 2. 42–47 an innumerable company of Christian martyrs are crowned. This takes us beyond the 1st century. The young man of great stature has a parallel in the Gospel of Peter, in the Acts of Perpetua and Felicitas, and also in the Shepherd of Hermas. This feature points to the second century, but, since the argument with Judaism still clearly possesses significance, we ought not to place the writing too late. We may adhere to a date around A.D. 200.

It is different with the appendix, chs. 15–16. In this a persecution is assumed, stretching over the entire eastern half of the Roman empire, a persecution in which the Christians, driven from their homes, robbed of their goods and imprisoned, were compelled to eat flesh offered to idols. For this there is available the long space of time from about 120 to the end of the persecutions under Constantine. On the basis of some particular features which it has been thought possible to fix in time, the writing has been dated in the 3rd century. But a precise decision as to the time of writing is no more possible than is a fixing of the place of origin, although the western regions of the Orient have the greatest degree of probability.

4. SIGNIFICANCE. The extent to which the apocalyptic material of 5th Esra attracted Christians in later times can be seen—in addition to other references and reminiscences in the official Roman Catholic liturgy—in the fact that in a fragment of a Missal from the 11th century the passage 2. 42–48 is communicated in complete text as the epistle for the Mass *de communi plurimorum martyrum*. Many separate points as well have special significance: the twelve angels with flowers 1. 40; the people of God who come from the east, 1. 38; the tree of life in Paradise, 2. 12; the twelve fruit-trees in 2. 18; the resurrection in 2. 31 and the exceedingly tall son of God in 2. 43 (on the growth-motif, cf. the material in E. Hammerschmidt, *Studies in the Ethiopic Anaphoras*, 1961, p. 98).

On the other hand, 6th Esra provides threats of judgment, comfort and exhortation within the definite circumstances of a period of persecution. Everything is earth-bound here. Nevertheless this work also seemed suitable for use in warning and exhortation, as is shown by the letter of the Anglo-Saxon writer Gildas (dated in the 7th or 6th century), in which the text of ch. 15. 21–27 and 16. 3f., 5–12 is reproduced.

5. LITERATURE. O. F. Fritzsche, *Libri apocryphi Veteris Testamenti*, Leipzig, 1871 (pp. 640ff.); R. L. Bensly, *The Fourth Book of Ezra* (with an introduction by M. R. James), Texts and Studies III. 2, 1895; the above-mentioned Fragment of 4 Esra 15. 57–59 in *The Oxyrhynchus Papyri*, Part VII (ed. A. Hunt), 1910, pp. 11ff.; older literature in E. Schürer, *The Jewish People in the time of Jesus Christ*, ET, Div. II, Vol. III, pp. 113f. (German ed.⁴ 1909, III. 330f.); in addition, M. J. Labourt, Le cinquième livre d'Esdras, *Rev. Bibl.* 17, 1909, pp. 412–434; D. de Bruyne, Fragments d'une apocalypse perdue, *Rev. Bénéd.* 33, 1921, pp. 97–109; A. Oepke, Ein bisher unbeachtetes Zitat aus dem 5. Buche Esra, *Coniect. Neotestament.* XI, 1947, pp. 179–195 (reprinted in *ZNW* 42, 1949, pp. 158–172); O. Plöger, Article "Das 5. und 6. Esrabuch" in *RGG³* II, 1958, cols. 699f.; also the introduction to 4 Esra (chs. 3–14) by B. Noack in *De Gammeltestamentlige Pseudepigrapher*, Heft 1, 1953, pp. 1–13.

FIFTH ESRA[1]

1. 4. The word of God which came to Esra, the son of Chusis, in the days of Nebuchadnezzar, thus: 5. Go and make known to my people their misdeeds, and to their sons the evil which they have committed against me, that they may recount it to their children's children. 6. For the sins of their fathers are increased in them (still); they have forgotten me and sacrificed to strange gods. 7. Have not I brought them out of the land of Egypt, out of the house of bondage? But they have provoked me to wrath and despised my counsels. 8. Shake thou therefore the hair of thy head and let all evils fall upon them, for they have not obeyed my law, the stiff-necked people!

9. How long shall I tolerate them? So many benefits have I shown to them! 10. Many kings have I overthrown for their sakes; Pharaoh and his servants and all his hosts have I thrown violently down. 11. Have I not for your sake destroyed the city of Bethsaida and burned with fire two cities in the east, Tyre and Sidon? 12. Speak thou then unto them: Thus saith the Lord: 13. Of a truth, I have brought you through the sea and in the pathless desert I provided for you prepared roads. As a leader I gave to you Moses and Aaron as a priest. 14. Light have I granted you by the pillar of fire and great wonders have I done among you. But you have forgotten me, saith the Lord.—15. Thus saith the Lord, the Almighty: The quails were for a sign to you; a camp did I give you for shelter; and there you murmured. 16. And you triumphed not in my name over the destruction of your enemies; no, even to this day, you still murmur. 17. Where are the benefits which I have shown to you? Have you not cried unto me in the desert, when you suffered hunger and thirst:—18. "Why hast thou brought us into this desert to kill us? Better that we had been slaves to the Egyptians than to die in this desert!" 19. Your sufferings made me sorrowful and I gave you manna for food; the bread of angels have you eaten. 20. When you suffered thirst, did I not cleave the rock and water flowed to your fill? Because of the heat I covered you with leaves of the trees. 21. Fertile lands

---

[1] No Biblical citations and references to the following section 1. 4–2. 9 are given, for the text is nothing but a mosaic of innumerable OT passages.

did I apportion to you; the Canaanites, the Perizites, the Philistines did I cast out before you. What shall I yet do for you? saith the Lord.—22. Thus saith the Lord, the Almighty: When you were in the wilderness, thirsting at the bitter waters and blaspheming my name, 23. there I let not fire rain upon you for your blasphemies, but casting a tree into the waters, I made the river sweet.—24. What shall I do to thee, Jacob? Thou wouldst not obey me, Judah! I will turn to other nations and give to them my name, that they may keep my statutes. 25. Since you have forsaken me, I will also forsake you. When you implore me for mercy, I will have no mercy upon you. 26. When you call on me, I will not hear. For you have defiled your hands with blood and your feet are swift to commit acts of murder. 27. You have not, as it were, left me in the lurch, but your own selves, saith the Lord.

28. Thus saith the Lord, the Almighty: Have I not admonished you with prayers, as a father his sons, as a mother her daughters, as a nurse her infants, 29. that you should be a people for me and I should be your God, that you should be sons to me and I a father to you? 30. I gathered you together as a hen gathereth her chickens under her wing.

But now, what shall I do to you? I will cast you forth from my presence! 31. When you bring offerings to me, I will turn my face from you; for your feasts and new moons and circumcisions of the flesh have I not asked. 32. I sent to you my servants the prophets, whom you have taken and slain and torn their bodies in pieces. Their blood will I visit upon you again, saith the Lord.—33. Thus saith the Lord, the Almighty: Your house is desolate; I will cast you forth as the wind does stubble. 34. And your children will not produce offspring, for they have despised my commandment to you and done that which is evil in my sight.

35. I will give your dwellings to a people which shall come, who, though they have not heard of me, yet believe; to whom I have shown no wonderful signs. They will do what I have commanded. 36. They have not seen the prophets, but they will hold in remembrance their history. 37. I testify to the grace which shall meet the people to come, whose children jump for joy, though they see me not with the eyes of the body, yet in their spirit they believe

what I have said. 38. And now, O Father, behold in glory and see thy people who come from the rising of the sun! 39. To them will I give the dominion with Abraham, Isaac and Jacob, Elias and Enoch, Zachariah and Hosea, Amos, Joel, Micah, Obadiah, 40. Zephaniah, Nahum, Jonah, Mattathias, Habakkuk and the twelve angels with flowers.

2. 1. Thus saith the Lord: I have brought this people out of bondage and have given them commandments by my servants the prophets, but they would not hear them, but threw my counsel to the wind. 2. The mother who bare them saith to them, Go, my sons, for I am widowed and forsaken. 3. I have brought you up with joy, and with sadness and sorrow have I lost you, since you have sinned before the Lord and done what is evil in my sight.—4. But now, what shall I do to you? I am widowed and forsaken. Go, my children, and ask the Lord for mercy. 5. But I call upon thee, O Father, as a witness upon the mother of these children, for they would not keep my covenant: 6. Let destruction come upon them, and looting upon their mother, so that no offspring may come after them. 7. Let them be scattered among the heathen, let their names be banished from the earth, for they have despised my covenant. 8. Woe to thee, Asshur, who shelterest in thee the unrighteous. Wicked city, remember what I have done to Sodom and Gomorrah, 9. whose land lies in clods of pitch and heaps of ashes; thus will I do to those who have not listened to me, saith the Lord, the Almighty.

10. Thus saith the Lord unto Esra: Tell my people that I will give to them the kingdom of Jerusalem which I would have given to Israel. 11. I will take unto me the glory of these (the Israelites) and give to those (my people) *the everlasting tabernacles*[1] which I had prepared for them (Israel). 12. *The tree of life*[2] will be to them for an ointment of sweet fragrance and they shall not labour nor weary. 13. *Ask and ye shall* receive;[3] plead for few days for your-selves, that they may be shortened. The kingdom is already prepared for you: watch!

14. I call heaven and earth to witness: I have given up the evil and created the good for (=so surely as) I live, saith the Lord. 15. (Good) mother, embrace thy children, bring them up with

---

[1] Lk. 16:9.   [2] Rev. 22:2.   [3] Cf. Mt. 7:7 and par.

joy like a dove (CM: give them joy like a dove who tends her young), establish their feet; for I have chosen thee, saith the Lord. 16. I will raise up the dead from their places and bring them forth out of the tombs,[1] for I have known my name in them. 17. Fear thou not, O mother of the children, for I have chosen thee, saith the Lord. 18. I will send for thy help my servants Isaiah and Jeremiah (CM + and Daniel) according to whose counsel I sanctified (CM + thee) and have prepared for thee twelve trees, heavy laden with many kinds of fruit, 19. and as many fountains which *flow with milk and honey*,[2] and *seven* measureless *mountains*,[3] filled with roses and lilies, wherein I will fill thy children with joy.

20. Do right to the widow, assist the fatherless to his right; give to the needy; protect the orphan, clothe the naked; 21. tend the cripple and the feeble, laugh not at the lame, defend the frail and let the blind man behold my glory.[4] 22. Guard the aged and the young within thy walls, preserve thy little children, that thy slaves and freemen rejoice and thy whole company live in cheerfulness. 23. Wherever thou findest the dead, there commit them to a grave, marking it; so will I give to thee the first place in my resurrection. 24. Rest and be at peace, my people, for your repose will come.[5]

25. Good nurse, nourish thy children, and establish their feet. 26. The (SA: servants) which I have given thee—none of them shall perish,[6] for I will require them according to thy number. 27. Be not anxious; for when the day of affliction and anguish is come, others will weep and be sorrowful, but thou shalt be gay and rich. 28. The nations will envy thee, and prevail not against thee, saith the Lord. 29. My hands will shelter thee, that thy children see not Gehĕnna. 30. Be joyful, O mother, with thy children, for I will deliver thee, saith the Lord. 31. Remember thy sleeping children, for I will bring them from the hidden graves in the earth and show mercy to them: *for I am merciful, saith the Lord.*[7] 32. Embrace thy children till I come, and proclaim mercy to them, for my wells run over and my grace will not cease.

33. I, Esra, received the command of the Lord on the mountain

---

[1] Cf. Is. 26:19; Mt. 24:22; 24:42. [2] Exod. 3:8, etc. [3] Enoch 24.
[4] Cf. Is. 1:17; 58:6f.; Jer. 7:5f.; James 1:27; Tob. 1:17. [5] Cf. Heb. 4:9.
[6] Cf. Jn. 17:12; also 10:28. [7] Jer. 3:12.

Horeb that I should go to Israel: when I came to them, they rejected me and received not the commandment of God. 34. Therefore I say unto you, ye nations (=heathen), you who hear and understand: Wait for your shepherd! He will give you everlasting rest, for he is near who shall come at the end of the world. 35. Be ready for the rewards of the kingdom, for everlasting light shall shine upon you for evermore. 36. Flee the shadow of this world; receive the joy of your glory; I call to witness my Saviour openly. 37. Receive that which is offered you by the Lord and be joyful, giving thanks to him *who has called you to his* heavenly *kingdom.*[1]

38. Arise and stand and behold the number of those who are sealed at the banquet of the Lord.[2] 39. Those who have withdrawn from the shadow of this world have received shining garments from the Lord.[3] 40. Receive, O Zion, thy number (see 26) and embrace *those who are clothed in white,*[4] who have fulfilled the law of the Lord. 41. The number of thy children, whom thou desirest, is complete; beseech the rule of the Lord that thy people, whom I have called from the beginning, may be sanctified.

42. I, Esra, saw upon mount Zion a great company, which I could not number, and they all praised the Lord with songs. 43. In the midst of them was a young man, tall of stature, towering above all the rest, and he set a crown upon the head of each one of them and he waxed ever taller. But I was absorbed by the wonder.[5] 44. So I asked the angel, saying, "Who are these, Lord?" 45. He answered and said to me, "These are they who have laid aside their mortal clothing and put on the immortal and have confessed the name of God.[6] Now are they crowned and receive *palms.* 46. And I said to the angel, "Who is that young man who setteth crowns upon them and giveth them *palms in their hands?*" 47. He answered me and said, "This is the Son of God whom they have confessed in the world." And I began to praise them who had appeared so valiant for the name of the Lord.

48. Then the angel said unto me, "Go! Proclaim to my people what wonders of the Lord thy God thou hast seen and how great they are."

[1] 1 Thess. 2:12. [2] Cf. Rev. 7:4ff.; Lk. 14:15. [3] Cf. Rev. 6:11; 7:9.
[4] Cf. *ibid.* [5] Cf. Hermas, Sim. IX. 6. 1. [6] Cf. Rev. 7:13f.

SIXTH ESRA

15. 1. Behold, speak thou in the ears of my people words of prophecy which I will put in thy mouth, saith the Lord, 2. and let them be written on paper, for they are faithful and true. 3. Fear not the schemes (which are devised) against thee; let not the unbelief of the adversary perplex thee, 4. for he who is unbelieving will die in his unbelief.

5. Behold I will bring evils on the whole round earth, saith the Lord, sword, famine, death and destruction, 6. since wickedness has covered the whole earth and their abominable works are completed. 7. Therefore saith the Lord: 8. No more will I be silent on their wickedness which they outrageously commit, nor will I tolerate the unrighteousness they practise. Behold innocent and righteous blood cries out unto me, and the souls of the righteous cry unceasingly. 9. Terrible vengeance will I exact from them and all innocent blood will I visit upon them. 10. Behold my people is led like a flock to the slaughter. No longer will I let them dwell in the land of Egypt, 11. but I will bring them out with a strong hand and an upraised arm, and will visit Egypt with plagues as before, and destroy its entire land. 12. Let Egypt mourn and her foundations for the shock of the chastisement and punishment which the Lord will bring upon her. 13. Let the husbandmen mourn who till the soil, for their grain shall fail and their trees be destroyed by burning and hail and a terrible storm. 14. Woe to the world and all who dwell therein! 15. For the sword and its destruction draws near. And one nation shall rise up against another in battle with their swords in their hands. 16. For dissension shall break out among men: they shall rise up one against another, and in the consciousness of power they will not be concerned for their king and the leader of their rulers. 17. For a man shall desire to go into a city and he will not be able to do so. 18. For on account of their arrogance will the cities be brought into confusion, their houses will be destroyed, the men afraid. 19. No man shall show pity to his neighbours, but will break into their houses with the sword to plunder their goods by reason of hunger for bread and great tribulation.

20. Behold, saith the Lord, I call together all kings of the earth,

to rouse those who come from the north and from the south, and from the east and from the west, that they may turn against one another and give back (in recompense) what they have given to the former. 21. As they have done till this present to my chosen, so will I do and recompense in their bosom. Thus saith the Lord God: 22. My right hand will not spare the sinners and my sword will not cease from those who shed innocent blood on the earth. 23. And a fire shall go forth from his wrath and consume the foundations of the earth, and sinners like kindled straw.

24. Woe to them that sin and keep not my commandments, saith the Lord. 25. I will not spare them. Away from me, rebellious sons! Defile not my sanctuary! 26. For the Lord knoweth all who trespass against him; therefore hath he delivered them to death and destruction. 27. For now hath evil come upon the whole round earth and ye must remain therein, for God will not deliver you, since you have trespassed against him.

28. Behold a vision, and it was terrible! And the appearance of it came from the East. 29. And the nations of the dragon of Arabia shall set forth in many chariots, and from the day of their setting forth, their hissing shall sound over the earth, so that all who hear them fear and tremble. 30. The raging Carmonians shall break forth in fury, like a boar from the wood; they shall come with great power and struggle with them in a conflict and shall waste a part of the land of the Assyrians. 31. And then shall the dragons, remembering their origin, have the upper hand, and if they shall turn to pursue them, snorting with great power, 32. then these latter shall be troubled and shall keep silent before their power and turn their feet to flight. 33. And from the land of the Assyrians shall he who lies in wait for them lay an ambush and shall destroy one of them. Then will fear and trembling fall on their hosts and powerlessness on their kings.

34. Behold—clouds from the east and from the north right to the south! And their appearance was exceeding terrible, full of wrath and storm. 35. And they will dash against one another and they shall pour a mighty storm over the earth. And the blood from the swords shall reach even to the belly of the horses, 36. to the thighs of a man, to the hocks of a camel. And great fear and trembling will be upon the earth. 37. All who see that wrath shall

be terrified and fear shall take hold of them. And after that many clouds 38. from the south and from the north and another part from the west shall rise up. 39. But mighty winds will come from the east and shall shut it up and the clouds which he had allowed to rise in wrath; and the storm which arose from east and west to cause destruction will be damaged. 40. And there shall rise up great and strong clouds, full of wrath and storm, to destroy the whole earth and its inhabitants. They will pour out over every high and exalted one terrible storms, 41. fire, hail, flying swords and great streams of water, so that all fields and valleys are filled with the abundance of their waters. 42. And they will destroy cities and walls, mountains and hills, the trees of the wood, the hay of the meadows and their corn. 43. And they will rush on their course even unto Babylon and destroy it. 44. They shall be gathered about it, and shall encircle it and pour out all their storm and all their anger upon it till they rase it to the ground. Then will the dust and smoke rise to the heaven and all around will bewail it. 45. And those who survive will be the servants of those who have destroyed it.

46. And thou, Asia, who sharest in the splendour of Babylon and in the glory of her station, 47. woe to thee, thou wretch! For thou hast become like to her, thou hast decked thy daughters for works of obscenity that thou might be pleased and praised among thy lovers who always desire thee. 48. The hateful harlot hast thou copied in all her works and devices. Therefore saith God: 49. I will send evils upon thee, widowhood, poverty, famine, sword and pestilence, which will waste thy houses, will destroy and slay. 50. And the glory of thy power will fade like a flower, when the heat shall arise which is sent against thee. 51. Thou wilt become weak and miserable by blows and bruised by stripes, so that thou wilt not be able to receive thy mighty ones and lovers. 52. Would I have been jealous against thee, saith the Lord, 53. if thou hadst not on every occasion slain my chosen, exulting with clapping of hands, and laughing at their death, when thou wast drunken? 54. Deck out the beauty of thy countenance; 55. the reward of harlotry dost thou bear in the bosom of thy raiment; therefore shalt thou receive recompense in thy bosom! 56. As thou doest to my chosen, saith the Lord, so will God do to thee

and will cast thee down into suffering. 57. Thy children will die of hunger, thou wilt fall by the sword, thy cities will be destroyed and all thy servants shall fall by the sword in the field. 58. And all who are in the mountains shall perish of hunger; they shall eat their own flesh and drink their own blood, because of hunger for bread and thirst for water. Unhappy one! 59. Miserable shalt thou become above all others, and suffering shall fall upon thee for recompense. 60. As they pass by, they will fall on the hated city and will destroy a portion of thy land and a portion of thy glory, when they return again from Babylon. And when thou art destroyed 61. and wasted, thou wilt be to them as straw, and they to thee as fire! 62. They will consume thee and thy cities, thy land and thy mountains, all thy woods and thy fruit trees will they burn with fire. 63. Thy children will be carried away captive, thy treasure will they take for booty and destroy the glory of thy splendour.

16. 1. Woe to thee, Babylon and Asia! woe to thee, Egypt and Syria! 2. Gird yourselves with sackcloth and fabric of hair, and bewail your children, and lament, for your destruction is near. 3. The sword is sent against you! 4. Who is there that shall ward it off? The fire is sent against you, 5. and who is there that shall quench it? Sufferings are sent against you, and who is there that shall drive them away? 6. Can a man drive away the hungry lion in the wood, or quench the fire when the straw is kindled? 7. Can a man turn back the arrow which is shot by a strong archer? 8. God the Lord sends the evils and who can drive them away? 9. Fire shall go forth from his wrath and who is there that may quench it? 10. He shall send his lightning, and who will not be afraid? He shall thunder and who will not be alarmed? 11. The Lord shall threaten and who will not utterly dissolve before his face? 12. The earth and its foundations quake, and the sea rises up from the deep, its waves will be troubled and its fish, at the presence of the Lord and the glory of his power. 13. For strong is his right hand which bends the bow! Sharp the arrows which are sent by him! They shall not turn back when he begins to send them upon the earth. 14. Behold, evils are sent forth and shall not return till they come upon the earth. 15. Fire has been kindled and will not be quenched till it consumes the foundations of the

earth. 16. As the arrow, shot by the mighty archer, turns not back, so will the evils not turn back which are sent on the earth.

17. Woe is me! woe is me! who will deliver me in these days? 18. The beginning of sorrows (comes)—and many groan; the beginning of famine—and many will perish; the beginning of wars—and powers are alarmed; the beginning of evils—and all will tremble. 19. What will they do (then) when the suffering (itself) comes? 20. Behold, hunger and plagues, confusion and affliction, are sent as scourges to bring amendment. 21. But in all this, they will not turn from their wickedness, nor ever remember the scourges.

Behold corn will be cheap in the earth, so that they will believe that peace has been granted them. 22. But then will evils spring forth on the earth, sword, famine and great confusion. 23. Most of the inhabitants of the earth will die of hunger, and the sword will destroy the others who have survived the famine. 24. The dead will lie on the streets like dung and no one will be there to lament (?) them. For the earth will be left desolate and its cities will be cast down. 25. There will be no one left to till the soil and sow seeds in it. 26. The trees will yield their fruit, but who will harvest it? 27. The grapes will ripen, but who will tread them? For there will be deep desolation everywhere. 28. For a man will passionately desire to see another man, and to hear his voice. 29. For of a city there shall be ten left surviving, and of a hamlet two who had hidden themselves in thick woods and in the clefts of the rocks. 30. As three or four olives remain on the several trees in an olive-garden, 31. and as in a vineyard, after the harvesting, some berries are left by those who carefully search through the yard, 32. so in these days, three or four will be left by those who search their houses with the sword. 33. And the land will be left desolate and its fields will be for briers; its paths and its ways let thorns grow up, for no flock of sheep will pass through any more. 34. The young women will weep because they have no fiancés; the women will weep because they have no husbands; their daughters will weep, because they are robbed of their helpers. 35. The fiancés will be destroyed in the war and the husbands will be destroyed by famine.

36. But hear this and understand it, ye servants of the Lord.

37. Behold, a word of the Lord (it is); receive it! Do not doubt what the Lord has said. 38. Behold, evils come and are not long time in coming! 39. As a woman who is pregnant with child in the ninth month, when the hour of her delivery draws near, for two or three hours before feels woeful pains in her body, and when the child leaves her body, there is not a moment of delay—40. so shall the evil not tarry to come upon the earth. And the world will suffer misery and sorrows will encompass it.

41. Hear the word, O ye my people! Prepare yourselves for the struggle, and in the evils behave yourselves as strangers on the earth. 42. He that selleth, let him be as one in flight; he that buyeth as he who is about to lose; 43. he that dealeth as he who has no more profit; he that builds as he who will not inhabit; 44. he that soweth as he that will not reap; likewise he that prunes (his vines) as he that will not gather the harvest; 45. they that marry as those who will not beget children; and they that marry not as those who are widowed. 46. Hence they that work, work in vain. 47. Strangers will harvest their fruits and they will deprive them of their property, destroy their houses and take their children into captivity. Therefore those who marry should know that they will bring forth their children in captivity and famine. 48. Those who traffic in business do it as those who plunder. For the more they adorn their cities and houses and their possessions and their persons, 49. the more will I be angry with them because of their sins, saith the Lord. 50. For as a beautiful and noble woman hates a harlot, 51. so shall righteousness hate iniquity when she adorns herself, and accuses her to her face, when he comes that defends her, seeking out every sin on the earth. 52. Therefore be not like to them and their works! 53. For behold, a moment, and iniquity will be destroyed from the earth and righteousness will reign among us. 54. Let not the sinner say that he has not sinned, nor the unrighteous man that he has acted righteously; for coals of fire will burn on the head of him who says, "I have not sinned, before God and his glory!" Behold the Lord knoweth all the works of men, 55. their imaginations, their aspirations, their thoughts and their hearts. 56. (He) who said, "Let the earth be made" and it was made, "let the heaven be made" and it was made, 57. through whose word the stars were

701

established, who knoweth the number of the stars—58. who searches the deeps and their treasures—who hath measured the sea and its contents—59. who has shut up the world in the midst of the waters and hath hung the earth over the waters by his word—60. who has stretched out the heaven like a chamber and founded it upon the waters—61. who has made in the desert springs of water and pools on the peaks of the mountains, to send forth rivers from on high to water the earth—62. who has formed man and given him a heart in the midst of the body, and has poured into him breath and life and understanding, 63. even the breath of Almighty God who made all things and has sought out the hidden things in hidden places: 64. surely he knoweth our imaginations and aspirations and what you think in your hearts! Woe to the sinners and to those who would hide their sins. 65. For the Lord will certainly search out all your works and openly put you all to shame. 66. And you will be put to confusion when your sins are brought before the eyes of men and your iniquities will rise up as accusers on that day. 67. What will ye do? How will you hide your sins before God and his angels? 68. Behold, God is the judge! Fear him! Cease from your sins and forget your iniquities to do them now for ever, so God will lead you forth and deliver you from all tribulation. 69. For behold, the wrath of a great multitude will burn against you and they will carry away captive some of you and make you eat food that is offered to idols. 70. And those who are led astray by them will be ridiculed, reproached and mistreated. 71. For there shall be . . . in adjoining cities a great rebellion against those who fear God. 72. For men will suffer want and, through their need, will be like madmen, sparing none, that they may plunder and destroy those who fear God. 73. For they shall destroy and plunder their goods, and banish them from their homes. 74. Then shall the tried quality of my elect come to the light, like gold which is tried by fire.

75. Hear, my elect, saith the Lord! Behold, the days of tribulation are near and I will deliver you from them. 76. Fear not and flinch not; for God is your leader. 77. And you who observe my commandments and precepts, saith the Lord God, let not your sins gain the upper hand over you, nor your iniquities lord it

over you. 78. Woe to them that are bound fast by their sins and over-run by their iniquities, like as a field, to which no one goes, is fast bound with bushes, and its corn overgrown with thorns: it is rooted out and thrown into the fire, that it may be utterly consumed.

2. CHRISTIAN SIBYLLINES
(*A. Kurfess*)

1. LITERATURE. Rzach, Pauly-Wissowa-Kroll II A, 2073–2183 (with full literature to 1920); K. Prüm, *Lex. f. Theol. u. Kirche* IX. 525ff. (with more recent literature). Editions: Rzach, 1891 (best critical edition); J. Geffcken, *GCS* 8, 1902 (important because of the religio-historical apparatus). Text with German translation: P. Lieger, *Christus im Munde der Sibylle, Progr. Schottengymn.* Wien 1911; A. Kurfess, Munich 1951 (this improved text is the basis of the translation in the German edition of the present work). Studies: H. Erbse, *Fragmente griechischer Theosophien*, 1941; H. Diels, *Sibyllinische Blätter*, 1890; J. Geffcken, *TU* 23. 1, 1902; Max. J. Wolff, Sibyllen und Sibyllinen, *Archiv f. Kulturgesch.* 24, 1934, 312–325; H. Fuchs, *Der geistige Widerstand gegen Rom in der antiken Welt*, 1938; A. Kurfess, *ZNW* 40, 1941, 151–165 (B. I/II); 38, 1939, 171–181 (Ps. Phokylides; B. II. 34 to 153); *id., Mnemosyne* 1941, 195ff.; *id., Würzburger Jahrb.* 2, 1947, 373ff. (B. VII); *id., Pastor Bonus,* Trier 1930, 262–271 (Virgil the prophet). On Hystaspes (source for B. II): H. Windisch, Verh. Akad. Amsterdam, 1929; Bidez-Cumont, *Les mages hellénisés,* Paris, 1931, I. 215–223; II. 359–377. On the Tiburtine Sibyl: E. Sackur, *Sibyllinische Texte und Forschungen,* 1898, 126–187; F. Kampers, *Die tiburtinische Sibylle im Mittelalter,* 1894; *id., Vom Werdegang der abendländischen Kaisermystik,* 1924. On the statue of Thea Sibylla recently found in Rome: R. Herbig, *Jahrb. d. Deutsch. Arch. Inst.* 59/60, 1944/45 (1949), 141ff. Further literature: A. Kurfess, Wie sind die Fragmente der Oracula Sibyllina einzuordnen? Ein Beitrag zu ihrer Überlieferung, *Aevum* 26, 1952, 228–235; *id.,* Sibyllarum carmina chromatico tenore modulata, *ibid.,* 385–394; *id.,* Zu den Oracula Sibyllina, *Colligere Fragmenta,* Beuron 1952, 75–83; *id.,* Ad Oracula Sibyllina (ed. J. Geffcken 1902), *Symbolae Osl.* 24, 1952, 54–77; *id.,* Alte lateinische Sibyllinenverse, *Theol. Quartalschr.* 133, 1953, 80–96; *id.,* Juvenal und die Sibylle, *Judaica* 10, 1954, 60–63; *id.,* Horaz und die Sibyllinen, *ZRGG* 8, 1956, 253–256; *id.,* Zum 5. Buch der Oracula Sibyllina, *Rhein. Museum f. Philologie* 29, 1956, 225–241; J. B. Bauer, Die Gottesmutter in den Oracula Sibyllina, *Marianum* 18, 1956, 118–224; *id.,* Or. Sib. I 323ab, *ZNW* 47, 1956, 284f.; *id.,* Das Sprichwort Or. Sib. III. 737, *Rhein. Mus. f. Philol.* 29, 1956, 95f.; A. Kurfess, Juvenal und die Sibylle, *Histor. Jahrb.* 76, 1957, 79–83; *id.,* Dies irae. Zum sog. 2. Buch der Or. Sibyll., *Histor. Jahrb.* 77, 1958, 328–338.

2. "SIBYL" AND SIBYLS. By Sibyls people in antiquity meant women who in a state of ecstasy proclaimed coming events,

generally unpleasant, spontaneously and without being asked or being connected with any particular oracle-site. This kind of prophecy came to the Greeks from the East; perhaps its oldest cultic centre is to be sought in the Persian or Iranian region. The Sibyl is brought into association with the flood (= the Zoroastrian cosmic winter) and proclaims the universal conflagration (=the cosmic summer); thereafter for the pious and faithful the universe is renewed once more. The name "sibyl" is not Greek, and as yet has not been explained; Varro's interpretation (in Lactantius) deriving it from Διὸς βουλή is naturally popular etymology. Originally there was only *the* Sibyl, the term being used as a proper name (Heraclitus, Vorsokr. fr. 92 Diels, from Plutarch, de Pyth. or. 6. 397A: "The Sibyl, with frenzied mouth uttering things not to be laughed at, unadorned and rough, yet reaches to a thousand years with her voice by aid of the god"). The Sibyl's influence reached its highest point in the period from the 8th to the 6th centuries (cf. E. Rohde, Psyche II[11], 63ff. (ET 1925, pp. 292f.)), and her activities extended chiefly over the area of the Greek colonies in Asia Minor. A distinctive feature is her great age, to which reference is made elsewhere also (e.g. in Pausanias 10. 12; Eusebius, Chronik ed. Helm[2], GCS 47, 1956, p. 89b; Augustine, de Civ. Dei 18. 23, Corp. Christian. ser. lat. 48, 1955, p. 613). Hence comes the idea that she made extensive journeys and prophesied at different places.

The Sibyl seems originally to have been a legendary demonic being. On a coin (cf. B. V. Head, *Historia numorum*, Oxford 1887, p. 499; enlarged in Roscher 4. 798) she is actually designated as a goddess ('Thea Sibylla'). Out of the one Sibyl (cf. Arrian, FHG 3. 598. 64) several later developed, after the rise of different collections of oracles or of different cultic centres (Buchholz). The proper name became the generic name, and the several Sibyls received names of their own, e.g. the Erythraean Herophile, the Samian Phyto, the Cumaean Demo or Demophile (cf. Diels, *op. cit*, 51[1]f.).

The oldest Hellenic Sibyl is that of Marpessos, about whom Tibullus still had information (II. 5. 71; cf. *Wurzb. Jb.* 2, 1948, 402ff.). The most important of her competitors is that of Erythrae (cf. the inscription of A.D. 162 found there in 1891; text in Rzach, *op. cit.*, 2085). Her statue has been found in Rome, and R. Herbig (*op. cit.*) has described it as a replica of the cultic statue in Erythrae. On her extensive travels the Erythraean Sibyl came also to Delphi, where (according to Pausanias 10. 12. 2) she described herself in her verses as Artemis and also as the lawful wife of Apollo, and then further as his sister or daughter. The beginning of this oldest *carmen Sibyllinum* has been handed on by

Clement of Alexandria (*Strom*. I. 108, from Heracleides Ponticus, 4th century B.C., who first mentions several Sibyls—ultimately, through Varro (in Lactantius) ten became the canonical number, but in the Middle Ages two others were added—and seeks to bring into order the reports about the Sibyl; cf. A. Tesp, *Die Fragmente d. griech. Kultschriftsteller*, 1914, 177ff.); the continuation is provided by Phlegon of Tralles, a contemporary of the emperor Hadrian (Macrob. 4. 7=FHG III. 610); according to this she was slain out of jealousy and compassion by Apollo's arrow. In her efforts to compete with the Pythia she was thus defeated (cf. Geffcken, *N.Jbb*. 15, 1912, 594). It is however important that the Sibyl took over the hexameter from Delphi as the metre for her prophecies.

The Sibyl appears to have come to Cumae at an early date (from Euboea; cf. Diels, *op. cit.*, 98). Of all the Sibyls of later times the Cumaean, next to the Erythraean, has become the most famous. She is said to have lived for a thousand years, and finally to have floated about as simply a whispering sound in the volcanic grotto which was the site of her oracle (on her connection with the Erythraean Sibyl cf. ps.-Aristotle, mirab. 1. 108; Servius on Virgil Aen. 6. 321). Her legend is chiefly associated with the famous Sibyl's cave at the foot of the citadel at Cumae, described by Virgil in the sixth book of the Aeneid (on the excavations there in 1920 cf. *Gnomon* 2, 1926, 366 and 747; *Mnemosyne* 55, 1927, 370ff.). On the legend according to which the Sibyl offered to King Tarquinius Priscus, at a high price, first nine and then three books, cf. W. Hoffmann, *Wandel und Herkunft der Sibyll. Bücher in Rom*, Diss. Leipzig 1933 (*Gnomon* 10, 1934, 387f.). The historical core of the legend is that the oracular sayings from Cumae probably reached Rome as early as the period of the kings, and there the oracle was put under state control and "Sibylline" oracles composed after the Cumaean pattern. The sayings preserved in the Capitoline temple were entrusted to the care of an official commission, originally of two and finally of fifteen members. In 83 B.C. the Sibylline Books were destroyed in the burning of the Temple of Jupiter. At that time new sayings were collected from every quarter on the orders of the government, and especially from Erythrae, and they continued to be the subject of official attention until Stilicho had them burned shortly after A.D. 400. It was in accordance with one such oracle, preserved for us in Phlegon (cf. Diels, *op. cit.*, 133ff.), that Augustus in 14 B.C. organized the great Ludi Saeculares. The Cumaean Sibyl however attained her greatest fame through Virgil's Fourth Eclogue, which foretold a saviour (40 B.C.) and from which numerous Christian writers drew single verses (esp. v. 7) and applied them to Christ; the emperor Constantine in his first address to the assembly of the saints, recorded in Eusebius, after quoting the famous acrostic (Or. Sib. VIII. 217–250), interpreted the whole poem with reference to Christ in chapters 19–21.

The latest Sibyl is the Hebrew, erroneously identified by Pausanias with the Babylonian, Sabbe or Sambethe by name. In the Hellenistic period there seems however to have been a Chaldean Sibyl, who in Greek hexameters recited Babylonian legends embodying Hellenistic ideas. She was called the daughter of Berossus since she drew upon the latter's historical work. Parts of this Chaldean Sibylline poetry were taken over by the original Jewish Sibyl (= Or. Sib. B. III; cf. P. Schnabel, *Berossos und die babylon.-hellenist. Lit.*, Leipzig 1923, 69–93, esp. 78ff.; A. Peretti, *La Sibilla Babilonese nelle propaganda hellenistica*, Florence 1943).

3. JEWISH AND HELLENISTIC SIBYLLINES. The great boom in Sibylline composition probably set in soon after the death of Alexander the Great. Lycophron's Alexandra (= Cassandra), from which the Sibylline writers took over the narration of history in the guise of prophecy, made its appearance about 270 B.C. Chance has presented us with a lengthy, although admittedly fragmentary, portion of a heathen Sibylline oracle (cf. Crönert, *Symbol. Osl.* 6, 1928, 57; *Pap. Osl.* fasc. 2, 1931, 27ff.). It shows the same style and the same technique as our collection of the Oracula Sibyllina, in which there are indeed plenty of heathen (Erythraean) oracles, inserted into their prophecies by the Jewish writers in order to secure a greater authority among the heathen for their Jewish propaganda and to prove that their forgeries were genuine verses of old and recognized Sibyls. For all that, the prophecies of doom uttered by the heathen Sibyls, especially the Erythraean, against cities, islands and countries bore a certain similarity to the threatenings of the OT prophets. The core of the Sibyllines is formed by the description of the end of the world. The historical sections which reach back to the past are developed into an interpretation of history from the point of view of the revelation of the sovereign power of the one true God and from that of the Messianic expectation.

The composition of Jewish Sibyllines had its centre in Alexandria. A Jew there wrote the first truly literary Sibylline book (= Or. Sib. III in its original form; the expanded version which we now have was compiled about 140 B.C.), and thereby created a new literary form. "The Jewish Sibyl . . . not only has no need to fear comparison with contemporary Alexandrian compositions, but has a claim to a conspicuous place among them" (P. Lieger).

The hatred felt for the Romans in the time of Vespasian and Titus is reflected in Or. Sib. IV and V (cf. H. Fuchs, *op.*

cit.). The last Sibylline books, which are all Jewish apart from a few interpolated verses (see below), stand on a footing of loyalty to the empire (there is no book missing between VIII and XI. That the last books are numbered XI–XIV instead of IX–XII is due to the numbering in the Ω branch of the tradition, in which Book VIII was divided into three, and these then counted as three books). Books VI, VII and VIII are purely Christian. Books I/II, which form a unity, are originally Jewish, but have been subjected to later Christian revision. In Book I verses 1–323 are Jewish (apart from the interpolation of the riddle, 137–146: the counterpart to 326–330); after a considerable lacuna, which is by no means made good by the four verses newly recovered from the so-called Sibylline theosophy (323 a–d), 324–400 are Christian (appearance and nature of Christ, Israel's sin against Christ and her fall). In the present Book II it is scarcely possible to separate the Christian element from the Jewish (on II. 34–153 cf. *ZNW* 38, 1939, 171ff.); the following verses I consider certainly Christian: 179–181; 190–192; 241–244; 263–267; 311f. (the original (Jewish) Book II probably began with the so-called Prologue (fr. 1–3, transmitted by Theophilus); the conclusion stands at the beginning of our present Book III, vv. 1–92, translated by Blass in Kautzsch, *Die Apokryphen und Pseudepigraphen des AT*, 1900; English trans. by Lanchester in Charles, *Apoc. and Pseud.* II, 1913).

4. CHARACTER OF THE CHRISTIAN SIBYLLINES, DATE OF COMPOSITION, AND SURVIVAL. If the Shepherd of Hermas (Vis. II. 4) shows acquaintance with the Jewish Sibyl, sacred also to the Christians, we soon learn of independent Christian Sibyls also, originating probably in the 2nd century. As the Jewish Sibylline literature arose out of the propaganda of the Jews, so the Christian was the result of the struggle of Christianity against heathenism. In Book VIII we have a fierce hatred against Rome, kindled by persecution; no longer is sinful Babylon the target, but Rome itself is mentioned by name; with a ghastly exultation the writer already sees the spectral Nero-Anti-Christ threatening to make an end of the abominable city. Even Rome's destiny hereafter is a subject for his attention. Book VIII, therefore, and certainly its first part, may still derive from the period before A.D. 180.

Book VII presents gnosticizing views: on v. 71 Geffcken compares the Acts of Thomas, caps. 17–23 (see above, pp. 451ff.) and Hermas, Vis. III. 4. 1; on Uranus as a mythological person: Epiphanius, *Haer.* 31. 1. 3; on God's noble "mothers" (Hope, Piety, Fear of God): Irenaeus I. 5. 2f. (p. 45f. Harvey), with similar figures in Hermas, Vis. III. 8, and Epiphanius 31. 5 (on the Valentinians); vv. 139f. "gnosticizing concepts", cf. Pistis Sophia

244f.; on the Ogdoad, Epiphanius, *Haer.* 31. 6. Geffcken consequently placed the book in the 3rd century, yet such "gnosticizing" seems to me to be possible already at the end of the 2nd century. In Book VII use is made of Book VI, a hymn to Christ (VI. 6 corresponds to VII. 84, the "baptism of fire").

While the Jewish "Urgedicht" originated shortly before or after the birth of Christ, Books I/II, which in their final form despite some gaps and roughnesses constitute a beautiful whole, presuppose the composition of the Revelation and Gospel of John. Jerusalem and the Temple are in ruins; the Hebrews wander abroad as adversaries of the faithful. On the other hand heathenism is not yet overcome. All this leads us to the period shortly after Hadrian; the date of composition is thus about 150 (soon after the appearance of the Gospel of the Egyptians, but before Books VII and VIII, since I and II are used in them, cf. *ZNW* 40, 1941, 151–165).

Rome could not tolerate such revolutionary occultism as makes itself felt in Book VII; hence the reading of such writings became a capital offence (Justin, Apol. I. 44).

The Christians however saw in the Sibyl, who for them always remained an ally in the heathen camp, one of the direct witnesses to the *gesta Dei*. After Hermas and Justin, who knew Sibyllines without making much use of them, we find them quoted in Athenagoras, Theophilus, Pseudo-Melito, Tertullian, Clement of Alexandria, Commodian, Lactantius, Eusebius (Constantine's speech, cap. 18/29), in the pseudo-Justinian Cohortatio ad Graecos, the questions and answers to the orthodox, the Apostolic Constitutions, in Gregory of Nazianzus, Sozomen, Augustine, ps.-Augustine. Then later the Sibylline vaticination ends in the prosaic prophecy of the Byzantines; in the West the Tiburtine Sibyl makes her appearance. The much-vaunted prophecy of the Lehnin monastery also goes back ultimately to the composition of the Sibyls.

5. THE TIBURTINE SIBYL. In the Middle Ages this Sibyl was especially celebrated; in Varro's catalogue of the Sibyls (Lactant., div. inst. I. 6. 8) she stands in the last place (tenth). Of her prophecy, certainly composed originally in Greek, we know a Latin version, the nucleus of which Sackur sets in the 4th century A.D. (*op. cit.*, 155ff., text 177ff.), and some Oriental versions (trans. by Schleifer, *Denkschrift d. Wien. Akad.* 2. III, 1910, 1ff.) which probably go back as far as the 3rd century. The essential content is formed by the interpretation of a dream which 100 Roman senators had in one and the same night, by the Sibylla Tiburtina, a daughter of King Priam (=Cassandra!), bearing the Latin name of Albunea. The Senators had dreamed of nine suns with

different aspects. The Sibyl explains the nine suns to them as nine ages; in the fourth (according to the oriental versions, in the sixth) Christ was born. The last (ninth) age is full of the confused conflict of various potentates; we feel ourselves vividly reminded of the narration by the Jewish Sibyls (XI–XIV) of events from Roman imperial history, which was the model for the predictions of German and Lombard rulers which are here inserted. In Sibylline fashion these princes are alluded to by the initial letters of their names. According to the date when the manuscript was written, the lists of rulers are completed and altered to match the historical course of events. In the oldest manuscript, the Escorialensis of 1047, the last ruler is a king *E nomine Salicus de Francia*, i.e. Enricus, the Henry III of the lineage of the Salic Franks who was at that time ruling (1039–1052; Sackur 134). After the conclusion of the series, the appearance of the Messianic King is described, the King who achieves the Christian world-empire: *rex Romanorum et Graecorum, cuius nomine Constans; hic erit statura grandis, aspectu decorus, vultu splendidus atque singula membrorum lineamenta decenter conpositus.* The Greek original has been discovered by S. G. Mercati (*Mélanges Grégoire,* 1949, pp. 473–481).

B. Bischof (*Mélanges J. de Ghellinck,* Gembloux 1951, pp. 121–147) has published a Latin Prophetia Sibillae magae (*Mundus origo mea est*) from three manuscripts, two of which derive from the 9th century. The poem begins with three distiches, and the rest is in hexameters with appalling versification and a thoroughly rampant text (there is no indication of a Greek *Vorlage*). It shows in its Christology a moderate Monarchianism (cf. vv. 20, 29 and 61ff.); a Patripassian formulation is avoided (4th century?).

ORACULA SIBYLLINA
End of Book I[1]

323 a ⟨When the maid shall give birth to the Logos of God Most High,

b But as wedded wife shall give to the Logos a name,

c Then from the east shall a star shine forth in the midst of the day

d Radiant and gleaming down from the heaven above,

e Proclaiming a great sign to poor mortal men.⟩

[1] The following translation is based on the Greek text as printed in the editions of Kurfess and Geffcken, with constant reference of course to the German version. The text of the opening lines is printed in Kurfess's article, *ZNW* 40, 1941, pp. 156f.
323a–e from the Sibylline Theosophy, cf. Erbse *op. cit..* v. 291; on 323a cf. Hennecke, Apokr. 2, p. 388 (Ezekiel apocryphon).

324 Yea, then shall the Son of the great God come to men,
325 Clothed in flesh, like unto mortals on earth.
   Four vowels he has, twofold the consonants in him,
   And now will I declare to thee also the whole number:
   Eight monads, and to these as many decads,
   And eight hundreds also his name will show
330 To unbelieving men; but think thou in thy heart
   Of Christ, the Son of the immortal, most high God.
   He will fulfil God's law, and not destroy,
   Offering a pattern for imitation, and will teach all things.
   To him shall priests bring and offer gold
335 And myrrh and frankincense; for indeed all these he will make.
   But when a voice shall come through a desert place
   Bringing tidings to men, and shall call upon all
   To make straight the ways and to cast out
   All evil from the heart, and that every body among men
340 Be illumined by the waters, that born anew
   They may no more in any way at all forsake the paths of right,
   Then one of barbarous mind, ensnared by the dancer's art,
   Shall give in reward the head of him that cried, and a sudden
       portent
   Shall be to men, when from the land of Egypt
345 Shall come, safe guarded, a precious stone; upon it
   The people of the Hebrews shall stumble, but Gentiles shall
       gather
   By his guidance; for indeed God who rules on high
   They shall come to know through him, and a path in a
       common light.
   For he shall show eternal life to men
350 Elect, but on the lawless he will bring the inextinguishable
       fire.
   Then shall he heal the sick and all the afflicted,
   As many as put their trust in him.
   And the blind shall see, and the lame walk,
   And the deaf shall hear, and they that speak not shall speak;

331 cf. I. 137–146. *332* cf. Mt. 5:17. *332–382* cf. VIII. 269–320. *334f.* cf. Mt. 2:11. *336* Mt. 3:3 and par. *339* cf. VIII. 247. *340* Jn. 3:3. *342f.* cf. Mt. 14:6ff. *345* cf. 1 Pet. 2:4. *346* Rom. 9:33 (Is. 8:14; 28:16). *346f.* cf. 384. *353* cf. Mt. 11:5 and par. *353–355* cf. VIII. 205–207.

355 Demons he shall drive out, and there shall be resurrection of
      the dead;
    On the waves he shall walk, and in a desert place
    From five loaves and fish from the sea
    Shall feed five thousand; and the remains of these
    Shall fill twelve baskets for the holy maiden.

*   *

*

360 Then Israel in her intoxication shall not perceive,
    Nor yet, weighed down, shall she hear with delicate ears.
    But when the wrath of the Most High comes on the Hebrews
    In raging fury and takes away faith from them,
    Because they ill-used the heavenly Son of God,
365 And then indeed blows and poisonous spitting
    Shall Israel give him with their polluted lips,
    And for food gall, and for drink unmixed vinegar
    They shall impiously give him, smitten they by evil frenzy
    In breast and heart; but not seeing with their eyes,
370 Blinder than moles, more dreadful than creeping beasts
    That shoot poison, shackled in deep slumber.
    But when he stretches out his hands and measures all things,
    And wears the crown of thorns, and his side
    They pierce with spears for the sake of the law, three whole
      hours
375 There shall be night of monstrous darkness in the midst of the
      day.
    And then shall Solomon's temple show to men
    A mighty wonder, when to the house of Aidoneus
    He goes down, proclaiming a resurrection to the dead.
    But when in three days he comes again to the light,
380 And shows to mortals a token, and teaches all things,
    Ascending in clouds will he journey to the house of heaven,
    Leaving to the world the ordinance of the Gospel.

356 cf. Mk. 6:48 and par. *357ff.* cf. VIII. 275–278; Mk. 6: 38ff.; Mt. 14:17ff.; Jn.
6:7ff. *360–380* cf. VIII. 287–320. *365* cf. Mt. 26:67 and par. *369ff.* cf. Is. 6:9f.; Mt.
13:14; Mk. 4:12; Lk. 8:10; Jn. 12:40; Acts 28:26. *375ff.* cf. VIII. 305ff.; Mt. 27:54;
Mk. 15:38; Lk. 23:44f.

Called by his name, a new shoot shall blossom forth
From the Gentiles guided by the law of the Mighty.
385 And moreover after this there shall be wise guides,
And then shall be thereafter a cessation of prophets.
Then when the Hebrews reap the bitter harvest,
Much gold and silver shall a Roman king carry off
In plunder. And thereafter other kingdoms
390 Shall follow without remission, as kingdoms perish,
And shall afflict men. But there shall be to those men
A mighty fall, when they rule in unrighteous arrogance.
But when Solomon's temple falls to the holy earth,
Cast down by men of barbarian speech
395 And brazen breastplates, and the Hebrews are driven from the
land
Wandering and plundered, and they mingle many tares
With the wheat, then shall there be an evil discord
For all men; and the cities despoiled on either side
Shall mourn each other, since they transgressed by an evil
deed,
And received the wrath of great God to their bosoms.

Book [II]

And then shall God thereafter make a great sign.
35 For like a radiant crown a star shall shine,
Radiant and brightly beaming from the brilliant heaven
For not a few days; for then he will show from heaven
A victor's crown for men who contend in the contest.
And then shall come the time of the great triumphal entry
40 Into the heavenly city, and it shall be universal
For all men, and have the renown of immortality.
And then shall every people in immortal contests
Contend for glorious victory; for there shall none
Be able shamelessly to purchase a crown for silver.
45 For Christ the holy shall adjudge to them just rewards,
And crown the excellent, and a prize immortal he will give
To martyrs who endure the contest even unto death.

384 cf. 346f. *387* cf. Mt. 24:32; Mk. 13:28; Lk. 21:30; Rev. 14:15; Hermas, Sim.
IV. 2. *389f.* cf. Mt. 24:7. *396f.* cf. Mt. 13:28. *37ff.* cf. 1 Cor. 9:24; Heb. 12:1; 2
Tim. 4:7. *47f.* cf. Rev. 2:10.

And to virgins who run their course well a prize incorruptible
He will give, and to all among men who deal justly
50 And to nations from far-distant lands
Who live holy lives and recognize one God.
And those who love marriage and abstain from stolen unions,
Rich gifts will he give to them also, and eternal hope.
For every soul of men is a gift of God,
55 And it is not lawful for men to defile it with all manner of
shame.

This is the contest, these the prizes, these the awards;
150 This is the gate of life and entry to immortality
Which the heavenly God appointed for righteous men
As guerdon of victory. They who receive
The crown nobly shall enter in by it.
But when this sign appears throughout all the world,
155 Children grown grey at the temples from birth,
And afflictions of men, famines and plagues and wars,
And change of seasons, lamentations, many tears—
Ah, how many children in all lands, bitterly wailing,
Shall devour their parents, wrapping the flesh
160 In shrouds, and foul with blood and dust
Bury them in earth, the mother of peoples! Poor wretches,
Men of the last generation, dreadful transgressors,
Children who do not understand that, when the race of
women
Do not give birth, the harvest of mortal men is come!
165 Near is the end, when instead of prophets
False deceivers approach, spreading reports on earth.
And Beliar too shall come and do many signs
For men. Then indeed a confusion among holy men,
Elect and faithful, and there shall be a plundering
170 Of them and the Hebrews. Dread wrath shall come upon
them,
When a twelve-tribe people shall come from the East
Seeking a people which Assyria's shoot destroyed,

48 cf. 1 Cor. 9:25. *150* cf. Mt. 7:13; Jn. 10:7. *155* cf. 4 Esd. 6. 21. *157* cf. VIII.
214f. *163f.* cf. Gospel of the Egyptians, Vol. I, pp. 166f. *165f.* cf. Mt. 24:11; Did.
16:3. *167f.* cf. 2 Cor. 6:15; Asc. Is. 4:2 (p. 648). *171* cf. 4 Esd. 13. 39.

Their kindred Hebrews; thereupon nations shall perish.
Later again shall rule over men exceeding mighty
175 Elect and faithful Hebrews, when they have brought them
To slavery as of old, for power shall never leave them.
And the Most High, the all-surveying who dwells in the ether,
Shall send sleep upon men, veiling their eyelids.
O blessed servants, whom the master when he comes
180 Shall find wakeful, who all kept watch,
Ever expectant with sleepless eyes.
Come he at dawn or dusk, or in the midst of the day,
Yet come he will for certain, and it shall be as I declare.
He shall appear to the sleepers, when from the starry heaven
185 All the stars shall be seen of all in the midst of the day,
With the two great lights as time presses on.
And then the Tishbite, speeding the heavenly chariot
From heaven and descending to earth, shall show three signs
To all the world, signs of a life that is perishing.
190 Woe to all those who in that day are found to be
Great with child, all those who give milk
To infant children, all those who dwell upon the wave;
Woe to all those who look upon that day!
For a murky cloud shall cover the boundless earth,
195 From East and West and North and South.
And then a great river of burning fire
Shall flow down from heaven and consume every place,
Earth and great ocean and the grey-blue sea,
Lakes and rivers, springs and relentless Hades
200 And the heavenly sphere. And the lights of heaven
Shall be dashed together into a form all-desolate;
For the stars shall all fall from heaven into the sea.
And all souls of men shall gnash with their teeth,
Burning in the river of pitch and the raging fire
205 On a glowing plain, and ashes shall cover all things.
[And then shall all the elements of the world be desolate,
Air, earth and sea, light, heaven, days and nights.]

179 cf. Mt. 24:46; Lk. 17:37. *180f.* cf. Lk. 12:46; Mt. 24:42. *184ff.* cf. VIII.
203ff.; 4 Esd. 5. 4. *187* cf. Mal. 4:5; Mt. 11:14; 16:14; 17:10. *188* cf. Did. 16. 6.
190f. cf. Mk. 13:17; Mt. 24:19; Lk. 21:23. *196–213* cf. VIII. 337–350; Apoc. Petri
c. 5 (above, p. 671). *196* cf. 256; VII. 120; VIII. 243. *200–213* cf. 305ff. *202* cf. VIII.
190.

No more shall unnumbered birds fly in the air,
No more the swimming creatures swim the sea,
210 Nor laden ship voyage upon the waves,
Nor guided cattle plough the earth;
No sound of trees beneath the wind. But in an instant all
Shall fuse together, and be separated into purity.
But when the undying messengers of the immortal God,
215 Michael and Gabriel, Raphael and Uriel shall come,
Who know full well what evils a man did before,
They shall bring the souls of men from the cloudy darkness
To judgment all, at the seat of God
Great and immortal; for one only is undying,
220 The Almighty himself, who shall be the judge of mortals.
And then to those beneath shall the heavenly give souls
And breath and speech, bones fitted together
With all manner of joints, flesh and nerves,
And veins and skin about the flesh, and hair of the head.
225 Divinely compacted, breathing and set in motion,
Bodies of earthly men shall rise on one day.
Cruel, unbreakable and inflexible are the monstrous bars
Of the gates of Hades, not forged of metal;
Yet Uriel, the great angel, shall burst and fling them open,
230 And shall bring all the shapes deeply mourning unto judg-
ment:
The phantoms especially of Titans, born long ago,
And giants too, and all whom the Flood carried off,
And whom on the deep the wave of the sea destroyed,
And all whom beasts and creeping things and birds
235 Devoured, all these shall he call to the judgment-seat;
And again, whom the flesh-devouring fire destroyed in flame,
These too shall he gather and set before God's judgment-seat.
But when he raises the dead, loosing the bond of destiny,
And Sabaoth Adonai the high-thundering shall sit
240 On a heavenly throne and establish a great pillar,
There shall come on a cloud to the eternal, eternal himself,

---

213 cf. VIII. 412. *215* cf. Enoch. c. 9f.; Apoc. Mos. R. 27. *216* cf. Ps. 69:28 (Rev.
17:8; Phil. 4:3); Enoch 108:7. *221ff.* cf. Ezek. 37:5ff.; Apoc. Petri c. 4 (above, p. 670).
227ff. cf. Apoc. Elias, p. 45. 6. 18 (ed. Steindorff). *233ff.* cf. Enoch 61:5. *241ff.* cf.
Mt. 25:31; 19:28; Apoc. Petri c. 6 (above, pp. 671f.).

Christ in glory with his blameless angels,
And shall sit on the right hand of Majesty, judging on his
throne
The life of the pious and the ways of impious men.
245 There shall come also Moses, the great friend of the Most
High,
Clothed in flesh; great Abraham too shall come,
Isaac and Jacob, Joshua, Daniel and Elias,
Habakkuk and Jonah, and they whom the Hebrews slew.
[And those after Jeremiah, all, he shall destroy at the throne,
250 Hebrews indicted, that they may receive fitting works
And pay the price for all that any did in mortal life.]
And then shall all pass through the burning river
And unquenchable flame; and the righteous
Shall all be saved, but the impious shall perish
255 For whole ages, as many as wrought evil aforetime
And committed murders, and all their accomplices,
Liars and thieves, the treacherous, grim destroyers of houses,
Parasites and adulterers, spreaders of evil reports,
The wickedly insolent, the lawless, the idolaters;
260 And all those who forsook the great immortal God,
And became blasphemers, ravagers of the pious,
Destroyers of faith and slayers of righteous men;
And all those who with crafty and shameless dissembling
As presbyters and reverend deacons looked
265 To the person and wealth of the suppliant and judged un-
justly (?),
Doing injustice to others, relying on false reports . . .
More deadly than leopards and wolves . . .
And all inordinately proud, and usurers,
Who heaping up usury out of usury in their houses
270 Wrought sore harm to orphans and to widows;
And all who give to widows and to orphans
From ill-gotten gains, and all who giving for their own labours
Revile as they give; and all who forsook their parents
In old age, not requiting at all nor as children to parents

245ff. cf. Apoc. Elias, p. 59. 14. 10ff.; Apoc. Esr. p. 30; Apoc. Paul (below, p. 556).
248 cf. Mt. 23:34. 252f. cf. VIII. 411. 255–283 cf. VIII. 419ff.; Mk. 7:21f.; Rom.
1:29; 1 Cor. 6:9; Gal. 5:20; Did. 3. 5; Apoc. Petri c. 6–12 (above, pp. 671ff.).

275 Supplying in their turn; and those who did not obey,
But answered savage words to them that begat them;
And all who receiving pledges denied it,
And all servants who turned against their masters,
And again those who defiled their flesh with lewdness,
280 And all who loosed the maiden girdle
In stealthy union, and women who slay the burden
Of the womb, and all who lawlessly cast out their offspring;
Wizards and witches with them, them also
The wrath of the heavenly and incorruptible God
285 Shall bring to the pillory, where in circle all about
Flows unwearied the fiery stream, and all of them together
The angels of the immortal, everlasting God
Shall punish fearfully with flaming whips,
Binding them tightly about with fiery chains
290 And unbreakable fetters; then in the dead of night
Shall they be flung into Gehenna among the beasts of
Tartarus,
Many and fearful, where darkness has no measure.
But when they have laid many torments upon all
Whose heart was evil, later again the fiery wheel
295 From the great river shall close in upon them,
Because wicked works were all their concern.
Then shall they lament, one here, one there, from afar
At their piteous lot, fathers and infant children,
Mothers too, and little ones weeping at the breast.
300 Neither shall there be for them surfeit of tears, nor shall the
voice
Of them that wail bitterly, now here, now there, be hearkened
to,
But far beneath Tartarus dark and dank
Afflicted they shall howl; in places unhallowed
They shall pay threefold for every evil deed they wrought,
305 Burning in a mighty fire. They shall gnash with their
teeth,
All wasting away with violent and consuming thirst,
And shall call death fair, and it shall flee from them.

286 cf. 196. *295* cf. Apoc. Petri c. 12 (above, p. 678). *305–312* cf. VIII. 350–358.

For neither death nor night shall give them rest any more.
Many an appeal, but in vain, shall they make to God who
    rules on high,
310 And then will he openly turn away his face from them.
For seven age-long days of repentance did he give
To erring men, by the hand of a holy virgin.
But the others, all who took thought for justice and noble
    works,
And piety and righteous ways of thinking,
315 Angels shall bear them through the burning river
And bring them to light and to a carefree life,
Where runs the immortal path of great God
And there are threefold springs of wine and milk and honey.
Earth the same for all, not divided by walls
320 And fences, will then bear fruits more abundant
Of its own accord; livelihood held in common, wealth
    unapportioned!
No pauper is there, no rich man, nor any tyrant,
No slave, nor again any great, nor shall any be small,
No kings, no rulers; but all share in common.
325 No longer shall any say "Night fell", nor again "Tomorrow"
Nor "It happened yesterday", nor be concerned with many
    days,
Nor spring nor harvest, nor winter nor autumn,
Nor marriage nor death, nor buying nor selling,
Nor sunset and sunrise; for all is one long day.
330 And for them will almighty, eternal God provide yet more.
To the pious, when they ask eternal God,
He will grant them to save men out of the devouring fire
And from everlasting torments. This also he will do.
For having gathered them again from the unwearying flame
335 And set them elsewhere, he will send them for his people's sake
Into another life and eternal with the immortals,
In the Elysian plain, where are the long waves
Of the ever-flowing, deep-bosomed Acherusian lake.

311f. cf. 4 Esdr. 5. 75ff. *318–321* cf. VIII. 208–212. *322ff.* cf. VIII. 110f., 121. *325ff.*
cf. VIII. 424ff. *330ff.* from Hystaspes? (cf. Lact. VII. 18. 2). *337f.* cf. Apoc. Petri c.
14 (above, p. 679).

Ah, unhappy me, what will become of me in that day!
340 For that in my folly, labouring more than all,
I sinned, taking thought neither for marriage nor for reason;
Yea more, in my house I shut out the inferiors
Of a wealthy man; and lawless things I did aforetime
Knowingly. But thou, Saviour, deliver me the shameless
345 From my scourgers, though I have wrought unspeakable
    things!
And I pray thee, let me rest a little from my song,
Holy Giver of manna, king of a great kingdom.

Book VI: Hymn to Christ

I sing from the heart the great son and famous of the Immortal,
To whom the Most High, his begetter, gave a throne to take
Ere he was born; for according to the flesh he was raised up
The second time, after he had washed in the stream of the
    river
5 Jordan, which is borne along on silvery foot, drawing its waves.
Who first, escaping from fire, shall see God
Coming in sweet spirit, on the white wings of a dove.
And a pure flower shall blossom, and springs gush forth.
He shall show ways to men, he shall show heavenly paths;
10 And he shall teach all with wise speeches.
He shall bring to judgment and persuade a disobedient people,
Proudly declaring the praiseworthy race of his heavenly
    Father.
He shall walk the waves, and deliver men from sickness,
He shall raise up the dead, and banish many pains.
15 And from one wallet there shall be sufficiency of bread for men
When David's house puts forth its shoot. In his hand
Is all the world, and earth and heaven and sea.
He shall flash like lightning on the earth, as at his first
    appearance
Two saw him, begotten from each other's side.
20 It shall be, when earth shall rejoice in the hope of a Son.

340–344 cf. VII. 151ff. *4f.* cf. VII. 66f. *6* cf. VII. 84; Gospel of the Ebionites fr. 4 (Vol. I, p. 157). *7* cf. Mt. 3:16; Mk. 1:10. *8* cf. Is. 11:1. *13* cf. Mt. 14:26; Mk. 6:48; Jn. 6:19. *14f.* cf. I. 353ff.; VIII. 205ff.; Mt. 11:5 and par. *15* cf. I. 357ff.; VIII. 275ff.; Mk. 6:43; Mt. 14:20; Jn. 6:13. *16* cf. VII. 31. *18* cf. Mt. 24:27. *20* cf. Protev. Jac. 18 (Vol. I, pp. 383ff.).

But for thee alone, land of Sodom, evil woe lies waiting;
For thou in thy folly didst not perceive thy God
When he came in the eyes of men. But from the thorn
Thou didst weave a crown, and bitter gall didst thou mingle
25 For an insulting drink. This will bring thee evil woe.
   O tree most blessed, on which God was stretched out,
Earth shall not have thee, but thou shalt see a heavenly home,
When thy fiery eye, O God, shall flash like lightning.

Book VII

O Rhodes, unhappy thou; for thee first, thee shall I weep.
Thou art first of cities, and first shalt thou perish,
Widowed of men and utterly bereft of life.
Delos, thou shalt set sail and be unstable on the water.
5 Cyprus, thee shall the wave of the grey-blue sea one day
      destroy.
Sicily, the fire that blazes beneath thee shall burn thee up.

*   *
   *

This, I say, is God's terrible oncoming water.
Noah alone of all men came forth and escaped.
Earth swims, the mountains swim, the ether also swims,
10 All things shall be water, and all shall perish in the waters.
The winds shall stand still, and there shall be a second age.
Phrygia, thou first shalt shine above the surface of the water;
But first for impiety thou shalt deny God,
Pleasing dumb idols which, unhappy one,
15 Shall destroy thee as many years go round.
   Unhappy Ethiopians, still suffering bitter pains,
Ye shall be smitten with swords, deep wounded in your flesh.
And fertile Egypt, ever concerned for its grain,
Which the Nile waters freely with its seven-fold flooding
      streams,
20 Intestine discord shall destroy; bereft of hope
Men then shall drive out Apis, baneful to men.

21 cf. Rev. 11:8. 24f. cf. VIII. 303 (Ps. 69:21). 27 cf. Gospel of Peter 39f. (Vol. I, p. 186). 28 cf. Rev. 1:7; 19:12. 7 cf. I. 183. 8 cf. I. 125. 9–11 = I. 193–195. 12 cf. I. 196.

Woe, Laodicea, thou that hast never seen God!
Audacious, thou liest; but the wave of Lycus surges over thee.

*   *

*

Great God himself, the Begetter, shall create many stars,
25 And hang the axis in the midst of the ether,
And shall set up, a great dread for men to behold, on high
A pillar gigantic in great fire, whose sparks
Shall destroy races of men who have wrought evil mischief.
For there shall be that occasion, once and for all, when men
30 Shall propitiate God, but shall not put end to their fruitless
troubles.
But through David's house shall all be accomplished,
For to him God himself gave a throne for his own possession
But the messengers shall lie down to sleep beneath his feet,
They who bring fires to light and pour forth rivers,
35 Who keep safe cities and send the winds.
But upon many men shall harsh life come,
Entering into their souls and changing the hearts of men.

*   *

*

40 This shall be in the fulness of time. But when others
Rule, the race of the warlike Persians, there shall be forthwith
Awesome bridals in consequence of lawless deeds.
For mother shall have her son as husband; son
Shall unite with mother; daughter lying with father
45 Shall sleep according to this barbarian use. But later
The Roman Ares shall flash upon them from many a lance,
And with human blood they shall knead much earth to a
bloody paste.
But then shall Italy's leader flee from the force of the spear,
But they shall leave on the ground the lance inlaid with gold
50 Which ever in the onset bears ahead the sign of destiny.
Verily the time shall be when the wicked, woefully ill-fated

33–35 cf. Hermas, Vis. III. 4. 1.

Ilias shall celebrate burial, not a wedding, where deeply
The brides shall mourn, because they knew not God
But ever with drums and cymbal gave forth sound.

55   Prophesy, Colophon; for a great and terrible fire hangs over
    thee.
    Thessaly ill-wedded, thee shall earth see no more,
    Nor yet thine ashes, but thou shalt set sail alone, an exile from
    the mainland;
    Thus, poor wretch, thou shalt be the sorry refuse of war,
    Falling to swift-flowing streams and to swords.

60 O wretched Corinth, grievous war shalt thou have about thee,
    Unhappy one, and ye shall perish at each other's hand.
    Tyre, thou so great shalt be found alone; for of pious men
    Widowed, thou shalt be distracted by them of small under-
    standing.

64   O Coelesyria, last abode of Phoenician men,

66 Wretch, thou didst not know thy God, whom once Jordan
    Washed in its streams, and the Spirit flew like a dove;
    Who was aforetime master both of earth and the starry
    heavens,
    Logos with the Father and the Holy Spirit,

70 And putting on flesh he flew swiftly to the house of the Father.
    Three towers did great Heaven establish for him,
    Therein now dwell the noble mothers of God,
    Hope and Piety and Holiness much desired,
    Who delight not in gold or silver but in reverence,

75 And the offerings of men and righteous thoughts.
    Thou shalt sacrifice to God, immortal, great and lordly,
    Not by melting a lump of incense in fire, nor with the knife
    Slaying the shaggy ram, but together with all
    Who bear thy blood thou shalt take a wild dove,

80 And having prayed thou shalt send it forth, straining thine
    eyes to heaven.
    Water then shalt thou pour on pure fire, crying out thus:
    "As the Father begot thee as Logos, I send forth the bird,
    Swift messenger of words, as Logos, with holy water

6of. cf. VI. 4ff. *68f.* cf. VIII. 264. *71* cf. Hermas, Vis. III. 4. 1. *73* cf. Hermas,
Vis. III. 8.

Sprinkling thy baptism, through which thou didst come out
  of fire."
85 Nor shalt thou shut thy door when a stranger shall come to
  thee
Begging thee to ward off poverty and hunger from him.
But taking this man's head and sprinkling with water
Pray three times; cry to thy God in such fashion:
"I do not lust after riches; but, a suppliant, I received a
  suppliant."
90 And at the threshold: "Father, thou provider, hearken!
Thou wilt give to him who prays." When the man has gone
  out:
"Afflict me not, holy and righteous majesty of God,
Hallowed, indomitable greatness, tested even in Gehenna!
Strengthen my poor heart, Father; unto thee have I looked,
95 Unto thee the immaculate, whom no hands wrought."

*   *
*

Sardinia, powerful now, thou shalt be changed into ashes;
Thou shalt no more be an island, when the tenth Time comes.
Sailing on the waters they shall seek thee that art no more,
Sea-birds shall wail over thee a bitter lamentation.
100   Rugged Mygdonia, hard-to-pass beacon of the sea,
Thou shalt plume thyself for an aeon, through aeons shalt thou
  perish
All in a hot breath, and be maddened by many sufferings.
  Land of the Celts, by the great mountain, the impassable Alp,
Deep sand shall cover thee altogether; no more shalt thou pay
  tribute,
105 No grain, no fodder; all-desolate shalt thou be of people
For ever, but thick with icy crystals
Thou shalt pay, unholy one, for the outrage thou didst not
  perceive.
  Rome the stout-hearted, after Macedonian warfare
Thou shalt hurl lightning upon Olympus; but God shall make
  thee utterly

84 cf. VI. 6. 89 cf. II. 56, 109.

110 Unheard of, when thou thinkest to stand firm
    For a yet greater onset. Then will I cry to thee thus:
    "Perishing, thou shalt lift up thy voice, thou that once gleamed
        in splendour.
    A second time, O Rome, a second time again will I cry against
        thee."
    And now, unhappy Syria, thee do I bitterly deplore.
115 Thebes of ill counsel, an evil sound is upon you
    Of piping flutes, for you the trumpet shall sound
    An evil sound; ye shall see all the land destroyed.
    Woe to thee wretched, woe malevolent sea!
    Thou shalt be wholly consumed by fire, and with brine shalt
        destroy a people.
120 For there shall be as much fire raging upon earth
    As water, it shall rush and destroy all the land.
    It shall burn up mountains, set rivers afire, empty the springs.
    The world shall be no world, when men are destroyed.
    Dreadfully burning, then shall the wretches look
125 To heaven, lit no more with stars but with fire.
    Nor shall they perish quickly, but dying in the flesh
    Yet burning in spirit for years of ages
    They shall know that God's law is not to be deceived,
    And other things hard to be borne, and that earth is oppressed
130 Because greatly daring she received the altars of the gods
    And deceived by the smoke grown dark in the ether
    ⟨Did not obey the noble commands of great God.⟩
    But those shall undergo great hardship, who for the sake of
        gain
    Utter base prophecies, prolonging an evil time,
    Who putting on the shaggy hides of sheep
135 Falsely call themselves Hebrews, although that is not their
        race;
    Inveterate talkers, profiting only in sorrows,
    They will not change their life nor will they persuade the
        righteous,
    Who faithfully propitiate God in their hearts.
    But in the third assignment as the years go round

120 cf. II. 196. *134* cf. Mt. 7:15. *139f.* cf. Apokr. 2, p. 19*.

140 Of the first Ogdoad, again another world is seen.
   Night shall be everywhere over earth, long and hateful.
   And then shall the dread odour of brimstone spread around,
   Announcing murders, when those shall perish
   In a terror of the night. Then will he beget a pure mind
145 Of men, and set up thy race as it was before.
   No more shall any cut the deep furrow with the crooked
       plough,
   No cattle plunge the guiding iron downward;
   No vine-twig shall there be, nor cluster, but at the same time
       all
   Shall eat with white teeth the dewy manna.
150 Then God too shall be with them and shall teach them
   As he taught unhappy me! What evils did I do aforetime
   Knowing! And many other things I wrought wickedly, taking
       no thought.
   Countless couches have I known, but never recked of marriage.
   Upon all I, utterly faithless, imposed the holy oath.
155 Suppliants I shut out, and in my halls
   Sinned against blood-relatives, disregarding the word of God.
   Wherefore fire shall devour and consume me. For I myself
   Shall not live, but an evil time will destroy me. Then
   Men shall come and prepare a grave for me thrice-wretched,
160 Or destroy me with stones; for of my own father conceiving
   I abandoned the dear child. Stone me, stone me, all of you!
   For thus shall I pay the penalty, and fix my eyes on heaven.

Book VIII

   The great wrath that is coming on a disobedient world
   At the last age, the outburst of God's anger, I show forth,
   Prophesying from city to city to all mankind.
   Since the tower fell, and the tongues of mortal men
5 Were divided into many dialects, first there arose
   The royal house of Egypt, then of the Persians,
   Medes and Ethiopians, Assyria, Babylon,
   Then of Macedonia, vaunting great pride,
   Then fifth the small and lawless kingdom of Italians

140f. cf. Virgil, Ecl. 4:40f. 151–155 cf. II. 343f. 1 cf. 1 Thess. 1:10. 4 cf. Gen. 11.

10 Last of all shall display to all mortals many evils,
And shall expend the labours of every land of men.
It shall lead unwearied kings of nations to the west,
Appoint ordinances for peoples, and subdue all things.
The mills of God grind slowly, but they grind exceeding small.
15 Fire then will crush all things, and reduce to fine powder
The high-crested peaks of mountains and all flesh.
For all, the beginning of evils is love of money and want of
understanding.
For there shall be desire for treacherous gold and silver;
For nothing do mortals prefer more than these.
20 Not the light of the sun, nor heaven, nor sea,
Nor earth broad-backed, whence all things spring,
Nor God the all-giver, the begetter of all,
Not faith and piety do they prefer to these.
This is the source of impiety and vaunt-courier of disorder,
25 Contriver of wars, grievous foe of peace,
Making parents hostile to children, children to parents.
Nor shall marriage ever be held in honour apart from gold.
Earth shall have bounds, and every sea its watchers,
Each craftily partitioned among all those who have gold.
30 And as if they wished to hold for ages the earth that feeds many
They shall despoil the poor, that procuring more land
They may themselves become slaves to vainglory.
And did not the wide earth have its seat
Afar from the starry heaven, the light would not be common
to men,
35 But bought for gold would belong to the rich
And for the beggars God would be preparing another aeon.
But on thee one day shall come from above, proud Rome,
A like heavenly stroke, and thou shalt first bow the neck;
Thou shalt be rased to the ground, and fire shall consume thee
wholly,
40 Laid low to thy foundations; and wealth shall perish,
And the foundations shall be the home of wolves and foxes.
And then shalt thou be wholly deserted, as if thou hadst never
been.

27 cf. Heb. 13:4.

Where then the Palladium? What manner of god shall save
    thee,
Of gold or stone or brass? Or where then thy Senate's
    decrees?
45 Where the race of Rhea and of Cronos,
And of Zeus and all whom thou didst reverence?
Lifeless demons, phantoms of the dead departed,
Whose tombs ill-fated Crete shall have for a boast,
Solemnly celebrating enthronement for the unfeeling dead.
50   But when thou, the voluptuous, hast had thrice five kings,
Who enslaved the world from the east unto the west,
There shall be a ruler grey-headed having the name of the
    near-by sea,
Touring the world with nimble foot, furnishing gifts,
Possessed of abundant gold and silver and from his foes
55 Gathering more; having stripped them he will return.
He will have part in all mysteries of forbidden magic,
Displaying a boy as a god, and cast down all objects of worship,
And open to all the mysteries of ancient error.
Then follows a woeful time, when the "woeful" himself shall
    perish,
60 And the people one day shall say: "Thy great power, O city,
    shall fall",
Knowing straightway that the evil day to come is upon them.
Then shall they mourn together, fathers and infant children,
Foreseeing thy most lamentable destiny.
Plaintive dirges shall the mournful raise by the banks of Tiber.
65   After him three shall rule in the last day of all,
Fulfilling the name of heavenly God
Whose power is both now and to all ages.
One, an old man, shall wield the sceptre far and wide,
A most pitiable king, who shall shut up and guard in his house
70 All the wealth of the world, that when from the ends of the
    earth
The fugitive fierce mother-slayer shall come again
Giving these to all he may set great wealth in Asia.
Then shalt thou mourn, stripping off the purple-bordered

64 cf. Ps. 136:1.

Patrician robe and wearing a mourning garment,
75 Thou haughty queen, offspring of Latin Roma;
No more shalt thou have fame for thine arrogance.
Nor shalt thou ever, ill-starred, be set upright, but bowed
    down;
For indeed the glory of the eagle-bearing legions shall fall.
Where then is thy power? What land shall be ally,
80 Lawlessly enslaved to thy frivolities?
For then shall there be confusion among men of all the earth,
When he comes, the Almighty himself, to judge on his throne
The souls of living and dead, and all the world.
Nor shall parents be dear to children, nor children
85 To parents, because of impiety and hopeless affliction.
Then shall be gnashing of teeth, dispersion and captivity,
When comes the fall of cities, and chasms in the earth;
And when the purple dragon comes upon the waves
With a host in its belly, and afflicts thy children,
90 While there is famine, yea, and civil war,
Near is the end of the world and the last day,
And judgment of immortal God for the proved elect.
But first there shall be implacable wrath of the Romans,
A time blood-drinking and a wretched life shall come.
95 Woe to thee, land of Italy, thou great barbarian nation,
Thou didst not know whence thou didst come, naked and
    unworthy,
To the light of the sun, that to the same place again
Thou mightest naked go, and later come to judgment
As having judged unjustly . . .
100 By giant hands alone against all the world
Descended from the height thou shalt dwell beneath the earth.
With naphtha and asphalt, brimstone and abundant fire,
Thou shalt be utterly destroyed and shalt be dust burning
For ages; and every one who beholds shall hear a bellowing
105 Great and mournful out of Hades, and gnashing of teeth,
And thee beating godless breasts with thy hands.
Upon all there shall be night, alike to those who have riches

84 cf. Enoch 56:7; 99:5; 100:2. *86* cf. 105, 125; Mt. 8:12; Lk. 13:28. *88* cf. Rev.
12:3f. *91* cf. Rev. 1:3; 22:10. *92* cf. Jn. 12:31; Rev. 14:7. *96* cf. Job 1:21; Eccl. 5:15;
Rev. 17:16; Jn. 5:24. *102* cf. Rev. 18:8; 19:20; 20:10; 21:8. *103* cf. Rev. 19:3.

And to the beggars; naked from earth, and naked again to
  earth,
They come, and end their life, when they have completed the
  time.
110 None is a slave there, nor lord, nor tyrant,
No kings, no princes swollen with conceit,
No orator skilled in the law, no ruler judging for money;
They pour no blood on altars in sacrificial libations;
Drum does not sound, nor cymbal clash,
115 Nor much-pierced flute with its frenzied note,
No sound of pipe bearing likeness to crooked serpent,
No trumpet, messenger of wars, with barbaric sound;
No drunkards in lawless revels or in dances,
No sound of lyre, no mischievous device;
120 No strife, no wrath of many forms, no sword
Is there among the dead, but a new age common to all.
  . . . ⟨All and sundry are dragged by⟩
122 The keeper of the keys from the great dungeon to God's
  throne.
⟨Go on now building, ye cities, and adorn yourselves nobly
With temples and market-places and circuses;⟩
123 With statues of gold and silver and of stone
Make yourselves beautiful, that ye may come to the bitter day,
125 Beholding thy punishment first, O Rome, and gnashing of
  teeth.
No more beneath thine enslaving yoke shall bow the neck
Syrian or Greek or barbarian or any other race.
Thou shalt be utterly ravaged, and done by as thou hast done;
Lamenting thou shalt give in fear, until thou hast paid in full.
130 Thou shalt be a triumph-spectacle for the world, and a reproach to all.

*   *

*

139 Again when the limit of time comes on of the phoenix,
140 There will come the ravager of a race of peoples, countless
  tribes, (and)

108 cf. 96. 110ff. cf. II. 322–324, VIII. 424ff. 112 cf. II. 62. 113 cf. II. 96.

The Hebrew nation. Then shall Ares lead Ares captive,
The presumptuous threat of the Romans he himself will
    destroy.
Ended is Rome's dominion, once so flourishing,
Ancient mistress to neighbouring cities.
145 No more shall the land of luxuriant Rome be victorious
When from Asia he comes in sovereign power with Ares.
And when he has wrought all this he will come booted to the
    city.
Thrice three hundred and forty and eight
Years shalt thou fulfil, when upon thee shall come ill-fated
150 A destiny violent fulfilling thy name.
    Alas, thrice unhappy me, when shall I see that day,
Bringing to thee destruction, Rome, bitter especially to the
    Latins?
Sing in his honour, if thou wilt, that man of hidden origin,
From the land of Asia riding on a Trojan chariot
155 With the heart of a lion. But when he cuts through the isthmus,
Gazing about, ready to go against all, exchanging the sea,
Then shall black blood follow after the great beast.
But the lion that destroyed the herds a dog pursued.
The sceptre they will take away, and he will pass to Hades.
160   To Rhodes also shall come a final evil, but the greatest,
And for Thebes there waits hereafter a dire captivity.
Egypt shall be destroyed by the wickedness of rulers.
[But when thereafter mortals escaped utter ruin,
Thrice happy was that man, and fourfold blessed.]
165 Rome shall be an alley, Delos invisible,
Samos a sandheap. . . .
Later again thereafter, evil shall lay hold on the Persians
Because of arrogance, and all wanton insolence shall perish.
    Then shall a holy ruler wield the sceptre of all earth
170 For all ages, he who raised up the dead.
Three shall the Most High bring at Rome to a pitiful fate,
And all men shall perish in their own halls.
But they will not be obedient, which would be far better.
But when for all the evil day grows longer
175 Of famine and plague intolerable, and of the din of war,

730

Then once again the wretched ruler of old time
Summoning a council shall deliberate how he may destroy . . .

*   *
*

The dry shall blossom, appearing with leaves together.
But the heavenly floor shall bring on the solid rock
180 Rain and fire and violent wind upon earth,
And abundance of rust-ruined crops throughout every land.

*   *
*

But again they will do shameless things, full of boldness,
Not fearing the wrath of God or of men,
Abandoning modesty, yearning for effrontery,
185 Rapacious tyrants and violent sinners,
Liars, faithless friends, evil-doers, in nothing true,
Breakers of faith, inventive of words, pouring out slander;
Nor will they know any surfeit of wealth, but shamelessly
Gather yet more; under the sway of tyrants shall they perish.
190   The stars shall all fall headlong into the sea;
Many new stars shall come forth, and a radiant comet
Men call the star, sign of much trouble
Yet impending, of war and mortal conflict.
    Might I live no more when the polluted woman shall reign,
195 But at the time when heavenly grace shall rule,
And when a holy child one day shall utterly destroy
All wickedness, opening for baleful mortals the abyss,
And suddenly a wooden house shall compass about the pious.
But when the tenth generation goes down to the house of
    Hades,
200 Thereafter shall be great power of woman; to whom many
    evils
Will God himself increase, when crowned she has obtained
A royal honour; but the whole year is half an aeon.
The sun shall appear by night, running its arid course;

190 cf. 341; II. 202; Is. 34:4; Mk. 13:25; Mt. 24:29; Rev. 6:13. *196ff.* cf. Rev.
12:5; 20:2f.; Virgil, Ecl. 4:14f.

The stars shall leave heaven's vault; and raging with many a gale

205 He shall make earth desert. But there shall be resurrection of the dead,

And swift running of the lame, and the deaf shall hear
And the blind see, and they that speak not shall speak,
And to all shall life be common, and riches too.
Earth the same for all, not divided by walls

210 Or fences, will bear fruits more abundant.
Springs of sweet wine and white milk
And of honey will it give . . .
Then the judgment of immortal God, the great King.
But when God changes the seasons . . .

215 Making winter summer, then are all the oracles fulfilled.
But when the world has perished ⟨and then the Eternal comes,
Fire shall hold sway in the darkness, and silence in the midst of the night.⟩

JESUS CHRIST, SON OF GOD, REDEEMER, CROSS[1]

Earth shall sweat, when the sign of judgment shall appear.
From heaven shall come the eternal king who is to be;
When he comes, he shall judge all flesh and the whole world.

220 And mortals, faithful and faithless, shall see God
Most High with the saints at the end of time.
He shall judge on his throne the souls of flesh-clothed men
When all the world becomes dry land and thorns.
Men shall cast down their idols and all their wealth.

225 And the fire shall burn up earth, heaven and sea,
Ranging abroad, and shall break the gates of Hades' prison.
Then shall all flesh of the dead come to the light of freedom,
That is, the saints; the lawless the fire shall torment for ages.
Whatever a man wrought secretly, then shall he speak all openly;

230 For God will open dark breasts with his lights.

---

[1] Lines 217–250 form an acrostic, of which the initial letters in the Greek make up the words Ἰησοῦς Χρειστὸς Θεοῦ Ὑιὸς Σωτὴρ Σταυρός. Retention of the acrostic form proved impossible to reconcile with accuracy in translation, and has therefore not been attempted (R. McL. W.).
224 Is. 2:18.

There shall be wailing from all, and gnashing of teeth.
The light of the sun shall be eclipsed, the dances of the stars;
Heaven he will roll up; and the light of the moon shall perish.
He will raise aloft the chasms, lay low the high places of the hills;
235 No more shall baneful height be seen among men.
Mountains shall be level with plains, and all the sea
Shall no more have voyages. For earth shall then be parched
With its springs, and the foaming rivers run dry.
A trumpet from heaven shall send forth a sound of great
    lamentation,
240 Mourning defilement of limbs and a world's calamity.
Then shall a gaping earth display the abyss of Tartarus.
All kings shall come to God's judgment seat.
From heaven shall flow a river of fire and brimstone.
Then shall be a sign for all mortals, a notable seal,
245 The wood among the faithful, the horn long desired,
Life for pious men, but a stumbling-block for the world,
With its waters enlightening the elect in twelve springs;
A staff of iron, shepherding, shall hold sway.
This is our God now proclaimed in acrostics,
250 Saviour, immortal King, who suffered for our sakes.
Whom Moses typified, extending holy arms,
Conquering Amalek by faith, that the people might know
That with God the Father elect and precious is
The staff of David, and the stone which he promised,
255 He who believes on which shall have eternal life.
For not in glory but as a mortal shall he come into the world,
Pitiable, dishonoured, unsightly, to give hope to the pitiable.
And to corruptible flesh he will give form, and heavenly faith
To the faithless, and he will give shape to the man
260 Moulded in the beginning by God's holy hands,
Whom the serpent led astray by guile, to go to a destiny
Of death and receive knowledge of good and of evil,
So that forsaking God he was subject to mortal customs.

231 cf. 350; II. 305; Mt. 8:12; Lk. 13:28. *234ff.* cf. Is. 40:3ff.; Bar. 5. 7; Asc. Mos. 10. 4. *236f.* cf. 348. *239* cf. Mt. 24:31; 1 Thess. 4:16; 1 Cor. 15:52. *243* cf. II. 196. *244* cf. Rev. 7:2f. *245* 1 Sam. 2:10; Ps. 132:17; Lk. 1:69. *246* cf. Rom. 9:33. *248* Ps. 2:9; Rev. 2:27; 12:5; 19:15. *251* cf. Exod. 17:11. *254* cf. Is. 11:1; 1 Pet. 2:6. *255* cf. Jn. 3:36. *257* cf. Is. 53:2ff.

For him first of all did the Almighty take as counsellor
265 In the beginning, and say: "My child, let us two make
The tribes of mortals, modelling them from our image!
Now I with my hands, and thou thereafter with the logos,
Shall tend our figure, that we may produce a common
    creation!"
Mindful of this resolve, then, will he come into the world
270 Bringing a corresponding copy to a holy virgin,
At the same time enlightening with water by older hands,
Doing all with a word and healing every disease.
With a word shall he make the winds to cease, and calm the
    sea
While it rages walking on it with feet of peace and in faith.
275 And from five loaves and fish of the sea
He shall feed five thousand men in the desert,
And then taking all the fragments left over
He will fill twelve baskets for a hope of the people.
He shall call the souls of the blessed, and love the pitiable,
280 Who when scoffed at return good for evil,
Beaten and scourged and yearning for poverty.
Perceiving all and seeing all and hearing all
He shall spy out the inmost parts and lay them bare for
    scrutiny;
For he himself of all is hearing and understanding and vision.
285 And the Word that creates forms, whom all obey,
Saving the dead and healing every disease,
Shall come at the last into the hands of lawless and unbeliev-
    ing men,
They shall give to God blows with their unclean hands
And with their polluted mouths poisonous spitting.
290 Then shall he expose his back and submit it to the whips,
292 And buffeted shall keep silence, lest any should know
Who and of whom he is and whence he came to speak to the
    dying.
And he shall wear the crown of thorns; for of thorns

264ff. cf. 439ff.; Hermas, Sim. IX. 12. 2. *266* Gen. 1:26. *272* cf. Mt. 15:30. *273* cf. Mk. 6:48; Jn. 6:18f. *275–278* cf. I. 357–359; VI. 15. *275* cf. Mk. 6:38ff. par. *287–320* cf. I. 360–380. *288* Mt. 26:67 par. *291* is doubtful, and is here omitted. *294* Mt. 27:29.

295 Is the crown of the elect, their eternal glory.
They shall pierce his sides with a reed because of their law ...
299 But when all these things are accomplished which I have
spoken,
300 Then in him shall all the law be dissolved, which from the
beginning
Was given to men in ordinances because of a disobedient
people.
He shall stretch out his hands and measure the whole world.
But for food they gave him gall, and to drink, sour wine;
This table of inhospitality will they display.
305 But the veil of the temple was rent, and in the midst of day
There shall be night dark and monstrous for three hours.
For no longer by secret law and in hidden temple to serve
The phantoms of the world, the hidden truth was again
revealed
When the eternal Master came down upon earth.
310 But he shall come to Hades, announcing hope to all
The saints, the end of ages and the final day,
And shall fulfil death's destiny when he has slept the third day;
And then returning from the dead he shall come to the light,
The first to show them that are called the beginning of
resurrection,
315 Having washed away the former iniquities in the waters
Of an immortal spring, that born from above
They may no more be in thrall to the lawless customs of the
world.
First to his own did the Lord then openly appear
In flesh, as he was before, and show in his hands and feet
320 Four nail-prints pierced in his own limbs,
East and west and south and north;
So many kingdoms of the world shall accomplish
The lawless, blameworthy deed as our example.
Rejoice, holy daughter of Sion, that hast suffered so much!
325 Thy king himself shall come, mounted on a gentle colt.
Meek, behold, he will come to take away our yoke

296 cf. Mt. 11:7. *297f.* corrupt, and hence omitted. *300* cf. Rom. 7:4ff. *303* Ps.
69:21. *305ff.* cf. I. 376ff. *310ff.* cf. 1 Pet. 3:19; 4:6. *316* Jn. 3:3, 7. *324ff.* Zech. 9:9
(Mt. 21:4ff.; Jn. 12:15). *325f.* Mt. 11:29.

Of slavery, hard to bear, that rests upon our neck,
And godless ordinances will he dissolve, and oppressive fetters.
Him know thou for thy God, who is God's Son.
330 Glorifying him and having him in thy breast
Love him with all thy soul and exalt his name!
Put away the old ways and wash thyself of his blood;
For he is not propitiated by thy songs or by thy prayers,
Nor gives he heed to corruptible sacrifices, being incorruptible.
335 But offering a holy hymn from understanding mouths
Know who this is, and then shalt thou see thy begetter.

*　　*

*

Then shall all the elements of the world be desolate,
Air, earth and sea, and the light of blazing fire;
And the heavenly sphere, and night, and all the days
340 Shall be dashed together into one, into a form all-desolate.
For the stars of the luminaries shall all fall from heaven.
No more shall the plumed birds fly on the air
Nor is there step on earth; for the wild beasts shall all perish.
No sounds of men or beasts or winged things.
345 A world in disorder shall hear no useful echo;
But the deep sea shall ring forth a great sound of menace
And the swimming creatures of the sea shall all trembling die;
And ship bearing cargo shall no more sail upon the waves.
But earth shall bellow, blood-stained by wars,
350 And all souls of men shall gnash with their teeth,
352 Consumed with thirst and hunger, pestilence and slaughters,
And they shall call death fair, and it shall flee from them;
For no more shall death give them rest, nor night.
355 Many an appeal, but in vain, shall they make to God who
     rules on high,
And then will he openly turn away his face from them.
For seven age-long days of repentance did he give
To erring men, by the hand of a holy virgin.

331 cf. Acts 9:15. 334 cf. Hos. 6:6; Mt. 9:13. 335 cf. 498ff. 337 cf. II. 200ff., 305–312. 341 cf. 190; II. 202. 342–348 cf. 4 Esd. 5:6. 348 cf. 236f. 350–358 cf. II. 305–312. 353 cf. Rev. 9:6. 355f. cf. Mt. 25:41ff.

God himself has made known to me all these things in my
    mind,
360 And he will accomplish all that is spoken by my mouth:
"I know the number of the sand and the measures of the sea,
I know the inmost parts of earth, and murky Tartarus,
I know the numbers of the stars, the trees, and how many
    tribes
Of things four-footed and swimming and of winged birds,
365 And of men, that are and shall be, and of the dead.
Myself I moulded the forms and the mind of men,
And gave them right reason, and taught them knowledge;
I who formed eyes and ears, seeing and hearing
And perceiving every thought, and privy to all,
370 Lurking within I keep silence, and later myself will convict
    them.

*   *
*

373 The dumb I understand, he that speaks not I hear,
And how great is the whole height from earth to heaven,
375 Beginning and End I know, I who made heaven and earth.
377 For I alone am God, and other god there is none.
They seek oracles of my image, wrought from wood,
And shaping with their hands a speechless idol
380 They honour it with prayers and unholy ritual.
Forsaking the Creator, they render service to wantonness;
Worthless the gifts men have, to useless beings they give them,
And as it were for my honour they think all these useful,
Celebrating a steaming banquet, as for their own dead.
385 For they burn flesh, and bones full of marrow,
Sacrificing on their altars, and to the demons pour out blood;
And lights they kindle for me, the giver of light,
And as if God were athirst men pour libations of wine
On their useless idols, getting drunk to no purpose.
390 I need no sacrifice or libation at your hand,
No foul reek of fat, no hateful blood.
For these things will they do in memory of kings

368 cf. Ps. 94:9. *387* cf. Is. 1:11; Micah 6:6ff. *390* cf. 333f.; II. 82. *392f.* cf. 46ff.

And tyrants, for dead demons, as if they were heavenly,
Performing a ritual godless and destructive.
395 And gods do the godless call their images,
Forsaking the Creator, thinking that from them they have
All hope and life, trusting to their hurt
In the dumb and speechless, that know not the good end.
I myself set forth two ways, of life and death,
400 And I set it in their mind to choose the good life;
But they turned eagerly to death and eternal fire.
Man is my image, possessed of right reason.
For him set thou a pure and bloodless table,
Filling it with good things, and give to the hungry bread
405 And to the thirsty drink, and to the naked body clothing,
Of thine own labours providing it with holy hands!
Receive the afflicted, come to the aid of the weary,
And present this living sacrifice to the living God,
Sowing now on the water, that I one day may give thee
410 Immortal fruits, and thou shalt have light eternal
And life unfading, when I bring all men to proof by fire.
For I shall smelt all things, and separate them into purity.
Heaven I shall roll up, earth's crannies I shall open,
And then shall I raise up the dead, destroying fate
415 And death's sting, and later shall I come to judgment,
Judging the life of pious and of impious men;
And I will set ram with ram, shepherd with shepherd,
And calf with calf, hard by one another for the testing.
All who were exalted, convicted in the trial,
420 And stopped the mouth of every man, that they full of envy
Might enslave all alike those who act in holy fashion,
Bidding them keep silence, eager for gain,
All these shall then depart, as not approved in my presence.
No more thereafter shalt thou say in sorrow "Will it be
  tomorrow?"
425 Nor "It happened yesterday"; thou art not concerned for
  many days,
Nor spring nor winter, nor harvest nor autumn,

399 cf. Did. 1: *402f.* cf. Gen. 1:26. *403* cf. II. 96; Lev. 17:10; Acts 15:20; 21:25. *403ff.* cf. 480ff. *404f.* cf. II. 83f.; Is. 58:7f., 10. *408* Rom. 12:1. *415* (Hos. 13:14); 1 Cor. 15:55. *417* cf. (Ezek. 34:17); Mt. 25:32f. *419ff.* cf. II. 255ff. *424ff.* cf II. 325ff.

Nor sunset and sunrise; for I will make day long.
But the light of Majesty shall be desired for ever.

*   *

*

429 Self-begotten, immaculate, everlasting and eternal,
430 He is able to measure the fiery breath of the heaven,
Wields thunder's sceptre with the flaming chariot,
And softens the peals of crashing thunders,
Convulsing the earth, he holds in check the tossing ⟨of the
    sea⟩,
Tempers the fiery scourges of the lightning;
435 Incessant streams of rain he has, and storms of hail
Ice-cold, the discharge of the clouds, the assaults of winter
    storms.
. . . .
439 Born before all creation in thy bosom,
440 Counsellor, moulder of men and founder of life,
Whom thou didst address with the first sweet sound of thy
    mouth:
"Behold, let us make man all like to our semblance,
And let us give him life-supporting breath to possess;
Him, mortal though he be, shall all earthly things serve,
445 And to him, moulded of earth, shall we subject all things."
Thus didst thou speak to the Logos, and all was done to thy
    purpose.
447 The elements were all alike obedient to thy command,
. . . .
449 Heaven, air, fire, earth, land and the flow of the sea,
450 Sun, moon, the choir of the heavenly stars,
Night and day, sleep and waking, spirit and impulse,
Soul and understanding, craft, voice and strength;
And the wild tribes of animals, the swimming and the winged
And those of the land, the amphibious, the creeping and
    those of double nature;
455 For in all respects he was in concord with thee beneath thy
    guidance.

442 Gen. 1:26; 2:7. 447ff. cf. Prov. 8:22ff.

And in the last times he changed his abode, and coming as
    a child
From the womb of the virgin Mary he arose, a new light.
From heaven he came, and put on mortal form.
First then the holy, mighty form of Gabriel was displayed.
460 And second the archangel addressed the maiden in speech:
"In thine immaculate bosom, virgin, do thou receive God."
Thus speaking, God breathed grace into the sweet maiden.
But she then was seized with alarm and wonder together as
    she listened,
And stood trembling; her mind was in turmoil,
465 Her heart leaping, at such unheard-of tidings.
But again she rejoiced and her heart was warmed by the
    saying,
And the maiden laughed, her cheeks flushed scarlet,
Gladly rejoicing and touched in her heart with shame;
Then took she courage. The Word flew into her body,
470 Made flesh in time and brought forth to life in her womb,
Was moulded to mortal form and became a boy
By virgin birth-pangs; this, a great wonder to mortals,
Is no great wonder to God the Father and to God the Son.
When the child was born, delight came upon the earth,
475 The heavenly throne laughed, and the world rejoiced,
A new-shining star, God-appointed, was revered by the Magi.
478 Bethlehem was chosen the homeland, divinely elect, of the
    Logos
477 And the swaddled child was shown to God's obedient in a
    manger,
479 To herdsmen of cattle and goats and shepherds of sheep.

*   *
*

480 To be lowly in heart, and hate malignant deeds,
And wholly to love one's neighbour as oneself;
To love God with all one's soul, and serve him.
Wherefore we, sprung of the holy race of Christ

476 cf. Mt. 2:2. *477f.* Lk. 2:7ff. *480ff.* cf. 403ff. *481f.* Mt. 22:39, 37 and par. *482* cf.
II. 60.

In heaven, are surnamed brethren,
485 Having the remembrance of gladness in our rituals
And walking the paths of piety and justice.
Never are we allowed to approach the inner shrines of temples
Or pour libations to images, or honour them with prayers,
Or with the manifold fragrance of flowers or with the gleam
490 Of torches, nor yet to furnish them with offerings of loaves;
Nor to send up the flame of the altar with vapours of incense,
Nor upon libations of bull-sacrifice to send the blood of
slaughtered sheep,
Rejoicing in deliverance, to atone for earthly penalty,
Nor with reeking smoke from the flesh-devouring pyre
495 And with foul vapours to pollute the light of ether;
But with holy understandings, rejoicing with merry heart,
With abundant love and with generous hands,
In gracious psalms and songs meet for God
To hymn thee the immortal and faithful are we bidden,
500 God, the Creator of all, the Omniscient . . .

Prophetia Sibillae magae (4th/5th cent.)
(*Mundus origo mea est*)

The world is my origin, but soul have I drawn from the stars.
My body inviolate God makes to tremble altogether.
⟨What God sets in my heart, that will I proclaim to men⟩,
If abundant faith adjudge truly devout.
5 Many a song have my songs uttered aforetime,
But the songs which now I write, these God knows.
The heavenly homeland's citadel first God created with a
word
[As a divine and perfect work and a great service,]
At the beginning of light, before chaos, God himself.
10 Beginning without end is God, God author of all.
He set chaos aside, separate from kindly night,
Commanded the day to stand, and night and day
To exchange in succession with their lights and move with the
stars
By which the ages of all things are renewed in cycle.

498 cf. Eph. 5:19f.; Col. 3:16f. 498ff cf. 335f.

15 A deluge he poured on earth, and a gift from above.
But after God had confined the waters by banks
The first born of heaven in his own right
To earth came down as man, the child of a virgin inviolate,
Bearing on purple neck for ever the crown.
20 And the Father himself drew near to his own self at the birth,
And one was the soul, one the spirit of his Son,
The name divided, undivided the sovereign power.
The Magus told of his birth in the name of the stars,
And the Lamb descended, whom scarce earth's circle could
contain.
25 He willed to assume the limbs of a human body,
But vigorous in strength of soul and a chaste body
Ever in the bloom of youth he knows not how to grow old.
Alone all-powerful, he shall himself rid the world of sin,
And the shoot is the Father himself; in the two one spirit,
30 One power, one will, nor any division of will.
He shall rule a world pacified by his father's virtues,
Thereafter returning to heaven and his father's golden house.
Praise him fervently with a loud voice, the Mighty!
Me he allows to speak, he who encompasses all the sea.
35 Most High God, Father, ⟨refuge⟩ and hope of thine own,
Most High Son of the Father, whose origin is seed of the word,
Who graciously bestow your commands on souls,
In mortal hearts secret things are spoken by you.
The wisdom of the Most High forbids us know—they are too
great—
40 What is and has been, and what is foretold for the future,
What fear stirs which heart, what spirit afflicts the soul,
What fortune rules kings, or divine power.
The souls of kings also are controlled by your dominion,
That peoples and nations may fall, nor times of peace arise,
45 But pestilence and fever and baneful heat of climate,
And waning as of the moon, eclipses of the sun,
And inroads of the surging sea with its ebb and flow.
You have given names to the stars and signs to the constella-
tions,

31 = Virgil, Ecl. iv. 17.

You command the hot springs to boil in the depths of the
    earth,
50 The burning rivers flow over fiery meadows (?).
To you is known the fire of the sun, you who can know
The thoughts of men, and crimes but contemplated.
Say, what doest thou, mortal man, who dost lose part of the
    body?
God Most High, only leave me not to blood and fire!
55 While thou savest the soul, in what body dost thou perish!
And I know that my form returns to me again.
I look for the fire, and fire does not suffice for fire;
Twice burning I bear threats and mighty wrath.
Fear him, when he arises, whom highest air shall serve.
60 That day shall come, whose hour the Most High knows,
Which ⟨the Father⟩ forbids us to know, and denied to the Son.
Nor shall I say so much, for himself too knows the day;
Who father to himself is not at variance with the Father,
The same can know, because the power is decreed.
65 Then we all pay the varied penalties, to our deserts.
Then shall many a father (?) fear the Most High and raise up
    tears
When he sees his son (?) tortured in the eddy of flame,
Fuel fed to the fire (?) and no end set to the punishment.
Then are kingdoms of no avail, nor all the purples
70 And dyed robes of kings, nor crowns adorned with jewels,
Nor sceptres entrusted to their hands for a whole century (?).
Of no avail the arts, no soothsayer comes to assist.
All things wearily stumble: honour, power, kingship.
The Father himself, hidden in the realm of the snowy world,
75 Shall give to his saints splendour for their abode.
All implore in supplication that the wrath may cease.
A few gather together, saints of proven heart,
Who ever with upright heart worshipped almighty God,
In whose mind dwelt the nursling spirit,
80 And who with sincere intent willed to fulfil his precepts.
Thee ever did they name as God, and humbly they prayed

60 f. cf. Mk 13:32. *65 ff.* cf. II. 284ff. *77–83* In the Latin the initial letters of these
lines form the acrostic KRISTUS.

With their voices, and day and night they groaned to thee.
Thus he addresses you, ye saints, with a gracious heart:
"Lo, I am he who made the frame of heaven and the stars,
85 Who commanded the world to shine with a twofold light,
Who founded earth and the seas, and poured forth souls,
Who with my hands led limbs through the members,
Added body to bones, and in the bones marrow,
Made firm the sinews, and veins filled with blood,
90 Who formed the gleaming skin from glutinous mud
And inserted souls and added senses to minds,
Who gave nourishment to souls and food for the body,
And riches I gave to the streams, and to the fields metals,
And pure springs, and waters meet for fountains,
95 And cattle, the race of flocks, the natures of birds,
Who shut up milk in the udders, separating the blood,
Who willed the grass to grow green in the furrows on the dry
    ground,
Who enclosed the fragile grain in spiked seed,
Who painted the earth with flowers in varied bud,
100 Who cared for the sweet souls of bees and their homes,
Who commanded the globes on the fruit-trees to swell with
    moisture,
Who gave vineyards, and made veins in the body.
These I provided and gave to man, nor denied him invention.
Yet am I unthanked, these thanks another receives.
105 This work is compared with deserts, rewards with deeds.
They worship mountains, rocks, sheep, bulls and caves,
Statues, springs, altars and an empty sepulchre!
Birds give augury, they acknowledge sun and moon,
The author of the works they despise, and forsake the great
    (Lord).
110 Look upon me; why have I redeemed all with my blood
If they have exchanged the kingdom for an earthly seat of
    men?
Their greed was greater than their terror of the darkness.
That the soul may be mine, it will seek me in due time (?)."

84ff. cf. VIII. 361ff. *87ff.* cf. II. 221ff. (after Posidonius, as Prof. H. Mommel of Berlin informed me by letter).

Receive these precepts with righteous heart in a pure body!
115 You who shed tears, prove yourselves worthy of reward!
The years press on, the centuries run to their end,
Which God knows, and refused to let me know.
This alone I know, what is and what is foretold for the future.
All that is ours diminishes; the stars grow dim,
120 Earth is dissolved, the poor air overturned.
If the blood is withdrawn, the whole race is scattered (?).
Deeds burden men, (crimes) planned destroy the guilty;
But he perishes exulting, that faith may purge his crimes.
Then all the race shall renew what it restores from itself (?).
125 The pure he will command to abide in eternal splendour,
To the chaste who merit the palm he appoints habitations.
Under such a Lord the rich shall have no place;
The poor man shall be rich, who believed in the depth of his
   heart.
Sinners find no grace, receive no reward (?).
130 To have done well beyond measure, this is the short way to
   life,
To say what is dear and the great Author loves (?),
To strive (?) after what the simple nature has for nourishment.
Lo, a mortal, I have sung the songs I knew.
Let not the awful day and the last avenging hour (?),
135 If I be worthy, snatch them away, and let it set my soul in
   heaven.
Short is man's life, and when ended dissolves with the years.

3. THE BOOK OF ELCHASAI
(J. Irmscher)

1. NAME AND TRADITION. Hippolytus (Ref. 9. 13–17 and 10. 29),
Epiphanius (*Haer.* 19 and 30) and Origen (ap. Eusebius *HE*
VI. 38) all mention the book of a certain Elchasai, which was
used by several sects and in particular by the Elchasaites, who
were named after this Elchasai. Hippolytus and Epiphanius, the
latter clearly uninfluenced by the former, adduce extracts from
this book, the only remains that we possess. One of these fragments (No. 9) contains a cryptogram which, reading outwards
from the middle word and inverting the order of the letters, produces an Aramaic formula; such a play upon words pre-supposes

readers who understood Aramaic, and makes it probable that the book in its original form was written in that language. The author's name is given as Elchasai by Hippolytus or his authority Alcibiades, the disciple of Elchasai, and also later by the Arabic writer en Nedîm in the Fihrist (cf. D. Chwolson, *Die Ssabier und Ssabismus* 2, 1856, 543), while Epiphanius has Elxai; the first and better-attested form deserves the preference. Both forms of the name go back to the Aramaic היל כמי, which Epiphanius (*Haer.* 19. 2. 10) correctly translates as "hidden power". It is not possible to decide whether Elchasai was his own name or a sobriquet (like that, for example, of Simon Magus in Acts 8:10).

2. CONTENT. When Hippolytus states (Ref. 9. 14. 3) that he intends to go through the Book of Elchasai, we may conclude that he presents his extracts in the sequence in which he found them in his source. Checking through these extracts, we come upon a meaningful and progressive development of thought; thus the Book of Elchasai must have been more than a mere collection of aphorisms. The introduction may have related that it was imparted to Elchasai by divine revelation. Following this vision and connected with it was the proclamation of a remission of sins. This is valid in particular for even the gross sinners, and is linked to a re-baptism. Ritual immersions are also commended as a means of healing for all kinds of sickness, and in addition a Jewish legalistic way of life is prescribed. Sacrifice and the sacerdotal actions associated with it are forbidden. Thereafter the apocalyptist promises a war among the powers of godlessness; if the adherents of Elchasai should fall into danger during it, an outward denial will be forgiven them provided only that they remain constant at heart. In such a case one need only pray a magic formula, Elchasai's promise: "I will be witness over you on the day of the great judgment." For the rest, it is essential to keep the book hidden from the eyes of intruders.

3. THE BASIC CHARACTER of the book is Jewish, but it is a syncretistic and not a pure Judaism. Jewish elements are in particular the requirements of circumcision, of sabbath observance, and of prayer in the direction of Jerusalem (Epiph., *Haer.* 19. 3. 5). Contrary to Judaism are the rejection of sacrifice and also the criticism of the OT associated with it (*ib.* 19. 3. 6). Christian with a strong tinge of Gnosticism are the ideas of the Son of God or Christ and the Holy Spirit as heavenly beings (see frags. 1 and 2), and in addition the promises of the forgiveness of sins and of eternal salvation, as well as the ethical requirements of sanctification. Contrary to the usage of ecclesiastical Christianity is the prescription of a second baptism. Of heathen origin are the

immersions with the invocation of the seven elements (see frags. 2 and 4), and also the astrological conceptions of the influence of malevolent stars.

4. ORIGIN AND DISSEMINATION. According to his own account (frag. 2) Elchasai came forward with his message in the third year of Trajan (101); he seems to have composed his book during the reign of the same emperor, as is suggested by the prophecy, given in frag. 7 but not fulfilled, of a universal conflict blazing up three years after the Parthian war (114–116) but still under Trajan's rule. The reports about Elchasai's homeland are contradictory; the most worthy of credit are some references in Epiphanius (*Haer.* 19. 2. 10ff.; 53. 1. 1ff.), which point to the region east of Jordan. The work was dedicated to the "Sobiai" the "baptized" (from צבע), as the adherents of Elchasai called themselves (not a person of that name, as Hippolytus Ref. 9. 13. 1–3 = Frag. 1a wrongly assumed). It was however disseminated also among other religious groups, both Jewish and Jewish-Christian, and for this Epiphanius once again affords the evidence (*Haer.* 19. 1; 30. 18; 53). It was brought to the congregation of Callistus in Rome about 220, and that in a Greek version, by the above-mentioned Alcibiades of Apamea, who was active as a missionary in the imperial capital. A propagandist advance by the sect to Caesarea in the year 247 is mentioned by Eusebius (*HE* VI. 38). It seems to have met with only slight success, and in general the sect's proselytizing power soon flagged, although it lingered on in isolated places for centuries to come.

5. LITERATURE. Fragments and testimonia in A. Hilgenfeld, *Novum Testamentum extra canonum receptum* III 2², 1881, pp. 227–240; W. Brandt, *Elchasai, ein Religionsstifter und sein Werk*, 1912 (a comprehensive monograph, but not to be used without Harnack's review in ThLZ 37, 1912, cols. 683ff.); H. Waitz, Das Buch des Elchasai, *Harnack-Ehrung*, 1921, pp. 87–104; J. Thomas, *Le mouvement baptiste en Palestine et Syrie*, 1935; H. J. Schoeps, *Theologie und Geschichte des Judenchristentums*, 1949, pp. 325ff.; *id.*, article *Elkesaiten* in *RGG*³ II, col. 435; G. Strecker, article *Elkesai* in RAC V, cols. 1171–1186.

Fragments

1. A certain Alcibiades, who lived in Apamea in Syria . . . came to Rome and brought with him a book. Of it he said that Elchasai, a righteous man, had received it from Seres in Parthia and had transmitted it to a certain Sobiai. It had been communicated by an angel, whose height was 24 schoinoi, which is 96 miles, his breadth four schoinoi, and from shoulder to shoulder six schoinoi, and the tracks of his feet in length 3½ schoinoi, which

is 14 miles, and in breadth 1½ schoinoi, and in height half a schoinos. And with him there was also a female figure, whose measurements Alcibiades says were commensurate with those mentioned; and the male figure was the Son of God, but the female was called Holy Spirit.

(Hippol., Ref. 9. 13. 1–3)

"And whence," he said, "did I know the measurements?" "Because," he said, "I saw from the mountains that their heads reached up to them, and when I had learned the measure of the mountain I knew the measurements both of Christ and of the Holy Spirit."

(Epiph., *Haer.* 30. 17. 7)

2. He affirms the following: That the gospel of a new forgiveness of sins was preached to men in the third year of Trajan's reign. And he appoints a baptism . . . of which he says that through it anyone who is defiled by any licentiousness and pollution and lawlessness receives forgiveness of sins . . . if he be converted and listen to the book and believe in it.

(Hippol., Ref. 9. 13. 3–4)

" If then, children, anyone has had relations with any animal whatsoever, or a male or a sister or a daughter, or has practised adultery or fornication, and wishes to receive forgiveness of his sins, let him, as soon as he has heard this book, be baptized a second time in the name of the great and most high God, and in the name of his Son, the great king. And let him purify himself and sanctify himself, and call to witness the seven witnesses written in this book, heaven and water and the holy spirits, and the angels of prayer, and the oil and the salt and the earth."

(Hippol., Ref. 9. 15. 1–2)

3. Again I say, ye adulterers, adulteresses and false prophets, if you wish to be converted, that your sins may be forgiven you, to you also there will be peace and a share with the righteous, from the time you hear this book and are baptized a second time with your clothing.

(Hippol., Ref. 9. 15. 3)

4. If then any man or woman or youth or maid is bitten, torn or touched by a mad and raving dog, in which is a spirit of destruction, let him run in the same hour with all he wears, and go down into a river or spring, wherever there may be a deep place, and let him baptize himself with all he wears and pray to the great and most high God with a faithful heart. Then let him call to witness the seven witnesses written in this book: "Behold, I call to witness the heaven and water and the holy spirits, and the angels of prayer and the oil and the salt and the earth. These seven witnesses I call to witness, that I will no more sin, nor commit adultery, nor steal, nor do wrong, nor claim more than is due, nor hate, nor transgress, nor take pleasure in any wickedness." Let him, then, say this and baptize himself with all he wears, in the name of the great and most high God. . . . The consumptive also are to baptize themselves in cold water forty times in seven days, and likewise also those possessed by demons.

(Hippol., Ref. 9. 15. 4–16. 1)

5. He forbids prayer towards the east, saying that one ought not to pray thus, but from every region have one's face towards Jerusalem,[1] those in the east to turn westwards to Jerusalem, those in the west eastwards to the same place, those in the north southwards, and those in the south northwards, so that from every quarter the face may be opposite Jerusalem.

(Epiph., *Haer.* 19. 3. 5)

6. He rejects sacrifices and priestly rites as being alien to God and never offered to God at all according to the fathers and the law. . . . But that water is acceptable to God and fire alien, he explains in the following words: "Children, go not according to the form of the fire,[2] because ye go astray; for such is error. For you see it, he says, very near and yet it is far away. Go not according to its form, but go rather according to the sound of the water."

(Epiph., *Haer.* 19. 3. 6f.)

[1] Cf. Dan. 6:10; Ezek. 8:16ff.; Berakoth 4. 5.
[2] Greek τέκνα, μὴ πρὸς τὸ εἶδος τοῦ πυρὸς πορεύεσθε. Perhaps "follow not the will-o'-the-wisp of the fire"? (R. M. W.).

7. These are evil stars of godlessness. This now is spoken to you, ye pious and disciples: Beware of the power of the days of their dominion, and do not make a start to your works in their days! Baptize neither man nor woman in the days of their authority, when the moon passes through from them and travels with them. Await the day when it departs from them, and then baptize and make a beginning with all your works! Moreover, honour the day of the Sabbath, for it is one of these days! But beware also not to begin anything on the third day of the week, for again when three years of the emperor Trajan are complete, from the time when he subjected the Parthians to his own authority, when these three years are fulfilled, the war between the godless angels of the north will break out; because of this all kingdoms of godlessness are in disorder.

(Hippol., Ref. 9. 16. 2–4)

8. He says that it is not a sin even if a man should chance to worship idols in a time of imminent persecution, if only he does not worship in his conscience, and whatever he confesses with his mouth he does not in his heart. . . . Phineas,[1] a priest of the tribe of Levi and Aaron and the ancient Phineas, in Babylon in the time of the captivity worshipped Artemis in Susa, and so escaped death and destruction in the time of Darius the king.

(Epiph., *Haer*. 19. 1. 8–9)

9. Let none seek after the interpretation, but let him only say in his prayer these words . . .: "Abar anid moib nochile daasim ana daasim nochile moib anid abar. Selam."

(Epiph., *Haer*. 19. 4. 3)

If we read from the middle outwards in either direction, the result is an Aramaic sentence:

אנא מסהד עליכון ביום דינא רבא

"I am witness over you on the day of the great judgment." Cf. M. A. Levy, *ZDMG* 12, 1858, p. 712.

10. Do not read this word to all men, and keep these commandments carefully, because not all men are faithful, nor all women upright.

(Hippol., Ref. 9. 17. 1)

---

[1] Cf. Num. 25:7; Eccles. 45:23.

750

XVIII

LATER APOCALYPSES

INTRODUCTION
(*W. Schneemelcher*)

It has already been stated above (pp. 598ff.) that Jewish Apocalyptic lived on vigorously in Christianity and that the literary form of Apocalypse continued into the period of the Church. The longer this went on the more this literary form was limited in its themes to descriptions of the other world, Anti-Christ and judgment. Insistence on repentance was necessarily also a constituent of these works.

There are a large number of later Apocalypses which are based in part on Jewish sources but in part only work up traditional material independently, and have been put into circulation under a name from the OT or NT. A short analysis of the more important texts is found in H. Weinel, 'Die spätere christliche Apokalyptik' (*EYXAPIΣTHPION. Studien zur Religion und Literatur des AT und NT*, Gunkel Festschrift 1923, II, pp. 141–173). For more information see also: *Lexikon für Theologie und Kirche*, 2nd edn. Vol. I, article 'Apokalypsen' (H. Gross and J. Michl). From the abundance of texts, we have presented below in their entirety two of the older (Apocalypses of Paul and Thomas); we append here brief references to some of the others.

I. APOCALYPSE OF SOPHONIAS (ZEPHANIAH)

A Book of the Prophet Sophonias (Zephaniah), or a Revelation of S., is rejected as apocryphal in the Stichometry of Nicephoros and in the Catalogue of the Sixty Canonical Books (cf. Vol. I, pp. 49ff.). Clement of Alexandria gives a quotation out of a Book of Sophonias in *Strom.* V. 11. 77. We cannot ascertain from what work this quotation came because the Coptic text of the Apocalypse of Sophonias does not contain it. Probably the quotation of Clement came from a Jewish writing, whereas the Coptic text represents a Christian redaction (of this Jewish text?). The description of the place of punishment occupies a great part of the existing Coptic text. Harnack in the course of his discussion asserts that its relationship to the Apocalypse of Paul is one of dependence on the part of the latter (*Gesch. der altchristl. Lit.*, II. 1, p. 573). This however requires further examination; equally the assigning of the 'anonymous apocalypse' (in Steindorff) to the

751

Apocalypse of Sophonias is not above doubt. The Coptic text cannot have been composed before A.D. 400—Text and Translation: G. Steindorff, *Die Apokalypse des Elias, eine unbekannte Apokalypse und Bruchstücke der Sophonias-Apokalypse* (*TU* 17. 3a) 1899; P. Riessler, *Altjüdisches Schrifttum ausserhalb der Bibel*, 1928, pp. 168–177.—Harnack, *op. cit.*, I. 2, p. 854; II. 1, pp. 572f.; Weinel, *op. cit.*, pp. 163f.

2. APOCALYPSE OF ELIJAH

The Apocalypse of Elijah is also rejected in the Stichometry of Nicephorus and in the Catalogue of the Sixty Books (Vol. I, pp. 49ff.). The other references in early Church literature to the Apocalypse of Elijah occur mostly in relation to two passages in Paul, 1 Cor. 2:9 and Eph. 5:14 (for the connection cf. Harnack, *op. cit.*, I. 2, pp. 853f.). Because Eph. 5:14 is a Christian hymn (cf. M. Dibelius, *Handbuch z. NT*, ad loc.) it can be left out of account here. With regard to 1 Cor. 2:9 we may observe that this text was undoubtedly a widespread logion (cf. Vol. I, p. 300, in reference to Logion 17 of the Gospel of Thomas) and for that reason assertions about the Apocalypse of Elijah can hardly be drawn from it. It is not even found in the Coptic text which contains the fragments of the Apocalypse of Elijah. In this Apocalypse, which has been at least edited by Christians (Weinel puts it at the end of the 4th century; Riessler considerably earlier), there are exhortations, predictions, descriptions of Anti-Christ, etc. The relationship to a Jewish Apocalypse of Elijah which is preserved in Hebrew needs further clarification.—Text: Steindorff, *op. cit.* (see above on 1.); P. Riessler, *op. cit.*, pp. 114–125 and 234–240.—Harnack, *op. cit.*, I. 2, p. 853; II. 1, pp. 571f.; Weinel, pp. 164ff.; M. Buttenwieser, *Die hebräische Eliasapokalypse*, 1897.

3. APOCALYPSE OF ZECHARIAH

In the early canonical lists (cf. Vol. I, pp. 49ff.) a book is mentioned in connection with Zechariah the father of John. It is indeed remarkable that this book is reckoned among the OT Apocrypha, Zechariah being identified with the prophet of that name. A. Berendts believed that there is not sufficient evidence for an OT Apocryphon and would prefer to see behind this title an account of the murder of Zechariah, the son of Barachiah, inspired by Mt. 23:35 (Lk. 11:51); this has then been referred to the Baptist's father and embellished with legend. Such a legend (3rd or 4th century?) may then have been the source for the account in the Protevangelium of James, chaps. 22–24 (Vol. I, pp. 387f.: this portion is clearly an addition to the Protevangelium), and for a Slavonic legend about the birth of John the forerunner and the death of his father Zechariah. A re-examination is required to see if this solution of a very intricate problem is correct. It is certain that there was a writing, perhaps of an apocalyptic nature, connected to the name of Zechariah. We cannot precisely say what it looked like.—A. Berendts, *Studien über Zacharias-Apokryphen und Zacharias-Legenden*, 1895; *Die handschriftliche Überlieferung der Zacharias- und Johannes-Apokryphen* (*TU* 26. 3), 1904. Cf. also H. Wall, 'A Coptic Fragment concerning the Childhood of John the Baptist', *Revue d'Égyptologie* 8, 1951, pp. 207–214.

4. APOCALYPSES OF JOHN

Three later apocalypses are known under the name of John.

(*a*) Ἀποκάλυψις τοῦ ἁγίου Ἰωάννου τοῦ θεολόγου (Text in Tischendorf, *Apa*, pp. 70–94). This is a disclosure by means of question and answer of many details of the next world: Anti-Christ is described, the fate of individuals in the resurrection is discussed in detail, the punishments of Hell and the joys of Heaven are represented. The writing probably makes use of Ephraem (cf. Bousset, *Der Antichrist*, 1895, p. 26) and consequently was probably first composed in the 5th century. The oldest testimony to it comes from the 9th century.—Cf. Weinel, *op. cit.*, pp. 149–151.

(*b*) F. Nau has published a shorter Apocalypse of John: 'Une deuxième Apocalypse apocryphe grecque de S. Jean' (*Rev. Bibl.* 23, 1914, pp. 209–221). According to Nau this Apocalypse had its origin in Cyprus between the 6th and 8th centuries.

(*c*) A third apocalyptic writing under the name of John has been preserved in a Coptic manuscript of the 11th century which E. A. W. Budge has published (*Coptic Apocrypha in the Dialect of Upper Egypt*, 1913, pp. 59–74; English translation, pp. 241–257). The work is entitled 'The mysteries of Saint John the Apostle and Holy Virgin'. On a heavenly journey John sees the mysteries of the world. Up to now there has been no careful investigation whether this Coptic writing goes back to a Greek substratum; similarly the date of its composition is unknown.

5. APOCALYPSES OF MARY

There are two writings ascribed to Mary the mother of God which concern us:

(*a*) Ἀποκάλυψις τῆς ἁγίας θεοτόκου περὶ τῶν κολάσεων; this is preserved in Greek, Armenian, Ethiopic and Old Slavonic versions. Its nature is that of a revelation in which Mary is shown the tortures of the damned, for whom she then asks pardon. The book "represents an attempt to draw into a more rigid system the tortures of Hell of the older Apocalypses" (Weinel, *op. cit.*, p. 156). It appeared probably in the 9th century and is dependent on the Apocalypses of Paul and Peter.—Text: M. R. James, *Apocrypha anecdota*, 1893, pp. 115–126; there is an examination of the text in Tischendorff, *Apa*, pp. xxvii–xxx.—Cf. Weinel, *op. cit.*, pp. 156f. A Cretan version in R. M. Dawkins, Κρητικὴ 'Αποκάλυψις τῆς Παναγίας (Κρητ. Χρονικά 2, 1948, pp. 487–500).

(*b*) Likewise dependent on the Apocalypse of Paul is the Ethiopian *Apocalypsis sen Visiso Mariae Virginis*, which may have originated in the 7th century, but is probably later. Latin translation by M. Chaine, *CSCO*. Script. Aeth. Ser. I, Vol. VII, 1909, pp. 43–68.

The *Liber Johannis de dormitione Mariae* which Tischendorff reproduces (*Apa*, pp. 95–112) is not an apocalypse but a legend.

6. APOCALYPSE OF STEPHEN

A *Revelatio sancti Stephani* is rejected as apocryphal in the so-called Decretum Gelasianum (cf. Vol. I, pp. 46f.). Nothing more is known about this apocalypse. It has been suggested, perhaps correctly, that there is a misunderstanding here: the reference in the Decr. Gel. does not relate to an apocalypse but to an account of the discovery of the relics of Stephen which was composed in Greek by the Presbyter Lucian of Kaphar Gamala in the year 415 and afterwards translated into Latin in two different recensions, of which one was made by Avitus of Braga.—Text of this account: *PL* 41, 805–815; S. Vanderlinden, 'Revelatio S. Stephani' (*Revue des études byzantines* I, 1946, pp. 178–217). Cf. also Altaner, p. 72.

7. APOCALYPSE OF BARTHOLOMEW

The Apocalypse of Bartholomew which continues to reappear in modern literature is not an apocalypse. The texts in question are rather later compilations belonging to the category of Gospels, even though many pieces may derive from apocalyptic tradition. These texts have therefore already been dealt with in Vol. I, pp. 484ff.

For the gnostic so-called Apocalypses in Coptic from Nag-Hammadi, cf. *supra* p. 599 and the particulars given by H.-Ch. Puech, 'Les nouveaux écrits gnostiques découverts en Haute-Égypte', *Coptic Studies in Honor of W. E. Crum*, 1950, pp. 91–154.

1. APOCALYPSE OF PAUL
(H. Duensing)

ATTESTATION. In his *Nomocanon* VII. 9 Barhebraeus introduces a quotation from Origen according to which the Apocalypse of Paul, with other Apocalypses and other early Christian writings which are there enumerated, was accepted by the Church. We can also assume from his *Homil. in Psalmos* (ed. Lommatzsch XII, 233) a knowledge at least of the subject-matter of our Apocalypse for he describes the destiny of the soul after death in a way closely related to chs. 13ff. in it; this pre-supposes that we accept the quotation as genuine as it stands and do not alter it with Zahn so as to read 'Peter' instead of 'Paul'. That however he cannot have had our recension before him, follows not only on the basis of the contents, but also from Sozomen; in relation to the Apocalypse of Paul he says (*Hist. eccl.* VII. 19, ed. Bidez-Hansen, *GCS* 50, 1960, 331) that none of the ancients knew it, that rather it supposedly appeared under the Emperor of the time, alluding to the story contained in it of its own discovery, and that after an inquiry from an ancient Presbyter in Tarsus it had turned out to be a fraud. If Origen knew a writing of this title it cannot have been the Apocalypse in the form in which we have it. We meet a more trustworthy testimony to its existence in Augustine (*In Ioh. tract.* 98. 8, ed. R. Willems, *Corp. Christ.* 36, 1954, 581) who says that some have concocted an Apocalypse of Paul which the true church does not accept. And when in the *Enchiridion* (112-113, *PL* 40, 284-285) he expounds the idea of the relaxation of the fate of damned souls in the day of the Lord, he will have drawn that from our writing; for at almost the same time (around 402) Prudentius produces this conception in his *Cathemerinon* (V. 125ff., ed. J. Bergman, *CSEL* 61, 1926, 30). The Apocalypse of Paul appears in the Decretum Gelasianum among the apocryphal books which were not accepted (ed. v. Dobschütz, *TU* 38. 4, 1912, 12). Later testimony only evidences continued knowledge of the Apocryphon and the eventual extension of its influence.

TRANSMISSION. The original Greek text has only come down to us in abbreviated form like a summary (cf. *infra*). As the versions show it has received additions, e.g. in 62. 5ff. there are statements directed against the Nestorians. The most complete and at the same time oldest witness is the Latin translation as published by M. R. James in accordance with a Parisian Manuscript; as a torso it is found in similar form in Cod. 317 of the Stadtbibliothek of St. Gall and has been published by Silverstein (*Studies and Documents* IV, London, 1935). Besides these there is a whole series of Latin recensions. A Syrian translation was first made public in an English translation from a manuscript in Urmiah; a German translation has been published by Zingerle (in *Heidenheims Vierteljahrsschrift* IV, 1871, 139-183) from the text printed later in 1933 by Ricciotti of Cod. Vatican. Syriacus 180. Like so many others this text travelled from Syria to Armenia and was preserved there in 4 forms. Slavonic editions of the work have also been preserved; of these the best is that of an old Russian translation. Next to the Latin the most important witness is a Coptic text which Budge published in 1915 with an English translation; this text begins with ch. 15 and has been expanded in places. The Ethiopic Apocalypse of Mary the Virgin which Chaine has published presents an adapted translation of chs. 13–44 (cf. *supra* p. 754).

The differences between the various texts are so great that it is impossible to put them adequately together. We have to keep to that recension which is most complete and has been transmitted comparatively well, and then use the others to complete and correct it; this means using the Latin text published by James. Casey says correctly (p. 5): "For most purposes it is sufficient to know the content of the work."

CONTENT AND SOURCES. In 2 Cor. 12 Paul tells of being caught up into Paradise and this gave someone who was familiar with the apocalyptic tradition the opportunity of putting in Paul's mouth what he himself knew or thought about the next world. He gets over the difficulty that Paul had described what he heard as unutterable by distinguishing between some things which Paul could not tell and others which he was permitted to relate (cf. ch. 21). The introductory report of the discovery of these important revelations serves to explain how it happened that they were not made public earlier, possibly even in the time of Paul himself. If this account comes from the (first) author himself the date of the work is fixed as the end of the fourth or beginning of the fifth century. In any case the recension which we have must date from that period. After this introduction, placed in the Syriac at the end, we have the rapture to the third heaven (ch. 3); here Paul is told of the complaints which creation has brought against sinning mankind and about the reason for the delay of final punishment, namely, the divine forbearance (chs. 3–6). In chs. 7–10 we are told of the reports about the deeds of men which the angels give to God every evening and morning. Ch. 11 brings a change of locality so that the apostle may see the souls of the righteous and of sinners at and after their death and observe where they live. So he is able to see how a righteous man dies and what happens to him and to a sinner and a soul which denies but then is confronted with those whom it has sinned against during its life in the body (chs. 11–18). Paul is now brought to Paradise where the doors with golden inscribed tables are the occasion for a question, which the *angelus interpres* answers by saying that the names of the righteous are on it. Both Enoch and Elijah greet Paul at his entrance. From heaven he sees the ocean surrounding the earth, the land of promise and Lake Acherusia, whiter than milk, in which the archangel Michael baptizes repentant sinners so that they can enter the city of Christ. He reaches this city by a voyage in a golden ship over Lake Acherusia. Among other things there are four rivers to be seen, one of honey, one of milk, one of wine, one of oil. At the first the prophets live, at the second the children of Bethlehem and those like them, at the third the Patriarchs, Lot, Job and other saints, at the fourth figures rejoicing and singing Psalms. In the city he also sees and hears David singing Hallelujah (chs. 19–30). In ch. 31 there commences the visitation of Hell with its various places of punishment. Among the damned are found presbyters (ch. 34), bishops (ch. 35), deacons and readers (*anagnosti*) (ch. 36). At the request of Michael and other angels and for the sake of Paul Christ gives to the damned freedom from torture on Sundays (chs. 31–44). Then another visit to Paradise follows (ch. 45). Here a strange sight is seen at the beginning, viz. a tree on which rested the Spirit of Gen. 1, at whose movement the waters of the four rivers of Paradise flow (ch. 45). Paul again meets the Patriarchs (ch. 47), Moses (ch. 48), the prophets, Lot, Job (ch. 49), Noah (ch. 50), Elijah and Elisha (ch. 51); only the meeting with Mary (ch. 46) was not mentioned earlier. The text breaks off suddenly in ch. 51 with the words "I will send rain on the earth". The Coptic alone goes on. In it Paul is yet again carried up into the third heaven (cf. the summary *infra*, pp. 795f.).

The many doublets in this carelessly compiled work show at once that the author has used material which was already in existence before him. His own individuality appears only in his high estimation of the life of monks and nuns, to whose circle evidently he himself belonged. If his own imagination provides the material relative to this life, he is elsewhere dependent on apocalyptic tradition; this, enriched with Greek ideas of the after-life, e.g. Tartarus, Lake Acherusia, the boat journey, permeated the early church, and then also the Church of the Middle Ages, in an ever-broadening stream. It is clear that he knew the contents of the *Apocalypse of Peter*; this is seen above all in the description of the places of punishment and especially in that for those guilty of abortion; this conclusion could not be denied at all provided the Coptic has preserved the original ending, in which after his heavenly journey Paul returns to the circle of Apostles gathered on the Mount of Olives. The author would then only have altered his source in so far as he replaces Clement as in the *Apocalypse of Peter* by Mark and Timothy as those who wrote down what Paul saw; this alteration would have been quite natural. Other borrowings are Lake Acherusia (cf. *supra*), the encounter with the Patriarchs, the fiery stream, the angel Tartaruchus or Temeluchus. The ferrying over Lake Acherusia occurs also in the *Apocalypse of Zephaniah* (G. Steindorff, *TU* 17. 3a, 1899); in it we have also the recording angel with the manuscript (chirographon—agreeing in the Greek expression!) and the encounter with all the righteous in the heavenly world, in particular with the Patriarchs, Enoch, Elijah and David. There is a striking contact with the Apocalypse of Elijah (*TU* 17. 3a) at the very beginning in ch. 3, where with very little variation the sentence is repeated: The word of the Lord came to me thus: "O son of man, say to this people, 'Why do you heap sin on sin and anger God the Lord, who made you'." (Steindorff, p. 155) If the additional material at the end of the Coptic is original, then the author copied from the *Apocalypse of Zephaniah*, where it says, "Be strong that you may conquer and be mighty that you may overcome the accuser and come up out of the underworld." (Steindorff, p. 170; cf. *ibid.* p. 55, ch. 12, lines 12ff. of the *Apocalypse of Elijah*, and p. 153: "Be triumphant and strong, for you are strong and are overcoming the accuser and coming up out of the underworld and the abyss." Cf. also the last four lines on the same page.) Casey (pp. 22ff.) draws attention to an agreement with Slavonic Enoch, chs. 8–9 (Morfil-Charles, pp. 7–9), in the description of Paradise; James (p. 552 n. 1) likewise draws attention to a contact with the *Testament of Job*. It is impossible to say from where the author may have drawn his fantastic representation of the colossal fruitfulness of eternity (ch. 22), which corresponds with the description of Papias (in Irenaeus, V. 33. 3f.). All these borrowings render a later date probable.

LITERATURE. All the relevant literature up to 1935 is listed in *Studies and Documents* (ed. Lake), Vol. IV: *Visio sancti Pauli*, ed. Th. Silverstein, 1935, pp. 219–229. This work carefully clarifies the branches of the Latin tradition and reproduces MS. 317 of the Stadtbibliothek of St. Gall. The remaining most important publications are: Tischendorf's edition of the abridged Greek text in his *Apocalypses apocryphae*, 1866, pp. 34–69; M. R. James' edition of the oldest Latin Version[1] in *Texts and Studies*, Vol. II. 3, 'Apocrypha Anecdota', Cambridge 1893 (on pp. 4–7 there is a comparison of the Greek, Syriac and Latin); the edition of the Syriac in *Orientalia* II, 1933, 'Apocalypsis Pauli syriace' ed. G. Ricciotti, pp. 1–24 and pp. 120–149, with a Latin translation; it consists of the Syriac text according to Cod. Vatic. syr. 180 compared with and completed according to Cod. Borgianus syr. 39. Zingerle had translated the former into German in 1871; the edition of the Coptic in *Miscellaneous Coptic Texts* ed. E. A. Wallis Budge (with an English translation, pp. 1043–1084), 1915.—R. P. Casey in *JThSt*, 1933, pp. 1–32, gives an excellent examination of pertinent questions. The archivist of the Cathedral in Barcelona, José Oliveras Caminal, has published in *Scriptorium*, I, 1946/7, pp. 240–242, from Codex 28 of the Cathedral a text coinciding in essentials with the section of the Vienna Cod. 362 printed by Silverstein (pp. 153–155). More recent literature in Altaner, p. 72. Since the appearance of the basic work of Silverstein the following studies of this theme may be picked out: A. Landgraf, *ZkTh*, 1936, 299–370; Th. Silverstein, 'Did Dante know the Vision of St. Paul?' *Harvard Studies and Notes in Philology and Literature* 19, 1937, pp. 231–247; B. Fischer, *Vig. Chr.*, 5, 1951, pp. 84–87 (use by Caesarius of Arles).[2]

Silverstein's greatest service lies in his most thorough examination of the Western tradition of our Apocalypse. In this tradition he has discovered the best representatives of the alleged original Greek text (Paris, B. N., MS. Nouv. acq. lat. 1631 and St. Gall, Stadtbibliothek—Bibl. Vadiana, Cod. 317). Similar work on the individual oriental versions would be exceedingly valuable for the recovery of the original text. James made use of the Syriac and Coptic versions in his transla-

---

[1] It will be denoted by L[1].
[2] Since the appearance of Silverstein's magnum opus, *Visio Pauli* (1935), eight new Latin texts of the Apocalypse have become known. He has examined these new documents and edited five of them: Th. Silverstein, 'The Vision of St. Paul. New Links and Patterns in the Western Tradition' (*Archives d'histoire doctrinale et littéraire du Moyen Age* 34, 1959, pp. 199–248). The new material throws light on the transmission of the text from the eleventh to the sixteenth centuries in Italy. On the basis of these texts the development of the abridged forms can be followed more exactly [A. de Santos Otero].

tion of the Latin text of Paris. It is important that the Slavonic tradi-
tion should be thoroughly examined. The available material is mostly
listed by N. Bonwetsch in Harnack, *Geschichte der altchristlichen Literatur*,
I. 2, 910f. On newly discovered manuscripts to be added cf. I. Ja.
Jacimirskij, Opisanie južno-slavjanskich i russkich rukopisej zagranič-
nich Bibliotek, Vol. I, St. Petersburg 1921; A. P. Konusov–V. F.
Pokrovskaja, Opisanie rukopisnogo Otdelenija Biblioteki Akademii
Nauk SSSR, Vol. IV, Moscow–Leningrad, 1951.

H. Ch. Puech has shown in *Coptic Studies in Honor of Walter Ewing
Crum* (pp. 134f.) that our Apocalypse of Paul has nothing to do with
the Coptic Apocalypse of Paul discovered recently at Nag Hammadi.

Abbreviations for the readings: L = Latin; Gr. = Greek; St. G. = text
of St. Gall; C = Coptic; S = Syriac; A = Armenian. Where readings
of the Latin text of the St. Gall MS. are preferred to those of the text
published by James or confirm amendments to it, attention is drawn
to this in the footnotes.

APOCALYPSE OF PAUL

The revelation of the holy apostle Paul: the things which were
revealed to him when he went up even to the third heaven
and was caught up into Paradise and heard unspeakable
words.[1]

1. In the consulate of Theodosius Augustus the Younger and of
Cynegius[2] a certain respected man was living in Tarsus in the
house which had once belonged to St. Paul; during the night an
angel appeared to him and gave him a revelation[3] telling him to
break up the foundations of the house and to make public what
he found. But he thought this was a delusion.

2. However the angel came the third time and scourged him
and compelled him to break up the foundations. And when he
had dug he discovered a marble box which was inscribed on the
sides; in it was the revelation of Saint Paul and the shoes in which
he used to walk when he was teaching the word of God. But he
was afraid to open the box (itself?) and brought it to a judge;
the judge accepted it and sent it as it was, sealed with lead, to
the emperor Theodosius; for he was afraid it might be something
else. And when the emperor received it he opened it and found
the revelation of Saint Paul. After a copy had been made he sent

[1] So Gr. Instead of this L¹ quotes 2 Cor. 12:1–5 and connects with what follows
by means of the question "At what time was it made public?".
[2] Thus correctly restored by James and calculated as A.D. 388.
[3] Gr. passive: "(the angel) was revealed": doubtless better.

the original manuscript to Jerusalem.[1] And it was written in it as follows:

3. The word of the Lord came to me thus:[2] Say to this people: "How long will you transgress and add sin to sin[3] and tempt the Lord who made you, saying[4] that you are Abraham's children[5] but doing the works of the devil? Walking[6] in confidence towards God (L[1]: Christus), boasting only because of your name, but poor because of the substance of sin?[7] Remember therefore and understand, children of men, that the whole creation is subject to God but that mankind alone sins. It rules over every creature and sins more than all nature.

4. For often the sun, the great light, has protested to the Lord, saying: O Lord God Almighty, I watch the ungodliness and unrighteousness of men; permit me to deal with them according to my powers so that they may know that thou alone art God. And a voice came to it, saying: I know all these things; for my eye sees and my ear hears, but my patience bears with them until they are converted and repent. But if they do not return to me I will judge them all.

5. Sometimes indeed the moon and the stars have protested to the Lord, saying: O Lord God Almighty, thou hast given us power over the night;[8] how long shall we watch the ungodliness and fornications and murders which the children of men commit? permit us to deal with them according to our powers so that they may know that thou alone art God. And a voice came to them, saying: I know all these things and my eye sees and my ear hears, but my patience bears with them until they are converted and repent. But if they do not return to me, I will judge them.

6. And the sea has frequently cried out, saying: O Lord God Almighty, men have defiled thy holy name in me; permit me to

---

[1] The last two sentences of this chapter are from Gr. L[1] has it the other way round: "He sent a copy of it to Jerusalem and retained the original." This account of the discovery appears as a postscript in the Syriac translation. The differences between the Syriac translations have generally been left unconsidered as leading too far afield.

[2] L[1] prefixes this with a secondary addition: "While I was in the body in which I had been caught up into the third heaven."

[3] Is. 30:1.

[4] This word is lacking in L[1], which in consequence has the meaningless sentence: "You are sons of God."

[5] Cf. Jn. 8:33ff.   [6] Lacking in L[1].   [7] In accordance with Gr.

[8] Cf. Jer. 31:35.

rise up and cover every wood and thicket and all the world that I may blot out all the children of men from before thy face, so that they may know that thou art God alone. And a voice came again and said: I know everything; for my eye sees everything and my ear hears, but my patience bears with them until they are converted and repent. But if they do not return, I will judge them. Sometimes the waters have also protested against the sons of men, saying: O Lord God Almighty, all the children of men have polluted thy holy name. And a voice came saying: I know everything before it happens for my eye sees and my ear hears everything, but my patience bears with them until they are converted. And if not, I will judge. Often the earth has also cried out to the Lord against the children of men, saying: O Lord God Almighty I suffer more harm than all thy creatures for I (must) bear the fornications, adulteries, murders, robberies, false oaths, sorceries and evil enchantments of men, and every evil which they commit, so that the father rises up against the son and the son against the father, and stranger against stranger, each to defile his neighbour's wife. The father mounts up on the bed of his son and the son likewise mounts up on the couch of his father; and those who offer a sacrifice to thy name have defiled thy holy place with all these evil deeds. Therefore I suffer more harm than every creature and although I do not wish to, I give[1] to the children of men my wealth and fruit. Permit me to destroy the strength of my fruit. And a voice came and said: I know everything and there is no one who can hide himself from his sin. And I know their ungodliness, but my holiness endures them until they are converted and repent. But if they do not return to me, I will judge them.[2]

7. Behold, children of men, creation is subject to God; but mankind alone sins. Therefore, children of men, bless the Lord God unceasingly every hour and every day; but especially at sunset. For at that hour all the angels go to the Lord to worship him and bring before him all the deeds of men, whether good or evil, which each of them does from morning until evening. And one angel goes forth rejoicing from the man he indwells but

[1] So in accordance with S[1].

[2] Gr omits the complaint of the waters and the earth; S unites sea and rivers; the Armenian versions are different again.

another goes with sad face.[1] When then the sun has set at the first hour of the night, in the same hour (come)[2] the angel of each people and the angel of each man and woman, (the angels) which protect and preserve them, because man is the image of God: and similarly at the hour of morning which is the twelfth hour of the night all the angels of men and women meet God to worship him and to bring before him every deed which each man has done, whether good or evil. Every day and (every) night the angels present to God an account of all the actions of mankind. Therefore I tell you, children of men, bless the Lord continually every day of your life.

8. Therefore at the appointed hour all the angels, every one rejoicing, go forth together before God that they may meet to worship at the hour arranged. And, behold, suddenly at the time there was a meeting (?),[3] and the angels came to worship before God, and the Spirit went to meet them; and a voice came forth and said, Whence have you come, our angels, bringing burdens of news?

9. They answered and said: We have come from those who have renounced this world on account of thy holy name; they wander as strangers and live[4] in a (the) cave(s) of the rocks; they weep every hour they dwell on earth, and they are hungry and thirst for the sake of thy name; their loins girt, they hold in their hands the incense of their hearts; they pray and bless at every hour; they are distressed and subdue themselves. More than all others who live on earth they are weeping and mourning. And we, their angels, mourn with them; wherever then it may please thee, command us to go and serve. Command them, Lord, to abide even to the end in righteousness.[5] And the voice of God came to them saying: Know that to you here my grace is established now, and my help, who is my dearly beloved Son, will be with them and guide them every hour; he will also serve them and never forsake them because their place is his dwelling. (*In Gr the Divine voice speaks briefly at the end of ch. 8*: I have kept them and shall keep them void of offence in my Kingdom.)

1 The last few words in accordance with Gr A[1] A[2].
2 Here we should probably insert "to meet God".   3 The text is in disorder.
4 'live' inserted in accordance with S.
5 This sentence is taken from Gr in place of the incomprehensible Latin words: ne et alii fecerint sed inopes pr(ae)caeteris qui sunt in terra.

10. When these angels had retired, behold, other angels who were weeping came into the meeting to worship in the presence of the Majesty. And the Spirit of God went forth to meet them; and the voice of God came, saying: Whence have you come, our angels, bearing burdens as servants of the world's news? And they answered and said in the presence of God: We have come from those who have called on thy name, whom the difficulties of the world have made miserable; for every hour they devise many opportunities, not making one pure prayer, not even with the whole heart, all the time they live; why therefore must we be present with men who are sinners? And the voice of God came to them: You must serve them until they are converted and repent:[1] but if they do not return to me, I shall judge them. Understand then, children of men, that whatever you do, whether it is good or evil, these angels report (it) to God.

11. And after that I saw one of the spiritual beings beside me and he caught me up in the Holy Spirit and carried me up to the third part of Heaven, which is the third[2] heaven.[3] And the angel answered and said to me: Follow me and I shall show you the place of the righteous where they are brought when they are dead; and after that I shall take you to the abyss and I shall show you the souls of sinners and the kind of place to which they are brought when they are dead. And I went behind the angel and he led me to heaven and I saw the firmament and I saw there the Power,[4] and the forgetfulness which deceives and seduces to itself the hearts of men, and the spirit of slander and the spirit of fornication and the spirit of wrath and the spirit of presumption were there, and the princes of wickedness were there. These I saw under the firmament of heaven. And again I looked and I saw angels who were pitiless, who had no compassion; their faces were full of wrath and their teeth projected from their mouths; their eyes flashed like the morning star in the east, and from the hairs of their head and out of their mouth went forth sparks of fire. And I asked the angel, saying: Who are these, sir? And the angel answered and said to me: These are those who are appointed

---

[1] Heb. 1:14.   [2] Cf. 2 Cor. 12:2.

[3] This sentence, which is indispensable for the understanding of the scene, is added in accordance with the Syriac, ed. Ricciotti, p. 9.

[4] We should expect the plural, "the powers", as in the Syriac.

for the souls of the wicked in the hour of need, for those who did not believe that they had the Lord for their helper and did not hope in him.

12. And I looked into the height and I saw other angels with faces shining like the sun; their loins were girt with golden girdles and they had palms in their hands, and the sign of God;[1] and they were clothed in raiment on which was written the name of the Son of God; and they were filled with all gentleness and pity. And I asked the angel and said: Who are these, sir, who have so much beauty and pity? And the angel answered and said to me: These are the angels of righteousness; they are sent to lead in the hour of their need the souls of the righteous who believed God was their helper. And I said to him: Must the righteous and the sinners meet the witnesses when they are dead? And the angel answered and said to me: There is one way by which all pass over to God, but the righteous, because they have a holy helper with them, are not troubled when they go to appear before God.

13. And I said to the angel: I wish to see the souls of the righteous and of sinners as they leave the world. And the angel answered and said to me: Look down at the earth. And from heaven I looked down on earth, and I saw the whole world and it was as nothing in my sight. And I saw the children of men as if they were nothing and growing weaker; and I was amazed and I said to the angel: Is this the size of men? And the angel answered and said to me: It is, and these are those who do harm (*Syr.*: sin) from morning to evening. And I looked and I saw a great cloud of fire spread out over the whole world, and I said to the angel: What is this, sir? And he said to me: This is the unrighteousness which is mixed by the princes of sinners (?) (*Gr.*: with the destruction of sinners. *Syr.*: with the prayer of men.)

14. And when I heard this, I sighed and wept; and I said to the angel: I wish to wait for the souls of the righteous and of sinners and observe in what way they go out of the body. And the angel answered and said to me: Look down again at the earth. And I looked and I saw the whole world, and men were as nothing and growing weaker; and I looked and saw a man at

[1] Cf. Rev. 7:9; 22:4.

the point of death. And the angel said to me: This man whom you
see is righteous. And again I looked and I saw all his deeds which
he had done for the sake of the name of God; and all his desires,
which he remembered and which he did not remember, all of
them stood before him in the hour of need. And I saw that the
righteous man had progressed and found refreshing and confidence; and before he left the world holy and wicked angels
stood together by him; and I saw them all; however the wicked
found no dwelling in him, but the holy had power over his soul,
directing it until it left the body. And they roused the soul, saying:
Soul, take knowledge of your body which you have left, for in the
day of resurrection you must return to that same body to receive
what is promised to all the righteous. They received therefore the
soul from the body and at once kissed it just as if they had known
it every day, and said to it: Be of good heart, for you did the will
of God while you were on the earth. And the angel that watched
over it day by day came to meet it and said to it: Be of good
heart, soul; for I rejoice over you because you did the will of
God on earth; for I have reported to God of what kind all your
deeds were. In the same way also the spirit advanced to meet it
and said: Soul, neither be afraid nor troubled until you come
to a place which you never knew; I however will be your helper,
for I found in you a place of refreshing during the time I dwelt
in you while I (?) was on earth. And its spirit strengthened it
and its angel took it up and led it into heaven. [And the angel
said][1]: And there went to meet it the evil powers who are under
heaven,[2] and the spirit of error came to it and said (to it; L[1]:
Whither, soul, do you hasten and dare to enter heaven? Wait
and let us see if there is anything of ours in you.) (S alone continues as follows:) And the soul was bound there. And there was
a fight between the good angels and the evil angels.[3] And when
that spirit of error saw (it), he wailed with a (loud) voice and
said: Alas for you, because we have found nothing of ours in you.
And behold! every angel and spirit helps you against me, and
behold, all these are with you and you have passed over from

[1] The bracketed words should be omitted. What follows is given as in the Syriac.
[2] The detailed description of the powers of darkness which the Coptic here introduces is secondary according to the evidence of the other versions.
[3] Cf. Rev. 12:7.

765

us.[1] And there came forth another spirit, a slandering spirit, and a spirit of fornication, and they came to meet it. But when they saw it, they wept over it and said: How did this soul escape us? It did the will of God on earth. And, behold, the angels indeed helped it and allowed it to pass over from us.—And all the powers and evil spirits came to meet it, even up to it. But they did not find anything of their own in it. And they were not able to do anything for themselves. And they gnashed their tooth (teeth) against this soul and said: How did it escape us? And the angel which led it answered and said to them: Be turned to confusion. There is no way for you to it. Indeed you were very cunning; you flattered it while it was on earth, but it paid no heed to you.

And then I heard the voice of myriad upon myriad of holy angels as they said: Rejoice and exult, O soul, be strong and do not tremble!—And they were greatly amazed at that soul because it had held fast by the sign of the living God.[2] And so they encouraged it and called it happy and said: We all rejoice over you because you have done the will of your Lord.[3]—And they led it until it worshipped in the presence of God. And when it had ceased,[4] at once Michael and all the host of angels fell down and worshipped the footstool of his feet and displayed the soul, saying: This is the God of all[5] who made you in his image and likeness. However an angel ran on ahead of it and declared, saying: Lord, remember its works; for this is the soul on whose deeds I reported to thee daily, acting according to thy judgment. And in the same way the spirit said: I am the spirit of quickening, breathing on it and dwelling in it. For I was refreshed in it during the time I dwelt in it. It behaved according to thy judgment. And the voice of God came and said: As this soul has not grieved me, so I shall not grieve it; as it has had compassion, so I shall have compassion on it. Let it therefore be handed over to Michael, the angel of the covenant, and let him lead it into the paradise of

[1] L[1] has: 'And behold, we have found nothing in you. I see also divine help and your angel, and the spirit rejoices with you because you have done the will of God on earth.' What follows is in accordance with S and St. G.

[2] St. G.: the cross of the Son of God.

[3] From here on again in accordance with L[1] and St. G.

[4] Either restore the singular or correct St. G. to: *Quam cum audissent*, when they had heard this.

[5] What follows is mostly in accordance with St. G.

jubilation, that it may be there until the day of resurrection and become also a fellow-heir with all the saints. And after that I heard the voices of a thousand times a thousand angels and archangels and the cherubim and the twenty-four elders who sang hymns and glorified God and cried: Righteous art thou, O Lord, and righteous are thy judgments; there is no respect of persons with thee and thou dost requite every man according to thy judgment.[1] And the angel answered and said to me: Have you believed and understood that whatever each of you has done, he sees it in the hour of his need? And I said: Yes, sir.

15. And he said to me: Look down again at the earth and wait for that[2] other soul of an ungodly man as it comes forth from the body, a soul which has provoked the Lord day and night by saying: I know nothing other than this world; I eat and drink and enjoy[3] what is in the world. For who has gone down into the underworld and coming up has told us that there is a judgment there? And I looked and saw all the scorn of the sinner and all that he had done and that stood before him in the hour of his need. And I saw that that hour was more bitter to him than the future judgment. And that man said: O that I had not been born nor been in the world![4] And then holy and wicked angels came together and the soul of the sinner saw both, and the holy angels found no place in it. The wicked angels had power over it; and when they led it out from the body, the angels admonished it three times, saying: O unfortunate soul, look at your flesh, which you have left. For on the day of resurrection you will have to return into your flesh to receive what is fitting to your sins and your ungodliness.

16. And when they led it out, its familiar angel went before it and said to it: O unfortunate soul, I am the angel who clung to you and reported daily to the Lord the evil deeds which you did night and day. And if it had been in my power I would not have served you one single day, but I was not able to do that (anything of those things). For[5] God is merciful and a righteous judge and

1 Cf. Rev. 4:10; 5:8, 14; 11:16; 19:4.
2 What follows is mostly in accordance with St. G.
3 Cf. Is. 22:13; 1 Cor. 15:32; Lk. 17:26f.
4 The last two sentences after S. Cf. Job. 3:3; Jer. 20:14.
5 What follows is mostly in accordance with St. G.

he has ordered us not to cease to serve a soul until you repent. But you have wasted the time for repentance. And today I am become a stranger to you, and you to me. Let us then go to the righteous judge; I will not discharge you before I know that from the present day I am become a stranger to you. And the spirit afflicted it and the angel troubled it. However when it had reached the powers, as already it went to enter heaven, there was laid on it one evil burden after another. For error and forgetfulness and tale-bearing met it and the spirit of fornication and the rest of the powers and they said to it: Where are you going, unfortunate soul? do you dare to rush on into heaven? Stop and let us see if we have any of our possessions in you, for we do not see any holy helper with you.

(S:) And when they had inspected it, they rejoiced and said: Yes, indeed, there is in you and you belong wholly to us; now we know that even your angel cannot help you and wrest you from us.—But the angel answered and said: Understand that it is a soul of the Lord, and he does not leave it and I also do not leave the image of God[1] in the hands of the evil. For he who supported me all the days of the life of this soul can support and help me and it. And I shall not leave it until it goes up to the throne of God on high. And when he sees it he will have power over it and send it wherever he wishes.[2]

And after that I heard voices in the height of heaven which said: Present the unfortunate soul to God that it may know there is a God whom[3] it has despised. Therefore when it had entered heaven, all the angels, thousands of thousands of them, saw it (and) they all cried with one voice saying: Woe to you, unfortunate soul, for the deeds which you did on earth; what answer will you give God when you approach to worship him? And the angel which was with it answered and said: Weep with me, my beloved ones, for I found no rest in this soul. And the angels answered him and said: Let such a soul be sent away from our midst; for since it came in, its foul stench has[4] gone through to all the angels. And then it was taken away to worship in the presence of God, and the angel showed to it the Lord God who

---

[1] Cf. Gen. 1:26.   [2] The special material belonging to the Syriac ends here.
[3] St. G.   [4] In what follows mostly in accordance with St. G.

had made it after his own image and likeness.[1] But its angel ran on ahead and said: Lord God Almighty, I am the angel of that soul on whose deeds I reported to thee day and night (not behaving according to thy judgment). Deal with it according to thy judgment. And in the same way the spirit said: I am the spirit which dwelt in it from the time when it was made in the world, and it did not follow my will. Judge it, Lord, according to thy judgment. And the voice of God came forth to it and said: Where is your fruit[2] which you have brought forth corresponding to the good things you received? Did I set even the difference of one day between you and the righteous? Did I not make the sun to rise over you just as over the righteous?[3] It however kept silent because it had nothing to say. And again a voice came saying: God's judgment is righteous and there is no respect of persons with him.[4] For whoever has shown mercy, to him will mercy be shown,[5] and whoever has not been merciful, God will not have mercy on him. Let him therefore be handed over to the angel Tartaruchus,[6] who is appointed over punishments, and let him send him into outer darkness where there is wailing and gnashing of teeth,[7] and let him remain there until the great day of judgment. After that I heard the voice of the angels and archangels who said: Righteous art thou, O Lord, and righteous is thy judgment.[8]

17. I looked again and behold two angels were leading a soul which was weeping and saying: Have mercy on me, O God, righteous judge.[9] For it is seven days today[10] since I came out of my body and was handed over to these two angels and they have led me to places which I had never seen. And God the righteous judge said to it: What have you done? You never showed mercy, and for that reason you have been handed over to such angels as have no mercy; and because you did not do what was right they have not treated you compassionately in the hour of your need. Confess therefore the sins which you committed while you were set in the world. And it answered and said: Lord, I have not sinned. And the Lord God, the righteous judge,[11] burned with

[1] Cf. Gen. 1:27; 9:6.   [2] Cf. Lk. 13:6ff.   [3] Cf. Mt. 5:45.
[4] Cf. Acts 10:34f.   [5] Cf. Mt. 5:7.   [6] St. G.: of Tartarus; Gr.: Temeluchos.
[7] Cf. Mt. 8:12; 22:13.   [8] Cf. Rev. 16:7; 19:2.   [9] St. G.
[10] Cf. Sir. 22. 13.   [11] St. G.

anger when it said, "I have not sinned", because it was lying; and God said: Do you think that you are still living in the world, where each of you sins and conceals it and hides it from his neighbour? Here, however, nothing is hidden. For if souls have come to worship in the presence of the throne then the good works of each and his sins are revealed.[1] And when the soul heard this, it kept quiet, for it had no answer. And I heard the Lord God, the righteous judge, speaking again: Come, angel of this soul, and stand in the middle. And the angel of the sinful soul came and he had a document in his hands and he said: This, Lord, in my hands is (the account of) all the sins of this soul from its youth up to the present day, from the day of its birth onward; and if thou order (it), Lord, I shall recount its deeds from when it was fifteen years old.[2] And the Lord God, the righteous judge, said: I tell you, angel, that I do not expect from you an account from the time when it was fifteen years old, but set forth its sins for the five years before it died and came here. And again, God, the righteous judge, said: I swear by myself and by my holy angels and my power, that if it had repented five[3] years before it died, because of a conversion one year old the evils which it had formerly done would now be forgotten and it would have remission and pardon of sins;[4] now however let it perish. And the angel of the sinful soul answered and said: Command, Lord, that angel to bring forth those souls.

18. And in that same hour the souls were brought out into the middle and the soul of the sinner recognized them. And the Lord said to the soul of the sinner: I say to you, soul, confess the deeds which you committed against these souls which you see, when they were in the world.[5] And it answered and said: Lord, it is not a full year since I slew this soul and shed its blood on the ground, and with (that) other I committed fornication; but that is not all, for I also injured it greatly by taking away its property. And the Lord God, the righteous judge said: Or did you not know that whoever has done violence to another, if the person who has suffered violence should die first, he is kept in this place until the one who has committed the offence dies and then both stand

---

[1] Sir. 39. 24.   [2] St. G.   [3] St. G.: 'one'.   [4] Cf. Ezek. 18:21.
[5] St. G.: you (sing.) were . . .

before the judge, and now each has received (*St. G. and L.*: 'will receive') according to what he did? And I heard the voice of one who said: Let that soul be handed over into the hands of Tartarus,[1] and it must be led down to the underworld. Let it be led into the prison of the underworld and be cast into torments and be left there until the great day of judgment. And again I heard thousands of thousands of angels who were singing a hymn to the Lord and crying: Righteous art thou, Lord, and righteous are thy judgments.[2]

19. The angel answered and said to me: Have you understood[3] all this? And I said: Yes, sir. And he said to me: Follow me again, and I will take you and show you the places of the righteous. And I followed the angel and he lifted me up to the third heaven[4] and he set me at the door of a gate. And I looked at it and saw that it was a golden gate and that there were two golden pillars before it[5] and two golden tables above the pillars full of letters. And again the angel turned to me and said: Blessed are you if you enter in by these gates, because only those are allowed to enter who have goodness and purity of body. And I asked the angel and said: Sir, tell me, for what reason are these letters set on those tables? The angel answered and said to me: These are the names of the righteous who while they dwell on earth serve God with a whole heart. And again I said:[6] Are then their names written in heaven while they are still on earth? And he said: Not only their names but also their faces are written, and the likeness of those who serve God is in heaven, and the servants of God, who serve him with a whole heart, are known to the angels before they leave the world.

20. And when I had entered within the gates of Paradise there came to meet me an old man whose face shone as the sun. And he embraced me and said: Hail, Paul, dearly beloved of God. And with joyful face he kissed me. And then he began to weep.[7] And I said to him: Father,[8] why are you weeping? And he sighed and wept again, and said: Because we are injured by men and they trouble us much; for there are many good things which

---

[1] Gr.: Tartaruchos. C: Temeluchos.   [2] Cf. Rev. 19:2.
[3] Gr., St. G. 'seen'.   [4] Cf. 2 Cor. 12:2, 4.   [5] St. G., Gr.
[6] In what follows mostly in accordance with St. G.
[7] St. G.   [8] St. G., C, Gr.

the Lord has prepared and his promise is great, but many do not accept them. And I asked the angel and said: Who is this, sir? And he said to me: This is Enoch,[1] the scribe of righteousness. And I entered within that place and immediately I saw Elijah[2] and he came and greeted me with gladness and joy. And when he had seen (me),[3] he turned away and wept and said to me: Paul, may you receive the reward[4] for the work which you have accomplished among mankind. As for me, I have seen the great and numerous good things which God has prepared for all the righteous, and the promises of God are great, but the majority do not accept them; but even with difficulty through many labours do a few (one and another) enter into these places.

21. And the angel answered and said to me: Whatever I now show you here and whatever you will hear, do not make it known to anyone on earth. And he brought me and showed me *and I heard there words which it is not lawful for a man to speak.*[5] And again he said: Follow me further and I shall show you what you ought to tell openly and report.

And he brought me down from the third heaven and he led me into the second heaven and he led me again to the firmament, and from the firmament he led me to the gates of heaven. And he opened an aperture[6] and there was the beginning of its foundation over a river which watered the whole earth. And I asked the angel and said: Sir, what is this river of water? And he said to me: This is the Ocean. And suddenly I came out of heaven and perceived that it is the light of heaven which gives light to the whole land there.[7] That land, however, was seven times brighter than silver. And I said: Sir, what is this place? And he said to me: This is the land of promise. Have you not yet heard what is written, "Blessed are the meek, for they will inherit the earth"?[8] The souls of the righteous, however,[9] when they have come out of the body are sent for a while to this place. And I said to the angel: Will then this land come to be seen after[10] a time? The

---

[1] Cf. the apocryphal Letter of Titus, *supra*, p. 153.
[2] Reading 'Elijah' with S and Vienna Codex 362. The *solem* or *solum* (St. G.) of other manuscripts is explained by the reading of the Greek *Helias* as *Helios*; cf. Silverstein, p. 37.
[3] Cf. the apocryphal Letter of Titus, *ibid.*
[4] Inserting *merces* with Vienna Cod. 362.   [5] 2 Cor. 12:4.   [6] St. G.
[7] St. G.   [8] Mt. 5:5.   [9] St. G.   [10] St. G.

angel answered and said to me: When Christ whom you preach comes to reign, then by the fiat of God the first earth will be dissolved and this land of promise will then be shown and it will be like dew or a cloud; and then the Lord Jesus Christ, the eternal king, will be revealed and he will come with all his saints[1] to dwell in it and he will reign over them for a thousand years[2] and they will eat of the good things which I shall now show you.

22. And I looked round that land and I saw a river flowing with milk and honey;[3] and at the edge of the river were planted trees full of fruit. And each tree was bearing twelve times[4] twelve fruits in the year, various and different. And I saw the creation of that place and all the work of God. And I saw there palm trees, some of twenty cubits and others of ten cubits. Now that land was seven times brighter than silver. And the trees were full of fruit from root (up) to tree-top. (L[1] is incomprehensible here and we replace with C:) From the root of each tree up to its heart there were ten thousand branches with tens of thousands of clusters [and there were ten thousand clusters on each branch] and there were ten thousand dates in each cluster. And it was the same with the vines. Each vine had ten thousand branches, and each branch had on it ten thousand bunches of grapes, and each bunch had ten thousand grapes.[5] And there were other trees there, myriads of myriads of them, and their fruit was in the same proportion. (L:) And I said to the angel: Why does each single tree yield thousands of fruits? And the angel answered and said to me: Because the Lord God of his abundance gives gifts profusely to the worthy, for they, while they were in the world, afflicted themselves of their own will and did everything for his holy name's sake.

And again I said to the angel: Sir, are these the only promises which the Lord God has promised to his saints? And the angel replied and said: No! for there are those which are seven times greater.

I tell you however that when the righteous have come forth from the body and[6] see the promises and good things which God

---

[1] Cf. 2 Thess. 1:10. [2] Rev. 20:2. [3] Cf. Exod. 3:8.
[4] St. G. is better: twelve times in the year various and different fruits.
[5] Cf. the description of Papias (Irenaeus, V. 33. 3f.).
[6] 'and' inserted in accordance with S.

has prepared for them, they will sigh and weep yet again, saying: Why did we utter a word from our mouth to irritate our neighbour even for a single day? I however asked and said again: Are these the only promises of God? And the angel answered and said to me: What you now see is for the married who have kept the purity of their marriages in acting chastely. But to virgins and to those *who hunger and thirst after righteousness*[1] and afflict themselves for the name of the Lord, God will give things seven times greater than what I shall now show you.

And after that he took me up away from that place where I had seen these things and, behold, a river whose waters were very white, whiter than milk. And I said to the angel: What is this? And he said to me: This is Lake Acherusia where the city of Christ is, but not every man is allowed to enter into that city. For this is the way which leads to God; and if there is anyone who is a fornicator and ungodly and who turns and repents and brings forth fruit worthy of repentance, first when he has come forth from the body he is brought and worships God and (he) is handed over from there at the command of God to the angel Michael and he baptizes him in Lake Acherusia. Thus he leads him into the city of Christ with those who have not sinned. And I marvelled and blessed the Lord God because of all I had seen.

23. And the angel answered and said to me: Follow me and I shall lead you into the city of Christ. And he stood by Lake Acherusia and put me in a golden boat and about three thousand angels were singing a hymn before me until I reached the city of Christ. Now the inhabitants of the city of Christ rejoiced greatly over me as I came to them, and I entered and saw the city of Christ;[2] and it was completely golden and there were twelve walls around it and twelve towers in it (C: a tower on each wall; S: and twelve thousand fortified towers are in its midst), and the individual walls as they encircled were distant from one another a stadium.[3] And I said to the angel: Sir, how much is one stadium? The angel answered and said to me: It is as great as between the Lord God and men on earth, for indeed the city of Christ is uniquely great. And in the circuit of the city there were

---

[1] Mt. 5:6.   [2] On what follows cf. Rev. 21:10ff.

[3] S Urmiensis: 'and between each of them was a stadium'. C: 'The circumference of each was a hundred stadia.'

twelve gates of great beauty, and four rivers which encircled it.[1] Now there was a river of honey and a river of milk and a river of wine and a river of oil. And I said to the angel: What are these rivers which encircle this city? And he said to me: These are the four rivers which flow abundantly for those who are in this land of promise; as for their names: the river of honey is called Phison, and the river of milk Euphrates, and the river of oil Gihon and the river of wine Tigris.[2] As therefore the righteous when they were in the world did not use their power over these things but went hungry without them and afflicted themselves for the name of the Lord God, therefore when they enter into this city the Lord will give them these above number[3] or measure.

24. And when I entered in through the gate I saw before the doors of the city trees which were big and very high and which had no fruit (but) only leaves. And I saw a few men scattered about among the trees and they wept greatly when they saw anyone enter into the city. And the trees did penance for them by abasing themselves and bowing down and by raising themselves up again. And I saw it and wept with them and asked the angel and said: Sir, who are these who are not allowed to enter into the city of Christ? And he said to me: These are those who fasting day and night have zealously practised renunciation, but they have had a heart proud beyond that of other men in that they have glorified and praised themselves and done nothing for their neighbours. For some they greeted in a friendly way, but to others they did not even say "Greetings": and to whom they wished they opened the doors of the monastery,[4] and if they did some small good to their neighbour they became puffed up. And I said: What then, sir? Has their pride prevented them from entering into the city of Christ? And the angel answered and said to me: Pride is the root of all wickedness. Are they better than the Son of God who came to the Jews in great humility? And I asked him and said: Why is it then that the trees abase themselves and raise themselves up again? And the angel answered and said to me: All the time these spent on earth serving God they humbled themselves shamefacedly during that time because men confounded and reproached them, but they were not sorry nor did

---

[1] St. G. without 'which'   [2] Cf. Gen. 2:11ff.   [3] St. G.   [4] St. G.

they repent in order to desist from the pride which was in them. This is why the trees abase themselves and rise up again. And I asked and said: For what reason are they allowed into the gates of the city? The angel answered and said to me: Because of the great goodness of God and because the entrance of all his saints who enter into this city is here. Therefore they have been left in this place so that when Christ the eternal king enters with all his saints, all the righteous at his entry may pray for them; and then they will enter with them into the city; yet none of them can have the same confidence as those who humbled themselves by serving the Lord God all their life.

25. And with the angel leading me I went on, and he brought me to the river of honey; and I saw there Isaiah and Jeremiah and Ezekiel and Amos and Micah and Zechariah, the major and minor prophets, and they greeted me in the city. I said to the angel: What is this way? And he said to me: This is the way of the prophets. Everyone who has grieved his own soul and on account of God has not done his own will, when he has come forth from the world and been led to the Lord God and has worshipped him, then at God's command he is handed over to Michael who leads him into the city to this place of the prophets; and they greet him as their friend and neighbour because he did the will of God.

26. Again he led me where the river of milk was; and there I saw in that place all the infants whom king Herod had slain[1] for the name of Christ, and they greeted me. And the angel said to me: All who preserve their chastity and purity,[2] when they come forth from their bodies, are handed over to Michael after they have worshipped the Lord God, and they are brought to the children and they greet them saying, "You are our brothers and friends and associates (members)". Among them they will inherit the promises of God.

27. Again he took me up and brought me to the north of the city and he led me where the river of wine was, and I saw there Abraham, Isaac and Jacob, Lot and Job and other saints; and they greeted me. And I asked and said: What is this place, sir? The angel answered and said to me: All those who have given

1 Cf. Mt. 2:16.   2 St. G.

776

hospitality to strangers, when they come forth from the world, first worship the Lord God and are handed over to Michael and by this route are led into the city, and all the righteous greet them[1] as sons and brothers and say to them, "Because you have kept humanity and hospitality for strangers, come, receive an inheritance in the city of our God." And each righteous man will receive the good gifts of God in the city in accordance with his own behaviour.

28. And again he brought me to the river of oil to the east of the city. And I saw there men who rejoiced and sang psalms, and I said: Who are these, sir? And the angel said to me: These are those who dedicated themselves to God with the whole heart and had no pride in themselves. For all who rejoice[2] in the Lord God and sing praises to him with the whole heart are brought here into this city.

29. And he brought me into the middle of the city close to the twelfth[3] wall. Now at this place it was higher than the others. And I asked and said: Is there a wall in the city of Christ surpassing this spot in honour? And the angel answered and said to me: The second is better than the first and similarly the third than the second because each one surpasses the other right up to the twelfth wall. And I said: Why, sir, does one surpass another in glory? Explain to me. And the angel answered and said to me: From all who in themselves have only a little slander or envy or pride something is taken away from their glory, although they appear to be in the city of Christ.[4] Look behind you.

And I turned and saw golden thrones which were set at the several gates, with men on them who had golden diadems and gems. And I looked and saw within, between the twelve men, thrones set in another rank which appeared (to be) of greater glory, so that no one was able to declare their praise. And I asked the angel and said: Sir, who are those who shall sit on the thrones?[5] And the angel answered and said to me: These are the thrones of those who had goodness and understanding of heart and (yet) made themselves fools for the Lord God's sake in that they neither knew the Scriptures nor many Psalms but paid heed

[1] In what follows St. G. has been mostly used. [2] Cf. Ps. 68:4.
[3] St. G and C.
[4] 'Although . . . Christ' according to St. G. L¹ differs. [5] St. G.

to one chapter concerning the commandments of God and hearing them acted with great carefulness in conformity to these (commandments) and have (thereby) shown a true zealousness before the Lord God. And admiration of these lays hold on all the saints before the Lord God, for they discuss with one another and say: Wait and see these unlearned men who understand nothing more, how they have merited such a great and beautiful robe and such glory because of their innocence.

And I saw in the midst of the city a great and very high altar; and there was standing alongside the altar one whose face shone like the sun and who held in his hands a psaltery and a harp and who sang saying, "Hallelujah!"[1] And his voice filled all the city. And as soon as all who were on the towers and at the gates heard him they replied, "Hallelujah!", so that the foundations of the city were shaken. And I asked the angel and said: Who, sir, is this here with such great power? And the angel said to me: This is David; this is the city of Jerusalem. But when Christ, the king of eternity, shall have come with the confidence (?) of his kingdom, then he will again step forward to sing and all the righteous will sing in reply at the same time, "Hallelujah". And I said: Sir, why is it that David alone begins the singing before all the other saints? And the angel answered and said to me: Because (?) Christ, the Son of God, sits at the right hand of his Father, this David will sing psalms before him in the seventh heaven; and just as it is done in the heavens, so it is done below, because it is not permitted to offer to God a sacrifice without David, but it is necessary for David to sing psalms at the time of the offering of the body and blood of Christ; as it is carried out in the heavens, so also on earth.

30. And I said to the angel: Sir, what is "Hallelujah"? And he answered and said to me: You search and inquire into everything. And he said to me: Hallelujah is a word in Hebrew, the language of God and angels. And the meaning of Hallelujah is this: tecel. cat. marith. macha. And I said: Sir, what is tecel. cat. marith. macha? And the angel answered and said to me: Tecel. cat. marith. macha is this: Let us bless him all together. I asked the angel and said: Sir, do all who say "Hallelujah" bless the

[1] Cf. Ps. 57:8.

Lord? And the angel answered and said to me: That is so; and again, if anyone should sing Hallelujah and there are some present who do not sing (it) at the same time, they commit sin because they do not join in the singing. And I said: Sir, does someone who is doting or very old sin in the same way? And the angel answered and said to me: No, but whoever is able, and does not join in the singing, you know that he is a despiser of the word. And it would be proud and discreditable that he should not bless the Lord God his maker.

31. And when he had ceased speaking to me, he led me forth out of the city through the midst of the trees and back from the sites of the land of good things, and he set me above the river of milk and honey. And then he led me to the ocean that bears the foundations of the heavens. And the angel answered and said to me: Do you understand that you are going away from here? And I said: Yes, sir. And he said to me: Come, follow me, and I shall show you the souls of the godless and sinners that you may know what the place is like. And I set out with the angel and he brought me towards the setting of the sun, and I saw the beginning of heaven, founded on a great river of water, and I asked: What is this river of water: And he said to me: This is the ocean which encircles the whole earth. And when I was beyond the ocean I looked and there was no light in that place, but darkness and sorrow and distress; and I sighed.

And there I saw a river boiling with fire, and in it was a multitude of men and women immersed up to their knees, and other men up to the navel, others up to the lips, and others up to the hair. And I asked the angel and said: Sir, who are these in the river of fire? And the angel answered and said to me: They are those who are neither hot nor cold[1] because they were found neither among the number of the righteous nor among the number of the godless. For these spent the period of their life on earth in passing some days in prayers but other days in sins and fornications right up to their death. And I asked and said: Who are these, sir, who are immersed up to the knees in fire: And he answered and said to me: These are those who when they have come out of church occupy themselves in discussing (in) strange

[1] Cf. Rev. 3:16.

discourses. Those, however, who are immersed up to the navel are those who when they have received the body and blood of Christ go away and fornicate and do not cease from their sins until they die. And those who are immersed up to the lips are those who when they meet in the church of God slander one another. Those immersed up to the eyebrows are those who give the nod to one another and (in that way) secretly prepare evil against their neighbour.

32. And I saw to the north a place of varied and different punishments which was full of men and women, and a river of fire poured over them.[1] And I looked and saw very deep pits and in them there were very many souls together; and the depth of that place was about 3,000[2] cubits, and I saw them sighing and weeping and saying: Lord, have mercy on us. But no one had mercy on them. And I asked the angel and said: Who are these, sir? And the angel answered and said to me: These are those who did not hope in the Lord that they would be able to have him for a helper. And I asked and said: Sir, if these souls remain through thirty or forty generations thus one above another, I believe the pits will not hold them unless[3] they are made to go deeper. And he said to me: The abyss has no measure; moreover there also follows on it the (gulf, void?) which is below it. And it is as if perhaps someone takes a stone and throws it into a very deep well and after many hours it reaches the ground; so is the abyss. For when these souls are thrown in they have scarcely reached the bottom after five hundred years.

33. Now when I had heard that, I wept and sighed for the race of men. The angel answered and said to me: Why do you weep? Are you more compassionate than God?[4] For since God is good and knows that there are punishments, he bears patiently the race of men, permitting each one to do his own will for the time that he lives on earth.

34. And I looked yet again at the river of fire and I saw there a man being strangled by angels, the guardians of Tartarus, who had in their hands an iron instrument with three prongs with which they pierced the intestines of that old man. And I asked

[1] St. G.   [2] St. G.: 30,000 stadia.
[3] Altering *si* to *nisi*.   [4] Cf. 4 Ezra 8:19.

the angel and said: Sir, who is that old man on whom such torments are inflicted? And the angel answered and said to me: He whom you see was a presbyter who did not execute his ministry properly. While he ate and drank and fornicated he offered to the Lord the sacrifice on his holy altar.[1]

35. And not far away I saw another old man whom four evil angels brought running in haste and they immersed him up to his knees in the river of fire and they struck him with stones and they wounded his face like a storm and they did not allow him to say: Have mercy on me. And I asked the angel and he said to me: He whom you see was a bishop but he did not execute his episcopal office properly; he did indeed receive a great name but he did not enter into the holiness of him who gave to him that name all his life, for he did not give righteous judgments and he had no compassion on the widows and orphans. But now he is being requited according to his iniquity and his deeds.

36. And I saw another man up to his knees in the river of fire. And his hands were stretched out and bloody, and worms came out of his mouth and from his nostrils and he was groaning and weeping and crying, and he said: Have mercy on me, for I suffer more than the rest who are in this punishment. And I asked: Who is this, sir? And he said to me: He whom you see was a deacon who ate up the offerings and committed fornication and did not do right in the sight of God. Therefore unceasingly he pays this penalty.

And I looked and saw at his side another man who was brought with haste and thrown into the river of fire, and he was (in it) up to the knees. And the angel came who was (appointed) over the punishments and he had a great blazing razor with which he lacerated the lips of that man and in the same way his tongue. And sighing I wept and asked: Who is that, sir? And he said to

[1] C and S are more original here. C: Then I looked at the river of fire; I saw an old man who was dragged (Gr: by two). They immersed him up to his knees. And the angel Aftemelouchos came with a great fork of fire which had three prongs and with it he dragged his entrails out of his mouth. (St. G. to practically the same effect) —S: And I looked and saw again a river of fire which flowed very much more rapidly than those other rivers and an old man whom angels brought and immersed in this river of fire up to his knees. And a servant of the angels came and he had in his hand a rod of iron on which there were three teeth. And he drew the entrails of that old man out of his mouth.

me: He whom you see was a reader (lector) and he read to the people; but he himself did not keep the commandments of God. Now he also pays his own penalty.

37. And in that place I saw another set of pits and in the middle of it a river full of a multitude of men and women whom worms were devouring. I then wept, and with a sigh I asked the angel and said: Sir, who are these? And he said to me: They are those who exacted usury at compound interest and trusted in their riches[1] and did not hope in God that he would be a helper to them.

And then I looked and I saw another place which was very confined, and there was as it were a wall and fire in its bounds. And in it I saw men and women chewing at their tongues. And I asked: Who are these, sir? And he said to me: They are those who reviled the Word of God in church, paying no attention to it, but counting God and his angels as nothing. Therefore in the same way they now pay their own special penalty.

38. And I looked and I saw another hole below in the pit,[2] and it had the appearance of blood. And I asked and said: Sir, what is this place? And he said to me: All (the) punishments flow together into this pit. And I saw men and women submerged up to their lips and I asked: Who are these, sir? And he said to me: These are magicians who dispensed magical charms to men and women and made it impossible for them to find peace until they died. And again I saw men and women with very black faces in the pit of fire; and sighing and weeping I asked: Who are these, sir? And he said to me: These are fornicators and adulterers who although they had their own wives committed adultery; and similarly the women committed adultery in the same way, though they had their own husbands. Therefore unceasingly they pay the penalty.

39. And there I saw girls wearing black clothing and four dreadful angels who had blazing chains in their hands. And they set them (the chains) on their necks and led them into darkness. And again weeping I asked the angel: Who are these, sir? And he said to me: They are those who although they were appointed as virgins defiled their virginity unknown to their parents. For

---

[1] Cf. Sir. 5:1.   [2] Reading 'hole' with Gr instead of 'man' as in L[1].

that reason they pay their own particular penalty unceasingly.[1]

And again I saw there men and women set[2] with lacerated hands and feet (*or* with hands and feet cut off) and naked in a place of ice and snow, and worms consumed them. And when I saw it I wept and asked: Who are these, sir? And he said to me: They are those who harmed orphans and widows and the poor,[3] and did not hope in the Lord; therefore they pay their own particular penalty unceasingly.

And I looked and saw others hanging over a channel of water and their tongues were very dry and much fruit was placed within their sight and they were not allowed to take of it; and I asked: Who are these, sir? And he said to me: They are those who broke their fast before the appointed hour; therefore they pay these penalties unceasingly.

And I saw other men and women suspended by their eyebrows and hair, and a river of fire drew (?) them; and I said: Who are these, sir? And he said to me: They are those who did not give themselves to their own husbands and wives but to adulterers, and therefore they pay their own particular penalty unceasingly.[4]

And I saw other men and women covered in dust, and their faces were like blood, and they were in a pit of tar and brimstone, and they were running in a river of fire. And I asked: Who are these, sir? And he said to me: They are those who have committed the iniquity of Sodom and Gomorrah, men with men.[5] Therefore they pay the penalty unceasingly.

40. And I looked and saw men and women clothed in bright clothing, whose eyes were blind, and they were set in a pit of

---

[1] The reason for the punishment is given more clearly in C and Gr. C: They are those who defiled their virginity before they were given to (their) husbands; before they were grown up, they defiled (it), even their parents did not know about them. Gr: They are those who did not obey their parents but before marriage defiled their virginity.

[2] One would expect 'set' to go with 'in a place of ice and snow'.

[3] Cf. Zech. 7:10.

[4] The better Coptic text of this paragraph runs: And I saw other men and women suspended head downwards; and great torches of fire were burning before their faces, and dragon-serpents were wound round their bodies and were devouring them. And I said to the angel: Who are these, my Lord, who are suffering in this fearful way? And the angel said to me: They are those who were in the habit of beautifying themselves with the devil's cosmetics and then going to church for the sake of adultery and not because of their husbands. They made God their enemy through their deceitful cosmetics. Therefore they will receive this punishment which will endure for ever.

[5] Cf. Gen. 19:4ff.

fire;[1] and I asked: Who are these, sir? And he said to me: They are the heathen who gave alms and did not know the Lord God; therefore they pay unceasingly their own particular penalty.

And I looked and saw other men and women on a fiery pyramid and wild animals were tearing them to pieces, and they were not allowed to say: Lord have mercy on us. And I saw the angel of punishments[2] laying punishments most vigorously on them and saying: Acknowledge the judgment of[3] the Son of God! For you were forewarned; when the divine Scriptures were read to you, you did not pay attention; therefore God's judgment is just; for your evil deeds laid hold on you and have led you into these punishments. But I sighed and wept; and I asked and said: Who are these men and women who are strangled in the fire and pay the penalty? And he answered me: They are the women who defiled what God had fashioned in that they gave birth to children from the womb and they are the men who went to bed with them. However their children appealed to the Lord God and the angels who are (set) over the punishments, saying: Defend us[4] from our parents,[5] for they have defiled what is fashioned by God; they have the name of God but they do not keep his commandments, and they gave us for food to dogs and to be trampled by pigs;[6] and they threw others into the river. But those children were handed over to the angels of Tartarus,[7] who were over the punishments, so that they should lead them into a spacious place of mercy. However their fathers and mothers were strangled in an everlasting punishment. And after this I saw men and women clothed in rags full of tar and sulphurous fire, and dragons were wound about their necks and shoulders and feet; and angels with fiery horns confined them and struck them and closed up their nostrils, saying to them: Why did you not know the time in which it was right for you to repent and to serve God, and did not do it? And I asked: Who are these, sir? And he said to me: They are those who seemed to renounce the world[8] by wearing

[1] St. G.   [2] C: Aftemelouchos.   [3] Thus C.   [4] St. G.
[5] Gr.: Grant us our rights against our mothers.
[6] C adds: and they did not permit us to grow up into righteous men and to serve God. Apoc. Mariae: they did not permit us to grow up to do good or evil.
[7] Gr.: 'an angel'. St. G.: 'the angel guarding Tartarus'. Apoc. Mariae: Temliaqos = Temeluchos.
[8] St. G.

our raiment, but the tribulations of the world made them miserable so that they did not arrange a single[1] Agape and had no compassion on the widows and the orphans; they did not take in the stranger and the pilgrim nor present a gift (oblation) nor show mercy to their neighbour. Not even for one day did their prayer go up pure unto the Lord God. But the many tribulations of the world held them back and they were not able to do right in the sight of God. And angels went round[2] with them to the place of punishments. And those who were being punished saw them and said to them: We, while we were living in the world, neglected God; why have you done the same? And they led them to another place and these also spoke in the same way to them: We, while we were in the world, knew that we were sinners; we saw you in holy clothing and we called you happy and said, "These are the righteous and the servants of God." But now we have recognized that in vain were you called by the name of God; therefore you pay the perpetual penalty.

And I sighed and wept and said: Woe to men! woe to sinners! Why were you born? And the angel answered and said to me: Why are you weeping? Are you more compassionate than the Lord God, who is blessed for ever, who has appointed judgment and allowed every man to choose good or evil and act as he wishes? Again I wept even very vehemently, and he said to me: Are you weeping, when you have not yet seen the greater punishments? Follow me and you will see those that are seven times greater than these.

41. And he brought me to the north, to the place of all punishments,[3] and he placed me above a well and I found it sealed with seven seals.[4] And the angel who was with me[5] answered and spoke to the angel of that place: Open the mouth of the well that Paul, God's dearly beloved, may look in, because power has been given him to see all the punishments of the underworld. And the angel said to me: Stand at a distance, for you will not be able to bear the stench of this place. Then when the well was opened there came up immediately a disagreeable and very evil smell which surpassed all the punishments. And I looked into the well

---

[1] St. G., C.   [2] In what follows mostly after St. G.   [3] St. G., C., S.
[4] Cf. Rev. 5:1.   [5] In the succeeding St. G. is often followed.

and saw fiery masses burning on all sides, and the narrowness of the well at its mouth was such that it was only able to take a single man. And the angel answered and said to me: If some one is sent into this well of the abyss and it is sealed above him, reference is never made to him before the Father and the Son and the Holy Spirit and the holy angels. And I said: Who are these, sir, who are sent into this well? And he said to me: They are those who have not confessed that Christ came in the flesh[1] and that the Virgin Mary bore him, and who say[2] that the bread of the Eucharist and the cup of blessing are not the body and blood of Christ.

42. And I looked from the north towards the west and I saw there the worm that never rests,[3] and in that place there was gnashing of teeth.[4] Now the worm was a cubit in size[5] and it had two heads. And I saw there men and women in the cold and gnashing of teeth. And I asked and said: Sir, who are these in this place? And he said to me: They are those who say that Christ has not risen from the dead and that this flesh does not rise.[6] And I asked and said: Sir, is there neither fire nor heat in this place? And he said to me: In this place there is nothing other than cold and snow. And again he said to me: Even if the sun were to rise over them they would not become warm because of the excessive coldness of the place and the snow.

When I heard this, I stretched out my hands and wept and with a sigh I said again: It would be better for us if we who are all sinners had not been born.

43. However when those who were in this very place saw me weeping with the angel, they cried out and themselves wept, saying: O Lord God, have mercy on us! And after that I saw heaven opened and the archangel Michael coming down from heaven, and with him the whole host of angels, and they came to those who were placed in the punishments. And seeing him they cried out again with tears, and said: Have mercy on us, archangel Michael, have mercy on us and on the human race, for because of your prayers the earth continues. We have now seen the judgment and known the Son of God. It was impossible for us to

---

[1] Cf. 1 Jn. 4:3.　　[2] Gr, cf. also St. G.　　[3] Cf. Mk. 9:48.
[4] Cf. Mt. 8:12, etc.　　[5] St. G.　　[6] Cf. 1 Cor. 15:12ff.

786

pray for this[1] previously before we came to this place. For we
did hear that there was a judgment before we came forth from
the world, but tribulations and a worldly-minded life did not
allow us to repent. And Michael answered and said: Listen when
Michael speaks: It is I who stand in the presence of God every
hour.[2] As the Lord lives,[3] in whose presence I stand, for one
day or one night I do not cease from praying continually for the
human race, and I pray for those who are (still) on earth. They,
however, do not stop committing iniquity and fornication and
they do not help me in what is good while they are placed on
earth. And the time during which you ought to have repented
you used up in vanity. But I have always thus prayed and now
I beseech that God may send dew and that rain may be appointed
over the earth, and I continue to pray until the earth bring forth
its fruit; and I say that if anyone has done even only a little
good I will strive for him and protect him until he escapes the
judgment of punishments. Where are your prayers? Where is
your repentance? You have squandered time contemptibly. But
now[4] weep, and I will weep with you, and the angels who are
with me together with the dearly beloved Paul, if perchance the
merciful God will show mercy and give you ease. And when they
heard these words they cried out and wept much and said all
together: Have mercy on us, Son of God. And I, Paul, sighed and
said: Lord God, Have mercy on what thou hast fashioned, have
mercy on the children of men, have mercy on thine own image.

44. And I looked and I saw heaven move[5] as a tree shaken by
the wind. And they suddenly threw themselves on their faces
before the throne; and I saw the 24 elders and the 4 beasts worshipping God,[6] and I saw the altar and the veil and the throne,
and all were rejoicing; and the smoke of a good odour rose up
beside the altar of the throne of God, and I heard the voice of
one who said: For what reason do you pray, angels and ministers
of ours? And they cried out and said: We pray because we see
thy great goodness to the race of men. And after that I saw the

[1] St. G. goes: (Now have we known judgment), because it was possible for us
previously to meet the Son of God before . . .
[2] Cf. Dan. 12:1.   [3] Thus after Gr, S, C.   [4] St. G.
[5] Perhaps the passive (moveri instead of movere) should be restored in agreement
with the Greek.
[6] Cf. Rev. 4:9f.

Son of God coming down from heaven, and a diadem was on his head. And when those who were placed in the punishments saw him, they all cried out together: Have mercy on us, Son of the most High[1] God; it is thou who hast granted ease[2] to all in heaven and on earth; have mercy likewise on us; for since we have seen thee, we have had ease. And a voice went forth from the Son of God throughout all the punishments, saying: What[3] work have you done, that you ask me for ease? My blood was poured out for your sakes and even so you did not repent. For your sakes I bore the crown of thorns on my head;[4] for you I was slapped on the cheeks, and even so you did not repent. Hanging on the cross I begged for water, and they gave me vinegar mingled with gall;[5] with a spear they laid open my right side.[6] For my name's sake they killed my servants, the prophets and the righteous,[7] and in all these things I gave you the opportunity for repentance, and you were not willing. Now, however, for the sake of Michael, the archangel of my covenant, and the angels who are with him, and for the sake of Paul, my dearly beloved, whom I would not sadden, and for the sake of your brethren who are in the world and present offerings, and for the sake of your children, because my commandments are in them,[8] and even more for my own goodness—on the very day on which I rose from the dead I grant to you all who are being punished a day and a night of ease for ever.[9] And they all cried out and said: We bless Thee, Son of God, because thou hast granted to us ease for a day and a night. For one day's ease is better for us than all the time of our life which we were on earth: and if we had clearly known that this (place) was appointed for those who sin we would have done no other work at all, have practised nothing,[10] and have committed no evil. What need was there for us to be born into the world?[11] For here is our pride compre-

---

[1] St. G.   [2] St. G.: 'dost grant'.
[3] Gr adds 'good'. Similarly C and Cod. Mon. 2625.
[4] Cf. Mk. 15:17 and pars.   [5] Cf. Mt. 27:34.
[6] Jn. 19:34.   [7] Cf. Mt. 5:11f.
[8] St. G. 'and for the sake of your friends who do my commandments'. Similarly C.
[9] Cf. Isr. Lévi, 'Le repos sabbatique des âmes damnées', Revue des études juives XXV, 1892, pp. 1–13 and XXVI, 1893, pp. 131–135 (Jewish parallels). For Christian material: Merkle, 'Die Sabbatruhe in der Hölle', in Röm. Quartalschrift, 1895, pp. 489–505. Worthy of note are Prudentius, Cathemerinon V. 125ff. and Augustine, Enchiridion, ch. 112; on this cf. supra p. 755.
[10] = carried on no trade.   [11] nasum is a corruption of natum esse as C shows.

hended, which rose up out of our mouth against our neighbours. Discomfort and our exceptionally great anguish and tears and the worms which are under us, these are worse for us than the punishments which . . . us.[1] When they said this, the wicked angels and those in charge of the punishments were angry with them and said: How long have you wept and sighed? For you have shown no mercy. This indeed is the judgment of God on him who has shown no mercy. However you have received this great grace—ease for the day and night of the Lord's day for the sake of Paul, the dearly beloved of God, who has come down to you.

45. And after this the angel said to me: Have you seen everything? And I said: Yes, sir. And he said to me: Follow me and I will lead you into paradise, and the righteous who are there will see you: for behold, they hope to see you and are ready to come to meet you with joy and exultation. Impelled by the Holy Spirit I followed the angel and he transferred (*lit.* 'set') me to (in) Paradise, and said to me: This is Paradise where Adam and his wife sinned.[2] And I entered into Paradise and I saw the origin of the waters; and the angel beckoned to me and said to me: See, he said, the waters; for this is the river Pison which encircles the whole land of Evila, and this other is the Gihon which encircles the whole land of Egypt and Ethiopia, and this other is the Tigris which is opposite Assyria, and this other is the Euphrates which waters the land of Mesopotamia.[3] And going in further I saw a tree planted out of whose roots waters flowed, and the source of the four rivers was in it. And the Spirit of God rested over that tree and when the Spirit breathed the waters flowed.[4] And I said: Sir, is it this tree itself which makes the waters flow? And he said to me: Because in the beginning before heaven and earth appeared everything was invisible, the Spirit of God hovered[5] over the waters; but since the commandment of God brought to light[6] heaven and earth, the Spirit rests over this tree. Therefore when the Spirit has breathed, the waters flow from the tree. And

---

[1] The passage is corrupt from 'For here'; C gives no assistance.
[2] Cf. Gen. 3:1ff.   [3] Cf. Gen. 2:11ff.
[4] In accordance with a textual emendation.
[5] The expression is from the Vulgate of Gen. 1:2.
[6] An impossible translation. Perhaps a *per* has fallen out before *praeceptum*; then we could translate 'came' instead of 'brought', taking 'heaven and earth' as the subject.

he took me by the hand and led me to the tree of the knowledge of good and evil[1] and said: This is the tree through which death entered into the world, and Adam receiving from his wife ate of it and death came into the world. And he showed to me another tree in the middle of paradise, and he said to me: This is the tree of life.[2]

46. While I still considered the wood (=the tree), I saw a virgin coming from a distance, and two hundred angels singing hymns before her. And I asked and said: Sir, who is this who comes in such great glory? And he said to me: This is the Virgin Mary, the Mother of the Lord. And when she had come near, she greeted me and said: Greetings, Paul, of God and angels and men dearly beloved. For all the saints have implored my son Jesus, who is my Lord, that you might come here in the body so that they might see you before you depart out of the world; and the Lord said to them: Wait and be patient. Just a short time and you will see him and he will be with you for ever. And again all together they said to him: Do not sadden us for we wish to see him while he is in the flesh; through him thy name has been greatly glorified in the world,[3] and we have seen that he has taken on himself all the works both of little and great. From those who come here we inquire saying: Who is it who guided you in the world? And they answer us: There is a man in the world whose name is Paul; he in his preaching proclaims Christ, and we believe that because of the power and sweetness of his speech many have entered into the Kingdom. Behold, all the righteous are behind me coming to meet you. But I say to you, Paul, that I come first to meet those who have done the will of my Son and Lord Jesus Christ, I go first to meet them and I do not leave them to be as strangers until they meet my beloved Son[4] in peace.

47. While she was still speaking I saw coming from a distance three very beautiful men, in appearance like Christ, with shining forms, and their angels; and I asked: Who are these, sir? And he said to me: Do you not know them? And I said: I do not, sir. And he answered: These are the fathers of the people, Abraham, Isaac and Jacob. And when they had come near to me they

---

[1] Cf. Gen. 2:17.   [2] Cf. Gen. 2:9.   [3] Cf. Acts 9:15.
[4] 'my beloved son' added from C.

greeted me and said: Greetings, Paul, dearly beloved of God and men; blessed is he who endured violence for the sake of the Lord. And Abraham answered me and said: This is my son Isaac, and Jacob my dearly beloved. And we knew the Lord and followed him. Blessed are all those who believed your word, that they might inherit the kingdom of God through work, renunciation and holiness and humility and love and gentleness and right faith in the Lord. And we also have devoted ourselves to the Lord whom you preach, covenanting that we will assist and serve all the souls that believe in him, just as fathers serve their sons.

While they were still speaking I saw twelve others coming in honour from a distance, and I asked: Who are these, sir? And he said: These are the patriarchs. And they stepped up and greeted me and said: Greetings, Paul, dearly beloved of God and men. The Lord has not saddened us, so that we see you while you are still in the body before you leave the world. And in accordance with their order each of them gave me his name, from Reuben to Benjamin; and Joseph said to me: I am the one who was sold;[1] and I tell you, Paul, that for all that my brothers did against me, I have not behaved in any way badly towards them, not even in all the labour that they laid on me, nor have I hurt them in any thing for that reason[2] from morning until evening. Blessed is he who for the Lord's sake has been injured in something and has endured, for the Lord will repay him many times when he has come forth from the world.

48. While he was still speaking I saw another beautiful one coming from a distance and his angels were singing hymns, and I asked: Who is this, sir, who is beautiful of face? And he said to me: Do you not know him? And I said: No, sir. And he said to me: This is Moses the lawgiver, to whom God gave the law. And when he had come near me he immediately began to weep, and then he greeted me. And I said to him: Why are you weeping? for I have heard that you excel all men in meekness. And he answered and said: I weep over those whom with trouble I planted, because they have borne no fruit and none of them has

---

[1] Cf. Gen. 37:23ff.

[2] C: I have never kept any evil feeling in my heart against them, even for a single day. Accordingly *eos* should be elided and it should be translated: nor have I in any way been harmed by them = have I felt myself harmed, etc.

made progress. And I saw that all the sheep whom I pastured were scattered and become as those who had no shepherd[1] and that all the labours which I endured for the children of Israel were considered[2] of no value and how many mighty deeds I had done among them and they had not understood; and I am amazed that aliens and uncircumcised and idol-worshippers are converted and have entered into the promises of God, but Israel has not entered. And I tell you, brother Paul, that at that hour when the people hanged Jesus, whom you preach, that the Father, the God of all, who gave me the law, and Michael and all the angels and archangels and Abraham and Isaac and Jacob and all the righteous wept for the Son of God as he hung on the cross. And all the saints turned their attention to me at that time, looking at me and saying: See, Moses, what those of your people have done to the Son of God. Therefore you are blessed, Paul, and blessed is the generation and people who have believed your word.

49. While he was still speaking twelve[3] others came, and when they saw me they said: Are you Paul, who are extolled in heaven and on earth? And I answered and said: Who are you? The first answered and said: I am Isaiah whose head Manasseh cut off with a wooden saw.[4] And the second likewise said: I am Jeremiah who was stoned by the children of Israel[5] and killed. And the third said: I am Ezekiel whom the children of Israel dragged by the feet over the rocks on the mountain until they dashed out my brains. And we bore all these trials because we wished to save the children of Israel. And I tell you that after the trials which they inflicted on me, I threw myself on my face before the Lord, praying for them, bending my knees until the second hour of the Lord's Day, until Michael came and lifted me up from the earth. Blessed are you, Paul, and blessed the people who have believed through you.

When these had passed on I saw another with a beautiful face and I asked: Who is this, sir? [When he had seen me he rejoiced][6]

---

[1] Cf. Mt. 9:36.   [2] *disputati* ⟨*sunt*⟩.   [3] Gr. 'three'.
[4] Cf. Heb. 11:37; Ascension of Isaiah 1:7; 5:1ff., cf. *supra* pp. 650f.
[5] Cf. the Spanish Bible of St. Pere of Roda (11th century).
[6] The words in square brackets I have transposed to the beginning of the following sentence, where they appear in round brackets.

And he said to me: This is Lot who was found righteous in Sodom. (When he had seen me he rejoiced), and coming up to me he greeted me and said: Blessed are you, Paul, and blessed the generation which you have served. And I answered and said to him: Are you Lot, who was found righteous in Sodom? And he said: I received angels into my house as strangers, and when the men of the city wished to violate them, I offered to them my two virgin daughters who had never known men, and gave to them saying: Use them as you wish, so long as you do nothing evil to these men; for this reason they have entered under the roof of my house.[1] We ought therefore to have confidence and understand that whatever anyone has done God will repay it to him many times over when they come to him. Blessed are you, Paul, and blessed the race which has believed your word.

When then he had ceased speaking to me I saw coming from a distance another man with a very beautiful face and he was smiling, and his angels were singing hymns; and I said to the angel who was with me: Does then each of the righteous have an angel as his companion?

And he said to me: Each of the saints has his own angel who helps him and sings a hymn, and the one does not leave the other. And I said: Who is this, sir? And he said: This is Job. And he approached and greeted me and said: Brother Paul, you have great honour with God and men. For I am Job who suffered much through thirty years from the suppuration of a wound. And at the beginning the sores that came out on (from) my body were like grains of wheat; on the third day, however, they became like an ass's foot; and the worms which fell were four fingers long. And the Devil appeared to me for the third time and said to me: Speak a word against the Lord and die.[2] I said to him: If it is the will of God that I continue in affliction all the time I live until I die, I shall not cease to praise the Lord God and shall receive greater reward. For I know that the trials of this world are nothing in comparison to the consolation that comes afterwards.[3] Therefore, Paul, you are blessed, and blessed is the race which has believed through your agency.

50. While he was still speaking another man came from a

---

[1] Cf. Gen. 19:1ff.   [2] Cf. Job 2:9f.   [3] Cf. Rom. 8:18.

distance crying and saying: You are blessed, Paul, and I am
blessed because I have seen you, the beloved of the Lord. And I
asked the angel: Who is this, sir? And he answered and said to
me: This is Noah from the time of the flood. And immediately
we greeted one another.[1] And with great joy he said to me: You
are Paul, the dearly beloved of God. And I asked him: Who are
you? And he said: I am Noah who lived in the time of the flood.
And I tell you, Paul, that I spent a hundred years making the
ark[2] when I did not take off the shirt I wore nor cut the hair of
my head. Moreover I strove after continence, not coming near
my wife; and in those hundred years the hair of my head did not
grow in length nor were my clothes dirty. And I implored the
men of that time, saying: Repent, for a flood of water will come
upon you. But they ridiculed me and mocked at my words. And
again they said to me: This time is rather for those who can play
and would sin as they please,[3] for him to whom it is possible to
commit fornication not a little; for God does not see and does
not know what is done by us all, and a flood of water will certainly
not come on this world. And they did not cease from their sins
until God destroyed all flesh which had the spirit of life in itself.
But know, God cares more for one righteous man than for a
whole generation of the ungodly. Therefore you, Paul, are blessed,
and blessed is the people who believed through your agency.

51. And I turned and saw other righteous men coming from a
distance and I asked the angel: Who are these, sir? And he
answered me: They are Elijah and Elisha. And they greeted me.
And I said to them: Who are you? And one of them answered
me and said: I am Elijah, the prophet of God. I am Elijah
who prayed and because of my word heaven did not rain for three
years and six months on account of the unrighteousness of men.[4]
God who does the will of his servants is righteous and true. For
often the angels prayed the Lord for rain, and he said: Be patient
until my servant Elijah prays and begs for this, and I will send
rain on the earth. . . .[5]

---

[1] Reading *nos* instead of *vos*.   [2] Cf. Gen. 6:14ff.
[3] Cf. Mt. 24:38 and pars.   [4] Cf. 1 Kings 17:1ff.
[5] At this point the text underlying L, S, and Gr broke off suddenly. What follows
is the continuation as found in the Coptic.
For the way in which the Syriac continues at this break after the words 'And the
angels have often prayed that he would give them rain' see the end of the section.

The suffering which each endures for God's sake, God will repay him twofold. Blessed are you, Paul, and blessed is the people who will believe through you. And as he was speaking another, Enoch, came and greeted me and said to me: The sufferings which a man endures for the sake of God, God does not afflict him when he leaves the world.

As he was speaking to me, behold, two others came up together and another was coming after them crying out to them: Wait for me, that I may come to see Paul the beloved of God; there will be deliverance for us (?) if we see him while he is still in the body. I said to the angel: My lord, who are these? He said to me: This is Zacharias and John his son.[1] I said to the angel: And the other who runs after them? He said: This is Abel whom Cain killed.[2] They greeted me and said to me: Blessed are you, Paul, you who are righteous in all your works. John said: I am he whose head they took off in prison for the sake of a woman who danced at a feast.[3] Zacharias said: I am he whom they killed while I was presenting the offering to God; and when the angels came for the offering, they carried up my body to God, and no man found where my body was taken.[4] Abel said: I am he whom Cain killed while I was presenting a sacrifice to God.[5] The sufferings which we endured for the sake of God are nothing; what we have done for the sake of God we have forgotten. And the righteous and all the angels surrounded me, and they rejoiced with me [because] they had seen me in the flesh.

And I looked and saw another who surpassed them all, very beautiful. And I said to the angel: Who is this, my lord? He said to me: This is Adam, the father of you all. When he came up to me, he greeted me with joy. He said to me: Courage, Paul, beloved of God, you who have brought a multitude to faith in God and to repentance, as I myself have repented and received my praise from the Compassionate and Merciful One.

James considers it possible that the Apocalypse ended here. On the other hand a real conclusion is lacking. When C continues now with a fresh visit to the third heaven with many doublets, this is secondary. However perhaps the conclusion of C with the return of the Apostle to the circle of fellow-apostles on the Mount of Olives contains the

---

[1] Cf. Lk. 1:5ff.   [2] Cf. Gen. 4:8.   [3] Cf. Mk. 6:24, 25 and pars.
[4] Cf. *The Protevangelium of James* 24:3 (Vol. I, p. 388).   [5] Cf. Gen. 4:8.

original conclusion and would lead us to assume that the rapture also took place on the Mount of Olives. In what follows we give an abstract of C, with the conclusion, however, in a full translation.

Paul is caught up in a cloud into the third heaven. There he receives the command to reveal to no one the things which he will see. Nevertheless he tells about a seal and an altar with seven angels to its right and left. Many thousands of angels sing to the Father. When Paul falls prostrate the angel who accompanies him raises him up and promises to show him his place. He is now brought into Paradise with its shining inhabitants and its glorious thrones. At his request he is shown his own throne in a tabernacle of light; before it there are two singing angels who are presented as Uriel and Suriel. He is greeted by the inhabitants; the angel explains that these are the plants which Paul planted in the world. After further information from the angel he sees Paradise. Three concentric walls surround it, two of silver and in the middle between them one of gold. In the description of Paradise a remarkable feature is its trees which praise God three times daily, morning, noon and evening. The angel argues Paul out of the idea that he might not be worthy to dwell in Paradise: he will win the victory over the Accuser in the underworld (Amente). Moreover he will have great honour on his return to the world. And whenever the whole human race hears the words of this Apocalypse then it will repent and live. Paul then gets a sight of the clothes and crowns of his fellow-apostles on thrones, and yet once more meets David who is singing with his harp. After that he sees the place of the martyrs.

The angel of the Lord took me up and brought me to the Mount of Olives. There I, Paul, found the apostles gathered together. I greeted them and made known to them everything which had happened to me and what I had seen and the honours which would be for the righteous and the ruin and destruction which would be for the ungodly. Then the apostles were glad and rejoiced and blessed God, and they commanded us together, i.e. myself, Mark and Timothy, the disciples of Saint Paul(!) the teacher of the Church, to put in writing this holy apocalypse for the benefit and help of those who will hear it. While the apostles were talking with us the Saviour Christ appeared to us out of the chariot of the cherubim, and he said to us: Greetings, my holy disciples, whom I have chosen out of the world! Greetings, Peter, crown of the apostles! Greetings, John, my beloved! Greetings to all (you) apostles! The peace of my good Father be with you. Then he turned to our father and said to him: Greetings, Paul, honoured letter writer![1] Greetings, Paul, mediator of the coven-

[1] Literally *Letterbearer*.

ant! Greetings, Paul, roof and foundation of the Church! Are
you convinced by the things which you have seen? Are you fully
convinced by the things which you have heard? Paul answered:
Yes, my Lord. Thy grace and thy love have accomplished for me
a great good. The Saviour answered and said: O beloved of the
Father, Amen, Amen, I tell you that the words of this apocalypse
will be preached in the whole world for the benefit of those who
shall hear it. Amen, Amen, I tell you, Paul, that whoever will take
care of this apocalypse, and will write it and set it down as a
testimony for the generations to come, to him I shall not show
the underworld with its bitter weeping, until the second generation of his seed. And whoever reads it with faith, I shall bless him
and his house. Whoever scoffs at the words of this apocalypse,
I will punish him.[1] And men are not to read therein except on
the holy days because I have revealed the whole mystery of my
deity to you, O my holy members. Behold, I have already made
known everything to you. Now go and go forth and preach the
Gospel of my kingdom because indeed your course and your holy
contest has drawn near. But you yourself, Paul, my chosen one,
will finish your (sing.) course with Peter, my beloved, on the fifth
day of the month Epeph.[2] You (sing.) will be in my kingdom for
ever. My power will be with you.—And he immediately commanded the clouds to take up the disciples and lead them to the
country which he had allotted to (each of) them. And they were
to preach the Gospel of the kingdom of heaven in every place
for ever because of the grace and love for man of our Lord Jesus
Christ, our Saviour, to whom be glory and to his gracious Father
and to the Holy Spirit for ever and ever. Amen.

After the words 'And the angels have often prayed that he would
give them rain' at the break in ch. 51 the Syriac continues:

until I invoked him anew, and then he gave to them. But you
are blessed, Paul, that your generation and all whom you teach
are children of the kingdom. And understand, Paul, that everyone
who believes through you is blessed and blessedness is preserved
for him.—Then he parted from me. And when he had gone away
from me the angel who was with me led me out and said with

[1] Cf. Rev. 22:18f. [2] = the eleventh Coptic month beginning the 25th June.

great seriousness: Paul, the mystery of this revelation has been given to you; as it pleases you, make it known and reveal it to men.—I, Paul, however, came to myself and I knew and understood what I had seen and I wrote it in a roll. And while I lived, I did not have rest to reveal this mystery, but I wrote it (down) and deposited it under the wall of a house of that believer with whom I was in Tarsus, a city of Cilicia. And when I was released from this temporal life (and stood) before my Lord, he spoke thus to me: Paul, have I shown everything to you so that you should put it under the wall of a house? Rather send and reveal it for its sake so that men may read it and turn to the way of truth that they may not come into these bitter torments.

And thus this revelation was discovered.

Then the account of the discovery follows.

2. APOCALYPSE OF THOMAS
(*A. de Santos Otero*)

For centuries the Apocalypse of Thomas was known only through the notice of it in the *Decretum Gelasianum* (Item 27, cf. Vol. I, p. 48). In 1908 C. Frick (*ZNW* 9, 1908, 172) drew attention to another reference which is contained in the Chronicle of Jerome of the *Codex Philippsianus No. 1829* in Berlin. In this it says in reference to the 18th year of Tiberius Caesar: *in libro quodam apocrypho qui dicitur Thomae apostoli scriptum est dominum iesum ad eum dixisse ab ascensu suo ad celum usque in secundum adventum eius novem iobeleus contineri.*

Today two versions of the Apocalypse of Thomas exist.

The longer is represented by: (*a*) Cod. Clm 4585 fol. 66ᵛ–67ᵛ (9th cent.) of Benediktbeuern. This text has been edited by Fr. Wilhelm in his book: *Deutsche Legenden und Legendare*, 1907; (*b*) a manuscript from the Library of the Chapter of Verona (8th cent.) which has been published by M. R. James in *JTS* 11, 1910, pp. 288–290; (*c*) Cod. Vatic. Palat. No. 220, discovered by E. v. Dobschütz and used by Bihlmeyer in his edition of Cod. Clm 4563. An early English form of this version is found in the fifteenth sermon of the famous Anglo-Saxon manuscript of Vercelli (9th cent.), cf. M. R. James, *Apoc. NT*, pp. 556ff. This version consists of two different parts. The first is concerned with the events and signs which are to precede the last judgment. In this it reveals a close dependence on similar descriptions of other Apocrypha of an apocalyptic nature, e.g. the Assumption of Moses, the Ascension of Isaiah and the Sibylline Books. This part should be regarded as an interpolation; its origin can be dated to the first or second half of the 5th century because of some historical references in the text (e.g. to the Emperor Theodosius and his two sons Arcadius and Honorius). Cf. Bihlmeyer in *Rev. Bénéd.* 28, 1911, p. 277.

The second part corresponds in range and content with the shorter version of the Apocalypse of Thomas. This version is represented by: (*a*) Cod. Vindob. Palatinus 16 (formerly Bobbiensis) fol. 60^r-60^v from the 5th century. This text was first discovered by J. Bick (*SWA* 159, 1908, 90–100) and identified by E. Hauler (*Wiener Studien* 30, 1908, 308–340) as a fragment of the Apocalypse of Thomas. It is the oldest witness of all to our Apocalypse; (*b*) Cod. Clm 4563 fol. 40^r-40^v (11th/12th century) from Benediktbeuern, discovered and edited by Bihlmeyer (*Rev. Bénéd.* 28, 1911, 272–276). This text agrees basically with Vindob. Palat. 16, has been fully preserved and reveals no interpolations.

The shorter version is our oldest witness to the original Apocalypse of Thomas, which would have been subject in the course of time to various orthodox and heretical revisions. We must associate this development above all with Manichaean and Priscillianist currents of thought. In favour of that there is not only the mention of the Apocalypse of Thomas in the Decretum Gelasianum but also some parallel places in Priscillianist writings; cf. De Bruyne (*Rev. Bénéd.* 24, 1907, 318–335) and Bihlmeyer, *ibid.*, 28, 1911, p. 279). Some typical Manichaean ideas, e.g. that of light, appear again and again in our Apocalypse. In this connection Bihlmeyer (*ibid.*, p. 282) points to the name *Thomas* which (according to the Acta Archelai of Hegemonius) was borne by one of the three greatest disciples of Mani. Both the longer and shorter versions (Cod. Vindob. Palat. 16 dates from the 5th century) suggest the conjecture that the Apocalypse of Thomas originated prior to the 5th century. Closely dependent on the canonical Revelation of John, it is the only apocryphal apocalypse which apportions the events of the End into seven days. This clearly recalls the seven seals, the seven trumpets and the seven bowls of the Revelation of John (Rev. 5–8:2; 8:2–11; 16). The numerous variants of the Latin codices point to different versions of an original Greek text.

The basis of our translation is the Latin text of Cod. Clm 4563 in the edition of Bihlmeyer (*Rev. Bénéd.* 28, 1911, 272–276) in which he takes into account the variants of the other codices. There is a complete English translation of both versions in M. R. James.

Hearken, Thomas,[1] for I am the Son of God the Father[2] and I am the father of all spirits.[3] Hear from me the signs which will

---

[1] Almost all the representatives of the longer version introduce this piece of writing with the words: *incipit epistula domini ad Thomam.* This is succeeded by a long description of the events which will take place in the last days. This description constitutes the first part of the version and is to be considered an interpolation; it concludes with a series of anathemas and cries of *Vae.* Following on this the description of the last seven days begins. With some variations it takes a similar course to the shorter version.

[2] Bihlmeyer (*ibid.*, p. 280) has seen traces of monarchian influence in the prominent place which the person *Dei Patris* occupies in the course of the work.

[3] Cf. Priscillian, *Tract.*, 11: *tu animarum pater . . . tu operatio spirituum, tu principum archangelorum, tu angelorum opus* (ed. Schepss, *CSEL* 18, 104).

be at the end of this world, when the end of the world will be fulfilled before my elect come forth from the world.

I tell you openly what now is about to happen to men.[1] When these are to take place the princes of the angels[2] do not know, for they are now hidden from them. Then the kings will divide the world among themselves;[3] there will be great hunger, great pestilences and much distress on the earth.[4] The sons of men will be enslaved in every nation and will perish by the sword.[5] There will be great disorder on earth. Thereafter when the hour of the end draws near there will be great signs in the sky for seven days and the powers of the heavens will be set in motion.[6] Then at the beginning of the third hour of the first day there will be a mighty and strong voice in the firmament of the heaven; a cloud of blood[7] will go up from the north and there will follow it great rolls of thunder and powerful flashes of lightning and it will cover the whole heaven. Then it will rain blood on all the earth. These are the signs of the first day.

And on the second day a great voice will resound in the firmament of heaven and the earth will be moved from its place.[8] The gates of heaven will be opened in the firmament of heaven from the east. The smoke of a great fire[9] will burst forth through the gates of heaven and will cover the whole heaven as far as the west. In that day there will be fears and great terrors in the world.[10] These are the signs of the second day.

And on the third day at about the third hour there will be a great voice in heaven and the depths of the earth will roar out from the four corners of the world.[11] The pinnacles of the firmament of heaven will be laid open and all the air will be filled with pillars of smoke. An exceedingly evil stench of sulphur will last until the tenth hour.[12] Men will say: We think the end is upon us so that we perish. These are the signs of the third day.

[1] The text appears to be corrupt at this point. The longer version offers no parallel.
[2] Cod. Vindob. Palat. No. 16: *principes angelorum*. Cod. Clm 4563: *principes, angeli*. Cf. Mk. 13:32 and pars.
[3] Cod. Clm. 4563: *Tunc erunt participationes in saeculo inter regem et regem*. This can be understood in dependence on Mk. 13:8, as an allusion to the struggles and wars for world dominion.
[4] Cf. Lk. 21:11; Mt. 24:7ff.   [5] Cf. Lk. 21:24.
[6] Cf. Lk. 21:11, 26; Mt. 24:29; Mk. 13:24f.   [7] Cf. Rev. 6:12; Joel 2:30.
[8] Cf. Rev. 6:12ff.   [9] Cf. Rev. 9:2.   [10] Cf. Luke 21:26.
[11] Cf. Rev. 7:1; Ezek. 7:2; 37:9; Mt. 24:31; Lk. 21:25; 4 Ezra 5:7.
[12] Cf. Rev. 9:17.

And at the first hour of the fourth day the Abyss will melt and rumble from the land of the east; then the whole earth will shake before the force of the earthquake. In that day the idols of the heathen[1] will fall as well as all the buildings of the earth before the force of the earthquake. These are the signs of the fourth day.

But on the fifth day at the sixth hour suddenly there will be great thunderings in the heaven and the powers of the light (will flash) and the sphere of the sun will be burst[2] and great darkness will be in the (whole) world as far as the west.[3] The air will be sorrowful without sun and moon. The stars will cease their work. In that day all nations will so see as (if they were enclosed) in a sack,[4] and they will despise the life of this world. These are the signs of the fifth day.

And at the fourth hour of the sixth day there will be a great voice in heaven. The firmament of heaven will be split from east to west[5] and the angels of the heavens will look out on the earth through the rents in the heavens and all men who are on earth will see the angelic host looking out from heaven. Then all men will flee into the tombs[6] and hide themselves from before the righteous angels, and say, "Oh that the earth would open and swallow us". For such things will happen as never happened since this world was created.[7] Then they will see me as I come down from above in the light of my Father with the power and honour of the holy angels.[8] Then at my arrival the restraint on the fire of paradise will be loosed, for paradise is enclosed with fire.[9]

[1] The *adornamenta* of Cod. Clm 4563 is replaced by *idolas* in Cod. Clm 4585 and by *monumenta* in Vatic. Palat. No. 220. The meaning at any rate is clear. Cf. Is. 2:18; pseudo-Matthew 22:2; 23 (Santos, pp. 234f.); Ev. Infantiae Arab. 10 (translated *ibid.*, p. 333).

[2] Clm 4563 has *et rota solis aperietur*. Bihlmeyer (*op. cit.*) proposes *operietur* instead of *aperietur*.

[3] Cf. Mt. 24:29; Rev. 6:12.

[4] Clm 4563 has, *In illa die omnes gentes ita videbunt, velut in sacculo*. James (p. 560) replaces *sacculo* with *speculo* and translates: "in that day shall all nations behold as in a mirror", though he does not rule out *sacculo* as a possibility. The manuscripts offer no clue for the understanding of this obscure passage.

[5] Cf. Copt. Apocalypse of Elijah (ed. Steindorff, p. 154) and Apocalypse of John, ch. 17 (ed. Tischendorf, *Apa*, p. 85).

[6] Vat. Palat. No. 220 has *speluncas montium* instead of the *monumentis* of Clm 4563. Cf. Rev. 6:15.

[7] Cf. Mt. 24:21; Mk. 13:19; Rev. 16:18; Dan. 12:1.

[8] Cf. Mt. 24:30; Mk. 13:26f; Lk. 21:27; Dan. 7:13. Mt. 25:31; Lk. 9:26; 1 Thess. 3:13 also refer to the presence of the angels at the Parousia. Cf. Dan. 7:10.

[9] It is not clear whether there is an allusion here to the expulsion of Adam from paradise (Gen. 3:24) or rather to the conception of the throne of God as surrounded by fire (cf. Dan. 7:9; Ezek. 1:4; Rev. 4:5). A Priscillianist Apocryphon also speaks of 'walls of fire' (*Rev. Bénéd.* 24, 1907, p. 323). There however they surround 'hell'.

And this is the eternal fire which devours the earthly globe and all the elements of the world.[1] Then the spirits and souls of the saints will come forth from paradise and come into all the earth, and each go to its own body where it is laid up; and each of them will say, "Here my body is laid up". And when the great voice of those spirits is heard there will be an earthquake everywhere in the earth and by the force of that earthquake the mountains will be shattered above and the rocks beneath. Then each spirit will return to its own vessel[2] and the bodies of the saints who sleep will rise.[3] Then their bodies will be changed into the image and likeness and honour of the holy angels and into the power of the image of my holy Father.[4] Then they will put on the garment of eternal life:[5] the garment from the cloud of light[6] which has never been seen in this world; for this cloud comes down from the upper kingdom of the heavens by the power of my Father, and will invest with its glory every spirit that has believed in me. Then they will be clothed and, as I said to you before, borne by the hands of the holy angels.[7] Then they will be carried off in a cloud of light into the air,[8] and rejoicing go with me into the heavens and remain in the light and honour of my Father. Then there will be great joy for them in the presence of my Father and in the presence of the holy angels. These are the signs of the sixth day.

And at the eighth hour of the seventh day there will be voices in the four corners[9] of heaven. All the air will be set in motion and filled with holy angels. These will make war among themselves for the whole day.[10] In that day the elect will be delivered by the holy angels from the destruction of the world.[11] Then all men will see that the hour of their destruction is come near. These are the signs of the seventh day.

And when the seven days are finished, on the eighth day at the

---

[1] Cf. 2 Pet. 3:7.   [2] Cf. 1 Thess. 4:4.   [3] Cf. Mt. 27:52.

[4] Cf. Gen. 1:26; 1 Cor. 15:49; 2 Cor. 3:18.

[5] Cf. Ascension of Isaiah 9:2 (Translation *supra* p. 656).

[6] Cf. Acts of Thomas, chs. 108–114 (*supra* pp. 498ff.). The important role which light plays in our apocalypse reminds us of Manichaean and Gnostic circles where as is well known the theme of light was very popular. Cf. Bihlmeyer, p. 281.

[7] Cf. Apoc. Moses, ch. 37 (ed. Tischendorf, *Apa*, p. 20); Story of Joseph the Carpenter, 23:2 (S. Morenz, *TU*, 56, 1951).

[8] Cf. 1 Thess. 4:17.   [9] Cf. Rev. 7:1.   [10] Cf. Rev. 12:7.

[11] Palat. Vatic. 220 has *querent electi de toto animo ut liberentur de perditione.* Cf. Rev. 7:3; Mt. 24:31; Mk. 13:27.

sixth hour there will be a gentle and pleasant voice in heaven from the east. Then that angel who has power over the holy angels will be made manifest. And there will go forth with him all the angels sitting on my holy Father's chariots of clouds, rejoicing and flying around in the air under heaven, to deliver the elect who believed in me; and they will rejoice that the destruction of the world has come.

The words of the Saviour to Thomas about the end of this world are finished.

POETIC COMPOSITIONS

1. THE NAASSENE PSALM
(*W. Bauer*)

INTRODUCTION. In his refutation of the Gnostic Naassenes, Hippolytus (V. 6ff.) incorporates the so-called *Naassenerpredigt* (V. 7. 3ff., ed. Wendland (*GCS* 26) 1916, pp. 79ff.), which according to Reitzenstein's demonstration[1] is an originally pagan address, or perhaps more correctly a syncretistic formation, the basic pagan content of which has from the beginning been enriched by a few Jewish additions. The Christian additions to this nucleus are at any rate easily detachable, and what remains is in all essentials a pagan sermon, an allegorizing interpretation of the hymn to Attis appended at the end (V. 9. 8f.) which—intended in the first place for recitation in the theatre—rests upon archaic forms (J. Kroll, *Die christliche Hymnodik bis zu Klemens von Alexandreia*, 1921, p. 93). Whether the Christian Naassenes also made use of it for purposes of worship, or merely in support of their speculations, can no longer be determined.

Cultic use is much more credible in the case of a two-part hymn which Hippolytus includes in connection with the sermon as a Psalm of the Naassenes (V. 10. 1ff., ed. Wendland, pp. 102ff.). Except for the first lines, which have an expanded metre, this hymn is in anapaests, the most common metre of the imperial period. Its poetic form has attracted numerous scholars (cf. Kroll, *op. cit.*, p. 96 note, and the literature here mentioned). The psalm is really entirely pagan. Only at one point has it been clearly Christianized by the insertion of the name *Jesus* instead of the deity originally there named.

On the content cf. Kroll, *op. cit.*, pp. 94–97.

THE NAASSENE PSALM (Hippol., Ref. V. 10. 2ff.)

Primal principle of all things was the first-born Mind;
The second, poured forth from the first-born, was Chaos;
The third, which received ⟨being and form from both⟩, is the soul.
And it is like the timid deer[2]
Which is hunted upon the earth
By death, which constantly
Tries its power upon it.
Is it today in the Kingdom of Light,
Tomorrow it is flung into misery,
Plunged deep in woe and tears.

---

[1] *Poimandres*, 1904, pp. 82ff.; *Studien zum antiken Synkretismus*, 1926, pp. 104ff.; 161–173.

[2] So according to the text transmitted: διὰ τοῦτο ἔλαφον μορφὴν περικειμένη. H. Jonas, *Gnosis und spätantiker Geist* I, 1954, p. 343, would conjecture: . . . ἔλαφ⟨ρ⟩ον . . . This conjecture has much in its favour. Jonas translates: "Therefore clothed in an insignificant form/It toils painfully in death's power."

On joy follow tears,[1]
On tears follows the judge,
On the judge follows death.
And wandering in the labyrinth
It seeks in vain for escape.
Jesus said: Look, Father,
Upon this tormented being,
How far from thy breath
It wanders sorrowful upon earth.
It seeks to flee the bitter chaos,
But knows not how to win through.
For its sake send me, Father;
Bearing the seals will I descend,
Whole aeons will I travel through,
All mysteries will I open,
And the forms of gods will I display;
And the hidden things of the holy way
—Gnosis I call it—I will bestow.

This translation has been made direct from the Greek, with the aid of Bauer's version, itself based on Harnack (*Lehrbuch der Dogmengeschichte* I, 5th ed., 1931, p. 257; *Apokr.* 2, p. 436).

2. THE ODES OF SOLOMON
(*W. Bauer*)

INTRODUCTION AND LITERATURE. The Odes of Solomon were formerly known only from two old Canon catalogues which mention the name, from a quotation in Lactantius (Inst. IV. 12. 3: Ode 19. 6f.), and through the circumstance that the Gnostic writing Pistis Sophia, preserved in Coptic, incorporates five Odes (1; 5; 6; 22; 25). In 1909 J. Rendel Harris discovered the collection itself in a Syriac manuscript about 400 years old, in which it was followed by the Psalms of Solomon, and in the same year he provided us with the Editio princeps. On his manuscript (H) in the first instance our knowledge of the Odes still rests today. A second Syriac codex (B) was found by F. C. Burkitt in 1912. Admittedly it only begins at Ode 17. 7, but on the other hand it possibly belongs as early as the 10th century.

H too, however, is incomplete, since it begins in the course of the third Ode. Here the Pistis Sophia comes to our assistance, at least so far as the first Ode is concerned. In cap. 59 we read: "But (δέ)[2] Mary, the Mother of Jesus, answered and said: 'My Lord, thy power of light once prophesied (προφητεύειν) concerning these words through

[1] The text in this and the two following lines is corrupt.
[2] The words in brackets are Greek loan-words in the Coptic text.

Solomon in the 19th Ode (ᾠδή) and said'." Then follows a hymn in five couplets. That it is our Ode is shown by the number 19, which is explained by the fact that in the *Vorlage* the 'Odes' were evidently appended to the 18 'Psalms' of Solomon, with a consecutive numbering.

The Coptic text of the Pistis Sophia was finally published by C. Schmidt, *Coptica II*, 1925. From him derives also the German translation in *GCS* 13, 1905.[1] The Odes of Solomon also have appeared in a sterling edition: R. Harris and A. Mingana, *The Odes and Psalms of Solomon*, I and II, 1916, 1920. On the material here collected and edited is based: *Die Oden Salomos*, edited by W. Bauer, *KlT* 64, 1933, the basis of our treatment of the subject. This in the translation lays emphasis only upon accuracy and, where at all feasible, preserves the word order. Retouching for the attainment of a clearer or aesthetically more satisfying wording has been deliberately avoided. Recently the Greek text of at least one Ode has also become known: *Papyrus Bodmer* X–XII (X: Apocryphal correspondence of the Corinthians and the Apostle Paul; XI: Eleventh Ode of Solomon; XII: Fragment of a liturgical hymn), a 3rd-century manuscript published by M. Testuz, Cologny-Genève (Bibl. Bodmeriana) 1959.

The original language of the Odes was almost certainly Greek,[2] but from the first notable scholars have argued for a Syriac original.[3] The idea that the Odes assumed their form through the redaction of older material by someone of different opinions has not been widely accepted (G. Kittel, Die Oden Salomos: überarbeitet oder einheitlich? Beitr. z. Wissenschaft vom AT und NT 16, 1914). Nor have most of the proposals which immediately after the appearance of the new discovery sought to determine its place in the history of religions (literature to 1920 in Harris-Mingana II, 455ff.; later the production slackened considerably). Harris conjectured a Jewish-Christian origin as early as the 1st century. A. von Harnack (*Ein jüdisch-christliches Psalmbuch aus dem 1. Jahrh.*, *TU* 35. 4, 1910) and F. Spitta (*ZNW* 11, 1910, pp. 193–203, 259–290) assumed Jewish origin with a Christian redaction. Th. Zahn (*Neue kirchl. Zeitschr.* 1910, pp. 667–701, 747–777) thought of a Christian about 120–150, while J. Labourt and P. Batiffol (*Les Odes de Salomon*, 1911) defined him more precisely as a Gentile Christian. Frankenberg (*op. cit.*) noticed connections with the Alexandrian theology. J. H. Bernard (*The Odes of Solomon*, 1912) believed the hymns to be intended for instruction prior to Baptism. The Montanists too make their appearance: F. C. Conybeare (*ZNW* 12, 1911, pp. 70–75), S. A. Fries (*ibid.*, pp. 108–125). But more and more the view became established that we have to do with a Gnostic hymn-book from the 2nd century: H. Gunkel (*ZNW* 11, 1910, pp. 291–328;

---

[1] For English translations of the Pistis Sophia see Vol. I, p. 250.

[2] F. Schulthess, *ZNW* 11, 1910, pp. 251f., and on the whole the majority. Attempts to recover the (original) Greek text in W. Frankenberg, *Das Verständnis der Oden Salomos* (*BZAW* 21) 1911. Cf. also the summary of the arguments for and against, and especially on the works of Connolly, in A. Adam, Die ursprüngliche Sprache der Salomo-Oden, *ZNW* 52, 1961, pp. 141–156.

[3] Thus A. Adam has recently pronounced in favour of a Semitic original (*ZNW* 52, pp. 141ff.), although admittedly for an Aramaic "which was close to the Edessene Syriac" (p. 156).

*RGG*² V, 1931, cols. 87–90), W. Stölten (*ZNW* 13, 1912, pp. 29–58), H. Gressmann (*Apokr.* 2, p. 437), J. Kroll (*Die christliche Hymnodik*, Verzeichnis der Vorlesungen an der Akademie Braunsberg 1921/22, pp. 70ff.), R. Abramowski (*ZNW* 35, 1936, pp. 44–69). Here 'Gnostic' must be understood in a broad sense. An exact identification of the poet is impossible. Neither for Bardesanes (W. R. Newbold, *JBL* 30, 1911, pp. 161–204) nor even for Valentinus (E. Preuschen, *ZNW* 11, 1910, p. 328 n. 3) are the reasons advanced decisive. Even the assumption of Edessa (J. de Zwaan, The Edessene Origins of the Odes of Solomon, *Quantulacumque*, Festschr. K. Lake, 1937, pp. 285–302; R. M. Grant, The Odes of Solomon and the Church of Antioch, *JBL* 63, 1944, pp. 363–377) or Antioch (Harris-Mingana, etc.) as the home of the Odes remains a conjecture, the former linked with the assumption of an original Syriac form. The attainment of certain knowledge here is difficult also because of the fact that Semitic poetry, in particular through the medium of the Greek OT, once exercised an influence on men of Greek speech too. J. Wellhausen (*GGA* 1910, p. 642) observed in the Odes probable Biblicisms, but no Semitisms. On the other hand Syrians of the stamp of Bardesanes were guided in their poetic efforts by Greek influence (J. Kroll, *Die christliche Hymnodik bis zu Klemens von Alexandreia*, 1912, referring to the Church History of Sozomen, who reports this about Harmonius, the son of Bardesanes (III. 16), and on the basis of his own observations).

Further Literature: H. J. E. W. Holstijn, *Oden van Salomo* (Zangen van Rust in den Heere), Zutphen 1942; A. Omodeo, Le Odi di Salomone, *Parola del Passato* 1, 1946, pp. 84–118; M. Mar Josip, Oldest Christian Hymnbook, Temple (Tex.) 1948; B. Steidle, 15. Ode Salomos, *Benedikt. Monatschr.* 24, 1948, pp. 241f.; C. Charlier, in *Esprit et Vie* (Paris) 1, 1948, pp. 239–244 (Ode 1; 11; 12; 17; 35; 42 Celtic); H. E. del Medico, La Lamelle Virolleaud, Παγκάρπεια, *Mélanges H. Grégoire* (Annuaire de l'Inst. de Philol. et d'Hist. Orientales et Slaves 9, Brussels 1949) pp. 179–192; O. Casel, in *Archiv. für Liturgiewissenschaft* 1, 1950, pp. 297ff. (survey of literature); W. Baumgartner, Das trennende Schwert in den Oden Salomons 28. 4, *Festschr. Bertholet*, 1950, pp. 50–57; A. Vööbus, *Celibacy, A Requirement for Admission to Baptism in the Early Syrian Church* (Papers of the Esthonian Theol. Society in Exile 1), Stockholm 1951; A. Ehrhardt, The Birth of the Synagogue and R. Akiba, *Studia Theologica* IX. 2, 1955, pp. 88f. (the Odes of Jewish origin. Kinship with the psalms from the Dead Sea); J. Daniélou, Odes de Salomon, *Dict. de la Bible*, Suppl. 32, cols. 677–684; F. M. Braun, L'énigme des Odes de Salomon, *Rev. Thomiste* 57, 1957, pp. 597–625; E. Fabbri, El tema de Cristo vivificante en las Odas de Salomón, Ciencia y Fe (Buenos Aires) 14, 1958, pp. 483–498; H. M. Schenke, *Die Herkunft des sog. Evangelium Veritatis*, 1959 (in terms of content the Odes and Ev. Veritatis belong together; both are non-Valentinian); F. M. Braun, in *Jean le Théologien et son Évangile dans l'Église ancienne* (Études bibliques) 1959, pp. 224–251.

[With reference to the omission of the Odes from this translation, see Preface to the English edition, page 12.]

INDEX OF NAMES AND SUBJECTS

The numbers refer to the pages, Vol. II being indicated by the prefixed Roman numeral.

Numbers or an asterisk in the upper register following the page number indicate the corresponding notes.

Numbers in **heavy** type indicate the main sections in which the subject is discussed in detail. In the case of authors or texts, numbers in *italics* refer to passages where verbatim quotations are presented.

Andrew: 156; 187; 192; 256; 258f.; 342f.; 492f.; II37; II39; II46; II50; II64; II78; II161; II179; II181; II225; II442
Andrew, Acts of: 266; II161[1]; II178; II181f.; II184f.; **II390ff.**; II576. Ch. 6: 275
Andrew, Gospel of: II50
Andronicus (Rom. 16:7): II67. (Acts of John): II199; II207f.; II210f.; II222; II224; II235; II238; II243–254
'Anēslasejā (Elysium): II679
Angaeus: 445; 462f.; 467f.
Angel: 198; 326; 337; 472; 488f.; 493ff.; 499; II250; II310; II366; II374; II387; II454; II649; II652–658; II669; II674f.; II679; II683; II686; II693 (Twelve A. with flowers); II747; II759ff. A. of the covenant: II766. A. of repentance: II632; II634f.; II641. A. of the firmament: II662. Princes of the A.: II800. A. of the (holy) Spirit: II647; II654; II658f.; II661f. A. of the Church: II647. A. of deficiency: 327. A. of the North: II750. A. of Light: II796. A. of the Sun: II649. A. who guard Tartarus: II780f. A. of Death: II657; II659. A. in the realm of the dead: II659. A. of the Underworld: II662
Angel of Satan: II645; II653. A. of Satan = Simon Magus: II272f.; II286; II300[2]; II316
angelus interpres: II623; II634f. (Cf. interpreting angel)
Anna: 374ff.; 427f.
an-Nadim: 348
Annas, high priest: 152; 382; 393; 450; 453f.; 463; 465; 467ff.; 478–482
Annubion: II558; II562
anointing with oil: II455
Anonymity: II89
Anselm: 152

Antichrist: 475; II148; II546; II600; II612–615; II625f.; II707 (Nero)
Antigonus: II602
Antioch: II328–330; II352f.; II360; II364
Antiochenes: II360
anti-Paulinism: II108
Antiquity, fictitious: II583; II623
Antonius: 453
Antulus: II298
Apamea: II747
Aparktias: 498
Apelles: 88; 349f.
Aphrodite: II560
Apis: II720
Apocalypse, Apocalypses: II142; II581ff.; II599 (Christian-Gnostic); II627 (Did. 16); II630 and 634 (Hermas); II795f.
Apocalypse, anonymous: II751
Apocalypse in the name of Abraham: 318
Apocalypse of Bartholomew: II754
Apocalypse of Elias, ch. 43:10: 200[5]
Apocalypses of James: 334
Apocalypses of John, apocryphal: II753. A. in the name of John: 319. A. of John (Interrogatio Johannis): 320
Apocalypses, later: **II751ff.**
Apocalypses of Mary: II753f.
Apocalypses from Nag Hammadi: II754
Apocalypse of Paul: II74; II599; II610; II638; II667; II751; **II755ff.**
Apocalypse of Paul, Coptic, from Nag Hammadi: II759
Apocalypse of Peter: **II663ff.** (See also, Peter, Apocalypse of)
Apocalypse of Sophonias (Zephaniah): II751f.
Apocalypse of Stephen: II754
Apocalypse, Synoptic: **II616ff.**
Apocalypse of Zechariah: II752f.

Gospel, Gospels—Cont.
II711; II797. Apocryphal G.:
62; **8off.**; 351; II33f. G. in
dialogue form: 249; 258. The
Four G.: 169; 231; 350
Gospel 'ālaph: 357–359. (Cf. G.
of the 22)
Gospel of Apelles: 346; **349ff.**
Gospel acc. to the Apostles,
Jewish-Christian: 131f.; 153
Gospel 'ārab ('ālaph): 357
Gospel of Bardesanes: **350**
Gospel of Bartholomew: *see* Barth-
olomew, Gospel of
Gospel of Basilides: 263; 279;
346ff.; 349
Gospel of Cerinthus: **345f.**
Gospel Edition, Zion: 136; *147*;
148; *149*; *150*
Gospel of Eve: **241ff.**; 342
Gospel of the Four Heavenly
Regions or of the Four corners
of the World): **231f.**
Gospel of Gamaliel: 485; **508ff.**
Gospels, Gnostic: **231ff.**; 338f.
Gospel, the great (from Alpha to
Omega), of Mani: 355f.; 361.
(Cf. Gospel, Living; Gospel of
Mani; Gospel of 22)
Gospel Harmony: 352
Gospel of James the Elder (from
Sacro Monte de Grenada): 334
Gospels, Jewish-Christian: 81f.;
117ff. (Cf. Ebionites, Gospel of;
Hebrews, Gospel of; Nazareans,
Gospel of)
Gospel of Judas: **313f.**
Gospel, Living, of Life, of the
Living One (of Mani): 269f.;
352; 355f.; 359f. (Cf. Gospel of
Mani)
Gospel of Mani: **350ff.** (Cf.
Gospel, the Great; Gospel,
Living; Gospel of 22)
Gospel of Marcion: **348f.**; 350
Gospel according to Mary: 244;
314; **340ff.**
Gospel according to Matthias:
263; 278; **308ff.**; 349

Gospel of Perfection: **232f.**
Gospel Preaching of John (Acts of
John 87ff.): *II224f.*; II264
Gospel of the Seventy: **269ff.**;
351
Gospel tau: 357. (Cf. Gospel of
22)
Gospel of Truth: 83; **233ff.**;
245; 335; **523ff.**
Gospel of the Twelve (Jewish-
Christian) 131; 153; 228; **263f.**;
279; 349
Gospel of the Twelve Apostles
(Manichaean): **268f.**; 351
Gospel of the Twelve (Kukean):
154; **264f.**
Gospel of the Twelve (acc. to
Revillout): 504
Gospels of the Twelve Apostles,
other: **271**
Gospel of the 22: 357. (Cf.
Gospel of Mani)
Governor: II357–362; II369f.
Gozan (river): II646
Grace: II229; II422[1]
Graphathas: 499
Graves of the Apostles: II43
Greek conception of God: II558f.
Greeks: II99f.; II560; II729
Gregory Nazianzus Ep. 20; Orat.
17. 5: *II98*
Gregory of Tours, Liber de mira-
culi b. Andreae: II391; II397
Grenada, leaden boxes in the
Sacro Monte: 334
Groomsmen, seven: II446
Grundschrift (basic Writing) of
Ps.-Clementines: II533
Guardian: II461
Gundaphorus: II443; II451;
II456

Habakkuk: II645; II650; II693;
II716
Hades: 471–474; 479ff.; 487;
489f.; 501; 531; II454; II515;
II679[3]; II714; II731. (Cf. Hell;
Dead, Realm of; Underworld)

Stephanus (of Corinth): II374
Stephen: (martyr, "deacon"):
  II53.
Story of the birth of Mary: 406
Story (syriac) of the holy Apostle
  Paul: II575
Strangers: II476
Stratiotics: 317²
Stratocles: II402; II412f.; II417;
  II420–423
Stratonice: II375
Succession: II75 (Apostolic); II86
Συγγενής: II393
Sun: II649
Σύναξις: 360
Superman: II686
Suriel: II796
Susa: II750
Susanna: II152
Symbolic Utterances: II586
Symeon, the Greek: 388
  (Simeon); 449; 468–470; 476f.
Synagogue, rulers of: 461; 464f.
Synoptics: 75ff.
Syria: 214; 330; II192; II427;
  II533; II699; II724; II747.
Syrian: II729
Systematizing of apocalyptic ex-
  pectations: II624
Syzygies: II533; II545; II553.
  Series of S.: II108. (Cf. Pairs
  of opposites)

Tabor: 164
Tarsus: II71f.; II759: II798
Tartaruchus (angel): II769
Tartarus: II460; II559; II717;
  II737; II771; II780; II784
Tatian: 125; 168; II54; II349;
  II395
Tatirokos (angel = Tartaruchus):
  II679
Tau: 357
Teacher(s): 467; II485; II605
teacher-ship: II569
Teachings of Adam: 318
Temlakos (angel): II675
Temple (of Apollo at Sidon):
  II368

Terracina: II316
Tertia: II431; II513ff.; II522–
  528; II530
Tertullian: II686; II688
—, De anima 23: 323
—, Apol. 5, 21: 444
—, De bapt. 17: II323. 20. 2: 89
—, De carne 7: 350
—, Exhort. 10.5: II687
—, De fuga 9. 4: II686f.
—, Adv. Marc. IV. 5. 3f.: II68
—, De praescr. 25: 233; II76
—, De pud. 21. 7: II686
—, De resurr. 11. 2: II687
—, Adv. Valent. 2: 245. 4: 331
Pseudo-Tertullian, Adv. omnes
  haer. 2: 324. 4: 233
Testament of Job: II758
Testamentum Domini: 298; 301;
  II599
Thaddaeus: 156; 438; 442f.; 507;
  II36f.; II59; II162; II166
Thaddaeus, Acts of: II577f.
Thamyris: II355–358; II360;
  II364
Thebes: II724; II730
Thecla: II155; II199; II355ff.
Thecla, Acts of: II332. (Cf. Paul
  and Thecla, Acts of)
Thecla cult: II333
Thecla traditions: II332
Theocleia: II355f.; II358; II364
Theocracy: II598
Theodas: 234; II72; II185
Theodicy: II587
Theodor Abū Qurra, Tractate on
  the Creator, par. 24: 268
Theodor bar Konai, Book of
  Scholia: 318; 324
Theodoret of Cyrus, haer. fab.
  comp. 1. 13: 317². 1. 15: 313
Theodosius II: 450; II759
Theodotus, apud Clem. Alex.,
  Exc. ex Theodoto 2. 2: 88.
  c. 14. 3: 172. c. 21. 3. 303. c.
  51. 3: 172. c. 66: II76. c.
  67: 169. c. 67. 2: 361
Theon: II284–287; II346
Theonoe: II374